Parenting A *to* Z

IRENE FRANCK
DAVID BROWNSTONE

HarperCollins*Publishers*

HarperCollins books may be purchased for educational, business, or sales promotional use. For information, please write to: Special Markets Department, HarperCollins*Publishers*, Inc., 10 East 53rd Street, New York, New York 10022.

SECOND EDITION

First edition published as the PARENT'S DESK REFERENCE.

Library of Congress Cataloging-in-Publication Data
Franck, Irene M.
Parenting A to Z/Irene M. Franck and David M. Brownstone.—2nd ed.
p. cm.
Revised and updated ed. of: The Parent's Desk Reference. 1991.

ISBN 0-06-271598-4

1. Child rearing—United States—Handbooks, manuals, etc. 2. Parenting—United States— Handbooks, manuals, etc. 3. Children—United States—Handbooks, manuals, etc. 4. Children— Health and development—United States—Handbooks, manuals, etc. 5. Child development—United States —Handbooks, manuals, etc. I. Franck, Irene M. II. Brownstone, David M. The Parent's Desk Reference. III. Title.
HQ769.F7165 1996
649'.1—dc20 96-6311

---

98 99 ❖/RRD 10 9 8 7 6 5 4 3

Preface to Second Edition

Parenting A to Z is the second edition of the *Parent's Desk Reference.* In this edition, the book remains, in essence, what it was: a unique conception-to-college encyclopedia and resource book for parents, providing information, guidance, and sources for further help on a wide range of personal, educational, medical, social, and legal matters that affect parents and their children. Among the topics included are:

- *Pregnancy and childbirth,* including infertility treatments and prenatal screening tests, such as *in vitro* fertilization and amniocentesis.
- *Child development,* including key skills and stages of development, and techniques and activities for developing those skills.
- *Nutrition and infant care,* including breastfeeding and proper diet.
- *Genetic and other common disorders of childhood or pregnancy,* such as Down syndrome, gestational diabetes, sudden infant death syndrome (SIDS), and chicken pox.
- *Education and special educational concerns,* such as learning disabilities, gifted children, several schooling alternatives, and the multiple impacts of the Family Educational Rights and Privacy Act, the Individuals with Disabilities Education Act, and other laws.
- *Educational, medical, and psychological tests,* including several general kinds of tests and such key specific tests as the Gesell Developmental Schedules, chorionic villus sampling, and the California Achievement Tests.
- *Family law and social services,* such as parents' rights, adoption, and the Parent Locator Service for child support disputes.
- *Key social problems relating to children,* such as drug and alcohol abuse, child abuse, and custody.

The main part of the book is an A-Z section consisting of over 2,500 entries on an extraordinarily wide range of matters of concern to parents today. Within each entry, words or phrases in SMALL CAPITAL LETTERS act as cross-references, indicating that the reader can find more information, if desired, under that heading.

In many of the most important entries, parents will also find descriptions of private and public organizations that provide help and further information, as well as a sampling of recent publications on the topic. These will allow parents to tap into the now-vast network of organizations that has developed around the particular needs and interests of parents and their children—from mainstream organizations concerned with parenting in general, such as the National Institute for Child Health and Development or the New Parents' Network, to small groups relating to very special interests, such as those for families with rare genetic disorders or for single women who wish to have children by artificial insemination.

For most serious children's disorders, there is at least one major national association—often run by and for affected families. These can be lifelines for parents who need ongoing support and information as they face difficult decisions about their children's health and future. Note, however, that this is very much a book for *all* parents—for those raising normal children without major special problems and for those raising normal children *with* major special problems. For us, as for their parents, all children are "normal"; some just require more help than others.

Many of the book's A-Z entries are accompanied by special boxed materials:

- *Sidelights* on what to expect, such as an explanation of the usual pattern of prenatal care or why new parents should not worry about a baby's "funny-looking legs."
- *Checklists* for possible trouble, such as signs of child abuse or observation checklists for learning disabilities or hearing problems.
- *Practical advice,* such as how to perform the Heimlich maneuver on a choking child, or how much and how often to feed a baby.
- *Evaluation guidelines,* such as what to look for in examining a child's school record or what to consider in choosing a doctor or clinic.
- *Tips for parents,* such as how to make visitation work for kids and divorced parents or how to prepare for a parent-teacher conference.
- *Related medical information,* such as the Apgar score for assessing the health of newborns or tips for avoiding foodborne illness.
- *Other special information,* such as illustrations of basic life-support procedures or a safety checklist for baby's first year.

Following the A-Z portion of the book is a Special Help section that includes additional materials, many too extensive to fit elsewhere. For example:

- *Basic Exercises for During and After Pregnancy,* to help women keep in optimum shape for themselves and their babies.
- *Chart of Normal Development,* outlining the year-by-year development of key skills (such as motor, language, self-help, social, and cognitive skills) from birth through age six.

- *Tips for parents* on choosing a school and resource materials on substance abuse.
- *Help on Learning and Education, Help for Special Children, Help Against Substance Abuse,* and *Help Against Child Abuse and Neglect,* all including organizations and other resources to help parents focus on these key areas.

A complete listing of all the special material in the book is given on page ix.

While the basic approach and structure of the book remains the same, much has been added and changed in this second edition. Indeed, it is striking how much has changed in the five short years since the first edition. The following are among the many notable changes reflected in the new edition:

- Managed care and HMOs have mushroomed, changing the character of health care and insurance.
- Doctors now recommend that most infants be put to sleep on their backs, changing a long-standing guideline.
- New medical technology allows even men who have had a vasectomy to have biological children and even women past menopause to bear children from others' eggs.
- Genetic discoveries have offered new hope for parents who carry—or fear they may carry—genetic disorders.
- The Family and Medical Leave Act has finally formalized a parent's right to maternity and family leave.
- The Individuals with Disabilities Education Act (IDEA) and the Americans with Disabilities Act (ADA) have expanded the services for and rights of children (and adults) with disabilities—and simultaneously made the parent's role as advocate for the child even more important.
- The Scholastic Aptitude Test has changed its format and its scoring method for the first time in decades; many schools are now offering SAT preparation courses; and many children are taking the SAT from the seventh grade and even earlier.
- Computer technology has spurred new ways of learning about the world—very much affecting parents and children.

New and revised entries and special boxes deal with these and many more topics.

Several major general entries are new to this edition, notably HEALTH CARE, HEALTH INSURANCE, SAFETY, SPORTS, VIOLENCE, REPRODUCTIVE SYSTEM, and DIVORCE, though specific related entries continue to be treated separately (in the case of divorce, they include CHILD SUPPORT, CUSTODY, VISITATION RIGHTS, and another new entry, SEPARATION AGREEMENT). Other notable new entries include HOSPICE, ADVOCACY, FAMILY AND MEDICAL LEAVE, PAIN AND PAIN TREATMENT, LICE, MOTION SICKNESS, ADVANCE DIRECTIVE, AU PAIR, NANNY, SERVICE DOGS, SUPPORTED EMPLOYMENT, PARENT TRAINING AND INFORMATION CENTERS, TECHNICAL ASSISTANCE FOR PARENTS PROGRAM (TAPP), SCABIES, TRANSITION, VOCATIONAL REHABILITATION SERVICES, and REPRODUCTIVE TECHNOLOGY, as well as separate entries on several new techniques, such as ASSISTED FERTILIZATION, EMBRYO BIOPSY, and INTRACYTOPLASMIC SPERM INJECTION. New special boxed materials include WHAT DO YOU NEED TO ASK ABOUT HEALTH INSURANCE AND MANAGED CARE?, TIPS FOR PROTECTING YOUR CHILDREN AGAINST ABDUCTION, YOUR BABY'S FIRST YEAR: A SAFETY CHECKLIST, SPECIAL HELP FOR SPECIAL COLLEGE STUDENTS, and TIPS FOR AVOIDING FOODBORNE ILLNESS.

Some new materials draw heavily on our own *What's New for Parents* (Prentice Hall/Simon and Schuster, 1993), which was a kind of interim update of the first edition of the *Parent's Desk Reference;* these include LEAD POISONING, SKIN CANCER, and the special boxes GET THE LEAD OUT! and WHEN DO KIDS NEED PROTECTION FROM THE SUN? We have also drawn on our *Women's Desk Reference* (Viking Penguin, 1993) for some new entries, such as RAPE, MORNING AFTER PILL, RU-486, FEMALE CIRCUMCISION, SEXUAL IDENTITY, and the new box WHAT HAPPENS DURING PREGNANCY?

We did not, in fact, realize what a massive undertaking this revision would be. We have personally contacted each of the hundreds of organizations in the book, updating information about their activities and publications as well as current address and contact information. An astonishing number of them have changed their names, merged with other organizations, or moved to new quarters, sometimes clear across the continent. To help readers keep up with changes that may take place after publication of this book, we have also included HOW TO FIND HOTLINES AND HELPLINES: A QUICK GUIDE.

As in the first edition, readers who want further information, help, or support will find organizations listed under the topic of interest, such as CUSTODY or POSTPARTUM DEPRESSION. A full write-up on the organization will be found under the entry where it best fits. Often, however, an organization provides information and services on many topics and may be useful to a wide range of parents. So briefer, cross-referenced entries will be found under other appropriate topics, providing pertinent information and a key phone number, while referring back to the full write-up for complete information.

For example, the main entries for The Arc and the Epilepsy Foundation of America are found under MENTAL RETARDATION and EPILEPSY, respectively. However, both organizations have materials on advocacy so brief cross-reference entries describing those materials are provided under ADVOCACY. Readers seeking help should look under the main topic of their concern, where they will find a general write-up, listings of organizations and other resources of interest, and cross-references to related topics.

For this second edition, we have also added new kinds of contact information for organizations. At the time of the first edition, faxes were just coming on; now almost every organization has a fax number. And more recently, as online access has boomed, many organizations have set up e-mail addresses and sometimes online services such as forums or resource libraries. So we now include, when an organization has them, fax numbers as well as e-mail addresses and other online addresses on the Internet and on online services (such as on America Online, Prodigy, or CompuServe).

We have also added information on many other online resources (many of them not linked with specific organizations) that provide information and support for parents, such as Moms Online and the Parents' Information Network (PIN) on America Online; Homework Helper on Prodigy; or the ADD-parents mailing list on the Internet, for parents of children with attention deficit hyperactivity disorder. We have not attempted to explain arcane Internet abbreviations or instructions—readers should not look here for an explanation of *http* or *html*—but the Internet-savvy will find access information to sites of interest. One caveat: the Internet is fast-changing, and names, sites, and codes may well be different from those given in the book. However, searchers will be able to find them or their equivalents by checking with online indexes.

Computer users should note that much of the material in this book appears in the Moms Online Desk Reference, part of the Moms Online service on America Online, along with material from *The Women's Desk Reference* and *What's New for Parents.* This material is searchable by key word online. Note, however, that this book contains many materials not available online, such as checklists, tables, and illustrated materials. On the other hand, the online version contains some materials for which we did not have room in the book.

Please note that although many matters related to health and legal issues are discussed in this book, we strongly feel that no book should be used as a substitute for on-the-spot professional advice. We urge parents to quickly see their doctor, lawyer, or other appropriate professional when problems arise.

Our thanks go to our editor Rob Kaplan, who has so capably shepherded the book through the production process at its new publisher. Thanks again to Gene Hawes for his always valued counsel and to Mary Racette for her expert typing and clerical help. As always, we also thank the staff of librarians throughout the northeastern library network, in particular the staff of the Chappaqua Library—Director Mark Hasskarl; the expert reference staff, including Martha Alcott, Teresa Bueti, Maryanne Eaton, Sue Farber, Carolyn Jones, Jane Peyraud, Paula Peyraud, and Carolyn Reznick; and the circulation staff, including Marilyn Coleman, Lois Siwicki, and Jane McKean—for fulfilling our wide-ranging research needs.

We also wish to thank the scores of people in public and private organizations all over the country, who so freely gave of their time and resources. In particular, we thank Betty Jean Lifton, American Adoption Congress; Seth Rockmuller, Alliance for Parental Involvement in Education; Karen Storek, New Parents' Network; Chrissie Bamber, Center for Law and Education (formerly of the now-dissolved National Committee for Citizens in Education); Polly Arango, Family Voices; Jim Sinclair, Autism Network International; Judy Ceusa, National Vaccine Injury Compensation Program; Mac Wimbish, National Water Safety Congress; Randy Swart, Bicycle Helmet Safety Institute; Wendy Sachs, International Nanny Association; Mary Jane Garcia, National Down Syndrome Congress; Charles Eichhorn and Nicholas Gattuccio, Foundation for Ichthyosis and Related Skin Types (FIRST); Jane Honikman, Postpartum Support International; Barbara MacDonald, Children's Rights Project; Pat Farmer and Barb VanHerreweghe, Support Organization for Trisomy 18, 13, and Related Disorders (SOFT); Gloria Roberts, Planned Parenthood; Martina Darrah, National Center for Education and Child and Maternal Health (NCEMCH); Gail Johnson, National Association for Sick Child Daycare Centers; Barbara Lincoln, Coordinator, Tripod Grapevine; Kenneth Pangborn, Parents and Children's Equality (PACE); Tammy Fortune, Division of Adult Education and Literacy Clearinghouse; Cindy Heider, National Programs Coordinator, People Against Rape; Jill Brensinger, The Johns Hopkins Hospital; Carol Yeh, Telecommunications for the Deaf; Kenneth Nathanson, Citizens for Safe Drivers Against Drunk Drivers and Chronic Offenders (CSD); Willy Prip and Deborah Kaufman, Choice in Dying; Jennifer L. Geipe, Adoptive Family Network; Gail Johnson, National Parent Network on Disabilities (NPND); Alice Gilgoff, National Association of Postpartum Care Services (NAPCS); Brian Graff, North American Vegetarian Society; Kim Bruno, FEMALE (Formerly Employed Mothers at the Leading Edge); Kay Damba, Mothers of Preschoolers (MOPS) International; Sharon Broom, American Social Health Association; Ann Wasserman and Suzanne L. Ramirez, Nursing Mothers Counsel; Sue Lehr, Facilitated Communication Institute; Judy Hammes, American Association for Gifted Children; Carol Gray, The Seeing Eye; Dallas Bubemyre, Find the Children; Charlene Waldman, Paget Foundation for Paget's Disease of Bone and Related Disorders; Jack Mayhew, American Council on Rural Special Education (ACRES); Janis Heil, Unite, Inc., Grief Support; Esther Ehrenberg, The Compassionate Friends; Eileen Ceskaden, Very Special Arts; Jany Levy, Cancer Care, Inc.; Howard Ruppel and Linda Lotz, American Association of Sex Educators, Counselors, and Therapists (AASECT); Amy Liss, Resource Center on Substance Abuse Prevention and Disability; Glennis McNeal, National Psoriasis Foundation; Christa Bucks, Mobility

International U.S.A.; Rebecca Jeffords, National Women's Resource Center; Tammy De Martino, Mothers at Home; Esther Zorn, International Cesarean Awareness Network; Lisa Reed, National Association of Postpartum Care Services; Dana Polsey, Latin America Parents Association; Cherie Sintes, Ambiguous Genitalia Support Network; Roslyn Brilliant, Disabled and Alone/Life Services for the Handicapped; and Anna El-Qudsi, Myasthenia Gravis Foundation. They and many others offer beacons of support, advice, counsel, and information for people facing the many and varied challenges of parenting.

IRENE FRANCK
DAVID BROWNSTONE

List of Special Materials

The main body of this work consists of A-Z entries; it also includes numerous boxed and other special materials, which are listed below.

SPECIAL BOXED MATERIAL

A

abandonment, in relation to family rights and responsibilities, leaving behind someone with whom one has legal rights and ties, and expressing no intention of returning.

A parent can be charged with abandonment if a child is deserted or if the parent leaves the child for too long a time without effective supervision and providing for basic needs. The age of the child, the nature of the supervision (or lack of it), and the length of the unsupervised period all affect legal judgment as to whether abandonment has occurred, and state laws vary on these matters. But if a parent is found to have abandoned a child, the child might be placed in FOSTER CARE and a lawsuit may be brought to terminate PARENTS' RIGHTS; in the absence of another parent, the child could then be placed for ADOPTION without parental permission. Courts vary in their handling of such questions. Traditionally, many have followed the "flicker of interest" rule of not terminating parents' rights when a parent has shown even the smallest degree of interest in the child's welfare. Others, especially more recently, have judged that a parent who has demonstrated a desire to be rid of all parental obligations has effectively abandoned the child.

Abandonment proceedings are sometimes initiated by stepparents or foster parents who wish to adopt a child, but cannot locate the BIOLOGICAL PARENTS to obtain legal permission. If a child, especially an infant, is physically abandoned, for instance on a doorstep or in a garbage can, the parent can be liable to criminal prosecution. In history, such abandonment was a common form of infanticide and still is in some cultures, especially when the child has DISABILITIES, parentage is disputed, or the child is female. Sometimes, however, such abandonment can be an attempt to make better provision for the child than the parent could do, such as when a parent leaves the child at a hospital or an orphanage.

One marriage partner leaving the other may also be called abandonment or desertion, traditionally one of the grounds for DIVORCE. Abandonment is said to have occurred when it is voluntary (that is, not provoked by the deserted spouse), when arrangements have not been made for a SEPARATION, when attempts at reconciliation have failed, and when the couple has actually parted (they no longer have sexual relations if living apart, for example). Traditionally, whatever her ties to her original home, a woman who failed to relocate with her husband to a new home might be charged with abandonment, though the husband was obliged to provide her with sufficient time and resources to make the move. In more recent years, such rulings have been challenged as sexually discriminatory, and women have been seeking—with some success—equal rights under the law.

Where more liberalized "no-fault" divorce laws prevail, questions of abandonment are no longer vital in divorce proceedings, but they can still have significant implications for parents. A parent who has left children with the remaining parent may lose CUSTODY, as well as possible ALIMONY or CHILD SUPPORT that might be arranged in a separation agreement. In addition, the spouse who leaves may lose rights to a partner's pension or insurance, or the right to contest a will or act as administrator. Married or not, a parent seeking to leave a parenting partner will want to seek advice from a legal professional who specializes in marital and family law, to ensure that parenting and financial rights are protected.

ABC Inventory, a type of individually administered READINESS TEST used in assessing the general maturity and school readiness of preschoolers, ages 3½ to 6½. In the test's four different types of tasks, the child is asked to draw a man (as in the GOODENOUGH-HARRIS DRAWING TEST), answer language questions such as "What has wings?", answer thought questions such as "What is ice when it melts?", and perform motor tasks, such as folding paper, copying a figure, or counting items. Results are scored according to the test manual. Schools often use the ABC Inventory for class placement. It may also be used as a kind of DEVELOPMENTAL SCREENING TEST, to identify children with learning problems, who may require further evaluation and services. (See TESTS.)

ability test, a type of TEST designed to measure performance of a particular skill or skills, such as a typing test; also an alternate term for INTELLIGENCE TEST. (See TESTS.)

abortion, the termination of a PREGNANCY, whether involuntarily or deliberately. Many abortions occur naturally, often because of GENETIC DEFECTS in the EMBRYO that are incompatible with life; medically these are called *spontaneous abortions* or MISCARRIAGES. At least 10 percent, and perhaps more like 30 percent, of all pregnancies are thought to end in spontaneous abortions, often before the woman realizes she is pregnant.

It is the deliberate termination of a pregnancy—*elective* or *induced abortion*, which people opposed to abortion often call *feticide* or *infanticide*—about which controversy rages. Long illegal (and still so in many parts of the world), abortions, for centuries, were performed in back alleys and other nonsterile settings, often by ill-trained practitioners or by the women themselves, using toxic substances or dangerous tools such as knitting needles and coat hangers. Even under the best circumstances, in

HOSPITALS or hospital-like settings, women having abortions have always faced the risk of life-threatening hemorrhages or infections. But the health risks have been magnified in back-alley settings, and those who most often faced those risks have been women too poor to travel to places where abortions were performed legally and relatively safely. Images of women dead or terribly damaged by abortions gone wrong and recognition of the unequal burden placed on poor women have led many countries to liberalize their laws regarding abortions.

In the United States the law changed in 1973, when, in the case of *Roe v. Wade,* a Supreme Court ruling allowed for unrestricted abortion in the first TRIMESTER (three months) of pregnancy. The ruling also provided for state regulation of abortion in the second trimester and state regulation or prohibition of abortion in the third trimester, except when the mother's life or health are threatened (a so-called *therapeutic abortion*). After *Roe v. Wade,* abortions became legal and widely available for the first time in the United States, sought by teenagers, single women, and married women for a wide variety of personal, social, and economic reasons. Since 1973, millions of abortions have been carried out, many at women's clinics, which offer both abortions and BIRTH CONTROL advice.

However, many people oppose abortions, seeing them as the murder of living beings—tiny, generally (until late in pregnancy) incapable of independent life, but recognizably human forms. They often argue that life begins at CONCEPTION and that the right of the FETUS to life takes precedence over the mother's right to choose whether or not to bear a child. Their protests have placed great pressure on clinics offering abortions, even leading to violence—including murder—against abortion-providers. Some who oppose abortions have also set up dummy clinics, ostensibly to offer abortions, but in fact to induce women to continue their pregnancies. In some cases these clinics use coercion, though others provide counseling, support, and help in placing a baby for ADOPTION.

Various federal and state laws have limited the use of public funds for abortion, and in recent years, the Supreme Court, while reaffirming the legality of abortion stated in *Roe v. Wade,* has allowed more restrictions to be placed by states, as long as they do not place what the court would consider an "undue burden." In some states, a teenage girl can only have an abortion if she obtains consent from a parent, though the Supreme Court ruled that an alternative, such as obtaining consent from a judge, must be provided. Some other states require that a woman be given a presentation about fetal development and the details of the abortion procedure, and then wait for twenty-four hours before being able to have an abortion.

All of these factors have limited practical access to abortions, especially to poor, adolescent women in rural areas, where the nearest clinic might be hundreds of miles away, and have put pressure on the concept of *abortion on demand.* Though few individuals would ever describe themselves as "pro-abortion," many people are active in the "pro-choice" movement, seeking to secure the woman's right to choose and wider dissemination of birth control alternatives to prevent unwanted pregnancies. Some women, fearing they will lose the right to legal abortion, have even formed self-help groups to perform abortions on each other, though many regard the "homemade" methods as hazardous because they have not been tested for safety and efficacy and could damage a woman's REPRODUCTIVE SYSTEM. These "self-help" abortions are also risky because the women who perform them are not trained to handle medical complications. Some women, especially teenage girls, faced with seemingly insuperable obstacles, have again turned to self-induced or back-alley abortions. A delayed abortion can cause an increased financial burden; an early abortion in a clinic is less expensive, but a late abortion legally can be provided only in a hospital.

Parents may sometimes find themselves in a difficult spot, supporting an anti-abortion or "pro-life" position, that may come up against the reality of the situation of their pregnant teenage daughter. In one poignant case, a model young woman, not wanting to "disappoint" her parents by telling them about her pregnancy, died after a botched abortion. Her parents later led a fight against parental consent laws, noting that their daughter died "because of a law we would have voted for."

In fact, abortions continue to be widespread. With the rise of various GENETIC SCREENING tests, such as AMNIOCENTESIS, CHORIONIC VILLUS SAMPLING, ALPHA FETOPROTEIN (AFP), and ULTRASOUND SCANS, many couples today routinely screen their fetus for possible GENETIC DEFECTS and CHROMOSOMAL ABNORMALITIES. Many choose to have an abortion if severe defects are found. This approach has been criticized, especially by people born with birth defects and genetic disorders who would not be living today had their parents chosen to have an abortion.

Some people also use genetic screening and abortion for sex selection of their children. Occasionally, this may lead to the abortion of a male fetus, when a couple wants a daughter instead of a son, but more often the reverse is true. In many places, notably in India and China, where sons are more desirable than daughters, female fetuses are aborted. Many women's rights supporters there are anti-abortion activists, noting that pregnant women in those countries often have little "choice" in the matter. In the United States, however, the Supreme Court ruled in 1976 that a woman could not be required to obtain her husband's consent, affirming a woman's right to choose an abortion, particularly when she already has more children than she can provide for or when she is in an abusive family situation.

Doctors may recommend therapeutic abortions in some occasions when the mother has a condition that might become life-threatening during pregnancy, such as HEART PROBLEMS, KIDNEY PROBLEMS, and CANCER, especially of the BREASTS or CERVIX, or when the mother is exposed to or carrying an infection that can seriously damage the baby, such as RUBELLA (German measles) or AIDS.

In contrast to the social and philosophical questions, abortion—removal of the fetus and the PLACENTA that nourishes it—is a relatively simply operation, in physical terms. It is vital to remove all pregnancy-related tissues from the uterus to avoid potentially life-threatening infection.

Abortions in the first trimester are often carried out by VACUUM EXTRACTION, literally sucking out the contents of the uterus. Sometimes this procedure is combined with an operation called a D & C (*dilatation and curettage*), a widening of the cervix and scraping of the lining of the UTERUS to be sure no tissue remains, a procedure performed under general or local ANESTHESIA. Some women's self-help groups have developed a "homemade" version of the procedure, using a syringe and thin tube (*cannula*) fed through the cervix into the uterus.

Abortions in the second trimester, though more hazardous and difficult, may be performed in much the same way they are in the first trimester. In this later stage, the combination of vacuum extraction and a D & C is called *dilatation and evacuation.* More often, especially after the fifteenth week, a saline solution or HORMONE injection into the AMNIOTIC SAC is used to induce CONTRACTIONS in the uterus, a procedure called *amnioinfusion, amniocentesis abortion,* or *intra-amniotic infusion.* Usually the fetus is expelled in about twelve hours; the woman normally remains in the hospital for one to two days afterward.

When performed under hospital or clinic conditions, the MORTALITY RATE for abortions is relatively low, less than 1 in 100,000 abortions in the first trimester, but the mortality rate rises later in the pregnancy. Women who have had an abortion, especially multiple abortions, also carry an increased risk of later miscarriage or INFERTILITY.

Some drugs can be taken extremely early in pregnancy, in fact even before it is known if a pregnancy exists (see MORNING AFTER PILL; RU–486). One of these is the so-called "abortion pill," RU–486, which its developers prefer to call a "preconception" pill. In the past, DES was sometimes given as a morning after pill, especially on college campuses, despite knowledge of its long-term adverse side effects.

A preliminary 1995 study showed that two drugs—*methotrexate* and *misoprostol*—could be administered to produce abortion during the first eight weeks of pregnancy, though further testing was needed before the approach could be pronounced safe for widespread use. In this approach, methotrexate (normally used in higher doses to treat CANCER, PSORIASIS, or ARTHRITIS) operates to block VITAMIN B (folic acid) and so hinder growth of the EMBRYO and PLACENTA. The drug has been used for some years to end ECTOPIC PREGNANCIES in a way that does not harm future ability to conceive.

In the study, after a woman was examined, given an ULTRASOUND scan to check the stage of the pregnancy, and counseled, she was given an injection of methotrexate. She then returned five to seven days later for insertion of a vaginal suppository containing misoprostol. Approximately two days later, cramping and bleeding occurred—essentially an induced early MISCARRIAGE. When it did not occur, a woman sometimes was given a second suppository; in a few cases, a vacuum extraction abortion was required. An examination was needed to ensure that the abortion was complete.

Though the two drugs are already widely available by prescription, they are approved for other uses. And though doctors may legally prescribe them for so-called "off-label" uses, many may be reluctant to do so, because their malpractice insurance may not cover them should complications arise. Side effects in this study were minor, primarily cramps and bleeding, but much is unknown about the long-term effects of the drugs, notably on a woman's MENSTRUAL CYCLE and future FERTILITY. If this two-drug approach proves safe, however, it may revolutionize abortions, which can then be secured in the privacy of a doctor's office or clinic, not subject to protests and disputes that have been occurring at abortion-providing clinics.

Many couples who have decided to have no more children choose STERILIZATION as a permanent form of birth control rather than face the question of possible abortion later on. Parents of sexually active children, especially daughters, may want to discuss birth control as part of home SEX EDUCATION, in an attempt to forestall the question of abortion. If they are not unalterably opposed to abortion for religious or other reasons, parents may also want to discuss abortion to open the lines of communication with their teenagers, rather than risking the possibility that their children may attempt to deal with an unwanted pregnancy on their own.

FOR HELP AND FURTHER INFORMATION

Planned Parenthood Federation of America (PPFA), 800–230–7526. Operates nationwide network of counseling and health services centers; publishes pamphlets *What if I'm Pregnant?* and *Abortion: Questions and Answers.* (For full group information, see BIRTH CONTROL.)

National Abortion Federation (NAF)
1436 U Street NW, Suite 103
Washington, DC 20009
202–667–5881; Hotline: 800–772–9100, U.S. except DC
Fax: 202–667–5890
Vicki Saporta, Executive Director
Organization concerned with abortion rights; sets standards and guidelines; provides information and referrals; acts as advocate; operates the NAF Legal Clearinghouse; publishes advocacy bulletins *Legal Abortion Is Safe Abortion* and *Judicial Bypass Procedure* and other materials for professionals and the public, including fact sheets such as *What Is Abortion?, Safety of Abortion, Abortion After 12 Weeks, Economics of Abortion, Women Who Have Abortions, Teenage Women,* and *Abortion and the Law*; books or booklets such as *Having an Abortion?: Your Guide to Good Care, Unsure About Your Pregnancy?: A Guide to Making the Right Decision for You*; and works on legal and medical issues.

National Abortion Rights Action League (NARAL)
1156 15th Street NW, Suite 700
Washington, DC 20005
202–973–3000

Fax: 202–973–3096
Kate Michelman, Executive Director
Organization of people seeking to retain women's rights to legal abortion; seeks to educate public and influence government policy; publishes membership newsletter and state-by-state review of abortion rights.

American Association of University Women (AAUW), 202–785–7700. Publishes *Teen Women and Abortion: Myth vs. Reality*. (For full group information, see HELP ON LEARNING AND EDUCATION on page 659.)

American College of Obstetricians and Gynecologists (ACOG), 202–638–5577. Publishes *Induced Abortion: Important Medical Facts*. (For full group information, see PREGNANCY.)

International Association of Parents and Professionals for Safe Alternatives in Childbirth (NAPSAC), Phone and fax: 314–238–2010. Publishes *Abortion and Clarification of Related Questions*. (For full group information, see CHILDBIRTH.)

National Institute of Child Health and Human Development (NICHD), 301–496–5133. (For full group information, see PREGNANCY.)

ABORTION ALTERNATIVE GROUPS

The Nurturing Network (TNN), 800–866–4666. Offers alternatives to abortion for women with crisis pregnancies. (For full group information, see PREGNANCY.)

National Adoption Information Clearinghouse (NAIC), 301–231–6512. Provides referrals to adoption agencies and crisis pregnancy centers; publishes *Are You Pregnant and Thinking About Adoption?* (For full group information, see ADOPTION.)

Bethany Christian Services, 800–238–4269. Provides information on abortion alternatives. (For full information, see ADOPTION.)

Concerned United Birthparents (CUB), 515–263–9558. Publishes *Closed Adoptions Promote Abortions*. (For full group information, see ADOPTION.)

ANTI-ABORTION GROUPS

National Right to Life Committee (NRLC)
419 Seventh Street NW, Suite 500
Washington, DC 20004–2293
202–626–8800
Fax: 202–737–9189 or 202–347–5907
Wanda Franz, President
Organization opposing abortion, euthanasia, and infanticide; acts as advocate; provides information; publishes biweekly *National Right to Life News* and other materials, including books *To Rescue the Future, Restoring the Right to Life, Abortion: The Silent Holocaust, Abortion Questions and Answers*, and *School-Based Clinics: The Abortion Connection*; brochures and booklets *Abortion: Some Medical Facts, Abortion: The Hard Cases, They're Forgetting Someone, New Technology Brings Clearer View of Life, Their Lives—A Single Issue?, When Does Life Begin?*, and *The Challenge to Be Pro-Life*; videos *A Matter of Choice* and *The Silent Scream;* and various materials on postabortion trauma.

Americans United for Life (AUL)
343 South Dearborn, Suite 1804
Chicago, IL 60604
312–786–9494
Fax: 312–786–2131
E-mail: 74507.3172@compuserve.com (CompuServe: 74507,3172)
Organization that seeks to protect life, opposing abortion and euthanasia; supports AUL Legal Defense Fund; maintains library; publishes various materials, including newsletter *Lex Vitae*.

Birthright, United States of America
686 North Broad Street
Woodbury, NJ 08096
Abortion Alternative Hotline: 800–848-LOVE [848–5683]; 609–848–1819
Fax: 609–848–2380
Denise Cocciolone, Executive Director
Network of groups seeking to convince women with unplanned pregnancies to seek alternatives to abortion; offers classes in childbirth and parenting; publishes various printed materials, including newsletter *Life-Guardian*.

Human Life International (HLI), 800–549–5433. Publishes pamphlet *From Conception to Abortion*. (For full group information, see BIRTH CONTROL.)

Couple to Couple League (CCL), 513–471–2000. Publishes brochure *From Contraception to Abortion* and booklet *Silent Abortions*, on the Pill and IUD. (For full group information, see NATURAL FAMILY PLANNING.)

National Woman's Christian Temperance Union (WCTU), 800–755–1321. Publishes leaflet *Silent Holocaust*. (For full group information, see HELP AGAINST SUBSTANCE ABUSE on page 703.)

ONLINE RESOURCES

Internet: Abortion directory. Provides access to library catalogs, databases, and servers. http://gopher.well.sf.ca.us

Internet: Usenet newsgroup. For information and discussion. To subscribe, send e-mail message to: news:table.abortion

OTHER RESOURCES

GENERAL WORKS

The Facts on Abortion. John Ankerberg and John Weldon. Harvest House, 1995.

Abortion: How and Where to Find Facts and Get Help. Robert D. Reed and others. R & E Publishers, 1993.

Abortion: A Doctor's Perspective—a Woman's Dilemma. Don Sloan and Paula Hartz. Fine, 1993.
Abortions. Otakar J. Pollak. Carlton, 1993.
A Woman's Book of Choices: Abortion, Menstrual Extraction, RU–486. Rebecca Chalker and Carol Downer. Four Walls Eight Windows, 1992.
Abortion: A Positive Decision. Patricia Lunneborg. Greenwood, 1992.
Common Sense about Abortion. Yuda Molk. Common Sense, 1992.
Abortion: A Rational Look at an Emotional Issue. R. C. Sproul. NavPress, 1990.

For preteens and teens

Roe vs. Wade (1973): Abortion. Susan D. Gold. Macmillan, 1994.
Roe v. Wade: The Abortion Question. D. J. Herda. Enslow, 1994.
Abortion: Beyond Personal Choice: Looking at Life. Center for Learning Network, 1992.
Abortion. Joan Nelson. Lucent, 1992.
The Abortion Debate. Claudia M. Caruana. Millbrook Press, 1992.
Abortion: A Serious Issue. Mark Siegel. Information Plus, 1991.
Choose Life! Unborn Children and the Right to Life. Francis D. Kelly, ed. National Catholic Education, 1991.
Abortion: Opposing Viewpoints. Charles P. Cozic and Stacey Tipp, eds. Greenhaven, 1991.
Abortion. Carl N. Flanders. Facts On File, 1990.

On postabortion effects

Post-Abortion Aftermath: A Comprehensive Consideration. Michael T. Mannion, ed. Sheed & Ward, 1994.
Beyond the Hidden Pain of Abortion. Patricia A. Bigliardi. Aglow Communications, 1994.
Five Steps Toward Post-Abortion Healing. Holly Francis. St. Paul Books, 1992.
Post-Abortion Trauma. Jeanette Vought. Zondervan, 1991.
The Mourning After: Help for Post Abortion Syndrome. Terry L. Selby. Baker, 1990.
Finding Peace after Abortion. Loraine Allison. Abbey, 1990.
Does Anyone Else Feel Like I Do? Pam Koerbel. Doubleday, 1990.

Personal experiences

Bitter Fruit: Women's Experiences of Unplanned Pregnancy, Abortion, and Adoption. Ann Perkins and Rira Townsend. Hunter House, 1992.
Our Choices: Women's Personal Decisions about Abortion. Sumi Hoshiko. Harrington Park/Haworth, 1992.
The Choices We Made: 25 Women and Men Speak Out about Abortion. Angela Bonavoglia, ed. Random, 1991.

On rights and status of the fetus

Life Before Birth: The Moral and Legal Status of Embryos and Fetuses. Bonnie Steinbock. Oxford University Press, 1992.
When Does Life Begin?: And Thirty-Nine Other Tough Questions about Abortion. John Ankerberg and John Weldon. Wolgemuth & Hyatt, 1990.
The Vatican, the Law and the Human Embryo. Michael J. Coughlan. University of Iowa Press, 1990.

(See also RU–486; ADOLESCENT PREGNANCY; PREGNANCY; SEX EDUCATION; BIRTH CONTROL; ADOPTION.)

abruptio placentae, a disorder in which the PLACENTA that nourishes a FETUS separates prematurely from the UTERUS wall, threatening continuation of the PREGNANCY. (See PLACENTA.)

absent parent, a parent who does not live with a child, including a parent who has lost CUSTODY of a child, a parent who has abandoned a child (see ABANDONMENT), and a FATHER who has never acknowledged paternity. Unless PARENTS' RIGHTS have been terminated, such parents retain PARENTS' RESPONSIBILITY for providing support for a child; various CHILD SUPPORT agencies spend great effort in locating them.

abused parent, an adult who was subjected to abuse as a child (see CHILD ABUSE AND NEGLECT; INCEST). Such parents are considered at higher-than-normal risk of inflicting child abuse, and many programs are designed to prevent the continuation of such a cycle of abuse.

accelerated programs, in EDUCATION, programs proceeding at a faster-than-usual pace, as when a student covers course material more quickly than usual, perhaps two years' work in one year, or skips a year's course work altogether, to take more advanced courses. In decades past, GIFTED CHILDREN commonly skipped grades, but today they more often attend faster-paced programs, often with ENRICHMENT, though in special cases they may do both. Students who finish required HIGH SCHOOL course work early, by the end of the junior year, for instance, may apply for *accelerated college entrance.* In some COLLEGES, EARLY ADMISSION policies allow some students to enter college without having completed secondary school course work. The COLLEGE ENTRANCE EXAMINATION BOARD administers a special program, the Accelerated College Enrollment Program (ACE), which allows students to take college courses on campus for credit, even before they formally leave high school and enter college.

accreditation, a citation that a school's program of studies meets established standards set by the evaluating agency, such as a state department of education, regional associations assigned to evaluate educational standards, or an association attempting to set standards in an area, as in PRESCHOOL education. Among the aspects of a school that might be examined in an accreditation evaluation are the quality of the teachers (their level of training for the subjects and age of students they are teaching), the nature of the CURRICULUM, the adequacy of the school's resources (such as classroom and other facilities, the library, and laboratory equipment), the record of the school's students on STANDARDIZED TESTS, the STUDENT-TEACHER RATIO, the school's ADMISSION requirements, and its general reputation. Parents who are sending their children to PRIVATE SCHOOLS or ALTERNATIVE SCHOOLS should look carefully at a school's accreditation as some measure of the school's educational performance. (For a parent's checklist for evaluating schools, see CHOOSING A SCHOOL FOR YOUR CHILD on page 659.) Accreditation is especially important on the COLLEGE level because, without it, a student may not be eligible for federal financial aid or be able to transfer credits to another college, if desired. (See EDUCATION.)

Accutane (isotretinoin), a prescription drug, a synthetic derivative of VITAMIN A, used to treat types of severe cystic ACNE unresponsive to other medications. Though Accutane has long been known to cause BIRTH DEFECTS, it was used by many women in the first weeks after CONCEPTION, before they realized they were pregnant. Among the defects associated with fetal exposure are HYDROCEPHALY (increase in the amount of fluid in spaces in the BRAIN), *microcephaly* (a very small head), various ear and facial abnormalities, HEART defects, and MENTAL RETARDATION. To avoid these, women are now advised to have a PREGNANCY TEST performed at least two weeks before starting Accutane therapy, to start the therapy on the second or third day of their next MENSTRUAL PERIOD, and to use two reliable forms of CONTRACEPTION simultaneously during therapy, if they do not abstain from sexual intercourse completely.

FOR HELP AND FURTHER INFORMATION

March of Dimes Birth Defects Foundation (MDBDF), 914–428–7100. Publishes information sheet *Accutane.* (For full group information, see BIRTH DEFECTS.)

National Institute of Child Health and Human Development (NICHD), 301–496–5133. (For full group information, see PREGNANCY.)

(See also ACNE; DRUG REACTIONS AND INTERACTIONS; VITAMIN A.)

achievement test, a type of educational TEST that measures how much knowledge or what level of skills a student has gained, often after specific instruction, as opposed to an APTITUDE TEST or INTELLIGENCE TEST. Test scores are often given in comparative terms, relating a student's score to widely established norms; the result is called an EDUCATIONAL AGE. Among the achievement tests commonly used in schools are the CALIFORNIA ACHIEVEMENT TESTS, IOWA TESTS OF BASIC SKILLS, METROPOLITAN ACHIEVEMENT TESTS, SEQUENTIAL TESTS OF EDUCATIONAL PROGRESS (STEP), SRA ACHIEVEMENT SERIES, STANFORD ACHIEVEMENT TESTS, TESTS OF ACHIEVEMENT AND PROFICIENCY™ (TAP), and WIDE RANGE ACHIEVEMENT TEST-REVISED. Some achievement tests are also READINESS TESTS, designed to see if a child has learned information basic to planned new learning, such as READING. (See TESTS; STANDARDIZED TESTS; EDUCATIONAL AGE; and the specific tests mentioned.)

achondroplasia, a type of BONE DISORDER that leads to abnormal GROWTH of the skull and the long bones of the arms and legs, resulting in short stature, or DWARFISM, though the trunk is closer to normal size. In achondroplasia, also called *chondrodystropy* or *fetal rickets,* the tip of the long bones, known as the *epiphysis,* is blocked from further growth because connecting cartilage prematurely turns to bone. In severe cases, this premature hardening even begins during fetal development, resulting in short, thick, often bowed arms and legs, a protruding forehead, SPINAL DISORDERS such as LORDOSIS (swayback) and KYPHOSIS (humpback), short stubby fingers widely separated between the third and fourth fingers (called *trident fingers*), and loose joints.

Many children affected by achondroplasia die in the fetal stage or in early childhood; those who survive have a nearly normal life expectancy. They have a tendency to develop EAR AND HEARING PROBLEMS from frequent ear infections, LUNG AND BREATHING PROBLEMS from constriction of the chest, TEETH AND DENTAL PROBLEMS from overcrowding, and pain and PARALYSIS in the lower body because of pressure on the spinal cord, which may require surgery. Skeletal abnormalities make the children slow to develop MOTOR SKILLS, such as walking and standing, but they generally have normal intelligence. They face formidable psychological problems, however, since neither the physical world nor the other people in it are geared to people of small and disproportionate body size.

Achondroplasia occurs in about 1 out of every 10,000 births. Many cases result from a GENETIC DISORDER of the AUTOSOMAL DOMINANT type, in which a parent carrying the defect has a 1 in 2 chance of passing it on to his or her child. But over 80 percent of the cases occur in children of parents without the disorder, the defect apparently resulting from a new mutation in either the egg (OVUM) or SPERM. How or why this happens is unclear, but older fathers are somewhat more likely to have children with the disorder.

Parents with achondroplasia will want to seek GENETIC COUNSELING when planning a PREGNANCY, but most cases cannot be anticipated and prevented. The condition can sometimes be diagnosed during pregnancy using ULTRASOUND. Treatment with HUMAN GROWTH HORMONE (hGH) is of little help for achondroplasia, but researchers are exploring other HORMONES that might act on the problematic cartilage cells as well as possible GENE THERAPY.

FOR HELP AND FURTHER INFORMATION

Human Growth Foundation (HGF), 800–451–6434. Publishes pamphlet *Achondroplasia.* (For full group information, see GROWTH AND GROWTH DISORDERS.)

Short Stature Foundation, 800–243–8273. Publishes newsletter *LPA Today* and booklet *My Child is a Dwarf.* (For full group information, see GROWTH AND GROWTH DISORDERS.)

March of Dimes Birth Defects Foundation (MDBDF), 914–428–7100. Publishes information sheet *Achondroplasia.* (For full group information, see BIRTH DEFECTS.)

National Arthritis and Musculoskeletal and Skin Diseases Information Clearinghouse (NAMSIC), 301–495–4484. (For full group information, see ARTHRITIS.)

National Institute of Child Health and Human Development (NICHD), 301–496–5133. (For full group information, see PREGNANCY.)

National Organization for Rare Disorders (NORD), 800–999–6673. (For full group information, see RARE DISORDERS.)

(See also BONE AND BONE DISORDERS; GROWTH AND GROWTH DISORDERS; HUMAN GROWTH HORMONE.)

acknowledged father, legal term for a man who has admitted or stipulated that he is the biological FATHER of a child whose BIRTH PARENTS are unmarried.

acne, an outbreak of pimples; a common, often CHRONIC type of skin disorder. The bane of adolescence, often triggered by hormonal changes, as during PUBERTY or before MENSTRUATION, acne results when the skin's oil (sebaceous) glands work overtime; in some gland ducts, dead cells and oil form a plug called a *comedo.* If the plug is below the skin's surface, it is medically a *whitehead* (*closed comedo*); if the plug emerges at the top of the duct, it is a *blackhead* (*open comedo*), the color resulting from buildup of the dark pigment called *melanin.* Acne can also be triggered by some cosmetics, chemicals, bacteria, food ALLERGIES, and DRUGS, including BIRTH CONTROL PILLS (though in some people, they act *against* acne).

A person's likelihood of getting acne seems to depend largely on GENETIC INHERITANCE, though other factors may contribute as well. One common form of acne, *acne vulgaris,* primarily affects ADOLESCENTS. A rare form, *infantile acne,* affects male infants, who are especially likely to experience acne vulgaris later on. Dermatologists recommend that patients *not* squeeze or pick at pimples, since this can injure the skin; instruments called *comedo extractors* may be used to remove them.

No cures for acne exist, but several treatments are available, including topical ointments, ANTIBIOTICS, and retinoids, a class of drugs derived from VITAMIN A, including ACCUTANE. Adolescent and adult women being treated for severe *cystic acne* need to be sure to check for possible PREGNANCY before beginning therapy, since some medications, notably Accutane, are associated with a wide range of BIRTH DEFECTS.

FOR HELP AND FURTHER INFORMATION

National Arthritis and Musculoskeletal and Skin Diseases Information Clearinghouse (NAMSIC), 301–495–4484. Publishes information package *Acne.* (For full group information, see ARTHRITIS.)

American Academy of Pediatrics (AAP), 800–433–9016. Publishes brochure *Acne Treatment and Control.* (For full group information, see HEALTH CARE.)

National Organization for Rare Disorders (NORD), 800–999–6673. Provides reprints on acne. (For full group information, see RARE DISORDERS.)

OTHER RESOURCES

Treating Acne: A Guide for Teens and Adults. Consumer Reports Books eds. and Richard A. Walzer. Consumer Reports, 1992.

Overcoming Acne: The How and Why of Healthy Skin Care. Alvin Silverstein and others. Morrow, 1990.

(See also ACCUTANE; SKIN AND SKIN DISORDERS.)

acoustic neuroma, a benign TUMOR involving the *auditory nerve,* which transmits electrical signals from the ear to the brain; also called *eighth nerve tumor, acoustic neurinoma,* or *Schwannoma.* If detected early, the tumor can be removed without hearing damage; but if diagnosed late, an acoustic neuroma (though not malignant) can be life-threatening or, when surgically removed, can at least involve hearing loss, disturbance of the sense of balance (related to the inner ear), and loss of feeling or paralysis in the face. Symptoms associated with acoustic neuromas are hearing loss in one or both ears (see EARS AND HEARING DISORDERS), ringing in the ears (*tinnitus*), headache, dizziness, and numbness in the face. Acoustic neuromas are sometimes associated with the GENETIC DISORDER called NEUROFIBROMATOSIS.

FOR HELP AND FURTHER INFORMATION

Acoustic Neuroma Association
P.O. Box 12402
Atlanta, GA 30355
404–237–8023
Fax: 404–237–8023
Linda Kees, Executive Director
Organization concerned with acoustic neuromas or other tumors of the cranial nerves; publishes various materials, including quarterly newsletter.

National Institute on Deafness and Other Communication Disorders (NIDCD), 800–241–1044. Publishes *Fact Sheet on Acoustic Neurinoma.* (For full group information, see COMMUNICATION SKILLS AND DISORDERS.)

National Organization for Rare Disorders (NORD), 800–999–6673. (For full group information, see RARE DISORDERS.)

(See also BRAIN TUMOR.)

acting out, a type of DEFENSE MECHANISM, in which a person expresses powerful inner feelings through behavior rather than words. When a child is troubled or in a stressful situation, acting out may seem disruptive, but can be a way of dealing with feelings too painful or confusing to handle otherwise.

active vocabulary, words that a child can use in his or her own speaking or writing, as opposed to the PASSIVE VOCABULARY of words he or she can recognize or understand in context in READING MATTER. Because children, like adults, understand much more than they can express, their passive vocabulary is always much larger than their active vocabulary.

activity learning, a type of LEARNING STYLE in which the child is participating fully, using various sensory modes, as in building a model or conducting an experiment, not just sitting and listening.

ACT Tests, a set of multiple-choice STANDARDIZED TESTS given to HIGH SCHOOL students, named for the American College Testing Program sponsoring it. Unlike the SCHOLASTIC APTITUDE TEST, which intends to assess a student's likely degree of success in college, the ACT tests seek to assess the level of skills attained by the student. The set of four tests covers English, mathematics, reading and scientific reasoning.

The student receives scores for the four main tests and additional subscores for seven areas within those four: under English, usage/mechanics and rhetorical skills; under mathematics, prealgebra/elementary algebra, intermediate algebra/coordinate geometry, and plane geometry/trigonometry; under reading, social studies/sciences and arts/literature. The four main tests each result in a score between 1 and 36; the seven subtests yield scores on a 1–18 scale; the scores are combined by a formula into a composite score, on a 1–36 scale. In 1995, among nearly one million high school seniors taking the ACT, the average composite score was 20.8.

Special arrangements can be made for children with DISABILITIES, such as LEARNING DISABILITIES, EAR AND HEARING PROBLEMS, and EYE AND VISION PROBLEMS, including those who are DEAF-BLIND; these may include untimed testing or use of a scribe (see SPECIAL HELP FOR SPECIAL COLLEGE STUDENTS on page 366). (See also TESTS; also HELP FOR SPECIAL CHILDREN on page 689.)

acute, a medical term indicating a condition that is of limited duration and often sharp or severe, such as a FEVER, rather than continuing or CHRONIC.

adapted education, instruction modified for children who are unlikely to be able to handle a regular school program, notably students with various DISABILITIES; more generally, it refers to instruction that has been tailored to a child's individual needs.

adaptive behavior, the range of skills needed to function normally in everyday settings, including SELF-HELP SKILLS, COMMUNICATIONS SKILLS, and SOCIAL SKILLS. Development of these skills begins in infancy, as a baby makes "contact" with and begins to communicate with those around him or her, and learns from others how to do all the things that will—years down the line—result in that baby becoming an independent person. In relation to DEVELOPMENTAL SCREENING TESTS and other tests for young children, such as the GESELL PRESCHOOL TESTS, the term "adaptive behavior" is often used to mean behavior indicating that a child can learn how to approach new tasks by watching how others do the tasks and then imitating them.

Among children with MENTAL RETARDATION, the development of adaptive behavior is vital to their functioning with relative independence as adults. A widely accepted current definition of mental retardation includes low IQ from childhood on and significant limitation in two or more adaptive skills, defined as communication, self-care, home living, social skills, leisure, health and safety, self-direction, functional academics, community use, and work. (See MENTAL RETARDATION.)

Adaptive Behavior Scale for Infants and Early Childhood (ABSI), an individually administered TEST used to evaluate the development of infants and young children, from birth to age six, by looking at general maturation, learning, and social adjustment. Using a standard interview and check sheet, a test administrator interviews a parent, teacher, or other adult close to the child. Among the areas covered by the test are independent functioning (including SELF-HELP SKILLS such as reaching and grasping, eating and drinking, toilet skills, and dressing), physical development (including both control of the body and locomotion, such as WALKING), COMMUNICATIONS SKILLS, conceptual skills (such as awareness of quantity, shapes, or time), play (types of play performed, such as SENSORIMOTOR), self-direction (including initiative and ATTENTION SPAN), and personal responsibility and socialization (such as consideration for others and personal interaction). The level of a child's skills in various areas is compared with NORMS established based on large populations. The test can be used with children who have MENTAL RETARDATION or developmental or physical DISABILITIES, and may help identify possible brain damage or other problems. (See TESTS.)

adaptive test, a test in which the sequence of questions and, to some extent, the actual questions themselves vary according to the way the student performs during the test, as opposed to traditional tests in which every student receives an identical test. An adaptive test is interactive—in the manner of a video or computer game or a children's mystery book in which the story is individualized by the reader's choices. As a student answers correctly in an adaptive test, the questions get progressively more difficult; an incorrect answer leads to an easier line of questions, designed to more clearly demonstrate the student's skills, abilities, and limitations. Questions are weighted according to their difficulty. The actual number of questions asked depends on the student's performance. In general, because of the customization, such tests are considerably shorter than their "static" counterparts; in the future, students may be able to complete in one day or less testing that presently takes several days.

Adaptive tests have been made possible by the advent of computers. Adaptive versions of the SCHOLASTIC APTITUDE TESTS are under development by the College Entrance Examination Board, and may be introduced before the year 2000. Early tests taken via the computer, such as those introduced in some graduate record examinations in the early 1990s, were essentially paper-and-pencil tests presented on screen. But adaptive versions of these examinations have been offered since 1992, and students report that they are much easier to take. Computerized adaptive tests could theoretically be given at an infinite variety of times and places (rather than on a few restricted days at a few restricted sites, as is now the case) and could produce scores immediately on completion. The customized nature of the test is also expected to give a more accurate and reliable test result.

However, students unfamiliar with computers will be at a disadvantage, at least in the first few years of this type of testing. Another disadvantage of computerized adaptive testing, at least in early versions, is that students do not have available to them some basic working methods they have been used to in paper-and-pencil tests: they can't scratch out wrong answers before deciding on the final answer in a multiple choice; they can't underline key words or sentences in text passages; and they can't go back to review previous problems, all of which help students achieve better test results. Some of these problems with adaptive tests are being addressed in later versions, however. (See also TESTS; SCHOLASTIC APTITUDE TEST.)

adenoids, two small masses of tissue in the throat above the TONSILS that act as filters in the *lymphatic system*, the network through which the body's IMMUNE SYSTEM operates. Situated near the back of the nose, adenoids generally shrink from about age five on, often disappearing by PUBERTY. But in some children, adenoids enlarge, obstructing the air passages, which causes snoring, a "nasal" voice, and breathing through the mouth; it also sometimes affects the Eustachian tube, resulting in EAR AND HEARING PROBLEMS. If a child has recurrent, severe infections, the adenoids may be removed in an *adenoidectomy*, often performed at the same time as a *tonsillectomy*. The adenoidectomy is a routine and normally very simple operation; however, on rare occasions children can experience life-threatening hemorrhages in the first week or two after the procedure. If a child shows signs of postoperative problems and does not seem to be recovering properly, parents should not hesitate to take the child back to the doctor—more than once, if necessary. (See TONSILS.)

adenoma, a TUMOR arising from a gland, usually BENIGN but capable of causing various diseases by triggering overproduction of certain HORMONES. (See TUMOR.)

adjustment disorder, a type of MENTAL DISORDER in which a person fails to adapt to a major stressful event in life, so much so that normal functioning (at home, school, or work) and social relationships are noticeably impaired. Adjustment disorders can occur at any age; among children, they often emerge around events such as DIVORCE or SEPARATION, death or serious illness in the family, loss of a job or home, and going to school. To psychiatrists, "adjustment disorder" is often referred to "maladaptive reactions" seen within three to six months of the onset of the stressful event, but that do not primarily stem from other kinds of mental disturbances. (See MENTAL DISORDERS.)

Administration for Children, Youth, and Families (ACYF), federal arm of the Department of Health and Human Services that supports social services in such areas as CHILD CARE, ADOPTION, and FOSTER CARE, especially with regard to finding temporary homes for children with SPECIAL NEEDS. This Federal office also coordinates the HEAD START program and many welfare mandates; as such, it has been the target of attacks on federal spending for social programs.

administrative procedure, a method used in administering and enforcing laws, especially those that affect benefits, including Social Security and CHILD SUPPORT. Administrative agencies—for instance those that govern child support—make orders directly rather than work through the court system. If individuals wish to protest an agency's order, ruling, or decision, they can ask for an *administrative hearing*, often held before an administrative law judge, to review the case. These hearings are less formal than court hearings—sometimes deceptively so. Witnesses may be called, but parties often have no legal representation, even though the resulting *administrative order* may have substantial effects on the persons involved. Generally, an order can be further reviewed within the agency or in court, if a parent so desires.

admission, in EDUCATION, when a student is formally accepted for enrollment in a course of study at a school, after having met the various entry requirements, such as an acceptable score on an ADMISSIONS TEST. From KINDERGARTEN to graduate school, some basic information about the student must be provided for admission, including identification and AGE (as attested by a BIRTH CERTIFICATE or BAPTISMAL CERTIFICATE). At every level beyond kindergarten, students must also provide TRANSCRIPTS of previous school work. For PRIVATE SCHOOLS and for private and public COLLEGES, students also generally need to have recommendations, as from former teachers or local community leaders.

In public schools, admissions tests are normally for SCREENING and diagnostic purposes, to help educators assess where in the school the student might fit best and to see if the student has any special learning problems to be addressed. But most private schools and colleges of any type base their admission decision at least partly the student's scores on required entrance tests. Many schools also have students fill out applications, ranging from brief to lengthy, that provide much personal information, used in the admissions decision. Some colleges today accept a common application, partly cutting down on the number of forms students must fill out.

Admissions policies of colleges and universities vary widely. Some public colleges have an *open admissions* policy, meaning they will accept any applicant (sometimes limited by state) regardless of previous academic record, sometimes including students with a GENERAL EQUIVALENCY DIPLOMA. Such nonselective policies give many students a second chance academically, but open admissions students often drop out at a high rate, unless the students have strong motivation to succeed (see DROPOUT) and the colleges have special programs to help them strengthen their basic skills. Colleges that pick and choose, on the basis of their particular requirements, among the students who apply, are said to have *selective admissions*; those that select the best-qualified applicants are said to have *competitive admissions*.

Normally, students applying for admissions send applications to colleges and universities by a specified date and hear the colleges' decisions in early spring, at which point the student decides which admission offer to accept. Under the CANDIDATES REPLY DATE AGREEMENT, sponsored by the COLLEGE ENTRANCE EXAMINATION BOARD, many colleges agree not to require students to give them a decision before May 1, the date by which students know which colleges have accepted and which have rejected them.

Some special admissions programs also exist. Under the *early decision plan*, a student can apply to an appropriate college early, usually in autumn of her or his senior year, and the college agrees to respond quickly, usually in December. The student agrees to accept admission to that school, if offered; if not offered, the student may apply to the same or other schools at the normal time, without prejudice. Some colleges have *rolling admissions*, which means that a student's application is evaluated whenever it is received and the decision communicated immediately, rather than on a set date.

For students in ACCELERATED PROGRAMS, some other options exist, including:

- EARLY ADMISSION to college before completing high school.
- Accelerated college entrance at the end of the junior year, if all high school requirements have been met.
- The ACCELERATED COLLEGE ENROLLMENT PROGRAM (ACE), which allows students to take COLLEGE courses on campus for credit, even before they formally leave high school and enter college.
- ADVANCED PLACEMENT, in which students gain college credit for work done before admission, through taking special high school courses, for instance, or passing a special examination.

(See EDUCATION; COLLEGE; PRESCHOOL; ADMISSION TEST; also HELP ON LEARNING AND EDUCATION on page 659.)

admission test, a TEST required for acceptance and ADMISSION to a particular school. An acceptable score on the SCHOLASTIC APTITUDE TEST is required of many college-bound students or a good score on the GESELL PRESCHOOL TEST may be required for entrance into a selective KINDERGARTEN or PRESCHOOL. (See ADMISSION; TESTS.)

adolescence, the stage between childhood and adulthood; a turbulent period in which the child goes through the massive set of psychological and social changes that accompany the physical changes of PUBERTY. During this period, roughly the teen years, adolescents begin to establish their own identity apart from their family and parents, to understand themselves as sexual beings with physical drives, and to begin shaping themselves as the adults they would like to be, often in imitation of local or celebrity role models.

Modern society has somewhat stacked the deck against adolescents. While in affluent Western countries, puberty is arriving sooner than in the past, adolescents are expected to postpone full adulthood ever longer, as COLLEGE is increasingly the norm. So the period during which adolescents desire and feel ready for independence but must remain dependent on their families, financially and to some extent emotionally, extends for years. For some, the result is increasingly strong rebellion against parents, schools, and other authority figures; at the other extreme, some remain dependent, indecisive, and unable to move fully into adulthood.

Adolescence is often a difficult period for parents and children both. While adolescents are experimenting and trying uncertainly to discover who they are, parents are often hurt and resentful of the adolescents' rebellion, sometimes seeing it as personal rejection. Parents also frequently disapprove of the ideas, people, and styles the adolescents are "trying on." Experts in parent-adolescent relationships stress the importance of being supportive and keeping open the lines of communication. They especially emphasize that parents should distinguish between their continuing love and respect for their adolescents and their possible disapproval of their children's behavior. Breakdown in communications can lead to escalating conflicts and, in the worst cases, to children becoming runaways or "throwaways." (See MISSING CHILDREN.)

Many psychological and social problems arise during adolescence. Some, triggered at least partly by the physical changes of puberty, include some MENTAL DISORDERS, such as SCHIZOPHRENIA. Others problems, such as ALCOHOL ABUSE, DRUG ABUSE, and ANOREXIA NERVOSA, arise from the experimentation, uncertainty, and rebellion of the teenagers, sometimes combined with peer pressure. Parents can find help in dealing with problems by looking elsewhere in this book, under the specific problem. (See GENERAL PARENTING RESOURCES on page 634.)

Adolescent and Adult Psychoeducational Profile (AAPEP), an individually administered examination used to evaluate the learning abilities of adolescents and adults with severe DISABILITIES, including AUTISM, many of them previously seen as untestable. The task-performance test, which develops a picture of the individual's strengths and weaknesses, is used as the basis for INDIVIDUALIZED EDUCATION PLANS and further plans on into adulthood. (See TESTS.)

adolescent pregnancy, pregnancy in a teenage girl, which presents special problems that affect both mother and child. In the United States today, approximately 1 out of every 8 births are by adolescent mothers. Most adolescent girls become pregnant without intending to do so. Some do not wish to keep the baby and so are faced with the difficult choice of having an ABORTION or placing the child for ADOPTION. In the past, many people have stressed that bearing the child for adoption was the better course, thinking it less traumatic for the teenage girl. However, some recent studies have indicated that having an abortion may be less traumatic for many young girls than giving up a baby to other parents, and less disruptive to their education and to their lives in general. Those who choose to bear and keep their child often fail to finish school and lack essential job skills for later in life.

Teenagers who choose to give birth face very special health problems. Often they have not yet completed their own growth, have poor NUTRITION, have used CONTRACEPTIVES around the time of CONCEPTION, take medications that can cause BIRTH DEFECTS (before knowing they are pregnant), and do not receive any PRENATAL CARE until after the crucial first TRIMESTER has passed, if then. They often also have habits dangerous to the baby (such as SMOKING, drinking alcohol, or taking drugs). As a result, they face an increased risk of high BLOOD PRESSURE, difficult LABOR, and death from complications of pregnancy (see MATERNAL MORTALITY). Their babies are more likely to be born PREMATURE and of LOW BIRTH WEIGHT, and to have increased risk of MENTAL RETARDATION, various medical problems, and INFANT MORTALITY. Parents will be wise to ensure that their sexually active teenagers are well-informed about the various methods of BIRTH CONTROL, through SEX EDUCATION at home as well as at school. A teen who does become pregnant and chooses to bear the child should be urged to seek PRENATAL CARE early, so that she and the developing baby can have the best support possible, including NUTRITION.

FOR HELP AND FURTHER INFORMATION

General organizations

Child Welfare League of America (CWLA), 202–638–2952. Publishes *Facing Teenage Pregnancy: A Handbook for the Pregnant Teen* and *That's What Drugs Took Me To ... A Story of Addiction and Teen Pregnancy* (video and discussion guide). (For full group information, see FOSTER CARE.)

March of Dimes Birth Defects Foundation (MDBDF), 914–428–7100. Publishes *Facts You Should Know About Teenage Pregnancy* and the video *Clear Vision*, on a male teen becoming pregnant. (For full group information, see BIRTH DEFECTS.)

Healthy Mothers, Healthy Babies National Coalition (HMHB), 202–863–2458. Publishes *Adolescent Pregnancy*. (For full group information, see PREGNANCY.)

Educational Equity Concepts (EEC), 212–725–1803. Publishes video *Mixed Messages: Teens Talk About Sex, Romance, Education, and Work.* (For full group information, see HELP ON LEARNING AND EDUCATION on page 659.)

National Maternal and Child Health Clearinghouse (NMCHC), 703–821–8955. Publishes *Comprehensive Adolescent Pregnancy Services: A Resource Guide.* (For full group information, see PREGNANCY.)

On prevention

National Organization on Adolescent Pregnancy, Parenting, and Prevention (NOAPP)
4421A East-West Highway
Bethesda, MD 20814
301–913–0378
Fax: 301–913–0380
Kathleen Sheeran, Executive Director
Organization concerned with teenage pregnancy and parenting; acts as advocate; publishes various materials, including quarterly *NOAPP Network Newsletter* and *Directory of Adolescent Pregnancy and Parenting Programs.*

Children's Defense Fund (CDF)
25 E Street NW
Washington, DC 20001
202–628–8787; 800–CDF–1200 [233–1200]
Fax: 202–662–3510

Black Community Crusade for Children (BCCC): 800–ASK-BCCC [275–2222]
Marian Wright Edelman, President and Founder
Organization acting as advocate for children and their rights, in such areas as child health and welfare, child care, child development, family services, and prevention of adolescent pregnancy; conducts research; assists local community groups; sponsors programs such as the Child Watch Visitation Program, the Black Community Crusade for Children (BCCC), and the Cease Fire! antiviolence campaign. Publishes monthly *CDF Reports*, BCCC quarterly newsletter *Necessary*, the annual *The State of America's Children, America's Children Falling Behind: The U.S. and the Convention on the Rights of the Child, Progress and Peril: Black Children in America, A Black Community Crusade and Covenant for Protecting Children*, state-by-state fact sheets on children's status, and numerous materials on adolescent pregnancy, such as *What About the Boys?: Teenage Pregnancy Prevention Strategies, Opportunities for Prevention: Building After-School and Summer Programs for Young Adolescents, Preventing Adolescent Pregnancy: What Schools Can Do*, and *Evaluating Your Adolescent Pregnancy Program: How to Get Started.*

Women's Action Alliance (WAA), 212–532–8330. Publishes *T.A.P.P. Sources: A National Directory for Teenage Pregnancy Prevention Programs.* (For full group information, see HELP ON LEARNING AND EDUCATION on page 659.)

American Association of University Women (AAUW), 202–785–7700. Publishes *Coping with Teen Pregnancy: Community Strategies.* (For full group information, see HELP ON LEARNING AND EDUCATION on page 659.)

Council for Exceptional Children (CEC), 800–328–0272. Publishes *Double Jeopardy: Pregnant and Parenting Youth in Special Education.* (For full group information, see HELP ON LEARNING AND EDUCATION on page 659.)

Home and School Institute (HSI), 800–634–2872. Publishes *Get Smart: Advice for Teens.* (For full group information, see HELP ON LEARNING AND EDUCATION.)

OTHER RESOURCES

FOR PARENTS AND OTHER ADULTS

Mom, I'm Pregnant: Understanding and Guiding the Teenage Mother. Teresa L. Wolff. Sulzburger and Graham, 1994.
You Can Help Pregnant and Parenting Teens. Jeanne W. Lindsay. Morning Glory, 1993.
Mom, I'm Pregnant: A Parent's Guide to the Pregnant Teen. Lovely Free-Smith and Melissa Baker. Skidmore Roth, 1991.

FOR PRETEENS AND TEENS

Promises: A Teen's Guide to Pregnancy. Ginny Brinkley and Sherry Sampson. Pink, 1993.
Pregnancy. Cathie Cush. Raintree Steck-Vaughn, 1993. Discusses the physical facts and options.
Teen Pregnancy: Why Are Kids Having Babies? Laurie Rozakis. 21st Century, 1993.
Teenage Pregnancy, rev. ed. Cathryn Jakobson. Walker, 1993.
Teen Pregnancy and Parenting Handbook. Patricia G. Mathes and Beverly J. Irby. Research Press, 1993.
Teenage Pregnancy. Gisela Meier. Marshall Cavendish, 1993.
Everything You Need to Know about Teen Pregnancy, rev. ed. Tracy Hughes. Rosen, 1992.
Kids Still Having Kids: People Talk about Teen Pregnancy. Janet Bode. Watts, 1992.
Teen Pregnancy. Judy Berlfein. Lucent, 1992.
Surviving Teen Pregnancy: Your Choices, Dreams and Decisions. Shirley M. Arthur. Morning Glory, 1991.
Facing Teenage Pregnancy: A Handbook for the Pregnant Teen. Patricia Roles. Child Welfare, 1990.
Teen Guide to Childbirth. Fern G. Brown. Watts, 1990.
Coping with an Unplanned Pregnancy. Carolyn Simpson. Rosen, 1990.

BACKGROUND WORKS

Young, Poor, and Pregnant: The Psychology of Teenage Motherhood. Judith S. Musick. Yale University Press, 1993.
Adolescent Pregnancy and Parenthood: An Annotated Guide. Ann Creighton-Zollar. Garland, 1990.

(See also PREGNANCY; SEX EDUCATION; BIRTH CONTROL; also GENERAL PARENTING RESOURCES, on page 634, under "For Teen Parents.")

adoption, taking into one's home and raising as one's own a child born to others, who are that child's BIOLOGICAL PARENTS, also called *birth parents* or *natural parents.* Formal adoption involves transfer of legal CUSTODY of a child to the adoptive parents. This procedure makes the adoptee legally part of the new family and means that the new FATHER and/or MOTHER have PARENTS' RIGHTS and PARENTS' RESPONSIBILITIES toward the adopted child. The adopted child also then legally has certain inheritance rights, under WILLS and insurance; these vary widely, however, so adoptive parents need to be sure that family legal documents—especially in such references as NEXT OF KIN, descendants, heirs of the body, born to, or issue—are changed, if necessary, to specifically include legally adopted children as well as biological children.

Although historically adoption has been arranged in a variety of ways, the standard American route in the late twentieth century has been *sealed or closed adoption,* in which adoptive parent and child are brought together by a neutral organization, generally a public or private adoption agency. The agency conducts an intensive HOME STUDY to assess the prospective parents' suitability to adopt a child and often provides counseling to adoptive and birth parents. Once the child has been placed for adoption, the BIRTH CERTIFICATE and other personal records are kept strictly confidential and are generally unavailable to biological parents, adoptive parents, or the adopted child, except by court order. The adoptive parents, the birth parents, and the child make up what are sometimes called the *adoption triangle.*

Under sealed adoption, adoptive parents learn only very general information about birth parents, such as age, race, ethnic background, religion, educational and occupational background, general medical and psychiatric history, information on intellect and personality, and some circumstances surrounding the birth and planned adoption, including whether the child is born outside marriage. Other information may be kept from adoptive parents, such as whether one or both birth parents are imprisoned or whether INCEST is involved.

Sealed adoption is intended to provide a clean break with the past, to give the child one home and family instead of a possibly confusing two, and to protect the identity of all involved. But the decision to seal adoption records has been the source of considerable dispute in recent decades. Some adoptees have made long, difficult searches to try to identify their birth parents. Conversely, some birth parents, regretting their decision to give a child up for adoption, have sought to find their children, though not all birth parents wish to be found. Various organizations (see the list that follows) have been formed to aid adopted children or birth parents in their search. Some groups maintain confidentiality of searchers, providing information only when both parties wish to be known to one another.

Aside from the desire for information about family background, people today are increasingly aware of GENETIC DISORDERS, which has also spurred the drive for more information about birth parents. Those who have been adopted need to have detailed health information on their BLOOD RELATIONS for GENETIC COUNSELING As a result, some organizations have tried to make more of such information available, while still protecting the privacy of birth parents, if desired. Some states also have laws allowing adopted people, once they become adults, to obtain certain information, though often only with the consent of the birth parents.

Some states gather extensive information on the medical and psychiatric backgrounds of the birth parents of an adopted child; in Wisconsin, for example, social workers must prepare reports on:

- The medical and genetic history of the birth parents, along with any available genetic information from them about other blood relations, such as grandparents, aunts, uncles, and brothers or sisters.
- Any medical examinations the birth parents had within the year before the proposed TERMINATION OF PARENT'S RIGHTS.
- The child's PRENATAL CARE and medical condition at birth.
- Any other information relevant to the child's medical and genetic history.

In addition, if either birth parent is found to have a genetically transferable disease, social workers are required to notify the child's adoptive parents, GUARDIAN, or (if over 18) the child.

Years after the adoption, many adopted children and birth parents desire to contact each other or other members of their family broken up through the adoption. Because of this trend, some states have opened adoption records to adult adopted children. However, allowing adopted children to view these records breaks a promise of confidentiality made to the birth parent at the time of adoption. And not all adopted children or birth parents wish to be "found." To try to partly meet the conflicting needs of those involved, some organizations (such as the International Soundex Reunion Registry, below) have established confidential mutual consent registries, where people desiring to meet can register. If both parties registered desire a meeting, a match is made and a meeting is arranged. Some states also have confidential intermediaries—trained individuals or agencies—who arrange meetings between consenting birth parents and adopted children.

Partly in response to unhappiness with traditional closed adoption, some parents and adoption professionals have, in recent decades, been experimenting with alternatives. The most popular of these is *open adoption,* in which birth parents and adoptive parents meet and get to know one another, often during the pregnancy. At its most open, the two sets of parents maintain full contact through letters, photographs, and perhaps meetings, as the child grows. In some variants, the birth and adoptive parents meet early on, but there is no exchange of full names, addresses, and phone numbers and no contact later. Alternatively, confidential exchange of letters and photographs between the adoptive parents of the child and the birth parents may be made through the adoption agency.

Adoption of older children is more likely to be open, as some have living relatives, such as a grandparent or siblings, with whom they want to stay in touch. Children adopted from abroad often want to keep in touch with family members in their homeland.

Critics of open adoption are concerned about the child being torn between two sets of parents and about changes of heart by birth parents leading to disruptive attempts to reverse the adoption. They say it was precisely the defects of historically open adoption that sealed adoption was meant to remedy.

Before the twentieth century, adoptions were mostly arranged privately, and many *private, independent,* or *direct adoptions* are still made. Often these are among relatives or friends, as when someone adopts a brother, a stepdaughter, a goddaughter, or a nephew. In other cases, would-be adopters may send out feelers among friends, acquaintances, doctors, or lawyers, or even put personal advertisements in local newspapers, seeking a child to adopt.

Such arrangements bypass traditional adoption agencies, and are especially attractive to would-be adopters who wish to shortcut the home study and adoption-agency evaluation procedure or who feel that some elements of their life-style would cause them difficulty in such a traditional adoption. Single people, older people, poor people, homosexuals, or people who already have large families, for example, often choose to adopt independently, since they have more difficulty obtaining a child for adoption through agencies, given the limited number of children available. Such private adoptions must be registered with a court to be official.

In an independent adoption, the child is normally brought to the adoptive home directly from the hospital. For the adoptive parents, the hazard is that the birth parents may reverse their decision and later remove the child, during a specified period, before the adoption becomes permanent. States have varying restrictions about independent or direct adoptions. The two sets of parents often make arrangements through a lawyer, but some states forbid intermediaries, making it mandatory for adoptive and birth parents to deal with each other directly. These legal but nontraditional adoptions are sometimes called *gray market adoptions.*

Beyond independent adoptions are illegal or *black market adoptions,* which involve payment of large amounts of money to intermediaries and to the birth parents or guardians. In the late twentieth century, in the wake of the ROE V. WADE decision on ABORTION, fewer infants have been available for adoption, so some would-be adopters have chosen to pay for babies (over and above paying the birth mother's living, medical, and legal expenses). The whole process is known as *baby brokering.* Because these adoptions are illegal, they can lead to heartbreak for all involved, as when an adoption is later contested or voided and the family torn apart.

A different alternative has developed for some adoptions that originate privately: *identified* or *designated adoption.* Here the prospective parents contact an adoption agency, which then handles the details of the adoption. These include making a home study, counseling the birth parents, obtaining adoption consent papers from the birth parents, and arranging for the adoptive parents to pay for the birth mother's living and medical expenses.

Another alternative form of adoption is *legal risk adoption* or *foster/adoption,* in which a child is placed in the home of would-be adopters on a FOSTER CARE basis while the final adoption is arranged, a process that can take months or even years, in extreme cases. This approach is designed to move children into permanent homes as quickly as possible, but can be risky for the adoptive parents, because they may end up losing the child if the birth mother or other relatives (once located) fail to sign the papers releasing the child for legal adoption.

In truth, there is no shortage of children to adopt, but many unplaced children are less attractive to would-be adopters because they are older, have siblings and the children wish to stay together, are of a different ethnic, religious, or racial background than the potential adoptive parents, or have SPECIAL NEEDS. To encourage adoption of special-needs children and other HARD-TO-PLACE CHILDREN, states have developed *adoption subsidies* or *adoption assistance plans,* partly funded by federal grants, to cover some of the costs incurred by adoptive parents, with no MEANS TEST involved. The Adoption Assistance and Child Welfare Act of 1980 (P.L. 96–272) describes such children as those who have "a specific factor or condition (such as ethnic background, age, membership in a minority or sibling group, or the presence of medical conditions, such as physical, mental, or emotional handicaps) that make it reasonable to conclude that the child could not be placed in an adoptive family without financial assistance."

Such plans may, for example, pay parents a monthly sum or cover specified medical, psychiatric, and other costs. Children receiving federal adoption assistance payments are also eligible for Medicaid benefits. Since state plans vary widely, parents who have made such a *subsidized adoption* can have difficulty continuing to receive their payments if they move from one state to another. However, some states belong to an Interstate Compact on Adoption and Medical Assistance, aimed at easing such a transition and assuring continuity of coverage.

People who wish to adopt sometimes look abroad. Such a course is long, involved, and fraught with difficulties and frustration. Each country has its own rules and regulations, usually with complicated and stringent requirements that must be met by would-be parents, and sometimes corrupt officials, as well. Questions of adoption can become entangled with those of nationalism, too, and many parents have gone almost to the end of the adoption process in a foreign country, only to find the national policy change to bar adoptions by people of other countries.

Even if prospective parents succeed in arranging to adopt a foreign child, they will find that they need to meet numerous requirements of the U.S. government, specifically the Immigration and Naturalization Service (which publishes *The Immigration of Adopted and Prospective Adoptive Children,* outlining the conditions would-be parents must meet to complete an adoption), and by the family's intended state of residence. Because the process is so complicated, various organizations (see the list of organizations that follows) have formed to pass on counsel, experience, and support. Parents are strongly advised not to "go it alone," but to work through various organizations and agencies that have some experience in foreign adoptions.

Whether at home or abroad, anyone who wishes to adopt must be prepared to handle an enormous amount of paper. ADOPTION PAPERWORK (on page 15) summarizes the main kinds of documents that must generally be gathered, often in multiple copies. Obtaining certified copies of birth, marriage, divorce, and death certificates is not always easy. The government publication *Where to Write for Vital Records: Births, Deaths, Marriages, and Divorces,* published by the Public Health Service, National Center for Health Statistics, tells where to start the process.

Parents who do adopt a child, especially an infant, may receive *adoption leave* from their employers, the equivalent of MATERNITY LEAVE, now more widely called FAMILY

Adoption Paperwork

Adoption involves an enormous amount of paperwork, both in connection with the initial home study and later to complete actual adoption applications. Most adoptions require *at least* the following documents. Some of these can take weeks or months to obtain, so prospective parents would be well advised to start the process early. Since you may need multiple copies for various applications, and often at least three copies for international adoption, you should probably order multiple copies.

BASIC DOCUMENTS FOR AN ADOPTION HOME STUDY AND APPLICATION:

- Birth certificate (certified copy)
- Marriage certificate (certified copy)
- Divorce record (certified copy)
- Death record of former spouse, if any (certified copy)
- Medical statement on physical and perhaps mental health from physician, including information on infertility (often on agency-supplied forms)
- Financial statements, such as bank statements, accountant's reports, or federal income-tax returns (notarized copies)
- Employment statements, including position, length of service, salary, stability of job.
- Birth certificates of other children, if applicable (certified copies).
- Personal autobiographies.
- Photographs of yourself, other children, and your home.
- Proof of naturalization, if applicable.
- Police files check to make sure parents have a clear police record, especially regarding child abuse (check normally performed by agency).

OTHER DOCUMENTS NEEDED FROM THE ADOPTION AGENCY OR BIRTH PARENTS

- Consent of birth parents to adoption or (if impossible) consent of GUARDIAN, NEXT OF KIN, NEXT FRIEND, or agency appointed by court.
- Medical consent giving you legal right to provide medical treatment for child.
- Petition for adoption, to be filed in state court.
- Final order of adoption from court (sometimes preceded by temporary, or interlocutory, order).
- New birth certificate for adopted child, with new name and parents.

ADDITIONAL DOCUMENTS REQUIRED FOR ADOPTION FROM OUTSIDE U.S.

- Translations of basic documents (above), notarized, verified, and authenticated at consulate of child's country.
- I–600 petition, "Petition to Classify Orphan as an Immediate Relative," to be filed with the Immigration and Naturalization Service (INS).
- I–600A, "Application for Advance Processing of Orphan Petition," to be filed with the INS before a specific child has been identified, to speed processing.
- Form FD–258, showing adoptive parents' fingerprints.
- Birth certificate (or other proof of age) of child (certified copy, with translation).
- Death certificate of child's birth parents (certified copy, with translation).
- Formal evidence of the child's surviving parent's inability to provide for child (certified copy, with translation).
- Release of the child by surviving parent, formally consenting to emigration and adoption (certified copy, with translation).
- Evidence of child's unconditional abandonment to an orphanage by parents (certified copy, with translation).
- Adoption decree (certified copy, with translation), if child was adopted abroad.
- Evidence that child has met preadoption requirements of proposed state of residence, such as posting bond.
- Passport for child.
- Alien registration for child in U.S.
- Application for readoption of child in U.S.
- Form N–402, "Application to File Petition for Naturalization in Behalf of Child," including less than 30–day-old photographs of the child or (if both adoptive parents are U.S. citizens) Form N–600, "Application for Certificate of Citizenship.
- Form G–641, "Certification of Birth Data," to act as birth certificate.

AND MEDICAL LEAVE. Even when employers are not required by the Family and Medical Leave Act to grant such leaves, some have standard maternity leave policies that also apply to adoptions. If the policy is unclear, adoptive parents may have time to "lobby" their personnel or human resources department to change the policy to cover their adoption or to make an exception for this special case. New adoptive parents also need to check beforehand to see if company or private plans, including HEALTH CARE plans, HEALTH INSURANCE, and life insurance, automatically cover an adopted child or if special arrangements must be made. They should also verify if any of the expenses associated with adoption are covered.

FOR HELP AND FURTHER INFORMATION

On adoption in general

National Adoption Information Clearinghouse (NAIC)
5640 Nicholson Lane, Suite 300
Rockville, MD 20852
301–231–6512
Fax: 301–984–8527
Organization concerned with adoption and unplanned pregnancies; provides information and referrals to adoption agencies, crisis pregnancy centers, and other support services; publishes numerous materials, including:

- general information: *Adoption—Where Do I Start?, The Adoption Home Study Process, The Value of Adoptive Parent Groups, Open Adoption, After Adoption: The Need for Services, Answers to Children's Questions About Adoption, Explaining Adoption to Your Child, Providing Background Information to Adoptive Parents, Adoption Benefits: Employers as Partners in Family Building, The Impact of Adoption on Birth Parents, Searching for Birth Relatives,* and *Adoption Laws: Answers to the Most-Asked Questions.*
- on special adoption situations: *Intercountry Adoption, Minority Adoptions, Single Parent Adoption: What You Need to Know, Foster Parent Adoption: What Parents Should Know, Transracial and Transcultural Adoption, Adoption and the African-American Child: A Guide for Parents, Military Families: New Hope for Waiting Children,* and *Issues Facing Adult Adoptees.*
- *National Adoption Directory, National Directory of Crisis Pregnancy Centers,* a catalog of audiovisual materials on adoption, copies of state laws on adoption, and other reference works and government reports.

National Council for Adoption (NCFA)
1930 Seventeenth Street NW
Washington, DC 20009
202–328–1200; Hotline 202–328–8072
Fax: 202–332–0935
William L. Pierce, Executive Director
Organization concerned with adoption; formerly National Committee for Adoption; supports confidentiality of adoption information; acts as advocate for traditional adoptions, working against private, nonstandard adoptions; provides information; publishes various materials for professionals and individuals, including *Adoption Factbook: United States Data, Issues, Regulations and Resources* and materials on search and consent laws.

American Adoption Congress (AAC)
1000 Connecticut Avenue, NW, Suite #9
Washington, DC 20036
206–483–3399
Betty Jean Lifton, Communications Contact
212–877–4086; summer: 508–349–3544
Fax: 212–873–0044; summer: 508–349–9601
Organization that acts as advocate for adoption reform; supports open records, open adoption, and family preservation; provides legislative advocacy and training, information, and referrals; publishes various materials, including quarterly newsletter *Decree* and regional newsletter.

Adoptive Family Network (AFN)
P.O. Box 7
Columbia, MD 21045–0007
301–984–6133
Jennifer L. Geipe, President
Organization of current and prospective adoptive families and adoption professionals; a MD-DC-based successor to Families Adopting Children Everywhere (FACE); offers information and support; acts as advocate; publishes quarterly *Network News,* booklet *The Adopted Child in Elementary School,* and a guide for educating teachers about adoption.

Adoptive Families of America (AFA)
3333 Highway 100 North
Minneapolis, Minnesota 55422
612–535–4829; 800–372–3300
Fax: 612–535–7808
Susan Freivalds, Director
Organization of adoptive and prospective adoptive parents; formerly OURS (Organization for United Response); acts as advocate; fosters support groups; provides information; provides grants for programs "working for children in need of permanence"; publishes various materials, including bimonthly *Adoptive Families, How-to-Adopt* information packet, and parenting resources catalog.

Child Welfare League of America (CWLA), 202–638–2952; Fax: 202–638–4004. Publishes *The Adoption Resource Guide: A National Directory of Licensed Agencies, Being Adopted* (for children), *Homeworks: At-Home Training Resources for Foster Parents and Adoptive Parents, Saying Goodbye to a Baby, A Book About Loss and Grief in Adoption* (for birth parents giving up a child for adoption), and *Adoption and Disclosure: A Review of the Law.* (For full group information, see FOSTER CARE.)

The Nurturing Network (TNN), 800–866–4666. Arranges for children to be adopted. (For full group information, see PREGNANCY.)

American Academy of Child and Adolescent Psychiatry (AACAP), 202–966–7300. Publishes information sheet *The Adopted Child.* (For full group information, see MENTAL DISORDERS.)

Center on Children and the Law, 202–662–1720. Publishes *Overcoming Barriers to Permanency: An Annotated Bibliography* and *Judicial Implementation of Permanency Planning Reforms: One Court that Works.* (For full group information, see HELP AGAINST CHILD ABUSE AND NEGLECT on page 680.)

Bethany Christian Services
800–238–4269
Internet: gopher://gopher.bethany.org/11
Pro-life organization for prospective adopters and women with unplanned pregnancies; offers counseling, housing, and other services; provides information on abortion alternatives; maintains directory of adoption-related resources.

ON ADOPTING CHILDREN FROM ABROAD

One Child at a Time
4040 Crabapple Lake Court
Roswell, GA 30076–4253
770–552–0415
Fax: 770–552–0129
Jodie Darragh, Executive Director
Organization of individuals and groups, including adoptive families, interested in aiding children abroad, especially in south and east Asia, Africa, and Latin America; formerly Americans for International Aid (AIA); assists families in arranging for adoptions; publishes quarterly newsletter.

International Social Service, American Branch (ISS/AB)
390 Park Avenue S.
New York, NY 10016
212–532–6350, ext. 323
Fax: 212–532–8558
Wells C. Klein, Executive Director
International network of social work agencies to aid families separated by national boundaries, as by migration; helps arrange for custody and care of children, reunion of family, access to services, and adoptions; represents interests of children in public discussion of international migration.

Latin America Parents Association (LAPA)
National Capital Region Chapter
P. O. Box 4403
Silver Spring, MD 20914–4403
301–431–3407
Organization for parents who have adopted a child from Latin America or who wish to; provides information and support, including seminars and workshops on Latin American culture and adoption processes; publishes newsletter.

ABOUT ADOPTION OF CHILDREN WITH SPECIAL NEEDS

National Adoption Exchange
1500 Walnut Street, Suite 701
Philadelphia, PA 19102
215–735–9988
Fax: 215–735–9410
Marlene Piasecki, Contact
Adoption referral service that seeks to match parents who have an approved home study with appropriate children, especially those who are hard to place, including siblings and children who are older, have disablilities, or are of an ethnic, religious, or racial background different from most potential adopters; provides information packets for parents, depending on their state and the type of child they wish to adopt; operates National Adoption Center; publishes newsletter.

North American Council on Adoptable Children (NACAC)
970 Raymond Avenue, Suite 106
St. Paul, MN 55104
612–644–3036
Fax: 612–644–9848
For groups of adoptive parents, especially those of hard-to-place children, and related adoption professionals and interested parties; encourages close ties between parent groups and adoption agencies, acts as clearinghouse for adoption information, and holds seminars and support programs; publishes newsletter and other materials, including *Self-Awareness, Self-Selection and Success: A Parent Preparation Guidebook for Special Needs Adoptions* and *Adopting Children with Special Needs: A Sequel.*

AASK (Adopt a Special Kid)
221 Broadway, Suite 702
Oakland, CA 94612
510–451–1748
Fax: 510–451–2023
Harriet Finck, National Director
Network of private, no-fee, full-service adoption agencies, with parent-led boards, focusing on adoption of children in the United States public welfare system; formerly AASK America (Aid to Adoption of Special Kids).

National Association for Families and Addiction Research and Education (NAFARE), 800–638–2229. Publishes brochure *Guidelines for Adopting Drug-Exposed Infants and Children,* including an explanation of risk factors and a checklist of essential information for prospective adoptive parents. (For full group information, see HELP AGAINST SUBSTANCE ABUSE on page 703.)

American Association on Mental Retardation (AAMR), 800–424–3688. Publishes *Parents for Children, Children for Parents: The Adoption Alternative.* (For full group information, see MENTAL RETARDATION.)

About adoption by people in special situations

Committee for Single Adoptive Parents (CSAP)
P.O. Box 15084
Chevy Chase, MD 20825
202–966–6367
Hope Marindin, Executive Director
Organization for current or prospective single adoptive parents; provides information and makes referrals; offers support and assistance in dealing with agencies; publishes *Handbook for Single Adoptive Parents.*

Lavender Families Resource Network, 206–325–2643, voice/TT. Publishes pamphlet *Second-Parent Adoptions for Lesbian and Gay Families, Adoption and Foster Parenting for Lesbians and Gay Men: Creating New Traditions in Family,* and *Memorandum in Support of Adoption Petition* (for second-parent adoption). (For full group information, see HOMOSEXUALITY.)

Single Mothers by Choice (SMC), 212–988–0993. Publishes resource packet on adoption. (For full group information, see General Parenting Resources on page 634.)

RESOLVE, Inc., HelpLine: 617–623–0744. Publishes fact sheets on adoption: *Overview, Parent-Initiated Adoption in the U.S.*, and *Perspectives.* (For full group information, see INFERTILITY.)

Lambda Legal Defense and Education Fund (LLDEF), 212–995–8585. Provides legal counsel for homosexuals wishing to adopt. (For full group information, see HOMOSEXUALITY.)

About later relationships between adoptees and birth parents

ALMA Society (Adoptees' Liberty Movement Association)
P. O. Box 727
Radio City Station
New York, NY 10101–0727
212–581–1568
Florence Anne Fisher, President and Founder
Organization that seeks to aid adoptees (over 18) and birth parents in finding each other; maintains ALMA International Reunion Registry Databank; works to establish adoptees legal rights to birth and adoption records; publishes newsletter *The ALMA Searchlight* and *The Official ALMA Searchers' Guide.*

Concerned United Birthparents (CUB)
2000 Walker Street
Des Moines, IA 50317
515–263–9558
Janet Fenton, President
Organization of people concerned with adoption reform; seeks to open birth and adoption records; maintains reunion registry; publishes monthly newsletter *The Communicator*; booklets *Thoughts for Birthparents Newly Considering Search, Child Abuse and Adoption, Birthparents' Perspective on Adoption, The Post Adoption Experience of Surrendering Parents, Why Won't My Birthmother Meet Me?, Uniform Adoption Act, Choices, Chances, Changes,* and *A Time for Sweeping Change: Re-examining Adoption*; and CUB papers: *Birthparents and Pride, Birthparents Searching: You Can't Have It Both Ways, Comments on Open Adoption, Adoption Abuse: The Eternal Punishment of Women, Are Adoptees Cutting Their Own Throats?*, and *On Language.*

International Soundex Reunion Registry (ISRR)
P.O. Box 2312
Carson City, NV 89702–2312
901 East 2nd Street
Carson City, NV 89701
702–882–7755
Anthony Vilardi, Registrar
Computerized system to match blood relations, registrants (over 18) who have been separated, as by adoption, foster care, divorce, or acts of war; maintains privacy of registrants, but notifies both parties if a match exists: they can agree to a reunion if mutually desired; forwards requests for confidential medical and genetic information to appropriate agencies or parties; does not perform search or give search advice.

Origins
P.O. Box 556
Whippany, NJ 07981
201–428–9683
Mary Anne Cohen, Cofounder
Organization for women whose children have been adopted by others; provides support; assists them and other relatives in searching for information about their children; publishes newsletter.

ONLINE RESOURCES

Internet: Adoption mailing list. Forum for discussion of all aspects of adoption. To subscribe, send this message "SUB adoption [your first name] [your last name]" to: mailto:listserv@think.com

Internet: Birthmother. Mailing list for women who have given up a child for adoption. To subscribe, send e-mail to: mailto:nadir@acca.nmsu.edu

Internet: Adoptees mailing list. Forum for discussion among adult adoptees. To subscribe, send e-mail to: mailto:adoptees-request@ucsd.edu

OTHER RESOURCES

For prospective parents

How to Adopt a Child: A Comprehensive Guide for Prospective Parents. Connie Crain and Jan Duffy. Nelson, 1994.
Keys to Adopting a Child. Kathy Lancaster. Barron's, 1994.
Adoption, 2nd ed. Kelly A. Sifferman. Career Press, 1994.

The Essential Adoption Handbook. Colleen Alexander-Roberts. Taylor, 1993.

Adopting Your Child: Options, Answers, and Actions. Nancy T. Reynolds. Self-Counsel Press, 1993.

Getting Ready for Adoption. Theresa McCoy. Adoption World, 1993.

The Penguin Adoption Handbook: A Guide to Creating Your New Family, rev. ed. Edmund B. Bolles. Viking Penguin, 1993.

The Adoption Resource Book, 3rd ed. Lois Gilman. HarperCollins, 1992.

The Complete Adoption Handbook. Kay M. Strom and Douglas R. Donnelly. Zondervan, 1992.

To Love a Child: Adoption, Foster Parenting, and Other Ways to Share Your Life with Children. Marianne Takas and Edward Warner. Addison-Wesley, 1992.

Adopt the Baby You Want. Michael R. Sullivan and Susan Schultz. Simon & Schuster, 1992.

How to Adopt Your Baby Privately: The Nationwide Directory of Adoption Attorneys. Christine Adamec, ed. Adoption Advocates Press, 1992.

Loving Journeys Guide to Adoption. Elaine L. Walker. Loving Journeys, 1992.

The Golden Cradle: How the Adoption Establishment Works—and How to Make It Work for You. Arty Elgart and Claire Berman. Carol, 1991.

Lifeline: The Action Guide to Adoption Search. Virgil L. Klunder. Caradium, 1991.

Adoption Choices: A Guidebook to National and International Adoption Resources. E. Paul. Visible Ink Press, 1991.

General works

Adoption: Opposing Viewpoints. Greenhaven, 1995.

The 125 Most Asked Questions about Adoption. Paul Baldwin. Morrow, 1993.

Adopting after Infertility. Patricia Irwin Johnston. Perspectives, 1992.

There Are Babies to Adopt. Christine A. Adamec. Windsor, 1991.

On special circumstances

How to Adopt Your Stepchild. Frank Zagone. Nolo Press, 1994.

Adopting or Fostering a Sexually Abused Child. Catherine Macaskill. Trafalgar, 1992.

Special-Needs Adoption: A Study of Intact Families. James A. Rosenthal and Victor K. Groze. Praeger/Greenwood, 1992.

Formed Families: Adoption of Children with Handicaps. Laraine M. Glidden. Haworth Press, 1990.

On open adoption

The Open Adoption Experience: A Complete Guide for Adoptive and Birth Families—From Making the Decision Through the Child's Growing Years. Lois R. Melina and Sharon K. Roszia. HarperCollins, 1993.

The Open Adoption Book: A Guide to Adoption Without Tears. Bruce M. Rappaport. Macmillan, 1992.

Cooperative Adoption: A Handbook, 2nd ed. Mary Jo Rillera and Sharon Kaplan. Pure, 1991.

Children of Open Adoption. Kathleen Silber and Patricia Martinez Dorner. Corona, 1990.

On international or transracial adoption

International Adoption: Sensitive Advice for Prospective Parents. Mary-Kate Murphy and Jean Knoll. Chicago Review, 1994.

How to Adopt Internationally: A Guide for Agency-Directed and Independent Adoption. Jean Nelson-Erichsen and Heino R. Erichsen. Los Ninos, 1993.

The Case for Transracial Adoption. Rita J. Simon and others. American University Press, 1993.

How to Adopt a Child from Another Country. Eileen M. Wirth and Joan Worden. Abingdon, 1993.

Transracial Adoption: Children and Parents Speak. Constance Pohl and Kathleen K. Harris. Watts, 1992.

"Are Those Kids Yours?": American Families with Children Adopted from Other Countries. Cheri Register. Free Press, 1991.

Parenting an adopted child

The Whole Life Adoption Book: Realistic Advice for Building a Healthy Adoptive Family. Jayne Schooler. Pinon Press, 1993.

Real Parents, Real Children: Parenting the Adopted Child. Holly Van Gulden and Lisa M. Bartels-Rabb. Crossroad, 1993.

Talking with Young Children about Adoption. Mary Watkins and Susan M. Fisher. Yale University Press, 1993.

Communicating with the Adopted Child. Miriam Komar. Walker, 1991.

For children

Tell Me a Real Adoption Story. Betty Jean Lifton. Knopf, 1994.

Did My First Mother Love Me?: A Story for an Adopted Child. Kathryn M. Miller. Morning Glory, 1994. Includes "Talking with Your Child About Adoption."

My Special Family: A Children's Book about Open Adoption. Kathleen Silber and Debra M. Parelskin. Open Adoption, 1994.

Adoption Stories for Young Children. Randall B. Hicks. Wordslinger, 1994.

Why Didn't She Keep Me: The Question Every Adopted Child Asks. Barbara Burlingham-Brown. Langford/Diamond Communications, 1993.

Adoption Controversies. Karen Liptak. Watts, 1993.

Zachary's New Home: A Story for Foster and Adopted Children. Geraldine M. Blomquist and Paul B. Blomquist. Gareth Stevens, 1993.

Adoption. Fred Rogers. Putnam, 1993.

A Forever Family: A Book About Adoption. Roslyn Banish. HarperCollins, 1992.

Steven's Baseball Mitt: A Book about Being Adopted. Kathy Stinson. Annick/Firefly, 1992.
A Family for Jamie: An Adoption Story. Suzanne Bloom. Clarkson Potter/Crown, 1991.
Oliver: A Story About Adoption. Lois Wickstrom. Our Child Press, 1991.
Families Are Different. Nina Pellegrini. Holiday, 1991.

For preteens or teens

Mario's Big Question: A Child's Guide to Adoption. Carolyn Nystrom. Lion, 1994.
Where Are My Birth Parents?: A Guide for Teenage Adoptees. Karen Gravelle and Susan Fischer. Walker, 1993.
Adopted from Asia: How It Feels to Grow up in America. Frances M. Koh. EastWest Press, 1993.
What My Sister Remembered. Marilyn Sachs. Dutton, 1992.

On searches and reunions for birth parents and adoptees

The Adoption Searchers' Handbook: A Guidebook for Adoptees, Birth Parents and Others Involved in the Adoption Search. Norma Tillman. Diane, 1994.
Birthright: The Guide to Search and Reunion for Adoptees, Birthparents, and Adoptive Parents. Jean A. Strauss. Viking Penguin, 1994.
Adoption Reunions: A Book for Adoptees, Birthparents and Adoptive Families. Michelle McColm. InBook, 1993.
Search: A Handbook for Adoptees and Birthparents, 2nd ed. Jayne Askin with Molly Davis. Oryx Press, 1992.
Birth Mother Search: Some Day I'll Find Her. E. B. Schumacher and others. Larksdale, 1992.
The Adoption Searchbook: Techniques for Tracing People, 3rd ed. *Adoption Encounter: Hurt, Transition, Healing.* Mary J. Rillera. Pure, 1991.
Lifeline: The Action Guide to Adoption Search. Virgil L. Klunder. Caradium, 1991.

Personal stories of adoptees and adoptive families

So Here I Am! But Where Did I Come From?: An Adoptee's Search for Identity. Mary R. Wotherspoon. Pate, 1994.
Dialogues about Adoption: Conversations Between Parents and Their Children. Linda Bothun, ed. Swan, 1994.
Gift Children: A Story of Race, Family, and Adoption in a Divided America. J. Douglas Bates. Ticknor and Fields, 1993.
Second Choice: Growing Up Adopted. Robert Andersen. Badger Hill, 1993.
Stories of Adoption: Loss and Reunion. Eric Blau. NewSage Press, 1992.
An Adopted Son: The Story of My Life. Norman Anderson. InterVarsity, 1991.
Letters to My Birthmother: An Adoptee's Diary of Her Search for Her Identity. Amy E. Dean. World Almanac, 1991.
I Wish You Didn't Know My Name: The Story of Michele Launders and Her Daughter Lisa. Michele Launders and Penina Spiegel. Warner, 1990.

Personal stories of birth parents of adopted children

Giving Away Simone: A True Story of Daughters, Mothers, Adoption, and Reunion. Jan L. Waldron. Times Books, 1995.
To Prison with Love: The True Story of Sandy Musser's Indecent Indictment and America's Adoption Travesty. Sandra K. Musser. Adoption Awareness Press, 1995. Author of *I Would Have Searched Forever* (1979).
A Crying Shame: A Moving, True Story of One Mother's Life-long Unwavering Love for the Son She Was Forced to Surrender to Adoption. Carol J. Tieman. Sleepy Hollow, 1994.
Birthmothers: Women Who Have Relinquished Babies for Adoption Tell Their Stories. Merry B. Jones. Chicago Review, 1993.
Shattered Dreams—Lonely Choices: Birthparents of Babies with Disabilities Talk about Adoption. Joanne Finnegan. Bergin & Garvey/Greenwood, 1993.
Letter to Louise: The Story of the Daughter She Gave for Adoption More Than Twenty-Five Years Ago. Pauline Collins. HarperCollins, 1992.
The Other Mother: A Woman's Love for the Child She Gave Up for Adoption. Carol Schaefer. Soho Press, 1991.
Wanted: First Child: A Birth-Mother's Story. Rebecca Harsin. Fithian Press, 1991.

Background works

The Journey of the Adopted Self: A Quest for Wholeness. Robert J. Lifton and Betty J. Lifton. Basic, 1994. Betty Lifton also wrote *Lost and Found: The Adoption Experience,* rev. ed. (1988) and the classic *Twice Born: Memoirs of an Adopted Daughter* (1977).
Adoption Crisis: The Truth Behind Adoption and Foster Care. Carole A. McKelvey and JoEllen Stevens. Fulcrum, 1994.
Being Adopted: The Lifelong Search for Self. David M. Brodzinsky and others. Doubleday, 1993.
Family Bonds: Adoption and the Politics of Parenting. Elizabeth Bartholet. Houghton Mifflin, 1993.
The Adoption Life Cycle: The Children and Their Families Through the Years. Elinor B. Rosenberg. Free Press, 1992.
Encyclopedia of Adoption. Christine A. Adamec and William Pierce. Facts on File, 1991.

adrenal glands, a pair of small glands that sit on top of the kidneys (ad + renal). The outer part (the *adrenal cortex)* produces a variety of HORMONES, including STEROIDS and some male sex hormones; the inner part (*adrenal medulla*) acts as part of the NERVOUS SYSTEM, responding to stress by producing other hormones, including *adrenaline,* which readies the body for action.

Among the disorders that may affect the adrenal gland in young people are:

- *Adrenogenital syndrome (congenital adrenal hyperplasia)*, in which the adrenal glands are unable to produce sufficient hormones. This may result in FAILURE TO THRIVE and sometimes causes development of male sex attributes in female babies. It is treated with administration of hormones.
- TUMORS, which can cause excess production of *hydrocortisone*. This may result in *Cushing's syndrome*, which involves wasting muscles, OBESITY, and excess male sex hormones in both sexes. In adults, these can lead to INFERTILITY.
- AUTOIMMUNE DISORDERS, in which the body mistakenly attacks its own tissue in the adrenal glands, leading to *Addison's disease*, a rare disorder in children. In CHRONIC form, this can lead to weight loss, weakness, and darkened skin. But in ACUTE form, the disease, if untreated, may result in confusion, COMA, and death.

Among the MEDICAL TESTS used to diagnose adrenal gland disorders are BLOOD TESTS or URINE TESTS, testing for hormone levels, and various SCANS, such as CT SCANS.

FOR HELP AND FURTHER INFORMATION

National Cushing's Association
4645 Van Nuys Boulevard, Suite 104
Sherman Oaks, CA 91403
818–788–9235; 818–788–9239
Andrea Hecht, President
Organization concerned with Cushing's syndrome; provides referrals; publishes various materials, including brochure *Cushing's Syndrome.*

National Kidney and Urologic Disease Information Clearinghouse (NKUDIC), 301–654–4415. (For full group information, see DIGESTIVE SYSTEM AND DISORDERS.)

National Institute of Child Health and Human Development (NICHD), 301–496–5133. (For full group information, see PREGNANCY.)

advance directive, a general term for oral or written instructions specifying a person's wishes regarding future HEALTH CARE, such as accepting or rejecting certain kinds of treatment. It is designed to go into effect only in the event that the individual is unconscious or unable to communicate, and (depending on state law) sometimes only at the end of life. The two best-known forms of advance directives are the *living will* and the *durable power of attorney for health care*, more popularly called a *health care proxy.*

Under a durable power of attorney for health care, the person empowered to make medical decisions on another's behalf is called a *health care agent, proxy, surrogate,* or *attorney-in-fact.* The actual legal details vary state by state (see Choice in Dying, under DEATH AND DYING, for information); in some cases, the proxy is only activated at the end of life, but in many states the person can act at any time you are unable to make those decisions yourself, such as if you are unconscious or in a coma.

A living will, on the other hand, concerns medical treatment for people who are dying. By law, an individual has the right to refuse medical treatment, such as artificial NUTRITION and hydration, and use of a VENTILATOR (respirator); the living will takes effect only if they are unable to communicate their wishes. Again, the legal details vary from state to state as to when the living will takes effect and which types of treatment it covers.

Since the passage of the 1991 Patient Self-Determination Act (PSDA), health care facilities receiving Medicare or Medicaid funds have been required to inform patients of their right to refuse medical treatment and to sign advance directives.

FOR HELP AND FURTHER INFORMATION

Choice in Dying, 800–989–9455. Publishes *You and Your Choices, Advance Directives,* and *Advance Directives and End-of-Life Decisions.* (For full group information, see DEATH AND DYING.)

National Kidney Foundation (NKF), 800–622–9010. Publishes *Advance Directives: A Guide for Patients and Their Families,* advance directive checklists, and other materials. (For full group information, see KIDNEY AND UROLOGICAL DISORDERS.)

OTHER RESOURCES

Living Wills and Wills. Harold Goldfluss. Random House, 1994.

The Living Will and Other Life-and-Death Medical Choices. Joseph E. Beltran. Nelson, 1994.

Take Control of Your Own Health Care Decisions: A State by State Guide to Preparing Your Living Will and Appointing Your Health Care Agent, with Forms. Phillip Williams. P. Gaines, 1994.

Advance Directives and the Pursuit of Death with Dignity. Norman L. Cantor. Indiana University Press, 1993.

You Decide: Using Living Wills and Other Advance Directives to Guide Your Treatment Choices. Evelyn J. Van Allen. Irwin, 1993.

Planning for Uncertainty: A Guide to Living Wills and Other Advance Directives for Health Care. David J. Doukas and William Reichel. Johns Hopkins, 1993.

Decide for Yourself: Life Support, Living Will, Power of Attorney for Health Care. Carolyn Brown and others. Pritchett and Hull, 1993.

Final Passages: Positive Choices for the Dying and Their Loved Ones. Judith Ahronheim and Doron Weber. Simon & Schuster, 1992.

To Live and Die with Dignity: A Guide to Living Wills. Samuel L. Peluso. Vista, 1991.

The Living Will Handbook: The Right to Decide Your Own Fate. Alan D. Lieberson. Hastings, 1991.

The Essential Guide to a Living Will: How to Protect Your Right to Refuse Medical Treatment. B. D. Colen. Prentice Hall, 1991.

Easing the Passage: Medical and Legal Steps, Including "the Living Will," to Guarantee a Tranquil and Pain-Free Death for Yourself and Loved Ones. David E. Outerbridge and Alan R. Hersh. HarperCollins, 1991.

Write Your Own Living Will. Bradley E. Smith and Jess M. Brallier. Crown, 1991.

advanced placement, in EDUCATION, granting a student a position higher than that of most entrants, usually after demonstration of proficiency in some aspects of course work; also called *advanced standing*. In one common type of advanced placement, students receive college credit for passing set examinations, such as those offered under the ADVANCED PLACEMENT PROGRAM, COLLEGE-LEVEL EXAMINATION PROGRAM, or PROFICIENCY EXAMINATION PROGRAM. Students who transfer to a new school receive advanced placement on the basis of their work at their old school. Some students, especially adults returning to college, can gain either college credit or waivers for required basic courses, if they have gained special knowledge on their own; this is sometimes called *experiential learning* or *life-experience credit*.

Advanced Placement Program (APP), national program operated by the COLLEGE ENTRANCE EXAMINATION BOARD, under which HIGH SCHOOL students take college-level courses in high school and, if they pass set examinations, are granted college CREDIT in those subjects, for ADVANCED PLACEMENT.

advocacy, actions designed to obtain something, such as services, payments, or rights, for another person; when an individual is acting on his or her own behalf, it is called *self-advocacy*. Advocacy is a major but rather unsung movement that has developed in the last few decades and has accelerated in the last few years. As public and private bureaucracies have grown, individuals have had to develop skills to obtain information, help, and support to meet their needs.

Many individuals have banded together to form advocacy and support groups, such as those described in this book. These organizations act as advocates for a general purpose, such as obtaining insurance coverage for a particular medical procedure or attempting to pass a law guaranteeing rights to people with DISABILITIES. These groups also provide information for individuals who act as advocates, such as parents acting on behalf of their children or others acting on their own behalf. A number of these organizations have developed expertise not only on the specific topic they focus on—such as EDUCATION, EPILEPSY, or MENTAL RETARDATION—but also in advocacy itself, providing parents with the tools they need to establish their own local support and advocacy groups.

The federal government has also recognized the need for and the importance of advocacy, especially for children with special needs. Under various federal laws, Protection and Advocacy (P&A) organizations, staffed primarily by lawyers and social workers, have been established to protect the civil rights of people with MENTAL DISORDERS, MENTAL RETARDATION, and other DISABILITIES, and to ensure that they—and their families—get the legal aid, information, referrals, and advocacy services to which they are entitled. Federally funded but independently operated, a P&A agency is found in every state.

The courts have also recognized the need of advocates to act on behalf of a child in certain situations. A COURT APPOINTED SPECIAL ADVOCATE (CASA), sometimes also called *guardian ad litem* (see GUARDIAN), is a specially trained volunteer who will represent the interests of the child in certain types of court cases. In cases of contested DIVORCE, for example, a CASA may be appointed to speak for the child's interests, which are not the same as those of either the mother or the father. A CASA may also be appointed for a child in a case of CHILD ABUSE AND NEGLECT or FOSTER CARE, and sometimes in judicial or administrative hearings in which no parent or GUARDIAN is available to speak for the child, such as when an INDIVIDUALIZED EDUCATION PLAN is being developed for a child with SPECIAL NEEDS.

But in most cases, whatever other advocates and support groups might be available, the parent must act as an advocate for a child—indeed, in our modern society, that has become part of the definition of the role of parent. This is especially so when children have DISABILITIES or other special needs. The EDUCATION FOR ALL HANDICAPPED CHILDREN ACT and its successor, the INDIVIDUALS WITH DISABILITIES EDUCATION ACT, call for evaluation and assessment of a child's needs from an early stage on.

The parent is involved from the start as part of the social service team that decides what kinds of evaluation or testing are needed and desired. If special needs are found, the team shapes the Individualized Education Plan (IEP), which outlines the educational and other services to be provided for the child, a plan that is periodically reevaluated as the child grows. If the plan is not properly implemented, if the parent disagrees with the plan, or if the plan does not work but fails to be changed, the parent may need to become a strong advocate for the child through various appeals. In many such cases, the parent is advised to bring in a trained advocate for technical advice and support during the appeals process.

Similarly, parents may find themselves needing to become strong advocates in obtaining HEALTH CARE and HEALTH INSURANCE benefits they feel are due to the child and family. In this case (as in so many others), a good offense may be the best defense—meaning it is wise to know your rights and entitlements before you engage in any discussion or confrontation with HOSPITAL or insurance company staff. Make informed health care and insurance choices; know beforehand what is covered and what is not; and have trained advocates with you if you need to fight for medical care or coverage. (For more on this, see HEALTH CARE; HEALTH INSURANCE; also WHAT DO YOU NEED TO ASK ABOUT HEALTH INSURANCE AND MANAGED CARE? on page 288.)

Parents of children with disabilities will need to educate their children to become advocates on their own behalf as they move into adulthood and beyond parental care. Again, many of the organizations in this book are extremely useful in helping such children gradually assume self-advocacy; indeed, some large organization have special affiliates for young people moving into adulthood, providing them with mutual support and guidance.

Parents of children with severe disabilities that will make them dependent into adulthood need to take a different route, often by appointing someone to be a GUARDIAN to act as advocate for the child if the parent has died or is for some reason not available or unable to act, as during cases of serious illness.

FOR HELP AND FURTHER INFORMATION

GENERAL ORGANIZATIONS

Children's Defense Fund (CDF), 800–233–1200. Publishes *A Parent's Guide to Child Advocacy, Your Family's Rights Under the New Fair Housing Law: Protecting Families with Children from Discrimination, Information for Action: An Advocate's Guide to Using Maternal and Child Health Data, Welcome the Child: A Child Advocacy Guide for Churches* (book and video), rev. ed., and a series of "Advocate's Guides." (For full group information, see ADOLESCENT PREGNANCY.)

Family Resource Coalition (FRC), 312–341–0900. Publishes *Starting and Operating Support Groups: A Guide for Parents.* (For full group information, see GENERAL PARENTING RESOURCES on page 634.)

Child Care Action Campaign (CCAC), 212–239–0138. Publishes *How to Advocate for Child Care: A Guide for Parents, Speaking with Your Employer About Child Care Assistance,* and materials on community action. (For full group information, see CHILD CARE.)

Center for Law and Education, 202–986–3000. Publishes "Information for Parents" brochure, *Parents Organizing,* and various works on advocacy in the school system. (For full group information, see HELP ON LEARNING AND EDUCATION on page 659.)

National Black Child Development Institute (NBCDI), 800–556–2234. Publishes the periodical *Black Child Advocate, Child Care Power,* and a series of "Community Empowerment Workbooks." (For full group information, see HELP ON LEARNING AND EDUCATION on page 659.)

National Association for the Education of Young Children (NAEYC), 800–424–2460. Publishes book *Speaking Out: Early Childhood Advocacy* and brochure *Building Principles for the Development, Analysis, and Implementation of Early Childhood Legislation.* (For full group information, see PRESCHOOL.)

Parent Care (PC), 317–872–9913. Publishes *Strategies: A Practical Guide for Dealing with Professionals and Human Service Systems, Peer Support Training Manual,* and *Developing Parent Support Programs: A How-to Guide.* (For full group information, see PREMATURE.)

Center on Children and the Law, 202–662–1720. Publishes *Lawyers for Children, A Review of Bar Sponsored Child Advocacy Projects, Establishing Ombudsman Programs for Children and Youth: How Government's Responsiveness to Its Young Citizens Can Be Improved,* and *Children's Rights in America: U.N. Convention on the Rights of the Child Compared with United States Law.* (For full group information, see HELP AGAINST CHILD ABUSE AND NEGLECT on page 680.)

National Mental Health Association (NMHA), 800–969–6642. Publishes pamphlet *Your Rights to Housing: A Consumer's Guide to the Fair Housing Act of 1988.* (For full group information, see MENTAL DISORDERS.)

American Adoption Congress (AAC), 206–483–3399. Provides legislative advocacy and training. (For full group information, see ADOPTION.)

Parents Without Partners (PWP), 800–637–7974. Publishes brochure *Single Parents and Legislative Action.* (For full group information, see GENERAL PARENTING RESOURCES on page 634.)

ON ADVOCACY FOR SPECIAL NEEDS

PACER Center (Parent Advocacy Coalition for Educational Rights), 612–827–2966, voice/TT. Publishes *How to Get Services by Being Assertive, How to Organize an Effective Parent Advocacy Group and Move Bureaucracies, Speak Up for Health Parent Handbook, Speak Up for Health: Training Package for Adolescents with Developmental Disabilities;* brochures *Effective Advocacy: Guidelines to Help Parents Help their Children* and *Basic Rights Workshop,* and other materials. (For full group information, see HELP FOR SPECIAL CHILDREN on page 689.)

Center on Human Policy (CHP), 315–443–3851. Publishes numerous materials on Self-Determination and advocacy reports *Negotiation: A Tool for Change* and *Principles of Whistleblowing.* (For full group information, see HELP FOR SPECIAL CHILDREN on page 689.)

National Association for Gifted Children (NAGC), 202–785–4268. Publishes *Advancing Gifted and Talented Education: An Educator and Parent Guide to Advocacy.* (For full group information, see GIFTED CHILD.)

National Mental Health Consumer Self-Help Clearinghouse, 800–553–4539. Publishes *Nuts and Bolts: A Technical Assistance Guide for Mental Health Consumer/Survivor Self-Help Groups;* pamphlets *Getting Money for Your Self-Help Group, How to Develop a Consumer-Run Newsletter, How to Start a Self-Help/Advocacy Group,* and *Making Our*

Voices Heard; and reprints on self-advocacy. (For full group information, see MENTAL DISORDERS.)

National Mental Health Association (NMHA), 800–969–6642. Publishes *Hope Is Not Enough: A Guide for Becoming an Advocate for Children's Mental Health Services, Organizing a Self-Help Advocacy Group for Children and Adolescents with Severe Emotional Problems: A Working Manual, Protection and Advocacy for Mentally Ill Individuals Act—As Amended Through 1992*, and *Operation Help: A Mental Health Advocate's Guide to Medicaid.* (For full group information, see MENTAL DISORDER.)

The Arc, 817–261–6003. Publishes *The Self-Advocacy Movement, Directory of Self-Advocacy Programs, Building Self-Advocacy in the Community, A Call to Action: The Roles of People with Mental Retardation in Leadership, Self-Advocacy/ Supporting the Vision* (video), and *The ADA Training Program for Self-Advocates, A Simplified Training on Titles II and III of the Americans with Disabilities Act.* (For full group information, see MENTAL RETARDATION.)

National Information Center for Children and Youth with Disabilities (NICHCY), 800–695–0285, voice/TT. Publishes *Accessing Parent Groups, Planning a Move, Mapping Your Strategy, Technical Assistance Guide: Operating a Local Information and Referral Center*, and *Special Education and Related Services: Communicating Through Letter Writing.* (For full group information, see HELP FOR SPECIAL CHILDREN on page 689.)

American Association on Mental Retardation (AAMR), 800–424–3688. Publishes *The Self-Advocacy Movement by People with Developmental Disabilities: A Demographic Study and Directory of Self-Advocacy Groups in the United States.* (For full group information, see MENTAL RETARDATION.)

Epilepsy Foundation of America (EFA), 800–332–1000. Publishes "Speaking Out: Partners in Advocacy" series: *Understanding the Process, Tools and Resources*, and *Family Action Guide.* (For full group information, see EPILEPSY.)

Rural Institute on Disabilities, 800–732–0323, voice/TT. Publishes *A Guide to Writing Letters to Public Officials: Contributing to Important Decisions Affecting You and Others.* (For full group information, see HELP FOR SPECIAL CHILDREN on page 689.)

Council for Exceptional Children (CEC), 800–328–0272. Publishes *Supporting Gifted Education Through Advocacy, CEC Special Education Advocacy Handbook*, and *Preparation for Special Education Hearings: A Practical Guide for Lessening the Trauma of Due Process Hearings.* (For full group information, see HELP ON LEARNING AND EDUCATION on page 659.)

National Federation of the Blind (NFB), 410–659–9314. Publishes *Blind Parents and the Courts, Legalized Kidnapping: State Takes Child Away from Blind Mother, Let's Hear It for Benign Neglect: The Cheadles Fight the System for the Right to Have Their Son Learn Braille*, and *A Federation Victory: Blind Parent Wins Unrestricted Child Care License.* (For full group information, see EYE AND VISION PROBLEMS.)

National Fragile X Foundation, 800–688–8765. Publishes *Ways to Build a Self-Help Group* and *Fighting for a School Program for a Child with Fragile X.* (For full group information, see FRAGILE X SYNDROME.)

National Institute of Child Health and Human Development (NICHD), 301–496–5133. Publishes research report *Learning Disabilities, Advocacy, Science and the Future of the Field.* (For full group information, see PREGNANCY.)

National Clearinghouse on Child Abuse and Neglect Information (NCCAN), 800–394–3366. Publishes annotated bibliography on abuse in *Foster Care.* (For full group information, see HELP AGAINST CHILD ABUSE AND NEGLECT on page 680.)

ON LEGAL CONCERNS

National Court Appointed Special Advocates Association (National CASA Association, or NCASAA)
2722 Eastlake Avenue, East, Suite 220
Seattle, WA 98102
206–328–8588; 800–628–3233
Fax: 206–323–8137
Michael S. Piraino, Chief Executive Officer
Organization of court appointed special advocates (CASAs); provides training; publishes quarterlies *CASA Connection* and *Feedback*, semiannual directory, and *NCASAA Communications Manual.*

Lavender Families Resource Network, 206–325–2643, voice/TT. Maintains volunteers to act as child advocates or guardians *ad litem* in custody disputes. (For full group information, see HOMOSEXUALITY.)

National Center on Child Abuse and Neglect (NCCAN), 202–205–8586; Fax: 202–260–9351. Publishes annotated bibliography *Child Advocacy.* (For full group information, see HELP AGAINST CHILD ABUSE AND NEGLECT on page 680.)

National Legal Resource Center For Child Advocacy and Protection, 202–331–2200. (For full group information, see HELP AGAINST CHILD ABUSE AND NEGLECT on page 680.)

C. Henry Kempe National Center for the Prevention and Treatment of Child Abuse and Neglect, National Association of Counsel for Children, 303–322–2260. Provides training for child advocates; publishes newsletter *The Guardian.* (For full group information, see HELP AGAINST CHILD ABUSE AND NEGLECT on page 680.)

National Center for Women and Family Law, 212–674–8200. Publishes *Guide to Interstate Custody: A Manual for Domestic Violence Advocates*, 2nd ed. and *Media-*

tion—A Guide for Advocates and Attorneys Representing Battered Women. (For full group information, see CUSTODY.)

OTHER RESOURCES

For parents

Your Child and Health Care: A "Dollars & Sense" Guide for Families with Special Needs. Lynn Robinson Rosenfeld. Paul H. Brookes, 1994.

How to Organize Prevention: Political, Organizational and Professional Challenges to Social Services. Hans-Uwe Otto and Gaby Flosser, eds. De Gruyter, 1992.

Turning the Tide: How to Be an Advocate for the ADD—ADHD Child. Karen K. Richards and John Leoter. Media Publications, 1992.

Attention Deficit Disorder and the Law—A Guide for Advocates. Peter S. Latham and Patricia S. Latham. JKL Communications, 1992.

On child advocates

I Speak for This Child: The True Stories of a Child Advocate. Gay Courter. Crown, 1995.

Who Speaks for the Children?: The Handbook of Individual and Class Child Advocacy. Jack C. Westman, ed. Pro Resource, 1991.

Advocating for the Child in Protection Proceedings: A Guide for Child Advocates. Donald N. Duquette. Free Press, 1990.

(See also COURT APPOINTED SPECIAL ADVOCATE; GUARDIAN; also organizations under specific concerns.)

affect, a psychological term for face, vocal, and body behaviors that express felt emotion, such as sadness, euphoria, or anger. The type of expressive behavior found in most of the population, regarded as "normal," is called a *broad affect.* However, people with MENTAL DISORDERS often have a narrower range of facial expression, pitch, or voice, and hand and body movements becomes gradually lessened. These are described and ranked in stages from *restricted* or *constricted affect* to *blunt affect* and finally to *flat affect,* in which the voice is a monotone and the face and body are virtually immobile. People who show abrupt mood swings are said to have *labile affect,* while those who exhibit behavioral expression that clashes with the situation (as when a child laughs while in great pain) are said to have *inappropriate affect.*

affective domain, one of three key categories of instructional content and learning objectives described by Benjamin Bloom, referring to feelings, emotions, values, and attitudes. (See DOMAIN.)

affinity, a formal term for the family relationships created by marriage, as with one's father-in-law or sister-in-law.

afterbirth, popular name for PLACENTA, the organ literally expelled from the UTERUS after CHILDBIRTH.

after-born, the legal designation for a child born after the death of its birth parent; also a child born after the signing of a parent's will. Even if not specifically covered in a parent's will, an after-born child in most states is entitled to a share in that parent's property, unless the parent is shown to have intended to give the child nothing.

against medical advice (AMA), actions contrary to a physician's orders. In cases of possible CHILD ABUSE AND NEGLECT, this may mean removing a child from the hospital without medical consent. A woman with a HIGH-RISK PREGNANCY who fails to heed medical cautions about her life-style may also be said to be going against medical advice.

age, in the simplest terms, the number of years in a person's life, called the *chronological age,* as measured from a birthdate, often attested to on a BIRTH CERTIFICATE or other acceptable certificate. But in education, psychology, medicine, law, statistics, and many other disciplines, a variety of other special definitions of *age* have emerged, some reflecting laws relating to age. Among these are:

- COMPULSORY SCHOOL AGE, the starting and ending ages between which a child is required to attend school; the specifics ages vary, but are usually between about six and sixteen.
- AGE OF CONSENT, the age at which a person can legally marry without obtaining consent from a parent or GUARDIAN.
- *Voting age,* the age at which a person can vote as a citizen.
- *Age of* MAJORITY, the age at which a MINOR becomes an adult for legal purposes; it varies, according to law, but is often around age 18.
- *Age of onset,* the age at which a disease or DISABILITY first appeared or was recognized.
- *Anatomical age,* the relationship between a child's growth and the statistical average age for a child of the same size; if a child of six has a degree of skeletal maturation normally seen in a seven-year-old, that child's anatomical age is seven. Similarly, a child's *grip age* would reflect a child's maturity in MOTOR SKILLS involving gripping; *dental age* would reflect the maturity of TEETH and jaw formation; and so on.

Definitions of age involving comparison of a person's growth or performance to some standard are also widely used in education. The EDUCATIONAL AGE (EA) reflects how the child's score relates to a wide range of other scores on an ACHIEVEMENT TEST; if an eight-year-old child's score is the score normally achieved by children half a year older, that child's educational age will be eight years, six months. That general type of comparison is called an *age equivalent, age norm,* or *developmental age,* and is used in many areas in education.

A child's MENTAL AGE (MA) reflects comparative performance on a mental ability or INTELLIGENCE TEST, while *reading age* reflects a child's performance on READING tests as compared to established norms. The highest age at which a child is consistently able to correctly answer all the items on a STANDARDIZED TEST is called the *basal age.* Sometimes a whole range of age comparisons—including educational, mental, dental, carpal (wrist), height, weight, social—are averaged together to give a child's *organismic age.*

age-appropriate, a general term describing skills, activities, toys, and behavior that are considered appropriate for a child of a certain age. The term sometimes refers to CHRONOLOGICAL AGE and sometimes to DEVELOPMENTAL AGE. (See also AGE.)

age-eligible, refers to a child who is eligible to enter school on the basis of CHRONOLOGICAL AGE, measured from the birthdate. With increasing use of DEVELOPMENTAL SCREENING TESTS, some children who are age-eligible may be barred from school or their parents may be advised not to enter them into KINDERGARTEN if their DEVELOPMENTAL AGE is considered too low. They will, of course, enter school in any case when they reach COMPULSORY SCHOOL AGE, but may be placed in special READINESS CLASSES or *transition programs.* Alternatively, some schools choose to enter the child with the regular class, sometimes planning to HOLD BACK the child another year, if necessary. On a few occasions, parents have successfully gone to court to have their age-eligible child allowed to enter kindergarten over the school's protest.

age equivalent, general term for a numerical summary expressing a student's general development by comparison with average scores for other students, using the same or similar TESTS, such as EDUCATIONAL AGE, DEVELOPMENTAL AGE, or MENTAL AGE. (See AGE.)

age of consent, the age (often 18) at which a person can legally marry without obtaining consent from a parent or GUARDIAN; also the age (variable according to state) at which a person can legally agree to have sexual intercourse. Someone who has sex with an *under-age person*—someone under the age of consent—is liable to a charge of STATUTORY RAPE.

agnosia, partial or total inability to recognize previously familiar objects, people, or other occurrences by using one's senses. Although the senses are unimpaired, the brain apparently "short-circuits" information received from normal sense organs; the condition may result from certain kinds of brain damage, as from a BRAIN TUMOR or TRAUMATIC BRAIN INJURY. If only one sense is affected, the agnosia may be labeled according to the name of the SENSORY MODE involved: *auditory, visual, olfactory* (smell), *gustatory* (taste), or *tactile* (touch). Children with LEARNING DISABILITIES or other DEVELOPMENTAL DISORDERS often have partial agnosia involving the VISUAL SKILLS and AUDITORY SKILLS. Inability to recognize or localize parts of one's own body is called *autopagnosia.* (See BRAIN AND BRAIN DISORDERS.)

agraphia, loss of the ability to write, a form of APHASIA often resulting from damage to the BRAIN, such as a BRAIN TUMOR or TRAUMATIC BRAIN INJURY. By contrast, difficulty in writing is called DYSGRAPHIA.

AIDS, a deadly infectious disease that drastically weakens the IMMUNE SYSTEM; its full name is *acquired immunodeficiency syndrome.* AIDS is caused by the *human immunodeficiency virus* (HIV), which attacks vital white blood cells called *helper T cells* that help produce disease-fighting ANTIBODIES. (For an explanation of how T cells work, see IMMUNE SYSTEM.) With the T cells crippled, the person becomes prey to CANCER and various infections described as "opportunistic" because they spread when the body loses its normal ability to fight them off. Different strains of HIV exist, some stronger than others. Some other organisms—perhaps including microbes called *mycoplasmas*—may sharply increase the ability of HIV to spread. People with various SEXUALLY TRANSMITTED DISEASES are also more susceptible to AIDS, possibly because of open sores on the body.

The HIV exists in various bodily fluids, including blood, SEMEN, saliva, tears, tissue in the NERVOUS SYSTEM, breast MILK, and secretions from female GENITALS. Studies of the known cases indicate that it is not spread by casual contact, as in home, office, school, or other public places. Activities such as touching, closed-mouth kissing, hugging, and giving blood, for example, are regarded as no-risk activities.

The HIV is spread by exchange of bodily fluids, apparently in just a few ways, notably by sexual intercourse, especially rough and/or anal intercourse; by reusing unsterilized needles from an infected person; by BLOOD TRANSFUSIONS with infected blood; by semen from sperm banks used in ARTIFICIAL INSEMINATION; and from mother to child by way of the PLACENTA, during CHILDBIRTH, or during BREASTFEEDING. Testing of blood; testing of mothers before, during, and after PREGNANCY; testing of sexual partners; use of CONDOMS during sexual intercourse (so-called "safe sex," better called "safer sex"); and similar measures can all cut the risks of exposure to HIV, though complete avoidance of any of these activities is the only sure way to avoid exposure to AIDS.

Most young children with AIDS are infected by their mothers (most of whom are unaware that they carry the virus) in the UTERUS, during CHILDBIRTH, or from later breastfeeding. For reasons as yet unknown, nearly two-thirds of the babies of infected mothers are born free of HIV infection. Some older children contract AIDS from blood transfusions, though far fewer than before 1985, when screening tests began to be used. A few have been infected as a result of sexual abuse (see CHILD ABUSE AND NEGLECT). Other young children are rarely exposed to AIDS, but they surely have fears about the disease, many of them based on ignorance, so parents will want to talk with children to clarify which activities are safe and which are not. (See WHAT CAN YOU (OR YOUR CHILD) DO TO AVOID STDS? on page 541.)

By contrast, somewhat older children and teenagers are at great risk for exposure to HIV, given widespread sexual activity and DRUG ABUSE in their age groups. Parents need to be sure children understand the risks involved in these activities and the ways to minimize those risks. However reluctant parents may have been in the past to undertake SEX EDUCATION with their children, in the 1990s it is a life-saving activity.

In particular, children need to understand that AIDS can happen to anyone, no matter what their age, sex, or socioeconomic background. They also need to be told that they cannot tell, just by looking at someone, if that person is free of HIV infection. If they are sexually active, children must protect themselves all the time, every time, and if they use drugs, they should *never* share needles. (See CONDOMS: WHAT EVERYONE NEEDS TO KNOW on page 143.)

Infection with HIV often appears first with signs of mild impairment of the immune system, such as swollen lymph nodes, skin disorders, weight loss, FEVER, DIARRHEA, common infections such as CANDIDIASIS (thrush), and increased susceptibility to other diseases such as HERPES or TUBERCULOSIS. This mild condition is called *AIDS-related complex* or *ARC*. As the infection progresses, full-blown AIDS develops, which often involves rare cancers such as Kaposi's sarcoma and lymphoma of the brain or infections such as TOXOPLASMOSIS, CYTOMEGALOVIRUS, and pneumonia (see LUNG AND BREATHING PROBLEMS), caused by a usually innocuous organism, *Pneumocystis carinii.*

Also characteristic of AIDS is a wasting syndrome, involving loss of more than 10 percent of body weight, chronic DIARRHEA, and persistent fever. Though some of these symptoms may result from inadequate diet or poor absorption of nutrients (see DIGESTIVE SYSTEM AND DISORDERS), metabolic changes also take place, some of them causing the body to seek energy in muscle and lean body mass, rather than FAT. Aggressive nutritional treatment is recommended, including small frequent meals, liquid nutritional supplements, easy-to-prepare foods, and easy-to-eat, easy-to-digest foods, avoiding hard, dry, rough, spicy, acidic, fatty, greasy, and gas-inducing foods.

If AIDS is suspected, various tests may be carried out, generally involving BLOOD TESTS for antibodies to HIV. Given the nature of the disease, a positive result is often checked with a second test, and a negative result is followed up by another test some months later. Such tests are also carried out on possible blood donors and donations, to screen the AIDS virus from the blood supply. A newer test, using fluid from the mouth, may be used for screening, but is less accurate and unsuitable for diagnosis.

AIDS was identified in Western countries only in the early 1980s, and so much is still unknown about the disease. Once contracted in its full form, the disease seems to have virtually a 100 percent MORTALITY RATE. However, it is unclear if people who show signs of antibodies to the AIDS virus will inevitably develop either ARC or AIDS, or if some will be able to fight off the disease altogether. It is also unclear whether ARC always progresses to full-blown AIDS or whether some people are able to stave off the deadly progression. Some people known to have been exposed to the virus in the 1980s have not developed AIDS. Scientists are studying such people to try to understand whether something in their bodies enabled them to fight off the disease or whether the strain to which they were exposed was a weak one and a possible candidate for use in a VACCINE.

While researchers are exploring many possible treatments and possible preventive vaccines, various antiviral drugs are being used in attempts to slow development of the disease. Early reports suggested that the earlier AIDS is recognized and treatment begun, the longer the survival and the better the quality of life; however, later reports were less clear. Little research has been done on the course and effects of AIDS in children, though the disease affects children somewhat differently, especially in the way it affects their nervous systems. Medications for adults were not made available for use with children until 1990 and then only after pressure from various organizations (see list of groups that follows). As of 1996, however, no cure exists.

FOR HELP AND FURTHER INFORMATION

GENERAL INFORMATION

National AIDS Hotline, 800–342–2437. Makes AIDS specialists available for free Classroom Call program; publishes brochures *HIV/AIDS, HIV Negative: When Are You Free from HIV?*, and *Positive Living*. (For full group information, see American Social Health Association, under SEXUALLY TRANSMITTED DISEASES.)

CDC National AIDS Clearinghouse
P.O. Box 6003
Rockville, MD 20849–6003
301–217–0023; 800–458–5231; 800–243–7012, TT
Fax: 301–251–5343
E-mail: aidsinfo@cdcnac.aspensys.com
Internet website: http://www.cdcnac.org
Federal organization providing information on AIDS; publishes numerous materials, including:

- general materials: *Facts About Adolescents and HIV/AIDS* and *Facts about the Scope of the HIV/AIDS Epidemic in the United States.*
- on prevention and testing: *HIV Infection and AIDS: Are You at Risk?, AIDS Prevention Guide: The Facts about HIV Infection and AIDS, Voluntary HIV Counseling and Testing: Facts, Issues, and Answers, Taking the HIV (AIDS) Test: How to Help Yourself,* and *Facts About CDC HIV/AIDS Prevention Activities.*

- "How to Help Yourself" guides on specific problems: *Testing Positive for HIV, Infections Linked to AIDS, AIDS-Related CMV, AIDS-Related MAC, The Brain Infection TOXO, HIV-Related TB*, and *The Lung Infection PCP.*
- numerous materials on treatment and services and technical reports.

National Institute of Allergy and Infectious Diseases (NIAID), 301–496–5717. Publishes *AIDS: Finding Better Treatments with Your Help.* (For full group information, see ALLERGY.)

Sexuality Information and Education Council of the United States (SIECUS), 212–819–9770. Publishes booklet *How to Talk to Your Children About AIDS*, reprint packets *AIDS* and *HIV/AIDS*, and annotated bibliography *HIV/AIDS.* (For full group information, see SEX EDUCATION.)

American College of Obstetricians and Gynecologists (ACOG), 202–638–5577. Publishes *Practicing Safe Sex* and *HIV Infection and Women.* (For full group information, see PREGNANCY.)

Agency for Health Care Policy and Research Clearinghouse, 800–358–9295. Publishes *HIV and Your Child: Consumer Guide, Understanding HIV: Consumer Guide*, and InstantFAX materials on HIV. (For full group information, see HEALTH INSURANCE.)

Planned Parenthood Federation of America (PPFA), 800–230–7526. Operates nationwide network of counseling and health services centers; publishes pamphlets *Kids and AIDS: A Guide for Parents, AIDS and HIV: Questions and Answers*, and *Sex—Safer and Satisfying.* (For full group information, see BIRTH CONTROL.)

American Council for Drug Education (ACDE), 800–488–3784. Publishes pamphlet *AIDS.* (For full group information, see HELP AGAINST SUBSTANCE ABUSE on page 703.)

Women's Action Alliance (WAA), 212–532–8330. Publishes *Women's Centers and AIDS Projects: A Guide to Educational Materials* and *Women, AIDS and Communities: A Guide for Action.* (For full group information, see HELP ON LEARNING AND EDUCATION on page 659.)

National Organization for Rare Disorders (NORD), 800–999–6673. (For full group information, see RARE DISORDERS.)

National Woman's Christian Temperance Union (WCTU), 800–755–1321. Publishes booklet *AIDS—What You Don't Know Can Kill You* and leaflet *AIDS Kills.* (For full group information, see HELP AGAINST SUBSTANCE ABUSE on page 703.)

Centers for Disease Control (CDC), 404–639–3311. (For full group information, see IMMUNIZATION.)

Healthy Mothers, Healthy Babies National Coalition (HMHB), 202–863–2458. Publishes *Women and HIV/AIDS.* (For full group information, see PREGNANCY.)

National Mental Health Consumer Self-Help Clearinghouse, 800–553–4539. Publishes reprint packet on AIDS and mental health. (For full group information, see MENTAL DISORDERS.)

ON CHILDREN AND AIDS

Pediatric AIDS Foundation (PAF)
1311 Colorado Avenue
Santa Monica, CA 90404
310–395–9051
Fax: 310–395–5149
Kathy Harmon, President
Organization concerned with AIDS in children; acts as advocate; sponsors research, especially on transmission of HIV from mother to infant; supports creation of special hospital programs for children.

National Pediatric HIV Resource Center (NPHRC)
Children's Hospital of New Jersey
15 South Ninth Street
Newark, NJ 07107
201–268–8251; 800–362–0071
Fax: 201–485–2752
Carolyn Burr, Associate Director
Federally funded program providing information on HIV in children through adolescence; provides technical assistance to HIV programs; publishes various materials (some available through National Maternal and Child Health Clearinghouse [NMCHC]; see PREGNANCY), including *Children and Families and HIV/AIDS*, a directory of educational materials; *HIV and AIDS in Children: Questions and Answers*; *Parent Information Booklets*; videos *What's Best for You: Families Talk About Disclosure* and *You're in Charge*; *Jimmy and the Eggs Virus* (for children); *My Child's Care* (notebook for tracking care information); and materials for health professionals.

National Clearinghouse for Alcohol and Drug Abuse Information (NCADI), 301–468–2600. Publishes *How Getting High Can Get You AIDS* and *How Not to Get High, Get Stupid, Get AIDS: A Guide to Partying* (both for teens), and Drug Abuse and AIDS Campaign for Teens "AIDS: Another Way Drugs Can Kill." (For full group information, see HELP AGAINST SUBSTANCE ABUSE on page 703.)

March of Dimes Birth Defects Foundation (MDBDF), 914–428–7100. Publishes pamphlet *AIDS: What We Need to Know* and information sheet *Perinatal AIDS.* (For full group information, see BIRTH DEFECTS.)

Child Welfare League of America (CWLA), 202–638–2952. Publishes *Caring at Home: A Guide for Families* (on caring for children with AIDS); four-video set: *Caring for Infants and Toddlers with HIV Infection, Caring for School-aged Children with HIV Infection, Adolescents: At Risk for HIV Infection*, and *Living with Loss: Children and*

HIV; and materials on community care for children with AIDS. (For full group information, see FOSTER CARE.)

The Children's Foundation (TCF), 202–347–3300. Publishes *Caring for an HIV-Infected Child in Family Day Care: Myths and Facts.* (For full group information, see CHILD CARE.)

Children's Defense Fund (CDF), 800–233–1200. Publishes *Teens and AIDS: Opportunities for Prevention.* (For full group information, see ADOLESCENT PREGNANCY.)

Child Care Law Center (CCLC), 415–495–5498. Publishes *Legal Aspects of Caring for Sick and Injured Children, Caring for Children with HIV or AIDS in Child Care,* and *HIV and AIDS: Employment Issues in Child Care.* (For full group information, see CHILD CARE.)

The Arc, 817–261–6003. Publishes fact sheet *HIV/AIDS and Mental Retardation* and materials for training people with mental retardation, including *HIV and AIDS Prevention Guide for Parents, Learn To Be Safe!,* and *SAFE: Stopping AIDS through Functional Education.* (For full group information, see MENTAL RETARDATION.)

American Academy of Child and Adolescent Psychiatry (AACAP), 202–966–7300. Publishes information sheet *Children and AIDS* and *HIV/AIDS Information Sheet-Resource Guide* for caregivers of children or adolescents with HIV/AIDS. (For full group information, see MENTAL DISORDERS.)

National Adoption Information Clearinghouse (NAIC), 301–231–6512. Publishes *Policy and Practice Issues for Adoption and Foster Care of HIV-Affected Children.* (For full group information, see ADOPTION.)

Association for Childhood Education International (ACEI), 800–423–3563. Publishes reprint *What Every Teacher Should Know About AIDS.* (For full group information, see HELP ON LEARNING AND EDUCATION on page 659.)

OTHER SOURCES OF INFORMATION

National Hospice Organization (NHO), 800–658–8898. Publishes brochures *What Everyone Should Know About AIDS* and *Caring for People with AIDS,* and book *Be a Friend,* paintings and drawings by children with HIV or who have a family member with HIV. (For full group information, see HOSPICE.)

National Safety Council (NSC), 800–621–7615. Publishes *AIDS: Facts, Choices, Prevention* (program with video, teacher's guide, and booklets for students and parents). (For full group information, see SAFETY.)

Association of Family and Conciliation Courts (AFCC), 608–251–4001. Publishes *AIDS and Family Law.* (For full group information, see DIVORCE.)

National Organization on Legal Problems of Education (NOLPE), 913–273–3550. Publishes *The Formulation of AIDS Policies: Legal Considerations for Schools* and *Health Related Legal Issues in Education.* (For full group information, see HELP ON LEARNING AND EDUCATION on page 659.)

National Maternal and Child Health Clearinghouse (NMCHC), 703–821–8955. (For full group information, see PREGNANCY.)

ONLINE RESOURCES

Internet: AIDS/HIV Information. Online information clearinghouse.
http://vector.casti.com.QRD/.html/AIDS.html

Internet: AIDS Treatment News. Online newsletter on current treatment and research.
gopher://odie.niaid.nih.gov/aa/aids

Internet: AIDS. Mailing list providing discussion forum about AIDS, especially about medical aspects but also about political and social concerns. To subscribe, send e-mail to: mailto:aids-request@cs.ucla.edu

Internet: AIDSLINE. Bibliographic database on medical and social issues. telnet://cdplus@cdplus.com

OTHER RESOURCES

FOR PARENTS AND OTHER ADULTS

Could Your Kid Die "Laughing"?: AIDS and Today's Adolescent. Carole Marsh. Gallopade, 1994.
AIDS-Proofing Your Kids: A Step-By-Step Guide. Loren E. Acker and others. Beyond Words, 1992.
Take These Broken Wings and Learn to Fly: The AIDS Support Book for Patients, Family and Friends, 2nd ed. Steven D. Dietz and M. Jane Parker Hicks. Harbinger, 1992.

GENERAL WORKS

AIDS, rev. ed. Carol D. Foster, ed. Information Plus, 1994.
HIV Prevention: Health Facts. Lucas Stang and Kathleen R. Miner. ETR Associates, 1994.
Uncovering the Mystery of AIDS: A Scientist Helps You Understand HIV. John J. Medina. Nelson, 1993.
201 Things You Should Know about AIDS and Other Sexually Transmitted Diseases. Jeffrey Nevid. Allyn, 1993.

PRACTICAL GUIDES

HIV—AIDS and Hepatitis: Everything You Need to Know to Protect Yourself and Others. Douglas D. Schoon. Milady, 1994.
The Woman's HIV Sourcebook: A Guide to Better Health and Well-Being. Patricia Kloser and Jane M. Craig. Taylor, 1994.
What You Can Do to Avoid AIDS. Earvin "Magic" Johnson. Times Books, 1992.
Understanding and Preventing AIDS: A Book for Everyone, rev. ed. Chris Jennings. Health Alert Press, 1992.

For children, on understanding and prevention

AIDS. Mark McCauslin. Crestwood/Macmillan, 1995.
Know about AIDS, 3rd ed. Margaret O. Hyde and Elizabeth H. Forsyth. Walker, 1994.
Lets Learn about AIDS. W. Gladden, 1994.
You Can Call Me Willy: A Story for Children to Learn about AIDS. Joan C. Verniero. Magination Press, 1994.
AIDS: Examining the Crisis. Tom Flynn and Karen Lound. Lerner, 1994.
Creating Compassion: Activities for Understanding HIV-AIDS. Phyllis Vos Wezeman. Pilgrim, 1994.
AIDS Questions and Answers for Kids, rev. ed. Linda Schwartz. Learning Works, 1993.
Putting the Brakes on AIDS: The Story of Macho McKar. Peter Enns. Kids International, 1992. Includes cassette.
AIDS: How It Works in the Body. Lorna Greenberg. Watts, 1992.
Let's Talk about AIDS and Sex. Rodney Gage. Broadman, 1992.

For children, on dealing with AIDS

Daddy and Me. Jeanne Moutoussamy-Ashe. Knopf, 1993. About Arthur Ashe and his daughter, Camera, as he was dying of AIDS.
Uncle Jerry Has AIDS. Jim Boulden. Boulden, 1992.
Alex, the Kid with AIDS. Linda Walvoord Girard. Albert Whitman, 1990.

For preteens and teens, on understanding and prevention

AIDS. Barbara Lerman-Golomb. Raintree Steck-Vaughn, 1995.
Drugs and AIDS. Barbara H. Draimin. Rosen, 1994.
First AIDS: Frank Facts for Kids. Carole Marsh. Gallopade, 1994.
AIDS: Trading Fear for Facts; A Guide for Young People, 3rd ed. Karen Hein. Consumer's Union, 1993.
Lynda Madaras Talks to Teens About AIDS: An Essential Guide for Parents, Teachers and Young People, rev. ed. Lynda Madaras. Newmarket Press, 1993.
AIDS Answers for Teens, rev. ed. Linda Schwartz. Learning Works, 1993.
The First Time Club: An AIDS Awareness Play. K.T. Curran. I. E. Clark, 1993.
100 Questions and Answers about AIDS: A Guide for Young People. Michael T. Ford. New Discovery/Macmillan, 1992.
100 Questions and Answers about AIDS: What You Need to Know Now. Beech Tree/Morrow, 1993.
AIDS: What Does It Mean to You?, 4th ed. Margaret O. Hyde and Elizabeth Forsyth. Walker, 1992.
Later with the Latex: AIDS. Armando B. Rico. Veracruz, 1992.
Safe Sex in the Age of AIDS. C. Everett Koop. Times Books, 1992.
Everything You Need to Know about AIDS, rev. ed. Barbara Taylor. Rosen, 1992.
What You Don't Know Can Kill You. Fran Arrick. Bantam, 1992.
AIDS: Deadly Threat, rev. ed. Alvin Silverstein and Sylvia Silverstein. Enslow, 1991.

For preteens and teens, on dealing with AIDS

Everything You Need to Know When a Parent Has AIDS. Working Together Against AIDS. (1994) *Coping When a Parent Has AIDS.* (1993) Barbara H. Draimin. Rosen.
My Brother Has AIDS. Deborah Davis. Atheneum/Macmillan, 1994.
It Happened to Nancy: A True Story from the Diary of a Teenager. Beatrice Sparks, ed. Avon, 1994. A teenage girl contracts AIDS after being raped.
Doomed to Die: A Lonely Walk. Kevin Dounuts. Old Country Books, 1993.
Teens with AIDS Speak Out. Mary Kittredge. Messner/Simon & Schuster, 1992.
Touched by AIDS. Margaret A. Cummings. Woman's Mission Union, 1992.

(See also IMMUNE SYSTEM; SEXUALLY TRANSMITTED DISEASES; BLOOD TRANSFUSIONS.)

Aid to Families with Dependent Children (AFDC), a state-administered federal welfare program providing financial assistance to needy MINOR children deprived of support from one of their parents, as through death, disability, unemployment, or ABANDONMENT; sometimes called Aid to Dependent Children (ADC), the program is established under SOCIAL SECURITY. The assistance may go to the remaining parent or to another person who has assumed CUSTODY, such as a grandparent, stepparent, or other relative. Application is made through a county department of social services or human resources.

The requirements for eligibility vary, each state having its own *need standard.* In some states, AFDC payments are made whenever need exists, even if both parents are employed but still living below the poverty level. In others, payments are made only when neither parent at home is employed. Most AFDC payments are made to women who are SINGLE PARENTS with young children. By law, the state is required to find the children's FATHER and obtain reimbursement of the CHILD SUPPORT for which he is legally responsible. In order to continue receiving payments due, the mother must help in this effort, which for unmarried mothers often includes instituting a PATERNITY SUIT to establish the legal father of the child.

As of 1995, the AFDC was one of the programs most heavily under fire in the U.S. Congress, and the long-term nature and even existence of the program was unclear.

albinism (hypopigmentation), a rare GENETIC DISORDER involving lack of the pigment *melanin*, caused when the skin cells (*melanocytes*) that normally produce melanin fail to work properly. (Another disorder, VITILIGO, involves lack of melanocytes.) Children born with albinism often have snow-white hair and skin, though these may darken slightly with age. People with albinism are subject to severe sunburn and tend to develop skin CANCERS; their eyes are often extremely sensitive to bright light; and they often have other EYE AND VISION PROBLEMS, such as STRABISMUS (crossed eyes), NYSTAGMUS (jerky, involuntary movements of the eyes), and MYOPIA (nearsightedness).

A genetic disorder of the AUTOSOMAL RECESSIVE type, albinism is passed on to a child only if both parents contribute the defective gene; if parents have one child with albinism, the chances are 1 in 4 that a later child will also have albinism. *Ocular albinism* affects only the eyes, and may be either autosomal recessive or X-LINKED. In addition to physical problems, children with albinism often face social problems, ranging from teasing to outright discrimination; these are often compounded among children of Black African descent by rejection within the family and community.

FOR HELP AND FURTHER INFORMATION

National Organization for Albinism and Hypopigmentation (NOAH)
1530 Locust Street, Suite 29
Philadelphia, PA 19102–4415
215–545–2322; 800–473–2310
Jennifer George and Connie Curry, Copresidents
Organization concerned with albinism and hypopigmentation; provides support and information; fosters research; publishes semiannual *NOAH News* and information bulletins such as *What Is Albinism?*, *Resources for Persons with Albinism*, *Assisting Students with Albinism*, *Ocular Albinism*, *Low Vision Aids*, *Sun Protection*, *Social and Emotional Aspects of Albinism*, and *African Americans and Albinism*.

National Organization for Rare Disorders (NORD), 800–999–6673. (For full group information, see RARE DISORDERS.)

National Association for Parents of the Visually Impaired, Inc. (NAPVI), 800–562–6265. Publishes *The Student with Albinism in the Regular Classroom*. (For full group information, see EYE AND VISION PROBLEMS.)

National Eye Institute (NEI), 800–869–2020. (For full group information, see EYE AND VISION PROBLEMS.)

(See also SKIN AND SKIN DISORDERS.)

alcohol abuse, physical and psychological dependence on alcohol, characterized by long-term excessive drinking, a felt need to continue drinking, and/or withdrawal symptoms that occur when drinking is discontinued. A major social problem, long thought to be primarily an adult phenomenon, alcohol abuse has become increasingly widespread among adolescents, often in conjunction with DRUG ABUSE, a combination called *cross-addiction*. Drunk driving, by both adults and adolescents, is also a major, life-threatening hazard for many young people.

Young children are also affected by alcohol abuse, as many of them live with a parent who is an alcoholic. The result may often be CHILD ABUSE AND NEGLECT. Many babies, in fact, are affected before birth by FETAL ALCOHOL SYNDROME, a result of their mother's drinking during PREGNANCY. Babies can also inherit a susceptibility to alcohol addiction.

Various organizations (see HELP AGAINST SUBSTANCE ABUSE on page 703) provide aid, support, and counsel to young children affected by alcohol abuse or who are themselves abusers. Many schools, too, have instituted programs to help children cope with the facts of alcoholism. Unfortunately, many children are left in limbo because state laws deny counseling without consent of the parent, who may be part of the problem.

Children of Alcoholics estimates that seven million children under age eighteen have an alcoholic parent and that some twenty-one million adults grew up in alcoholic families. They stress that it is vital for children of alcoholic families to understand they are not alone, that they did not cause the parent's drinking problem, that they can neither control nor cure it, that they are at increased risk of themselves becoming alcoholics, and that they deserve help for themselves, whether or not the alcoholic parent seeks help. (For an overview of the effects and signs of alcohol and other substance abuse, plus organizations, reference works, and recommendations for parents, see HELP AGAINST SUBSTANCE ABUSE on page 703.)

alexia (word blindness), inability to read, despite unimpaired vision and intelligence; an extreme form of DYSLEXIA.

allegation, in a law suit, a statement of what one party expects or hopes to prove during a trial. In a case of CHILD ABUSE OR NEGLECT, for example, the allegation would describe specific acts of mistreatment to be discussed at the trial, and it is up to the judge (or in some criminal cases, the jury) to decide whether the alleged facts are proved.

allergy, an excessive response by the IMMUNE SYSTEM to some foreign substance, called an *antigen* or more specifically, an *allergen*. Allergy is a general term that encompasses a wide range of problems, including ASTHMA, reaction to FOOD ADDITIVES, and some kinds of FOOD INTOLERANCE, as well as hypersensitivity to many other substances such as pollen, mold spores, insects, insect bites, animal dander, latex, and injected drugs, such as penicillin. Why some people suffer from allergies and others do not is unclear, but some sensitivities seem to be inherited.

Allergic reactions range from the barely noticeable to the life-threatening. When the immune system mobilizes against a foreign substance, the body goes through various changes. A chemical called *histamine* is released, blood vessels widen, tissues fill with fluid, and muscles go into spasm. (A common medication to counter allergy, *antihistamine*, is aimed at blocking just such effects.) Other parts of the body may also be involved, especially a rash or swelling on the skin, inflammation of the eyes and breathing passages (as in asthma), and digestive upset, including VOMITING and DIARRHEA. These are common reactions in, for example, *hay fever* or *allergic rhinitis*.

Most seriously, as in reactions to some drugs, insect venom, and foods, the body may go into anaphylactic SHOCK, a severe, life-threatening drop in BLOOD PRESSURE, which requires immediate treatment, notably injection of *epinephrine*, to counteract the effects. People who have once suffered such a severe reaction must avoid such triggering allergens, if possible, and carry with them a dose of the medication, to be injected if the reaction starts. The dose should be carried *on their person*; the reaction can occur so quickly that the person may be incapacitated and die before reaching the house or car for the medication. If any family member is subject to such reactions, parents and older children should know how give such a life-saving injection.

Sometimes the offending allergen is obvious, such as a bee sting or a penicillin injection. But more often, the precise substance causing the problem is unknown. Then physicians may perform a *patch test*, in which samples of various substances are taped to the skin; those that trigger the person's allergic reactions will cause the skin to be raised and red. BLOOD TESTS may also be used to measure levels of antibodies to particular allergens. Once the problem allergens are identified, the person can avoid them as much as possible. (See CONTROLLING THE HOME ENVIRONMENT FOR THE ASTHMATIC CHILD on page 51 for examples of how to minimize exposure.)

Where appropriate, physicians may try *immunotherapy* (popularly called *allergy shots*). This involves injections of small, diluted doses of the allergen under the patient's skin once or twice a week over a period of three to four years, gradually increasing the size of the dose and the time between doses, to build up tolerance to the allergen. This is a long, expensive process that requires careful monitoring, and the injections themselves can cause allergic reactions. But for some the treatment works well.

Latex allergy can be identified by a test introduced in 1995. This is especially important for people with medical problems, health care workers, and any others whose activities bring them into frequent contact with latex products. Though only about 1 percent of the population has sensitivity to latex, the allergy is found in 15 percent of health care workers and in 34 to 100 percent of people with SPINA BIFIDA, who are exposed repeatedly during enemas using bottles with latex tips.

FOR HELP AND FURTHER INFORMATION

National Institute of Allergy and Infectious Diseases (NIAID)
Office of Communications
31 Center Drive, MSC 2520
Building 31, Room 7A50
Bethesda, MD 20892
301–496–5717
Fax: 301–402–0120
E-mail: ocpostoffice@/niaid.nih.gov
Internet: gopher://gopher.niaid.nih.gov/1
One of the U.S. National Institutes of Health. Sponsors research; provides information; maintains network of Asthma and Allergic Disease Centers; publishes various brochures, including *NIAID: The Edge of Discovery*, and research reports for professionals.

Allergy and Asthma Network/Mothers of Asthmatics (AAN•MA), 800–878–4403. Publishes books *Breathing Easy with Day Care: A Guide About Asthma and Allergies for Parents and Caregivers*, *Sneezing Your Head Off? How to Live with Your Allergic Nose*, *Your Food-Allergic Child: a Parent's Guide*, and *The Allergy Cookbook*, and the video *Allergies: Medicine for the Public*.

Asthma and Allergy Foundation of America (AAFA)
1125 15th Street NW, Suite 502
Washington, DC 20005
202–466–7643; 800–7ASTHMA [727–8462]
Fax: 202–466–8940
Mary Worstell, Executive Director
Organization concerned with allergy and asthma; supports research; provides information; publishes various materials, including a bimonthly newspaper.

American Allergy Association (AAA)
P.O. Box 7273
Menlo Park, CA 94026
For catalog, send stamped, self-addressed envelope to:
1100 Industrial #9
San Carlos, CA 94070
Allergy Line: 415–855–8036
Internet: gopher//gopher.hooked.net:70/11/gophers/nonprofit/allergy
Organization offering information and resources relating to allergy and asthma; maintains database; publishes various materials, including:

- General materials: *Living with Allergies*, *Food Families* (for identifying cross-reactions), *Traveling with Allergies*, *Pollen Times—By State, By Month*, allergy recipe books, and allergy alerts, on special problems such as dyes in medications, drug interactions, food additives, latex, and problem foods.
- Allergy information sheets: *The Differences Between Egg Subsitutes and Egg Replacers*, *Milk Allergy*, *Lactose Intolerance*, and *FDA Bans Sulfite*.

- *Allergy Products Directory*, rev. ed.: Vol. 1: *Controlling Your Environment*, Vol. 2: *Asthma Resources Directory*, Vol. 3: *Allergy/Asthma Finding Help*, and Vol. 4: *Protecting Your Skin.*

American Academy of Pediatrics (AAP), 800–433–9016. Publishes brochure *Allergies in Children.* (For full group information, see HEALTH CARE.)

Food and Drug Administration (FDA), 800–332–1088 (to receive form for reporting adverse reactions). (For full group information, see DRUG REACTIONS AND INTERACTIONS.)

National Jewish Center for Immunology and Respiratory Medicine, 800–222–5864. (For full group information, LUNG AND BREATHING DISORDERS.)

American Council on Science and Health (ACSH), 212–362–7044. Publishes *Hay Fever* and *Unproven "Allergies": An Epidemic of Nonsense.* (For full group information, see SAFETY.)

OTHER RESOURCES

For parents and other adults

Ward Lock Family Health Guide: Asthma and Allergies. Anne Kent. Sterling, 1994.
The Best Guide to Allergy, 3rd ed. Nathan D. and others. Humana, 1994.
A Parent's Guide to Allergies and Asthma. Marion Steinmann. Dell, 1992.
Keys to Dealing with Childhood Allergies. Judy L. Bachman. Barron's, 1992.
Allergies: Complete Guide to Diagnosis, Treatment, and Daily Management. Consumer Reports, 1992.
Is This Your Child? Discovering and Treating Unrecognized Allergies. Doris J. Rapp. Morrow, 1991.
How to Identify—and Control—Your Child's Food Allergies. Jane McNicol. Wiley, 1991. Paperback title: *Your Child's Food Allergies: Detecting and Treating Hyperactivity, Congestion, Irritability and Other Symptoms Caused by Common Food Allergies* (1992).

General works

Allergic Reactions. David Nitka, II. Champion Books, 1994.
Allergies A-Z. Tova Navarra and Myron Lipkowitz. Facts on File, 1994.
What's New in Allergy: New Developments and How They Can Help You Overcome Allergy and Asthma, 3rd ed. Stephen Astor. Two A's, 1992.
Allergies. Gerald Newman and Eleanor Newman Layfield. Watts, 1992.
Allergy Overload: Are Foods and Chemicals Killing You? Stephen Griffiths, HarperCollins, 1992.
All about Asthma and Allergy. H. Morrow Brown. Trafalgar Square, 1991.

On dealing with allergies

You Can Do Something about Your Allergies. Nelson L. Novick. Macmillan, 1994.
Empty Your Bucket: Practical Steps to Overcome Allergy and Allergic Asthma. Stephen Astor. Two A's, 1993.
Living Allergy Free: How to Create and Maintain An Allergen- and Irritant-Free Environment. M. Eric Gershwin and Edwin L. Klingelhofer. Humana, 1992.
What's New in Allergy: New Developments and How They Can Help You Overcome Allergy and Asthma, 3rd ed. *Take Charge of Your Allergy: Professional Secrets You Need to Know to Obtain the Best Allergy Care.* Stephen Astor. Two A's, 1992.
Sneezing Your Head Off?: How to Live with Your Allergic Nose. Peter B. Boggs. Simon & Schuster, 1992.
No More Allergies: Identifying and Eliminating Allergies and Sensitivity Reactions to Everything in Your Environment. Gary Null. Villard/Random, 1992.
Relief from Hayfever and Other Allergies. Lesley Sussman. Dell, 1992.
Random House Personal Medical Handbook: For People with Allergies. Paula Dranov. Random, 1991.
The Whole Way to Allergy Relief and Prevention: A Doctor's Complete Guide to Treatment and Self-Care. Jacqueline Krohn and others. Hartley & Marks, 1991.

On food allergies

The Complete Guide to Food Allergy and Intolerance. Jonathan Brostoff and Linda Gamlin. Crown, 1992.
Dr. Braly's Food Allergy and Nutrition Revolution. James Braly. Keats, 1992.
The Complete Guide to Food Allergy and Intolerance. Jonathan Brostoff and Linda Gamlin. Crown, 1992.
The Allergy Discovery Diet: A Rotation Diet for Discovering Your Allergies to Food. John E. Postley and Janet M. Barton. Doubleday, 1990.
Healthier Children. Barbara Kahan. Keats Publishing, 1990. On behavior problems linked to food sensitivity and other environmental factors.

For children

Determined to Win: Children Living with Allergies and Asthma. Thomas Bergman. Gareth Stevens, 1994.
All about Allergies. Susan N. Terkel. Dutton, 1993.

For preteens and teens

Allergies. Elaine Landau. Twenty-First Century Books, 1994.
Plants That Make You Sniffle and Sneeze. Carol Lerner. Morrow, 1993.
Allergies. Gerald Newman and Eleanor N. Layfield. Watts, 1992.

(See also ASTHMA; CELIAC SPRUE; IMMUNE SYSTEM; LUNG AND BREATHING DISORDERS; FOOD ADDITIVES; FOOD INTOLERANCE.)

allogenic, in medicine, a general term referring to a type of TRANSPLANT or BLOOD TRANSFUSION that comes from a DONOR, a person whose tissues are different, yet similar enough to be given. By contrast, a transplant using tissues from elsewhere in the person's own body is called AUTOLOGOUS.

alpha fetoprotein (AFP), a protein produced in a FETUS's liver that is passed into the mother's blood, where it can be sampled and tested, generally about sixteen to nineteen weeks into a PREGNANCY. Abnormally high AFP levels are often associated with NEURAL TUBE DEFECTS, such as SPINA BIFIDA, and with other ailments such as KIDNEY PROBLEMS, while low levels can be linked with DOWN SYNDROME; testing is done when family history warrants it. But the *maternal serum alpha-fetoprotein test* (MSAFP) is only a general screen; abnormal AFP levels do not necessarily signal abnormalities, but rather the advisability of more precise GENETIC SCREENING procedures, such as AMNIOCENTESIS and ULTRASOUND. A high AFP level may also appear when a pregnant woman is carrying twins. The MSAFP test has been found somewhat unreliable in dealing with low AFP levels. (See GENETIC DISORDERS; GENETIC SCREENING.)

alpha 1-antitrypsin deficiency (a1AT), a GENETIC DISORDER, identified by a BLOOD TEST, that results from lack of the liver protein *alpha 1-antitrypsin.* The deficiency affects both the liver and the lungs, causing cirrhosis of the liver (see LIVER AND LIVER PROBLEMS) and emphysema (see LUNG AND BREATHING DISORDERS). No treatment currently exists, but liver TRANSPLANTS offer hope of survival to people with the deficiency.

FOR HELP AND FURTHER INFORMATION

National Organization for Rare Disorders (NORD), 800–999–6673. (For full group information, see RARE DISORDERS.)

National Digestive Disease Information Clearinghouse (NDDIC), 301–654–3810. (For full group information, see DIGESTIVE SYSTEM AND DISORDERS.)

National Heart, Lung, and Blood Information Center (NHLBIC), 301–251–1222. (For full group information, see HEART AND HEART PROBLEMS.)

American Liver Foundation (ALF), 800–223–0179. (For full group information, see LIVER AND LIVER PROBLEMS.)

alternative school, a school that offers nontraditional educational approaches. An alternative school is sometimes called a SCHOOL OF CHOICE and is often a type of MAGNET SCHOOL. Approaches vary widely. For example, children may work primarily in small, informal groups or in UNGRADED classes, rather than in the usual classrooms in a TRACKING system. They may work at INDEPENDENT STUDY, rather than each doing the same homework assignment. Though some alternative schools are public schools, most are PRIVATE SCHOOLS. Alternative schools hold attractions for many parents, but they should make sure that the school is properly staffed and equipped and has some recognizable ACCREDITATION. The U.S. Department of Education's CHOOSING A SCHOOL FOR YOUR CHILD, reproduced on page 659, includes a checklist for evaluating schools. Some parents who are dissatisfied with schools in general opt for HOME SCHOOLING.

FOR HELP AND FURTHER INFORMATION

National Coalition of Alternative Community Schools (NCACS)
58 School House Road
Summertown, TN 38483
615–964–3670
Michael Traugot, National Office Coordinator
Organization concerned with alternative schools; acts as advocate; provides information and referrals; publishes various materials, including quarterly *National Coalition News*, semiannual journal *Skole, National Directory of Alternative Schools*, and video *Alternative School Sampler.*

National Association for Legal Support of Alternative Schools (NALSAS)
P.O. Box 2823
Santa Fe, NM 87501
505–471–6928
Fax: 505–474–3220
Ed Nagel, Coordinator
Organization concerned with alternatives to public school education; provides information on legal issues relating to nonpublic education; serves as accrediting agency for alternative schools; sponsors Home Study Exchange, linking home-study students, often through pen-pal contacts; publishes semiannual *Tidbits.*

(See specific topics highlighted in entry; also EDUCATION.)

ambidextrous, type of HANDEDNESS in which a person uses both hands with equal proficiency and skill, with neither hand having DOMINANCE over the other.

amelia, a BIRTH DEFECT that involves the absence of one or more limbs. If all four limbs are missing, it is called *tetramelia*, while nearly absent limbs, with hands or feet attached almost directly to the body, is called PHOCOMELIA. *Amelia* is also a psychological term for the apathy and indifference sometimes associated with PSYCHOSIS.

amelogenesis imperfecta, a GENETIC DISORDER that causes the TEETH to have thin enamel, deficient in CALCIUM. The child's teeth are mottled and susceptible to tooth decay and require careful dental care.

Americans with Disabilities Act (ADA), a 1990 federal law (Public Law 101–336) ensuring individuals with DISABILITIES access to the full range of public and private services (but excepting religious organizations and private clubs), including retail stores, private schools, public transportation, restaurants, museums, hotels, places of work, and the like. The law requires that "auxiliary aids and services," such as wheelchair access to bathrooms, lifts on buses, and doors that open with electronic eyes, be provided where necessary. The ADA applies to all sites operated by state and local government and to all sites of private employers of fifteen or more people.

In defining "disabilities," the ADA adopted the functional approach long since established (see SECTION 504 of the Rehabilitation Act of 1973), so that people covered are those who have physical or mental impairment, who have a record of such impairment, and are regarded as having such an impairment. In general, physical impairment is defined as "any physiological disorder or condition, cosmetic disfigurements, or anatomical loss affecting one or more of the following body systems: neurological; musculoskeletal; special sense organs; respiratory, including speech organs; cardiovascular; reproductive; digestive; genito-urinary; hemic and lymphatic; skin; and endocrine," also covering communicable diseases, except when they "pose a direct threat to the health and safety of others...that cannot be eliminated by reasonable accommodations."

A mental impairment is defined as "any mental or psychological disorder, such as mental retardation, organic brain syndrome, emotional or mental illness, and specific learning disabilities." Though the law has some exceptions, such as airplanes and buildings of fewer than three stories, the aim throughout has been to secure full access and inclusion in every part of life for people with disabilities and chronic illnesses.

This overarching law seeks to cover most aspects of life. For parents of children with disabilities from birth to age twenty-one, many other laws, such as the INDIVIDUALS WITH DISABILITIES EDUCATION ACT, may have more immediate practical significance.

FOR HELP AND FURTHER INFORMATION

The Arc, 817–261–6003. Publishes fact sheets *The American with Disabilities Act of 1990* and *The Americans With Disabilities Act of 1990 and Employment*, and *The ADA Title III—A Guide for Making Your Business Accessible to People with Mental Retardation.* (For full group information, see MENTAL RETARDATION.)

National Mental Health Association (NMHA), 800–969–6642. Publishes pamphlet *Americans with Disabilities Act of 1990.*

Candlelighters Childhood Cancer Foundation (CCCF), 800–366–2223. Publishes *Introduction to the ADA.* (For full group information, see CANCER.)

Child Care Law Center (CCLC), 415–495–5498. Publishes brochures *The Americans with Disabilities Act and Child Care: Information for Parents*, booklet *Child Care and the ADA: Highlights for Parents.* (For full group information, see CHILD CARE.)

National Mental Health Consumer Self-Help Clearinghouse, 800–553–4539. Publishes reprint packet on the ADA. (For full group information, see MENTAL DISORDERS.)

(See also ADVOCACY; CHILD CARE; HELP FOR SPECIAL CHILDREN on page 689.)

amino acids, a group of chemical compounds that make up all PROTEINS and are therefore vital to proper NUTRITION. Approximately 20 amino acids are found in the human body, in proteins and also elsewhere in the body, where they aid in biochemical reactions. Some amino acids, termed *nonessential,* can be manufactured within the body; others, called *essential,* can only be obtained from a proper diet. Animal sources generally give a wider range of amino acids than do plant sources, so parents who choose a VEGETARIAN diet for their families must be sure that the selection of foods includes all of the essential amino acids. (See NUTRITION; VEGETARIAN.)

amniocentesis, a GENETIC SCREENING procedure that involves withdrawing AMNIOTIC FLUID from the sac surrounding the FETUS, using a needle (guided by ULTRASOUND) inserted through the abdomen. The fetal cells in the fluid can then be analyzed for many possible disorders, such as DOWN SYNDROME, SPINA BIFIDA, and GLYCOGEN STORAGE DISEASES; tests also show the sex of the fetus, which is required to assess the risk of X-LINKED GENETIC DISORDERS. Amniocentesis is performed at about fourteen to sixteen weeks into the pregnancy—later than other procedures such as CHORIONIC VILLUS SAMPLING—and the laboratory analysis takes longer; it also carries some risk of MISCARRIAGE and of fetal or maternal hemorrhage. Even so, amniocentesis is often recommended for women over thirty-five, for those with abnormally high ALPHA FETOPROTEIN levels, and for those whose family history indicates a higher-than-normal possibility of genetic disorders. (See GENETIC DISORDERS; GENETIC SCREENING; REPRODUCTIVE TECHNOLOGY.)

amniotic fluid, the clear fluid that surrounds the FETUS in the UTERUS, which is held within a membrane called an *amniotic sac* that protects the fetus from pressure from the mother's internal organs and injury from outside. The fetus swallows the circulating fluid, absorbs it into the bloodstream, and then excretes urine into it; the developing being does not drown because the lungs are not used for breathing until after birth. Mostly water, the fluid also contains other substances, such as

FATS (lipids) and waste fetal cells. It is such substances that are examined in the PRENATAL SCREENING test called AMNIOCENTESIS.

The amniotic fluid in its sac is the "bag of waters" that breaks just before, during, or after CHILDBIRTH. Too little amniotic fluid, called *oligohydramnios*, and too much fluid, called *hydramnios* or *polyhydramnios*, can both signal problems for the developing fetus. If a fetus has difficulty swallowing, as in cases of anencephaly (see SPINA BIFIDA) or ATRESIA in the esophagus, amniotic fluid will accumulate in the amniotic sac. The liquid may also accumulate in a woman with DIABETES or MULTIPLE BIRTHS. Hydramnios is associated with higher risk of PREMATURE delivery and abnormal FETAL PRESENTATION. On the other hand, oligohydramnios can occur if the fetus has KIDNEY AND UROLOGICAL PROBLEMS, if the PLACENTA is malfunctioning, if the mother has PREECLAMPSIA or ECLAMPSIA, or if delivery is overdue (beyond about forty-one weeks). Too little amniotic fluid is associated early with MISCARRIAGE and later with some physical deformities, such as CLUBFOOT. (See CHILDBIRTH; AMNIOCENTESIS.)

analysis-level thinking, developing conclusions after study of the various aspects of a situation or event. One of the main kinds of thinking or learning processes described by Benjamin Bloom, the others being KNOWLEDGE-LEVEL, COMPREHENSION-LEVEL, APPLICATION-LEVEL, SYNTHESIS-LEVEL, and EVALUATION-LEVEL.

analytic learning, a type of LEARNING STYLE that focuses on the general rule or concept first, then on the parts or supporting details.

anaphylactic shock, a type of SHOCK induced by an allergic reaction to an injected substance, such as bee's venom or penicillin. (See ALLERGY; SHOCK.)

anatomical age, numerical summary of the relationship between a child's growth and the statistical average for a child of the same size and sex; if a child of six has a degree of skeletal maturation normally seen in a seven-year-old, that child's anatomical age is seven. (See AGE.)

anemia, a condition in which a person has a deficiency in the red blood cells, which contain the *hemoglobin* that carries the all-important oxygen throughout the body. Red blood cells, originally formed in the BONE MARROW, live for about 120 days in the blood stream; older red cells are gradually trapped in the filtering tissues of the *lymphatic system* (see IMMUNE SYSTEM) and destroyed, often in the spleen. Anemia can result when more red blood cells are destroyed than are formed, when red blood cells self-destruct in the bloodstream (a process called *hemolysis*), when large amounts of blood have been lost (from injury, surgery, or internal bleeding), or when blood cells themselves are defective and incapable of carrying oxygen as they should.

Anemia can range from a mild condition to a severe, life-threatening one. Symptoms include headaches, fatigue, breathing difficulty during EXERCISE, paleness, and in more severe cases dizziness from too little oxygen to the brain, pain from too little oxygen to the heart, heart palpitations, and sometimes jaundice from an excess of the yellow pigment *bilirubin*, formed when red blood cells are destroyed (see LIVER AND LIVER PROBLEMS). Anemia is normally diagnosed by standard BLOOD TESTS, especially a complete blood count (CBC), which measures the number and proportion of the various types of blood cells in a sample of the patient's blood.

In general, treatment aims to restore the proper balance and effectiveness of the person's red blood cells, often by providing BLOOD TRANSFUSIONS and, where possible, attempting to treat the underlying cause of the anemia. The success of the treatment depends partly on the severity of the condition, how long the condition existed before it was diagnosed (and therefore how much the body was weakened or damaged), and the underlying cause.

Blood is the basic "transport system" of the body and is in contact with every organ and tissue, so anemia can have many causes. Among the main types found in children are:

- *Iron-deficiency anemia*, by far the most widespread type of anemia, generally resulting from a diet insufficient in IRON, a key mineral needed in the synthesis of hemoglobin. Iron-deficiency anemia is uncommon in breastfed infants, but may often occur if introduction of SOLID FOODS is delayed or if a toddler is allowed to subsist mostly on MILK. If children are not eating iron-bearing foods at the usual age (see SOLID FOODS), parents are advised to add an iron supplement to the diet. During their GROWTH SPURT, young boys may also need extra iron to prevent anemia, as may girls once MENSTRUATION starts, but older boys generally do not and risk having excess iron, which can build up in and damage body organs if they take a supplement.
- *Sickle cell anemia*, a GENETIC DISORDER of the AUTOSOMAL RECESSIVE type, in which the hemoglobin is abnormal, causing the red blood cells to be distorted into a sickle or crescent shape. Not only are these blood cells less effective at carrying oxygen, but their abnormal shape sometimes causes small blood vessels to become clogged, a painful, potentially life-threatening condition called a *sickle cell crisis*, which can badly damage organs involved, such as brain, kidney, liver, lungs, and spleen. Such a crisis is often treated with BLOOD TRANSFUSIONS, sometimes partial *exchange transfusions*, ANTIBIOTICS to fight infection, and oxygen.

  In the past, sickle cell anemia was often fatal before age three, with children dying suddenly from overwhelming infections. Screening of infants and advances in medical treatment, including giving preventive penicillin treatments in the first two years of life (until children have received all their basic vaccinations), has greatly increased life expectancy. However, the highest MORTALITY RATE is still found among children, who are also at great risk for stroke (see TRAUMATIC BRAIN INJURY).

The sickle-cell trait is found most often among Blacks and to some extent among people of Mediterranean origin. Children affected are those who have inherited the trait from both parents; those who inherit the trait from only one parent are usually symptom-free, but are CARRIERS. Prospective parents with sickle-cell anemia in their family history may want to seek GENETIC COUNSELING. Various PRENATAL TESTS can tell if a FETUS has the trait.

- *Thalassemia,* a genetic disorder of the autosomal recessive type, in which the red blood cells are fragile and smaller than usual and prematurely self-destruct. Thalassemia, found most often among people of Mediterranean origin, is also called *Mediterranean anemia* (thalassa = sea), but it also occurs among people of southeast Asian ancestry. Either of two chains of PROTEINS in hemoglobin, the *alpha* chain or the *beta* chain, may be involved. The severity of the disorder varies from mild to life-threatening.

  The most severe form is *beta-thalassemia,* also called *thalassemia major* or *Cooley's anemia.* Symptoms often appear in infancy, including slow physical development; susceptibility to infections, often leading to jaundice (see LIVER AND LIVER PROBLEMS); and enlargement of the SPLEEN and bone marrow, which can cause abnormal bone growth. If it is undiagnosed and untreated, death normally occurs before age three. Blood transfusions are often given, but these cause excess iron to be stored in body organs (*hemosiderosis*), which can in turn cause cirrhosis of the liver, DIABETES, heart problems, and early death.

  This iron build-up can be counteracted with painful eight- to twelve-hour nightly infusions of a medication, using a battery-operated pump and a needle inserted into the abdomen to remove accumulated iron. Researchers are exploring the possibility of using an oral drug to replace the pump. BONE MARROW TRANSPLANTS can cure Cooley's anemia, but the operation carries high risks and is available to limited numbers of patients. Prospective parents will want to consider genetic counseling and prenatal testing. GENE THERAPY holds promise for the future.
- *Megaloblastic anemia,* in which deficiency of key VITAMINS, specifically VITAMIN B12 and FOLIC ACID, leads to production of abnormally large, deformed red blood cells (*macrocytes).* Sometimes the deficiency results from the body's inability to absorb VITAMIN B12, a condition called *pernicious anemia.* But megalobastic anemia can also result from poor NUTRITION or from MALABSORPTION, especially with disorders such as CROHN'S DISEASE or CELIAC SPRUE; it is also associated with diabetes and hypothyroidism (see THYROID GLAND). If possible, the underlying problem is treated, but beyond that, treatment may require regular injections or supplements of the missing vitamins.
- *Aplastic anemia,* in which the blood has too few blood cells of all types, because of damage to the bone marrow where the cells are produced. Though aplastic anemia can result from some kinds of viral infections, it often stems from external sources, such as therapies using radiation and chemotherapy (see CANCER) or exposure to some kinds of chemicals (see ENVIRONMENTAL HAZARDS). A rare CONGENITAL form of aplastic anemia is *Fanconi's anemia.* In some cases, aplastic anemia may be treated by bone marrow transplant. If severe and irreversible, it can be fatal.

Anemia can also result when a child has long-term CHRONIC illness. In cases of RH INCOMPATIBILITY between mother and child, anemia may develop in the FETUS. Anemia may also develop during PREGNANCY and is best prevented by a diet of foods rich in iron, including liver, red meats, dried beans, leafy green vegetables, and iron-fortified cereals. During PRENATAL CARE and WELL-BABY EXAMINATIONS, anemia is routinely tested for, so that any developing problems can be treated most effectively before damage is done. Some doctors routinely prescribe iron supplements during pregnancy, since more iron is required than is found in the average diet. Iron supplements tend to make bowel movements darker and harder, so—especially during pregnancy—women are advised to increase the amount of fluids and roughage in their diet.

FOR HELP AND FURTHER INFORMATION

National Heart, Lung, and Blood Information Center (NHLBIC), 301–251–1222. (For full group information, see HEART AND HEART PROBLEMS.)

National Maternal and Child Health Clearinghouse (NMCHC), 703–821–8955. Publishes *Parents' Handbook for Sickle Cell Disease, Part I: Birth to Six Years of Age, Part II: Six to Eighteen Years of Age, Problem Oriented Management of Sickle Syndromes,* and *Sickle Cell: A Resource Guide for Families and Professionals,* 2nd ed. (For full group information, see PREGNANCY.)

Sickle Cell Disease Association of America (SCDAA)
200 Corporate Pointe, Suite 495
Culver City, CA 90230–7633
301–216–6363; 800–421–8453
Fax: 301–480–0868
Linda Anderson, Executive Director
Organization concerned with sickle cell disease; formerly the National Association for Sickle Cell Disease (NASCD); provides information; acts as advocate; sponsors local chapters; publishes various materials, including:

- quarterly *Sickle Cell News, SCDAA Record,* and *SCDAA Annual Report.*
- fact sheets: *Sickle Cell Trait and Anemia, Hemoglobin C Trait, Thalassemia Trait, Pregnant Women with Sickle Cell*

Trait, Parents of Newborns with Sickle Cell Trait (or *Sickle Cell Anemia*), *Parents of Newborns with Sickle Cell Hemoglobin C Disease* (or *Thalassemia Disease*), *Questions and Answers About How to Provide Your Child with Sickle Cell Disease with the Best Chance*, and *Questions and Answers About What Parents Should Do When Their Child Has Pain.*

- booklets: *How to Help Your Child to Take It in Stride, Parent/Teacher Guide, SCA—Tell the Facts, Help! A Guide to Sickle Cell Disease Programs and Services*, and *Highlights of the Sickle Cell Story.*
- "viewpoints" on promising treatments and discoveries, and materials on community organizations and programs.

Cooley's Anemia Foundation
129–09 26th Avenue
Flushing, NY 11354
718–321-CURE [2873]; 800–522–7222
Fax: 718–321–3340
Gina Cioffi, Executive Director
Organization concerned with Cooley's anemia; provides information and referrals; operates **Thalassemia Action Group (TAG)** for patient support; encourages research; publishes various materials, including quarterly newsletter *Lifeline*; brochures *The Fight Against Thalassemia* and *Thalassemia—It's Your Choice*; booklets *What Is Cooley's Anemia, All You Need to Know About Being a Carrier of Thalassemia*, and *My Coloring Book on Thalassemia* (for children); and videos *TAG You're It* and *Precious Gift of Time.*

Fanconi Anemia Support Group
1902 Jefferson Street, Suite 2
Eugene, OR 97405
503–687–4658
Fax: 503–687–0548
Linda De Spain, Executive Coordinator
Lynn Frohnmayer or David Frohnmayer, Contacts
Organization of families of children who have Fanconi anemia; provides information; supports research; publishes *FA Family Newsletter and Scientific Supplement, FA Family Bulletin, FA Family Director*, and *Fanconi Anemia: A Handbook for Families and Their Physicians*, 2nd ed.

March of Dimes Birth Defects Foundation (MDBDF), 914–428–7100. Publishes information sheets *Sickle Cell Anemia* and *Thalassemia.* (For full group information, see BIRTH DEFECTS.)

National Organization for Rare Disorders (NORD), 800–999–6673. (For full group information, see RARE DISORDERS.)

Parents Helping Parents (PHP), 408–727–5775. Publishes information packet *Sickle Cell Anemia.* (For full group information, see HELP FOR SPECIAL CHILDREN on page 689.)

Agency for Health Care Policy and Research Clearinghouse, 800–358–9295. Publishes *Sickle Cell Disease in Newborns and Infants: A Guide for Parents* and InstantFAX materials on sickle cell disease. (For full group information, see HEALTH INSURANCE)

OTHER RESOURCES

GENERAL WORKS

Back to Our Roots: Cooking for Control of Sickle Cell Anemia and Cancer Prevention, 2nd ed. Dawud Ujamaa. Al Mai Dah, 1995.

Anemia: A Guide to Causes, Treatment and Prevention. Jill Davies. Thorsons, 1994.

What You Can Do about Anemia. Marilyn Larkin. Dell, 1993.

Sickle Cell Anemia: A Source Guide. Gordon, 1991.

FOR PRETEENS OR TEENS

Sickle Cell Anemia. George Beshore, ed. Watts, 1994.

(See also BLOOD AND BLOOD DISORDERS; GENETIC COUNSELING; GENETIC DISORDERS.)

anesthesia, treatment to block sensation of pain during a medical procedure; literally, absence of feeling. Anesthesia may be topical, local, regional, or general. *Topical anesthesia* is the most minimal, involving application of a sense-deadening substance to a surface such as the skin, a membrane, or the cornea of the eye. *Local anesthesia* is applied to just a small area of the body, as in dental surgery or some minor surgical procedures. It is often administered by INJECTION, though sometimes a surface anesthetic may be used. It is local anesthesia that is now commonly used in CIRCUMCISION, though many doctors still use no anesthesia at all for children (for a discussion of why, see below and PAIN AND PAIN TREATMENT).

Regional anesthetic deadens feeling in a whole area of the body, generally by means of a *nerve block*, an injection to anesthetize the main nerve serving that area of the body. The nerve block allows physicians to anesthetize areas that are very large or hard to reach directly by injection. Among the main kinds of regional anesthetic are:

- *Epidural anesthesia*, in which anesthetic is injected into the spine—more precisely, into the epidural space between the vertebrae and the spinal cord—during surgery or CHILDBIRTH—to anesthetize the area around the pelvis, lower abdomen, and GENITALS. Often a CATHETER (a thin, flexible tube) is left in place, so more anesthetic or *analgesics* (pain-killers) can be given as needed.
- *Pudendal block*, in which anesthetic is injected into the VAGINA wall, to anesthetize the area of the VULVA during LABOR (especially during FORCEPS DELIVERY), without affecting the contractions of the UTERUS.
- *Paracervical block*, in which the anesthetic is injected into the CERVIX during childbirth without adversely affecting labor.
- *Spinal anesthesia*, in which the anesthetic is injected between the vertebrae into the CEREBROSPINAL FLUID,

using a technique similar to a LUMBAR PUNCTURE; used for surgery involving the lower limbs and abdomen, alternatively with epidural anesthesia.

- *Caudal block*, in which anesthetic is injected into the bottom part of the spinal cord through the sacrum (just above the "tail bone", during childbirth or surgery in the genital or rectal area; often epidural anesthesia is used instead, since caudal block is less reliable and, during childbirth, carries the risk of reducing the force of the contractions and of accidental injection of the FETUS.
- *Intercostal anesthesia*, involving injection between two ribs.
- *Brachial plexus anesthesia*, involving injection into the set of nerves that serves each arm.

Use of regional anesthesia has very much changed childbirth (as well as many forms of surgery), allowing a woman to have relief from pain, while retaining consciousness during the birth itself. As part of the planning for childbirth, women and their partners will want to explore and discuss with their physician the advantages and disadvantages of the various kinds of anesthesia and whether some forms may slow labor by weakening contractions or may adversely affect the baby.

Beyond regional anesthesia is *general anesthesia*, in which the patient not only loses feeling but also consciousness as well. Still common in many kinds of surgery, it is rarely used today during childbirth, because it can cause LUNG AND BREATHING PROBLEMS for the baby. Before an operation, the ANESTHESIOLOGIST normally meets with the patient to assess the patient's physical condition and to discuss the kind of anesthesia to be used. The type of anesthesia will depend on the kind and length of the procedure being performed, which might range from a twenty-minute surgical BIOPSY to a many-hours-long organ TRANSPLANT.

Before leaving for the operating room, a patient is generally given an injection of a muscle relaxant and perhaps some other drugs through a vein in the hand; the needle is left in place for administration of other drugs later as needed. The anesthesia itself may be given by injection or by inhalation of gases, sometimes breathed in through a mask (as when a muscle relaxant has been given) or through breathing tubes.

Anesthesia is not risk-free. A small number of people have allergic, sometimes life-threatening reactions to anesthetics. This condition is a GENETIC DISORDER called *malignant hyperthermia,* involving extremely high temperature and rigid muscles. If such reactions appear anywhere in a family's medical history, parents should be sure their doctor knows about the problem before childbirth or other kinds of treatment. On rare occasions, nerves can be damaged also by injections of regional anesthetics, and general anesthesia can bring on dangerous and even fatal heart irregularities, breathing problems, low BLOOD PRESSURE, and other kinds of problems.

When time permits before an operation, and especially when a child is being operated on, parents should explore carefully the pros and cons of various forms of anesthesia. They must, in particular, act as advocates for their children (see ADVOCACY). Many doctors practicing today were trained in the belief that babies and young children feel no pain, the assumption being that their CENTRAL NERVOUS SYSTEMS are not sufficiently developed. That mistaken belief was disproved by at least the early 1970s, but even into the late 1980s surgery was frequently performed on infants and young children with *no anesthesia.* The picture is changing in the 1990s—but still slowly. Even when anesthesia is used during surgery, pain in infants and young children is often not treated after surgery (see PAIN AND PAIN TREATMENT). Recent studies have shown that operations performed on infants who received anesthesia and sedation had fewer postoperative complications, while infants who underwent surgery with "minimal" anesthesia had more postoperative complications and a higher death rate.

FOR HELP AND FURTHER INFORMATION

Pediatric Projects, 800–947–0947. Publishes reprint *Presence of Parents in the Anaesthetic Room.* (For full group information, see HOSPITAL.)

National Institute of General Medical Sciences (NIGMS)
45 Center Drive
MSC 6200
Bethesda, MD 20892–6200
301–496–7301
Fax: 301–402–0224
One of the National Institutes of Health, researching areas of general medical concern; provides information; publishes general materials and technical reports for specialists.

(See MALIGNANT HYPERTHERMIA.)

anesthesiologist (anesthetist), a physician who specializes in administering anesthetics, drugs that produce local or general loss of sensation, usually in preparation for some form of surgery. In some situations, a *nurse anesthetist,* a registered nurse with advanced training, may handle ANESTHESIA. If you or your child are scheduled for any procedure that may require anesthesia, you should meet with the anesthesiologist beforehand to discuss the various options and the risks and benefits of each.

angiogram (arteriogram), a MEDICAL TEST in which a contrasting material (usually a dye) is injected into a deep artery in the body, such as in the groin or neck, and X-RAYS are taken as the material flows through the body. Angiograms can be used in many situations. In diagnosing BRAIN TUMORS, they may help a physician to see the precise pattern of blood vessels in the brain and the amount of blood that may be feeding into a tumor. In diagnosing heart problems, angiography often involves insertion of a CATHETER through the groin or arm to check for abnormalities in the blood vessels, in various body organs, and in sites of blood clots or internal bleeding. In diagnosing EYE AND VISION PROBLEMS, OPTHALMOLOGISTS sometimes use a technique called *fluorescein retinal angiography* or *eye angiography*, in which X-rays are taken of the eye, after INJECTION of a dyed fluid and use of eyedrops to dilate (open) the pupils of the eye. (See MEDICAL TESTS.)

anorexia nervosa, a type of MENTAL DISORDER, psychiatrically classified as an *eating disorder*, that involves self-starvation, through dieting and also often through induced VOMITING and use of laxatives (characteristic of the related eating disorder, BULIMIA NERVOSA). People with anorexia nervosa have not "lost their appetite," as the term *anorexia* implies; they are, in fact, often obsessed with food, sometimes hoarding or concealing it, but their intense fear of gaining weight and "being fat" leads them to drastically reduce their food intake. They also have a distorted BODY IMAGE, imagining that they are fat, even when they are emaciated. Those who suffer from the disorder often take their body weight down to 15 to 25 percent below normal body weight for their age. Even before onset, only about a third of those afflicted are even mildly overweight, rarely obese.

The disorder can affect young children, adolescent boys, or adults of both sexes, but is most common among adolescent girls ages twelve through twenty-one. The first sign (even before dramatic weight loss) is often cessation of MENSTRUATION. The drastic drop in weight and the resulting toll on the body cause a variety of other bodily changes, including lowered temperature, slowed heartbeat, lowered BLOOD PRESSURE, EDEMA, CONSTIPATION, slowing of sexual maturation (in both boys and girls), loss of HAIR on the head, and development of *lanugo* (hair like that on newborns) on the body. Often associated disorders are DEPRESSION and OBSESSIVE COMPULSIVE DISORDER.

The causes of anorexia nervosa are unknown, but the National Institute of Child Health and Human Development (NICHD) notes, "a combination of psychological, environmental, and physiological factors are associated with development of the disorder." Psychologists note that many people with anorexia nervosa come from White middle- and upper-class families who emphasize high achievement and that before onset of the disorder they were often good students and "model children." Some feel that the normal adolescent feelings of rebellion were suppressed and that anorexia nervosa is somehow a result of desire for independent control and perfection.

Others are researching possible physical causes. The HYPOTHALAMUS, which affects many of the body's key functions, is abnormal in people with anorexia nervosa, and researchers are exploring the possibility that malfunctions in the hypothalamus precede and help trigger the disorder.

The most important concern, once the disorder is recognized, is to get the patient to eat and gain weight; stressing the urgency, the NICHD notes "about 10 to 15 percent of anorexia nervosa patients die, usually after losing at least half their normal body weight." In addition to nutritional therapy, treatment often involves both individual psychotherapy and family counseling, sometimes in the family setting, but often in a hospital. If the patient is hospitalized, arrangements (called a *behavioral contract*) are often made for the patient to have privileges (such as outings) in return for weight gain. That keeps control in the patient's hands. Family counseling focuses on how not to make eating become a source of family tension. Support groups (see the following list) can be helpful to both parents and anorexics, immediately and in the years that follow. Relapses sometimes occur, even after a patient has completed treatment and regained normal weight, so the NICHD recommends that follow-up therapy be maintained for three to five years. Parents should be aware that many HEALTH CARE programs and HEALTH INSURANCE policies do not cover therapy for MENTAL DISORDERS. However, at least one family in recent years has won a claim for coverage for the hospital care given to their daughter, which focused on physical therapy.

Beyond the question of actual anorexia, many parents are concerned about how teenagers (and many adults) view *body image*. Though many American children are medically considered obese because they weigh 20 percent more than the normal weight for their height (see OBESITY), many people who diet strenuously, including most of those with anorexia and bulimia, are not overweight, but only *think* themselves to be so. They have an unrealistic image of an "ideal" weight, for people in general and for themselves in particular. Often this ideal is fostered by social images, such as the unrealistic figures of the Barbie and other "fashion" dolls.

Children also exaggerate or even imagine defects in themselves as part of a general fear of being unattractive. This is especially true in adolescence, notably among girls, some of whom fight the normal and healthy changes in their body proportions, as they seek to emulate svelte, skinny, and often downright anorexic figures in the media. Interestingly, one recent study of 3,000 adolescents found that while most teenage boys were trying to *gain* weight, to have a body shape more like an adult's, approximately two-thirds of the teenage girls were attempting to *lose* weight; these were typically girls who were of normal weight. Some other studies have suggested that girls with eating disorders are often copying their mothers' behavior toward dieting and eating and her view of bodily perfection. The eating disorders bulimia and anorexia are found only among 2 to 4 percent of teenage girls (and a much smaller percentage of boys), but clearly the number of children who have a distorted body image is much higher.

FOR HELP AND FURTHER INFORMATION

National Association of Anorexia Nervosa and Associated Disorders (ANAD)
P.O. Box 7
Highland Park, IL 60035
Hotline 847–831–3438
Fax: 847–433–4632
Vivian Meehan, President

Organization concerned with anorexia and other eating disorders; provides support, information, and referrals; publishes various materials, including newsletter *Working Together* and *When Image Becomes an Obsession, It's Time to Take a Closer Look!*.

American Anorexia Bulimia Association (AABA)
293 Central Park West, 1-R
New York, NY 10024
212–501–8351
Randi Wirth, Executive Director
Network of professionally led support groups for people with eating disorders; offers information, counseling, and referrals; links new members with recovered member; publishes various materials, such as newsletter, fact sheets, and pamphlets, including bibliography.

National Institute of Child Health and Human Development (NICHD), 301–496–5133. Publishes *Facts About Anorexia Nervosa.* (For full group information, see PREGNANCY.)

National Institute of Mental Health (NIMH), 301–443–4513. Publishes *Eating Disorders.* (For full group information, see MENTAL DISORDER.)

American Academy of Child and Adolescent Psychiatry (AACAP), 202–966–7300. Publishes information sheet *Teenagers with Eating Disorders.* (For full group information, see MENTAL DISORDERS.)

Food and Nutrition Information Center (FNIC), 301–504–5414. Publishes resource list *Anorexia Nervosa and Bulimia Nutri-Topics.* (For full group information, see NUTRITION.)

National Mental Health Consumer Self-Help Clearinghouse, 800–553–4539. Publishes reprint packet on eating disorders. (For full group information, see MENTAL DISORDERS.)

OTHER RESOURCES

For parents and other adults

The No-Nonsense Parents' Guide: What You Can Do about Teens and Alcohol, Drugs, Sex, Eating Disorders and Depression. Sheila Fuller and others. Parents Pipeline, 1992.

A Parent's Guide to Eating Disorders: Prevention and Treatment of Anorexia Nervosa and Bulimia. Brett Valette. Avon, 1990.

Anorexia, Bulimia, and Compulsive Overeating: A Practical Guide for Counselors and Families. David Swift and Kathleen Zraly. Continuum, 1990. Paperback title: *Overcoming Eating Disorders: Recovery from Anorexia, Bulimia, and Compulsive Overeating* (1992).

General works

Eating Disorders: The Facts, 3rd ed. Suzanne Abraham and Derek Llewellyn-Jones. Oxford University Press, 1992.

Eating Disorders. Steven Spotts. Rapha, 1991.

Eating Disorders. L. George Hsu. Guilford Press, 1990.

For children

Eating Disorders. Don Nardo. Lucent Books, 1991.

About Weight Problems and Eating Disorders. Joy Berry. Children's, 1990.

For preteens and teens

When Food's a Foe: How to Confront and Conquer Eating Disorders, rev. ed. Nancy J. Kolodny. Little, Brown, 1992.

Straight Talk about Eating Disorders. Michael Maloney and Rachel Kranz. Facts on File, 1991.

Everything You Need to Know about Eating Disorders. Rachel Kubersky. Rosen, 1991.

Coping with Eating Disorders. Barbara Moe. Rosen, 1991.

Eating Disorders. John R. Mathews. Facts on File, 1990.

Eating Habits and Disorders. Rachel Epstein. Chelsea House, 1990.

On treatment and recovery

The Deadly Diet: Recovering from Anorexia and Bulimia, 2nd ed. Terence J. Sandbeck. New Harbinger, 1993.

Beyond Chaotic Eating: A Way Out of Anorexia, Bulimia, and Compulsive Eating. Helena Wilkinson. Zondervan, 1993.

Anorexia Nervosa and Recovery: A Hunger for Meaning. Karen Way. Haworth, 1992.

Controlling Eating Disorders with Facts, Advice, and Resources, Raymond Lemberg, ed. Oryx Press, 1992.

The Thin Disguise: Understanding and Overcoming Anorexia and Bulimia. Pam Vredevelt. Nelson, 1992.

It's Not Your Fault: Overcoming Anorexia and Bulimia Through Biopsychiatry. Russell Marx. Random, 1991.

Living with Anorexia and Bulimia. James Moorey. St. Martin's, 1991.

Personal experiences

Diary of an Anorectic: A Young Woman's Struggle With Anorexia and Her Journey Toward Recovery. Kelly A. Phillips. Palm Bay, 1995.

The Withering Child. John A. Gould. University of Georgia Press, 1993. On a self-starving young son.

Feast of Famine: A Physician's Personal Struggle to Overcome Anorexia Nervosa. Joan Johnston. RPI Publishing, 1993.

Hope and Recovery: A Mother-Daughter Story about Anorexia Nervosa, Bulimia, and Manic Depression. Becky T. Markosian and Emma L. Thayne. Watts, 1992.

Starving for Attention: A Young Woman's Struggle with and Triumph over Anorexia Nervosa, 2nd ed. Cherry Boone O'Neill. Hazelden, 1992.

Hope and Recovery: A Mother-Daughter Story about Anorexia Nervosa, Bulimia, and Manic Depression. Becky Thayne Markosian and Emma Lou Thayne. Watts, 1992.

Conversations with Anorexics. Hilde Bruch and others. Basic Books, 1989.

BACKGROUND WORKS

Starving in the Silences: An Exploration of Anorexia Nervosa. Matra Robertson. New York University Press, 1992.
Starving to Death in a Sea of Objects: The Anorexia Nervosa Syndrome. John A. Sours. Aronson, 1992.
The Beauty Myth. Naomi Wolf. Morrow, 1991.
Anorexia and Bulimia: Anatomy of a Social Epidemic. Richard A. Gordon. Blackwell, 1990.

(See also BULIMIA; MENTAL DISORDERS.)

anovulation, failure of the OVARIES to develop, mature, and release an egg (OVUM) for fertilization, a possible cause of INFERTILITY. A woman who has a MENSTRUAL PERIOD without release of an egg is said to have had an *anovulatory period* (see OVULATION).

anoxia, deficiency in or stoppage of oxygen supply to the body, as may happen during PREGNANCY, during difficult LABOR, or in some cases of high FEVER and accidents, such as near-drowning. It can also result from ANEMIA, in which the blood is unable to carry oxygen to body tissues, or from internal toxic conditions in which the tissues are unable to absorb oxygen from the blood. However it occurs, anoxia can cause damage to affected tissues. The brain is especially susceptible, and oxygen starvation has been implicated in numerous DEVELOPMENTAL DISORDERS, such as LEARNING DISABILITIES.

antibodies, substances created by the IMMUNE SYSTEM to fight *antigens,* which are matter that the body perceives as foreign. In IMMUNIZATION, various VACCINES are used to trigger production of antibodies without the person actually getting and having to fight off the disease itself. (See IMMUNE SYSTEM; IMMUNIZATION.)

antidiuretic hormone (ADH), a HORMONE produced by the PITUITARY GLAND, which controls how much fluid remains in the body and how much is excreted in urine. Lack of ADH can trigger *diabetes insipidus* (see DIABETES).

antigen, a substance that the body perceives as "foreign" and that therefore triggers a response from the IMMUNE SYSTEM, which (among other things) produces ANTIBODIES to fight the substance. If the antigen is involved in ALLERGY or ASTHMA, it is often called an *allergen.*

antioxidant, a substance that works in the body to help prevent oxygen from destroying other substances; VITAMIN K is a common antioxidant in the body. When used as FOOD ADDITIVES, antioxidants work as preservatives, to stave off spoilage.

anxiety, a feeling of uneasiness, tension, worry, and fear, that often includes physical changes, such as disturbed breathing, rapid heartbeat, and sweating; a common symptom in many MENTAL DISORDERS. Anxiety and AVOIDANCE behavior are especially characteristic of the disorders classified as *anxiety disorders,* including PANIC DISORDERS, *phobic disorders* (see PHOBIA), OBSESSIVE COMPULSIVE DISORDER, SEPARATION ANXIETY DISORDER, AVOIDANT DISORDER, and OVERANXIOUS DISORDER.

Apgar score, an evaluation of the condition of a newborn; a summary using a five-factor rating scale, with each factor given zero, one, or two points and a top score of ten points. The evaluation is normally done a minute after birth and then again five minutes after birth, with both scores noted on the baby's medical record. The aim of the Apgar score is to identify as quickly as possible babies with special problems that may call for immediate treatment or transfer to a NEONATAL INTENSIVE CARE UNIT (NICU). A newborn with a score of seven to ten is regarded as being in excellent condition. A score of five to seven suggests some mild problems, while a lower score indicates need for immediate intervention, such as RESUSCITATION. Sometimes the second score is much higher because a problem, such as mucus obstructing the air passage, is only temporary. (See APGAR SCORING SYSTEM on page 43.)

aphasia, loss or impairment of the ability to use words and to understand language symbols in reading, writing, or speaking, usually resulting from TRAUMATIC BRAIN INJURY, disease, or delayed development of the CENTRAL NERVOUS SYSTEM, in which case it is called *developmental aphasia.* Impairment of language ability is also called *dysphasia.* A type of aphasia involving the inability to recall the names of people, objects, and places is called *anomia*; difficulty in producing handwriting is called DYSGRAPHIA, while total inability to write is *agraphia.* Children with LEARNING DISABILITIES or other DEVELOPMENTAL DISORDERS may sometimes have aphasia; they experience great frustration when they know what they want to say, but are unable to say it.

FOR HELP AND FURTHER INFORMATION

National Institute on Deafness and Other Communication Disorders (NIDCD), 800–241–1044. Publishes *Aphasia Treatment: Current Approaches and Research Opportunities* and *Language Disorders Organizational Resources.* (For full group information, see COMMUNICATION SKILLS AND DISORDERS.)

American Speech-Language-Hearing Association, 800–638–8255, voice/TT. Publishes brochure *Questions About Adult Aphasia.* (For full group information, see COMMUNICATION SKILLS AND DISORDERS.)

American Heart Association (AHA), 800–242–8721. Publishes *Caring for the Person with Aphasia.* (For full group information, see HEART AND HEART PROBLEMS.)

OTHER RESOURCES

Understanding Aphasia. Harold Goodglass. Academic Press, 1993.

(See also LEARNING DISABILITIES.)

apnea of prematurity (AOP), brief cessation of breathing, normally found in SLEEP APNEA, but of special danger among PREMATURE infants and overweight children; also called *apnea of infancy* (AOI).

Apparent Life-Threatening Event (ALTE), a frightening episode in which an observer thinks someone has died or is dying and needs RESUSCITATION. In cases of infants with pathologic SLEEP APNEA, this is sometimes called *aborted crib death* or *near-miss SIDS* and seems to be associated with increased risk of SUDDEN INFANT DEATH SYNDROME (SIDS).

appeal, in the court system, a formal request for a higher court to review the judgment of a lower court; if errors are found in the conduct of the earlier trial, the lower court may be overruled and possibly a new trial granted. The right of appeal was not always available outside the traditional court system, in administrative areas such as those involving EDUCATION and family law, but in recent years it has been extended to many such areas. If parents disagree with the INDIVIDUALIZED EDUCATION PROGRAM proposed for a child, for example, they can follow an established appeal procedure. This is often called DUE PROCESS, the legal term for the constitutional right that is now being applied to noncourt areas.

appendicitis, inflammation of the APPENDIX, a small projection off the large intestine; an ACUTE and highly dangerous disorder that can occur at any age, but is most common among children (though not infants) and young adults, especially males. Appendicitis has various causes, including obstruction by hardened feces or an undigested foreign body or infestation by parasites, that lead to inflammation and infection. Early symptoms include generalized, sometimes intermittent pain around the mid-abdomen, gradually localizing in the lower right quarter of the abdomen; nausea and VOMITING; low-grade FEVER; increased white blood count; and decreased bowel activity and CONSTIPATION. Because these symptoms can be found with other disorders, appendicitis is not easy to diagnose. However, a child with some of these symptoms should be examined by a doctor immediately.

If appendicitis is diagnosed, emergency surgery—an *appendectomy* (removal of the appendix)—is indicated. If treatment is delayed, the appendix will generally rupture, at first causing cessation of pain, but quickly spreading infection to the abdominal (*peritoneal*) cavity. The result is *peritonitis,* a life-threatening infection, though now often treatable if caught early. (See APPENDIX; IMMUNE SYSTEM; DIGESTIVE SYSTEM AND DISORDERS.)

appendix, a small projection off the large intestine that contains tissue that acts as a filter in the *lymphatic system,* the network through which the body's IMMUNE SYSTEM operates. If the appendix itself becomes infected and inflamed, the resulting acute APPENDICITIS can be life-threatening and requires emergency surgery.

application-level thinking, use of previously learned information in a new, unfamiliar context. The term comes from Benjamin Bloom's description of the various kinds of thinking or learning processes, the other main types being KNOWLEDGE-LEVEL, COMPREHENSION-LEVEL, ANALYSIS-LEVEL, SYNTHESIS-LEVEL, and EVALUATION-LEVEL.

appropriate gestational age (AGA), a description applied to an infant who is small and of LOW BIRTH WEIGHT, but whose size and stage of development is appropriate to his or her stage of GESTATION, meaning the number of weeks since CONCEPTION; often refers to a PREMATURE baby. By contrast, an infant who is *small for gestational age* (SGA) grew more slowly than normal. (See GESTATIONAL AGE.)

Apgar Scoring System

RATING FACTOR	0 POINTS	1 POINT	2 POINTS
Color	Blue or pale	Trunk pink, extremities blue	All pink
Heart rate	None	Slow (under 100 beat per minute)	Over 100 per minute
Muscle tone	Limp	Some movement of limbs	Active movement of limbs
Reflex irritability (on being "poked") in nose)	No response	Grimace when stimulated	Cry, cough, or sneeze
Respiratory effort	None	Irregular, with weak cry	Regular with strong cry

apraxia, inability to produce in sequence the movements necessary to draw shapes and figures or to copy words and letters, because of inadequate development of FINE MOTOR SKILLS.

aptitude test, a general type of test that is designed to predict a student's success in various kinds of learning before any instruction has taken place, as opposed to an ACHIEVEMENT TEST, given after instruction. How well aptitude tests succeed in doing this is a point of considerable controversy that focuses on VALIDITY. Many aptitude tests—probably the best-known is the SCHOLASTIC APTITUDE TEST—attempt to measure academic aptitude.

Mechanical aptitude tests attempt to assess how well a student is likely to do in learning skills involving mechanical devices. They normally test reasoning in relation to mechanical things and SPATIAL RELATIONS. In the widest sense, READINESS TESTS and DEVELOPMENTAL SCREENING TESTS are kinds of aptitude tests, but they generally purport to test not general learning success, but whether the child has the necessary PREREQUISITE skills and behavioral development needed to benefit fully from instruction. (See TESTS.)

arbitration, a procedure under which two parties submit their dispute for resolution to a neutral third party; that person (often someone from the American Arbitration Association) is either selected by the disputing parties or appointed by the court. The procedure is informal, though each side can present evidence and bring witnesses; however, unlike with MEDIATION, the arbitration decision is binding on both parties. The main advantages of arbitration are that it avoids the cost, delay, hard feelings, and even trauma involved in court cases. In some cases mediation, in which the mediator attempts to help the disputants themselves solve their problem, may be preferable; many turn to arbitration only if mediation fails. Many SEPARATION AGREEMENTS and cohabitation (living together) agreements include mediation and arbitration clauses. (See CUSTODY.)

architectural barriers, obstacles, such as stairs, narrow doorways, and inaccessible bathrooms, that bar people with physical DISABILITIES from free access to buildings. Many older buildings are completely inaccessible to people with physical disabilities, but various laws require that at least some be modified for free access. The EDUCATION FOR ALL HANDICAPPED CHILDREN ACT, for example, requires that school buildings be made accessible to students with disabilities. New construction of many kinds, especially schools and buildings supported by federal funds, must be designed for easy access.

arrearages, back payments that have accumulated on a debt, such as unpaid, overdue CHILD SUPPORT payments; also called *arrears*. The term is sometimes also used to refer to "unpaid" visits, when VISITATION RIGHTS have been denied.

arthritis, inflammation of the joints, often with swelling, pain, stiffness, and redness, a condition that can have a wide variety of causes and can affect just one part of the body or many. Most forms of arthritis affect primarily older people, as the joints wear down over the years, but some forms affect children.

Juvenile rheumatoid arthritis (JRA), also called *Still's disease*, generally attacks children, causing not only the usual pain and stiffness, but also sometimes muscle ATROPHY and deformity. If damage affects the *epiphyses*, the "growth plates" at the end of the long bones, the child's overall growth may be impaired. The severity of JRA depends to some extent on which parts of the body are affected; the systemic form of JRA can affect the heart and liver as well as the joints. JRA is thought to be a type of AUTOIMMUNE DISORDER, in which the body mistakenly attacks its own tissue. Some research suggests that it may result from a GENETIC DEFECT. The most common time of onset is ages one to three or ages eight to twelve. Unlike with adult forms of the disease, which usually persist, juvenile rheumatoid arthritis in some children may pass by the age of PUBERTY.

A related form of rheumatic disease affecting children is *ankylosing spondylitis*, which affects most severely the joints of the spine and the pelvis (*sacroiliac joints*). Another rheumatic disease sometimes appearing in children is LUPUS ERYTHEMATOSUS.

Children can also have forms of arthritis as a result of injury to a joint; bacterial infection, as from GONORRHEA, TUBERCULOSIS, or LYME DISEASE; or other disorders, such as ANEMIA. A related disorder is ARTHROGRYPOSIS MULTIPLEX CONGENITA (AMC).

FOR HELP AND FURTHER INFORMATION

American Juvenile Arthritis Organization (AJAO)
Arthritis Foundation
1314 Spring Street NW
Atlanta, GA 30309
404–872–7100; 800–283–7800
Fax: 404–872–0457
Don Riggin, Director and Chief Executive Officer
Patricia Harrington, Vice President for AJAO and Special Projects, Contact
Organization concerned with juvenile arthritis and related diseases; an arm of the Arthritis Foundation; provides information and referrals; publishes many materials; AJAO materials include quarterly *AJAO Newsletter*, bimonthly magazine *Arthritis Today* and booklets *Arthritis in Children*, *We Can: A Guide for Parents of Children with Arthritis*, *Understanding Juvenile Rheumatoid Arthritis*, *Growing Up with a Rheumatic Disease* (slide/tape program), *JRA and Me* (for children), *Ankylosing Spondylitis*, and *Directory of Pediatric Rheumatology Service*.

National Institute of Arthritis and Musculoskeletal and Skin Diseases (NIAMS)
1 AMS Circle
Bethesda, MD 20892–3675

301–495–4484
Fax: 301–480–6069
One of the National Institutes of Health, sponsoring research on arthritis, lupus, scleroderma, and other musculoskeletal and skin diseases; provides information, primarily through National Arthritis and Musculoskeletal and Skin Diseases Information Clearinghouse (NAMSIC) (see next organization listed)

National Arthritis and Musculoskeletal and Skin Diseases Information Clearinghouse (NAMSIC)
Box AMS
9000 Rockville Pike
Bethesda, MD 20892
301–495–4484
Fax: 301–480–6069
A service of the National Institute of Arthritis and Musculoskeletal and Skin Diseases (NIAMS) (see previous organization listing); publishes various materials, including information packages *Arthritis*, *Arthritis in Children*, *Juvenile Arthritis*, *Rheumatoid Arthritis*, *Arthritis and Diet*, *Osteoarthritis*, and related disorders; and research reports.

American Academy of Orthopaedic Surgeons (AAOS), 800–346–2267. Publishes brochure *Arthritis.* (For full group information, see BONE AND BONE DISORDERS.)

National Chronic Pain Outreach Association, Inc. (NCPOA), 301–652–4948. Publishes *Arthritis and Bradykinins.* (For full group information, see PAIN AND PAIN TREATMENT.)

National Organization for Rare Disorders (NORD), 800–999–6673. (For full group information, see RARE DISORDERS.)

Resources for Rehabilitation, 617–862–6455. Publishes brochure *Living with Arthritis.* (For full group information, see EYE AND VISION PROBLEMS.)

OTHER RESOURCES

For parents and other adults

Ward Lock Family Health Guide: Arthritis and Rheumatism. Lee Rodwell. Sterling, 1994.
Parenting a Child with Arthritis: A Practical, Empathetic Guide to Help You and Your Child Live with Arthritis. Earl Brewer, Jr. and Kathy C. Angel. Lowell House, 1992.
If It Runs in Your Family, Arthritis: Reducing the Risk. Mary D. Eades. Bantam, 1992.

General works

The Arthritis Sourcebook: Everything You Need to Know. Earl J. Brewer, Jr. and Kathy C. Angel. Lowell House, 1993.
Arthritis: Questions You Have, Answers You Need. Ellen Moyer. People's Medical Society, 1993.
The Duke University Medical Center Book of Arthritis. David S. Pisetsky and Susan F. Trien. Fawcett, 1992.

For teens

Arthritis. Dale C. Garell and Solomon H. Snyder, eds. Chelsea House, 1992.

Background works

All about Arthritis: Past, Present, Future. Derrick Brewerton. Harvard University Press, 1992.
Bees Don't Get Arthritis. Fred Malone. Academy Books, 1992.

(See also IMMUNE SYSTEM; LYME DISEASE.)

arthrogryposis multiplex congenita (AMC), a CONGENITAL disorder in which various joints of the body have a limited range of motion or *joint contracture.* Sometimes only a few joints are affected and the motion limitation is minimal. More often hands, wrists, elbows, shoulders, hips, knees, and feet are affected, the joints being stiff and contracted and sometimes fixed in painful awkward positions. In the most severe cases, virtually every joint, including jaw and spine, are affected. Often, accompanying muscle weakness further limits movement.

AMC is present at birth, and although some cases may have a genetic basis, most are believed to result from conditions in the UTERUS during PREGNANCY. In some cases, a FETUS may be constricted and unable to move; in such a case, it is theorized, unwanted connective tissue grows and fixes the joint in place, and unstretched tendons are shortened, limiting movement. In others cases, the muscles fail to develop properly or ATROPHY, possibly because of illness in the mother during pregnancy or perhaps because of some GENETIC DISORDERS such as MUSCULAR DYSTROPHY. Some cases of AMC may also result from malformation of the CENTRAL NERVOUS SYSTEM and spinal cord or from abnormal connections between tendons, bones, joints, and joint linings. Intelligence is not generally affected by AMC, but other abnormalities occasionally associated with AMC include CLEFT LIP AND PALATE, CLUBFOOT, and undescended testicles (CRYPTORCHIDISM).

AMC is not PROGRESSIVE and tends to improve as an infant grows. The disorder is often helped by physical therapy, to enhance mobility, and sometimes surgery or use of ORTHOPEDIC DEVICES to attempt to change the angle of the joint. Often, however, surgery needs to be repeated, as problems recur. Parents considering surgery for their child should carefully explore the likely benefits and their permanence. Surgery and follow-up rehabilitation should be handled by medical specialists experienced in dealing with this relatively rare disorder.

FOR HELP AND FURTHER INFORMATION

AVENUES (National Support Group for Arthrogryposis Multiplex Congenita)
P.O. Box 5192
Sonora, CA 95379
209–928–3688
E-mail: avenues@sonnet.com

Mary Anne Schmidt and Jim Schmidt, Executive Directors
Organization concerned with arthrogryposis multiplex congenita; provides information and referrals; publishes newsletter *Avenues* and *What Is Arthrogryposis?*

National Arthritis and Musculoskeletal and Skin Diseases Information Clearinghouse (NAMSIC), 301–495–4484. (For full group information, see ARTHRITIS.)

National Organization for Rare Disorders (NORD), 800–999–6673. (For full group information, see RARE DISORDERS.)

arthroscopic surgery, inspection and repair of the inside of a joint, using a flexible viewing tube called an *endoscope*, inserted through a small incision. The technique is most commonly used on knee joints and allows ORTHOPEDISTS to remove damaged material, repair torn tissues, and do other procedures. Arthroscopic surgery allows people—notably athletes—to resume normal activity quickly, unlike a traditional operation, in which the whole kneecap is exposed. (See BONE AND BONE DISORDERS.)

artificial insemination (AI), introduction of SEMEN into a woman's VAGINA through a tube or other instrument rather than through sexual intercourse, to achieve FERTILIZATION. To maximize the chances of conception, the woman normally uses various methods, such as NATURAL FAMILY PLANNING techniques, to pinpoint when OVULATION occurs. Using a HOME MEDICAL TEST (see OVULATION), she can normally identify the time of ovulation, which is the optimum time for insemination.

There are two main kinds of artificial insemination:

- *Artificial insemination-husband (AIH)*, also called *homologous insemination*, in which sperm from a woman's husband or sexual partner is used. On the appropriate day, the man provides semen, normally produced by MASTURBATION in a doctor's office and placed in a sterile container. The semen is generally injected near the woman's CERVIX using a syringe or plastic tube. Sometimes a small cup is used to hold the semen in place for a few hours. AIH may be used when the man has a physical disability that prevents normal intercourse, when there is a problem with the SPERM (as when there is a low sperm count or when the sperm need special treatment before being introduced), or when the fluids in the woman's vagina are hostile to the sperm (this procedure largely bypasses the vaginal fluids). A man's semen may also sometimes be stored ahead of time, if he will be undergoing medical treatment, such as radiation or chemotherapy (see CANCER), that can cause STERILITY. The procedure itself is simple, and some couples choose to perform insemination by themselves at home, though with a lower success rate. They should take care, however, not to introduce infection or to damage the genital tissues. To increase the success rate, the procedure may be repeated over the several days of highest fertility.
- *Artificial insemination-donor (AID)*, also called *heterologous insemination*, in which the semen used is from a donor, usually an anonymous one. Semen is obtained ahead of time from donors, sometimes for a fee. If the semen is collected at a SPERM BANK, donors must be in good general health and have been screened for known physical and mental disorders, though no amount of screening can guarantee that the man does not unknowingly carry a defective gene. Semen is frozen in liquid nitrogen and stored; before use, it is tested for common infections. Since AIDS and hepatitis (see LIVER AND LIVER PROBLEMS) can be transmitted through donor sperm, SPERM BANKS today are advised to use sperm only from donors who have tested negative for these viruses on two widely spaced tests. People considering AID—including single heterosexual or lesbian women who want to use the sperm of a known donor—are advised to explore protections very carefully. They are especially urged not to use fresh sperm; sperm should be frozen and stored until two negative AIDS and hepatitis tests have been obtained.

Couples may use AID when they have a history of GENETIC DISORDERS or RH INCOMPATIBILITY and in cases of INFERTILITY, such as when the man has too few or defective sperm. The identity of donors to sperm banks generally remains confidential, unless *both* the donor and the inseminated woman agree to have the information revealed. Women without male sexual partners can also choose to have a child through AID, using sperm from a personally chosen donor, such as a friend or, in the case of a lesbian couple, often a partner's brother or other male relative (she should be sure to arrange for testing, however, as noted earlier in this entry). Some states have implicitly or explicitly limited artificial insemination to married women, though some single women have successfully challenged such laws. Physically, the procedure is much the same as in AIH, with no apparent increase in BIRTH DEFECTS. Frozen sperm has a somewhat shorter life span, however, so timing is even more crucial. The woman (or the couple) is sometimes able to choose the donor, on the basis of anonymous information about the person's health and abilities, perhaps attempting to match characteristics of the donor with her (or their) own.

Anonymous sperm is often ordered from a sperm bank elsewhere in the country, to minimize the likelihood that a child will later unknowingly meet and marry another child with the same BIOLOGICAL FATHER. Women should get very specific information from their doctor on the source of the sperm. In one notorious case, a doctor who had performed artificial insemination on over 180 women had used his *own* sperm rather than sperm from a bank, so that many children in one region had, genetically, been fathered by a single man.

With AIH, the legal father is also the biological father, so legal questions are at a minimum. With AID, the law generally regards the woman's husband as the legal father. The anonymous biological father does not have PARENTS' RIGHTS. Legal problems and special wrinkles still remain, however. In one recent case, a woman became inseminated with what was supposed to be semen from her husband (who had since died of cancer). In fact, she received someone else's semen, as genetic analysis confirmed. Women without male sexual partners who use sperm from known male friends may also face uncertainty about who the child's legal father is, depending on the laws of the state where the women and their friends live. Similar legal problems surround SURROGATE PARENTING, which often uses artificial insemination.

With lesbian couples, the partner who actually bears the child is the biological MOTHER; the other partner may have no legal parental rights and, if the couple splits, may have no basis for CUSTODY or VISITATION RIGHTS. Couples can attempt to cover such eventualities by making preinsemination agreements, but these may or may not stand up in court, depending on the law in the state they live in at the time. They may well want to consult lesbian rights specialists before having a child on this basis.

FOR HELP AND FURTHER INFORMATION

RESOLVE, Inc., HelpLine: 617–623–0744. Publishes fact sheet *Husband Insemination (including IUI).* (For full group information, see INFERTILITY.)

Single Mothers by Choice (SMC), 212–988–0993. Publishes resource packet on donor insemination. (For full group information, see GENERAL PARENTING RESOURCES on page 634.)

Lavender Families Resource Network, 206–325–2643, voice/TT. Publishes pamphlet *Donor Insemination Basics* and resource packet on donor insemination. (For full group information, see HOMOSEXUALITY.)

National Institute of Child Health and Human Development (NICHD), 301–496–5133. (For full group information, see PREGNANCY.)

Donor's Offspring
P.O. Box 37
Sarcoxie, MO 64862
417–673–1906; 417–548–3679
Candace Cay Turner, Executive Director
Organization for people using, considering, or conceived through donor insemination. Publishes newsletter.

American Society for Reproductive Medicine (ASRM), 205–978–5000. (For full group information, see INFERTILITY.)

OTHER RESOURCES

GENERAL WORKS

Challenging Conceptions: Planning a Family by Self-Insemination. Lisa Saffron. InBook, 1994.

Donor Insemination. Christopher L. Barratt and Ian Cooke, eds. Cambridge University Press, 1993.

Lethal Secrets: The Psychology of Donor Insemination Problems and Solutions, rev. ed. Annette Baran and Reuben Pannor. Amistad, 1993.

FOR CHILDREN

Let Me Explain: A Story about Donor Insemination. Jane T. Schnitter. Perspectives, 1995.

(See also INFERTILITY.)

artificial respiration, attempting to restart or maintain breathing for someone whose breathing has stopped or is inadequate to maintain functioning; also called *rescue breathing* (if done mouth to mouth) or *ventilation* (especially if by a machine called a VENTILATOR or respirator). In *cardiopulmonary resuscitation* (CPR), *chest compressions* are also used, to stimulate the heart. The Public Health Service recommmends that parents take first aid and cardiopulmonary resuscitation courses locally, from the Red Cross or a nearby "Y," and review them periodically. They offer general guidelines for maintaining basic life support in an infant. (See IF YOUR INFANT IS NOT BREATHING on pages 48 and 49.)

FOR HELP AND FURTHER INFORMATION

Child Welfare League of America (CWLA), 202–638–2952. Publishes *CPR for Infants and Children: A Guide to Cardiopulmonary Resuscitation.* (For full group information, see FOSTER CARE.)

asphyxia, a severe kind of HYPOXIA (lack of oxygen). In the period just before, during, and after delivery, PERINATAL ASPHYXIA is a leading cause of infant death.

aspiration, withdrawal of fluid through a hollow needle, as in an ASPIRATION BIOPSY; also the act of breathing in or inhaling. In young children, foreign objects or substances can sometimes be inhaled directly or aspirated as vomit into the lungs, causing pneumonia. (See LUNG AND BREATHING DISORDERS.)

aspiration biopsy, a type of BIOPSY that uses a hollow *aspiration needle* to obtain a sample of suspect material, such as a possible TUMOR, from the body for laboratory analysis; also the technique of removing BONE MARROW from a patient, as part of a BONE MARROW TRANSPLANT.

assault, in the law, a threat to cause deliberate or reckless physical injury to someone, as opposed to BATTERY, which is actual physical violence or offensive contact. In general, *simple assault* is a threat the person did not seriously intend to carry out or an uncompleted attempt at injury. *Aggravated assault* refers to threat with intention to do physical injury or to commit other crimes. In general usage, as in discussions of child abuse (see CHILD ABUSE AND NEGLECT) or RAPE, the term is often used more loosely, as in "sexual assault," but such actions are legally considered battery.

assessment, a general term for evaluation, most often used to refer to testing, as in DIAGNOSTIC ASSESSMENT TESTS. Written evaluation of students—instead of or in addition to number or letter GRADES—is sometimes called INFORMAL ASSESSMENT or *summative evaluation.*

assessment center, in EDUCATION, an area of a school or a separate facility primarily devoted to administering various kinds of TESTS, generally to individual children, such as INTELLIGENCE TESTS, DEVELOPMENTAL SCREENING TESTS, DIAGNOSTIC ASSESSMENT TESTS, or READINESS TESTS.

assignment of support rights, an agreement made by a CUSTODIAL PARENT who has not been receiving court-ordered CHILD SUPPORT payments. The assignment of support rights normally specifies that such payments (including ARREARAGES) will be paid to the state, in exchange for various benefits, including a grant from AID TO FAMILIES WITH DEPENDENT CHILDREN.

assisted fertilization, general term for a range of technologies that use MICROMANIPULATION to help the SPERM and egg (OVUM) join to achieve FERTILIZATION, when more conventional forms of REPRODUCTIVE TECHNOLOGY, such as IN VITRO FERTILIZATION, have failed. Among these newer and still highly experimental techniques—all variations on in vitro fertilization—are INTRACYTOPLASMIC SPERM INJECTION (ICSI), PARTIAL ZONA DISSECTION (PZD), and SUBZONAL SPERM INSERTION (SZI). These methods are especially suitable for the most severe cases of male-related infertility, especially ICSI and SZI, which can be used on some men who have no active or normally shaped sperm. The two techniques can even be used on some men who have no sperm in their semen, as when their VAS DEFERENS are blocked, as long as they have some sperm-producing tissue in their TESTES.

These techniques are still in their early stages of development and testing, but there is some suggestion that FETUSES and babies born as a result of these new approaches may have a higher rate of CONGENITAL abnormalities. To check for possible BIRTH DEFECTS, people using such techniques are advised to have various PRENATAL TESTS performed, such as AMNIOCENTESIS, ULTRASOUND SCANS, or CHORIONIC VILLUS SAMPLING. Another still highly experimental prenatal test is EMBRYO BIOPSY, used with various reproductive technologies to check for GENETIC DISORDERS before the embryo is implanted in the woman. (See INFERTILITY; REPRODUCTIVE TECHNOLOGY.)

If Your Infant Is Not Breathing

BASIC LIFE SUPPORT

If your baby is not breathing, no matter what the reason, or has no pulse (his or her heart has stopped beating), you must provide life support until help arrives. This means that [after calling for emergency help] you must try to stimulate the baby to start breathing again, and the heart to start pumping again, by the following steps:

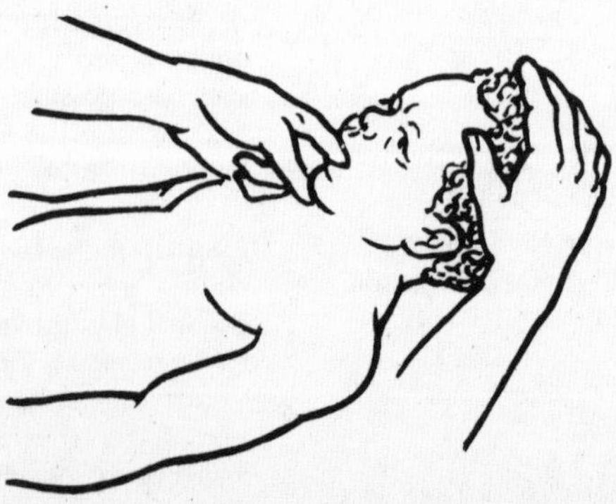

RESCUE BREATHING (VENTILATION)

1. Clear the mouth with your finger, quickly removing any mucus, vomit, food, or object.
2. Place the baby face up on the floor, table, or other firm surface.

3. If neck or spine has not been injured, tilt baby's head back slightly with chin up. Place your hand on baby's forehead to keep head in this position.

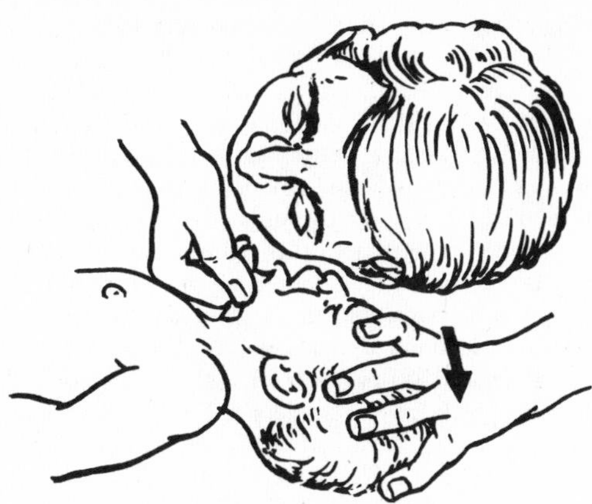

4. Cover mouth and nose with your mouth and blow gently until you see baby's chest rise.

5. Remove your mouth and let baby's lungs empty.
6. Take a quick breath yourself.
7. Repeat steps 4 and 5.

8. After breathing twice, check to be sure baby's heart is beating by feeling with your index and middle finger for pulse in the inside of baby's upper arm between the elbow and shoulder.

IF NO PULSE, YOU MUST TRY TO STIMULATE THE HEART BY PERFORMING CHEST COMPRESSIONS (see below).

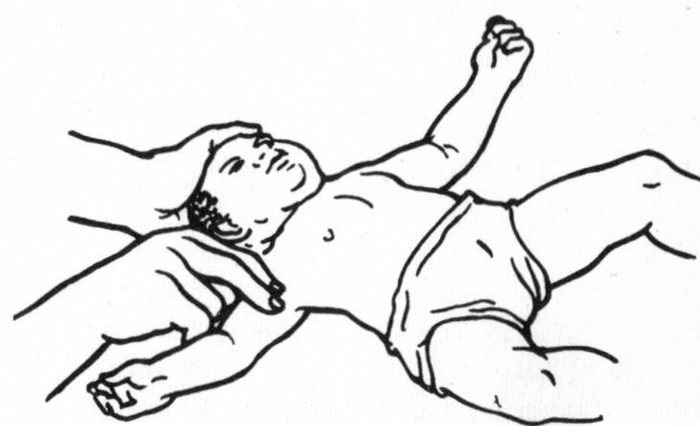

9. If there is a pulse, continue rescue breathing at the rate of once every three seconds. Check to be sure baby's chest is rising — a sign the baby's airway is clear and air is entering freely. If air is not moving, quickly check the position of your baby's head, and try it again.
10. IF STILL NO MOVEMENT, THERE IS PROBABLY SOMETHING BLOCKING THE BABY's AIRWAY. TO CLEAR THE AIRWAY, FOLLOW STEPS UNDER CHOKING.

CHEST COMPRESSIONS

1. Follow an imaginary line across the baby's chest from one nipple to the other. Place three fingers just below the middle of that imaginary line.
2. Lift the finger closest to the line, and with the two remaining fingers, press down to 1/2 to 1 inch.
3. Keeping fingers in place, press, relax, press, relax for a total of five compressions.
4. Do one ventilation (rescue breathing).
5. Then repeat five compressions and one ventilation rapidly (the entire cycle should take less than 5 seconds to complete) 10 times.
6. Feel again for a pulse; if there is none, do 10 more cycles.
7. Repeat entire procedure until help arrives.

Source: Infant Care (1989). Prepared for the Public Health Service by the Health Resources and Services Administration, Bureau of Maternal and Child Health and Resources Development.

assisted hatching, a form of REPRODUCTIVE TECHNOLOGY that uses MICROMANIPULATION to help overcome INFERTILITY. More precisely, microtools are used to help the EMBRYO shed the ZONA PELLUCIDA, its protective outer layer. This process, called *hatching*, normally occurs a week or so after FERTILIZATION, just before the embryo implants itself in the UTERUS. Hatching is inhibited in some women, for as yet unknown reasons, one of which may be maternal age. This is a new and highly experimental technique, still in the early stages of development and testing. It remains to be seen if the technique damages the embryo. (See INFERTILITY; REPRODUCTIVE TECHNOLOGY.)

assistive technology, general name for the range of devices and services that have been designed to help people with DISABILITIES develop their skills and to allow independent living, both to the greatest extent possible. Assistive technology is a broad term that includes ORTHOPEDIC DEVICES such as wheelchairs, braces, and canes; various devices to aid in seeing and hearing (see EAR AND HEARING PROBLEMS; EYE AND VISION PROBLEMS); and, in the widest sense, also covers SERVICE DOGS. Computers offer many possibilities for assistive technology; many applications for people with disabilities are already widely available, but some can be custom-developed for people in special situations. (See HELP FOR SPECIAL CHILDREN on page 689, under "On Techniques and Services for Independent Living.")

associate degree, the DEGREE awarded by most two-year COLLEGES to students who successfully complete their program of study; an Associate in Arts (A.A.), Associate in Science (A.S.), Associate in Applied Science (A.A.S.), or Association in Occupational Studies (A.O.S.) are associate degrees.

associative learning, a type of LEARNING STYLE that focuses on relating new knowledge, skills, and concepts to prior learning.

asthma, a condition involving recurrent bouts of breathlessness, wheezing, and coughing; a kind of LUNG AND BREATHING DISORDER that is closely related to ALLERGY. In an asthma attack, the bronchial tubes become constricted from muscle spasms and swelling in the bronchial tissue, and mucus clogs the smaller tubes, so fresh oxygen-bearing air cannot enter. In severe cases, the person may turn pale or blue (CYANOSIS), especially around the lips and NAILS; have a rapid heartbeat (*tachycardia*); break out in a cold sweat; and indicate general distress. Though not generally fatal, asthma kills hundreds of people each year, with hundreds more dying from asthma-related complications. Many of those who die are people who have developed the disease as adults, for whom the attacks are most severe. However, children are also at risk and, in severe cases, should receive prompt medical care.

Precisely what causes asthma is not clear. Attacks can be triggered by widely varying factors at different times in different people, including respiratory infections; excitement or emotional stress; vigorous EXERCISE; aspirin and some other anti-inflammatory drugs; weather changes and climate extremes, including sudden drafts; some kinds of foods (such as peanut butter, eggs, shellfish, chocolate, and foods containing sulfites); and a very wide range of substances carried in the air. Among these airborne substances (called *allergens*) are dust, animal hair and skin (*dander*), tobacco smoke, pollen, mold, aerosol sprays, cooking smoke, and feathers, in the home, and various kinds of pollutants such as automobile exhaust, industrial fumes and vapors, traces of metals and chemicals, cotton and wood dust, and the like, outdoors and at work and school (see ENVIRONMENTAL HAZARDS). Asthma triggered by outside factors such as those just mentioned is sometimes called *extrinsic asthma*. Evidence is also increasing that sensitivity to allergens that cause asthma attacks is increased by ozone pollution from automobile exhausts and industrial emissions, a major problem in cities.

In general, people are more likely to develop asthma if there is a family history of allergies. Except when the asthma begins before age two, the National Institute of Allergy and Infectious Diseases (NIAID) reports, the earlier the onset of asthma in a child, the less severe and long-lasting it will probably be. Some children do "outgrow" the condition by mid-adolescence, but what percentage is not clear.

Asthma cases are on the rise, most sharply among children under age eighteen; hospitalizations and fatalities from asthma are up sharply as well. Asthma is a special problem for children, partly because their immature respiratory systems and narrow breathing passages make them especially vulnerable to an asthmatic attack. In addition, asthma is often not diagnosed in children. Parents and doctors alike may attribute their wheezing to a respiratory infection or to some other condition. Asthma experts have urged doctors to test the breathing capacity of all patients suspected of having asthma, using a device called a *spirometer*. Parents should be alert to the possibility of asthma and raise it with the child's pediatrician or the family doctor. The NIAID recommends that treatment should begin as soon as the disease is recognized, to minimize damage to the respiratory system.

The main treatment is to identify the causes of asthma attacks in a particular child and avoid them whenever possible. That may take some considerable detective work and then sometimes considerable work to keep an environment free of allergens (see CONTROLLING THE ENVIRONMENT FOR THE ASTHMATIC CHILD on page 51). Where the allergens are unavoidable, the child may need to undergo standard allergy treatment (see ALLERGY). Depending on the child, a doctor may also prescribe cough medicines (*expectorants*), drinking water and breathing moist air to clear air passages, *postural drainage* that uses gravity to clear mucus, drugs to relax the muscles of the air passages (*bronchodilators*), and newer drugs to reduce inflammation and so prevent further attacks.

While traditional therapies have focused on relaxing constricted muscles that blocked airflow to the lungs, asthma experts have more recently come to understand that several hours *after* the initial tightening, cells in the airways release chemicals that caused inflammation. Among the new medications for countering inflammation of air passages are inhaled STEROIDS. Because steroids have adverse side effects (see STEROIDS), these inhalants are used with caution, generally for more severe cases, and patients must be carefully taught to use them safely. Their long-term effects on the body remain to be seen.

Parents with asthmatic children should seek the best and most current information available, from government and private organizations (see the list of organizations that follows). At least one study of asthma treatment, published in 1991, strongly suggests that asthma patients are not being *over*treated, but rather *under*treated. Researchers found that many nonspecialist doctors were unaware of the shift in focus from bronchodilators to treating inflammation, which is often implicated in asthma deaths. However, *over*treatment can also be a problem. Another 1991 study indicates that overuse of other anti-inflammatory drugs, called *beta–2 agonists*, might increase the risk of fatal asthma attacks. All in all, effective asthma treatment involves vigilance and a careful balancing act. Some asthma experts suggest that asthma patients should use a spirometer every day to test their breathing, to get timely therapy when needed, to prevent further attacks, and to help control chronic symptoms.

FOR HELP AND FURTHER INFORMATION

Allergy and Asthma Network/Mothers of Asthmatics (AAN/MA)
3554 Chain Bridge Road, Suite 200
Fairfax, VA 22030–2709

Controlling the Home Environment for the Asthmatic Child

Here are some tips on how parents can help keep the home environment clear of problems that can trigger or exacerbate asthma attacks:

- Avoid contact with pets and other animals.
- Avoid tobacco smoke.
- Control humidity, but beware belt-type humidifiers, which provide good growing places for fungi and bacteria.
- Install ventilator fans for stoves.
- Use air conditioners to screen particles from the air, and change filters frequently.
- Keep doors and windows closed to keep out unwanted particles, such as pollen.
- Make sure household odors are well vented.
- See that the heating system and its filters are properly maintained.
- If possible, use electric heat rather than a forced-air heating system.
- Vacuum rooms when children are elsewhere, to avoid dust inhalation.
- Keep closet doors shut to minimize spreading of dust, and keep wool clothing in plastic garment bags.
- Use and store household chemicals carefully.
- Avoid dustcatchers like rugs, stuffed toys, cushions, pleated lampshades, venetian blinds, and cotton or wool blankets.
- Instead use bare wood or tile floors; plain, simple furniture; washable pillows and blankets of synthetic materials; and washable window shades.
- Air new mattresses packed in plastic until the odor is gone.
- Use nonallergenic cleaning agents, such as:
  - plain ammonia for general household cleaning.
  - baking soda for general household cleaning and deodorizer (sprinkle on rugs before vacuuming).
  - oils such as beeswax, lemon oil, raw linseed oil, mineral oil, wax, and olive oil (though not on pewter)—be sure they have not turned rancid.
  - nonchlorine bleaches for household and laundry cleaning.
  - charcoal packets as room and refrigerator deodorizers; close off rooms briefly.
  - club soda as a spot remover for clothing or rugs; pour on spot, let set, and sponge up.
  - salt as a kitchen cleaner, to loosen burned-on foods.
  - unscented, mild soaps; avoid scented deodorant soaps.
  - white or apple cider vinegar mixed with water to remove mold, mineral deposits, crayon marks, wallpaper.

Source: Adapted from Allen & Hanbury's flyer based on "Helping Asthmatic Patients Control Their Environment," by J.C. Selner. Journal of Respiratory Disorders (1986) 7:83–104.

703–385–4403; Helpline: 800–878–4403
Fax: 703–352–4354
E-mail: aanma@aol.com (America Online: AANMA)
Internet Website: http://www.podi.com/health/aanma
Nancy Sander, President and Founder
Organization concerned with asthma and allergy; operates Learning Resource Center; maintains registry of support groups and research, operates LegiNet, on related legislation; provides medications and treatment devices at discount; publishes numerous materials, including:

- monthly: *The MA Report*, *Kids Newsletter*, and *School Information Packet*, for parents and school administrators.
- books: *A Parent's Guide to Asthma*, 2nd ed., *Consumer Update on Asthma*, *Breathing Easy with Day Care: A Guide About Asthma and Allergies for Parents and Caregivers*, *The Asthma Organizer*, rev. ed., *Asthma and Exercise*, *Asthma: The Complete Guide*, *Best of the MA Report*, rev. ed., and materials on treatments and treatment devices.
- "What Everyone Needs to Know About" booklets *Asthma*, *Bronchodilators*, *Exercise-Induced Asthma*, *Theophylline*, *Corticosteroids*, and *Cromolyn Sodium*.
- videos: *Asthma: What You Need to Know*, *Aerobics for Asthmatics*, *Managing Childhood Asthma*, and (for children) *Breathe Easy: Young People's Guide to Asthma*, *Wheeze World*, *Free to Breathe*, *So You Have Asthma Too!*, and *I'm a Meter Reader*.

American Allergy Association (AAA), 415–322–1663. Publishes *Asthma in Your Family?* and multivolume *Allergy Products Directory*, rev. ed. (Vol. 1: *Controlling Your Environment*; Vol. 3: *Allergy/Asthma, Finding Help)*. (For full group information, see ALLERGY.)

American Academy of Pediatrics (AAP), 800–433–9016. Publishes video-and-booklet set *Managing Childhood Asthma: A Parent's Guide.* (For full group information, see HEALTH CARE.)

National Heart, Lung, and Blood Information Center (NHLBIC), 301–251–1222. (For full group information, see HEART AND HEART PROBLEMS.)

National Institute of Allergy and Infectious Diseases (NIAID), 301–496–5717. (For full group information, see ALLERGY.)

Asthma and Allergy Foundation of America (AAFA), 800–727–8462. Publishes *Taming Asthma and Allergy by Controlling Your Environment: A Guide for Patients.* (For full group information, see ALLERGY.)

National Jewish Center for Immunology and Respiratory Medicine, 800–222–5864. (For full group information, see LUNG AND BREATHING DISORDERS.)

Asthma Information Center
P.O. Box 790
Springhouse, PA 19477–0790
800–727–5400
Provides information on asthma, including a list of support groups, in response to written requests.

American Lung Association (ALA), 800–586–4872. (For full group information, see LUNG AND BREATHING DISORDERS.)

OTHER RESOURCES

For parents and other adults

A Parent's Guide to Asthma: How You Can Help Your Child Control Asthma at Home, School, and Play. Nancy Sander. NAL-Dutton, 1994.
Ward Lock Family Health Guide: Asthma and Allergies. Anne Kent. Sterling, 1994.
Keys to Parenting the Asthmatic Child. Barron's, 1994.
Childhood Asthma: A Guide for Parents. Candace Hollinger and Debra Neill-Mareci. HIN, 1993.
A Parent's Guide to Allergies and Asthma. Marion Steinmann. Dell, 1992.
Breathing Easy: A Parent's Guide to Dealing with Your Child's Asthma. Maryann Stevens. Prentice Hall, 1991.
Childhood Asthma: A Doctor's Complete Treatment Plan. Mike Whiteside. Thorsons, 1991.

General works

Asthma: Questions You Have, Answers You Need. Paula Brisco. People's Medical Society, 1994.
Asthma. A. J. Wardlaw. Coronet Books, 1993.
Children and Asthma: The New Epidemic and How to Treat It. Bob Lanier. Summit, 1992.
All about Asthma and Allergy. H. Morrow Brown. Trafalgar Square, 1991.
One Minute Asthma: What You Need to Know. Thomas F. Plaut. Pedipress, 1991.

On dealing with asthma

Living with Asthma. Anthony R. Rooklin and Shelagh R. Masline. NAL-Dutton, 1995.
Understand and Control Your Asthma. Helene Boutin and Louis-Philippe Boulet. University of Toronto Press, 1994.
Asthma: A Concise Guide to Alternative Treatments. Roy Ridgeway. Element, 1994.
Empty Your Bucket: Practical Steps to Overcome Allergy and Allergic Asthma. Stephen Astor. Two A's, 1993.
Asthma: Stop Suffering, Start Living, 2nd ed. M. Eric Gershwin and E. L. Klingelhofer. Addison-Wesley, 1992.
Asthma Self-Help Book: How to Live a Normal Life in Spite of Your Condition, 2nd ed. Paul J. Hannaway. Prima, 1992.
A Handbook for Asthma Self-Management: A Patient's Guide to Living with Asthma. Thomas L. Creer and others. Ohio University Press, 1991.
Asthmatic's Action Plan: Practical Advice for Gaining Relief from Distressing Symptoms. John Chapman. Thorsons, 1991.

Open Airways: An Asthma Self-Management Program. Gordon, 1991.
The Asthma Self-Care Book: How to Take Control of Your Asthma. Geri Harrington. HarperCollins, 1991.
What You Can Do about Asthma. Nathaniel Altman. Dell, 1991.

For children

Taking Asthma to School. Kim Gosselin. JayJo Books, 1995.
Breathe Easy: Young People's Guide to Asthma. Jonathan H. Weiss. Magination Press, 1994.
Determined to Win: Children Living with Allergies and Asthma. Thomas Bergman. Gareth Stevens, 1994.
The Lion Who Had Asthma. Jonathan London. Albert Whitman, 1992.

For teens

Living with Asthma. Margaret O. Hyde and Elizabeth H. Forsyth. Walker, 1995.

Personal experiences

The Asthma Storm: One Family's Journey from Asthma Diagnosis to Control. Barbara L. Westmoreland. Lane Press, 1994.
Catching My Breath: An Asthmatic Explores His Illness. Tim Brookes. Times Books, 1994.

(See also ALLERGY; LUNG AND BREATHING PROBLEMS.)

ataxia, lack of coordination and balance, often resulting in a staggering, awkward, uncertain gait. A person with ataxia generally walks with legs too far apart, lifted jerkily, and steps abnormally high, then drops the sole of the foot so that it strikes the ground flat. Jerky eye movements called NYSTAGMUS are often associated. Ataxia generally indicates some kind of damage or disorder in the SPINAL CORD or the part of the BRAIN called the *cerebellum*; causes may include damage during CHILDBIRTH, a severe infection, TRAUMATIC BRAIN INJURY, BRAIN TUMOR, response to some toxin (poison), or some other disorder that causes degeneration in the CENTRAL NERVOUS SYSTEM, including MULTIPLE SCLEROSIS and GENETIC DISORDERS such as *Friedreich's ataxia* or *ataxia telangiectasia.* Recent discovery of a gene that causes ataxia was a major breakthrough, promising hope for better understanding, diagnosis, and possibly a cure.

Friedreich's ataxia is a rare inherited form of ataxia, resulting from an AUTOSOMAL RECESSIVE trait, which involves muscle weakness and loss of muscle control, especially of the lower limbs but sometimes of the upper limbs as well. It generally appears between ages five and twenty, most often at PUBERTY, and progresses to severe disability and premature death. Among associated symptoms are SCOLIOSIS, tremors of the head, slurred speech, and heart problems, which are often the cause of death. Pneumonia is another often fatal complication. BABINSKI'S REFLEX and ROMBERG SIGN may signal the presence of Friedreich's ataxia.

Another rare PROGRESSIVE genetic disease of autosomal recessive origin, ataxia telangiectasia (also called *Louis-Bar syndrome*) is associated with unusually large and numerous blood vessels (*telangiectasias*, sometimes mistakenly referred to as "broken" blood vessels) in areas of the skin, causing redness, especially around the ears and face. It appears in infancy and gradually worsens, and is often associated with sinus and pulmonary infections and with increased risk of MALIGNANT TUMORS, especially LEUKEMIA.

FOR HELP AND FURTHER INFORMATION

National Ataxia Foundation (NAF)
750 Twelve Oaks Center
15500 Wayzata Boulevard, Suite 750
Wayzata, MN 55391
612–473–7666
Fax: 612–473–9289
E-mail: nbxu87a@prodigy.com (Prodigy: NBXU87A)
Donna Gruetzmacher, Executive Director
Organization concerned with hereditary ataxia and related disorders such as Charcot-Marie-Tooth syndrome, hereditary spastic paraplegia, and ataxia telangiectasia; provides information and referrals; publishes various materials, including quarterly newsletter *Generations, Hereditary Ataxia, Ataxia Telangiectasia, Spastic Paraplegia, Hereditary Ataxia: The Facts, Hereditary Ataxia: A Guidebook for Managing Speech and Swallowing Problems, Frenkel's Exercises, Students with Friedreich's Ataxia* (for teachers), video *Together ... There Is Hope*, a pen-pal directory, and lists of resources.

National Institute of Neurological Disorders and Stroke (NINDS), 800–352–9424. Publishes fact sheet *Friedreich's Ataxia.* (For full group information, see BRAIN AND BRAIN DISORDERS.)

National Spinal Cord Injury Association (NSCIA), 800–962–9629 (For full group information, see SPINAL CORD INJURY.)

Immune Deficiency Foundation (IDF), 800–296–4433. (For full group information, see IMMUNE SYSTEM.)

National Organization for Rare Disorders (NORD), 800–999–6673. (For full group information, see RARE DISORDERS.)

(See also GENETIC DISORDERS; MUSCULAR DYSTROPHY; also HELP FOR SPECIAL CHILDREN on page 689.)

at risk, having an increased likelihood of developing a certain disease or condition. (See RISK FACTORS.)

athetosis, slow, involuntary, writhing movements, resulting from disturbances deep within the brain, often associated with the quick, jerky movements of CHOREA; the combination is called *choreoathetosis.* The condition is often found in people who have HUNTINGTON'S DISEASE, CEREBRAL PALSY, ENCEPHALITIS, or BRAIN DISORDERS. It can also be a side effect of certain drugs.

athletic scholarship, a type of SCHOLARSHIP offered to students with outstanding SPORTS abilities, who are expected to make a major contribution to a school's athletic program. Many highly talented athletes are actively recruited and often offered FINANCIAL AID and other material inducements to attend a particular COLLEGE. Too often, the focus is only on the sport, with EDUCATION getting insufficient attention. As a result, some athletes, who have been passed through school and college on the basis of their athletic ability, find themselves retired in their late twenties and early thirties with few other skills to fall back on. Some of them are actually functionally ILLITERATE. (See SPORTS; also HELP ON LEARNING AND EDUCATION on page 659.)

atrophy, the shrinking, weakening, and "wasting away" of a part of the body, because of disease, disuse, or damage from MUSCULAR DYSTROPHY, SPINAL CORD INJURY, or prolonged hospitalization. In MOTOR NEURON DISEASES, for example, the muscles waste away because the nerves supplying communication with them are damaged.

attachment, a partial synonym for BONDING, but with a wider focus. A child forms an attachment not only with the primary CAREGIVER but also with other people, such as other family members or a NANNY, with whom there is a significant link.

attendance, in EDUCATION, the presence of a student in school or in a school-sponsored activity on a day when the school is considered in session. Under COMPULSORY ATTENDANCE laws, children are required to be present when school is in session, except when they have a valid excuse. An attendance or TRUANT officer is normally assigned in the school to seek out students and parents who fail to comply.

attention deficit hyperactivity disorder (ADHD), a complex of behavioral problems generally marked by DISTRACTIBILITY, impulsiveness, short ATTENTION SPAN, mood changes, disorganization, often SLEEP DISORDERS, and physical restlessness called HYPERACTIVITY (hyperkinetic syndrome), beyond what is considered normal for the person's chronological and mental AGE. When hyperactivity is not found or has been outgrown, as is often the case in older adolescents or adults, the term generally used is *attention deficit disorder* (ADD). Formerly the condition went under other names, including *minimal brain dysfunction* (MBD) or *hyperkinetic reaction of childhood.* Definitions and names have varied over the years partly because the range of behaviors exhibited varies and the disorder is so hard to pin down. ADHD is not a learning disability; rather children with ADHD have problems learning because of difficulties with attention, distraction, and organization; however, many children with ADHD have LEARNING DISABILTIES, further complicating diagnosis. ADHD behaviors are also often found in children with other problems, such as TOURETTE SYNDROME, MENTAL RETARDATION, CEREBRAL PALSY, EPILEPSY, childhood SCHIZOPHRENIA, and other neurological or psychiatric disorders.

Children with ADHD have difficulty finishing a task, following through a set of instructions, organizing work for completion, sometimes even watching a television program clear through. They will frequently jump into a task before instructions have been finished, interrupt others, and not wait for their turn in school or at home. In PRESCHOOL, children with ADHD are constantly or excessively on the move, often in a disorganized or disruptive way; in older children, the disorder is more likely to show itself in squirming, fidgeting, and general restlessness, as well as in messy work and inability to complete assigned tasks. ADHD children frequently act impulsively, without reflecting on consequences, sometimes in such a way as to endanger themselves or others (such as grabbing a hot pan or riding a skateboard down a steep incline). Such behaviors interfere with learning and lead to both academic failure and low self-esteem, often accompanied by emotional instability and mood swings (LABILITY) and spurts of temper. This may be complicated in young children by inability to fully control bowels and bladder, resulting in BEDWETTING (*enuresis*) and SOILING (*encopresis*).

ADHD behaviors are not evident in all settings. They are most obvious in settings (such as a classroom) that require quiet, sustained listening but contain many distractions. In fact, ADHD often is not recognized until a child enters school. But ADHD behaviors can be minimal in a one-to-one setting or where distracting stimuli are limited. In EDUCATION, therefore, one common approach is to arrange for highly structured tutorial or small-group teaching situations for ADHD children.

Children with ADHD often have problems with MOTOR SKILLS, VISUAL SKILLS, AUDITORY SKILLS, and COMMUNICATIONS SKILLS, including difficulty in conceptualizing, using language, and memory. (Subscribers to the America Online computer service can find information on techniques for helping young children with ADHD, including such techniques as MODELING, BEHAVIOR MODIFICATION, and breaking instructions into small steps, in the Moms Online Desk Reference section of Moms Online, under "Teaching Young Children.")

ADHD probably stems from a variety of causes, as yet ill-understood. It is presumed to result from damage or malfunctioning of the brain (see BRAIN AND BRAIN DISORDERS) and CENTRAL NERVOUS SYSTEM, but not from major brain or neurological damage, since many people with ADHD are of average or above average intelligence. GENETIC INHERITANCE, biochemical problems, injury or damage during birth, and possibly ALLERGY to certain foods or food additives have all been implicated in causing ADHD, though how and to what extent is unclear. ADHD is three to nine times more likely among boys than among girls. The behaviors may also be triggered by an unsettled or chaotic home environment, especially one involving CHILD ABUSE AND NEGLECT, and may sometimes be linked with family history of ALCOHOL ABUSE and psychiatric problems.

Children whose hyperactivity interferes with their learning are often treated with a medicine such as Ritalin, which is paradoxically a stimulant. This medication increases brain activity and control, in the process decreasing hyperactivity and distractibility and increasing attention and muscular coordination. Among the medication's occasional side effects are INSOMNIA, diminished appetite, CONSTIPATION, and less often stomachaches and headaches. Antidepressant medications are also sometimes prescribed. Some of these can cause heart problems and need to be carefully monitored (see HEART AND HEART PROBLEMS).

Both types of medications also can have potentially serious DRUG REACTIONS AND INTERACTIONS with other drugs such as BIRTH CONTROL PILLS and some cold medications, but also with alcohol and drugs that are abused, increasing the possibility of respiratory failure and the likelihood of a drug overdose. Some people have expressed concern about the prescription of medications such as Ritalin, which is after all a controlled substance of the amphetamine type; past research has not shown increased DRUG ABUSE among children or teens who were given Ritalin, but more recently some have found that Ritalin itself can be an abused drug. Such drugs may cause a slight slowing of growth during early years of use (see GROWTH AND GROWTH DISORDERS), but research suggests that growth "catches up" overall.

Various types of psychological therapies have also been employed with ADHD children, in particular *self-control therapy*, also called *cognitive therapy*, which teaches the child strategies for relaxing and controlling impulsive behaviors, including anger, while also aiming to increase the child's self-esteem.

Special diets and mega-vitamin therapies have also been tried. Most notable of these is the *Feingold diet*, a type of *elimination diet*, which excludes any foods (or medicines) that contain artificial flavorings or colorings, salicylates (as in aspirin), and certain food preservatives.

Though the diet apparently helps some people with ADHD, notably those with associated ALLERGIES, others seem to derive little or no benefit from it. Large doses of VITAMINS and MINERALS can also be harmful. Before placing their child in any special diet, parents should consult with a PEDIATRICIAN to be sure that the child will get proper NUTRITION with a restricted diet. A balanced diet and moderate EXERCISE may be more beneficial to many children.

Among some children, ADHD behaviors, especially hyperactivity, disappear during ADOLESCENCE, but in others they continue, though perhaps masked, into adulthood. The natural rebellion of adolescence can also lead teenagers to stop taking medications, therapies, and special tutoring, increasing their problems.

Without recognition, diagnosis, and support, the frustration and lack of success experienced by people with ADHD can result in social, psychological, and educational problems, such as low self-esteem or DEPRESSION, sometimes leading to JUVENILE DELINQUENCY. But in both children and adults, the behaviors associated with ADHD can be turned to advantage in work that requires high energy level, intense bursts of activity, and considerable freedom and independence, as in outdoor work or the arts.

In recent decades, civil rights have been extended to cover individuals with DISABILITIES, in areas such as education and later employment. ADHD children have legal rights to due process and equal opportunity for an education (see EDUCATION FOR ALL HANDICAPPED CHILDREN; INDIVIDUALS WITH DISABILITIES EDUCATION ACT; AMERICANS WITH DISABILITIES ACT). In 1990, for example, a North Carolina school district was found to have violated the law for failing to identify and evaluate ADHD in a child and failing to provide a free public education appropriate to the disorder. ADHD teens heading toward college can, today, often get help to accommodate their special needs (see SPECIAL HELP FOR SPECIAL COLLEGE STUDENTS on page 366).

FOR HELP AND FURTHER INFORMATION

Challenge, Inc.
P.O. Box 488
West Newbury, MA 01985–0688
508–462–0495 (For Fax, Press 5* after the tone); 800-ADD–2322 [233–2322]
Jean Conner Harrison, Contact
Organization concerned with ADD/ADHD; formerly Attention Deficit Disorder Association (ADDA); provides information and referrals; offers prescription discounts to members; publishes bimonthly newsletter *Challenge* and tape *Don't Give Up—Don't Let Go.*

Children and Adults with Attention Deficit Disorder (CHADD)
499 Northwest 70th Avenue, Suite 308
Plantation, FL 33317
305–587–3700
Fax: 305–587–4599
JoAnne Evans, President
Organization of parent support groups concerned with attention deficit disorders; disseminates information; publishes newsletter *Chadderbox*, semiannual magazine *Chadder*, and CHADD fact sheets, including *The Disability Named ADD, Parenting a Child with ADD, Educational Rights of Children with ADD*, and *Medical Management of ADD.*

PACER Center (Parent Advocacy Coalition for Educational Rights), 612–827–2966, voice/TT. Publishes *Living with ADHD: A Practical Guide to Coping with Attention Deficit Hyperactivity Disorder, ADHD Federal Clarification Policy*, and video *Why Won't My Child Pay Attention?* (For full group information, see HELP FOR SPECIAL CHILDREN on page 689.)

Council for Exceptional Children (CEC),
800–328–0272. Publishes brochure *Children with ADD: A*

Shared Responsibility; special-topic reports, such as *ADHD and Children Who Are Gifted* and *Providing an Appropriate Education to Children with Attention Deficit Disorder*; and materials on teaching ADHD children. (For full group information, see HELP ON LEARNING AND EDUCATION on page 659.)

National Fragile X Foundation, 800–688–8765. Publishes *Managing Attention Deficits and Hyperactivity*. (For full group information, see FRAGILE X SYNDROME.)

American Academy of Child and Adolescent Psychiatry (AACAP), 202–966–7300. Publishes information sheet *Children Who Can't Pay Attention*. (For full group information, see MENTAL DISORDERS.)

American Academy of Pediatrics (AAP), 800–433–9016. Publishes brochure *Understanding the ADHD Child*. (For full group information, see HEALTH CARE.)

National Institute of Mental Health (NIMH), 301–443–4513. Publishes *Attention Deficit Hyperactivity Disorder*. (For full group information, see MENTAL DISORDER.)

Association for Children with Down Syndrome (ACDS), 516–221–4700. Publishes *Attention Deficit Hyperactivity Disorder (ADHD) in Children with Down Syndrome*. (For full group information, see DOWN SYNDROME.)

National Institute of Child Health and Human Development (NICHD), 301–496–5133. (For full group information, see PREGNANCY.)

National Information Center for Children and Youth with Disabilities (NICHCY), 800–695–0285, voice/TT. Publishes *Attention Deficit Disorder*. (For full group information, see HELP FOR SPECIAL CHILDREN on page 689.)

HEATH Resource Center, National Clearinghouse on Postsecondary Education for Individuals with Disabilities, 800–544–3284, voice/TT. Publishes *Attention Deficit Disorder*. (For full group information, see HELP FOR SPECIAL CHILDREN on page 689.)

Parents Helping Parents (PHP), 408–727–5775. Publishes information packet *Attention Deficit Disorder—Hyperactivity*. (For full group information, see HELP FOR SPECIAL CHILDREN on page 689.)

National Alliance for the Mentally Ill (NAMI), 800–950–6264. Publishes brochure *Attention Deficit Hyperactivity in Children*; online forum and library covers ADHD. (For full group information, see MENTAL DISORDERS.)

American Association of University Affiliated Programs for Persons with Developmental Disabilities (AAUAP), 301–588–8252. (For full group information, see HELP FOR SPECIAL CHILDREN on page 689.)

Association for Childhood Education International (ACEI), 800–423–3563. Publishes reprint *Attention Deficit Disorder: Help for the Classroom Teacher*. (For full group information, see HELP ON LEARNING AND EDUCATION on page 659.)

Feingold Association of the United States
Drawer AG
Holtsville, NY 11742
516–369–9340
Organization of parents and professionals supporting use of the Feingold diet with children; sponsors local self-help groups; provides information and referrals; publishes various materials, including monthly newsletter *Pure Facts*, *Feingold Handbook*, food lists, shopping guide, and cookbook.

National Woman's Christian Temperance Union (WCTU), 800–755–1321. Publishes booklet *Coping with Hyperactive Children*. (For full group information, see HELP AGAINST SUBSTANCE ABUSE on page 703.)

Resource Center on Substance Abuse Prevention and Disability, 202–628–8442. Publishes *A Look at Alcohol and Other Drug Abuse Prevention and Attention Deficit Disorder*. (For full group information, see HELP FOR SPECIAL CHILDREN on page 689.)

ONLINE RESOURCES

ADD Forum (CompuServe), international 24-hour-a-day support group for people with ADD and their families; holds conferences for adults and kids; maintains online library files on topics such as parenting, schools and learning, ADD theories and studies, Tourette syndrome, autism, and publications.

Internet: ADD-parents. Mailing list providing support and information to parents of children with ADHD. To subscribe, send e-mail to: mailto:add-parents-request@mv.mv.com

Issues in Mental Health (America Online: IMH). Provides discussion forum and online library covering attention deficit disorder. (Location: Lifestyles and Interests, Issues in Mental Health) (For full information, see MENTAL DISORDERS.)

OTHER RESOURCES

FOR PARENTS AND OTHER ADULTS

Is Your Child Hyperactive?: Inattentive, Impulsive, Distractible. Stephen Garber. Villard, 1995.

Helping Your Hyperactive—Attention Deficit Child, 2nd ed. John F. Taylor. Prima, 1994.

Managing Attention Deficit Disorder in Your Family: Discovering and Coping with ADD. Bill Cooper. MasterMedia, 1994.

The ADHD Parenting Handbook: Practical Advice for Parents from Parents. Colleen Alexander-Roberts. Taylor, 1994.

Attention Deficit Disorders, Hyperactivity and Associated Disorders: A Handbook for Parents and Professionals, 6th ed. Wendy S. Coleman. Calliope Books, 1993.

Maybe You Know My Kid: A Parent's Guide to Identifying, Understanding and Helping Your Child with Attention Deficit Hyperactivity Disorder, rev. ed. Mary Cahill Fowler. Birch Lane/Carol, 1993.
The Hyperactive Child Book: Treating, Educating and Living with an ADHD Child—Strategies That Really Work, from an Award-Winning Team of Experts. Patricia Kennedy and others. St. Martin's, 1993.
The Parents' Hyperactivity Handbook: Helping the Fidgety Child. D. M. Paltin. Plenum, 1993.
Attention Deficit Hyperactivity Disorder: What Every Parent Wants to Know. David L. Wodrich, ed. Paul H. Brookes, 1993.
Keys to Parenting Children with Attention Deficit Disorders. Barry E. McNamara and Francine J. McNamara. Barron's, 1993.
Hyperactivity: Why Won't My Child Pay Attention? Sam Goldstein and Michael Goldstein. Wiley, 1992.
Dr. Larry Silver's Advice to Parents on Attention-Deficit Hyperactivity. Larry B. Silver. American Psychiatric Press, 1992.
The Hyperactive Child. Grant Martin. Victor/SP Publications, 1992.
Lord, Help Me Love This Hyperactive Child. Evelyn Langston. Broadman, 1992.
Help for the Hyperactive Child. William G. Crook. Future Health, 1991.
Attention Deficit Hyperactivity Disorder: Questions and Answers for Parents. Gregory S. Greenberg and Wade Horn. Research Press, 1991.

General works

Driven to Distraction: Attention Deficit Disorder in Children and Adults. Edward M. Hallowell and John Ratey. Pantheon, 1994.
Sit Down and Pay Attention: Coping with Attention-Deficit Disorder Throughout the Life Cycle. Ronald Goldberg. PIA Press, 1991.
Attention Deficit Disorder. Juan Garcia. Rapha, 1991.

For children

Putting on the Brakes: Young People's Guide to Understanding Attention Deficit Hyperactivity Disorder (ADHD). Patricia O. Quinn and Judith M. Stern. Magination Press, 1991. Also *The "Putting on the Brakes" Activity Book for Young People with ADHD* (1993).
Eagle Eyes: A Child's View of Attention Deficit Disorder. Jeanne Gehret. Verbal Images Press, 1991.
Shelley, the Hyperactive Turtle. Deborah Moss. Woodbine House, 1989.

For preteens and teens

I Would If I Could: A Teenager's Guide to ADHD-Hyperactivity. Michael Gordon. GSI Publications, 1992.
My Brother's a World-Class Pain: A Sibling's Guide to ADHD-Hyperactivity. Michael Gordon. GSI Publications, 1992.
Making the Grade: An Adolescent's Struggle with ADD. Roberta N. Parker and Harvey C. Parker. Special Press, 1992.

For college students

ADD and the College Student: A Guide for High School and College Students with Attention Deficit Disorder. Patricia O. Quinn, ed. Magination Press, 1994.
Survival Guide for College Students with ADD or LD. Kathleen G. Nadeau. Magination Press, 1994.

On ADD in adults

Out of the Fog: Treatment Options and Coping Strategies for Adults with Attention Deficit Disorder. Kevin Murphy and Suzanne LeVert. Hyperion, 1995.
The Attention Deficit Disorder in Adults Workbook. Lynn Weiss. Taylor, 1994.
You Mean I'm Not Lazy, Stupid or Crazy?!: A Self-Help Book for Adults with Attention Deficit Disorder. Kate Kelly and Peggy Ramundo. Tyrell and Jerem, 1993.
Attention Deficit Disorder in Adults: Support and Practical Help for Sufferers and Their Spouses. Lynn Weiss. Taylor, 1991.

Background works

A.D.D. from A-Z: A Comprehensive Guide to Attention Deficit Disorder. William N. Bender and Philip J. McLaughlin. Sopris, 1994.
Attention Deficit Disorder: Hyperactivity Revisited, rev. ed. H. Moghadam and Joel Fagan. Temeron Books, 1994.
Alphabet Soup: A Recipe for Understanding and Treating Attention Deficit Disorder. James Javorsky. Minerva, 1994.
Attention Deficit Disorder and Learning Disabilities: Reality, Myths, and Controversial Treatments. Barbara D. Ingersoll and Sam Goldstein. Doubleday, 1993.
Attention Deficit Disorder: A Different Perception. Thomas Hartmann. Underwood-Miller, 1993.

(See also ADVOCACY; LEARNING DISABILITIES; ALLERGIES.)

attention span, the amount of time someone can concentrate on a task without losing interest in it or being distracted from it. Attention span is one of the "skills" a young child develops gradually; however, children with LEARNING DISABILITIES and some other DEVELOPMENTAL DISORDERS may have heightened DISTRACTIBILITY, often as part of a complex of problems known as ATTENTION DEFICIT HYPERACTIVITY DISORDER (ADHD).

audiologist, a health professional who specializes in screening for and diagnosing hearing problems, often in schools or clinics. Audiologists use HEARING TESTS to assess the amount of hearing loss, if any; to show just what a child can and cannot hear; and to judge if a HEARING AID might help. If so, the audiologist will prescribe and fit the hearing aid and also recommend any other appropriate special devices or programs. It is wise to have children's hearing tested early and regularly, so that hearing problems can be detected and treated before they cause communication problems. If COMMUNICATION DISORDERS have resulted from hearing loss, the child is generally referred to a SPEECH-LANGUAGE PATHOLOGIST. Audiologists are not physicians; problems treatable by drugs or surgery are referred to medical specialists, such as OTOLARYNGOLOGISTS. (See EARS AND HEARING PROBLEMS.)

auditory brainstem response (ABR), a type of HEARING TEST, also called *brain stem auditory evoked responses* (BSAER). It uses electrodes attached to the scalp to record the brain's response to sounds and is a common test in assessing EAR AND HEARING PROBLEMS, especially for use with infants and in checking for a possible ACOUSTIC NEUROMA.

Auditory Discrimination Test, Wepman's, a widely used DIAGNOSTIC ASSESSMENT TEST focusing on AUDITORY SKILLS, used with children ages four to eight. In the individually administered test, the child is presented with pairs of spoken words and asked to tell if they are the same or different. The results, rated against standardization tables, are designed to highlight possible problems with READING and COMMUNICATIONS SKILLS. Other forms of the test are sometimes used for follow-up testing after REMEDIAL INSTRUCTION. (See TESTS.)

auditory nerve (eighth nerve), the nerve that carries electrical signals representing sound vibrations from the inner ear to the brain. Malfunctioning of the auditory nerve leads to *sensori-neural loss*, a significant EAR AND HEARING PROBLEM.

auditory skills, a set of overlapping skills that involve the ears and hearing; closely related to COMMUNICATIONS SKILLS.

Auditory discrimination is the ability to distinguish one sound from another. Children with hearing problems, LEARNING DISABILITIES, or some other DEVELOPMENTAL DISORDERS may have trouble telling the difference between words that sound similar, such as *pale* and *bale*. They also may have trouble distinguishing between a familiar and an unfamiliar voice or recognizing familiar nonverbal sounds, such as an alarm clock or siren. This is a form of auditory AGNOSIA. Such problems can cause confusion and frustration in learning, as a child may miss the point of what is being said or be confused about who is saying it.

Auditory memory is the ability to remember for a short time what you have heard. Children with learning disabilities or some other developmental disorders often have difficulty with short-term auditory memory. No matter how hard they concentrate, they may only be able to remember three or four words in a row, often forgetting the beginning of a sentence before the end has been reached. They may also confuse the order of sounds heard; *basket* might become *bakset*, for example. Such children frequently ask for things to be repeated and may repeat them out loud to themselves, trying to remember them.

Localization is the ability to identify where a sound is coming from. Some children have great difficulty with this; such children may look all around the room on hearing their names called.

The CHART OF NORMAL DEVELOPMENT (see page 637) indicates when, between birth and age six, children first *on the average* begin to develop the main COMMUNICATION SKILLS. Children grow and learn at individual and varying paces, but every child can benefit from activities designed to enhance their natural development. (See EAR AND HEARING PROBLEMS.)

au pair, a person, usually a young woman, who lives with a family, assisting with CHILD CARE and light housework. *Au pair* means *on par*, implying that the person is intended to live as an equal member of the family, not as an employee. *Au pairs* may have no formal training, though they commonly have had experience as BABYSITTERS, and may receive some child care and development training from the agency that places them with a family. *Au pairs* generally assist parents in child care, rather than taking full responsibility for the child. Traditionally *au pairs* have been young people from other countries seeking to experience American life, though the term may be applied to young Americans as well. *Au pairs* are usually paid only a modest salary or allowance and given a private room and sometimes other benefits, such as use of a car. Those caring for children under age two, who are usually required to have more experience, are generally paid more than regular *au pairs*. (See CHILD CARE; also CHECKLIST FOR CHOOSING CHILD CARE on page 114.)

FOR HELP AND FURTHER INFORMATION

Au Pair Homestay/Au Pair Homestay Abroad
World Learning
1015 15th Street, NW, Suite 750
Washington, DC 20005
202–408–5380
Fax: 202–408–5397
Karen Wayne, Executive Director
Organization that screens and sponsors *au pairs* to stay with American families; a cultural exchange program of World Learning (formerly U.S. Experiment in International Living); matches American families with *au pairs* screened in Europe and given child care and first aid training (including CPR); AuPair Homestay Abroad similarly matches young Americans as au pairs with European families; provides community coordinator; publishes information packet.

Au Pair in America
102 Greenwich Avenue
Greenwich, CT 06830

203–869–9090; 800–9-AU PAIR [927–2437]
Fax: 203–863–6180
Organization that provides *au pairs* for American families in 170 "clusters," each served by a Community Counselor; cosponsored by American Institute for Foreign Study and American Heritage Association; screens both au pairs and family applicants; provides child care and development training; publishes brochure.

autism, a type of MENTAL DISORDER that appears in early childhood, generally before age three. Though the severity of the disorder differs from child to child, the disorder is generally marked by lack of normal social interaction with parents and others. The autistic child resists physical and eye contact and developmentally impaired in many areas, including SOCIAL SKILLS, LANGUAGE SKILLS, SELF-HELP SKILLS, and communication skills (see COMMUNICATION SKILLS AND DISORDERS). The child often exhibits sharply restricted activities and interests, with insistence on sameness in environment and routine. Repetitive movements, such as rocking, spinning, head-banging, and hand-twisting, are characteristic, as are standardized or stereotypical responses to social situations. MENTAL RETARDATION is common, and some of the most severely affected autistics tend to develop SEIZURES. This puzzling disorder is presently classified by psychiatrists as *autistic disorder*, a type of *pervasive developmental disorder*, but it has previously gone under a variety of other names, including *atypical development*, *symbiotic psychosis*, *childhood psychosis*, and *childhood schizophrenia*. Though once assumed to have resulted from poor parental environment, recent studies have indicated nothing of the sort. The causes of the disorder are obscure, though it has been associated with various physical disorders, including maternal RUBELLA, untreated PHENYLKETONURIA, CELIAC SPRUE, ENCEPHALITIS, tuberous sclerosis, FRAGILE X SYNDROME, and lack of oxygen at CHILDBIRTH.

FOR HELP AND FURTHER INFORMATION

Autism Society of America (ASA)
7910 Woodmont Avenue, Suite 650
Bethesda, MD 20814
301–657–0881; 800–3-AUTISM [328–8476]
Fax: 301–657–0869; Fax-on-Demand (24 hours) 800-FAX–0899 [329–0899]
Organization concerned with autism; provides information and makes referrals; publishes quarterly newsletter *Advocate* and other materials, including:

- general brochures and booklets: *What Is Autism*, *Autism Primer: Twenty Questions and Answers*, and *General Information Resource List*; and books *Autism: Explaining the Enigma*, *Children with Autism*, *Laughing and Loving with Autism*, *Case Studies in Autism* (follows a 4-year-old autistic child), and *Holistic Interpretation of Autism*.
- books for adults: *A Parent's Guide to Autism*, *Introduction to Autism: A Self Instructional Module*, rev. ed., *After the Tears*, *Autism: A Practical Guide for Those Who Help Others*, *Record Book for Individuals with Autism*, *Helping People with Autism Manage Their Behavior*, rev. ed., and *High-Functioning Individuals with Autism*.
- for children: *Joey and Sam* and *Kristy and the Secret of Susan*.
- personal experiences: *Hearing Equals Behavior*, *The Sound of a Miracle*, *Turning Every Stone*, *Until Tomorrow: A Family Lives with Autism*, *When Snow Turns to Rain*, *Winter's Flower*, *Without Reason*, and *Silent Words* (on facilitated communication).
- materials for health professionals.

Autism Network International (ANI)
P.O. Box 448
Syracuse, NY 13210–0448
315–476–2462
Fax: 315–425–1978.
E-mail: jisincla@mailbox.syr.edu
Internet discussion list: ANI-L. To subscribe, send this message: "subscribe ani-l [your first name] [your last name]" to: listserv@utkvm1.utk.edu
Jim Sinclair, Coordinator
Self-help, self-advocacy organization run by and for people with autism; offers forum for sharing information, support, and coping tips; provides information and referrals; publishes quarterly *Our Voice* and pen-pal directories for people with autism and related developmental neurological abnormalities, such as hydrocephalus and Tourette syndrome; one directory is for people who use assistance in communicating.

American Academy of Child and Adolescent Psychiatry (AACAP), 202–966–7300. Publishes information sheet *The Autistic Child*. (For full group information, see MENTAL DISORDERS.)

Council for Exceptional Children (CEC), 800–328–0272. Publishes *Social Skills for Students with Autism* and special report *Peer Tutoring and Small-Group Instruction for Students with Autism and Developmental Delays*. (For full group information, see HELP ON LEARNING AND EDUCATION on page 659.)

Parents Helping Parents (PHP), 408–727–5775. Has division focusing on autism. (For full group information, see HELP FOR SPECIAL CHILDREN on page 689.)

National Information Center for Children and Youth with Disabilities (NICHCY), 800–695–0285, voice/TT. Publishes *Autism*. (For full group information, see HELP FOR SPECIAL CHILDREN on page 689.)

National Organization for Rare Disorders (NORD), 800–999–6673. Provides reprints on autism. (For full group information, see RARE DISORDERS.)

ONLINE RESOURCES

ADD Forum (CompuServe). Maintains discussions and online libraries on autism. (For full group information, see ATTENTION DEFICIT HYPERACTIVITY DISORDER.)

Internet: Autism list. To subscribe send this message "sub autism [your first name] [your last name]" to: mail to:listserv@juvm.stjohns.edu

(See also major online services for bulletin boards related to autism.)

OTHER RESOURCES

For parents and other adults

Keys to Parenting the Child with Autism. Marlene T. Brill. Barron's, 1994.
Educating Children with Autism: A Guide to Selecting an Appropriate Program. Michael D. Powers. Woodbine House, 1994.
Siblings of Children with Autism: A Guide for Families. Sandra L. Harris. Woodbine House, 1994.
A Parent's Guide to Autism. Charles Hart. Simon & Schuster, 1993.
Autism: Information and Resources for Parents, Families, and Professionals. Richard L. Simpson and Paul Zionts. PRO-ED, 1992.
Handbook of Autism: A Guide for Parents and Professionals. Maureen Aarons and Tessa Gittens. Routledge, 1991.

For children

Joey and Sam: A Heartwarming Storybook about Autism, a Family, and a Brother's Love. Illana Katz and Edward Ritvo. Real Life Storybooks, 1993.
Russell Is Extra Special: A Book about Autism for Children. Charles A. Amenta. Magination Press, 1992.

Personal experiences

I Don't Want to be Inside Me Anymore: Messages from an Autistic Mind. Birger Sellin. Basic, 1995.
Out of Silence: An Autistic Boy's Journey into Language and Communication. Russell Martin. Penguin, 1995.
Somebody Somewhere: Breaking Free from the World of Autism. Donna Williams. Times Books, 1994. Sequel to her *Nobody Nowhere: The Extraordinary Autobiography of an Autistic* (1992).
Son-Rise: The Miracle Continues, rev. ed. Barry N. Kaufman. H. J. Kramer, 1994. Sequel to *Son-Rise* (1976), describing the family's intensive personalized education program; here introduced by that son, Raun.
Laughing and Loving with Autism: A Collection of "Real Life" Warm and Humorous Stories. R. Wayne Gilpin. Future Education, 1993. Sequel: *More Laughing and Loving with Autism* (1994)
News from the Border: A Mother's Memoir of Her Autistic Son. Jane T. McDonnell. Ticknor and Fields, 1993.
When Snow Turns to Rain: One Family's Struggle to Solve the Riddle of Autism. Craig B. Schulze. Woodbine House, 1993.
Let Me Hear Your Voice: A Family's Triumph over Autism. Catherine Maurice. Knopf, 1993.
Little Boy Lost. Bronwyn Hocking. Trafalgar, 1993.
The Sound of a Miracle: A Child's Triumph over Autism. Annabel Stehli. Doubleday, 1991.

Background works

Autism: From Tragedy to Triumph. Carol Johnson and Julia Crowder. Branden, 1994.
Autism: The Facts. Simon Baron-Cohen and Patrick Bolton. Oxford University Press, 1993.
Autism: Explaining the Enigma. Uta Frith. Basil Blackwell, 1989.

(See also MENTAL RETARDATION; COMMUNICATION DISORDERS; MENTAL DISORDERS; also HELP FOR SPECIAL CHILDREN on page 689.)

autistic fantasy, a type of DEFENSE MECHANISM, in which a child (or adult) substitutes persistent daydreaming for human contact or for dealing directly with personal problems.

autoimmune disorders, disorders that result when the body's IMMUNE SYSTEM malfunctions and attacks the body's own tissues or organs, mistakenly identifying them as foreign invaders. Among the autoimmune disorders that are commonly found among young people are rheumatoid ARTHRITIS, DIABETES (Type I), LUPUS, a disorder of the THYROID GLAND (*Hashimoto's thyroiditis*), a disorder of the ADRENAL GLANDS (*Addison's disease*), and pernicious ANEMIA. Problems with autoimmunity are also involved in some kinds of ALLERGY. (See IMMUNE SYSTEM and specific disorders.)

autologous, in medicine, a general term referring to a type of TRANSPLANT or BLOOD TRANSFUSION that comes from the person's own body. Tissue, BONE MARROW, or blood are often taken days or weeks earlier and stored for use in a specific operation. By contrast, a transplant or transfusion from a DONOR is called ALLOGENIC.

autonomic nervous system, the part of the CENTRAL NERVOUS SYSTEM that controls the actions that the body makes "automatically" or "involuntarily," such as heartbeat, breathing, production of substances by various glands, and the like.

autosomal dominant (AD), a pattern of GENETIC INHERITANCE in which only one copy of a particular gene needs to be present for a trait (such as brown eyes) to be expressed. Though a person may carry two genes for the same dominant trait, only one is needed. In general, autosomal dominant disorders usually affect an average of 50 percent of each generation (males and females equally) and rarely skip a generation. A person without the disorder cannot pass it on to his or her children, though a new mutation can occur in any child.

Among the GENETIC DISORDERS that are of the autosomal dominant type are ACHONDROPLASIA, HUNTINGTON'S CHOREA, POLYDACTYLY, and NEUROFIBROMATOSIS. These disorders may affect individuals in widely varying ways; one may show mild signs of a disease, while others may have a severe form of the disorder. Even if a child is not seriously affected, it is important to diagnose a mild form of the disorder to help prevent damage from cumulative or later possible effects and also to help parents and their genetic counselors judge the likelihood that another child may be seriously affected. (See also GENETIC COUNSELING; PEDIGREE.)

autosomal recessive (AR), a pattern of GENETIC INHERITANCE in which both copies of a particular gene pair are needed for the same trait (such as blue eyes) to be expressed. Autosomal recessive disorders do not appear in every generation. Where both parents carry a gene for the disorder, an average of one in four of their children will be affected, males and females equally. Among the GENETIC DISORDERS that are of the autosomal recessive type are PHENYLKETONURIA, GALACTOSEMIA, ALBINISM, Tay-Sachs disease (see LIPID STORAGE DISEASES), sickle cell ANEMIA, CYSTIC FIBROSIS, and WILSON'S DISEASE. (See also GENETIC COUNSELING; PEDIGREE.)

autosomes, the twenty-two pairs of genes that, with the SEX CHROMOSOMES, make up the complete set of chromosomes that form each individual's GENETIC INHERITANCE. If both of the paired genes are alike (both for blue eyes, for example), the person is said to be a HOMOZYGOTE for that gene; if they differ (as with one gene for blue eyes and one for brown eyes), the person is called a HETEROZYGOTE for that gene. If only one copy of a gene must be present for a trait to be expressed (regardless of what the other gene in the pair is), it is called DOMINANT, and the pattern of inheritance is called AUTOSOMAL DOMINANT. But if the two paired genes need to be alike for a trait to be expressed, the inheritance pattern is called AUTOSOMAL RECESSIVE.

average, a number intended to give a general picture of a group of numbers, such as test scores; in statistics, the average is called a *measure of central tendency*. The most common type of average is the *mean*, which is calculated by adding the scores and dividing by the number of scores, as in calculating a GRADE-POINT AVERAGE or CUMULATIVE AVERAGE. But average may sometimes refer to a *median*, the score precisely in a middle when the scores are ranked in order (for example, in the scores 73, 82, 87, 88, and 95, 87 is the median), or to a *mode*, the score that appears most often, as when five people got 75 on a test, and no more than two people have any other test score.

avoidance, a type of DEFENSE MECHANISM in which the person tries to steer clear of people, situations, or objects perceived as threatening to the self, especially if related to unconscious impulses and imagined punishment for such impulses. A common type of behavior in ANXIETY disorders.

avoidant disorder of childhood or adolescence, a type of ANXIETY DISORDER in which children (girls more than boys) shrink excessively from contact with strangers. AVOIDANCE in children under two or two-and-a-half, popularly called *stranger anxiety*, is quite normal. But if it appears after that, especially in the early school years, it can lead to impaired SOCIAL SKILLS, isolation, and DEPRESSION. In severe cases, the child may be so shy and anxious he or she becomes inarticulate or even MUTE. If avoidance persists into adulthood, the condition is classified by psychiatrists as *avoidant personality disorder*. It may also be associated with some other disorders, such as SEPARATION ANXIETY DISORDER, OVERANXIOUS DISORDER, or PHOBIA. (See MENTAL DISORDERS.)

B

Babinski's reflex, upward flexion of the big toe and fanning of the other toes, when a child's foot is firmly stroked on the outside of the sole. Babinski's REFLEX is normal in newborns, but its presence in children and adults can indicate brain or spinal cord disorders. The normal postnewborn response to such stroking, called the *plantar response,* is to curl the toes.

Baby Doe Law, legislation designed to protect the right of infants with DISABILITIES to receive medical care, whether or not the parents wish it; named after a New York case in which an anonymous baby, dubbed "Baby Jane Doe," was given life-saving surgery for SPINA BIFIDA and other defects, despite her parents' objections. As part of the Child Abuse Amendments of 1984, Public Law 98–457, the Baby Doe Law requires that if states are to continue to receive federal grant money for CHILD ABUSE AND NEGLECT programs, they must institute programs to investigate suspected cases of "withholding of medically indicated treatment from disabled infants with life-threatening conditions."

More specifically, the law requires that a handicapped infant must always be given appropriate NUTRITION, hydration (fluids), and medication, and should be given "medically indicated treatment" unless the infant is in a CHRONIC and irreversible COMA; the treatment would merely prolong dying, while not improving life-threatening conditions; or the treatment would be inhumane and futile in terms of survival.

To be in compliance with the law, under Department of Health and Human Services' (HHS) regulations, states must require that a state agency be informed of cases in which it is suspected that medical treatment is being withheld; that agency then investigates such alleged "medical neglect," a process that includes gaining access to medical records, and may initiate court proceedings to obtain medical treatment for disabled infants.

The Baby Doe regulations cover infants under 1 year old and also children who have been continuously hospitalized since birth, were born extremely PREMATURE babies, or have long-term disabilities. The HHS also made clear that the decision to give or withhold treatment should not be based on the child's anticipated "quality of life" but on "reasonable medical judgment," the decision being one "that would be made about the case and the treatment possibilities with respect to the medical conditions involved."

FOR HELP AND FURTHER INFORMATION

National Information Clearinghouse (NIC) for Infants with Disabilities and Life-Threatening Conditions, 800–922–9234, ext. 201, voice/TDD. Publishes *Summary of Child Abuse Amendments of 1984, Legal Issues* and a bibliography on care of infants with disabilities. (For full group information, see HELP FOR SPECIAL CHILDREN on page 689.)

Spina Bifida Association of America (SBAA), 800–621–3141. (For full group information, see SPINA BIFIDA.)

babysitter, a person who cares for a child on an irregular basis, generally part-time, often a young girl or boy, but sometimes an older person, such as a neighbor or relative. No special training is required of babysitters, though many communities have established programs to provide basic training in CHILD CARE, first aid, and handling emergencies for young people planning to work as babysitters. During holidays or summers, babysitters may be employed on a more regular basis as a PARENT'S HELPER or AU PAIR. (See CHILD CARE; also CHECKLIST FOR CHOOSING CHILD CARE on page 114.)

bachelor's degree, the DEGREE awarded by most four-year COLLEGES and universities to students who successfully complete their program of study, usually a Bachelor of Arts (B.A.) or Bachelor of Science (B.S.). Bachelor's degrees are sometimes also awarded for longer courses of study, such as architecture or pharmacy, or for some kinds of graduate study, such as theology.

back to basics, a late–twentieth-century phrase calling for a return to the focus on teaching fundamental skills—especially the so-called "three R's": reading, 'riting, and 'rithmetic—and de-emphasizing supposedly "softer" subjects, such as music, art, and social studies. (See EDUCATION.)

balanitis, inflammation of the glans and foreskin of the PENIS, often from infections such as *candidiasis.* Prevention of this inflammation has traditionally been one of the medical reasons advanced for male CIRCUMCISION.

baptismal certificate (church certificate), a written form indicating the date of birth and of baptism of a child issued by a church. Such a certificate can sometimes be used as proof of age—for entering school, for example—when the BIRTH CERTIFICATE is unavailable.

barium X-ray examination, a medical procedure, often called a *GI (gastrointestinal) series,* to help diagnose DIGESTIVE DISORDERS involving the use of barium as a contrasting medium, so that details of the digestive system will show up clearly on X-RAYS. For examination of the upper part of the system (an *upper GI series*) or the whole system, the patient is given a "barium milkshake" to drink and X-rays are taken at intervals as the barium passes through the system. For examination of the small intestine, a tube is fed into the system through the mouth or nose and the barium introduced directly at the site to be X-rayed. For examination of the large intestine, the patient's system is made as empty as possible, then a tube fed through the anus introduces barium into the body, a procedure popularly called a "barium enema." (See DIGESTIVE SYSTEM AND DISORDERS.)

basal age, the highest age at which a child is consistently able to correctly answer all the items on a STANDARDIZED TEST. In a STANFORD-BINET INTELLIGENCE TEST, the age level at which a child can complete all questions correctly; the opposite is known as the *ceiling age.*

Basic Skills and Educational Proficiency Program, a federal program set up with the passage of Public Law 95–561, the Educational Amendments of 1978; an expansion of the earlier RIGHT TO READ program. Its aim is to upgrade basic skills among both children and adults, especially in the areas of READING, mathematics, speaking, and writing.

basic skills, skills learned in ELEMENTARY SCHOOL, such as READING, spelling, and adding and subtracting, that are fundamental to all other later learning. Acquisition of such skills is often tested by ACHIEVEMENT TESTS, such as the IOWA TESTS OF BASIC SKILLS.

battered child syndrome, a pattern of physical and other signs, including FRACTURES, BURNS, bruises, welts, cuts, and internal damage, indicating that a child's internal and external injuries were inflicted by someone, generally a parent, other CAREGIVER, or older SIBLING, using a hand, fist, or object such as a belt, pan, or pipe. This was the name given by the medical professional to cases of child abuse when it was first formally recognized in 1961, but it is now seen as just one type of CHILD ABUSE, which is often intended as DISCIPLINE or punishment. (See HELP AGAINST CHILD ABUSE AND NEGLECT on page 680.)

battery, in testing, a series of two or more TESTS, such as ACHIEVEMENT TESTS, given to a person within a short period. Also a group of STANDARDIZED TESTS that have been developed and tested on the same general population and so are considered comparable to one another.

In the law, battery often refers to physical VIOLENCE or contact that is offensive to and without the consent of the victim, as in cases of CHILD ABUSE. An unintentional action causing no severe harm is commonly called *simple battery,* while intentional violence is generally termed *aggravated battery.* By contrast, ASSAULT is the legal term that often refers to the threat of, or sometimes an uncompleted attempt at, injury or VIOLENCE. Battery is often (though it need not be) preceded by threats, hence the common phrase "assault and battery." What does, or does not, constitute battery in the schools, in the home, and in other settings is a matter of intense dispute.

Bayley Scales of Infant Development, an individually administered test that attempts to measure the development of mental processes and MOTOR SKILLS in infants ages two to thirty months. The test administrator uses various items as stimuli to evoke responses from the child. The infant's reactions, which may include early attempts to communicate and the use of gross and fine MOTOR SKILLS, are then described in the Infant Behavior Record. The Bayley Scales are often used to determine whether a child is developing normally or has a DEVELOPMENTAL DELAY and may be in need of special services. (See TESTS.)

bedwetting, inability to exercise full control of urination, especially during the night but also sometimes during the day. Medically called *enuresis,* bedwetting is a common problem in otherwise normal children of school age; preschool-age children are seen as still developing control of urinary functions. By contrast, children who have physical disorders, such as SPINA BIFIDA or PARALYSIS, which prevent them from exercising control, are said to have INCONTINENCE.

Primary enuresis is when a child has never developed the ability to stay dry reliably through the night; *secondary enuresis* is when a child begins to wet the bed again after being dry for months or years. Secondary enuresis can result from diseases, disorders, or upset in a child's life, such as hospitalization or the birth of a SIBLING. Parents should have a physician thoroughly examine the child for possible physical problems.

The causes of primary enuresis are less clear, but it often seems to run in families. Smaller bladders, delay in development of the nerves and muscles involved, insufficiency of ANTIDIURETIC HORMONE, and other such subtle factors often found in enuretic children may be part of a child's GENETIC INHERITANCE. Problems with TOILET TRAINING, passed on from one generation to the next, can exacerbate the problem. If a child is still wetting the bed by school age (or earlier, if the child is anxious about or socially restricted by the bedwetting), parents may want to seek help among the network of health professionals in their community.

One of the most commonly used approaches to ending bedwetting is a buzzer-alarm, triggered by the first few drops of urine, which is used to help children gradually train themselves to wake up during the night to urinate. This is effective for many children, though it may be counter-productive for others who already feel anxiety and stress. Medications can also help sometimes, though some are dangerously toxic. One promising new approach is a nasal spray (desmopressin acetate) that stimulates production of antidiuretic hormone. When emotional disturbance is involved, psychological therapy may be recommended—for psychiatrists, enuresis is labeled an *elimination disorder*, a kind of MENTAL DISORDER. Whatever approach is taken, children with enuresis require considerable understanding and support from their families.

FOR HELP AND FURTHER INFORMATION

National Mental Health Association (NMHA), 800–969–6642. Publishes *Coping with the Bed-Wetting Problem.* (For full group information, see MENTAL DISORDERS.)

American Academy of Child and Adolescent Psychiatry (AACAP), 202–966–7300. Publishes information sheet *Bedwetting.* (For full group information, see MENTAL DISORDERS.)

OTHER RESOURCES

GENERAL WORKS

Dry All Night: The Picture Book Technique That Stops Bedwetting. Alison Mack. Little, Brown, 1989.

Toilet Training and Bed Wetting: A Practical Guide for Today's Parents. Heather Welford. Harper and Row, 1988.

FOR CHILDREN

Sammy the Elephant and Mr. Camel: A Story to Help Children Overcome Enuresis While Discovering Self-Appreciation. Joyce C. Mills and Richard J. Crowley. Magination Press, 1988.

BACKGROUND BOOKS

Nocturnal Enuresis: The Child's Experience. Richard J. Butler. Butterworth-Heinemann, 1994.

(See also TOILET TRAINING; INCONTINENCE; KIDNEY AND UROLOGICAL DISORDERS; MENTAL DISORDERS.)

behavior modification, teaching and guidance technique used to mold and change behavior by rewarding desired actions and ignoring—that is, withholding reward for—unwanted actions. Such rewards are sometimes material, but often are simply recognition and warm praise, and they are offered not only when a child has complete success at a task but also when the child has made honest effort or has come a step closer to success (what psychologists call *successive approximation).* The underlying principle of behavior modification is that POSITIVE REINFORCEMENT—rewards, including praise for effort—encourages children (and adults!) to continue to improve their skills and learn new ones, while punishment and criticism tend to discourage them from making the effort to improve and try new things. (Subscribers to the America Online computer service can find a fuller discussion of using behavioral modification techniques with young children, in the Moms Online Desk Reference section of Moms Online, under "Teaching Young Children.") Behavior modification is also widely used with teenagers and adults in programs that focus on changing behavior, such as SMOKING, regardless of its causes. (See DISCIPLINE.)

Behavior Rating Instrument for Autistic and Other Atypical Children (BRIACC), an individually administered observational inventory, a type of DIAGNOSTIC ASSESSMENT TEST, used to evaluate children with AUTISM or other children who cannot or do not cooperate with more formal testing procedures. A trained examiner takes an inventory of behaviors over two days of observations, focusing especially on eight areas: communication, vocalization or speech, reception of sound and speech, relationships with adults, social responsiveness, body movement, drive for mastery, and psychobiological development. These are then graded on separate scales, and the results are compared against NORMS set by normal children aged 3½ to 4½. (See TESTS.)

Bender Visual Motor Gestalt Test (Bender-Gestalt), a type of DIAGNOSTIC ASSESSMENT TEST that is used to help identify possible LEARNING DISABILITIES, BRAIN DISORDERS, MENTAL RETARDATION, MENTAL DISORDER, or general DEVELOPMENTAL DELAY for children beginning at age three and for adults. The person is given a series of cards, each bearing a design, and is asked to reproduce designs on blank paper. The drawings are scored by test professionals based on various aspects of form, shape, pattern, and orientation on the paper. Though often individually administered, the test can also be given to groups. (See TESTS.)

benign, in medicine, a general term referring to a mild condition or form of a disease, especially a TUMOR, that is not expected to progress to the point of being life-threatening. In contrast, something regarded as life-threatening is called MALIGNANT.

Benton Visual Retention Test, a type of individually administered DIAGNOSTIC ASSESSMENT TEST used with children beginning at age eight and also with adults. It is used to help identify possible disorders in visual memory, such as those that occur in people with LEARNING DISABILITIES. Given ten designs one by one, the child is asked to reproduce each on plain paper. The results are professionally scored. (See TESTS.)

best interests of the child, in family law, a general principle guiding the court in determining such matters as CUSTODY and VISITATION RIGHTS that gives precedence to the emotional and financial stability of the child; also called the *least detrimental alternative.* In cases of CHILD ABUSE AND NEGLECT, the court has traditionally assumed that it is in the child's best interests to remain in the home while the case is being studied or while the parents undergo treatment, except when the child's life is threatened or the parents have proven unable to respond to treatment. The principle of the best interests of the child acts as a brake on overuse of institutional placement by the state, but can have the unwanted result of leaving the child in danger.

binge eating disorder, a pattern of compulsive eating behaviors; a type of eating disorder. It is characterized by recurrent episodes of excessive, out-of-control eating, often lasting hours at a time and involving large amounts of food, frequently over 2,000 calories—more than an adult should need for an entire day. Unlike the occasional "splurge" that most people have—gobbling a quart of ice cream, for example—binge eating disorder is characterized by compulsive eating phases that often involve:

- Eating far more rapidly than usual.
- Eating until uncomfortably full.
- Eating large amounts of food even when not physically hungry.
- Eating large amounts throughout the day, not in distinct meals.
- Eating alone because of feeling embarrassed over the amount being consumed.
- Feeling unable to stop eating or control consumption, once a binge starts.
- Feeling distress, disgust, guilt, or depression about the overeating.

People with this disorder do not attempt to purge their bodies of excess calories, as in BULIMIA, but simply gain weight from their compulsive eating. As yet, this disorder has not been recognized as an "official diagnosis" in the psychiatric and medical community, so specific therapies are still being developed. Until therapies are recognized, treatment for many patients may not be eligible for coverage under their HEALTH CARE or HEALTH INSURANCE plans.

FOR HELP AND FURTHER INFORMATION

Hazelden Foundation (HF), 800–262–5010. Publishes *Compulsive Overeater, Recovery from Compulsive Eating: A Complete Guide to the Twelve Step Program,* and other materials for compulsive eaters. (For full group information, see HELP AGAINST SUBSTANCE ABUSE on page 703.)

OTHER RESOURCES

Silent Hunger: Overcoming Eating Compulsions with Dignity and Grace. Judy Halliday and Arthur Halliday. Revell, 1994.

Fat and Furious: Women and Food Obsession. Judi Hollis. Ballantine, 1994.

Freedom from Food: The Secret Lives of Dieters and Compulsive Eaters. Elizabeth Hampshire. Prentice Hall, 1990.

Compulsive Eating. Donna LeBlanc. Health Communications, 1990.

(See also OBESITY; BULIMIA; ANOREXIA NERVOSA.)

biological parents, the male and female whose genes actually make up the GENETIC INHERITANCE of a child and who are therefore the child's immediate ancestors and nearest BLOOD RELATIONS; also called *birth parents* or *natural parents.* The term is most widely used when a child has more than one set of parents, to distinguish between the parents whose genes the child carries and those who have legal CUSTODY of the child, such as adoptive parents, foster parents, or stepparents. Biological parents generally have PARENTS' RIGHTS and PARENTS' RESPONSIBILITIES, including the right to see the children and the duty to contribute to their support, except in cases of TERMINATION OF PARENTAL RIGHTS. (See FATHER; MOTHER.)

In at least one situation, the biological parent is not the same as the birth parent—when a *host surrogate mother* bears a baby developed from the fertilized egg that contains the genes of the couple who employed the surrogate. (See SURROGATE MOTHER.)

biopsy, the taking of tissue or cells from the body to examine in a laboratory, often for diagnostic purposes, as when assessing whether a person has CANCER or MUSCULAR DYSTROPHY. Most biopsies involve removing a small piece of skin or muscle under local ANESTHESIA. For an accessible TUMOR or internal organ, a hollow *aspiration needle* may be inserted into the body to suck up cells, sometimes with the aid of ULTRASOUND or other types of SCANS. If a tumor or internal organ is not readily accessible, a biopsy may be obtained under a general anesthetic by pushing an ENDOSCOPE (long viewing tube) with forceps attached into the body. Biopsy samples may also be obtained as part of a regular operation under general anesthesia, although sometimes a whole tumor is removed and sent for analysis. (See MEDICAL TESTS.)

biotin, a VITAMIN once called vitamin H but now considered part of a group of vitamins known as vitamin B complex. It is important in the METABOLISM of CARBOHYDRATES, PROTEINS, and FATS. Symptoms of deficiency include fatigue, DEPRESSION, nausea, insomnia, and muscle pain. Deficiency is rare, because bacteria produce biotin in the intestinal tract, but can occur with long-term use of ANTIBIOTICS or sulfa drugs. Biotin is abundant in eggs, milk, and meats, though raw egg white contains a factor that destroys biotin. Possible results of excess biotin are unknown because it is water-soluble and excess is normally excreted in urine and feces. (See RECOMMENDED DAILY ALLOWANCES; VITAMINS.)

bipolar disorder, a type of MOOD DISORDER that involves episodes of strong DEPRESSION and mania (a state of high energy, irritability, and impulsiveness) as a person swings from "highs" to "lows," generally with intervening periods of more normal moods. Bipolar disorder is a form of MENTAL DISORDER previously called *manic-depressive illness.* Bipolar disorder often goes unrecognized, unless one of the episodes is severe enough to require temporary hospitalization. Once diagnosed, it often responds to medication, such as lithium; psychotherapy and electroshock therapy may also be used. The causes of bipolar disorder are unknown, though it may be a kind of GENETIC DISORDER. In 1987, scientists found what they thought was a defective gene that causes bipolar disorder, but later studies cast doubt on that conclusion. (See MENTAL DISORDERS.)

birth canal, the widened CERVIX and VAGINA through which a baby passes on its way from the UTERUS during CHILDBIRTH.

birth certificate, a formal written document stating a person's name and date of birth, generally based on a report by the doctor who attended at the birth, which is filed in a government office of vital statistics. A child who has been adopted will generally be issued a new birth certificate showing the date of birth, new name, and new parents, though usually not showing the fact of adoption. A HOSPITAL form showing a child's name and date of birth may also be called a birth certificate. A birth certificate is a key personal document required for several purposes, such as entering school (to attest the AGE of the child), obtaining a passport, during ADOPTION procedures, and in establishing information for a PEDIGREE in GENETIC COUNSELING. The government publication *Where to Write for Vital Records: Births, Deaths, Marriages, and Divorces*, published by the Public Health Service, National Center for Health Statistics, tells where to write for copies of birth certificates, if needed.

birth control, exercise of deliberate choice over when one will conceive and bear a child, in this sense also called *family planning*. In practice, two choices may be involved: first, whether or not to allow CONCEPTION to take place unimpeded; second, if conception occurs, whether to continue the PREGNANCY or have an ABORTION. The latter decision may be based on many personal factors in the life of the woman and her partner, but it may also depend partly on the results of various PRENATAL TESTS. In a wider sense, birth control also refers to a social goal of limiting family size, and therefore population growth, by limiting conception.

Birth control also refers to various methods for preventing undesired pregnancies, encompassing:

- *Contraception*, which focuses on preventing CONCEPTION, including methods such as the CONDOM, SPERMICIDES, DIAPHRAGM, CERVICAL CAP, INTRAUTERINE DEVICE (IUD), DEPO-PROVERA, NORPLANT, VAGINAL POUCH, DOUCHING, CERVICAL SPONGE, and BIRTH CONTROL PILLS (oral contraceptives).
- STERILIZATION, surgical procedures intended to be permanent, including VASECTOMY and TUBAL LIGATION.
- ABORTION, the termination of a pregnancy, once begun, which may be achieved by surgical methods or by drugs, such as RU–486 or the newer *methotrexate-misoprostol* combination, both still experimental in the United States.
- NATURAL FAMILY PLANNING, including the calendar (rhythm) method, the basal body temperature method, vaginal (cervical) mucus (or Billings) method, and the symptothermal method.
- MORNING AFTER PILL, a drug given after sexual intercourse that is designed to block a pregnancy by preventing a fertilized egg (OVUM) from implanting in the UTERUS or by expelling the contents of the uterus.

Parents who want to plan when and at what intervals to have their children will want to review the merits and demerits of various birth control methods and discuss them with their doctor or other health professional. The methods that have the least risk and the most effectiveness are the best choices. Sexually active ADOLESCENTS should also be introduced to birth control, preferably by their parents. Whatever other form of birth control teenagers use for contraception, they should also use CONDOMS for protection from various SEXUALLY TRANSMITTED DISEASES, such as GONORRHEA, HERPES, and AIDS.

FOR HELP AND FURTHER INFORMATION

Planned Parenthood Federation of America (PPFA)
810 Seventh Avenue
New York, NY 10019
212–541–7800; 800–230-PLAN [230–7526]
Fax: 212–245–1845
Gloria Feldt, President
Organization concerned with access to birth control methods and infertility services; sponsors research; provides information and referrals; acts as advocate; publishes various materials, including bimonthly newsletters *LINK Line, The Planned Parenthood Women's Health Letter*; pamphlets *Facts About Birth Control, Your Contraceptive Choices, You and the Pill, Norplant® and You, The Condom: What It Is, What It Is For, How to Use It, Diaphragms and Cervical Caps, Understanding IUDs, Is Depo-Provera® for You?, Smoking or the Pill, Your Key to Good Health: The Gynecological Exam,* and *What if I'm Pregnant?*; and training and reference materials for health professionals.

Human Life International (HLI)
7845 Airpark Road, Suite E
Gaithersburg, MD 20879
301–670–7884; 800–549-LIFE [5433]
Fax: 301–869–7363
Matthew Habiger, President
Organization opposing intervention into the reproductive processes; fosters natural family planning; provides information; operates Magdalene Rescue and Rehabilitation program; publishes various materials, including monthly *HLI Reports*; *Pro-Life/Family Catalog*; occasional special reports; pamphlets *From Conception to Abortion* and *The "Alternative" to Secular Sex Education*; and numerous reprints.

American College of Obstetricians and Gynecologists (ACOG), 202–638–5577. Publishes *Birth Control Pills.* (For full group information, see PREGNANCY.)

Couple to Couple League (CCL), 513–471–2000. Publishes brochures *The Pill: How Does It Work? Is It Safe?*, *The Pill and the IUD: Some Facts for an Informed Choice, From Contraception to Abortion, The Legacy of Planned Parenthood, Not in the Public Interest: The Planned Parenthood Version of Sex Education*, and other materials. (For full group information, see NATURAL FAMILY PLANNING.)

Choice
1233 Locust Street, 3rd Floor
Philadelphia, PA 19107
215–985–3355
Hotline for health information: 215–985–3300
Hotline for day-care information: 215–985–3302
Lisa Shulock, Executive Director
Organization providing information on reproductive health care; provides telephone counseling and referrals; publishes various materials.

National Family Planning and Reproductive Health Association (NFPRHA)
122 C Street NW, Suite 380
Washington, DC 20001
202–628–3535
Fax: 202–737–2690
E-mail: judithdesarno@msn.com
Judith M. De Sarno, President and CEO
Organization concerned with family planning and reproductive health; acts as advocate; publishes various materials.

American Social Health Association (ASHA), 800–227–8922. Publishes brochure *Condoms, Contraceptives and STDs* and *Condoms in the Prevention of Sexually Transmitted Disease.* (For full group information, see SEXUALLY TRANSMITTED DISEASES.)

Sexuality Information and Education Council of the United States (SIECUS), 212–819–9770. Publishes fact sheet *The Truth About Latex Condoms.* (For full group information, see SEX EDUCATION.)

Women's Legal Defense Fund, 202–986–2600. Publishes *Norplant Legislation and Litigation.* (For full group information, see FAMILY AND MEDICAL LEAVE.)

OTHER RESOURCES

General works

Contraception: A User's Handbook. Anne Szarewski and John Guillebaud. Oxford University Press, 1994.
Understanding the Pill: A Consumer's Guide to Oral Contraceptives. Greg Juhn. Haworth Press, 1994.
Contraception: Your Questions Answered, 2nd ed. John Guillebaud. Churchill, 1993.
The Complete Guide to Fertility and Family Planning. Sarah Freeman and Vern L. Bullough. Prometheus Books, 1992.
Questions and Answers about Birth Control. M. Sanger. Gordon, 1992.
The Contraceptive Handbook: A Guide to Safe and Effective Choices for Men and Women. Consumer Reports, 1992.
The Fertility and Contraception Book. Julia Mosse and Josephine Heation. Faber and Faber, 1991.
Family Planning. Tim Parks. Grove Weidenfeld, 1991.

On Natural Family Planning

The Ovulation Method of Natural Family Planning: An Introductory Booklet for New Users, rev. ed. Thomas W. Hilgers. Pope Paul Sixth, 1993.
Natural Fertility: The Complete Guide to Avoiding or Achieving Conception. Francesca Naish. Sterling, 1992.
Fertility: A Comprehensive Guide to Natural Family Planning. Elizabeth Clubb and Jane Knight. Sterling, 1992.
Your Fertility Signals: Using Them to Achieve or Avoid Pregnancy, Naturally. Merryl Winstein. Smooth Stone Press, 1990.
The Billings Method. Evelyn Billings and Ann Westmore. Ballantine, 1989.

For preteens and teens

I Con ... If You Con(dom): The Ins and Outs of Contraception for the Sexually Active Girl or Boy. Carole Marsh. Gallopade, 1994.
Margaret Sanger: Every Child a Wanted Child. Nancy Whitelaw. Dillon/Macmillan, 1994.
Coping with Birth Control, rev. ed. Michael Benson. Rosen, 1992.

Background Books

Pregnancy: Private Decisions, Public Debates. Kathlyn Gay. Watts, 1994.
Family Planning and the Law. Kenneth M. Norrie. Ashgate, 1991.
Woman's Body, Woman's Right: Birth Control in America, rev. ed. Linda Gordon. Viking Penguin, 1990.

(See SEX EDUCATION; NATURAL FAMILY PLANNING; ADOLESCENT PREGNANCY; ABORTION; SEXUALLY TRANSMITTED DISEASES; also specific types of birth control.)

birth control pill, drugs that use various HORMONES to block CONCEPTION; also called *oral contraceptives.* "The pill" is a popular form of temporary BIRTH CONTROL (as opposed to permanent STERILIZATION), though its side effects make a poor choice for some women. In general, these pills act by maintaining steady levels of key female sex hormones, which block release of an egg (OVUM) from a woman's OVARIES, because the rising and falling levels of these hormones normally trigger OVULATION during the MENSTRUAL CYCLE.

Birth control pills come in two main forms:

- *Combination pills,* made from ESTROGEN and progestin, a synthetic form of PROGESTERONE; both are hormones similar to those produced in a woman's own body). The Food and Drug Administration (FDA) rates combination pills as 99 percent effective as contraceptives. Among the side effects experienced are nausea, high BLOOD PRESSURE, and blood clots, which at worst can cause severe problems, including blindness and death. Newer *biphasic* and *triphasic* forms of the pills, designed to more closely approximate a woman's normal hormonal variations, may lessen such side effects.
- *Mini-pills,* made only of progestin, which are rated by the FDA as 97 percent effective in contraception. Less commonly used, these also act to make the CERVIX and UTERUS more hostile to SPERM. Among the side effects are spotting and bleeding between periods.

Oral contraceptives must be taken every day for twenty-one days, regardless of how often a woman has SEXUAL INTERCOURSE, and then discontinued for seven days. If a woman misses a period while on the pill, she is advised to take a PREGNANCY TEST. If she is not pregnant and periods continue to be missed, she may need a pill with a different balance of hormones. Some women who experience side effects such as growth of facial HAIR, ACNE, or oily skin (see SKIN AND SKIN DISORDERS) also may switch to a different kind of pill.

Since its introduction in the 1960s, "the pill" has been the contraceptive of choice for many sexually active women. However, individual women and their doctors should carefully weigh their personal and family medical histories against the health pros and cons of the pill. In general, the FDA recommends that women who smoke, are over 35, or have high blood pressure, DIABETES, heart problems, blood clots, unexplained vaginal bleeding, CANCER (especially of the BREASTS or UTERUS), or high CHOLESTEROL should *not* take birth control pills, because of increased risk of heart attack and stroke. Also, women who are or may be pregnant should not take them, because they can cause BIRTH DEFECTS. Combination pills also carry increased risk of gall bladder problems, liver problems, and possible cancer of the CERVIX; studies have produced conflicting results about possible increased risk of breast cancer.

Some people who take combination pills also experience VOMITING, severe headaches, DEPRESSION, dizziness, EDEMA (water buildup), missed menstrual periods, and problems with contact lenses (see EYE AND VISION PROBLEMS). Birth control pills also cause adverse interactions with some other common medications, including some BARBITURATES and ANTIBIOTICS (see DRUG REACTIONS AND INTERACTIONS).

However, oral contraceptives carry some health benefits. MENSTRUATION is usually lighter and less painful, formation of cysts in breasts and OVARIES is less common, and so is PELVIC INFLAMMATORY DISEASE. If a pregnancy does occur, ECTOPIC PREGNANCY is less likely, and the pills may afford some protection against cancer of the ovaries or the endometrium (lining of the uterus). A 1991 study from the Alan Guttmacher Institute, balancing the risk of death against the likelihood of death being prevented by use of the pill, concluded: "The average women who has ever used the pill is less likely to get cancer and die as a result before age 55 than a woman who has never used the pill."

Parents of sexually active teenagers may well want to explore with their daughters and doctors the best type of birth control to use. If the pill is adopted, the FDA advises: "Women prescribed birth control pills should acquaint themselves with the information in the patient package insert accompanying the prescription. They should also have their blood pressure checked and should have physical examinations and PAP TESTS at least yearly. Because the risk of serious side effects in many cases decreases with a reduced hormone dose, patients should discuss with their physicians using the lowest effective dose."

But women should be warned that the pill provides protection against contraception only. It offers no protection against SEXUALLY TRANSMITTED DISEASES (STDs), such as AIDS, PELVIC INFLAMMATORY DISEASE, and the viruses linked with cervical cancer. Women are advised to also use a barrier method, such as the CONDOM or VAGINAL POUCH. (See BIRTH CONTROL.)

birth defects, malformations, malfunctions, and other CONGENITAL disorders that appear in newborns, including GENETIC DISORDERS and CHROMOSOMAL ABNORMALITIES, as well as problems resulting from other causes, such as exposure to radiation (see ENVIRONMENTAL HAZARDS), drugs (see DRUG REACTIONS AND INTERACTIONS), disease, or injury during PREGNANCY or CHILDBIRTH. Some defects—at least 10 to 30 percent—are so lethal that the FETUS fails to develop and a spontaneous ABORTION (MISCARRIAGE) occurs, sometimes so early in pregnancy that the woman does not even know she is pregnant. With some defects, such as ANENCEPHALY, babies die shortly after birth. Of those babies who survive, perhaps 5 to 9 percent have some sort of birth defect—perhaps more because some congenital disorders (such as HUNTINGTON'S DISEASE) only appear later in life.

Some birth defects can now be spotted with PRENATAL TESTS, given as part of GENETIC SCREENING early in pregnancy. This gives the parents the option of choosing for the mother to have a selective abortion, having the defect repaired through IN UTERO SURGERY (an option available only in a few special situations), or preparing to raise a child with SPECIAL NEEDS. Physicians who specialize in birth defects are called TERATOLOGISTS, from the Greek word "teras" meaning monster.

Though there are many thousands of known or suspected defects, any single type of birth defect is rare and their causes are generally unknown. Most birth defects seem to result from a combination of GENETIC INHERITANCE and environmental factors. Two couples with similar life-styles and home settings, exposed to the same

ENVIRONMENTAL HAZARDS, may be differently affected, depending on their genetic predisposition. So one couple's child may be born with a birth defect, but not the other's. For unknown reasons, birth defects also appear at widely varying rates in different parts of the world. SPINA BIFIDA, for example, occurs in roughly 1 of every 575 births in Northern Ireland, but only in 1 every 20,000 births in Japan, while in the United States the rate is about 1 in every 3,333 births. Recent studies have suggested that if a woman has a child with a birth defect, her chances of having another child with a birth defect are increased if she continues to live in the same area, but are reduced if she moves to a different area. This finding tends to support theories that the defects are triggered by exposure to some substances in the immediate environment.

In some cases, however, researchers can identify specific causes for a birth defect, such as a chromosomal abnormality, exposure to a specific disease (such as RUBELLA) or drug (such as ACCUTANE), or the pregnant mother's shortage of an essential VITAMIN or MINERAL. As a result, much emphasis has been placed on the mother getting good PRENATAL CARE, avoiding known *reproductive hazards* (environmental hazards that have direct effects on a developing fetus), and getting proper NUTRITION.

Some drugs can cause birth defects at any stage during a pregnancy, including in the early weeks before a woman realizes she is pregnant, so a woman who may be pregnant or is considering a pregnancy should take no medications—prescription or over-the-counter—without first consulting her GYNECOLOGIST/OBSTETRICIAN about the possible effects on a developing fetus. Fathers taking strong medications may also want to check with a physician before a planned conception. Other reproductive hazards include toxic chemicals, SMOKING, alcohol, CHRONIC illness in either parent, SPERMICIDES used around the time of pregnancy, rubella, TOXOPLASMOSIS, viral diseases such as hepatitis (see LIVER AND LIVER PROBLEMS), X-RAYS (not only in medicine or industry, but also in high-altitude flying), ANESTHESIA, and stress.

Experts in GENETIC COUNSELING can help prospective parents review their genetic and personal histories and assess the risk of their having a child with a birth defect. Best consulted before pregnancy, genetic counselors can also advise on any life-style changes that can help parents reduce their risk of having a child with birth defects. This is important because the fetus is most vulnerable to damage during the first TRIMESTER (three months) of pregnancy.

FOR HELP AND FURTHER INFORMATION

National Maternal and Child Health Clearinghouse (NMCHC), 703–821–8955. Provides information on specific genetic diseases and support groups; publishes *Genetic Screening for Inborn Errors of Metabolism* and *Learning Together: A Guide for Families with Genetic Disorders.* (For full group information, see PREGNANCY.)

March of Dimes Birth Defects Foundation
1275 Mamaroneck Avenue
White Plains, NY 10605
914–428–7100 (local chapters in telephone directory white pages)
Fax: 914–428–8203
Jennifer Howse, President
Organization concerned about birth defects; provides information and referrals; some local chapters have available certified midwives; publishes numerous materials, including book *Birth Defects: A Brighter Future*; pamphlet *When Baby Needs Extra Care*; education kit *You, Me and Others* (on basic genetics, in three levels: Grades K–2, 3–4, and 5–6); videos: *Inside My Mom, Same Inside* (on children with birth defects), and *It's Up to Me*; and numerous information sheets and professional education materials.

Association of Birth Defect Children (ABDC)
827 Irma Avenue
Orlando, FL 32803
407–245–7035; Birth Defect Registry Hotline
800–313-ABDC [313–2232]
Betty Mekdeci, Executive Director
Organization focusing on birth defects; acts as advocate; provides in-depth Health Resource reports on specific birth defects, disabilities, and treatment options; publishes quarterlies *ABDC News* and *Environmental Birth Defects Digest.*

Center for Safety in the Arts (CSA), 212–227–6220. Publishes fact sheet *Reproductive Hazards in the Arts and Crafts.* (For full group information, see ENVIRONMENTAL HAZARDS.)

American College of Obstetricians and Gynecologists (ACOG), 202–638–5577. Publishes *Maternal Serum Screening for Birth Defects.* (For full group information, see PREGNANCY.)

National Organization for Rare Disorders (NORD), 800–999–6673. (For full group information, see RARE DISORDERS.)

OTHER RESOURCES

GENERAL WORKS

Birth Defects. Chelsea House, 1993.
The Encyclopedia of Genetic Disorders and Birth Defects. Mark D. Ludman and James Wyndbrandt. Facts on File, 1990.
Environmental Causes of Human Birth Defects. T. V. Persaud. C. C. Thomas, 1990.

FOR PRETEENS AND TEENS

Drugs and Birth Defects. Nancy Shniderman and Sue Hurwitz. Rosen, 1994.
Understanding Birth Defects. Karen Gravelle. Watts, 1991.

(See also GENETIC COUNSELING; GENETIC DISORDERS; PREGNANCY; DES; CLEFT LIP AND PALATE; other specific disorders.)

birthing chair, a chair designed to use gravity to ease CHILDBIRTH. Traditional in many cultures until modern times, the birthing chair, often a simple high-backed stool with a hole in the center, has come back into use in recent decades in modern designs that allow women to sit up or recline. A section of the chair can drop during delivery. The chair is not used when ANESTHESIA is required. (See PREGNANCY; CHILDBIRTH.)

birthing room, a homelike, relaxed setting—often attached to a HOSPITAL, but sometimes in a freestanding MATERNITY CENTER—where a woman gives birth. Developed largely in response to the impersonality of traditional hospital DELIVERY ROOMS, birthing rooms often have home-style furniture, allow birth to take place in one place (without the usual shift from LABOR ROOM to delivery room), and sometimes allow family members (not just the BIRTH PARTNER) to attend the birth, if desired. Some birthing rooms provide special birthing beds or BIRTHING CHAIRS that allow a woman to give birth from a sitting or semi-reclining position, often with a lower section of the chair or bed being dropped down during actual delivery. Birthing rooms are used only for low-risk pregnancies. If complications occur, the mother and child will need to be moved into a regular delivery rooms, which in some emergency situations can result in dangerous loss of time. (See PREGNANCY; CHILDBIRTH; MATERNITY CENTER; CERTIFIED NURSE-MIDWIFE.)

birth order, the position a child occupies in a family, based on the order of arrival and the number of other children. Only child, first-born, second-born, middle child, and youngest are examples of birth order. Traditionally, many people have believed that birth order has a strong influence on a child's development and personality. Theories abound, among them that first-born or only children are strong, self-directed, capable leaders; that second-born or middle children are more relaxed, spontaneous compromisers; and that third-born or youngest children are more gentle, passive, withdrawn followers. Some assert that first-born or only children tend to support the status quo, while second and later children are more likely to challenge established views. Though popular, such views are highly controversial. Some studies tend to support influence of birth order on personality, but critics charge that supposed influence of birth order often turns out, on closer analysis, to actually be due to other factors, such as the family's social and economic status, the educational level, or AGE.

OTHER RESOURCES

For parents

A Parents' Guide to Raising an Only-Child. Michael K. Meyerhoff. W. Gladden, 1993.
Birth Order Book. Kevin Leman. Dell, 1992.
Keys to Preparing for Your Second Child. Meg Zweiback. Barron's, 1991.
Parenting an Only Child: The Joys and Challenges of Raising Your One and Only. Susan Newman. Doubleday, 1990.

On being a first-born or only child

Growing Up Firstborn: The Pressure and Privilege of Being Number One. Kevin Leman. Delacorte, 1989.
The Only Child: Being One, Loving One, Understanding One, Raising One. Darrell Sifford. Putnam, 1989.

On a second child

Second Child. John Saul. Bantam, 1990.
The Second Child: Family Transition and Adjustment. Robert B. Stewart, Jr. Sage, 1990.

For children

The Birth-Order Blues. Joan Drescher. Viking, 1993.
Only Child. H. M. Hoover. Dutton, 1992.

(See also GENERAL PARENTING RESOURCES on page 634.)

birth partner, the person who is designated by a pregnant woman to be her "coach" during CHILDBIRTH. The birth partner is generally the FATHER, but can be a friend or relative. The birth partner is someone who has attended PREPARED CHILDBIRTH classes with the woman. A DOULA may also be brought in to help the mother and birth partner during the birth and sometimes afterwards. (See CHILDBIRTH.)

Blacky Pictures, a type of PROJECTIVE TEST for use with children five and up, to attempt to gain information on the child's personality. The child is given a set of twelve cartoon pictures featuring a dog named Blacky and is asked to make up a story about them, answer questions for each picture, and sort them by preference. The test is usually administered individually, but may be given to groups with the pictures on slides. (See TESTS.)

Bliss symbols, a set of standardized symbols developed for use with young children who are not able to

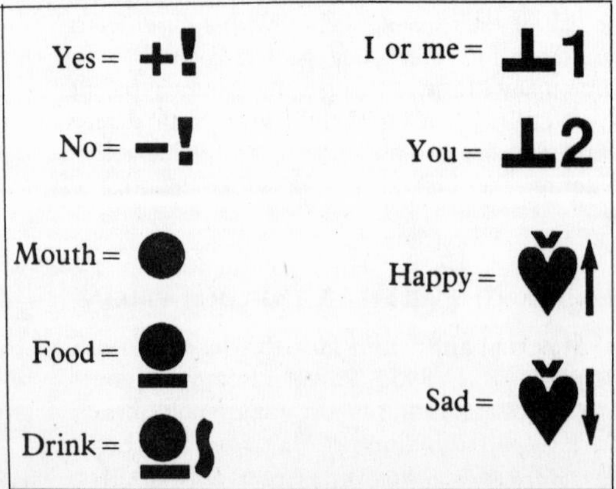

Bliss Symbols

speak clearly enough to express themselves. Children who have ORTHOPEDIC DISABILITIES that affect their speaking apparatus and who have not yet learned to read and write fall into this category. The child moves symbols around (see samples on page 70) on CONVERSATION BOARDS to "converse" with others.

block parents, individuals in a community, often identified by a sign in a window or on a house, who are designated as people to whom children (and adults) can go when they need help. When an urban school community is divided into "blocks" for ease of communication, the block parent may be the person responsible for communication between the neighborhood and the school.

blood and blood disorders, the vital, red fluid that circulates in the body's veins and arteries and problems associated with it. Most of blood is made up of blood cells, all formed in the BONE MARROW, including:

- *Red blood cells* (RBCs) or *erythrocytes*, which transport oxygen from the lungs, exchanging it for the waste product carbon dioxide. Inside the RBCs is the pigment *hemoglobin*, which carries the vital oxygen.
- *White blood cells* (WBCs) or *leukocytes*, larger but less numerous than RBCs. These are the blood's infection-fighters and come in various types, including *lymphocytes*, which are important in the IMMUNE SYSTEM.
- *Platelets* or *thrombocytes*, the smallest blood cells, control bleeding through blood clotting and speed repair of injured blood vessels.

The balance of the blood volume is a fluid called *plasma*, which contains a variety of dissolved substances it transports throughout the body, including PROTEINS, MINERALS, VITAMINS, HORMONES, FATS, and sugars for use in tissues, as well as waste products such as bilirubin (see LIVER AND LIVER PROBLEMS).

The blood is the body's barometer and often gives early indications of many health problems, not just blood disorders. One of the basic kinds of BLOOD TESTS, the CBC or *complete blood count*, measures the number of each of these kinds of cells in proportion to one another. Other forms of blood tests often measure the amount and proportion of other substances carried in the blood.

Among the main kinds of blood disorders are:

- ANEMIA, too few red blood cells.
- *Polycythemia*, too many red blood cells.
- LEUKEMIA, too many white blood cells, a form of CANCER.
- HEMOPHILIA, various bleeding disorders resulting from defective platelets and ineffective clotting.
- *Thrombosis*, overactive clotting that can cause heart problems.

Some blood disorders are caused by GENETIC DISORDERS, some by poor NUTRITION. Poisons, TUMORS, radiation, and drugs can all have adverse effects on the proper functioning of the blood. Bacteria can enter the blood (for example, through injury) and multiply, producing *septicemia*; when bacteria produce toxins—substances that act as poisons within the body—the infection is called TOXEMIA. Both are commonly called *blood poisoning* and are potentially life-threatening.

Blood also comes in different types, distinguished by differing ANTIGENS (protein markers). The two main kinds of markers are A and B, and the four main kinds of blood are A (with only A markers), B (with only B), AB (with A and B), and O (with neither).

Another distinguishing characteristic of blood is the presence or absence of a complex marker called an *Rh factor*. Approximately 85 percent of the population has the factor (Rh positive), but 15 percent do not (Rh negative). During a PREGNANCY this can cause problems, because of RH INCOMPATIBILITY, which leads to *erythroblastosis fetalis*, also known as *hemolytic disease of the newborn*. Rh incompatibility can also lead to problems during BLOOD TRANSFUSIONS.

FOR HELP AND FURTHER INFORMATION

National Heart, Lung, and Blood Information Center (NHLBIC), 301–251–1222. Publishes *Check Your Blood I.Q.*, *Check Your Platelet I.Q.*, *Immune Thrombocytopenic Purpura (ITP)*, and professional materials. (For full group information, see HEART AND HEART PROBLEMS.)

National Organization for Rare Disorders (NORD), 800–999–6673. (For full group information, see RARE DISORDERS.)

OTHER RESOURCES

GENERAL WORKS

The Blood Book: All about Blood and Blood Tests. B. Birkner and G. Hoffmann. Hartley and Marks, 1992.

FOR CHILDREN AND PRETEENS

The Heart and Blood, rev. ed. Steve Parker. Watts, 1991.

(See also ANEMIA; HEMOPHILIA; LEUKEMIA; BLOOD PRESSURE; BLOOD TRANSFUSIONS; HEART AND HEART DISORDERS.)

blood pressure, the force blood exerts on the walls of the blood vessels (arteries and veins) and the heart as it circulates in the body. Using a device called a *sphygmomanometer*, in which an inflated rubber cuff is wrapped tightly around the upper arm, the force of the blood moving from the heart to the main artery in the arm can be measured; this is the *systolic pressure*. As the cuff is deflated and the blood begins to flow freely, the *diastolic pressure* is taken. The two figures are given together, so a typical reading for a young adult might be 110/75 and for a mature adult more like 120/80.

Blood pressure is quite variable and may rise or fall for many reasons, including activity, time of the day, or the action of drugs. But people who have blood pressure that is consistently way below normal, because of illness, certain drugs, blood loss, SHOCK, heart attack, or problems with the ADRENAL GLANDS, are said to have *hypotension.* This can lead to reduced blood flow to the brain, resulting in dizziness or fainting.

Conversely, those with abnormally high blood pressure—normally above 140/90—are said to have *hypertension.* This may be in response to physical activity, stress, excess salt, certain drugs, SMOKING, and various kinds of disorders, including KIDNEY AND UROLOGICAL PROBLEMS, problems with the ADRENAL GLANDS, some heart problems, and OBESITY. Hypertension can sometimes develop when a woman is taking BIRTH CONTROL PILLS. If unchecked, it can increase the risk of stroke, heart failure, kidney damage, and EYE AND VISION PROBLEMS, notably retinopathy. In general, it can be controlled by life-style changes, supplemented with drugs, if necessary.

Hypertension can also develop during PREGNANCY and can increase the risk of serious complications, especially PREECLAMPSIA and ECLAMPSIA, if not treated promptly. It is especially likely among pregnant adolescents under age fifteen; first-time mothers, especially older ones; women who are underweight; or those who are from low socioeconomic backgrounds. The causes of pregnancy-induced hypertension are unclear, but a tendency toward it can run in families. A woman who has hypertension before CONCEPTION has a high risk of complications during pregnancy.

FOR HELP AND FURTHER INFORMATION

National Heart, Lung, and Blood Information Center (NHLBIC), 301–251–1222. Publishes booklets *High Blood Pressure: Treat It for Life*; fact sheets *High Blood Pressure: A Common But Controllable Disorder, Facts About How to Prevent High Blood Pressure,* and *High Blood Pressure and What You Can Do About It*; and other general and professional materials. (For full group information, see HEART AND HEART PROBLEMS.)

Citizens for Public Action on Blood Pressure and Cholesterol
P.O. Box 30374
7200 Wisconsin Avenue, Suite 1002
Bethesda, MD 20814
301–770–1711
Fax: 301–770–1713
Gerald Wilson, Executive Director
Organization seeking to prevent heart disease; advocates screening and prevention programs; publishes *High Blood Pressure and Your Health.*

American Heart Association (AHA), 800–242–8721. Publishes *About High Blood Pressure in Children: What Parents Should Know, About High Blood Pressure in Teenagers* (for teens), *About High Blood Pressure, About High Blood Pressure in African Americans, High Blood Pressure, What Every Woman Should Know About High Blood Pressure, What to Ask About High Blood Pressure, How You Can Help Your Doctor Treat Your High Blood Pressure,* and recipe booklets for lowering blood pressure. (For full group information, see HEART AND HEART PROBLEMS.)

National Kidney Foundation (NKF), 800–622–9010. Publishes *High Blood Pressure and Your Kidneys* and "Living with High Blood Pressure" brochures, including *The Role of the Family.* (For full group information, see KIDNEY AND UROLOGICAL DISORDERS.)

National Organization for Rare Disorders (NORD), 800–999–6673. (For full group information, see RARE DISORDERS.)

National Safety Council (NSC), 800–621–7615. Publishes *High Blood Pressure* (guide and video). (For full group information, see SAFETY.)

OTHER RESOURCES

Blood Pressure: Questions You Have, Answers You Need. Ed Weiner. People's Medical Society, 1992.
Lower Your Blood Pressure and Live Longer. Marvin Moser. Berkley, 1992.
Toward Better Blood Pressure. Linda Pietz and others. Park Nicollet, 1992.
The H.A.R.T. Program—Hypertension Autonomic Relaxation Treatment: A Comprehensive Guide to Lowering Your Blood Pressure Without Drugs. D. Ariel Kerman and Richard Trubo. HarperCollins, 1992.

(See also BLOOD AND BLOOD DISORDERS.)

blood relations, people who share some close GENETIC INHERITANCE and therefore have an increased risk of passing on various traits, including GENETIC DISORDERS. Blood relations are said to have CONSANGUINITY and may be barred from marriage and sexual relations by law and societal prohibitions (see INCEST). When someone dies INTESTATE (without a will), the court determines the specific blood relations of KIN to decide INHERITANCE RIGHTS, in accordance with the law at that time, a question that may be muddied by the increasing use of REPRODUCTIVE TECHNOLOGY. In the absence of ADVANCE DIRECTIVES, life-or-death medical decisions are often made by blood relations, as provided under the prevailing law.

blood tests, a wide variety of MEDICAL TESTS done on samples of blood taken from a vein (VENIPUNCTURE) to assess the health of the body and its major systems. *Hematological tests* look at aspects of the blood itself; among such tests are *complete blood count* (see BLOOD AND BLOOD DISORDERS) and THROMBIN TIME, which measures blood-clotting ability. *Microbiological tests* search for infectious organisms carried in the blood and for ANTIBODIES that may have formed to counteract them. Often these tests take the form of attempting to grow a CULTURE in the laboratory. *Biochemical or blood chemistry tests* examine substances carried in the blood, such as SODIUM and other elements, VITAMINS, gases, drugs, and bilirubin (see LIVER AND LIVER PROBLEMS). Using medical shorthand, doctors may refer to different groups of tests by the organ whose health is being examined, such as KIDNEY FUNCTIONS TESTS or LIVER FUNCTION TESTS, or by the information sought, such as BLOOD GASES or the thyroid-stimulating hormones T_4 and T_3. (See specific tests mentioned above or MEDICAL TESTS.)

blood transfusions, the introduction of large quantities of blood or blood components (such as red blood cells) into a patient's body to replace blood lost or weakened through injury, surgery, or disease. Blood is stored in blood banks by ABO type and Rh factor (see BLOOD AND BLOOD DISORDERS), and is used only for people whose blood type is compatible. Even so, except in emergency situations, blood for transfusions is generally tested against a sample of the patient's blood to be sure no compatibility problems exist. People with blood type O, Rh factor negative are called *universal donors*, because their blood can be used in emergencies for most other people with little risk of incompatibility; otherwise fluids without actual blood cells might be used. If blood is incompatible, donor cells may self-destruct by bursting (*hemolysis)*, leading to possibly severe reactions, such as SHOCK or kidney failure, in the recipient.

Blood transfusions are commonly given after severe bleeding, as from an accident, operation, hemorrhage, or bleeding ulcer. They also often are given to people with blood disorders such as ANEMIA or LEUKEMIA. When a child is born with *hemolytic disease of the newborn*, a result of RH INCOMPATIBILITY, an *exchange transfusion* may be performed, in which virtually all of the infant's blood is replaced to prevent permanent damage. Usually, the blood is dripped slowly into the infant's vein, at the rate of about a pint over one to four hours, during which time the infant is checked for any sign of a reaction. In an emergency, a pint of blood may be given in minutes.

A serious problem with blood transfusions is the possibility of being infected by disease from the donor's blood. Blood banks routinely test for infections such as AIDS, hepatitis B (see LIVER AND LIVER PROBLEMS), and SYPHILIS, but some risk remains from these diseases as well as from rarer or unknown ones. The vulnerabilty of the blood system was demonstrated when AIDS came on the scene. Numerous people, many of them children, contracted the disease before it was recognized as a major threat and tests were put into place to screen blood for it. To cut down on the risk of disease, many hospitals have programs allowing people to donate some of their own blood during the weeks before a planned operation. This is called an AUTOLOGOUS blood transfusion. Family and friends also donate blood designated for use by a particular patient, though some studies have shown this blood is not necessarily safer than that from blood banks.

FOR HELP AND FURTHER INFORMATION

National Heart, Lung, and Blood Information Center (NHLBIC), 301–251–1222. Publishes *Your Operation, Your Blood* and professional materials. (For full group information, see HEART AND HEART PROBLEMS.)

blood-brain barrier (BBB), a physiological protective screen surrounding the brain that keeps many substances from the blood from passing into the brain or slows their passage. Normally a protective mechanism, the blood-brain barrier can sometimes have negative effects, as when it keeps some kinds of drugs from reaching diseased portions of the brain. In such cases, medications may be given as intrathecal INJECTIONS directly into the CEREBROSPINAL FLUID or as intraarterial injections directly into an artery feeding a BRAIN TUMOR. Some medications, given beforehand, can also temporarily allow passage of other medications through the barrier.

bloody show, in PREGNANCY, the bloody mucus that appears just before the onset of LABOR.

blue babies, babies born with congenital heart defects, causing characteristic CYANOSIS (blueness around the lips and NAILS). (See HEART AND HEART PROBLEMS.)

boards, nickname for various kinds of ADMISSIONS TESTS. In relation to children, boards often refer to DIAGNOSTIC ASSESSMENT TESTS (nicknamed *baby boards*) or the dreaded precollege tests offered by the College Board (see COLLEGE ENTRANCE EXAMINATION BOARD).

body image (body identity), an awareness of one's body as being separate from the environment, of its parts and their relationship to one another and to the outside environment, and of the possibilities of body movement and action. Young children must develop a sense of the body and learn to identify the parts of their own bodies. Gradually they learn to recognize how they relate to objects around them and how they can avoid running into objects or how they can move them without awkwardness. But some children, such as those with SCHIZOPHRENIA, lack a clear body image. For example, a schizophrenic girl may not be aware that her hand is attached to her body, causing her to lack coordination and the ability to work with objects in a predictable way. People with some eating disorders may also have distorted body images; for example, those with ANOREXIA NERVOSA often see themselves as fat when, in fact, they are grotesquely thin. A child's sense of body is sometimes tested using PROJECTIVE TESTS such as the HOUSE-TREE-PERSON TEST or DRAW-A-PERSON TEST.

Boehm Test of Basic Concepts, a type of READINESS TEST administered individually or to small groups of children from grades K–2 that attempts to assess a child's grasp of the basic concepts used in classroom teaching. The examiner poses a series of questions and the child marks in a multiple-choice picture booklet which one of several pictures fits each question, generally relating to quantity, space, and time. The fifty-item test is then scored by a hand key and the SCORE may be included in a report to be used in a PARENT-TEACHER CONFERENCE, if desired. In an individually administered preschool version for children ages three through five, a similar approach is used, but the child is asked to respond to oral instructions by pointing to one or several pictures, and each concept is tested twice. (See TESTS.)

bonding, the forming of special emotional ties between a baby and his or her primary CAREGIVER, often the MOTHER, but also sometimes the FATHER, another adult, or another child; also called *maternal-infant attachment.* After CHILDBIRTH, the newborn is often placed on the mother's abdomen to start the process of bonding between the two. Considered key to the normal development of the baby, bonding is the process of interaction by which the child develops trust and security vital for "making contact" with the world and for learning the SOCIAL SKILLS, COMMUNICATIONS SKILLS, VISUAL SKILLS, and AUDITORY SKILLS needed to function in the world. Psychologists sometimes call this early close relationship between mother and child the SYMBIOTIC STAGE.

PREMATURE or HIGH-RISK BABIES who need to stay in HOSPITALS for some days or weeks after birth are in special need of bonding. Indeed, children who lack such bonding and stimulation often have retarded physical and mental development, leading to a variety of problem conditions including FAILURE TO THRIVE, MATERNAL DEPRIVATION SYNDROME, and REACTIVE ATTACHMENT DISORDER OF INFANCY. Mothers who fail to bond with their children are AT RISK for later CHILD ABUSE AND NEGLECT.

When bonding is disrupted between a child and his or her primary caregiver, children may experience phases of grief similar to those common in response to death: first, *protest,* showing anger and anguish, while seeking to reestablish the bond; then *despair,* on recognizing that the bond will not be reestablished quickly; finally *detachment,* involving social withdrawal, defensiveness, and indifference, which may survive even if the bond is reestablished.

FOR HELP AND FURTHER INFORMATION

National Committee for Prevention of Child Abuse (NCPCA), 800–835–2671. Publishes *Parent-Child Bonding: The Development of Intimacy.* (For full group information, see HELP AGAINST CHILD ABUSE AND NEGLECT on page 680.)

Twin Services, TWINLINE: 510–524–0863. Publishes *Bonding with Multiples.* (For full group information, see MULTIPLE BIRTH.)

OTHER RESOURCES

Pregnancy, Birth and Bonding: A Guide for the Mother-to-Be. Longmeadow Press Staff. Longmeadow, 1993.

Mother-Infant Bonding: A Scientific Fiction. Diane E. Eyer. Yale University Press, 1993.

The Earliest Relationship: Parents, Infants, and the Drama of Early Attachment. T. Berry Brazelton and Bertrand Cramer. Addison-Wesley, 1990.

bone and bone disorders, The skeleton that makes up the hard but resilient framework of the body, which is vital for the ability to move at will, and problems relating to it. In general, bone consists of three main layers. On the outside is a thin membrane (*periosteum*) containing blood vessels and nerves; below that is the dense hard shell we normally think of as bone, which gets its rigidity from large amounts of CALCIUM and PHOSPHATE; inside the shell is spongy tissue, including the BONE MARROW, where vital BLOOD cells are produced.

An EMBRYO has no bone, only cartilage; in a process called *ossification,* this tough, resilient material begins to turn into bone in the FETUS at about the seventh or eighth week of development. But ossification proceeds very slowly and is not completed in early adulthood, which is why calcium is so important all through childhood and ADOLESCENCE and is one of the reasons why ADOLESCENT PREGNANCY takes such a physical toll on a young girl's still-growing body. (See BUILDING STRONG BONES below.)

At birth, a baby's skull is soft in some places and has gaps called FONTANELLES, which later are closed with bone. In the long bones of the arms and legs, growth takes place primarily at the ends, called EPIPHYSES; if these epiphyses ossify prematurely, for whatever reason, GROWTH stops and short stature results.

Like all parts in the body, bone is constantly undergoing change. Cells called *osteoclasts* remove calcium from the bone, while other cells called *osteoblasts* deposit calcium phosphate in the bone. In a healthy body, the destruction of old, worn-out cells and the formation of new ones is well balanced, with the calcium level in blood regulated by various HORMONES, including key hormones from the PITUITARY, ADRENAL, and THYROID GLANDS and the sex hormones ESTROGEN and TESTOSTERONE. If the body is not healthy, however, the process will go awry, sometimes resulting in bones that are too hard or too soft.

In the healthy body, calcium is deposited into bone faster than it is taken out, with the calcium deposition peaking at about age 35. This is the time of *peak bone mass,* when the bones are most dense and strong. It is important for children—and especially for young women—to build strong bones in youth and young adulthood, because after that peak their bones gradually lose calcium and density.

Bones may be subject to several kinds of disorders:

- FRACTURE, as from direct injury or overuse.
- Infection, as in OSTEOMYELITIS.
- GENETIC DISORDERS, such as OSTEOGENESIS IMPERFECTA, ACHONDROPLASIA, and OSTEOPETROSIS.
- Nutritional deficiencies, such as lack of VITAMIN D and CALCIUM, which can cause RICKETS in children.
- Hormone disorders, such as OSTEOPOROSIS or pituitary disorders.
- TUMORS, including CANCER.
- Degeneration, or wearing down, as in *osteoarthritis*, primarily in older adults.
- AUTOIMMUNE DISORDERS, such as rheumatoid ARTHRITIS.
- Other diseases of unclear origin, such as CRANIOSYNOSTOSIS.

If the bone marrow is damaged or defective, a BONE MARROW TRANSPLANT may be attempted. If the bone is weakened or excessively hardened, a child may have trouble developing MOTOR SKILLS; ORTHOPEDIC DEVICES may sometimes be used as aids and to protect the bone from use after fracture or surgery.

FOR HELP AND FURTHER INFORMATION

American Academy of Orthopaedic Surgeons (AAOS)
6300 North River Road
Rosemont, IL 60018–4262
708–823–7186; 800–346–2267
William W. Tipton, M.D., Executive Vice President
Professional organization of orthopedic surgeons; publishes journal, videos, books, and courses for health professionals; publications of public interest include: brochures *Sprains and Strains, Fractures, Cast Care, Shoulder Pain, Neck Pain, Common Foot Problems, Shoes, Arthroscopy, Orthopaedics, Total Joint Replacement,* and *Carpal Tunnel Syndrome*; patient education newsletter *Orthopaedic Perspectives*; and numerous videos.

National Arthritis and Musculoskeletal and Skin Diseases Information Clearinghouse (NAMSIC), 301–495–4484. Publishes information packages *Neck and Cervical Pain, Back Pain, Heel Spurs, Knee Replacement, Hip Replacement,* and *Osteomyelitis.* (For full group information, see ARTHRITIS.)

Shriner's Hospitals for Crippled Children
P.O. Box 31356
Tampa, FL 33631–3356
813–281–0300
Patient referral line: 800–237–5055 (8 A.M.–5 P.M., ET)
Network of hospitals—nineteen orthopedic hospitals and three burn institutes—providing free medical care for children (through age seventeen) with orthopedic problems, whether congenital, accident-related, or related to diseases of the bones, joints, and muscles. The hospitals also provide care for severe burns and spinal cord injuries. The organization publishes triannual magazine *Between Us*; operated and funded by the Shrine of North America; patient referral line (see 800 number given after address) confirms that the child's condition is one treated by the Shriners Hospitals and sends application forms, also available from any Shriner or Shrine organization.

National Cancer Institute (NCI), 800–422–6237. Publishes "What You Need to Know About" brochure on bone cancer. (For full group information, see CANCER.)

American Cancer Society (ACS), 800–227–2345. Publishes materials on bone cancer. (For full group information, see CANCER.)

Center for Safety in the Arts (CSA), 212–227–6220. Publishes fact sheets *Musculoskeletal Problems in Dancers* and *Musculoskeletal Problems in Musicians.* (For full group information, see ENVIRONMENTAL HAZARDS.)

OTHER RESOURCES

FOR CHILDREN AND PRETEENS

A Book about Your Skeleton. Ruth B. Gross. Scholastic, 1994.
Your Bones: An Inside Look at Skeletons. Peter Murray. Child's World, 1992.
Muscles and Bones. Jane Saunderson. Troll, 1992.

(See also MOTOR SKILLS; GROWTH AND GROWTH DISORDERS; ORTHOPEDIC DEVICES; SPINE AND SPINAL DISORDERS; and other specific disorders.)

bone marrow, blood-producing tissue within the bones of the body; the factory for oxygen-carrying red blood cells, disease-fighting white blood cells, and platelets, important in blood clotting. At birth, the most productive "red" bone marrow is present in all bones, but by ADOLESCENCE it generally becomes confined to the large central bones, including the spine, skull, chestbone (*sternum*), ribs, shoulderbone (*clavicle*), shoulder blades (*scapulae*), and hip bones. Normally well-protected in its bony housing, bone marrow can be affected by infections such as OSTEOMYELITIS or by TUMORS; it can also malfunction, producing too few of some blood cells, as in aplastic ANEMIA, or too many, as in LEUKEMIA. When bone marrow has been damaged, surgical removal of diseased marrow and replacement with healthy marrow may be attempted in a BONE MARROW TRANSPLANT. (See BLOOD AND BLOOD DISORDERS; BONE AND BONE DISORDERS; BONE MARROW TRANSPLANT.)

bone marrow transplant (BMT), a surgical operation to replace diseased or defective BONE MARROW with healthy bone marrow, generally performed when the person faces a life-threatening disorder, such as severe aplastic ANEMIA, LEUKEMIA, CANCER, or certain serious GENETIC DISORDERS. First, the patient's defective bone marrow is destroyed by drugs or radiation (see CANCER). Then in the actual operation, a hollow *aspiration needle* is inserted into the affected bones and is used to remove the old bone marrow. Afterward new bone marrow cells are fed into the patient intravenously; these find their way into the aspirated cavities, where they will—if all goes as planned—begin to produce blood.

The problem of finding compatible bone marrow is a formidable one. In an *allogenic BMT* the healthy bone marrow is provided by someone whose tissue is similar to the patient's, such as a SIBLING, but the chance of finding a match even in a close relative is only one in four and is much less likely in strangers. In certain situations, when parts of the patient's own body has healthy bone marrow, some is taken and frozen until ready for use in a later TRANSPLANT; this is called an AUTOLOGOUS BMT. The autologous BMT shows considerable promise in the treatment of TUMORS that previously might have been considered untreatable.

The BMT is a difficult, delicate, and dangerous operation, and the failure rate is relatively high, but it offers hope to people who might in earlier decades have had no chance of survival. The autologous BMT, especially, holds wide hope for people with cancers so severe as to have been previously untreatable, since the heavy doses of radiation required would kill the bone marrow.

FOR HELP AND FURTHER INFORMATION

National Marrow Donor Program
3433 Broadway Street, NE, Suite 400
Minneapolis, MN 55413
800–654–1247
Fax: 612–627–5899
Registry of potential bone marrow donors; publishes various materials.

Candlelighters Childhood Cancer Foundation (CCCF), 800–366–2223. Publishes *The Candlelighters Guide to Bone Marrow Transplants in Children.*

National Cancer Institute (NCI), 800–422–6237. Publishes *Bone Marrow Transplantation.* (For full group information, see CANCER.)

National Heart, Lung, and Blood Information Center (NHLBIC), 301–251–1222. (For full group information, see HEART AND HEART PROBLEMS.)

(See also TRANSPLANTS; CANCER.)

bottlefeeding, supplying an infant with nutrients in a modified MILK or milk-like fluid called FORMULA fed through a bottle with a nipple similar to that on a BREAST. Public health experts recommend BREASTFEEDING when possible, because the mother's milk provides more completely balanced NUTRITION and temporary IMMUNIZATION against various kinds of diseases. But many women find breastfeeding too inconvenient, unattractive, or difficult to arrange, especially in a world where both parents often work. Also not all women who might like to breastfeed can do so, because they may not produce enough milk—or milk nutritious enough—to meet their baby's needs, or other physical problems, may bar breastfeeding (in the mother or the infant). Bottlefeeding, though a second choice for doctors, is a perfectly good alternative to breastfeeding. Mothers (and also fathers) are equally able to establish the close BONDING relationship with the baby if they cuddle, rock, and talk with the child while bottlefeeding.

Some kinds of commercially available formulas come in a ready-to-use liquid form; less expensive liquid concentrates or dry powders need water added to approximate breast milk. The preparation of the formula and the sterilization of the bottles and other equipment used are extremely important, because germs can grow very quickly in warm milk, causing digestive disorders in infants, some of which can be very serious and hinder the absorption of nutrients needed for proper growth (see DIGESTIVE SYSTEM AND DISORDERS; also FIXING FORMULA on page 77). The storage of formula is equally important. The Public Health Service recommends: "Don't feed any formula that has been left at room temperature in a nursing bottle or open can for more than an hour, or in the refrigerator for more than 2 days."

Properly prepared formula contains all the nutrients needed by a baby. The Food and Drug Administration monitors the nutrient content of commercially prepared formulas under the Infant Formula Act of 1980, but parents will be wise to check with their doctor about the choice of formula, because some labeled as "nutritionally complete" actually may lack some amino acids and minerals. Parents should also note that, in some recent cases, incomplete formula has been packaged under fraudulent labels, purporting to be bestselling brands.

Parents are advised not to give their babies additional VITAMINS or IRON, unless the doctor specifically recommends it, to avoid overtaxing the baby's immature digestive system and kidneys. However, if the child fails to thrive on the formula, they should check with the doctor to be sure the baby is getting—and absorbing—all the necessary nutrients. Parents should also not try to change a child's bowel movements (see DIGESTIVE SYSTEM AND DISORDERS) or spitting up (see REGURGITATION) by changing formulas. If they have concerns in this area, they should consult the doctor or clinic.

The Public Health Service's booklet *Infant Care* provides the following guidelines for bottlefeeding:

- Hold your baby close to you in your arms, with the head a little higher than the rest of the body.
- Tilt the bottle to be sure that milk is in the nipple. Touch the nipple next to the baby's mouth and the baby will turn and grasp the nipple. Hold the bottle so that it sticks straight out at a right angle to the baby's mouth.
- The nipple's holes should be large enough so that milk drops slowly (about one drop per second) from the bottle when it is held with the nipple down.
- You should see air bubbles entering the bottle as the baby drinks (except when using plastic-lined bottles that collapse as the bottle empties). If no air bubbles appear, milk will stop flowing. Check to see that the cap is not on too tight.

Fixing Formula

Parents who have decided to bottlefeed their baby should consult with their doctor or clinic before the birth about the form and perhaps the brand of formula recommended. Choose a formula with iron unless there are medical reasons why you should not. Always check the expiration date, and do not buy formula or use it if that date has passed.

EQUIPMENT NEEDED FOR BOTTLE-FEEDING

- *Nursing bottles with caps.* Six to eight 8-ounce bottles, or fewer if you wash them more than once a day. You may choose reusable bottles or disposable bottles with sterile plastic liners.
- *Nipples.* One for each bottle, plus a few spares. Those made of silicone will last longer.
- *A bottle brush and a nipple brush.*

STEP-BY-STEP PREPARATION

Once you have chosen and brought home the formula, follow these easy steps to prepare it:

- Always wash your hands before preparing baby's formula and bottles to prevent infection.
- Use bottles, caps, and nipples that have been washed in clean water and dishwashing soap or detergent, or in the dishwasher if you have one. (You may wash them with the family dishes). If you wash them by hand, use a bottle brush. Squeeze water through the nipple holes to be sure that they are open. Rinse well to remove all detergent, and let them stand in a rack to dry; (Check the package to see if they should be boiled before you use them the first time.)
- When you are ready to feed your baby, clean the top of the formula can (if the formula you've chosen is canned) with soap and water. Rinse.
- Open the can with a clean punch-type opener.
- Using the directions that came with the formula, pour it into the bottle. *Mix it with water if it is a concentrate or powder.* Use only fresh water directly from the cold water tap (that is, not hot water; you may wish to use a water filter).
- Put the nipple and the cap on the bottle.
- No warming is necessary. Babies can take cold formula, although they may prefer it warm when they are young.
- Try to feed your baby the formula within thirty minutes of the time you prepare it. If it isn't used up within about an hour, throw it away and start again *with a clean bottle.*
- Keep any opened can of liquid formula, covered, in the refrigerator (powdered formula does not need to be kept cold until it is mixed with water).

IF YOU USE WATER FROM A WELL

If you use water from a well instead of from a community water supply, you should have it tested to make sure that it is safe before you use it for your baby. Call your local health department—they may test it or tell you how to find a company that will do it for you.

If your well water is not pure (or if you are not sure of its purity), you may choose to breastfeed or to feed your infant ready-to-use formula. If you use powdered or concentrated formula, you will need to take a few extra steps to make the water safe for your baby:

- *Boil* each day's supply of water for twenty minutes.
- Pour the boiling water into a clean jar (that has been boiled or washed in a dishwasher).
- Be sure to cool the water before you use it.
- Keep the jar covered in the refrigerator for use in making formula.
- Wash the jar daily.

Note: If someone else will be feeding your baby, make sure that person knows exactly how to prepare the formula. Adding water when it's not needed and not adding water when it's essential can hurt your baby.

Source: Infant Care (1989). Prepared by the Bureau of Maternal and Child Health and Resources Development for the Public Health Service.

- Halfway through the bottle and again when your baby is finished eating, burp your baby on your shoulder by patting him or her gently on the back until you hear a burp. (Another way is to hold your baby face down on his or her stomach in your lap over your hand or knee and pat his or her back.) Your baby will usually burp up some air and often a little of the formula.
- Don't leave a bottle containing formula—or *anything else*—with your baby to calm or help him or her sleep. Your baby's teeth are developing and milk, formula, juices, or other liquids that remain in your baby's mouth can lead to cavities. [See NURSING BOTTLE SYNDROME.] In addition, propping a bottle may result in baby choking or developing an ear infection.

Infants are generally fed solely on formula for the first six months or so (see FEEDING BABY: HOW OFTEN? HOW MUCH? on page 248). Then some SOLID FOODS—at first not literally solids, but usually cooked cereals and purees—should begin to be added to the diet.

FOR HELP AND FURTHER INFORMATION

National Maternal and Child Health Clearinghouse (NMCHC), 703–821–8955. (For full group information, see PREGNANCY.)

American Allergy Association (AAA), 415–322–1663. Publishes *Infant Formulas for Allergic Infants.* (For full group information, see ALLERGY.)

Cleft Palate Foundation, 800–242–5338. Publishes *Feeding an Infant with a Cleft.* (For full group information, see CLEFT LIP AND PALATE.)

(See also FORMULA; MILK; BREASTFEEDING; FEEDING; NUTRITION; SOLID FOODS.)

botulism, a rare but often fatal form of poisoning that results from eating food contaminated with the bacterium *Clostridium botulinium.* In adults, botulism is rare, and most often results from improperly canned or preserved foods. But infants can contract botulism if the bacteria enter the body in water or other foods (notably honey, which should not be fed to infants), or through injury that breaks the skin. The bacteria then grow in the intestinal system, producing a toxin (poison) that attacks and paralyzes the NERVOUS SYSTEM, which affects breathing. One early symptom of the infection is HYPOTONIA, or floppy muscles. Other symptoms including difficulty swallowing or speaking, nausea, VOMITING, and double vision. Untreated, more than two out of three people will die from botulism. Early treatment with an antitoxin can lower that rate, but recovery will be slow.

FOR HELP AND FURTHER INFORMATION

National Institute of Allergy and Infectious Diseases (NIAID), 301–496–5717. (For full group information, see ALLERGY.)

National Organization for Rare Disorders (NORD), 800–999–6673. (For full group information, see RARE DISORDERS.)

brain and brain disorders, the command center of the body that, with the spinal cord and the network of nerves that feed information to and from every part of the body, controls every voluntary and involuntary reaction we make; an amazingly complex and delicate system subject to a variety of diseases and injuries.

The brain itself has three main parts:

- The *brain stem*, which connects the spinal cord and the brain, controls key functions such as heartbeat and breathing, and is the source for the important cranial nerves that serve the eyes, ears, mouth, and other areas of the face and throat. A person in a COMA, with substantial damage to various parts of the brain, may still continue to breathe if the lower part of the brain stem is still functioning. If the brain stem totally ceases to function, physicians conclude that BRAIN DEATH has occurred.
- The *cerebrum*, the largest part of the brain, made up of billions of nerve cells and divided into two hemispheres, each containing a central cavity, or VENTRICLE, filled with cerebrospinal fluid (CSF). The cerebrum is where most conscious and "thoughtful" activities occur. In relation to the senses or to motor activities, the left half of the brain generally controls the right side of the body and vice versa. For most people—right-handers and many left-handers—the so-called "left brain" is DOMINANT. This left hemisphere focuses on word comprehension, language, speech, and numbers. The "right brain" focuses more on spatial relationships and feelings. Some parts of the cerebrum focus on quite specific functions, such as seeing, hearing, or smelling. If these parts are damaged, the senses they serve may be dulled or lost. Other activities, such as memory, are carried on more generally and in both halves of the brain.
- The *cerebellum*, the second largest portion of the brain, connected to the brainstem and lying underneath the cerebrum. The cerebellum controls many subconscious activities, especially those involving balance and coordination of movement. Among the disorders that are linked with disease or damage to the cerebellum are ATAXIA and DYSARTHRIA. The *medulloblastoma*, a BRAIN TUMOR common in children, grows in the cerebellum.

Covering the brain is a membrane called the *meninges.* The brain itself is housed in a rigid bony skull, or *cranium*, that provides protection but little room for expansion. As a result, any injury or disease that causes brain inflammation can readily cause damage, as the brain swells and presses against its casing.

Brain damage can result from a number of different causes, among them:

- GENETIC DISORDERS, including CHROMOSOMAL ABNORMALITIES, that affect the brain. Among the common results are MENTAL RETARDATION, as in DOWN SYNDROME or Tay-Sachs disease (see LIPID STORAGE DISORDERS); structural defects, such as very small head (*microcephaly*), ANENCEPHALY (absence of a brain), and HYDROCEPHALUS (water on the brain); and degeneration of brain tissue, as in HUNTINGTON'S CHOREA.

- Infection and resulting inflammation, especially ENCEPHALITIS (inflammation of the brain) and MENINGITIS (inflammation of the meninges), sometimes as part of another disease such as MEASLES or CHICKEN POX.
- Lack of blood and the vital oxygen it provides to the brain cells. Many children suffer HYPOXIA (lack of oxygen) during CHILDBIRTH, drowning, SLEEP APNEA, or CHOKING; among the resulting conditions are CEREBRAL PALSY and perhaps LEARNING DISABILITIES.
- TUMORS, which are abnormal growths in or around the brain, and can be either BENIGN or MALIGNANT (see BRAIN TUMORS).
- Degeneration of nerve or brain tissue, often for unknown causes, in such illnesses as MULTIPLE SCLEROSIS and Alzheimer's disease.

Many kinds of MENTAL DISORDERS, sleep disorders, and eating disorders are clearly linked with brain functioning, but how and why they occur is unknown. In many cases, as with DEPRESSION and SCHIZOPHRENIA, physicians believe that the underlying cause is related to disorders in the brain chemistry. Such diseases are sometimes called *organic brain syndromes.* Misfunctions of the brain can also cause SEIZURES, as in EPILEPSY.

The billions of cells in the brain pass information by means of tiny electrical impulses. They can be measured by an ELECTROENCEPHALOGRAPH (EEG), which depicts electrical activity in the brain. Physical damage to or abnormalities in the brain and surrounding structures can be "seen" through various imaging techniques, such as the CT SCAN and MRI. In checking for signs of bleeding or infection, a physician may perform a LUMBAR PUNCTURE, to sample cerebrospinal fluid.

FOR HELP AND FURTHER INFORMATION

National Institute of Neurological Disorders and Stroke (NINDS)
P.O. Box 5801
Bethesda, MD 20824
301–496–5751; 800–352–9424
Fax: 301–402–2186
Zach Hall, Director
One of the National Institutes of Health, focusing on brain and nervous system disorders; publishes various materials, including *Know Your Brain, Dizziness, NINDS Fact Sheet,* and directory *Neurological Disorders: Voluntary Health Agencies and Other Patient Resources.*

National Organization for Rare Disorders (NORD), 800–999–6673. (For full group information, see RARE DISORDERS.)

Council for Exceptional Children (CEC), 800–328–0272. Publishes report *Brain Research.* (For full group information, see HELP ON LEARNING AND EDUCATION on page 659.)

OTHER RESOURCES

GENERAL WORKS

How Your Brain Works. Anne Novitt-Moreno. Ziff-Davis, 1995.

Human Brain: Its Capacities and Functions, 2nd ed. Isaac Asimov. NAL-Dutton, 1994.

The Brain: An Introduction to the Psychology of the Human Brain and Behavior. Christine Temple. Viking Penguin, 1994.

The Brain Has a Mind of Its Own: Insights from a Practicing Neurologist. Richard Restak. Harmony/Crown, 1991.

The Brain and Nervous System. Charles B. Clayman, ed. Reader's Digest, 1991.

The Three-Pound Universe: Revolutionary Discoveries about the Brain—From the Chemistry of the Mind to the New Frontiers of the Soul. Judith Hooper and Dick Teresi. Tarcher, 1991.

The Amazing Brain. Robert Ornstein and Richard F. Thompson. Houghton Mifflin, 1991.

ON BRAIN DISORDERS AND SURGERY

Brain Surgery: What to Know and Ask. Elaine B. LePage. Pritchett and Hull, 1994.

The Healing Blade: Neurosurgery on the Edge of Life and Death. Edward J. Sylvester. Simon & Schuster, 1993.

Psychosurgery: Damaging the Brain to Save the Mind. Joann E. Rodgers. HarperCollins, 1992.

FOR CHILDREN AND PRETEENS

Brain Surgery for Beginners: And Other Major Operations for Minors. Steve Parker and David West. Millbrook, 1995.

It's All In Your Head. Sylvia Funston. Putnam, 1995.

Your Brain: How You Got It and How It Works. Tabitha M. Powledge. Macmillan, 1994.

Mind and Matter. Jenny Bryan. Dillon/Macmillan, 1993.

Looking Inside the Brain. Ron Schultz. John Muir, 1992.

Brain. Douglas Mathers. Troll, 1992.

BACKGROUND WORKS

The Cognitive Brain. Arnold Trehub. MIT Press, 1994.

The Creative Loop: How the Brain Makes a Mind. Erich Harth. Addison-Wesley, 1993.

(See also NERVOUS SYSTEM; SPINE AND SPINAL DISORDERS; TRAUMATIC BRAIN INJURY; BRAIN TUMOR; EPILEPSY; and other specific diseases or disorders or medical tests.)

brain death, total cessation of all activity in the brain, generally measured by lack of electrical signals on ELECTROENCEPHALOGRAPH readings taken over a period of at least twelve to twenty-four hours, even though heart and lungs may still continue to function (with machine assistance). The time period is important because some conditions, such as some kinds of poisoning or drug reactions, can suppress brain activity. Brain death (sometimes called irreversible COMA) has been variously defined and interpreted in different states and settings, but generally the patient has ceased to have reflexes, movements, and independent breathing. The definition of death has become important in several respects, notably with regard to the question of whether a patient should be maintained in a VENTILATOR and whether the patient's organs might be used for TRANSPLANTS. Organs intended for transplant must be removed after brain death but while heart and lungs are still functioning to keep organs supplied with blood and oxygen. Some of these issues can be dealt with before an emergency, in ADVANCE DIRECTIVES. (See BRAIN AND BRAIN DISORDERS; DEATH AND DYING.)

brain tumor, TUMORS, either MALIGNANT or BENIGN, that occur in or around the BRAIN. *Primary brain tumors,* which originate in the brain itself, are the most common in children and are the second most common cause of CANCER death in children under fifteen years old. Less common are *secondary brain tumors,* which arise from malignant cells originating elsewhere.

The causes of brain tumors are unclear, but GENETIC INHERITANCE, ENVIRONMENTAL HAZARDS, and viruses are among the many possibilities being investigated. The size and growth of tumors is affected by some events; they often increase during a PREGNANCY, for example, probably as a result of HORMONE stimulation.

Among the most common types of brain tumors affecting children are:

- *Medulloblastoma,* a rapidly growing, invasive, malignant tumor of the *cerebellum,* the part of the BRAIN governing balance and coordination of movement. Medulloblastomas tend to spread to other parts of the body through the cerebrospinal fluid in the NERVOUS SYSTEM. Treatment may include surgery—involving complete removal, if the tumor's location is favorable, but partial otherwise—followed by radiation therapy and sometimes chemotherapy (see CANCER for both).
- *Astrocytoma,* a tumor of the brain (glial) tissue which can be either benign or malignant. Severe tumors (Grade III—see TUMOR for grading system) are called *anaplastic astrocytomas*; even more severe forms (Grade IV) are sometimes called *glioblastomas.* Treatment may include surgery—complete, if the tumor's location is favorable, but partial otherwise—followed by radiation therapy and sometimes chemotherapy.
- *Glioblastoma (glioblastoma multiforme or GBM),* a malignant Grade IV tumor, the most common and most destructive type of brain tumor. Glioblastoma is also a name given to the most serious astrocytomas. Because of their varied, invasive, and spreading nature, glioblastomas are more difficult to treat surgically and to control through radiation and chemotherapy than many other tumors.
- *Ependymoma,* a benign or malignant tumor deep inside the brain, generally in the region of the cerebellum and the small central VENTRICLE, usually not fully treatable by surgery. Treatment may include radiation therapy, SHUNTS to relieve fluid pressure on the brain, and sometimes chemotherapy.
- *Craniopharyngioma,* a benign, cystlike tumor that may appear in various parts of the brain region. It may be removed completely if it is in a favorable location; if not, radiation therapy is often used.

Symptoms of a brain tumor vary widely depending on the location of the tumor, its size, and how fast it is growing. Because symptoms are so general, they may seem to be indicative of other disorders, which is why brain tumors are not readily diagnosed until other possibilities are eliminated. Among the most common symptoms experienced are:

- ATAXIA, or lack of coordination.
- Persistent VOMITING.
- Weakness of the facial muscles.
- *Dysphagia,* or difficulty in swallowing.
- DYSARTHRIA, or difficulty in speaking.
- EYE AND VISION PROBLEMS, such as *nystagmus* or *strabismus.*
- Tilting of the head.
- Headache.
- Drowsiness.
- EAR AND HEARING PROBLEMS.
- PARALYSIS or weakness (*paresis*) on one side of the body (*hemiparesis*).
- Personality changes.

The nature of some symptoms, such as loss of vision in one eye or paralysis of a particular area of the body, can give physicians an early clue to the location of a possible tumor.

A wide variety of medical tests can be used to diagnose brain tumors, including a MYELOGRAM, ANGIOGRAM, brains scans (such as CAT SCANS, MRI, and PET SCAN), LUMBAR PUNCTURE (spinal tap), ELECTROENCEPHALOGRAM (EEG), and BIOPSY.

FOR HELP AND FURTHER INFORMATION

American Brain Tumor Association (ABTA)
2720 River Road, Suite 146
Des Plains, IL 60018
708–827–9910; Patient Line: 800–886–2282
Fax: 708–827–9918
E-mail: abta@aol.com (America Online: ABTA)
Naomi Berkowitz, Executive Director
Organization concerned with brain tumors; formerly Association for Brain Tumor Research (AFBTR); sponsors peer-support groups; operates pen-pal program; provides information and referrals; publishes triannual newsletter *Message Line* and other materials, including:

- basic materials: *A Primer of Brain Tumors, A Brain Tumor—Sharing Hope, Using a Medical Library,* and *Coping with a Brain Tumor, Part I: From Diagnosis to Treatment, Part II: During and After Treatment.*

- on children: *When Your Child Is Ready to Return to School* and *Alex's Journey: The Story of a Child with a Brain Tumor*, for readers ages nine to thirteen.
- on specific tumors: *About Ependymoma, About Glioblastoma Multiforme and Anaplastic Astocytoma, About Medulloblastoma/PNET, About Meningioma, About Metastatic Tumors to the Brain and Spine, About Oligodendroglioma and Mixed Glioma*, and *About Pituitary Turmos.*
- on treatments: *Chemotherapy of Brain Tumors, Immunotherapy of Brain Tumors, Radiation Therapy of Brain Tumors* (Parts I & II), and *Shunts.*

Brain Tumor Foundation for Children
2231 Perimeter Park Drive, Suite 9
Atlanta, GA 30341
404–458–5554
Fax: 404–458–5467
Organization that sponsors local support groups; publishes newsletter for parents of children with brain tumors.

National Cancer Institute (NCI), 800–422–6237. Publishes *What You Need to Know About Cancer of the Brain.* (For full group information, see CANCER.)

American Cancer Society (ACS), 800–227–2345. Publishes materials on brain cancer. (For full group information, see CANCER.)

National Institute of Neurological Disorders and Stroke (NINDS), 800–352–9424. Publishes brochure *Brain and Spinal Cord Tumors: Hope Through Research.* (For full group information, see BRAIN AND BRAIN DISORDERS.)

Epilepsy Foundation of America (EFA), 800–332–1000. Publishes materials on seizures and seizure medications. (For full group information, see EPILEPSY).

National Organization for Rare Disorders (NORD), 800–999–6673. (For full group information, see RARE DISORDERS.)

OTHER RESOURCES

Navigating Through a Strange Land: A Book for Brain Tumor Patients and Their Families. Tricia A. Roloff, ed. Indigo Press, 1994.

Brainstorm. Karen Osney Brownstein. Avon, 1984.

(See also TUMORS; CANCER; DEATH AND DYING; also HELP FOR SPECIAL CHILDREN on page 689, including "On wishes for terminally or chronically ill children.")

breaking of the bag of waters, in PREGNANCY, the breaking of the sac holding the AMNIOTIC FLUID that protects the baby, generally just before the onset of LABOR.

breast, either of the pair of hemispheric structures on the chest of mature females composed largely of fatty tissue surrounding fifteen to twenty milk-secreting glands (physiologically modified sweat glands) that funnel milk into the nipple in the middle. Physiologically, breasts are called *mammary glands.* Men and children of both sexes have undeveloped breasts. Under some conditions, as when taking female HORMONES, a child's or a male's breasts can develop, a condition called GYNECOMASTIA. Newborns sometimes also may have enlarged breasts, in response to the mother's hormones, and may even produce breastmilk, popularly called *witch's milk.*

At PUBERTY, a girl's breasts begin to swell and the nipple and the *areola* (the brownish area around the nipple) both enlarge. Breasts are key SECONDARY SEX CHARACTERISTICS that develop with the onset of sexual maturity, and their sensitivity is closely associated with sexual pleasure. The size and shape of the breasts vary widely from person to person, though often the left one is slightly larger than the right. During PREGNANCY, the breasts prepare to meet their main physiological function when the hormones ESTROGEN and PROGESTERONE activate the milk-producing glands and cause the whole breast, including the nipple, to enlarge, in preparation for BREASTFEEDING.

Most breast disorders affect adult women. Nursing mothers sometimes may develop *mastitis,* or inflammation of the breast. TUMORS are common, especially between ages thirty and fifty; some tumors are BENIGN, but many are MALIGNANT. In fact, breast cancer is the most common kind of CANCER in women, affecting an estimated one in eight during a lifetime, and is a main cause of death for women ages thirty to fifty. On rare occasions, breast cancer also occurs in males, especially in those with KLINEFELTER'S SYNDROME. Increased risk of cancer is associated with women who have early MENARCHE (onset of MENSTRUATION) and late MENOPAUSE (cessation of menstruation); have their first child in their late twenties and thirties (or bear no children); have a history of radiation exposure to the breasts, as from multiple X-rays for SCOLIOSIS; have a family history of breast cancer; have a personal history of benign tumors; are tall and heavy (as opposed to short and thin); and have a diet high in FATS. It is unclear what effect, if any, the BIRTH-CONTROL PILL has on the risk of breast cancer. Scientists have recently discovered a defective gene linked with breast cancer. Originally thought connected to only a small proportion of breast cancers, the gene was later linked to almost all breast cancers. This raises the possibility of developing a genetic screening test to identify those women most at risk for breast cancer or for the most aggressive and dangerous types of breast cancer. In the meantime, women with a family history of breast cancer will want to be especially careful as to cancer risk factors, to have periodic checkups, and to educate their daughters to be likewise vigilant.

Sexually mature women of whatever age can best protect themselves by conducting regular breast self-examinations and can best protect their teenage daughters by teaching them how to do so as well (see BREAST SELF-EXAMINATION on page 82). *Mammography,* a type of X-RAY using minimal radiation and therefore posing little risk, is recommended for adult women. They should check with their doctor as to the periodicity, depending on their particular history.

FOR HELP AND FURTHER INFORMATION

American College of Obstetricians and Gynecologists (ACOG), 202–638–5577. Publishes *Detecting and Treating Breast Problems* and *Mammography.* (For full group information, see PREGNANCY.)

American Cancer Society (ACS), 800–227–2345. Publishes *How to do Breast Self Examination*, video *Something Very Special* (on BSE), and *Nowhere to Hide* (on breast cancer and mammography) for teens. (For full group information, see CANCER.)

American Institute for Cancer Research (AICR), 800–843–8114. Publishes *Questions and Answers about Breasts Lumps and Breast Cancer, What Do You Need to Know about Breast Cancer?*, and *Reducing Your Risk of Breast Cancer.* (For full group information, see CANCER.)

National Cancer Institute (NCI), 800–422–6237. Publishes *Understanding Breast Changes: A Health Guide for All Women, Chances Are You Need a Mammogram, Questions and Answers About Choosing a Mammography Facility*, and *What You Need to Know About Breast Cancer.* (For full group information, see CANCER.)

National Institute of Child Health and Human Development (NICHD), 301–496–5133. (For full group information, see PREGNANCY.)

Food and Drug Administration (FDA), 301–443–3170; Breast Implant Hotline: 800–532–4440. (For full group information, see DRUG REACTIONS AND INTERACTIONS.)

OTHER RESOURCES

GENERAL WORKS

Dr. Susan Love's Breast Book, rev. ed. Susan M. Love with Karen Lindsey. Addison-Wesley, 1995.

In Touch with Your Breasts. James Davidson and Jan Ninebrenner. WRS Group, 1994.

The Informed Woman's Guide to Breast Health: Breast Changes That Are Not Cancer, rev. ed. Kerry A. McGinn. Bull, 1992.

Healthy Breasts: Every Woman's Birthright!. Iris A. Michael. Clarke, 1991.

Breast Care Options for the 1990's, rev. ed. Paul Kuehn. Newmark, 1991.

ON BREAST SELF-EXAMINATION

How to Examine Your Breasts: A Guide to Breast Health Care. Judith Tetzleff and Prabharathie G. Nama. Budlong, 1991

Breast Self Examination and You. P.G. Nama. Budlong, 1991.

ON BREAST CANCER

Breast Cancer: A Family Survival Guide. Lucille M. Pederson and Janet M. Trigg. Bergin and Garvey/Greenwood, 1995.

Breast Cancer: A Guide for Every Woman. Michael Baum and others. Oxford University Press, 1994.

Breast Self-Examination

The purpose of the breast self-examination is to identify any changes in the way the breasts look and feel. It is best performed at about the same time each month, preferably after a period, so the body will be at about the same stage of the menstrual cycle and any abnormalities can be most easily detected.

The woman should first stand or sit in front of a mirror with arms down at her sides, then with each arm raised in turn. In each position, she is looking for any changes in the shape, size, or appearance of the skin (including the appearance of or changes to any kind of moles or other marks) or for edema (fluid buildup). Still standing or sitting, the women should then feel the breast surface for any peculiarities and squeeze the nipple to test for soreness and discharge.

In the second stage of the examination, she should lie on her back with a pillow under shoulders and head. With her left arm down at her side, she should move her fingers, keeping her right hand flat and open, in a circular direction around the nipple of the left breast, working slowly outward in ever-widening circles, feeling for lumps or any other kind of abnormality. She should then raise her left arm over her head and repeat the procedure on the same breast, extending the circular feeling (in medical terms, *palpation*) up to the collarbone and into the armpit. She should then repeat this whole second stage on the other breast. Any abnormality should be reported to the doctor immediately, since if detected early enough, breast cancer can be treated effectively before it has spread.

The Breast Cancer Handbook: Taking Control—Knowing the Options—Making Decisions. Joan Swirsky and Barbara Balaban. HarperCollins, 1994.

Breast Cancer: What Every Woman Should Know. Rita Baron-Faust and others. Hearst, 1994.

Breast Cancer: What Your Doctor Won't Tell You about Prevention, Diagnosis, and Treatment. Steve Austin and Cathy Hitchcock. Prima, 1994.

Straight Talk about Breast Cancer: From Diagnosis to Recovery. Suzanne Braddock and others. Addicus, 1994.

Your Breast Cancer Treatment Handbook: A Patient's Guide to Understanding the Disease, Treatment Options, and Physical and Emotional Recovery from Breast Cancer. Judy C. Kneece. EduCare, 1994.

The Breast Cancer Companion: From Diagnosis, through Treatment, to Recovery, Everything You Need to Know for Every Step along the Way. Kathy LaTour. Morrow, 1993.

Breast Cancer: The Complete Guide. Yashar Hirshaut and Peter Pressman. Bantam, 1992.

Beating the Odds Against Breast and Ovarian Cancer: Reducing Your Hereditary Risk. Mary M. Kemeny and Paula Dranov. Addison-Wesley, 1992.

The Race Is Run One Step at a Time: Every Woman's Guide to Taking Charge of Breast Cancer. Nancy Brinker and Catherine M. Harris. Simon & Schuster, 1991.

For preteens and teens

Will I Get Breast Cancer?: Questions and Answers for Teenage Girls. Carole G. Vogel. Simon & Schuster, 1995.

breastfeeding, feeding a newborn on human MILK from a mother's BREASTS, the natural and traditional method of feeding infants. Breast milk is produced in response to a variety of HORMONES, but especially PROLACTIN, which itself is produced by the PITUITARY GLAND in response to the infant's SUCKING on the breast and is maintained as long as nursing continues.

Breastfeeding has a significant number of advantages, as summarized in the Public Health Service's publication *Infant Care*:

- Mother's milk normally has just the right amount of the right nutrients to help the baby grow, with no worry about whether it is "too rich" or "too thin".
- It is easy for the baby's immature system to digest.
- Mother's milk contains ANTIBODIES that give the baby a temporary IMMUNIZATION, protecting against viruses and bacteria.
- Breastfeeding lessens the likelihood that a child will later develop ALLERGIES.
- Mother's milk is clean, uncontaminated, and served at the right temperature.
- Mother's milk is ready when the baby is hungry, needing no equipment, preparation, or cleanup.
- Breastfeeding is inexpensive; it costs less than BOTTLEFEEDING with FORMULA.
- Mother's milk is the only food a baby needs for the first four to six months.
- Breastfeeding uses some of the extra FAT stored for this purpose in the body during PREGNANCY, which helps mothers to lose weight.
- Breastfeeding also helps the UTERUS resume its normal size more quickly.
- Breastfeeding helps with BONDING, the building of the special emotional and physical relationship between mother and child.

Given this array of advantages, it is no wonder that many doctors and clinics recommend that mothers breastfeed their children, if possible.

According to the Public Health Service, over half of all babies now born in the United States are breastfed. Breastfeeding is not an automatic choice, however. In a world where many mothers return to work outside the home soon after giving birth, breastfeeding requires very special kinds of arrangements, such as special CHILD CARE arrangements at work, so that the baby can be breastfed periodically through the day, or use of a BREAST PUMP to extract milk from the breasts. The milk can then be stored and fed to the baby in a bottle later by others, while the mother is gone. Parents need to explore the pros and cons of breastfeeding vs. bottlefeeding as part of their preparation for the new child, so that they are prepared before the child arrives.

Breastfeeding, though natural, needs to be learned. Before the birth, prospective mothers will want to gather information on breastfeeding from organizations like those listed following this entry, from LACTATION SPECIALISTS, from postpartum DOULAS or *postpartum and breastfeeding childbirth assistants*, and also from friends or relatives who have recently breastfed a baby and can give practical advice on getting started. BREASTFEEDING: TIPS FOR FIRST-TIME MOTHERS (on page 84) should also help. See also FEEDING BABY: HOW OFTEN? HOW MUCH? on page 248.

Sometimes, although the mother follows dietary recommendations, the milk supply seems inadequate. This can sometimes be remedied by nursing the baby more often, to stimulate the body to produce more milk. If the baby does not seem to thrive, the doctor should be consulted. On rare occasions, infants who were breastfed received such inadequate nutrition and fluids that they died of malnutrition and dehydration.

Not all women who choose to breastfeed are able to do so. Various problems can occur. Breastfeeding mothers can develop breast infections (*mastitis*), which can sometimes be treated early enough for nursing to continue. The baby may develop breast milk jaundice (see LIVER AND LIVER PROBLEMS) and need to be taken temporarily off breastfeeding. Some babies also have physical problems, such as CLEFT LIP AND PALATE, that make nursing difficult to impossible. Some mothers also find that breastfeeding conflicts with their sexual image or requires too great a time commitment in their busy schedules. These mothers may turn to bottlefeeding,

Breastfeeding: Tips for First-Time Mothers

Following these steps may help first-time new mothers to get started breastfeeding.

- It helps you and the baby learn how to breastfeed if you begin in the first few hours after birth when the baby is alert.
- Find a chair that is comfortable for you and your baby, such as a chair with arms, a footstool, and a pillow.
- Hold your baby comfortably across your lap, with his or her head in the crook of your arm, so that his or her mouth directly faces your nipple. Tuck baby's arms out of the way so they don't get between baby's mouth and your nipple. Support your breast with your thumb *above* the areola (the dark part of the breast) and the rest of your fingers *below* the areola, out of the way of your baby's mouth.
- Touch your baby's cheek or lower lip with your nipple to start. The baby will open his or her mouth wider, and the tongue will move downward [see ROOTING REFLEX]. Once this happens, move your baby quickly onto your breast.
- Allow baby to grasp the darkly-colored part of the breast in his or her mouth. Your baby gets milk by pressing the areola with tongue, gums, and cheek, as well as by suction. Baby's grasp on your nipple should not hurt if baby is properly attached to your breast. (Baby's nose should be pressed against the breast. Even though his or her nose appears buried, your baby should be able to breathe easily. If there is a problem, press lightly on your breast to move it away from the baby's nose and make breathing easier.)
- When you want to stop nursing, break the suction by putting your finger in the corner of your baby's mouth, between the gums. This will help prevent sore nipples.
- Feed the baby at both breasts. You will probably nurse your baby for at least ten to twenty minutes per side, about every two to three hours or *more often* during the first several weeks. If you finish feeding on the right breast, start the next feeding on the left breast. Alternate breasts in this way each time you feed your baby. It is normal for newborns to eat eight to twelve or more times every twenty-four hours. This need to eat so often may taper off after several months.
- Because there is a tighter seal between baby's mouth and your nipple than there is with a bottle, breastfed babies do not swallow as much air. That means that they do not need to burp as much after feeding. Still, you should try to burp your baby halfway through and again when your baby is finished eating by placing him or her on your shoulder and patting gently on the back until you hear a burp.
- If you have less milk than your baby seems to want, try nursing more often. This will increase your supply of milk, usually within three to four days.

Receiving advice and practicing are the best ways to learn to breastfeed. If you have questions or need help after you leave the hospital, find someone who is experienced and sympathetic to teach you. Most obstetric and nursery nurses are good helpers. Other mothers who have breastfed their babies and enjoyed it can help you and provide valuable support. "Lactation specialists" may be available in many areas, as are chapters of the La Leche League. In many communities, mothers have organized La Leche League chapters or other groups especially to help new mothers with breastfeeding. Your doctor, clinic, hospital staff, or other mothers should be able to help you find such a group.

Your breasts only need to be cleaned with plain water, which may be done during your daily shower or bath. Keep yourself rested, well nourished, and relaxed, if possible. You will need to drink more liquids (eight to twelve glasses daily), eat more protein, and ingest some extra calories when you are nursing. Be sure you eat at least three servings of lean meat, fish, poultry, eggs, dried beans or peas each day (for protein) and four glasses of milk or servings of cheese or yogurt (for calcium.) Fruits, juices, and green leafy vegetables will give you extra vitamins and minerals.

There are no special foods that will insure successful breastfeeding. Likewise, there is no basis for avoiding garlic, curry, strong-flavored vegetables, or any other nourishing food. Remember, it takes several hours for a food flavor to appear in your milk. If a particular food seems to cause you or your baby discomfort, omit that food to see if it is the cause. Do not use alcohol, drugs, and cigarettes. Ask your doctor, nurse, or pharmacist before you take any medicines.

Most women find that a good nursing bra (one with wide straps, good support, and that opens easily for feeding) makes breastfeeding easier and more comfortable. Many women even wear a nursing bra during their last weeks of pregnancy.

Milk may leak from your breasts between feedings. Place a small, clean absorbent pad in your bra, and change it as necessary, to keep your nipples dry and clean.

If your entire breast becomes swollen and painful, try letting your baby nurse more often. Also try warm towels or a warm shower, massaging milk from the edges of your breast toward the nipple, and expressing some milk to make yourself more comfortable.

Early signs of breast infection include a tender, red area as well as flulike symptoms: body aches, headache, nausea, and fever. If any of these symptoms appear, contact your doctor or clinic promptly.

Sometimes it may be necessary to be away from your baby for one or more feedings. If you want to continue fully breastfeeding, you should express your milk either by hand or by using a breast pump during the time when your baby would normally feed. You can save breastmilk and have it fed to your baby while you are away—it can safely be left at room temperature for forty minutes, in the refrigerator for forty-eight hours, or in your freezer for up to three months. Store it in a sterile glass or a hard plastic container (such as a bottle) or in a disposable bottle. If the milk is cooled or frozen, bring it to room temperature by placing it in warm water. Don't heat breastmilk in a microwave or over boiling water.

If you are away from your baby and facilities aren't available for you to keep your expressed breastmilk, you may need to discard it. Or, if you can't express your milk, nurse your baby as soon as you get home.

Breastfeeding is recommended as the only food for baby for the first four to six months. After that, other foods are added while breastfeeding may continue through the first year or longer. In addition to being the most healthful way of feeding your baby, it will help mother and baby develop a special bond, or closeness. Remember, mothers and babies *learn* breastfeeding. Don't get discouraged. Soon you and your baby will be on the way to a pleasing and successful breastfeeding experience.

Source: Infant Care (1989). Prepared by the Bureau of Maternal and Child Health and Resources Development for the Public Health Service.

either temporarily or permanently. If they wish to resume breastfeeding, they need to continue to express the milk during the days when the baby is on the bottle, to maintain milk production.

If, for whatever reason, breastfeeding is stopped early, doctors recommend infant FORMULA as the best substitute and parents may want to be prepared with at least minimal provisions for BOTTLEFEEDING, in case of problems. Infants should not, however, be given cow's MILK, which doesn't have complete nutrition for babies and can overtax their young digestive systems. In any case, after about six months, the baby needs more than breastmilk or formula and should begin eating SOLID FOODS.

FOR HELP AND FURTHER INFORMATION

La Leche League International (LLLI)
1400 North Meacham Road
Schaumburg, IL 60173
847–519–7730; 800-LALECHE [525–3243]
Fax: 847–519–0035
E-mail: lllol@library.unmed.edu
Lee Ann Deal, Executive Director
International network concerned with breastfeeding; provides information and referrals; maintains resource centers; trains group leaders; publishes and distributes numerous materials.

Nursing Mothers Counsel
P.O. Box 50063
Palo Alto, CA 94303
415–599–3669
Suzanne L. Ramirez, Executive Director
Organization offering support to breastfeeding mothers; has breast pumps for rental and accessories for purchase; provides free packet of breastfeeding information, including *Breastfeeding Your Baby, Nursing Twins, Maintaining a Milk Supply for the Premature or Ill Infant, Proper Positioning Techniques for Breastfeeding, The Baby Who Won't Breastfeed, The Working Nursing Mother*, and *Manual Expression of Breast Milk.*

American Academy of Pediatrics (AAP),
800–433–9016. Publishes brochure *Breastfeeding: A Gift of Love* and video-and-booklet set *Breastfeeding: The Art of Mothering.* (For full group information, see HEALTH CARE.)

American College of Obstetricians and Gynecologists (ACOG), 202–638–5577. Publishes *Breast-Feeding Your Baby.* (For full group information, see PREGNANCY.)

National Maternal and Child Health Clearinghouse (NMCHC), 703–821–8955. Publishes many materials, including *Art and Science of Breastfeeding* (Manual and Slide Set) and *Nutrition During Lactation.* (For full group information, see PREGNANCY.)

International Lactation Consultant Association (ILCA)
201 Brown Avenue
Evanston, IL 60202–3601
708–260–8874
Fax: 708–475–2523
Organization of professional lactation consultants; provides information and referrals; publishes quarterly newsletter *ILCA Globe* and *Journal of Human Lactation.*

Human Lactation Center (HLC)
666 Sturges Highway
Westport, CT 06880
203–259–5995
Dana Raphael, Director
Organization that supports breastfeeding; conducts research and consults on lactation and nutrition for infants and mothers; maintains library and museum; publishes various materials.

Couple to Couple League (CCL), 513–471–2000. Publishes brochure *Breastfeeding: Does It Really Space Babies?* (For full group information, see NATURAL FAMILY PLANNING.)

Children's PKU Network (CPN), 619–569–9881. Publishes reprint on breastfeeding babies with phenylketonuria (PKU). (For full group information, see PHENYLKETONURIA.)

Twin Services, TWINLINE: 510–524–0863. Publishes *Breastfeeding Twins.* (For full group information, see MULTIPLE BIRTH.)

International Association of Parents and Professionals for Safe Alternatives in Childbirth (NAPSAC), Phone and fax: 314–238–2010. Publishes *Tru-Breast.* (For full group information, see CHILDBIRTH.)

Healthy Mothers, Healthy Babies National Coalition (HMHB), 202–863–2458. Publishes *What Gives These Companies a Competitive Edge?: Worksite Support for Breastfeeding Employees, A Guide to Establishing a Lactation Room at the Worksite,* and resource list *Breastfeeding/Nutrition.* (For full group information, see PREGNANCY.)

Cleft Palate Foundation, 800–242–5338. Publishes *Feeding an Infant with a Cleft.* (For full group information, see CLEFT LIP AND PALATE.)

OTHER RESOURCES

GENERAL WORKS

The Experience of Breastfeeding, rev. ed. Sheila Kitzinger. Viking Penguin, 1995.
The Nursing Mother's Guide to Weaning. Kathleen Huggins and Linda Ziedrich. Harvard Common Press, 1994.
Breast Milk, Nature's Perfect Formula: More Than 100 Answers to the Most Frequently Asked Questions About Breast Milk. Margaret B. Salmon. Techkits, 1994.
Breastfeeding Your Baby: A Guide for the Contemporary Family. Carl Jones and Ruth A. Lawrence. Macmillan, 1993.
Breastfeeding Secrets and Solutions. Janis Graham. Pocket Books, 1993.
Doctor Discusses Breast Feeding. Marie P. Warner and Miriam Gilbert. Budlong, 1992.
The Nursing Mother's Companion, rev. ed. Kathleen Huggins. Harvard Common Press, 1991.
Breastfeeding Today: A Mother's Companion, 2nd ed. Candace Woessner and others. Avery, 1991.
Keys to Breast Feeding. William Sears. Barron's, 1991.
A Practical Guide to Breastfeeding. Janie Riordan. Jones & Bartlett, 1991.

FOR CHILDREN

Maggie's Weaning. Mary J. Deutschbein. Moon Gold, 1994.
Mommy Breastfeeds Our Baby. Teresa P. Carroll. NuBaby, 1990.

BACKGROUND WORKS

The Nature of Birth and Breastfeeding. Michel Odent. Bergin & Garvey/Greenwood, 1992.
Breastfeeding: Something Special for Mother and Baby, rev ed. Toni Berg. New Futures, 1992.
Women's Experience of Breast Feeding. Heather Maclean. University of Toronto Press, 1990.

(See also MILK; BOTTLEFEEDING; FORMULA; SOLID FOODS; NUTRITION; DRUG REACTIONS AND INTERACTIONS.)

breast pump, a device used to draw, or *express,* milk out of the BREASTS, as when a BREASTFEEDING mother is going to be away from her baby for a few hours and wants to store some breastmilk to enable someone else to feed the baby during her absence. The breast pump may also be used to relieve pressure when the breasts are too full. The device itself is simple; a rubber suction cup is placed over the nipple and an attached rubber bulb is pumped (by hand or electricity) to draw out milk that is funneled into the connected glass or plastic bottle. Women who use breast pumps should be sure that all parts are carefully sterilized before use. (See BREASTFEEDING; also BREASTFEEDING: TIPS FOR FIRST-TIME MOTHERS on page 84, which includes information on how and how long to store breastmilk safely.)

Brigance® Diagnostic Inventory of Early Development, an individually administered test that attempts to measure general development in children from birth to age seven. The test includes a variety of paper-and-pencil, oral-response, and direct-observation sections, focusing on MOTOR SKILLS, SELF-HELP SKILLS, COMMUNICATIONS SKILLS, general knowledge and comprehension, and academic skills. Tasks are arranged in the order in which such skills are generally developed. The resulting SCORES are given in terms of DEVELOPMENTAL AGE. The Brigance Inventory is widely used as a READINESS TEST and a DEVELOPMENTAL SCREENING TEST, especially in diagnosing DEVELOPMENTAL DELAYS and in developing INDIVIDUALIZED EDUCATION PLANS. The child often is tested periodically to monitor development. Similar approaches are used in the Brigance® Preschool Screen, the Brigance® K & 1 Screen, and the Brigance® Inventory of Essential Skills (for grades four through twelve), which are used to test for readiness skills, placement, and possible special services. (See TESTS.)

Brudzinski's sign, involuntary flexing in a patient's limbs and hips when the head is flexed; a SIGN that generally indicates the existence of MENINGITIS.

bruxism, grinding of teeth (see TEETH AND DENTAL PROBLEMS), especially at night. A bad bite, or MALOCCLUSION, can cause children to grind their teeth. A dentist may recommend a bite plate to protect the teeth from damage at night or may refer the patient to an ORTHODONTIST to correct the problem. Bruxism can also result from tension and from worms.

bulimia (bulimia nervosa), a type of eating disorder that involves binge eating—intake of large amounts of food in a short time—followed by induced VOMITING, use of laxatives, dieting, or fasting to avoid gaining weight. This is commonly called the *binge-purge cycle.* By contrast, people with BINGE EATING DISORDER simply gain wait, without purging after binges. These binges, when the eating patterns are quite out of control, often take place secretly and are halted only by abdominal pain, vomiting, sleep, or outside interruption. Sometimes associated with ANOREXIA NERVOSA, bulimia is not, by itself, generally a life-threatening disease. But it wreaks enormous havoc on the body all the same. Stomach acid from vomiting causes dental decay, persistent vomiting sometimes causes tears and ruptures in the stomach and esophagus, and disturbance of the body's ELECTROLYTES and DEHYDRATION lead to severe physical problems, including heart irregularities, which can sometimes trigger death. The disorder usually occurs during adolescence or early adulthood, is more prevalent among females than males, and may persist for years. As with anorexia nervosa, the causes are unknown.

FOR HELP AND FURTHER INFORMATION

National Organization for Rare Disorders (NORD), 800–999–6673. (For full group information, see RARE DISORDERS.)

National Institute of Mental Health (NIMH), 301–443–4513. Publishes *Eating Disorders.* (For full group information, see MENTAL DISORDER.)

Food and Nutrition Information Center (FNIC), 301–504–5414. Publishes resource list *Anorexia Nervosa and Bulimia Nutri-Topics.* (For full group information, see NUTRITION.).

OTHER RESOURCES

Bulimia: Disease of Addiction. Judith C. Food Addicts, 1993.
Bulimia: A Guide to Recovery: Understanding and Overcoming the Binge-Purge Syndrome, rev. ed. Lindsey Hall and Leigh Cohn. Gurze, 1992.
Bulimia: A Guide for Family and Friends. Robert T. Shermand and Ron A. Thompson. Free Press, 1990.
Eating without Fear: A Guide to Understanding and Overcoming Bulimia. Lindsey Hall. Bantam, 1990.

(See also ANOREXIA NERVOSA for works on eating disorders in general; also BINGE EATING DISORDER; MENTAL DISORDERS.)

burn, damage to skin from heat above 120°F, which may be caused by a source of heat, hot water, fire, chemicals, electricity, or gases. Because of their tender skin, children are very vulnerable to burns, most of which occur in the home and are preventable. Though fires are the largest and best known cause of burns, many skin burns are caused by simply having the hot water heater set too high, when children are placed in exceedingly hot water (by mistake or through CHILD ABUSE AND NEGLECT), or when children accidentally turn on the hot water themselves.

In the 1970s, water heaters were often set at 140°F–150°F, which could produce third-degree burns in a child in two to five seconds. Since then, many states have established guidelines to lower the settings to 120°F, resulting in a marked decrease in tap-water burns. Parents may well want to check the temperature setting on their water heater to be sure it is set at no more than 120°F. They can also buy antiscalding devices, which prevent too-hot water from being released at the faucet or shower-head.

Parents should also make sure their children are aware of the hazards in cooking—this is important with so many LATCHKEY CHILDREN home alone for some hours while parents are working. Most children are well aware of the dangers posed by burners and boiling water, but many parents let even very young children use the microwave, thinking it is safe. The U.S. Department of Agriculture (USDA), however, warns that "... *severe burns can and do occur from improper microwave usage.* Special packaging for kids' favorite foods like popcorn, pizza, and french fries can get too hot for them to handle. Steam from popcorn bags can burn the eyes, face, arms, and hands. Jelly donuts, pastries, hot dogs, and other foods can reach *scalding* temperatures in seconds."

Each year, hundreds of children under age fifteen receive microwave-related burns. The USDA recommends that *only children who can read be allowed to use the microwave*, and that, if you give permission for your child to use the microwave, you should *start by holding a training session with the child.* The USDA offers these tips for kids on safe microwaving:

- Never turn on an empty oven. This can cause the oven to break.
- Read package directions carefully. Make sure you know how to set the microwave oven controls (for example, ten seconds, rather than ten minutes).
- Use only microwave-safe cookware. Mark specific utensils and containers for microwave use and keep them in a certain place. Never reuse cold storage containers such as margarine tubs.
- Rotate food in the microwave and stir halfway through cooking, if possible.
- Use pot holders to remove items from the microwave. Microwavable dishes get hot from cooked food. Do not use the microwave if you have to reach up to remove food from the oven.
- If a dish is covered with plastic wrap or wax paper, turn up one corner to let excess steam escape. Pull plastic wrap off foods so steam escapes away from hands and face. Steam can burn.
- Never pop any food right from the microwave into your mouth. Allow the food to cool for several minutes before eating.

SPECIFIC TIPS FOR KIDS' FAVORITE FOODS

- *Hotdogs and Baked Potatoes.* Pierce before cooking. This keeps them from exploding.
- *Jelly Donuts and Fruit Pastries.* Break open before eating. The jelly or fruit inside can get very hot and burn your mouth.
- *Popcorn.* Let the bag sit for several minutes before opening. Steam from the bag can burn the face, eyes, arms, and hands.

Burns are classed by their degree of severity. *First degree burns* are those that involve only the upper layer of the skin, the *epidermis.* For these, the Public Health Service's booklet *Infant Care* recommends:

- Rinse with cold water for five to ten minutes. Don't use ointments or greases.
- Do not break blisters.
- Cover with sterile dressing or clean cloth held in place by a nonadhesive material such as aluminum foil.
- A cold pack made by putting ice cubes in a plastic bag and covering with several layers of cloth may relieve the pain of a fresh burn. Leave in place for about fifteen minutes.

In many first-degree burns, such as sunburns, the damaged skin peels away in a few days.

If the burn is caused by lye, oven cleaner, pesticides, or other strong chemicals coming into contact with the baby's skin or eyes, the Public Health Service recommends that it be washed off with "large amounts of water immediately and for a long time." More specifically:

- Remove any contaminated clothing.
- Place the affected area directly under a faucet, garden hose, or shower, and keep rinsing for fifteen minutes.
- Use a bottle, cup, or gentle faucet to wash out eyes; keep the eyelids open as much as possible and continue to flush out for at least thirty minutes.
- Call your doctor or clinic immediately.

Second-degree burns, affecting the upper and second layers of the skin, are more serious, but may heal without scarring, unless widespread. *Third-degree burns* involve all three layers of skin (see SKIN AND SKIN DISORDERS), exposing the body to infection and loss of fluids, which can quickly bring on SHOCK and possibly death, unless the patient is given intravenous fluids. Second-degree burns over more than 30 percent or third-degree burns over more than 10 percent of the body can be critical and life-threatening.

If a child has been burned, parents are advised (after dousing the child with water) to cover exposed burned areas with dry, clean, lint-free cloth, but not to try to remove clothing stuck to wounds, then to get medical attention as quickly as possible. When fire is involved, heated smoke may also cause inflammation of the lungs and damage to the eyes. When electricity is involved, phys cians need to check for heart damage.

In a HOSPITAL or specialized *burn center,* a burn victim will be given PARENTERAL NUTRITION, including ANTIBIOTICS and *analgesics* (painkillers), and the wounds will be either covered with antibacterial dressing or left exposed in a specially controlled antiseptic setting. Skin grafts and PLASTIC SURGERY, sometimes in several operations, may be required. (See SAFETY.)

FOR HELP AND FURTHER INFORMATION

Shriner's Hospitals for Crippled Children,
800–237–5055. Provides free medical care for children with severe burns. (For full group information, see BONE AND BONE DISORDERS.)

Phoenix Society
11 Rust Hill Road
Levittown, PA 19056
215–946-BURN [946–2876]; 800–888-BURN [946–2876]
Fax: 215–946–4788

Network of peer-support groups of burn victims and their families; provides information; publishes materials, including newsletter *Icarus File.*

National Burn Victim Foundation
3234 Scotland Road
Orange, NJ 07050
201–676–7700
Fax: 201–673–6353
Organization to aid burn victims; sponsors peer-support groups and educational programs; offers professional counseling and special programs for burned children.

OTHER RESOURCES

GENERAL WORKS

Severe Burns: A Family Guide to Medical and Emotional Recovery. Baltimore Regional Burn Center Staff and Andrew M. Munster. Johns Hopkins, 1993.

Journeys Through Hell: Stories of Burn Survivors' Reconstruction of Self and Identity. Dennis J. Stouffer. Rowman, 1994.

burping, the audible return of air from the stomach; in an adult called *belching.* Babies swallow a good deal of air while they are feeding, more during BOTTLEFEEDING than BREASTFEEDING because the baby's mouth generally fits more closely around the breast. Burping a baby two or three times during a feeding can help reduce the amount of REGURGITATION (spitting up) of food and fluid.

busing, in EDUCATION, transporting children who live beyond a certain distance to school. In recent decades, busing has often come to mean longer-distance transporting of children to schools outside their neighborhoods as part of efforts to achieve racial balance and DESEGREGATION. Busing has often been mandated by federal courts, and proponents of the approach applaud the judiciary's attempt to provide equality of opportunity to students of all races, when schools and other branches of government have failed to do so. Critics, however, charge that court action amounts to government by the judiciary, usurping the prerogatives of the legislative and executive branches. On a personal level, some parents openly prefer a segregated school system, while many parents (regardless of their feelings about desegregation) have been concerned about the effect of the disruptive busing on young children, some of whom are transported for long distances, when they might otherwise have walked to their neighborhood school. In reaction to busing, many parents opted out of the PUBLIC SCHOOL system altogether, choosing instead to place their children in PRIVATE SCHOOLS or to try HOME SCHOOLING. In recent years, many school districts have tried alternative voluntary approaches to desegregation instead of involuntary busing; SCHOOLS OF CHOICE, especially MAGNET SCHOOLS, are often key features of such programs. (See EDUCATION; DESEGREGATION.)

C

calcification, formation of bone through deposits of CALCIUM, which show up on X-RAYS, such as the SKELETAL SURVEYS often done in cases of possible CHILD ABUSE AND NEGLECT. The amount of calcium deposited shows how well a newly broken bone is healing and also marks the location of old healed FRACTURES.

calcium, a MINERAL vital to the building and maintenance of strong bones and teeth, also important in the proper functioning of nerves and muscles, in blood clotting, and in the body's METABOLISM. Calcium is the most abundant mineral in the body and one of the most important elements overall. Each adult body contains over two pounds of calcium. The most important sources of calcium are milk and other dairy products, eggs, fish (especially sardines and shellfish), green leafy vegetables, dried peas and beans, and fruits (especially citrus fruits).

The level of calcium in the blood is controlled by VITAMIN D in the body and by various HORMONES, produced by the THYROID and parathyroid glands. Problems with these glands, KIDNEY AND UROLOGICAL PROBLEMS, lack of sufficient calcium in the diet, and other disorders can lead to calcium deficiency (*hypocalcemia*). In infants, this can lead to TETANY or RICKETS. Too much calcium can cause harmful calcium deposits in tissue and DEPRESSION. Calcium is added to bone in youth and young adulthood, peaking at about age thirty-five. Women should be sure to get sufficient calcium during PREGNANCY and BREASTFEEDING, especially during ADOLESCENT PREGNANCY, to avoid loss of calcium from bones during these draining periods and lessen their later risk of OSTEOPOROSIS. (See MINERALS; NUTRITION, VITAMIN D; LACTATION; BONE AND BONE DISORDERS; TEETH AND DENTAL PROBLEM.)

California Achievement Tests (CAT), a series of group-administered, multiple-item, paper-and-pencil tests used to assess basic academic skills in children from grades K–12. The tests, available in different forms and at overlapping levels through the thirteen grades, measure knowledge and skills appropriate to each, especially in the areas of READING, spelling, language, reference, mathematics, and sometimes STUDY SKILLS, science, social studies, and computer literacy. Tests in specific subjects are also available for end-of-course use, as in algebra or chemistry. Tests may be scored by hand or computer, and the SCORES themselves may be expressed in various ways. The CAT is widely used as a READINESS TEST, to assess whether the student is ready for PROMOTION to more advanced classes and to help in class placement decisions. (See TESTS.)

Callier-Azusa Scale, an individually administered test widely used with children who have multiple, severe, or profound disabilities, including DEAF-BLIND children, to assess their capacity in such areas as MOTOR SKILLS, perceptual skills (including VISUAL, AUDITORY, and TACTILE SKILLS), SELF-HELP SKILLS, COMMUNICATION SKILLS, cognitive skills, and SOCIAL SKILLS. The focus in each area is on DEVELOPMENTAL MILESTONES as they occur among children with disabilities (the CHART OF NORMAL DEVELOPMENT on page 637 shows when various skills are usually developed). One or preferably several people familiar with the child's behavior keep an observational inventory of behaviors in a classroom setting over at least two weeks. The presence or absence of specific behavior is noted and the results are expressed very generally in AGE-EQUIVALENTS. This is called the G-Edition of the scale; an H-edition is used to assess communication skills in children and adolescents with severe or multiple disabilities. (See TESTS.)

cancer, a general name for a wide variety of diseases all characterized by unchecked growth of cells in one or more parts of the body. The resulting abnormal growths, called TUMORS or *neoplasms,* crowd out normal cells and eventually kill the tissue or organs involved. Any part of the body can be affected, not just the major organs such as the heart and lungs, but also skin (see SKIN DISORDERS), the lymphatic system, as in Hodgkin's disease (see IMMUNE SYSTEM), and BONE MARROW (see LEUKEMIA).

Not all tumors are cancerous. Many grow so slowly that they are not considered life-threatening, and are labeled BENIGN. Tumors that grow rapidly enough to threaten life are called MALIGNANT or cancerous. Some otherwise benign tumors can still be life-threatening if they occur in a sensitive area, such as the brain. (For an overview of the different kinds of tumors, see TUMOR and BRAIN TUMOR.)

Cancers are relatively rare among children; some 8,000 new cases are diagnosed annually in the United States. Even so, cancer is the leading cause of death by disease for children ages one through fourteen, accounting for approximately 1,600 deaths annually in the United States, about one-third of them from leukemia. The most common cancer sites for children are the blood and BONE MARROW, bone, lymph nodes, brain, NERVOUS SYSTEM, kidneys, and soft tissues. According to the American Cancer Society, the most common childhood cancers are:

- LEUKEMIA, unchecked production of white blood cells in the bone marrow, a cancer increasingly common in children, for unknown reasons.

- *Brain cancers,* the first symptoms of which are often headaches, blurred or double vision, dizziness, nausea, and difficulty in walking and handling objects (see BRAIN TUMOR). This type of cancer has sharply increased among children in the last two decades.
- *Osteogenic sarcoma,* a bone cancer that is often painless at first. The initial sign is often a swelling in the area of the tumor.
- *Ewing's sarcoma,* a *myeloma,* or tumor of the bone marrow.
- *Neuroblastoma,* a tumor of embryonic nerve cells, most common in the abdominal area.
- *Rhabdomyosarcoma,* the most common type of soft tissue cancer (*sarcoma*); it may occur in the head or neck area, genito-urinary area, trunk, or limbs.
- *Lymphoma* and *Hodgkin's disease,* which affect the lymph nodes (see IMMUNE SYSTEM), but may also involve bone marrow and other organs. Symptoms include general weakness, fever, and possibly swelling of the lymph notes in the neck, armpits, or groin.
- *Retinoblastoma,* a cancer of the eye most common in children under age four. It can often be cured with early detection and appropriate treatment (see EYE AND VISION PROBLEMS).
- *Wilms' tumor,* a cancer of the kidney (*nephroblastoma*) often signaled by a lump or swelling in the abdomen.

Cancers in children are often hard to detect. Many physicians recommend that (in addition to regular medical checkups) parents should routinely—at least once a month—lightly feel over a young child's body, especially the abdomen, the head or neck area, and the armpits; if they find any changes or abnormalities, take the child to the doctor immediately. They should be alert to any persistent, unusual symptoms, including an unusual swelling or mass; an increased tendency to bruise; unexplained paleness and loss of energy; persistent, localized pain or limping; prolonged, unexplained fever or illness; frequent headaches, often with VOMITING; sudden eye or vision changes; and excessive, rapid weight loss. As with all cancers, the sooner it is detected, the better the chance of a cure.

Two other kinds of cancer are of particular concern to parents: *breast cancer,* the most common type of cancer among American women and the main cause of death for women ages thirty to fifty (see BREASTS), and *testicular cancer,* the most common cancer among American men ages fifteen to thirty-five (see TESTES). Both of these forms of cancer can affect relatively young men and women. That means that young parents may be faced with cancer in a partner and may also need to help their children deal with the questions of cancer, its treatment, and possible death. Parents should prepare their sons and daughters to perform self-examinations beginning during PUBERTY, to reduce their exposure to RISK FACTORS for cancer (see the list that follows). Parents should also make their children aware at puberty of any family history of cancer, so that they can protect themselves as much as possible in the future (see BREAST SELF-EXAMINATION on page 82; TESTICULAR SELF-EXAMINATION on page 590).

In addition, parents will want to be alert to the risks for SKIN CANCER, which is triggered largely by childhood exposure to sun. (See SKIN CANCER; SKIN AND SKIN DISORDERS; also WHEN DO KIDS NEED PROTECTION FROM THE SUN? on page 548.)

At the most basic level, cancer begins when *oncogenes* (genes that control cell growth and duplication) become abnormal, sometimes due to the presence of cancer-inducing substances called *carcinogens.* The growth at the original site of the cancer is called *primary,* but cancers "shed" cells that enter the blood stream and the lymphatic system. The body's immune system attacks and kills some of these cells, but if the cancer goes undetected and untreated, some cancerous cells will survive to establish cancerous growths elsewhere in the body, called *secondary tumors* or *metastases.*

What causes cells to become cancerous in the first place is a question with no clear and simple answers. Cancers are not directly inherited, but some people can inherit a susceptibility or tendency to develop cancer; several genetic markers have been identified with cancers. Nor is cancer directly contagious, though some forms may be triggered by viruses. But a person's likelihood of getting cancer is known to be increased by a variety of risk factors. Though no one yet knows how to prevent cancer, some general guidelines for reducing the risk of getting it are:

- Avoid SMOKING, which is considered responsible for most cases of lung cancer today, as well as being implicated in numerous other health problems. Nonsmoking tobacco, such as snuff and chewing tobacco, is also dangerous. It has been linked to cancers of the mouth, larynx, throat, and esophagus. Damage is magnified if smoking is combined with heavy drinking (see ALCOHOL ABUSE).
- Avoid direct exposure to sunlight, which is implicated in almost all cases of skin cancer (see references above).
- Avoid exposure to radiation, which can can cause cell damage and increase cancer risk (though it can also be used as a therapy; see discussion of cancer treatments in this entry). Medical and dental X-rays are designed to give minimal exposure to radiation. Radiation from nuclear activities is a concern, as is the gas radon (see ENVIRONMENTAL HAZARDS).
- Avoid exposure to carcinogenic chemicals, which can also cause unknown damage; the main problem is that the cancer-triggering risk of specific chemicals is often unknown, and when those chemicals are mixed in the "chemical stews" of polluted environments, new and unintended chemicals can form, creating wholly unknown risks (see ENVIRONMENTAL HAZARDS).
- Avoid foods that have been smoked or cured in nitrites or salt; these have been linked to cancers of the esophagus and stomach. Many other known carcinogenic

food additives have been removed from the market (see FOOD ADDITIVES).

- Eat a low-fat, high-fiber diet, which is believed to lower the risk of breast, colon, and prostate cancers. Diets heavy in FATS are linked with a higher rate of cancers overall.
- Eat plenty of fruits and vegetables, which are associated with lessened risk of cancer in general and of some forms of cancer in particular, such as lung, bladder, esophagus, and stomach cancers. The cabbage and broccoli family has been found particularly good in protecting against cancer.
- Maintain a weight in the proper range for your age and height, since OBESITY is linked with increased risk of many cancers, especially those of the colon, breast, gall bladder, OVARIES, and UTERUS.
- Consult carefully with your doctor about the possible cancer risks of any medications you are taking.
- Practice safe sex, since some viruses passed during sexual activity have been linked with cancers; for instance, hepatitis B has been connected with liver cancer (see LIVER AND LIVER PROBLEMS). Sexual and reproductive history has some effect on cancer risk overall; for example, women who have children early in life are at less risk for some forms of cancer than women who have no children or who have them late in life. Men and women who have many sexual partners are at greater risk of cancer, possibly because of viruses passed during sexual activity (see SEXUALLY TRANSMITTED DISEASES).

Parents will want to cut down on such risk factors to lessen the risk for themselves and their children of developing cancer later on. But, in many cases, the causes of the cancer are unknown and develop extremely rapidly. This is often the case with cancers in children, such as leukemia, brain tumors, and abdominal tumors.

Cancer can be detected in several ways. Sometimes, the growth can be seen—externally, as in cases of skin cancers, or internally, as in cancer of the CERVIX—or felt, as in breast or testicular cancer. Various SCANS, such as ULTRASOUND, MRI, or CT SCANS, can also provide visual information about possible tumors. BLOOD TESTS, laboratory analysis of blood samples, can sometimes provide clues to the existence of cancer. When indicated, the doctor may perform a BIOPSY to take a sample of the suspect tissue, a procedure that can require an operation if an internal organ is involved. Laboratory tests will then confirm if the sample cells are benign—as they are in most cases—or malignant.

Treatment varies with the type of cancer, the part of the body involved, and the general medical condition of the patient. Physicians will generally develop a medical treatment plan, called a *protocol,* to be followed in a particular case. Such a plan may include a variety of therapies, such as:

- *Surgery,* complete excision, if the tumor's location allows it, but partial removal otherwise. Surgical removal at least diminishes the number of malignant cells to be treated by other therapies. In some cases, the location of the tumor—as in the thigh—may require amputation of a limb or formation of a new body opening (OSTOMY). If the tumor is located in an inaccessible position, such as deep in the brain or in another vital structure, surgery may be considered impossible.
- *Radiotherapy,* use of radiation (often X-rays or gamma rays) in as concentrated a form as possible to destroy malignant cells without causing other, potentially deadly health problems in the patient. With *interstitial radiation* (*brachytherapy*), radioactive materials are implanted directly into the tumor.
- *Chemotherapy,* use of poisonous chemicals to kill tumor cells, which are generally more vulnerable to toxins than are healthy cells. As with radiation, the difficulty is often to obtain sufficient concentration to destroy tumor cells without poisoning the rest of the body. If the tumor is in the brain, special techniques may be required to breach the BLOOD-BRAIN BARRIER.
- BONE MARROW TRANSPLANTS (BMT), subjection of a patient to massive doses of radiation or chemotherapy; both treatments kill the cancer but also the bone marrow which is then replaced by new bone marrow. In cases of leukemia, this procedure has long been used when patients have been unable to find donors with bone marrow similar enough to their own to replace the marrow that has been destroyed. In a more recent variation, when the patient has health marrow, some of it is removed before the therapy, carefully cultured, and injected back into the bone after therapy. This procedure is called an *autologous bone marrow transplant.* A BMT is a painful and dangerous procedure, best performed on people whose bodies are otherwise strong and healthy, but it holds promise for otherwise untreatable or unresponsive life-threatening tumors.
- *Immunotherapy,* activation or stimulation of the body's own immune system to fight tumors; a focus of considerable research, though not yet used as a major standard therapy.
- *Steroid therapy,* administration of various kinds of STEROIDS, as in cases of brain tumors, to hold down *edema* (fluid accumulation and resulting swelling), which can damage tissues such as the brain.
- *Hyperthermia,* use of heat to kill cancer cells or to make them more susceptible to radiation therapy; still an experimental approach.
- *Photoradiation,* administration of a light-sensitive drug, after which the patient is placed under a special light; also still an experimental technique.

Other approaches are being developed experimentally, such as genetically engineered cells that target cancer cells for destruction or self-destruction (see GENE THERAPY). Some drugs, such as *taxol,* have shown promise against some cancers but cause serious and potentially life-threatening side effects in some patients and are still under review.

Because of these and other techniques, many more people have been able to beat cancer and go on to live normal lives. But the treatments themselves often have severe side effects, including loss of appetite (*anorexia*), severe weight loss and wasting of body tissues (*cachexia*), VOMITING, water retention (EDEMA), DIARRHEA, CONSTIPATION, DEHYDRATION, HAIR loss, mouth sores, loss or distortion of taste and smell (mouth blindness or ANOSMIA), dry mouth (XEROSTOMIA), and tooth decay. These side effects are difficult enough for adults to deal with, but even more difficult for children, who are sometimes too young to fully understand what is occurring.

In dealing with cancer in their children, parents can turn for help to many organizations and resources (see the list that follows). For example, they should note the National Cancer Institute's *Talking With Your Child About Cancer* on when and what to tell children of different age groups. For information on facing a possibly terminal illness, see DEATH AND DYING; ADVANCE DIRECTIVE. For more on different types of hospitals and arrangements for children, see HOSPITALS; HOSPICE.

FOR HELP AND FURTHER INFORMATION

National Cancer Institute (NCI)
9000 Rockville Pike
Building 31, Room 10A16
Bethesda, MD 20892
Cancer Information Service: 800–4-CANCER [422–6237]
Federal arm concerned with cancer research and policy; gathers and disseminates information; maintains regional directories of cancer-related services and programs, and computerized database of currently funded experimental treatments; publishes numerous print and audiovisual materials, including:

- general information: *What You Need to Know About Cancer, Questions and Answers About Metastatic Cancer,* and "What You Need to Know About Cancer" brochures, such as *Hodgkin's Disease, Multiple Myeloma,* and *Non-Hodgkin's Lymphoma.*
- on children and cancer: *Young People with Cancer: A Handbook for Parents, Talking with Your Child About Cancer, When Someone in Your Family Has Cancer* (for young people whose parent or sibling has cancer), *Managing Your Child's Eating Problems During Cancer Treatment.*
- numerous materials on treatments and research, such as *Facing Forward: A Guide for Cancer Survivors, Chemotherapy and You: A Guide to Self-Help During Treatment, Help Yourself During Chemotherapy: 4 Steps for Patients, Radiation Therapy and You: A Guide to Self-Help During Treatment,* and *Taking Time: Support for People with Cancer and the People Who Care About Them.*

American Cancer Society (ACS)
30 Glenn Street
White Plains, NY 10603
914–949–4800; 800–227–2345
Fax: 914–949–4279
John R. Seffrin, Executive Vice President and Chief Staff Officer
Organization working against cancer; sponsors research, education, and support services, including programs such as I Can Cope, for cancer patients and their families; provides information; publishes newsletter *Cancer News* and other materials, including:

- General materials: *Answering Your Questions About Cancer, Cancer: Assessing Your Risks (A Personalized Test), Cancer Facts for Women, Cancer Facts for Men, Cancer-Related Checkups,* and *Cancer Word Book.*
- For children: video *Janey Junkfood's Fresh Adventure*; and educational kit *Early Start to Good Health.*
- For preteens and teens: videos *The Intricate Cell*; educational kits *Nature of Cancer, Right Choices, Health Myself* and *Health Network*; and *Health Decisions* (computer game).
- Many other titles on childhood cancer, cancer treatment, nutrition and cancer, and specific cancers, such as Hodgkin's disease and lymphomas.

Candlelighters Childhood Cancer Foundation (CCCF)
7910 Woodmont Drive, Suite 460
Bethesda, MD 20814–3015
301–657–8401; 800–366–2223
Fax: 301–718–2686
E-mail: 75717.3513@compuserve.com (CompuServe: 75717,3513)
James R. Kitterman, Executive Director
Organization focusing on support and services for families of children with cancer; supported by the American Cancer Society (see previous organization entry); maintains library; provides information and referrals; acts as advocate; publishes various materials, including *The Candlelighters Quarterly* (for adults), quarterlies *CCCF Youth Newsletter* and *The Phoenix* (for adult survivors of childhood cancer), list of camps for children with cancer and their siblings, packets of reprints on specific topics, research reports, bibliographies, and resource guides.

Cancer Care, Inc. and the National Cancer Care Foundation
1180 Avenue of the Americas
New York, NY 10036
212–221–3300; Counseling Line: 800–813-HOPE [813–4673]
Fax: 212–719–0263
Diane Blum, Executive Director
Organization supporting cancer patients and families, primarily in the northeast and Florida; offers services such as counseling and financial assistance; maintains special programs for children, adolescents, AIDS patients, the bereaved, and other groups; publishes various pamphlets, including *Helping Children Understand Cancer, Helping Children Cope, Guide to Cancer Care Services,*

Adolescent Outreach Program, and *African-American Outreach Program*.

Children's Hospice International (CHI), Helpline: 800–242–4453. Publishes children's books *They Never Want to Tell You: Children Talk About Cancer* and *Letter to a Child with Cancer*. (For full group information, see HOSPICE.)

American Institute for Cancer Research (AICR)
1759 R Street NW
Washington, DC 20009
202–328–7744; 800–843–8114
Marilyn Gentry, President
Organization devoted to cancer research; publishes AICR Information Series of booklets and pamphlets, including *Cancer Information: Where to Find Help*, *The Cancer Process*, *Everything Doesn't Cause Cancer*, *Reducing Your Risk of Prostate Cancer*; and works for health professionals.

The Hereditary Colorectal Cancer Registry
550 N. Broadway, Suite 108
The Johns Hopkins Hospital
Baltimore, MD 21205
410–614–4038 Jill Brensinger, Genetic Counselor
410–755–3875 Judy Bacon, Coordinator of Registry
International registry for people with family history of G.I. polyposis and hereditary colon cancer; formerly the G.I. Polyposis and Hereditary Colon Cancer Registry; seeks to identify families at risk and to educate them and health professionals; provides information and makes referrals; maintains family study center; publishes various materials, including quarterly newsletter *GI Polyposis & Related Conditions*, quarterly *Ostomy*, *Family Studies in Genetic Disorders*, and Johns Hopkins Guides for Patients and Families: *Familial Adenomatous Polyposis* and *Hereditary Non-polyposis Colorectal Cancer*.

Food and Nutrition Information Center (FNIC), 301–504–5414. Publishes resource list *Nutrition and Cancer Nutri-Topics*. (For full group information, see NUTRITION.)

American Brain Tumor Association (ABTA), 800–886–2282. (For full group information, see BRAIN TUMOR.)

DES Action, 800–337–9288. Publishes *Breast Cancer: Risk, Protection, Detection and Treatment*. (For full group information, see DES.)

National Oral Health Information Clearinghouse (NOHIC), 301–402–7364. Publishes *What You Need to Know About Oral Cancer*, *Chemotherapy and Oral Health*, and *Radiation Therapy and Oral Health*. (For full group information, see TEETH AND DENTAL PROBLEMS.)

National Clearinghouse for Alcohol and Drug Abuse Information (NCADI), 301–468–2600. Publishes *Alcohol and Cancer: Estimating the Cost of Alcohol Abuse*. (For full group information, see HELP AGAINST SUBSTANCE ABUSE on page 703.)

Agency for Health Care Policy and Research Clearinghouse, 800–358–9295. Publishes *Things to Know About Quality Mammograms: A Woman's Guide*, *Managing Cancer Pain: Patient Guide*, and InstantFAX materials on cancer pain. (For full group information, see HEALTH INSURANCE.)

Corporate Angel Network
Westchester County Airport
Building 1
White Plains, NY 10604
914–328–1313
Priscilla Blum, President
Organization that coordinates free flights to NCI-approved treatment centers for cancer patients (and one family member or attendant) on corporate airplanes, when seats are available; there is no financial need requirement.

American Council on Science and Health (ACSH), 212–362–7044. Publishes *Diet and Cancer* and *Cancer Clusters*. (For full group information, see SAFETY.)

RESOLVE, Inc., HelpLine: 617–623–0744. Publishes *Cancer and Infertility*. (For full group information, see INFERTILITY.)

National Safety Council (NSC), 800–621–7615. Publishes *Diet and Cancer Prevention* guide and video. (For full group information, see SAFETY.)

National Organization for Rare Disorders (NORD), 800–999–6673. (For full group information, see RARE DISORDERS.)

National Woman's Christian Temperance Union (WCTU), 800–755–1321. Publishes leaflet *Marijuana and Cancer*. (For full group information, see HELP AGAINST SUBSTANCE ABUSE on page 703.)

OTHER RESOURCES

FOR PARENTS AND OTHER ADULTS

When Someone You Love Has Cancer. Dana R. Pomeroy. IBS Press, 1991.
Coping Magazine, for cancer patients and families, on cancer research, services, and personal experiences. Available from 2019 North Carothers, Franklin, TN 37064; 615–790–2400.
The Child with Cancer. Jennifer Thompson. Ishiyaku Euro, 1990.

GENERAL WORKS

Understanding Cancer, 4th ed. Mark Renneker. Bull, 1994.
Cancer. Robert M. McAllister and others. Basic, 1993.
Understanding Cancer. Jay S. Roth. Academic Press, 1991.
Cancer: Your Questions Answered. Charles Dobree. Trafalgar Square, 1990.

ON PREVENTION

The Complete Guide to Preventing Cancer: How You Can Reduce Your Risk. Elizabeth Whelan. Prometheus, 1994.

Fifty-Two Ways to Protect Yourself from Cancer. Terry T. Shintani and J. M. Miller. Nelson, 1993.
Women's Cancers: How to Prevent Them, How to Treat Them, How to Beat Them. Kerry A. McGinn and Pamela J. Haylock. Hunter House, 1993.
Cancer Preventions and Remedies. John J. Williams and Laurie Williams. Consumertronics, 1993.
A Family Doctor's Guide to Understanding and Preventing Cancer. S. R. Kaura. Health Press, 1990.

ON DEALING WITH CANCER

Choice in Healing: Integrating the Best of Conventional and Alternative Approaches to Cancer. Michael Lerner. MIT Press, 1994.
Everyone's Guide to Cancer Therapy, 2nd ed. Malin Dollinger. Andrews and McMeel, 1994.
How to Fight Cancer and Win, rev. ed. William L. Fischer. Fischer, 1994.
You Can Conquer Cancer: Prevention and Management. Ian Gawler. Seven Hills, 1994.
Your Defense Against Cancer. H. Dreher. HarperCollins, 1994.
If the President Had Cancer: Cancer Care, How to Find and Get the Best There Is. Gary L. Schine. Sandra, 1993.
Fifty Essential Things to Do When the Doctor Says It's Cancer. Greg Anderson. NAL-Dutton, 1993.
Coping with Chemotherapy, rev. ed. Nancy P. Bruning. Ballantine, 1993.
Fight Cancer: How to Prevent It and How to Fight It. Karol Sikora and Hilary Thomas. Parkwest, 1992.
Get Help, Get Positive, Get Well: The Aggressive Approach to Cancer Therapy. Sarah Winograd. Rainbow, 1992.
Diagnosis Cancer: Your Guide Through the First Few Months. Wendy S. Harpham. Norton, 1992.

(See also NUTRITION, under "On cancer-fighting nutrition.")

FOR CHILDREN

An Alphabet about Kids with Cancer. Rita Berglund. Children's Legacy, 1994. (Address: P.O. Box 300305, Denver, CO 80203; 303–830–7595)
Understanding Cancer. Susan N. Terkel and Marlene L. Brazz. Watts, 1993.
About Cancer. Cynthia Moritz. New Readers, 1993.
My Mommy Has Cancer. Carolyn S. Parkinson. Solace, 1992.
A Boy and His Baseball: The Dave Dravecky Story. Judy Gire. Zondervan, 1992.

FOR PRETEENS OR TEENS

Cancer. Elaine Landau. Twenty-First Century Books, 1994.
C Word: Teenagers and Their Families Living with Cancer. Elena Dorfman. NewSage Press, 1993.
Living with Cancer. Simon Smail. Watts, 1990.
Cancer. Joann Rodgers. Chelsea House, 1990.
Coping When a Parent Has Cancer. Linda Leopold Strauss. Rosen, 1988.

PERSONAL EXPERIENCES OF TEENS

I'll Never Walk Alone. Carol Simonides. Continuum, 1983. Autobiography of a teenager with cancer.
No Dragons To Slay. J. Greenberg. Farrar, Straus & Giroux, 1983. A 17-year-old boy with a tumor.
On With My Life. P. Trull. Putnam, 1983. Autobiography of girl whose leg was amputated to cure cancer.
Too Old to Cry ... Too Young to Die. Edith Pendleton, ed. Thomas Nelson, 1980. By and for terminally ill teenagers.

OTHER PERSONAL EXPERIENCES

Autobiography of a Face. Lucy Grealy. Houghton Mifflin, 1994.
David's Legacy. Barbara Wallschlaeger. 1994. (Order from the author: P.O. Box 657, Lac de Flambeau, WI 54538)
Mommy Isn't Sick; She's Just Dying. Ernest N. Bigelow. Bigelow, 1993.
Recovery from Cancer: A Personal Story of Sickness and Health. Elaine Nussbaum. Avery, 1992.
Healing Journey. O. Carl Simon. Bantam, 1992.
Life in the Shadow. Bill Soiffer. Chronicle Books, 1991.
The Power Within: True Stories of Exceptional Patients Who Fought Back with Hope. Wendy Williams. Harper Collins, 1990.

BACKGROUND WORKS

Confronting Cancer: The Disease, the Treatment, the Future. M. M. Sherry. Plenum, 1994.
The Cancer Puzzle: An Indepth Exploration to Its Many Causes, Treatments and Prevention. Alan Young. F. Amato, 1993.
The Cancer Book: A Guide to Understanding the Causes, Prevention, and Treatment of Cancer. Geoffrey M. Cooper. Jones and Bartlett, 1993.
The Road Back to Health: Coping with the Emotional Aspects of Cancer, rev. ed. Neil A. Fiore. Celestial Arts, 1991.

(See also LEUKEMIA; TUMOR; BRAIN TUMOR; BONE MARROW TRANSPLANT; ACOUSTIC NEUROMA; DEATH AND DYING; HOSPITAL; OSTOMY; also HELP FOR SPECIAL CHILDREN, on page 689, under "On wishes for terminally or chronically ill children.")

Candidates Reply Date Agreement, an agreement, sponsored by the COLLEGE ENTRANCE EXAMINATION BOARD, that colleges will not require students to accept or reject an offer of ADMISSION or of FINANCIAL AID before May 1. The aim is to allow the student to learn of all the possible offers open, before choosing one of them.

candidiasis, infection by the fungus *candida albicans.* The fungus fluorishes in moist parts of the body, such as the mouth, the VAGINA, or under the FORESKIN of an uncircumcised male's PENIS, but it is normally kept in check by bacteria in the body, unless something upsets the body's balances. ANTIBIOTICS, in killing bacteria, can allow candidiasis to spread; drugs that suppress the IMMUNE SYSTEM can also encourage candidiasis growth, as can the disease AIDS. Pregnant women, women on BIRTH CONTROL pills, and people with DIABETES may, because of changes in the body's chemical balances, be susceptible to candidiasis. Symptoms include itchiness; a thick, white discharge from the vagina; yellowish patches in the mouth; and white, flaky patches on moist skin. Babies with diaper rash are susceptible to candidiasis, and the fungus can cause BALANITIS, inflammation of the tip of the penis. Treated with antifungal medications, candidiasis is best combatted by keeping skin dry.

carbohydrates, a group of naturally occurring, organic compounds, including sugar, starch, and cellulose, that provide the main source of energy for all body functions. The average American adult is estimated to eat approximately half a pound of carbohydrates each day in such common and inexpensive foods as bread, potatoes, pastries, candy, soft drinks, rice, spaghetti, fruits, and vegetables. Nutritionists recommend getting carbohydrates primarily from unprocessed (unrefined) foods, such as whole-grain cereals and fresh fruits, because they have more nutrients and FIBER than refined foods, such as sugar and white flour. (See NUTRITION.)

carcinoma, general term for a kind of MALIGNANT TUMOR, or CANCER, that arises from skin covering the body or lining organs (notably the liver and kidneys) or systems (such as the digestive, respiratory, urological, and reproductive systems). (See TUMOR; CANCER.)

cardiac monitor, a type of electronic machine that monitors heartbeat, often used to alert parents or medical staff to dangerous irregularities in the heartbeat of a PREMATURE infant, such as one susceptible to SLEEP APNEA or thought at risk for SUDDEN INFANT DEATH SYNDROME. Sometimes a *cardiorespiratory monitor* is used to monitor both heartbeat and breathing.

caregiver, a person responsible for a child's health and welfare, and for meeting the child's basic physical and psychological needs. Caregivers include those who have full-time legal responsibility for the child, such as MOTHER, FATHER, or GUARDIAN; others in the home, such as SIBLINGS or COPARENTS; and others who have short- or longer-term care of the child, such as BABYSITTER, NANNY, AU PAIR, PARENT'S HELPER, or other CHILD CARE worker. More widely, the terms *caregiver* and *caretaker* refer to anyone who meets the physical, emotional, and social needs of others, though "caretaker" is more often used in relation to care for heavily dependent people past infancy, such as adults with severe disabilities.

carrier, someone who carries something that can cause a disease or a disorder, such as bacteria or a malfunctioning RECESSIVE gene, and is unaffected by it, but may pass it on to others. A woman who passes on an X-LINKED GENETIC DISORDER to her sons is a carrier, as is someone who passes on a hepatitis virus (see LIVER AND LIVER PROBLEMS).

catastrophic reaction, unrestrained actions in response to an apparently minor situation that to a child is frightening, threatening, frustrating, overstimulating, or otherwise upsetting. The child may, for example, scream uncontrollably, bang his or her head on the floor, throw things, or cry unconsolably. Children with LEARNING DISABILITIES or MENTAL DISORDERS are especially susceptible to this kind of reaction, but many children will occasionally respond with a catastrophic reaction to unexpected or disturbing changes in routine or to pressure to achieve more than their present skills allow.

categorical aid, governmental financial assistance given to people who fit into a certain category, such as children with DISABILITIES, rather than people who pass a MEANS TEST. Much assistance under SOCIAL SECURITY is categorical; an example is the AID TO FAMILIES WITH DEPENDENT CHILDREN program.

catheter, a hollow, flexible tube that can be inserted into the body through a blood vessel or natural body opening to withdraw or remove fluid and sometimes to aid in diagnosis of a disorder. Using a technique called CLEAN, INTERMITTENT CATHETERIZATION, some children, such as those with SPINA BIFIDA, learn at a very early age to insert a catheter into themselves to drain urine from their bladders, to prevent kidney damage or infection.

cathexis, powerful concentration of emotion on a particular person, place, or thing, or on one's self. When such a concentration becomes painful or troubling, DISPLACEMENT may occur, in which the emotion becomes focused on another person or object instead.

Cattell Infant Intelligence Scale, an individually administered INTELLIGENCE TEST used to assess the mental development of children aged three to thirty months. Various objects, such as cubes, pencils, and pegboards, are used as stimuli to assess the child's motor control. The test administrator takes notes on the responses and also on the infant's attempts to communicate. (See TESTS.)

ceiling age, in an INTELLIGENCE TEST, notably the STANFORD-BINET INTELLIGENCE TEST, the age level at which a child cannot complete any questions correctly. The opposite is the *basal age*.

celiac sprue (celiac disease), a type of FOOD INTOLERANCE involving a sensitivity to *gluten*, the insoluble PRO-

TEIN that is part of wheat, rye, barley, and some other grains; also called *gluten-induced enteropathy* (GSE), literally an ailment of the intestine caused by gluten. Celiac sprue runs in families, and so may be a form of GENETIC DISORDER, but its exact pattern of inheritance is not fully known. Sensitized and damaged by contact with gluten, the intestines become unable to properly absorb other kinds of nutrients, the result being MALABSORPTION and often severe MALNUTRITION. Also characteristic is an itchy rash on limbs, back, and buttocks, called *dermatitis herpetiformes* (DH). Other symptoms of celiac sprue include pale, fatty, foul-smelling feces, DIARRHEA, VOMITING, DEHYDRATION, and buildup of acids in the body, which can be severe and even life-threatening in infants, and can stunt both physical and intellectual development.

In its classic form, celiac sprue has its onset between ages six and eighteen months, but in many cases symptoms do not emerge until years later. Until properly diagnosed, it can sometimes be mistaken for other disorders, such CYSTIC FIBROSIS or various food ALLERGIES, and is sometimes associated with LACTOSE INTOLERANCE, sensitivity to milk. Parents with a family history of food allergies and a child with puzzling symptoms may wish to have the child checked for celiac sprue. It is generally diagnosed by a BIOPSY of the intestinal lining. Some kinds of BLOOD TESTS can also be used as screening for asymptomatic celiac sprue.

The treatment is a gluten-restricted diet, avoiding all products made from wheat, rye, barley, and sometimes oats, including breads, cereals, and pasta; rice and corn are then the main grains in the diet, with the rest of the food groups all available. The symptoms generally begin to recede within a few weeks, though when the intestine has been severely damaged recovery may be slow.

FOR HELP AND FURTHER INFORMATION

Celiac Sprue Association/United States of America (CSA/USA)
P.O. Box 31700
Omaha, Nebraska 68131
402–558–0600
Leon R. Rotmann, Executive Director
Organization concerned with celiac sprue and dermatitis herpetiformis; provides information and referrals; publishes various materials, including quarterly *Lifeline*; *A Basic Primer on Celiac Sprue* (video); *Handbook: On the Celiac Condition*; *Basics for the Gluten-Free Diet*, information sheets *Celiac Sprue, Parents of Children with Celiac Sprue, Your Student Has Celiac Disease*, and *Dermatitis Herpetiformis*; listing of gluten-free products; and cookbooks.

American Celiac Society/Dietary Support Coalition (ACS/DSC)
58 Musano Court
West Orange, NJ 07052–4114
201–325–8837
Annette Bentley, Executive Director
Organization concerned with celiac sprue, gluten (wheat) intolerance, Crohn's disease, lactose intolerance, food allergies, and related dietary disorders; provides information and referrals; publishes newsletter and bulletins.

Gluten Intolerance Group of North America (GIG)
P.O. Box 23055
Seattle, WA 98102
206–325–6980
Elaine I. Hartsook, Executive Director
Organization concerned with celiac sprue or dermatitis herpetiformis; provides information, counseling, and referrals; maintains library of videos for rental or purchase; publishes various materials, including quarterly *GIG Newsletter*, *GIG Cookbook*, foreign-language travel aids, cookbooks, and patient packets, including resource guides, diet instructions, and bread recipes.

National Digestive Disease Information Clearinghouse (NDDIC), 301–654–3810. (For full group information, see DIGESTIVE SYSTEM AND DISORDERS.)

National Organization for Rare Disorders (NORD), 800–999–6673. (For full group information, see RARE DISORDERS.)

American Allergy Association (AAA), 415–322–1663. Publishes *Eating Without, Guide to Gluten-Free Diets, Allergic to Wheat?*, and *Allergy Alerts*. (For full group information, see ALLERGY.)

(See also METABOLIC DISORDERS; DIGESTIVE SYSTEM AND DISORDERS.)

centesis, a type of SPECIMEN TEST in which a fluid sample is taken from the body using a hollow needle (*aspiration needle*), as in the MEDICAL TEST called AMNIOCENTESIS.

central nervous system (CNS), in anatomy, the system made up of the brain and spinal cord that receives information from, interprets, and transmits information to the rest of the body, served by a network of nerves called the PERIPHERAL NERVOUS SYTEM (PNS). The CNS is extremely sensitive to injury, and damage to it is generally irreparable, causing long-term DISABILITY. By contrast, the effects of injury to nerves in the outlying peripheral nervous system are more local and responsive to surgery.

FOR HELP AND FURTHER REFERENCE

The Central Nervous System: Structure and Function. Per Brodal. Oxford University Press, 1992.
Nervous System. Alvin Silverstein and others. Twenty First Century Books, 1994. For children.

(See also BRAIN AND BRAIN DISORDERS; SPINE AND SPINAL DISORDERS.)

central register, in relation to CHILD ABUSE AND NEGLECT, a collection of reports held in some central agency. Arrangements vary by state, but the purpose of the central register is to provided a place for SOCIAL WORKERS and others to check, in cases of suspected child abuse, to see if any previous such reports have been filed. Critics warn that such files are not always kept fully confidential and that unverified reports are not always cleared from the register.

cephalopelvic disproportion, a condition in which a baby's head is too large for the mother's pelvis, leading to difficult and sometimes impossible LABOR.

cerebral palsy (CP), a disorder caused by damage to the brain, especially affecting ability to control movement and posture. *Palsy* is a synonym for PARALYSIS, although a more accurate description of the usual muscular symptoms might be weakness (*paresis*) and inability to make voluntary movements and suppress involuntary ones. Depending on the location and extent of the damage, cerebral palsy can be mild, revealing itself as a kind of awkwardness, or severe, largely incapacitating a child from infancy. It is sometimes associated with other problems such as SEIZURES (EPILEPSY), MENTAL RETARDATION, EAR AND HEARING PROBLEMS, EYE AND VISION PROBLEMS, communication problems (see COMMUNICATION SKILLS AND DISORDERS), and impairment of other senses. Some of the children most severely affected with cerebral palsy may not survive infancy, but most will have a normal life span.

Cerebral palsy is not contagious. It is not PROGRESSIVE—it does not get worse as time passes and may instead improve somewhat with therapy (see discussion of treatment later in this entry). It is not inherited, except in rare cases in which it is associated with a GENETIC DISORDER, notably LESCH-NYHAN SYNDROME. Most cases, caused by brain damage during PREGNANCY, CHILDBIRTH, or the neonatal period (just after birth), are called *congenital cerebral palsy*, because the disorder is present at or around the time of birth. However, approximately 10 percent of the cases are *acquired cerebral palsy*, in which CP has been triggered by events after birth: TRAUMATIC BRAIN INJURY, infections such as MENINGITIS, and other types of brain damage, including injury from CHILD ABUSE AND NEGLECT.

Just why CP occurs is far from clear. Approximately 58 percent of the cases of cerebral palsy occur in children who are born at full term and full weight and in whom doctors can discern no cause of brain damage, given the present state of knowledge and technology. However, studies have shown that numerous conditions are RISK FACTORS for cerebral palsy. These factors don't necessarily lead to the disorder, but increase the risk that a child will have it. Among the main risk factors are:

- Infections in the mother during pregnancy, including RUBELLA (German measles); SEXUALLY TRANSMITTED DISEASES such as GONORRHEA, CHLAMYDIA, and SYPHILIS; and various other bacterial and viral infections, some of which attack the baby's NERVOUS SYSTEM.
- PREMATURE birth.
- LOW BIRTH WEIGHT, though some infants who weigh under two pounds at birth and spend months in neonatal intensive care have been unimpaired.
- Difficult or abnormal delivery, especially awkward FETAL PRESENTATION (position at birth), lengthy or too abrupt labor, or obstruction of the UMBILICAL CORD.
- HYPOXIA, or insufficient oxygen, in the brain, for a variety of reasons, such as premature separation of the PLACENTA during delivery or swelling of the brain due to illness.
- Incompatability between parents' and fetus's blood types, especially RH INCOMPATIBILITY.
- Jaundice of the newborn or hyperbilirubinemia (see LIVER AND LIVER PROBLEMS), sometimes associated with Rh incompatibility.
- Medications taken and DRUG ABUSE by the mother.
- LEAD POISONING.
- SMOKING by the mother.
- ALCOHOL ABUSE by the mother.

With increased knowledge, developing technology, and enhanced PRENATAL CARE, the risks of CP can be much diminished, even if the condition cannot be completely prevented. Precise figures are hard to come by because of wide variations in the disorder and because doctors are not required to report it. But the United Cerebral Palsy Association estimates that approximately 3,000 infants are born with cerebral palsy each year, and some 500 other preschool-age children later acquire the condition.

Cerebral palsy is generally recognized in a child's early years, as DEVELOPMENTAL DELAY becomes apparent. Though various kinds of medical SCANS can help doctors identify some brain abnormalities, the disorder is most often diagnosed from its symptoms. These may include:

- Retention of PRIMITIVE REFLEXES, involuntary reactions to particular stimuli that are normally found only in newborns.
- Muscular weakness and "floppiness" (HYPOTONIA).
- Assumption of abnormal, awkward positions, which (if uncorrected) can lead to skeletal disorders.
- Favoring one side of the body over the other.
- Poor muscle control and lack of coordination.
- Muscle spasms or seizures.
- Problems with sucking, chewing, and swallowing.
- Unusual tenseness and irritability in infancy.
- Inability to control bladder and bowels (INCONTINENCE).
- Difficulty in speaking.
- Difficulty in concentrating, which has adverse effects on learning.
- Trouble in interpreting sense perceptions, such as inability to identify objects by touch.
- Other problems with the senses, especially with hearing and vision.

Some children may show serious symptoms at birth; some may not show any clear signs for a long time. Most children with cerebral palsy are diagnosed by age five. It is important to diagnose the disorder early so that therapy can minimize handicaps, learning is not hindered, and the child (and parents) can adjust more readily.

Doctors classify cerebral palsy in two ways: by the affected limbs and by the nature of the movement disturbance.

BY AFFECTED LIMBS

- *Diplegia*, when limbs on opposite sides are affected, such as both legs.
- *Hemiplegia* or *hemiparesis*, when the arm and leg on one side are affected.
- *Quadriplegia* or *quadriparesis*, when all four limbs are affected.

BY THE NATURE OF THE MOVEMENT DISTURBANCE

- *Spastic cerebral palsy*, when muscles are tense, contracted, and resistant to movement; the most common form of cerebral palsy, especially in infants whose birth weight is low or in premature babies.
- *Athetoid cerebral palsy*, when the affected parts of the body perform involuntary writhing movements, such as turning, twisting, facial grimacing, and drooling, often associated with jerky, abrupt, flailing motions (CHOREA). This form of cerebral palsy generally involves damage only to the motor centers, not to other parts of the brain. But those unfamiliar with the disorder often take "strange" and "unnatural" movements, such as flailing and grimacing, as signs of mental or emotional disturbance.
- *Ataxic cerebral palsy*, when the main characteristic is lack of balance and coordination and disturbed depth perception, due to damage to the cerebellum. ATAXIA involves trouble maintaining balance and swaying when standing.
- *Rigidity*, when muscles are extremely tight and resistant to movement.
- *Tremor*, when muscles shake uncontrollably, interfering with coordination.

Sometimes several areas of the brain are involved, so the description of a particular child's condition may incorporate several of the above terms and symptoms.

No cure exists for cerebral palsy, but various kinds of therapies are used to help each child do as much as he or she is capable of. Among these are:

- *Physical therapy*, the use of therapeutic exercises and activities to extend the child's range of controlled movement, generally focusing on gross MOTOR SKILLS. Some of these use the *Bobath technique*, in which exercises first focus on countering primitive reflexes. Therapy then aims at extending the range of voluntary movement, sometimes with the help of BEHAVIOR MODIFICATION, which offers positive reinforcement to help the child act against the body's awkward inclinations. Physical therapists also help children learn how to use ORTHOPEDIC DEVICES, such as wheelchairs and walkers.
- BIOFEEDBACK, in which a child is given information about the functioning of a particular part of the body. Often the body is hooked up to an electrical machine that produces visual or auditory signals; the child is taught to concentrate on changing the visual picture or sound. Through such techniques, children with cerebral palsy can gain increased control over movements and are sometimes able to do things like drink from a cup or control their bladder—things previously beyond their range of skills.
- *Occupational therapy*, the use of therapeutic exercises and activities to extend the child's range of controlled movement, generally focusing on fine motor skills, many of which are SELF-HELP SKILLS. For children, that may mean learning how to dress themselves, comb their hair, brush their teeth, drink from a cup, or hold a pen or pencil. For young adults, the skills include preparation for living as self-sufficiently and independently as possible (see VOCATIONAL REHABILITATION SERVICES).
- *Speech and language therapy*, which can help children overcome some speech and hearing impairments and also help them learn to use the great variety of mechanical and electronic devices that have been developed to aid them, such as voice synthesizers or specially adapted computers (see EAR AND HEARING PROBLEMS; COMMUNICATION SKILLS AND DISORDERS).
- *Drugs*, including muscle relaxants for spastic muscles and antiseizure drugs if epilepsy is involved. Drugs are best used sparingly, however, since the long-term side effects on the already-damaged and still-developing nervous system are unknown.
- *Surgery*, which can be helpful in dealing with certain specific problems, such as those involving eyes, ears, and gait; brain surgery may help some, but is still experimental.
- ORTHOPEDIC DEVICES, such as wheelchairs, walkers, page-turners, specially equipped automobiles, and the like.

Many physical therapists stress that a varied and stimulating environment is in itself a powerful "treatment" for the child. Also important to both child and family are counseling, which can offer emotional support and relief of stress, advice on handling practical problems, and training to prepare for the future as the child grows into an adult. Many public and private organizations also provide financial assistance, diagnostic and treatment centers, vocational training and guidance, RESPITE CARE for families of children with cerebral palsy, special recreational facilities, adapted work settings, and adapted living arrangements. (See also HELP FOR SPECIAL CHILDREN on page 689.) (Subscribers to the America Online computer service can find "Will My Child Ever Walk?" in the Moms Online Desk Reference section of Moms Online, under "cerebral palsy.")

FOR HELP AND FURTHER INFORMATION

United Cerebral Palsy Association (UCPA)
1660 L Street NW, Suite 700
Washington, DC 20036–5602
202–776–0406; 202–973–7197, TT; 800-USA–5UCP [872–5827] voice/TT
Fax: 202–776–0414
E-mail: ucpa@aol.com (America Online: UCPA)
John D. Kemp, Executive Director
Organization concerned with cerebral palsy and related handicaps; provides information and referrals; acts as advocate; sponsors research; publishes many materials, including *Children with Cerebral Palsy: A Parents' Guide, Handling the Young Cerebral Palsied Child at Home, After the Tears: Parents Talk About Raising a Child with a Disability, Each of Us Remembers: Parents of Children with Cerebral Palsy Answer Your Questions, I Wish: Dreams and Realities of Parenting a Special Needs Child, I Raise My Eyes to Say Yes: A Memoir, A Mother's Touch: The Tiffany Callo Story* (about a woman with CP and her fight to raise her own children), and *Walk with Me* (by an 8-year-old with CP).

National Institute of Neurological Disorders and Stroke (NINDS), 800–352–9424. Publishes brochure *Cerebral Palsy: Hope Through Research.* (For full group information, see BRAIN AND BRAIN DISORDERS.)

Shriner's Hospitals for Crippled Children, 800–237–5055. Provides free medical care for children with orthopedic problems. (For full group information, see BONE AND BONE DISORDERS.)

Pediatric Projects, 800–947–0947. Publishes reprint *Raising a CP Child in a Rural Area.* (For full group information, see HOSPITAL.)

National Information Center for Children and Youth with Disabilities (NICHCY), 800–695–0285, voice/TT. Publishes *Cerebral Palsy.* (For full group information, see HELP FOR SPECIAL CHILDREN on page 832.)

National Easter Seal Society, 800–221–6827. Publishes *Understanding Cerebral Palsy.* (For full group information, see HELP FOR SPECIAL CHILDREN on page 689.)

American Association of University Affiliated Programs for Persons with Developmental Disabilities (AAUAP), 301–588–8252. (For full group information, see HELP FOR SPECIAL CHILDREN on page 689.)

National Organization for Rare Disorders (NORD), 800–999–6673. (For full group information, see RARE DISORDERS.)

OTHER RESOURCES

FOR PARENTS

Coping with Cerebral Palsy: Answers to Questions Parents Often Ask, 2nd ed. Jay Schleichkorn. PRO-ED, 1993.

Children with Cerebral Palsy: A Parents' Guide. Elaine Geralis, ed. Woodbine House, 1991.

FOR CHILDREN AND PRETEENS

Yes, I Can: Challenging Cerebral Palsy. Doris Sanford. Questar, 1992.

Going Places: Children Living with Cerebral Palsy. Thomas Bergman. Gareth Stevens, 1991.

Arnie and the New Kid. Nancy Carlson. Viking, 1990.

FOR TEENS

Cerebral Palsy. Nathan Aaseng. Watts, 1991.

BACKGROUND BOOKS

Cerebral Palsy: The Child and Young Person. L. Cogher. Chapman and Hall, 1992.

(See also ORTHOPEDIC DEVICES; also HELP FOR SPECIAL CHILDREN on page 689.)

cerebrospinal fluid (CSF), the fluid that circulates throughout the brain and spinal cord. In some kinds of MEDICAL TESTS, such as the LUMBAR PUNCTURE or *cisternal puncture*, samples of CSF may be taken for analysis or removed and replaced by a dyed fluid that shows up in images, as in MYELOGRAM. In some cases of BRAIN TUMORS, a SHUNT may be inserted in the skull to allow the cerebrospinal fluid to flow freely past an inoperable obstruction. (See BRAIN AND BRAIN DISORDERS; SPINE AND SPINAL DISORDERS.)

certificate of attendance, a document confirming that a student attended school during certain specified periods. Such a certificate is often given to a student who will not be obtaining either a DIPLOMA or a CERTIFICATE OF COMPLETION, such as a student with MENTAL RETARDATION who has passed beyond normal school age, but has attended school regularly, taking a CURRICULUM focusing on FUNCTIONAL SKILLS.

certificate of completion, a document confirming that a student has successfully completed a course of study, usually courses that do not carry credit toward GRADUATION; sometimes called a *certificate of training.*

certificate of high school equivalency, a document awarded to a student who has achieved passing scores on TESTS OF GENERAL EDUCATIONAL DEVELOPMENT or their recognized equivalents; also called GENERAL EQUIVALENCY DIPLOMAS. Such certificates, given by a state education department or other authorized agency, are accepted as the equivalent of a high school DIPLOMA by employers and in postsecondary schools, such as COLLEGES or PROPRIETARY SCHOOLS. High school DROPOUTS who do not return to finish their schooling in a formal way, may study on their own, as through INDEPENDENT STUDY, and obtain a high school equivalency certificate.

certified nurse-midwife (CNM), a registered nurse with special training in advising women during normal PREGNANCY as part of PRENATAL CARE, counseling on such matters as NUTRITION, EXERCISE, and preparation for CHILDBIRTH. The certified nurse-midwife assists during LABOR, DELIVERY, and PERINATAL CARE and provides after-birth instruction on self-care and infant care, including BREASTFEEDING or BOTTLEFEEDING. However, a woman with a HIGH-RISK PREGNANCY would be referred to a physician—usually to an OBSTETRICIAN-GYNECOLOGIST or FETAL AND MATERNAL SPECIALIST—early in her pregnancy. Also, if complications develop during the birth, a doctor may be called in or the woman and baby transported on an emergency basis to a HOSPITAL.

Unlike traditional *lay midwives*, who may have experience in assisting at childbirth but no formal training or certification, CNMs must meet certain training and licensing requirements. Most CNMs (approximately 85 percent) work in hospitals or HEALTH MAINTENANCE ORGANIZATIONS (HMOs) as part of the obstetrical team delivering babies in normal or low-risk pregnancies, often in hospital-connected birthing center. Approximately 11 percent of CNM-attended births take place in MATERNITY CENTERS (alternative birthing centers) and some 4 percent are HOME BIRTHS.

In some states, certified nurse-midwives can practice independently, but in many states they must practice in association with a doctor. In areas where midwifery is discouraged, however, their activities are restricted because they have difficulty finding doctors and hospitals who will associate with them to provide required backup medical care. This can mean that backup hospitals are not close by, a potential danger if an emergency occurs during delivery. Parents who wish to be attended by a CNM at delivery should carefully examine the backup arrangements, in case emergency medical care is needed. Often parents themselves must provide emergency transportation to the hospital. Fees for CNMs (but not for lay midwives) are covered by many HEALTH INSURANCE plans, public and private.

The midwifery movement has much expanded in recent decades, partly in reaction to hospital birthing practices, which many people came to see as cold, impersonal, and invasive. In response, the hospitals themselves have changed somewhat. CNMs have been recognized for their role in providing prenatal care, especially for women at high risk of have low birth weight babies in underserved rural and inner-city areas. They are often employed by public health departments for that purpose.

FOR HELP AND FURTHER INFORMATION

American College of Nurse-Midwives (ACNM)
1522 K Street NW, Suite 1000
Washington, DC 20005
202–728–9860
Ronald E. Nitzsche, Chief Operating Officer
Organization of certified nurse midwives; seeks to educate public; serves as accrediting agency for nurse-midwife education programs; provides information and referrals.

March of Dimes Birth Defects Foundation (MDBDF), 914–428–7100. Some local chapters have available certified midwives. (For full group information, see BIRTH DEFECTS.)

OTHER RESOURCES

Choosing a Nurse-Midwife: Your Guide to Safe, Sensitive Care During Pregnancy and the Birth of Your Child. Catherine Poole and Elizabeth Parr. Wiley, 1994.

A Nurse-Midwife's Guide to Pregnancy and Childbirth. Budlong, 1994.

The Midwife's Pregnancy and Childbirth Book: Having Your Baby Your Way. Marion McCartney and Antonia Van der Meer. Holt, 1990.

cervical cap, a form of BIRTH CONTROL that consists of a rubber cup, used with SPERMICIDE cream or jelly, that fits tightly over the cervix. Used widely in Europe, the cervical cap was approved for use in the United States in 1988. Here it must be fitted by a doctor and is available only by prescription. The cap is harder to insert and remove than a DIAPHRAGM, but the Food and Drug Administration (FDA) rates both as having roughly the same effectiveness—between 90 and 98 percent. The cervical cap is inserted before sexual intercourse and can remain in place for forty-eight hours. Unlike the diaphragm, it does not require additional spermicide for repeated intercourse.

Women and their sex partners can have allergic reactions to the rubber or to the spermicide, and they are warned to discontinue use and see a doctor in case of any genital burning or irritation. (For information on other possible problems, such as BIRTH DEFECTS, see SPERMICIDE.)

The cervical cap carries some increased risk of an abnormal PAP SMEAR, TOXIC SHOCK SYNDROME, and infections of the VAGINA, cervix, or UTERUS. The cap should not be inserted or used during MENSTRUATION or just after CHILDBIRTH or ABORTION. Used with spermicide, the cervical cap gives some protection against SEXUALLY TRANSMITTED DISEASES, though it should not be regarded as protection against AIDS.

Several alternative forms of cervical cap are being explored. The *Fem cap*, also of silicone rubber, has a "brim" that helps create an airtight seal with the vaginal walls; it would require fitting by a doctor. Two over-the-counter alternatives are the *Oves cervical cap*, made of clear, flexible silicone rubber and disposable, and *LEAs Shield*, a silicone rubber cap, with a special loop to allow for easy insertion and removal, that can be reused more than twenty times. (See BIRTH CONTROL.)

cervical mucus method, a BIRTH CONTROL approach that involves monitoring changes in the mucus secreted by a woman's CERVIX to determine when OVULA-

TION has taken place; a type of NATURAL FAMILY PLANNING that employs periodic abstinence during a woman's fertile period as a means of CONTRACEPTION. The same techniques may be used to identify the most likely time for CONCEPTION in dealing with INFERTILITY. (See NATURAL FAMILY PLANNING.)

cervical sponge, an over-the-counter, single-use, disposable form of BIRTH CONTROL that consists of a soft, slightly cup-shaped sponge saturated with a SPERMICIDE that forms both a physical and chemical barrier to SPERM. The sponge is inserted into the VAGINA and positioned to cover the CERVIX before sexual intercourse. It should be left in place for at least six and up to twenty-four hours after intercourse. During that time intercourse can be repeated, if desired. After removal, the sponge should be thrown away and not reused. The Food and Drug Administration (FDA) rates the cervical sponge as 80 to 87 percent effective as a contraceptive. It gives some protection against SEXUALLY TRANSMITTED DISEASES, but should not be regarded as protection against AIDS.

Sometimes women or their sexual partners have allergic reactions to the sponge; the woman should discontinue use if either she or her partner experience irritation or burning. Although it requires no fitting, some women, especially those with ARTHRITIS, can have difficulty inserting, positioning, and removing the sponge. (See SPERMICIDE for other possible problems, including BIRTH DEFECTS.) The sponge can sometimes fragment on removal, causing infection, and has on rare occasions been linked with cases of TOXIC SHOCK SYNDROME. In 1995, the American maker of the cervical sponge ceased its manufacture after the FDA found bacterial contamination of the product resulting from problems the firm thought too costly to correct. (See BIRTH CONTROL.)

cervix, the small, fibrous neck of the UTERUS, which during CHILDBIRTH widens greatly to form (with the VAGINA) the *birth canal*, the passageway through which the baby is normally delivered. Blood also exits the uterus by way of the cervix during MENSTRUATION. After sexual intercourse, SPERM must pass through the cervix from the vagina into the uterus. The cervix secretes a mucus that sometimes makes that passage more difficult but around the time of ovulation often makes it easier. Changes in the cervical mucus at around the time of ovulation are used in some methods of BIRTH CONTROL (see NATURAL FAMILY PLANNING). During PREGNANCY, the cervix becomes longer and more muscular, helping to hold the developing FETUS in the uterus. Then, as a woman's body prepares for LABOR and DELIVERY, the cervix shortens and widens dramatically to form part of the birth canal.

The cervix is subject to a number of disorders that can affect the REPRODUCTIVE SYSTEM, including:

- *inflammation of the cervix (cervicitis)*, which can result from a variety of infections, especially SEXUALLY TRANSMITTED DISEASES such as CHLAMYDIA, GONORRHEA, HERPES, and GENITAL WARTS. These can readily spread to infect the uterus (*endometritis*) and FALLOPIAN TUBES (*salpingitis*), causing possible INFERTILITY; some viruses also increase the risk of cancer.
- TUMORS, a variety of growths that can appear in or on the cervix, many of them small BENIGN growths called *polyps*, but some MALIGNANT (see CANCER). The PAP SMEAR test involves checking cervical cells for signs of possible malignancy. Women who are sexually very active and who have multiple sex partners are at increased risk for cervical cancer, partly because of exposure to viruses.
- *Injury*, notably tears or strains sustained during CHILDBIRTH, especially after a long, difficult delivery or during a badly performed ABORTION. Sometimes injuries are substantial enough to cause internal bleeding and require major surgery. In most cases, the injuries heal, but they may leave the muscle weakened, so that in a future pregnancy the cervix cannot hold the FETUS properly in place, a condition called INCOMPETENT CERVIX. If not recognized and treated, this condition could lead to MISCARRIAGE or PREMATURE delivery.

If a woman has cervicitis at the time of delivery, her baby can also be infected at birth, with serious consequences including possible blindness (see EYE AND VISION PROBLEMS) and pneumonia (see LUNG AND BREATHING DISORDERS). Symptoms of any such condition should be discussed with the doctor before the birth and treated, if possible; if not, a CESAREAN SECTION may be indicated.

FOR HELP AND FURTHER INFORMATION

American College of Obstetricians and Gynecologists (ACOG), 202–638–5577. Publishes *The Pap Test* and *Dilation and Curettage (D&C)*. (For full group information, see PREGNANCY.)

National Cancer Institute (NCI), 800–422–6237. Publishes *Having a Pelvic Exam and Pap Test, The Pap Test: It Can Save Your Life!*, and *What You Need to Know About Cancer of the Cervix*. (For full group information, see CANCER.)

(See also PREGNANCY; OVULATION; NATURAL FAMILY PLANNING.)

cesarean section (C-section), a surgical procedure to deliver a baby through an incision in a woman's abdomen, in cases when delivery through the VAGINA is impossible or dangerous to mother or child; also called an *abdominal delivery*. In decades past, the incision was usually a vertical cut made high on the abdomen, the so-called *classical uterine incision*. For various reasons, some doctors used a vertical incision low on the abdomen (*low vertical incision*) or two incisions, one vertical, one horizontal (*inverted-T incision*). These types of incisions carry the risk of causing the UTERUS to rupture during future pregnancies, which led to the once-widespread medical rule "once a cesarean, always a cesarean."

But in recent years, most physicians have instead used a horizontal incision low on the abdomen, called a *low transverse uterine incision* or *bikini cut.* With this approach, many women have been able to deliver a later child normally through the vagina rather than necessarily having repeat cesareans for any future children. Various organizations (see the list that follows) have been created to promote the idea of *vaginal birth after cesarean section* (VABC). Such births are possible because the conditions that indicate a cesarean section in one birth often are not present in a later one.

Generally a matter of medical choice, Cesarean sections are performed for a variety of reasons for the safety of mother and/or child; they are not usually chosen out of absolute necessity. Among the situations in which cesareans are often performed are:

- FETAL DISTRESS, in which the baby has insufficient oxygen during difficult labor.
- *Problems with the* PLACENTA, the organ that nourishes the fetus, including *placenta previa* and *abruptio placenta* (see PLACENTA).
- *Active infection in the mother,* which might damage the child, as when a HERPES infection in the genitals could cause blindness or other BIRTH DEFECTS.
- *Abnormal* FETAL PRESENTATION, such as *breech presentation* (feet or buttocks down) or *transverse lie* (horizontal position), rather than a vertical, head-down presentation.
- *Baby too large for mother's pelvis,* which may become apparent in late stages of labor.
- MULTIPLE BIRTHS, which often involve some of the above difficulties, especially abnormal presentation and fetal distress.
- PROLAPSE of the UMBILICAL CORD, in which the cord drops down into the VAGINA, possibly endangering the baby's oxygen supply.
- DYSTOCIA, or difficulties that cause labor to cease, often because the mother is overtired or because of abnormalities in the shape of her internal organs.
- *Previous cesarean section* with a vertical or other problem incision.

Today the C-section itself is often performed under local (epidural) ANESTHESIA. The bladder is emptied by a CATHETER, the AMNIOTIC FLUID drained off by suction, the baby delivered through the incision, and the placenta (afterbirth) removed. Though the cesarean using epidural anesthesia is still major surgery, recovery is generally faster than when general anesthesia is used.

The number of cesareans has risen dramatically in the past two decades, partly because it has become a safer operation and partly because OBSTETRICIANS are concerned about malpractice charges if mother or baby experience problems resulting from difficult labor. Some studies have found a wide variation in the frequency of cesarean sections, depending on the area, the doctor, and to some extent the socioeconomic level of the community; more C-sections generally are performed in affluent areas.

When choosing an obstetrician, prospective parents may want to discuss the question of C-sections and when they should and should not be used. They should be sure that they are comfortable with their chosen doctor's approach; if not, they should choose another doctor. In selecting a HOSPITAL, parents-to-be should find out the hospital's policies on allowing husbands to attend a C-section delivery. Some hospitals allow fathers to be present; others do not, because of increased risk of infection, crowded operating-room quarters, and the possibility of the father fainting. Since the mother is under only a local anesthetic, the father can give her emotional support.

For a subsequent birth after a previous C-section, parents may want to explore the hospital's policy of allowing at least a *trial of labor,* rather than automatically assuming that the next child will also be delivered by cesarean. One advantage of the trial of labor is that it indicates when the baby is ready to be born; otherwise, when the DUE DATE is uncertain, doctors may opt for a cesarean section when the baby is, in fact, PREMATURE, causing medical problems that need not have existed.

FOR HELP AND FURTHER INFORMATION

C/SEC (Cesareans/Support, Education, and Concern)
22 Forest Road
Framingham, MA 01701
508–877–8266
Organization concerned with cesarean deliveries, especially preventing unnecessary cesareans, encouraging family-centered birth and hospital care, and stressing vaginal birth after cesarean; provides information and referrals; publishes various materials.

American College of Obstetricians and Gynecologists (ACOG), 202–638–5577. Publishes *Cesarean Birth* and *Vaginal Birth After Cesarean Delivery.* (For full group information, see PREGNANCY.)

International Cesarean Awareness Network (ICAN)
c/o April Kubachka
1657 West 259th Place
Harbor City, CA 90710
310–530–5545
Organization concerned with increased rate of cesareans; formerly Cesarean Prevention Movement (CPM); provides referrals to physicians who support vaginal birth after a cesarean; publishes various materials, including quarterly newspaper and *Cesarean Facts.*

National Institute of Child Health and Human Development (NICHD), 301–496–5133. Publishes *Facts About Cesarean Childbirth.* (For full group information, see PREGNANCY.)

OTHER RESOURCES

Trust Your Body! Trust Your Baby!: Childbirth Wisdom and Cesarean Prevention. Andrea F. Henkart. Bergin and Garvey/Greenwood, 1995.

Having a Cesarean Baby: The Complete Guide for a Happy and Safe Cesarean Childbirth Experience, 2nd ed. Richard Hausknecht and Joan R. Heilman. NAL-Dutton, 1991.
Recovering from a "C" Section. Margaret Blackstone and Tahira Humayun. Longmeadow Press, 1991.
The Expectant Parent's Guide to Preventing a Cesarean Section. Carl Jones. Bergin & Garvey/Greenwood, 1991.
Birth After Cesarean: The Medical Facts. Bruce L. Flamm. Prentice Hall, 1990.

changed circumstance, in family law, a substantial change in a family situation, such as sharp drop or increase in income and hence in ability to pay, a geographical move, or an illness or DISABILITY in the child or in either parent. Such a substantial change is generally necessary before the court will consider reviewing such matters as CUSTODY, VISITATION RIGHTS, or CHILD SUPPORT.

Chapter 1, shorthand name for a federal program to fund educational programs for students primarily from low-income families, especially for those who have fallen below grade level in key skills such as mathematics, READING, and writing. The program was created under Chapter 1 of Title I of the Elementary and Secondary Education Act of 1965, as amended by Chapter 1 of the Education Consolidation and Improvement Act of 1981, and the Hawkins-Stafford Elementary and Secondary School Improvements Amendments of 1988. Under these laws, each year the federal government sends a grant of money to each state (to *state educational agencies,* or SEAs), which then distribute the money to school districts based on the number of low-income families they serve. Local school districts (sometimes called *local education agencies,* or LEAs) then select "target schools"—those with the most children from low-income families—and the students in those schools most in need of help, as indicated by TEST scores, school reports, and teachers' evaluations, whether these specific children are from low-income families or not.

The LEAs then develop programs to help those students, involving parents wherever possible, setting goals, and evaluating student progress along the way. These plans are reviewed and revised annually, if goals are not being met. Chapter 1 funds are often used to provide smaller classes, more teachers and teaching aides, extra REMEDIAL INSTRUCTION in key skills, and more varied teaching approaches and materials.

FOR HELP AND FURTHER INFORMATION

National Coalition of Title I/Chapter I Parents (NCTCP)
National Parent Center
Edmonds School Building
9th & D Streets NE, 2nd Floor
Washington, DC 20002
202–547–9286
Fax: 202–544–2813
Marilyn Aklin, Director
Organization of parents, educators, and others concerned with the education of children falling under federal Title 1 or Chapter 1 programs—primarily children who are educationally disadvantaged in reading or mathematics; provides information to parents and professionals; offers training and technical help to parents and local groups; runs National Parent Center, seeking to increase parent involvement in children's education; publishes various materials, including bimonthly newsletter and handbook.

Center for Law and Education, 202–986–3000. Publishes *Chapter 1 Advocacy Handbook: Making the Chapter 1 Program Work in the Schools.* (For full group information, see HELP ON LEARNING AND EDUCATION on page 659.)

(See also EDUCATION.)

chicken pox (varicella), a highly communicable disease caused by the *varicella-zoster virus* (VZV, a type of HERPES virus), generally characterized by a rash of fluid-filled blisters. It is spread from person to person in droplets from coughing, sneezing, or just talking, or by contact with fluid from broken blisters. The disease can be transmitted from one to two days before the rash appears and lasts until all the blisters have dried, usually about four to five days.

For most children, the disease takes a mild form, involving a slight fever and a rash of blisters, which children must be kept from scratching to avoid bacterial infection. However inconvenient, the disease is often so mild that some doctors used to recommend that children be exposed to chicken pox young when it will do them little or no harm. Most people have, in fact, had the disease by age ten, and so have lifelong IMMUNIZATION from further attacks.

But for adolescents, adults, or children with lowered resistance, for instance those with LEUKEMIA, chicken pox can be a very serious matter, sometimes involving PNEUMONIA, various breathing difficulties (partly from blisters in the throat), and on rare occasions ENCEPHALITIS (inflammation of the brain), REYE SYNDROME, hepatitis (see LIVER AND LIVER PROBLEMS), and THROMBOCYTOPENIA. Of the estimated 3.7 million cases in America each year, some 9,300 result in hospitalizations, and 50 to 100 people die, most of them young children. Like other herpes viruses, the varicella-zoster virus afterward lies dormant in the body's nerve tissues and later may cause attacks of *herpes zoster* (shingles) in elderly or debilitated people.

Pregnant women are especially at risk, not only for themselves but for their babies, for the disease can produce a complex of BIRTH DEFECTS called *congenital varicella syndrome.* Among these are muscle and bone defects, deformed limbs, scars, PARALYSIS, SEIZURES, and MENTAL RETARDATION. The March of Dimes reports that birth defects are most serious if the mother contracts the disease during the first

TRIMESTER (three months), with few defects resulting from the disease in the second and third trimesters. The baby is also at great risk if the mother contracts chicken pox in the few days just before delivery; then up to 3 out of 10 newborns will contract the disease, and perhaps 30 percent of them will die from it.

Pregnant women who have never, to their knowledge, had chicken pox can have a BLOOD TEST to check their IMMUNITY. If they are shown to be susceptible to chicken pox, they should avoid exposure to the disease, if at all possible. If they are exposed, they should see a doctor immediately, because an injection of IMMUNOGLOBULIN can offer temporary PASSIVE IMMUNITY to prevent or lessen chicken pox.

As of 1995, a vaccine had been approved for chicken pox, after ten years of study showed it to be 70 to 90 percent effective. Among those who still got the disease despite having had the vaccine, the symptoms were generally mild. For children ages one through twelve, a single injection is recommended, which for toddlers may be given along with the MEASLES-MUMPS-RUBELLA (MMR) VACCINE at about age fifteen months. Adolescents and adults who have not had the disease should receive two injections four to eight weeks apart. Adverse reactions to the vaccine—including redness, swelling, hardness at the site of the injection, fatigue, malaise, and nausea—were mild during the study. Testing continues on long-term effects and the possible necessity of a booster shot.

FOR HELP AND FURTHER INFORMATION

National Foundation for Infectious Diseases (NFID)
4733 Bethesda Avenue, Suite 750
Bethesda, MD 20814–5228
301–656–0003
Fax: 301–907–0878
E-mail: nfid@aol.com (America Online: NFID)
Internet: http://www.medscape.com/nfid
Leonard Novick, Executive Director
Organization focusing on causes, cures, and prevention for infectious diseases; sponsors research; educates public and professionals; publishes bimonthly newsletter *Double Helix* and brochures such as *What Parents Need to Know about Chickenpox.*

National Institute of Allergy and Infectious Diseases (NIAID), 301–496–5717. (For full group information, see ALLERGIES.)

National Institute of Child Health and Human Development (NICHD), 301–496–5133. (For full group information, see PREGNANCY.)

March of Dimes Birth Defects Foundation (MDBDF), 914–428–7100. Publishes information sheet *Chicken Pox and Fifth Disease.* (For full group information, see BIRTH DEFECTS.)

National Institute of Neurological Disorders and Stroke (NINDS), 800–352–9424. Publishes *Shingles (Herpes Zoster): Hope Through Research.* (For full group information, see BRAIN AND BRAIN DISORDERS.)

OTHER RESOURCES

For children

I've Got Chicken Pox. True Kelley. Dutton, 1994. Fiction.
Chicken Pox. Shen Roddie. Little, Brown, 1993.
Betsy and the Chicken Pox. Gunilla Wolde. Random, 1990.

child, a son or daughter of any age, though commonly a young person, especially a preteen; in law, as in the 1974 Child Abuse Prevention and Treatment Act, a MINOR, usually meaning someone under age eighteen.

child abuse and neglect (CAN), "the physical or mental injury, sexual abuse, negligent treatment or maltreatment of a child under 18 by a person who is responsible for the child's welfare," as defined in the 1974 federal Child Abuse Prevention and Treatment Act.

Child abuse refers to deliberate acts that harm or threaten to harm the child's health or welfare, including:

- *Physical abuse,* acts that result in internal and external physical injuries, most obviously FRACTURES, BURNS, BRUISES, welts, and cuts, inflicted by hand or fist or by an object such as a strap or pipe, often intended as DISCIPLINE or punishment. Some types of physical punishment long thought harmless, such as shaking a child, are now known to have specific and often serious physical effects. Internal and external injuries often form recognizable patterns such as the BATTERED CHILD SYNDROME or the WHIPLASH-SHAKEN INFANT SYNDROME, which Suspected Child Abuse and Neglect (SCAN) teams use as indicators of possible child abuse. Whether or to what extent CORPORAL PUNISHMENT is appropriate in either the family or school settings is hotly contested.
- *Sexual abuse,* acts of a sexual nature between a child and a parent or CAREGIVER, defined by the National Center on Child Abuse and Neglect (established by the 1974 act) as "contacts or interactions between a child and an adult when the child is being used for the sexual stimulation of the perpetrator or another person. Sexual abuse may also be committed by a person under the age of 18 when that person is either significantly older than the victim or when the perpetrator is in a position of power or control over another child." Such acts involving a young child are viewed with extreme gravity, as in a CHILD CARE setting, or within the family, such as INCEST between father and daughter, the most common type of sexual abuse. Sexual acts of consenting adolescents, though they are legally under the AGE

Indicators of Child Abuse and Neglect

Category	Child's appearance	Child's behavior	Caretaker's behavior
Physical abuse	Bruises and welts (on the face, lips, or mouth; in various stages of healing; on large areas of the torso, back, buttocks, or thighs; in unusual patterns, clustered, or reflective of the instrument used to inflict them; on several different surface areas) Burns (cigar or cigarette burns; glove- or socklike burns or doughnut-shaped burns on the buttocks or genitalia indicative of immersion in hot liquid; rope burns on the arms, legs, neck, or torso; patterned burns that show the shape of the item [iron, grill, etc.] used to inflict them) Fractures (skull, jaw, or nasal fractures; spiral fractures of the long [arm and leg] bones; fractures in various states of healing; multiple fractures; any fracture in a child under the age of two) Lacerations and abrasions (to the mouth, lip, gums, or eye; to the external genitalia) Human bite marks	Wary of physical contact with adults Apprehensive when other children cry Demonstrates extremes in behavior (e.g. extreme aggressiveness or withdrawal) Seems frightened of parents/caretaker Reports injury by parents/caretaker	Has history of abuse as a child Uses harsh discipline inappropriate to child's age, transgression, and condition Offers illogical, unconvincing, contradictory or no explanation of child's injury Seems unconcerned about child Significantly misperceives child (e.g., sees him as bad, evil, a monster, etc.) Psychotic or psychopathic Misuses alcohol or other drugs Attempts to conceal child's injury or to protect identity of person responsible
Neglect	Consistently dirty, unwashed, hungry, or inappropriately dressed Without supervision for extended periods of time or when engaged in dangerous activities Constantly tired or listless Has unattended medical problems or lacks routine medical care. Is exploited, overworked, or kept from attending school Has been abandoned	Is engaging in delinquent acts (e.g. vandalism, drinking, prostitution, drug use, etc.) Is begging or stealing food Rarely attends school	Misuses alcohol or other drugs Maintains chaotic home life Shows evidence of apathy or futility Is mentally ill or of diminished intelligence Has long-term chronic illnesses Has history of neglect as a child

CATEGORY	CHILD'S APPEARANCE	CHILD'S BEHAVIOR	CARETAKER'S BEHAVIOR
Sexual abuse	Has torn, stained, or bloody underclothing Experiences pain or itching in the genital area Has bruises or bleeding in external genitalia, vagina, or anal regions Has venereal disease Has swollen or red cervix, vulva, or perineum Has semen around mouth or genitalia or on clothing Is pregnant	Appears withdrawn or engages in fantasy or infantile behavior Has poor peer relationships Is unwilling to participate in physical activities Is engaging in delinquent acts or runs away States he/she has been sexually assaulted by parent/caretaker	Extremely protective or jealous of child Encourages child to engage in prostitution or sexual acts in the presence of caretaker Has been sexually abused as a child Is experiencing marital difficulties Misuses alcohol or other drugs Is frequently absent from the home
Emotional maltreatment	Emotional maltreatment, often less tangible than other forms of child abuse and neglect, can be indicated by behaviors of the child and the caretaker.	Appears overly compliant, passive, undemanding Is extremely agressive, demanding, or rageful Shows overly adoptive behaviors, either inappropriately adult (e.g. parents other children) or inappropriately infantile (e.g. rocks constantly, sucks thumb, is enuretic) Lags in physical, emotional, and intellectual development Attempts suicide	Blames or belittles child Is cold and rejecting Withholds love Treats siblings unequally Seems unconcerned about child's problem

Source: Interdisciplinary Glossary on Child Abuse and Neglect: Legal, Medical, Social Work Terms (1980). Prepared for the National Center on Child Abuse and Neglect, Children's Bureau, Administration of Children, Youth and Families, Department of Health and Human Services by the Midwest Parent-Child Welfare Resource Center (now Region V Child Abuse and Neglect Resource Center).

OF CONSENT, are viewed less seriously, though the acts may legally be considered STATUTORY RAPE.

- *Psychological and emotional abuse,* personal verbal abuse, persistent rejection, isolation, terrorization, encouragement of self-destructive behavior, or making unrealistic demands on a child that, often combined with other types of abuse, result in negative self-image and often behavioral problems and even MENTAL DISORDERS. Long-term verbal harassment and denigration of a child is a particularly insidious form of abuse and in some ways is more devastating than physical abuse alone.

All states have some sort of law requiring that child abuse be reported and filed in some CENTRAL REGISTER, though they have different definitions of what constitutes abuse, who must report it, and what action should then be taken. Reports of abuse are followed up, often by a specially deputed Suspected Child Abuse or Neglect (SCAN) team, usually including at least a PEDIATRICIAN, a SOCIAL WORKER, and a PSYCHIATRIST or PSYCHOLOGIST. Reports that are confirmed or verified are called *founded reports.* Critics have charged that too often warnings go unheeded, until damage is irreparable. However, critics charge that central registers fail to fully protect confidentiality and do not properly clear their files of unverified, *unfounded reports.*

By contrast, *child neglect* refers not to actions but to failures to act, especially to provide for the child's basic needs. Again, state laws and definitions vary and not all states require reporting of child neglect, but among the kinds of neglect are:

- *Physical neglect,* failure to provide the necessities of life, such as food, clothing, shelter, hygiene, and SUPERVISION, though financially able to do so; ABANDONMENT of a child; or rejection of a child that leads to expulsion from the home. In an infant or small child, physical neglect, especially failure to provide sufficient food, can lead to FAILURE TO THRIVE. There is, however, wide disagreement about what constitutes sufficient supervision of a young child; much depends on the age of the child, the time of day during which the child is unsupervised, the length of unsupervised time, and the arrangements the parent has made for the child's unsupervised time. The parent of a 12-year-old LATCHKEY CHILD, who has made thorough emergency plans for unsupervised time during the day, is unlikely to be charged with physical neglect.
- *Medical neglect,* failure to provide medical or dental care for a condition that, if untreated, could cause severe damage or death to a child. Often medical neglect is part of a wider picture of neglect. But among some religious groups who disavow medical treatment, charges of medical neglect sometimes bring before the courts and social agencies painful and difficult conflicts between the PARENTS' RIGHTS to make decisions about medical care and the PARENTS' RESPONSIBILITIES, as interpreted by the state, to provide essential medical care.
- *Educational neglect,* failure to provide for a child's COGNITIVE DEVELOPMENT, failure to enroll a child in school or obtain SPECIAL EDUCATION, and sometimes also failure to see that the child attends school regularly. Parents of chronic TRUANTS are legally liable, and in some areas government agencies are attempting to reduce or eliminate welfare payments for families whose children do not attend school regularly without a valid excuse.
- *Moral neglect,* failure to teach basic principles of right and wrong, what some call general social values. In practice, this general stricture most often applies to parents who knowingly allow their children to commit crimes, such as stealing or prostitution, or push them into doing so.
- *Psychological/emotional neglect,* failure to provide support and stimulation for the child's basic psychological growth and development; in essence, a lack of responsiveness to the child's needs, hopes, fears, and aspirations, a quality sometimes called *nurturance*; also a failure to obtain help for a child's resulting psychological problems. While such neglect undoubtedly exists, it is extremely difficult to prove and few states have laws regarding it.

When it was first formally recognized by the American medical profession in 1961, child abuse was called the BATTERED CHILD SYNDROME (see separate entry). But child abuse is now seen as wider and more various. It is also seen as far more widespread, with investigated and confirmed cases of child abuse in the United States averaging approximately one million a year in the 1990s, with three times that many investigated allegations of abuse (47 out of every 1,000 children, up nearly 63 percent from 1985). According to the National Resource Center on Child Abuse and Neglect, of the substantiated child abuse cases in 1994 (based on 36 of 52 states), approximately 49 percent involved neglect, 21 percent physical abuse, 11 percent sexual abuse, 3 percent emotional maltreatment, and 16 percent other forms of maltreatment (often multiple abuse). Fewer than 1 percent of the child abuse cases involved abuse in child care or FOSTER CARE settings. In 1994, at least 1,271 children died from abuse. Some 45 percent of those fatalities involved children who had previously been brought to the attention of local child protective service agencies. An estimated 35 percent involved cases of DRUG ABUSE or ALCOHOL ABUSE.

Child abuse may occur in all racial, ethnic, and socioeconomic groups, but physical abuse and neglect are especially common among people living in poverty. The effects on the children are pervasive and longlasting, affecting mental health and development during childhood, and have been linked with drops in IQS and increased likelihood of LEARNING DISABILITIES, DEPRESSION, substance abuse, SUICIDE, JUVENILE DELINQUENCY, and VIOLENCE during ADOLESCENCE and on into adulthood, when those who have been abused often perpetuate the cycle of abuse.

Parents need to be aware of the signs that might indicate possible child abuse or neglect, because their child may be in the care of many people at various times, including relatives and other people living in the household, former wives or husbands, friends, neighbors, BABYSITTERS, CHILD CARE workers, teachers, and others. It is only human to think that child abuse "can't happen here," but in fact it is far more common than most people recognize. Parents can best help their children by regularly taking a hardheaded look at the kinds of signs and symptoms that health, social, and other community officials look at (see INDICATORS OF CHILD ABUSE AND NEGLECT on page 106).

If child abuse—sexual or otherwise—is suspected, they will be wise to remain calm and collected and to take a cool look at the evidence rather than rushing to judgment. If a public accusation or formal charges are brought, the resulting furor can be damaging to all involved, including the parents and child as well as the accused, so parents want to be sure of their facts. This is especially true because children are impressionable and often say what they think adults wish to hear; they can be easily and inadvertently "led" to express fears or describe events that might not have occurred to them in the absence of leading questions. When child abuse cases go to trial, testimony by children can be traumatic in itself. In some cases, the child may be allowed to testify on video, rather than in the actual courtroom, though that violates the right of individuals to be confronted by their accusers.

Parents should also be aware that they themselves may be the targets of child abuse accusations. So much publicity has been given to child abuse in recent years that there is some danger of hysteria or overreaction. In rightly seeking to identify cases of child abuse, some people can be overzealous, catching innocent and unsuspecting parents and other caregivers in a complicated net of officialdom. Vindictive ex-spouses and others can also sometimes use charges of child abuse as part of some personal contest. Parents who share CUSTODY or have VISITATION RIGHTS with their children and any adults who work with children, for example in SPORTS, should take care not to place themselves in situations that could be misunderstood or misinterpreted and to be aware of their own rights in such situations (see discussion below). Parents can therefore also protect *themselves* by looking carefully at INDICATORS OF CHILD ABUSE AND NEGLECT (page 106), which describe the kinds of appearances and actions that make officials suspect child abuse, and the list of high-risk factors given later in the entry.

One of the main benefits of the growing awareness of child abuse is that many individuals have sought help to break the cycle by bringing the pain of their childhood out in the open, healing the hurts of the past, and moving beyond them. A considerable number of programs have developed to help child abusers—often mutual support groups they attend with other adult survivors of childhood abuse. While this recovery movement has been beneficial to many, it has created problems of its own.

Many people have only in adulthood "recovered" forgotten memories of childhood abuse of various kinds. Some of these cases are undoubtedly genuine, but in other cases patients seem to have been inadvertently induced under therapy to "recover" memories of events that turn out not to have existed, in what has been dubbed the *false memory syndrome.* This has led to painful disruptions within families, as children have accused their parents of childhood abuse, sometimes publicly bringing charges against them. When the memories have proved false, the whole process has also been extremely damaging to the person making them. It is extremely important that therapists and social workers not in any way *direct* their patients' memories, however inadvertently.

The procedure for handling suspected child abuse and neglect cases varies widely. In a model pattern, once a child abuse report or a suspect hospital admission is made, the child is removed from the situation. If a parent is being charged with abuse or neglect, the child is generally taken out of the home and put into protective or emergency CUSTODY, also called *detention.* Sometimes the whole family will be taken to a twenty-four-hour residential *family shelter,* for short-term diagnosis and treatment, as part of CRISIS INTERVENTION. Quickly—ideally within forty-eight hours—a social worker, PROBATION officer, or other official is supposed to file a *detention request;* this calls for a *detention hearing* to be held, usually within twenty-four hours of filing, to see whether the child should be kept apart from the family until a full court hearing takes place. Meanwhile, within the same seventy-two hour period, various workers evaluate the child, parent, family, and home environment and assess the validity of child abuse accusations. At a multidisciplinary *dispositional conference,* they then recommend what measures (if any) are needed to protect the child, what long-term treatment for family members is advisable, and whether the court needs to be involved.

At a *dispositional hearing,* a JUVENILE COURT or FAMILY LAW COURT will decide whether or not the child should be returned to the home (and if so, under what conditions) or whether she or he should be placed in a different setting, such as in FOSTER CARE, a GROUP HOME, or another relative's home. Following the general rule of the BEST INTERESTS OF THE CHILD, the child has usually been returned to the home, since that has traditionally been seen as giving the most emotional and financial stability. However, because of some recent, highly publicized deaths of children returned to or left with abusive families, decisions have been changing somewhat.

Generally the child and some or all family members are given *day treatment,* services that include psychological and social counseling, structured supervision, and activities designed to break the cycle of abuse and begin the process of repairing the damage. However, if the situation is regarded as sufficiently dangerous or destructive, the social workers may recommend a *dependency hearing,* in which the state takes temporary custody of the child, provides for counseling and therapy of the child and family, and aims to reunite the family. If this approach fails, however, the state may seek TERMINATION OF PARENTS' RIGHTS.

The procedure just described posits an ideal. In practice, in many cases—some studies suggest more than half of all cases—the child and family receive no service, treatment, or protection whatsoever; the case is closed on the day it was officially substantiated.

The National Center on Child Abuse and Neglect has recommended that people accused of child abuse or neglect—family members or other caregivers—should have their legal rights protected, including the rights to:

- Be informed of their legal rights.
- Receive written notice and information on legal rights regarding protective custody.
- Have a lawyer's counsel during any trial or ADMINISTRATIVE PROCEDURE.

- Appeal a decision.
- Have material in a child Ïabuse or neglect report kept confidential.

In essence, the Center is encouraging extension of rights to DUE PROCESS into areas in which they formerly seldom applied. The Center has also recommended that the government's child protective services have legal counsel and that the child's interests be represented independently, as by a court-appointed *guardian ad litem* (see GUARDIAN) or *court appointed special adovocate* (see ADVOCACY).

Social work professionals also seek to prevent child abuse and neglect before it happens or before it goes too far. They watch for signs of problems and practice EARLY INTERVENTION, trying to offer help or relieve stress before a family's problems become too severe. *Abused parents,* adults who were themselves subjected to abuse as a child, are considered at higher-than-normal risk of later inflicting child abuse. Among the factors that tag a family as at risk for child abuse are:

- Abused parents.
- ALCOHOL ABUSE or DRUG ABUSE.
- MENTAL DISORDER of a parent.
- MENTAL RETARDATION of a parent.
- Anomie, or personal alienation, of a parent.
- Social isolation of family.
- Parental unemployment or strong stress and dissatisfaction in work.
- Lack of maternal-infant BONDING.
- Lack of resources for child care.
- Parental ignorance of infant care and child development.
- Unwanted child.
- Immature parents.
- Child with DISABILITIES, including HYPERACTIVITY.
- Baby with COLIC.
- Parental discord.
- Sudden changes in family such as death, illness, or separation.

If a situation seems immediately threatening to a child's health or welfare, social workers make a crisis intervention. Some critics charge that the practice of early intervention is unwarranted meddling in family matters and is itself open to abuse.

Recognizing that family patterns can perpetuate child abuse and neglect many organizations and self-help groups (see the following list of organizations) also help families try to break the cycle of child abuse and neglect and deal with current problems. Families are linked with other families who share similar problems and learn new ways of interacting within a family, including nonviolent ways of training and disciplining children.

The concept of child abuse and neglect has also been applied to state institutions, such as jails or group homes that fail to properly care for children, and has been used to bring legal pressure to change institutional conditions. (For help and further information, see HELP AGAINST CHILD ABUSE AND NEGLECT on page 680.)

childbirth, the whole process of a baby's emergence from the UTERUS into independent life, which culminates after nine months of PREGNANCY in the intense activity of LABOR and DELIVERY. For most of history, women were attended at childbirth by midwives. Only in the last few centuries were men even allowed in the rooms where labor and delivery took place. But with the rise of modern medicine, OBSTETRICIAN/GYNECOLOGISTS became the main health-care providers for women giving birth and by the mid-twentieth century most births, especially in the United States, took place in HOSPITALS, which came to routinely use ANESTHESIA and painkillers (*analgesics*) and various kinds of medical technology and techniques, such as FETAL MONITORING, FORCEPS DELIVERY, VACUUM EXTRACTION, EPISIOTOMY, and CESAREAN SECTION. Each of these came as great advances in their day, freeing women from the great pain of childbirth and providing life- and health-saving alternatives in cases of difficult deliveries.

In recent decades, however, many people came to feel that medical technology was sometimes overused and that childbirth in the hospital was cold, impersonal, and invasive. So came the rise of the *natural childbirth* movement, often called *prepared childbirth, psychoprophylaxis,* or *psychophysical preparation for childbirth,* which stresses avoidance of intervention in the birth process unless absolutely necessary. Prepared childbirth emphasizes educational programs for pregnant women and their BIRTH PARTNERS, focusing on relaxation techniques for dealing with LABOR pains. The woman and her birth partner, usually the father, but sometimes a relative or friend, normally attend a series of classes, taught by CERTIFIED NURSE-MIDWIVES or other trained childbirth educators. These often focus on a set of breathing exercises to lessen tension in the body during labor, the aim being to enable women to diminish or better deal with pain and so require less in the way of anesthesia and analgesics.

Designed as well to diminish fear and anxiety through knowledge, the classes educate the couple about the anatomy and physiology of pregnancy and delivery, parenting skills, PRENATAL CARE, and some of the early choices that must be made regarding BREASTFEEDING or BOTTLEFEEDING and CIRCUMCISION. Many also stress EXERCISES that improve muscle tone and stamina in preparation for childbirth.

Among the best-known natural childbirth approaches are:

- *Lamaze method* or *Lamaze-Pavlov method,* the most widespread approach today, which spurred the natural childbirth movement in the 1960s in the United States. Breathing exercises stress concentrating on a focal point to ease consciousness of pain and to keep the all-important oxygen supply flowing to the baby and the muscles of the UTERUS. The birth partner coaches the process, sometimes offering massages to encourage relaxation.

- *Read (Dick-Read) method*, an approach developed in the 1930s by the man who coined the phrase "natural childbirth" and posited that much of the pain of labor and delivery was due to what he termed the *fear tension pain syndrome.* To counter this, he developed classes including physical exercises, stressing the development of different breathing patterns for different stages of labor.
- *LeBoyer method*, which stresses gentle delivery in a quiet, dimly lit, relaxing room with a minimum of interference (such as pulling on the baby's head). This method seeks to avoid overstimulating the baby's senses. To foster maternal-infant BONDING, the newborn is placed on the mother's abdomen and massaged immediately after birth, then gently washed by the father in warm water.
- *Bradley method*, which focuses heavily on the father as coach, is often called *husband-coached childbirth.* It encourages continuation of normal activities during the first stage of labor.

The choice of a childbirth approach is generally intertwined with the choice of health care providers and birth sites. Along with natural childbirth, the midwife movement has revived—practitioners are now generally trained certified nurse-midwives (CNMs). At first, CNMs worked mostly in MATERNITY CENTERS or attended at HOME BIRTHS, but many now work in hospitals as well. Many hospitals also now offer a much wider range of alternatives, such as BIRTHING ROOMS and LABOR/DELIVERY/RECOVERY ROOMS. For the first time, not only fathers but also, in some cases, other family members have been able to become active participants in the childbirth process. In addition to birth partners, women also sometimes have other people assisting them during delivery, variously called *childbirth assistants* and DOULAS. Some assistants focus on support and care for the mother in the immediate postdelivery period, support BONDING, and help with BREASTFEEDING, if desired.

Women also have more options in childbirth positions, too. Though lying flat on a bed has been the standard mode for delivery in recent centuries, the BIRTHING CHAIR—a high-backed chair with a hole or semicircular cut in the seat, a design that goes back to at least biblical times—has been revived. Other equipment, including a reclining chair or bed with a drop-down bottom, have also been used.

Parents-to-be will want to learn more about the birthing methods mentioned above and about the pros and cons of various birthing sites before deciding which approach best suits their needs and desires. Much will depend on the parents' personal inclinations. However, if the woman has a HIGH-RISK PREGNANCY, choices will be more limited.

FOR HELP AND FURTHER INFORMATION

General Information

National Maternal and Child Health Clearinghouse (NMCHC), 703–821–8955 (For full group information, see PREGNANCY.)

National Institute of Child Health and Human Development (NICHD), 301–496–5133. (For full group information, see PREGNANCY.)

American College of Obstetricians and Gynecologists (ACOG), 202–638–5577. Publishes *ACOG Guide to Planning for Pregnancy, Birth, and Beyond, You and Your Baby: Prenatal Care, Labor and Delivery and Postpartum Care, How to Tell When Labor Begins,* and *Vaginal Birth After Cesarean Delivery.* (For full group information, see PREGNANCY.)

International Association of Parents and Professionals for Safe Alternatives in Childbirth (NAPSAC)
Route 1, Box 646
Marble Hill, MO 63764
Phone and fax: 314–238–2010
David Stewart, Executive Director
International organization of childbirth professionals promoting alternatives to traditional hospital-based births; provides information and referrals; publishes booklet *Home Birth and Midwifery—Safer Than We Thought*; books *Safe Alternatives in Childbirth, The Five Standards for Safe Childbearing, Emergency Childbirth, 21st Century Obstetrics Now!, The Childbirth Activists' Handbook, NAPSAC Directory of Alternative Birth Services and Consumer Guide*; and videotapes and reprints.

International Childbirth Education Association (ICEA)
P.O. Box 20048
Minneapolis, MN 55420
612–854–8660
Fax: 612–854–8772
Trudy Keller, President
Organization concerned with family-centered maternity care, including educating parents for childbirth and breastfeeding; provides information and referrals; supports safe, low-cost alternatives and parental choice; publishes various materials, including quarterly *International Journal of Childbirth Education, ICEA Membership Directory,* and discount catalog of books.

Childbirth Education Foundation (CEF)
P.O. Box 5
Richboro, PA 18954
215–357–2792
E-mail: jperon@delphi.com (Delphi: JPERON)
James E. Peron, Executive Director
Organization of people concerned with reform of childbirth methods and treatment of newborns; promotes certified nurse-midwives, birthing centers, and

similar alternatives; provides training for childbirth educators in such techniques as the Lamaze method and training for La Leche instructors; publishes various materials.

American Academy of Husband-Coached Childbirth (AAHCC)
P.O. Box 5224
Sherman Oaks, CA 91413
818–788–6662
Marjie Hathaway, Executive Director
For-profit organization dedicated to spreading use of the Bradley Method® of natural childbirth; trains instructors; provides information and referrals; operates Pregnancy Hotline; publishes various print and audiovisual materials.

American Society for Prophylaxis in Obstetrics (ASPO/Lamaze)
1200 19th Street NW, Suite 300
Washington, DC 20036–2401
202–857–1128; 800–368–4404
Fax: 202–223–4579
Linda Harmon, Executive Director
Organization of health professionals, parents, and others interested in the Lamaze method of natural childbirth; trains and certifies instructors; provides information and makes referrals.

Read Natural Childbirth Foundation (RNCF)
P.O. Box 150956
San Rafael, CA 94915–0956
415–456–8462
Margaret B. Farley, President
Organization of health professionals and others interested in the Grantly Dick-Read approach to natural childbirth; publishes various materials, including *Preparation for Childbirth* and film *A Time to Be Born.*

National Association of Childbirth Assistants (NACA)
205 Copco Lane
San Jose, CA 95126
408–225–9167; 800–868–6222
Claudia Lowe, President
Organization of professional childbirth assistants; provides information and referrals; offers training and certification; publishes various materials, including *Childbirth Assistant Journal, You and Me: Becoming a Family, Becoming a Childbirth Assistant, Postpartum and Breastfeeding Assistant, 292 Labor Support Techniques, Confident Childbirth: Parents-to-Be Workbook and Resource Guide, Prayers and Passages for Childbirth and Beyond, Guided Self-Hypnosis for Childbirth and Beyond: A Woman's Workbook, Planning for a Positive Birth Experience: a Consumer Guidebook, Marketing Tips for Birth Support Providers,* and *The Birth Ball Newsletter,* about using a specially developed ball for exercise before and after pregnancy.

Birth Support Providers, International (BSPI)
4 David Court
Novato, CA 94947
800–818-BSPI [818–2774]
Claudia Lowe, President
International organization with which National Association of Childbirth Assistants (organization listed in previous paragraph) is affiliated; conducts training programs; publishes quarterly newsletter *BSP International* and *The Childbirth Companion Directory.*

Doulas of North America (DONA)
1100–23rd Avenue East
Seattle, WA 98112
500–448-DONA
Fax: 206–325–0472
E-mail: pennyinc@aol.com (America Online: PENNY-INC)
Penny Simkin, Founder
Organization of birth doulas; provides information, referrals, and certification; runs conferences and workshops; publishes quarterly newsletter and video *Introducing the Doula.*

National Association of Childbearing Centers (NACC), 215–234–8068. (For full group information, see MATERNITY CENTER.)

Maternity Center Association (MCA), 212–369–7300. (For full group information, see MATERNITY CENTER).

United Cerebral Palsy Association (UCPA), 800–872–5827. Publishes *Mother to Be: A Guide to Pregnancy and Birth for Women with Disabilities.* (For full group information, see CEREBRAL PALSY.)

ONLINE RESOURCES

Internet: Midwifery Resources on the Net. Resource file. gopher://una.hh.lib.umich.edu

OTHER RESOURCES

GENERAL WORKS

Childbirth Choices Today: Everything You Need to Know to Plan a Safe and Rewarding Birth. Carl Jones. Citadel/Carol, 1995.

Childbirth Without Fear. HarperCollins, 1994.

Six Practical Lessons for an Easier Childbirth, 3rd ed. Elisabeth D. Bing. Bantam, 1994.

An Easier Childbirth: A Mother's Guide for Birthing Normally, 2nd ed. Gayle Peterson. Shadow and Light, 1993.

Pregnancy and Childbirth. Charles B. Clayman, ed. Reader's Digest, 1993.

Wellness: Pregnancy, Childbirth and Parenting. Robert Kime. Dushkin, 1992.

A Good Birth, a Safe Birth: Choosing and Having the Childbirth Experience You Want, 3rd ed. Diana Korte and Roberta Scaer. Harvard Common Press, 1992.
Guide to Pregnancy and Childbirth. William G. Birch. Budlong, 1991.
Childbirth with Love. Niels H. Lauersen. Berkley, 1991.
Methods of Childbirth: The Completely Updated Version of a Classic Work for Today's Woman, rev. ed. Constance A. Bean. Morrow, 1990.
A Wise Birth: Bringing Together the Best of Natural Birth with Modern Medicine. Penny Armstrong and Sheryl Feldman. Morrow, 1990.
Good Birth: A Safe Birth, rev. ed. Diana Korte. Bantam, 1990.
The Illustrated Book of Pregnancy and Childbirth. Margaret Martin. Facts on File, 1991.
Childbirth Choices in Mothers' Words. Kim Selbert. Mills Sanderson, 1990.

On natural childbirth

All about Childbirth: A Manual for Prepared Childbirth, 4th ed. Alice T. MacMahon. Family Publications, 1994.
Doctor Discusses Prepared Childbirth. Lou Joseph and Ulisse Cucco. Budlong, 1993.
The Working Woman's Lamaze Handbook: The Essential Guide to Pregnancy, Lamaze and Childbirth. O. Robin Sweet and Patty Bryan. Hyperion, 1992.
Open Season: A Survival Guide for Natural Childbirth in the 1990s. Nancy W. Cohen. Greenwood, 1991.
The Lamaze Ready Reference Guide for Labor and Birth, 2nd ed. Harriet R. Shapiro and others. Shapiro Kuba, 1990.
Doctor Discusses Prepared Childbirth. Lou Joseph and Ulisse Cucco. Budlong, 1990.
Birth Without Violence. Frederick Leboyer. Fawcett, 1990.
Partners in Birth: Your Complete Guide to Helping a Mother Give Birth. Kathy Cain. Warner, 1990.
(See also CERTIFIED NURSE-MIDWIFE.)

On alternative approaches

Preparing for Birth with Yoga: Exercises for Pregnancy and Childbirth. Janet Balaskas. Element, 1994.
Creative Childbirth: The Leclaire Method of Easy Birthing Through Hypnosis and Rational-Intuitive Thought. Michelle L. O'Neill. Papyrus, 1993.
Unassisted Childbirth. Laura K. Shanley. Greenwood, 1993.
The Water Birth Handbook: Everything You Need to Know about Waterbirths. Roger Lichy and Eileen Herzberg. Atrium, 1992.
Alternative Birth: The Complete Guide. Carl Jones. Tarcher, 1991.

Background books

Psychology of Pregnancy and Childbirth. Lorraine Sherr. Blackwell, 1994.
The A-to-Z of Pregnancy and Childbirth: A Concise Encyclopedia. Nancy Evans. Hunter House, 1993.
The Nature of Birth and Breastfeeding. Michel Odent. Bergin & Garvey/Greenwood, 1992.
Understanding Pregnancy and Childbirth, rev. ed. Sheldon H. Cherry. Macmillan, 1992.
Illustrated Dictionary of Pregnancy and Childbirth. Carl Jones. Simon & Schuster, 1991.

(See also PREGNANCY; LABOR; DELIVERY; CESAREAN SECTION; MATERNITY CENTER; CERTIFIED NURSE-MIDWIFE; HOME BIRTH; EXERCISE.)

child care, care and supervision of infants and children by people other than their parents. In past decades, when many women stayed at home with their young children, child care usually meant bringing in a babysitter or relative for a few hours on an evening. But today, with many more single parents and working couples having children, child care means a much more major commitment for many families, often for over forty hours a week. Some employers, church and community organizations, and schools (as in the 21ST CENTURY SCHOOL) have begun to meet this enormous need locally. However, state and federal governments have so far failed to address the issue in any comprehensive way, so parents are generally on their own in arranging for child care.

The three main alternatives for temporary babysitting or longer-term child care are:

- *In the family home*—a babysitter (often a teenager, an older woman, or a relative) may come to care for a child on an occasional, temporary basis; more regular, though not necessarily full-time care may be provided for by a relative (such as a grandmother), a PARENT'S HELPER, an AU PAIR. A full-time caregiver may be a NANNY, an AU PAIR, or a housekeeper.
- *In someone else's home*—child care provided in a family setting, often with five or six other children, is often called *family day care.* This arrangement offers flexible hours and individual attention in a home setting and is often less expensive than a child care center, though if the caregiver or her own family is ill, parents will need to make temporary alternative arrangements. Some women who wish to be with their young children, but also wish and/or need to keep working, establish their own small family day care centers.
- *In a separate child care center*—care provided for larger groups of children in centers that are sometimes connected with the workplace or a community center but are often private, for-profit organizations. Parents should seek licensed child care centers wherever possible; though no one can absolutely guarantee the safety of a center, licensing at least attempts to ensure that a center meets some minimum standards. Unlike family day care, child care centers generally have backup staff, but often have less flexible hours, though some are extending hours to supply coverage for parents who work evenings and nights.

For many parents, just finding affordable day care is a major problem. They need to start planning months ahead of time to be sure that they have arrangements in place when they need them. Certainly they should not rely on vague "we can always take one more" promises. Friends and relatives in the neighborhood, other families with young children, local newspapers, organizations such as those listed later in this entry, and community agencies such as local offices of the Department of Health or Social Services, can all help parents locate local child care workers, family day care, or day care centers. In calculating costs, parents should take into account that some centers charge a sliding fee depending on family income and that federal and state income tax credits may be available for some child care expenses, depending on current laws.

In making choices about child care, parents should see that the caregiver has compatible views on such crucial matters as offering babies stimulation; developing various skills, such as LANGUAGE SKILLS and MOTOR SKILLS; using DISCIPLINE; concern for health and safety; TOILET TRAINING; and the like. Ideally, the caregiver will have some basic training in child development and emergency procedures such as first aid and ARTIFICIAL RESPIRATION; in some communities, even young babysitters are offered courses leading to "certification." The CHECKLIST FOR CHOOSING CHILD CARE on (below) can help parents in assessing whether a particular person or center is the right one for their child.

Once child care decisions have been made, parents should periodically reassess how the arrangement is working for the child, in particular if the child feels happy and comfortable with the caregiver and if the caregiver is responsive to parents' needs and concerns. Parents should also be aware of the possibilities of CHILD ABUSE AND NEGLECT, though less than 1 percent of child abuse takes

Checklist for Choosing Child Care

For care both inside and outside of your home:

- Do you think the person who would care for your baby will really care about him or her?
- Are your suggestions for the care of your baby welcomed and listened to?
- Has the caregiver had a medical examination to show that he or she has no disease that your baby could catch and is strong and healthy enough to care for children?
- Has he or she taken first-aid and cardiopulmonary resuscitation (CPR) courses recently? Are first-aid supplies available?
- Is there a telephone which the caregiver can use to reach you or call for help in an emergency?
- Would you feel at ease leaving your baby in the person's care?
- Does the caregiver treat each baby as his or her own—talking to each while bathing or changing, holding each child while feeding, and paying attention to each child's needs?
- How does the caregiver deal with behavioral issues (such as tantrums)?

For care outside of your home:

- Is there at least one person to care for each four or five babies at all times during the day?
- Is the home or center safe and clean, with room for play and sleep, and fresh air?
- Are there age-appropriate toys to play with?
- Do the caregivers and children seem to be happy, alert, and enjoying themselves?
- Are you welcome to visit at any time, with or without telling them in advance that you are coming?
- Will care be available for all of the hours and days (including holidays) you will need it?
- What happens if your baby becomes ill or hurt?
- Is the facility registered or licensed by the state or by another agency?
- How long has the facility been in operation, and how long have the present caregivers been on staff?
- Will they give you regular reports about how your baby is doing?
- Will they tell you about any accidents your baby may have, or any contagious disease in the group?
- Will appropriate snacks and meals be available on a regular schedule?

Before you make a final decision, ask for and check references. Talk with other parents whose children have been cared for by the individuals or centers you are considering. Ask whether they are satisfied or have any complaints.

Source: Infant Care (1989). Prepared for the Public Health Service by the Health Resources and Services Administration, Bureau of Maternal and Child Health and Resources Development.

place in child care or FOSTER CARE facilities. In particular, they should also be alert to unusual or unexplained accidents or injuries, or to a child's discomfort, disquiet, fear, or upset in the caregiver's presence, apart from initial STRANGER ANXIETY and normal SEPARATION ANXIETY (see INDICATORS OF CHILD ABUSE AND NEGLECT on page 106). Infants and young children, especially, may be unable to communicate if a problem exists, but even with older children parents must be sensitive to problems in the relationship between child and caregiver; they should act decisively to make a change, if appropriate. They should not, however, change caregivers lightly, because each such change is a major disruption in a young child's life.

Most child care programs are only for well children; those with infectious diseases must stay home until they are well, to avoid spreading the illness to others. That means that a parent must stay home with the child, often losing time from work, or that other special interim arrangements need to be made, such as having a trusted relative, neighbor, or babysitter come in to care for the child. But sick child day care centers are being established in many areas of the country. These are sites where parents can bring their mildly (not seriously or chronically) ill children on a temporary basis. These centers are usually more expensive, since they have somewhat specialized facilities, to keep infection from spreading among the children, and have at least one registered nurse on staff, but they are a godsend for working parents where they exist.

FOR HELP AND FURTHER INFORMATION

GENERAL ORGANIZATIONS

American Academy of Pediatrics (AAP), 800–433–9016. Publishes brochures *Child Care: What's Best for Your Family* and *Baby Sitting Reminders*, computer program *Safety First: A Guide to Safe Child Care for Baby-Sitters*. (For full group information, see health care.)

National Maternal and Child Health Clearinghouse (NMCHC), 703–821–8955. Publishes numerous materials on child care programs, such as *Improving the Quality of Out-of-Home Child Care—National Resource Center for Health and Safety in Child Care*. (For full group information, see PREGNANCY.)

Child Care Aware Resource Referral Line, 800–424–2246 (9 A.M.–5 P.M., CT). Information and referral service sponsored by a group of organizations.

National Association for Sick Child Daycare Centers (NASCDC)
10950 Three Chopt Road
Richmond, VA 23233
804–747–0100
Fax: 804–740–0893
Gail Johnson, President
Organization concerned with child care for mildly ill children; acts as a clearinghouse for information, including state-by-state information on facilities and regulations; conducts research; provides information and referrals; publishes period newsletters.

The Children's Foundation (TCF)
725 15th Street NW, Suite #505
Washington, DC 20005
202–347–3300
Fax: 202–347–3382
Kay Hollestelle, Executive Director
Organization concerned with improving the lives of children, focusing on areas such as welfare reform, food assistance, health care, child care, and collecting child support; acts as advocate; sponsors National Family Day Care Project and National Child Support Project; provides training to caregivers and parents; provides accreditation for family day care centers; publishes various materials, including bimonthly newsletter *The Family Day Care Bulletin*; annual *Directory of Family Day Care Associations and Support Groups*; *A Guide for Parents Using or Seeking Home-Based Child Care, Who Should Care for Infants and Toddlers? A Family Day Care Perspective, Checklist of Toys, Books, and Materials* (guidelines for choosing appropriate materials); *Fact Sheet on Family Day Care, General Information on Child Care in the United States*, and numerous materials for family day care providers.

Child Care Action Campaign (CCAC)
330 Seventh Avenue, 17th Floor
New York, NY 10001
212–239–0138
Fax: 212–268–6515
Barbara Reisman, Executive Director
Coalition of individuals and organizations seeking to improve provision of child care; conducts Family Support Watch, Parents' Agenda, and Education Campaign; publishes various materials, including *Caring for Your Child: Making the Right Choice, Family Day Care, School Age Child Care, How to Use the Federal Child Care Tax Credit, Questions and Answers About Infant and Toddler Care, Infectious Disease and Child Care, Finding Good Child Care: A Checklist, Finding and Hiring an Qualified In-Home Caregiver, Temporary Care of the Mildly Sick Child, Is Day Care Good for Children?, Facts About the Child Care Crisis, Current Child Care Legislation, Where Are the Dollars for Child Care?*, and numerous materials on employer-provided child care and on starting and running child care programs.

Families and Work Institute (FWI), 212–465–2044. Publishes *The Role of Child Care Centers in the Lives of Parents, Education Before School: Investing in Quality Child Care*, and numerous studies on child care and improvement of child care programs. (For full group information, see GENERAL PARENTING RESOURCES on page 634.)

National Association for the Education of Young Children (NAEYC), 800–424–2460. Publishes various materials, including brochures: *Finding the Best Care for Your Infant or Toddler, How to Choose a Good Early Childhood Program, What Are the Benefits of High Quality Programs, Where Your Child Care Dollars Go*, and *Keeping*

Healthy: Parents, Teachers, and Children; book-and-video *What Is Quality Child Care?*; and numerous materials on child care programs, including appropriate activities and policies. (For full group information, see PRESCHOOL.)

Zero to Three National Center for Clinical Infant Programs
2000 14th Street North, Suite 380
Arlington, VA 22201–2500
703–528–4300; Publications order: 800–899–4301
Fax: 703–528–6848
Matthew Melmed, Executive Director
Organization concerned with the development of infants and toddlers; acts as advocate; offers training programs; publishes numerous materials, including bimonthly newsletter *Zero to Three*; *Heart Start: The Emotional Foundations of School Readiness*; *Caring for Infants and Toddlers in Violent Environments: Hurt, Healing and Hope*; works on infant and family services; audiocassettes *Infant/Toddler Child Care* and *Parent/Professional Collaboration*, and other materials for professionals.

National Black Child Development Institute (NBCDI), 800–556–2234. Publishes *Selecting Child Care: A Checklist* and *Child Care Power*, on community-based advocacy. (For full group information, see HELP ON LEARNING AND EDUCATION on page 659.)

Child Welfare League of America (CWLA), 202–638–2952. Publishes *Older Adults Caring for Children: Intergenerational Child Care*, *First Steps Toward Cultural Difference: Socialization in Infant/Toddler Day Care*, and materials for child care providers. (For full group information, see FOSTER CARE.)

Child Care Law Center (CCLC)
22 2nd Street, 5th Floor
San Francisco, CA 94105
415–495–5498; Parent questions: Tu & Th 9 A.M.–12 P.M., PT
Fax: 415–495–6734
Deena Lahn, Executive Director
Organization focusing on legal aspects of child care, such as expanding child-care options for low-income families and children with special needs, changing zoning laws for family day care, drafting "whistleblower" legislation for reporting licensing violations, and providing due process for child care workers; provides information, support, education, and legal aid; publishes brochure *The Americans with Disabilities Act and Child Care: Information for Parents*; booklets *Child Care and the ADA: Highlights for Parents* and *Child Care Contracts: Information for Parents*; and various materials for child care providers (for other titles, see AIDS; CUSTODY).

Association for Childhood Education International (ACEI), 800–423–3563. Publishes book *Personalizing Care with Infants, Toddlers and Families* and position paper *The Right to Quality Child Care*. (For full group information, see HELP ON LEARNING AND EDUCATION on page 659.)

Institute for Childhood Resources (INICR)
220 Montgomery Street, #2811
San Francisco, CA 94104
415–864–1169
Fax: 510–540–0171
Stevanne Auerbach, Director
Organization focusing on needs of children from birth to school age; operates information clearinghouse and resource center; consults with individuals and groups on topics such as parenting, childhood education, child care, and toys and games; publishes various materials, including book *Keys to Choosing Child Care* and audiotape *Tips on Choosing Child Care*.

High-Scope Educational Research Foundation, 800–407–7377. Publishes video *The High-Scope Curriculum: Its Implementation in Family Childcare Homes* and various materials for child care programs. (For full group information, see PRESCHOOL.)

Children's Defense Fund (CDF), 800–233–1200. Publishes *Child Care: An Essential Service for Teen Parents*, *Child Care and Development: Key Facts*, and works of social analysis. (For full group information, see ADOLESCENT PREGNANCY.)

National Association for Family Day Care (NAFDC)
725 15th Street NW, Suite 505
Washington, DC 20005
202–347–3356; 800–359–3817
Linda Geigle, Contact
For parents, caretakers, and others interested in improving provision of children's day care in household settings and in setting standards for day care centers; publishes newsletter and other publications, including the brochure *What Is Family Day Care?*

Division of Child and Youth Services, American Psychological Association (APA), 202–336–6013. Publishes *When You Need Child Day Care*. (For full group information, see MENTAL DISORDERS.)

American Association of Family and Consumer Sciences (AAFCS), 703–706–4600. Publishes *Developmentally Appropriate Practice in School-Age Child Care Programs* and *Beyond the Latchkey: Expanding Community for School Age Care—A Community Training Program*. (For full group information, see GENERAL PARENTING RESOURCES on page 634.)

Division of Child and Youth Services c/o American Psychological Association (APA), 202–336–6013. Publishes *When You Need Child Day Care*. (For full group information, see MENTAL DISORDERS.)

Mothers at Home (MAH), 703–827–5903. Publishes public policy packet *Mothers Speak Out on Child Care*. (For full group information, see GENERAL PARENTING RESOURCES on page 634.)

International Nanny Association (INA), 402–691–9628. (For full group information, see NANNY.)

ERIC (Educational Resources Information Center) Clearinghouse on Elementary and Early Childhood Education, 800–583–4135. (For full group information, see HELP ON LEARNING AND EDUCATION on page 659.)

ON SAFETY CONCERNS

Sudden Infant Death Syndrome Alliance (SIDS Alliance), 800–221–7437. Publishes *What Childcare Facilities Should Know.* (For full group information, see SUDDEN INFANT DEATH SYNDROME.)

National Safety Council (NSC), 800–621–7615. (For full group information, see SAFETY.)

National Sudden Infant Death Syndrome Clearinghouse (NSIDSC), 703–821–8955, ext. 474. Publishes *When Sudden Infant Death Syndrome (SIDS) Occurs in Childcare Settings.* (For full group information, see SUDDEN INFANT DEATH SYNDROME.)

ON CHILDREN WITH SPECIAL NEEDS

American Academy of Child and Adolescent Psychiatry (AACAP), 202–966–7300. Publishes information sheet *Making Day Care a Good Experience.*

Rural Institute on Disabilities, 800–732–0323, voice/TT. Publishes newsletter *Child Care Plus +, Integrated Child Care: Meeting the Challenge,* and reprints on child care. (For full group information, see HELP FOR SPECIAL CHILDREN on page 689.)

Epilepsy Foundation of America (EFA), 800–332–1000. Publishes *When Seizures Don't Look Like Seizures: Facts for Those Who Care for Children, Children and Seizures: Information for Babysitters,* and other educational materials. (For full group information, see EPILEPSY.)

National Federation of the Blind (NFB), 410–659–9314. Publishes *Baby-Sitting* and *A Federation Victory: Blind Parent Wins Unrestricted Child Care License.* (For full group information, see EYE AND VISION PROBLEMS.)

ON CARE FOR CHILDREN WITH SPECIAL NEEDS

PACER Center (Parent Advocacy Coalition for Educational Rights), 612–827–2966, voice/TT. Publishes *Child Care for Children with Special Needs* (For full group information, see HELP FOR SPECIAL CHILDREN on page 689.)

Parents Helping Parents (PHP), 408–727–5775. Publishes *Daycare for Children with Special Needs.* (For full group information, see HELP FOR SPECIAL CHILDREN on page 689.)

The Arc, 817–261–6003. Publishes fact sheet *Child Care Settings and the Americans with Disabilities Act* and *All Kids Count: Child Care and the Americans with Disabilities Act (ADA).* (For full group information, see MENTAL RETARDATION.)

ONLINE RESOURCES

Internet: ACS Gopher. Resource file on children, families, and child care, from Administration for Children and Families of the U.S. Department of Health and Human Services. gopher://spike.acf.dhhs.gov

OTHER RESOURCES

FOR PARENTS

Fifty-Two Ways to Evaluate Your Childcare Options. Jan L. Dargatz. Nelson, 1994.

Choosing Schools and Child Care Options: Answering Parents' Questions. Nancy H. Phillips. C. C. Thomas, 1994.

Sourcebook on Parenting and Child Care. Kathryn H. Carpenter, ed. Oryx, 1994.

What Every Parent Should Know about Child Care. Karla Satchwell. R & E Publishers, 1993.

It Works for Us: Proven Child Care Tips from Experienced Parents Across the Country. Tom McMahon and Claire Zion. Pocket Books, 1993.

Child Care for the 'Nineties: An Owner's Manual. Alfredo O. Santesteban. ABC and F Press, 1993.

Nolo's Law Form Kit: Hiring Child Care and Household Help. Barbara K. Repa. Nolo, 1993.

A Parent's Guide to Ensuring a Successful Day Care Experience for an Infant or Toddler. Michael K. Meyerhoff. W. Gladden, 1992.

Choices in Child Care: What's Best for Your Child. Suzanne Laird. Temeron, 1992.

Shopping for Quality Daycare. Claudia Bischoff. Round Lake, 1992.

Nothing but the Best: Making Day Care Work for You and Your Child. Diane Lusk and Bruce McPherson. Morrow, 1992.

Speaking of: Child Care: Everything You Wanted To Know. Suraj Gupte. Sterling/Apt, 1991.

All about Child Care, rev. ed. Marilyn Segal. Nova University Family Center, 1991.

Child Care: A Parent's Guide. Sonja Flating. Facts on File, 1991.

Keys to Choosing Child Care. Stevanne Auerbach. Barron's, 1991. By the director of the Institute for Childhood Resources.

Junior Citizens: An Owner's Manual: Child Care for the Computer Generation. Peter Hartman. Great Bear, 1991.

Sharing the Caring. Amy L. Dombro. Simon & Schuster, 1991.

FOR CHILDREN

Gracias, Rosa. Michelle Markel. Albert Whitman, 1995. A young girl and her Latina babysitter.

Good Job! Moms at Work, Kids at Play. Fifteen-minute video for preschoolers. Brandeis University Office of Student Affairs, 1994.

Nobody Asked If I Wanted a Babysitter. Martha Alexander. Puffin, 1993.

Babysitting with Big Bird. Liza Alexander. Golden/Western, 1993.

Babysitting for Benjamin. Valiska Gregory. Little, Brown, 1993.

My New Baby-Sitter. Christine Loomis. Morrow, 1991.

Eleanor and the Babysitter. Susan Hellard. Little, Brown, 1991.

For preteens and teens

Day Care: Looking for Answers. Kathlyn Gay. Enslow, 1992.

For teen babysitters and child care workers

The New Complete Babysitter's Handbook. Carol Barkin and Elizabeth James. Houghton Mifflin, 1995.

Babysitter's Companion. Mary Jayne Fogerty. Happy Trails, 1994.

Dynamite Counselors Don't Explode!: A Complete Survival Course for Child-Care Workers and Camp Counselors. Michael Pastore. Zorba, 1993.

The Babysitting Co-op Guidebook: Building a Community Support Network. Patricia McManus. Diane, 1993.

Kid Sitter Basics: A Handbook for Babysitters. Celeste Stuhring. Westport, 1992.

Our Family Babysitting Guide. Julie Young and Woody Young. Joy Publishing, 1992. Originally titled: *Babysitting Wise.*

How to Make More Money Babysitting: What Works, What Doesn't, and Why. Richard D. O'Keef. Diamond, 1992.

How to Be a Super Sitter. Lee Salk and Jay Litvin. VGM Career/NTC, 1991.

Babysitting. Frances S. Dayee. Watts, 1990.

On starting family day care programs

Start Your Own At-Home Child Care Business, 2nd ed. Patricia C. Gallagher. Gallagher Jordan, 1994.

How to Open and Operate a Home-Based Day Care Business: An Unabridged Guide. Shari Steelsmith. Globe Pequot, 1994.

Start and Run a Profitable Home Daycare: Your Step-by-Step Business Plan. Catherine Pruissen. Self-Counsel Press, 1993.

Better Baby Care: A Book for Family Day Care Providers, rev. ed. M. Nash and others. Children's Foundation, 1993.

Caring for Other People's Children: A Complete Guide to Family Day Care. Frances K. Alston. Teachers College, 1992.

The Home Day Care Manual: How to Set up and Operate a Successful Home Day Care. Michelle Landry, ed. Adlai House, 1991.

Little People: Big Business: A Guide to Successful In-Home Day Care. Margaret M. Gillis and others. Betterway, 1991.

Background works

Are Our Kids All Right?: Lessons for the Child Care Generation. Susan B. Dynerman. Peterson's Guides, 1994.

Daycare, rev. ed. Alison Clarke-Stewart. Harvard University Press, 1993.

Scenes from Day Care: How Teachers Teach and What Children Learn. Elizabeth Platt. Teachers College, 1992.

A Child's Place: A Year in the Life of a Day Care Center. Ellen R. Shell. Little, Brown, 1992.

The Day Care Dilemma: Critical Concerns for American Families. Angela Browne Miller. Plenum/Insight, 1990.

(See also NANNY; SAFETY; FAMILY AND MEDICAL LEAVE; HELP ON LEARNING AND EDUCATION on page 659.)

Childfind, a government-sponsored program to identify young children AT RISK for having a LEARNING DISABILITY or other DISABILITY that could affect learning. The purpose of these and similar programs, mandated by the EDUCATION FOR ALL HANDICAPPED CHILDREN ACT and its successor, the INDIVIDUALS WITH DISABILITIES EDUCATION ACT, is to identify as early as possible (preferably before KINDERGARTEN or first grade) children who need EARLY INTERVENTION or special services to be fully prepared for school.

child prodigy, a child who demonstrates unusual and superior talent at a very early age, especially in music or the arts, such as a child who begins composing music on the piano at age three (see GIFTED CHILD).

childproofing, careful examination of any setting in which a young child will spend any amount of time to remove and place out of reach (in a closed closet or on an upper shelf, for example) anything that might prove a danger to the child or anything that the child might damage. Marbles or nuts, which the child might swallow, are examples of dangerous items that need to be removed; a beautiful bowl or a fine book are objects that a child could easily damage. Anything else dangerous, such as electrical outlets to fiddle with or toilet bowls to drown in, should be secured. More children die in avoidable accidents each year from hazards seen and unseen than from life-threatening diseases, according to the National Safety Council. Parents of an infant will need to periodically analyze what their child is capable of doing and what new dangers might emerge as the child develops. (For an outline of what the baby can do at various stages in the first twelve months, see YOUR BABY'S FIRST YEAR: A SAFETY CHECKLIST on page 520.) When parents go visiting with the child, they should also keep a watchful eye out and (if the social situation allows it) temporarily childproof the room they and the child will be in.

No parent can watch a child every minute of every day. Anticipation is the key to preventing injury, but too few parents—especially first-time parents—have the ability to identify the many potential hazards to their young child, much less know how to remove or modify them so as to reduce or eliminate the danger. For every hazard they might spy, another might go unnoticed and pose a threat to the child's SAFETY. Hence the emergence of a new service for parents: babyproofing.

Babyproofing services are hired to come into the home, evaluate its dangers from a *child's* point of view, and remove, replace, or install what is necessary to make the home safe. They offer the advantages of experience in spotting potential dangers and ready access to the devices and skills for the necessary changes, modifications, or installations. These include not just the familiar gates for stairways, shields for electrical outlets, or coverings for balcony railings (now often of plexiglass), but also less-familiar items such as latches on drawers, locks on refrigerators, corner guards on glass or stone coffee tables, latches on toilets, and metal attachments to keep windows from opening so far that a child might fall out. Though many such devices are available to everyone and could be installed by do-it-yourselfers, the sheer inconvenience of trying to get devices from a couple of dozen different suppliers makes many people turn instead to babyproofing services—especially because charges for services at a modest-sized apartment or home may be little more than the cost of a visit or two to the emergency room, in case of an accident, to say nothing of the anguish saved.

Parents who choose to do their own babyproofing will have to shop around for the right devices to install in their homes. Among the many child-resistant or childproof products the firm offers are outlet plugs or covers, locks for switches (as for a garbage disposal unit), cabinet and drawer latches, oven and cabinet locks, stove knob covers, stove guards, velcro-type appliance latches, VCR locks, edge-and-corner bumpers, balcony guards, door stoppers (to protect children's fingers), cord shorteners, window locks, and even a small-object tester, to see if an object is small enough to fit into a child's mouth. (See also SAFETY; ENVIRONMENTAL HAZARDS).

Children's Apperception Test (CAT), a type of individually administered PROJECTIVE TEST similar to and modeled on the THEMATIC APPERCEPTION TEST, but designed for children ages three through ten. In the CAT-A version, a child is given a series of pictures, often of animals in human settings, one at a time and is asked to make up stories about them. The aim is to reveal the child's personality and maturity. The CAT-H version uses humans in family situations, while the CAT-S version shows animals in family situations, often ones including stressful elements, such as parental separation, disability, illness, or a mother's pregnancy. (See TESTS.)

child support, money that parents must pay for the care of their child, to cover expenses for such things as food, clothing, shelter, medicine, education, and insurance; part of the responsibilities associated with PARENTS' RIGHTS. Whether the child's parents are married or unmarried, the legal MOTHER and FATHER both have support obligations. The support obligation extends at least until the child reaches legal adulthood, often age eighteen, or becomes formally an EMANCIPATED MINOR. In practice, most parents continue to support their children well beyond age eighteen, through college and sometimes beyond, especially if the child has severe DISABILITIES. Before then, child support obligations end only with the permanent TERMINATION OF PARENTAL RIGHTS, as when a child is given up for ADOPTION and in cases of ABANDONMENT.

For most families, child support is accepted as a matter of course. Even if parents separate or divorce, they generally recognize that support must continue to be provided for the children. Where separating parents generally disagree is over what level of support should be provided. On this question parents have historically had very little uniform guidance, since the amount of child support varies widely. Celebrity divorces to the contrary, a mother and children are almost invariably poorer than before a separation—and so, generally, is the father. Couples trying to make an equitable child support arrangement on their own are a relative rarity, and many contact organizations of various kinds (see list of organizations that follows) to help them. When separating or divorcing parents can agree between themselves (generally with advice from lawyers) on how much child support is reasonable, the court will generally accept their decision as part of their SEPARATION AGREEMENT.

When they cannot agree on child support (and the related issue of alimony), the issue is taken to the courts. Specialist divorce lawyers, enlisted by each side, attempt to gain every monetary, tax, and other advantage possible for their respective clients. The 1984 Child Support Enforcement Act encouraged the formation of state guidelines on what is a fair amount of child support. But, in fact, the guidelines have been ill-defined and open to quite different interpretations about what is fair, based on the two parties' ability to earn and ability to pay.

To some extent, the amount of child support awarded hinges on who has CUSTODY of the child. In most cases—90 percent in the United States—the mother gets custody and the father is asked to pay child support; the reverse is rarer. Joint custody is becoming increasingly common, but one substantial problem for women is that child support payments are often much lower in joint custody, based on the assumption that the child will spend much time with the father. However, that fails to take into account the mother's cost in maintaining the child's home full-time. In practice, some fathers use joint custody only as a ploy to lower support payments, and the woman often ends up with full-time custody anyway—but with less money to cover expenses.

The person who receives a court order to pay child support—generally the father, but sometimes the mother—is called the *obligated parent* or *responsible parent.* It is extremely important for both partners to have advice from separate experienced attorneys in this court proceeding, because court ruling on child support, once made, is not easily changed, though it can later be modified, temporarily or permanently, if the court is convinced that CHANGED CIRCUMSTANCES, such as a sharp rise or decrease in income or a change in a child's health requiring expensive medical care, warrant it.

It is also important to have fair child support payments at the start, because in some cases low child support payments have, in an odd twist, caused later loss of custody. When child support payments are so low that a woman, as custodial parent, goes to work to better support the child, she has in some cases later lost custody to a remarried husband on the court's assumption (correct or incorrect) that the new stepmother will stay at home to care for the children.

Many reopened custody disputes have also resulted from a woman's attempt to get promised child support payments—a far wider and more serious problem. In fact, over 41 percent of custodial mothers in America receive *no* support at all from the child's father. Of those who do receive support, only half receive the full amount. Some fathers, even when they are able to pay, also end support when the child is 18 (leaving children feeling—not surprisingly—abandoned), though most continue to provide support for a child's COLLEGE education. Nonpayment stretches across all education and socioeconomic brackets and is not linked to either the amount of child support granted or to the father's ability to pay. Well over a third of separated or divorced families therefore exist below the poverty level, and many depend on government assistance.

Various federal and state programs have been put into place to try to ease the strain on custodial mothers and to get noncustodial fathers to pay their proper share of child support. The federal Office of Child Support Enforcement (OCSE) works through regional and state agencies to find the DELINQUENT parent, often using its PARENT LOCATOR SERVICE (PLS). The PLS uses computers on the federal level to search through income tax records, Social Security earnings and benefit records, and the like. Its counterparts on the state level scan voter registration, motor vehicle, driver's license, welfare, prison, Worker's Compensation, and similar records. While the PLS has had some success in locating missing parents, some custodial parents also use friends, relatives, colleagues, and knowledge of interests and associations to try to find the delinquent parent.

The Child Support Enforcement Amendments also give women ways of collecting support (through the OCSE), once the delinquent parent is found. These include:

- Withholding child support payments automatically from paychecks.
- Withholding tax refunds to pay overdue child support (ARREARAGES).
- Requiring that the delinquent parent post bonds or securities to guarantee payment.
- Government seizure of property, or *sequestration*, for sale to cover arrears.
- Reporting delinquent parents to credit agencies when amounts are over $1,000.

Like the comparable act regarding custody, the Uniform Reciprocal Enforcement of Support Act (URESA) and its revised form (RURESA) provide for enforcement of child support payments when the obligated parent lives in a different state than the custodial parent and children. If the father ignores court orders to pay, he is held in contempt of court and can be sent to jail, though that is, in fact, rarely done.

Another approach applied to the problem is WAGE ATTACHMENT, under which the obligated parent's employer is notified of any child support order and the required amount is "attached" or taken from the paycheck and sent as child support. In some states, the wage attachment law applies automatically to everyone who has been ordered to pay child support. Sometimes the obligated parent may have wages voluntarily withheld to pay for child support.

Some families not receiving child support are eligible for aid under the AID TO FAMILIES WITH DEPENDENT CHILDREN program; if so, they are required by law to cooperate in the state's search for the delinquent parent to obtain reimbursement for child support payments. If the ABSENT PARENT is found, the custodial parent will be asked to sign an ASSIGNMENT OF SUPPORT RIGHTS, specifying that court-ordered back child support payments will be paid to the state, in exchange for AFDC grants and other benefits. If the absent parent is an unwed FATHER, the state may initiate a PATERNITY SUIT to establish his legal status as father.

FOR HELP AND FURTHER INFORMATION

National Center for Women and Family Law, 212–674–8200. Publishes *Child Support and You*; *Custody, Visitation, and Child Support*; and various reference and legal materials. (For full group information, see CUSTODY.)

Parents Without Partners (PWP), 800–637–7974. Publishes information sheets *What Custodial Parents Should Know About Child Support* and *What Noncustodial Parents Should Know About Child Support.* (For full group information, see GENERAL PARENTING RESOURCES on page 634.)

Association of Family and Conciliation Courts (AFCC), 608–251–4001. Publishes pamphlet *Child Support.* (For full group information, see DIVORCE.)

Lavender Families Resource Network, 206–325–2643, voice/TT. Publishes article reprint *Custody and Visitation: Their Relationship to Establishing and Enforcing Support.* (For full group information, see HOMOSEXUALITY.)

Women's Legal Defense Fund, 202–986–2600. Publishes *Report Card on State Child Support Guidelines.* (For full group information, see FAMILY AND MEDICAL LEAVE.)

National Committee for Fair Divorce and Alimony (NCFDAL), 212–766–4030. (For full group information, see CUSTODY)

Academy of Family Mediators (AFM), 617–674–2663. (For full group information, see CUSTODY.)

Help Abolish Legal Tyranny (HALT), 202–347–9600. (For full group information, see CUSTODY.)

National Organization for Women's Legal Defense and Education Fund, 212–925–6635. (For full group information, see CUSTODY.)

National Center for Women and Family Law, 212–674–8200. (For full group information, see CUSTODY.)

CALM, Inc. (Custody Action for Lesbian Mothers), 610–667–7508. (For full group information, see CUSTODY.)

Father's Rights of America (FRA), 818–888–0378. (For full group information, see CUSTODY.)

National Congress for Men and Children (NCFC), 800–733–3237. (For full group information, see CUSTODY.)

Center on Children and the Law, 202–662–1720. Publishes *Toward a Common Goal: Tribal and State Intergovernmental Agreements for Child Support Cases.* (For full group information, see HELP AGAINST CHILD ABUSE AND NEGLECT on page 680.)

Children's Defense Fund (CDF), 800–233–1200. Publishes *Enforcing Child Support: Are States Doing the Job?* (For full group information, see ADOLESCENT PREGNANCY.)

OTHER RESOURCES

Child Support: How to Get What Your Child Needs and Deserves. Carole A. Chambers. Summit, 1991.

How to Do Better at Collecting Child Support and Alimony. Robert S. Sigman. Legovac, 1991.

How to Modify and Collect Child Support, 3rd ed. Joseph Matthews et al. Nolo Press, 1990.

(See also CUSTODY; DIVORCE; SEPARATION AGREEMENT.)

chiropractor, a health professional with the degree of Doctor of Chiropractic, or D.C., who is not trained or licensed in the use of drugs or surgery, but works within the system of chiropractic medicine, which sees diseases and disorders as resulting from malfunctioning of the NERVOUS SYSTEM and uses physical manipulation of the spine as the main form of treatment.

chlamydia, infection by the bacterium *Chlamydia trachomatis,* the most common SEXUALLY TRANSMITTED DISEASE, infecting an estimated four million people each year in the United States alone. Chlamydia is spread through vaginal or anal, and sometimes oral, sex; babies can also be infected by the mother at birth.

Chlamydia is nicknamed the "silent STD," because initial symptoms are mild or even absent altogether in some 75 percent of women and 25 percent of men. As a result, many people are unaware that they have the disease before complications have set in. Most seriously, chlamydia can cause permanent damage to the reproductive organs in both men and women, leading to INFERTILITY and possibly even STERILITY. In women, the most serious complication is PELVIC INFLAMMATORY DISEASE (PID), which is also linked to potentially deadly ECTOPIC PREGNANCY. In men, infection can cause inflammation in the urinary tract (medically called *nongonococcal urethritis* [NGU] or *nonspecific urethritis* [NSU]) or other parts of the reproductive system. In severe cases, infection can cause STERILITY in men or women. Chlamydia may also cause infection elsewhere in the body, such as in the rectum, in the lining of the eye (*conjunctivitis*) (see EYE AND VISION PROBLEMS), or in the lymph nodes in the groin (*lymphogranuloma venerum* or LGV). In babies, chlamydia can also lead to pneumonia (see LUNG AND BREATHING PROBLEMS) and to eye or ear infections.

Men and women who do have symptoms (generally starting one to three weeks after exposure) may have pain during urination, a discharge of mucus or pus from the PENIS or VAGINA, and a low-grade FEVER; women may also have lower abdominal pain and nonmenstrual vaginal bleeding, while men may have burning or itching at the opening of the penis and pain and swelling in the TESTICLES. People experiencing such symptoms should see a doctor promptly. If chlamydia is diagnosed, the patient's partners should also be tested and treated, and they should avoid sex until the treatment is completed.

Chlamydia is sometimes confused with, and often occurs with, GONORRHEA; both are treated with ANTIBIOTICS. Chlamydia infections can be detected by any of several quick office tests, and many doctors recommend that anyone who has multiple sex partners, especially a woman of childbearing age, should be tested annually. Many doctors also recommend that all pregnant women be routinely tested to prevent infection of babies. (For help and further information, including how to avoid infection, see SEXUALLY TRANSMITTED DISEASES.)

chloride, a MINERAL, generally found in a compound with SODIUM as table salt, that is important in the body's digestive juices (such as forming hydrochloric acid in the stomach). Either too much or too little chloride can upset the chemical balance of the body. (See MINERALS; NUTRITION.)

choking, partial and complete blockage of the air passages, generally because the person has swallowed food or a foreign object that has lodged in the throat.

What If an Infant Is Choking?

If your baby's airway is blocked, follow these steps:

- *If someone is nearby, first call for help; if you are alone, try the procedures below for a minute or so before you phone for emergency help.*
- Place the baby face down on your forearm, with his or her head lower than the body and the head and neck stable or supported. Support your forearm firmly against your body. (If your baby is large, you may lay him or her face down on your lap, with head lower than body.)
- Slap the baby rapidly between the shoulder blades four times, with the heel of your hand.
- Turn the baby over and thrust into the chest (just below baby's nipples—the same location as for chest compression [see RESCUE BREATHING])—with two fingers four times rapidly.
- If something is completely blocking the windpipe and the baby still is not breathing, open the

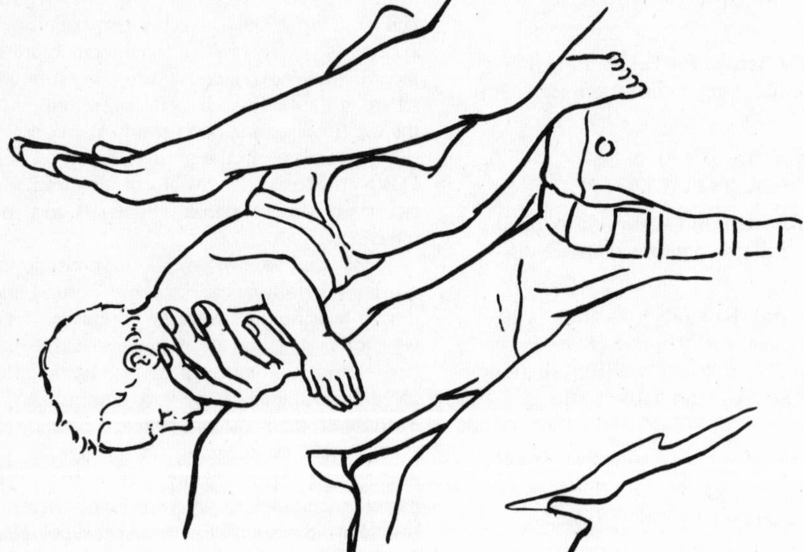

mouth by grasping both tongue and lower jaw between your thumb and finger and lift. This should move the tongue away from the back of the throat and may help open the throat. IF YOU CAN SEE something blocking the windpipe, try to remove it by carefully sweeping your finger from back to front.

- If breathing does not start again, try giving two ventilations [rescue breathing; see ARTIFICIAL RESPIRATION; also IF YOUR INFANT IS NOT BREATHING on page 48].
- If airway is still blocked, repeat entire procedure until help arrives.

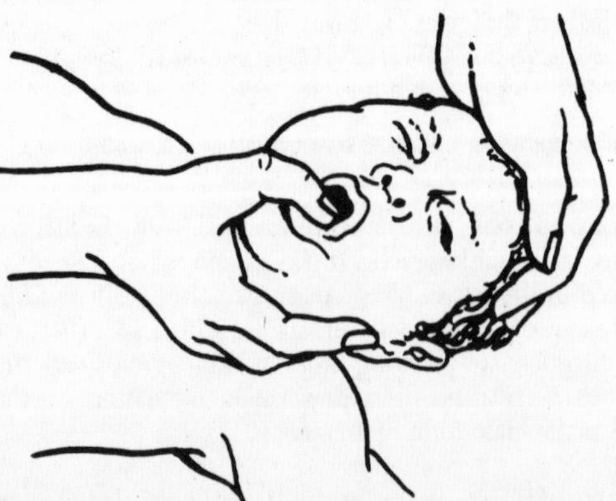

Source: Infant Care (1989). Prepared for the Public Health Service by the Health Resources and Services Administration, Bureau of Maternal and Child Health and Resources Development.

What If a Child Is Choking?

When food or a foreign body is sucked into the windpipe, the victim is unable to talk, turns blue, and can die within minutes. The technique described below forces air from the lungs up the windpipe to dislodge whatever is blocking the windpipe and thereby restore breathing. *If someone is nearby, first call for help; if you are alone, try the procedures below for a minute or so before you phone for emergency help*:

1. *If the child is standing,* support his or her chest with one hand, and with the heel of the other give the child four rapid, forceful blows between the shoulder blades. *If the child is lying down,* place your knee against his or her chest for support, and administer blows.

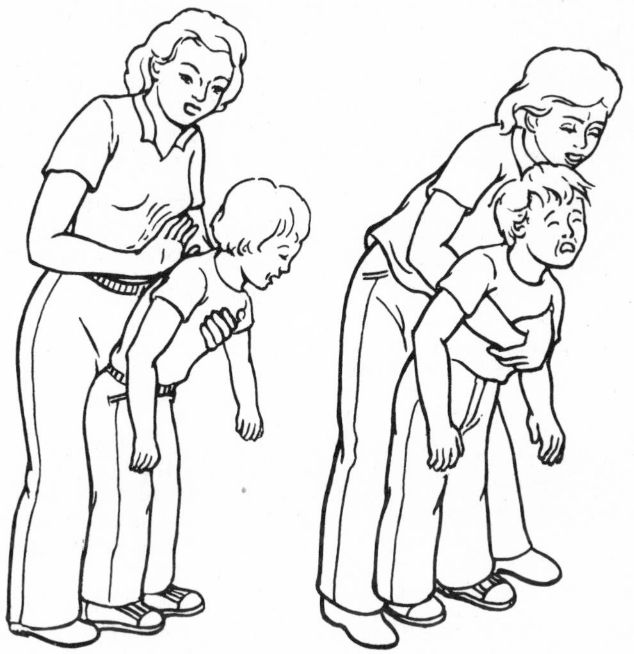

2. *If the obstruction is not cleared,* wrap your arms around the child, with the thumb side of your fist against his or her stomach between the navel and the rib cage. Grasp your fist with your other hand and make four quick, upward thrusts. Repeat if necessary. Watch breathing closely.

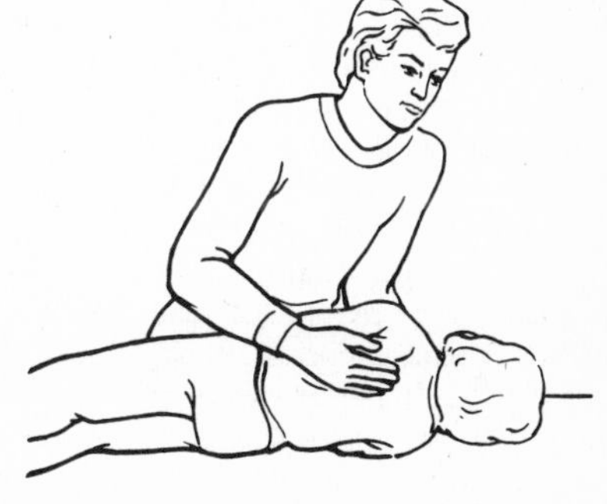

Source: Mainstreaming Preschoolers: Children with Orthopedic Handicaps by Shari Stokes Kieran, Frances Partridge Connor, Caren Saaz von Hippel, and Sherry Harris Jones (1986). Prepared for the Department of Health and Human Services by the Administration for Children, Youth and Families, Head Start Bureau.

Partial obstruction, with some air flow, can often be cleared by coughing, but total obstruction will lead to ASPHYXIA unless the airways are opened. Children are especially vulnerable to choking because their air passages are narrower than those of adults and because very young children cannot recognize that they should not try to swallow small items, such as jelly beans or buttons. The danger is increased if the children have physical problems with the muscles of the mouth and neck that affect speaking, breathing, and eating.

Prevention is the best approach to avoiding choking problems. Keeping dangerous items out of the reach of young children is an important part of CHILDPROOFING. Young children should never be fed small foods or pieces of food that can cause choking, such as nuts, raisins, popcorn, hard candy, or carrots. Hot dogs should not be fed to children under age four unless they have been sliced lengthwise and then crosswise into small pieces.

If, despite a parent's watchfulness, a child does swallow something and begin to choke, immediate action is needed to prevent suffocation, brain damage, and death. The parent may pound the child on the back, use the HEIMLICH MANEUVER (see WHAT IF AN INFANT IS CHOKING? on page 122; WHAT IF A CHILD IS CHOKING? on page 123). If results are not immediate, parents should call for emergency medical help. If medically trained personnel are readily available, an emergency TRACHEOSTOMY may be performed.

FOR HELP AND FURTHER INFORMATION

American Academy of Pediatrics (AAP), 800–433–9016. Publishes brochure *Choking Prevention and First Aid for Infants and Children.* (For full group information, see HEALTH CARE.)

cholesterol, a group of fatty substances present in foods from animal sources (including meat, poultry, eggs, and dairy products) but not from plant sources. The body makes sufficient cholesterol for its own needs, which include helping in the formation of VITAMIN D and various HORMONES. But excessive amounts that are ingested in high-fat diets are carried in the blood stream and cause a buildup of fatty tissue in the arteries (called *atherosclerosis*), and therefore a risk of heart disease (see HEART AND HEART PROBLEMS). Cholesterol can also crystallize in the gall bladder to form gallstones. Not all forms of cholesterol are the same. *High-density lipoproteins* (HDLs)—so-called "good cholesterol"—seem to help protect against arterial buildup, while *low-density lipoproteins* (LDLs) and *very-low-density lipoproteins* (VDLs) tend to increase the buildup. Though the effects are normally not seen until adulthood, recent studies have shown that atherosclerosis starts in childhood, so parents will be wise to watch the cholesterol content of meals for all family members (see FATS).

FOR HELP AND FURTHER INFORMATION

National Heart, Lung, and Blood Information Center (NHLBIC), 301–251–1222. Publishes booklets *Parent's Guide: Cholesterol in Children: Health Eating Is a Family Affair, Eat With Your Heart in Mind* (for children ages seven through ten), *Heart Health . . . Your Choice* (for ages eleven through fourteen), *Heart Habits: Don't Eat Your Heart Out* (for ages fifteen through eighteen), *So You Have High Blood Cholesterol,* and *Step by Step: Eating to Lower Your High Blood Cholesterol*; fact sheets *Facts About Blood Cholesterol*; and professional materials.

Citizens for Public Action on Blood Pressure and Cholesterol, 301–770–1711. Publishes *Cholesterol and Kids: A Parent's Guide, A Physician's Handbook: Cholesterol in Children and Adolescents,* and *Your Cholesterol Test Results and Treatment Plan.* (For full group information, see BLOOD PRESSURE.)

American Academy of Pediatrics (AAP), 800–433–9016. Publishes brochure *Growing Up Healthy—Fat, Cholesterol, and More.* (For full group information, see HEALTH CARE.)

American Heart Association (AHA), 800–242–8721. Publishes *Cholesterol and Your Heart* and diet manuals. (For full group information, see HEART AND HEART PROBLEMS.)

National Safety Council (NSC), 800–621–7615. Publishes *Cholesterol* (guide and video). (For full group information, see SAFETY.)

OTHER RESOURCES

Beating the Odds Against Heart Disease and High Cholesterol: Reducing Your Hereditary Risk. C. Richard Conti and Diana Tonnessen. Addison-Wesley, 1992.

Your Child and Cholesterol. Eugene Eisman and Diane Batshaw Eisman. Fell, 1990.

chordee, a CONGENITAL defect in which a male's PENIS curves downward; often association with HYPOSPADIAS.

chorea, unpredictable, involuntary, jerky movements, especially in the face and limbs, resulting from disturbances deep within the brain; formerly called *St. Vitus's dance.* The condition is most often found in two diseases, HUNTINGTON'S DISEASE and SYDENHAM'S CHOREA. It also sometimes appears during pregnancy, as *chorea gravidarum*; as a side effect from some kinds of drugs, including BIRTH CONTROL PILLS; or in CEREBRAL PALSY, often associated with the slow writhing of ATHETOSIS, in a combination called *choreoathetosis.*

chorionic villus sampling (CVS or chorionic biopsy), a GENETIC SCREENING procedure that involves removing some cells from tiny, fingerlike projections (*villi*) on the PLACENTA's outer membrane, the *chorion.* These cells, identical to those of the FETUS, can be used to identify some GENETIC DISORDERS, such as DOWN SYNDROME. Usually a flexible tube (CATHETER), guided by ULTRASOUND, is inserted through the pregnant woman's VAGINA, though sometimes a needle may be inserted through the abdomen. CVS can be done eight to twelve weeks into a pregnancy, much earlier than AMNIOCENTESIS, and its results are received more quickly, making an ABORTION easier, if desired. But CVS can identify fewer genetic problems and carries a higher risk of MISCARRIAGE than amniocentesis, while its long-term effects on the fetus are not yet known. Some studies have also linked CVS with BIRTH DEFECTS affecting the fingers and limbs, such as stunted or missing digits. But other larger studies found no such effects. Some researchers have suggested that, for safety, women might want to have CVS after ten weeks of pregnancy rather than earlier, since such injuries are less likely to occur later in fetal development. They also advise women considering chorionic villus sampling to be sure that the doctor has substantial experience with the procedure. (See GENETIC DISORDERS; GENETIC SCREENING.)

chromosomal abnormalities, problems resulting from mistakes in the duplication of the chromosomes that carry an individual's GENETIC INHERITANCE. Normally a baby is born with twenty-three pairs of chromosomes, twenty-two pairs called AUTOSOMES and one pair of SEX CHROMOSOMES (XX for a female and XY for a male). But due to errors in duplication of the chromosomes, occasionally some babies will have too many chromosomes, some too few, some will be missing pieces of chromosomes, some will have extra pieces, and some will have chromosomes separated and then rejoined in the wrong places (*translocation*). Many of these errors are so serious that the FETUS cannot develop and a spontaneous ABORTION (MISCARRIAGE) occurs, or the chromosome errors cause the death of the child just before or soon after birth.

Having one or more extra full sets of chromosomes, a condition called *polyploidy*, is lethal. So, in many cases, is having a triplet in place of a chromosome pair, a condition called TRISOMY. However, some babies with trisomy survive, including many who have a triplet for chromosome 21. Their disorder is called DOWN SYNDROME or *trisomy 21*. Other, rarer trisomies include PATAU'S SYNDROME or *trisomy 13*, and EDWARDS' SYNDROME or *trisomy 18*. Syndromes resulting from deletion of all or part of a chromosome are rare, but include the CRI DU CHAT SYNDROME.

Problems with the sex chromosomes lead to other common chromosomal abnormalities, including TURNER'S SYNDROME, in which a girl has only one X chromosome, instead of two, and KLINEFELTER'S SYNDROME, in which a boy has extra X chromosomes. Sometimes the chromosomal abnormality has only slight effects and can go undetected, but may be passed on to the next generation. The older the prospective parents, especially after the woman is over 30, the greater the chance of having chromosomal abnormalities, so GENETIC COUNSELING and GENETIC SCREENING are often recommended. (See GENETIC DISORDERS.)

chronic, a medical term for a condition that exists for a long period of time, often a lifetime, rather than being ACUTE, meaning limited in time and sharp or severe.

chronological age (CA), a child's age as measured from the birth date, which must often be attested to by showing a BIRTH CERTIFICATE or other acceptable certificate, as when a child enters school. A child's age is often used in comparisons of performance, skills, or behavior with others of the same chronological age, as in a child's EDUCATIONAL AGE or MENTAL AGE. (See TEST; AGE.)

circumcision, removal of the foreskin, a loose fold of skin that covers the head, or *glans*, of the PENIS; a brief operation generally performed on newborns. Long performed for religious reasons by Jews and Muslims, circumcision became widespread throughout the United States by the mid-twentieth century, but today is somewhat less universal and for many controversial. In the United States today, somewhat under 60 percent of babies are circumcised.

People who recommend circumcision note that:

- The circumcised penis is easier to keep clean.
- In uncircumcised penises, secretions tend to be trapped under the foreskin and become infected, causing problems such as BALANITIS, an inflammation of the glans and foreskin.
- Circumcision avoids the painful possibilities of PHIMOSIS, in which a foreskin is too tight, cannot be fully drawn back, and impedes free urination, and PARAPHIMOSIS, in which the retracted foreskin is too tight and becomes a tourniquet.
- Cancer of the penis and of the CERVIX are found more often among uncircumcised men and their wives.
- The operation is less painful and less traumatic when performed on a newborn than on an older child or an adult.

Those against circumcision regard the operation as an unnecessary surgical intervention that creates as many problems as it is designed to prevent, carrying some risk of injury to the penis and URETHRA, infection, hemorrhage, and, in rare cases, severe damage to the penis. They argue that the foreskin protects the glans from urine, feces, and abrasions from clothing, keeping the glans soft and moist and protecting it from injury throughout life, and that circumcised males lose sensitivity in the glans. Those strongly opposed to circumcision regard it as genital mutilation, as much as is FEMALE CIRCUMCISION, and as a form of CHILD SEXUAL ABUSE.

In the operation itself, the child is generally laid on a board with his arms and legs strapped down. The genitals are cleaned and covered with antiseptic. The foreskin is then cut away from the glans. After the operation, parents are advised to put some petroleum jelly and a strip of gauze over the penis each time they change the baby's diaper for a week to ten days, until the area has healed. They should not clean the area with alcohol.

An additional major controversy surrounding circumcision is that many doctors still perform the operation without giving the infant any ANESTHESIA, despite decades of work that has disproved long-held notions that newborns feel no pain (see PAIN AND PAIN TREATMENT). The use of topical anesthetic on the area and often an injection at the base of the penis (though that in itself is painful) are increasingly becoming standard. However, many babies are still given no pain medication during the recovery period, when the raw wound comes into contact with urine.

Parents should read about circumcision, discuss it between themselves and with their doctor, and come to a decision before the actual birth. If they decide to have the child circumcised, that is best done while the child is still in the HOSPITAL. However, circumcision would be postponed if the child has any CONGENITAL defect of the penis such as HYPOSPADIAS, since the foreskin tissue might be needed during a later surgical reconstruction.

FOR HELP AND FURTHER INFORMATION

General organizations

National Maternal and Child Health Clearinghouse (NMCHC), 703–821–8955 (For full group information, see PREGNANCY.)

National Perinatal Association (NPA), 813–971–1008. (For full group information, see PERINATAL CARE.)

National Perinatal Information Center, 401–274–0650. (For full group information, see PERINATAL CARE.)

American College of Obstetricians and Gynecologists (ACOG), 202–638–5577. Publishes *Circumcision.* (For full group information, see PREGNANCY.)

American Academy of Pediatrics (AAP), 800–433–9016. Publishes brochure *Newborn: Care of the Uncircumcised Penis.* (For full group information, see HEALTH CARE.)

Organizations against circumcision

National Organization of Circumcision Information Resource Centers (NOCIRC)
P.O. Box 2512
San Anselmo, CA 94979–2512
415–488–9883
Fax: 415–488–9660
Marilyn Fayre Milos, Executive Director
Network focusing on both male and female circumcision; formerly Informed Consent; publishes *NOCIRC Newsletter*, brochures *Answers to Your Questions About Infant Circumcision* and *Answers to Your Questions About Your Young Son's Intact Penis*; and reprints.

Newborn Rights Society (NRS)
P.O. Box 48
St. Peters, PA 19470
610–323–6061
Paul Zimmer, Contact
Organization of people opposing routine medical procedures such as circumcision and silver nitrate in the eyes as invasive and against the rights of the newborn; gathers and disseminates data.

Non-Circumcision Educational Foundation (NCEF)
P.O. Box 5
Richboro, PA 18954
215–357–2792
E-mail: jperon@delphi.com (Delphi: JPERON)
James E. Peron, Executive Director
Organization of parents, medical personnel involved in childbirth, and others who are interested in seeking to end routine circumcision and other medical treatments regarded as invasive, such as putting silver nitrate in the newborn's eyes as a preventative; runs seminars and workshops, and publishes print and film materials.

Remain Intact Organization (RIO)
Rural Route 2-Airport, Box 86
Larchwood, IA 51241
712–477–2256
Russell Zanggner, Director
Organization opposing routine circumcision, regarding circumcision as criminal genital mutilation and child sexual abuse; distributes numerous materials, including *The Case Against Circumcision* and *Breaking the Silence... Circumcision... The Ultimate Sexual Assault.*

OTHER RESOURCES

The Joy of Being a Boy. Elizabeth Noble and Leo Sorger. New Life Images, 1994. Includes discussion of circumcision.

Circumcision: A Parent's Decision for Life. Aaron J. Fink. Kavanah, 1988.

cisternal puncture, a type of MEDICAL TEST in which a small amount of fluid is removed from the base of the brain. It is used as an alternative or complement to a LUMBAR PUNCTURE.

civil proceeding, any noncriminal legal action, such as cases in which two parties disagree over rights. Most cases in JUVENILE COURTS, FAMILY COURTS, or DOMESTIC RELATIONS COURTS are civil proceedings and (unlike criminal court) do not involve the right to a jury trial. Rules about what kinds of evidence are admissible are also much looser than in criminal court.

class parent, the parent, often the MOTHER, who helps in a child's classroom, on field trips, and at other special events, generally in rotation with other parents for a specified period, though sometimes for a whole school year; also called a *room parent.*

clean hands doctrine, in family law, the general rule that a party who has acted in bad faith is judged with disfavor in future disputes. A parent who has resorted to PARENTAL KIDNAPPING is, for example, highly unlikely to later gain CUSTODY of the child, except in very special circumstances.

clean, intermittent catheterization (CIC), a medical technique for emptying the bladder that involves temporarily inserting a drainage tube (CATHETER) into the URETHRA, the passage through which urine flows out of the bladder. The tube, usually of plactic, is inserted every three to four hours, then taken out again and washed with soap and water. It has been found that, with proper care, sterilization of the tube is not necessary. Since the 1970s, CIC has generally replaced the earlier procedure of making a surgical opening into the abdomen and collecting the urine in an external bag.

Some children, such as those with spina bifida, cannot control the nerves and muscles that normally handle emptying of the bladder, so CIC is used to handle that function. Parents or caregivers handle the catheterization until children are able to do it themselves. Some of them learn to do it as young as ages three or four, often practicing on a special doll before performing the procedure on themselves. According to a 1984 Supreme Court ruling (Irving Independent School District vs. Tatro), a school nurse or a trained layperson must be provided in schools, including preschools, to perform CIC, if a child with disabilities is unable to do so. Commenting that "Services like CIC that permit a child to remain in school during the day are no less related to the effort to educate than are services that enable a child to reach, enter, or exit the school," the Court likened CIC to transportation, regarding it as a related educational service rather than a medical service. (Subscribers to the America Online computer service can find "Why Clean, Intermittent Catherization?" in the Moms Online Desk Reference section of Moms Online, under "catherization.")

cleft lip and palate, a type of BIRTH DEFECT involving a split in the lip and in the roof of the mouth (*hard palate*), sometimes extending back to the soft palate at the back of the mouth and the nostrils. During PREGNANCY, the two parts of the FETUS's face and palate develop separately; these normally fuse by birth, but fail to close in approximately 1 of every 700 babies. Sometimes this incomplete closure is part of a syndrome—a set of physical characteristics that tend to occur together—such as PIERRE ROBIN SYNDROME. But often isolated cleft appear, for reasons that are unclear, but may be linked to genetic and environmental factors, such as ALCOHOL and DRUG ABUSE, use of some medications, and DIABETES in the mother. Recent studies also indicate that MALNUTRITION, especially lack of proper VITAMINS, during the first few weeks of pregnancy are associated with significantly higher risk of having a child with cleft lip or palate.

Clefts of both lip and palate affect twice as many boys as girls, though cleft of the palate alone occur slightly more often in girls. Clefts are also twice as common among Whites as among Blacks, and occur infrequently among people of Asian ancestry. Women AT RISK, or those with a family history including cleft lip or palate, may well want to seek GENETIC COUNSELING when considering a pregnancy.

Babies with cleft lips are generally able to feed normally, but those with cleft palates must generally be bottlefed, sometimes with the help of an *obturator*, a device that covers the cleft palate during feeding. Cleft lips can be surgically repaired, generally within the first three months of life. A small scar will remain, though it will fade over time. Surgical repair of a cleft palate is normally done later, between twelve and eighteen months of age, and may require more than one operation and perhaps a BLOOD TRANSFUSION. Parents should discuss how to arrange for a safe blood transfusion. The surgical team often includes several specialists, such as a PEDIATRICIAN, a PLASTIC SURGEON, and dental specialists.

Before and after surgery SPEECH-LANGUAGE PATHOLOGISTS and AUDIOLOGISTS (hearing specialists) are also consulted often. Even after surgery, people with cleft palates often have EAR AND HEARING PROBLEMS that require special attention to prevent hearing loss and speech problems. They are also more likely to have TEETH AND DENTAL PROBLEMS, and may require help from an ORTHODONTIST.

FOR HELP AND FURTHER INFORMATION

Cleft Palate Foundation
1218 Grandview Avenue
University of Pittsburgh
Pittsburgh, PA 15211
412–481–1376; CLEFTLINE: 800–24-CLEFT [242–5338]
Fax: 412–481–0847
Nancy C. Smythe, Executive Director
Organization concerned with cleft lip and palate and other craniofacial birth defects; provides information and makes referrals; seeks to shape public policy; publishes various materials, including:

- brochures: *For Parents of Newborn Babies with Cleft Lip/Palate* and *Cleft Lip, Palate, and Craniofacial Birth Defects.*
- booklets: *Feeding an Infant with a Cleft, Cleft Lip and Cleft Palate: The First Four Years, Cleft Lip and Cleft Palate: The Child from Three to Twelve Years, Information for the Teenager Born with a Cleft Lip and/or Palate,* and *The Genetics of Cleft Lip and Palate: Information for Families.*
- "Information About" sheets: *Choosing a Cleft Palate or Craniofacial Team, Crouzon Syndrome (Craniofacial Dysostosis), Dental Care, Financial Assistance, Submucous Cleft, Treacher Collins Syndrome,* and *Treatment for Adults with Cleft Lip and Palate.*

(For other titles, see CRANIOSYNOSTOSIS; PIERRE ROBIN SYNDROME.)

Prescription Parents
P.O. Box 426
Quincy, MA 02269
617–479–2463

Laura I. Cohen, Executive Director
Organization of parents of children with cleft lip or palate and health professionals who work with them; encourages formation of parent support groups; publishes various materials, including newsletter.

AboutFace
USA:
P.O. Box 727
Warrington, PA 18976
Canada:
123 Edward Street, Suite 1405
Toronto, Ontario M5G 1E2
416–593–1448; 800–225-FACE [225–3223]
Fax: 215–491–0603
E-mail: abtface@aol.com (America Online: ABTFACE)
Pamela Onyx, Director
International organization of parents and professionals concerned with cleft palate and facial disfigurement. Provides support and information; encourages formation of local groups and linking of parents with similar experiences; publishes various materials, including the brochure AboutFace and pamphlets on facial disfigurement and other disorders, such as craniosynotosis.

March of Dimes Birth Defects Foundation (MDBDF), 914–428–7100. Publishes information sheet *Cleft Lip and Palate.* (For full group information, see BIRTH DEFECTS.)

Parents Helping Parents (PHP), 408–727–5775. Has division focusing on cleft lip and palate; publishes information packet *Cleft Lip and Palate.* (For full group information, see HELP FOR SPECIAL CHILDREN on page 689.)

National Institute of Dental Research (NIDR), 301–496–4261. (For full group information, see TEETH AND DENTAL PROBLEMS.)

FACES—The National Association for the Craniofacially Handicapped, 615–266–1632. (For full group information, see PLASTIC SURGERY.)

National Foundation for Facial Reconstruction
317 East 34th Street, Room 901
New York, NY 10016
212–263–6656; 800–422-FACE
Fax: 212–263–7534
Calliope K. Ligelis, Executive Director
Organization concerned with reconstructive facial surgery; provides information; publishes newsletter.

National Organization for Rare Disorders (NORD), 800–999–6673. (For full group information, see RARE DISORDERS.)

OTHER RESOURCES

A Parent's Guide to Cleft Lip and Palate. Karlind T. Moller et al. University of Minnesota Press, 1989.

(See also COMMUNICATION SKILLS AND DISORDERS.)

clinodactyly, abnormal bending (to the side or toward the middle) of one or more fingers or toes, a BIRTH DEFECT found in some disorders, such as CORNELIA DE LANGE SYNDROME.

clitoris, a small organ lying in the upper part of the VULVA; the main organ of sexual pleasure in women. A button of tissue similar to that in a man's PENIS, the clitoris is extremely sensitive to the touch, especially at the tip, being richly supplied with blood vessels and nerve endings. When stimulated, it fills with blood and become erect, though still less than an inch long. The SKIN covering the clitoris is a moist mucous membrane, and the structure itself is protected by a partly retractable hood, called a *foreskin* or *prepuce*, formed by the meeting of the small inner LABIA ("lips") of the vulva, the *labia minora.* The clitoris is also somewhat protected by the pubic bone and its associated fatty tissue, called the *mons veneris* or mound of Venus, which lies above it.

Direct or indirect stimulation of the clitoris brings sexual pleasure, sometimes leading to the climactic sensations known as an ORGASM. Over the centuries, people in some cultures have disliked or feared the idea of a woman having an orgasm or, indeed, any sexual pleasure. This has led some peoples to practice surgical removal of the clitoris and other parts of the GENITALS, a form of sexual mutilation called FEMALE CIRCUMCISION.

closed captions, captions on film or television that are invisible except to people with special captioning decoders, as opposed to captions superimposed on the picture for all to see. The technique, which is encouraged and partly subsidized by government funding, allows people with EAR AND HEARING PROBLEMS to have readier access to news, arts, and entertainment programs.

clubfoot (talipes), a CONGENITAL deformity in which the foot or ankle is twisted and somewhat fixed in an awkward position; a common BIRTH DEFECT affecting approximately 1 in every 400 babies, boys twice as often as girls. By far the most common and most severe kind of clubfoot is *talipes equinovarus,* in which one or both feet are twisted downward and inward, or "clubbed," often with the heel cord so tight that the foot cannot be easily moved into a normal position. Less severe and more easily treatable forms of clubfoot are *talipes calcaneal valgus,* in which the foot is sharply angled upward and outward, and *talipes metatarsus varus,* in which the front part of the food is twisted inward.

The causes of clubfoot are complex and unclear, but apparently involve both genetic and environmental factors, including drugs, infection, or other disease; it is sometimes associated with other birth defects, such as SPINA BIFIDA. Couples with clubfoot in their family history may wish to seek GENETIC COUNSELING when considering a pregnancy. Though once thought true of all forms of clubfoot, only the mildest cases are now thought to be caused by constriction within the UTERUS. Milder cases of clubfoot may respond to exercises starting shortly after birth, but more severe cases may also require plastic casts or surgery, especially to stretch or lengthen the heel cord. Mild or severe, clubfoot is best treated early.

FOR HELP AND FURTHER INFORMATION

March of Dimes Birth Defects Foundation (MDBDF), 914–428–7100. Publishes information sheet *Clubfoot.* (For full group information, see BIRTH DEFECTS.)

Shriner's Hospitals for Crippled Children, 800–237–5055. Provides free medical care for children with orthopedic problems. (For full group information, see BONE AND BONE DISORDERS.)

National Maternal and Child Health Clearinghouse (NMCHC), 703–821–8955 (For full group information, see PREGNANCY.)

National Institute of Child Health and Human Development (NICHD), 301–496–5133. (For full group information, see PREGNANCY.)

National Organization for Rare Disorders (NORD), 800–999–6673. (For full group information, see RARE DISORDERS.)

cochlear implant, a device using a microprocessor to simulate the functions normally performed by the *cochlea*, a structure in the inner ear, to aid people whose EAR AND HEARING PROBLEMS are so severe that they cannot be signficantly helped by a HEARING AID. A tiny electrical receiver and transmitter is surgically implanted into the inner ear; there it receives electrical signals from an external microphone and speech processor and transmits them to the brain. At its present state of development, the cochlear implant does not allow for normal hearing, but used in conjunction with LIPREADING, it can allow for much greater understanding of speech. It is most successful with POSTLINGUAL deaf people, who have some experience of spoken language.

Cognitive Abilities Test™ (COGAT), a series of paper-and-pencil, multiple-choice, group-administered STANDARDIZED TESTS for children from grades K–12 that are designed for assessment of verbal, quantitative, and nonverbal cognitive skills. The Primary Battery covers grades K–3, with two levels (K–1 and 2–3), focusing on oral vocabulary, verbal classification, relational concepts, figure classification, figure matrices, and quantitative concepts. For older children, separate Multilevel Editions exist for each grade, 3–12. These focus on three areas: verbal skills, such as sentence completion, verbal classification, and verbal analogies; quantitative skills, including quantitative relations, number series, and building equations; and nonverbal skills, such as figure classification, figure analogies, and figure analysis. The COGAT tests may be used in diagnosing possible LEARNING DISABILITIES, in planning INDIVIDUALIZED EDUCATION PLANS, and more generally in identifying students who need help in developing certain kinds of thinking skills. The NORMS for the COGAT tests were developed on the same population of students as those for the IOWA TESTS OF BASIC SKILLS and the TESTS OF ACHIEVEMENT AND PROFICIENCY™ (TAP), and they are often used to compare actual and anticipated achievement test scores.

cognitive development, the process by which an infant gains knowledge and becomes a thinking being, developing the whole range of perceptual and conceptual skills needed for organizing and understanding experience of the world, including memory, discrimination, sequencing, concept formation, generalization, reasoning, and problem-solving. Psychologist Jean Piaget, pioneer in studying cognitive development, proposed that children pass through four stages of cognitive learning:

- *sensory motor* (or *sensori-motor*): During roughly the first two years of life, a child becomes aware of sense perceptions and uses this knowledge in developing MOTOR SKILLS. Children learn OBJECT PERMANENCE and cause and effect, as they begin to understand and somewhat control the environment.
- *preoperational*: Between roughly ages two to seven, a child acquires language skills, begins to use symbols (words and images), and develops reasoning ability, but is as yet unable to deal with abstract concepts and deductive reasoning.
- *concrete operations*: Between roughly ages seven and eleven, a child begins to develop systematic reasoning and can apply logic to concrete, physical problems, but is not yet able to deal with abstract questions. That is, children at this stage may begin to solve problems in their heads, by thinking rather than doing, but the problems still relate to concrete things.
- *formal operations*: Between roughly ages eleven and sixteen, a child develops the ability to think and apply logic to and solve problems about abstract ideas, not just about concrete objects that can be readily perceived. This, for Piaget, marked the development of adult thinking, a stage at which a child begins to be able to hypothesize what might have been or what might be and to plan for the future.

Piaget's thinking on cognitive development has been enormously influential. However, many psychologists now feel that individual variations in the timing, sequence, and style of learning, especially among children who come from widely varying environments, are considerably greater than Piaget recognized. Piaget did, however, spur considerable observation and research as to just what and how children learn and when. A CHART OF NORMAL DEVELOPMENT (on page 637) indicates when between birth and age six children first *on the average* begin to develop the main cognitive skills.

Children with LEARNING DISABILITIES or other DEVELOPMENTAL DISORDERS may have malfunctions that inhibit their cognitive development. They often think in concrete terms, taking words quite literally rather than generalizing. For example, if you tell a group of children to get into a circle, a learning disabled child may step into a circle drawn on a carpet, rather than joining hands in a ring. They may take much longer to learn real-life connections, such as that grass needs rain to grow.

Children develop at individual and varying paces, but every child can benefit from activities designed to enhance their natural development. (Subscribers to the America Online computer service can find activities designed to help develop children's skills, including cognitive skills, in the Moms Online Desk Reference section of Moms Online, under "Teaching Young Children," and also some general suggestions in "How Parents Can Help a Child's Mind to Grow," under "cognitive development.")

FOR HELP AND FURTHER INFORMATION

Jean Piaget Society (JPS)
c/o William M. Gray, Treasurer
Department of Educational Psychology
University of Toledo
Toledo, OH 43606–3390
E-mail: fac0002@uoft01.bitnet
Internet: Piaget-L list-server. To subscribe, send this message "subscribe PIAGET-L [your first name] [your last name]" to: mailto:listserver@nic.umass.edu
Organization of people interested in Piaget's ideas on cognitive development; fosters research; publishes quarterly newsletter *The Genetic Epistemologist* and proceedings of annual symposia.

National Association for the Education of Young Children (NAEYC), 800–424–2460. Publishes books *The Child's Construction of Knowledge: Piaget for Teaching Children, Number in Preschool and Kindergarten: Educational Implications of Piaget's Theory*, and *Group Games in Early Education: Implications of Piaget's Theory.* (For full group information, see PRESCHOOL.)

High-Scope Educational Research Foundation, 800–407–7377. (For full group information, see PRESCHOOL.).

cognitive domain, one of three key categories of instructional content and learning objectives described by Benjamin Bloom, referring to thinking skills such as problem-solving, memory and recall, comprehension, reasoning, and judgment. (See DOMAIN.)

cognitive style, the type of approach that a person generally takes toward learning activities and problem-solving. One person may carefully analyze a task, break it down, and put the smaller steps in order, while another may jump impulsively into the middle of a new activity. (See LEARNING STYLE.)

colic (infantile), a condition in which an otherwise happy, healthy, alert young baby has attacks of crying and screaming—often quite different from the cries for food or attention—nearly every day, often in the evening, and at about the same hour of the day. Precisely what causes the attacks is unknown, though many people think it involves severe, painful spasms in the intestines; it is often associated with gas rumbling through the intestines. The crying may last for just a few minutes or may go on for twenty minutes or more, then end sud-

Tips for Parents With Colicky Babies

If your baby has an attack of colic, holding him or her across your knees on the stomach often will give some comfort. Some colicky babies cry less if they are kept in motion—try rocking or pushing in a carriage.

There is little you can do except try to comfort the baby until the attack stops. Make sure your baby isn't crying for some other reason (he or she is hungry, wet, lonely, or wearing clothing that is uncomfortable). It is important to remember that if your baby has colic, it does not interfere with his or her general health and growth. Your baby should grow out of it by the time he or she is twelve to sixteen weeks old.

"Colicky" babies do annoy and distress their mothers and fathers and anybody living in the household. Remind everyone that it is not the baby's fault, it is not your fault, and the baby will get over it. If the crying becomes too much to bear, put baby safely in the crib and walk into another room for a few minutes of relief. If the colic becomes a real problem, it is worth a special trip to your doctor.

Source: Infant Care (1989). Prepared for the Public Health Service by the Bureau of Maternal and Child Health and Resources Development.

denly, perhaps tailing off into a soft whimper, and may start up again just before sleep. Luckily, the condition generally disappears in a few weeks, having done no harm except to the parents' nerves.

It is wise for parents to be sure from the baby's medical checkups that the crying does not reflect some physical problem that requires attention. Beyond that, the parents' main role is to try to soothe the child—but not with feeding, for that may exacerbate the problem—and maintain their own composure. Some experts recommend against overstimulating the child or conveying any sense of anxiety, which could only make the problem worse. One option during such attacks is for parents or others in the household to take turns being with the baby, giving each other a break.

OTHER RESOURCES

Parents Books of Infant Colic. Phyllis Schneider. Ballantine, 1990.

Stopping Baby's Colic. Ted Ayllon and Mori Freed. Putnam, 1989.

college, in general, a school offering education beyond the HIGH SCHOOL level, but most often one that offers academic education leading to the lower-level postsecondary DEGREES. Two-year colleges (junior or community colleges) normally grant ASSOCIATE DEGREES, while four-year colleges award BACHELOR'S DEGREES. One or more colleges, graduate schools, and professional schools grouped together make up a UNIVERSITY, which often focuses on research in addition to teaching.

Once open to relatively few people, a college education has in recent decades become available to a much wider segment of the population and has become increasingly necessary for individuals. A college degree is a PREREQUISITE for many jobs, since the complexity of the modern technological world requires more highly skilled people than in the past. The need for more sophisticated job skills is reflected in the rapid spread of two-year community colleges, which provide advanced training in many occupational, technical, and cultural areas. Today, many students, who in earlier decades would have finished their schooling at twelfth grade or earlier, attend community colleges.

Many two- and four-year public colleges and universities have been far better funded in recent decades than most private colleges and universities, and therefore often have more modern and extensive libraries, laboratory equipment, and other facilities and can often attract high-quality professors by paying better salaries. As a result, many of the highest-ranking colleges and universities in recent surveys of the professors themselves have been public universities, with some public schools (such as the University of Michigan and top branches of the University of California) sometimes edging out IVY LEAGUE schools like Harvard and Yale for top honors. Parents considering both academic excellence and their own pocketbooks may well focus early on sending their children to public colleges rather than automatically aiming for the far more expensive private colleges. They should, however, also carefully assess the current situation; draconian tax cuts in California, for example, have diminished the quality of programs in that state's once-vaunted higher education system.

A college education is not necessary or even advisable for everyone. Many people have neither the interest, the aptitude, nor the basic skills to pursue academic education beyond the high school level. Their occupational options may be somewhat circumscribed by the lack of a college degree, but if they have other kinds of skills and interests to pursue, they may be perfectly happy to forego college.

But for those who choose to attend college, some of the main questions are:

- Identifying what they want in a college—small or large, competitive or easygoing, urban or rural, public or private, whether it offers special programs, and so on.
- Identifying which colleges will offer what they want.
- Gaining ADMISSION to the schools that interest them.
- Arranging to finance college costs.
- Selecting which of the schools that offer them admission best fits their needs.

With all the focus on admissions and financing and on the prestige of this school or that, students sometimes lose sight of their own personal preferences. But it is worth analyzing colleges very early and carefully choosing to apply to those that suit a student's individual needs, for those colleges are likely to make for the most successful and satisfying college career.

One of the key precollege hurdles are STANDARDIZED TESTS such as the SCHOLASTIC APTITUDE TEST. The PRELIMINARY SCHOLASTIC APTITUDE TEST, offered in the junior year of high school, can give the student an idea of where he or she stands relative to other students. Students and parents should use this information wisely in selecting which colleges to apply to, a process in which a school's guidance counselor can be helpful. The important point is to apply to schools that will suit the student's needs and desires, but which are not so competitive that the application is likely to fail. If students (or parents) still prefer to try for riskily competitive schools, they should be sure to have one or more *safety schools*, to which admission is almost guaranteed.

Parents and college-bound teens will want to pick up the current edition of one of the standard college handbooks, such as that published by the College Board or one of the many others. They may also find the materials listed in this entry of assistance in planning, choosing possibilities, making applications, surviving the admissions process, and achieving success in college.

FOR HELP AND FURTHER INFORMATION

GENERAL ORGANIZATIONS

American Association of University Women (AAUW), 202–785–7700. Publishes *College Admissions Tests: Opportu-*

nities or Roadblocks. (For full group information, see HELP ON LEARNING AND EDUCATION on page 659.)

HEATH Resource Center, National Clearinghouse on Postsecondary Education for Individuals with Disabilities, 800–544–3284, voice/TT. Publishes *College Admissions Tests.* (For full group information, see HELP FOR SPECIAL CHILDREN on page 689.)

Alliance for Parental Involvement in Education (ALLPIE), 518–392–6900. Publishes *College Admissions: A Guide for Homeschoolers.* (For full group information, and more titles, see HELP ON LEARNING AND EDUCATION on page 659.)

FOR SPECIAL STUDENTS

HEATH Resource Center, National Clearinghouse on Postsecondary Education for Individuals with Disabilities, 800–544–3284, voice/TT. Publishes *How to Choose a College: Guide for the Student with a Disability, College Freshman with Disabilities, Community College and Students with Disabilities, Resources for Students with Severe Disabilities on Campus, Make the Most of Your Opportunities, Vocational Rehabilitation Services—A Postsecondary Student Consumer's Guide, Student Consumer Speaks Up, Students with Disabilities and Law School, Access to the Science and Engineering Lab and Classroom,* and *Section 504—The Law and Its Impact on Postsecondary Institutions.* (For full group information, see HELP FOR SPECIAL CHILDREN on page 689.)

Alexander Graham Bell Association for the Deaf (AGBAD), 202–337–5220, voice/TT. Publishes *How the Student with Hearing Loss Can Succeed in College: A Handbook for Students, Families and Professionals.* (For full group information, see EAR AND HEARING PROBLEMS.)

National Information Center on Deafness (NICD), 202–651–5051; 202–651–5052, TT. Publishes *Students Who Are Deaf and Hard of Hearing in Postsecondary Education.* (For full group information, see EAR AND HEARING PROBLEMS.)

Self-Help for Hard of Hearing People (SHHH), 301–657–2248; 301–657–2249, TT. Publishes *Guide for Students with Hearing Loss* (on college). (For full group information, see EAR AND HEARING PROBLEMS.)

ONLINE RESOURCES

College and Adult Students Forum (CompuServe: STUFOB). Provides information on college admissions and funding from the U.S. Department of Education, as in *The Student Guide* from the Admissions/Financing Library.

College Forum (CompuServe). Provides discussions and online libraries on all areas of college and campus life; includes school rankings, information on graduate schools, and career centers; offers conferences with guest experts.

Career Resource Library (American Online: Career). Provides information on resources in all media to help in planning further education, job search, business plans, and personal and social development; includes searchable Occupational Profiles Database.

OTHER RESOURCES

FOR PARENTS AND TEENS

The College Guide for Parents, 3rd ed. Charles J. Shields. College Board, 1994.

Preparing Your Child for College: A Resource Book for Parents. Diane, 1993.

How to Get into and Graduate from College in Four Years with Good Grades, a Useful Major, a Lot of Knowledge, a Little Debt, Great Friends... Martin J. Spethman. Westgate, 1993.

College Shoppe!: The One-Stop List of Helpful Tips for Students and Their Parents. Mike Sicar. Midnight Oil, 1993.

You Can Survive College—We Did!: A Guide for Kids and Their Parents. Beverly P. Faaborg and Tony Faaborg. Educational Media, 1992.

When Kids Go to College: A Parent's Guide to Changing Relationships. Barbara Newman and Philip Newman. Ohio State University Press, 1992.

What to Expect from College: A University President's Guide for Students and Parents. Dennis O'Brien. St. Martin's, 1991.

ON NOT GOING TO COLLEGE

But What If I Don't Want to Go to College? Harlow Unger. Facts on File, 1992.

What Do You Mean You Don't Want to Go to College? by Liliane Quon McCain and Larry Strauss. Lowell House/Contemporary, 1990.

ON CHOOSING A COLLEGE

College Selection Workbook. Barry Beckham. Beckham House, 1994.

Making a Difference College Guide: Exciting Choices for Students Who Want to Make A Better World, 3rd ed. Miriam Weinstein. Sage, 1994.

Widen Your Choices. College Board, 1993. Video for middle school students.

College Planning-Search Book, 17th ed. American College Testing, 1991.

Choosing a College: The Student's Step-by-Step Decision-Making Workbook. Gordon Porter Miller. College Board, 1990.

Looking Beyond the Ivy League: Finding the College That's Right for You. Loren Pope. Penguin, 1990.

Campus Visits and College Interviews: A Complete Guide for College-Bound Students and Their Families. Zola Dincin Schneider. College Board, 1987.

ON ADMISSIONS

College Times. College Board. Annual magazine.

A Student's Guide to College Admissions: Everything Your Guidance Counselor Has No Time to Tell You, 3rd ed. Harlow G. Unger. Facts On File, 1995.

USA Today Getting Into College. Pat Ordovensky. Peterson's, 1995.

Playing the Selective College Admissions Game. Richard Moll. Viking Penguin, 1994.

College Admissions Crash Course. Sally Rubenstone. Preferred Marketing, 1994.

Behind the Scenes: An Inside Look at the Selective College Admission Process, 10th ed. Edward B. Wall. Octameron, 1994.

The Princeton Review: The Student Access Guide to College Admissions. Adam Robinson. Random, 1993.

Opening College Doors: How to Make the Admission Process Work for You. Pat Ordovensky and Robert Thornton. HarperCollins, 1992.

The College Admissions Game ... How to Play and Win. Judith C. Bowen. College Information Service, 1992.

The Best Guide to the Top Colleges: How to Get into the Ivies or Nearly Ivies. Joyce S. Mitchell. Garrett, 1991.

Other Routes into College: Alternative Admission. Stacy Needle. McKay/Random, 1991. On colleges who accept students who can show college potential, but do not meet the usual admission standards.

College Admissions: Cracking the System. Villard, 1990.

50 College Admission Directors Speak to Parents. Sandra F. MacGowan and Sarah M. McGinty. Harcourt Brace Jovanovich, 1990.

(See also SPORTS.)

On applications

Applications: A Guide to Filling Out All Kinds of Forms. Jeffrey Shniderman and Sue Hurwitz. Rosen, 1993.

College Applications and Essays: A How-To Handbook, 2nd ed. Susan D. Van Raalte. Prentice Hall, 1993.

Write Your Way into College, 2nd ed. George Ehrenhaft. Barron's, 1993.

How to Write a Winning College-Application Essay. Michael Mason. Prima, 1991.

Your College Application. Scott Gelband and others. College Board, 1991.

Writing Your College Application Essay. Sarah Myers McGinty. College Board, 1991.

On college transfers

Your Transfer Planner: Strategic Tools and Guerilla Tactics. Carey E. Harbin. Wadsworth, 1995.

The Transfer Student's Guide to Changing Colleges. Sidonia Dalby and Sally Rubenstone. Prentice Hall, 1993.

On preparing for college

Summer on Campus: College Experiences for High School Students, 2nd ed. College Board, 1996.

College Knowledge: What You Need to Know Before You Go. Jennifer Trussell. Carnegie, 1995.

College Planning Calendar for Juniors and Seniors. College Board, 1994.

Mitchell Express: The Fast Track to the Top Colleges. Joyce S. Mitchell. Garrett, 1993.

Reading Lists for College-Bound Students, 2nd ed. Doug Estell and others. Prentice Hall, 1993.

College Countdown: A Planning Guide for High School Students. Helen H. Heron. Heron, 1992.

College Transitions: A First-Year Guide for Parents and Students. Kent D. Beeler. Kendall-Hunt, 1991.

On early years in college

Getting Oriented. Rhonda H. Atkinson and Debbie G. Longman. West, 1994.

The First Year Experience, 2nd ed. Rebecca Leonard. Kendall-Hunt, 1992.

Starting College. Robert V. Iosue. Wellspring, 1992.

College: The First Two Years. Washington Shannon. Ginn, 1992.

Transition: An Introduction to Urban College Student Life. Robert DeLucia, ed. Ginn, 1992.

After the SATs: An Insider's Guide to Freshman Year. Michele A. Paige. Barron's, 1991.

College Smarts: The Official Freshman Handbook. Joyce S. Mitchell. Garrett, 1991.

On the general college experience

College: Your Complete Guide to the Best Five Years of Your Life. Clark Benson and Alex Gordon. Picket Fence, 1994.

The College Survival Guide. Bruce M. Rowe. West, 1994.

College Undercover: What Every Student Needs to Know. Merrick J. Marion. Wharton, 1994.

College Survival, 3rd ed. Greg Gottesman. Prentice Hall, 1994.

So This Is College Too. Marlene F. Blumin. Kendall-Hunt, 1993.

College Survival Guide: Doing It Smarter. Nicholas V. Haan. R & E Publishers, 1993.

The College Survival Kit Handbook: The Official Handbook for the College Survival Kit. Steven Fink. Sterman, 1993.

Your College Experience: Strategies for Success. A. Jerome Jewler and John N. Gardner. Wadsworth, 1993.

Starting from Scratch: Strategies for the Successful College Experience. Bonita S. Jacobs and others. Kendall-Hunt, 1993.

Student Success: How to Succeed in College and Still Have Time for Your Friends. Timothy L. Walter. Harcourt Brace, 1993.

Bruce Stuart and Kim Stuart's College 101. Bruce S. Stuart and Kim Stuart. Macmillan, 1993.

The Undergraduate Almanac: A Low Life Guide to Higher Education. Jon Sbar. Crazed Rodent, 1992.

You Can Master the Maze of College. John Van Brunt. Washington, 1992.

College Life. Ellen Rosenberg. Viking Penguin, 1992.

College Survival: A Crash Course for Students by Students, 2nd ed. Greg Gottesman. Prentice Hall, 1992.

On self-management

Fifty-Two Ways to Get Along with Your College Roommate. C. E. Rollins. Nelson, 1994.

Princeton Review: Surviving Without Your Parents' Money. Geoffrey Martz. Random, 1993.
The Student Body: A Survival Guide to College Eating and Weight Control. Jill Brown and Jane Myers. Two-J Books, 1993.
Self-Management for College Students: The ABC Approach, rev. ed. Edward J. O'Keefe and Donna S. Berger. Partridge Hill, 1993.
Beating the College Blues: A Student's Guide to Coping with the Emotional Ups and Downs of College Life. Paul Grayson and Philip Meilman. Facts on File, 1992.
Inside College: New Freedom, New Responsibility. Henry C. Moses. College Board, 1990.
Campus Health Guide: The College Student's Handbook for Healthy Living. Carol L. Otis and Roger Goldingay. College Board, 1989.

For specific groups

The College Woman's Handbook. Rachel Dobkin and Shana Sippy. Workman, 1995.
*The Complete Handbook for College Women: Making the Most of Your College Experience.*Carol Weinberg. NYU Press, 1994.
University Success: The Christian Perspective. Josephine Shangkuan-Ong. Kendall-Hunt, 1994.
The Black Student's Guide to College Success. Ruby D. Higgins, ed. Greenwood, 1993.
The Hillel Guide to Jewish Life on Campus: The Most Comprehensive Guide to a Quality College Experience, rev. ed. Ruth F. Cernea, ed. B'nai B'rith-Hillel, 1993.

On succeeding in college

Majoring in Success: Make College Easier, Beat the System and Get a Very Cool Job. Patrick Combs. Ten Speed Press, 1995.
Orientation to College Learning. Dianna L. Van Blerkom. Wadsworth, 1995.
Getting the Most Out of College. Arthur W. Chickering and Nancy K. Schlossberg. Allyn, 1994.
Coping with College: A Guide for Academic Success. Alice L. Hamachek. Allyn, 1994.
Toolkit for College Success. Daniel R. Walther. Wadsworth, 1994.
Making the Most of College, rev. ed. Spencer A. Rathus and Lois Fichner-Rathus. Prentice Hall, 1994.
College Study Skills: Becoming a Strategic Learner. Dianna L. Van Blerkom. Wadsworth, 1994.
The College Success Book: A Whole-Student Approach to Academic Excellence. James E. Groccia. Glenbridge, 1994.
College Success Strategies: Workbook, 2nd ed. Linda M. Gubbe. Kendall-Hunt, 1993.
Simple Rules for Success in College. Alan S. Cirlin. Kendall-Hunt, 1993.
Becoming an "A" Student, 2nd ed. Harriet L. Whyte. Kendall-Hunt, 1993.
Strategies for College Success, 2nd ed. Mary C. Starke. Prentice Hall, 1993.
Learning Skills for College and Career. Paul Hettich. Brooks-Cole, 1992.
Opening Doors to College Success. Karen Bergher. Kendall-Hunt, 1992.
Conquering College: The Most Fun You Can Have Learning the Things You Need to Know. Howard Scott Warshaw. EduQuest, 1992.
Doing It Right: Improving College Learning Skills. Ben E. Johnson. Heath, 1992.
College Student's Handbook for Better Grades, Job Search, and Career Success. S. A. Swami. Minibook, 1991.
Truth about College: How to Survive and Succeed As a Student in the Nineties. Scott Edelstein. Carol, 1991.
Acing College: A Professor's Guide to Beating the System. Joshua Halberstam. Viking Penguin, 1991.
Becoming a Master Student. David B. Ellis. College Survival, 1991.
College Basics: How to Start Right and Finish Strong, 2nd ed. Marvin Lunenfeld and Peter Lunenfeld. Semester, 1991.

Personal experiences

Taking Charge of My Life: Personal Essays by Today's College Students. Townsend, 1993.
Letters from the College Front. Doug Hutchcraft and Ronald P. Hutchcraft. Baker, 1993. ("Girls' Edition" and "Guys' Edition.")

(See also ADMISSIONS; FINANCIAL AID; SCHOLASTIC APTITUDE TEST; ACT TESTS.)

college boards, popular name for precollege tests, especially the SCHOLASTIC APTITUDE TEST, offered by the COLLEGE ENTRANCE EXAMINATION BOARD.

College Entrance Examination Board (College Board or CEEB), a nonprofit organization providing services to hundreds of colleges, universities, agencies, and other groups, primarily offering widely used tests for college-bound students, among them:

- SCHOLASTIC APTITUDE TEST (SAT), a student ADMISSIONS TEST for COLLEGE;
- PRELIMINARY SCHOLASTIC APTITUDE TEST/National Merit Scholarship Qualifying Test (PSAT/NMSQT), a "warm-up" for the SAT that is also used for the National Merit Scholarships;
- ADVANCED PLACEMENT PROGRAM (APP), for high school students seeking college credits;
- COLLEGE LEVEL EXAMINATION PROGRAM (CLEP), for college students seeking noncourse credit.

The College Board also operates the College Scholarship Service for students seeking FINANCIAL AID. Though its testing services are clearly valued by colleges and universities, critics have often complained that such TESTS distort the evaluation process, giving preference to those who are good at taking tests over those who may have other, equally valuable but less easily measurable skills and abilities.

College-Level Examination Program (CLEP), a series of STANDARDIZED TESTS offered by the COLLEGE ENTRANCE EXAMINATION BOARD in dozens of subjects to students who are studying in EXTERNAL DEGREE PROGRAMS or who wish to gain college CREDIT through self-study before entering, or while enrolled in, a regular campus-based college program. Students would be wise to confirm beforehand that their college will accept CLEP results for credit and ADVANCED PLACEMENT.

College Work-Study (CWS), a federally funded WORK-STUDY PROGRAM, open to undergraduate and graduate students, offering jobs on and off campus. Undergraduates are paid by the hour, graduates by the hour or by salary. All participants are paid at least monthly, but the amount earned cannot exceed demonstrated need. (See FINANCIAL AID.)

colonoscope, a type of ENDOSCOPE, passed through the anus, used by doctors in visually examining the colon (large intestine). (See DIGESTIVE SYSTEM AND DISORDERS.)

colostrum, a yellowish fluid that is produced by the BREASTS in the last part of PREGNANCY and the first few days after CHILDBIRTH, before the normal LACTATION begins. The colostrum contains white blood cells, ANTIBODIES, PROTEIN, MINERALS, FATS, and sugars. Women may wish to place a small, clean, cotton pad in a bra to prevent clothes from becoming stained. They should wash the breasts with mild soap and water, as necessary, to avoid infection.

coma, a state of deep unconsciousness from which the person cannot be aroused; the term is generally applied when this sleeplike state lasts for more than an hour. The depth of a coma varies, but in general, the person does not respond either to external stimuli (such as shouts or pinches) or to internal cues (such as the sensation of a full bladder). People in a coma generally have eyes closed or, if open, their eyes are unfocused, and they may have sleep-wake cycles. Unlike conditions of BRAIN DEATH, some types of brain activity remain. Even severely comatose patients can sometimes breathe on their own, move their eyes, and make other facial movements. Patients in less severe comas may even have some modest response to external stimulation, even though still unconscious. Coma can result from a variety of problems, including TRAUMATIC BRAIN INJURY, BRAIN TUMOR, severe cases of DIABETES, kidney problems, liver problems, ENCEPHALITIS, MENINGITIS, SHOCK, and HYPOXIA.

If feeding, breathing, and other vital functions are maintained, people can sometimes exist for years in a coma, in what is called a persistent vegetative state. In some cases, however, no real chance for recovery exists; it is in some of these cases that families have faced the difficult right-to-die questions (see DEATH AND DYING).

FOR HELP AND FURTHER INFORMATION

Brain Injury Association, 800–444–6443. Publishes information packet *Coma, The Catastrophe of Coma: A Way Back, Coma: Its Treatment and Consequences, The Care and Rehabilitation of the Patient in Persistent Vegetative State, Family Reactions to Persistent Vegetative State, Law and Medicine: The Persistent Vegetative State.* (For full group information, see TRAUMATIC BRAIN INJURY.)

National Institute of Neurological Disorders and Stroke (NINDS), 800–352–9424. (For full group information, see BRAIN AND BRAIN DISORDERS.)

comfort habits, actions or objects adopted by young children to enhance their feeling of comfort, safety, and security. These include SUCKING a thumb, finger, or PACIFIER, adopting a TRANSITIONAL COMFORT OBJECT such as a teddy bear or old blanket, and repetitive, rhythmic activities such as rocking or HAIR twisting. Sucking and comfort objects generally cause no concern (unless the object is accidentally lost!), but repetitive physical activities can interfere with the child's developing relationship with the world, becoming a sort of self-hypnosis. If a child seems to be withdrawing from other activities into rhythmic habits (rather than falling into them when bored, as at sleeptime) and especially if the activities are potentially dangerous (such as head-banging), parents may want to consult their PEDIATRICIAN for ways to counteract or divert the habits before they become ingrained. These can develop into a psychological condition called *stereotypic habit disorder*, which may require treatment. Often, however, substantial amounts of loving attention and playtime with parents can turn the child away from rhythmic habits, if they have not already become well-established.

communication skills and disorders, the skills involved in and the problems arising from using speech and language, which become obvious in early childhood as children learn to communicate with others. Speech is just one method of communicating with language, which is the ability to use symbols to represent objects and ideas. These symbols may include written characters and words used in WRITING, the gestures used in SIGN LANGUAGE, standardized BLISS SYMBOLS moved on a CONVERSATION BOARD, or the spoken sounds used in speech.

Children learning to communicate must master two different kinds of language skills. The first is *receptive language*, the ability to understand or comprehend what is heard. The other is *expressive language*, the ability to express oneself verbally. Most children (like most adults) understand more than they are able to express. Many perfectly normal young children have difficulty imitating sounds and language clearly enough to be understood, but many outgrow such problems during the early grades of school.

The process starts early. Researchers have found that babies learn language sounds far earlier than was previ-

Observation Checklist for Possible Communication Disorders in Preschoolers

RECEPTION

	Often or Always	Rarely or Never
After 24 months, the child cannot point to common objects that are named.	☐	☐
After 24 months, the child cannot understand simple one-part directions, such as "Bring me the ball."	☐	☐
After 36 months, the child repeats questions rather than answering them. For example, when asked, "What did you do yesterday?" the child responds "Do yesterday."	☐	☐
After 48 months, the child cannot follow two-part directions, such as "Put the book away and get a chair."	☐	☐
After 48 months, the child is unable to respond, even with appropriate gestures, to a slightly complex question such as "What do you do when you're thirsty?"	☐	☐
After 48 months, the child seems confused when asked a question or when the class is given instructions. The child waits to see what the other children are doing when directions are given.	☐	☐

EXPRESSION

	Often or Always	Rarely or Never
After 24 months, the child has not yet started talking.	☐	☐
After 36 months, the child cannot put words together to make simple sentences such as "Give me more juice."	☐	☐
After 48 months, the child cannot tell a recent series of events.	☐	☐
After 48 months, there are unusual word confusions or substitutions of words when the child talks. For example, the child may say "I want a crayon" for "I want a pencil," or "Give me the stove thing" for "Give me a pot."	☐	☐
After 60 months, most of the child's grammar and sentence structure seems noticeably faulty and is unlike the communication pattern used in the child's home.	☐	☐

ARTICULATION

	Often or Always	Rarely or Never
After 24 months, the child uses mostly vowel sounds (oo, ah, ee) and gestures when talking.	☐	☐
After 36 months, the child leaves out the first sound in many words (says "at" for "cat" or "es" for "yes").	☐	☐
After 42 months, friends, neighbors, and teachers cannot understand most of what the child says.	☐	☐
At any age, the child seems embarrassed or disturbed about his or her speech.	☐	☐
At any age, speech sounds are more than a year late in developing.	☐	☐

RHYTHM

	Often or Always	Rarely or Never
The child has noticeable difficulty and seems to struggle trying to say words or sounds.	☐	☐
The child is aware of this difficulty.	☐	☐
There is an abnormal amount of hesitation, repetition of sounds ("cuh-cuh-can") or words ("but-but-but"), and/or prolongation of sounds ("ssssomething") or words ("mmmmeeee") in the child's speech and the child seems aware of it.	☐	☐

VOICE

	Often or Always	Rarely or Never
The child's voice is so soft that he or she can barely be heard.	☐	☐
The child's voice is extremely loud.	☐	☐
The child's pitch is inappropriate (too high or too low) for the child's sex and age.	☐	☐
The child's voice sounds hoarse, strained, or unusual in some way.	☐	☐
The child's speech is nasal (sounds as if he or she has a cold or sinus condition).	☐	☐
The child's speech is hypernasal (sounds seem to be spoken through the nose rather than through the mouth).	☐	☐

Many of the items in this checklist were obtained from *Getting a HEAD START on Speech and Language Problems* by Susan Hansen. Copyright 1974 Meyer Children's Rehabilitation Institute, 444 South 44 Street, Omaha, Nebraska 68131.

Source: Mainstreaming Preschoolers: Children with Speech and Language Impairments: A Guide for Teachers, Parents, and Others Who Work with Speech and Language Impaired Preschoolers. Jacqueline Liebergott and others. Government Printing Office (1978). Prepared for the Head Start Bureau, Administration for Children, Youth and Families.

ously thought. A 1992 study, for example, suggests that by the age of six months, babies have learned the basic sounds of the language spoken by the people around them. The finding was surprising because previous studies have indicated that it normally takes *another* six months before babies understand that sounds are used to convey word meanings. Such studies underline the importance of recognizing and quickly treating chronic ear infections in babies, since they may hinder language development. The studies also highlight the role of parents and CAREGIVERS as early language tutors of their children and emphasize the importance of communicating with infants, such as PREMATURE babies or those with severe health problems, in HOSPITALS. And they confirm the usefulness of talking to babies—as so many parents and other adults do—with a relatively high-pitched voice, clear pronunciation, and marked intonation. By doing so, researchers suggest, they are providing their babies with the basics of language. Even nonsense sounds such as "goo-goo" have value, since infants are learning sounds even if they do not yet recognize that a meaning may be attached to them. (Subscribers to the America Online computer service can find a fuller discussion, "Your Baby Hears You Talking," in the Moms Online Desk Reference section of Moms Online, under "communication skills and disorders.")

The CHART OF NORMAL DEVELOPMENT on page 637 indicates when, between birth and age six, children generally first develop the main communication skills and other skills. Parents should be cautioned that children develop at individual and widely varying paces. If they have real concerns about a child's development, they should by all means have the child professionally evaluated, but many perfectly normal children do not begin to speak until *long* after the averages say they should.

Some children have continuing problems. They are said to have a language disorder if their difficulty is in understanding language or putting words together to make sense. In such cases, the cause is generally some kind of malfunction of the brain. The National Institute of Deafness and Other Communication Disorders (NIDCD) notes that such problems may show themselves in several ways:

- Children may have trouble giving names to objects and using those names to formulate ideas about how the world is organized. For example, they cannot learn that a toy they play with is called "car" and that a toy car of another color or a real car can also be called "car."
- They may have trouble learning the rules of grammar. Such children might not learn, for example, how to use prepositions and other small words like "in" and "the."
- They may not use language appropriately for the context; for example, they might respond to a teacher's question by reciting an irrelevant jingle heard on television.

Children are said to have *speech disorders* if they have trouble actually producing the sounds of the language. Such problems may stem from a malfunction in the brain or an inability to properly control the muscles needed to produce the sounds. Speech is actually a highly complex activity, directed by the brain, using various muscles in the tongue, lips, jaw, palate, larynx and face to change the shape of the mouth. The mouth forms the sound made by air being pushed from the lungs through the vocal cords in the larynx, while other consonants ("stop" sounds) are produced by the lips, the teeth, and the roof of the mouth. Children with certain kinds of physical problems, such as CEREBRAL PALSY or CLEFT LIP AND PALATE, have special difficulty with speech.

Speech problems are far more widespread than language problems, affecting twice as many boys as girls. The NIDCD estimates that speech disorders affect approximately 10 to 15 percent of preschoolers and 6 percent of children in grades 1–12. By contrast, language disorders affect 2 to 3 percent of preschoolers and 1 percent of older children. In both cases, an affected child will be significantly behind other children of the same age, background, and ability in their rate of speech and language development. Professionals in the field use a wide variety of phrases to describe the kind of slowed development shown in these children, including *developmental language disorder, delayed speech, impaired language, motor disorder,* and *idiopathic speech and language disorders* (meaning "of no known cause").

Children with communication disorders often have other kinds of problems, such as EAR AND HEARING PROBLEMS, MENTAL RETARDATION, CRI DU CHAT SYNDROME, TOURETTE SYNDROME, and AUTISM, which can magnify the effects of communications problems. For example, children who have trouble with AUDITORY SKILLS—auditory discrimination, auditory memory, or localization—also have trouble developing receptive language skills, because they misunderstand or forget words. They may have trouble learning some of the key action words (such as the verbs *put, jump,* or *run*) and words showing position (such as the prepositions *in, on, behind,* or *under*). If so, they are unable to understand seemingly simple directions, such as "Put the ball in the box."

Children with LEARNING DISABILITIES and some other DEVELOPMENTAL DISORDERS may also have problems in learning the forms of the language, such as singular or plural, or past and present tense of verbs. They may often forget the words they want to say, substitute one word for another (such as *table* for *chair*), or substitute sound effects for a word (such as *meow* for *cat*). Such children often cannot imitate movements of the tongue or lips for actions such as blowing, and they may experience equal difficulty in copying body language or nonverbal communication, as in using gestures, mime, or facial expression.

But apart from these multiple problems, there are several different kinds of speech and language problems that may affect children:

- *Phonological impairment,* or *misarticulation,* in which a child says the sounds wrong or omits or duplicates sounds within a word, as in *wabbit* for *rabbit, thnake* for *snake, dood* for *good,* and *poo* for *spoon.* The problem might be poor neurological motor skills, an error in learning, or difficulty in identifying some speech sounds. A child might also drop an unstressed syllable, as in *nana* for *banana* or *te-phone* for *telephone.* Many young children do this early in speech development, but when this type of pronunciation persists unduly, brain dysfunction is considered the cause. Some of these misarticulations are popularly called "baby talk" or *lisping*; to make sure a child does not learn to speak improperly, experts recommend that parents avoid using "baby talk" altogether.
- *Stuttering,* or *stammering,* in which the the speech rhythms are disrupted. A stuttering child repeatedly hesitates, stumbles, prolongs, or spasmodically pronounces certain problem sounds, which vary from person to person. Stuttering is common among children, especially boys, but many outgrow it or receive therapy in early childhood to help overcome it. Professionals advise parents to be patient and calm, not to make the child anxious about the stuttering and so exacerbate it, and to seek therapy early on so that the speech pattern does not become set for life. Parents should also be aware that stuttering comes and goes for unknown reasons. The causes of stuttering are unclear, but there is strong evidence of a genetic factor; it seems to run in families, and some feel it results from some subtle brain dysfunction. Some regard the triggers as psychological, but others suggest that emotional problems are often a result, not a cause, of stuttering. Recent researchers have found that while, in most people, one set of vocal muscles relaxes and the other contracts during speech, in stutterers both sets of muscles contract very hard. As the NIDCD puts it, the muscles are "setting up a virtual tug of war for control of the cords."
- *Dyspraxia,* which is the inability to properly coordinate in sequence the movements required for speech. In dyspraxia, the vocal instruments seem to be in perfectly good working order, but there is a disruption in the instructions from the brain to the muscles involved in speech. Children with verbal dyspraxia make many of

the same errors as in phonological impairment, but may also speak using only vowels, making their speech virtually unintelligible.

- DYSARTHRIA, involves problems with controlling the muscles used in speaking and often characterized by the mouth being open all the time and the tongue protruding. This disorder is often associated with others affecting the NERVOUS SYSTEM; the child may have trouble eating, as well.
- APHASIA, lack of expressive or receptive language function. When resulting from TRAUMATIC BRAIN INJURY that has damaged the brain area involved in speech after the child had begun to develop communications skill, the condition is called *acquired aphasia.*
- *Chronic voice disorders,* in which the voice is unusually loud, soft, high, low, raspy, strained, hoarse, nasal, monotone, and in other ways abnormal.

The OBSERVATION CHECKLIST FOR POSSIBLE COMMUNICATION DISORDERS IN PRESCHOOLERS (page 136) can alert parents or teachers to an undiagnosed speech or language problem in a preschooler. For each item in the five areas, parents should check either the "often or always" or the "rarely or never" column. Young children are still developing, so the age covered by the various questions is important. One or more checks in the "often or always" column could signal a communication problem, so parents should have the child evaluated.

Whatever the type of communication disorder, therapy is generally in the hands of a SPEECH-LANGUAGE PATHOLOGIST, also called a *speech therapist,* working with various medical specialists, including:

- AUDIOLOGIST, to assess any association with hearing problems.
- OTOLARYNGOLOGIST, to examine whether there are physical conditions in the speech-making apparatus that need medical treatment, including surgery.
- NEUROLOGIST, to detect, if possible, any brain abnormalities.
- PSYCHOLOGIST, to assess the child's mental abilities, through various TESTS.

Together these specialists will develop a program of exercises that the speech-language pathologist will use to lessen or eliminate the speech disorders. Often these involve a variety of techniques, including tapes and headphones that help the child hear his or her own speech and begin to shape the sounds more appropriately. Pathologists also rely on a wide variety of exercises designed to enhance COGNITIVE DEVELOPMENT. For people who stutter, various exercises are used to teach how to relax the larynx muscles and slow the rate of speech.

In school and in prechool programs such as HEAD START, children with communication disorders are often entitled to special help under the EDUCATION FOR ALL HANDICAPPED CHILDREN ACT and its successor the INDIVIDUALS WITH DISABILITIES EDUCATION ACT. Various descriptions are used to identify who is regarded as having a DISABILITY under these laws, but Head Start's definition is:

> A child shall be reported as speech impaired with such identifiable disorders as receptive and/or expressive language impairment, stuttering, chronic voice disorders, and serious articulation problems affecting social, emotional and/or educational achievements; and speech and language disorders accompanying conditions of hearing loss, cleft palate, cerebral palsy, mental retardation, emotional disturbance, multiple handicapping conditions, and other sensory and health impairments. This category excludes conditions of a transitional nature consequent to the early developmental processes of the child.

More generally, children are considered to have disabilities if they fit a definition like that in the previous paragraph and so require SPECIAL EDUCATION and related services.

Every young child can benefit from activities designed to enhance their natural development, as in imitating speech and body language. (Subscribers to the America Online computer service can find activities designed to develop children's communication skills in the Moms Online Desk Reference section of Moms Online, under "Teaching Young Children.")

FOR HELP AND FURTHER INFORMATION

National Institute on Deafness and Other Communication Disorders (NIDCD)
9000 Rockville Pike
Building 31, Room 3C–35
Bethesda, MD 20892
800–241–1044; 800–241–1055, TT
Fax: 301–402–0018
James B. Snow, Director
One of the U.S. National Institutes of Health, sponsoring research on deafness and other communicative disorders as well as smell and taste disorders; provides information; publishes various materials, including research reports for professionals and brochures on topics such as *Update on Developmental Speech and Language Disorders, Update on Stuttering, Speech Disorders Organizational Resources, Voice Disorders Organizational Resources,* and professional materials.

American Speech-Language-Hearing Association
10801 Rockville Pike
Rockville, MD 20852
301–897–5700, voice/TT; HELPLINE:
800–638–8255, voice/TT (U.S. except MD, AK, HI)
Fax: 301–571–0457
Frederick T. Spahr, Executive Director
Organization of professional speech-language patholo-

gists and audiologists; provides information and referrals; offers certification and accreditation programs; publishes various materials, including *Asha—The Monthly Magazine* and four professional journals; general brochures: *How Does Your Child Hear and Talk?, Recognizing Communication Disorders, Speech and Language Disorders and the Speech-Language Pathologist,* and *Do Your Health Benefits Cover Audiology and Speech-Language Pathology Services?*; "Questions About" brochures: *Child Language, Otitis Media, Hearing, and Language Development, Stuttering, Articulation Problems, Voice Problems,* and *Adult Aphasia*; materials on adults with speech, language, or hearing disorders; and professional materials.

National Easter Seal Society, 800–221–6827. Publishes *Are You Listening to What Your Child May Not Be Saying? Understanding Stuttering,* and *Understanding Speech-Language Pathology.* (For full group information, see HELP FOR SPECIAL CHILDREN on page 689.)

Facilitated Communication Institute
Syracuse University
370 Huntington Hall
Syracuse, NY 13244–2340
315–443–9657
Fax: 315–443–2274
E-mail (Sue Lehr, Contact): slehr@mailbox.syr.edu
Douglas Biklen, Director
Organization concerned with facilitated communication; provides information, consultation, and training; conducts research; publishes various materials, including quarterly newsletter *The Facilitated Communication Digest*; brochure *Making the Point: New Developments in Facilitated Communication*; videos *We Have a Lot to Offer: An Introduction to Facilitated Communication, A Part of Our Life: Facilitated Communication with Preschool Age Children, Facilitated Communication: In the School Years, A New Beginning: Facilitated Communication for Adults, Facilitated Communication for Family and Friends,* and *Every Step of the Way: Toward Independent Communication.*

National Information Center for Children and Youth with Disabilities (NICHCY), 800–695–0285, voice/TT. Publishes *Speech and Language Impairment.* (For full group information, see HELP FOR SPECIAL CHILDREN on page 689.)

Scottish Rite Foundation
Southern Jurisdiction, U.S.A., Inc.
1733 Sixteenth Street NW
Washington, DC 20009–3199
202–232–3579
Fax: 202–376–1843
Masonic organization that operates a network of centers for childhood speech and language disorders; publishes pamphlet listing centers.

Council for Exceptional Children (CEC), 800–328–0272. Includes Division for Children with Communication Disorders (DCCD), which publishes semiannual *DCCD Newsletter* and *Journal of Childhood Communication Disorders,* and other materials. CEC also publishes special-topic report *Children with Communication Disorders.* (For full group information, see HELP ON LEARNING AND EDUCATION on page 659.)

Brain Injury Association, 800–444–6443. Publishes *Language and Communicative Disorders Following Pediatric Head Injury* and *Speech and Language Disorders: Impairment of Communication Following Head Injury: Information Guide for Families.* (For full group information, see TRAUMATIC BRAIN INJURY.)

Autism Society of America (ASA), 800–328–8476. Publishes *Some Social Communication Skill Objectives and Teaching Strategies for People with Autism* and *Teaching Spontaneous Communication to Autistic and Communication Handicapped Children.* (For full group information, see AUTISM.)

Blind Children's Center, 800–222–3566. Publishes *Dancing Cheek to Cheek* on early social, play, and language interactions and language guides *Talk to Me* (books I and II). (For full group information, see EYE AND VISION PROBLEMS.)

National Fragile X Foundation, 800–688–8765. Publishes *Speech and Language Skills.* (For full group information, see FRAGILE X SYNDROME.)

Association for Children with Down Syndrome (ACDS), 516–221–4700. Publishes *Utilizing Computers to Facilitate Language in Preschool Children with Down Syndrome.* (For full group information, see DOWN SYNDROME.)

ON STUTTERING

Stuttering Foundation of America
3100 Walnut Grove Road, Suite 603
P.O. Box 11749
Memphis, TN 38111
901–452–0995; 800–992–9392
Fax: 901–452–3931
E-mail: stuttersfa@aol.com (America Online: STUTTERSFA)
Organization concerned about stuttering; formerly Speech Foundation of America; fosters research; provides information and referrals; publishes various materials, including:

- brochures: *If You Think Your Child is Stuttering, The Child Who Stutters at School: Notes to the Teacher, Using the Telephone: A Guide for People Who Stutter, How to React When Speaking With Someone Who Stutters, Turning On to Therapy,* and fact sheets *Did You Know . . . .*
- books: *Stuttering and Your Child: Questions and Answers, If Your Child Stutters: A Guide for Parents, Self-Therapy for the Stutterer, Stuttering Therapy: Prevention and Intervention with Children, Do You Stutter? A Guide for Teens, To the Stutterer, Stuttering Words, Treatment of the Young Stutterer in the School, Stuttering: Success and Failures in Therapy,* and materials for health professionals.

- videos: *Stuttering and Your Child: A Videotape for Parents, Prevention of Stuttering: Identifying the Danger Signs, Prevention of Stuttering: Family Counseling,* and *Therapy in Action.*

National Center for Stuttering (NCS)
200 East 33 Street
New York, NY 10016
212–532–1460; 800–221–2483
E-mail: schwrtz@is.nyu.edu
Lorraine Schneider, Director
Organization providing information to families of children who stutter. Provides treatment for children and adults; maintains computerized database on new approaches and theories; publishes quarterly newsletter and annual review of published literature.

National Stuttering Project (NSP)
2151 Irving Street, Suite 208
San Francisco, CA 94122–1609
415–566–5324; 800–364–1NSP [364–1677]
John Ahlbach, Executive Director
Organization concerned with stuttering; provides information and referrals; acts as advocate; publishes various materials, including monthly newsletters *Letting Go;* brochures and pamphlets *A Guide for Parents of Children Who Stutter, A Brochure for Teachers of Children Who Stutter, Notes to Listeners—What to Do and What to Know When Talking with a Person Who Stutters, To My Friends Who Stutter: Some Considerations,* and *Daddy to Make It Better?* (on stuttering in a 2-year-old); books *Understanding and Controlling Stuttering, Not Good at Talking, A Stutterers' Story, A Taste of Freedom: Essays on Life and Stuttering, How to Conquer Your Fears of Speaking Before People;* and videos *A Message for Teenagers* and *Stuttering Is Not Funny.*

International Foundation for Stutterers (IFS)
P.O. Box 462
Belle Mead, NJ 08502
201–359–6469
Arthur Maurice, President
Organization of people who stutter, their friends and families, speech-language therapists, and concerned others. Encourages establishment of mutual-support, self-help groups to supplement and reinforce speech therapy; gathers and disseminates information on stuttering, its causes, and treatments; publishes quarterly newsletter *Look Who's Talking.*

National Mental Health Association (NMHA), 800–969–6642. Publishes *Coping with a Child's Stuttering Problem.*

ONLINE RESOURCES

Internet: Stutt-L. Site for discussion. To subscribe, send this message: "SUB Stutt-L [your first name] [your last name] to: mailto:listserv@vm.temple.edu

OTHER RESOURCES

For parents

Talking Together: A Parent's Guide to the Development, Enrichment, and Problems of Speech and Language. Katherine F. Schetz and Stuart K. Cassell, Jr. Pocahontas, 1994.

Helping Baby Talk: A Pressure-Free Approach to Your Child's First Words from Birth to 3 Years. Lorraine Rocissano and Jean Grasso Fitzpatrick. Avon, 1990.

Practical guides

Coping with Speech Anxiety. Joe Ayres and Tim Hopf. Ablex, 1993.

Help Me Talk Right: How to Correct a Child's Lisp in 15 Easy Lessons. Mirla G. Raz. Gersten Weitz, 1993.

Coping for Kids Who Stutter. John C. Weber. Speech Bin, 1993.

Speech Sports: Games for Speech and Language Fun. Janet M. Shaw. Speech Bin, 1991.

For children

The Staff. Newsletter for children eleven and under, and for their families and teachers; encourages pen-pals. Available from: Janice Westbrook, Aaron's Associates, 6114 Waterway, Garland, TX 75043; 214–226–9855.

How You Talk, rev. ed. Paul Showers. HarperCollins, 1992.

Tootsie Tanner, Why Don't You Talk? Patricia Reilly Giff. Dell, 1990.

General background works

Growing up with Language: How Children Learn to Talk. Naomi S. Baron. Addison-Wesley, 1993.

The Child's Path to Spoken Language. John L. Locke. Harvard University Press, 1993.

The Transition from Infancy to Language: Acquiring the Power of Expression. Lois Bloom. Cambridge University Press, 1993.

Background works on communication disorders

Language Disorders in Children and Adolescents. Rhea Paul. Mosby, 1995.

Language Disorders in Older Students: Preadolescents and Adolescents. Nancy McKinley. Thinking Publications, 1995.

Communication Unbound: How Facilitated Communication Is Challenging Traditional Views of Autism and Ability-Disability. Douglas Biklen. Teachers College, 1993.

An Introduction to Children with Language Disorders, 2nd ed. Vicki Reed. Macmillan, 1993.

Language and Communication Disorders in Children, 3rd ed. Deena K. Bernstein and Ellenmorris Tiegerman. Macmillan, 1992.

(See also Help for Special Children on page 689.)

community control, a decentralized approach to handling educational and related questions concerning neighborhood schools generally found in large cities. The decentralization is a reaction to previously highly centralized school administrations, which were felt to be unresponsive to local needs. Critics charge that decentralization too often leads to lack of control and accountability and opens the door to fraud and corruption. Programs such as SCHOOLS OF CHOICE are attempts to make schools more responsive and to involve parents in the educational process, while retaining the overall centralized planning felt necessary in large cities.

compensatory education, a type of SPECIAL EDUCATION to make up lacks or deficiencies in a child's experience and skills, notably in children who are socioeconomically or culturally disadvantaged. Compensatory education especially targets members of minority groups, so that they will be on a more equal footing with other students.

comprehension-level thinking, understanding of relationships between two pieces of previously learned information or between an old and a new piece of information; one description of the various kinds of thinking or learning processes is described by Benjamin Bloom. The other main types are KNOWLEDGE-LEVEL, APPLICATION-LEVEL, ANALYSIS-LEVEL, SYNTHESIS-LEVEL, and EVALUATION-LEVEL.

compulsory attendance, the legal requirement that all children attend school when it is in session, with the student's precise starting age (generally five or six) and minimum leaving age (often sixteen) specified by the individual states. Students who fail to attend schools are considered TRUANTS and parents who fail to send their children to school are legally liable and may be compelled to do so by the school's ATTENDANCE or truant officer.

compulsory school age, the ages during which a child is required to attend school; the specifics ages vary, but are usually between five and six and sixteen. (See COMPULSORY ATTENDANCE.)

conception, in relation to PREGNANCY, the entry of a SPERM into an egg (OVUM), forming a ZYGOTE. It is an alternative term for FERTILIZATION but has a broader definition, encompassing the man and woman's efforts to conceive, as well as the biological union of sperm and egg. Attempts to avoid conception are often called *contraception, family planning*, or BIRTH CONTROL. In cases of INFERTILITY, a variety of methods are used to achieve conception. (See INFERTILITY.)

conceptualization, the process of developing a general idea from specific observations, as when a child sees apples, peaches, and pears and recognizes that they are all fruits.

conceptus, in physiology, the result of CONCEPTION, encompassing the whole range of development from when the egg (OVUM) is first fertilized by the SPERM through the complete PREGNANCY and birth, including the stages called ZYGOTE, EMBRYO, and FETUS.

condom, a form of BIRTH CONTROL that uses a thin, stretchable sheath over the PENIS to trap the SPERM during sexual activity and prevent exchange of body fluids; also called *prophylactic, rubber*, or *safe*. The term generally refers to a sheath worn by males; the *female condom* is more precisely called a VAGINAL POUCH.

The Food and Drug Administration (FDA) rates condoms as 64 to 97 percent effective as contraceptive devices; studies show that they fail, through tearing or slippage, 1 to 12 percent of the time. They also provide much-needed protection (though not 100 percent) against SEXUALLY TRANSMITTED DISEASES (STDs), such as AIDS. Rubber condoms are far more effective for that purpose, since those made of natural material (lamb intestines) have pores large enough for viruses to pass through. A condom made of natural material may be needed when either partner has an ALLERGY to rubber, but natural-material condoms provide far less protection against STDs. Some manufacturers have added a SPERMICIDE to the condoms to increase their effectiveness in CONTRACEPTION.

During sexual activity, the condom should be placed on the man's penis as soon as it is erect, before it touches any part of his partner's body. Except when used during oral sex, condoms generally require lubrication; however, only *water-based* lubricants should be used, as oil-based lubricants—including Vaseline, vegetable oil, baby oil, hand lotion, massage oils, and dairy oils—can damage condoms, making them more susceptible to tearing and ineffective for any kind of protection. Condoms should be stored in cool, dark, and dry places, opened only when about to be used, and *never* reused. If the condom slips during or after sex, it should be held in place at the rim until withdrawal. If it breaks during sex, the penis should be withdrawn immediately and the condom removed; the penis and surrounding area should be washed, and a new condom put on before continuing intercourse. (See CONDOMS: WHAT EVERYONE NEEDS TO KNOW on page 143.)

Parents of sexually active children will want to urge them to use a condom during any sexual contact. It is best for parents to discuss protection before a child has his or her first sexual contact, though government and schools are also attempting to spread the word through SEX EDUCATION. Many women today, from their teens on, carry condoms for use during sex. Indeed, they account for 25 percent of the condom sales in the United States. However, many men still resist wearing condoms. An alternative adopted by some women is the relatively new vaginal pouch. (See BIRTH CONTROL.)

conduct disorder, a type of MENTAL DISORDER, classified by psychiatrists as a DISRUPTIVE BEHAVIOR DISORDER, which commonly develops (more often among boys than girls) in late childhood or ADOLESCENCE and which involves persistent, long-term violation of the rights of others and of usual social NORMS. This often includes physical aggression and cruelty to people and animals, deliberate destruction of property (including arson), violent stealing, assault, and sometimes rape and murder, often associated with (but not necessarily caused by) DRUG ABUSE or ALCOHOL ABUSE. Such children often have great trouble at school, at home, and socially; they may be labeled OUT OF CONTROL children or if they are in legal trouble JUVENILE DELINQUENTS and so may find themselves in FOSTER CARE or in other institutions. Among the children AT RISK for developing the disorder are those who have ATTENTION DEFICIT HYPERACTIVITY DISORDER, low self-esteem, REJECTION by parents, extremely rigid DISCIPLINE from parents, and lack of stable home life. If the pattern of behavior persists into adulthood, it is often called *anti-social personality disorder*. (See MENTAL DISORDERS.)

confidentiality, the practice among professionals, such as lawyers, doctors, and psychologists, of regarding conversations with their clients or patients as private. They consider that information imparted by the patient or client is not to be revealed to other unauthorized parties. If this confidentiality is protected by law, as it commonly is with lawyers (laws are more variable regarding other professionals), the conversation is sometimes called a PRIVILEGED COMMUNICATION. Confidentiality of educational records, including those of children with DISABILITIES, has also been covered by various laws, including the FAMILY EDUCATIONAL RIGHTS AND PRIVACY ACT and the EDUCATION FOR ALL HANDICAPPED CHILDREN ACT.

Condoms: What Everyone Needs to Know

Both men and women should know how to select and use condoms for their own self-protection.

CONDOM SHOPPING GUIDE

Use this handy shopping guide as a reminder of what to look for when buying condoms, lubricant, and spermicides:

Be sure to choose:

☑ latex
☑ disease prevention claim on package label

Also consider:

☐ with spermicide
☐ separate spermicide
☐ gel
☐ cream
☐ foam
☐ with lubricant
☐ separate lubricant. (Select only *water-based* lubricants made for this purpose.)

GUIDELINES FOR USING A CONDOM

For maximum safety, both for disease prevention and birth control, the U.S. Public Health Service has developed these guidelines for men using condoms:

- Use a new condom for every act of intercourse.
- If the penis is uncircumcised, pull the foreskin back before putting the condom on.
- Put the condom on after the penis is erect (hard) and before *any* contact is made between the penis and any part of the partner's body.
- If using a spermicide, put some inside the condom tip.
- If the condom does not have a reservoir tip, pinch the tip enough to leave a half-inch space for semen to collect.
- While pinching the half-inch tip, place the condom against the penis and unroll it all the way to the base. Put more spermicide or lubricant on the outside.
- If you feel a condom break while you are having sex, stop immediately and pull out. Do not continue until you have put on a new condom and used more spermicide.
- After ejaculation and before the penis gets soft, the male should grip the rim of the condom and carefully withdraw from his partner.
- To remove the condom from the penis, pull it off gently, being careful semen doesn't spill out.
- Wrap the used condom in a tissue and throw it in the trash where others won't handle it. Because condoms may cause problems in sewers, don't flush down the toilet. Afterwards, wash your hands with soap and water.
- Finally, beware of drugs and alcohol! They can affect your judgment, so you may forget to use a condom. They may even affect your ability to use a condom properly.

Source: Adapted from Condoms and Sexually Transmitted Diseases . . . Especially AIDS, Department of Health and Human Services, Public Health Service, Food and Drug Administration, Center for Devices and Radiological Health (1990).

congenital, something present at birth, usually problems such as BIRTH DEFECTS, including GENETIC DISORDERS or CHROMOSOMAL ABNORMALITIES, and those resulting from other causes, such as exposure to radiation, drugs, or injury (see ENVIRONMENTAL HAZARDS).

congenital dislocation of the hip, a CONGENITAL abnormality in which the "ball" or head of the thigh bone (*femur*) does not sit properly into its appointed socket, a cavity in the pelvis, but instead sits outside it. Why congenital dislocation occurs is unknown, though it is more common in girls than in boys, especially when the child is born from a BREECH position. If not discovered during routine WELL-BABY EXAMINATIONS, congenital dislocation of the hip generally becomes apparent through a limp when a baby starts WALKING. The condition is treated in infants by using splints or traction to hold the ball in the socket for a few months; that usually solves the problem with no adverse effects. But if the disorder is not discovered or treated until later in childhood, surgery, hospitalization, and long-term casts are usually required and some problems may remain.

FOR HELP AND FURTHER INFORMATION

National Institute of Child Health and Human Development (NICHD), 301–496–5133. (For full group information, see PREGNANCY.)

Shriner's Hospitals for Crippled Children, 800–237–5055. Provides free medical care for children with orthopedic problems. (For full group information, see BONE AND BONE DISORDERS.)

consanguinity, a formal term describing the relationship of BLOOD RELATIONS, who share a common GENETIC INHERITANCE. As KIN, individuals with blood relationships have certain legal INHERITANCE RIGHTS in the absence of a will.

consent agreement, in relation to CHILD SUPPORT, a voluntary written statement from an unwed FATHER that acknowledges a child as his own and recognizes his responsibility to provide child support.

conservator, A kind of GUARDIAN, usually a person appointed by a court to manage the affairs of someone incapable of managing his or her own property, often an adult with severe DISABILITIES or an otherwise incapacitated adult (especially one with considerable assets). In some places, a public or private agency may be appointed to act as conservator. To avoid court involvement in appointing a conservator, parents who wish to secure the future of a child with disabilities may instead prepare a durable POWER OF ATTORNEY (see ADVANCE DIRECTIVE) giving a chosen person the power to act if the parents are incapacitated.

constipation, infrequent or difficult bowel movements characterized by hard and dry feces. Constipation can result from physical causes, such as narrowing of parts of the digestive system, painful tears (fissures) in the skin around the anus, inflammation of the intestines, and suppression or disruption of the normal bowel activity because of some disorder, such as IRRITABLE BOWEL SYNDROME. Problems in diet can also contribute, especially lack of FIBER in older children. For treating constipation in infants, see BABY'S BOWELS—WHAT'S NORMAL, WHAT'S NOT (on page 176). Sometimes constipation can result from repeatedly ignoring signals that bowels should be moved, perhaps because of misunderstandings during TOILET TRAINING. In pregnant women, constipation and associated hemorrhoids are common (see CONSTIPATION DURING PREGNANCY, on page 145). (See DIGESTIVE SYSTEM AND DISORDERS.)

contempt of court, defiance of a court's authority, either directly and disruptively by challenging officials in court or indirectly, as in violating a court order. A parent who fails to provide court-ordered CHILD SUPPORT may be in contempt of court, as may be a parent who denies court-ordered VISITATION RIGHTS. Such contempt can call for a fine, jail, or both, but in family law situations, the court is generally reluctant to impose punishment that may be seen as causing harm to children in the family.

contraception, a form of BIRTH CONTROL that focuses on preventing CONCEPTION, including methods such as the CONDOM, SPERMICIDES, CERVICAL SPONGE, DIAPHRAGM, CERVICAL CAP, INTRAUTERINE DEVICE (IUD), DEPO-PROVERA, NORPLANT, VAGINAL POUCH, DOUCHING, and BIRTH CONTROL PILLS.

contractions, powerful, spasmodic, painful, rhythmic squeezing of the walls of the UTERUS during LABOR.

controllable disease, an illness or disorder that has no CURE but that can be treated—with medicines, physical therapy, and a wide variety of other treatments—so as to hold the disease's symptoms in check. Among the common diseases that are controllable with current medical technology are DIABETES and PHENYLKETONURIA.

conversation board, a flat surface that can be used for communication. Children who are unable to speak clearly enough to be understood, such as those who have ORTHOPEDIC DISABILITIES affecting their speech apparatus and who are not able to write, can communicate by means of a conversation board. For young children who have not yet learned to read, a set of standardized symbols called BLISS SYMBOLS have been developed. Once children are able to read and spell, they can move letters and words into position on the board to "converse" with others.

convulsion, violent muscular contractions that accompany some kinds of SEIZURES, especially the most disruptive seizures that go under the umbrella of EPILEPSY.

Cooperative English Tests, a group-administered test of LANGUAGE SKILLS for children in grades nine through college; a paper-and-pencil test covering reading comprehension (including vocabulary level and speed of comprehension) and expression (both in conveying exact meaning and in using mechanics of grammar and punctuation). The tests are available in two levels and are often used for class placement, especially to identify those who may benefit from REMEDIAL INSTRUCTION or ACCELERATED PROGRAMS. (See TESTS.)

cooperative, type of PRESCHOOL or NURSERY SCHOOL in which parents supply much or all of the staffing and assistance, sometimes managing and financing the entire operation.

co-parent, a person who does not have legal CUSTODY of a child and has no formalized legal PARENTS' RIGHTS and PARENTS' RESPONSIBILITIES, but who shares in the care, support, and custody of the child, along with the CUSTODIAL PARENT. A woman sharing a household with a man and the child in his custody is called a co-parent; so is a stepfather who has not legally adopted his stepchildren. The term is commonly used among homosexual couples, in which generally only one of them has legal responsibility for a child, through birth, custody, or ADOPTION.

copper, a MINERAL vital to the body, though only in trace amounts, to help form PROTEINS and enzymes that manage biochemical functions and to help form red blood cells. Copper is found in organ meats (such as liver, kidneys, and heart), shellfish, dried beans and peas, nuts, fruits (especially raisins), and mushrooms. Copper deficiency is rare, but excess can cause nausea, VOMITING, and DIARRHEA, as when people eat food cooked in unlined copper pots or drink alcohol distilled with copper tubing. Excess copper can lead to serious health problems, such as hepatitis or cirrhosis of the liver (see LIVER AND LIVER PROBLEMS). Copper can also build up in the body as a result of certain diseases, such as WILSON'S DISEASE. (See MINERALS; NUTRITION.)

coprolalia, a rare condition in which a person involuntarily utters words seen as vulgar or obscene; literally, "fecal speech." Coprolalia often results from a brain dysfunction, or a MENTAL DISORDER such as SCHIZOPHRENIA, or a condition such as TOURETTE SYNDROME.

cordocentesus (percutaneous umbilical cord sampling or PUBS), a relatively new GENETIC SCREENING procedure that involves drawing a sample of blood identical to that of the FETUS from the UMBILICAL CORD, using a needle guided by ULTRASOUND that is inserted into the abdomen of a pregnant woman. The sample can then be quickly analyzed for some serious genetic blood disorders, such as HEMOPHILIA, THALASSEMIA, or sickle-cell ANEMIA. (For organizations and reference works offering help and further information, see GENETIC DISORDERS; GENETIC SCREENING.)

Cornelia de Lange syndrome (CdLS), a type of CONGENITAL disorder characterized by a wide variety of physical signs; also called *Amsterdam syndrome* or *Brachmann-de Lange Syndrome.* Common characteristics of children with CdLS include LOW BIRTH WEIGHT; MENTAL RETARDATION and developmental delay; delayed growth and short stature; small head (*microcephaly*), with low forehead and ears; heavy eyebrows that meet at midline; short, upturned nose; small jaw; and thin lips. Other characteristics frequently linked with CdLS include one or more limbs somewhat shortened (*micromelia*) or nearly nonexistent with hands or feet attached almost directly to the body (PHOCOMELIA); thumb placed low on the hand; abnormal bending of some fingers or toes (*clinodactyly*); limited extension of the arm at the elbow; webbing of the second and third toes; and unusually large amounts of

Constipation During Pregnancy

Constipation is due to hormonal changes that tend to relax the muscles of your digestive system. Late in pregnancy, constipation may be caused by the growing uterus pressing on the lower intestine. There are several things you can do to relieve constipation. Drink six to eight glasses of liquids a day. A glass of cold water or juice before breakfast is often effective. Eat foods that provide fiber, such as whole grain cereals and breads and raw fruits and vegetables. Get some exercise every day and make a habit of going to the bathroom every day at the same time. If you continue to be troubled after trying these things, tell your doctor. Do not take enemas, laxatives, or home remedies unless recommended by your doctor.

Source: Prenatal Care (1983). Prepared for the Public Health Service by the Bureau of Health Care Delivery and Assistance, Division of Maternal and Child Health.

body hair (HIRSUTISM). A child with CdLS is also more likely to have bowel abnormalities or gastroesophagel reflux (see DIGESTIVE SYSTEM AND DISORDERS), SEIZURES, heart defects (see HEART AND HEART PROBLEMS), CLEFT LIP AND PALATE, and feeding difficulties. Some researchers distinguish between a short-statured, large-featured form of the syndrome (called *Brachman-de Lange or dwarf type*) and a larger form (*Bruck-de Lange type*), characterized by a heavily muscular, wrestlerlike appearance, with broad neck and shoulders. The cause of de Lange syndrome is unknown, but researchers suspect a CHROMOSOMAL ABNORMALITY. However, it is believed to stem from a rare mutation and is not inherited like a typical GENETIC DISORDER. Prospective parents with a history of the syndrome in their family may want to seek GENETIC COUNSELING for information on current PRENATAL TESTS. High resolution ULTRASOUND can allow detection of some limb abnormalities.

FOR HELP AND FURTHER INFORMATION

Cornelia de Lange Syndrome (CdLS) Foundation
60 Dyer Avenue
Collinsville, CT 06022
203–693–0159; 800–753-CdLS [753–2357];
800–223–8355
Fax: 203–693–6819
Julie A. Mairano, Executive Director
Organization concerned with Cornelia de Lange syndrome; provides information; aids families in making decisions about child's future; publishes various materials, including bimonthly *Reaching Out, Facts about CdLS, Facing the Challenges: A Family's Guide to CdLS, Dealing with Doctors*; video *Speech and Language Acquisition in CdLS*; and numerous other materials.

National Institute of Child Health and Human Development (NICHD), 301–496–5133. (For full group information, see PREGNANCY.)

National Organization for Rare Disorders (NORD), 800–999–6673. (For full group information, see RARE DISORDERS.)

corporal punishment, physical blows or hurts to the body, defined by Parents and Teachers Against Violence in Education (PTAVE) as "hitting, paddling, spanking, grabbing, shaking, forced exercise, and any other means of inflicting pain as punishment." Once thought almost synonymous with DISCIPLINE, corporal punishment is now under considerable attack because it can easily escalate into child abuse, especially when it results from an adult's frustration or a MENTAL DISORDER.

Some social workers and psychologists believe that corporal punishment is always destructive and to be avoided; others believe that no harm is done if parents on occasion resort to a light spanking. But almost all believe that corporal punishment is unnecessary and usually represents a failure of the adult's patience and imagination in developing alternative forms of positive discipline.

Corporal punishment in the schools is also widely criticized as physically and psychologically harmful to the child and as contributing to (not lessening) behavioral problems, reducing the ability to learn, and causing SCHOOL PHOBIA. Many medical, social work, educational, and other professionals have called for a complete ban on physical punishment in schools, and many states and cities have formally abolished the practice. In fact, though, many teachers and principals continue to adminster physical punishment, and the courts have upheld the school's right to do so in some circumstances. Unfortunately, school-administered corporal punishment can cause serious injuries or medical problems—serious enough that, if administered by a parent, they would be considered child abuse. School officials, though, are seldom challenged by parents, social workers, or legal authorities. Various organizations (see the list that follows) have been fighting to protect children from VIOLENCE in schools.

FOR HELP AND FURTHER INFORMATION

End Violence Against the Next Generation (EVAN-G)
977 Keeler Avenue
Berkeley, CA 94708
415–527–0454
Adah Maurer, Executive Director
Organization devoted to ending corporal punishment, as in schools and institutes; acts as advocate; supports research and development of alternatives; provides information and counsel to schools; publishes various materials, including quarterly *The Last Resort* and other materials.

Parents and Teachers Against Violence in Education (PTAVE)
P. O. Box 1033
Alamo, CA 94507–7033
510–831–1661
Fax: 510–838–8914
Jordan Riak, President
Organization seeking to end corporal punishment and other child abuse in schools and institutions; advises parents and educators; publishes various materials, including pamphlets *Plain Talk About Spanking* and *The Sexual Dangers of Spanking Children* and reprints *Should We Outlaw Spanking?* and *An Alternative to Spanking*.

National Center for the Study of Corporal Punishment and Alternatives in the Schools (NCSCPAS)
253 Ritter Hall South
Department of School Psychology
Temple University
Philadelphia, PA 19122
215–204–6028
Irwin A. Hyman, Director
Organization concerned with psychological and educational effects of corporal punishment in schools; acts as advocate; conducts research; provides information and

counseling services for parents and teachers; publishes journal *Discipline* and other materials.

C. Henry Kempe National Center for the Prevention and Treatment of Child Abuse and Neglect, 303–321–3963. Publishes *Think Twice: The Medical Effects of Physical Punishment.* (For full group information, see HELP AGAINST CHILD ABUSE AND NEGLECT on page 680.)

National Committee for Prevention of Child Abuse (NCPCA), 800–835–2671. Publishes *A Future Filled with Healthy Minds and Bodies: A Call to Abolish Corporal Punishment in Schools.* (For full group information, see HELP AGAINST CHILD ABUSE AND NEGLECT on page 680.)

National Organization on Legal Problems of Education (NOLPE), 913–273–3550. Publishes *Corporal Punishment in Schools: Reading the Law* and *The Principal's Decision (A Teaching Monograph on Corporal Punishment).*

Center for Law and Education, 202–986–3000. Publishes "Information for Parents" brochure *Corporal Punishment* and *Corporal Punishment: Legal Research Guide.* (For full group information, see HELP ON LEARNING AND EDUCATION on page 659.)

Association for Childhood Education International (ACEI), 800–423–3563. Publishes position paper *The Banning of Corporal Punishment in Child Care, School and Other Educative Settings in the United States.* (For full group information, see HELP ON LEARNING AND EDUCATION on page 659.)

OTHER RESOURCES

Beating the Devil Out of Them: Corporal Punishment in American Families. Murray A. Straus. Free Press, 1994.

Fine Line: When Discipline Becomes Child Abuse. David A. Sabatino. TAB, 1991.

Spare the Child: The Religious Roots of Punishment and the Psychological Impact of Physical Abuse. Philip Greven. Random, 1991.

For Your Own Good: Hidden Cruelty in Child Rearing and the Roots of Violence. Alice Miller. Farrar, Straus and Giroux, 1983.

(See also HELP AGAINST CHILD ABUSE AND NEGLECT on page 680; DISCIPLINE; EDUCATION.)

cosmetic surgery, a surgical operation performed primarily to change shape and appearance, rather than for medical reasons, which is generally called *reconstructive surgery.* Two common kinds of cosmetic surgery performed on children, especially teenagers, are *rhinoplasty* on the nose and *otoplasty* on the ears. (See PLASTIC SURGERY.)

court appointed special advocate (CASA), a specially trained volunteer who will represent the interests of an otherwise unrepresented child in certain types of court cases, such as judicial hearings involving CHILD ABUSE AND NEGLECT. (For help and more information, see ADVOCACY.)

court of conciliation, an offshoot of the DOMESTIC RELATIONS COURT, staffed by professional counselors rather than legal personnel, that in some states is charged with trying to facilitate reconciliations in divorce cases.

cradle cap, harmless, waxy, yellowish scales that develop on the scalp and forehead of infants, generally in their first year; a BENIGN kind of SKIN DISORDER that is related to the adult condition *seborrhea.* Though it does not result from poor hygiene, washing with mild soap and water may help, perhaps after putting mineral oil on the scalp. If that doesn't help or if the area is inflamed, a doctor should be consulted.

craniosynostosis, a condition involving premature closing of or absence of joints, or *sutures,* in the skull. A baby with this condition is born without FONTANELLES, or spaces between the plates of the skull to allow for growth. Causes of the disorder are unclear. Craniosynostosis is associated with some bone disorders such as RICKETS and with some BIRTH DEFECTS or an abnormally small brain, but the condition can occur in babies with no other obvious disorders. To prevent brain damage, the plates of the skull need to be separated surgically within a few months after birth.

FOR HELP AND FURTHER INFORMATION

National Arthritis and Musculoskeletal and Skin Diseases Information Clearinghouse (NAMSIC), 301–495–4484. (For full group information, see ARTHRITIS.)

National Institute of Dental Research (NIDR), 301–496–4261. (For full group information, see TEETH AND DENTAL PROBLEMS.)

AboutFace, 800–225–3223. Publishes pamphlet on craniosynostosis. (For full group information, see CLEFT LIP AND PALATE.)

Cleft Palate Foundation, 800–242–5338. *Choosing a Cleft Palate or Craniofacial Team* and *Crouzon Syndrome (Craniofacial Dysostosis).* (For full group information, see CLEFT LIP AND PALATE.)

(See also BONE AND BONE DISORDERS.)

creative thinking, mental processes that are original, flexible, and imaginative, often producing unusual and novel approaches to problems. Often thought of as the province of the arts, where creativity is essential, creative thinking is also important and valued in many other areas of work as well, such as science and technology. Though creative thinking is hard to define, a child who has it is often deemed a GIFTED CHILD.

creativity test, a type of test that attempts to measure CREATIVE THINKING, sometimes used to assess the thinking abilities of a child who comes from a disadvantaged or non-English-speaking background. Such a test might, for example, ask a child to think of new uses for a familiar object, such as a broom.

credit, in EDUCATION, recognition of a student's successful completion of work in a course; more specifically, a unit of value awarded by a school for such work. In HIGH SCHOOLS, each course is generally worth one credit unit, and the student must accumulate a specified number of these credits, with an appropriate number of credits from various areas of study (such as English, mathematics, or science), in order to qualify for GRADUATION. At the COLLEGE level, varying numbers of credits are awarded to courses, generally based on the number of hours per week that a student is scheduled to spend in the class. A literature class that meets for one hour on Mondays, Wednesdays, and Fridays, for example, would generally carry three credits. But an organic chemistry class that meets for the same three hours but also has two scheduled hours of laboratory work might carry five credits. At the end of the SEMESTER, a student's GRADE for the course and the credits—sometimes called *credit-hours*—carried by the course are used to calculate his or her GRADE-POINT AVERAGE.

credit by examination, COLLEGE credit gained by passing a test, even though the student did not take a college course or reside on campus. Some students study in special classes during HIGH SCHOOL that prepare them for tests in the ADVANCED PLACEMENT PROGRAM (APP); others may study on their own or through INDEPENDENT STUDY to prepare for tests in the COLLEGE-LEVEL EXAMINATION PROGRAM (CLEP) or the PROFICIENCY EXAMINATION PROGRAM (PEP).

cri du chat syndrome, a CONGENITAL condition resulting from a CHROMOSOMAL ABNORMALITY in which part of chromosome 5 has been lost; also called *cry of the cat syndrome* or *5p- syndrome.* Infants with the syndrome are marked by a kitten-like mewing cry, which disappears after the first few weeks. They suffer from physical and MENTAL RETARDATION, along with other problems such as SYNDACTYLY and heart problems.

FOR HELP AND FURTHER INFORMATION

5p- Society
11609 Oakmont
Overland Park, KS 66210
618–687–3006
Joan Steele, Contact Person
Mutual-support, self-help organization for families who have a child with cri du chat or 5p- syndrome; provides information to public and professionals; publishes various materials, including quarterly *5p- Newsletter* and *North American 5p- Syndrome Listing.*

(See also GENETIC DISORDERS; GENETIC COUNSELING; HEART AND HEART PROBLEMS.)

criminal court, a court adjudicating prosecutions initiated by the government for violations of criminal law. Those being prosecuted in criminal courts are judged innocent unless proven guilty beyond a reasonable doubt and strict rules apply about what evidence is admissible. Most JUVENILES charged with crimes come before a CIVIL COURT, such as a JUVENILE COURT or FAMILY COURT, and are subject to less severe penalties, although there is an increasing tendency to try MINORS as adults when they are accused of serious crimes. Many minors, if found guilty, are treated as juvenile DELINQUENTS rather than as criminals.

crisis intervention, action taken to help relieve an immediately threatening or serious situation, the short-term aim being to remove a threat to health or welfare, and the longer-term aim to help the person or family recognize the problem and learn how to cope with it. The term may, for example, refer to a social worker who provides emergency services to relieve stress within a family or removes a child from a possible abusive setting, or to a parent who confronts and provides help for a child on drugs. Similar action taken before an immediate threat exists is called EARLY INTERVENTION. (See HELP AGAINST CHILD ABUSE AND NEGLECT on page 680; HELP AGAINST SUBSTANCE ABUSE on page 703.)

criterion-referenced, a type of TEST in which the student's performance is measured against a specific standard, such as 75 out of 100 questions correct, ability to solve a set problem, or ability to type fifty words a minute with no more than five errors, as opposed to a NORM-REFERENCED TEST in which performance is compared with that of a larger group. (See TESTS.)

croup (acute laryngotracheobronchitis or LTB), a common disease of young children, in which viral infection (sometimes complicated by bacteria and ALLERGIES as well) causes inflammation and narrowing of the breathing passages, with resulting hoarseness, distinctive harsh coughing, and rough breathing (STRIDOR). It often occurs in dry houses and at night and is generally helped by humidity, as from a humidifier, vaporizer, the mist from a shower or pot of boiling water, or moist night air. Soothing of the child may help the muscles relax and ease breathing. But if the child has severe difficulty breathing or begins to turn blue around the lips and NAILS (CYANOSIS), hospitalization may be indicated to prevent brain damage from lack of oxygen (HYPOXIA). The alternative treatments include being placed in a tent with humidified oxygen or temporary insertion of a breathing tube, either through the mouth (using a hollow, flexible tube called an ENDOSCOPE) or through an artificial opening in the throat (in an operation called a TRACHEOSTOMY). Children generally recover in a few days, though some are subject to recurrence. Croup usually does not appear after about age four, because by then the breathing tubes are larger and firmer and so less liable to constrict. (See LUNG AND BREATHING DISORDERS.)

crown, an artifical "cap" to replace the natural crown of a tooth, the enamel-coated part above the gum. Crowns are used when a tooth's natural crown has been damaged beyond repair but also for cosmetic reasons, as when a tooth turns grayish after ROOT CANAL THERAPY. Crowns in the front of the mouth are normally made of porcelain or other materials that can be given a shade to match the surrounding natural teeth. Crowns on the grinding teeth—bicuspids and especially molars—are generally made of an alloy of gold or other metal, or at least have metal on the upper surface, for strength. In recent decades, dentists have developed several alternatives to artificial crowns for cosmetic use, when the natural crown of the tooth is intact. (See TEETH.)

crowning, the first glimpse of a baby's head through the VAGINA during LABOR and DELIVERY.

CT scan (computerized tomography), a type of MEDICAL TEST that involves a high-speed X-RAY machine linked to a computer, so that a series of pictures taken at different planes are combined into computer-simulated three-dimensional views; also called *computerized axial tomography* or *CAT scan.* In a CT scan, air and liquid show up as black, the most dense bones as white, and tissues as various shades of gray. The CT scan gives far more precise pictures than ordinary X-ray photographs and ULTRASOUND, involves low exposure to X-rays, can be used to view any internal organs (including the brain). These types of scans are especially useful in detecting CALCIUM deposits (often signs of old healed FRACTURES), bone displacements in new fractures, accumulations of fluid, and TUMORS, sometimes giving enough detail so physicians can judge whether the tumor is likely to be BENIGN or MALIGNANT. Because X-rays can damage a FETUS, women who are or suspect they may be pregnant are advised not to have a CT scan. (For help or further information, see MEDICAL TESTS.)

cued speech, enhancement of speech, by making lip movements clear and using finger signs for particular sounds that are otherwise easily confused, such as "p" and "b," to ease SPEECHREADING by people with hearing impairment. It has proven especially helpful for communication between hearing family members or friends and a person who is deaf or hard-of-hearing. This technique has also significantly aided children who were born deaf, after cochlear implant surgery. (For help or further information, see EAR OR HEARING PROBLEMS.)

culture, a type of MEDICAL TEST in which microorganisms or material taken from the body, in procedures such as BLOOD TESTS, URINALYSIS, or BIOPSY, are grown and cultivated in the laboratory. The aim is often to identify bacteria or other infectious organisms, so that proper treatment can be given. Cells in laboratory cultures may also be examined as part of PRENATAL TESTING to check for CHROMOSOMAL ABNORMALITIES or signs of possible GENETIC DISORDERS. Sometimes tissue may be grown, or cultured, for later use in grafts or tissue TRANSPLANTS.

culture-fair (culture-free), a term describing a TEST that attempts to avoid bias in favor of children of White, comfortably middle-class, English-speaking, two-parent family backgrounds. Many tests used with children—especially INTELLIGENCE TESTS, which purport to measure "pure" mental ability—have been criticized for discriminating unfairly against children of other backgrounds in the content, vocabulary, and assumptions of their questions. Many testing organizations have attempted to respond to these criticisms by rewriting their tests or by making other tests for children of differing backgrounds. But controversy still remains. Parents whose family backgrounds are in any way nontraditional, especially in the areas of language and culture in the home, should try to see that school officials are aware of any special circumstances in a child's background that might affect test performance. If a particular test or set of tests produces results parents feel may be biased, they should call for retesting.

cumulative average, the AVERAGE of a student's GRADES from entry into a school or COLLEGE up to a given point, or GRADUATION. In HIGH SCHOOLS, the cumulative average means an average of the letter or numerical grades handed out during the period. In college it often refers to a GRADE POINT AVERAGE that takes into account the number of CREDITS granted to each particular course.

cure, in medicine, to treat a disease so as to achieve total disappearance of its SIGNS and SYMPTOMS, restoring the patient to normal health. A temporary halt in the advance of a PROGRESSIVE disease or the spontaneous temporary lessening or disappearance of symptoms (REMISSION) is not generally considered a cure. Many diseases today are not curable, but they are CONTROLLABLE, meaning that the symptoms can be held in check with regular treatment.

curriculum, the range of programs offered to students in a school, developed in a deliberate sequence, with the content, materials, and approaches geared to the abilities of the students and the established goals of the school. A school's curriculum is generally established according to prevailing standards in the region or state and can vary widely from place to place. Partly because of this wide variation, there has been increasing discussion of establishing NATIONAL STANDARDS.

The curriculum may vary within a school, such as a HIGH SCHOOL where students have a wide range of abilities and educational aims. College-bound students would take an *academic curriculum*, but students seeking less-demanding courses, who are perhaps unsure of their future direction, might follow a *general curriculum*. Students who are not college-bound, but want to learn skills that will help them get a job, might follow a *vocational curriculum*.

However, students with severe DISABILITIES might follow a *functional curriculum*, designed to help them learn the skills basic to everyday life, the aim being to help them become as independent as possible. This kind of *adapted* or *differentiated* curriculum for students with SPECIAL NEEDS has in recent years helped prepare some students (such as those with MENTAL RETARDATION), who would once have been fully dependent as adults, to instead take minimally demanding, carefully structured jobs in the adult world (see SUPPORTED EMPLOYMENT). By law, students with disabilities will have an INDIVIDUALIZED EDUCATION PROGRAM tailored to their individual skills and potential.

Within a particular program, the group of courses taken by all students is called the *core curriculum*; other optional courses are termed *electives*. When the same kinds of subjects are taught, but with increasing depth and detail over several years, the school is employing a *spiral curriculum*. When the same material is taught to different groups of students at different rates—for example, over five years for one group and over six years for another—the result is called a *parallel curriculum*. If the school's courses heavily focus on content, rather than on the way a student learns or is taught, it is called a *subject-centered curriculum*. A *classical curriculum* is one that emphasizes the traditional liberal arts, including literature, art, music, philosophy, history, and foreign languages, normally on the college level. When the subject matters of two different types of courses, such as literature and history, are taught together, the result is called a *fused curriculum*. (See EDUCATION.)

custodial parent, the parent who has been awarded sole legal CUSTODY of a child, as in a DIVORCE case in which shared custody has not been granted. The term sometimes also applies to a nonparent who has custody, such as a friend or a relative. When parents have shared custody, the parent with whom the child is staying at any one particular time is considered the custodial parent.

custody, in family law, the right and duty to care for and control basic decisions regarding children who are MINORS, as well as adults with DISABILITIES severe enough to make them unable to take charge of basic tasks for themselves, such as a grown child with MENTAL RETARDATION. Custody is part of both PARENTS' RIGHTS and PARENTS' RESPONSIBILITIES and includes provision of food, clothing, shelter, basic HEALTH CARE, EDUCATION, and DISCIPLINE. *Legal custody* refers to the rights to make basic decisions about a child in such matters as education and medical care; it may be exercised by one person alone or jointly. *Physical custody* refers to where the child lives and who provides day-to-day care and control. When both parents share a home with the children, both legal and physical custody is fully shared by both parents; when a single parent raises a child alone beginning at the time of birth or ADOPTION, that person has *sole custody*, including both legal and physical custody. Parents in a stable marriage share *joint custody* of their children, which also includes both legal and physical custody.

Custody problems arise in cases of separation or DIVORCE, when parents must agree between themselves—or the court must decide for them—who will have custody and with what limitations. In general, the *custodial parent* will be the parent the child lives with. The *noncustodial parent* still has CHILD SUPPORT obligations, but may or may not have the legal right to participate in major decisions regarding the child, depending on the agreement reached. Among the main types of arrangements between parents are:

- *Sole custody*, in which one parent has both physical and legal custody of the child. The other parent has VISITATION RIGHTS, but generally no legal right to participate in major decisions, though he or she may often do so informally.
- *Shared* or *joint custody*, in which the parents generally share custody and the child spends a substantial amount of time with each parent. Actual arrangements vary, but may include spending the school year with one parent and most of the holidays with the other; or spending alternate weeks, months, or years with each parent. Many courts—and many parents—favor joint custody because a child has continuing contact with and support from both parents during the crucial childhood years. Some states routinely award joint legal custody, while giving one parent physical custody. One disadvantage to shared physical custody is that children's lives, and their network of friends and contacts, are so frequently disrupted, a special problem during the teens.

  Ideally, joint custody—with its ideally shared responsibility—can ease the parental burdens of the custodial parent by dividing the responsibility, but any form of joint custody requires substantial cooperation between parents and so has little chance of working well if the relationship is acrimonious. Joint custody can also work out very badly for the custodial parents, especially women. Some noncustodial men seek joint custody for the purpose of lowering CHILD SUPPORT payments, arguing before the court that lower amounts are justified because the children will spend much of their time with them. The result is often that the women end up with *de facto* sole custody, but with less money for support. Also, with joint custody, the custodial parent does not have the sole authority to make key decisions in a timely way, especially if the couple is unable to agree on questions affecting the children.

- *Bird's nest custody* or *nesting*, a less common form of joint custody designed to ease disruption of children's lives. Here children stay in their home, and the parents shuttle in and out at agreed-upon intervals, such as one during the week and the other on weekends. This provides a more stable base for the children, but disrupts the parents' lives. It is also expensive and complicated, since each parent must maintain separate living quarters or have temporary living arrangements outside the family home.
- *Splitting*, also a less common option, for families with several children, in which the family is divided, with some children in the sole custody of the MOTHER full time and the others in the sole custody of the FATHER. This avoids some of the abrasions of joint custody and eliminates shuttling back and forth by all. But the absolute breaking up of the family is disruptive, and often *all* children feel short-changed by missing contact with the other parent and siblings. The two sets of siblings can also develop strong resentment and rivalries, over such matters as the perceived advantages and disadvantages of each home.

Often arguments over custody are continuations of the battles that caused the split in the first place and are further complicated when—as is common today—one or both parents have new partners, and often new children or stepchildren as well.

If the parents are unable to agree on custody, the court, often a FAMILY COURT or DOMESTIC RELATIONS COURT, will decide for them. In the nineteenth century, the court decision was almost always that the father should be given custody of the children. Later, the equal rights of both parents were more often recognized and custody was awarded to the "most fit" parent, the one who could best provide for the emotional and material needs of the child. Then in the twentieth century, under the popularly dubbed TENDER-YEARS DOCTRINE, courts began to award custody of children routinely to the mother, except in special circumstances, such as when she was shown to be clearly less fit than the father. In recent decades, at least since the 1960s, the court has tended to take a somewhat less dogmatic view of custody questions. In fact, in some states the court is even forbidden to take into account the parent's sex in awarding custody. Mothers are still commonly granted custody—in the United States, approximately 90 percent of the time—but this is often because fathers do not object. When fathers *do* choose to contest custody, today they often are favored, some estimate by a ratio of two to one. In fact, some women's groups argue that the current court approach takes insufficient account of the special relationship that normally exists between mother and child.

Sometimes the custody fight is not between two parents but between one parent and a relative or friend. A single mother may contest custody with a grandmother who has been caring for the child for several years, for example. Or after the death of a child's mother, the court may need to decide whether to award custody to the stepfather, with whom the child has been living for years, or to the child's BIOLOGICAL FATHER.

The court generally assesses custody questions in light of the BEST INTERESTS OF THE CHILD—sometimes, more realistically, choosing the *least detrimental alternative*—and may award sole custody to one parent and visitation rights to the other, joint custody, or custody to a GUARDIAN. When sharply contested custody questions are before a court, a *guardian ad litem* (at law) or child advocate (see ADVOCACY) may be appointed to act in the child's behalf. Among the areas the court explores in determining custody are:

- *Established living pattern*: The court will tend to favor the parent or arrangement that provides the most continuity and stability for the child, especially the parent who will remain in the same family home and keep current school, community, and religious ties, as opposed to a parent who is moving away. The court also tends to keep siblings together, rather than divide them.
- *Emotional ties*: The court tends to favor the parent or guardian perceived to have the strongest emotional ties with the child; this is the PSYCHOLOGICAL PARENT, the person who has been closest to the child's day-to-day hopes and fears.
- *Child's age, sex, health, and physical condition*: The court tends to favor the person perceived as being able to deal best with a child's needs, including any special health needs (see HEALTH CARE).
- *Parent's health and physical condition*: The court tends to favor the parent who is physically best equipped to care for the child, but a parent's disability is not supposed to stand in the way of a custody award.
- *Parent's ability to supply basic necessities*: The court will need to be assured that the child's basic needs for food, clothing, shelter, and medical care are met, but will not necessarily choose the more affluent parent, since financial arrangements can be made through CHILD SUPPORT. Failure to provide for the child can later lead to loss of custody.
- *Parent's plans for education*: The court tends to favor the parent who has formulated plans for the child's education, especially COLLEGE, though the parent's own level of education or skills are not a major factor to consider.
- *Parent's behavior*: The court tends to favor the parent whose behavior has been the most circumspect and traditionally "moral" and who has regular religious involvement. Adultery during the marriage can weigh heavily against custody, especially for the mother; later on, living unmarried with another sexual partner can, in some states, also cause a parent to lose custody. Parents who have, after the marriage relationship, openly acknowledged HOMOSEXUALITY and live with a partner of the same sex have special difficulty in custody fights. Various groups (see the list of organizations that

follows) have been formed to help parents fight custody battles, especially by urging that parents' activities should be evaluated by the court only in terms of whether there is any direct harm to the child. Problems with drugs, alcohol, money-handling, and the like can also count against a parent in a custody decision.

- *Parental acrimony*: The court tends to favor a parent who wishes to ensure continuing contact between the child and the other parent, looking with disfavor on a parent who tries to sever such contact by making active personal attacks on the other parent, by trying to break down the child's love and respect for the other parent (a practice called the *parental alienation syndrome*), by denying visitation rights, by taking the child to an undisclosed location, or by outright PARENTAL KIDNAPPING. Such actions can also lead to loss of custody later on.
- *Blood ties*: The court tends to favor the person with the strongest blood ties to the child—a mother over a grandmother or a father over a stepfather—when other considerations do not tip the balance. Among unmarried couples with no legally recognized relationship, the mother tends to be favored in custody disputes. With lesbian couples in which one woman actually bore the child, she tends to be favored in a custody dispute as a BIOLOGICAL PARENT.
- *Citizenship*: For children born outside the U.S. and with only one parent a U.S. citizen, who need to live in the U.S. for a specified period in order to retain citizenship, the court tends to rule against awarding custody to a parent who intends to take the child out of the country, risking the loss of valuable U.S. citizenship.
- *Child's preference*: The court tends to give some weight to an older child's preference for a parent or guardian, but less to a younger child's views, except as they reflect on other aspects of the child's relationship to the parents. The judge may have a private interview with the child IN CAMERA (in chambers), with the record of the conversation sealed to anyone else.

On reviewing the child's total situation, the judge may also, in some special situations, override the parents' agreement and decide on a different custody arrangement.

Once the court has made a custody decision, it is not lightly changed. CHANGED CIRCUMSTANCES, such as the temporary hospitalization of a parent, may cause a temporary change in the custody arrangement. But permanent changes are seldom ordered, except when the changed circumstances directly and adversely affect the child. If the custodial parent loses a job because of alcoholism (see ALCOHOL ABUSE; DRUG ABUSE) or is convicted of a crime, the court may make a permanent change. But individuals who have lost custody for such reasons should not assume that because they "reform" they will be able to reverse a custody decision, since stability and continuity for the child continue to be regarded as major principles.

One of the major custody problems of recent decades has been parental kidnapping of children by a parent who feels unjustly deprived of custody or visitation rights. Hundreds of thousands of children have been abducted by parents or other family members in recent years, causing a great deal of personal anguish and public furor. Often the children are returned within a week, but sometimes the parent and child go underground, breaking all communication with the other parent or the court system for long periods, or disappear permanently. Many parents have resorted to kidnapping in the hope that a court in a different jurisdiction would award them custody. To prevent that, the federal government passed the Parental Kidnapping Prevention Act and many states have adopted the UNIFORM CHILD CUSTODY JURISDICTION ACT (UCCJA); under these laws, the new state will enforce the original order, rather than modify it, except in some very special circumstances. The parent who has once resorted to kidnapping may also irreparably damage chances to later gain custody, under the CLEAN HANDS DOCTRINE. The parent will not be charged with kidnapping, however; a federal law labeled Title 18, Section 1201A, exempts parents from such charges. Many custodial parents who have lost their children to kidnapping are attempting to change the law, however, and some states have laws against parental kidnapping.

Another serious problem is that, in no-holds-barred custody fights, some parents have taken to making allegations of child abuse, especially sexual abuse (see CHILD ABUSE AND NEGLECT). While many cases of child abuse are legitimate and are right to bring up in court, a substantial minority have been found to be fabricated by vindictive ex-spouses. Parents in that kind of custody fight should be wary of putting themselves in any situation—however innocent in fact—that might be twisted or misconstrued. And any parent who considers making such a charge should get counsel before raising such a question and be very sure of the facts—understanding that children are very impressionable and easily led to say what they think interviewers wish them to say. A parent should consider how best to protect the child's interests in deciding how to handle the situation.

Some women have hidden their children from authorities to prevent the father from having visitation rights when they have suspected or alleged sexual abuse. In one highly publicized case, young Hilary Foretich was the subject of a massive search and was found months later in New Zealand in the care of her maternal grandparents. In that particular case, she was allowed to remain in the New Zealand, since the court in that country is not bound by any kind of uniform code for handling custody disputes.

In cases of suspected CHILD ABUSE AND NEGLECT, when SOCIAL WORKERS or other health or public officials fear that parents are hurting children or failing to properly care for them, the state may temporarily take the child into *protective custody* or *emergency custody* and place the child in FOSTER CARE. The foster home may be a private home, a GROUP HOME, or another facility; the child stays there until a hearing has been held on the charges.

Custody decisions primarily concern children, because by law children are regarded as unable to make such decisions for themselves. But parents can also find themselves in a fight over custody of an unmarried, grown child who is judged incompetent to handle everyday self-care. Unmarried adults who live together, even for many years, do not automatically have the legally recognized right to care for each other. If one of them becomes so seriously disabled through accident or illness as to be unconscious or unable to communicate desires regarding medical care, the partner often has no legal standing to make the necessary medical decisions or other decisions. These can only be made by the nearest legally recognized relative, even if the person who is ill and the relative have been long estranged. Some of the most bitter and poignant cases of recent years have involved fights over custody of a severely disabled person between parents and an unmarried partner.

FOR HELP AND GENERAL INFORMATION

About custody of children in general

Parents Without Partners (PWP), 800–637–7974. Publishes information sheets *What Noncustodial Parents Should Know About Child Visitation* and *Rights of Noncustodial Parents to Examine School Records.* (For full group information, see General Parenting Resources on page 634.)

Association of Family and Conciliation Courts (AFCC), 608–251–4001. Publishes pamphlets *Preparing for Your Custody Evaluation, Joint Custody: A New Way of Being Related,* and *Child Visitation/Parent Access—A Relationship That Lasts Forever,* booklet *Joint Custody and Shared Parenting;* videotapes on difficult mediation situations; and various legal materials.

Parents and Children's Equality (PACE)
3980 Orchard Hill Circle
Palm Harbor, FL 34684
813–786–6911
E-mail: ken.pangborn@mercopus.com
Kenneth R. Pangborn, Executive Director
For parents and professionals, such as lawyers and counselors, involved in divorce and custody questions; seeks the child's best interests during divorce; counsels partners who divorce and aids them in gaining access to their children in cases of parental abduction or other interference with custody or visitation rights; counsels parents in cases of child abuse, including sexual abuse; conducts seminars and attempts to influence public policy; publishes *Directory of Divorce Reform Organizations.*

National Congress for Men and Children (NCFC)
851 Minnesota Avenue
P.O. Box 171675
Kansas City, KS 66117–0675
913–281–9943; 202-FATHERS [328–4377]; 800–733-DADS [733–3237]
Fax: 913–342–1414
E-mail: ncfc@primenet.com
Travis Ballard, President
Organization concerned with fathers' rights, men's rights, and divorce reform; acts as advocate; supports joint custody and equity in custody and child support litigation; publishes newsletter *NetWORK* and membership manual.

About shared or joint custody

Joint Custody Association (JCA)
10606 Wilkins Avenue
Los Angeles, CA 90024
310–475–5352
Fax: 310–474–4859
James A. Cook, President
Organization concerned with joint custody and related legal and financial concerns; provides information and referrals; publishes *Joint Custody and Family Law* and information kits for parents.

National Legal Resource Center For Child Advocacy and Protection, American Bar Association, 202–331–2200. (For full group information, see Help Against Child Abuse and Neglect on page 680.)

HALT: An Organization of Americans for Legal Reform
1319 F Street NW, Suite 300
Washington, DC 20004
202–347–9600
Fax: 202–347–9606
E-mail: haltfry@aol.com (America Online: HALTFRY)
Organization of people interested in citizens acting as their own lawyers (termed *pro se*); formerly Help Abolish Legal Tyranny; publishes *You, Your Family and the Law: A Legal Guide for Today's Families, Everyday Law Series, Using the Law Library: A Nonlawyer's Guide, Dancing with Lawyers: How to Take Charge and Get Results, Using a Lawyer … And What to Do If Things Go Wrong, If You Want to Sue a Lawyer: A Directory of Legal Malpractice Attorneys, Everyday Contracts: Protecting Your Rights,* and works on other topics such as real estate, probate, and small claims courts.

National Organization for Women's Legal Defense and Education Fund
99 Hudson Street
New York, NY 10036
212–925–6635
Fax: 212–226–1066
Organization focusing on legal problems and needs of women; runs family law program; provides referral services.

National Center for Women and Family Law
799 Broadway, Suite 402
New York, NY 10003

212–674–8200
Fax: 212–533–5104
HANSNET: 1193
Nechama Masliansky, Director
Organization that gathers and disseminates information on women's relationship to family law; publishes numerous materials, including bimonthly newsletter *The Women's Advocate, Custody, Visitation, and Child Support, The Primary Caretaker Factor, Joint Custody Resource Packet, Joint Custody and Public Benefits, Battered Women and Custody, Visitation: Denial, Supervision or Suspension, Friendly Parent Provisions in Custody Determinations, Moving Restrictions on Custodial Parents, Modification of Custody Awards, Interstate Child Custody Disputes and Parental Kidnapping: Policy, Practice, and Law, Confronting Economic Factors in Child Custody Disputes, AIDS as a Factor in Visitation Cases,* and *Gender Bias in the Courts.*

Parents Sharing Custody (PSC)
420 South Beverly Drive, Suite 100
Beverly Hills, CA 90212–4410
310–286–9171
Linda Blakeley, Director
For divorced parents who have joint custody of children and others interested in such arrangements; aims to educate others about shared custody through seminars and other programs.

About handling custody problems

Academy of Family Mediators (AFM)
4 Militia Drive
Lexington, MA 02173
617–674–2663
Fax: 617–674–2690
Ericka Gray, Executive Director
Organization of attorneys and mental health professionals supporting the use of mediation in family disputes; provides information and makes referrals; supports mediation standards; publishes quarterly *Mediation News,* journal *Mediation Quarterly,* membership directory, and other materials.

Mothers Without Custody (MWOC)
P.O. Box 56762
Houston, TX 77256
713–840–1622
Angie Mease, Executive Director
Cathy Knapp, Contact
Network of mutual-support, self-help groups for mothers who do not live with their children for whatever reason, whether by choice or because of judicial or social agency intervention, loss of custody, or abduction of the child by an ex-husband; provides information, referrals, and legal help; publishes newsletter *Mother-to-Mother.*

Center on Children and the Law, 202–662–1720. Publishes *Sexual Abuse Allegations in Custody and Visitation Cases: A Resource Book for Judges and Court Personnel.* (For full group information, see Help Against Child Abuse and Neglect on page 680.)

Committee for Mother and Child Rights (CMCR)
210 Ole Orchard Drive
Clear Brook, VA 22624
703–722–3652
ElizaBeth Owen, National Coordinator
Organization for mothers without custody or with custody problems; provides support; seeks to shape public policy.

Child Care Law Center (CCLC); 415–495–5498. Publishes *Child Custody Disputes: With Whom Can the Child Go Home.* (For full group information, see child care.)

National Legal Resource Center For Child Advocacy and Protection, 202–331–2200. (For full group information, see Help Against Child Abuse and Neglect on page 680.)

About custody problems of lesbians and gay men

Lavender Families Resource Network, 206–325–2643, voice/TT. Publishes pamphlet *Custody Advice for Lesbian and Gay Parents* and article reprints *Child Custody and the Homosexual Parent, Assessing Children's Best Interests When a Parent Is Gay or Lesbian, Social Attitudes, Legal Standards and Personal Trauma in Child Custody Cases, The Impact of Parental Homosexuality in Child Custody Cases: A Review of the Literature, Grandparents and Psychological Parents: Rights and Remedies, How to Choose and Deal with a Lawyer, Expert Testimony in Custody Cases, Custody and Visitation: Their Relationship to Establishing and Enforcing Support,* and *Lesbian Mothers: Psychosocial Assumptions in Family Law.* (For full group information, see homosexuality.)

Lambda Legal Defense and Education Fund (LLDEF), 212–995–8585. Defends homosexuals' rights in child custody cases. (For full group information, see homosexuality.)

CALM, Inc. (Custody Action for Lesbian Mothers)
P.O. Box 281
Narberth, PA 19072–0281
610–667–7508
Fax: 610–667–0978
Rosalie G. Davies, Coordinator
Organization providing free legal counseling services to lesbian mothers facing child custody, child support, or visitation battles; provides information and referrals; offers emotional support; acts as advocate.

ONLINE RESOURCES

Internet: Children's Rights. Resources from various organizations, including Children's Rights Council, Central Ohio Organization, Father and Children for Equality, and National Congress of Men and Children.
telnet://cwgk4.chem.cwru.edu

OTHER RESOURCES

FOR PARENTS

Child Custody: How and Where to Find Facts and Get Help. Robert D. Reed and Danek S. Kaus. R & E Publishers, 1993.

Mother's Guide to Child Support, Custody and Visitation and *Father's Guide to Child Support, Custody and Visitation.* Sal Fariello and Vera Fariello. SFT, 1992.

Separate Houses: A Practical Guide for Divorced Parents. Robert B. Shapiro. Prentice-Hall, 1991.

The Joint Custody Handbook, rev. ed. Miriam G. Cohen. Running Press, 1991.

Divorce and Child Custody: Your Options and Legal Rights. Richard L. Strohm and Deanna Peters. Makai, 1991.

ON CUSTODY DISPUTES

Win Your Child Custody War: Custody Winning Strategies. C. Hardwick. Pale Horse, 1994.

How to Win Your Child Custody Dispute. Jonathan Gould. Sulzburger and Graham, 1994.

Don't Settle for Less: A Woman's Guide to Getting a Fair Divorce and Custody Settlement. Bev Pekala. Doubleday, 1994.

A Parent's Guide to Legal Violence: The Pawning of Our Children. Louise Wallace. PineTree, 1992.

Parent vs. Parent: How You and Your Child Can Survive the Custody Battle. Stephen P. Herman. Pantheon, 1990.

FOR OR BY CHILDREN OR TEENS

Understanding Child Custody. Susan N. Terkel. Watts, 1991.

BACKGROUND BOOKS

From Father's Property to Children's Rights: The History of Child Custody in the United States. Mary A. Mason. Columbia University Press, 1994.

Dividing the Child: Social and Legal Dilemmas of Custody. Eleanor E. Maccoby and Robert H. Mnookin. Harvard University Press, 1992.

Humanizing Child Custody Disputes: The Family's Team. Gordon B. Plumb and Mary E. Lindley. C. C. Thomas, 1990.

(See also VISITATION RIGHTS; MISSING CHILDREN; HELP AGAINST CHILD ABUSE AND NEGLECT on page 680; also GENERAL PARENTING RESOURCES on page 634, for more help and information on divorce and stepfamilies.)

cutoff score (cutting score), on an ADMISSION TEST, a SCORE a student must reach or risk being rejected by a school—even though test professionals always stress that no one should accept, reject, or make any other key decision on the basis of any single test score alone. If parents feel their child was unfairly rejected on the basis of a single test, they should seek a retest.

cyanosis, blueness, especially around the lips and NAILS, indicating lack of oxygen; a common symptom among infants that appears in RESPIRATORY DISTRESS SYNDROME or PERSISTENT FETAL CIRCULATION and in many other kinds of LUNG AND BREATHING DISORDERS and heart problems (see HEART AND HEART PROBLEMS).

cystic fibrosis (CF), a GENETIC DISORDER, also called *mucoviscidosis,* the leading killer of children and young adults among genetic diseases in the United States. CF is a METABOLIC DISORDER in which the body's *exocrine* (externally secreting) glands, including the sweat and salivary glands, produce not the normal clear, free-flowing fluid but a thick, sticky mucus; this mucus accumulates in various parts of the body, notably the lungs and pancreas, interfering with vital functions, such as breathing and digestion.

CF is not infectious, but is a genetic disorder of the AUTOSOMAL RECESSIVE type, so a child inherits it only if both parents—often symptomless CARRIERS—carry the defective gene, as an estimated twelve million Americans do. CF affects approximately 1 in every 2,500 newborns, most often those of Caucasian ancestry, less often Blacks, and only rarely those of Asian background.

The generalized symptoms of cystic fibrosis are easily mistaken for respiratory disorders such as pneumonia and ASTHMA, so it can sometimes be difficult to diagnose accurately. The three main symptoms are:

- *Pancreatic insufficiency*: The pancreas secretes enzymes necessary for proper digestion, but in CF, mucus tends to block the passageways by which the enzymes reach the small intestine. As a result, the digestive process is seriously disrupted; much food passes through the body undigested, so despite a very large intake of food, a person with CF may show signs of MALNUTRITION. Early signs of this are fatty, foul-smelling stool and abdominal pain. Lack of digestive enzymes in the small intestines is one clue to a diagnosis of cystic fibrosis.
- *Respiratory problems*: Chronic LUNG AND BREATHING DISORDERS are common among people with CF, because thick mucus obstructs the air passages of the lung and bronchial tubes, causing labored breathing and chronic cough. Worse, the mucus is a prime breeding ground for bacteria, which often become resistant to treatment by ANTIBIOTICS, producing chronic respiratory infections. Breathing problems lead to poor circulation and increased BLOOD PRESSURE, which in turn can cause damage to the lungs and heart, further weakening the body's ability to resist infection. It is this pattern of complications that the Public Health Service estimates causes 90 percent of all deaths from CF.
- *Excessive loss of salt*: People with CF lose large amounts of SODIUM and CHLORIDE in their sweat, causing weakness and listlessness and, in summer, increased risk of DEHYDRATION or heat exhaustion. The most commonly used diagnostic test for CF is, in fact, the *sweat test,* which tests for abnormal concentrations of salt in sweat.

Other symptoms seen in severe cases of CF are short, stubby ("clubbed") fingers and bluish lips (CYANOSIS). For unknown reasons, not all people are affected with equal severity. Some people show serious symptoms in infancy, while others with lesser symptoms may be diagnosed only later in childhood. And some experience primarily breathing difficulties, without much digestive involvement, while others experience the reverse.

Researchers are working hard to develop more accurate diagnostic tests, because it is vitally important to begin treatment early, before great damage has been done. The main treatments include:

- Use of antibiotics to combat infections.
- Aerosal inhalation to clear air passages.
- Physical therapy, especially *postural drainage,* a technique that uses gravity and "pounding" of the chest to help dislodge and drain mucus from the lungs and bronchial tubes.
- Pancreatic extracts, taken to replace missing enzymes.
- Additional quantities of food, though well-balanced and relatively low in fat.
- Supplemental salt to replace that lost in perspiration.

Until recently, few people with cystic fibrosis reached school age. Treatment techniques developed in recent decades have greatly improved both the quality and length of life for CF patients, with many living into their 20s and 30s and even beyond. Among the recently developed treatments is a new mucus-thinning drug introduced only in 1993.

Most important, in 1989, researchers identified the CF gene and a year later were able to correct CF cells in the laboratory, holding out hopes that GENE THERAPY might actually cure the disease sometime in the future. In promising, though still highly experimental studies, scientists have been attempting to introduce into patients' bodies enough genetically corrected CF genes to ease or eliminate the symptoms of the disorder. A modified cold virus is being used to "deliver" normal genes by various means, including nose drops and a *bronchoscope,* a flexible tube that drizzles the virus directly into the bronchial tubes. Other delivery systems are also being explored. Patients are then monitored to see if the normal genes "turn on" and begin to function, though only a small part of the body is being reached in these early experiments.

Increasing knowledge of the gene should also help researchers understand precisely what causes CF and lead them to other ways to correct the defect. At present, however, there is no preventive or cure for CF, only treatments to alleviate symptoms of the disease.

Since the CF gene was identified, GENETIC SCREENING tests such as CHORIONIC VILLUS SAMPLING and AMNIOCENTESIS have been used to see if a FETUS has CF. Tests for CF are still in early stages, however, and lack RELIABILITY, giving a great many FALSE POSITIVES and FALSE NEGATIVES—so some doctors question their value. Prospective parents who have any family history of CF will want to seek GENETIC COUNSELING.

FOR HELP AND FURTHER INFORMATION

Cystic Fibrosis Foundation (CFF)
6931 Arlington Road
Bethesda, MD 20814
301–951–4422; 800-FIGHT-CF [344–4823], U.S. except MD
Fax: 301–951–6378
Robert Beall, President and Chief Executive Officer
Organization concerned with cystic fibrosis; funds research; helps fund CF medical centers; acts as advocate; provides information and referrals; offers discounts on drugs and home infusion; publishes quarterly newsletter *Commitment* and fact sheets *Facts About CF, Gene Therapy and CF, Progress in CF Research,* and *Foundation Facts.*

National Digestive Disease Information Clearinghouse (NDDIC), 301–654–3810. (For full group information, see DIGESTIVE SYSTEM AND DISORDERS.)

National Organization for Rare Disorders (NORD), 800–999–6673. (For full group information, see RARE DISORDERS.)

OTHER RESOURCES

General works

Cystic Fibrosis: The Facts, 2nd ed. Ann Harris and Maurice Super. Oxford University Press, 1993.

A Parent's Guide to Cystic Fibrosis. Burton L. Shapiro and Ralph C. Heussner, Jr. University of Minnesota Press, 1990.

For children

CF in His Corner. Gail Radley. Four Winds Press, 1984.

Alex: The Life of a Child. Frank Deford. Viking, 1983.

For teens

Cystic Fibrosis. Virginia Alvin and Robert Silverstein. Watts, 1994.

(See also GENETIC COUNSELING; HELP FOR SPECIAL CHILDREN on page 689.)

cytomegalovirus (CMV) infection, a kind of SEXUALLY TRANSMITTED DISEASE caused by the cytomegalovirus (CMV), but one that is spread not only by sexual contact but also by other forms of bodily contact, including kissing. A member of the HERPES family, CMV is a common virus, infecting most mature adults. Like its relatives, CMV often lies dormant in the body, becoming reactivated from time to time. In most healthy adults, CMV has few serious consequences, causing flu-like symptoms, such as FEVER, fatigue, and swollen lymph glands, similar to those of INFECTIOUS MONONUCLEOSIS.

But CMV can be quite dangerous to infants, whose IMMUNE SYSTEMS are not yet fully developed; to people whose immune systems are damaged or being suppressed, such as those who have AIDS or are undergoing chemotherapy; and to pregnant women, who can pass the virus on to the FETUS, with resulting BIRTH DEFECTS, such as MENTAL RETARDATION, EAR AND HEARING PROBLEMS, EPILEPSY, various deformities, and even death. The National Institute of Allergy and Infectious Diseases estimates that CMV is the "leading cause of congenital infection," affecting 6,000 babies a year. Various diagnostic tests exist but are not very reliable, nor are there yet any effective drugs to treat the virus, though some are being tested. Some doctors have cautioned pregnant women who work in CHILD CARE that they are at increased risk of catching the infection from the young children in their care, but they also note that the virus is so widespread and readily transmitted that it is hard to avoid. (For help and further information, including how to avoid infection, see SEXUALLY TRANSMITTED DISEASES.)

D

day treatment, treatment given to people while they remain living in their own homes rather than in a hospital or other live-in care facility. In cases of CHILD ABUSE AND NEGLECT, day treatment services for the child and some or all family members may include psychological and social counseling, structured supervision, and activities designed to break the cycle of abuse and begin the process of repairing the damage.

deaf, a term applied to people whose hearing is so severely impaired that it cannot be used for the ordinary purposes of life, with or without a HEARING AID. When hearing is impaired but can be used for the ordinary purposes of life with the use of a hearing aid, a person is generally termed *hard of hearing*. (See EAR AND HEARING PROBLEMS.)

deaf-blind, a term applied to a person who has significant loss of both sight and hearing. Deaf-blindness can be caused by GENETIC DISORDERS, by the mother contracting RUBELLA (German measles) during PREGNANCY, or by other illnesses, disorders, DRUG REACTIONS OR INTERACTIONS, or accidents. People with this dual DISABILITY have often had less support and attention than those with a single disability. Frequently children who are recognized as deaf are sent to schools for the deaf, and their vision loss often goes undetected, sometimes for years, slowing their intellectual development. Early recognition, treatment, and training are vital.

Most people who are deaf-blind are not totally lacking in sight or hearing. They may be able to understand some speech with a HEARING AID and have some sight, but their disabilities are such that they have difficulty in communication, mobility, and daily living skills. Those who are born deaf-blind are most disadvantaged, because they have had no direct experience of the hearing or sighted world. It is somewhat easier for those who have had some sight and hearing, especially for a long enough period during childhood to have learned to speak.

Communication is vital if the deaf-blind child or adult is not to be left in terrible isolation. When deaf-blind people have sufficient sight, they may be able to read in large print or in braille and to communicate with others using SIGN LANGUAGE. Long-distance communication can be achieved through TEXT TYPEWRITER (TT) machines, sometimes employing relay services when only one of the two people communicating has a TT. When deaf-blind people do have have sufficient sight, they can communicate with others using a print-on-palm method or fingerspelling using a *manual alphabet*, the kind that Annie Sullivan taught so memorably to deaf-blind Helen Keller. They can also communicate with others using machines such as a braille typewriter or a computer that produces text in print or braille or records what has been typed on the keyboard using voice synthesis. A reverse process allows individuals who are deaf-blind to read standard print. The material is scanned into a computer with optical character recognition programs. The material can then be read in braille or through a device called an *Optacon*, which converts the image of a printed letter into a vibrating tactile form that can be felt with a finger.

Mobility and daily living are more difficult for the deaf-blind. Many deaf-blind people rely on SERVICE DOGS to help them in these areas. Ultrasonic mobility enhancement systems have been developed; deaf-blind people also often use a long cane and sometimes wear buttons describing their condition and asking people to help them cross the street.

FOR HELP AND FURTHER INFORMATION

Helen Keller National Center for Deaf-Blind Youths and Adults (HKNC)
111 Middle Neck Road
Sands Point, NY 11050–1299
516–944–8900; 516–944–8637, TT
National Family Association for Deaf-Blind:
800–255–0411, ext. 275
Fax: 516–944–7302
Joseph McNulty, Director
Organization established by Congress to serve people with significant loss of both sight and hearing; operates National Training Center, National Training Team (NTT), and Technical Assistance Center (TAC), focusing on transition to adulthood; sponsors National Family Association for Deaf-Blind (NFADB) acting as advocate for families on national level; provides evaluation, rehabilitation, personal adjustment training, job preparation, and placement; publishes *NAT-CEN News*, *NPN Newsletter*, *Directory of Agencies Serving People Who Are Deaf-Blind*, and other materials; NFADB also publishes a newsletter.

American Association of the Deaf-Blind (AADB)
814 Thayer Avenue
Silver Spring, MD 20910
301–588–6545
Rod Macdonald, President
Organization of deaf-blind people and their families; provides information and makes referrals; encourages independent living for the deaf-blind; publishes quarterly *Deaf-Blind American* in large print and braille.

National Information Center on Deafness (NICD), 202–651–5051; 202–651–5052, TT. Publishes *Information on Deaf-Blindness.* (For full group information, see EAR AND HEARING PROBLEMS.)

ONLINE RESOURCES

Internet: Disability-Related Resources. Collection of resources, including deaf-blind concerns. gopher://hawking.u.washington.edu

(See also EAR AND HEARING PROBLEMS; EYE AND VISION PROBLEMS)

dean's list, a list prepared at the end of each term (traditionally by the dean's office) indicating which students at the COLLEGE or university achieved a GRADE POINT AVERAGE of B or better, or, if number GRADES are used, generally 90 or better; the college equivalent of a high school's HONOR ROLL.

death and dying, the gradual or abrupt cessation of life, traditionally indicated by lack of heartbeat and breathing; what some medical professionals now call *apparent death.* In recent decades, with the development of VENTILATORS and other technology to assist in maintaining heart and lung functions, a new definition of death has emerged—BRAIN DEATH, which focuses on the lack of activity in the brain. Definitions vary from state to state, however, and the specific definition recognized in a particular area is sometimes called *legal death.*

Although children are a symbol of life, some 100,000 die each year in the United States alone, according to Children's Hospice International. Another one million children have severe CHRONIC illness. For parents, a child's dying is a nightmare come true. Such a death may come suddenly, as a result of an accident (see SAFETY; VIOLENCE), but many children die as a result of terminal illness, such as CANCER, AIDS, or untreatable GENETIC DISORDERS. If all medical treatments have been tried and exhausted, terminally ill patients and their families often favor the HOSPICE approach over HOSPITALS, since it focuses on maintaining the quality of the patient's remaining life, rather than continuing aggressive therapy in a hospital regardless of all other concerns.

Questions of death and the use of medical technology in cases of irreversible COMA and TERMINAL illness have raised grave problems for the families of people lingering on the edge of death. If a terminally ill child is considered so severely ill that death is inevitable and imminent, parents may be asked to decide if the child should be placed on a ventilator, in case heart and lungs fail, or if the child should be allowed to die without intervention. If they decide upon the latter, the physician may write *no code* or *do not resuscitate (DNR)* on the child's medical chart.

Once a child is placed on an artificial breathing machine, the decision as to when (if ever) the child is later taken off is extremely difficult, since many health personnel feel that their professional standards call for doing everything possible to maintain life. Parents have in some cases endured lengthy court cases to win the right to remove their child from a machine—in effect, to win the child's right to die. The legal questions in these areas have only begun to be explored.

Health professionals once routinely allowed the next of kin to make HEALTH CARE decisions for family members, including adults unable to make those decisions themselves and children, who are legally considered unable to make such decisions. However, because of controversy over the use of ventilators and other life-support services and increasing concerns over liability, many hospitals and doctors have begun to require families to go to court to obtain legal authority to refuse life support on behalf of the patient. To avoid this cumbersome process, many states have passed statutes establishing a list of people, ranked in priority, who are legally empowered to act on behalf of the patient in accordance with known wishes or, if the person's wishes are unknown, in the "best interest" of the patient. The list varies, but generally includes, in order: a patient's spouse, an adult child, a parent, and a sibling.

For many parents, the questions of death are bound up with PREGNANCY and CHILDBIRTH, as in cases of MISCARRIAGE or STILLBIRTH, when a child dies before birth, or MATERNAL MORTALITY, in which the mother dies from complications of the pregnancy. For babies born alive, the first year—and especially the first month—are the most dangerous time. The rate of death in infants varies widely from country to country, depending on various factors, including medical care, PRENATAL CARE, and socioeconomic conditions. In the United States, the INFANT MORTALITY RATE—the number of infants per 1,000 who die in their first year—is 10 per 1,000 for White infants and 19 per 1,000 for Black infants. Of these, two-thirds die in the first month.

In that first month, babies are most at risk from RESPIRATORY DISTRESS SYNDROME, complications associated with PREMATURE birth and LOW BIRTHWEIGHT, CONGENITAL abnormalities (such as SPINA BIFIDA), and effects of maternal complications of pregnancy. In the second month through the twelfth month of life, death most often occurs because of SUDDEN INFANT DEATH SYNDROME, congenital abnormalities, and infections (bacterial or viral) such as pneumonia, influenza, bronchitis (see LUNG AND BREATHING PROBLEMS), septicemia (see BLOOD AND BLOOD DISORDERS), and MENINGITIS, followed by injuries and murder.

Among older children, ages one through nineteen, by far the main cause of death is injuries, followed by congenital abnormalities, CANCER, HEART PROBLEMS, and murder. During ADOLESCENCE, SUICIDE becomes a major cause of death and murder an increasingly important one.

Though death may come suddenly and unexpectedly, sometimes families must together face the impending loss of a parent, grandparent, sibling, or other close relative or friend—or the possibility of their own death. Death and dying were, for centuries, almost unmentionables. Often

Somehow Children Know

Children sense the truth. Some parents who tried to "spare" their children from knowing that a family member had a terminal illness later voiced regret at not discussing the truth during the course of the disease. Children have amazing capabilities when they understand a situation. However, when their normal world is turned upside down and whispered conversations go on behind closed doors, they often imagine situations that are worse than reality. Young children dwell on "terrible" things *they* have done or said that place responsibility for the upheaval in the household on themselves. This is especially true if the child is going through a period of testing parental authority or in some other way is in disagreement with family members. Children—especially young ones—tend to view themselves as the center of the universe and see many situations only in direct relationship to themselves.

The children's ages and emotional maturity should suggest what and how much to disclose. It might help to realize that it comforts children to know when someone is dying because it confirms their belief that something is amiss within the family....

The most compelling reason for sharing the diagnosis with adults and children alike is that cancer [and other terminal illnesses] can be so terribly lonely. No one need try to bear the knowledge alone.

Source: Taking Time: Support for People with Cancer and the People Who Care About them (1987). Prepared for the Public Health Service by the National Cancer Institute.

doctors did not tell patients when they were dying, and family members pretended that nothing was wrong. No one was fooled, however, and the very great tragedy was that because no one acknowledged death and discussed it openly, family members were cut off from the possibility of support from one another. Today, there is a much greater understanding that all humans face the same questions of death and dying, that they have many of the same reactions in response to it, and that by sharing their thoughts and feelings they can all be helped to face questions of death, to come to terms with it, and with love and support from others to learn to move beyond.

This very much includes young children, because when death occurs in a family (as noted in SOMEHOW CHILDREN KNOW above), young children, who are sensitive to changes in the home, may readily come to feel that they have caused those changes, a classic example of MAGICAL THINKING. Like doctors with their patients, parents need to be sensitive to how much a child wants to know. The basic guideline is to be forthcoming and responsive, but not to force unwanted knowledge on a child. Without frank acknowledgment that something is wrong, the child is left to deal alone with terrible fears and felt "responsibilities."

Many groups have been formed by parents who have experienced the death of a child (or other family member) and by people who have worked with them. These organizations provide help, information, and support to families facing death or terminal illness. Other children in the family, as well as parents, suffer enormous stress and pain when a sibling is seriously ill or dies. Organizations have also been formed to help them. (See the list of organizations that follows, including those relating to specific diseases, such as CANCER or AIDS; also see HELP FOR SPECIAL CHILDREN on page 689, under "On wishes for terminally or chronically ill children.") Even some funeral homes have begun to provide supportive services, called *bereavement counseling*, to people surviving a death in the family. So have HOSPICE organizations.

It is also a sad fact of life that today many children experience the death of a family member or friend because of DRUG ABUSE, VIOLENCE, or SUICIDE. Many communities, schools, churches, and other local organizations may arrange for counselors to be brought in to help children deal with the fact of death.

After the death of a family member or friend, children may experience the same kind of wide range of responses felt by adults. They may feel anxious and fearful, worried that they may die, that something is wrong with them, or concerned about who will take care of them now. They may feel angry at the person who died or at God for allowing the person to die. They may also feel abandoned and lash out at others in anger. Or they may feel guilty because of something they said or did toward the person who died, feeling that somehow their behavior caused harm or even caused the death. Children may also resent attention focused on the dead person, especially if it is another child, and may feel even more guilt about that. They may regress to earlier behaviors, to thumbsucking, BEDWETTING, pressing to sleep with parents, or being fearful of being left with a babysitter or in CHILD CARE. They may experience physical symptoms, such as headaches, stomachaches, changes in eating habits, sleeping problems, and nightmares (see SLEEP AND SLEEP DISORDERS). Children, particularly younger ones, may react with shock and disbelief, acting as though the death did not happen. They may show no emotion, especially when they do not understand the concept of death. They may experience sadness, expressed in crying, quietness, introspection, daydreaming, and sometimes DEPRESSION.

Parents, who are often experiencing many of the same feelings, are strongly advised to bring children promptly and openly into the grieving process, rather than let them be "forgotten mourners," the role children have tradtionally been given. Parents are advised to accept the child's responses, whatever they may be; to try to respond to their spoken or unspoken fears; and to be honest in saying they cannot explain some things about death because they themselves do not understand them. Above all, especially for parents who are dealing with their own grief, it is important to show visible, physical, and verbal love, affection, and support to the mourning child. Many children are helped by expressing their memories of the dead person in a diary, journal, set of drawings, album of photos, or box of mementos. Children who are old enough or who express a desire to do so should be included in memorial services. However, parents should prepare the child by explaining what a funeral is and how it serves as a way for family and friends to say good-bye. If the child's grief seems excessive or prolonged, parents should not hesitate to seek out counselors.

FOR HELP AND FURTHER INFORMATION

The Compassionate Friends (TCF)
P.O. Box 3696
Oak Brook, IL 60522
708–990–0010
Therese Goodrich, Executive Director
Nondenominational network of mutual-support, self-help groups of and for parents who have lost a child; seeks to counsel and support surviving family members, including siblings; links grieving families with "telephone friends" to talk with; publishes newsletter and other materials.

Sudden Infant Death Syndrome Alliance (SIDS Alliance), 800–221–7437. Publishes *Grief After SIDS, Parents and the Grieving Process, Sudden Infant Death Syndrome: Siblings and Grief, For Grandparents...A Double Grief, A Child's Understanding of Death, Notes from Krisit's Mom, Grief of Children,* and *Couples and Grief.* (For full group information, see SUDDEN INFANT DEATH SYNDROME.)

Children's Hospice International (CHI), 800–242–4453. (For full group information, see HOSPICE.) Publishes various materials, including:

- On children's death: *There Is a Rainbow Behind Every Cloud: The Center for Attitudinal Healing, Shira—A Legacy of Courage, Am I Still a Sister?,* and *O Susan! Looking Forward with Hope after the Death of a Child.*
- For children and teens: *Tell Me Papa* and *Mango Days: A Teenager Facing Eternity Reflects on the Beauty of Life.*
- On grief and bereavement: *Approaching Grief, Sibling Grief,* and video "*When I Die, Don't You Cry*".

Pediatric Projects, 800–947–0947. Publishes *Preschoolers' Experience with Loss and Death* and *Can You Love Someone You Never Knew?* on newborn death. (For full group information, see HOSPITAL.)

Parents of Murdered Children (POMC)
100 East Eighth Street, B–41
Cincinnati, OH 45202
513–721–5683
Fax: 513–345–4489
Sharon Tewskbury, Executive Director
Mutual-support, self-help group of parents of a murdered child or other survivors of homicide victims; disseminates information about the grieving process and about dealing with the criminal justice system; publishes newsletter *Survivors,* the books *Path Through the Criminal Justice System,* and *Thanks for Asking: Collections of Remembrances,* and the pamphlets *Truth in Sentencing, Sibling Grief: The Forgotten Mourners, The Courage to Grieve: A Weekend of Hope and Healing, DNA Finger Printing,* and *Memorial Wall,* POMC's traveling memorial plaques honoring dead children.

SHARE—Pregnancy and Infant Loss Support
St. Joseph's Health Center
300 First Capitol Drive
St. Charles, MO 63301–2893
314–947–6164
Fax: 314–947–7486
Catherine A. Lammert, Executive Director
Network of support groups for families who have experienced stillbirth, miscarriage, or infant death; provides information and referrals; publishes various materials, including newsletter *Share, Bittersweet...hellogoodbye: A Resource in Planning Farewell Rituals When a Baby Dies,* perinatal bereavement bibliography, *Starting Your Own SHARE Group,* and books and audiovisual materials for adults working with bereaved children.

National Sudden Infant Death Syndrome Clearinghouse (NSIDSC); 703–821–8955, ext. 474. Publishes *Parents and the Grieving Process, The Grief of Children,* and *After Sudden Infant Death Syndrome (SIDS): Facing Anniversaries, Holidays, and Special Events.* (For full group information, see SUDDEN INFANT DEATH SYNDROME.)

Johnson Institute, 800–231–5165, U.S. except MN. Publishes *Helping Children Cope with Separation and Loss, I Wish I Could Hold Your Hand...A Child's Guide to Grief and Loss,* and *Children Who Grieve: A Manual for Conducting Support Groups.* (For full group information, see HELP AGAINST SUBSTANCE ABUSE on page 703.)

American Academy of Child and Adolescent Psychiatry (AACAP), 202–966–7300. Publishes information sheet *Children and Grief.* (For full group information, see MENTAL DISORDERS.)

Parents Without Partners (PWP), 800–637–7974. Publishes reading list *Annotated Bibliography and Resource*

List for the Widowed. (For full group information, see GENERAL PARENTING RESOURCES on page 634.)

Cancer Care, Inc. and the National Cancer Care Foundation, 800–813–4673. (For full group information, see CANCER.)

Twin Services, TWINLINE: 510–524–0863. Publishes *Multiple Birth Loss.* (For full group information, see MULTIPLE BIRTH.)

Pregnancy and Infant Loss Center (PILC)
1415 East Wayzata Boulevard, Suite 30
Wayzata, MN 55391
612–473–9372
Fax: 612–473–8978
Gail Steltes, Executive Director
Organization for parents who have experienced miscarriage, stillbirth, or infant death; provides information and referrals; encourages formation of mutual-support parent groups; publishes newsletter *Loving Arms, Bereavement Support Group Guide,* and other materials, including:

- For parents: *Empty Arms, Unsung Lullabies: A Parents' Guide to Healing After Childbearing Loss, Newborn Death, When Hello Means Goodbye, Empty Cradle, Broken Heart, For Better or Worse* (on couple's problems after a child's death), and *Pregnancy Heartbreak: Unfulfilled Promises, A Mother's Dilemma.*
- On grief and bereavement: *Planning a Precious Goodbye, Self-Care and the Griever, Free to Grieve, Grieving Grandparents, What Family and Friends Can Do, Loving and Letting Go, Men and Grief, The Rocking Horse Is Lonely—And Other Stories of Fathers' Grief, Stolen Joy—Healing after Infertility and Infant Loss, Remembering with Love: Messages of Hope for the First Year of Grieving and Beyond.*
- For children: *No New Baby, Timothy Duck, Where's Jess, Talking With Young People About Death, Thumpy's Story* (with coloring book and workbook for older children), *Sibling Grief,* and *Our Baby Died. Why?* (on a stillborn sibling).

Unite, Inc., Grief Support
c/o Jeanes Hospital
7600 Central Avenue
Philadelphia, PA 19111–2499
215–728–3777
Janis Heil, Executive Director
Organization "offering grief support following miscarriage, stillbirth, and infant death" through support groups in Pennsylvania and New Jersey; publishes national bimonthly newsletter *UNITE Notes.*

National Mental Health Association (NMHA), 800–969–6642. Publishes *Coping with Bereavement.* (For full group information, see MENTAL DISORDERS.)

National Association for the Education of Young Children (NAEYC), 800–424–2460. Publishes book *Caring: Supporting Children's Growth,* on dealing with problems such as divorce, abuse, and death. (For full group information, see PRESCHOOL.)

National Institute of Child Health and Human Development (NICHD), 301–496–5133. (For full group information, see PREGNANCY.)

National Hospice Organization (NHO), 800–658–8898. Publishes brochures: *When Someone You Love Dies, About Dying, About Grief, About Widowhood, About Funeral Planning, About Stress, About Depression,* and *About Anger.* (For full group information, see HOSPICE.)

Good Grief Program
Judge Baker Children's Center
295 Longwood Avenue
Boston, MA 02115
617–232–8390
Organization to provide crisis intervention in schools, hospices, and community groups to aid children when a friend becomes terminally ill or dies; provides training; publishes various materials.

ON CHOICES IN DYING

Choice in Dying
200 Varick Street
New York, NY 10014
212–366–5540; 800–989-WILL [989–9455]
Fax: 212–366–5337
Karen Orloff Kaplan, Executive Director
Organization concerned with the rights of the dying; formed by the joinder of Concern for the Dying and Society for the Right to Die; provides information and counseling on living wills (which it pioneered) and other advance directives, and on life-sustaining technology, pain management, and other issues surrounding critical care dying; helps shape public policy; publishes "Question-and-Answer" booklets: *You and Your Choices, Advance Directives, Advance Directives and End-of-Life Decisions, Dying at Home,* and *Artificial Nutrition/Hydration*; videos *Choices* (with accompanying *Values History* booklet), *Life Support Decisions, An Act of Self-Determination, A Time to Choose, In Sickness or in Health,* and *Dax's Case*; state-specific living will forms; and materials for legal and health professionals.

National Right to Life Committee (NRLC), 202–626–8800. Publishes *Withholding Food and Fluid* and *Active Euthanasia and Assisted Suicide.* (For full group information, see ABORTION.)

Better Health and Medical Forum (America Online: Health, Medicine) Provides discussion areas and libraries covering patients' rights. (For full information, see health care.)

OTHER RESOURCES

FOR PARENTS

Grief as a Family Process. Ester R. Shapiro. Guilford, 1994.
Death Is Hard to Live With: Teenagers and How They Cope with Death. Janet Bode. Delacorte, 1993.

Mothers in Mourning. Nicole Loraux. Routledge, 1992.
Not Just Another Day: Families, Grief, and Special Days. Missy Lowery. Centering Corp., 1992.

General works

How We Die: Reflections on Life's Final Chapter. Sherwin B. Nuland. Knopf, 1994.
Questions and Answers on Death and Dying. Elisabeth Kübler-Ross. Macmillan, 1993. By the author of *On Death and Dying.*
Looking at Death. Barbara Norfleet. Godine, 1993.
When Someone Dies. Sharon Greenlee. Peachtree, 1992.
Understanding Death and Grief. David M. Lindsey. Personal Growth, 1991.
Dying. John Hinton. Viking Penguin, 1991.
When Your Spouse Dies: A Concise and Practical Source of Help and Advice. Cathleen L. Curry. Ave Maria Press, 1990. For surviving adults and children.

On helping children deal with death

After Goodbye: How to Begin Again after the Death of Someone You Love. Ted Menten. Running Press, 1994.
When I Die, Will I Get Better? Joeri Breebaart and Piet Breebaart. P. Bedrick, 1993.
Mommy, What Does Dying Mean? Kim Tott-Rizzuti. Dorrance, 1992.
Living with Death—Primary. Mary J. Cera. *Living with Death—Middle School.* Judith Bisnignano. Good Apple, 1991.
Talking About Death: A Dialogue Between Parent and Child, rev. ed. Earl A. Grollman. Beacon, 1990.

On pregnancy or infant loss

Life Line: A Journal for Parents Grieving a Miscarriage, Stillbirth or Early Infant Death. Joanie Reid. Pineapple, 1994.
Gone Too Soon: The Life and Loss of Infants and Unborn Children. Sherri D. Wittwer. Covenant Communications, 1994.
Coping with Infant or Fetal Loss: The Couple's Healing Process. Kathleen R. Gilbert and Laura S. Smart. Brunner-Mazel, 1992.
A Silent Sorrow. Ingrid Kohn and others. Bantam, 1992.
Newborn Death, rev. ed. Joy Johnson and Marvin Johnson. Centering Corp., 1992.
Waiting: A Diary of Loss and Hope in Pregnancy. Ellen J. Reich. Haworth Press, 1991.
Sudden Infant Death: Enduring the Loss. John DeFrain and others. Free Press, 1991.
Hidden Loss: Miscarriage and Ectopic Pregnancy. Valerie Hey. Quartet, 1990.

On loss of a child

A Child Dies—A Portrait of Family Grief. Joan Hagan Arnold and Penelope Bushman Gemma. Charles Press, 1994.
The Lessons of Love: Rediscovering Our Passion for Life When It All Seems Too Hard To Take. Melody Beattie. HarperCollins, 1994. On recovering from the death of a son.
Lori... Where Are You?: A Mother's Experience of Grief and Loss. Elaine Visitacion. E. Visitacion, 1993.
Goodbye My Child. Sara Rich Wheeler and Margaret Pike. Centering Corporation, 1992.
How to Survive the Loss of a Child: Filling the Emptiness and Rebuilding Your Life. Catherine Sanders. Prima, 1992.
Gone but Not Lost: Grieving the Death of a Child. David W. Wiersbe. Baker, 1992.
Children Die, Too, rev. ed. Joy Johnson and Marvin Johnson. Centering Corp., 1992.

On death by violence

Just Us: Homicidal Bereavement. Wanda Henry-Jenkins. Centering Corp., 1993.
No Time for Goodbyes, 4th ed. Janice H. Lord. Pathfinder, 1991.
Who Lives Happily Ever After?: For Families Whose Child Has Died Violently. Sharon Turnbull. Centering Corp., 1990.

On death from AIDS

Recovering from the Loss of a Loved One to AIDS. Katherine F. Donnelly. St. Martin's, 1994.
After You Say Goodbye: When Someone You Love Dies of AIDS. Paul K. Froman. Chronicle, 1992.

On a pet's death

Forever Friends: Resolving Grief after the Loss of a Beloved Animal. Joan Coleman. J. C. Tara, 1993.
The Loss of a Pet. Wallace Sife. Howell, 1993.

For children

The Three Birds: A Story for Children about the Loss of a Loved One, 3 vols. Marinus Van Den Berg. Gareth Stevens, 1994.
I Heard Your Mommy Died. Mark Scrivani. Centering Corp., 1994.
I Wish I Could Hold Your Hand: A Child's Guide to Grief and Loss. Pat Palmer. Impact, 1994.
Growing up When Someone You Love Has Died. Rona D. Schenkerman. Bureau for At-Risk Youth, 1993.
Something Happened in My House: A Journey of Children's Grief. Karen Carpenter and Susie Howard. Byte Size, 1993.
Am I Still a Sister?, 3rd ed. Alicia M. Sims. Big A, 1993.
A Bunch of Balloons: A Book—Workbook for Grieving Children. Dorothy Ferguson. Centering Corp., 1992.
The Secret Places: The Story of a Child's Adventure with Grief. James A. Campbell. Centering Corp., 1992.
My Daddy Died and It's All God's Fault. Sue Holden. Word, 1991.
Death. Gail Stewart. Crestwood, 1990.

FOR PRETEENS AND TEENS

How Teenagers Cope with Grief: Something I've Never Felt Before. Doris Zagdanski. Seven Hills, 1994.
Straight Talk About Death for Teenagers: How to Cope with Losing Someone You Love. Earl A. Grollman. Beacon, 1993.
Death Is Hard to Live With: Teenagers and How They Cope with Death. Janet Bode, ed. Delacorte, 1993.
Death and Beyond: Answers to Teens' Questions about Death, Reincarnation, Ghosts, and the Afterlife. Jim Watkins. Tyndale, 1993.
Everything You Need to Know about Grieving. Rosen, 1993.
Teenagers Face to Face with Bereavement. Karen Gravelle and Charles Haskins. Messner, 1989.
Remember the Secret. Elizabeth Kübler-Ross. Celestial Arts, 1988. Useful for children facing life-threatening illness or death of a loved one.
How It Feels When a Parent Dies. Jill Krementz. Knopf, 1981.
Too Old to Cry... Too Young to Die. Edith Pendleton, ed. Nelson, 1980. By and for terminally ill teenagers.

ON GRIEF, MOURNING, AND RECOVERY

Your First Year of Grief. Meg Woodson. Zondervan, 1994.
I'm Grieving As Fast As I Can: How Young Widows and Widowers Can Cope and Heal. Linda Feinberg. New Horizon, 1994.
Gentle Closings: How to Say Goodbye to Someone You Love. Ted Menten. Running Press, 1992.
Understanding and Coping with Bereavement. Warner F. Bowers. Carlton, 1992.
Grief Is a Process. Margie Kennedy-Reeves. Harbor House West, 1992.
Afterloss: A Recovery Companion for Those Who Are Grieving. Barbara H. LesStrang. Nelson, 1992.

BACKGROUND WORKS

Alone among the Living. Richard G. Hoard. University of Georgia Press, 1994. On the death of a father during the author's teens.
Motherless Daughters: The Legacy of Loss. Hope Edelman. Addison-Wesley, 1994.
Exploring Life's Last Frontier: The World of Death, Dying and Letting Go. Heather A. Harder. Channel One, 1993.
The Dying and the Bereaved Teenager. John D. Morgan, ed. Charles, 1990.

(See also ADVANCE DIRECTIVE [for living wills and health care proxies]; MISCARRIAGE; SUICIDE; SUDDEN INFANT DEATH SYNDROME; STILLBIRTH; HOSPITALS; HOSPICE.)

decoding, the process of extracting meaning from symbols, such as written, spoken, or signed words or numbers. An important intellectual skill, a PREREQUISITE to much learning, decoding poses significant problems for many people with brain dysfunction. A child with LEARNING DISABILITIES—especially DYSLEXIA—may see printed words upside down, backwards, or distorted in a variety of ways and may have trouble decoding the symbols. Similarly, a child with DYSCALCULIA may have trouble decoding and working with mathematical symbols. Such children may also have trouble with the reverse process, ENCODING.

decree, in law, a court order, as in cases of rulings on questions such as CHILD SUPPORT or CUSTODY. A provisional decree is often termed *interlocutory*, as in cases when a DIVORCE is granted but only becomes final after a specified waiting period.

de facto, in the law, a phrase applied to situations that exist, regardless of intention, such as SEGREGATION in a neighborhood or school; Latin for "in fact."

de jure, in the law, a phrase applied to practices that are open, deliberate, formal, and written into statutes; Latin for "by law." Before the 1950s, for example, much SEGREGATION was *de jure* (by law). When the civil rights movement began, many discriminatory laws were swept from the books, and the segregation that remains today is often *de facto* (in fact).

deductive learning, a LEARNING STYLE in which a teacher or parent presents a general rule or concept and the child learns to apply it to specific situations; also called *expository learning.*

default judgment, a decision made by the court when someone fails to respond to a charge, such as nonpayment of CHILD SUPPORT, or to appeal a case.

defense mechanism, in psychology, a generally involuntary pattern of thoughts, behavior, and feelings that serve to protect the self from perceived threats, including ANXIETY and guilt. Among the common defense mechanisms found among children are ACTING OUT, AUTISTIC FANTASY, DISPLACEMENT, IDEALIZATION, PASSIVE AGGRESSION, and REACTION FORMATION.

deficiency diseases, disorders resulting from lack of some essential nutrients in the diet, such as PROTEINS, CARBOHYDRATES, MINERALS, or VITAMINS; a vitamin deficiency condition is also sometimes called *avitaminosis.*

degree, a title conferred on a COLLEGE student who has successfully completed a course of undergraduate or graduate study; also an alternative term for DIPLOMA. The main kinds of degrees are ASSOCIATE DEGREE, BACHELOR'S DEGREE, MASTER'S DEGREE, or DOCTOR'S DEGREE.

degree requirements, the number and type of courses in various areas of study that a student must complete to be eligible for a DIPLOMA or DEGREE from a school. Degree requirements vary, depending on the school, state, and type of CURRICULUM the student is following.

Degrees of Reading Power, a TEST that measures a student's ability to comprehend READING matter of a determined level of difficulty.

dehydration, a condition involving a dangerously low water level in the body's tissues, generally also involving loss of key substances called ELECTROLYTES that are normally dissolved in the body fluids. When water is available and the person is conscious, powerful sensations of thirst generally prevent dehydration. But infants, small children, and adults who are severely ill may be vulnerable to serious, even life-threatening damage from dehydration. Because they have a larger skin area in proportion to their size than adults do, infants lose proportionately more water by evaporation; their kidneys also do not function as well as an adult's. As a result, infants are vulnerable to water imbalance. Normal BREASTFEEDING and BOTTLEFEEDING should provide adequate water, though the baby may require some additional water in very hot weather.

But DIARRHEA, VOMITING, and FEVER can cause sudden dehydration, which can quickly put a baby's life at risk, so medical help should be sought immediately. Women who breastfeed should also be sure that they baby is getting enough food; in two recent cases, babies died of dehydration when the breast milk dried up without the mother realizing it. If parents have any question about whether their baby is getting enough fluids, they should ask their doctor.

In addition to thirst, symptoms of dehydration include dry lips and tongue, dizziness and confusion, rapid heart beat and breathing, and eventual COMA. Parents should be alert to possible dehydration and call a doctor immediately if the child has had no wet diapers for three hours or more, is hard to waken or unusually fussy, has sunken eyes, has a high fever, or will not drink fluids.

Treatment involves replacing not only water but also vital electrolytes, using *rehydration* mixtures, also called oral electrolyte solutions, available in drugstores) to resupply the fluid and balance necesary for recovery. This is called *oral rehydration therapy* (ORT); in hospitals, it is part of PARENTERAL NUTRITION. Under a doctor's guidance, parents should feed the baby the rehydration solution, continuing until the stool is back to normal. If the baby vomits or spits up the solution, they should try giving smaller amounts more often, calling the doctor again if vomiting continues. Between electrolyte feedings, they should also continue BREASTFEEDING, BOTTLEFEEDING, or giving solid food, as appropriate. They should, however, avoid soft drinks, fruit juices, or sports drinks, which can worsen the diarrhea.

delinquent, a term applied to behavior or acts that lead to the conviction of a MINOR in JUVENILE COURT—often behavior that would, if performed by an adult, be labeled criminal. The term *delinquent* is also often used to refer to JUVENILES who have violated social standards or are considered UNSOCIALIZED. More generally, the term refers to a person's failure to perform required duties or obligations, so a parent who fails to make CHILD SUPPORT payments may be called delinquent.

delirium, a confused, turbulent mental state, often including HALLUCINATIONS, DELUSIONS, LABILITY (emotional swings), and ANXIETY, generally an ACUTE reaction in cases of ORGANIC MENTAL DISORDER, as may be caused by infection, METABOLIC DISORDERS, or TRAUMATIC BRAIN INJURY. Delirium is usually reversible once the underlying condition is treated. In cases of ALCOHOL ABUSE, the state caused by withdrawal is often called *delirium tremens* (DTs).

delivery, in PREGNANCY, the bringing forth of a baby from the mother's UTERUS and also the expulsion of the PLACENTA (afterbirth), which are the second and third stages of LABOR. Delivery is a general term for the variety of ways in which a child appears in or is brought out into the world, including normal vaginal birth, assisted vaginal birth such as FORCEPS DELIVERY and VACUUM EXTRACTION, extraction of a child through an incision in the abdomen (CESAREAN SECTION), or the various methods of natural or prepared CHILDBIRTH. It also refers to the birth of a child from an abnormal FETAL PRESENTATION, such as a *breech delivery*. (See PREGNANCY; LABOR; CHILDBIRTH.)

delivery room, in traditional HOSPITAL births, the room where a woman gives birth after she is transferred from a LABOR ROOM. In look and furnishings, a delivery room is much like an operating room. It has the advantage of containing medical equipment that is readily at hand should it be needed if complications develop during CHILDBIRTH. But many people in recent decades have found the delivery room cold and forbidding, so some women (except for those with HIGH-RISK PREGNANCIES) have preferred to give birth in a more homelike setting, such as a MATERNITY CENTER or a hospital-attached BIRTHING ROOM, or to have a HOME BIRTH.

Hospitals have different rules about who will or will not be allowed in the delivery room, and prospective parents should inquire about these rules in making choices about where their baby will be delivered. These days, the BIRTH PARTNER generally will be allowed to remain with the woman during delivery. But some hospitals require that the birth partner have taken childbirth preparation classes, and the hospital staff may ask the partner to leave in case of emergencies or complications, especially a CESAREAN SECTION. Some hospitals have gone to an all-in-one *labor/delivery/recovery room* (LDR), to avoid the often-unsettling shift from labor room to delivery room. Others have gone even further, developing the *labor/delivery/recovery/postpartum room* (LDRP), where a mother stays from her arrival at the hospital, through labor and delivery, and until discharge.

delusion, a false belief, firmly held though contradicted by physical reality or common sense, as when a child believes a control box has been implanted in his head, or a seventy-pound anorexic girl insists she is obese. (See MENTAL DISORDERS.)

dementia, a long-term or irreversible deterioration of intellectual functioning affecting memory, personality, VISUAL SKILLS, SPATIAL RELATIONS, and general thinking ability. Dementia may result from some kinds of ORGANIC MENTAL DISORDERS, as from illness or injury, or may accompany some other kinds of mental disturbances, such as SCHIZOPHRENIA. (See MENTAL DISORDERS.)

dental age, a summary of the relationship between a child's growth and the statistical average for a child of the same size and sex. If a child of six has a maturity of TEETH and jaw formation normally seen in a seven-year-old, that child's dental age is seven. (See AGE.)

dentist, the dental equivalent of the family physician, the health professional who has primary care of the teeth and gums. Modern dentists focus on prevention not just treatment, and are oriented toward early detection and handling of dental problems before much damage has been done. Among the dental specialists to whom a patient might be referred are the ORTHODONTIST, ENDODONTIST, PERIODONTIST, and ORAL SURGEON. (See TEETH AND DENTAL PROBLEMS.)

dependency hearing, a hearing at which the court assesses whether or not the state should take temporary CUSTODY of a child, as in extreme cases of CHILD ABUSE AND NEGLECT.

Depo-Provera, an injectable form of BIRTH CONTROL, a STEROID (*depo-medroxy progesterone acetate*) that mimics the effects of progestin, the synthetic form of PROGESTERONE used in BIRTH CONTROL PILLS and NORPLANT. The drug is contained in tiny crystals which, after they are injected in a water-based solution, release it into the woman's body. Its main effect is to suppress OVULATION, the release of a woman's egg (OVUM), so preventing PREGNANCY.

The main advantages of Depo-Provera are that it is injected only four times a year, eliminating BIRTH CONTROL concerns for the rest of the year; it is as effective as birth control pills in preventing PREGNANCY, with nearly 99 percent effectiveness; and it can be used privately, without a sexual partner's knowledge. When a woman is on Depo-Provera, her MENSTRUAL CYCLES are likely to stop, which some women regard as an advantage.

Though used in other countries earlier, Depo-Provera was not approved for use in the United States until 1993, although panels of experts had recommended approval twice in the 1970s. The concern has been that some international studies have indicated that women using Depo-Provera have an increased risk of BREAST CANCER. However, a World Health Organization (WHO) international study reported that among *all* women, no additional breast cancer risk was found. They study also concluded that although risk of breast cancer in women under thirty-five was slightly increased, risk of CANCER of the endometrium (the lining of the UTERUS) was lessened, leading overall to a decreased risk of cancer. (See BIRTH CONTROL.)

depression, a condition characterized by feelings of hopelessness, worthlessness, dejection, apathy, pessimism, fatigue, and general lack of well-being. People of all ages can experience minor and temporary depression in particular circumstances, often in stressful events and situations such as bereavement (see DEATH AND DYING), SEPARATION, DIVORCE, and CHRONIC illness. Such cases of depression are generally temporary, and people are able to recover on their own, with the support of friends and family.

But sometimes the depression is so deep or longlasting as to qualify as a MENTAL DISORDER. In general, the National Institute of Mental Health (NIMH) indicates that a clinical case of depression may exist if at least four of the symptoms below are apparent nearly every day for at least two weeks:

- Change in appetite or weight.
- Changes in sleeping patterns, such as inability to sleep through the night or unusually long sleep.
- Speaking or moving with unusual speed or slowness (motor agitation or retardation).
- Loss of interest or pleasure in usual activities.
- Decrease in sexual drive.
- Fatigue and loss of energy.
- Depressed or irritable mood.
- Feelings of worthlessness, self-reproach, or guilt.
- Diminished ability to think or concentrate, slowed thinking, or indecisiveness.
- Thoughts of death, suicide, wishing to be dead, or suicide attempt.

The NIMH notes that most people who attempt SUICIDE are depressed, though many people who are depressed never attempt or even consider suicide. In some people, depression alternates with a hyperactive, manic state, the resulting condition being called *manic-depression* or a *bipolar disorder*. Research suggests that this condition may be linked to a genetic defect (see GENETIC DISORDER).

The causes of depression are still obscure. Recent studies do make some things clear—most importantly, that depression is not triggered solely by emotional or social factors in the person's life. Indeed, researchers are finding more and more evidence that major depression is associated with biochemical changes leading to abnormal brain functioning, which can actually be seen on certain kinds of brain scans. These changes can be caused by genetic or environmental factors, illnesses such as stroke, side effects of medications (such as those used to control high blood pressure), or genetic, environmental, or other as-yet-unknown factors. Often if a person experiences one episode of depression, more will follow. Indeed, some doctors think of clinical depression as a chronic disease, with periodic episodes of acute symptoms.

Among women, one major trigger for depression is CHILDBIRTH (see POSTPARTUM DEPRESSION). Other kinds of depression may appear at any time. Though long thought a condition primarily affecting adults, depression is now understood to be common among young people as well, especially among adolescent girls, and often linked with other disorders. Among adult women, especially those living alone, depression is often associated with ALCOHOL ABUSE or DRUG ABUSE.

Various medications have been developed that can ease the symptoms of depression by altering brain chemistry, though how they work is not clear. Several major kinds of antidepressants exist; which one a doctor prescribes depends on a particular patient's medical condition, what other medications the person is taking, and the likelihood of side effects. The drugs work slowly and can take weeks—perhaps three to six weeks among younger adults, but six to twelve weeks in older people—to build up in the body sufficiently to reduce symptoms. Many people fail to take the full prescribed dose of the medications needed to be effective. Medication levels may be slowly reduced after symptoms have subsided, though at least one recent study has shown that patients kept on the steady level of medication had fewer recurrent bouts of depression.

When antidepressant medications fail to work, one controversial approach is electroconvulsive therapy (ECT), in which electrical currents are sent through the brain while the patient is anesthetized, the aim being to produce a brain SEIZURE, to "shock" the brain back into proper functioning. Once widely used and abused, ECT fell into disfavor in the mid-twentieth century, though it is still sometimes employed. The Food and Drug Administration and many others have expressed concern about side effects such as confusion, memory lapses, headaches, muscle soreness, nausea, and more serious effects such as heart disturbances and possible loss of memory, short- or long-term. Another concern is that psychiatrists need no special license or certification to use ECT.

Depression is also treated with therapy, counseling, and sometimes temporary hospitalization. Whether they are recovering from major or minor depression, many people are substantially aided by mutual-support groups (see the list of organizations that follows).

FOR HELP AND FURTHER INFORMATION

National Institute of Mental Health (NIMH), 800–421–4211. Publishes *Plain Talk About Depression, What to Do When a Friend Is Depressed: Guide for Students, Helpful Facts About Depressive Disorders, Let's Talk About Depression, Bipolar Disorder, Depressive Illness: Treatments Bring New Hope, Depression: What You Need to Know, Depression: Effective Treatments Are Available, Helping the Depressed Person Get Treatment, Depression: Patients Get Younger as Rx Options Increase*, and materials on campaigns against depression.

Depression and Related Affective Disorders Association (DRADA)
Meyer 3–181, 600 North Wolfe Street
Baltimore, MD 21287–7381
410–955–4647; 202–955–5800
Fax: 410–614–3241
E-mail: drada@welchlink.jhu.edu
Organization concerned with affective disorders such as depression and manic depression; aids self-help groups; provides information and referrals; publishes numerous materials, including newsletter *Smooth Sailing*; pamphlets *Adolescent Depression: A Counselor's Guide, How to Evaluate Your Psychiatrist or Other Therapist If You Have (Or Possibly Have) a Depressive Disorder, "I Wish I Was Never Born. I Really Hate Myself,"* and *"I Am the Greatest. I Am Depressed"*; and videos *Depressive Illness: What You Need to Know, Carrie's Story* (about a teen with depression), *A Patient's Perspective—Dick Cavett*, and *A Patient's Perspective—Mike Wallace.*

National Mental Health Association (NMHA), 800–969–6642. Publishes *Answers to Your Questions About Clinical Depression* and *Depression: What You Should Know About It.* (For full group information, see MENTAL DISORDERS.)

National Alliance for the Mentally Ill (NAMI), 800–950–6264. Publishes brochures *Depressive Disorders in Children and Adolescents, Understanding Depression: What You Need to Know About This Medical Illness, Understanding Manic Depression: What You Need to Know About This Medical Illness,* and books *Helping Your Depressed Child, The Depression Workbook, Manic Depressive Illness,* and *You Mean I Don't Have to Feel This Way?*, about a daughter's successful treatment; online forum and libraries cover depression and medications. (For full group information, see MENTAL DISORDERS.)

American Academy of Child and Adolescent Psychiatry (AACAP), 202–966–7300. Publishes information sheet *The Depressed Child.* (For full group information, see MENTAL DISORDERS.)

American Academy of Pediatrics (AAP), 800–433–9016. Publishes brochure *Surviving: Coping with Adolescent Depression and Suicide.* (For full group information, see HEALTH CARE.)

Agency for Health Care Policy and Research Clearinghouse, 800–358–9295. Publishes *Depression Is a Treatable Illness* and InstantFAX materials on depression. (For full group information, see HEALTH INSURANCE.)

National Mental Health Consumer Self-Help Clearinghouse, 800–553–4539. Publishes reprint packet on depressive disorders and manic depression. (For full group information, see MENTAL DISORDERS.)

National Chronic Pain Outreach Association, Inc. (NCPOA), 301–652–4948. Publishes *Depression and*

Chronic Pain and *Up from Depression: My Story.* (For full group information, see PAIN AND PAIN TREATMENT.)

American College of Obstetricians and Gynecologists (ACOG), 202–638–5577. Publishes *Depression.* (For full group information, see PREGNANCY.)

Hazelden Foundation (HF), 800–262–5010. Publishes *Dealing with Depression in 12 Step Recovery.* (For full group information, see HELP AGAINST SUBSTANCE ABUSE on page 703.)

Council for Exceptional Children (CEC), 800–328–0272. Publishes Depression and Suicide: Special Education Students At Risk. (For full group information, HELP ON LEARNING AND EDUCATION on page 659.)

OTHER RESOURCES

For parents

Helping Your Depressed Teenager: A Guide for Parents and Caregivers. Gerald D. Oster and Sarah S. Montgomery. Wiley, 1995.

A Parent's Guide to Depression in Children and Adolescents. Patricia G. Shapiro. Dell, 1994.

Helping Your Depressed Child: A Reassuring Guide to the Causes and Treatments of Childhood and Adolescent Depression. Lawrence Kerns and Adrienne Lieberman. Prima, 1993.

The No-Nonsense Parents' Guide: What You Can Do about Teens and Alcohol, Drugs, Sex, Eating Disorders and Depression. Sheila Fuller and others. Parents Pipeline, 1992.

Depression: What Families Should Know. Ballantine, 1991.

I Want to Kill Myself: Helping Your Child Cope with Depression and Suicidal Thoughts. T.K. Shamoo. Lexington, 1990.

General works

Overcoming Depression rev. ed. Demitri F. Papolos and Janice Papolos. HarperCollins, 1994.

Depression: The Mood Disease, rev. ed. Francis Mark Mondimore. Johns Hopkins, 1993.

Straight Talk About Anxiety and Depression. M. Maloney and R. Kranz. Dell, 1993.

Winter Blues: Seasonal Affective Disorder: What It Is and How to Overcome It. N.E. Rosenthal. Guilford, 1993.

The Depression Workbook: A Guide for Living with Depression. M.E. Copeland. New Harbinger, 1992.

Awakening from Depression: A Mind-Body Approach to Emotional Recovery. Jerome Marmorstein and Nanette Marmorstein. Woodbridge, 1992.

Feel Well Again: Three Hundred Fifty Questions and Answers about Depression and Anxiety. Mercedes Leidlich. Maupin House, 1991.

You Mean I Don't Have to Feel This Way?: New Help for Depression, Anxiety, and Addiction. Colette Dowling. Bantam, 1991.

Encyclopedia of Depression. Roberta Roesch. Facts on File, 1990.

For preteens or teens

Straight Talk about Anxiety and Depression. Michael Maloney and Rachel Kranz. Facts on File, 1991.

Dont Be S. A. D.: A Teenage Guide to Handling Stress, Anxiety and Depression. Susan Newman. Messner/Simon & Schuster, 1991.

Teenage Depression. Herma Silverstein. Watts, 1990.

Personal experiences

Undercurrents: A Therapist's Reckoning with Her Own Depression. Martha Manning, HarperCollins, 1995.

What of the Night?: A Journey Through Depression and Anxiety. Jeffrey J. Knowles. Herald Press, 1993.

I Don't Know Who You Are Anymore: A Family's Struggle with Depression. Kellie Branson and Dale A. Babcock. Legendary, 1992.

(See also MENTAL DISORDERS; POSTPARTUM DEPRESSION.)

dermatologist, a physician specializing in treatment of SKIN AND SKIN DISORDERS.

DES (diethylstilbestrol), a synthetic form of ESTROGEN, the female HORMONE. Between 1941 and 1971, DES was given to many pregnant women, especially those with DIABETES or a history of MISCARRIAGE, PREMATURE delivery, or slight bleeding during PREGNANCY. Only later was the drug found to have significant adverse effects on women and their children. However, many women did not remember taking the drug, so they and their children were often unaware of the possible long-term side effects.

DES mothers have increased risk of breast CANCER. DES daughters are more likely have miscarriages, ECTOPIC PREGNANCY, or premature delivery. They may also have some structural changes in their bodies, especially in the VAGINA and CERVIX, that can make conception more difficult (see INFERTILITY) and are at increased risk of having a rare cancer of the vagina or cervix (*clear-cell adenocarcinoma*). DES sons are more likely to have underdeveloped or undescended TESTES, low SPERM counts, and other genital problems.

Many DES sons and daughters have had normal, healthy children, with no problems for the mothers during pregnancy. But women once exposed to DES during gestation are advised to have regular medical checkups to screen for possible changes in the body. Many doctors also advise that DES daughters should avoid BIRTH CONTROL PILLS containing estrogen, which might increase cancer risk.

Prospective parents who are unsure if they were exposed to DES should check with their mothers regarding medications (including some prescription vitamins) and problems during pregnancy. They may also want to check medical records from their mother's doctor, pharmacy, or hospital; DES Action (see the list of organizations that follows) gives advice on how to do this. A third generation of children—DES grandchildren—are now appearing, but it is still too early to know if they are also affected.

Despite knowledge of its side effects, in some places DES was given as a "morning after" pill on college campuses as late as 1980. Women who remember being given such medications should check their medical records and consult their current doctors for advice.

FOR HELP AND FURTHER INFORMATION

DES Action
1615 Broadway, Suite 510
Oakland, CA 94612
510–465–4011; 800-DES–9288 [337–9288]
Fax: 510–465–4815
E-mail: desact@well.sf.ca.us
Organization concerned with the effects of DES (diethylstilbestrol); gathers and disseminates information; offers support; publishes various materials, including quarterly *Voice, DES Exposure: Questions and Answers for Mothers, Daughters and Sons, Preventing Preterm Birth: A Parent's Guide, Every Woman's Guide to Tests During Pregnancy,* and research findings.

RESOLVE, Inc., HelpLine: 617–623–0744. Publishes facts sheet *DES: Its Impact on Infertility.* (For full group information, see infertility.)

(See also CANCER; BIRTH DEFECTS; GENETIC COUNSELING; INFERTILITY; PREMATURE.)

desegregation, in EDUCATION, the transfer of students from one school to another to achieve racial balance or to end other kinds of discrimination (such as separation of children with DISABILITIES from other children), often mandated by the court in cases of SEGREGATION, whether DE JURE (deliberate and written into law) or DE FACTO (in fact, often enforced by informal social pressures). One major court-mandated approach to de facto segregation has been BUSING, but more recently some school districts have tried various voluntary methods for achieving desegregation, through SCHOOLS OF CHOICE and MAGNET SCHOOLS.

OTHER RESOURCES

The Carrot or the Stick for School Desegregation Policy: Magnet Schools or Forced Busing Christine H. Rossell. Temple University Press, 1992.

School Desegregation, Enough Is Enough. William R. Ross. Danmo, 1992.

(See EDUCATION; SCHOOL OF CHOICE.)

detention, in government social services, protective or emergency CUSTODY; in cases of CHILD ABUSE OR NEGLECT, social workers generally file a *detention request,* calling for a *detention hearing* to be held, usually within twenty-four hours of filing, to see whether the child should be kept apart from the family until a full court hearing takes place. In education, detention refers to the practice of holding a child temporarily after school or during what would normally be recess time, often as punishment for infractions of school rules.

developmental age (DA), in general, an alternate term for EDUCATIONAL AGE, but more specifically a child's score on the GESELL PRESCHOOL TEST; sometimes called *maturational age* (MA).

developmental delay (maturation lag), a significantly longer-than-normal length of time before a child learns certain skills or begins to be able to do certain key kinds of activities, called DEVELOPMENTAL MILESTONES. Federal laws require states to have EARLY INTERVENTION programs for children from birth to age two who show developmental delays in various areas. States have the option of whether to provide programs for children who are considered AT-RISK for developmental delay because of conditions at or during CHILDBIRTH or in infancy, such as LOW BIRTH WEIGHT, inadequate NUTRITION or HEALTH CARE, and exposure to alcohol or drugs in the UTERUS. (See EARLY INTERVENTION; INDIVIDUALS WITH DISABILITIES EDUCATION ACT.)

developmental disorders, a general term used in some quite different ways, referring variously to:

- The characteristic behaviors a child shows at each stage of emotional development, such as crying, stranger anxiety, and separation anxiety, which are not in fact disorders at all.
- Generally slow development (see DEVELOPMENTAL DELAY) and retention of infantile behavior.
- Conditions that are characterized by slower-than-normal development or whose characteristics cause development to be slowed because of increased difficulty, as in MENTAL RETARDATION, AUTISM, EPILEPSY, and some speech and language disorders (see COMMUNICATIONS SKILLS AND DISORDERS).
- Conditions appearing in childhood characterized by delay in development of specific skills or functions, but not related to mental problems or inadequate teaching, including communication disorders and various LEARNING DISABILITIES; sometimes called *specific developmental disorders.*
- Any medical condition that becomes apparent in youth or adolescence; also called a *developmental disability* (DD).

Because the term is used in so many different ways, parents will be wise to try to get more precise descriptions from educational, psychological, or medical professionals who are evaluating their children.

developmental milestones, key kinds of activities that are used as indicators of a child's development, notably activities in the areas of MOTOR SKILLS, COGNITIVE DEVELOPMENT, SELF-HELP SKILLS, SOCIAL SKILLS, and COM-

MUNICATIONS SKILLS. The CHART OF NORMAL DEVELOPMENT on page 637 indicates when between birth and age six children first *on the average* begin to do certain things. Note (as the materials accompanying the chart explain) that children may vary widely from the average as to when they reach certain milestones and still be quite normal. But if a child is seriously delayed (called *developmental delay*) in one or more skills areas, parents may want to consult the family doctor to see if there is a problem, especially one that might benefit from early diagnosis and treatment (see EARLY INTERVENTION).

developmental schedules, tables of behavior considered appropriate to various age levels for children being tested with the GESELL PRESCHOOL TEST or the Gesell School Readiness Test—Complete Battery.

developmental screening test, a type of TEST given to help identify children who may have LEARNING DISABILITIES or other DISABILITIES that could affect learning. Such tests are used to survey a child's abilities and skills in a wide range of areas, including LANGUAGE SKILLS, reasoning, gross and fine MOTOR SKILLS, SOCIAL SKILLS, and general personal development, though the testing itself may last no longer than fifteen to twenty minutes. Among the most common developmental screening tests are the GESELL PRESCHOOL TEST, the ABC INVENTORY, BRIGANCE® DIAGNOSTIC INVENTORY OF EARLY DEVELOPMENT, EARLY SCREENING INVENTORY, JORDAN LEFT-RIGHT REVERSAL TEST, MEETING STREET SCHOOL SCREENING TEST, and SPECIFIC LANGUAGE DISABILITY TESTS. Screening sometimes includes a DRAW-A-PERSON-type test for indications as to the child's emotional development. Parents may be asked to fill out a questionnaire on the child's medical and developmental background.

For the results to be most reliable, such tests should be individually administered to the child by a psychologist, teacher, or assistant; it is important that the person be sensitive to children, that children be prepared for testing (see books listed in the bibliography at the end of this entry), and that the tests chosen be appropriate for the child's cultural and linguistic background. If not, or if parents disagree with the results of the test—for example, it they feel it wrongly identifies problems or failed to identify problems—they may want to try to arrange for retesting, since key decisions will made on the basis of test results. Parents should understand that the testing of young children is a very uncertain affair, and that many tests used for developmental screening were not originally designed for that purpose and lack RELIABILITY (see TESTS). Certainly, if a child was not well on the day of the testing, or if the test was disrupted or disturbed in any way, retesting may well be indicated. If results are on a borderline, retesting after eight to ten weeks of further development is often appropriate.

Developmental screening tests are the first step in an evaluation process mandated by the EDUCATION FOR ALL HANDICAPPED CHILDREN ACT and its successor, the INDIVIDUALS WITH DISABILITIES EDUCATION ACT (IDEA). States are required, through school systems and social services, to have in place programs (such as CHILDFIND) to identify children AT RISK for having such problems and arrange for developmental screening tests to be given. If the tests indicate that children may have a problem, they are then referred for DIAGNOSTIC ASSESSMENT TESTS to provide more detailed information on the nature of the problem. Children with obvious disabilities are generally referred directly for diagnosis.

Developmental Test of Visual-Motor Integration (VMI or Beery-Buktenica Test), a test designed to identify people who have problems with VISUAL SKILLS, fine MOTOR SKILLS (especially use of hands), and EYE-HAND COORDINATION. The multiple-item, paper-and-pencil test offers increasingly difficult geometric figures for the child to copy and may be administered individually or to groups. A short form is used only for children aged three through eight, while a longer form is used for ages three through eighteen and for adults with DEVELOPMENTAL DELAY. Tests are scored according to a manual, which contains NORMS by age; the results are given in converted SCORES and PERCENTILES. (See TESTS.)

diabetes, a disorder in which a person's body is unable to use sugar as it should to provide for energy needs; its formal medical name is *diabetes mellitus* (DM), to distinguish it from the far rarer *diabetes insipidus* (see the description later in this entry). The disorder occurs when the pancreas produces too little or no *insulin,* the HORMONE that is needed to break down the sugar GLUCOSE, the body's main form of energy, into usable form. As a result, the level of sugar in the blood becomes abnormally high, causing a characteristic set of symptoms, including great thirst and hunger, very frequent urination, fatigue, and weight loss.

There are two main types of diabetes mellitus:

- *Insulin-dependent (type I),* in which the pancreas makes little or no insulin. This form appears quite suddenly, at any age, but usually before the age of thirty, especially in the teens, affecting about two in every thousand people under age twenty. To control this form of diabetes, the person must carefully monitor the amount of glucose in the blood, eat a planned diet, get plenty of exercise, and have an injection of insulin each day. This form is also called *juvenile-onset diabetes, insulin-dependent diabetes mellitus (IDDM)* or *ketosis-prone diabetes.*
- *Noninsulin-dependent (type II),* in which the pancreas makes some insulin; this is the common type of diabetes, affecting approximately 20 out of every 1,000 people. For some people with type II diabetes, a careful diet and regular exercise may be sufficient to control the disease. Others may need to take insulin or other medications as well. Type II diabetes can also appear at

any age, but it most commonly emerges after age forty. People with type II tend toward obesity and their bodies are thought to resist the effects of insulin. This form is also called n*oninsulin-dependent diabetes mellitus (NIDDM), adult-onset diabetes, maturity-onset diabetes,* or *ketosis-resistant diabetes.*

Both main forms of diabetes seem to have some hereditary component, but not everyone who inherits a predisposition toward the disorder actually gets the disease. In type I, the disease may result when, after a viral infection, the person's body mistakenly attacks and destroys insulin-producing parts of the pancreas (see AUTOIMMUNE DISORDER). In type II the triggering mechanism most often seems to be excessive weight.

If unrecognized or untreated, insulin-dependent diabetes can have serious effects. In the absence of glucose for energy, the body begins to break down its stores of fat, releasing acids (*ketones*) into the blood. The result is *diabetic ketoacidosis,* which can lead to diabetic COMA and death, if not reversed.

While no cure exists, diabetes is a CONTROLLABLE DISEASE. People with insulin-dependent diabetes carefully watch their diets and generally give themselves INJECTIONS one to four times a day with insulin of animal or synthetic (genetically engineered) origin. Alternatively, some people with hard-to-control diabetes use a device called an *insulin pump,* with a needle inserted under the skin, which pumps a continuous low level of insulin between meals and an extra dose (when the person presses the appropriate buttons) at mealtimes. The aim is to avoid extremes in the levels of glucose in the blood. Too much glucose (*hyperglycemia*) causes symptoms of diabetes to recur. Too little glucose—called *hypoglycemia* or *insulin shock*—can lead to weakness, dizziness, confusion, and sometimes unconsciousness and SEIZURES. To avoid these extremes, people with type I diabetes monitor their glucose levels carefully, generally using a type of HOME MEDICAL TEST. With a blood glucose monitoring home medical kit, for example, the person pricks a finger or earlobe to obtain a drop of blood. That is placed on a strip specially treated with a chemical that reacts with the glucose to produce a color that varies with the glucose concentration. The resulting color is compared with a color guide or read by an electronic monitor. Urine glucose tests are also available but are not as accurate.

When the disease is not well controlled, diabetes can have serious complications. These include RETINOPATHY (a type of EYE AND VISION PROBLEM involving damage to the retina resulting from pressure on the blood vessels), *neuropathy* (damage to peripheral nerve fibers), ulcers (raw sores) on the feet that can turn gangrenous, KIDNEY AND UROLOGICAL PROBLEMS, and periodontal problems (see TEETH). People with diabetes are also at some increased risk of later developing high BLOOD PRESSURE, CATARACTS, atherosclerosis (constriction of the arteries), and other circulatory disorders. Most people with diabetes can lead relatively normal lives, though there is a slightly reduced life expectancy. Women with diabetes can generally have a normal PREGNANCY.

During PREGNANCY, some women may develop a form of diabetes, called *gestational diabetes mellitus (GDM)* or *type III diabetes.* It is important to recognize the diabetes and bring it under control early to lessen the risk of damage to the child and complications in the mother. In most cases, this form of diabetes disappears after CHILDBIRTH, though in some cases it may signal future onset of diabetes or previously undiagnosed diabetes.

Infants whose mothers have diabetes are at increased risk of PREMATURE birth, BIRTH DEFECTS, excessively high birth weight, RESPIRATORY DISTRESS SYNDROME, and other conditions that give them a higher-than-usual INFANT MORTALITY rate, especially if blood glucose levels are high throughout the pregnancy. The mothers are also at higher risk of complications before, during, and after CHILDBIRTH. Because of this, screening for diabetes is a common part of PRENATAL CARE, especially for any woman who shows possible signs of diabetes, such as a FETUS unexpectedly large for its GESTATIONAL AGE; excess AMNIOTIC FLUID; sugar in urine; increased thirst or urination; frequent or persistent vaginal or urinary trace infections; or previous history of gestational diabetes.

A far rarer form of diabetes, *diabetes insipidus,* is a METABOLIC DISORDER of entirely different origin than diabetes mellitus, but with similar symptoms in the early stages, especially excessive thirst (*polydipsia*) and production of great quantities of urine (*polyuria*). Most cases of diabetes insipidus result from the PITUITARY GLAND's inadequate production of the *antidiuretic hormone* (ADH), which controls the amount of water excreted from the body as urine. Diabetes insipidus can be a sign of a TUMOR in or damage to the pituitary. Lack of sufficient water intake to match the enormous output can lead to serious DEHYDRATION, ultimately resulting in COMA and possible serious damage, especially in infants and small children. This form of diabetes insipidus can be treated with a synthetic form of ADH. A rarer form of the disorder, *nephrogenic diabetes insipidus,* can result from a failure of the kidneys to respond to the ADH in the body. This can be a CONGENITAL disorder or may result from kidney infection (*pyelonephritis*). It cannot be treated with ADH, but requires careful control of diet and water intake, with medication to suppress some thirst symptoms.

FOR HELP AND FURTHER INFORMATION

National Diabetes Information Clearinghouse (NDIC)
Box NDIC
Bethesda, MD 20892–3560
301–654–3327
Fax: 301–267–6080
Federal information clearinghouse on diabetes, a service of the National Institute of Diabetes and Digestive and Kidney Diseases (see DIGESTIVE SYSTEM AND DISORDERS);

maintains online database for health professionals; publishes quarterly newsletter *Diabetes Dateline* and other materials, including:

- Information packets: *General Information About Diabetes, Hypertension and Diabetes, Self-Monitoring of Blood Glucose,* and *Employment, Discrimination, and Diabetes.*
- Fact sheets: *Diabetes Overview, Diabetes in Blacks, Diabetes in Hispanics, Diabetic Neuropathy, Diabetes Statistics,* and *Directory of Diabetes Organizations.*
- Books and booklets: *Insulin-Dependent Diabetes, Noninsulin-Dependent Diabetes, Understanding Gestational Diabetes. Pregnancy and Diabetes* (bibliography), *The Diabetes Dictionary,* and *Diabetic Retinopathy.*
- Reprints and literature searches from online database and materials for health professionals.

American Diabetes Association (ADA)
National Service Center
1660 Duke Street
Alexandria, VA 22314
703–549–1500; 800–232–3472
Fax: 703–836–7439
America Online: American Diabetes
John Graham, Executive Vice President
Organization concerned with diabetes; maintains online forum (see America Online keyword, above), including information, articles, message boards, conference rooms, and searchable online database; provides information and services; publishes numerous materials, including:

- Magazines *Diabetes Forecast* and *Kid's Corner* and five journals for health professionals.
- For parents: *Children with Diabetes* and *Caring for Children with Diabetes.*
- For pregnant women: *Diabetes and Pregnancy: What to Expect* and *Gestational Diabetes: What to Expect.*
- General materials: *Right From the Start* (on newly diagnosed diabetes patients), *101 Tips for Improving Your Blood Sugar, Type II Diabetes: Your Healthy Living Guide, The Fitness Book for People with Diabetes, The Take-Charge Guide to Type I Diabetes, Diabetes A to Z, Necessary Toughness* (on professional football player with diabetes), *The "Other" diabetes* (Type II), *Diabetes: A Positive Approach* (video), *Diabetes and How You Can Manage It Easily* (audiocassette), *Diabetes and Exercise* (video), *The Human Side of Diabetes: Beyond Doctors, Diets, and Drugs, A Diabetic Doctor Looks at Diabetes: His and Yours.*
- For children: *Grilled Cheese at Four O'clock in the Morning, Terry Ryder Rides Again!, The Right Time,* and *It's Time to Learn About Diabetes.*
- Annual guide to diabetes products, numerous cookbooks and nutrition books, and materials for health professionals.

Juvenile Diabetes Foundation International (JDFI)
c/o Diabetes Research Foundation
432 Park Avenue South, 16th Floor
New York, NY 10016–8013
212–889–7575; 800-JDF-CURE [533–2873] or 800–223–1138
Fax: 212–725–7259
Kenneth Farber, Executive Director
Organization for people with juvenile diabetes or insulin-dependent diabetes; funds research; provides information and services through local affiliates; publishes many materials, including quarterly newsletter *Tie Lines*; magazine *Countdown*; books *Parenting a Diabetic Child* (also a video), *Managing Your Child's Diabetes,* and *The Kids, Food and Diabetes Family Cookbook*; and booklets such as *Your Child Has Diabetes, A Child With Diabetes Is in Your Care, What You Should Know About Diabetes, Information About Insulin,* and *Oral Medications and Type II Diabetes.*

Joslin Diabetes Center (JDC)
One Joslin Place
Boston, MA 02215
617–732–2400; For orders: 800–344–4501
Fax for orders: 617–732–2562
Private center specializing in research and treatment of diabetes; provides information; publishes various materials, including:

- *The Basic Pak for Insulin Users* (including *Diabetes Treated with Insulin: A Short Guide,* written at a fourth grade reading level, and *Menu-Planning—Simple!*).
- *The Type II Two-Pack* (including *Managing Your Diabetes Without Insulin* and *Menu-Planning—Simple!*).
- Booklets *Good Health with Diabetes Through Exercise, Eating Well, Living Better, Fighting Longterm Complications, The Foot Book,* and *Weight Loss—A Winning Battle.*
- Books *A Guide for Women with Diabetes Who Are Pregnant…or Plan to Be, A Guide for Parents of Children and Youth with Diabetes, Outsmarting Diabetes, Joslin's Diabetes Mellitus, Joslin Diabetes Manual, The Joslin Diabetes Gourmet Cookbook, Everybody Likes to Eat.*

Resources for Rehabilitation, 617–862–6455. Publishes brochures *Living with Diabetes* and *Living with Diabetic Retinopathy.* (For full group information, see EYE AND VISION PROBLEMS.)

March of Dimes Birth Defects Foundation (MDBDF), 914–428–7100. Publishes information sheet *Diabetes During Pregnancy.* (For full group information, see BIRTH DEFECTS.)

National Institute of Child Health and Human Development (NICHD), 301–496–5133. Publishes *Facts About Gestational Diabetes.* (For full group information, see PREGNANCY.)

National Federation of the Blind (NFB), 410–659–9314. Publishes quarterly *Voice of the Diabetic, Diabetes, Complications, Options, Diabetics, Don't Give Up on Braille, Diabetes—Without High Blood Sugar,* and *Scientists Discover Diabetes Hormone.* (For full group information, see EYE AND VISION PROBLEMS.)

National Kidney Foundation (NKF), 800–622–9010. Publishes *Diabetes and Kidney Disease, Preventing Diabetic Kidney Disease,* and *Living with High Blood Pressure and Diabetes.* (For full group information, see KIDNEY AND UROLOGICAL DISORDERS.)

National Organization for Rare Disorders (NORD), 800–999–6673. (For full group information, see RARE DISORDERS.)

National Eye Institute (NEI), 800–869–2020. Publishes brochure *Don't Lose Sight of Diabetic Eye Disease, Diabetic Retinopathy,* and *Educating People with Diabetes Kit.* (For full group information, see EYE AND VISION PROBLEMS.)

Food and Nutrition Information Center (FNIC), 301–504–5414. Publishes resource list *Nutrition and Diabetes Nutri-Topics.* (For full group information, see NUTRITION.)

OTHER RESOURCES

For parents

Parenting a Diabetic Child: A Practical, Empathetic Guide to Help You and Your Child Live with Diabetes. Gloria Loring. Lowell House, 1993.

Everyone Likes to Eat: How Children Can Eat Most of the Foods They Enjoy and Still Take Care of Their Diabetes, 2nd ed. Hugo Hollerorth and Debra Kaplan. Chronimed, 1993.

Managing Your Child's Diabetes. MasterMedia, 1992.

If Your Child Has Diabetes: An Answer Book for Parents. Perigee/Putnam, 1990.

General works

Diabetes: Questions You Have—Answers You Need. Paula Brisco. People's Medical Society, 1993.

It's Time to Learn about Diabetes. Jean Betschart. Chronimed, 1991.

A Doctor Discusses Diabetes. Lou Joseph and John J. Lynch. Budlong, 1991.

The Human Side of Diabetes: Beyond Doctors, Diets and Drugs. Mike Raymond. Noble Press, 1991.

The Diabetic's Book: All Your Questions Answered, rev. ed. June Biermann and Barbara Toohey. Tarcher, 1990.

Practical guides

Outsmarting Diabetes: A Breakthrough Approach for Reducing the Effects. Richard S. Beaser. Chronimed, 1994.

Diabetes 101: A Pure and Simple Guide for People Who Use Insulin, 2nd ed. Richard Dolinar and Betty P. Brackenridge. Chronimed, 1993.

Diabetes: Your Complete Exercise Guide. Neil F. Gordon. Human Kinetics, 1993.

Balance Your Act: A Book for Adults with Diabetes. Maria A. Ludi and Nancy Hull. Pritchett and Hull, 1993.

Living with Diabetes. Arlan L. Rosenbloom and Diana Tonnessen. NAL-Dutton, 1993.

Diabetes: Beating the Odds: The Doctor's Guide to Reducing Your Risk. Elliot J. Rayfield and Cheryl Solimini. Addison-Wesley, 1992.

The Diabetic's Total Health Book, 3rd ed. June Biermann and Barbara Toohey. Tarcher, 1992.

Charting: The Systematic Approach to Achieving Control. Janice L. Roth. R. A. Rapaport, 1991.

A Touch of Diabetes: A Guide for People Who Have Type II, Noninsulin-Dependent Diabetes. Lois Iovanovic-Peterson and others. Chronimed, 1991.

Reversing Diabetes. Julian M. Whitaker. Warner, 1990.

The Diabetes Sourcebook: Today's Methods and Ways to Give Yourself the Best Care. Diana W. Guthrie and Richard A. Guthrie. Lowell House, 1990.

The Diabetes Self-Care Method: The Breakthrough Program of Self-Management That Will Help You Lead a Better, Freer, More Normal Life, rev. ed. Charles M. Peterson and Lois Jovanovic-Peterson. Lowell House, 1990.

Diabetes: Actively Staying Healthy: Your Game Plan for Diabetes and Exercise. Marian Franz. Chronimed, 1990.

For children

Diabetes. Carol Semple. Crestwood/Macmillan, 1995.

Taking Diabetes to School. Kim Gosselin. JayJo, 1994.

Meeting the Challenge: Children Living with Diabetes. Thomas Bergman. Gareth Stevens, 1992.

Even Little Kids Get Diabetes. Connie Pirner. A. Whitman, 1991.

For teens

Diabetes. Elaine Landau. Twenty-First Century Books, 1994.

Diabetes. Alvin Silverstein and others. Enslow, 1994.

Diabetes Care Made Easy: A Simple Step-by-Step Guide for Controlling Your Diabetes. Allison Nemaneic and others. Chronimed, 1992.

Diabetes. Marjorie Little. Chelsea House, 1991.

Diabetes. Paul Almonte and Theresa Desmond. Crestwood/Macmillan, 1991.

diagnostic assessment test, a type of test designed to identify specific problems and needs. In education, such tests are often given after DEVELOPMENTAL SCREENING TESTS have indicated the possible existence of LEARNING DISABILITIES or other DISABILITIES. Diagnostic assessment tests are then used to provide more detailed information about the potential problem; information from these tests are used to help plan INDIVIDUALIZED EDUCATION PROGRAMS for the child under the EDUCATION FOR ALL HANDICAPPED CHILDREN ACT and its successor, the INDIVIDUALS WITH DISABILITIES EDUCATION ACT (IDEA). Among the most common diagnostic assessment tests are the GESELL PRESCHOOL TEST, ILLINOIS TEST OF PSYCHOLINGUISTIC ABILITIES, KAUFMAN ASSESSMENT BATTERY FOR CHILDREN (K-ABC), MCCARTHY SCALES OF CHILDREN'S ABILITIES (MSCA), STANFORD-BINET INTELLIGENCE SCALE, and WECHSLER PRESCHOOL AND PRIMARY SCALE OF INTELLI-

GENCE (WPPSI), while other tests used for special children include the BEHAVIOR RATING INSTRUMENT FOR AUTISTIC AND OTHER ATYPICAL CHILDREN (BRIACC), PSYCHOEDUCATIONAL PROFILE (PEP), and ADOLESCENT AND ADULT PSYCHOEDUCATIONAL PROFILE (AAPEP).

Diagnostic assessment tests such as these are also often used, for placement purposes, as ADMISSION TESTS (popularly dubbed "Baby Boards") for selective PRESCHOOLS, for example, or for indications of the type of class most appropriate for a child. (See also TESTS and specific tests noted in this entry.)

Diagnostic Reading Scales (DMR or Spache), an individually administered TEST of READING skills for children, a verbal test focusing on word recognition, reading comprehension (oral and silent), PHONICS, and word analysis, as well as auditory comprehension. The DMR is used as a DIAGNOSTIC ASSESSMENT TEST to identify a student's specific strengths and weaknesses in reading, for purposes of class placement and possible REMEDIAL INSTRUCTION. (See TESTS.)

dialysis, use of an artificial machine to filter waste products from the blood when a person's kidneys are unable to function, either temporarily or permanently. The two main kinds of dialysis are *hemodialysis* and *peritoneal dialysis.*

For hemodialysis, surgeons implant a connection (SHUNT) between an artery (A) and vein (V) in a patient. In an AV shunt, connected tubes outside the body (covered with a sterile bandage when not in use) link an artery and vein, with blood flowing through it; during dialysis, the connector is removed, and blood flows into the dialysis machine, is cleansed, and then flows out and back into the body. In an AV *fistula*, an artificial connection is surgically created between a vein and an artery inside the body (with no part of it exposed, and so no need to wear a bandage); during dialysis, the machine is connected to the fistula by needles, to do the necessary cleansing. Hemodialysis must be done two to three times during a week, and takes about four to six hours per visit. The patient must also follow a carefully restricted diet and take various drugs and VITAMINS.

While performing the same function as hemodialysis, *peritoneal dialysis* differs in that the process is continuous and takes place in the patient's abdomen (*peritoneal cavity*), using the peritoneal membrane itself as the filter. A hollow tube (CATHETER) is surgically implanted in the patient's abdomen. With *intermittent peritoneal dialysis* (IPD), a patient is hooked up to a machine several times a day, in a procedure that can be performed at home. But peritoneal dialysis can also be done in ways that allow greater freedom of movement and life-style.

With *continuous ambulatory peritoneal dialysis* (CAPD), a bag of a special dialysate solution is connected to the catheter and allowed to drain by gravity into the abdomen. The still-connected empty bag is then tucked inside the patient's clothing and, while normal everyday activities continue, the blood's waste products are filtered out; then after four to five hours, the bag is taken out and the fluid with the filtered waste products drains into the bag, which is then discarded. This kind of exchange is made four to six times a day, while the person is able to go to school, work, or otherwise live a normal life. And because dialysis is continuous, diet is not restricted. It does, however, carry the risk of *peritonitis,* a dangerous infection of the lining of the peritoneal cavity, so sterility is very important in carrying out this procedure. An alternate form, called *continuous cycling peritoneal dialysis* (CCPD), uses filtering during the day as in CAPD, but the actual exchange of fluids is made only at night, with a machine recycling solutions several times each night. (See KIDNEY AND UROLOGICAL DISORDERS.)

diaphragm, a muscle dividing the chest from the abdomen that helps move air in and out of the lungs (see LUNG AND BREATHING DISORDERS); more generally, a membrane that separates two areas.

As a form of BIRTH CONTROL, a diaphragm is a slightly cup-shaped disk of soft rubber with a flexible rim that fits over the CERVIX. Filled with a SPERMICIDE jelly or cream before insertion, the diaphragm forms both a physical and chemical barrier to SPERM. The spermicide or the rubber in the diaphragm can sometimes cause allergic reactions in the woman or her partner. In that case, use should be discontinued and a doctor consulted in case of any genital burning or irritation. (See ALLERGIES; for other possible problems, such as BIRTH DEFECTS, see SPERMICIDE.)

Unlike the CERVICAL SPONGE, the diaphragm is a prescription device that must be fitted by a physician, though it is looser-fitting than a CERVICAL CAP. It should be inserted within an hour before sexual intercourse and left in place for at least six to eight hours afterward. If intercourse is repeated during that period, more spermicide should be added to the VAGINA (the diaphragm itself should not be moved). The Food and Drug Administration (FDA) rates the diaphragm as 80 to 98 percent effective as a contraceptive. Some women also wear diaphragms if they wish to have sex during MENSTRUATION, to hold back the flow.

Diaphragms must be kept clean and stored in a cool, dry place to retain their effectiveness and prevent damage to the rubber. Women also need to be careful not to damage the rubber during handling or insertion with sharp nails or rings. Only water-based lubricants should be used; oil-based lubricants—including Vaseline, vegetable oil, baby oil, hand lotion, massage oils, and dairy oils—can damage the rubber.

The main disadvantage of the diaphragm-and-spermicide combination is that it must be inserted ahead of time, which detracts from sexual spontaneity, or after the preliminaries to intercourse have already begun, when insertion of the diaphragm may not always be convenient. In that respect, diaphragms may be less suitable for sexually active teens than for more settled adult couples.

Diaphragms have also been associated with increased risk of bladder infections, CONSTIPATION, and on rare occasions TOXIC SHOCK SYNDROME. The devices are also messy and sometimes difficult to remove, especially for women with ARTHRITIS.

The diaphragm and spermicide provide some protection against SEXUALLY TRANSMITTED DISEASES (STDs), but should not be considered protection against AIDS. For that, some women also ask the man to use a CONDOM or themselves use a VAGINAL POUCH, which combines features of the diaphragm and condom. (See BIRTH CONTROL.)

diaphragmatic hernia, a kind of BIRTH DEFECT in which an abnormal hole in the diaphragm allows some abdominal organs, especially the intestines, to move into the space normally occupied by the lungs, a situation that can be identified by some kinds of PRENATAL TESTS, notably ULTRASOUND. Often the chest space becomes so crowded that the lungs cannot develop normally, so that, after birth, a baby is unable to breathe independently and soon dies. New experimental techniques allow this defect to be corrected with IN UTERO SURGERY.

diarrhea, excessively loose, watery, and frequent bowel movements. Diarrhea often results from gastrointestinal infection, but may be a symptom of a wider disorder, such as LACTOSE INTOLERANCE or IRRITABLE BOWEL SYNDROME. Whatever the cause, the result can be DEHYDRATION (loss of body fluids), which in children and especially infants can be extremely dangerous and possibly fatal—even from a single explosive watery bowel movement. Treatment of dehydration involves giving a special fluid mixture containing ELECTROLYTES (available in drugstores), to replace what has been lost; this is called *oral rehydration therapy* (ORT). (See DEHYDRATION; DIGESTIVE SYSTEM AND DISORDERS; also BABY'S BOWELS—WHAT'S NORMAL, WHAT'S NOT on page 176.)

digestive system and disorders, the system that processes food in the body, extracting substances to be used and eliminating the rest, and the problems and diseases affecting it.

In the digestive system, food is taken in at the mouth, where is it chewed and softened with saliva, beginning the digestive process. The food is then swallowed, passing through the throat and the tube-like *esophagus* into the stomach. There it is mixed by muscle action for two to four hours with hydrochloric acid and various digestive enzymes. Once it is semiliquid, it is then moved on to the *duodenum*, the first part of the small intestine, where more digestive enzymes (from the liver, gallbladder, and pancreas) are added, and then on through the small intestine, which produces more enzymes to further the digestive process and also absorbs nutrients through its lining. The undigested matter is moved on from the last part of the small intestine (*ileum*) into the large intestine (*colon*), where most remaining fluid and some vital chemicals are absorbed. The remainder is then moved into the last part of the large intestine, the *rectum*, to be excreted through the *anus* as *feces* or *stool*.

All along the way, the food is propelled by muscle contractions (*peristalsis*), while ring-like muscles called *sphincters* temporarily halt the movement of food between parts of the system during processing. The body produces various HORMONES that direct digestive operations, including muscular contractions and production of enzymes by different organs.

The digestive process can go awry in a number of ways. If food passes too quickly through the system, the body is unable to obtain necessary nutrients and fails to absorb much of the water and vital chemicals. The result is DIARRHEA, which in children can result in a possibly fatal loss of body fluids (see DEHYDRATION). But if the food passes too slowly through the system, too much water will be absorbed, and the stool will be so dry it cannot be readily moved, the result being CONSTIPATION. This is often a problem in pregnant women (see CONSTIPATION DURING PREGNANCY on page 145) and can also result from various other medical problems, especially chronic diseases (see descriptions later in this entry).

While changing diapers for infants and toddlers, parents should be alert to changes in bowel movements as indicators of possible physical problems (see BABY'S BOWELS—WHAT'S NORMAL, WHAT'S NOT on page 176). Bowel movements will differ somewhat depending on whether the baby is fed by BREASTFEEDING or BOTTLEFEEDING. Among the choices parents must make, at least provisionally, before a birth is what kind of diapers to use. Traditional cloth diapers have largely been replaced by chemically treated, usually plastic-coated disposable paper diapers. Certainly disposables are more convenient for parents and are often required in CHILD CARE facilities. However, they are not "disposable" in an environmental sense, and many babies have more—and more serious—diaper rashes with disposables, though that may vary with the brand. As a result some parents have returned to using cloth diapers, which have themselves been made more convenient by the use of velcro tabs and sometimes safety buckles (so the baby can't undo them), and more attractive with various colors and designs; they may be used with nylon pull-on diaper covers as "outerwear" and some come in all-in-one styles that include nylon outer covers.

Young children need to be taught to control bowel movements and urination (see TOILET TRAINING). Inability to control bowel movements, for instance because of neurological impairment, is called INCONTINENCE. If the lack of control seems without physical cause or occurs after toilet training, it may be called SOILING or *encopresis*.

The digestive system can also be upset, causing a queasiness called *nausea* and sometimes VOMITING, which is expulsion of partially digested food from the stomach through the mouth. Vomiting is especially common in pregnant women as MORNING SICKNESS and in young children (see VOMITING IN PREGNANCY on page 623; VOMITING AND YOUR BABY on page 623). It can also be a sign of various physical problems and so should be actively explored (see VOMITING). Deliberate vomiting is part of the binge-purge syndrome called BULIMIA. Many people, especially children and preteens, are also affected by MOTION SICKNESS (see TIPS FOR FIGHTING MOTION SICKNESS on page 413). Nausea and vomiting can also be caused by the body's sensitivity to or inability to properly digest certain foods, as in FOOD INTOLERANCE; LACTOSE INTOLERANCE; CELIAC SPRUE (gluten intolerance); and various METABOLIC DISORDERS, such as ALPHA–1 ANTITRYPSIN DEFICIENCY and GLYCOGEN STORAGE DISEASE.

Children and adults are also subject to various gastrointestinal infections, often viruses. Persistent vomiting or diarrhea can also cause dehydration or chemical imbalance, which should be treated. In general, for parent or child, if a stomach upset lasts more than a few days, a doctor should be consulted, since self-treatment can mask a more serious condition. But a doctor should be called immediately if symptoms are severe, such as:

Baby's Bowels—What's Normal, What's Not

Babies' first bowel movements, which usually occur in the hospital, are sticky and greenish-black. After a week or two, they will become lighter, gradually turn yellow, and become less sticky, remaining that way for the next year. A baby may have anywhere from four to ten movements a day to one movement every three or four days. After the first month, the number of bowel movements decreases to three or four times a day or to as few as once a week. As long as the bowel movements are soft, your baby is not constipated.

Movements may be as firm as those of a normal adult or as soft as loose scrambled eggs and may be yellow, green, or brown. The color, consistency, and odor will be different depending on whether the baby is fed breastmilk or different kinds of formulas.

For a breastfed infant, the bowel movements usually look yellow or yellow-green and are soft to runny in consistency. Generally, your baby should have at least two to three bowel movements a day for the first few weeks. This is a sign that your baby is getting enough milk.

Your baby may turn red in the face and cry with each bowel movement or may seem totally unaware of them. All of these behaviors are normal.

Soiled diapers should be changed soon after a bowel movement to keep the baby as clean and comfortable as possible.

CONSTIPATION

Constipation is when the bowel movements are hard, dry, and difficult to pass, no matter how frequent or infrequent they may be. Constipation should not be a problem if you breastfeed. If you bottlefeed, 1 tablespoon of light corn syrup in a 4–ounce bottle of water (for infants younger than three months) or 1 tablespoon prune juice added to one of the baby's bottles (for older babies) may soften the bowel movements. If not, ask your doctor or clinic staff what to do. Do *not* use mineral oil, castor oil, adult laxatives or enemas without medical advice.

DIARRHEA

Sometimes your baby will have frequent loose or watery bowel movements. Watery bowel movements can cause a baby to lose more fluid than he or she is drinking. This "dehydration" (loss of liquid) can be a true medical emergency. Even a single, huge, explosive, watery bowel movement can be an emergency in an infant one to two months old, especially if he or she has a poor appetite or is vomiting. *Call or visit your doctor or clinic right away when the child has one or more large, watery bowel movements.*

BLOOD IN BOWEL MOVEMENT

Slight blood streaking on the outside of a bowel movement is usually caused by a small sore or tear ("fissure") in the anus and is not a cause for alarm. The tear and the bleeding can often be cured by keeping the stools soft with light corn syrup or prune juice or a remedy from your doctor.

Do not delay calling or going to your doctor or to the clinic right away if there is bloody diarrhea or if fresh blood or blood clots are passed with the bowel movements.

Source: Infant Care (1989). Prepared for the Public Health Service by the Bureau of Maternal and Child Health and Resources Development.

- Continuous vomiting or diarrhea.
- Extreme pain or discomfort in the gastrointestinal tract.
- Black stool (unless it follows treatment with a drug containing bismuth subsalicylate, such as Pepto-Bismol).
- Visible blood in the stool.
- Vomiting of blood or matter resembling coffee grounds (which may be partly digested blood).

Among the more serious problems that commonly affect children's digestive systems are:

- Infection and inflammation anywhere in the system, but especially in:
  - The esophagus, which can become inflamed and sometimes even torn or ruptured if there is frequent vomiting (as in bulimia or some KIDNEY UROLOGICAL PROBLEMS), if a foreign body is swallowed, or if corrosive chemicals are swallowed. This can cause narrowing of the esophagus, making swallowing difficult.
  - The stomach, which is normally protected by various acids, but is still prey to various gastrointestinal infections (*gastroenteritis*), sometimes with associated infections of the ileum (*ileitis*) and colon (*colitis*). These may be caused by bacteria, viruses, worms, or parasites, such as the protozoa *giardiasis* and *amebiasis*. Some of these come under the rough heading of "food poisoning," and some can be quite serious, including cholera, typhoid fever, and BOTULISM. It is important to seek medical help and treat such infections actively, because continuing inflammation and infection can seriously weaken the body. (See TIPS FOR AVOIDING FOODBORNE ILLNESS on page 178, including numbers to call for information on food safety.)
- Infections in localized areas, such as APPENDICITIS (inflammation of the appendix, a tiny projection off the small intestine).
- INFLAMMATORY BOWEL DISEASE (*Crohn's disease* and *ulcerative colitis*), affecting the digestive tract, especially the small intestine.

Congenital abnormalities: A child can be born with malformations of the digestive system, such as:

- CLEFT LIP AND PALATE, making feeding difficult.
- *Atresia* (abnormal closure), as in *esophageal atresia,* where the esophagus reaches a dead end before reaching the stomach, a condition requiring immediate surgical correction. Atresia may also affect the intestines. In biliary atresia (see liver and liver problems), openings for the liver's bile ducts are absent or malformed.
- *Stenosis* (abnormal narrowing), as in *pyloric stenosis,* where the stomach outlet (controlled by the *pyloric sphincter* ring-muscle) is narrow so that food cannot freely pass into the small intestine, a condition often requiring surgical correction. Stenosis can also affect the intestines; in *anal stenosis,* the passage is too small to allow for excreting stool.
- *Meckel's diverticulum,* a small hollow sac near the end of the small intestine, a common disorder which can sometimes cause infection, obstruction, or severe bleeding, requiring surgery and BLOOD TRANSFUSIONS. Symptoms of an inflamed diverticulum are similar to those of APPENDICITIS.
- *Imperforate anus,* in which the anus has no opening; this condition must be surgically corrected immediately after birth.
- *Other disorders,* including rarer problems such as:
  - *Achalasia,* in which the muscle that controls the passage between the esophagus and the stomach fails to relax, sometimes causing difficulty in vomiting and swallowing.
  - *Peptic ulcer,* a raw sore in the gastrointestinal tract, generally in the stomach, esophagus, or duodenum; when serious, considerable bleeding may result and surgery may be required. However, in recent years, doctors have discovered that most peptic ulcers are caused by a bacterial infection, which can be treated with antibiotics. Peptic ulcers, which mostly affect adults but can also affect children—are exacerbated by alcohol, coffee, tea, aspirin, large meals, and general stress.
  - Telescoping (*intussusception* or *prolapse)* or twisting (*volvulus*) of the small intestine, sometimes linked with Meckel's diverticulum, a small polyp, or volvulus, of the stomach. These disorders are most often found in young children, leading to COLIC-like reactions, vomiting, and blood in the stool. Often diagnosed by BARIUM X-RAY, surgery may be required to clear the painful and potentially life-threatening obstruction.
  - *Familial polyposis,* a rare inherited disease in which many polyps grow in the colon; associated with later high risk of colon CANCER.
  - *Malabsorption,* impaired ability to digest food, especially to absorb nutrients from it, as in cases of METABOLIC DISORDERS or other types of digestive problems.
  - IRRITABLE BOWEL SYNDROME, also called *spastic colon.*

Many other kinds of disorders are closely related to digestive disorders, including pernicious ANEMIA, DIABETES, CYSTIC FIBROSIS, and HEMATOCHROMATOSIS; see also KIDNEY AND UROLOGICAL PROBLEMS, and LIVER AND LIVER PROBLEMS.

Among the specialists who work with the digestive system are the GASTROENTEROLOGIST and PROCTOLOGIST. Various kinds of MEDICAL TESTS, devices, and procedures may be used in relation to digestive disorders, including the COLONOSCOPE, GASTROSCOPE, PROCTOSCOPE, SIGMOIDOSCOPE, OSTOMY (including *colostomy* and *ileostomy*), and BARIUM X-RAY EXAMINATIONS.

FOR HELP AND FURTHER INFORMATION

GENERAL ORGANIZATIONS

Digestive Disease National Coalition
711 Second Street NE, Suite 200
Washington, DC 20002
202–544–7497

Tips for Avoiding Foodborne Illness

A major area of safety concern from infancy throughout life is foodborne illness, commonly called *food poisoning* (see DIGESTIVE SYSTEM AND DISORDERS). Parents can cut their family's risk of food poisoning by adopting some simple rules of good hygiene in the kitchen—and teaching their children to follow their example:

- Set your refrigerator temperature at 40° F or less. Surveys show that most refrigerators are set much higher, even above 50° F. Even at 40° F, bacteria are not killed, but their growth is slowed and sickness is less likely.
- Defrost meat, poultry, and fish products by thawing them in the refrigerator or in a microwave oven (following package directions). Alternatively, enclose the meat or fish in a water-tight plastic bag and thaw it in cold water, changing the water every thirty minutes. Never thaw on the counter or in the sink at room temperature, since bacteria can multiply rapidly.
- Marinate meat in the refrigerator, not at room temperature.
- Wash hands, utensils, and cutting boards thoroughly with hot, soapy water and clean cutting board with a mild chlorine bleach solution or commercial sanitizing agent *after* preparing raw meat and *before* preparing any other foods, such as vegetables. Afterward, wash all counters and surfaces that have come into contact with any foods.
- Cook meat thoroughly, especially pork, ground beef, and chicken. In these days of widespread bacterial contaminants, such as *Salmonella* and *E. coli*, which can cause serious and in some cases life-threatening intestinal infections, the days of "rare" meat should be past. Today meat should be cooked until it is no longer red in the middle and the juices run clear. The internal temperature should reach at least 160° F. Poultry should be 180° F. Fish should flake with a fork. Uncooked meat products such as salami should also be avoided, since they have also recently been found to spread bacteria.
- Cover food with a lid or vented plastic wrap so steam can help make microwaving more thorough; but make sure the wrap does not touch the food.
- If your microwave has no turntable, rotate your food dish once or twice by hand during the cooking period.
- For microwaved food, be sure to follow directions as to standing time; microwaving creates pockets of heat, and standing allows heat to spread more evenly to all parts.
- Cook eggs thoroughly, so both yolk and white are firm, not runny. Even fresh, unbroken eggs can be contaminated with *Salmonella* bacteria. Do not use recipes that call for raw or only partially cooked eggs, and do not taste or "lick the bowl" if batter is made with raw eggs. If you or your children can't resist tasting—consider buying pasteurized eggs, which have been treated to kill bacteria; these are used in commercial cookie mixes.
- Never taste food that looks moldy or smells strange, to see if you can still use it; even a small amount of spoiled food can cause illness. Just throw it away.
- Use clean dishes and utensils for food, not those used for storage or preparation of raw or leftover food.
- Do not leave leftovers standing at room temperature; cover and refrigerate them as soon as possible. When possible, divide large portions of food into small, shallow containers; that allows safer, quicker cooling in the refrigerator. Remove stuffing from poultry and refrigerate it separately.
- Throw away food that has been standing at room temperature for more than two hours. The danger of food poisoning is too great for the small amount of food to be saved. Fresh-cooked food is especially hazardous, since it does not have the preservatives found in commercially prepared foods (see FOOD ADDITIVES). The watchword is: When in doubt, throw it out.
- Throw away any baby formula that has been left at room temperature in a nursing bottle or open container for more than an hour or in the refrigerator for more than two days.
- Do not overpack your refrigerator. Cool air must be able to circulate to keep food safe.
- Heat leftovers thoroughly; be especially careful with microwaves, which can heat unevenly. Bring sauces, soups, and gravy to a boil. Heat other leftovers to 165° F.

- Pack children's lunches in insulated carriers with a cold pack. Caution children against leaving the lunch bags in direct sunlight or on a warm radiator.
- Carry picnic food in an insulated carrier with a cold pack. Keep it in the shade and keep the lid closed as much as possible.
- For parties, keep food on ice or replenish platters from food stored in the refrigerator. Divide hot food into small servings, which can be refrigerated until time to heat them for serving.
- Do not let dirty dishes sit in water for a long time, which creates a "bacterial stew." Wash them by hand within two hours or wash them in a dishwasher. Either way, let them air dry; avoid handling them while they're wet.
- Wash kitchen towels, cloths, and sponges often, replacing sponges every few weeks, since bacteria live in them.
- Sanitize the kitchen sink drain, disposal unit, and connecting pipe periodically with a solution of 1 teaspoon of chlorine bleach in 1 quart of water or with a commercial sanitizing product, to halt bacterial growth in trapped particles.
- In case of a power outage, a full freezer (a separate chest-sized unit or a refrigerator freezer) will keep food frozen for about two days; a half-full freezer will keep food frozen for about one day. If it seems unlikely that power will be back on before the food defrosts, take your food to a friend's freezer, if possible, or use dry ice (but handle carefully: do not touch it or breathe the fumes). Keep the freezer door shut as much as possible.
- Without power, your refrigerator will keep food safely cool for four to six hours, depending on the kitchen temperature. Block ice (not dry ice) can be put on shelves to keep food cooler.
- Food that still contains ice crystals or that feels refrigerator-cold can be refrozen. But any thawed food that has risen to room temperature and has been there for two hours or more should be thrown away, as should anything with a strange odor or color.

Avoiding foodborne illness also requires some care in shopping. Following a few tips will help:

- Buy only food in good condition. Refrigerated food should be cold to the touch. Frozen food should be rock-solid. Packages should have no holes, rips, or punctures. Canned goods should be free of dents, cracks, or bulging lids, which can indicate a serious food poisoning threat. Some screw-top containers have a "safety button" that pops up if food is spoiled; check these before opening.
- Check expiration dates and do not buy anything that is past its date or that you do not expect to use before the date indicated on the package.
- Make the grocery store your last stop, taking food straight home to the refrigerator. Never leave food in a hot car.
- If you won't be using fish, meat, or poultry within a few days, freeze it immediately.
- Store packages of raw meat, poultry, or fish on plates, so they will not contaminate other foods with their juices, which often contain bacteria (that will be killed by proper cooking).

With young children in the home, infections are spread more readily. Some general hygiene recommendations can help reduce the spread of infections, both at home and in child care facilities:

- See that eating surfaces are properly cleaned and sanitized.
- Make sure diaper-changing is done in a place quite separate from food areas. In evaluating child care facilities, see that running water is readily available in the changing area.
- Whoever is changing diapers should wash their hands after each diaper change and also after helping a child in the bathroom or with a tissue.
- If a child is ill, keep the child home from child care or school and encourage other parents to do the same. (Note that some regions have sick child day care programs; see CHILD CARE.)
- If children or adults have contact with house or neighborhood pets, they should wash their hands very carefully.

Source: Adapted in part from various food-safety materials of the Food and Drug Administration [FDA] and the U.S. Department of Agriculture [UDSA].

Fax: 202–546–7105
Dale P. Dirks, Washington Representative
Network of organizations focusing on improving health of people with digestive disease problems; seeks to educate public and shape public policy; distributes various materials.

National Institute of Diabetes, Digestive and Kidney Diseases (NIDDK)
131 Center Drive, MSC
Bethesda, MD 20892–2560
301–496–3583
One of the U.S. National Institutes of Health, sponsoring research on diabetes, digestive diseases, kidney diseases, and related ailments; provides information, notably through the National Diabetes Information Clearinghouse (NDIC; see DIABETES), National Kidney and Urologic Disease Information Clearinghouse (NKUDIC; see KIDNEY AND UROLOGICAL DISORDERS) and National Digestive Disease Information Clearinghouse (NDDIC; see following organization listing).

National Digestive Disease Information Clearinghouse (NDDIC)
2 Information Way
Bethesda, MD 20892–3572
301–654–3810
Federal clearinghouse for information on digestive diseases, a service of the National Institute of Diabetes and Digestive and Kidney Diseases (NIDDK; see preceding organization listing); provides information and referrals; publishes various materials, including numerous brochures on digestive disorders.

Crohn's and Colitis Foundation of America, Inc. (CCFA)
386 Park Avenue South, 17th Floor
New York, NY 10016–8804
212–685–3440; 800–932–2423
Fax: 212–779–4098
Prodigy: CCFA
Barbara T. Boyle, Executive Director
Organization concerned with Crohn's disease and colitis; provides information and referrals; offers medications at discount; some chapters offer financial aid; publishes newsletters; books *Managing Your Child's Crohn's Disease and Ulcerative Colitis, People…not Patients: A Source Book for Living with IBD,* and *Treating IBD: A Patient's Guide to the Medical and Surgical Management of Inflammatory Bowel Disease*; and "Questions and Answers about" brochure: *Crohn's Disease and Ulcerative Colitis* (including a glossary of IBD terms), *Diet and Nutrition, Pregnancy, Emotional Factors, Complications,* and *Surgery.*

Child Health Foundation
10630 Little Patuxent Parkway, Suite 325
Columbia, MD 21044
410–992–5512; 301–596–4514
Fax: 410–992–5614
Charlene Dale, Executive Vice President
Organization focusing on dissemination of inexpensive medical technologies to treat the most common causes of illness and death in children internationally; publishes newsletter and information sheets *When Your Baby Has Diarrhea* and *ORT: Oral Rehydration Therapy Facts.*

National Cancer Institute (NCI), 800–422–6237. Publishes "What You Need to Know About Cancer" brochures on cancer of the colon and rectum, esophagus, stomach, and pancreas. (For full group information, see CANCER.)

American Cancer Society (ACS), 800–227–2345. Publishes materials on colorectal cancer and cancer of the stomach and esophagus. (For full group information, see CANCER.)

American Celiac Society/Dietary Support Coalition (ACS/DSC), 201–325–8837. (For full group information, see CELIAC SPRUE.)

National Foundation for Ileitis and Colitis (NFIC), 800–932–2423. (For full group information, see INFLAMMATORY BOWEL DISEASE.)

Accent, 800–787–8444. Publishes *Bowel Management: A Manual of Ideas and Techniques.* (For full group information, see HELP FOR SPECIAL CHILDREN on page 689.)

American Institute for Cancer Research (AICR), 800–843–8114. Publishes *Reducing Your Risk of Colon Cancer* and *Diet, Nutrition, and Cancers of the Colon and Rectum.* (For full group information, see CANCER.)

The Hereditary Colorectal Cancer Registry, 410–614–4038. (For full group information, see CANCER.)

United Ostomy Association (UOA), 800–826–0826. (For full group information, see OSTOMY.)

National Organization for Rare Disorders (NORD), 800–999–6673. (For full group information, see RARE DISORDERS.)

ORGANIZATIONS ON FOOD SAFETY

U.S. Department of Agriculture (USDA) Meat and Poultry Hotline (twenty-four hours): 202–720–3333; 800–535–4555. Provides recorded messages twenty-four hours a day; home economists and registered dietitians are available to answer questions 10 A.M.–4 P.M., M-F, ET.

Food and Drug Administration (FDA), 301–443–3170.

FDA Seafood Hotline (twenty-four hours): 202–205–4314; 800-FDA–4010 [332–4010]. (For full group information, see DRUG REACTIONS AND INTERACTIONS.)

Food and Nutrition Information Center (FNIC), 301–504–5414. Operates Foodborne Illness Education Information Center. (For full group information, see NUTRITION.)

OTHER RESOURCES

GENERAL WORKS

A Healthy Digestion. Charles B. Clayman, ed. RD Assn, 1992.

Understanding Your Digestive System. Michael F. Elmore. Creative Ideas, 1991.

ON DEALING WITH OR PREVENTING PROBLEMS

Correct Food Combining for Easy Digestion: How to Get Rid of Indigestion, Gas, Bloating, Belching and Bad Breath. Gordon Press, 1992.

Food Combining and Digestion: How to Get More Out of What You Eat, 2nd ed. Steve Meyerowitz. Sprout House, 1992.

Indigestion: Living Better with Upper Intestinal Problems. Henry D. Janowitz. Oxford University Press, 1992.

The IBD Nutrition Book. Jan K. Greenwood. Wiley, 1992.

Gastrointestinal Health: A Self-Help Nutritional Program. Steve R. Peikin. HarperCollins, 1991.

Complete Guide to Digestive Disorders: End Poor Digestion with This Self-Help Plan. Kathleen Mayes. Thorsons, 1990.

The Complete Book of Better Digestion: A Gut-Level Guide to Gastric Relief. Michael Oppenheim. Rodale, 1990.

Eating Right for a Bad Gut: The Complete Nutritional Guide to Ileitis, Crohn's Disease and Inflammatory Bowel Syndrome. James Scala. NAL, 1990.

The Wellness Book of I. B. S.: A Guide to Lifelong Relief from Symptoms of One of America's Most Common and Least-Talked-About Ailments: Irritable Bowel Syndrome. Deralee Scanlon and Barbara Cottman Becnel. St. Martin's, 1990.

Uninvited Guests: Intestinal Parasites and Your Health. Ann Louise Gittleman and Albert R. Salem. Pioneer Books, 1990.

FOR CHILDREN

Digestive System and Excretory Systems. Alvin Silverstein and others. Twenty-First Century Books, 1994.

The Digestive System. Merce Parramon. Chelsea House, 1994.

Digestion: The Digestive System. Jenny Bryan. Macmillan, 1993.

Eating. Anita Ganeri. Raintree Steck-Vaughn, 1994.

Eating a Meal: How You Eat, Drink and Digest. Steve Parker. Watts, 1991.

Food and Digestion, rev. ed. Steve Parker. Watts, 1991.

BACKGROUND WORKS

Anorectal Malformations: A Surgeon's Experience. Subir K. Chatterjee. Oxford University Press, 1993.

(See also CONSTIPATION; DIARRHEA; DIABETES; INFLAMMATORY BOWEL DISEASE; IRRITABLE BOWEL SYNDROME; KIDNEY AND UROLOGICAL PROBLEMS; LIVER AND LIVER PROBLEMS; METABOLIC DISORDERS; OSTOMY.)

dilation, during LABOR, the widening of the CERVIX, generally to about four inches, in preparation for the actual DELIVERY of a baby.

diphtheria, a bacterial illness that was once a major childhood killer but is now extremely rare in areas where most people have received IMMUNIZATION. The diphtheria vaccine is usually given in a combination DTP VACCINE, which also immunizes against TETANUS (lockjaw) and WHOOPING COUGH (*pertussis*).

Passed through droplets in the air from coughing or sneezing, from infected people or unaffected CARRIERS, the diphtheria bacteria cause a membrane to form in the throat that may obstruct swallowing and breathing and sometimes requires a TRACHEOSTOMY to maintain breathing. Diphtheria is generally responsive to ANTIBIOTICS such as penicillin in the early stages, but if the disease takes hold, the bacteria produces a powerful, life-threatening toxin (poison) in the body. This can sometimes be treated with ANTITOXINS, but causes PARALYSIS, heart failure, and bronchial pneumonia in many. One out of ten patients dies. The diphtheria vaccine does not provide lifelong protection, and a booster is recommended every ten years, generally combined with tetanus in the TD VACCINE.

FOR HELP AND FURTHER INFORMATION

National Institute of Allergy and Infectious Diseases (NIAID), 301–496–5717. (For full group information, see ALLERGIES.)

National Institute of Child Health and Human Development (NICHD), 301–496–5133. (For full group information, see PREGNANCY.)

(See also DTP VACCINE; IMMUNIZATION.)

diploma, a formal document certifying that a student has successfully completed a course of study, generally offered at GRADUATION from a HIGH SCHOOL, COLLEGE, or GRADUATE SCHOOL; sometimes called a *degree, parchment* or *sheepskin*, especially at the college level. Colleges that give degrees too easily or even fraudulently, for no work at all, are sometimes called *diploma mills* or *degree mills.*

disabilities, a general term referring to a wide range of minor or major physical or mental impairments in people who have some degree of difficulty in activities such as walking, seeing, hearing, speaking, and learning. The term has come to largely replace the designation HANDICAPPED, except where that term has been written into law. DEVELOPMENTAL DISORDERS or disabilities are those impairments that emerge or become evident during early growth and development, as a child shows significant delay in reaching key DEVELOPMENTAL MILESTONES.

In the past three decades, numerous laws have been passed to ensure that children with disabilities, including those with CHRONIC illnesses, have equal opportunity to education and self-development. In addition to the more general AMERICANS WITH DISABILITIES ACT, the key federal laws in this area include:

- SECTION 504, a portion of the Civil Rights Act for Handicapped Persons, which bars any organization or institution receiving federal funds from discriminating in any way against qualified people with disabilities. It established a "functional" view of disability.
- EDUCATION FOR ALL HANDICAPPED CHILDREN ACT of 1975, which established the rights of children with disabilities to a free and appropriate EDUCATION, and which was amended in 1983, 1986, and 1990.
- INDIVIDUALS WITH DISABILITIES EDUCATION ACT (IDEA), which incorporated and reauthorized the Education for all Handicapped Children Act and its amendments.

Though the education mandates initially covered children from ages six to twenty-one, the EHC required the establishment of programs (such as CHILDFIND) to try to identify such children as early as possible, to provide treatment and other special services quickly and to minimize the impact of the disabilities (see EARLY INTERVENTION).

Whatever the child's age, the parent must be closely involved in the evaluation, assessment, and planning processes. The parent may call for an initial evaluation or someone else may suggest that the child be tested. But the parent must be informed at every stage and must agree to any evaluation or testing. Then—if the child is indeed shown to have special needs—the parent must approve of the plan to meet those needs.

The evaluation will include a review of the child's educational history (provided by a school adminstrator), a current educational assessment (by the child's classroom teacher), and assessment of specific areas that seem to pose difficulty. The parent or others may also call for additional information, including assessments of the child's medical and health status, the home and family history, and a psychological evaluation of the child. Parents have the right to be informed of the assessments to be discussed before any evaluation meeting, but they may need to specifically request that information to be provided to them.

Any school-age child who is found to have SPECIAL NEEDS is provided with an INDIVIDUALIZED EDUCATION PROGRAM (IEP) outlining what staff at the school will be teaching the child, how they will go about it, how they will evaluate progress and measure success, and what special educational services will be provided.

Given the wide definition of the word, many children are seen to have some kind of disability. Also, with modern medical technology, many children are surviving with severe disabilities who might not have done so in the past. Partly as a result, many organizations have been formed to support, educate, and act as advocates for children with disabilities and their parents (see ADVOCACY), especially to ensure that the children's rights are respected. Also, many books have been written to help maximize the independence of children with disabilities. Many of these organizations and works are listed in this book under specific disabilities, notably under these headings: EAR AND HEARING PROBLEMS, EYE AND VISION PROBLEMS, LEARNING DISABILITIES, MENTAL RETARDATION, MENTAL DISORDERS, and COMMUNICATION SKILLS AND DISORDERS. Many other organizations and written works deal with overarching general needs of many kinds of disabled people—so many that we have listed them separately under HELP FOR SPECIAL CHILDREN, on page 689.

discipline, guidance and training to help someone—usually a child or someone less experienced—to develop self-control and conduct appropriate to given situations. Within the family, discipline is both a PARENT'S RIGHT and a PARENT'S RESPONSIBILITY, given that the primary training of a child is a parental prerogative and that the state requires the parent to exercise SUPERVISION and control in the process of teaching the child self-control.

Discipline was long considered almost synonymous with punishment, especially CORPORAL PUNISHMENT. But today the line between acceptable corporal punishment and child abuse is in considerable flux. Social norms are changing and state laws now have various definitions of what constitutes child abuse. More importantly, some crucial distinctions are now made between discipline and punishment, with discipline seen as a positive, corrective approach and punishment a negative, often destructive one (see COMPARISON OF DISCIPLINE AND PUNISHMENT on page 183).

One key underlying idea in the modern view of discipline is *positive reinforcement*, an idea taken from psychology: in essence, that you should focus on rewarding children for doing things you want them to keep on doing or for making attempts in the right direction. The rewards are often smiles, hugs, and attention, though sometimes they can be more tangible treats. The corollary is to withhold reinforcement (rather than negatively punish) for behavior that you do not wish to see. Reserve sharp "No's" or punishment, if necessary, for dangerous situations in which first you must protect the child before guiding his or her behavior for future situations. Such positive reinforcement approaches are widely used in schools, as well, where discipline is also a prime concern.

Among the many alternatives to punishment, perhaps the most important, if the child's behavior is unruly, is a brief TIME-OUT, a cooling-off period during which the child is separated from general activity, but without humiliation or great fuss. Parents sometimes need a time-out, too. Punishment given in frustration or anger can escalate to child abuse or at least damage the parent-child relationship. Wise parents will not act in anger, but will cool off in another room, after first seeing that a young child is in a safe setting, such as a crib or playpen.

Beyond that, experts agree, it is important to set basic rules for behavior, make sure the child is clear as to what they are, and be consistent about reminding the child of the rules. No matter what the child's age, but especially

Comparison of Discipline and Punishment

DISCIPLINE	PUNISHMENT
Can be given before, during, or after an event	Is usually given after an event
Focuses on developing internal controls to affect future behavior	Focuses on external control, which may or may not affect behavior
Stresses generalizing learning	May focus only on past event
Has a rational, educational purpose	May result from frustration or anger, and irrationally inflicts pain
Recognizes individual worth and capabilities	Is often dehumanizing and denigrating of abilities
Can forge stronger interpersonal bonds	Usually causes deterioration of relationships
Uses authority figure as role model	Stresses submission to authority figure

with very young children, parents should try to make very clear precisely what behavior they are focusing on and should be consistent in their approach. Effective discipline also benefits from some foresightedness—such as forestalling problems before they begin by distracting the child or by planning a situation to avoid the problem in the first place—and creativity in coming up with alternatives.

Ideally, parents should involve children in discussing and developing alternatives to problem behavior, which, incidentally, also helps improve the children's problem-solving skills. Parents can help children see the longer-term consequences of their behavior, aiding the children's SOCIAL SKILLS and COGNITIVE DEVELOPMENT. Parents are ROLE MODELS for their children, who will tend to copy parental behavior, so the parent's most important role is to guide the child in developing rules of action. Many schools have developed programs that will supplement parents' efforts (or substitute for them, if parental control is lacking) in helping children develop self-control, consider the consequences of their behavior, and learn other alternatives to unruly or violent behavior.

FOR HELP AND FURTHER INFORMATION

National Association for the Education of Young Children (NAEYC), 800–424–2460. Publishes book *A Guide to Discipline*; brochures *Helping Children Learn Self-Control* and *Love and Learn: Discipline for Young Children*; and videos *Discipline* and *Discipline: Appropriate Guidance of Young Children.* (For full group information, see PRESCHOOL.)

American Academy of Child and Adolescent Psychiatry (AACAP), 202–966–7300. Publishes information sheet *Discipline.* (For full group information, see MENTAL DISORDERS.)

Childhelp USA, 818–953–7577. Publishes pamphlet *Discipline Is Love.* (For full group information, see HELP AGAINST CHILD ABUSE AND NEGLECT on page 680.)

Effectiveness Training International, 800–628–1197. Publishes *Teaching Children Self-Discipline at Home and at School.* (For full group information, see GENERAL PARENTING RESOURCES on page 634.)

National Congress of Parents and Teachers (National PTA), 312–670–6782. (For full group information, see HELP ON LEARNING AND EDUCATION on page 659.)

National Center for the Study of Corporal Punishment and Alternatives in the Schools (NCSCPAS), 215–204–6028. (For full group information, see CORPORAL PUNISHMENT.)

Alliance for Parental Involvement in Education (ALLPIE), 518–392–6900. Publishes *Teaching Children Self-Discipline At Home and At School: New Ways Parents and Teachers Can Build Self-Control, Self-Esteem and Self-Reliance.* (For full group information, see HELP ON LEARNING AND EDUCATION on page 659.)

Alexander Graham Bell Association for the Deaf (AGBAD), 202–337–5220, voice/TT. Publishes *Parenting with Love and Logic: Teaching Children Responsibility.* (For full group information, see EAR AND HEARING PROBLEMS.)

National Committee for Prevention of Child Abuse (NCPCA), 800–835–2671. Publishes *Child Discipline: Guidelines for Parents.* (For full group information, see HELP AGAINST CHILD ABUSE AND NEGLECT on page 680.)

Toughlove
P.O. Box 1069
Doylestown, PA 18901

215–348–7090
Fax: 215–348–9874
Julene Burch, Executive Director
Network of mutual-support groups for parents of problem adolescents; encourages setting of basic behavior standards and withdrawal of privileges for breaking rules; in extreme cases, advises barring children from home, with members providing shelter until rules are agreed to; publishes various materials.

Center for Law and Education, 202–986–3000. Publishes *School Discipline and Students Rights: An Advocate's Manual, School Discipline Case Law, Isolation as a Discipline Technique,* and *Disciplinary Exclusion of Students with Disabilities Under Federal Law: An Overview.* (For full group information, see HELP ON LEARNING AND EDUCATION on page 659.)

National Mental Health Association (NMHA), 800–969–6642. Publishes *A Close Look at Development and Discipline.* (For full group information, see MENTAL DISORDERS.)

OTHER RESOURCES

GENERAL WORKS FOR PARENTS

The Thoughtful Art of Discipline: Teaching Responsibility When Your Child Misbehaves. Dale R. Olen. Life Skills, 1994.

Love and Limits: Guidance Tools for Creative Parenting. Elizabeth Crary. Parenting Press, 1994.

Kids Are Worth It: Giving Your Child the Gift of Inner Discipline. Barbara Coloroso. Morrow, 1994.

Assertive Discipline for Parents. Lee Canter. HarperCollins, 1993.

Positive Discipline for Single Parents: A Practical Guide to Raising Children Who Are Responsible, Respectful, and Resourceful and *Positive Discipline A-Z.* Jane Nelsen and others. Prima, 1993.

Five Thousand Ways to Say No to Your Child. Walt Peterson. Mendocino Coast, 1993.

Playful Parenting: Turning the Dilemma of Discipline into Fun and Games. Denise Chapman Weston and Mark S. Weston. Tarcher, 1993.

NO is a Love Word: How to say "NO" to Children of All Ages Firmly, Fairly, Consistently and Without Guilt. Lonnie Carton. Learning Center, 1992.

Positive Parental Discipline. Marvin Goldstein and others. Bureau for At-Risk Youth, 1992.

When Kids Bend the Rules—One Hundred One Creative Discipline Ideas. Elizabeth W. Crisci. Accent, 1992.

Discipline: A Sourcebook of 50 Failsafe Techniques for Parents. James Windell. Collier, 1991. By a child and family psychotherapist.

Good Kids, Bad Behavior: Helping Children Learn Self-Discipline. Peter A. Williamson. Simon & Schuster, 1990.

ON DISCIPLINE FOR TODDLERS AND PRESCHOOLERS

The Discipline Book: Everything You Need to Know to Have a Better-Behaved Child—from Birth to Age 10. William Sears and Martha Sears. Little, Brown, 1995.

Eight Weeks to a Well-Behaved Child: A Failsafe Program for Toddlers Through Teens. James Windell. Macmillan, 1994.

Disciplining Your Preschooler and Feeling Good about It, rev. ed. Mitch Golant and Susan K. Golant. Lowell House, 1993.

Keys to Disciplining Your Child: From Infant to Toddler. Linda Siegel and Eleanor Siegel. Barron's, 1993.

Without Spanking or Spoiling: A Practical Approach to Toddler and Preschool Guidance, 2nd ed. Elizabeth Crary. Parenting Press, 1993.

Time-Out for Toddlers: Positive Solutions to Typical Problems in Children. James W. Varni and Donna G. Corwin. Berkley, 1991.

Teach Your Child to Behave: Disciplining with Love from 2 to 8 Years. Charles E. Schaefer and Theresa F. DiGeronimo. NAL-Dutton, 1991.

Discipline from Birth to Three: How to Prevent and Deal with Discipline Problems with Babies and Toddlers. Jeanne W. Lindsay and Sally McCullough. 1991.

ON DISCIPLINE FOR OLDER CHILDREN

Positive Discipline for Teenagers: Resolving Conflict with Your Teenage Son or Daughter. Jane Nelson and Lynn Lott. Prima, 1994.

Stop Struggling with Your Child: Quick Tip Parenting Solutions That Will Work for You—and Your Kids Ages 4–12. Evonne Weinhaus and Karen Friedman. HarperCollins, 1991.

How to Discipline Your 6 to 12 Year Old without Losing Your Mind. Jerry L. Wyckoff and Barbara C. Unell. Doubleday, 1991.

BACKGROUND WORKS

Discipline with Dignity. Merrill Harmin, NEA, 1994.

Managing Misbehaviour in Schools. Tony Charlton and Kenneth David, ed. Routledge, 1993.

Permissiveness in Child Rearing and Education—A Failed Doctrine?: New Trends for the 1990s. E. Lakin Phillips. University Press of America, 1993.

Spoiled Rotten: Today's Children and How to Change Them. Fred G. Gosman. Random, 1992.

(See also CORPORAL PUNISHMENT; VIOLENCE; CHILD ABUSE AND NEGLECT; also GENERAL PARENTING RESOURCES on page 634.)

disclosing tablets, in dental care, tablets that harmlessly tint areas of the teeth that have not been brushed thoroughly. Such tablets are especially useful for young children, up to perhaps age eight, as they are learning to brush their own teeth. (See TEETH AND DENTAL PROBLEMS.)

discovery learning, a LEARNING STYLE in which a child is given information or materials about a variety of specific situations and learns to draw a general conclusion or rule from them; also called *inductive learning.*

disinhibition, a pattern of responding to situations without constraint often found in children with LEARNING DISABILITIES or MENTAL DISORDERS, who are unable to stop themselves from responding to the variety of distracting stimuli in their environment.

displaced child syndrome, a pattern of responses sometimes seen in a child after the birth of a SIBLING, including jealousy, feelings of rejection by others, irritability, and easy discouragement; related to SEPARATION ANXIETY.

displacement, a type of DEFENSE MECHANISM, in which a child (or adult) transfers emotional focus (CATHEXIS) away from a troubling thought or feeling to a less frightening or painful one.

dispositional conference, a multidisciplinary meeting, often involving a SOCIAL WORKER, PEDIATRICIAN, and PSYCHOLOGIST or PSYCHIATRIST, at which decisions are made about short-term CUSTODY of a child in cases of possible CHILD ABUSE AND NEGLECT. At a later *dispositional hearing*, a court or administrative official may decide longer-term questions about the child's CUSTODY.

dissociative disorders, a class of MENTAL DISORDERS characterized by disturbance and sometimes fracturing (dissociation) of consciousness, memory, and identity; also called *hysterical neuroses, dissociative type*. Among those commonly affecting children is MULTIPLE PERSONALITY DISORDER. (See MENTAL DISORDERS.)

distance education, enrollment in an educational institution that has, instead of classes, sequenced lesson materials for a student to study and work on at home. Distance education is a relatively recent term that has replaced the older "home study" or "correspondence courses," but which has a broader meaning that includes courses involving lectures on television networks and on closed-circuit television. The student's completed lessons are mailed or otherwise conveyed to the school, where they are evaluated, corrected, and graded by school instructors and returned to the student with appropriate comments. Distance education courses vary widely. They may be part of degree programs (as for a HIGH SCHOOL or COLLEGE degree), combined with on-the-job training—courses to upgrade job skills without lost time from work, or standalone courses to gain certain skills or enhance interests. Some can be completed in a few weeks; others require several years of intensive study. Home study courses have traditionally been taken by adults or by former DROPOUTS. However, distance education now is widely used to teach children (or adults) who have DISABILITIES or CHRONIC ILLNESS so severe as to prevent them from attending normal classes. It is also used to bring educational resources to widely separated and often isolated settings, such as rural schools. Children studying at home under their parents' supervision are generally said to be in HOME SCHOOLING.

FOR HELP AND FURTHER INFORMATION

Distance Education and Training Council (DETC)
1601 18th Street NW
Washington, DC 20009–2529
202–234–5100
Fax: 202–332–1386
Michael Lambert, Executive Director
Organization that establishes standards and supplies accreditation for home study or correspondence schools, formerly National Home Study Council (NHSC); acts as information clearinghouse; publishes various materials, including semiannual *News*, *Directory of Accredited Institutions*, brochures *Is Home Study for You?*, *What Does Acreditation Mean to You?*, *Earning an Academic Degree Outside the Classroom*, and *Facts About the Distance Education and Training Council*.

ONLINE RESOURCES

Internet: Distance Education. Computer-based learning systems from TeleEducation, New Brunswick Department of Advanced Education and Labor.
gopher://gopher.ollc.mta.ca

OTHER RESOURCES

Personal Computers for Distance Education: The Study of an Educational Innovation. Anne Jones and others. St. Martin's, 1992.

distractibility, inability to focus for very long on any single task, instead tending to shift attention to new sights, sounds, or activities in the environment; a common problem among children with LEARNING DISABILITIES, especially ATTENTION DEFICIT HYPERACTIVITY DISORDER.

divorce, the termination of a marriage, a formal dissolution of the legal bonds between two people who feel they can no longer continue as a couple. A divorce is actually the end of a process that, legally, begins with a physical separation and is generally first codified in a SEPARATION AGREEMENT. This is the document that lays out the new rights and responsibilities of the two parties on continuing matters between them, including CUSTODY of any children, CHILD SUPPORT, alimony, division of marital property, insurance, and possible INHERITANCE RIGHTS or what share each may have in the other's estate at death.

Ideally, the parties should come to their own agreement on such issues. When they cannot, many turn to ARBITRATION or MEDIATION. Indeed, in some states, the parties are required to attempt mediation of their disputes. However, if they still cannot agree on such issues, a civil trial may be held, with attorneys for both sides calling witnesses and presenting evidence to a judge and in some cases a jury.

Until recent decades, divorces were generally granted only in limited situations when one of the parties offered legal bases, or *grounds*, for divorce, such as adultery or

ABANDONMENT. Divorce was therefore formally an adversarial proceeding, even when wife and husband agreed that the marriage was beyond repair. In more recent years, many states have begun to offer nonadversarial proceedings called *no-fault divorces*, in which partners can mutually agree to dissolve the marriage, based on incompatibility, irreconcilable differences, or irretrievable breakdown of the marital relationship. The precise terms of divorce vary from state to state, but some offer virtual *divorce on demand*, in which both parties (or sometimes just one party) say that the marriage is unsalvageable and often when the parties have lived apart voluntarily for a period of time.

Unfortunately, adversarial approaches have continued. Some couples have strong animosity over the split, as when only one party wishes to get a divorce. And in many divorces, the parties disagree on key issues, including custody, child support, alimony, and division of marital property. Adversarial stances have also continued partly because the so-called "guilty" party often fares less well in court decisions on contested issues.

Divorce has become so common that approximately two children in five now grow up in families in which there has been a divorce. The traditional stigma of divorce has lessened, but the pain and trauma for children shows no sign of abating. It is made worse in cases of acrimonious, adversarial disputes, which sometimes involve publicly smearing the other party, as with charges of child abuse. Many parents also actively try to break down a child's love and respect for the ex-partner, in what is called the *parental alienation syndrome.*

In attempts to confront parents with the damage they may be doing to their children (not to mention themselves) in vicious divorces, courts in some parts of the country are requiring divorcing parents to attend seminars about the effects their children may face and ways to avoid them. One such model program in Georgia uses a mix of lectures, films, and role-playing by paired leaders to give a child's-eye view of divorce, often through dramatizations of parental conflict scenarios. The program is designed to get parents to think about how their actions affect their children.

Many young children mistakenly assume that they have somehow caused the parental conflict and separation. Both younger and older children of divorce often experience behavioral and academic problems, as well as difficulty in establishing lasting relationships themselves. Contrary to earlier assumptions, some evidence suggests that older children are most affected in the long run, possibly because they are caught in the pre-separation battleground for longer than younger children. Indeed, conflict itself is responsible for much of the damage—before, during, and after the divorce.

Remarriage of one or both parents adds even more complicating elements to the equation. For children, the success and stability of the new "blended" families depends greatly on the level of continuing conflict among their parents and stepparents. In fact, when parental conflict persists, some studies indicate that the pattern of switching children back and forth from one parent's residence to the other's may do more harm than good. Indeed, some studies have shown that when parents are in sharp conflict, children in families that are still intact can suffer effects similar to those from divorced families.

Beyond the conflict, divorce brings massive disruption to children's lives, and often results in the children effectively losing one parent. A 1991 national survey of over 1,400 children from divorced families found that an astonishing 23 percent of the fathers had had no contact with their children for the previous five years and another 20 percent of fathers had not seen their children at all during the preceding year. Many fathers fail to maintain child support payments; even when they do, the level of support for the mother and children is generally lower than when the family was together. Many children of divorce also feel abandoned when, as often happens, the support payments stop at age 18; many divorced fathers—even professionals with comfortable incomes—fail to contribute to their children's college education.

Because divorce adversely affects so many children, some schools are running special support groups and counseling programs for "divorced kids" modeled on a program established in Ballston Spa, New York, in 1978. In the "Banana Splits" program, children from divorced families gather weekly, under the leadership of school psychologists, to share their experiences and provide support and encouragement for each other. Across the United States, such programs operate in elementary schools, with different age groups meeting separately, and increasingly in high schools as well. Programs are voluntary and often require parental consent. Matters discussed are generally confidential, but the adult leader may ask a child's permission to discuss a particular matter that warrants special attention with a parent.

In the end, it is up to parents themselves to help children deal with the myriad questions surrounding divorce, remarriage, and single parenting.

FOR HELP AND FURTHER INFORMATION

Association of Family and Conciliation Courts (AFCC)
329 W. Wilson
Madison, WI 53703
608–251–4001
Fax: 608–251–2231
Interdisciplinary organization of professionals concerned with constructive resolution of family disputes; provides information and referrals; publishes various materials, including pamphlets *Parents Are Forever*, *Twenty Questions Divorcing Parents Ask About Their Children*, and *Guide for a Successful Marriage*; booklet *Children and Divorce*; videos *Children in the Middle* (for group use), *It's Still Your Choice*, *You're Still Mum and Dad*, and *The Economic Impact of Divorce—It's More Than Dollars and Cents*; and numerous professional materials.

Johnson Institute, 800–231–5165, U.S. except MN. (For full group information, see HELP AGAINST SUBSTANCE ABUSE on page 703.) Publishes various materials, including:

- For parents: *Parenting Alone: Raising Your Children After One Parent Leaves, The Divorce Workbook: A Guide for Kids and Families, Helping Children Cope with Separation and Loss, Changing Families: A Guide for Kids and Grown-ups, When One Parent Leaves: Surviving the Loss Without Alcohol and Other Drugs.*
- For children: *Thomas Barker Talks About Divorce and Separation, I Wish I Could Hold Your Hand...A Child's Guide to Grief and Loss,* and *My Kind of Family: A Book for Kids in Single-Parent Homes.*
- Materials for support programs.

Parents Without Partners (PWP), 800–637–7974. Publishes book *My Mom and Dad Are Getting a Divorce* and reading lists for children and parents. (For full group information, see GENERAL PARENTING RESOURCES on page 634.)

National Association for the Education of Young Children (NAEYC), 800–424–2460. Publishes book *Caring: Supporting Children's Growth,* on dealing with problems such as divorce, abuse, and death. (For full group information, see PRESCHOOL.)

National Mental Health Association (NMHA), 800–969–6642. Publishes *Coping with Separation and Divorce, Helping a Child Cope with Separation and Divorce,* and *Helping a Child Build a Full Life with One Parent.* (For full group information, see MENTAL DISORDERS.)

American Academy of Pediatrics (AAP), 800–433–9016. Publishes brochure *Divorce and Children* and *Single Parenting.* (For full group information, see HEALTH CARE.)

National Center for Women and Family Law, 212–674–8200. Publishes *Studies on the Economic Impact of Divorce on Women and Children.* (For full group information, see CUSTODY; for more titles, see BATTERED WOMEN; CHILD SUPPORT.)

American Academy of Child and Adolescent Psychiatry (AACAP), 202–966–7300. Publishes information sheet *Children and Divorce.* (For full group information, see MENTAL DISORDERS.)

Help Abolish Legal Tyranny (HALT), 202–347–9600. (For full group information, see CUSTODY.)

CALM, Inc. (Custody Action for Lesbian Mothers), 610–667–7508. (For full group information, see CUSTODY.)

National Woman's Christian Temperance Union (WCTU), 800–755–1321. Publishes booklet *Divorce in the Family.* (For full group information, see HELP AGAINST SUBSTANCE ABUSE on page 703.)

ONLINE RESOURCES

Issues in Mental Health (America Online: IMH). Provides discussion forum and online library covering divorce and separation. (Location: Lifestyles and Interests, Issues in Mental Health.) (For full information, see MENTAL DISORDERS.)

OTHER RESOURCES

GENERAL WORKS

Divorce Help Sourcebook. Margorie Engel. Gale, 1994.
The Divorce Book. Harriet N. Cohen and Ralph Gardner, Jr. Avon, 1994.
Healthy Divorce. Sandra V. Everett and Craig A. Everett. Jossey-Bass, 1994.
Good Divorce. C. Ahrons. HarperCollins, 1994.
The Divorced Dad Dilemma: A Father's Guide to Understanding, Grieving and Growing Beyond the Losses of Divorce and to Developing a Deeper, Ongoing Relationships with His Children. Gerald S. Mayer. Desert City Press, 1994.
Divorce Wars No More. Stephen K. Erickson. CPI, 1993.
Divorce, a Four Letter Word. Peter L. Grieco, Jr. and Michael J. Termini. PT Publications, 1993.
Divorce Dirty Tricks. Joan Brovins and Thomas Oehmke. Lifetime, 1993.
Divorce and New Beginnings: An Authoritative Guide to Recovery and Growth, Solo Parenting, and Stepfamilies. Genevieve Clapp. Wiley, 1992.
Between Love and Hate: A Guide to Civilized Divorce. L. Gold. Plenum, 1992.
Vicki Lansky's Divorce Book. Vicki Lansky. NAL-Dutton, 1991.
Divorce Without Guilt. Robert Preston and Cheryl Preston. Center for Dynamic Living, 1991.
On Divorce. Louis De Bonald. Transaction Publishers, 1991.
Answers: A Divorce—Separation Survival Handbook. Divorce Support, 1991.
Long-Distance Parenting: A Guide for Divorced Parents. Miriam G. Cohen. NAL-Dutton, 1991.
Divorce Yourself: The National No-Fault Divorce Kit, rev. ed. Daniel Sitarz. Nova, 1991.

ON TRYING TO AVOID DIVORCE

Divorce Busting. Michele Weiner-Davis. Simon & Schuster, 1993.
Reconcilable Differences: Mending Broken Relationships, rev. ed. Jim Talley. Nelson, 1991.
Divorce Won't Help, rev. ed. Edmund Berlger. International Universities Press, 1991.
Alternative to Divorce, 4th ed. James R. Hine. Interstate, 1990.

On divorce mediation

Mediate Your Divorce and Save Attorneys' Fees. Paula Latimer. P. Latimer, 1993.

A Guide to Divorce Mediation: How to Reach a Fair, Legal Settlement at a Fraction of the Cost. Gary J. Friedman. Workman, 1993.

Divorcing with Dignity: Mediation: the Sensible Alternative. Tim Emerick-Cayton. Westminster John Knox, 1993.

On helping children deal with divorce

Helping Your Grandchildren Through Their Parents' Divorce. Joan S. Cohen. Walker, 1994.

Helping Children Cope with Divorce. Jane C. Sacknowitz. Bureau for At-Risk Youth, 1992.

Helping Children Cope with Divorce. Edward Teyber. Free Press, 1992.

For the Sake of the Children: How to Share Your Children with Your Ex-Spouse—in Spite of Your Anger. Kris Kline and Stephen Pew. Prima, 1992.

Divorced Kids: What You Need to Know to Help Kids Survive a Divorce. Laurene Johnson and Georgelyn Rosenfeld. Nelson, 1990.

For children

My Life Turned Upside Down but I Turned It Rightside Up. Mary B. Field and Hennie Shore. Center for Applied Psychology, 1994.

Mike's Lonely Summer: A Child's Guide to Divorce. Carolyn Nystrom. Lion, 1994.

Growing up with Divorce. Rona D. Schenkerman. Bureau for At-Risk Youth, 1993.

I Have Two Dads. Linnea Schulz. Centering Corp., 1993.

My Parents Got a Divorce. Gary Sprague. Chariot Family, 1992.

When is Daddy Coming Home?: A Workbook for Children of Divorce. Darlene Weyborne. Aronson, 1992.

Safely Through the Storm: Divorce Recovery for Kids. Dan Quello. Harvest House, 1992.

Living with Divorce. Elizabeth Garigan and Michael Urbanski. Good Apple, 1991.

At Daddy's on Saturdays. Linda Walvoord Girard. Albert Whitman, 1991.

D Is for Divorce. Lori Peters Norris. Health Communications, 1991.

For preteens and teens

Pulling Yourself Together When Your Parents Are Pulling Apart. Angela E. Hunt. Tyndale, 1995.

How to Survive Your Parents' Divorce. Nancy O. Bolick. Watts, 1994.

How to Survive Your Parents' Divorce: Kids' Advice to Kids. Gayle Kimball. Equality Press, 1994.

If My Parents Are Getting Divorced, Why Am I the One Who Hurts? Jeanie Gordon. Zondervan, 1993.

Divorce Recovery for Teenagers. Steve Murray and Randy Smith. Zondervan, 1991.

On effects of divorce on children

Innocent Victims: Understanding the Needs and Fears of Your Children. Thomas Whiteman. Nelson, 1993.

Growing up Divorced. Diane Fassell. Pocket Books, 1992.

Divorced Kids. Laurene Johnson and Georgelyn Rosenfeld. Fawcett, 1992.

Parents Whose Parents Were Divorced. R. Thomas Berner. Haworth, 1992.

Children of Divorce. Debbie Barr. Zondervan, 1992. Originally titled: *Caught in the Crossfire.*

Divided Families: What Happens to Children When Parents Part. Frank F. Furstenberg, Jr. and Andrew J. Cherlin. Harvard University Press, 1991.

Your Child: Living with Divorce. Better Homes and Gardens Editors. Meredith, 1990.

Background works

The Responsible Parent: A Study in Divorce Mediation. Christine Piper. Prentice Hall, 1994.

The Parental Alienation Syndrome: A Guide for Mental Health and Legal Professionals. Richard A. Gardner. Creative Therapeutics, 1992.

DNA, complex molecules that make up genes and carry the basic information about a person's GENETIC INHERITANCE; essentially the building blocks of life. DNA is an abbreviation for *deoxyribonucleic acid.*

doctoral degree (doctor's degree or doctorate), the highest degree offered for GRADUATE studies, beyond the MASTER'S DEGREE. A doctorate, often a *Ph. D.* (doctorate of philosophy), is awarded to a student who has successfully completed a specified program that normally requires at least three or four years of study beyond the BACHELOR'S DEGREE.

domains, in EDUCATION, a general term for areas of learning and behavior that refers to three key categories of instructional content and learning objectives described by Benjamin Bloom in the 1950s: *affective domain, cognitive domain,* and *psychomotor domain.* The affective domain refers to feelings, emotions, values, and attitudes (AFFECT being a psychological word for shown feelings). The cognitive domain covers thinking skills such as problem-solving, memory and recall, comprehension, reasoning, and judgment. The psychomotor domain refers to a child's physical and muscular functioning. These domains are often referred to by educators planning CURRICULUM, such as the courses in an INDIVIDUALIZED EDUCATION PLAN for a child with DISABILITIES, which has specific learning objectives planned for each area. The term *domain* has also been used to refer to other categories of learning.

domestic relations court, the type of civil court that handles DIVORCE and CUSTODY cases resulting from divorce or separation. In some states, the role of the domestic relations court is taken over by the FAMILY COURT. Some domestic relations courts also have an affiliated COURT OF CONCILIATION, staffed by professional counselors rather than legal personnel, to facilitate reconciliations.

dominance, the tendency of a person to rely most heavily on—and to be most easy and proficient at using—one eye, ear, hand, or foot over the other; sometimes called *sidedness.* In relation to preference for the right or left hand, dominance may be called HANDEDNESS. Dominance in hands, eyes, and feet is believed to reflect *cerebral dominance* of one hemisphere of the brain over the other, the right side of the brain corresponding to the left side of the body, and vice versa. Generally the preferred eye, hand, and foot are all on the same side of the body, left or right. But in some people, including many with LEARNING DISABILITIES, they are not. So a child might, for example, be right-footed and right-eyed, but left-handed. Such a condition is called *cross dominance* or *mixed dominance.* In some young children with learning disabilities, dominance (including handedness) is not fully established, and they often confuse left with right. A condition in which neither eye dominates is called *ambieyedness,* as an equally proficient use of the hands is called *ambidextrous.*

dominant, in GENETIC INHERITANCE, a gene that produces its effect regardless of the information coded on its paired gene. If one parent contributes a dominant gene for curly hair, for example, the child will have curly hair, no matter what gene the other parent contributed to the pair. With normal genes, this causes no problem, but if the dominant gene is defective, then the child will inherit a GENETIC DISORDER.

The expression of a gene may be modified by other genes, by a person's unique environment, sometimes even by which parent contributed the gene. In the case of a defective gene, this means that symptoms can range from severe to unnoticeable. Parents who have a family history including any genetic disorder may want to seek GENETIC COUNSELING, to see if they are unknowingly carrying a dominant gene for a genetic disorder. Among the common disorders carried by dominant genes are HUNTINGTON'S CHOREA, ACHONDROPLASIA, POLYDACTYLY, MARFAN'S SYNDROME, NEUROFIBROMATOSIS, OSTEOGENESIS IMPERFECTA (brittle bone disease), and hypercholesterolemia (high blood CHOLESTEROL). A parent who carries a gene for a dominant disorder has a 50 percent chance to passing that gene on to a child (see AUTOSOMAL DOMINANT), so GENETIC SCREENING of the FETUS may be advisable. (See GENETIC DISORDERS.)

douching, use of a fluid to rinse out a woman's VAGINA. Generally the fluid is placed in a bag held above waist height; it flows under pressure through a tube placed in the vagina. Douching is done for a variety of reasons, among them:

- *Hygiene,* the idea being that bathing the vagina is comparable to washing the rest of the body, as after MENSTRUATION or use of a SPERMICIDE. However, the vagina is self-cleansing, so douching is neither necessary nor medically recommended. Indeed, many health professionals note that douching reduces the natural acidity of the vaginal fluids, which may allow readier growth of infectious organisms. The pressure of the fluid used may push disease-causing organisms further into the UTERUS and FALLOPIAN TUBES, making PELVIC INFLAMMATORY DISEASE more likely.
- *Fighting disease,* as a home remedy for vaginal infections. However, the above concerns apply here as well. Also, except where a sterile disposable device is used, the douche tube can *introduce* infection into the vagina.
- *BIRTH CONTROL,* though it is quite unreliable for these purposes, its effectiveness in preventing PREGNANCY being rated at from 60 percent to zero. It is ineffective because SPERM can travel very quickly, often passing beyond the vagina and into the CERVIX in only a minute or two. The pressure of the douching fluid can even speed some sperm on their route. Women attempting to become pregnant should also realize that douching *before* sexual intercourse or ARTIFICIAL INSEMINATION can decrease the chances of CONCEPTION by washing away cervical mucus that helps draw sperm into and through the cervix.
- SEX SELECTION, attempts to alter the acidity-alkalinity balance of the vaginal fluids to favor sperm-carrying chromosomes for a baby of the desired sex.

Women who wish to douche for personal cleanliness should discuss with their doctor when, how, how often, and what fluids to use. Some over-the-counter sprays and douches can cause irritation or ALLERGIES and can mask symptoms of an infection, allowing it to spread internally unnoticed. If standard nondisposable douche bags are used, they should be washed carefully and stored clean and dry, so as not to provide a growing place for bacteria or other disease-causing organisms. Certainly women should not douche if they suspect they may be pregnant; after any gynecological procedure, such as an ABORTION; after CHILDBIRTH, until the doctor approves; and before a GYNECOLOGICAL EXAMINATION, since it may flush away signs of infection before they can be recognized and analyzed. (See VAGINA; BIRTH CONTROL.)

Down syndrome, a CONGENITAL condition resulting from a CHROMOSOMAL ABNORMALITY, usually the existence of three copies (TRISOMY) of chromosome 21, instead of the normal two; also called *Down's syndrome, trisomy 21, congenital acromicria,* or *mongolism.* Down syndrome is the most common cause of MENTAL RETARDATION, affecting about 1 in approximately 800 to 1,000 births in the

United States. What triggers the improper cell division is unknown; viral infections, hormonal abnormalities, IMMUNE SYSTEM problems, X-rays, DRUGS, and GENETIC DISORDERS are all being explored.

Women who are over thirty-five or have Down syndrome in their family history have long been known to be at special risk of having a child with the syndrome. More recently, research has suggested that FATHERS over fifty have an increased risk of having a child with Down syndrome. However, 80 percent of babies with Down syndrome were born to parents under those ages. Both parents may want to seek GENETIC COUNSELING before PREGNANCY or have GENETIC SCREENING during the early stage of pregnancy, using such tests as AMNIOCENTESIS and CHORIONIC VILLUS SAMPLING to see if the FETUS has Down syndrome. The results of these tests leave open the options of selective ABORTION or of preparing for a SPECIAL CHILD.

Children with Down syndrome characteristically have eyes that slope upward at the outer corners and are partly covered by *epicanthal folds*, folds of skin on the inner corners, giving them a supposedly "Asian" appearance (which gave rise to the earlier name *mongolism*). They also tend to have small facial features, a large tongue, a skull flattened in the back, hyperflexible joints, one bending site on the fifth fingers (instead of the usual two), and hands with a single horizontal palm crease. As newborns, they commonly lack the MORO REFLEX. Down syndrome children are unusually likely to have heart and circulatory defects (see HEART AND HEART PROBLEMS), ATRESIA (narrowing) in the intestinal system, EAR AND HEARING PROBLEMS, and LEUKEMIA—so much so that in previous decades relatively few reached full adulthood. However, many of these problems are now treatable with medication and surgery, and the average life expectancy of a person with Down syndrome is approximately fifty-five years.

No treatment is known to alter the course of Down syndrome. Some parents have tried a controversial *cell therapy*, using INJECTIONS of fetal sheep and rabbit cells, which its European developers claim improves MOTOR and SOCIAL SKILLS in Down syndrome children. This treatment has not been approved by the FOOD AND DRUG ADMINISTRATION, and scientific studies so far fail to support the claim. Reports of progress among some children may, some scientists suggest, be due to additional attention. Supporters of the therapy say the studies were flawed, since most children tested received only one shot, rather than repeated treatment.

In the past, many children with Down syndrome were placed in a LONG-TERM CARE facility from infancy. However, they have been shown to benefit greatly from EARLY INTERVENTION, as through sensory stimulation in infancy and exercises to develop their MOTOR SKILLS, language skills, COGNITIVE DEVELOPMENT, and SELF-HELP SKILLS. As a result, many are now raised at home, with their parents often receiving advice and help from organizations (such as those listed in this entry) and parent support groups. Down syndrome children do require special care, however, which can place a strain on a family; when a parent or FAMILY feels unable to raise the child, many are placed with adoptive families.

Children with Down syndrome develop more slowly; for example, they generally begin walking at eighteen to thirty-six months, rather than twelve to fourteen months. However, their range of development is far greater than was previously recognized. The reading level of adults with Down syndrome ranges between third-grade and twelfth-grade levels, averaging around sixth-grade level. Their average IQ is approximately 70 to 75. Fewer than 5 percent are severely or profoundly mentally retarded, requiring close care throughout their lifetimes. Others have benefited greatly from the EDUCATION FOR ALL HANDICAPPED CHILDREN ACT and its successor, the INDIVIDUALS WITH DISABILITIES EDUCATION ACT, and after completing their schooling are able to work in supportive, supervised employment settings. Today the aim is to help people with Down syndrome live as independently as possible, often with some assistance (see MENTAL RETARDATION; GROUP HOME; SUPPORTED EMPLOYMENT). The development of GROUP HOMES has provided comfortable living settings for many people with Down syndrome.

FOR HELP AND FURTHER INFORMATION

National Down Syndrome Society (NDSS)
666 Broadway, 8th Floor
New York, NY 10012–2317
212–460–9330; 800–221–4602
Fax: 212–979–2873
Myra Marnick, Executive Director
Organization concerned with Down syndrome; publishes various materials, including:

- Newsletter *Update* and magazine *News 'n Views*, written by and for young adults with Down syndrome.
- Fact sheets: *Down Syndrome, Questions and Answers About Down Syndrome, Down Syndrome: Myths and Truths, The Heart and Down Syndrome, The Neurology of Down Syndrome, Endocrine Conditions and Down Syndrome, Sexuality and Down Syndrome,* and *Alzheimer's Disease and Down Syndrome.*
- *Down Syndrome: Living and Learning in the Community, Project Child Respite Manual,* and *Home Based Computer Program for Children with Down Syndrome.*
- Videos: *Gifts of Love*—on raising young children with Down syndrome, its sequel *Opportunities to Grow, This Baby Needs You Even More*—for new parents of children with Down syndrome, *A World of Opportunities, Employability, Bittersweet Waltz,* on a boy's first year in a regular fifth grade class, and *Bernardsville Beginnings,* following a first-grader for a year in an inclusion program.
- List of suggested readings and health care materials for professionals.

National Down Syndrome Congress (NDSC)
1605 Chantilly Drive, Suite 250
Atlanta, GA 30324

404–633–1555; 800–232-NDSC [232–6372]
Fax: 404–633–2817
Frank Murphy, Executive Director
Organization concerned with Down syndrome; seeks to enhance the dignity and personal horizons of people with Down; advises parents; publishes *Down Syndrome News, Facts About Down Syndrome,* pamphlet *Down Syndrome,* parent groups alerts, and bibliography.

Association for Children with Down Syndrome (ACDS)
2616 Martin Avenue
Bellmore, Long Island, NY 11710
516–221–4700
Fax: 516–221–4311
Organization focusing on inclusion and programs for children with Down syndrome; encourages parental advocacy; publishes various materials, including bimonthly newsletter *Spot Lite*; books *Down Syndrome Developmental Milestones* and *Special Kids Make Special Friends* (on helping young children and new parents better understand Down syndrome); and videos *A Different Kind Of Beginning, Special Days with Special Kids, A Special Love,* and *A Day at ACDS.*

National Institute of Child Health and Human Development (NICHD), 301–496–5133. Publishes *Facts About Down Syndrome.* (For full group information, see PREGNANCY.)

March of Dimes Birth Defects Foundation (MDBDF), 914–428–7100. Publishes information sheet *Down Syndrome.* (For full group information, see BIRTH DEFECTS.)

Council for Exceptional Children (CEC), 800–328–0272. Publishes special report *Down Syndrome.* (For full group information, see HELP ON LEARNING AND EDUCATION on page 659.)

National Information Center for Children and Youth with Disabilities (NICHCY), 800–695–0285, voice/TT. Publishes *Down Syndrome.* (For full group information, see HELP FOR SPECIAL CHILDREN on page 689.)

The Arc, 817–261–6003. Publishes *An Overview of Down Syndrome* and fact sheets *Down Syndrome.* (For full group information, see MENTAL RETARDATION.)

PACER Center (Parent Advocacy Coalition for Educational Rights), 612–827–2966, voice/TT. Publishes *Princess Margaret's Adventures in Wonderland,* by a 17-year-old with Down syndrome. (For full group information, see HELP FOR SPECIAL CHILDREN on page 689.)

National Easter Seal Society, 800–221–6827. Publishes *Understanding Down Syndrome.* (For full group information, see HELP FOR SPECIAL CHILDREN on page 689.)

Parents Helping Parents (PHP), 408–727–5775. Has division focusing on Down syndrome; publishes information packet *Down Syndrome.* (For full group information, see HELP FOR SPECIAL CHILDREN on page 689.)

National Organization for Rare Disorders (NORD), 800–999–6673. (For full group information, see RARE DISORDERS.)

ONLINE RESOURCES

Internet: Down Syndrome. For discussion. To subscribe, send this message "SUB downs-syndrome [your first name] [your last name]" to: mailto:listserv@vm1.nodak.edu

("Chat rooms" or "forums" are also available on America Online, CompuServe, and Prodigy.)

OTHER RESOURCES

FOR PARENTS

Teaching Reading to Children with Down Syndrome: A Guide for Parents and Teachers. Patricia Oelwein. Woodbine, 1995.
Keys to Parenting a Child with Down Syndrome. Marlene Targ Brill. Barron's, 1993.
Differences in Common: Straight Talk on Mental Retardation, Down Syndrome and Life. Marilyn Trainer. Woodbine, 1991.
A Parent's Guide to Down Syndrome: Toward a Brighter Future. Siegfried M. Pueschel. Brookes, 1990.
Down Syndrome, Now What Do I Do? Anne F. Squires and Andrew C. Squires. Indian Orchard, 1990.
Down Syndrome: The Facts. Mark Selikowitz. Oxford University Press, 1990.

ON EDUCATION AND DEVELOPMENT

Teaching Reading to Children with Down Syndrome: A Guide for Parents and Teachers. P. Oelwein. Woodbine, 1995.
Time to Begin: Early Education for Children with Down Syndrome. Valentine Dmitriev. Penn Cove Press, 1994.
Communication Skills in Children with Down Syndrome. Libby Kumin. Woodbine, 1994.
Communicating Together. Bimonthly newsletter for parents and professionals about speech and language skills in children with Down syndrome. Address: P.O. Box 6395, Columbia, MD 21045–6395; 410–995–0722.

FOR CHILDREN

Thumbs Up Rico! Maria Testa. Whitman, 1994.
Are There Stripes in Heaven? Lee Klein. Paulie, 1994.
Chris Burke: He Overcame Down Syndrome. Gregory Lee. Rourke, 1993.
My Special Brother. Lena Schiff. CIS Communications, 1991.
We Can Do It! L. Dwight. Checkerboard Press, 1992.
Charlsie's Chuckle. Clara Widess Berkus. Woodbine, 1992.

FOR OR BY ADOLESCENTS

Count Us In: Growing Up with Down Syndrome. Jason Kingsley and Mitchell Levitz. Harcourt Brace, 1994. By two young men with Down syndrome.

A Special Kind of Hero. Chris Burke and Jo Beth McDaniel. Bantam, 1991. By the star of television's *Life Goes On,* now an editor of *News 'n Views,* from the National Down Syndrome Society.

Personal experiences

Down Is Up for Aaron Eagle: A Mother's Spiritual Journey with Down's Syndrome. Vicki Nobel. HarperCollins, 1993.
Our Special Child, 2nd ed. Bette M. Ross. Nelson, 1993.
Angel Unaware. Dale E. Rogers. Revell, 1992.

(See also GENETIC DISORDERS; GENETIC COUNSELING; MENTAL RETARDATION; and also HELP FOR SPECIAL CHILDREN on page 689.)

draw-a-person test, a type of PROJECTIVE TEST in which psychologists attempt to discern a child's personality characteristics from drawings of the self and others. Also, a general term for a draw-a-person task in various other tests, such as the GOODENOUGH-HARRIS DRAWING TEST or the ABC INVENTORY, where it may be used to measure nonverbal intelligence.

dropout, a student who has stopped attending school before graduating or completing a given course of study, whether the student is under COMPULSORY SCHOOL AGE or over. Considerable attention, effort, and analysis has gone into trying to understand why students drop out and how to keep them from doing so. Some schools have special programs to try to maintain students identified as potential dropouts or to bring back to school some who have already left. Dropouts who later wish to continue their schooling can study, on their own or in groups, to take a series of TESTS OF GENERAL EDUCATIONAL DEVELOPMENT. If they pass, they are awarded a certificate of high school equivalency, commonly called a GENERAL EQUIVALENCY DIPLOMA (GED).

drug abuse, physical and psychological dependence on chemical substances, including over-the-counter drugs, prescribed medications, or illicit substances, when the drugs are used primarily for the physical and emotional effects they produce, rather than for any therapeutic reasons. While some drug abuse results when a person becomes dependent on a drug initially used for therapeutic reasons, such as tranquilizers, drug abuse more often results from experimentation with so-called recreational drugs, especially during the vulnerable and uncertain period of ADOLESCENCE.

With regular or heavy use, various physical changes occur as the body becomes dependent on the drug, so that if use ends, severe physical and mental distress called *withdrawal symptoms* result. Once drug abuse is established, a person often needs to enter a special treatment program during the withdrawal period. Drug abuse is certainly one of the major social problems in the world today and one of the major challenges facing parents of young children, not only because of the abuse itself but also because of the possibly life-threatening infections that are often linked with drug use, notably AIDS and hepatitis (see LIVER AND LIVER PROBLEMS).

Because of its importance, many parents are working actively on prevention programs aimed at young children, hoping to head off drug use before it begins. Some parents have even begun to use home drug tests to try to see if their children are using drugs. However, this may have the unintended effect of driving parent and child further apart and short-circuiting the lines of communication that need to be kept open if parents are to be able to help their children avoid drugs—or to give them up, once started. Parents should also be wary about giving too much credence to HOME MEDICAL TESTS. (For an overview of the effects and signs of drug and other substance abuse, plus organizations, reference works, and recommendations for parents, see HELP AGAINST SUBSTANCE ABUSE on page 703.)

drug reactions and interactions, undesired effects on a person from a medication or effects that result from mixing two or more different drugs. Reactions or effects from interactions can range from a mild rash to life-threatening SHOCK, as in cases of penicillin ALLERGY. Drugs are powerful chemicals that can do much good, but can also cause unintended harm.

For the safety of children, the most important rule regarding drugs may be for pregnant women and for children to take *no* drugs without a doctor's supervision. During PREGNANCY, a fetus is enormously vulnerable to BIRTH DEFECTS, especially during the early months, so drugs should be avoided whenever possible. If medication is required, the doctor will prescribe only those drugs believed to have no adverse effects on the pregnancy. A pregnant woman should take medications only when absolutely necessary, because a medication may have an unusual effect on her and on her fetus; sometimes, despite careful testing, drugs can damage a fetus in previously unrecognized ways.

Children, too, are enormously vulnerable to damage from drugs. Parents should not assume that children are just "small adults" and give them small doses of adult medicines. In fact, the vital organs, such as the liver, kidneys, and intestinal tract of infants and young children mature only over some years. Before that maturation takes place, a child's body cannot break down, use, and eliminate drugs the way an adult's can, so drugs can build up in the body to toxic levels.

In general, parents should be aware of the known side effects of any medicines the child is taking. When a drug is prescribed, they should ask the doctors to explain possible side effects (see WHAT SHOULD YOU ASK YOU DOCTOR ABOUT A NEW MEDICATION? on page 193). Parents may also want to ask the druggist for a copy of the manufacturer's leaflet about the drug and possible side effects. For some drugs, such as contraceptives and estrogens, the FDA requires that a leaflet be provided to the patient. This information can also be found in a standard annual reference, *The Physician's Desk Reference*, available in many libraries. Nonprescription drugs are required to carry these labels on the package. For safety, it is important to read such labels carefully.

Parents also need to know if there are any warnings to be followed. A patient taking a particular medication might be warned to stay out of the sun, drink plenty of water, or avoid citrus juices, for example. Sometimes this is because the drug will work less effectively—for instance, dairy products may impair absorption of the antibiotic tetracycline—but sometimes it is to avoid unwanted side effects. In some cases, the drugs may have the effect of altering the body's handling of food; BIRTH CONTROL PILLS, for example, lower the level of FOLIC ACID in the blood, so women who are on the pill should eat plenty of dark green leafy vegetables, to ensure a sufficient amount of this important vitamin. Some pills should be taken before eating, some after, and some with food. Patients need to know when and how to take the medication for proper effectiveness—and to avoid unnecessary upset to the digestive system.

Many medications have dangerous interactions with alcohol. For example, taking Tylenol while continuing to drink alcoholic beverages has been linked with liver failure in some people, who subsequently required liver TRANSPLANTS for survival. Parents need to be aware of such possible hazards for themselves, but also for their young children and especially teens. This is a special problem when children have a kind of DISABILITY or CHRONIC illness that requires them to be on some kind of medication all the time. Since the temptation to try alcohol in their teens is great, children who take certain prescribed drugs can be endangered.

If parent or child is taking other medications (perhaps prescribed for a different condition by a different doctor), is on a special diet, is taking vitamin or mineral supplements, or is pregnant, the doctor needs to know that before prescribing a new medication. Sometimes if two drugs are taken together, one will partially block the action of the other. Or, conversely, sometimes two drugs together can have a more powerful impact. If this is by design, well and good; often, indeed, doctors will prescribe two drugs to be taken at once, such as an antihistamine and aspirin. However, if two noncomplementary drugs are taken together, the unintended effects can be dangerous, as when someone inadvertently takes two drugs that each depress the CENTRAL NERVOUS SYSTEM. It is this combination that makes alcohol and some drugs so deadly. SMOKING can also change the body's response to drugs, so if someone starts or stops smoking while on a long-term course of medication, the dosage may need to be changed.

Parents should also raise the question of generic drugs with their doctor. A company that discovers and develops a new medication receives a seventeen-year patent, giving it exclusive rights to market the drug under its *brand name* or *trade name*. After this seventeen-year period

What Should You Ask Your Doctor About a New Medication?

For safety, parents should ask the following questions about any new medication prescribed for themselves or their children.

- What is the name of the medication? Write it down so you won't forget it and will be able to research it, if appropriate.
- What is the medication supposed to do? For example, is it intended to make the pain go away? Treat the cause of the pain? Reduce fever? Lower blood pressure? Cure an infection?
- What side effects might occur? Are any of them potentially serious?
- How should you take the medicine? Does "three times a day" mean morning, noon, and night? Should you take it with meals, before meals, or after meals? If the directions say "every six hours," should you get up during the night to take the medicine on time?
- How long should you take the medicine? This is important to know because often people stop taking medication because they feel better but before the problem has been fully cured; in such cases it will recur.
- Are there other medicines, including vitamins and minerals, you should not take while you are taking this one?
- Are there any foods or beverages, including alcoholic drinks, that you should avoid while you are taking this medication?
- Should the prescription be filled with a brand name medication? Or is a generic medication equally effective?

Source: Adapted in part from "Here Are Some Things You Should Know About Prescription Drugs," FDA Consumer, *June, 1982.*

expires, other companies can manufacture and sell the drug under another brand name or under its common chemical name, called a *generic name.* Almost all states today allow pharmacists to fill a prescription with a generic drug, with the doctor's approval. In some cases, the pharmacist may even be required to fill the prescription with a generic drug, unless the doctor specified DAW—"dispense as written." Generic drugs are often much less expensive than brand name drugs. The problem is that they are often much less effective—in medical terms, "not therapeutically equivalent"—in some cases because their formulation is slightly different and in others because the company's products are highly variable. Studies have found that generic brands may vary by as much as 15 percent or more in their intended effects (and side effects) and in their rate of absorption from name brand drugs. Also, not all drugs are manufactured in a generic version. Parents should discuss with their doctor whether a generic drug is likely to be satisfactory. Many people prefer to avoid generic drugs, except for medications treating relatively minor problems.

Whenever they or their child begin taking a medication, parents should be alert for any possible side effects and consult a doctor quickly if any appear. Parents should also be extremely careful in dosage for children; a recent study found that many children were being given potentially dangerous overdosages of medicines, especially liquids, because parents failed to measure the dosage properly. In case of a reaction, a different medication or a different dosage may be recommended. Any serious reaction should be noted in the child's permanent medical record and also in the parent's personal health record for the child. These reactions should be mentioned to any future doctors before medication is prescribed.

During the course of treatment, the medication should be kept in its original container and stored safely out of reach of children. Many medications today come in child-resistant containers, but none is child*proof.* Children can do themselves great harm by opening medicine bottles and swallowing the contents; this includes nonprescription drugs such as iron pills, a very common danger. If some medication remains after the course of treatment is over, it should be stored as directed, often away from light or in the refrigerator. However, medications should never be given to someone for whom they were not prescribed. Those medications no longer needed should be flushed down the toilet and their containers thrown away.

Parents should also be wary of so-called "smart drugs" that are claimed to improve memory, concentration, or intelligence; elevate the normal brain to a higher-than-normal state; and even correct brain dysfunctions, such as EPILEPSY. The Food and Drug Administration (FDA) warns that no drugs or other products have been approved for these purposes. Such products, in many forms and from many sources, vary widely and may be made from a wide variety of ingredients. However, they have not been submitted to controlled scientific testing and no data supporting these claims has been submitted to the government. The FDA warns that using such drugs can be dangerous for several reasons:

- Imported drugs are not manufactured under the quality control standards of the United States, which are perhaps the strictest in the world.
- People are placing themselves at risk when they take prescription drugs without a doctor's supervision and when no evidence has shown that the drugs are either safe or effective.
- Even "healthful" and vital nutrients, such as vitamins and amino acids, can be harmful and sometimes toxic when taken in excess amounts.

Parents should not be misled by marketing claims and should alert their children to the possibility of misleading or misguided sales pitches.

FOR HELP AND FURTHER INFORMATION

Food and Drug Administration (FDA)
U.S. Department of Health and Human Services
Office of Consumer and Professional Affairs
5600 Fishers Lane
Rockville, MD 20857
Consumer Affairs Office: 301–443–3170 (1–3:30 PM ET); Medwatch (to receive form for reporting adverse reactions): 800–332–1088; Breast Implant Hotline: 800–532–4440; FDA Seafood Hotline (24 hours): 202–205–4314; 800-FDA–4010 [332–4010]
Internet Database: telnet://bbs@fdabbs.fda.gov
Federal department responsible for regulating foods, including labeling and safety; drugs, including approval, packaging, and prescription drug advertising; cosmetics, including safety; biological products, such as vaccines and blood; medical devices, including approval and registration; veterinary products, including foods, drugs, and devices; and radiological devices, providing safety standards and practices for such things as X-ray equipment, microwave ovens, television receivers, and lasers. Answers public queries about drug safety and proper drug use; collects information about adverse reactions to above products; publishes *The FDA Consumer,* alerts regarding recalls and product safety, and numerous materials for health professionals.

National Health Information Center
P.O. Box 1133
Washington, DC 20013–1133
301–565–4167; 800–336–4797
Federally sponsored service providing referrals to national nonprofit organizations or federal agencies best-suited to answer health questions, preferably in writing; maintains database, available to the public through DIRLINE, part of National Library of Medicine's MEDLARS system; publishes directories, resource guides, and bibliographies in print and electronic form, as well as *Healthy People 2000, Health Information Resources in the Federal Government,* and *Healthfinders,* resource lists on current concerns.

American Medical Association, 800–621–8335. Publishes *The AMA Guide to Prescription and Over-the-Counter Drugs.* (For full group information, see HEALTH CARE.)

American Allergy Association (AAA), 415–322–1663. Publishes allergy alerts about special problems such as dyes in medications, drug interactions, latex, and problem foods. (For full group information, see ALLERGY.)

National Chronic Pain Outreach Association, Inc. (NCPOA), 301–652–4948 Publishes *Avoiding an Adverse Drug Reaction* and materials on pain medications. (For full group information, see PAIN AND PAIN TREATMENT.)

National Clearinghouse for Alcohol and Drug Abuse Information (NCADI), 301–468–2600. Publishes *Alcohol Medication Interactions.* (For full group information, see HELP AGAINST SUBSTANCE ABUSE on page 703.)

National Institute of Child Health and Human Development (NICHD), 301–496–5133. Publishes *Transdermal Delivery of Drugs* (For full group information, see PREGNANCY.)

Self-Help for Hard of Hearing People (SHHH), 301–657–2248; 301-657–2249, TT. Publishes *Can Medication Affect My Hearing?* (For full group information, see EAR AND HEARING PROBLEMS.)

ONLINE RESOURCES

Recreational Pharmacology Server. Large collection of data sheets, answers to commonly asked questions, articles, and other resources, plus links to related sites. http://steinl.u.washington.edu:2012/pharm/pharm.html

OTHER RESOURCES

ON MEDICATIONS

Your Child's Medication: A Parent's Guide to Common Prescription and Over-the-Counter Medications. Karen S. Bond. Wiley, 1991.

The Pill Book Guide to Children's Medications. Michael Mitchell. Bantam, 1990.

The Complete Guide to Prescription and Non-Prescription Drugs, 7th ed. H. Winter Griffith. Body Press, 1990.

The Pill Book, 4th ed. Harold M. Silverman. Bantam, 1990.

The Intelligent Consumer's Pharmacy: The Complete User's Guide to Drugs, Vitamins and Other Chemical Products. Ellen Hodgson Brown and Lynn Paige Walker. Carroll & Graf, 1990.

The Essential Guide to Psychiatric Drugs. Jack M. Gorman. St. Martin's, 1990.

Psychiatric Drugs: A Consumer's Guide. Stuart Yudofsky and others. Grove Weidenfeld, 1990.

DTP vaccine, type of VACCINE given to provide IMMUNIZATION against three life-threatening childhood diseases: DIPHTHERIA, TETANUS (lockjaw), and WHOOPING COUGH (pertussis); also called the *DPT vaccine.* The vaccine is generally given as a series of five injections between the ages of two months and six years, with a sixth tetanus-diphteria (Td or DT) booster at ages eleven to twelve. All fifty states in the U.S. require children to be immunized against diphtheria before entering school; almost all require tetanus immunization, while about two-thirds require pertussis immunization.

Side effects from the diphtheria and tetanus vaccines are not common and usually consist only of soreness and slight fever. However, the pertussis vaccine has been controversial, since the traditional form, made from whole bacteria, can trigger some serious reactions. Most children will have a slight fever and will be irritable for one to two days after getting the DTP shot, and half will have soreness and swelling in the area of the injection. In approximately 1 case out of every 330, the child will have a temperature of 105°F or more. Perhaps 1 child in 100 will have continuous crying lasting three or more hours, and 1 in 900 will have unusual high-pitched crying. Convulsions or episodes of limpness and paleness occur in perhaps 1 of every 1,750 cases.

In general, parents are advised to check with the family doctor before a scheduled DTP vaccination if the child:

- Is sick at the time with something more serious than a cold.
- Has had a convulsion or is suspected of having a problem of the nervous system.
- Has had a serious reaction to any portion of the DTP vaccine, including any of the reactions described above.
- Is taking a drug or undergoing a treatment that lowers the body's resistance to infection, such as cortisone, prednisone, certain anticancer drugs, or irradiation, since they may diminish the effectiveness of the vaccine.
- Has a family history of convulsions in parents or siblings.

Depending on current public health guidelines, the doctor may consider that such children should not receive the pertussis portion of the vaccine, though they may still get a diphtheria-tetanus (DT) shot. However, because the risks of not receiving the vaccine are considerable (see WHOOPING COUGH), children are recommended to have the DTP vaccine whenever possible. On balance, then, the Public Health Service has continued to recommend the full DTP vaccine, with certain cautions. In the event of a convulsion at any time, including after the receipt of DTP, the child should be seen by a doctor as soon as possible. The doctor will determine whether the child should continue to receive the DTP vaccine or the DT instead.

Some large-scale studies have indicated that the risk of SEIZURES and CONVULSIONS is no greater among children receiving the pertussis vaccine than among those who do not receive it. In recent years, a new form of pertussis vaccine has been developed. This one does not include the whole cells of pertussis bacteria (unlike the traditional pertussis vaccines), so it produces fewer and milder reactions. However, as of mid-1996 the new vaccine (DTaP) was approved for use only for the first, fourth, and fifth shots of the DTP series, but not for the second and third.

A major 1991 study by the National Academy of Science's Institute of Medicine found that potentially life-threatening allergic reactions can occur in approximately 1 to 2 cases per 100,000 DTP vaccinations, though it is unclear whether those reactions are caused by the pertussis, diphtheria, or tetanus portions of the combination vaccine. It also found:

- Little or no evidence that would connect the DTP vaccine with adverse effects such as LEARNING DISABILITIES, HYPERACTIVITY, ANEMIA, or chronic nerve damage.
- No evidence linking the DTP vaccine with AUTISM.
- Little or no evidence linking the DTP vaccine to infantile spasms, REYE SYNDROME, and SUDDEN INFANT DEATH SYNDROME.
- Insufficient evidence of a link between the DTP vaccine and juvenile DIABETES, severe skin rashes, low blood platelet cell counts, and Guillain-Barré syndrome and other nerve illnesses.

The committee noted that many of these possible adverse effects "occur in the absence of vaccination, are clinically ill-defined, and are generally of unknown causation in the general population." They urged more research in many areas on which there was insufficient information. Since early 1991, the federal government has been monitoring serious side effects of childhood vaccinations through its Vaccine Adverse Events Reporting System, which requires physicians to report adverse reactions. Panel members concluded that the diphtheria-tetanus-pertussis vaccines are effective in protecting children against these diseases—and that the diseases themselves present greater dangers than the possible adverse reactions.

Partly in response to the above reports, the Public Health Service (PHS) in late 1991 modified its position relating to the DTP vaccine. In the past, it had said that any of the following reactions after a DTP shot should be an "absolute reason" for not giving a child the pertussis portion of the DTP shot:

- A temperature of 105°F within forty-eight hours of vaccination.
- Collapse or shock-like state within forty-eight hours of vaccination.
- Persistent, inconsolable crying lasting three hours and occurring within forty-eight hours of vaccination.
- Convulsions, with or without fever, occurring within three days of vaccination.

Under the new PHS guidelines, the reactions listed above are regarded only as precautions or warning signs, and physicians have more leeway in deciding whether to discontinue the pertussis component of future shots or to continue with the full DTP vaccine.

Parents whose children have had severe and damaging reactions from the DTP (and some other) vaccines may be able to claim compensation from the NATIONAL VACCINE INJURY COMPENSATION PROGRAM.

FOR HELP AND FURTHER INFORMATION

National Vaccine Information Center (NVIC), 800–909–7468. Publishes *Whooping Cough, the DPT Vaccine and Reducing Vaccine Reaction.* (For full group information, see IMMUNIZATION.)

National Vaccine Injury Compensation Program (NVICP), 800–338–2382. (For full group information, see CHILDHOOD VACCINE INJURY ACT.)

(See also IMMUNIZATION, for a recommended immunization schedule.)

dual grading system, in EDUCATION, an evaluative approach that gives two marks, one for achievement as compared to others in the class (the usual GRADE) and one for achievement relative to one's ability, sometimes popularly called "for effort."

due date, the date on which a baby's birth is expected, traditionally calculated by doctors as 280 days (forty weeks) from the beginning of the woman's last MENSTRUATION, even though FERTILIZATION probably did not take place until two weeks later, at the time of OVULATION. The due date is also medically called *expected date of confinement* (EDC). To calculate a due date, start with the day on which the last period began (say July 15), add nine months (making it April 15) and add seven days (making the due date April 22). By contrast, the average period of GESTATION is 266 days (thirty-eight weeks), figured from the date of fertilization. If the actual fertilization date is known, subtracting two weeks from the due date gives a more accurate expected delivery date. Because the forty-week due date calculation is imprecise, OBSTETRICIANS-GYNECOLOGISTS may give a more accurate due date toward the end of the PREGNANCY, guided by a variety of tests and examinations, including when the first heartbeat is heard.

due process, a person's right to be treated with fairness in any legal proceeding, one of the most basic rights of a United States citizen. The term comes from the phrase in the Constitution "no person shall be deprived of life, liberty, or property without due process of law." Due process often includes the rights to receive adequate notice of hearings, to receive notice of allegations or charges, to have a lawyer's counsel, to confront and cross-examine witnesses, to refuse to give self-incriminating testimony, to be presumed innocent, and to receive a jury trial. However, the precise details of what constitutes fairness in what settings, for what types of cases, and for what people is a complex matter that changes somewhat as courts rule on specific cases.

People involved in family law and many types of matters dealt with in ADMINISTRATIVE PROCEDURES were traditionally often not accorded the basic legal protection of due process. However, a series of cases over the years have resulted in due process safeguards gradually being extended into some of these areas, as in relation to separation and DIVORCE, schools, and social services, including CUSTODY and TERMINATION OF PARENT'S RIGHTS. Even so, in some circumstances, parents or children may be adversely affected by a hearing—or even a decision made without a hearing—at which they had no opportunity to be heard. To get a new, fair hearing, they may then be obliged to prove that they were denied due process.

Due process hearings are common in connection with the EDUCATION FOR ALL HANDICAPPED CHILDREN ACT and its successor, the INDIVIDUALS WITH DISABILITIES EDUCATION ACT, when parents disagree with the INDIVIDUALIZED EDUCATION PLAN the school prepares for their child. (For an outline of parents' rights in such cases, see INDIVIDUALS WITH DISABILITIES EDUCATION ACT; for a discussion of rulings regarding student suspensions or expulsions from school, see SUSPENSION.)

Durrell Analysis of Reading Difficulty, an individually administered TEST of READING skills for children in grades 1–6 that includes oral reading, silent reading, listening comprehension, listening vocabulary, spelling, word recognition/word analysis, auditory analysis of words and word elements, pronunciation of word elements, visual memory of words, and prereading PHONICS abilities. The Durrell test is often used as a DIAGNOSTIC ASSESSMENT TEST for the planning of REMEDIAL INSTRUCTION, as well as to attempt to predict a child's future reading skills. (See TESTS.)

dwarfism, abnormally short stature and general underdevelopment of the body, which may result from a wide variety of causes, among them:

- GENETIC DISORDERS, such as MUCOPOLYSACCHARIDOSES.
- Malfunctioning of some part of the ENDOCRINE SYSTEM, especially the PITUITARY GLAND or the THYROID GLAND.
- CHRONIC illnesses that sap strength and slow growth.
- Persistent MALNUTRITION, as in nutritional disorders such as RICKETS.
- Kidney failure (see KIDNEY AND UROLOGICAL DISORDERS).
- Defects in the digestive and absorptive systems (see DIGESTIVE SYSTEM AND DISORDERS).
- Psychosocial stress, as in MATERNAL DEPRIVATION SYNDROME.

Dwarfism is often associated with other problems or defects, such as MENTAL RETARDATION. (See GROWTH AND GROWTH DISORDERS).

dysarthria, difficult, often unclear speech resulting from malfunctioning of the muscles used in pronouncing words, often because of damage to the nerves serving the area. Dysarthria may result from a BRAIN TUMOR. Total inability to speak is called *anarthria.* (See COMMUNICATION SKILLS AND DISORDERS.)

dyscalculia, difficulty in working with mathematical symbols and functions, presumably because of some brain dysfunction; one kind of LEARNING DISABILITIES. Total inability to work with numbers is called *acalculia.*

dysfunctional, a general term applied to something that is not working properly. A FAMILY unable to cope with its problems and meet its responsibilities, such as one responsible for CHILD ABUSE AND NEGLECT, may be called dysfunctional. The term may also refer to a medical problem, such as kidney dysfunction.

dysgraphia, difficulty in WRITING, especially in producing handwriting legible to others, generally because of problems with *visual-motor integration,* one of the key VISUAL SKILLS. Total inability to write is called *agraphia,* a type of APHASIA.

dyslexia, difficulty in reading, despite unimpaired vision and intelligence; also called *partial word blindness.* This is a type of LEARNING DISABILITY relating specifically to reading problems. A dyslexic child may see printed words upside down, backwards, or otherwise distorted. Total inability to read—that is, to interpret written symbols—is called *alexia* or *word blindness.*

dysphasia, a kind of communication disorder involving inability to speak the words in one's mind or to find the correct words to speak, as well as inability to understand spoken or written words. The condition that may result from certain kinds of damage to the brain, such as a BRAIN TUMOR or TRAUMATIC BRAIN INJURY. (See BRAIN AND BRAIN DISORDERS; COMMUNICATION SKILLS AND DISORDERS.)

dystocia, medical term for difficult (sometimes impossible) LABOR, when labor fails to progress during CHILDBIRTH. It can occur when a mother is overtired or when her internal organs are abnormally shaped. Dystocia generally indicates the need for medical assistance, including FORCEPS DELIVERY, VACUUM EXTRACTION, or CESAREAN SECTION.

E

ear and hearing problems, the twin structures on either side of the head that are involved in receiving and registering sounds and transmitting information about those sounds to the brain for interpretation. Hearing problems are impairment in those functions. The *outer ear* (the visible part) acts as a funnel for sound and transmits it to the *eardrum*, a membrane that vibrates like a drum when sound strikes it.

This vibration is passed on to the *ossicles*, a set of tiny bones (the *malleus*, the *incus*, and the *stapes*) in the *middle ear* that amplify the sound. The middle ear is connected to the throat by a narrow canal called the *eustachian tube*, which helps protect the delicate eardrum and ossicles from too-rapid, potentially dangerous changes in pressure, as when a passenger is in an airplane that is taking off or landing, or from loud noises.

The amplified vibrations are then passed on to the *cochlea*, a fluid-filled, snail-shaped, bony shell in the *inner ear*. Within the cochlea is the actual organ of hearing, the *organ of Corti*, a minute duct filled with microscopic hair cells. These take the incoming sound vibrations and transform them into electrical signals that are picked up by nearby nerve cells and transmitted to the brain by way of the *auditory nerve*, also called the *eighth nerve*.

How the brain then takes these signals and interprets them is little known, but the process is the subject of much research. Scientists do know that different parts of the brain are primarily associated with various activities, such as interpreting speech and music, thinking, memory, and learning. But they do not yet know how we can focus on one sound in a noisy setting, "tuning out" other unwanted sounds, or how we identify the source of a sound from some distance away.

Clearly, such a delicate set of mechanisms and processes is easily disrupted, which can impair hearing. Many hearing problems are associated with problems in the outer and middle ear and involve the gathering and passing on of the sound vibrations; this type of hearing impairment is called *conductive loss*. By contrast, *sensori-neural loss* occurs when there is a problem in the inner ear, especially with the delicate hair cells or with the nerves that carry sound to the brain.

Both types of loss may occur either before or after birth. Hearing loss that is present at birth, when the child has no experience of sound or spoken language, is called *prelingual*, a term also used to refer to people who lost their hearing before age three, before they had fully learned how to speak. Hearing loss after a person has had some experience of sound and language, especially after age three, is called *postlingual*. Approximately 95 percent of people who are impaired are prelingual; they need considerable special training to develop fluent communication skills.

Conductive losses are less severe than sensori-neural losses, and can usually be reduced or eliminated through medical treatment. Sensori-neural losses are more severe and, at present, cannot be cured or even reduced by medical treatment. But most children with sensori-neural losses can be helped greatly by a HEARING AID. It is important that children with sensori-neural losses see a doctor regularly to make sure infections or other problems do not increase their hearing loss, or present a medical problem that may otherwise be physically damaging. Sometimes a child may have *mixed hearing loss*, involving problems both in the outer or middle ear and the inner ear.

Conductive losses may be caused by:

- Infections that fill the ear with fluid, the most common being the middle ear infection called *otitis media*. Researchers estimate that two out of three children have at least one episode of otitis media before reaching school age. Often during colds or other respiratory illnesses, mucus and pus drain into the middle ear, causing swelling, inflammation, pain, and temporary or sometimes permanent hearing impairment. The infection may also spread to the nearby mastoid bone causing inflammation, or *mastoiditis*. With modern ANTIBIOTICS, many infections can be cleared up leaving no lasting damage (and without the surgery once common for mastoiditis). But some children have five or six bouts a year of chronic otitis media, creating the risk of some permanent hearing loss. Then an OTOLOGIST or OTOLARYNGOLOGIST may make a tiny incision in the eardrum to drain built-up fluid; if fluid continues to build up, the surgeon may insert a minute drainage tube in the eardrum, in a procedure called a *tympanostomy*. Such an operation can ease the problem, but may result in thickening or scarring of the eardrum. If children (or parents) have middle-ear infections or colds, they should not fly, because the changes in pressure can cause ear damage. Though otitis media is often accompanied by fever and ear pain, sometimes the first sign of middle-ear infection is a child saying "huh?" more often or turning the radio or television volume up higher than usual. Parents should be especially alert to such signs in children who have problems communicating, such as those with AUTISM or very young children.
- Ruptured eardrum, which can result from an injury; a pressure drop that is too sudden or too drastic; or damage caused by a foreign object, such as a pencil, stick, or hairpin. Using the modern techniques of MICROSURGERY, ear specialists can now repair or rebuild an eardrum in

many such cases. Using a technique called *myringoplasty*, surgeons can close a hole in the eardrum using a tissue graft from elsewhere in the body.

- External blockage, such as a buildup of ear wax in the ear or the presence of a foreign object, such as a bead or a bug. Such blocks should be removed only by a medical specialist, such as an otologist or otolaryngologist, because the eardrum can be damaged in the process. Buildup of wax and other debris can, if the ear is often under water, serve as a medium for growth of bacteria, yeasts, fungus, or viruses. The result is the common ear ailment called *otitis externa* or *swimmer's ear*, which is infection or inflammation in the outer ear, often accompanied by MYRINGITIS, inflammation of the eardum. The debris needs to be professionally cleaned out and the area medicinally disinfected. Showers rather than baths are less conducive to otitis externa, and a child vulnerable to ear infections may need to limit swimming.
- Deformity in the ear structures, such as the hereditary hearing problem called *otosclerosis*, in which one or more of the bones in the middle ear have excess bone and so cannot transmit sound vibrations effectively. Modern surgery can remove excess bone and, if necessary, replace part of the bone with an artificial part.
- Missing or occluded (obstructed) ear canal, a rare condition.
- ALLERGIES.

In rare cases, a child may have a hearing loss that comes and goes. Such a child has normal hearing, but may occasionally suffer a significant hearing loss because of allergies and chronic colds. This kind of hearing loss can be very hard to detect and treat. One week you may notice inconsistent responses like those of a child with hearing impairment, who is unaware she is being talked to. The next week, the child will respond as though she has normal hearing. You should bring this kind of problem to the attention of a doctor.

Sensori-neural losses may be caused by many different things:

- Diseases during PREGNANCY. German measles (RUBELLA) and common MEASLES (rubeola) once caused numerous cases of hearing impairment at birth. Luckily vaccines now exist for both these diseases; any woman considering pregnancy should be sure to be vaccinated well before CONCEPTION. Other common infections that can cause hearing loss, but for which no vaccines currently exist, are CYTOMEGALOVIRUS, TOXOPLASMOSIS, and HERPES simplex type 2 virus, which causes genital infection.
- Heredity. Of the 4,000 babies born deaf in the United States each year, perhaps half have lost their hearing because of GENETIC DISORDERS. Many more have substantial hearing impairment, which only becomes apparent later. If prospective parents have hereditary deafness in their personal or family history, they may want to seek GENETIC COUNSELING to assess how great the risk might be that their child could have impaired hearing.
- Difficult LABOR and delivery, including APGAR SCORES of 0–4 at one minute after birth or 0–6 at five minutes after birth. If the baby's oxygen supply is temporarily cut off during labor, for example, hearing damage may result. Being on a VENTILATOR (respirator) for five or more days in the first month of life is also associated with hearing loss.
- Drugs taken by a pregnant woman during pregnancy, or by a child. Aspirin, some antibiotics (such as streptomycin or neomycin), and some diuretics (water-reducing pills) can on occasion damage hair cells or other parts of the inner ear; so can some antiCANCER drugs. Anyone taking such drugs who experiences change in hearing, dizziness, balance problems, or tinnitus (ringing in the ears; see below) should check promptly with a physician. Parents should be alert to such symptoms in their children.
- Childhood diseases, such as MUMPS, measles, and CHICKEN POX.
- Viral infections, such as MENINGITIS and ENCEPHALITIS.
- Prolonged high FEVER.
- TUMORS. Most common are ACOUSTIC NEUROMAS, also called *eighth nerve tumors*; associated symptoms are hearing loss in one or both ears, headaches, dizziness, tinnitus, and numbness in the face. If detected early, the tumor can be removed without hearing damage; but if diagnosed late, acoustic neuromas can be life-threatening or surgical removal can at least involve hearing loss, disturbance of the sense of balance (related to the inner ear), and loss of feeling or paralysis in the face.
- Physical damage to head or ear. A severe blow to the head, an accident, brain hemorrhage, or similar trauma may damage hearing ability (see TRAUMATIC BRAIN INJURY).
- Excessive or intense noise. Brief exposure to extremely loud, intense, explosive sound can cause temporary, but possibly reversible hearing loss. Continued exposure can cause permanent damage to the vital hair cells of the inner ear, causing irreversible hearing loss—a serious problem in a society that is surrounded by noise, not least in personal earphones.

Sometimes hearing impairment is associated with other diseases or disorders, among them HUNTER'S SYNDROME, ALBERS-SCHÖNBERG DISEASE, TREACHERS-COLLINS SYNDROME, and LOW BIRTH WEIGHT, such as when a newborn weighs under 3.3 pounds; see also THYROID GLAND.

Sensori-neural loss affects sound at some frequencies more than others, so that even with a hearing aid, a person with sensori-neural loss often hears distorted sounds, making use of an aid impossible. A COCHLEAR IMPLANT, which uses a microprocessor to simulate the functions performed by the cochlea, may help some such people.

Another type of ear and hearing problem is *tinnitus*, which is persistent ringing, whistling, buzzing, tinkling, or other annoying noises in the ears. The disorder commonly results from disturbances of the acoustic nerve, when it transmits to the brain electrical signals unrelated to external sounds. Tinnitus is a type of sensori-neural problem. The causes of that form of tinnitus are not fully known, but in children it is sometimes associated with traumatic brain injury, otosclerosis, allergies, infections, or ARTHRITIS. However, another form of tinnitus can be caused by wax buildup in the outer ear canal, by perforation of the eardrum, or by fluid accumulation behind the eardrum.

It is extremely important that any hearing impairment be identified early, so that a child can get treatment, aid, and training to minimize damage and loss. Because hearing problems are often among the complex of problems experienced by PREMATURE and seriously ill babies treated in NEONATAL INTENSIVE CARE UNITS (NICUs), many today are routinely screened with a test called the *auditory brainstem response* (ABR) or *brain stem auditory evoked responses* (BSAER). This involves sending test signals—clicks or pips—to the child through earphones; if the child hears the sound, a device similar to an ELECTROENCEPHALOGRAPH will display evoked brainwaves on a screen; this is far more accurate than guessing from a baby's movements whether or not the sound was heard.

Deafness itself does not affect intellectual capacity, but the language and sounds children hear from birth provide vital experience, and many aspects of learning depend on a child's communication skills (see COMMUNICATIONS SKILLS AND DISORDERS). As a result, children with undiagnosed hearing impairment may quickly fall behind in developing skills. Some kinds of hearing loss can be identified in newborns, but many cases of hearing impairment go undiagnosed for years, with children mistakenly thought to have MENTAL RETARDATION. Government agencies now have EARLY INTERVENTION programs to try to identify hearing and other such problems in infancy, but parents can often spot hearing loss best (see PARENTS ARE THE FIRST TO KNOW IF THEIR INFANTS CANNOT HEAR on page 201).

Sometimes hearing impairment, especially if it is mild, is not diagnosed until the child enters nursery school. The OBSERVATION CHECKLIST FOR POSSIBLE HEARING IMPAIRMENT IN PRESCHOOLERS on page 202 was designed to help Head Start teachers tell if children in their preschool classes might have an undiagnosed hearing problem, but parents can use the checklist to assess if their young child needs to be referred to an AUDIOLOGIST for HEARING TESTS. If a child is found to have a significant hearing loss, he or she will be entitled to special educational and other services under the EDUCATION FOR ALL HANDICAPPED CHILDREN ACT and its successor, the INDIVIDUALS WITH DISABILITIES EDUCATION ACT.

Hearing loss is defined in different ways by different people for various purposes. Government agencies use specific *categorical definitions* for administrative reporting purposes; these set out certain kinds of categories and test results that would make a child eligible for certain government services, as under the Education for All Handicapped Children Act. Mild impairments that can be readily corrected are not considered disabilities, unless they fall within specified governmental definitions and, because of the disability, they require special education and related services.

More important for parents and teachers is the *functional definition* of a child's impairment; this describes how an individual child can and cannot use hearing for the ordinary purposes of life. Few people have total loss of hearing. Most children commonly termed *deaf* have some level of hearing that is demonstrable on a hearing test. This is called *residual hearing.* How useful this residual (remaining) hearing is for functioning in life determines whether a person is considered deaf or hard of hearing. Being able to use hearing for the "ordinary purposes of life" means being able to understand speech through hearing alone or hearing combined with SPEECHREADING (lipreading), and being able to hear enough of ordinary sounds—such as telephones, traffic, and voices—to be able to make sense out of them. A child who functions this way is termed *hard of hearing*; a child who cannot use hearing to function this way is termed *deaf.*

A second type of functional definition is based on the degree of hearing loss and is determined by hearing tests, normally performed by an audiologist. In this definition, all children, whether they are categorized as deaf or hard of hearing, are referred to as *hearing impaired.* The government publication *Mainstreaming Preschoolers: Children with Hearing Impairment* explains it this way:

Hearing impairment covers the entire range of degree of hearing loss and is broken down into four categories: *mild, moderate, severe,* and *profound.* (For a fuller discussion, see HEARING TESTS.) Children who have the same degree of hearing loss may function quite differently from one another, however. One child with a severe hearing impairment may be functionally hard of hearing, while another child with a severe hearing impairment may be functionally deaf.

While audiometric testing tells how loud a sound must be to be heard by a hearing impaired child (without a hearing aid), it does not tell how distorted sounds may be for that particular child. Two children with the same measurable degree of hearing loss may hear sounds with differing degrees of clarity, which greatly affect what each is able to understand. Categories of loss also do not tell what a child's potential for hearing or listening may be. And they do not tell how a child will function on a daily basis.

For these reasons, the measured degree of hearing loss in a child (mild, moderate, severe, or profound) cannot be used to predict behaviors or functioning of that child. Many hearing impaired children can learn to use the hearing they have to understand and to speak, although these skills will vary from child to child.

Hearing impaired children have two different problems in receiving sound. First, sounds are not as loud as they are for children without hearing impairment. Sounds

Parents Are the First to Know If Their Infants Cannot Hear

When you check your baby's hearing, he or she should be happy and the room quiet.

DOES YOUR BABY SOMETIMES:

BETWEEN BIRTH AND THREE MONTHS

- Startle or jump when there is a sudden loud sound?
- Stir or wake up and cry when someone talks or makes a noise?
- Recognize the sound of your voice and is quieted and sometimes pacified by the sound of your voice?

BETWEEN THREE AND SIX MONTHS

- Turn his or her eyes toward an interesting sound?
- Respond to mother's or father's voice?
- Turn his or her eyes toward you when you call his or her name?

BETWEEN SIX AND TWELVE MONTHS

- Turn toward an interesting sound and toward you when his or her name is called from behind? (Sounds need NOT be loud.)
- Understand "no" and "bye-bye" and similar common words?
- Search or look around when hearing new sounds?

If your baby cannot do these things, check with your doctor. Parents must persist until their concerns are answered!

Source: U.S. Surgeon General's office.

may be slightly softer than normal, very soft, or even impossible for hearing impaired children to hear. Through testing, a professional can determine how loud a sound has to be for a child to be able to hear it.

Second, for children with more severe hearing loss, sounds may be distorted, as well as soft. When sounds are distorted they can be mistaken for other sounds or can be impossible to understand. The amount of distortion cannot be measured by a test, but it greatly affects how children function. It is necessary to be aware of these two problems—loudness and distortion—to understand fully the effects of hearing loss.

The results of audiological tests and of observations in the classroom and in the home allow teachers, in consultation with parents, to develop INDIVIDUALIZED EDUCATION PLANS for children with hearing impairment.

A hearing impaired child's central problem is learning to communicate. In order to communicate, children need to send and receive messages. Hearing impaired children have a harder time than other children learning to talk and to understand the conversation of others. This is because hearing impaired children may not hear a message clearly, may hear it at a reduced intensity, or may not hear it at all. Therefore, the ability to communicate through spoken language is developed more slowly in hearing impaired children than in other children. A CHART OF NORMAL DEVELOPMENT (on page 637) indicates when, between birth and age six, unimpaired children first *on the average* begin to perform the main communication skills and other basic skills.

Children with prelingual hearing loss—those who were deaf at birth and so had no experience of sound and spoken language or who lost their hearing before age three, before they learned how to speak—have the most difficulty. Such children—95 percent of the hearing-impaired children—need much more special training to develop fluent communications skills and special skills such as speechreading, SIGN LANGUAGE (such as American Sign Language), CUED SPEECH, and FINGERSPELLING.

Considerable dispute exists among people concerned with the deaf, between those who believe deaf people should avoid any form of MANUAL COMMUNICATION and focus totally on oral speech and those who believe that they should use any and all means of communication open to them—an approach called TOTAL COMMUNICATION. SPEECH AND LANGUAGE PATHOLOGISTS use a variety of approaches to teach speech to deaf children, including having the child learn to mimic the "voiceprint" that shows up on a computer screen and feeling the vibrations in the jaw, throat, and neck muscles (as Helen Keller learned from her teacher).

Various kinds of technical aids have also been developed to aid hearing-impaired people. Among these are:

- Text telephone (TT) devices that allow people with hearing impairment to use the telephone by typing on a computer, which then produces digital, print, large print, or braille readouts, and—if the particular device has speech synthesis capability—even voice transmissions; formerly called *Telecommunication Devices for the Deaf* (TDDs) or or *Teletypewriters (TTYs)*. Some such devices can also store and send messages, and answer the telephone automatically. Newer forms can communicate with regular computers, though some earlier ones, using TTY language, cannot. Where one person

Observation Checklist for Possible Hearing Impairment in Preschoolers

USING AN OBSERVATION CHECKLIST

The checklist of behaviors that follows can alert you to undiagnosed hearing loss in a child and help you know when to refer that child for professional evaluation. There are certain aspects of the child's medical history that are important to note on your checklist, in addition to observable behaviors. Look through the child's records or ask the child's doctor to help you answer the "medical history" questions. Then continue to fill in your checklist from your observations.

If a child displays one or two of the behaviors listed, watch him or her more closely and in a variety of situations. Look carefully for other listed behaviors. You may also want to ask teachers or child-care staff if they have observed any of the behaviors on the checklist. If you can't decide whether something is wrong, request that a specialist, such as a teacher in a special program for the hearing-impaired, observe the child, too.

MEDICAL HISTORY

	YES	NO
Is there a history of earaches or ear infections in the child's records?	☐	☐
Does the child complain of earaches, ringing, or buzzing in the ears?	☐	☐
Does the child have allergies or what appear to be chronic colds?	☐	☐
Has the child had a disease (mumps, measles) accompanied by a high fever?	☐	☐
Do parents say that they have wondered if the child has a hearing loss?	☐	☐

HEARING

	YES	NO
Does the child fail to respond to loud, unusual, or unexpected sounds?	☐	☐
Does the child fail to respond to communication that excites the other children? (For example, "Who wants ice cream?")	☐	☐
Does the child frequently fail to understand or respond to instructions or greetings when he or she doesn't see the speaker?	☐	☐
Does the child seem to watch other children rather than listen to the teacher in order to learn what to do next?	☐	☐
Does the child have difficulty finding the source of a sound?	☐	☐
Does the child constantly turn the television, radio, or record player up louder?	☐	☐
Does the child's attention wander or does the child look around the room while the teacher is talking or reading a story?	☐	☐

SPEECH

	YES	NO
Does the child frequently say "Huh?" or "What?" or show other signs of not understanding what has been said?	☐	☐
Does the child use very little speech?	☐	☐
Does the child have difficulty controlling how loudly or softly he or she speaks?	☐	☐
Does the child have trouble putting words together in the right order?	☐	☐
Does the child's voice seem too high-pitched, too low-pitched, or too nasal?	☐	☐
Is the child's speech full of words and sentences that cannot be understood or recognized?	☐	☐
Does the child have poor articulation?	☐	☐

OTHER BEHAVIOR

	YES	NO
Does the child have a short attention span?	☐	☐
Does the child seem frequently restless?	☐	☐
Does the child breathe with his or her mouth open?	☐	☐
Is the child seldom the first one to do what the teachers has asked the group to do?	☐	☐
Is the child easily frustrated or distracted in a group?	☐	☐
Does the child tend to play in the quietest group?	☐	☐
Does the child tend to play alone more than the other children do?	☐	☐
Does the child seem unaware of social conventions?	☐	☐
For example, does the child:		
■ never say automatically "thank you," "excuse me," or "sorry"?	☐	☐
■ generally tap or grab another person instead of calling his or her name?	☐	☐
■ not become quiet in quiet areas or activities (church, story corner, naptime)?	☐	☐
■ not ask permission to leave the room, go to the bathroom, get a drink?	☐	☐
■ appear unaware of disturbing others with noises?	☐	☐

Source: Mainstreaming Preschoolers: Children with Hearing Impairment—A Guide for Teachers, Parents, and Others Who Work with Hearing Impaired Preschoolers. Rita Ann LaPorta et al. 1978. Prepared for the Head Start Bureau, Administration for Children, Youth and Families.

does not have a TT, the other uses a relay service to convey the message, by voice or type, as appropriate. This relay service can be reached at 800–855–2881, voice, or 800–855–2880, TT.

- Alerting systems that use flashing lights or vibrations to signal particular sounds, such as the ringing of a phone, the crying of a baby, or the beep of a smoke detector.
- Electronic mail (e-mail), using typed messages on computers as a main avenue of communication, such as DeafNet (operated by the Deaf Communications Institute) and Disabilities Forum (on CompuServe).
- Interactive instruction, using computers or videodiscs, especially for speech and language development.
- Computers for word processing, making writing and corrections much easier.
- Computers for speech recognition, in which words spoken in a classroom are translated by a computer in print on a screen.
- SPEECH SYNTHESIS, computer programs that allow a deaf person to type in a computer and have the computer "speak" the words.
- FM systems, in which a parent or teacher wears a microphone and FM transmitter, and the child wears a receiver tuned to the same channel. This allows the child to hear the speaker's voice regardless of location or other background noise, and is often used to supplement, sometimes to replace, hearing aids. There are a variety of assistive listening devices (ALDs), systems that funnel sound directly into a hearing aid—and so deliver sound to the ear more efficiently—and also filter out background noise. These use various technologies, including electromagnetic fields, radio waves, and infrared systems.
- CLOSED CAPTIONS for visual materials.

Such devices and others surely to come are gradually increasing the independence of people who are deaf or hearing impaired. Among other special arrangements possible are use of specially trained dogs (see SERVICE DOGS) to act as "alerting systems," generally only for adolescents or adults who are old enough to care for the dog. In some test situations, as for the SCHOLASTIC APTITUDE TEST or the ACT TESTS, students may be allowed to use an interpreter or translator (see SPECIAL HELP FOR SPECIAL COLLEGE STUDENTS on page 366).

FOR HELP AND FURTHER INFORMATION

ABOUT HEARING PROBLEMS AND IMPAIRMENT

Alexander Graham Bell Association for the Deaf (AGBAD)
3417 Volta Place NW
Washington, DC 20007
202–337–5220, voice/TT; 800-HEARKID [432–7543]
E-mail: agbell@deaftek.sprint.com or agbell2@aol.com
(America Online: ABGBELL2)
Donna McCord Dickman, Executive Director
Susan Coffman, Director of Professional Programs and Services, Contact
Organization concerned with deafness and other hearing problems; provides information; maintains Parents' Section, Children's Rights Program, and Oral Hearing-Impaired Section; offers financial aid for children with hearing impairment; publishes various materials, including:

- Bimonthly magazine *Volta Voices* and quarterly journal *Volta Review*.

- For families: brochures *Can Your Baby Hear?, Speech and Hearing Checklist, A Parent's Guide to Middle Ear Infections, Understanding Ear Infection, Communication, Consistency, Caring: A Parent's Guide to Raising a Hearing-Impaired Child* and *Helping Your Hard-of-Hearing Child Succeed*; books *When Your Child Is Deaf: A Guide for Parents, Raising Your Hearing-Impaired Child: A Guide for Parents, Parents' Guide to Speech and Deafness, Families and Their Hearing-Impaired Children, The Language of Toys: Teaching Communication Skills to Special Needs Children, Listening to Learn: A Handbook for Parents with Hearing-Impaired Children, Talk With Me*, and *When a Hug Won't Fix the Hurt*; video *Part of This World*; and parent packets on age-related topics (for children from birth to age five, ages six through twelve, and teens and young adults).
- On general communication: *Choices in Deafness: A Parent's Guide, Auditory-Verbal Therapy for Parents and Professionals, Cued Speech Resource Guide for Parents of Deaf Children*, videos *I Can Hear!* and *Do You Hear That?*, and educational materials, including early intervention programs for children.
- On speechreading: brochure *Speechreading for Better Communication*, book *Lipreading for Children, The Lipreader's Calendar*, and various videotapes.
- On auditory training: *I Heard That! A Developmental Sequence of Listening Activities for the Young Child, Facilitating Hearing and Listening in Young Children, The Joy of Listening: An Auditory Training Program*, and works for adults and teachers.
- On language and speech development: *Listening and Talking: A Guide to Promoting Spoken Language in Young Hearing-Impaired Children*, video *Learning to Communicate: The First Three Years, Schedules of Development for Hearing-Impaired Infants and Their Parents, The Hearing-Impaired Child: Infancy Through High-School Years, Let's Converse: Developing and Expanding Conversational Skills of Children and Teenagers Who Are Hearing-Impaired, Communication Skills in Hearing Impaired Children, Curriculum Guide: Hearing-Impaired Children, Birth to Three Years and Their Parents, Parents and Teachers: Partners in Language Development*, and professional materials.
- On cochlear implants: *Cochlear Implants and Children: A Handbook for Parents, Teachers, and Speech and Hearing Professionals, Cochlear Implants, Pediatric Cochlear Implants: An Overview of Options and Alternatives in Education and Rehabilitation*, and professional works.
- Brochures and technical materials on other assistive technologies.
- Professional materials on education, curriculum, medical concerns, and legal issues, such as *Communication Access for Persons with Hearing Loss: Compliance with the Americans with Disabilities Act*.

National Information Center on Deafness (NICD)
Gallaudet University
800 Florida Avenue NE
Washington, DC 20002
202–651–5051; 202–651–5052, TT
Fax: 202–651–5051
E-mail: nicd@gallua.bitnet
Loraine DiPietro, Executive Director
Information clearinghouse on all aspects of hearing loss and deafness; provides information and referrals; publishes numerous materials, including:

- Annual *NICD Directory of National Organizations of and for Deaf and Hard of Hearing People* and *Professionals and Consumer Periodicals from Gallaudet University*.
- General materials: *Deafness: A Fact Sheet, Some Facts About Otitis Media, Genetics and Deafness, Noise and Hearing Loss, Info to Go* (on the NICD), *Questions and Answers About Cochlear Implants*, and *Questions and Answers About Tinnitus*.
- For parents: *Growing Together: Information for Parents of Deaf and Hard of Hearing Children, Hearing Children of Deaf Parents, Summer Camps for Deaf and Hard of Hearing Children.*
- For children: *The Ear and Hearing, Growing Up Without Hearing*, and *How Deaf People Communicate* (all in two versions, for grades 3–4 or for grades 5 and above).
- On assistive devices: *Alerting and Communication Devices for Deaf and Hard of Hearing People, Hearing Aids and Other Assistive Devices: Where to Get Assistance, Assistive Devices: A Consumer-Oriented Summary, Assistive Devices Demonstration Centers, Providers of Captioning Services for Video Productions*, and *What Are TDDs?*
- On communication and sign language: *Books for Learning Sign Language, Communicating with Deaf People: An Introduction, Resources to Develop Speechreading Skills, Learning Sign Language: Audio Visual/Computer Programs, Locating Sign Language Classes, Sign Language Specialty Items: Where to Get Them*, and *Communication Tips for Adults with Hearing Loss.*
- Other resources: *Leading National Publications of and for Deaf People, Making New Friends* (locating pen pals), *Travel Resources for Deaf and Hard of Hearing People, National Religious Organizations for Deaf and Hard of Hearing People, Performance Groups, Deaf Culture: Suggested Reading, A Resource List* (of free and inexpensive brochures), and *Deaf Culture Videotapes.*
- Materials on careers in the field and on hearing loss among older adults.

National Institute on Deafness and Other Communication Disorders (NIDCD), 800–241–1044. Publishes *Hearing and Hearing Loss Information Packet, Recent Research on Hereditary Deafness, Cochlear Implants, Early Identification of Hearing Impairment in Infants and Young Children, Because You Asked About Ménière's Disease, Update on Dizziness, Tinnitus Information Packet, Fact Sheet on Captioning*, and *Facts About Telecommunications Relay Services.* (For full group information, see COMMUNICATION SKILLS AND DISORDERS.)

National Association for Hearing and Speech Action (NAHSA)
10801 Rockville Pike
Rockville, MD 20852

301–897–8682, voice/TT; MD, AK and HI call collect
800–638-TALK [638–8255], voice/TT; U.S. except MD, AK, and HI
Russell Malone, President
Consumer affiliate of the American Speech-Language-Association (see COMMUNICATION SKILLS AND DISORDERS); provides information and referrals; publishes various materials, including brochures *How Does You Child Hear and Talk?, Hearing Impairment and the Audiologist, Do Your Health Benefits Cover Audiology and Speech-Language Pathology Services?*, and "Questions About" brochures *Otitis Media, Hearing and Language Development, Assistive Listening Devices, Tinnitus*, and *Noise and Hearing Loss.*

Better Hearing Institute (BHI)
Box 1840
Washington, DC 20013
5021-B Backlick Road
Annandale, VA 22003
703–642–0580; Hearing Helpline: 800-EAR-WELL [327–9355], voice/TT
Fax: 703–750–9302
Organization concerned with hearing impairments; provides information; publishes various print and audiovisual materials, including newsletter *Better Hearing News*; booklet *A Guide to Your Child's Hearing*; pamphlets *Overcome Hearing Loss Now!, Discover a World of Better Hearing, We Chose Better Hearing!, Answers to Common Questions about Assistive Technology, Tinnitus, or Head Noises, Nerve Deafness and You*, and *Your Guide to Better Hearing*; and videos *People vs. Noise, Overcoming Hearing Loss, A New Age for Better Hearing.*

National Association of the Deaf (NAD)
814 Thayer Avenue
Silver Spring, MD
301–587–1788, voice/TT
Bookstore: 301–587–6282
Gary Olsen, Executive Director
Nationwide organization acting as advocate for the deaf; provides information; publishes numerous materials, including magazine *Deaf American* and newsletter *NAD Broadcaster.*

Self-Help for Hard of Hearing People (SHHH)
7910 Woodmont Avenue, Suite 1200
Bethesda, MD 20814
301–657–2248; 301–657–2249, TT
Fax: 301–913–9413
Donna Sorkin, Executive Director
Organization for hard-of-hearing individuals, their families, and concerned professionals. Publishes bimonthly *SHHH Journal*, quarterly *SHHH News*, and other materials, including:

- General works: *Inheriting Hearing Loss, An Invisible Condition: The Human Side of Hearing Loss, I Think I Have a Hearing Problem! What Should I Do?, Hearing Loss: Personal and Social Considerations, Living Alone with a Hearing Loss, Sensorineural Hearing Loss, Tinnitus, Meniere's Disease, Stress Management, Persuading Your Spouse/Relative/Friend to Acknowledge a Hearing Loss and Seek Help*, and *Finding the Right Aural Rehabilitation Program.*
- On living with hearing loss: *Staying in Touch!, Communication Issues Related to Hearing Loss, Speak Out! Tips on Speaking in Public for Individuals with a Hearing Loss, Actions Speak Louder: Tips for Putting on Skits Related to Hearing Loss.*
- On communication options: *Lipreading Naturally, New Solutions to Old Problems, Telephone Strategies: A Technical and Practical Guide for Hard of Hearing People, Technical Assistance Resource Guide, Cued Speech*, audiotape *Getting Through*, and video *I See What You're Saying: A Practical Guide to Speechreading.*
- Video-and-manual packages *Relaxation Training for Hard of Hearing People, Communication Rules for Hard of Hearing People, Did I Do That?, Getting Along, Is That What You Think?*, and *A Newcomer's Guide to an Old Problem: Hearing Loss.*
- Materials on various assistive devices, videos on recent research, and materials on employment and for hospitals serving people with hearing loss.

American Association of the Deaf-Blind (AADB), 301–588–6545. (For full group information, see DEAF-BLIND.)

Deafpride
1350 Potomac Avenue SE
Washington, DC 20003
202–675–6700, voice/TT
Fax: 202–547–0547
Ann Champ-Wilson, Executive Director
Organization concerned with the human and civil rights of deaf people; acts as advocate; publishes quarterly newsletter *Deafpride Advocate Quarterly.*

National Center for Law and the Deaf
Gallaudet University
800 Florida Avenue NE
Washington, DC 20002
202–651–5373, voice/TT
Public service of Gallaudet University; aids hearing-impaired people with legal problems in many areas; publishes various materials.

Deaf-REACH
3521 12th Street NE
Washington, DC 20017
202–832–6681, voice/TT
Fax: 202–832–8454
Rebecca Clark, Executive Director
Organization of people who are deaf and also have other disabilities; formerly the National Health Care Foundation for the Deaf; offers counseling, education, referral, advocacy, housing; operates community programs, including supported employment services and residential programs for deaf adults with mental illness who need to learn independent living skills; provides internships to undergraduate and graduate students who have hearing-impairment.

House Ear Institute
2100 W. Third Street
Los Angeles, CA 90057–1902
213–483–4431; 213–484–2642, TT
Fax: 213–483–3716
John W. House, M.D., President
Organization that researches and develops new approaches to ear and hearing disorders. Operates Center for Deaf Children; runs support groups for parents of deaf children; trains and updates medical professionals; maintains professional library; publishes various materials.

National Cued Speech Association (NSCA)
P.O. Box 31345
Raleigh, NC 27622
919–828–1218
Fax: 919–828–1862
Mary Elsie Daisy, Executive Director
Organization concerned with use of cued speech; provides information; publishes bimonthly newsletter *On Cue* and journal *Cued Speech Annual.*

American Tinnitus Association (ATA)
P.O. Box 5
Portland, OR 97207–0005
503–248–9985
Fax: 503–248–0024
Gloria E. Reich, Executive Director
Organization of people concerned with tinnitus; encourages formation of local mutual-support groups; provides information and makes referrals; publishes various materials including the newsletter *Tinnitus Today*; books *When Silence Is a Stranger, Tinnitus: What Is That Noise in My Head,* and *Tinnitus—Living with the Ringing in Your Ears*; brochures *Information about Tinnitus, Coping with the Stress of Tinnitus, Tinnitus Family Information, Noise: Its Effects on Hearing and Tinnitus, TMJ the Self-Help Program,* and *Hyperacusis: A Life-Altering Supersensitivity to Sound*; audiotape *Sounds of Tinnitus*; and *Tinnitus Bibliography.*

Pediatric Projects, 800–947–0947. Publishes reprint *How to Use a Sign Language Interpreter.* (For full group information, see HOSPITAL.)

Relay Service, for communication when only one party has a TT (see TEXT TYPEWRITER): 800–855–2881, voice; 800–855–2880, TT.

Helen Keller National Center for Deaf-Blind Youths and Adults (HKNC), 516–944–8900; 516–944–8637, TT; **National Family Association for Deaf-Blind**, 800–255–0411, ext. 275. (For full group information, see DEAF-BLIND.)

Agency for Health Care Policy and Research Clearinghouse, 800–358–9295. Publishes *Middle Ear Fluid in Young Children: Parent Guide* and InstantFAX materials on otitis media. (For full group information, see HEALTH INSURANCE).

Resource Center on Substance Abuse Prevention and Disability, 202–628–8442. Publishes *A Look at Alcohol and Other Drug Abuse Prevention and Deafness and Hearing Loss.* (For full group information, see HELP FOR SPECIAL CHILDREN on page 689.)

Tripod
2901 North Keystone Street
Burbank, CA 91504–1620
818–972–2080, voice/TT
Tripod Grapevine 800–352–8888, voice/TT, U.S. except CA; 800–2-TRIPOD [287–4763], CA
Megan Williams and Michael Shamberg, Founders
Barbara Lincoln, Coordinator, TRIPOD Grapevine
Organization of people concerned with hearing impairment in children (name was originally an acronym for Toward Rehabilitation Involvement for Parents of the Deaf); provides information on raising and educating hearing-impaired children; has established model educational program focusing on Montessori approaches and integrating hearing and hearing-impaired children taught by teams of hearing and deaf instructors; publishes various materials, including newsletter *Sensen* and videos *We Can Do Anything*—featuring program students—and *Language Says It All* (both available on loan).

National Information Center for Children and Youth with Disabilities (NICHCY), 800–695–0285, voice/TT. Publishes *Deafness.* (For full group information, see HELP FOR SPECIAL CHILDREN on page 689.)

HEATH Resource Center, National Clearinghouse on Postsecondary Education for Individuals with Disabilities, 800–544–3284, voice/TT. Publishes *Students Who Are Deaf or Hard of Hearing in Postsecondary Education.* (For full group information, see HELP FOR SPECIAL CHILDREN on page 689.)

Resources for Rehabilitation, 617–862–6455. Publishes brochure *Living with Hearing Loss* and books *Resources for People with Disabilities and Chronic Conditions* and *A Woman's Guide to Coping with Disability.* (For full group information, see EYE AND VISION PROBLEMS.)

Brain Injury Association, 800–444–6443. Publishes *Hearing Loss Following Head Injury.* (For full group information, see TRAUMATIC BRAIN INJURY.)

National Organization for Rare Disorders (NORD), 800–999–6673. (For full group information, see RARE DISORDERS.)

Center for Safety in the Arts (CSA), 212–227–6220. Publishes fact sheet *Hearing Loss in Musicians.* (For full group information, see ENVIRONMENTAL HAZARDS.)

ON SPECIAL PROGRAMS AND AIDS FOR THE DEAF AND HEARING IMPAIRED

International Hearing Society (IHS), 800–521–5247. (For full group information, see HEARING AID.)

Registry of Interpreters for the Deaf, Inc. (RID)
8630 Fenton Street, Suite 324
Silver Spring, MD 20910
301–608–0050, voice/TT
Fax: 301–608–0508
Clay Nettles, Executive Director
Organization of professional interpreters, translators, and transliterators; trains and certifies interpreters for the deaf; maintains register of people trained in use of American Sign Language and other signing systems; provides information; publishes various materials, including professional texts.

Telecommunications for the Deaf, Inc. (TDI)
814 Thayer Avenue
Silver Spring, MD 20910
301–589–3786, voice; 301–589–3006, TT
E-mail: sonnytdi@aol.com (America Online: SONNYTDI)
Alfred Sonnenstrahl, Executive Director
Organization of hearing-impaired people and others who use text telephones (TTs) or TTYs, formerly called Telecommunications Devices for the Deaf (TDDs); publishes international telephone directory of TT-users; promotes closed captioning and provides necessary decoders; publishes various materials, including *National Directory of TTY Numbers, GA and SK Etiquette* (on using TTs), and *One Thing Led to the Next: The Real History of TTYs*; *E.A.S.E. Program*, the Emergency Access Self Evaluation program for emergency service providers; and videos *Now You See It: Visual Technologies for Deaf and Hard of Hearing People* and *Using Your TTY*.

Hear You Are, Inc. (HYAI)
4 Musconetcong Avenue
Stanhope, NJ 07874
Voice-TT-Fax: 201–347–7662; 800–278-EARS [278–3277], voice/TT
Dorinne Davis, President
Organization providing information about therapy and assistive technology devices for people with hearing impairment; publishes numerous materials, including:

- General works: *Say That Again, Please* (on the work of a child with hearing loss or deafness), *Hearing Loss, Living with a Hearing Problem: Coping Strategies and Devices for the Hearing Impaired, Better Hearing Through Lipreading*, and *Communication Therapy*.
- For parents and teachers: *Ear Infections in Your Child, A Parent's Guide to Middle Ear Infections, Understanding Ear Infections, Early Communication Skills*, and *Activities and Ideas*.
- Catalog of therapy books and games to stimulate communication in children with hearing impairment, including videotapes on speechreading and sign language.
- Catalog of items such as FM systems, telephone and doorbell devices, television amplifiers, smoke-alert devices, hearing protection, infrared systems, and closed captions devices.
- Books for adults with hearing loss.

Modern Talking Picture Service, Inc. (MTPS)
5000 Park Street North
St. Petersburg, FL 33709
813–545–8781; 800–237–6213, voice/TT
Fax: 813–545–8782
Free service for people with hearing impairment, loaning open-captioned educational and general interest films and videos (requiring no special decoder); funded by U.S. Department of Education.

National Captioning Institute (NCI)
5203 Leesburg Pike, Suite 1500
Falls Church, VA 22041
703–998–2400; 800–533–9673;
800–321–8337, TT
Fax: 703–917–9878
Philip W. Bravin, President
Organization providing captioned services for networks and program producers; distributes decoders free to low-income families; publishes *Caption*.

National Library Services for the Blind and Physically Handicapped, Library of Congress, 800–424–8567, U.S. except DC. Publishes guides *Deaf-Blindness: National Organizations and Resources*. (For full group information, see HELP FOR SPECIAL CHILDREN on page 689.)

ABOUT SPECIAL COLLEGE PROGRAMS FOR THE DEAF

College and Career Programs
Center for Assessment and Demographic Studies
Gallaudet University
800 Florida Avenue NE
Washington, DC 20002
202–651–5000
Fax: 202–651–5746
Publishes *College and Career Programs for Deaf Students*, describing U.S. community college and technical school programs for deaf students.

National Technical Institute for the Deaf (NTID)
Lyndon Baines Johnson Building
P.O. .Box 9887
Rochester, NY 14623–0887
716–475–6400, Voice/TT
Fax: 716–475–6500.
College for students with hearing impairments, largely federally funded; part of Rochester Institute of Technology; conducts research; operates NTID Center on Employment (NCE).

Scholastic Aptitude Test (SAT), Admissions Testing Program for Handicapped Students, 609–771–7137. Offers special testing arrangements for students with disabilties, including untimed tests or additional time, interpreter, and rest breaks. (For full group information, see HELP FOR SPECIAL CHILDREN on page 689; see also SPECIAL HELP FOR SPECIAL COLLEGE STUDENTS on page 366.)

ONLINE RESOURCES

Internet: DeafGopher. Collection of resources on deafness. gopher://cal.msu.edu/11/msu/dept/deaf

Internet: Disability-Related Resources. Collection of resources, including deafness. gopher://hawking.u.washington.edu

OTHER RESOURCES

FOR FAMILIES OF HEARING-IMPAIRED CHILDREN

For Hearing People Only: Answers to Some of the Most Commonly Asked Questions about the Deaf Community, Its Culture and the Deaf Reality, 2nd ed. Matthew S. Moore and Linda Levitan. MSM Productions, 1993.

World Around You. Five times a year. Address: Gallaudet University, KDES No. 6, 800 Florida Avenue NE, Washington, DC 20002–3695.

ON TINNITUS

Tinnitus: Dealing with the Ringing in Your Ears. Richard Hallam. Thorsons, 1994.

Living with Tinnitus. David W Rees and Simon D. Smith. St. Martin's, 1992.

ON SIGN LANGUAGE, FOR FAMILIES AND CAREGIVERS

Caring for Young Children: Signing for Day Care Providers and Sitters. S. Harold Collins. Garlic Press, 1993.

Meeting Halfway in American Sign Language: A Common Ground for Effective Communication among Deaf and Hearing People. Bernard Bragg and Jack Olson. MSM Productions, 1993.

Signs for Me: Basic Sign Vocabulary for Children, Parents and Teachers. Benjamin Bahan and Joe Dannis. Dawn Sign Press, 1990.

GENERAL WORKS ON SIGN LANGUAGE

Sign Language. Phil Schaaf. Masters, 1994.

Sign Language: In a Flash. Elizabeth Burchard and Kelley Higgens-Nelson. Flash Blasters, 1994.

Signing Made Simple. Nelson, 1994.

American Sign Language: A Comprehensive Dictionary. Martin L. Sternberg. HarperCollins, 1993.

Signing Exact English. Gerilee Gustason and Esther Zawolkow. Modern Signs, 1993.

Sign Language Primer. Nelson, 1993.

American Sign Language Dictionary and Thesaurus. Ron Houston. X-Pr Austin, 1992.

The Pocket Dictionary of Signing, rev. ed. Rod R. Butterworth and Mickey Flodin. Berkley, 1992.

Gallaudet Survival Guide to Signing, exp. ed. Leonard G. Lane. Gallaudet University Press, 1990.

FOR CHILDREN

I Hear. Helen Oxenbury. Candlewick, 1995. Baby board book.

Hearing. Lillian Wright. Raintree Steck-Vaughn, 1994.

The Silent Hero. George Shea. Random, 1994.

A First Book of Sign Language: Word Signs. Debby Slier. Checkerboard, 1993.

Hearing. Mandy Suhr. Carolrhoda, 1993.

Noni Hears. Cecile Bertrand. Western, 1993.

Ears. Douglas Mathers. Troll, 1992.

A Very Special Sister. Dorothy Hoffman Levi. K. Green/Gallaudet University Press, 1992.

Hearing Things. Allan Fowler. Children's, 1991.

Finding a Common Language: Children Living with Deafness. Thomas Bergman. Gareth Stevens, 1990.

Ears Are For Hearing. Paul Showers. Crowell/Harper, 1990.

FOR PRETEENS AND TEENS

HiP Magazine. Six times a year. For ages eight through fourteen. Address: 1563 Solano Avenue, #137, Berkeley, CA 94707.

Deafness. Elaine Landau. Twenty-First Century Books, 1994.

PERSONAL EXPERIENCES

Listening: Ways of Hearing in a Silent World. Hannah Merker. HarperCollins, 1994.

Silent Observer. Christy MacKinnon. Gallaudet University Press, 1993.

The Other Side of Silence. Arden Neisser. Gallaudet University Press, 1990.

Annie's World. Nancy Smiler Levinson. Gallaudet University Press, 1990.

Hometown Heroes: Successful Deaf Youth in America. Diane Robinette. Gallaudet University Press, 1990.

Children of Silence: The Story of My Daughter's Triumph over Deafness. Kathy Robinson. Dutton, 1988.

ON COMMUNICATION CONTROVERSIES

A Child Sacrificed to the Deaf Culture. Tom Bertling. Kodiak Media, 1994.

Mask of Benevolence: Disabling the Deaf Community. Harlan Lane. Knopf, 1992.

Manual Communication: Implications for Education. Harry Bornstein, ed. Gallaudet University, 1990.

BACKGROUND WORKS

Deafness, Deprivation and IQ. J. P. Braden. Greenwood, 1994.

Psychological Development of Deaf Children. Marc Marschark. Oxford University Press, 1993.

Language and Literacy Development in Children Who Are Deaf. Barbara R. Schirmer. Macmillan, 1993.

The Hearing-Impaired Child. Antonia B. Maxon and Diane Brackett. Andover/Butterworth-Heinemann, 1992.

Encyclopedia of Deafness and Hearing Disorders. Carol Turkington and Allen Sussman. Facts on File, 1992.

Legal Rights: The Guide for Deaf and Hard of Hearing People, 4th ed. National Center for Law and Deafness. Gallaudet University Press, 1991.

Dancing without Music: Deafness in America. Beryl Lieff Benderly. Gallaudet University, 1990.

(See also HEARING AIDS; HEARING TESTS; COMMUNICATION SKILLS AND DISORDERS; SERVICE DOGS; also HELP FOR SPECIAL CHILDREN on page 689.)

early admission, in education, formal acceptance of a student into COLLEGE, before completion of HIGH SCHOOL studies, a form of ACCELERATION. (See ADMISSION.)

Early and Periodic Screening, Diagnosis, and Treatment (EPSDT), a federal program established in 1967, as part of Title 19 of the SOCIAL SECURITY Act, to foster early detection of potentially disabling conditions in children up to age 21 on Medicaid. The program seeks, through early health care, to diminish the consequences of physical or mental problems and to lessen the later need for remedial services, which, in the long run, enhances the child's ability to live an independent life. Under EPSDT, each child on Medicaid should be screened at least once a year. The screening includes a full history of health, development, EDUCATION, NUTRITION, and IMMUNIZATION; an unclothed physical examination; laboratory tests; vision tests (see EYE AND VISION PROBLEMS), hearing tests (see EAR AND HEARING PROBLEMS), dental screening (see TEETH AND DENTAL PROBLEMS), and (between ages one and five) screening for LEAD POISONING.

Although initially too poorly funded to carry out its mission properly, EPSDT helped diagnose and obtain treatment for many otherwise undetected, potentially debilitating conditions. Under the Omnibus Budget Reconciliation Act (OBRA) of 1989, the program was expanded, notably requiring that state Medicaid programs pay for any "medically necessary" services (such as dental care, DEVELOPMENTAL SCREENING TESTS, and vision care, including eyeglasses) required by a child under Medicaid, whether or not that state's Medicaid plan normally covers that specific service. OBRA also allowed a wider range of professionals to perform evaluations, permitting some providers to administer part of the screening, even if others must perform the rest. Any child on Medicaid is automatically covered by the EPSDT program. States are urged by law to encourage participation of all eligible children, but a parent, GUARDIAN, or advocate (see ADVOCACY) must see that the child actually receives the required evaluation and services.

FOR HELP AND FURTHER INFORMATION

National Maternal and Child Health Clearinghouse (NMCHC), 703–821–8955. Publishes *EPSDT: A Guide to Educational Programs.* (For full group information, see PREGNANCY.)

Zero to Three National Center for Clinical Infant Programs, 703–528–4300. Publishes *Diagnostic Classification of Mental Health and Developmental Disorders of Infancy and Early Childhood, Screening and Assessment: Guidelines for Identifying Young Disabled and Developmentally Vulnerable Children and Their Families,* and *Warning Signals: Basic Criteria for Tracking At-Risk Infants and Toddlers,* and audiocassettes on *Screening Assessment* and *Diagnosis.* (For full group information, see CHILD CARE.)

National Information Center for Children and Youth with Disabilities (NICHCY), 800–695–0285, voice/TT. Publishes bibliography *Assessing Children for the Presence of a Disability.* (For full group information, see HELP FOR SPECIAL CHILDREN on page 689.)

ERIC (Educational Resources Information Center) Clearinghouse on Assessment and Evaluation, 800–464–3742. (For full group information, see HELP ON LEARNING AND EDUCATION on page 659.)

OTHER RESOURCES

Your Child and Health Care: A "Dollars & Sense" Guide for Families with Special Needs. Lynn Robinson Rosenfeld. Paul H. Brookes, 1994.

(See HELP FOR SPECIAL CHILDREN on page 689.)

early childhood education, a general term with varying meanings, sometimes referring to PRESCHOOL education, including NURSERY SCHOOL, HEAD START, or any other programs before KINDERGARTEN level; sometimes referring to any school-based education from PREPRIMARY LEVEL through PRIMARY SCHOOL.

early decision plan, in education, a program of early student application, usually in autumn of the senior year, and early response by a COLLEGE, usually in December. (See ADMISSION.)

Early Education for Children with Disabilities Program Projects (EEPCD), a network of federally funded projects conducting research on early EDUCATION of children with DEVELOPMENTAL DISORDERS and also providing outreach, technical assistance, and model programs; established under the INDIVIDUALS WITH DISABILITIES EDUCATION ACT (IDEA).

early intervention, an umbrella term for services provided for children who are experiencing, or are considered AT RISK of, DEVELOPMENTAL DELAY. Various government programs, such as CHILDFIND, have been established to try to identify children with developmental delay, so services can be provided as early as possible.

Amendments to the EDUCATION FOR ALL HANDICAPPED CHILDREN ACT and its successor, the INDIVIDUALS WITH DISABILITIES EDUCATION ACT, require states to have early intervention programs for children from birth to age two who show developmental delays in COGNITIVE DEVELOPMENT, physical development, communication (see COMMUNICATION SKILLS AND DISORDERS), social and emotional development, or ADAPTIVE BEHAVIOR, and also to children who have a diagnosed condition with a "high probability of resulting in developmental delays," including DOWN SYNDROME, EPILEPSY, CHROMOSOMAL ABNOR-

MALITIES, GENETIC DISORDERS, BIRTH DEFECTS, METABOLIC DISORDERS, FETAL ALCOHOL SYNDROME, and severe sensory impairments. Individual states may also provide such services to other children considered AT-RISK for developmental delay, including babies born with LOW BIRTH WEIGHT, RESPIRATORY DISTRESS SYNDROME, or PRENATAL exposure to harmful substances, such as COCAINE, and babies born of a teenage mother (see ADOLESCENT PREGNANCY), of a mother or father with a developmental disability, or into a family with a low educational level or living in poverty.

Services may be provided in the home or elsewhere in the community, but must include (as necessary) ASSISTIVE TECHNOLOGY devices, audiology, speech-language pathology services, vision services, diagnostic and evaluative medical services, nursing services, nutrition services, physical therapy, occupational therapy, social work services, family training and counseling, and transportation to and from services.

Whatever services the state elects to offer, an infant or toddler identified as "in need" must be promptly referred for evaluation and an INDIVIDUALIZED FAMILY SERVICE PLAN (IFSP) developed within forty-five days of referral. The state must also identify a lead agency to coordinate its early intervention program, have a coordinating council with parent participation, conduct public awareness programs about developmental delays, establish a central directory of early intervention services and experts in the state, including support groups, and maintain a database on children requiring services, their numbers, and the kind of services being provided.

Under the IDEA, states establish definitions of which children have developmental delay or which have conditions with a "high probability or resulting in developmental delay." The law stresses the importance of having the assessment of developmental delay made in the context of the child's home situation. Services are provided only with parental approval, and confidentiality of services to both child and parent are to be maintained. Parents and GUARDIANS are also allowed full access to all records and evaluations of the child, the family, and the child's progress under the IFSP.

FOR HELP AND FURTHER INFORMATION

Council for Exceptional Children (CEC), 800–328–0272. Includes Division for Early Childhood (DEC), which publishes newsletter *DEC Communicator*, *Journal of Early Intervention*, and other materials. CEC also publishes *Meeting Early Intervention Challenges: Issues from Birth to Three* and numerous special-topic reports. (For full group information, see HELP ON LEARNING AND EDUCATION on page 659.)

Center for Law and Education, 202–986–3000. Publishes "Information for Parents" brochures *Protecting Parents' Right to Privacy: The Significance of Consent and Confidentiality in the Provision of Early Intervention Services.* (For full group information, see HELP ON LEARNING AND EDUCATION on page 659.)

PACER Center (Parent Advocacy Coalition for Educational Rights), 612–827–2966, voice/TT. Publishes *Parents Can Play a Role in Local IEICs (Interagency Early Intervention Committees)* and *Parents and Professionals* (two articles). (For full group information, see HELP FOR SPECIAL CHILDREN on page 689.)

(See also specific disabilities; also HELP FOR SPECIAL CHILDREN on page 689.)

Early Screening Inventory (ESI), a DEVELOPMENTAL SCREENING TEST that attempts to assess ability to acquire new skills; it is administered individually or in groups to children ages four through six. Among the test's four sections are tasks calling for free drawing and copying figures, language comprehension and expression, reasoning and counting, and balancing and motor coordination. Parents are asked to fill out a questionnaire on the child's family background, including medical history. Scoring is done according to a manual, and results may be used to indicate that a child needs further evaluation, as with a DIAGNOSTIC ASSESSMENT TEST. (See TESTS.)

eating disorders, a group of MENTAL DISORDERS; a psychiatric classification, including ANOREXIA NERVOSA, BULIMIA NERVOSA, PICA, and RUMINATION DISORDER OF INFANCY; BINGE EATING DISORDER may also be included in this category.

echolalia, repetition of someone else's words or phrases, in a parrotlike, meaningless way. This behavior is found among some people with brain dysfunctions or MENTAL DISORDERS such as SCHIZOPHRENIA, or with conditions such as TOURETTE SYNDROME.

eclampsia, a rare but extremely serious condition affecting women late in PREGNANCY, during LABOR, and shortly after DELIVERY. It generally occurs following unchecked PREECLAMPSIA. Many symptoms of preeclampsia—such as hypertension (high BLOOD PRESSURE), EDEMA (fluid buildup), and PROTEIN in the urine (*proteinuria*)—become more severe and are often accompanied by SEIZURES that threaten both mother and baby, sometimes resulting in COMA or death. Emergency delivery is often performed, by CESAREAN SECTION, if necessary, because the condition generally clears soon after CHILDBIRTH; however, severe damage may already have been done to many body systems.

With proper PRENATAL CARE, preeclampsia need not progress to eclampsia, but once severe symptoms of eclampsia develop, perhaps 1 out of 4 babies and 1 out of 10 mothers will die. The cause is unknown, though some have suggested that preeclampsia and eclampsia are triggered by a toxin (poison) produced by the PLACENTA, the fetus-nourishing organ in the UTERUS. Indeed, preeclampsia and eclampsia are sometimes considered mild and severe forms of a condition called *toxemia of pregnancy*. (See PREGNANCY.)

ecological inventory, a type of survey performed by a SPECIAL EDUCATION teacher to identify skills that a child with DISABILITIES needs to develop in order to function successfully later as adult in work and in everyday living situations, such as stores, restaurants, parks, and buses.

ectopic pregnancy, any PREGNANCY that is implanted and develops outside the UTERUS, generally in the FALLOPIAN TUBES (called a *tubal pregnancy*) but sometimes in one of the OVARIES or, on rare occasions, in the CERVIX or elsewhere in the abdominal cavity. A woman who has previously had an operation on or infection in the Fallopian tubes is at increased risk for having an ectopic pregnancy; use of an IUD, congenital abnormalities, use of some kinds of BIRTH CONTROL PILLS, and earlier attempted STERILIZATION may also increase risk. Ectopic pregnancy is a common condition, affecting perhaps 1–2 out of 100 pregnancies. In some cases, the fertilized egg (CONCEPTUS) is not VIABLE and simply dies and is reabsorbed into body tissues at a very early stage.

Early signs of ectopic pregnancy often include missed menstrual periods, severe abdominal pain, and spotting (light bleeding) from the VAGINA. If the ectopic pregnancy is undiscovered and the tube or other location ruptures, hemorrhage can lead to SHOCK and in some cases to death. In addition to PREGNANCY TESTS, diagnosis is often made through ULTRASOUND and LAPAROSCOPY. If ectopic pregnancy is confirmed, an emergency operation (*laparotomy*) is performed to remove the developing EMBRYO and any associated tissues, and to repair (or remove) the tube or other nearby structures. Often BLOOD TRANSFUSIONS are needed if the tube has ruptured. Chances of normal conception are reduced after an ectopic pregnancy, but IN VITRO FERTILIZATION can bypass the tubes by implanting an embryo directly into the uterus. (See PREGNANCY.)

edema, abnormal accumulation of fluid in the body's tissues, causing swelling; a sign of imbalances and disruptions of the body's chemistry that can result from a wide variety of diseases and disorders, such as KIDNEY AND UROLOGICAL PROBLEMS. Drugs called *diuretics* are often prescribed and salt is restricted in the diet to lessen fluid retention.

education, the process by which a child (and later an adult) acquires new knowledge and skills, especially those necessary for independent living, whether by informal exposure to new data, ideas, and experiences, the semiformal teaching of a parent, or by formal, organized instruction in a school.

Parents are a child's first teacher, through whom the child begins to learn that the world is an interesting place and worth communicating with. They have the important task of establishing regular contact between the baby and the world from birth on and encouraging the baby's efforts to interact with the people and things in his or her environment. (Subscribers to the America Online computer service can find activities designed to develop children's skills in various areas, as well as general guidelines for teaching young children, in the Moms Online Desk Reference section of Moms Online, under "Teaching Young Children.") Working parents need to be sure that their baby receives the necessary attention and stimulation in CHILD CARE. Babies who do not get the required physical contact and sensory stimulation can lapse into a kind of apathy or DEPRESSION, ceasing attempts to make contact with the world. As a result, they can become retarded in development, a condition known medically as MARASMUS, or FAILURE TO THRIVE. Much teaching, of course, goes on under the heading of play. Many everyday household items can fruitfully be used as toys for babies. (For safety cautions, see CHILDPROOFING; SAFETY.)

BABY'S GROWTH AND DEVELOPMENT: THE FIRST YEAR (on page 212) gives some sense of what babies, *on the average*, learn to do at different stages within their first year. This chart will help parents adjust to their baby's development, rather than becoming frustrated themselves or making their baby uncomfortable by trying to teach the infant something most babies don't learn until they are older. Knowledge of how a baby grows and develops can also help parents plan ahead to keep a baby's environment safe. For guidance on doing so, depending on what the baby can do at each stage of development, see YOUR BABY'S FIRST YEAR: A SAFETY CHECKLIST (on page 520) and SAFETY.

Parents should not be concerned if their baby reaches a DEVELOPMENTAL MILESTONE later (or earlier!) than on the chart, but they should examine why this might be. Babies are individuals, and variations in the timing of development of skills does not mean that they have problems. If a child develops late in just one or two areas, and average or fast in others, this may be a mark of the child's individual learning pattern. But if the baby is late in developing most skills, parents should ask themselves the following questions.

- Have they been giving the child an opportunity to learn?
- Have they been praising and encouraging the child's efforts?
- Is the child a premature baby or physically ill?

If they do not see a reason for the late development, and the child does not improve, they should have a doctor or clinic staff check the child. If they say the baby will "grow out of it" but the child still does not seem to be developing, they should seek another opinion. If there is a health problem or some lack of opportunity to learn and develop, the sooner the problem is recognized and either corrected or dealt with, the better for the child's long-term development.

Baby's Growth and Development: The First Year

Here are some of the things you can usually expect your baby to do in the first year of life.

BY ABOUT SIX WEEKS:

- Holds head off of bed for a few moments while lying on stomach.
- Follows an object with eyes for a short distance.
- Pays attention to sounds.
- Makes a few vocal sounds other than crying.
- Looks at your face.
- Smiles when you smile or play with him or her.
- Moves arms and legs in an energetic manner.

BY ABOUT FIVE MONTHS:

- Holds head upright while lying on stomach.
- Holds head steady when held in a sitting position.
- Laughs, squeals, and babbles.
- Turns to your voice.
- Rolls over.
- Eyes follow an object that moves from side to side.
- Recognizes parents.
- Brings hands together in front of the body.
- Reaches for and holds objects.
- Passes object from one hand to the other.
- Begins to chew.
- Stretches out arms to be picked up.
- Smiles by himself or herself.

BY ABOUT EIGHT MONTHS:

- Sits without support when placed in sitting position.
- Takes part of weight on own legs when held steady.
- Creeps (moves body forward with arm movements and leg kicks).
- Starts to make recognizable sounds ("baa" or "daa").
- Responds to "no" and to his or her name.
- Grasps object off of flat surface.
- Eats crackers by himself or herself.
- Looks around for the source of new sounds.

BY ABOUT TEN MONTHS:

- Gets into sitting position on his or her own.
- Stands, holding on.
- Crawls.
- Picks up a small object with thumb and fingers.
- Tries to get an object that is out of reach.
- Pulls back when you try to pull a toy from his or her hand.
- Drinks from a cup when it is held to his or her mouth.
- Plays peek-a-boo.
- Uses voice to get attention.

BY ABOUT TWELVE MONTHS:

- Brings together two toys held in hand.
- Imitates your speech.
- Uses "Dada" or "Mama" to mean a specific person.
- Plays pat-a-cake.
- Can walk holding onto something.
- Finds one object under another.
- Waves bye-bye.
- Understands simple words and phrases ("Come here").

SOON AFTER BABY'S FIRST BIRTHDAY:

- Stands alone, then walks alone.
- Scribbles with a pencil or crayon.
- Drinks from a cup by self.
- Uses a spoon (spills a little!).
- Plays with a ball on the floor.
- Can say two or three words (may not be clear).

Don't worry if your baby is different—each baby develops in his or her own way. However, if you notice large variations from what you might expect, or if you have other concerns, ask your doctor or clinic staff. (Note: If your baby arrived early—was premature—he or she may develop a little later in some things and not in others.)

Source: Infant Care. Washington, DC: Government Printing Office (1989). Prepared for the Public Health Service, Bureau of Maternal and Child Health and Resources Development.

In families where the parent or parents work outside the home, an infant is likely to be in the care of others, such as a NANNY in the home or CHILD CARE in a variety of other settings, from a very early age on. During the day, in the parents' absence, these caregivers are responsible for teaching the baby. From ages two to three, many babies are part of PLAY GROUPS, where they begin to develop their social skills. From ages three to five, many children join somewhat more formal, organized groups and classes, in various PRESCHOOL programs, including NURSERY SCHOOLS, HEAD START programs, PREKINDERGARTEN, and MONTESSORI SCHOOLS. (For information on evaluating early childhood programs, see PRESCHOOLS.)

During these years, children develop a wide range of skills. The CHART OF NORMAL DEVELOPMENT (on page 637) indicates when between birth and age six children first *on the average* begin to develop the key skills: MOTOR SKILLS (gross and fine), communication skills (understanding and speaking language; see COMMUNICATION SKILLS AND DISORDERS), COGNITIVE SKILLS, SELF-HELP SKILLS, and SOCIAL SKILLS. Children develop at individual and varying paces, but every child can benefit from activities designed to enhance their natural development. (Subscribers to the America Online computer service can find activities designed to develop children's skills in various areas, as well as general guidelines for teaching young children, in the Moms Online Desk Reference section of Moms Online, under "Teaching Young Children.")

At about age five, many children enter the formal school system in KINDERGARTEN; where no kindergarten exists, some enter ELEMENTARY or PRIMARY SCHOOL at about age six in first grade. By law, children are required to be in COMPULSORY ATTENDANCE at a school between specified ages, usually six to sixteen. During this period, therefore, legal requirements, rights, and responsibilities impinge on the parent's educational choices.

Some parents choose to educate their children themselves, through HOME SCHOOLING; if they do, they need to meet whatever requirements have been set for children's education in their state of residence. Some parents educate their children at home in the early years, later sending the children to regular schools. Others follow home schooling through their children's ADOLESCENCE, often using correspondence materials for INDEPENDENT STUDY. Relatively few families take this very demanding approach.

A substantial minority of children—about one in eight—at this point enter PRIVATE SCHOOLS, for a variety of reasons, including differing parental views on DISCIPLINE (stricter or freer), more varied educational methods, desire for religious schooling, attempts to avoid DESEGREGATION, prestige (as with elite BOARDING SCHOOLS), and smaller classes. Parents who send their children to private schools are not exempt from taxes for PUBLIC SCHOOLS, a situation some wish to change with a VOUCHER SYSTEM, under which tax funds could be used for either public or private schools. Critics stress that this would run counter to separation of church and state, since many private schools are religiously oriented or affiliated. Many parents keep their children in private schools only until it is time to enter JUNIOR HIGH or HIGH SCHOOL, since public high schools are often better funded and therefore are likely to have the kinds of laboratory and other kinds of educational materials needed for high school classes, especially in the sciences.

The majority of students enter the public schools at age five or six and stay in them from elementary school through MIDDLE SCHOOL or junior high school and on to high school (secondary school). These schools vary widely around the country, in terms of CURRICULUM and resources, partly because Americans have long resisted any standardization of education. Recognition of the flaws and shortcomings of the current educational system, however, have led to increased discussion about instituting NATIONAL STANDARDS on curriculum and possibly national tests, to see how well those standards are met.

Certainly a major problem in education today is that the distribution of resources varies so widely. Rural schools, especially in poor, sparsely populated areas, and inner-city schools with limited resources often have trouble attracting high quality teachers, for example, and may not have the kind of equipment needed for a full science or technical program. On the other hand, children in some rural schools have the advantage of smaller classes and more personal education. Surburban schools may have resources for the physical plant and may attract good teachers, but may sometimes be impersonal and focus too heavily on achievement, rather than on developing the individual. Inner-city schools have the considerable cultural resources of the city itself to draw on, but many individual schools have been starved of funds, are wracked with VIOLENCE, and cannot attract and hold top teachers.

Under the circumstances, parents concerned with their children's education must look very carefully at the schools in their area. If they are moving into an area, they are well advised to learn as much as they can about the strengths and weaknesses of the various schools available and to make the school part of the decision about where to live. HELP ON LEARNING AND EDUCATION (on page 659) includes evaluative guides to public and private schools. The importance of schooling and the desire to provide more varied programs for many students have led to the popularity of SCHOOLS OF CHOICE, in which schools are deliberately varied to provide educational experiences among which parents and children can choose. The U.S. Department of Education's pamphlet CHOOSING A SCHOOL FOR YOUR CHILD, which includes a checklist for evaluating schools, is reproduced on page 659. Private schools are sometimes also considered "schools of choice," and certainly the same guidelines can be used in evaluating a private school.

Wherever they live, parents are advised to become actively involved in school life and help improve the quality of education in the area. Virtually every study of education indicates that the schools are improved and the

Parent Rights to Involvement in Public Schools

The National Committee for Citizens in Education (NCCE) believes parents should have a number of "rights" to become involved in the public schools their children attend. Most of those rights listed might better be classified as "expectations" parents have for their relationship with their child's school and specific tasks or activities parents can do to become active participants in the educational process. A few are based on the Constitution, federal or state laws, or Supreme Court rulings. Others have been identified by many research studies which show that any and all types of parent involvement have a positive effect on a child's success in school.

Many school districts afford these basic "rights" automatically to the parents and citizens in the community. Others do not yet feel comfortable with encouraging parents to become equal partners in the educational process. We urge parents to assert their right to participate in and be consulted about their children's education.

WHY PARENTS HAVE RIGHTS

It is the belief of NCCE that parents of children in the public schools have fundamental rights to become involved, based on the following:

- Children do better in school when their parents are involved.
- Public schools are supported by tax dollars.
- Teachers, principals, and other school personnel are public officials accountable to the school board, which in turn is accountable to the public.
- The public school system was organized to serve the citizens of the community, especially the children and their parents. As such, it should have an open atmosphere and be responsive to their needs.

PARENTS HAVE A RIGHT TO INFORMATION ABOUT:

- Teachers and principals—their background and experience.
- School policies, rules, and regulations in the areas of:
  - Health and medical regulations, such as:
    - Required examinations and inoculations.
    - Procedures if a child is sick at school.
  - Attendance regulations:
    - How many days may a student be absent or late without a penalty?
    - What should you do if your child is sick and cannot attend school?
    - Will the school inform you if your child is absent?
  - Disciplinary policy, behavior standards, grounds for suspension and exclusion, including procedures to be followed.
  - Schedule for the school year, such as:
    - Dates of parent/teacher conferences.
    - Holidays.
    - Parent meetings.
    - Report cards.
  - Sources of all rules and policies, whether state law, local district policy, or policy of the school principal.
- Grievance procedures—how you can appeal rules and regulations with which you disagree.
- Academic requirements, criteria for student evaluation, homework regulations, standards for promotion, problems your child may have with schoolwork or behavior.
- Curriculum—what is being taught, how the curriculum is organized, how students are grouped for instruction, and what methods are being employed in the classes.

PARENTS HAVE RIGHTS OF ACCESS TO:

- Review all records kept by the school about your child and to challenge inaccurate information or material that you believe is an invasion of privacy.
- Visit the school and your child's classroom after making arrangements with the school office and the classroom teacher.
- See your child's teacher and the school principal without "red tape" and delay.
- Have individual teacher conferences several times a year, in privacy, with a translator if needed, at a time convenient to both parent and teacher. The meeting may be at home if that is the only feasible way for the meeting to be held.

PARENTS HAVE RIGHTS TO PARTICIPATE AND BE CONSULTED:

- Before a change in placement, retention in grade, or assignment to a special classroom.
- To get help for a child who is not doing well.
- To appeal school decisions affecting your child.
- To organize and participate in parent organizations.
- To attend and speak at school board meetings.

WHAT RESEARCH REVEALS ABOUT PARENT INVOLVEMENT

The forty-nine studies annotated in the report, *The Evidence Continues to Grow*, document and corroborate that "when parents are involved, children do better in school, and they go to better schools."

Programs designed with strong parent involvement produce students who perform better than programs that are otherwise identical but without parent involvement. Children whose parents help them at home and stay in touch with the school score higher than children of similar aptitude and family background whose parents are *not involved*. Schools where children are failing improve dramatically when parents are called in to help.

Some of the major benefits of parent involvement are:

- High grades and test scores.
- Long-term academic achievement.
- Positive attitudes and behavior.
- More successful programs.
- More effective schools.

HOW SCHOOLS BENEFIT FROM PARENT INVOLVEMENT

When parents can expect the "rights" to information, access, and consultation to be honored by school personnel, an atmosphere of trust and collaboration will develop between school and home, children will perform at a higher level, and the educational system will benefit.

Source: National Committee for Citizens in Education (now dissolved; see Center for Law and Education).

children's learning benefits from strong parental involvement. Numerous laws and policy changes have, in fact, brought parents much more into the public education system than in the past.

The federal EDUCATION FOR ALL HANDICAPPED CHILDREN ACT and its successor, the INDIVIDUALS WITH DISABILITIES EDUCATION ACT, requires states and local school districts to actively seek out, beginning in infancy and then throughout the school years, any child with a DISABILITY that affects learning. Children who may have learning problems undergo DEVELOPMENTAL SCREENING and DIAGNOSTIC ASSESSMENT TESTS, depending on what kind of problem is suspected. If a problem is diagnosed, the child is entitled to special educational services and school officials must draw up an INDIVIDUALIZED EDUCATION PROGRAM designed to overcome, eliminate, or ameliorate the problem—but none of this can take place without the parent's knowledge and consent. Parents are involved at every stage, asking questions, getting answers, acting as advocates for their child (sometimes with other advocates to help; see ADVOCACY), monitoring the child's progress, and helping modify the program, if necessary. If school and parents disagree on what is appropriate, a whole process of appeals and hearings, many of them based on considerations of DUE PROCESS, have been developed that may eventually extend to the court system.

CHAPTER 1 (of Title I of the Elementary and Secondary Education Act of 1965) is another federal program, this one providing funds to students of low-income families who are performing below GRADE level. Parents in these programs are equally involved in the processes of selecting the schools and students within those schools who will be eligible for funds.

Another federal law that affects all parents of school-age children is the FAMILY EDUCATIONAL RIGHTS AND PRIVACY ACT OF 1974 (FERPA), which gives parents (and students after age 18) access to school records and control over who gets to see them, outside of the school system and court-mandated disclosures. See that entry, and the related CHECKLIST FOR REVIEW OF SCHOOL RECORDS on page 244 for guidelines on what to look for and how to act when reviewing and attempting to revise or correct school records. Under FERPA, too, a whole appeal system operates.

As parents have increasingly become active advocates of their children's educational rights and participants in the school system that teaches them, the once informal PARENT-TEACHER CONFERENCES have often been turned into multidisciplinary team discussions of test results and educational programs. Parents may also want to review a summary of PARENT'S RIGHTS TO INVOLVEMENT IN PUBLIC SCHOOLS (above) and notes for a recommended ANNUAL EDUCATION CHECKUP (on page 216).

Annual Education Checkup

Most parents are convinced of the importance of an annual medical checkup for their children, but what about an annual education checkup? The National Committee for Citizens in Education (NCCE) suggests that a good way to help assure a child's progress in school is for every parent of a school-aged child to conduct an annual educational checkup. This checklist tells you how.

Basic steps include reviewing home and school files kept on your child and interviewing your child's teacher and possibly other members of the school staff. If your child is having special problems in school, you may need to consult some of the school system's specialists.

If, after talking to your child's teacher or counselor and reviewing and correcting the school record, any aspect of your child's schooling remains unsatisfactory to you, there are some steps you can take toward resolving the situation. You can appeal to the principal, superintendent, or school board if you disagree with disciplinary action or school policies and practices. Keep in mind that when you request a hearing, it is your right to bring your own expert, a doctor, lawyer, interpreter, or parent advocate.

Working together with the school is the best way to help your child in school. It is NCCE's hope that this review will help discover school problems early and give parents and teachers a chance to work out a plan for each child to guarantee school success.

REVIEW OF MATERIAL AT HOME

Check on school-related materials sent home during the last year. It's a good idea to keep a separate file for each child. As you review the file, ask your child for his or her comments on school. You might ask "What do you like best? What least?" and "What would you like to change?" The checklist below lists other questions to consider.

CHECKLIST FOR REVIEW OF MATERIAL AT HOME

	YES	NO	NEED MORE INFO
Do I have all previously issued report cards?	☐	☐	☐
Does any correspondence with teachers and principal remain unanswered?	☐	☐	☐
If our school produces a handbook, do I have a copy? Does it clearly answer any questions I may have about school policies on such subjects as suspension, promotion, graduating procedures, attendance, and due process rights?	☐	☐	☐
If our school does not have a handbook, do I know to whom to go for answers to questions?	☐	☐	☐
Are my child's immunizations against contagious diseases up to date, and have I made an appointment for my child's annual school medical checkup for next fall?	☐	☐	☐
Have I made a list of questions I want to ask my child's teacher, and have I set aside materials from my home file that I plan to take with me?	☐	☐	☐

To complete the checkup, you should also review the TIPS FOR PARENT-TEACHER CONFERENCES on page 452 under PARENT-TEACHER CONFERENCE and the CHECKLIST FOR REVIEW OF SCHOOL RECORDS on page 244 under FAMILY EDUCATIONAL RIGHTS AND PRIVACY ACT.

Source: National Committee for Citizens in Education (now dissolved; see Center for Law and Education).

Numerous organizations (see HELP ON LEARNING AND EDUCATION on page 659) have developed to help parents prepare themselves for these new responsibilities. One of the roles of these groups is to explain to parents the nature and significance of the many and varied TESTS given to young children (many of which are described by name in separate entries in this book).

educational age (EA), a summary reflecting how a child's score relates to a wide range of other scores on the same ACHIEVEMENT TEST; also called *achievement age.* If an eight-year-old child's score on an achievement test is the score normally achieved by children half a year older, that child's educational age will be eight years, six months. (See TEST; NORM-REFERENCED TEST; AGE.)

Educational Amendments of 1978 (Public Law 95–561), the federal statute that included the GIFTED AND TALENTED CHILDREN'S ACT of 1978 and the BASIC SKILLS AND EDUCATIONAL PROFICIENCY PROGRAM.

Educational Testing Service (ETS), a company that prepares and offers many tests for other organizations, the best-known being the SCHOLASTIC APTITITUDE TEST written by the ETS for the COLLEGE ENTRANCE EXAMINATION BOARD.

Education for All Handicapped Children Act (EHC), the more formal name of this act is Public Law 94–142, a 1975 federal law that established the rights of children with DISABILITIES to a free and appropriate public EDUCATION, when previously many such children had received little or no benefit from the PUBLIC SCHOOL system. An earlier, related statute was SECTION 504 of the Rehabilitation Act of 1973 (part of the Civil Rights Act for Handicapped Persons), which barred any organization or institution receiving federal funds from discriminating in any way against qualified people with disabilities.

The EHC required schools to provide an appropriate education to children with disabilities and to ensure them access to educational services or risk losing all federal funds. (Private and parochial schools, which receive no federal funds, are not covered by the law.)

Amendments in 1986 (Public Law 99–457) required provision of appropriate PRESCHOOL programs for children from ages three to five and EARLY INTERVENTION programs for children from birth to age two. It also mandated establishment of PARENT TRAINING AND INFORMATION (PTI) CENTERS in each state to help parents understand the rights of their children with disabilities; these in turn established TECHNICAL ASSISTANCE FOR PARENTS PROGRAM (TAPP) agencies to help families take advantage of the programs for their children.

Provisions of the EHC were consolidated and reauthorized under the INDIVIDUALS WITH DISABILITIES EDUCATION ACT (IDEA) in 1991 (see separate entry).

Edwards' syndrome (trisomy 18), a CONGENITAL condition stemming from a CHROMOSOMAL ABNORMALITY that results from the existence of three copies (*trisomy*) of chromosome 18. Infants with Edwards' syndrome have severe MENTAL RETARDATION and often numerous defects, such as CLEFT LIP AND PALATE, SYNDACTYLY, CLUB FEET, and malformation of internal organs. Most die within a few months.

FOR HELP AND FURTHER INFORMATION

Support Organization for Trisomy 18, 13 and Related Disorders (SOFT)
2982 South Union Street
Rochester, NY 14624
716–594–4621
Barb VanHerreweghe, President
Organization concerned with trisomy 18 or 13 or related disorders; provides support; publishes various materials, including quarterly newsletter *S.O.F.T. Touch*; *Trisomy 18: A Book for Families*; *Care of the Childen and Infant with Trisomy 18 and Trisomy 13*; brochure *Trisomy 18*; and pamphlet *S.O.F.T.*

National Organization for Rare Disorders (NORD), 800–999–6673. (For full group information, see RARE DISORDERS.)

(See also GENETIC DISORDERS.)

effacement, in PREGNANCY, the softening and flattening of the CERVIX during LABOR and its merging with the UTERUS wall in preparation for the actual DELIVERY of a baby.

egg, in relation to PREGNANCY, the OVUM that unites with a SPERM at the point of CONCEPTION or FERTILIZATION.

egg donation, a treatment for INFERTILITY in which an egg (OVUM) from one woman is implanted into another woman, after being fertilized by SPERM from the second woman's partner or sperm donor. The procedure involves use of various forms of REPRODUCTIVE TECHNOLOGY, such as IN VITRO FERTILIZATION or GAMETE INTRA-FALLOPIAN TUBE TRANSFER.

Egg donation is less hazardous than EMBRYO TRANSFER, in which the donor is inseminated and the embryo implanted in her uterus is flushed out. However, it does involve some pain and risk for the donor, who must undergo hormonal stimulation and surgical removal of the eggs (see IN VITRO FERTILIZATION). This makes recruitment of donors difficult, especially since in the best programs donors are accepted only after they have undergone extensive screening for GENETIC DISORDERS, SEXUALLY TRANSMITTED DISEASES, and other medical problems, as well as psychological and social screening. In the past, eggs not used during in vitro fertilization were commonly donated into an egg donor "pool." However, with continued advances in freezing human eggs and embryos (*cryopreservation*), many woman prefer to save these for possible future attempts at pregnancy—which means that there are fewer eggs available. As a result, a large proportion of egg donations are from relatives or other people known to the couple. In one notable case using this process, a grandmother bore her grandchild, when her daughter was unable to do so herself. Egg donation is especially attractive to women who are over 40, who have prematurely failed ovaries or no ovaries at all, who have genetic disorders that bar them from using their own eggs, or who are facing therapies that would probably end their fertility, such as chemotherapy for CANCER.

A more general concern relating to egg donation is the long-term relationship between the donor (when that person is not anonymous) and the couple having the child. In particular, the couple needs to be concerned with whether the donor will interfere in the raising of the child or even attempt to gain CUSTODY at some later date. There are also some religious questions. The Roman Catholic church is opposed to *in vitro* fertilization and related reproductive technology approaches. Also, in Judaism, the baby's religion is determined by the mother's religion; but for these purposes, it is not clear who is regarded as the mother. (See INFERTILITY; REPRODUCTIVE TECHNOLOGY.)

ejaculation, the emission of SEMEN from a male's PENIS at the point of ORGASM. In response to rhythmic pressure on the penis, muscles in the area move the constituents of semen—SPERM from the EPIDIDYMIS through the VAS DEFERENS, fluids from the PROSTATE GLAND, and secretions from the SEMINAL VESICLES—into the EJACULATORY DUCT, prior to release, and then into the URETHRA, from which it is released during ejaculation. (A valve normally closes off the bladder, so urine does not leak into the semen.)

Ejaculation can sometimes occur too quickly, a condition called *premature ejaculation* that is common in ADOLESCENTS but also occurs in adults, frequently from overstimulation or anxiety. Sometimes ejaculation fails to occur at all. Referred to as *inhibited ejaculation*, it can happen because of drugs, disorders such as DIABETES, or psychological problems. If medical problems have been ruled out, sex therapy can sometimes help. Occasionally, especially in cases of neurological damage or pelvic surgery, the valve to the bladder fails to operate properly and semen is released into the bladder instead of into the penis. Adolescents often have ejaculations during sleep, called *nocturnal emissions* or *wet dreams*. These are quite normal, though they may cause anxiety or embarrassment to teenagers.

ejaculatory duct, a short tube in which SPERM from the EPIDIDYMIS (by way of the VAS DEFERENS) mixes with fluids from the PROSTATE GLAND and secretions from the SEMINAL VESICLES. The resulting mixture is SEMEN, which is released into the URETHRA during EJACULATION at the point of ORGASM.

elective, an optional course that a student may take, as opposed to the courses in a school's core CURRICULUM, which all students must take.

electrocardiograph (ECG or EKG), a MEDICAL TEST that records the electrical activity of the heart used in diagnosing heart disorders. Electrodes are attached painlessly to the chest, wrists, and ankles; these transmit information about the electrical changes in the heart as it undergoes each rest-contraction cycle. The information is usually recorded as a graph on a sheet of paper (sometimes also on a screen), which physicians analyze for information about possible abnormalities in the heart's functioning. An ECG can be done in a doctor's office, clinic, or hospital; in some cases, as in an INTENSIVE CARE UNIT, the ECG machine may remain attached for hours or days, until the need for such monitoring is passed. (See MEDICAL TESTS; HEART AND HEART PROBLEMS.)

electroencephalograph (EEG), a MEDICAL TEST that records the electrical activity of the BRAIN, an aid in the diagnosis of such disorders as EPILEPSY, BRAIN TUMORS, MENTAL RETARDATION, and MENTAL DISORDERS. Electrodes are painlessly attached to the patient's scalp, and as an extremely weak current is passed between them, the electroencephalograph records the brain's electrical activity during a variety of activities, including responses to bright lights, drugs, visual exercises, or sleep. A more recent type of test, *brain stem auditory evoked responses* (BSAER), uses EEG-type technology to test for EAR AND HEARING PROBLEMS. (See MEDICAL TESTS.)

electrolytes, substances that break up into electrically charged particles when dissolved or melted in fluids such as the blood and are vital to the normal functioning of the body. Some kinds of disorders, such as METABOLIC DISORDERS, and more general disorders, such as DEHYDRATION resulting from DIARRHEA, can cause loss of electrolytes or imbalance between them (*acid-base imbalance*), disrupting the body and sometimes even threatening life. Among the key electrolytes are SODIUM (important in maintaining fluid balance), CALCIUM (needed for the relaxation of skeletal muscle, contraction of heart muscle, and building bones), POTASSIUM (needed for contraction of skeletal muscle and relaxation of heart muscle), CHLORIDE, hydrogen, MAGNESIUM, bicarbonate, PROTEINS, PHOSPHATE, and sulfate.

electromyogram (EMG), a MEDICAL TEST in which the electrical activity in a set of muscles is recorded and analyzed. The electromyogram is a harmless test in which small electrodes are placed on or in the skin and the patterns of electrical activity are projected on a screen or over a loudspeaker. An EMG is used to test for muscle disorders, such as MUSCULAR DYSTROPHY.

elementary school, an institution providing EDUCATION to grades 1–5, and sometimes also to KINDERGARTEN and grades 6–8 if these are housed in the same set of buildings; also called a PRIMARY SCHOOL, *grade school,* or *grammar school.* From elementary school, children move either into MIDDLE SCHOOL or directly into HIGH SCHOOL. While KINDERGARTEN is largely preparatory, in the first grade children begin to learn the three R's—reading 'riting, and 'rithmetic—and are gradually introduced to material in science, geography, and history that is simplified at first, but becomes increasingly sophisticated as the grades progress. The U.S. Department of Education has also recommended that children have some exposure to foreign languages, computers, music, and art in elementary school.

Americans have in the past resisted any attempts at formulating a national curriculum for elementary schools and HIGH SCHOOLS, but in recent decades concern over the decline of some basic educational skills among students has inclined many to view the idea more favorably (see NATIONAL STANDARDS).

In general, children in elementary school spend most of their time in a single classroom with one teacher, going to other locations only for special activities, such as art or gym. The Department of Education has also increasingly recommended that parents exercise choice in finding the right school for their child; see CHOOSING A SCHOOL FOR YOUR CHILD (on page 659), which provides a checklist for evaluating schools. (See HELP ON LEARNING AND EDUCATION on page 659.)

elimination diet, a restrictive diet that eliminates all foods or additives thought to trigger or worsen the problem in question, such as an ALLERGY or digestive disorder (see DIGESTIVE SYSTEM AND DISORDERS). Also an alternate term for the *Feingold diet,* sometimes used in the treatment of ATTENTION DEFICIT HYPERACTIVITY DISORDER.

emancipated minors, a child generally under 18 who is classed as a MINOR, but who has become free of parental control and CUSTODY. Minors who leave home, join the military, or otherwise assume legal responsibility for themselves and show their full independence from parental support may legally be declared emancipated by a court; those who marry or who have a court-supervised legal agreement with their parents may be emancipated without court order, though in some states they will require a court order or their parents' consent to the marriage. Once emancipated, minors have all the legal rights and responsibilities of an adult, including the ability to sign a contract or make a will. In some circumstances, however, parents may still have CHILD SUPPORT responsibilities toward emancipated minors, unless they are formally canceled by the court.

embryo, a medical designation for the growing being early during a PREGNANCY, from the time of IMPLANTATION, when the fertilized egg attaches itself to the lining of the UTERUS, through the first eight weeks of GESTATION. After that point, the being is generally known as a FETUS. More generally, the term *embryo* is used for the fertilized egg from the point of FERTILIZATION, especially in the various types of REPRODUCTIVE TECHNOLOGY. The unfertilized egg and then the embryo have a protective outer layer, the ZONA PELLUCIDA, which it sheds just before implantation, a process called *hatching.* Techniques of ASSISTED FERTILIZATION focus on helping sperm penetrate the zona pellucida, while ASSISTED HATCHING focuses on helping the embryo shed that layer before implantation. In some cases, EMBRYO BIOPSY (also called *pre-implantation genetic diagnosis*) is used to screen an embryo for GENETIC DISORDERS before implantation.

Soon after implantation, some of the egg's cells begin to develop the nourishing PLACENTA. Also a sac filled with AMNIOTIC FLUID begins to form, cushioning the developing embryo. (It is this fluid that is sampled in the GENETIC SCREENING test called AMNIOCENTESIS.) These early weeks of embryonic development are crucial to the new being; it is during this period, by the fifth week, that all the major organs begin to develop. And it is also during this period, often before a woman even realizes that she is pregnant, that great damage can be done by ingesting alcohol or taking drugs and by exposure to radiation and other ENVIRONMENTAL HAZARDS that can lead to BIRTH DEFECTS. (See PREGNANCY; BIRTH DEFECTS.)

embryo biopsy, a GENETIC SCREENING approach that is used in conjunction with various forms of REPRODUCTIVE TECHNOLOGY on EMBRYOS created by IN VITRO FERTILIZATION or related laboratory techniques; also called *pre-implantation genetic diagnosis.* In this procedure, one or a few cells are removed from the embryo and examined in the laboratory for possible GENETIC DEFECTS, so that only embryos without obvious defects can be selected for transfer or freezing for later use. This is still a new and highly experimental technique, with potential to harm the fetus; the first twenty or so babies born by this technique showed no unusual problems, but the long-term effects remain to be seen. Like many of the new reproductive techniques, much depends on the skill and experience of the person actually performing the procedure. Among the genetic disorders and CHROMOSOMAL ABNORMALITIES that can currently be identified this way are CYSTIC FIBROSIS, DOWN SYNDROME, and Tay-Sachs disease (see LIPID STORAGE DISEASES); but many more should soon be identifiable, as each week seems to bring announcement of newly discovered genetic markers. (See IN VITRO FERTILIZATION; REPRODUCTIVE TECHNOLOGY; GENETIC DISORDER.)

embryologist, a health professional focusing on the study of EMBRYOS that are formed from the joinder of SPERM and egg (OVUM). Embryologists have become increasingly important as the field of reproductive technology has developed. In IN VITRO FERTILIZATION and related early reproductive techniques, their main work focused on maintaining optimum laboratory conditions for holding sperm and egg and the resulting embryo, until it was implanted into the MOTHER. But the embryologists have since developed newer, more revolutionary techniques, using MICROMANIPULATION to achieve FERTILIZATION.

embryo transfer, in general, the placement of a fertilized egg (EMBRYO) in a woman's uterus for possible IMPLANTATION; a procedure basic to IN VITRO FERTILIZATION and many other types of REPRODUCTIVE TECHNOLOGY. Embryo transfer is also a specific approach to INFERTILITY that involves a female egg (OVUM) donor, who volunteers to be inseminated with a man's sperm. After the fertilized egg has been implanted in her UTERUS for a few days, the developing EMBRYO is flushed out and implanted into the uterus of the man's wife or sex partner. For the procedure to work, the two women's MENSTRUAL CYCLES must be in unison. No surgery is involved, but the donor faces two potential physical problems: the embryo may resist flushing, leaving her pregnant, or it may be flushed up into the Fallopian tubes, causing a life-threatening ECTOPIC PREGNANCY and necessitating emergency surgery. Various legal questions need to be resolved, not the least of which is: Which woman is the legal mother? Though this technique has long been used with animals, it is still so new among humans that its success rate—and problem rate—is not yet clear. Because of the problems associated with it, other fertilization alternatives have come to be preferred, such as EGG DONATION. (See INFERTILITY; CHILDBIRTH.)

encephalitis, infection and inflammation of the BRAIN, most commonly by a virus but sometimes by bacteria, often in connection with MENINGITIS (inflammation of the membrane covering the brain) or other infections such as AIDS, MEASLES, MUMPS, or CHICKEN POX. The virus most often responsible is a form of HERPES, which causes cold sores. In *St. Louis encephalitis,* the virus is introduced to the body by a mosquito bite. Symptoms include FEVER, headache, confusion, disturbed perception and behavior, PARALYSIS and weakness, SEIZURES, and sometimes loss of consciousness, COMA, and death. Physicians may use a variety of methods to diagnose the disease, such as CT SCAN, LUMBAR PUNCTURE, ELECTROENCEPHALOGRAM, BLOOD TESTS, and even a BIOPSY. Little can be done to treat most forms of the disease, though an antiviral drug can be used against the herpes virus. Recovery depends on the patient's age and condition. Those who do recover often have some kinds of brain damage. (See MENINGITIS.)

encoding, the process of converting spoken or signed words or numbers into written symbols. An important intellectual skill basic to much learning, encoding poses significant problems for many people with brain dysfunction. A child with LEARNING DISABILITIES, especially DYSLEXIA, for example, may see printed words upside down, backwards, or distorted in a variety of ways and so may have trouble encoding the symbols. Similarly, a child with DYSCALCULIA may have trouble encoding and working with mathematical symbols. Such children may also have trouble with the reverse process, DECODING. (See WRITING.)

endocrine system, the set of glands that produce many of the key HORMONES needed to regulate the body's functioning, including the HYPOTHALAMUS, PITUITARY GLAND, THYROID GLAND, parathyroid glands, THYMUS, ADRENAL GLANDS, and the sex organs called GONADS (TESTES in the male and OVARIES in the female).

endodontist, a DENTIST who specializes in treating the living pulp of teeth, especially in doing ROOT CANAL THERAPY. (See TEETH AND DENTAL PROBLEMS.)

endometriosis, abnormal growth in the body of tissue (*endometrium)* that normally lines the UTERUS, which sometimes grows in other reproductive organs such as the OVARIES, the FALLOPIAN TUBES, the outside wall of the uterus, and the pelvic area between the uterus and rectum. Like the endometrium during a normal MENSTRUAL CYCLE, this tissue breaks down and bleeds monthly. However, because the blood has no outlet, blood-filled cysts form, which are both painful and a leading cause of INFERTILITY.

The cause of endometriosis is unknown, though some suggest that it may be triggered by a problem in the IMMUNE SYSTEM. It generally affects women between ages twenty-five and forty-five, becoming increasingly common as a woman grows older. The condition often causes painful sexual intercourse and painful or otherwise abnormal menstrual periods, the pain varying with the menstrual cycle. Where it is widespread, scar tissue can virtually bind reproductive organs in place, sometimes trapping eggs (see OVUM) within the ovaries.

The condition is normally confirmed by a LAPAROSCOPY, visual examination of the abdomen through a small incision, but requires treatment only if it is painful or if the woman wants to have children. The main treatment is a variety of HORMONES that cannot cure the disease but can bring it under control. If a woman does become pregnant, the symptoms of endometriosis decline sharply.

Unfortunately, only about half the women with endometriosis are able to conceive normally, and those who succeed in doing so suffer three times the normal rate of MISCARRIAGE and sixteen times the normal rate of ECTOPIC PREGNANCY. In some women, laparoscopic surgery can be used to burn, scrape, or otherwise remove abnormal endometrial tissue and restore fertility, sometimes also limiting adhesions and pain. Laser surgery can be used in an attempt to free ovaries to perform normally.

Women with endometriosis who wish to have children are advised to do so as early as possible, because it is a progressive condition, lessening only with MENOPAUSE. If before menopause the symptoms are too difficult to bear, HYSTERECTOMY—removal of the whole uterus—is an option.

FOR HELP AND FURTHER INFORMATION

Endometriosis Association (EA)
8585 North 76th Place
Milwaukee, WI 53223
414–355–2200; 800–992-ENDO [992–3636], US;
800–426–2END [462–2363], Canada
Fax: 414–355–6065
Mary Lou Ballweg, President
Organization concerned with endometriosis; provides information and referrals; publishes various materials, including bimonthly newsletter; brochures; books *Overcoming Endometriosis: New Help from the Endometriosis Association* and *Living with Endometriosis: How to Cope with the Physical and Emotional Challenges*; videotapes *You're Not Alone... Understanding Endometriosis* and *The Choice Is Ours: New Surgeries for Endometriosis*; and audiotapes on support and surgical options.

RESOLVE, Inc., HelpLine: 617–623–0744. Offers adoption services, along with infertility treatments. Publishes fact sheets *Endometriosis, Three Doctors Look at Endometriosis, Environmental Factors (Including Weight and Stress)*, and *Infections: Role in Infertility and Pregnancy Loss.* (For full group information, see INFERTILITY.)

National Institute of Child Health and Human Development (NICHD), 301–496–5133. Publishes *Facts About Endometriosis.* (For full group information, see PREGNANCY.)

American College of Obstetricians and Gynecologists (ACOG), 202–638–5577. Publishes *Important Facts About Endometriosis.* (For full group information, see PREGNANCY.)

National Organization for Rare Disorders (NORD), 800–999–6673. (For full group information, see RARE DISORDERS.)

OTHER RESOURCES

Alternatives for Women with Endometriosis: A Guide by Women for Women. Ruth Carol, ed. Third Side Press, 1994.
Fibroid Tumors and Endometriosis: A Self-Help Program. Susan M. Lark. National Nursing, 1993.

(See also INFERTILITY; UTERUS.)

endoscope, a hollow, generally flexible viewing tube, often fitted with a light, used by physicians to look at the body's internal organs directly, rather than indirectly as with a SCAN. The endoscope may be fed through one of the body's natural openings, such as the mouth, nose, anus, or VAGINA, or it may be passed through a surgical incision in the chest or abdomen or near a joint. An endoscope can also be used for a variety of other purposes, such as to assist in obtaining a BIOPSY, to aid in delicate operations such as FETAL SURGERY or ARTHROSCOPY, or to inflate internal cavities with air for better examination. *Endoscope* is a general term; often the tube is given a more specific name indicating the purpose for which it is being used, such as a *bronchoscope* for viewing the bronchial tubes or a *gastroscope* for looking at the stomach.

engagement, in PREGNANCY, the beginning of the baby's movement into the BIRTH CANAL in preparation for DELIVERY. This engaging, the "falling," or "dropping" of the baby, is often quite noticeable, since the mother can suddenly breathe much easier. In the most typical FETAL PRESENTATION, the head of the FETUS settles first into the pelvis; this may occur two to three weeks before the DUE DATE, but sometimes not until the beginning of LABOR. Abnormal presentation can prevent proper engagement and cause difficult delivery. (See LABOR; PREGNANCY; CHILDBIRTH; FETAL PRESENTATION.)

enrichment, in EDUCATION, use of special kinds of subject matter and experiences, often going beyond the basic content of the CURRICULUM, to expand and deepen the knowledge and understanding of students. Enrichment is often used with college-bound students, especially those who are GIFTED CHILDREN, to enhance their education and keep their interest, when the ordinary curriculum might not be sufficiently challenging and stimulating. In PRESCHOOL programs and in COMPENSATORY EDUCATION, enrichment might be used to help students gain experience and skills they might not have obtained from their home environment, as through field trips, audiovisual presentations, and visiting experts.

environmental hazards, substances in home, work, or community that can have adverse effects on health; when they affect the health of a FETUS during PREGNANCY, they are often called *reproductive hazards.* Some of these, such as radiation from the sun, occur naturally; many others result from human activities, often involving chemicals and human-induced radiation. The catalog of possible environmental hazards is enormous, but parents should be alert to some that pose particular hazards to children's growth and development. Among these are:

- *Radiation,* energy in the form of waves or particles that occurs all around us, which is actually vital to life. However, in some forms and concentrations, radiation can be highly dangerous, although it can be put to use in radiation therapy (see CANCER). Ultraviolet (UV) radiation, cosmic rays, X-rays, and gamma rays are all forms of high-frequency radiation called *ionizing radiation,* known to cause considerable damage within the human body. X-rays and gamma rays are the most penetrating and dangerous; excess exposure can cause genetic damage, seriously harm both the fetus and the growing child, and trigger CANCER and types of health problems. Prospective parents whose activities expose them to high doses of radiation, such as aviation or nuclear energy, may want to change work temporarily before conceiving a child. UV radiation is linked to increases in SKIN CANCER and some EYE AND VISION PROBLEMS. (See SKIN CANCER; also WHEN DO KIDS NEED PROTECTION FROM THE SUN? on page 548.)

Low-frequency electromagnetic radiation, or emissions, from computers, televisions, other appliances, and electrical power lines, has excited considerable concern in recent years. Though some suggest that it may be linked to childhood cancer and other problems, the scientific evidence is so far inconsistent. As a matter of caution, parents may wish not to live directly near major power lines. They will also want to be alert to news about other sources of radiation in daily life and to new studies clarifying where dangers may exist.

- *Radon*, an odorless, colorless, naturally radioactive gas that occurs in rocks, soil, and water. It dissipates quickly and without danger in the air, but can build up to dangerous levels indoors and can constitute a major cancer hazard. Though recognized as toxic since at least the 1960s, the scope of the contamination has become clear only in the 1980s and 1990s. It is a particular concern in new homes, especially those built in high-radon areas or using radon-producing building materials, and is worst in houses made "tight" to save energy. Parents may want to have an environmental engineer check radon levels in their homes or use a home kit designed for the purpose. Even older homes in areas not known to have high radon levels can have high radon readings.
- *Pesticides*, chemicals used on growing plants, especially food. These chemicals are designed to kill certain plants and insects and can also be extremely harmful and even deadly to people. Though many pesticides dissipate naturally in the environment without harming humans, the wrong chemical in the wrong concentration can trigger CANCER and damage to other major systems in the body, including the heart, lungs, kidneys, liver, and central nervous system. Pesticides are strongly regulated, and small residue in foods are well below the levels shown by testing to be dangerous. However, much is as yet unknown about the long-term effects of pesticides and about the results of chemicals mixing in the environment—laboratories do not test for the interaction of these chemicals. Recent studies have suggested that pesticides may be especially dangerous to children under age eight, whose developing bodies are less able to ward off harmful effects. Children are also at increased risk because their diet is made up of more pesticide-containing foods than adults. Parents will want to wash all fruit and vegetable products carefully before they are eaten by the family. Some may also prefer to buy produce produced by organic farming, without use of pesticides (though some contamination from the environment in general is unavoidable). Parents will also want to stay informed about food alerts relating to possible pesticide danger.

  Though much popular concern has focused on pesticide residues in food, the greatest danger often comes from use of pesticides in and around the home. Parents who use pesticides around the home or yard should follow instructions *exactly*, in terms of strength, timing, protective clothing, storage, and disposal. For pesticide use in the house, children, pets (including birds and fish), food items, dishes, and cooking utensils should all be removed, and the area should be ventilated for *at least* the amount of time prescribed on the label. When using pesticides outdoors, close the windows of the house and keep children and pets indoors. Do not use on a windy day, and avoid smoking, since some pesticides are flammable and also traces may be carried from hand to mouth. After applying pesticides, you should rinse your boots or shoes before entering your home, to avoid tracking the pesticide into the house, then shower and shampoo thoroughly and wash your clothing—separately from the family laundry. Stored pesticides should be *locked* away from children, prominently identified, and never stored in any containers associated with food or drink, such as an empty soda bottle. If a lawn firm uses chemicals, check with them to find out how long to wait before it will be safe for children to play on the lawn.
- *Asbestos*, a naturally occurring fibrous mineral that was widely used for insulation, especially around water pipes and electrical devices and in some building materials, in industry and also in many homes and schools, before its dangers were fully known. Only in recent decades has it become clear that asbestos exposure is linked with sharply increased risk of LUNG AND BREATHING PROBLEMS and cancer, especially of the lung and chest lining. Asbestos is now banned for almost all new products in the United States, though it continues to be widely used elsewhere. The problem is that, although much asbestos has been removed since the 1970s, much remains. Some recent studies indicate that unless it is exposed and breaking apart, asbestos may be better sealed off from the air but otherwise left alone, since removal causes the fibers to be widely disperse into the air, making them more dangerous. If asbestos is in the home, parents should not attempt to remove it themselves; they would be better advised to employ professionals who are trained and equipped to do the job or at least to thoroughly train and equip themselves before attempting the job.
- *Lead*, a widespread and dangerous environmental contaminant (see LEAD POISONING; also GET THE LEAD OUT! on page 354).

Beyond these environmental contaminants, parents will want to be especially aware of the potential dangers of ordinary household substances. Some of these are clearly marked "Poison," but many others are often not recognized as dangerous, including materials used as art supplies for children or adults (see Art Hazards Information Center under Center for Safety in the Arts, below).

Certainly, parents should post for themselves, their caregivers, and their children the phone numbers of the local poison control center in an accessible, highly visible location. They should also take steps to prepare themselves and their children to meet an environmental emergency, such as a toxic chemical spill. (Subscribers to the America Online computer service can find "Are You Ready?: Emergency Preparedness Checklist" in the Moms Online Desk Reference section of Moms Online, under "Emergnecy Checklist.")

FOR HELP AND FURTHER INFORMATION

American Council on Science and Health (ACSH), 212–362–7044. Publishes *Issues in the Environment, America's Water: Assessing the Quality, Asbestos, Biotechnology: An Introduction, Dioxin in the Environment, From Mice to Men: Benefits and Limitations of Animal Testing, Laboratory Animal Testing, Lawn Care Chemicals, The Health Effects of Low-Level Radiation, Multiple Chemical Sensitivity, PCBs: Is the Cure Worth the Cost?*, and *Pesticides: Helpful or Harmful?*

National Pesticide Telecommunications Network, 800–858–7378 (6:30 A.M.–4:30 P.M. PT). Service of the Environmental Protection Agency (EPA) and Oregon State University; answers questions on health and environmental risks of various pesticides.

National Safety Council (NSC), 800–621–7615. Publishes *Radon: What You Need to Know*. (For full group information, see SAFETY.)

Center for Safety in the Arts (CSA)
5 Beekman Street, Suite 820
New York, NY 10038
212–227–6220
Fax: 212–233–3846
E-mail: csa@tmn.com or mmccann@rdz.stjohns.edu or 71310.1217@compuserve.com (CompuServe: 71310,1217 [Michael McCann])
Angela Babin, Director
Organization concerned with hazardous chemicals used in arts and crafts, formerly Center for Occupational Hazards; operates Art Hazards Information Center; provides information and referrals; offers workshops and consultation; publishes various materials including quarterly newsletter *Arts Hazards News*; data sheets on specific types of art hazards and precautions, including *Children's Art Supplies Can Be Toxic, Hazards in the Arts, Smoke and Fog Hazards, Theatrical, Shared Make-up, and Cosmetic Aerosol Sprays, Ventilation, Woodworking Hazards, Oil Painting Hazards in Classrooms, Ceramic Glazes May Poison Food, Ceramics, Cadmium Hazards, Dyeing Safely*, and *Emergency Response to Spills and Leaks*; videos; reprints of articles; lists of acceptable arts and craft materials.

March of Dimes Birth Defects Foundation (MDBDF), 914–428–7100. Publishes information sheet *Video Display Terminals*. (For full group information, see BIRTH DEFECTS.)

National Organization for Rare Disorders (NORD), 800–999–6673. (For full group information, see RARE DISORDERS.)

National Organization on Legal Problems of Education (NOLPE), 913–273–3550. Publishes *Legal Aspects of Asbestos Abatement*. (For full group information, see HELP ON LEARNING AND EDUCATION on page 659.)

American Allergy Association (AAA), 415–322–1663. Publishes *Your Home Environment* and *Your Work Environment*. (For full group information, see ALLERGY.)

National Mental Health Consumer Self-Help Clearinghouse, 800–553–4539. Publishes reprint packet on environmental illness. (For full group information, see MENTAL DISORDERS.)

ONLINE RESOURCES

Better Health and Medical Forum (America Online: Health, Medicine) Provides discussion areas and libraries covering environmental hazards. (For full information, see HEALTH CARE.)

OTHER RESOURCES

Raising Healthy Children: Protecting Your Child from Common Environmental Health Threats. Herbert L. Needleman and Philip J. Landrigan. Farrar, Straus & Giroux, 1994.

The Nontoxic Home and Office: Protecting Yourself and Your Family from Everyday Toxics and Health Hazards, rev. ed. Debra Lynn Dadd. Tarcher, 1992.

Healthy Homes, Healthy Kids: Protecting Your Children from Everyday Environmental Hazards. Joyce M. Schoemaker and Charity Y. Vitale. Island Press, 1991.

Your Health and the Indoor Environment: A Complete Guide to Better Health through Control of the Indoor Atmosphere. Randall Earl Dunford and Kevin G. May. NuDawn Publishing, 1991.

(See also SAFETY; ALLERGY; LEAD POISONING; YOUR BABY'S FIRST YEAR: A SAFETY CHECKLIST on page 520.)

epidermolysis bullosa (EB), a rare condition in which skin and mucus membranes blister from injury or friction and, in severe cases, simply from normal activities, which may include internal blistering in the digestive system. Though one form can be acquired during ADOLESCENCE or later, most forms of epidermolysis bullosa are GENETIC DISORDERS, some of the AUTOSOMAL DOMINANT type, others AUTOSOMAL RECESSIVE, and some are apparent at birth. Blisters resemble serious BURNS, and must be treated as carefully to avoid infection. Some blisters form permanent scars, which can cause immobility and deformity. In severe forms, some infants can die during the first year of life from infections and loss of fluid, though sometimes the symptoms lessen in children who survive. EB can be detected during PREG-

NANCY using FETOSCOPY, BLOOD TESTS, and BIOPSY. Prospective parents with EB in their personal or family history may want to seek GENETIC COUNSELING.

FOR HELP AND FURTHER INFORMATION

National Arthritis and Musculoskeletal and Skin Diseases Information Clearinghouse (NAMSIC), 301–495–4484. Publishes *Living with Epidermolysis Bullosa.*

National Maternal and Child Health Clearinghouse (NMCHC), 703–821–8955 (For full group information, see PREGNANCY.)

National Organization for Rare Disorders (NORD), 800–999–6673. (For full group information, see RARE DISORDERS.)

(See also GENETIC COUNSELING; SKIN DISORDERS.)

epididymis, an area behind the TESTES, which includes a long coiled tube where a man's SPERM mature and are stored.

epididymo-orchitis, inflammation of one or both TESTES and the EPIDIDYMIS, the SPERM storage area behind the testes, by a variety of organisms often associated with CHLAMYDIA and GONORRHEA. It is treated with cold packs to reduce swelling, painkillers (*analgesics*), support for the SCROTUM, and ANTIBIOTICS. By contrast, ORCHITIS—inflammation of the testes alone—is generally caused by the MUMPS virus.

epilepsy, not a single disease, but a general term for a wide range of symptoms, most notable of which is the tendency to have recurring SEIZURES (convulsions), which are sudden periods of involuntary, uncontrolled electrical activity in the brain, often accompanied by violent muscular contractions. Instead of the normal generation of about eighty impulses a second, some of the brain's nerve cells might "fire" 500 times a second during an epileptic seizure, disrupting normal brain activities with electrical overload.

These various types of epileptic seizures are classed under two main headings: *generalized seizures*, which affect the whole brain, and *partial seizures* (*focal seizures*), which are localized in one part of the brain. Within these two categories, the main kinds of epileptic seizures are:

GENERALIZED SEIZURES

- *Tonic-clonic* (*grand mal*), the best-known type of seizure, though not the most common, involving involuntary, uncontrolled electrical activity in the brain, often (but not necessarily) accompanied by violent muscular contractions called CONVULSIONS. People having a tonic-clonic seizure may cry out hoarsely, then fall to the ground unconscious, their body stiffening and jerking. The person may lose control of the bladder and bowels, have a froth of saliva at the mouth, and turn somewhat bluish as oxygen intake is slowed. Then, after a minute or two, the brain restores normal activity, the jerking movements end, and the seizure is over, leaving the person confused and drowsy. After a period of sleep, the person can usually resume normal activity. A tonic-clonic seizure is sometimes presaged by an *aura*, a variable complex of unusual sensations such as an odd smell or taste, light, a slight sick feeling, or warmth; if recognized, it can give the person time to move away from any hazards nearby.
- *Absence* (*petit mal*), a seizure that lasts only a few seconds, involving brief loss of consciousness, often seeming like daydreaming or blank staring, sometimes with rhythmic twitching of the eyelids or facial muscles, but generally without any aura. A child may stumble and fall, then get up and continue running, with no one—including himself—realizing that he has had a seizure.

PARTIAL SEIZURES

- *Simple partial seizure* (*Jacksonian seizure*), a seizure involving disturbances in movement only, in which the person retains consciousness, but cannot control his or her movements, generally trembling or jerking an arm or leg, sometimes starting with just a finger. Another form of simple partial seizure involves seeing strange, illusory people or sounds, or having a strong, disconcerting feeling of *déjà vu*—that the events being experienced have happened before.
- *Complex partial seizure* (*psychomotor* or *temporal lobe seizure*), a seizure in which the person becomes trancelike and moves as in a daze through a set of motions, which are often much the same in each attack; not totally out of contact, the person can often respond to simple directions given calmly by a familiar voice, as of a friend or family member. The person returns to awareness in a minute or two, with no recollection of what happened, but only perhaps some confusion and irritability.
- *Secondarily generalized seizure*, a seizure that was initially partial but spreads to become generalized.

See WHAT SHOULD YOU DO IF SOMEONE HAS A SEIZURE? (on page 225).

Epilepsy can begin at any time of life, but generally appears first in childhood, normally between ages two and twenty. In at least half of the cases, the cause is completely unknown. In the rest, though the precise mechanism remains obscure, some of the disorder's many and various triggering factors can be identified, including TRAUMATIC BRAIN INJURY, BRAIN TUMOR, CONGENITAL damage or disorders of the BRAIN (such as MENTAL RETARDATION or CEREBRAL PALSY, sometimes as a result of difficult CHILDBIRTH), GENETIC DISORDERS, LEAD POISONING, poor NUTRITION, and severe infections, such as MENINGITIS, ENCEPHALITIS, TUBERCULOSIS, malaria, and MEASLES. To the extent that these and like causes can be reduced or elimi-

What Should You Do If Someone Has a Seizure?

CONVULSIVE SEIZURE

First aid for epilepsy is basically very simple. It keeps the person safe until the seizure stops naturally by itself. These are the key things to remember about a convulsive seizure:

- Keep calm and reassure other people who may be nearby.
- Clear the area around the person of anything hard or sharp.
- Loosen ties or anything around the neck that may make breathing difficult.
- Put something flat and soft, like a folded jacket, under the head.
- Turn person gently onto his or her side. This will help keep the airway clear. Do *not* try to force his mouth open with any hard implement or with fingers. It is not true that a person having a seizure can swallow his tongue. Efforts to hold the tongue down can injure teeth or jaw.
- Don't hold the person down or try to stop movements.
- Don't attempt artificial respiration, except in the unlikely event that a person does not start breathing again after the seizure has stopped.
- Stay with the person until the seizure ends naturally.
- Be friendly and reassuring as consciousness returns.
- Offer to call a taxi, friend, or relative to help the person get home if he seems confused or unable to get home by himself.

If you know the person has epilepsy, it is usually not necessary to call an ambulance unless the seizure lasts longer than a few minutes, unless another seizure begins soon after the first, or unless the person cannot be awakened after the jerking movements have stopped.

OTHER KINDS OF SEIZURES

You don't have to do anything if a person has brief periods of staring or shaking of the limbs. If someone has the kind of seizure that involves a dazed state and automatic behavior, the best thing to do is:

- Watch the person carefully and explain to others what is happening. Often people who don't recognize this kind of behavior as a seizure will think that the dazed person is drunk or on drugs.
- Speak quietly and calmly in a friendly way.
- Guide the person gently away from any danger, such as a steep flight of steps, a busy highway, or a hot stove. Don't grab hold, however, unless some immediate danger threatens. People having this kind of seizure are on "automatic pilot" so far as their movements are concerned and instinct may make them struggle or lash out at the person who is trying to hold them.
- Stay with the person until full consciousness returns, and offer help in returning home.

Source: Questions and Answers about Epilepsy. Epilepsy Foundation of America.

nated—as by PRENATAL CARE, SAFETY, and IMMUNIZATION against infections—many kinds of epilepsy are preventable.

Epilepsy is generally diagnosed by a PEDIATRICIAN, family PHYSICIAN, or NEUROLOGIST on the basis of a parent's descriptions of the seizures and a review of the child's medical history. Doctors may also use an ELECTROENCEPHALOGRAPH (EEG) to record the electrical activity of the brain. By comparing the record with normal brain waves, they may be able to diagnose epilepsy, but not all types of epilepsy show up on an EEG. Doctors may also use various kinds of SCANS to look for any kinds of physical abnormalities, such as TUMORS or signs of head injuries, that might be causing seizures.

Where epilepsy has a precise, treatable cause, the problem can sometimes be eliminated, as by surgery, a change in medications for other illnesses (see DRUG REACTIONS AND INTERACTIONS), or a special diet. But in many cases, epilepsy is best controlled by drugs. The precise medication used depends on the type of seizure and the response of the person. These drugs generally need to be taken regularly to keep a steady level in the body; if so, the Epilepsy Foundation of America estimates that seizures can be controlled in 4 out of 5 patients. More promising, there are some indications that, if children on medication have been seizure-free for some years, some might be very slowly withdrawn from the medication and remain free of symptoms. In any case, with some forms of epilepsy, especially absence seizures, many children tend to "grow out of it."

Other approaches tried in some situations include a special high-FAT diet, called a *ketogenic diet*; supplemental

VITAMINS; and biofeedback. But these are best tried, if appropriate, only under a doctor's direction.

Beyond that, people with epilepsy can often live quite normal lives. They have the normal range of intelligence and must only exercise caution in SPORTS, work, and other activities that involve potential hazards, such as drinking alcoholic drinks (which can bring on seizures in some), engaging in water activities (such as swimming and boating), exposure to heights, driving automobiles, and operating other dangerous machinery. If they are shown to have been seizure free for a certain time (depending on the state), they can usually get a driver's license. People with epilepsy may have difficulty getting insurance; where it is available, they may be subject to high rates and be placed in special risk "pools." Antidiscrimination laws protecting people with DISABILITIES apply to people with epilepsy; however, they often may have to fight discrimination in employment and social situations. Various organizations (see listing in this entry) can help in such areas.

Women with epilepsy would be wise to consult a doctor and perhaps receive GENETIC COUNSELING before becoming pregnant. Because PREGNANCY changes the balance of HORMONES in the body, it also changes the response of the body to medication, so in some women it can increase the number of seizures; in others, the reverse happens. More important, the Epilepsy Foundation of America estimates that women taking epilepsy medications have a two to three times greater risk of having a baby with a BIRTH DEFECT. It is unclear what proportion of the defects are caused by the epilepsy itself and what proportion by the medication, but because most such birth defects occur in the first three months of pregnancy, it is important to plan ahead. Certain medications seem to be associated with certain kinds of birth defects, including CLEFT PALATE, heart disorders (see HEART AND HEART PROBLEMS), FETAL HYDANTOIN SYNDROME, and SPINA BIFIDA. Women taking epilepsy medications may want to seek PRENATAL TESTING. Women planning on BREASTFEEDING should also discuss medications with their doctors beforehand, since some amount of the drugs in their system will be passed on in the milk.

FOR HELP AND FURTHER INFORMATION

Epilepsy Foundation of America (EFA)
4351 Garden City Drive, Suite 406
Landover, MD 20785
301–459–3700; 800–332–4050; Patient Information Service: 800-EFA–1000 [332–1000]; For materials in alternative media: 800–332–2070, TT
Fax: 301–577–4941
E-mail: efanel@capcon.net
William McLin, Executive Director
Organization concerned with seizure disorders; acts as advocate; provides information and referrals; sponsors research; publishes various materials, including:

- Newsletter *Epilepsy USA* and brochures about the EFA.
- Pamphlets for parents: *Thoughts on Parenting the Child With Epilepsy, Recognizing the Hidden Signs of Childhood Seizures, Epilepsy: Part of Your Life, Surgery for Epilepsy, Epilepsy and Learning Disabilities, The Child With Epilepsy at Camp, Medicines for Epilepsy,* and *Epilepsy Medicines and Dental Care.*
- "Issues and Answers" guides: three for parents (covering birth to age six, ages six through twelve, and teens and young adults) and *Exploring Your Possibilities: A Guide for Teens and Young Adults with Epilepsy.*
- Books for parents: *Children with Epilepsy: A Parents Guide, Seizures and Epilepsy in Childhood: A Guide for Parents, Parenting and You: A Guide for Parents with Seizure Disorders, Mom, I Have a Staring Problem, Does Your Child Have Epilepsy?, Brothers and Sisters: A Guide for Families of Children with Epilepsy,* and *Epilepsy Parent and Family Networks Resource Manual.*
- General pamphlets: *Epilepsy: Questions and Answers About Seizure Disorders, Finding Out About Seizures: A Guide to Medical Tests* (to help parents introduce tests to children), *Finding Out About Epilepsy: A Guide to Treatment, Seizure Recognition and First Aid, All About Partial Seizures, Seizure Record Form, Medicines for Epilepsy, Medication Record Form, Preventing Epilepsy,* and *Medical Aspects of Epilepsy.*
- General books: *The Legal Rights of Persons with Epilepsy, Living Well with Epilepsy, A Guide to Understanding and Living with Epilepsy, Brainstorms: Epilepsy in Our Words,* and *The Brainstorms Companion: Epilepsy in Our View.*
- Pamphlets for children: *Child's Guide to Seizure Disorders, Me and My World Storybook, Seizure Man, First Aid for Seizures, Because You Are My Friend, Spider-Man Battles the Myth Monster.*
- Books for children: *Lee the Rabbit with Epilepsy, Julia, Mungo, and the Earthquake, Alice, Dotty the Dalmatian Has Epilepsy,* and *When Mom or Dad Has Seizures: A Guide for Young People.*
- Pamphlet for teens: *Answers to Your Questions About Epilepsy.*
- Videos for parents: *Epilepsy: The Child and the Family, Epilepsy in the Teen Years, Epilepsy and the Family, The Rest of the Family, And Life Goes On: Severe Seizures of Early Childhood,* and *Planning for Today and Tomorrow.*
- General videos: *Understanding Seizure Disorders, Understanding Complex Partial Seizures, Epilepsy: Quality of Life, Seizure First Aid, Living with Epilepsy, Driving: Information for People with Seizure Disorders, How Medicines Work,* and *A Question of Epilepsy.*
- Videos for children: *I Have Epilepsy Too* and *Because You Are My Friend.*
- Numerous materials for health professionals and for adults with epilepsy, on everyday life, employment, treatment, and legal rights.

National Easter Seal Society, 800–221–6827. (For full group information, see HELP FOR SPECIAL CHILDREN on page 689.)

National Institute of Neurological Disorders and Stroke (NINDS), 800–352–9424. Publishes brochure *Epilepsy: Hope Through Research.* (For full group information, see BRAIN AND BRAIN DISORDERS.)

National Information Center for Children and Youth with Disabilities (NICHCY), 800–695–0285, voice/TT. Publishes *Epilepsy.* (For full group information, see HELP FOR SPECIAL CHILDREN on page 689.)

Brain Injury Association, 800–444–6443. Publishes *Head Trauma and Epilepsy* and *Post-traumatic Seizures and Post-traumatic Epilepsy in Children,* (For full group information, see TRAUMATIC BRAIN INJURY.)

Parents Helping Parents (PHP), 408–727–5775. Publishes information packet *Seizures.* (For full group information, see HELP FOR SPECIAL CHILDREN on page 689.)

National Organization for Rare Disorders (NORD), 800–999–6673. (For full group information, see RARE DISORDERS.)

National Mental Health Consumer Self-Help Clearinghouse, 800–553–4539. Publishes reprint packet on epilepsy seizures. (For full group information, see MENTAL DISORDERS.)

Resources for Rehabilitation, 617–862–6455. Publishes book *Resources for People with Disabilities and Chronic Conditions* and *A Woman's Guide to Coping with Disability,* both including sections on epilepsy. (For full group information, see EYE AND VISION PROBLEMS.)

OTHER RESOURCES

For parents and other adults

Seizures and Epilepsy in Childhood: A Guide for Parents. John M. Freeman and others. Johns Hopkins, 1990.

Does Your Child Have Epilepsy?, 2nd ed. James E. Jan. PRO-ED, 1991.

Mom, I Have a Staring Problem: A True Story of Petit Mal Seizures and the Hidden Problem It Can Cause: Learning Disability. Marian C. Buckel and Tiffany Buckel. M. C. Buckel, 1992.

General works

A Guide to Understanding and Living with Epilepsy. Orrin Devinsky. Davis, 1994.

The Parke-Davis Manual on Epilepsy: Useful Tips That Help You Get the Best Out of Life. Solomon Moshe and others, eds. KSF Group, 1992.

For children

Moments That Disappear: Children Living with Epilepsy. Thomas Bergman. Gareth Stevens, 1992.

Trick or Treat or Trouble. Barbara Aiello and Jeffrey Shulman. Twenty-First Century Books, 1988.

For preteens or teens

Epilepsy. Elaine Landau. Twenty-First Century Books, 1994.

Halsey's Pride. Lynn Hall. Scribners, 1990. About a girl with epilepsy.

Epilepsy. Tom McGowen. Watts, 1989.

(See also HELP FOR SPECIAL CHILDREN, on page 689.)

episiotomy, a controversial medical procedure in which a surgical incision is made in the tissue between a woman's VAGINA and anus during CHILDBIRTH to ease DELIVERY of the baby. It is generally used when the tissue is under pressure by the baby's head and seems likely to tear; almost always in cases of FORCEPS DELIVERY or breech FETAL PRESENTATION, where a larger opening is needed; and often when there are signs of FETAL DISTRESS. Advocates note that an episiotomy causes less pressure on the head of a PREMATURE baby and enlarges the vaginal opening neatly, preventing the tears in tissue that can otherwise occur, that are harder to repair afterward, and that can lead to complications. Critics say that episiotomies have been overused, with some obstretricians performing episiotomies almost routinely, and that the incision sometimes causes discomfort long after the birth. In exploring CHILDBIRTH alternatives, parents will want to find out a doctor's or hospital's policies on using episiotomies. (See CHILDBIRTH.)

erythema infectiosum, an infectious disease caused by a type of virus, which results in a striking red rash on the cheeks, giving it an alternate name, the *slapped cheeks disease.* It is also called the *fifth disease,* because it is the least well known of the common childhood diseases, the other main ones being MEASLES, MUMPS, CHICKEN POX, and RUBELLA (German measles). Erythema infectiosum causes only mild symptoms in children, but is presently being studied closely because some medical researchers suspect that it can cause BIRTH DEFECTS, especially a dangerous form of ANEMIA, in the babies of pregnant women who contract the disease.

FOR HELP AND FURTHER INFORMATION

March of Dimes Birth Defects Foundation (MDBDF), 914–428–7100. Publishes information sheet *Chicken Pox and Fifth Disease.* (For full group information, see BIRTH DEFECTS.)

National Institute of Allergy and Infectious Diseases (NIAID), 301–496–5717. (For full group information, see ALLERGIES.)

National Institute of Child Health and Human Development (NICHD), 301–496–5133. (For full group information, see PREGNANCY.)

estrogen, a key female HORMONE; actually a group of hormones that regulate female sexual development and the activities of the REPRODUCTIVE SYSTEM; one of the family of STEROIDS. Estrogen is produced by both females and males, in the OVARIES and TESTES respectively, but in only small amounts in boys, young girls, and men. In older girls, larger amounts of estrogen trigger the physical changes that take place during PUBERTY, most notably the development of distinctive female SECONDARY SEX CHARACTERISTICS.

From the time of a girl's first MENSTRUATION through MENOPAUSE, except during PREGNANCY or severe illness or stress, estrogen levels will rise and fall in a monthly MENSTRUAL CYCLE. FOLLICLE-STIMULATING HORMONE (FSH) triggers production of estrogen, as well as ripening of eggs in the OVARIES. Later in the cycle, if fertilization does not take place, estrogen production will decline, until the cycle comes around again. During pregnancy, estrogen is produced and maintained at high levels by the PLACENTA, the tissue that nourishes the developing FETUS. Some estrogen is also produced by the ADRENAL GLANDS and by fatty (*adipose*) tissue.

Both naturally derived and synthetic estrogen are used in treating women for a variety of symptoms and disorders, including menstrual irregularities, suppression of lactation after CHILDBIRTH, treating some forms of CANCER (though it fuels others), and menopausal problems (see ESTROGEN REPLACEMENT THERAPY). They also form the basis for various types of contraceptive medications, including BIRTH CONTROL PILLS, NORPLANT, and DEPO-PROVERA. Estrogen can cause significant side effects, however, and should be used only after careful consideration of a woman's total medical situation. Evidence from studies has suggested that men whose mothers took estrogen might be at increased risk from testicular CANCER (see TESTES).

etiology, the study of the causes of a disease, both in general and in specific cases, including investigation of a patient's susceptibility, the specific agent causing the disease, and the way in which the agent was introduced into the body. In cases of severe, communicable diseases, such as AIDS, examination of the means of transmission is important in preventing its spread to others.

evaluation-level thinking, making judgments on the basis of established criteria; one of the kinds of thinking or learning processes described by Benjamin Bloom. The other main types are KNOWLEDGE-LEVEL, COMPREHENSION-LEVEL, APPLICATION-LEVEL, ANALYSIS-LEVEL, and SYNTHESIS-LEVEL.

exacerbations, in medicine, flare-ups of a disease or disorder, when the symptoms temporarily increase in intensity, before once again subsiding or going into REMISSION, as in disorders such as MULTIPLE SCLEROSIS.

exercise, physical activity to improve the health and functioning of the body, as by increasing blood circulation and muscle strength. In response to concerns about being "unfit," many parents and children have turned to exercise, often establishing regular exercise programs. Both pregnant women and children should exercise some caution, however.

Ideally, women should have been exercising before becoming pregnant; that way they will start off relatively fit and be familiar with their body's response to exercise. In any case, women are advised to have a thorough medical examination before embarking on an exercise program during PREGNANCY. Doctors may suggest restrictions or recommend not exercising, as when a woman has heart problems, will have a MULTIPLE BIRTH, or shows signs indicating the possibility of MISCARRIAGE or PREMATURE DELIVERY.

Most women will want to do some basic exercises to prepare them for CHILDBIRTH and DELIVERY, like those in BASIC EXERCISES FOR DURING AND AFTER PREGNANCY (on page 634). These can serve as warm-up activities for a more extensive exercise program, if desired. The American College of Obstetrics and Gynecology suggests, however, that pregnant women should avoid:

- Strenuous activities calling for twisting, turning, deep flexion, extension, or bouncy, jerky motion.
- Competitive sports calling for stamina and endurance.
- Activities depending on balance, which might lead to a fall.
- Activities that raise body temperature too high (including sauna and whirlpool).
- Exercises done lying flat on the back, which can cut normal blood flow through the vena cava to the fetus (see HEART AND HEART PROBLEMS).
- High-risk activities such as diving or skiing.

They also recommend exercising no more than three times a week, with sessions of fifteen minutes tops (not counting warm-up and cool-down), and with a maximum heartbeat of 140 beats per minute. Women are advised to halt exercise if any sign of strain, fatigue, dizziness, bleeding, contractions, nausea, chest pain, and the like appear.

Some cautions are recommended for children, too. In their book *Pediatric Athlete*, the American Academy of Orthopaedic Surgeons notes that children are not miniature adults; rather, their bodies are still developing and have different needs and requirements than adults'. For example, they use more calories and tire faster; build up more body heat, and so have increased risk of heat-related illnesses; and breathe faster, making them more susceptible to pollution. The AAOS warns against using adult training programs for children, and suggests instead that SPORTS and activities should be chosen with the child's DEVELOPMENTAL AGE in mind, noting that before PUBERTY, boys and girls have generally equivalent athletic potential.

Many families these days are starting exercise early, by taking their children to developmental play programs starting in early infancy. These parent-infant classes often have specially trained instructors and use music, games, sights, sounds, and specially built play equipment to provide exercise and stimulation for babies. Parents also learn about exercises and games to play with children at home. The classes also provide a forum where parents of children who are the same age can meet and share experiences and resources. Many such programs have graded classes, for babies, toddlers, and children of different ages and skills, with exercises designed to enhance skills appropriate to the age. Programs for infants who have just learned, or are in the process of learning, to walk stress balance, exploration, spatial awareness, and other skills to build confidence in mobility and to refine body movement. Programs for preschoolers and older children are often drop-off programs, with parent participation optional. Some such child-oriented exercise centers also maintain resource centers and lending libraries on not just exercise but also general parenting and child care. Apart from the benefits of exercise, children also benefit from family participation, which is not generally available through participation in organized competitive sports.

Parents should, however, be aware of the potential dangers to children from exercise equipment. A 1992 research report found that of the more than 25,000 injuries from exercise equipment annually in the United States, more than half involved children under age fifteen. The most dangerous type of equipment was exercise bikes, involved in 55 percent of the accidents, which generally resulted in the amputation of a finger or a toe. Even more serious were jump ropes, involved in 25 percent of the accidents. In a majority of these, the rope user was strangled to death. Over 80 percent of the accidents involving children occurred when the children were playing or exercising alone or were unsupervised.

The obvious conclusions for parents are:

- Be careful of yourselves and your children when using exercise equipment.
- Do not let children use exercise equipment alone or unsupervised.
- Do not store exercise equipment in ways and places that might "attract" use by children.
- If it is possible to lock up or lock away exercise equipment to prevent possibly dangerous use by children, do so.

FOR HELP AND FURTHER INFORMATION

National Heart, Lung, and Blood Information Center (NHLBIC), 301–251–1222. Publishes booklet *Exercise and Your Heart: A Guide to Physical Activity* and *Check Your Physical Activity and Heart Disease I.Q.* (For full group information, see HEART AND HEART PROBLEMS.)

American Heart Association (AHA), 800–242–8721. Publishes *"E" Is for Exercise, Exercise and Your Heart, About Your Heart and Exercise, Walking...Natural Fun, Natural Fitness,* and "For a Healthy Heart" brochures: *Cycling, Dancing, Running,* and *Swimming.* (For full group information, see HEART AND HEART PROBLEMS.)

American Academy of Pediatrics (AAP), 800–433–9016. Publishes brochure *Better Health Through Fitness.* (For full group information, see HEALTH CARE.)

American College of Obstetricians and Gynecologists (ACOG), 202–638–5577. Publishes *Exercise and Fitness: A Guide for Women.* (For full group information, see PREGNANCY.)

National Arthritis and Musculoskeletal and Skin Diseases Information Clearinghouse (NAMSIC), 301–495–4484. Publishes information package *Arthritis and Exercise.* (For full group information, see ARTHRITIS.)

Center for Safety in the Arts (CSA), 212–227–6220. Publishes videos *Introduction to Dance Medicine: Keeping Dancers Dancing* and *Therapeutic Exercises for Musicians*; and fact sheets *Musculoskeletal Problems in Dancers* and *Musculoskeletal Problems in Musicians.* (For full group information, see ENVIRONMENTAL HAZARDS.)

Accent, 800–787–8444. Publishes *Conditioning with Physical Disabilities* and videos *Lisa Ericson's Seated Aerobic Workout* and *Anybody Can Sit and Be Fit.* (For full group information, see HELP FOR SPECIAL CHILDREN on page 689.)

National Safety Council (NSC), 800–621–7615. (For full group information, see SAFETY.)

ON EXERCISE DURING PREGNANCY

Positive Pregnancy and Parenting Fitness, 800–433–5523. (For full group information, see PREGNANCY.) .

C/SEC (Cesareans/Support, Education, and Concern), 508–877–8266. (For full group information, see CESAREAN SECTION.)

National Association of Childbirth Assistants (NACA), 800–868–6222. Publishes *The Birth Ball,* about using a specially developed ball for exercise before and after pregnancy. (For full group information, see CHILDBIRTH.)

March of Dimes Birth Defects Foundation (MDBDF), 914–428–7100. Publishes information sheet *Fitness for Two.* (For full group information, see BIRTH DEFECTS.)

ONLINE RESOURCES

Better Health and Medical Forum (America Online: Health, Medicine) Provides discussion areas and libraries covering exercise. (For full information, see HEALTH CARE.)

OTHER RESOURCES

GENERAL WORKS

Exercise. Don Nardo. Chelsea House, 1992.

The Safe Exercise Handbook. Toni T. Branner. Kendall-Hunt, 1991.

Living with Exercise. Steven N. Blair. American Health, 1991.
Exercise, Fitness, and Health. Charles B. Clayman, ed. RD Assn, 1991.
Surviving Exercise. Judy Alter. Houghton Mifflin, 1990.
Full Circle Fitness: Be Your Own Personal Trainer. Rebecca Eastman and Patricia Ryan. Morrow, 1990.

ON EXERCISE FOR CHILDREN

Kid Fitness—A Complete Shape Up Program from Birth Through High School. Kenneth Cooper. Bantam, 1991. By the "father of aerobics."
Weight and Strength Training for Kids and Teenagers. Ken Sprague and Chris Sprague. Tarcher, 1991.

ON EXERCISE DURING AND AFTER PREGNANCY

Shape up During Pregnancy. Swift. Thorsons, 1993.
The Pregnant Woman's Comfort Guide: Safe, Quick and Easy Relief from the Discomforts of Pregnancy and Postpartum. Sherry L. Jimenez. Avery, 1992.
Get into Shape After Childbirth. Gillian Fletcher. Trafalgar, 1992.
Easy Pregnancy with Yoga. Stella Weller. Thorsons, 1991.
Elisabeth Bing's Guide to Moving Through Pregnancy: Advice from America's Foremost Childbirth Educator on Making Pregnancy as Physically Comfortable as Possible, at Home and at Work. Elisabeth Bing. Noonday/Farrar, Straus & Giroux, 1991.
Fitness for Two: Guidelines for Exercise During Pregnancy. Gayle Brannon. R & M Press, 1990.

(See also MOTOR SKILLS, for movement programs for children; SPORTS; SAFETY.)

ex parte, a hearing in which only one party appears before a judge; from Latin, meaning "from one side." In cases of threatened VIOLENCE or PARENTAL KIDNAPPING, the judge may issue a TEMPORARY RESTRAINING ORDER, prior to a full hearing and a possible INJUNCTION.

expulsion, in EDUCATION, an order for a student to leave a school, generally only after repeated, serious misbehavior, though sometimes for grossly inadequate performance at school work. Unlike SUSPENSION, which is temporary, expulsion is long-term, either for the balance of the school year or permanently at that school, though the student may be enrolled elsewhere. Some states require that an expelled student be provided with alternate education, if they are under COMPULSORY SCHOOL AGE. Various Supreme Court rulings have affected the legal rights of students and schools in cases of suspension and expulsion.

expunged records, records that have been destroyed as if they had never existed. Documents of JUVENILE COURT proceedings are often restricted or even SEALED; then, after a specified number of years, the JUVENILE, parent, or GUARDIAN may apply for the records to be expunged, generally on showing that the problem behavior has been improved. An unverified report of possible CHILD ABUSE AND NEGLECT may also be—though sometimes is not—removed from a CENTRAL REGISTER.

external cephalic version, a medical procedure when there are problems with FETAL PRESENTATION, in which a doctor tries to turn (the meaning of "version") the baby to the normal position, head downward, for delivery.

external degree programs, in EDUCATION, especially at the COLLEGE level, programs that allow students to learn material and fulfill course requirements (such as TESTS, papers, and laboratory work) largely on their own, with little or no attendance at scheduled classes on a college campus. Some external degree students use INDEPENDENT STUDY via correspondence; others a form of Open University, combining correspondence study with learning via radio and television broadcasts or via computer transmission. Such students generally earn CREDIT for their courses by taking examinations, either tests offered by the individual school or STANDARDIZED TESTS such as those in the COLLEGE-LEVEL EXAMINATION PROGRAM. External degree programs are especially attractive to people who prefer to study on their own or those who have time commitments that preclude their attending regular classes, such as parents with children at home or adults whose jobs involve travel and irregular hours.

eye and vision problems, the organs of sight and the widely varied disorders that affect them. A number of vision disorders can affect children, some of which can permanently damage the child's vision if they are not diagnosed and treated in early childhood. Though newborns can see, their vision develops substantially in their early years, especially in the first few months, with development normally complete by about age nine. For the eyes to develop normally, they must both be used equally or the sight in the weaker eye may be impaired or totally lost.

The OBSERVATION CHECKLIST FOR POSSIBLE VISION PROBLEMS IN PRESCHOOLERS (on page 231) can help parents spot signs of possible vision problems. If glasses or other corrective measures, such as contact lenses or eye patches, are prescribed, it is extremely important for the child's future sight that they be worn regularly.

Parents will also want to protect their children from eye injuries by educating them from the time they are very young about the dangers of injuries, as from:

- Sharp, pointed objects, such as pencils, knives, and pieces of glass, metal, or wood, but also less hard but still dangerous items such as cards and straws.
- Projectile toys such as BB guns, bows and arrows, darts, and sling-shots.
- Fireworks.
- Unsupervised work in shop or laboratory, at home or in school, where goggles should always be worn.
- SPORTS accidents.

Observation Checklist for Possible Vision Problems in Preschoolers

The checklist that follows can help you identify if a child has a vision problem. Check any behavior that applies. If a child shows *any* of these symptoms, there *may* be eye trouble, and the child should be referred for evaluation.

BEHAVIOR	YES	NO
Rubs eyes excessively.	☐	☐
Shuts or covers one eye, tilts head, or thrusts head forward.	☐	☐
Has difficulty in work that requires close use of the eyes (such as putting puzzle parts together or matching identical shapes).	☐	☐
Blinks more than usual or is irritable when doing close work.	☐	☐
Holds objects close to eyes.	☐	☐
Is unable to see distant things clearly.	☐	☐
Squints eyelids together or frowns.	☐	☐
APPEARANCE		
Has crossed eyes.	☐	☐
Eyelids are red-rimmed, crusty, or swollen.	☐	☐
Eyes are inflamed or watery.	☐	☐
Has recurring styes (small inflamed swellings on the rim of the eyelid).	☐	☐
COMPLAINTS		
Eyes itch, burn, or feel scratchy.	☐	☐
Cannot see well.	☐	☐
Has dizziness, headaches, or nausea following close eye work.	☐	☐
Has blurred or double vision.	☐	☐

Source: Mainstreaming Preschoolers: Children with Visual Handicaps—A Guide for Teachers, Parents, and Others Who Work with Visually Handicapped Preschoolers. Lou Alonso and others. U.S. Government Printing Office (1984). Prepared for the Head Start Bureau. Adapted from "Signs of Possible Eye Trouble in Children from the National Society for the Prevention of Blindness."

The National Society to Prevent Blindness estimates that sports injuries alone affect approximately 11,000 children a year, with nearly one quarter of the injuries to children ages five through fourteen resulting from baseball injuries. They recommend that children protect their eyes by wearing safety eyeguards or industrial quality safety glasses, with either plain (*plano*) or corrective lenses, and helmets, when appropriate, for such sports as hockey or bicycle riding (see SPORTS). For older children, cosmetics are another hazard. They should be applied only with great care (and never in a moving vehicle) and should never be shared, since that can spread infection.

The eyes themselves are a pair of round structures set deep into a bony eye socket on either side of the nose. Each eye is protected largely by the whitish *sclera*; in the center of the sclera is the transparent *cornea*, which controls focusing. Behind the cornea is a depression filled with fluid (*aqueous humor*), in which is set the *iris* (the colored part of the eye). In the center of iris is the *pupil*, which widens (*dilates*) or contracts in response to dark or light, controlling the amount of light entering. Behind the iris is the *lens*, set in a ring of delicate muscles (the *ciliary body*), which changes the shape of the lens to help the eye focus. Behind the lens is a jelly-like substance called the *vitreous humor*.

Deep in the back of the eye is the *retina*, which receives the image gathered and focused by the cornea and lens. The retina's light-sensing structures (*rods* and *cones*) convert the light impulses into electrical impulses, which they transmit along the *optic nerve* to the brain. The rods, situated mostly around the edges of the retina, are light sensors; cones, the color sensors, are generally grouped more in the center of the retina. The retina itself is kept supplied with necessary oxygen and sugar by a network of blood vessels called the *choroid plexus*.

For rest and protection, the whole mechanism can be sealed off from the outside by closing the eyelids, to each of which is attached a thin, flexible membrane called the *conjunctiva*. This and the eyelid itself contain glands that secrete tears and mucus that continually coat the eye and keep it moist, a process helped by blinking.

For the brain to interpret the information transmitted along the optic nerve, and especially to blend the two separate images into a single image and to be able to judge distances, the two eyes must work together in a coordinated way. This *stereoscopic vision* or *binocular vision* is managed by a set of small muscles that align the eyes according to signals received from the brain. If the action of the eyes is at all abnormal, the brain cannot properly coordinate images from the two eyes, causing numerous problems.

Few of these problems involve total loss of sight, though many can result in legal blindness, if undiagnosed and untreated. Many involve vision impairment of various kinds and severity, some of which can be partly corrected, as through glasses (external lenses ground to correct vision defects), contact lenses (specially ground lenses placed directly over the cornea), drugs, or surgery, especially LASER SURGERY or MICROSURGERY.

Many eye disorders appear only with age, but many others affect young people, and some are present at birth. The most common of these involve the muscular coordination and structure of the eyes, including:

- *Strabismus*, or crossed eyes, in which one eye turns or squints, because of a muscle or neurological problem. Often the squinting eye has impaired vision. If that eye is turned toward the nose, the condition is called *esotropia*; if turned outward, it is *exotropia*. Children with this problem may use the eyes alternately, but if (as often happens) they use one eye continuously, they risk losing sight in the other eye, a condition *amblyopia* (see next definition in this entry). Opthalmologists may try to prevent this by using an eyepatch over the stronger eye. Glasses and surgery may also be required to treat the problem. Strabismus can be a sign of brain disorders, such as a brain tumor.
- *Amblyopia*, permanently impaired vision, though the eye shows no structural abnormality; the problem apparently lies in the nerves connecting the retina with the brain. Amblyopia can result from nutritional deficiency or toxic levels of alcohol, tobacco, or other poisons. But in children, amblyopia often results from use of a single eye in strabismus (see above), often called *suppression amblyopia*, *amblyopia ex anopsia*, or *lazy eye blindness*. Cataracts and astigmatism (see below) can also cause amblyopia. An eyepatch over the stronger eye, glasses, and surgery may be used to treat the problem.
- *Ametropia*, or errors in focusing the eye, which can occur in various forms, including:

  ▪ *Myopia*, or *nearsightedness*, in which near vision (within 8–20 inches) is strong but far vision is blurred. Children with uncorrected myopia often tire easily and may be restless or inattentive when doing work requiring distance vision. The problem is easily corrected with glasses.

  ▪ *Hyperopia*, or *farsightedness*, in which vision is blurred for near vision (and sometimes far vision as well). The condition is easily corrected with glasses. Children with uncorrected hyperopia may be fussy and irritable, and may tire easily doing work requiring near vision.

  ▪ *Astigmatism*, in which the cornea is slightly misshapen, causing blurring and distortion of vision. In mild cases, the distortion can be offset by specially ground lenses in glasses, but in severe cases, *contact lenses* are needed to provide a smooth, undistorted focusing surface.

  ▪ *Anisometropia* or *aniseikonia*, in which the two eyes vary markedly in what they see, because of unequal focusing power in the eyes or differences in the size and shape of the eyes. As a result, one eye sees an object of one size and shape, while the other sees the same object as a different size and shape, as when one eye is myopic and the other hyperopic. Glasses are not fully effective in treating this problem, though contact lenses are somewhat better.
- *Size defects*, including eyes smaller than normal (*microcornea*), larger than normal (*megalocornea*), or bulging (*buphthalmos*, or "ox-eye"), which can lead to *glaucoma* (see below).

In additional to structural problems, disorders may affect various parts of the eye. One of the most sensitive parts is the retina; among the retinal disorders found in young people (as well as adults) are:

- *Detachment of or damage to the retina*, when the light-sensitive membrane of the retina is torn or pulled away from the layer behind it, allowing vitreous humor to leak in between. This can occur after a major injury, but sometimes occurs spontaneously, especially in people with severe myopia. The first symptom is usually flashes of light at the edge of the *field of vision*, the area the eye sees when looking straight ahead, without shifting position. Retinal detachment is an emergency, requiring immediate surgical repair. Otherwise, if the central part of the retina (the *macula*) becomes detached, central vision may be lost, though some *peripheral vision* may remain from the edges of the field of vision. If surgery fails, an injectable silicone drug may be used to attempt reattachment.
- *Retinopathy*, a general disease or disorder of the retina. The term usually refers to retinal damage from long-term hypertension (high BLOOD PRESSURE) or DIABETES, which can lead to blindness. It is common among PREMATURE babies and is known as *retinopathy of prematurity* (ROP), which is now sometimes treated with lasers.
- *Retinitis pigmentosa* (RP), a PROGRESSIVE disease in which the rods of the retina degenerate and become pigmented. This sometimes starts in early childhood as poor night vision, but is not recognized until later, as vision is gradually reduced. Cones are less slowly affected, so central vision remains longer, but RP

sometimes leads to total blindness. RP is a GENETIC DISORDER, with an inheritance pattern that can be AUTOSOMAL RECESSIVE, AUTOSOMAL DOMINANT, or X-LINKED. Some children also have an inherited disposition for the center of the retina to degenerate, a condition called *macular degeneration.* Retinal degeneration may also accompany some other genetic disorders, such as LAURENCE-MOON-BEIDL SYNDROME and Tay-Sachs disease (see LIPID STORAGE DISEASES).

- *Retinoblastoma,* a MALIGNANT TUMOR that often occurs in very young children; susceptibility may be inherited. Often seen first in a whitened pupil, retinoblastoma may cause blindness in the eye and sometimes spreads along the optic nerve to the brain; it may be accompanied by strabismus (see above). Radiation therapy is the main treatment (see CANCER); the eye may be removed, if necessary. Any eye abnormality in an infant should be brought to a doctor's attention immediately. Tumors may also form elsewhere in the eye, some of them BENIGN, some secondary tumors from elsewhere in the body.
- *Retrolental fibroplasia,* in which a mass of scar tissue forms in back of the lens of the eye, usually affecting both eyes. Severe cases can lead to complete loss of sight.
- *Color blindness,* more accurately *color vision deficiency,* which involves reduced ability to perceive color differences, often especially in the red and green ranges. Absolute color blindness, which is very rare, involves seeing everything in shades of black and white. Color vision deficiency is a common GENETIC DISORDER of the X-linked type that affects primarily men. Women are mostly CARRIERS. It is not a serious problem, except when a child's inability to distinguish colors can be a SAFETY hazard.

The eye's other focusing part, the cornea, is also subject to various disorders, including:

- *Corneal abrasion,* or *scratching,* which can then become infected and ulcerated; the resulting scar can lead to some loss of vision.
- *Injury by corrosive substances,* in which the eye is splashed by substances such as acids or alkalis; the eye must be washed with large amounts of water to attempt to save sight.
- *Xerophthalmia* (*dry eye*), involving severe dryness of the cornea and conjunctiva, which may result from severe VITAMIN A deficiency. If uncorrected, it can result in *keratomalacia,* a softening of the cornea; that can often lead to perforation, a condition that can cause blindness.
- *Keratoconjunctivitis sicca* (*dry eye and conjunctiva*), in which the film of tears coating the eye is inadequate to protect the eye, as in some disorders, such as SJOGREN SYNDROME.
- *Uveitis,* inflammation of the *uveal tissues*—the iris, choroid, or ciliary body—often from infection, but sometimes in connection with an AUTOIMMUNE DISORDER.

If the cornea has become damaged beyond repair, a cornea TRANSPLANT may restore sight, using a donor's cornea stored in an *eye bank.* Cornea transplants are far easier and more often successful than other kinds of transplants, because the cornea is relatively insulated from the body's IMMUNE SYSTEM, making rejection less likely.

In addition, the eye is subject to other disorders, among them:

- *Infections,* as by bacteria, viruses, and also parasites, especially in people with weakened immune systems. Among the most common infections is *conjunctivitis* ("pink eye"), inflammation of the membrane that covers the eye when closed; this can also result from ALLERGY. Newborns often pick up a conjunctival infection called *opththalmia* from the mother during birth; this may be bacterial or related to various SEXUALLY TRANSMITTED DISEASES, such as GONORRHEA or HERPES, which can spread and damage vision. A severe form of conjunctivitis, called *trachoma,* is caused by CHLAMYDIA; if not effectively treated with ANTIBIOTICS, it can scar the cornea and reduce vision to light only. Use of silver nitrate and antibiotic ointments as part of routine PERINATAL CARE have made such infections rare. Inflammation and infection of the internal eye (*endophthalmitis*) can also be extremely serious. Inflammation of the eyelids (*blepharitis*) often involves itchiness and pus or mucus on the lids and lashes.
- *Glaucoma,* a condition involving abnormally high pressure on the aqueous fluid of the eye. This can damage the optic nerve and result in severe loss of sight or sometimes in *tunnel vision,* in which the child has only central vision, with no peripheral vision. In children, glaucoma is sometimes associated with *buphthalmos* (bulging eye); it can also result from injury, disease, or other disorders, such as PIERRE ROBIN SYNDROME. If diagnosed in time, the condition can be controlled with drugs, before damage occurs.
- *Cataracts,* loss of transparency in the lens at the back of the eye, gradually decreasing transmission of light to the retina. Most cases of cataracts occur in elderly people, but one form occurs in infants at birth. These congenital cataracts may result from the mother's infection with RUBELLA or ingestion of certain drugs during PREGNANCY; it is also associated with some GENETIC DISORDERS, such as DOWN SYNDROME. A child with GALACTOSEMIA is at risk for developing cataracts unless kept on a restricted diet. In most cases, surgery can be performed to remove the clouded lens and restore sight, replacing the lens with special glasses or lens implants.
- *Nystagmus,* sometimes called *dancing eyes,* in which the eyes make involuntary, rapid, jerky movements from side to side, often in combination with some other kind of visual DISABILITY or health disorder, such as a brain tumor or hereditary form of ATAXIAS. Young children with nystagmus may be able to focus more clearly if they are taught to put a finger on what they want to see and use a marker for close work.

- *Optic atrophy*, in which the optic nerve has been damaged, as by some causes noted above, impairing both central visual acuity and color vision. Children with optic atrophy have a much easier time perceiving black print on white paper than on colored paper. Handheld magnifiers can also help.
- *Hyphema*, hemorrhage in the front of the eye, often looking like a bloodshot eye, which can be caused by violent shaking or a blow to the head and is one sign of possible child abuse (see SHAKEN CHILD SYNDROME; CHILD ABUSE AND NEGLECT).
- *Papilledema (choked disc)*, a swelling of the optic nerve, as may result from a brain tumor increasing the fluid pressure inside the skull.
- *Diplopia*, or double vision, which may result from a variety of causes, including a brain tumor.

Various parts of the eye can also be damaged by poisons, such as methanol (see ENVIRONMENTAL HAZARDS); by MALNUTRITION; by heavy SMOKING and ALCOHOL ABUSE; by some metals (see LEAD POISONING); and by some kinds of drugs. Excess exposure to sunlight can also cause eye damage, including cataracts in the long term. Parents will want to be sure that their children's eyes are protected from the sun (see WHEN DO KIDS NEED PROTECTION FROM THE SUN? on page 548).

In checking a child's eyes, ophthalmologists generally first examine the physical appearance of the eyes and the surrounding skin, the movement of the eyes (checking for strabismus, for example), visual acuity (sharpness of vision), field of vision, and color vision. In the process they use a variety of techniques.

Best known is the *Snellen test*, the wall chart of letters, numbers, or symbols, often starting with a big "E" on the top; each row below it is smaller and labeled with the distance at which it can be read by people with normal vision. For preschoolers, the big "E" alone is used, placed in different positions. This tests *central visual acuity*, or sharpness of vision in the direct line of sight. It is generally used for testing vision at a distance of 20 feet, using one eye at a time. A child who, from 20 feet away, can read a line that people of normal vision can read from 20 feet away, is said to have 20/20 vision. If a child has 20/30 vision, that means that the child can read at 20 feet what people of normal vision can read from 30 feet away. A Snellen rating of 20/30 or less is one of the common descriptions of people with "reduced vision." A similarly graded test for near vision is called the *Jaeger test*. Where appropriate, *visual field tests* will be used to check peripheral vision.

In examining the inner part of the eye (which is possible because the main parts are transparent), the ophthalmologist will generally use a *slit-lamp microscope* and *ophthalmoscope* to provide magnification to check for possible abnormalities or damage, sometimes after the pupil has been widened (*dilated*) with eye drops. If infection is suspected, a sample of cells may be scraped off and a CULTURE made in the laboratory. If abrasions or ulcers are suspected, a dye may be put into the eye to show any damage. To check for possible glaucoma, pressure within the eye is measured by a test called *applanation tonometry*. Where appropriate, the doctor may also check *depth perception* (DP), the ability to perceive the distance of objects and their relative position in space, and *light perception* (LP), the ability to distinguish light from dark.

Finally, a variety of *refraction tests* will help the opthalmologist decide whether corrective lenses—glasses or contact lenses—are needed. Glasses are sufficient for many mild eye problems, such as myopia. Many people, however, prefer contact lenses of various kinds, which also have some advantages in correcting certain conditions (as noted above). Hard lenses are the most durable kind of contact lenses; softer lenses are more expensive, mold to the shape of the cornea, and can be worn longer. But therein lies a trap: if lenses are worn longer without proper cleansing, they may promote infection in the eyes, sometimes causing very serious damage. Contact lenses may also be damaged by exposure to some chemicals. In addition, some people's eyes are sensitive and irritated by contact lenses; have allergic reactions to the materials used in them; or have eyes too dry to wear them for long. If children are using contact lenses, parents should be very careful about how long at a time the lenses are worn and about STERILIZATION; at any sign of a problem—sensitivity, redness, mucus, discomfort—contact lenses should be removed and the child taken to the doctor. Women taking BIRTH CONTROL PILLS may also have problems with contact lenses.

When a child has serious vision problems, the ophthalmologist's report will be made available to the school, and often PRESCHOOL, where appropriate. Reports are sometimes rather technical; for example, ophthalmologists may use the abbreviations *OD* (*oculus dexter*) to refer to the right eye, *OS* (*oculus sinister*) for the left eye, *OU* (*oculus uterque*) if a condition affects both eyes, and *CC* (*cum correction*) meaning with corrective lenses, such as glasses. These reports are used in determining whether the child has a disability and therefore is eligible for SPECIAL EDUCATION assistance and, if so, of what kind.

In the HEAD START program, for example, various categories of visual impairment are described. In these, a child is considered *blind* when any *one* of the following exist:

- The child is sightless or has such limited vision that he/she must rely on hearing and touch as his/her chief means of learning.
- A determination of legal blindness in the state of residence has been made.
- Central (visual) acuity does not exceed 20/200 in the better eye, with correcting lenses, or it is greater than 20/200, but is accompanied by a limitation in the field of vision such that the widest diameter of visual field subtends an angle of no greater than 20 degrees (this is a physical description of tunnel vision).

As implied above, few children are totally sightless; most have some remaining sight, sometimes described as *low vision.*

The much wider category in Head Start is *visually impaired,* described as:

> A child shall be reported as visually impaired if central (visual) acuity, with corrective lenses, does not exceed 20/70 in either eye, but who is not blind; or whose visual acuity is greater than 20/70, but is accompanied by a limitation in the field of vision such that the widest diameter of visual field subtends an angle of no greater than 140 degrees, or who suffers any other loss of visual function that will restrict learning processes, e.g. faulty muscular action. *Not to be included in this category are persons whose vision with eyeglasses is normal, or nearly so.*

It is important for both parents and teachers, however, to focus not on the technical categories, which are used for reporting purposes, but on functional questions: For instance, how well can the child use remaining vision for everyday purposes? Some children are able to use their residual vision far more effectively than others, and some kinds of visual problems cause more difficulties in everyday life than others. A child's vision may also be affected by other factors, such as illness, fatigue, or stress, so that something they can do one week they might not necessarily be able to do the next.

Parents of children with low vision should talk to the child much more than normal, whenever going in or out of the room, for example, or when something unusual is happening. That will maximize the child's development by providing satisfying contact with the outside world and should start immediately after birth or as soon as blindness is recognized.

Children should be encouraged to use whatever vision capabilities they have, however slight they may be. The Head Start program recommends: "The eyes, especially in early childhood, benefit from use. You should encourage a child to look both far and near, and to examine objects close up. If necessary, encourage a child to hold objects close to the face, even if only part of the object is seen in this manner." In some programs, special assistants called *orientation and mobility instructors* or *peripatologists* are available to help a visually handicapped child learn the concepts and skills necessary to understand where they are and to move about safely and easily. With special assistance such as this and somewhat ADAPTED EDUCATION, many students with impaired vision are able to attend local schools, either in regular classrooms or special ones or both; some others may instead go to residential schools for children who are blind or have multiple disabilities.

Various kinds of services are available to help visually impaired children and adults. Many materials have been printed in *Braille,* a system of raised dots used to represent letters, numbers, musical notes and symbols, and other symbols. Large-print books and various video aids are available, including audio captioning of television programs (often on what is called a *second audio channel* on the television set), as are audio recordings of books on records and tape, including textbooks; many of these are available at little or no cost. Computers, some as small as pocket-size, can operate as talking word processors, producing output in braille; for people of low vision, computers with special software can print letters as large as a full screen for reading and working. (Subscribers to the America Online computer service can find activities designed to develop children's visual skills in the Moms Online Desk Reference section of Moms Online, under "Teaching Young Children.")

Though there are no separate colleges for the blind, many colleges and testing programs have special arrangements to accommodate blind or visually impaired students (see SPECIAL HELP FOR SPECIAL COLLEGE STUDENTS on page 366). SERVICE DOGS are often used to give people mobility when sight is extremely low. Government assistance and tax credits are also often available, as through SOCIAL SECURITY. Parents seeking help and assistance for their visually impaired child should see the organizations below (see also HELP FOR SPECIAL CHILDREN on page 689).

FOR HELP AND FURTHER INFORMATION

ORGANIZATIONS FOCUSING ON CHILDREN

The National Organization for Parents of Blind Children
410–659–9314
Barbara Cheadle, President
Affiliate of the National Federation of the Blind (see next organization listed); publishes quarterly *Future Reflections.*

National Federation of the Blind (NFB)
1800 Johnson Street
Baltimore, MD 21230
410–659–9314; Job Opportunity number: 800–638–7518
Fax: 410–685–5653
NFB NET 24-hour bulletin board: 410–752–5011
Organization concerned with vision impairment or loss; acts as advocate; operates National Blindness Information Center, International Braille and Technology Center for the Blind (which houses NFB NET, above), exploring use of computer-related technology, and JOB, a job listing and referral service; provides some postsecondary scholarships to students who are blind; publishes monthly *The Braille Monitor* and quarterly *Future Reflections* (for parents of blind children) and numerous other materials (in two or more formats: print, braille, recorded disk, or audiocassette), those of special interest to parents including:

- For parents: *Parents of Blind Children, Parents Find the National Federal of the Blind, Changing What It Means to Be Blind, Blind: Then and Now, Growing Up with Independence: The Blind Child's Use of the White Cane, Is Your*

Child Age-Appropriate?, Listen to Your Elders, Love, Dating, and Marriage: Blind Children Grow Up and Become Parents, Too, I Am a Blind Mother Fighting to Keep My Children from Corruption, I Remember, I Was a Young Mother Being Stifled by Blindness, Independence: To Have and to Hold, A Mother of Blind Children Addresses the Professionals, Do You Know a Blind Person?, Blindness and Disorders of the Eye, and *On Becoming a Wise Consumer of Low Vision Services.*

- For children and adolescents: *Serena Can Wait at the Bottom of the Hill, To Be a Parent,* and *The Voice of the Fourth Generation: Blind Kids Express Their Views.*
- On Braille: *Braille Literacy: Issues for Consumers and Providers, Why Not Braille, Braille: A Survival Skill for All Blind People, Braille: Pedagogy, Prejudice, and the Banner of Equality,* and *Braille: What Is It? What Does It Mean to the Blind.*
- Films and videocassettes, including *It's Not So Different: An Interview With Blind Parents, Kids with Canes,* and *We Know Who We Are,* about three students who are blind.
- Materials on daily living, such as *Comments on Clothing, Suggestions for the Blind Cook,* and *Why Use the Long White Cane,* and on other areas of life, such as accommodations, travel, careers, discrimination, history, philosophy, technology, and vending, and books for professionals and general reading.

National Association for Parents of the Visually Impaired, Inc. (NAPVI)
P.O. Box 317
Watertown, MA 02272–0317
617–972–7441; 800–562–6265
Fax: 617–972–7444
Susan LaVenture, Executive Director
Organization of and for parents of visually impaired children and others; seeks to educate public; has Choices for Children campaign to strengthen services to blind and visually impaired children; provides information and support; offers training and workshops; publishes various print and taped materials, including quarterly newsletter *Awareness,* books and booklets *Take Charge: A Guide to Resources for Parents of the Visually Impaired, Preschool Learning Activities for the Visually Impaired Child—A Guide for Parents, Legislative Handbook for Parents, Parents to the Rescue, Your Child's Information Journal, How to Pack 'Em In: A Guide to Planning Workshops,* and *A Guide to Library Resources for Teachers of the Visually Impaired,* and *The Student with Albinism in the Regular Classroom.*

Blind Children's Center
4120 Marathon Street
Los Angeles, CA 90029
213–664–2153, 800–222–3566, U.S. except CA,
800–222–3567, CA
Fax: 213–665–3828
Organization for parents of vision-impaired children; publishes various materials, including *First Steps: A Handbook for Teaching Young Children Who Are Visually Impaired, Heart to Heart* (for parents), and *Selecting a Program.*

International Institute for Visually Impaired and Blind Children's Fund, 0–7 (IIVI, 0–7)
2875 Northwind Drive, #211
East Lansing, MI 48823–5040
517–333–1425
Sherry Raynor, President
Organization concerned with vision-impaired children from birth to age seven; operates information center; consults and offers workshops; publishes various materials, including quarterly newsletter and materials for stimulating children at different stages and levels of impairment.

National Alliance of Blind Students (NABS)
1155 15th Street NW, Suite 720
Washington, DC 20005
202–467–5081; 800–424–8666 (3–5:30 P.M. ET)
Fax: 202–467–5085
Internet Listserv: NABS-L
To subscribe, send the message "subscribe NABS-L [your first name] [your last name]" to:
mailto:listserv@uscbvm.ucsb.edu
Student affiliate of the American Council of the Blind (see writeup later in this listing); provides information and referrals; offers scholarships to blind and visually impaired students; publishes quarterly newsletter *The Student Advocate.*

Council for Exceptional Children (CEC), 800–328–0272. Includes Division on Visual Handicaps (DVH), which publishes newsletter *DVH Quarterly* and other materials. CEC also publishes special report: *Visual Impairments.* (For full group information, see HELP ON LEARNING AND EDUCATION on page 659.)

Helen Keller National Center for Deaf-Blind Youths and Adults (HKNC), 516–944–8900; 516–944–8637, TT; **National Family Association for Deaf-Blind**: 800–255–0411, ext. 275. (For full group information, see DEAF-BLIND.)

Parents and Cataract Kids (PACK)
179 Hunter's Lane
Devon, PA 19333
610–352–0719
Julie Gerhardt, President
Organization of parents whose children have cataracts; encourages formation of local groups and parent-to-parent contact; publishes quarterly newsletter *In-Sight.*

Association for Children with Down Syndrome (ACDS), 516–221–4700. Publishes *Eyeglasses On,* on preparing very young children to wear eyeglasses. (For full group information, see DOWN SYNDROME.)

National Information Center for Children and Youth with Disabilities (NICHCY), 800–695–0285, voice/TT. Publishes *Visual Impairments.* (For full group information, see HELP FOR SPECIAL CHILDREN on page 689.)

American Academy of Pediatrics (AAP), 800–433–9016. Publishes brochures *Your Child's Eyes.* (For full group information, see HEALTH CARE.)

GENERAL ORGANIZATIONS

American Foundation for the Blind (AFB)
11 Penn Plaza, Suite 300
New York, NY 10001
212–502–7600; 212–502–7662, TTY; 800-AFBLIND [232–5463] (1 A.M.–12 P.M., 2 P.M.–4 P.M. EST)
Fax: 212–502–7777
E-mail: afbinfo@afb.org
Carl Augusto, Executive Director
Organization for people who are blind or visually impaired, their families, and professionals who work with them; provides information and referrals; helps blind people and their families develop self-help programs; sells technical aids for visually impaired people; maintains library and national consultant on early childhood; publishes extensive list of general materials in large type, recording, and braille, as well as basic guide to services for the blind from birth on, *Directory of Services for Blind and Visually Impaired Persons in the United States,* and numerous informative materials.

Prevent Blindness America
500 East Remington Road
Schaumburg, IL 60173–5611
312–843–2020; 800–221–3004; 800–331–2020
Fax: 708–843–8458
Richard Hellner, Executive Director
Organization concerned with blindness and preservation of sight; formerly National Society to Prevent Blindness (NSPB); provides information and referrals; supports research; operates screening programs; publishes various materials, including newsletter *Prevent Blindness News*; brochures *The Eye and How We See, Your Child's Sight, Signs of Possible Eye Trouble in Children, Preschoolers Home Eye Test, Understanding Conjunctivitis ("Pink Eye"), Amblyopia ("Lazy Eye"), Strabismus ("Crossed Eyes"), Signs of Possible Eye Trouble in Adults, Diabetic Retinopathy, Family Home Eye Test,* and other brochures relating to adult eye disorders; vision screening and teaching materials for health professionals; and materials on eye safety on the job.

American Council of the Blind (ACB)
1155 15th Street NW, Suite 720
Washington, DC 20005
202–467–5081; 800–424–8666, U.S. except DC
Legislative Information Hotline: 800–424–8666 (after 6 P.M.)
Fax: 202–467–5085
ASB On-Line Bulletin Board: 202–331–1058
Editor's e-mail: ncrabb@access.digex.net
Oral O. Miller, National Representative
Organization concerned with people who are blind or visually impaired; provides information and referrals; acts as advocate; records talking books and maintains library about vision problems; publishes various materials in large type, recording, and braille, including monthly *The Braille Forum, Journal of Visual Impairment and Blindness, Directory of Agencies Serving the Visually Handicapped in the U.S.,* catalog *Products for People with Vision Problems,* brochures on specific topics, and radio program *ACB Reports*; has numerous special-interest affiliates, such as ACB Parents, Council of Citizens with Low Vision, Guide Dog Users, Friends-In-Art, Library Users of America, and National Association of Blind Students.

Council of Citizens with Low Vision (CCLV)
1400 North Drake Road, #218
Kalamazoo, MI 49006
616–381–9566
Elizabeth Lennon, President
Organization concerned with people who have partial sight or low vision; encourages use of technical aids and services to enhance residual vision; acts as advocate; publishes quarterly large-print newsletter and pamphlets.

National Association for Visually Handicapped (NAVH)
22 West 21st Street
New York, NY 10010
212–889–3141
Fax: 212–727–2931
Lorraine H. Marchi, Director
Organization concerned with the partially seeing, or "hard of seeing®"; provides information and referrals; maintains lending library of large print materials; publishes large print children's newsletter *In Focus,* newsletter for adults *Seeing Clearly,* and other materials, including:

- For parents: *About Children's Eyes, About Children's Vision, Family Guide—Growth and Development of the Partially Seeing Child,* and *Heartbreak of Being "A Little Bit Blind."*
- General materials: *The Eye and Your Vision, Classification of Impaired Vision, Eye-Q Test, It's All Right to Be Angry, Sensitivity to People with Partial Eyesight, Problems of the Partially Seeing, What Every Low Vision Patient Should Know, A Patient's Guide to Visual Aids and Illumination, Communicating with People Who Have Trouble Hearing and Seeing,* and *How to Use Your Low Vision Glasses.*
- On specific problems: *Diabetic Retinopathy, Diseases of the Macula, Cataracts, Glaucoma—The Sneak Thief of Sight.*
- Large print loan library catalog and visual aids and information materials catalog, and materials for older people and for health professionals.

National Eye Institute (NEI)
1 Center Drive, MSC 2510
Bethesda, MD 20892
301–496–5248
Fax: 301–402–1065

NEI Publications Distribution Center
2020 Vision Place
Bethesda, MD 20892–3655
800–869–2020
One of the U.S. National Institutes of Health, sponsoring research on eyes and vision disorders; provides information; publishes various materials, including:

- Fact sheets: *The Cornea and Corneal Diseases, Glossary of Vision Terms, Selected National Eye Health-Related Organizations,* and *Selected Resources for People with Low Vision.*
- "Don't Lose Sight of" brochures: *Cataract, Glaucoma,* and *Age-Related Macular Degeneration.*
- Information packages: *Amblyopia and Strabismus, Behcet's Disease and the Eye, Blepharitis, Cataract Surgery, Dry Eye Syndrome, Graves' Disease and the Eye, Macular Holes, Radial Keratotomy, Retinitis Pigmentosa,* and *Sarcoidosis and the Eye.*
- Combined Health Information Database (CHID) searches on *Childhood Disorders, Eye Care and Eye Safety, Inherited Disorders, Low Vision, Materials for Parents of Visually Impaired Children, Rehabilitation, Glaucoma, Cataract,* and *Age-Related Macular Degeneration.*
- Combined Health Information Database (CHID) searches and technical reports.

The Foundation Fighting Blindness
1401 Mt. Royal Avenue, 4th Floor
Baltimore, MD 21217–4245
410–225–9400; 410–225–9409, TT;
800–683–5555
Eye Donation Hotline: 800–638–1818 (24 hours a day)
Fax: 410–225–3936
Robert Gray, Executive Director
Organization concerned with retinitis pigmentosa and related inherited degenerative diseases of the retina; formerly the RP (Retinitis Pigmentosa) Foundation Fighting Blindness; gathers and disseminates information; sponsors research and runs screening centers; publishes various materials, including *Fighting Blindness News, Information About RP, The Inheritance of RP, Information About Usher Syndrome, Information on Choroidermia, Information on Bardet Biedel Syndrome, Information on Stargardt Disease, Tips for Teachers,* and *Tips for Travelers.*

Association for Macular Diseases
210 East 64th Street
New York, NY 10021
212–605–3719
Nikolai Stevenson, President
Organization for people concerned with macular diseases; sponsors eye donor project.

National Organization for Rare Disorders (NORD), 800–999–6673. (For full group information, see RARE DISORDERS.)

Center for Safety in the Arts (CSA), 212–227–6220. Publishes fact sheet *Eye and Face Protection.* (For full group information, see ENVIRONMENTAL HAZARDS.)

Resource Center on Substance Abuse Prevention and Disability, 202–628–8442. Publishes *A Look at Alcohol and Other Drug Abuse Prevention and Blindness and Visual Impairments.* (For full group information, see HELP FOR SPECIAL CHILDREN on page 689.).

ON RESOURCES AND SPECIAL SERVICES

HEATH Resource Center, National Clearinghouse on Postsecondary Education for Individuals with Disabilities, 800–544–3284, voice/TT. Publishes *Students Who Are Blind or Visually Impaired in Postsecondary Education.* (For full group information, see HELP FOR SPECIAL CHILDREN on page 689.)

The Seeing Eye, 201–539–4425. Publishes *Choices: Living with Vision Loss* for newly blind people and their families. (For full group information, see SERVICE DOGS.)

Resources for Rehabilitation
33 Bedford Street, Suite 19A
Lexington, MA 02173
617–862–6455
Fax: 617–861–7517
Nonprofit organization that publishes large-print publications for people with disabilities, including books *Living with Low Vision: A Resource Guide for People with Sight Loss, Providing Services for People with Vision Loss: A Multidisciplinary Perspective, Meeting the Needs of People with Vision Loss: A Multidisciplinary Perspective, Rehabilitation Resource Manual: VISION, Resources for People with Disabilities and Chronic Conditions,* and *A Woman's Guide to Coping with Disability*; and brochures *Living with Low Vision, How to Keep Reading with Vision Loss, Aids for Everyday Living with Vision Loss, High Tech Aids for People with Vision Loss,* and *Living with Diabetic Retinopathy.*

National Library Services for the Blind and Physically Handicapped, Library of Congress, 800–424–8567, U.S. except DC. Publishes guides *Deaf-Blindness: National Organizations and Resources, Sports, Outdoor Recreation, and Games for Visually and Physically Impaired Individuals,* and *Library Resources for the Blind and Physically Handicapped*; brochures *Reading with Low Vision, Talking Books for People with Physical Disabilities, Facts: Music for Blind and Physically Handicapped Individuals, Braille An Extraordinary Volunteer Opportunity, Facts: About Braille,* and *Do You Know This Tune?* (on braille music). (For full group information, see HELP FOR SPECIAL CHILDREN on page 689.)

Recording for the Blind and Dyslexic (RFBD)
20 Roszel Road
Princeton, NJ 08540
609–452–0606; For book orders only:
800–221–4792
Fax: 609–520–7990
E-mail: info@rsb.org
Ritchie Geisel, President

Nonprofit organization providing taped educational materials, books on diskette, and other services for people who cannot read standard print because of visual or other disability; materials are free after a one-time application and registration fee; catalog and quarterly updates on audiotape or disk can be purchased.

ONLINE RESOURCES

Internet: BlindFam. Mailing list on blindness in everyday family life. To subscribe, send e-mail message to: mailto:listserv@sjuvm.stjohns.edu

Internet: Blind News Digest. Mailing list on visual loss. To subscribe, send e-mail message to: wtm@bunker.afd.olivetti,com or send this message "SUB BlindNws [your first name] [your last name]" to: mailto:listserv@vm1.nodak.edu

Internet: Disability-Related Resources. Collection of resources, including information on blindness. gopher://hawking.u.washington.edu

OTHER RESOURCES

GENERAL WORKS

20–20: A Total Guide to Improving Your Vision and Preventing Eye Disease. Mitchell H. Friedlaender and Stef Donev. Random House, 1994.
Preserve Your Sight: The Definitve Nutrition and Lifestyle Guide to Preventive Eye Care. Michael E. Lieppman and Bill Sardi. Eye Communications, 1994.
The Complete Guide to Eye Care, Eyeglasses, and Contact Lenses, rev. ed. Walter J. Zinn and Herbert Solomon. Lifetime, 1992.
Your Eyes!: A Comprehensive Look at the Understanding and Treatment of Vision Problems. Thomas L. D'Alonzo. Avanti, 1991.
Sight for Life. Lee T. Nordan. J.B. Media International, 1991.

FOR PARENTS AND OTHER ADULTS

Can't Your Child See?: A Guide for Parents and Professionals about Young Visually Impaired Children, 3rd ed. Eileen P. Scott and others. PRO-ED, 1994.
Living and Learning with Blind Children: A Guide for Parents and Teachers of Visually Impaired Children. Felicity Harrison and Mary Crow. University of Toronto Press, 1993.
Mainstreaming Preschoolers: Children with Visual Handicaps: A Guide for Teachers, Parents, and Others Who Work with Visually Handicapped Preschoolers. Lou Alonso and others. U.S. Government Printing Office, 1984.

ON VISION PROBLEMS

A Singular View: The Art of Seeing with One Eye, 5th ed. Frank B. Brady. Frank B Brady, 1994.
Encyclopedia of Blindness and Sight Impairments. Jill Sardegna. Facts on File, 1990.
Living with Blindness. Steve Parker. Watts, 1989.

FOR CHILDREN

I See, 2nd ed. Helen Oxenbury. Candlewick, 1995. Baby board book.
Seeing. Lillian Wright. Raintree Steck-Vaughn, 1994.
What Do You See? Patricia Lauber. Crown, 1994.
Why Do Some People Need Glasses? Isaac Asimov and Carrie Dierks. Gareth Stevens, 1993.
Sight. Mandy Suhr. Carolrhoda, 1993.
Look at Your Eyes, rev. ed. Paul Showers. HarperCollins, 1992.
You Won't Believe Your Eyes. Milan Tytla and Nancy Crystal. Firefly, 1992.
Eyes. Aleksander Jedrosz. Troll, 1992.
Seeing Things. Allan Fowler. Childrens, 1991.
Seeing in Special Ways. Thomas Bergman. Gareth Stevens, 1990.
The Eye and Seeing, rev. ed. Steve Parker. Watts, 1990.

FOR PRETEENS AND TEENS

Lifeprints, quarterly magazine for blind or visually impaired youth (junior and senior high school). Available from Blindskills, Inc., P.O. Box 5181, Salem, OR 97304.
Preparing for Adolescence. James Dobson. W. A. T. Braille, 1991. For visually impaired teens.

(See also SERVICE DOGS; VISUAL SKILLS; HELP FOR SPECIAL CHILDREN on page 689.)

F

fail, in EDUCATION, having a level of performance too low to be acceptable as evidence of learning, whether on a single TEST or piece of work, or for a whole course, in which case a teacher would not allow a student CREDIT for taking a course. Sometimes the failing level is a preset GRADE, such as a letter average below a "D" or a numerical average below 65 or 70. And sometimes the "fail" label simply distinguishes those who did not receive credit from those who did, in a PASS-FAIL SYSTEM.

failure to thrive, abnormally slow growth and development of a child, as compared to the usual pattern for children of their weight at birth. Failure to grow normally can result from a wide variety of causes, including:

- MALNUTRITION, which itself can result from a variety of causes, such as:

  Poverty in the family.
  Lack of knowledge by the MOTHER and FATHER about how and what to feed the child.
  CHILD ABUSE AND NEGLECT.
  Severe MATERNAL DEPRIVATION SYNDROME, as from outright rejection of the child by the mother and father or from allowing an infant to be left in a HOSPITAL without stimulation, warmth, or human contact.

- CHROMOSOMAL ABNORMALITIES, including TURNER'S SYNDROME, DOWN SYNDROME, and other TRISOMIES.
- ACUTE illness, such as an infection.
- CHRONIC illness or general health problems, which are sapping the child's ability to grow and develop (for example, see HEART AND HEART PROBLEMS; KIDNEY AND UROLOGICAL PROBLEMS; LIVER AND LIVER PROBLEMS).
- METABOLIC DISORDERS or malabsorption (see DIGESTIVE SYSTEM AND DISORDERS), which keep the child from getting the proper NUTRITION, even though the diet is sufficient.

If unrecognized and unreversed, failure to thrive can lead to permanent retardation of physical, mental, and social development. Extreme failure to thrive can lead to a severe condition called MARASMUS. That is a main reason why WELL BABY EXAMINATIONS include careful monitoring of height and weight and why, if the parent-child relationship seems deficient, social services attempt EARLY INTERVENTION. (See GROWTH AND GROWTH DISORDERS.)

Fallopian tubes, the pair of narrow tubes that arc around the lower abdomen from the two OVARIES to a woman's UTERUS. The ends of the Fallopian tubes, which lie above the ovaries, are like upside-down, flowerlike funnels. When a mature egg (OVUM) is released by an ovary, the petal-like ends (*fimbriae)* of the Fallopian tube open to receive it, drawing the powerless egg inside by the wavelike action of millions of hairlike cells (*cilia*). Once in the Fallopian tubes, the egg undergoes division (*meiosis*) once more; its 23 chromosomes, each made of double strands of DNA, reduce themselves to 23 single strands of DNA, ready for FERTILIZATION, with the duplicate strand passing out of the picture. The egg is propelled by muscular contractions to slowly move through the tube to the uterus, a journey that takes approximately four to five days. If FERTILIZATION takes place, it is during this journey, in the twelve to twenty-four hours when the egg is viable, if SPERM are present at the same time. If so, the fertilized egg will, on arriving in the uterus, implant itself in the *endometrium* (the uterine lining), becoming an EMBRYO. If not, the unfertilized egg will be expelled from the uterus in the next MENSTRUATION.

Several things can occur to hinder this delicate process taking place in the Fallopian tubes.

- The egg may not be able to cross the space between the follicle where it matured and the fimbriae that will sweep it into the Fallopian tubes.
- The Fallopian tubes may be inflamed, a condition called *salpingitis*, often as a result of infection. This is a very common cause of INFERTILITY.
- The fertilized egg may not be moved all the way into the uterus, often because the tube is too narrow or has been damaged, as from infection, previous operation, or use of an INTRAUTERINE DEVICE (IUD). Instead the fertilized egg may implant itself in the Fallopian tubes, resulting in an ECTOPIC (or tubal) PREGNANCY. As the embryo grows there, the tube will rupture, causing possibly life-threatening hemorrhaging, and possibly diminishing future chances for conception, though the other tube (if undamaged) may still be open for use.

Women whose Fallopian tubes are damaged or who are otherwise unsuitable for natural conception may turn to IN VITRO FERTILIZATION or other forms of REPRODUCTIVE TECHNOLOGY to become pregnant. Because the tubes are so vital to fertilization, women who wish to have no more children sometimes choose, as a permanent form of BIRTH CONTROL, to have their "tubes tied," an operation medically called a TUBAL LIGATION. One alternative is a *fimbriectomy*, in which the petal-like fimbriae are removed. (See PREGNANCY; INFERTILITY.)

false negative, a TEST result that wrongly indicates that a person does not have the characteristics being tested for. If a child is given a SCREENING TEST for hearing problems and it fails to identify an existing hearing impairment, the result is a false negative.

false positive, a TEST result that wrongly indicates that a person has the characteristics being tested for. If a child is given a SCREENING TEST that indicates he has DIABETES, when in fact he does not, the result is called a false positive.

family, two or more people living together, sharing common responsibilities and obligations, among them physical, emotional, social, and economic care, and related to each other by blood, ADOPTION, marriage, or mutual agreement. Families come in many shapes and forms. Some people restrict the term to people related by blood or marriage who live together. In a wider sense, a family may refer to all one's relatives, regardless of where they live, or to all the descendants of a common ancestor. Because family is so differently defined, laws relating often specify what does, and does not, constitute a family for legal purposes. Such legal definitions are increasingly being challenged by people in nontraditional relationships who regard themselves as a family, such as a LESBIAN couple or an unmarried heterosexual couple living together. At stake is not simply acceptance by society, but often very practical benefits, such as being able to share in HEALTH INSURANCE and pension benefits, or being able to rent a house in a single-family zone.

The most basic form is the *nuclear family*, consisting of two generations in one household. The classic type of nuclear family is made up of FATHER, MOTHER, and children, but single-parent families are also nuclear, as is a HOMOSEXUAL couple raising a child. The *head of the family* is the person who primarily supports one or more others in the family and has significant authority within the family; for income tax purposes, the head of the household is generally the person who contributes over half of the necessary support of a family member, other than a spouse. With many modern two-career families, the "head of household" description is not only less useful, but also runs counter to any egalitarian feelings of the couple.

One enormously significant change in the family in recent decades has been the number of women who act as heads of households; many of them are divorced women raising their children with little or no CHILD SUPPORT or single parents raising children on their own, as well as many single women, often elderly, living alone. Around the world such households headed by women are generally poorer than those headed by men, with the woman often being the sole working-age provider and often supporting not only children but also other ill or aging relatives.

A family that has never been through a DIVORCE or separation is sometimes called an *intact family*; conversely, a family that has been split is often termed a *broken family*, though many parents object to the term because it indicates that the family needs to be "fixed." Many broken families reform themselves into new nuclear *stepfamilies*, often made up of a previously married mother and father and the children from their respective marriages, plus any new children they may have together. Such *blended families* can have rather complicated living relationships, with ex-spouses having VISITATION RIGHTS or with other children from a previous marriage shuttling in and out of the house according to various CUSTODY arrangements. Relationships between step-SIBLINGS and half-siblings, and between step-parents and step-children, also often take some delicate handling.

Legal relationships in such families vary widely. Often a stepfather, despite having practical day-to-day authority in the house, will in fact have no formal legally recognized custody relationship with a stepchild. Such a father is sometimes called a CO-PARENT. Some stepparents clarify the legal relationship by formal adoption of their stepchildren, if the biological father consents or has abandoned the child. Many modern families involve co-parents. In a household where a man and woman live unmarried with her son from a previous marriage, the man is co-parent to the woman's son, but has no formal legal relationship to him. Similarly, in a household in which a lesbian couple has adopted a child, often (depending on applicable laws) only one woman can legally be the adoptive parent; the other would be a co-parent.

With far more freedom in choosing marriage partners, many families today are formed by couples from different religious, cultural, or racial backgrounds. *Interfaith* or *interracial* marriages sometimes pose special strains, most of all regarding the religious and cultural aspects of how the children should be raised; such problems are extremely painful and difficult in cases of separation and divorce, when the court often must decide questions parents are unable to resolve. In one notable case, for example, the court ruled that the child was to be raised by one parent, but educated in the religion of the other parent.

An *extended family* is one that includes people other than parents and their children, generally those relatives beyond parents and children who are living in the FAMILY HOME, such as grandparents, aunts, uncles, and cousins. However, the term sometimes refers to the whole network of relatives with whom the family is in regular contact. Extended families in a single home were the traditional norm and still are in many parts of the world. In the United States today, nuclear families predominate, though that trend may be slowing somewhat for economic and health reasons. Though many individuals may feel constrained by the conservatism and traditionalism typical of an extended family, it has the advantages of providing strong personal roots for family members, ideally with older people receiving respect and passing on their knowledge and experience to younger family members. Extended families also provide a support system for individuals that is lacking in more widely dispersed households. In truth, some of the social movements of recent decades have their roots in the desire to recreate such a support system.

Multi-parent families are one such approach. In the United States, these are found in some kinds of collective households or communes, where adults share the rearing of the children. They are also found in *polygamous* families—rare and generally illegal in the United States, but common in some parts of the world—in which a husband has several wives (*polygyny*), or a wife has several husbands (*polyandry*).

Another approach is to choose a *surrogate family*, a familylike network based on chosen friends and often shared work, culture, interests, or neighborhoods. The now-common mutual-support, SELF-HELP GROUPS may partly represent an attempt by some people to replace the support individuals once had from extended families. Many organizations have formalized these attempts to create a nonbiological family, such as Big Brother/Big Sister of America (see GENERAL PARENTING RESOURCES on page634).

Most families function more or less on their own, with occasional help from the government's social support system. But some families find themselves unable to cope with the problems they are faced with and in particular are unable to care for their children; such families are labeled *dysfunctional*. Health and social work professionals have studied the family intensively in the past decades, analyzing the dynamics of family relationships and trying to identify signals that a family is dysfunctional and at high risk for problems such as CHILD ABUSE AND NEGLECT. Their aim is to try to recognize signs of impending trouble and to prevent full-blown problems by means of EARLY INTERVENTION and CRISIS INTERVENTION. (See CUSTODY; CHILD SUPPORT; GRANDPARENTS' RIGHTS; MOTHER; FATHER; also GENERAL PARENTING RESOURCES on page 634, for range of books on various kinds of families and parenting.)

family and medical leave, provision of unpaid time off for *both* parents around a child's birth or ADOPTION or during other serious illness in the family, with job security, seniority, HEALTH INSURANCE, and sometimes other benefits continuing. Though some individual companies long had reasonable MATERNITY LEAVE programs, providing unpaid time off for a MOTHER before and after CHILDBIRTH, the United States for many years lagged behind other countries in both the more limited maternity leave and the wider family and medical leave. Several times during the 1980s and early 1990s, a family and medical leave act was passed by Congress, only to be vetoed.

However, under the Family and Medical Leave Act of 1993 (Public Law 103–3), an individual who works at least twenty-five hours a week at a company with fifty or more employees, and has worked there for at least one year, is entitled to twelve weeks of unpaid leave at the time of a child's birth, ADOPTION, or when FOSTER CARE begins, for personal illness, or for serious illness of a family member, such as a child, parent, or spouse (but not a parent-in-law or partner, if unmarried). The leave can be taken on a part-time basis, as in part of certain days or one day a week (though teachers are restricted as to when during the year leave can be taken), and health insurance benefits are continued. The individual's job, or its equivalent, is guaranteed on return to work.

The law has rationalized leave arrangements and in fact provides *minimum* provisions, which are bettered by many large companies. Parents—who in the past had to cobble together a patchwork of vacation time, sick days, and personal days to be with their children at crucial times—can now take leave without jeopardizing their jobs. Similarly, the law gives support and protection to men and women, especially single parents, who take leave when a child or other family member has a severe illness, a CHRONIC illness, or DISABILITIES.

Problems still exist, however. Both men and women may find they lose out on perks and promotions in some companies if they take family and medical leave. Most notably, many women who return to work after giving birth find that they have been moved out of their previous career line onto a slower promotion track, called the *mommy track*.

In smaller firms, not covered by the law, even basic maternity leave may not be guaranteed. Many a woman has found that on announcing her PREGNANCY, she was summarily fired. The PREGNANCY DISCRIMINATION ACT was designed to prevent this, but is hard to enforce and does not cover the smallest firms.

FOR HELP AND FURTHER INFORMATION

Women's Legal Defense Fund
1875 Connecticut Avenue NW, Suite 710
Washington, DC 20009
202–986–2600
Fax: 202–986–2539
Judith L. Lichtman, President
Organization concerned with issues involving women, such as family and medical leave, reproductive freedom, sex discrimination in the workplace, quality health care, child support, and custody disputes; acts as advocate; publishes various materials, including *The Women's Legal Defense Fund's Guide to the Family and Medical Leave Act, FMLA Fact Sheet, State Laws and Regulations on Family and Medical Leave, Working Families Speak*, and *Sexual Harassment Fact Sheet.*

Families and Work Institute (FWI), 212–465–2044. Publishes *The Implementation of Flexible Time and Leave Policies, Parental Leave and Productivity*, and *Beyond the Parental Leave Debate.* (For full group information, see GENERAL PARENTING RESOURCES on page 634.)

American Association of University Women (AAUW), 202–785–7700. Publishes *Family Leave: A Solution to Work and Family Conflicts.* (For full group information, see HELP ON LEARNING AND EDUCATION on page 659.)

9 to 5, National Association of Working Women, 800–522–0925. Publishes *Wage Replacement for Family Leave: Is It Feasible?* (For full group information, see PREGNANCY DISCRIMINATION ACT.)

OTHER RESOURCES

Everything A Working Mother Needs to Know about Pregnancy Rights, Maternity Leave, and Making Her Career Work for Her. Anne Cicero Weisberg and Carol A. Buckler. Doubleday, 1994.

Maternity Leave: The Working Woman's Practical Guide to Combining Pregnancy, Motherhood and Career. Eileen L. Casey. Green Mountain, 1992.

Family and Medical Leave: Strategies for Success. Lisa Sementilli-Dann. CPA Washington, 1991.

(See also PREGNANCY DISCRIMINATION ACT; CHILD CARE; MATERNITY LEAVE.)

family car doctrine, a legal rule, in some states, that the registered owner of a family car is responsible for any damage caused by a family member using the car with the owner's knowledge and consent.

family court, the type of civil court that in some states combines the functions of DOMESTIC RELATIONS COURT, JUVENILE COURT, and PROBATE COURT. On occasion, criminal cases involving families, such as CHILD ABUSE AND NEGLECT cases, also are handled in the family court.

Family Educational Rights and Privacy Act (FERPA), a 1974 law sometimes called the *Buckley Amendment,* under which schools risk loss of federal funds if they fail to give parents access to the STUDENT RECORD of their child under 18, including all recorded information about the child maintained anywhere and in any form by the school system. The law applies only to public schools, not to private, parochial, and other independent schools, though some voluntarily comply with its provisions.

Under FERPA, the school can release information from the student record to people outside the school system only with the parent's authorization, except when a child is transferring to another school, where authorized state and federal officials require access, in compliance with a court order, for accrediting organizations or certain school-sponsored studies, for some organizations providing student FINANCIAL AID, or in health or safety emergencies. After a divorce, NONCUSTODIAL PARENTS retain the right to examine the student's record, unless there is a legally binding document to the contrary; the school may inform the CUSTODIAL PARENT of such a request, but cannot ask permission. Over age eighteen, the student has control over access to the record and must authorize any access, including that by parents. Parents (and students over eighteen) also have the right to receive a list of those people who have been permitted to see the child's records and to request that the child's name, address, and phone number not be released to anyone outside the school system.

Under the law, the school is directed to inform parents at least once a year of their right to examine and challenge the child's school record and to provide a list of the types and locations of all records kept by the school in any media (including handwritten, print, tapes, computer disks, and microfiche). How this is done is up to each school—through a student handbook, newspaper article, PTA bulletin, or special letter to parents. Each school must adopt a written policy on FERPA compliance and provide a parent or eligible student with a copy on request.

If a parent requests (in writing or orally) to inspect the student's record, the school has forty-five days to respond and is barred from removing or destroying any material in the record after receiving the request. If the parent is unable to review the record at school, a copy must be provided to the parents, for a reasonable fee. The school is also obliged to respond to parents' reasonable requests for interpretations or explanations and may charge a nominal fee to cover time and expenses.

The law gives the parents the chance to request correction or deletion of inaccurate, outdated, harmful, or inappropriate information; clarifications of any misconceptions or skewed comments that may be entered into a child's records and mistakenly be passed on as gospel; and information that violates the privacy or other rights of you and your child. If parents have a problem with the child's school record, they should first meet with the principal and request that the document be removed or revised. If the principal does not agree to do so, parents should request an impartial hearing, as provided for in FERPA, and present their case to the assigned hearing officer. If the parents' request to amend the records is still denied, they have the right to place in the file a written statement describing their reasons for disagreeing with specific material or information in the record.

It is important for parents to review the record and attempt to correct it if necessary, because long after the people who wrote comments in the record are gone, other people will refer to that record in writing recommendations and reports, as when requested to do so by colleges or employers. Throughout the process they should keep copies of all letters and other materials received and careful notes on all conversations or conferences, including statements from specific persons, when appropriate.

If a school denies access to a child's records, releases student information without proper consent, or otherwise fails to comply with FERPA in other ways, the parent can file a complaint with the Family Policy Compliance Office (see listing later in this entry). This must be done *within 180 days of the alleged violation.* No standard complaint form is required, but their letter should include:

- The exact name and full address of the school and school district.
- The name, title, and telephone number of the person in charge of the school or school district (for example, superintendent, principal, president, or chancellor).
- The name and titles of the person with whom the parents have dealt.

Checklist for Review of School Records[1]

	Yes	No	Need more info
Have I received satisfactory answers to questions about the location and content of my child's school records?	☐	☐	☐
Has my child's entire school record been gathered in the school office? If not, where are the other parts of the record?	☐	☐	☐
Are parts of the record on tape, in a computer data bank, or on microfilm or microfiche?	☐	☐	☐
In looking through the record, are there any unexplained labels used to describe my child, like hyperactive, learning disabled, or antisocial?	☐	☐	☐
Have I seen the following parts of the record and had them explained to me? (Do not expect to see all of the following. Some entries may not apply to your child.)	☐	☐	☐
Grades, year by year	☐	☐	☐
Health records	☐	☐	☐
Attendance records	☐	☐	☐
Test scores	☐	☐	☐
Psychologist's and school social worker's reports to school staff or recommendations (Psychologist's and school social worker's notes as part of treatment may be held confidentially.)	☐	☐	☐
Reports from welfare and social service agencies	☐	☐	☐
Transcripts from other schools	☐	☐	☐
Guidance counselor's career or college recommendations	☐	☐	☐
Disciplinary actions	☐	☐	☐
Honors, awards	☐	☐	☐

Source: National Committee for Citizens in Education (now dissolved; see Center for Law and Education.)

[1] This checklist is recommended as part of the "Annual Education Checkup" described on page 216 under EDUCATION.

- The names of the student or students who are the subjects of the complaint.
- A concise but specific description of alleged violation, including dates, summaries of conversations and conferences, and statements from individuals. Note: If it concerns denial of access to the student records, the complaint cannot be filed until forty-five days have passed from the original request.
- Copies of any pertinent documents or memoranda.

FOR HELP AND FURTHER INFORMATION

Family Policy Compliance Office
U.S. Department of Education
600 Independence Avenue SW
Washington, DC 20202
202–260–3887
Fax: 202–260–9001
Federal office monitoring compliance with two laws: FERPA and PPRA (Protection of Pupil Rights Act); provides information on FERPA laws and regulations; in case of problems, will on receipt of a written request describing the problem, contact the school.

Children's Defense Fund (CDF), 800-CDF–1200 [233–1200]. Publishes *Your Child's School Records.* (For full group information, see ADOLESCENT PREGNANCY.)

Parents Without Partners (PWP), 800–637–7974. Publishes information sheet *Rights of Noncustodial Parents to Examine School Records.* (For full group information, see GENERAL PARENTING RESOURCES on page 634.)

Center for Law and Education, 202–986–3000. Publishes "Information for Parents" brochure *Access to School Records.* (For full group information, see HELP ON LEARNING AND EDUCATION on page 659.)

family home, in family law, the owned home in which a family lived before a DIVORCE or separation. In many states, the court will not allow the house to be sold as long as there are MINOR children living there or will award the NONCUSTODIAL PARENT with half of its estimated value, but only after the children leave the home or the CUSTODIAL PARENT moves or remarries. In cases of threatened CHILD ABUSE AND NEGLECT or PARENTAL KIDNAPPING, the offending parent may sometimes be barred from the family home by a TEMPORARY RESTRAINING ORDER.

family life education, courses that educate people about aspects of family living, such as parenting, child development, and communication skills. Such courses are increasingly taught in schools to prepare adolescents for adulthood and marriage, though these often focus primarily on SEX EDUCATION. Family life education has been recommended for parents who have been, or are at risk of, committing CHILD ABUSE AND NEGLECT, as part of the 21ST-CENTURY SCHOOL, for example.

family practice physician, an alternate term for *general practitioner*, a type of PHYSICIAN who provides medical care to people of all ages and either sex.

family practitioner (FP), a physician who specializes in providing general health care to the whole family, including children and women during PREGNANCY, though any family member having special problems will be referred to a specialist, such as an OBSTETRICIAN-GYNECOLOGIST.

family shelter, a residence to which many or all members of a family might go or be taken, as in cases of possible CHILD ABUSE AND NEGLECT. Often twenty-four-hour counseling, along with short-term diagnosis and treatment, is available as part of CRISIS INTERVENTION.

family-at-risk, a family that, in the opinion of social workers, is at increased risk of being DYSFUNCTIONAL, as in cases of child abuse. (See CHILD ABUSE AND NEGLECT for list of risk factors.)

fat, a type of compound that is a key source of energy for the body, and part of the structure of the body's cells. Fats (often called lipids) also carry the fat-soluble VITAMINS A, D, E, and K. Nutritionists recommend that fats should compose only 30 percent of daily caloric intake, but since most foods contain fats, most people in Western countries consume far too much fat. The major component of fats are fatty acids, which come in various types, including:

- *Saturated fatty acids*, which are solid or nearly so at room temperature, found most abundantly in food from animal sources. These are especially undesirable in the diet because they tend to increase the amounts of CHOLESTEROL in the blood.
- *Unsaturated fatty acids*, which are liquid at room temperature. These often come from plant sources and tend to decrease the amounts of cholesterol in the blood. The two types of unsaturated fatty acids are:
  - *Monounsaturated fatty acids*, such as olive oil and peanut oil.
  - *Polyunsaturated fatty acids*, such as safflower, sunflower, corn, soybean, and cottonseed oils, which tend to reduce cholesterol most effectively.

Nutritionists and others researching the relationship between diet and heart disease have reached wide agreement in recommending that the diet for adults should lean heavily toward polyunsaturated types of fats in the diet. This means not only in cooking—the so-called "visible fats"—but also in the choice of foods, since meat, fish, poultry, and dairy products all contain so-called "invisible fats." Recently, revised dietary guidelines for Americans recommend that no more than 30 percent of a person's daily calories should come from fat and no more than one-third of that from saturated fats. The guidelines have been extended to cover not just adults but also children. However, the American Academy of Pediatricians (AAP) cautions that fats should not be restricted before age two, when they are needed for proper growth. That means that in a 2,000-calorie daily diet—as might be normal for a full-grown adult of medium build—fat should make up a maximum of 67 grams, with less than 22 grams of that from saturated fats, such as butter. The problem is that Americans routinely have a far higher proportion of fat in their diet, an average of about 37 percent, according to some recent estimates.

Recent research has also found that not all calories are equal; while calories from other types of foods, such as CARBOHYDRATES and PROTEINS, are used by the body as fuel and stored only if there is excess at the moment, almost all fat calories are immediately stored and used only when the body's other sources of energy are depleted or unavailable. More than that, the amount of fat that can be stored seems limitless. Each fat cell can expand to more than ten times its original size, and new ones can be developed for additional storage. These are some of the reasons that, once it has been stored, fat is so hard to get rid of and why watching fat intake beginning with childhood is desirable.

Among the problems associated with fats are some METABOLIC DISORDERS, in which abnormal amounts of fats are stored in the body. These disorders are sometimes called LIPID STORAGE DISEASES (*lipidoses*), and include *Gaucher's disease, Krabbe's disease, Niemann-Pick disease,* and *Tay-Sachs disease.* Eating disorders such as OBESITY and BINGE EATING DISORDER often involve overconsumption of fat. (See also NUTRITION; CHOLESTEROL; LIPIDOSES; OBESITY.)

father, the male who has PARENTS' RIGHTS and PARENTS' RESPONSIBILITIES toward a child, especially a MINOR. The male whose GENETIC INHERITANCE contributed directly to the child and who is one of the child's nearest BLOOD RELATIONS is the child's BIOLOGICAL FATHER, also called the *natural father* or *birth father*.

Children generally have INHERITANCE RIGHTS from their father. However, this depends on the precise relationship between father and child at the father's death and on the current state of law and judicial interpretation on many new and complicated legal questions as to father-child relationships (see discussion below). If the father dies before the birth, the child is called a *posthumous child* and may inherit from the father at birth.

If the biological father gives up his parental rights and allows his child to be placed for ADOPTION, a male who adopts the child is called the *adoptive father*; if the placement is temporary or pending final adoption, the male may be called the *foster father*. If the biological father and the child's mother are married at the time of the birth, he is also the *legal father*. If the mother is married to someone other than the biological father, her husband is the child's *stepfather*; though he may have informal authority in the home, he does not become the child's legal father unless he adopts the child (see ADOPTION).

If the child's mother is unmarried, and the father recognizes the child as his, he is called the *acknowledged father*. If a child's mother is unmarried, and no male has acknowledged the child as his, the presumed biological father is often called the *unwed father* or may be legally known as the *putative father*. Before the child is actually born, the unwed father generally has no legal right to be involved in the unwed mother's decision on a possible ABORTION. But after the birth, an unwed father has at least the right to visit the child and the obligation to contribute to the child's support. If the unwed mother decides to place the child for ADOPTION, the unwed father can protest against TERMINATION OF PARENTS' RIGHTS. Whether or not he succeeds will depend on highly variable state laws; some may grant him CUSTODY, if he desires it, while others may allow the adoption, especially if the child is a newborn.

If an unwed mother is receiving benefits under the AID TO FAMILIES WITH DEPENDENT CHILDREN program and some other programs, the state will attempt to locate the father to have him reimburse the state for money paid for CHILD SUPPORT. The putative father, once located, may voluntarily sign a CONSENT AGREEMENT acknowledging the child and his responsibility for support; otherwise the state may institute a PATERNITY SUIT to establish that he is the *legal father* or *acknowledged father*.

Under the UNIFORM PARENTAGE ACT, enacted in some states, a man is generally presumed to be a child's father if:

- He has acknowledged the child as his own, as by raising the child in his own home as his child.
- He and the mother were married at the child's birth, or the child was born within 300 days of the marriage's end.
- He and the mother married, or tried to do so, after the child's birth, and he either acknowledged in writing that the child was his or allowed his name to appear on the birth certificate or has assumed child support obligations, either voluntarily or by court order.

Until recently, the husband of a child's mother was automatically considered to be the child's legal father, whatever anecdotal evidence there may have been to the contrary. But with the advent of BLOOD TESTS that can exclude paternity with high accuracy, even if they cannot always say with equal accuracy who the father was, courts have sometimes allowed the paternity of a legal father to be questioned.

Complications can arise with modern REPRODUCTIVE TECHNOLOGY, such as ARTIFICIAL INSEMINATION or IN VITRO FERTILIZATION. If a woman is inseminated with SPERM from her husband, then the biological father of the baby is also the legal father. If a married woman is inseminated with sperm from a donor—someone other than her husband—the woman's husband is generally considered the legal father, and the biological father is considered to have no legal rights, though this may not yet be fully established, as the law is still developing in this new area. That may not pose a problem when the sperm comes from an anonymous donor, but can produce complications if sperm was donated by a male known to the woman. In that case, laws may vary as to whether the known donor is the legal father or whether the child has *no* legal father.

In recent decades, many men have become far more active as fathers. Once generally barred from DELIVERY rooms (as they still are in some HOSPITALS), many men, with the rise of natural CHILDBIRTH, have become active coaches, supporters, masseurs, and general aides in their role as *birth partners*. Many of today's fathers also tend to be more closely involved with their children beginning at birth, often building a close relationship from the start and gaining the pleasure of knowing their children intimately as they grow—an experience earlier generations of fathers often missed. Some have actively sought *paternity leave* (see FAMILY AND MEDICAL LEAVE) and more flexible work schedules to allow more time with the new baby, though these are still often not practical alternatives for many.

Especially when both parents work, fathers today are more likely to be actively engaged in day-to-day care, from feeding and dressing their children to playing with them and putting them to bed. However, society provides little support for such activities. Employers rarely approve of fathers taking time off from work to care for a sick child or to visit a child's school, for example. Despite many societal changes, the primary responsibility for childrearing still tends to fall on the MOTHER.

That is especially so if the parents DIVORCE, in which case many fathers are able to see their children only when CUSTODY and VISITATION RIGHTS allow. Most fathers do not request custody, though courts will often grant it when they do. When the mother has custody—as 9 out of 10 do in the United States—many fathers fail to keep up a fatherly contact with their children, and many do not even regularly exercise VISITATION RIGHTS. A 1991 study of

1,400 children from divorced families found that 23 percent of fathers had had *no* contact at all with their children in the previous five years, and another 20 percent had not seen their children at all during the previous year. Many also fail to meet their CHILD SUPPORT obligations.

FOR HELP AND FURTHER INFORMATION

Fatherhood Project (FP)
c/o Families and Work Institute (FWI)
330 Seventh Avenue
New York, NY 10001
James A. Levine, Director
212–268–4846
Fax: 212–465–8637
International Fatherhood Network: E-mail:
levineja@aol.com (America Online: LevineJA)
Organization to promote fathers' participation in raising children; loosely affiliated with Families and Work Institute (see GENERAL PARENTING RESOURCES on page 634.); conducts research; maintains International Fatherhood Network; develops model programs such as Male Involvement Project; provides information and referrals; publishes reports such as *Getting Men Involved: Strategies for Early Childhood Programs, Fathers and Work, New Expectations: National Goals and Community Strategies for Responsible Fatherhood.*

March of Dimes Birth Defects Foundation (MDBDF), 914–428–7100. Publishes pamphlets *Dad, It's Your Baby, Too* and *Men Have Babies, Too.* (For full group information, see BIRTH DEFECTS.)

International Association of Parents and Professionals for Safe Alternatives in Childbirth (NAPSAC), phone and fax: 314–238–2010. Publishes *Fathering and Career.* (For full group information, see CHILDBIRTH.)

OTHER RESOURCES

The Passions of Fatherhood. Samuel Osherson. Fawcett, 1995.
Fathers and Toddlers: How Toddlers Grow and What They Need from You, from 18 Months to Three Years (1994) and *Fathers and Babies: How Babies Grow and What They Need from You, from Birth to 18 Months* (1993). Jean Marzollo. HarperCollins.
The Father Factor: What You Need to Know to Make a Difference. Henry B. Biller and Robert J. Trotter. Pocket Books, 1994.
Fathers. Jon Winokur, ed. NAL-Dutton, 1993.
Fourteen Keys to Successful Fathering. Ken Canfield. Moody, 1993.
Beside Every Great Dad. Ken R. Canfield and Nancy L. Swihart. Tyndale, 1993.
One Hundred One Ways to Be a Special Dad. Vicki Lansky. Contemporary, 1993.
Straight from a Dad's Heart. Robert Hamrin. Nelson, 1993.
Finding Time for Fathering. M. Golant and S. Golant. Ballantine, 1992.
How to Father. Fitzhugh Dodson. NAL-Dutton, 1992.
Father's Almanac. S. Adams Sullivan. Doubleday, 1992.
Your 30-Day Journey to Being a World-Class Father. C.W. Neal. Thomas Nelson, 1992.
Father and Child: Practical Advice for Today's Dad. Carolyn T. Chubet and others. Longmeadow Press, 1991.
Keys to Becoming a Father. William Sears. Barron's, 1991.

ON THE FATHER-CHILD RELATIONSHIP

The Search for Lost Fathering: Rebuilding Your Father Relationship. James L. Schaller. Revell, 1995.
Daddy, Daddy, Be There. Candy D. Boyd. Philomel/Putnam, 1995.
Father Hunger. Robert S. McGee. Vine/Servant, 1993.
Dear Dad: Thank You for Being Mine. Scott Matthews and Tamara Nikuradse. Bantam, 1993.
Fathers, Come Home: A Wake-up Call for Busy Dads. William D. Swindell. Greenlawn, 1993.
Fathers Are Like Elephants Because They're the Biggest Ones Around: But They Still Are Pretty Gentle Underneath. David Heller. Random, 1993.
Kids, Teens, and Wives: How to Live with Them—and Love Them. Dan Day. Pacific Press, 1992.
A Father's Gift: The Legacy of Memories. Ken Gire. Daybreak/Zondervan, 1992. Originally titled: *The Gift of Remembrance*
Like Son, Like Father: Healing the Father-Son Wound in Men's Lives. Gregory M. Vogt and Stephen T. Sirridge. Plenum, 1991.
Between Father and Child: How to Become the Kind of Father You Want to Be. Ronald F. Levant. Viking Penguin, 1991.
My Father's Shadow: Intergenerational Conflict in African American Men's Autobiography. David L. Dudley. University of Pennsylvania Press, 1991.
Daddy, Where Were You?: Healing for the Father-Deprived Daughter. Heather Harpham. Aglow Communications, 1991.

FOR CHILDREN

We're Very Good Friends, My Father and I. P. K. Hallinan. Ideals, 1990.
Dear Dad, Love Laurie. Susan Beth Pfeffer. Scholastic, 1990.
Martha's New Daddy. Danielle Steel. Delacorte, 1989.

(See also GENERAL PARENTING RESOURCES on page 634.)

fear tension pain syndrome, a complex of feelings and reactions that are believed to be the source of much of the pain of LABOR and DELIVERY; it was first described by Dr. Grantly Dick-Read, who went on to develop early approaches to natural CHILDBIRTH, now often called PREPARED CHILDBIRTH.

feedback, information about the results of previous actions, which can then be used as a guide to future action. In relation to one's body, for example, feedback may be the sense of motion or pain that comes from moving your arm; this information can then be used to decide whether or not to move the arm further or pull it back. Children with an improper BODY IMAGE get inadequate feedback or do not know how to interpret it; as a result, they often cannot judge the effect of their actions nor can they learn, for future reference, the likely result of an action. People with eating disorders, such as ANOREXIA NERVOSA, get faulty feedback, sometimes leading them to think they are obese, when in fact they are grotesquely thin. This misinformation can cause them to act in ways harmful to themselves. More generally, feedback refers to the response of others to us and our actions, which helps shape our view of how we feel about ourselves and how we will act in the future. In this sense, feedback can be used positively, to shape behavior, as in BEHAVIOR MODIFICATION, or negatively, to inhibit behavior.

feeding, the supplying of nutrients to someone who is unable to eat independently or in the normal way. The term generally applies to infants, who receive their NUTRITION either through BREASTFEEDING or BOTTLEFEEDING using FORMULA (see FEEDING BABY: HOW OFTEN? HOW MUCH? below).

In a HOSPITAL setting, the term *feeding* may also refer to providing nutrients through some means other than eating, by inserting a tube into the stomach or intestines, often through the mouth or nose, or by putting nutritional fluids directly into the bloodstream intravenously, a method called PARENTERAL NUTRITION or *intravenous feeding*. Such artificial feeding is often used for PREMATURE babies, whose SUCKING OR ROOTING REFLEX is insufficiently developed for normal feeding, as well as for children (and adults) who have various digestive disorders, KIDNEY AND UROLOGICAL PROBLEMS, brain disorders, high FEVER, or severe BURNS. (See BREASTFEEDING; BOTTLEFEEDING; SOLID FOODS; also STARTING ON SOLID FOODS on page 559.)

female circumcision, traditional mutilation of a woman's external GENITALS, the aim being to destroy a woman's capacity for sexual pleasure and so attempt to ensure chastity. The practice is not mentioned in the Koran and predates Mohammed, dating back to Egypt, and was even used in Western countries in the nineteenth and early twentieth centuries as a "treatment" for MASTURBATION and nymphomania. Today, however, it is mostly associated with Arab-Muslim cultures in Africa and West-

Feeding Baby: How Often? How Much?

HOW OFTEN TO FEED

Feed your baby when he or she seems hungry. Most babies will fall into a pattern of six to eight feedings about three to five hours apart. It is easier and better to get a regular schedule by working from the baby's own timing, than by just deciding to feed at certain times whether the baby is hungry or not. You will soon be able to tell from your baby's crying and fussing what his or her needs are.

After a few weeks, most babies will begin to sleep through one of the feedings. Most parents prefer to skip the night feeding rather than a daytime feeding. If your baby sleeps through a daytime feeding, wake and feed at the usual time so that the baby—hopefully—will give up one of the nighttime feedings.

HOW MUCH TO FEED

Don't worry about how much is taken at a single feeding; most babies will have times when they just aren't hungry and other times when they take more than you expect. If your baby is growing at a satisfactory rate, he or she is probably getting the right amount.

If you are breastfeeding, you don't have to concern youself about how much to feed—your baby decides. Most mothers who are breastfeeding worry at some time about whether they have enough milk. Actually, too little milk is unusual and *more frequent feeding naturally increases the supply.* The best reassurance is your baby's normal activity and growth.

If you are bottlefeeding, most babies, after the first few days, take 2 to 3 ounces of milk each day for each pound of their body weight. Most bottlefed babies want six or seven feedings each day. For a 7 pound baby, this would mean 14 to 21 ounces of formula a day (2 ½ to 3 ½ ounces in each six or seven feedings).

You might begin by offering 3 ounces in each bottle. When your baby begins to empty the bottle completely at two or three feedings a day, add an additional 1 ounce to the bottle. Stay a little ahead of the baby and let the baby decide how much to take. If your baby takes much more or less than 2 or 3 ounces per pound per day, talk with your doctor or clinic staff.

Source: Infant Care (1989). Prepared by the Bureau of Maternal and Child Health and Resources Development for the Public Health Service.

ern Asia, most intensively in Somalia, though it is widely condemned internationally. Some Western governments and immigrant families have come into sharp conflict over the family's desire to have a daughter circumcised.

There are three main kinds of female genital mutilation:

- *Sunna circumcision,* which involves removing the tip of the CLITORIS, the main organ of sexual pleasure in a woman, in that way similar to a man's PENIS. The term *circumcision* is something of a misnomer, since that term more properly refers only to removal of the FORESKIN, the partly retractable hood of skin over the clitoris, analogous to male CIRCUMCISION.
- *Clitoridectomy,* which involves removal of the entire clitoris and parts of the *labia minora,* the "small lips" that partly enclose it (see LABIA). Sometimes the *labia minora* are completely removed, and so are parts of the *labia majora,* the larger, outer lips; then the remaining tissue is stitched together, with an opening left for sexual intercourse and urination. In Western societies, clitoridectomy is rarely performed today, except in cases of CANCER of the VULVA.
- *Infibulation,* also called *Pharaonic* or *Sudanese circumcision,* which involves complete removal of the clitoris and also removal of the labia minora and majora, or their mutilation so that they adhere together in a lengthwise strip of scar tissue. In rural Sudan, for example, a local midwife uses a knife, razorblade, or other sharp (though generally rough and nonsurgical) instrument, to cut off the clitoris and scrape the skin off the labia majora, which are then stitched together with string using acacia thorns. She leaves a small opening at the base, through which a small stick or twig is inserted, to allow for passage of urine (see URINARY TRACT) and blood from MENSTRUATION. The girl's legs are then tied together down to her ankles, and remain so until the labia have healed so as to completely close over the genital area. At marriage, this scar will be cut open, generally with no ANESTHESIA, to allow for sexual intercourse and possible CHILDBIRTH. Sometimes the labia will be resutured after birth and cut open again later.

The most common of these operations is the *clitoridectomy,* the most dangerous *infibulation.* Such operations are performed at different times in different societies, as early as infancy and as late as shortly before marriage, but commonly between ages seven and thirteen, often as a rite of PUBERTY.

The health problems resulting from genital mutilation are extensive. The initial operation can cause life-threatening problems such as infections, hemorrhaging, or tetanus, apart from the pain itself, which also can cause severe psychological trauma. Longer-term health effects including ANEMIA, retention of menstrual blood and urine (which can lead to kidney or cardiovascular problems), and painful MENSTRUATION. In marriage, many circumcised women have difficult or painful intercourse, or *dyspareunia,* with scar tissue sometimes forming a virtually impenetrable barrier to vaginal intercourse. Infections can result in PELVIC INFLAMMATORY DISEASE (PID), which can lead to INFERTILITY and potentially life-threatening ECTOPIC PREGNANCY. Women who do become pregnant often have difficulty in CHILDBIRTH, with increased risk of STILLBIRTH, and sometimes are unable to give birth normally. With the repeated infibulation operations, some women become unable to have normal vaginal intercourse and are sometimes then cast aside by their husbands.

FOR HELP AND FURTHER INFORMATION

National Organization of Circumcision Information Resource Centers (NOCIRC), 415–488–9883. (For full group information, see CIRCUMCISION.)

OTHER RESOURCES

Psychological Effects of the Female Circumcision. Ahmed I. Ballal. Vantage, 1992.

fertility specialist, an OBSTETRICIAN/GYNECOLOGIST who specializes in the particular problems of INFERTILITY and ways to overcome them; also called a *sterologist.* This is a fairly new medical specialty on the cutting edge of that branch of medical technology, often working as part of a team of specialists, including physicians and counselors.

fertilization, the union of an egg (OVUM) and a SPERM, which normally takes place in a woman's FALLOPIAN TUBE, the sperm (one of millions released in an EJACULATION) having traveled from the VAGINA through the CERVIX and UTERUS to the tube; also called CONCEPTION, a somewhat wider term. In fertilization, the single sperm burrows through the two outer layers of the egg, at which point the egg's membrane immediately bars the way to other sperm. The resulting fertilized egg is technically called a ZYGOTE, though (especially since the development of reproductive technology) it is more commonly called an EMBRYO. If two sperm enter, the egg will not be VIABLE, having lethal duplication of DNA, and a spontaneous ABORTION will occur, so early that the tissue will probably simply be reabsorbed by the body or flushed out in MENSTRUATION. (The same is true of many other fertilized eggs that have defects so severe that they are clearly, at a very early stage, incompatible with life.) If two eggs are fertilized by two different sperm, the result will be *dizygotic, nonidentical,* or *fraternal* twins; if a zygote separates into two separate EMBRYOS, the result is *monozygotic* or *identical* twins (see MULTIPLE BIRTH).

Fertilization is the beginning of a PREGNANCY, but the end of a long process. Both egg and sperm have been formed by special subdivisions (*meiosis*) so that each has only half of the genetic material needed for a new individual (see GENETIC INHERITANCE; OVULATION), and is incomplete without the other. The egg is the single survivor of a group of eggs that begin ripening each month during a woman's fertile years, from the many hundreds of thousands of eggs existing in potential form at a woman's birth. The sperm is one of millions released in an EJACULATION at a man's orgasm.

During the woman's monthly MENSTRUAL CYCLE, various HORMONES trigger the ripe egg to burst out of her OVARIES and move into the Fallopian tubes, and cause the mucus in her VAGINA and CERVIX to change consistency and texture to allow for passage of sperm. The sperm cross the relatively vast expanse of the VAGINA, the usually hostile passageway of the CERVIX, the also vast UTERUS, and move on into the Fallopian tubes. Once there, a single sperm uses special chemicals in its head to penetrate the two outer protective layers of the egg; then the egg's membrane changes chemically in unknown ways to immediately bar other sperm from entering. The result is called a ZYGOTE or *fertilized egg.*

The fertilized egg, formed by an earlier cell division, undergoes another cell division on penetration by the sperm, producing 23 single strands of DNA in the main egg and leaving the rest (called a *polar body*) to wither away. The sperm's DNA and the egg's DNA now begin to pair up, to form 23 double strands of DNA, which then duplicate themselves to form the 46 chromosomes needed for a new human being. It is in cell divisions and in this pairing up process that some CHROMOSOMAL ABNORMALITIES can occur, as genetic material breaks apart and recombines not always perfectly.

With the joining of egg and sperm, a unique being has been created, and his or her sex determined (see SEXUAL IDENTITY). The egg carries an X SEX CHROMOSOME. If the sperm's sex chromosome is also an X, the baby will be a girl; if a Y, a boy.

The zygote quickly starts dividing to form new duplicate cells, as it travels slowly down the Fallopian tube. (Medically, the ball of cells, which soon develops a hollow center, is called a *blastocyte.*) On reaching the UTERUS (usually seven to ten days after fertilization), the egg sheds an outer protective layer, the ZONA PELLUCIDA, and implants itself in the uterus wall, where it begins to develop as an embryo.

Although fertilization normally takes place in the Fallopian tubes, sometimes it takes place in the OVARIES or elsewhere in the body. In other instances, the developing embryo fails to move into the uterus, instead implanting itself elsewhere in the body, notably in the Fallopian tubes. The result is a potentially life-threatening ECTOPIC PREGNANCY, which requires emergency surgery.

For a variety of reasons, fertilization sometimes cannot take place normally. Various alternatives have been developed for circumventing and treating this resulting INFERTILITY. (See INFERTILITY, for methods of achieving fertilization; see also PREGNANCY; GENETIC DISORDERS; BIRTH CONTROL.)

fetal alcohol syndrome (FAS), a combination of physical and mental BIRTH DEFECTS resulting from alcohol consumed by the mother during PREGNANCY. Only recognized in the early 1970s, FAS is now known to be one of the most common causes of MENTAL RETARDATION. Among the typical characteristics of an FAS baby are an abnormally small head and brain; small and wide-spaced eyes; short, upturned nose; flat cheeks; various irregularities or malformations of face, joints, and limbs; and malformations of internal organs, especially the heart. Babies with FAS are also shorter and weigh less than normal when born, and fail to "catch up," even when special POSTNATAL CARE is provided. They often continue to have poor coordination, HYPERACTIVITY, short ATTENTION SPAN, extreme nervousness, and behavioral problems. They are also more likely to have problems such as ASTHMA, BEDWETTING (*enuresis*), digestive sensitivity, and sleep problems.

In the United States, fetal alcohol syndrome affects perhaps 1 out of every 750 newborns (about 5,000 babies a year). Another 11,000–18,000 are born with only some characteristics of the syndrome, then called *fetal alcohol effects* (FAE). Pregnant women who drink during pregnancy are also at increased risk of having a STILLBIRTH or MISCARRIAGE; in the fourth month to the sixth month of pregnancy, a heavy drinker's risk of miscarriage is two to four times normal. Women who drink during pregnancy are also two to three times more likely to lose their baby from the twenty-eighth week of GESTATION through the first week after birth.

Precisely how the alcohol does all this damage is not yet entirely clear. It is known that the alcohol goes into the mother's bloodstream and quickly passes through the PLACENTA to the FETUS; but because a baby's organs are still developing, they cannot break down the alcohol as quickly as an adult's, so the alcohol is much more concentrated in the fetal bloodstream.

How much is too much? No one knows. In some women, the alcohol contained in six mixed drinks or cans of beer daily can produce the full fetal alcohol syndrome; in many women, the equivalent of two to five drinks daily also produces damage. But the individual women's system also apparently plays a significant role; some can drink heavily to no apparent effect on the fetus, while others can drink very little and still have babies with *fetal alcohol effects* (FAE). For this reason, the U.S. Surgeon General's office has said that the safest choice for women is to stop drinking totally from the time they are planning or anticipating possible CONCEPTION (or from the time they suspect they may be pregnant) through birth—and through BREASTFEEDING as well, for alcohol can continue to cause damage then.

Nor should women assume, because they have abstained for most of the time, that drinking heavily at a single party or celebration will be safe. In fact, some evidence suggests that sudden heavy drinking may be the most harmful of all. The main point to keep in mind is that fetal alcohol syndrome, unlike many other possible BIRTH DEFECTS, is entirely preventable.

FOR HELP AND FURTHER INFORMATION

National Association for Families and Addiction Research and Education (NAFARE), 800–638–2229. Publishes brochure *What You Need to Know About Fetal Alcohol Syndrome.* (For full group information, see HELP AGAINST SUBSTANCE ABUSE on page 703.)

National Clearinghouse for Alcohol and Drug Abuse Information (NCADI), 301–468–2600. Publishes *Fetal Alcohol Syndrome.* (For full group information, see HELP AGAINST SUBSTANCE ABUSE on page 703).

National Woman's Christian Temperance Union (WCTU), 800–755–1321. Publishes leaflet *Is FAS Worth the Risk?* (For full group information, see HELP AGAINST SUBSTANCE ABUSE on page 703.)

Family Empowerment Network (FEN): Support for Families Affected by FAS/FAE
University of Wisconsin-Madison
610 Langdon Street, Room 521
Madison, WI 53703
608–262–6590; Family Advocate Line:
800–462–5254
Fax: 608–265–2329
Raymond Kessel, Director
Georgianna Wilton, Coordinator
Organization concerned with families affected by fetal alcohol syndrome or fetal alcohol effects; acts as advocate; provides information and referrals; offers technical assistance in forming local support groups; provides training, including educational teleconference series; publishes quarterly newsletter *FEN Pen.*

National Organization on Fetal Alcohol Syndrome
1815 H Street NW, Suite 1000
Washington, DC 20006
202–785–4585; 800–66-NOFAS [666–6327]
Fax: 202–466–6456
Patti Munter, President
Organization concerned with fetal alcohol syndrome; send stamped, self-addressed envelope for information kit.

March of Dimes Birth Defects Foundation (MDBDF), 914–428–7100. Publishes pamphlet *Alcohol and Pregnancy: Make the Right Choice,* information sheet *Drinking During Pregnancy,* and video *Smoking, Drinking and Drugs.* (For full group information, see BIRTH DEFECTS.)

Johnson Institute, 800–231–5165. Publishes *You're Going to Have a Baby* and *What You Can Do to Prevent Fetal Alcohol Syndrome.* (For full group information, see HELP AGAINST SUBSTANCE ABUSE on page 703.)

Children of Alcoholics Foundation (CAF), 800–359–2623. Publishes *Fetal Alcohol Syndrome: The Impact on Children's Ability to Learn.* (For full group information, see HELP AGAINST SUBSTANCE ABUSE on page 703.)

National Council on Alcoholism and Drug Dependency (NCADD), 800–622–2255. Publishes fact sheet *Alcohol-Related Birth Defects.* (For full group information, see HELP AGAINST SUBSTANCE ABUSE on page 703.)

National Maternal and Child Health Clearinghouse (NMCHC), 703–821–8955 (For full group information, see PREGNANCY.)

National Institute of Child Health and Human Development (NICHD), 301–496–5133. (For full group information, see PREGNANCY.)

The Arc, 817–261–6003. Publishes fact sheets *Think Before You Drink* and *Facts About Alcohol Use During Pregnancy.* (For full group information, see MENTAL RETARDATION.)

National Organization for Rare Disorders (NORD), 800–999–6673. (For full group information, see RARE DISORDERS.)

OTHER RESOURCES

Prenatal Exposure to Drugs—Alcohol: Characteristics and Educational Implications of Fetal Alcohol Syndrome and Cocaine–Polydrug Effects. Jeanette M. Soby. C. C. Thomas, 1994.

Tad and Me: How I Found Out about Fetal Alcohol Syndrome. Betsy Houlton. Hazelden, 1991. For preteens and teens.

fetal distress, a general term for problems experienced by the FETUS, generally referring to difficulty in getting sufficient oxygen during the period of LABOR and DELIVERY. FETAL MONITORING seeks to identify early signs of fetal distress so death and damage can be avoided. If a sample of blood from the baby's scalp shows high acidity, that may also indicate insufficient oxygen (HYPOXIA). So can the presence of MECONIUM (fetal stool) in the AMNIOTIC FLUID. In cases of fetal distress, prompt delivery is indicated, often either by FORCEPS DELIVERY, VACUUM EXTRACTION, or CESAREAN SECTION. (See LABOR; CHILDBIRTH.)

fetal hydantoin syndrome (FHS), a group of BIRTH DEFECTS found in women with EPILEPSY who have taken antiseizure medications derived from the chemical hydantoin. Among the common characteristics are a small head (*microencephaly*), growth deficiency (see GROWTH AND GROWTH DISORDERS), abnormalities of the NAILS and fingers, and sometimes MENTAL RETARDATION.

fetal-maternal exchange, the exchange of nutrients and oxygen from the mother's blood for waste products from the baby's blood, accomplished through the PLACENTA.

fetal monitoring (electronic fetal monitoring or EFM), use of an electronic device that allows medical staff to track a FETUS's heart rate and the contractions of the mother's UTERUS. Monitoring can be done externally by using ULTRASOUND to detect the fetal heartbeat and by using a sensor placed on a woman's abdomen to register contractions. Internal monitoring involves the implantation of an electrode on the baby's scalp, by way of a CATHETER fed in through the VAGINA; a catheter also allows for internal detection of the uterine contractions. Physicians often use internal fetal monitoring when there are indications of possible problems, especially if the mother is two weeks past her DUE DATE, the aim being to detect problems—generically called FETAL DISTRESS—in time to save the baby's life and possibly to prevent damage.

In the past many doctors have thought such internal monitoring to be risk-free, though some parents have regarded it as needlessly invasive. More recently, however, research has suggested that use of internal fetal monitoring is associated with a higher risk of neurological problems, such as CEREBRAL PALSY and that signs of fetal distress are equally well detected using external means, including the stethoscope. (See CHILDBIRTH.)

fetal presentation, the orientation of the FETUS in the mother's pelvic cavity in preparation for CHILDBIRTH. The baby moves into this prebirth position in what is called ENGAGEMENT, often two to three weeks before the DUE DATE, though sometimes not until the beginning of LABOR. The main types of presentation include:

- *Cephalic presentation,* the usual head-first presentation. Often the fetus has been oriented head upward during the PREGNANCY, but in most cases (about 96 percent) the baby turns around with head downward in the pelvic cavity in the last weeks before delivery. A cephalic presentation may be described more precisely by the part of the head that first appears in the pelvis, such as:

  Vertex presentation, in which the top of the head (crown) shows first; the easiest and safest position for delivery.

  Brow presentation, with forehead first, which can cause difficulty in delivery.

  Chin presentation, with chin first, which can also complicate delivery.

- *Breech presentation,* with buttocks, or sometimes feet or knees, appearing first at the opening of the pelvis. A common position earlier in pregnancy, breech presentation occurs only in about 3 percent of babies at the time of delivery, especially in cases of MULTIPLE BIRTH. If the baby is in a breech position at about the thrity-eighth week, the doctor may try to maneuver the fetus around, working from the outside (*external cephalic version*), a delicate procedure because it risks premature separation of the PLACENTA. Sometimes this maneuver does not work, or it works but the baby returns to the breech position, perhaps because the mother's pelvis is too small or her UTERUS IS abnormally shaped. Breech birth makes for a considerably more difficult delivery, often requiring some assistance, such as FORCEPS DELIVERY, EPISIOTOMY, or VACUUM EXTRACTION; FETAL MONITORING may be used to check for signs of FETAL DISTRESS. Sometimes a CESAREAN SECTION may be indicated, especially if a woman has not previously borne a child. Breech presentations can be more precisely described:

  Complete breech, in which the legs are folded on the thighs, which are tucked up on the abdomen.

  Frank breech, in which the legs are straight and bent upward, so that the feet are near the shoulder; these newborns may retain this position for a few days after birth.

  Footling breech, in which one or both feet are tucked backward under the buttocks at the pelvic opening, with one foot being called *single footling* and both feet called *double footling.*

- *Compound presentation,* in which more than one part is placed first in the pelvis, such as a hand next to the head.

Cephalic and breech presentations may also be described as *longitudinal lies,* since the axis of the fetus is in the same direction as that of the mother, generally up and down. But in approximately 1 in every 500 presentations, a baby will lie crosswise, or horizontally, in the uterus, with a shoulder toward the pelvis. This is termed a *transverse lie.* If the baby cannot be turned, a transverse lie generally requires a cesarean section. In general, any type of presentation other than cephalic is termed *malpresentation* or *abnormal presentation.* (See CHILDBIRTH; DELIVERY.)

feticide, the killing of a living FETUS in the UTERUS, as through ABORTION. Some antiabortion activists use the term INFANTICIDE instead, for rhetorical purposes.

fetoscopy, a prenatal diagnostic procedure in which a flexible tube containing a periscopelike device called a *laparoscope* is inserted through a small incision in a pregnant woman's abdomen and the UTERUS wall. Using this special form of LAPAROSCOPY, physicians can then visually examine the fetus for signs of abnormal development and, in certain cases, repair defects through IN UTERO SURGERY. Samples of blood, fluid, and fetus cells can also be taken for testing, though other GENETIC SCREENING procedures are often used for this. (See GENETIC DISORDERS; PREGNANCY.)

fetus, the being that develops in the mother's UTERUS, a term applied from the eighth week through birth; literally "offspring" or "little one." (Before the eighth week, it is known as an EMBRYO.) The fetus floats in protective AMNIOTIC FLUID and is nourished by the PLACENTA, to which it is connected by the UMBILICAL CORD. In the eighth week, on the average, the fetus is only about 1–1½ inches long and weighs about two-thirds of an ounce, but by the fortieth week, at FULL-TERM, the baby on the average will measure 20 inches and weigh 7½ pounds. (See PREGNANCY for a description of month-by-month development.)

fever (pyrexia), an abnormally high body temperature, above the normal 98.6°F (37°C), generally due to infections caused by bacteria or viruses, but sometimes stemming from other types of problems within the body, including reaction to medications (see DRUG REACTIONS AND INTERACTIONS). Fever is a natural part of the body's reaction to invasion by disease organisms, but it can have serious effects, especially in young children. Most serious, very high fever can cause CONVULSIONS, COMA, and even death in some situations. Other common accompanying SYMPTOMS are confusion; delirium; shivering; headache; thirst; flushed, hot skin; rapid breathing; and alternating shivering and sweating.

Apart from treating the underlying cause, if possible, the main aim is to bring down the body temperature, as by giving a sponge bath with lukewarm water or giving acetaminophen. (Aspirin should not be given to children or teens, because of its link to REYE SYNDROME). Parents should consult a physician about any fever, especially in a very young child, so that the causative condition can be treated. Some serious diseases, such as MENINGITIS can progress extremely rapidly, so prompt attention is important.

In years past, infants and young children who had febrile SEIZURES—twitching or jerking and loss of consciousness associated with high fever—were routinely given daily doses of phenobarbital to prevent recurrence of seizures. But a study by the National Institute of Neurological Disorders and Stroke (NINDS) found that the drug is ineffective as an anticonvulsant, since children who took the drug had as many seizures as those who did not. Beyond that, those who took phenobarbital had significantly lower scores on intelligence tests, effects that lasted for at least some months after the drug was stopped. Longer-term effects are still being studied. However, some doctors are now questioning whether febrile seizures should be treated at all.

In taking temperatures, doctors and parents alike traditionally used the old standby, the mercury-in-glass thermometer, either orally, rectally, or under the arm. However, it has often been a problem to get young children to stay still for several minutes, and there have also been concerns about the thermometer breaking and injuring the child. As alternatives, some parents have tried temperature "strips" placed against the child's forehead, but these may not be as accurate and reliable as desired. In recent years, doctors have generally switched to a new type of instrument, a battery-powered hand-held thermometer (the Thermoscan) that, placed in the patient's ear, gives a reading in just one second. The device gauges heat by the infrared (heat) waves given off by tissue surrounding the eardum, converting this reading into an equivalent temperature displayed on a dial. These devices are expensive, but many parents have turned to them as well. Their main advantages are speed, safety, lack of discomfort, less vulnerability to environmental influences, and elimination of the struggle to keep children still long enough to take their temperature. They can even be used with a sleeping child and in a dimly lit room.

If parents decide (on consultation with a doctor) to use such a device, they are advised to take temperatures of all family members, when healthy, several times a day for a few days, to find the normal temperature range for each person. That is good advice in general, whatever temperature-taking device is used, since body temperature changes throughout the day, and both the average temperature and range of temperatures vary widely from one person to another. Doing this will also help parents become accustomed to using the new Thermoscan, before sickness strikes. (See FEVER AND BABIES below.)

Fever and Babies

Temperatures will vary during the day. However, if your baby feels particularly warm, take the baby's temperature. If your baby's temperature taken rectally is above 100°F, you should call your doctor or clinic.

Fever is the body's natural response to many infections. If your baby has a fever, there is something wrong. If your baby is less than two months old, call your doctor or clinic immediately. If an infant with a high fever (above 102°F) is playful and cheerful, the sickness is not likely to be serious, but you should call your doctor to be sure. An older baby with only a slight fever or no fever who appears to be sick and weak also needs medical attention. Fever should warn you to watch carefully, but it doesn't tell you how sick your child may be.

Many babies will have a fever with every cold. Many have a fever for a day or two with no other signs of illness except tiredness and fussiness.

Give plenty to drink and take off any extra sweaters or blankets. A "sponge bath" with a cloth dampened with lukewarm water may help if your baby's temperature is high. You may also try a bath in lukewarm water. If your baby seems uncomfortable or particularly jittery, call your doctor or clinic.

It will be helpful to take your baby's temperature before you call the doctor or clinic so that you can report the number to them.

Source: Infant Care (1989). Prepared by the Bureau of Maternal and Child Health and Resources Development, Public Health Service.

fiber, in the diet, that portion of plants that is indigestible by humans. It helps avoid CONSTIPATION and maintain normal bowel movements because it soaks up water and so eases passage of feces through the intestines. Dietary fiber, found in whole-grain products, fruits, and root vegetables, can also help ease problems associated with IRRITABLE BOWEL SYNDROME and cut the risk of developing CANCER. (See NUTRITION.)

figure-ground discrimination, the ability to distinguish between important and unimportant information in an environment, such as a child's ability to focus on a teacher's voice and ignore the singing in the next room. Children with a high degree of DISTRACTIBILITY are often unable to select and attend to one aspect of the environment and "tune out" others. Some psychological tests ask people to look at pictures and identify which is the "figure" and which the "background"; people with brain disorders often confuse the two.

financial aid, for students, a variety of programs providing help in handling the costs of attending a COLLEGE or PRIVATE SCHOOL. Some apply only to TUITION costs, but others cover additional expenses, such as room and board, books, and other supplies. Financial aid comes in many forms, including SCHOLARSHIPS, GRANTS, SUBSIDIZED LOANS, WORK-STUDY PROGRAMS, and (generally in graduate school) fellowships and assistantships. A school's financial aid administrator works with a student to put together a financial aid "package" consisting of several types of aid, to meet the student's needs. Many types of federally subsidized financial aid will be suspended or terminated if a student is convicted of possessing or distributing drugs.

FOR HELP AND FURTHER INFORMATION

Federal Student Aid Information Center
Office of Student Financial Assistance
Postsecondary Education
U.S. Department of Education
Washington, DC 20202
800–333-INFO [333–4630]; 800–433–3243; 800–730–8913, TT
Offers students information about federal student financial aid programs; publishes *Student Guide: Five Federal Financial Aid Programs* and other materials.

Citizens' Scholarship Foundation of America (CSFA)
Box 297
St. Peter, MN 56082
507–931–1682; 800–537–4180
Fax: 507–931–9168
Marlys C. Johnson, Vice President
Organization originated the Dollars for Scholars program under which local communities raise money (emphasizing small contributions from many people) for college and technical training for local students; aims to help average as well as top students and to fund technical as well as college education; helps local communities organize scholarship programs; publishes various materials, including monthly newsletter.

United Student Aid Funds (USA FUNDS)
11100 USA Parkway
Fishers, IN 46038
317–849–6510; 800–428–9250
Organization providing low-cost loans to college students needing financial aid; funded by corporations and foundations; operates toll-free number and WHIZ-KID online computer processing; publishes various materials, including quarterly newsletter and pamphlets.

National Scholarship Service and Fund for Negro Students (NSSFNS)
250 Auburn Avenue NE, Suite 500
Atlanta, GA 30303
404–577–3990
Fax: 404–577–4102
Geoffrey Heard, Executive Director
Organization providing college scholarships for low-income minority students; provides advice and referral to interested students, especially those in Talent Search and Upward Bound projects; arranges student-college interview sessions; advises guidance and admissions counselors; operates CASHE (Computer Assisted Scholarship for Higher Education) service; publishes brochure and annual report.

HEATH Resource Center, National Clearinghouse on Postsecondary Education for Individuals with Disabilities, 800–544–3284, voice/TT. Publishes *Financial Aid for Students with Disabilities.* (For full group information, see HELP FOR SPECIAL CHILDREN on page 689.)

OTHER RESOURCES

PLANNING AHEAD TO MEET COLLEGE COSTS

Paying for College: A Guide for Parents. Gerald Krefetz. College Board, 1994.
Bright Ideas: The Ins and Outs of Financing a College Education. Donna S. Carpenter. Simon & Schuster, 1992.
Investing Tips Grampa Taught Us: A Guide for Financing College Costs and More. Elizabeth Mason and Eric Eber. Financial Press, 1994.
Free Tuition: How to Beat the Soaring Cost of College Through Smart and Legal Tax Planning. Alexander A. Bove. Financial Planning Institute, 1993.
Planning to Finance Your Child's College Education: How Much to Save—Obtaining Financial Aid—Tax and Investment Strategies—Work Sheets, 2nd ed. J. Gibberman. Commerce, 1992.

GENERAL PLANNING GUIDES

The College Costs and Financial Aid Handbook. College Board. Includes worksheets and sample aid forms.
College Cost Explorer FUND FINDER. College Board. Computer software (MS-DOS).

College Financial Aid Annual. College Research Group, compilers. ARCO.
How to Obtain Maximum College Financial Aid, 4th ed. Edward Rosenwasser. Student College Aid, 1994.
College Check Mate: Innovative Tuition Plans That Make You a Winner, 8th ed. Debra Wexler. Octameron, 1994.
Financial Aid Fin-Ancer: Expert Answers to College Financing Questions, 6th ed. Joseph Re, ed. Octameron, 1994.
College Financial Aid Made Easy. Patrick L. Bellantoni. Tara, 1994.
USA Today's Financial Aid for College. Pat Ordovensky. Peterson's, 1994.
The McGraw-Hill College Handbook, 4th ed. Richard Marius and Harvey S. Wiener. McGraw-Hill, 1994.
Fund Your Way Through College: Uncovering 1,100 Great Opportunities in Undergraduate Financial Aid. Debra M. Kirby. Visible Ink, 1992.
Barron's Best Buys in College Education, 2nd ed. Lucia Solorzano. Barron, 1992.
College Funding Made Easy: How to Save for College While Maintaining Eligibility for Financial Aid. J. Grady Cash. Betterway, 1991.

Aid for specific groups

How to Find Money for College. Saryl Z. Schwartz. Pathfinders-College Affordability Productions. (*The Woman Student,* 1992; *The Graduate Student* and *The Minority Student,* 1993; *The Disabled Student,* 1994.)
Dollars for College: A Handbook of Financial Aid Sources for Minority Students. Sandra K. Williams and Mezell L. Williams, Jr. Educational Facilitators, 1991.

Working during college

Employment Guide for College Students, rev. ed. Scott E. Davis. Simsbury, 1993.
The Student Entrepreneur's Guide: How to Start and Run Your Own Business, rev. ed. Brett Kingstone. McGraw-Hill, 1990.

fine motor skills, the type of MOTOR SKILL that uses the small muscles of the fingers, toes, wrists, lips, and tongue to perform precision tasks, such as WRITING or tying shoes.

fingerspelling, use of hand shapes to stand for letters of the alphabet, to spell out words. Fingerspelling is often used by people with EAR AND HEARING PROBLEMS when they are being taught using a TOTAL COMMUNICATIONS approach or by people who are DEAF-BLIND, but is avoided by those teachers of the deaf who belief that no form of MANUAL COMMUNICATION should be used.

504 Accommodation Plan, a program under SECTION 504 of the Rehabilitation Act of 1973 that provides services to some children with DISABILITIES or CHRONIC illnesses who do not require SPECIAL EDUCATION and an INDIVIDUALIZED EDUCATION PLAN under the EDUCATION FOR ALL HANDICAPPED CHILDREN ACT and its successor, the INDIVIDUALS WITH DISABILITIES EDUCATION ACT.

floppy infant syndrome, a general term for a condition in which some babies, especially PREMATURE infants, have unusually limp, slack, or flaccid muscles (HYPOTONIA). This generally disappears as they mature, but in some children it remains and is associated with a variety of conditions, including CEREBRAL PALSY, MOTOR NEURON DISEASES, DOWN SYNDROME, heart disorders (see HEART AND HEART PROBLEMS), thyroid disorders (see THYROID GLAND), and MALNUTRITION. *Floppy infant syndrome* is sometimes used specifically to refer to SPINAL MUSCULAR ATROPHY. (See MUSCULAR DYSTROPHY.)

fluoridation, in dentistry, treatment of teeth with the chemical FLUORINE, which helps strengthen tooth's protective enamel and also reduces the cavity-causing acid formed by bacteria in the mouth. In the last few decades, fluoridation in the public water supply has helped cut tooth decay dramatically—so much so that approximately two-thirds of children age nine have never had a cavity in their permanent teeth.

The process is not without controversy. Some people have always criticized fluoridation as introducing risks of unknown magnitude into people's lives and cite some animal studies suggesting that large amounts of fluorine can increase the risk of CANCER. The main scientific community, however, has found no convincing data of such a risk to humans and continues to strongly recommend fluoridation. A major 1991 study involving over a dozen federal agencies concluded that fluoridating drinking water poses no detectable risk of causing cancer in humans and is not linked with DOWN SYNDROME, gastrointestinal problems, or disease of the genital, urinary, and respiratory systems. The study also found that the benefits of fluoridated water outweigh any risks, having cut the number of cavities among children by two-thirds in the last fifty years. Another study found no differences in the cancer rate between fluoridated areas and unfluoridated areas of New York State.

If the family water supply does not contain adequate fluoride, parents are advised to see that their children get daily fluoride supplements beginning in infancy, because it is most effective when teeth are forming. Fluoride may be administered in the form of drops (for infants) or tablets (once children are able to swallow pills), or can be applied directly to the teeth in a solution or gel, or in toothpaste or mouthwashes. Use should be continued at least through age fourteen.

Fluoride administration should be done under the direction of a dentist or physician, however, since too much fluoride can cause discoloration of teeth, called *dental fluorosis.* To avoid this, dentists recommend using only a pea-sized portion of fluoride toothpaste for preschoolers and suggest that mouthrinses not be used until age six, since younger children tend to swallow rather than rinse. Older children should be taught not to swallow either toothpaste or fluoridated rinses, both of which have high fluoride concentrations. Some schools conduct weekly fluoride mouth-rinsing programs for school-age children or provide tablets for students.

If the home water supply has the recommended amount of additional fluoride, the Food and Drug Administration (FDA) advises parents not to give their children additional fluoride. If the family physician or dentist still prescribes supplements, the FDA recommends that parents raise the question of possible excess fluoride. Parents should note, however, that even if the home water supply has sufficient fluoride, it will be of little or no benefit to BREASTFEEDING babies, who drink little or no water, or babies given ready-to-drink FORMULA.

Families who drink only bottled water may have difficulty assessing the level of fluoride they are getting. Despite advertising claims about "springs of remarkable purity," many bottled brands (perhaps 50 percent) obtain their water from municipal supplies, which may or may not be fluoridated, though some may have the fluoride content removed during the bottling process. (See TEETH AND DENTAL PROBLEMS.)

fluorine, a MINERAL vital to the body, though only in small amounts, for proper formation and maintenance of bone, especially in children. It is widely used in FLUORIDATION programs, to help prevent tooth decay. Some have suggested that fluorine used in fluoridation can *cause* health problems, such as increased risk of CANCER, but public health experts generally feel that current scientific data does not support that view (see FLUORIDATION). In large amounts, such as when pesticides containing fluorine are ingested, it can cause poisoning and even death. (See MINERALS; NUTRITION; TEETH AND DENTAL PROBLEMS; BONE AND BONE DISORDERS.)

fluoroscopy, a type of RADIOGRAPHY in which X-RAYS are used to give not still pictures, but moving ones. Fluoroscopy is especially useful as a guide to the physician in certain delicate procedures, such as when giving a BLOOD TRANSFUSION to a FETUS still in the UTERUS.

folic acid (folacin), a VITAMIN important in the manufacturing of red blood cells and in energy METABOLISM, the process that provides energy for the body's use, working closely with VITAMIN B12 and VITAMIN C. It is part of a group of vitamins known as the vitamin B complex; substances containing folic acid are called folates. Folic acid is abundant in liver, beans, and green leafy vegetables, and is also found in nuts, fresh oranges, and whole wheat products. It is very important in development of the FETUS, especially of the nervous system and red blood cells, and folic acid deficiency has been linked with increased risk of neural tube defects (see SPINA BIFIDA). Pregnant women are sometimes given folic acid supplements, especially during the last three months of pregnancy. Some researchers recommend folic acid supplements for smokers. Symptoms of folic acid deficiency are DIARRHEA and a form of ANEMIA, causing fatigue, pallor, and depression, while overconsumption can obscure the presence of pernicious anemia. (See VITAMINS.)

follicles, egg-producing structures in the OVARIES; the follicle that produces the "lead" egg is called the *graafian follicle*. Follicle is also a general name for the sites from which teeth or strands of HAIR emerge.

follicle-stimulating hormone (FSH), a HORMONE produced by the PITUITARY GLAND. In women, FSH production stimulates the OVARIES to ripen eggs (see OVUM) and to produce the female sex hormone ESTROGEN as part of the MENSTRUAL CYCLE. Later in the cycle, a fall in the levels of estrogen and PROGESTERONE triggers production of more FSH to begin the next cycle. In men, FSH is involved in the maturation of SPERM.

fontanelles, two soft spots in a baby's skull, which at birth are covered only by membranes. In these two areas, bones of the skull fuse and harden later, the rear one at about age two months and the top front one at about age eighteen months. The softness of a baby's skull allows the head to pass through the BIRTH CANAL during CHILDBIRTH. Some babies, especially those with DOWN SYNDROME, have more than two fontanelles. Abnormalities of the fontanelles are associated with some brain disorders. They may temporarily bulge when a baby cries, but persistent tension in the membrane can indicate physical problems, such as HYDROCEPHALUS. (See BRAIN AND BRAIN DISORDERS.)

food additive, any substance added to food during processing. In the United States and many other countries, such additives are regulated and tested for safety, though problems can still occur. Additives are used for a variety of reasons, including:

- *To preserve storage quality*: Preservatives retard growth of bacteria, molds, and yeasts that can spoil food and otherwise cause food poisoning (see DIGESTIVE SYSTEM AND DISORDERS; SAFETY); some ANTIOXIDANTS prevent other kinds of food changes, such as discoloration or rancidness, during normal storage life. One common group of preservative used in meats are NITRITES.
- *To improve texture*: These additives, including stabilizers, emulsifiers (to prevent separation), thickeners, and gelling agents, help make the food's texture more attractive.
- *To improve taste and color*: Colors and flavorings are added to enhance the food's original taste and color, to make up for qualities lost during processing, or to make foods appropriate for use by people with specific health problems, as artificial sweeteners used in products for people with DIABETES.

- *To enhance the food's performance*: Various additives are used to make the food respond in an enhanced or more standardized way during cooking, such as flour to be used for baking bread.

The Food and Drug Administration (FDA) is charged with ensuring the safety of food additives. For regulatory purposes, the FDA divides food additives into several groups:

- *Generally recognized as safe (GRAS) substances*, substances like sugar and salt, two of the most widespread food additives, and also many spices, herbs, and vitamins, which are considered "safe based either on a history of safe use before 1958 or on published scientific evidence." Though these may be considered safe, many parents will want to select foods not overloaded with sugar and salt, which can cause tooth decay and high BLOOD PRESSURE, even if they are not implicated in the more serious problems tested for.
- *Prior-sanctioned substances*, substances that were sanctioned before 1958 for use in a specific food by either the FDA or the U.S. Department of Agriculture. Nitrites, for example, are prior-sanctioned substances used as common preservatives in meats.
- *Food additives*, substances that have no proven track record. The artificial sweetener *aspartame* (brand name NutraSweet), for example, was simply unknown at the time it was proposed for use, so it had to undergo substantial testing before approval. Substances used in food packaging can also end up in food and so must be tested by the FDA.
- *Color additives*, dyes used in foods, drugs, cosmetics, and other medical products, which are subjected to testing similar to that for food additives. Those in use in 1960 were given provisional approval at that time; some were later dropped, because testing showed them unsafe or because manufacturers were no longer interested in using them. Food dyes have been suspected of triggering or exacerbating HYPERACTIVITY, but no real consensus on the question has developed in the scientific community.

Neither GRAS, prior-sanctioned substances, nor provisionally approved color additives remain on the FDA's approved list unreviewed. If later data indicates that a substance is unsafe, it is removed. Both saccharin and cyclamates were once on the GRAS list, for example, but evidence showed that they might cause cancer in animals. As a result, cyclamates were banned altogether and saccharin was kept only by special exemption from Congress because people with diabetes need the substance. Since then, aspartame has become the most widely used artificial sweetener.

Nitrites have come under some fire, because, in the intestines, they are converted into chemical compounds called *nitrosamines*, which have been shown to cause cancer in animals. Though nitrites have not been barred from use, partly because the scientific evidence is indirect and partly because no good substitute is readily available, many parents may wish to limit their family's consumption of nitrite-containing meats, such as sausages.

Some approved additives are safe for most people, but dangerous to a few, sometimes causing potentially life-threatening allergic reactions. The FDA collects information on complaints the department receives directly, through its *Adverse Reaction Monitoring System* (ARMS), or indirectly, from the manufacturer. The complaints are classified by the severity of the symptoms and the directness of the relationship between the product and the symptom. Among the additives about which complaints are most often received are aspartame, sulfites (a preservative), monosodium glutamate (MSG; a flavor-enhancer), nitrites, polysorbate (an emulsifier), and some color dyes. Some reactions are extremely severe—substances such as MSG can in some people induce deadly anaphylactic shock (see SHOCK; ALLERGY). According to the ARMS records, before sulfites were banned from salad bars in 1986, over two dozen people may have died from such allergic reactions to them. On the other hand, sometimes reactions are so widely diverse, general, or vague, that they cannot be substantiated. For example, while early studies indicated that some people have an allergic-type reaction to aspartame, at least one study showed reactions to aspartame were less than to a neutral placebo.

The FDA suggests that, if you or anyone in your family has an allergic reaction to a food additive, you should first contact your local physician for treatment. Then you or the doctor should contact the nearest FDA field office (in the blue pages of the telephone book) to report information about the reaction.

FOR HELP AND FURTHER INFORMATION

Food and Drug Administration (FDA),
301–443–3170; Medwatch (to receive form for reporting adverse reactions): 800–332–1088. (For full group information, see DRUG REACTIONS AND INTERACTIONS.)

OTHER RESOURCES

A Consumer's Dictionary of Food Additives, 3rd ed. Ruth Winter. Crown, 1989.

(See also NUTRITION; ALLERGY; ATTENTION DEFICIT HYPERACTIVITY DISORDER.)

food intolerance, a general term for a regular adverse reaction to a food or FOOD ADDITIVE that does not stem from food poisoning (see DIGESTIVE SYSTEM AND DISORDERS) or a psychological reaction. It can refer to a wide range of responses, from a mild upset stomach after eating fried foods to an ALLERGY involving possibly life-threatening anaphylactic shock (see SHOCK; ALLERGY), from a substance like monosodium glutamate (MSG).

Many forms of food intolerance are related to a biochemical deficiency, either inherited or environmentally triggered, that makes the body unable to digest certain foods. Among these are LACTOSE INTOLERANCE, CELIAC SPRUE (gluten intolerance), and even DIABETES mellitus (a sort of glucose intolerance). In a wider sense, some kinds of METABOLIC DISORDERS, involving the body's inability to break down and use for energy essential nutrients, might also be considered examples of food intolerance. When first starting a baby on SOLID FOODS, public health experts recommend that parents try one simple food at a time, for a few days each, to identify any possible adverse reactions to specific foods. (See NUTRITION; also specific topics noted above.)

food labels, information that the Food and Drug Administration (FDA) requires to be on all food products from manufacturers. Traditionally, food labels included information on the ingredients, the net contents or net weight (including liquid), the name and business address of the manufacturer, packer, or distributor, and (when appropriate) the date by which it should be sold. Under the 1990 Nutrition Labeling and Education Act, food labels were revised to provide more useful, more understandable, consumer-oriented information, and the FDA was charged with clarifying and regulating the use of health-related terms, to ensure that consumers obtain accurate nutritional information from food labels. Virtually all packaged foods are now required to show nutrition information and information on conditions for their use. In general, the food labeling program requires that:

- Ingredients be listed in descending order of predominance by weight. Manufacturers who wish to declare ingredients by percent of content must follow a uniform format.
- All sweeteners be grouped together under the collective term "sweeteners," with the various types listed in parentheses in descending order of predominance by weight.
- Labels list all ingredients of standardized foods, such as peanut butter, bread, ketchup, mayonnaise, and macaroni. These are foods for which the government has long set standards (recipes), but the ingredients may no longer be familiar to many shoppers. Standards were introduced in the 1930s to help consumers avoid being cheated by cheap substitutes and fraudulent packaging. If a product does not meet the minimum standard for a product, it cannot be called by that name. A peanut-butterlike product that does not contain 90 percent peanuts cannot, for example, be legally called peanut butter. Also, a less nutritious product resembling a standardized food must be called an imitation and given a different name.
- Color additives be listed on labels by name.
- Labels indicate whether the product includes monosodium glutamate (MSG) and protein hydrolysates (used as flavors or flavor enhancers), so consumers with special religious, medical, or cultural dietary requirements can identify the food source of the additive.
- Juice beverage labels state the percentage of actual fruit or vegetable juice in the drink, and the percentages of different types of juices, if the drink includes more than one.
- Caseinate be identified as a milk derivative when used in foods that are called "nondairy," such as coffee whiteners, since some people are allergic to milk.
- Sulfites used in foods be declared in foods for which ingredients are standardized, since some people are allergic to sulfites (see ALLERGY).
- Serving sizes be defined by the FDA in accordance with everyday norms, not arbitrarily set by manufacturers.
- Terms such as "light" and "low-fat" be defined by the FDA, so they cannot be used misleadingly in advertising, as in the past.

The FDA is also preparing materials for stores to display near counters for selling raw fruits, raw vegetables, and raw, minimally processed, or heat-treated fish and shellfish, to offer guidance to shoppers. These would initially be voluntary, but would become mandatory if not sufficiently widespread by May 1993. The U.S. Department of Agriculture (USDA) is making similar arrangement for the labeling of meat and poultry, which it regulates.

In addition, the new law has given the FDA for the first time the authority to allow food labels to carry claims relating food to specific health conditions; previously such claims were not allowed, since products with those claims were regarded as drugs. Among the food—health condition relationships immediately allowed to be shown on labels are:

- CALCIUM and OSTEOPOROSIS.
- SODIUM and hypertension (high BLOOD PRESSURE).
- FAT and cardiovascular disease.
- Fat and CANCER.

The FDA will explore other such claims of healthy relationships, such as FIBER and heart disease, fiber and cancer, FOLIC ACID and neural tube defects (such as SPINA BIFIDA), ANTIOXIDANT VITAMINS with cancer, ZINC with IMMUNE SYSTEM function in the elderly, or omega–3 fatty acids with heart disease. Such foods making health claims would also have to meet certain FDA guidelines. Specifically, those that contain more than a specified proportion of fat, saturated fat, cholesterol, or sodium would be barred from making any health claims.

The FDA has also attempted to make food labels more meaningful by indicating the maximum daily recommended amounts—called DAILY REFERENCE VALUES or DRVs—of substances such as fat, saturated fat, cholesterol, protein, fiber, sodium, potassium, and carbohydrates. The idea is to help consumers make nutritionally wise shopping decisions by allowing them to compare the amount of nutrients in the food with the maximum amount an "average" person should consume.

Beyond that, product dating is required by the FDA only on a very few products (such as an expiration date for infant FORMULA). Dating is widely used nevertheless, usually as "pull dates" (to be taken from the store shelf by that date) or "use by dates" (not to be used after that date). Most canned foods and other products with a long shelf life also are required to give information about the manufacturer and the place of packaging, should a recall be required.

FOR HELP AND FURTHER INFORMATION

Food and Drug Administration (FDA), 301–443–3170. (For full group information, see DRUG REACTIONS AND INTERACTIONS.)

American Institute for Cancer Research (AICR), 800–843–8114. Publishes *The New Food Labels.* (For full group information, see CANCER.)

forceps delivery, use of a hinged device with two curved arms; these are inserted into a woman's VAGINA during CHILDBIRTH, placed around a child's head, and then used to aid in DELIVERY. Forceps are generally removed as soon as the head is delivered, allowing the rest of the delivery to proceed normally, but they can leave some temporary marks on the head and face. They are used in some cases of FETAL DISTRESS, especially early in the delivery or when the mother is unable to push out the baby on her own. Forceps are used somewhat less often in recent years, as VACUUM EXTRACTIONS and CESAREAN SECTIONS have become more common. (See CHILDBIRTH.)

foreskin (prepuce), the loose fold of skin over the head, or glans, of the PENIS of a newborn male. It is often removed for medical or religious reasons in the operation called CIRCUMCISION.

form constancy, the ability to recognize an object or shape, regardless of slight changes in color, size, or the position or angle from which it is viewed. This is an important element in SPATIAL ORIENTATION and in VISUAL SKILLS, which often causes difficulty for children with LEARNING DISABILITIES or other DEVELOPMENTAL DISORDERS.

formula, a fluid preparation designed to simulate breast MILK in its balance and amount of nutrients (though it cannot give the natural IMMUNIZATION provided by mother to child). Commercially sold formulas can come in various forms:

- *Ready-to-use form,* the most expensive form, to which no water is added.
- *Liquid concentrate,* to which some water is added.
- *Dry powder,* the cheapest form, to which water is added.

Packages of formula are required to carry expiration dates as part of their FOOD LABELS; parents should always carefully check the expiration date, and if it has passed, throw the formula away unused. Parents who have decided to bottlefeed their baby should consult with their doctor or clinic before the birth about the form and perhaps the brand of formula recommended. Generally they will use one with added iron, unless there are medical reasons for avoiding iron.

Cow's milk, the basis of most formulas, is incomplete nutritionally, difficult for a newborn to digest, and has concentrations of some FATS and MINERALS that are too high. But in formula, some milk fats are replaced by vegetable oils, minerals are diluted, VITAMINS and some other minerals are added, and the resulting mixture is heated to make the PROTEIN more digestible. If a child proves to have LACTOSE INTOLERANCE (inability to digest milk properly) or sensitivity to something else in cow's milk, other formulas are available as substitutes, including some based on soy.

To ensure that infants get proper nutrition for normal growth and development, the Food and Drug Administration (under the Infant Formula Act of 1980) has set standards for the nutrient composition of commercially available infant formulas. It is vitally important, however, that formula be prepared and used precisely according to directions (see FIXING FORMULA on page 77). Too diluted a formula can lead to MALNUTRITION and serious imbalances in body chemistry, while too concentrated a formula can overtax the infant's immature system, causing other kinds of imbalances and sometimes severe KIDNEY AND UROLOGICAL PROBLEMS. (See BOTTLEFEEDING; MILK.)

foster care, the system of assigning a MINOR child to the home of adults other than relatives, to be temporarily cared for until the child can return home, reaches the legal age of adulthood, or is adopted. Foster parents, who are normally appointed GUARDIANS of those in their care, receive payments to help in supporting the children. In 1995, some 440,000 children were living in foster care, 62 percent more than a decade earlier, though in that same period the number of qualified foster parents had dropped from 134,000 to 100,000. The average stay for a child in foster care was 1.4 years, but 11 percent spend 5 years or more in foster care.

Children may be placed in foster care in a variety of situations, most notably when a parent has been acused of CHILD ABUSE AND NEGLECT or INCEST. Ideally, the child is not returned to the family home until the abusive parent has undergone therapy and has satisfied the court that the child is in no danger. In practice, the child is often returned home routinely, without any such assurance, sometimes because many social work agencies are grossly understaffed and underfunded and also because of a shortage of foster parents.

In cases of ABANDONMENT or TERMINATION OF PARENTAL RIGHTS, a child in foster care may become available for ADOPTION; in such cases, foster parents are often able to adopt the child, if they wish. Too often, however, a child languishes in limbo, continuing in foster care because the overburdened welfare system has failed even to process the papers necessary for adoption. Various organizations (see listings in this entry) have been established to act as advocates for children caught in the web of welfare system (see ADVOCACY). Some of these organizations have opened the activities of various agencies to scrutiny through lawsuits, in attempts to gain children the protection to which they are legally entitled.

Many children have been placed in the homes of foster parents who wish to adopt them, but cannot legally do so until the parents or other biological relatives have been located to give their consent. This is called *legal risk adoption* or *foster/adoption* (see ADOPTION). It is designed to move children into permanent homes as soon as possible, but may leave both the children and the foster parents waiting for months, sometimes years, for the adoption paperwork to be completed. It can also risk heartbreak, as when the child's relatives, once located, refuse to sign the papers legalizing the adoption.

For children with SPECIAL NEEDS and some adults judged to be INCOMPETENT, such as some who have severe DISABILITIES, MENTAL DISORDERS, or MENTAL RETARDATION, LONG-TERM CARE may be provided in a homelike setting, in what are called GROUP HOMES or *community living.* Some communities sponsor foster grandparents programs, in which retired older people (paid or as volunteers) develop a relationship with a child who has special needs, because of disabilities, for instance, or family problems at home. In an odd twist, in this age of ADOLESCENT PREGNANCY, sometimes children who are in foster care because they are not old enough to legally live independently, are MOTHERS themselves, who have legal responsibility for their children.

FOR HELP AND FURTHER INFORMATION

Child Welfare League of America (CWLA)
440 First Street NW
Washington, DC 20001
202–638–2952
Fax: 202–638–4004
David Liederman, Chief Executive Officer
Organization that aims to "guard children's rights and serve children's needs," especially for those deprived, abused, or neglected; provides information and referrals; acts as advocate; publishes newsletters *Children's Monitor* and *Washington Social Legislation,* bimonthly journal *Child Welfare,* quarterly magazine *Children's Voice* and various materials, many for professionals, others for the public, including:

- General works: *Children Can't Wait: Reducing Delays for Children in Out-of-Home Care, Kinship Care: A Natural Bridge, A Developmental Network Approach to Therapeutic Foster Care,* and *No More Partings: An Examination of Long-Term Family Foster Care.*
- For foster parents: *Foster Parenting in the 1990s* (video training curriculum), *Homeworks: At-Home Training Resources for Foster Parents and Adoptive Parents, Foster Parent Retention and Recruitment: State of the Art in Practice and Policy,* and *Conversations* (three booklets: *What You Always Wanted to Discuss About Foster Care But Didn't Have the Chance or the Time to Bring Up, What's So Special About Teenagers?,* and *Foster Parents and Social Workers: On the Job Together*).
- On parents of children in foster care: *Parents of Children in Placement: Perspectives and Programs, Walk a Mile in My Shoes: A Book about Biological Parents for Foster Parents and Social Workers, Together Again: Family Reunification in Foster Care,* and *Family Visiting of Children in Out-of-Home Care: A Practical Guide.*
- On teens in foster care: *Independence: A Life Skills Guide for Teens, Independent-Living Services for At-Risk Adolescents, Ready, Set, Go: An Agency Guide to Independent Living,* and *Preparing Adolescents for Life After Foster Care: The Central Role of Foster Parents.*
- For children: *My Foster Home: A Story for Children Entering Foster Care, I Miss My Foster Parents,* and *The Visit.*
- On troubled children in foster care: *Therapeutic Foster Care: Critical Issues, Troubled Youth in Treatment Homes: A Handbook of Therapeutic Foster Care, Quality Care for Tough Kids: Studies of the Maintenance of Subsidized Foster Placements in The Casey Family Program,* and *Son-Up, Son-Down* (novel of two troubled brothers in foster care).

Children's Rights, Inc.
132 West 43rd Street
New York, NY 10036
212–944–9800, ext. 714
Fax: 212–921–7916
Marcia R. Lowry, Executive Director
Organization seeking to strengthen services to and rights of children, to protect them from being harmed by agencies set up to protect them, especially child welfare systems and foster care; formerly the Children's Rights Project of the American Civil Liberties Union (ACLU); publishes *Children's Rights Fact Sheet, Proposal for a National Organization to Reform Services Provided to Poor Children,* and *A Force for Change: Children's Rights Project of the ACLU.*

National Black Child Development Institute (NBCDI), 800–556–2234. Publishes *Who Will Care When Parents Can't* and *Parental Drug Abuse and African American Children in Foster Care.* (For full group information, see HELP ON LEARNING AND EDUCATION on page 659.)

Center on Children and the Law, 202–662–1720. Publishes *Overcoming Barriers to Permanency: An Annotated Bibliography, Judicial Implementation of Permanency Planning Reforms: One Court that Works* and *How to Work with Your Court: A Guide for Child Welfare Agency Administrators.* (For full group information, see HELP AGAINST CHILD ABUSE AND NEGLECT on page 680.)

Children's Defense Fund (CDF), 800–233–1200. Publishes *Teens in Foster Care: Preventing Pregnancy and Building Self-Esteem.* (For full group information, see ADOLESCENT PREGNANCY.)

National Clearinghouse on Child Abuse and Neglect Information (NCCAN), 800-FYI-3366 [394–3366]. Publishes annotated bibliography on abuse *Foster Care.* (For full group information, see HELP AGAINST CHILD ABUSE AND NEGLECT on page 680.)

National Adoption Information Clearinghouse (NAIC), 301–231–6512. Publishes *The Sibling Bond: Its Importance in Foster Care and Adoptive Placement.* (For full group information, see ADOPTION.)

Lavender Families Resource Network, 206–325–2643, voice/TT. Publishes *Adoption and Foster Parenting for Lesbians and Gay Men: Creating New Traditions in Family.* (For full group information, see HOMOSEXUALITY.)

American Association on Mental Retardation (AAMR), 800–424–3688. Publishes *Foster Family Care.* (For full group information, see MENTAL RETARDATION.)

OTHER RESOURCES

GENERAL WORKS

When There's No Place Like Home: Options for Children Living Apart from Their Natural Families. Jan Blacher, ed. P. H. Brookes, 1994.
Families at Risk: A Guide to Understand and Protect Children and Care Givers Involved in Out-of-Home or Adoptive Care. Jodee Kulp. Better Endings, 1993.
Child Custody, Foster Care, and Adoptions. Joseph R. Carrieri. Free Press, 1991.

FOR FOSTER PARENTS

Adopting or Fostering a Sexually Abused Child. Catherine Macaskill. Trafalgar, 1992.
To Love a Child: Adoption, Foster Parenting, and Other Ways to Share Your Life with Children. Marianne Takas and Edward Warner. Addison-Wesley, 1992.
Lesbians and Gay Men As Foster Parents. Wendell Ricketts. University of Southern Maine, 1991.

FOR CHILDREN

Not Home: Somehow, Somewhere, There Must Be Love: A Novel. Ann Grifalconi. Little, Brown, 1995. Fiction.
The Long Journey Home. Richard J. Delaney and Terry McNerney. R. J. Delaney, 1994.
Pablo's Tree. Pat Mora. Macmillan, 1994. Fiction.
Zachary's New Home: A Story for Foster and Adopted Children. Geraldine M. Blomquist and Paul B. Blomquist. Gareth Stevens, 1993.
Onion Tears. Diana Kidd. Orchard/Watts, 1991. Fiction.
Where Is Home: Living Through Foster Care. E. P. Jones. Four Walls, Eight Windows, 1990.

FOR PRETEENS AND TEENS

Everything You Need to Know About Living in a Foster Home. Joseph Falke. Rosen, 1995.
Foster Care. Nancy Millichap. Watts, 1994.
Adam and Eve and Pinch-Me. Julie Johnston. Little, Brown, 1994. Fiction.
Out of Nowhere. Ouida Sebestyen. Orchard/Watts, 1994. Fiction.
Writing to Richie. Patricia Calvert. Macmillan, 1994. Fiction.
When the Road Ends. Jean Thesman. Houghton Mifflin, 1992. Fiction.
Coping As a Foster Child. Geraldine M. Blomquist. Rosen, 1992.
Foster Families. Jeanne Barmat. Crestwood/Macmillan, 1991.
The Golden Days. Gail Radley. Macmillan, 1991. Fiction.

BACKGROUND WORKS

Nobody's Baby: Foster Care in America. Deborah Chase. Wiley, 1994.
Adoption Crisis: The Truth Behind Adoption and Foster Care. Carole A. McKelvey and JoEllen Stevens. Fulcrum, 1994.
Raised by the Government: An Inside Look into America's Child Welfare System. Ira M. Schwartz and others. Free Press, 1994.
Life for Me Ain't Been No Crystal Stair. Susan Sheehan. Pantheon, 1993. On three generations raised in foster care, including a 14-year-old mother.

foster parents, adults who have been given legal authority to care for a MINOR in their home, sometimes only temporarily until a child returns to the birth parents, but sometimes in anticipation of adoption (see FOSTER CARE; ADOPTION).

fracture, a break in a bone, as from a fall or a blow, but sometimes during normal use, as in certain disorders such as OSTEOPOROSIS. Fractures may be classified by the nature of the break. *Simple fractures,* also called *closed fractures,* are those in which the two bone pieces are not displaced and so do not break the skin or damage surrounding tissue. Breaks in which the pieces of the bone are displaced and do break the skin and damage surrounding tissue are called *open or compound fractures.* Some other types of fractures include:

- *Comminuted fracture,* with bone shattered into more than two pieces, as in an automobile accident.
- *Transverse fracture,* with the two pieces of bones dislocated sideways by a sharp blow or from stress from excessive use.
- *Greenstick fracture,* common in young children, in which the bone bends and breaks only partway through—as with a young growing twig rather than an old dry stick.
- *Stress fractures,* resulting from overuse, as in overexercising as part of a SPORTS program.

X-RAYS or other SCANS are often used to give physicians a picture of the exact nature of the break. A major concern in childhood is that a fracture not damage the *epiphyses,* the growth centers at the ends of the bone, while the child is still growing (see GROWTH AND GROWTH DISORDERS). Some kinds and types of fractures can be indicators of physical abuse (see INDICATORS OF CHILD ABUSE AND NEGLECT on page 106).

The most serious kind of fracture is one that involves possible SPINAL CORD INJURY. People with such injuries should be moved only in extreme emergency and treated only by trained health professionals. Otherwise, the affected bone should be immobilized as well as possible, but without trying to force the bone back into position, and medical care should be sought immediately.

If the pieces of the bone have been displaced, they must be *reduced,* or put back into their original position, so that the bone can heal properly. Often the bones can be manipulated through the skin, in a procedure called a *closed reduction,* but sometimes surgery is necessary to expose the pieces for repositioning in what is called an *open reduction.* Once replaced, the bones are immobilized so that they can heal; new bone called *callus* grows at the point of the break. Often a plaster cast is used to immobilize the bones, but in some cases pins are temporarily inserted surgically, sometimes affixed to external metal rods, depending on the type of fracture. In general, fractures in children mend much more quickly than in adults, and fractures in nonweight-bearing bones, such as arms or collarbones (*clavicles*), heal more quickly than weight-bearing bones, such as legs. In some cases, the fracture fails to heal properly, and surgery may be necessary. PHYSICAL THERAPISTS may provide guidance in restoring full strength and mobility to the affected part, and ORTHOPEDIC DEVICES may be needed to provide mobility while protecting the healing bone. (See BONE AND BONE DISORDERS.)

fragile X syndrome (X-linked mental retardation), a CONGENITAL condition resulting from a CHROMOSOMAL ABNORMALITY in which the X SEX CHROMOSOME is malformed (termed *fragile* because it often breaks during chromosome analysis). It is one of the most common genetic mutations known—the National Fragile X Foundation estimates that 1 in every 300 females is a CARRIER of the mutation and 1 in every 1,000 males is affected by it. It is also one of the most common causes of MENTAL RETARDATION, though intellectual capacity of people with the syndrome can range from normal to severely retarded. Some developmental delay or retardation is found in approximately 50 percent of the females who carry the full-mutation (rather than premutation) form and in 80 percent of the males who inherit the gene. A woman with the gene has a 50 percent change of passing it on to each of her children; a man with the gene will pass it only to his daughters.

Among the physical characteristics linked with the syndrome are a long face, large or prominent ears, and large testicles in the males, and sometimes also flat feet, double-jointed fingers, and a heart murmur (caused by mitral valve prolapse; see HEART AND HEART DISORDERS). However, the range of physical characteristics is also wide and many people show few or only subtle manifestiations of these.

Many people with the syndrome are believed to be as yet undiagnosed, and many researchers believe that the syndrome is linked with many cases of LEARNING DISABILITIES, ATTENTION DEFICIT HYPERACTIVITY DISORDER, and language delays (see COMMUNICATION SKILLS AND DISORDERS). The 1991 discovery of the Fragile Mental Retardation (FMR–1) gene involved should lead to better understanding of the syndrome and its effects. The disorder can now be identified through GENETIC SCREENING, and prospective parents who suspect possible fragile X syndrome in their family may want to seek GENETIC COUNSELING.

FOR HELP AND FURTHER INFORMATION

National Fragile X Foundation
1441 York Street, Suite 303
Denver, CO 80206
303–333–6155; 800–688–8765
Fax: 303–333–4369
Dave Nommensen, Executive Director
Organization concerned with fragile X syndrome; provides information; publishes newsletter *Foundation Monthly, Boys with Fragile X Syndrome, Girls with Fragile X Syndrome, Behavioral Characteristics of Fragile X Syndrome, The Importance of Early Intervention, Calming Activities, "Needs" List for School Aged Children with Fragile X, Sensory Integration Techniques, Educational Interventions, Medical Management,* and various audiovisual and teaching aids.

The Arc, 817–261–6003. Publishes fact sheet *Fragile X Syndrome.* (For full group information, see MENTAL RETARDATION.)

National Organization for Rare Disorders (NORD), 800–999–6673. (For full group information, see RARE DISORDERS.)

(See also GENETIC DISORDERS.)

Frostig Developmental Test of Visual Perception (DTVP), a widely used type of DIAGNOSTIC ASSESSMENT TEST, administered individually or to groups of children from prekindergarten through grade 3. Used to help identify possible LEARNING DISABILITIES or neurological DISABILITIES, the Frostig test focuses on VISUAL SKILLS, covering five main areas: EYE-HAND COORDINATION, FIGURE-GROUND DISCRIMINATION, FORM CONSTANCY, SPATIAL RELATIONS, and SPATIAL ORIENTATION. Test results are compared to NORMS that are correlated with READING skill norms in first grade classes. (See TESTS.)

full-term, in relation to CHILDBIRTH, a baby who is born at the completion of GESTATION and so has had the normal amount of time to develop in the UTERUS, as opposed to a PREMATURE child, who is born without having the full nine months (medically, forty weeks) to develop.

functional skills, those skills necessary to everyday life; sometimes called *survival skills.* The term is especially used in SPECIAL EDUCATION to identify skills that a child with DISABILITIES must learn or forever be dependent on others to perform, such as brushing teeth or writing a check. A school program that focuses on such skills may be called a functional CURRICULUM. In EDUCATION in general, functional skills are those that can be immediately applied in daily life, such as typing or auto mechanics. Functional reading skills means reading ability sufficient for the purposes of daily life—reading signs, train schedules, application forms, and the like; people who are unable to read such materials are called functionally ILLITERATE.

G

galactosemia, a rare genetic disorder of the autosomal recessive type; a kind of metabolic disorder that results from the lack of a key liver enzyme (galactose–1-phosphate uridyl transferase), leaving the body unable to break down galactose, contained in the milk sugar lactose. If not quickly recognized and treated, galactosemia can soon cause failure to thrive and serious complications that can result in death for as many as three out of four children during infancy. The disorder can lead to cirrhosis of the liver, jaundice (see liver and liver problems), cataracts (see eye and vision disorders), and mental retardation. Various medical tests for galactosemia, especially blood tests and urine tests, can be performed, beginning in the child's first week of life. Many states require testing for the disorder from a drop of blood taken from a heel prick at birth.

Treatment of galactosemia involves lifelong avoidance of normal MILK, substituting lactose-free milk when available. However, if the condition is diagnosed late, some damage may be irreversible. Even with the restrictive diet, children with galactosemia may be more likely to have speech and language problems (see COMMUNICATIONS SKILLS AND DISORDERS), LEARNING DISABILITIES, and delay in developing MOTOR SKILLS. On maturation, a girl's OVARIES may also malfunction. The metabolic disorder can be diagnosed during prenatal screening through AMNIOCENTESIS.

FOR HELP AND FURTHER INFORMATION

Parents of Galactosemic Children (PGC)
2871 Stagecoach Drive
Valley Springs, CA 95252
209–772–2449
Gayle Dennis, Contact Person

Mutual support group for families of children with galactosemia; operates a parent help line; provides information; publishes newsletter.

National Institute of Child Health and Human Development (NICHD), 301–496–5133. Publishes *Galactosemia: New Frontiers in Research.* (For full group information, see PREGNANCY.)

National Digestive Disease Information Clearinghouse (NDDIC), 301–654–3810. (For full group information, see DIGESTIVE SYSTEM AND DISORDERS.)

National Organization for Rare Disorders (NORD), 800–999–6673. (For full group information, see RARE DISORDERS.)

(See also METABOLIC DISORDERS; LIVER AND LIVER PROBLEMS; DIGESTIVE SYSTEM AND DISORDERS; LACTOSE INTOLERANCE.)

gamete intra-fallopian tube transfer (GIFT), a treatment for INFERTILITY that involves removing eggs (see OVUM) from a woman's OVARIES and inserting them and a man's SPERM in her FALLOPIAN TUBE, allowing FERTILIZATION to take place in the normal environment with some scientific assistance. The procedure for maturing and removing eggs is similar to that in IN VITRO FERTILIZATION, but the eggs are immediately mixed with the ready sperm and (while the woman is still on the operating table) inserted into the Fallopian tubes by a CATHETER. If all goes well, fertilization takes place, and the fertilized egg moves down the Fallopian tube into the UTERUS, where the crucial IMPLANTATION occurs. It is vital to see that the fertilized egg does not implant itself in the Fallopian tubes (or anywhere other than the uterus), since that could lead to a life-threatening ECTOPIC PREGNANCY, which would require emergency surgery to remove. In a related procedure, *zygote intrafallopian transfer* (ZIFT), zygotes (newly fertilized embryos or "pre-embryos") are placed in the Fallopian tube a day after retrieval.

GIFT is still a fairly new technique, so its long-term success rate is not yet known. But some studies suggest that it has a higher pregnancy rate per egg retrieval than IVF, especially for women over 40. It is generally considered appropriate for women who have normal Fallopian tubes but who have ENDOMETRIOSIS, cervical mucus problems, or other unexplained causes for infertility. (See INFERTILITY; REPRODUCTIVE TECHNOLOGY.)

gargoylism, a combination of defects often found in (and an outdated term for) Hurler syndrome and Hunter's syndrome (see MUCOPOLYSACCHARIDOSES), but found in some other GENETIC DISORDERS as well. Among the characteristics of gargoylism are DWARFISM, MENTAL RETARDATION, large head with protruding tongue and prominent brows, thick arms, legs, hands, and ribs, along with various other skeletal deformities, enlarged liver and spleen, and some eye defects, such as clouded cornea (see EYE AND VISION PROBLEMS).

gastroenterologist, a PHYSICIAN who specializes in treating disorders of digestive system, especially the stomach and intestines.

gastroscope, a type of lighted ENDOSCOPE, swallowed by the patient, used by doctors in visually examining the stomach. (See DIGESTIVE SYSTEM DISORDERS.)

Gates-MacGinitie Reading Test (GMRT), a group-administered TEST of READING skills for children in grades K–12. A multiple-item, paper-and-pencil test, it focuses on reading comprehension and vocabulary development at various grade levels and letter recognition and letter sounds. The GMRT is often used as a DIAGNOSTIC ASSESSMENT TEST to identify students who need REMEDIAL INSTRUCTION or, conversely, ACCELERATED PROGRAMS, as well as to evaluate school instructional programs. (See TESTS.)

Gates-McKillop-Horowitz Reading Diagnostic Tests, an individually administered TEST of READING skills for children in grades 1–6, evaluating oral reading, recognition of isolated words, knowledge of word parts, recognition of common word parts and ability to blend them, reading words, giving letter sounds, naming letters, writing, and AUDITORY SKILLS such as identifying vowel sounds, auditory blending, and discrimination. The test is generally given for class placement purposes, and not all parts will be used with all students. (See TESTS.)

gender identity, a person's inner sense of being male or female, which some psychologists think is firmly established before age three. By contrast, SEXUAL IDENTITY is determined by one's physical attributes, though these can sometimes be ambiguous. Gender identity is an *internal* feeling, by contrast with gender roles, which are established externally for that person by others and are reflected in rearing, training, dressing, and societal expectations.

Many individuals stretch, bend, and rebel against their assigned gender roles, but even so, for most people, gender identity and gender role are identical. But some feel that their gender identity and gender role are totally contradictory. A child may have a girl's external GENITALS, for example, and have been dressed, trained, and raised as a girl, but still maintain the inner conviction of being a boy, and vice versa. Such feelings go under a variety of names, including *transsexualism, eonism, psychic hermaphroditism, metatropism,* and *severe intersexuality.* Psychiatrists sometimes class them as *gender identity disorders.* Many people in the gay and lesbian communities, however, react strongly against characterization of such feelings as *disorders.*

Such gender identity conflicts go far beyond the nonconformity of someone labeled a "tomboy" or "sissy" and are unrelated to suspected feelings of inadequacy about meeting societal expectations or to desires to have the presumed social advantages accorded to the other sex. People with differing gender identities feel that they *are,* in their innermost beings, a gender other than that assigned to them by society and experience intense distress over that assignment. Such feelings often emerge in childhood and involve rejection of clothing and activities thought proper for their assigned gender. Such children often insist that they will grow up to be the sex they feel themselves to be. Just recently, researchers have found some differences in the brains of transsexuals, which may be an underlying physical basis for such feelings.

Children with gender identity disorders can have significant social problems, often leading to or associated with DEPRESSION, SEPARATION ANXIETY, or general withdrawal. After PUBERTY, many develop a HOMOSEXUAL orientation and adopt the clothes of the "opposite"—for them, the true—sex, in what is termed *cross-dressing.* In adulthood, some feel so strongly about their gender identity that they undergo a sex change operation, called *sex reassignment surgery.* (See HOMOSEXUALITY; MENTAL DISORDERS.)

General Equivalency Diploma (GED), a certificate of HIGH SCHOOL equivalency given to a school DROPOUT who later takes and passes a series of TESTS OF GENERAL EDUCATIONAL DEVELOPMENT.

general practitioner (GP), a type of PHYSICIAN who provides medical care to people of all ages and either sex, today more commonly called a *family physician.* A general practitioner treats a wide variety of health problems, sometimes (especially in rural areas) treating children and women during PREGNANCY, though a patient having special problems will be referred to a specialist, such as an OBSTETRICIAN-GYNECOLOGIST.

gene therapy, a new, still largely experimental approach to treating GENETIC DISORDERS that involves inserting into the body (by various means) cells containing healthy genes to replace defective ones. Perhaps in the future this type of therapy will include actually manipulating the body's genes to correct defects. Though such approaches are still in their infancy, they hold great promise potentially for all genetic disorders. Among the diseases on which early experiments have focused are CYSTIC FIBROSIS; MUSCULAR DYSTROPHY; and *severe combined immunodeficiency,* a disorder for which the therapy was first tried in humans, with early indications of success (see IMMUNE SYSTEM). One main problem is to find means of delivering the genes to the body in sufficient amounts but in ways that will bypass the normal defenses of the body's immune system. The distance can be great between experiment and practical therapy, but new approaches and applications for gene therapy seem to come almost every day. Concerned families will want to keep in touch with breaking events, not only through newspapers and government health information lines, but also by joining one or more of the organizations relating to the particular genetic disorder affecting them.

genetic counseling, a guidance service, often offered by a PHYSICIAN with special training in medical genetics, that helps prospective parents assess their risk of having a child with a GENETIC DISORDER—or the likelihood that a disorder in one child might appear in other, later children. Counselors explain the pattern of GENETIC INHERITANCE that leads to such disorders and give parents the background information necessary for deciding whether or not to try to have a child.

People with a personal, family, ethnic, or racial history of genetic abnormalities are prime candidates for genetic counseling. So are older couples; those who are near BLOOD RELATIONS; those who have had a previous MISCARRIAGE or infant death; and those whose work exposes them to ENVIRONMENTAL HAZARDS that might adversely affect a pregnancy. All have a higher-than-normal risk of bearing a child with a genetic disorder.

Generally genetic counseling starts with the preparation of a PEDIGREE (see COMMON PEDIGREE SYMBOLS AND SAMPLE OF A PEDIGREE on page 456), a medical family tree that shows the inheritance patterns of traits and disorders in both families. If a couple had a previous child born with genetic problems, counselors might arrange for analysis of the CHROMOSOMES of the parents and child, seeking to identify abnormalities that might affect a future birth. In doing so, they would draw on the information currently being built up by scientific researchers as to the location and makeup of the tens of thousands of genes in the human body, including specific genes, called *markers,* linked with known disorders. Counselors would also explore environmental influences that might have contributed to the abnormality, such as exposure to radiation, injury, MALNUTRITION, or drugs (see DRUG REACTIONS AND INTERACTIONS; DRUG ABUSE).

Genetic counselors also advise on GENETIC SCREENING, including the variety of PRENATAL TESTS by which a FETUS can be tested to see if it has inherited some major genetic disorders. If so, the counselors can explain the outlook for a child with that abnormality and describe what special treatment might be necessary, so the couple can decide whether to prepare for a SPECIAL CHILD or have a selective ABORTION. In some cases counselors might also explore with the couple other alternatives, such as ADOPTION, ARTIFICIAL INSEMINATION using a donor's sperm, or even SURROGATE MOTHERHOOD.

FOR HELP AND FURTHER INFORMATION

National Society of Genetic Counselors (NSGC)
Division of Medical Genetics
Michael Reese Hospital and Medical Center
31st Street and Lakeshore Drive
Chicago, IL 60616
Beth A. Fine, President
Organization of professional genetic counselors; publishes quarterly newsletter *Perspectives in Genetic Counseling,* quarterly *Journal of Genetic Counseling,* and annual *NSGC Membership Directory*; provides referrals on written request; does not maintain or disseminate information on specific genetic disorders.

National Fragile X Foundation, 800–688–8765. Publishes *Genetic Counseling Issues and Information.* (For full group information, see FRAGILE X SYNDROME.)

OTHER RESOURCES

The Tentative Pregnancy: How Amniocentesis Changes the Experience of Motherhood. Barbara K. Rothman. Norton, 1993.

Before Birth: Prenatal Testing for Genetic Disease. Elena O. Nightingale and Melissa Goodman. Harvard University Press, 1990.

Backdoor to Eugenics. Troy Duster. Routledge, 1990.

(See also GENETIC DISORDERS; GENETIC SCREENING.)

genetic disorder, an abnormal trait or disease that results from mistakes in an individual's "genetic blueprint," such as a problem in the DNA coding of the genes or errors in duplication of the chromosomes. The defective gene may have been received from one or both parents, as part of the individual's GENETIC INHERITANCE, or it may stem from a MUTATION in the genetic material in the SPERM or egg (OVUM) that joined to form the new individual at the point of FERTILIZATION.

Disorders that result from a single gene or gene pair are known as *unifactorial disorders.* If the problem is on the pair of SEX CHROMOSOMES, that almost always means that it is on the X CHROMOSOME. Such disorders are called X-LINKED, *sex-linked,* or *sex-limited,* because they usually affect only male children, having been passed on by mothers who are usually unaffected CARRIERS. Among such X-linked diseases are HEMOPHILIA, COLOR BLINDNESS, MUSCULAR DYSTROPHY (Duchenne), G6PD DEFICIENCY, FRAGILE X SYNDROME, and spinal ATAXIA.

Single-gene disorders that appear on any of the other 22 pairs of chromosomes (AUTOSOMES) are called autosomal disorders. Some are DOMINANT, meaning that they need only be passed on by one parent to affect the child. Among these AUTOSOMAL DOMINANT disorders are HUNTINGTON'S CHOREA, MARFAN'S SYNDROME, NEUROFIBROMATOSIS, ACHONDROPLASIA, OSTEOGENESIS IMPERFECTA, and POLYCYSTIC KIDNEY DISEASE. A parent who carries the gene for an autosomal dominant disorder has a 50 percent chance of passing it on to a child.

Other single-gene disorders are RECESSIVE, meaning that a child must receive the gene from both parents to get the disorder. Among these AUTOSOMAL RECESSIVE disorders are CYSTIC FIBROSIS, PHENYLKETONURIA, sickle cell ANEMIA, GALACTOSEMIA, some LIPID STORAGE DISEASES, such as *Gaucher disease* and *Tay-Sachs disease,* Friedreich's ATAXIA, and Hurler syndrome (see MUCOPOLYSACCHARIDOSES). If both parents carry the gene for an autosomal recessive disorder, they have a 25 percent chance of having an affected child, with a 50 percent chance that their child will be a carrier of the recessive gene.

A great many genetic disorders, however, are not caused by a single gene, but by a mixture of various genes affected by environmental influences. Among these MULTIFACTORIAL DISORDERS are CLEFT LIP AND PALATE, CLUBFOOT, neural tube defects such as SPINA BIFIDA, EPILEPSY, DIABETES, ARTHRITIS, and CONGENITAL DISLOCATION OF THE HIP. Sorting out the relative importance of genetic and environmental factors in such diseases is extremely difficult, but genetic researchers are making ever more accurate estimates of the heritability of these diseases—the likelihood that they will appear in the next generation, apart from environmental effects. Such information is of great value in GENETIC COUNSELING. Serious genetic disorders can also result from CHROMOSOMAL ABNORMALITIES.

FOR HELP AND FURTHER INFORMATION

National Maternal and Child Health Clearinghouse (NMCHC), 703–821–8955. Provides information to public and professionals about general child and maternal health and specific genetic diseases; helps parents locate mutual-support groups; publishes *Understanding DNA Testing: A Basic Guide for Families, Genetic Support Groups: Volunteers and Professionals as Partners, Medical Genetics: A Legal Frontier, Genetic Family History: An Aid to Better Health in Adoptive Children,* and bibliographies. (For full group information, see PREGNANCY.)

National Institute of Child Health and Human Development (NICHD), 301–496–5133. Publishes *Genetics and Teratology.* (For full group information, see PREGNANCY.)

Alliance of Genetic Support Groups
35 Wisconsin Circle, Suite 440
Chevy Chase, MD 20815–7015
301–652–5553; 800–336-GENE [336–4363]
Fax: 301–654–0171
Coalition of support groups, professionals, and others concerned with genetic disorders; seeks to shape public policy; provides technical assistance to new and existing genetic support groups; publishes various materials, including monthly *ALERT, Directory of National Genetic Voluntary Organizations, Bibliography: Genetics for High School and College Students, Health Insurance Resource Guide, Peer Support Training Resource Guide, Chapter Resource Guide, Needs Assessment for Support Groups, Empty Pocket Syndrome: How to Get Funding, Starting a Support Group* (information packet), *Integrating Consumers into the Regional Genetics Networks, Informed Consent: Participation in Genetic Research Studies,* and *Guidelines for Media Reporting in the Genetic Age.*

March of Dimes Birth Defects Foundation (MDBDF), 914–428–7100. Publishes booklet *Genetic Counseling,* pamphlet *Genetic Testing and Gene Therapy,* and video *Our Genetic Heritage.* (For full group information, see BIRTH DEFECTS.)

National Organization for Rare Disorders (NORD), 800–999–6673. (For full group information, see RARE DISORDERS.)

National Foundation for Jewish Genetic Diseases (NFJGD)
250 Park Avenue, Suite 1000
New York, NY 10177
212–371–1030
Fax: 212–319–5808
George Crohn, Jr., President
Organization concerned with genetic diseases that particularly affect Jews; provides information; publishes fact sheet *You Have a Right to Know. . .About Jewish Genetic Diseases.*

Hereditary Disease Foundation (HDF), 310–458–4183. (For full group information, see HUNTINGTON'S DISEASE.)

National Clearinghouse for Alcohol and Drug Abuse Information (NCADI), 301–468–2600. Publishes *The Genetics of Alcoholism* and *Screening for Alcoholism.* (For full group information, see HELP AGAINST SUBSTANCE ABUSE on page 680).

OTHER RESOURCES

GENERAL WORKS

The Encyclopedia of Genetic Disorders and Birth Defects. Mark D. Ludman and James Wyndbrandt. Facts on File, 1990.
The Family Genetic Sourcebook. Benjamin A. Pierce. Wiley, 1990.
Family Diseases: Are You At Risk. Myra Vanderpool Gormley. Genealogical Publishing, 1989.

(See also GENETIC COUNSELING; BIRTH DEFECTS; PEDIGREE; PREGNANCY; specific diseases.)

genetic inheritance, the set of information that is passed from parents to child and that determines the physical characteristics of the unique individual created at FERTILIZATION. The basic units of inheritance are *genes,* which are DNA molecules in a cell's nucleus organized in linear sequence on 23 thread-like pairs of structures called chromosomes. One pair, the SEX CHROMOSOMES, determines the new being's gender. A normal female has two X chromosomes, a normal male has an X and a Y. The other 22 chromosome pairs, called AUTOSOMES, carry the majority of the being's genetic inheritance.

The complete set of genes for an individual is set at the point of CONCEPTION, when the father's SPERM and the mother's egg (OVUM) each contribute half of the paired genetic material for the new being. When the sperm and eggs first form, the chromosomes in the nucleus of each are first duplicated, then divided, creating four "daughter cells." This cell-dividing process, called *meiosis,* results in each daughter cell having half of the chromosomes needed by a new being—and each having a different selection of the genetic material. These differing selections are then incorporated into each parent's sperm and eggs.

Later, when a sperm and egg join, the half-selection of chromosomes from each parent combine to make a unique new being. The fertilized egg then created receives 50 percent of its genes from its mother and 50 percent from its father. And because the genetic inheritance of both parents was formed in the same way, 25 percent of the genes derived from each of its four grandparents.

The pattern of genes in that fertilized egg will be duplicated over and over as part of the nucleus of every cell in the new being. Given the tens of thousands of genes involved, it is not surprising that errors sometimes occur, which are passed on to the new being. Errors in the cell-division process of meiosis give rise to CHROMOSOMAL ABNORMALITIES; inherited mistakes in the coding of the genes themselves lead to GENETIC DISORDERS; some abnormalities arise from a spontaneous change in the genes of sperm or egg, called a *mutation.*

Most genetic information, however, is passed on normally. How the new pattern of genes will be expressed in the new being depends on the nature of each gene and its relation to other genes. Genes operate in pairs, with the paired genes for each site being called *alleles.* If a pair is identical, the person is called a *homozygote* for that gene; if the paired genes differ, the person is a *heterozygote.* If one gene is DOMINANT, it will affect the individual no matter what the other gene is. If either of the paired genes for eye color is brown, for example, the baby will have brown eyes, since brown eyes are dominant. If a gene is RECESSIVE, it will affect the individual only if its paired gene is identical. For a baby to have blue eyes, a recessive trait, both parents must give it a gene for blue eyes.

The exception to that is the genes that appear on the sex chromosomes. The Y chromosome is small and carries little genetic information apart from that relating to male sexual development; but the X chromosome carries a full complement of genetic information. So if a recessive gene is on a male's X chromosome, it will affect him, because no paired dominant gene is present; the same gene on a female's X chromosome would not affect her if the paired gene was dominant, only if both were recessive. That partly explains why many men, but few women, are partially bald; the gene relating to baldness is recessive and resides on the X chromosome. Traits and disorders that affect mostly males, because they appear on the X chromosome, are often called X-LINKED, *sex-linked,* or *sex-limited.* Traits and disorders that are controlled by a single gene are called unifactorial (see GENETIC DISORDERS); those that are affected by multiple genes, as well as by the individual's environment, are called MULTIFACTORIAL.

Each gene occupies a specific site on a particular chromosome, and considerable scientific research is being focused on mapping the position of genes, especially noting the site of malfunctioning genes that cause common genetic disorders. Such sites, or *genetic markers,* can then be used to identify carriers, people who though healthy themselves carry defective genes and could pass them on to their children. Researchers are exploring ways to correct such defects in the future, using developing techniques of GENE THERAPY. Physicians use genetic markers in GENETIC SCREENING, attempting to identify whether or not a FETUS has inherited a defective gene. All this new information has given rise, in recent decades, to GENETIC COUNSELING, a service that attempts to advise prospective parents on genetic risks.

OTHER RESOURCES

Voices in Your Blood: Discovering Identity Through Family History. G. G. Vandagriff. Andrews and McMeel, 1993.

Nature's Thumbprint: The New Genetics of Personality. Peter B. Neubauer and Alexander Neubauer. Addison-Wesley, 1990.

Discover It Yourself: Where Did You Get Those Eyes? Kay Cooper. Avon, 1993. For children.

(See also GENETIC DISORDERS; AUTOSOMAL DOMINANT; AUTOSOMAL RECESSIVE; X-LINKED; MULTIFACTORIAL DISORDER; also PEDIGREE; also GENERAL PARENTING RESOURCES on page 634, under "On family history.")

genetic screening, a range of TESTS aimed at identifying or ruling out possible GENETIC DISORDERS or BIRTH DEFECTS. Many are PRENATAL TESTS, given to women during PREGNANCY, to see if the FETUS has identifiable birth defects. Tests such as AMNIOCENTESIS, CHORIONIC VILLUS SAMPLING, CORDOCENTESUS, or ALPHA FETOPROTEIN generally involve taking samples of material shed by the FETUS and analyzing the genetic content for clues as to possible abnormalities. Other prenatal tests, such as FETOSCOPY or ULTRASOUND scans, look directly or indirectly at the fetus for visual signs of defects. If abnormalities are identified, parents may choose to prepare for a SPECIAL CHILD, attempt correction of the defect through IN UTERO SURGERY, or terminate the pregnancy with an ABORTION. Differing medical conditions and family histories call for the use of different tests, each with their own strengths and weaknesses, but no test, nor all the known tests combined, can identify all possible birth defects. A newer, still highly experimental technique, EMBRYO BIOPSY, is used in some forms of REPRODUCTIVE TECHNOLOGY to check a laboratory-fertilized embryo for abnormalities before it is implanted into the woman's uterus.

However, other kinds of genetic screening tests are given to prospective parents, as part of GENETIC COUNSELING, to see if they are carrying CHROMOSOMAL ABNORMALITIES or defective genes. Sometimes a child with a genetic disorder will also be tested for information that might shed light on whether a later child might have the same disorder. Discoveries of new *genetic markers,* identified with specific disorders, seem to be made weekly. As knowledge about these markers accumulates, tests are being developed to provide information about a person's GENETIC INHERITANCE. For example, the 1993 discovery of a gene linked to HUNTINGTON'S CHOREA has allowed development of a new test to tell whether or not a person carries the disease. Previously many people did not know they carried the gene until they were adults who had already had children and had possibly passed the defective gene on to them.

FOR HELP AND FURTHER INFORMATION

American College of Obstetricians and Gynecologists (ACOG), 202–638–5577. Publishes *Prenatal Testing for Genetic Disorders* and *Maternal Serum Screening for Birth Defects.* (For full group information, see PREGNANCY.)

National Fragile X Foundation, 800–688–8765. Publishes *Listing of DNA/Genetic Testing Centers.* (For full group information, see FRAGILE X SYNDROME.)

National Maternal and Child Health Clearinghouse (NMCHC), 703–821–8955. Publishes *State Laws and Regulations Governing Newborn Screening, Legal Liability and Quality Assurance in Newborn Screening, National Newborn Screening Report—1991, Final Report 1994, Newborn Screening for Sickle Cell Disease and Other Hemoglobinopathies*, and *Newborn Screening for Sickle Cell Disease: Issues and Implications.* (For full group information, see PREGNANCY.)

Pregnancy and Infant Loss Center (PILC), 612–473–9372. Publishes *Difficult Decisions* and *A Time to Decide, A Time to Heal: For Parents Making Difficult Decisions About Babies They Love*, both on prenatal diagnosis of a serious medical problems. (For full group information, see DEATH AND DYING.)

National Institute of Child Health and Human Development (NICHD), 301–496–5133. (For full group information, see PREGNANCY.)

Council for Responsible Genetics (CRG)
5 Upland Road, Suite 3
Cambridge, MA 02140
617–868–0870
Fax: 617–491–5344
Wendy McGoodwin, Executive Director
Organization focusing on the social implications of biotechnology and new reproductive technology; publishes newsletter *GeneWATCH* and various position papers.

(See also GENETIC COUNSELING; GENETIC DISORDERS; MEDICAL TESTS.)

genital warts, growths in the genital area caused by infection with one or more of the over 70 *human papillomaviruses* (HPV's); a kind of SEXUALLY TRANSMITTED DISEASE that needs to be dealt with quickly, because genital warts have been linked to an increased risk of some kinds of CANCERS, especially of the CERVIX, but also sometimes of the PENIS. Also called *concylomata acuminata* or *venereal warts*, genital warts often grow during PREGNANCY, making urination and later DELIVERY difficult. In addition, a child can be infected during the CHILDBIRTH process, developing warts in the throat (*laryngeal papillomatosis*), a possibly life-threatening condition sometimes requiring corrective surgery. The American Social Health Association estimates that 750,000 people develop genital warts each year in the United States alone.

Within three weeks to three months of contact with an infected person, small, hard, visible spots develop in many infected people. However, the National Institute of Allergy and Infectious Diseases found in one study that almost half of the infected women had no symptoms. Genital warts are generally diagnosed by visual examination, sometimes including a *colposcopy*, by means of a lighted magnifying instrument; sometimes a BIOPSY of cervical tissue may be taken and analyzed, along with other laboratory tests.

Once diagnosed, genital warts are treated with a chemical solution (except during PREGNANCY, since the medication can cause BIRTH DEFECTS) or the antiviral drug interferon, or sometimes are removed by freezing, burning, and if necessary surgery, including LASER SURGERY. However, the virus can persist after treatment, so those infected should check for recurrence of genital warts. In some cases the body's IMMUNE SYSTEM is able to fight off HPV without treatment. (For help and further information, including how to avoid infection, see SEXUALLY TRANSMITTED DISEASES.)

genitals, the reproductive organs, especially the external sex organs. In the male, these include the PENIS and the pouch called a *scrotum* containing the two TESTES (see REPRODUCTIVE SYSTEM). In the female, these are generally called the VULVA, and include the CLITORIS and the opening of the VAGINA, partly blocked by tissue called the HYMEN, enclosed by the LABIA, two sets of "lips," the outer (*labia majora*) and the inner (*labia minora*). The condition of having underdeveloped genitals is called HYPOGENITALISM.

genius, a person of extremely high intellectual ability, who has made or is considered likely to make a significant contribution in one or more fields. Despite the lack of RELIABILITY of INTELLIGENCE TESTS, a person with an IQ of 140 or over is often considered to be a genius. A child whose IQ is in that "genius" range is usually considered a GIFTED CHILD.

Gesell Preschool Test, a widely used, individually administered DEVELOPMENTAL SCREENING TEST, for assessing the emotional, physical, and behavioral development of children 2½ to 6 years old. The test includes various tasks (subtests), among them:

- Building increasingly more complex structures with cubes (sometimes following a demonstration), which tests for fine MOTOR SKILLS, EYE-HAND COORDINATION, ATTENTION SPAN, and other skills.
- An interview that tests accuracy of personal and family knowledge as well as LANGUAGE SKILLS.
- A pencil-and-paper test, in which a child is to write her or his name, which tests for DOMINANCE, NEUROMUSCULAR DEVELOPMENT, fine motor skills, and TASK-APPROPRIATE behavior; that is followed by tasks involving copying various geometric designs, writing numbers, and completing a picture of a partially drawn person.
- Naming animals and talking about favorite activities, which indicates attention and level of interests.
- Understanding prepositions, which tests both language skills and understanding of SPATIAL RELATIONS.
- Repeating numbers, which tests various memory and attention skills.

Other tasks include a picture vocabulary test, a "color forms" test to assess recognition of shapes, a formboard test, and other motor tests.

For children four-and-a-half, several other tests are added, forming the *Gesell School Readiness Test—Complete Battery*. Additional tasks include copying more complex forms, a labeling and naming exercise focusing on right or left orientation, and two visual tests, one involving matching cards and the other requiring the child to draw designs from memory after being shown cards. In the course of the test, the specially trained examiners make various notes about the child's behavior, including behavior not directly related to the task (called OVERFLOW BEHAVIOR). They then compare these behaviors with a variety of *developmental schedules* that outline what is considered the age levels for behaviors in each of the areas listed, based on observed NORMS in children's behavior. The child's behavioral scores are summarized to give an overall DEVELOPMENTAL AGE (DA). The school readiness test is generally used to assess a child's readiness for KINDERGARTEN or promotion to the next grade or to reassess grade level placement.

Many questions have been raised about the RELIABILITY and predictive VALIDITY of the Gesell tests. Children develop in highly individual and variable ways, and many children assigned a low developmental age turn out to have visual or other undiagnosed perceptual problems (as in much childhood testing). In addition, as Samuel Meisels commented in his *Developmental Screening in Early Childhood*, published under the auspices of the National Association for the Education of Young Children: "Classification data concerning predictive validity of these tests [including Gesell] is inadequate. As a result, they...cannot be recommended for use in a developmental screening program." Many others disagree, and in fact the Gesell materials are widely used. But a parent whose child runs into difficulty in school placement because of a developmental age that is too low should certainly explore, protest, retest, and do whatever is appropriate to right a situation, if it seems wrong.

OTHER RESOURCES

The Baby Boards: A Parent's Guide to Preschool and Primary School Entrance Tests. Jacqueline Robinson. Arco, 1988. Gives advice on preparing a child for a Gesell test.

(See TEST; INTELLIGENCE TEST; ADVOCACY.)

gestation, the period during which a FETUS is developing in the UTERUS, from CONCEPTION to CHILDBIRTH. If a baby is PREMATURE, its stage of development is indicated by its GESTATIONAL AGE, the number of weeks from the beginning of the mother's last MENSTRUATION. The average length of gestation is 266 days (38 weeks) from the date of FERTILIZATION. But since the date of fertilization is unknown or uncertain, doctors traditionally calculate the DUE DATE as being 280 days (40 weeks) from the beginning of the mother's last menstruation.

gestational age, the age of a FETUS still in the UTERUS or of a PREMATURE newborn, indicating the number of weeks of development, usually measured by physicians as the number of weeks from the beginning date of the mother's last MENSTRUATION (see DUE DATE; GESTATION). Gestational age is important because premature infants are less fully developed, and the younger they are, the more vulnerable to certain kinds of disorders or conditions. SLEEP APNEA, for example, occurs in about 35 to 50 percent of premature infants, but it occurs among nearly 90 percent of those who are below 29 weeks in gestational age (as opposed to the normal 40 weeks).

Gifted and Talented Children's Act (Public Law 95–561), a 1978 federal law intended to provide for the special educational needs of GIFTED CHILDREN; it is unevenly implemented because of widely differing definitions of "gifted."

gifted child, a child who has very superior abilities, especially in academic areas, but also sometimes in artistic or athletic fields. It is widely agreed that such children have SPECIAL NEEDS and benefit most from ADAPTED EDUCATION programs. However, the definition of "gifted" varies widely. The classic early description focused on a gifted child's special combination of high cognitive development, intellectual superiority, creativity, and motivation that set him or her off from peers and that give the child the potential of making significant contributions to society. The GIFTED AND TALENTED CHILDREN'S ACT of 1978 had a wider and more controversial definition of gifted and talented youngsters as:

> Children and, whenever applicable, youth, who are identified at the preschool, elementary, or secondary level as possessing demonstrated or potential abilities that give evidence of high performance capabilities in areas such as intellectual, creative, specific academic, or leadership ability, or in the performing and visual arts, and who by reason thereof, require services or activities not ordinarily provided by the school.

Though differing definitions and inadequate funding have meant that federal programs have not been made widely available, parents who believe that their child truly is gifted in one or more areas may still want to contact local school officials to get help in planning the child's program from PRESCHOOL on. They may also want to contact one of the organizations listed in this entry or the child-study unit of some nearby university. When necessary, they may need to become strong advocates for their children (see ADVOCACY).

Children develop at widely differing rates, however, and parents should beware of putting pressure on a child they proudly think is "gifted." Conversely, parents should not fear that their child is too precocious or "learning too fast." Both pushing a child and holding a child back can be harmful, and parents will be wise to let a child's talents develop naturally, providing all the stimulation and experiences that a child seems ready and eager for, without overwhelming the child. They will also have to be sensitive to the hazards of SIBLING RIVALRY, if other children in the family do not show similar gifts, and to the social problems faced by gifted children in finding friends of their own age and abilities.

In general, parents of bright children—whether or not they fit others' definition of "gifted"—may have to feel their way since opinions differ strongly about which approaches are best for gifted children: moving them into separate programs designed only for high-ability students, an approach that can have the hazard of cutting them off from many of their peers (see TRACKING), or keeping them in regular classrooms but providing them with special ENRICHMENT, which risks closing off the highest development of their potential.

FOR HELP AND FURTHER INFORMATION

National Association for Gifted Children (NAGC)
1707 L Street NW Suite 550
Washington, DC 20036
202–785–4268
Peter C. Rosenstein, Executive Director
Organization of parents and educators concerned with gifted children; provides information; advises on curriculum development and special programming; includes divisions on creativity, curriculum studies, future studies, global awareness, counseling and guidance, parent and community, early childhood, professional development, research and evaluation, special populations, special schools/programs, computers and technology, visual and performing arts, and conceptual foundations; publishes various materials, including:

- Newsletter *Communique, Gifted Child Quarterly, Directory of Special Schools/Programs,* and *"How to" Guide for Starting an NAGC Affiliate.*
- Parent Information Guides: *Suggestions for Stimulating the Minds of Infants* (birth to eighteen months), *Questions Most Asked on Identification of the Gifted/Talented, Some Thoughts on Acceleration, 25 Suggestions for Parents of Able Children,* and *Sharing Responsibility.*
- Books for parents: *Parents' Guide to Raising a Gifted Child; The Most-Asked Questions About Gifted Children; Bringing Out the Best; Guiding the Gifted Child; Smart Girls, Gifted Women; The Survival Guide for Parents of Gifted Kids; Underachievement Syndrome; Creative Talents: Their Nature, Uses and Development;* and *Mentor Relationships.*
- Books for children and teens: *Gifted Kids Speak Out, Perfectionism: What's Bad About Being Too Good,* and *The Gifted Kids Survival Guide* (three versions: one through age ten; another and a sequel for ages eleven through eighteen).
- Professional materials and research briefs.

Council for Exceptional Children (CEC),
800–328–0272. (For full group information, see HELP ON LEARNING AND EDUCATION on page 659.) Includes The Association for the Gifted (TAG), which publishes quarterlies *TAG Update* and *Journal for the Education of the Gifted,* and other materials. CEC also publishes:

- General works: *Gifted Education and the Middle School, Summer Programs for Gifted Students* (computer disk), and special report *Educating Exceptional Children.*
- For parents: *Your Gifted Child: How to Recognize and Develop the Special Talents in Your Child from Birth to Age Seven, College Planning for Gifted Students,* 2nd ed., and video *Being Gifted: The Gift.*
- Numerous special-topic reports, such as *Helping Your Highly Gifted Child, How Parents Can Support Gifted Children, Nurturing Giftedness in Young Children, Readings and Resources for Parents and Teachers of Gifted Children, Should Gifted Students Be Grade-Advanced?, Supporting Gifted Education Through Advocacy, Underachieving Gifted Students, Nurturing Social-Emotional Development of Gifted Students, Personal Computers Help Gifted Students Work Smart, ADHD and Children Who Are Gifted, College Planning for Gifted and Talented Youth, Discovering Interests and Talents Through Summer Experiences, Giftedness and the Gifted: What's It All About?, Guiding the Gifted Reader,* and *Helping Adolescents Adjust to Giftedness.*
- Materials on school reform and for teachers and counselors.

Gifted Child Society (GCS)
190 Rock Road
Glen Rock, NJ 07452
201–444–6530;
Parent Information line: 900–773-PING [773–7464]
Fax: 444–9099
Gina Ginsberg Riggs, Executive Director
Organization concerned with gifted children; acts as advocate; sponsors Saturday enrichment classes, special preschool programs, and Whiz Kids programs for multiethnic gifted children; provides support services, such as testing and counseling for gifted children, including the learning disabled; publishes various materials, including semiannual newsletter, periodic directory, and advocacy packets.

American Association for Gifted Children (AAGC)
1121 West Main Street, Suite 100
Durham, NC 27701
919–683–1400
Fax: 919–683–1742
E-mail: judyh@iluvatar.tip.duke.edu
Internet Website: http://www.jayi.com/jayi/aagc
Irving Alexander, President
Organization providing resources on developing the talents of gifted children; seeks to educate public; publishes newsletter and working papers.

Center for Talented Youth (CTY)
Johns Hopkins University
3400 North Charles Street
Baltimore, MD 21218
410–516–0337
Fax: 410–516–0804

Accelerated program for academically talented students at eleven residential sites; performs annual Talent Search; operates Young Students Program for children ages seven through eleven; offers information, advice, and advocacy; provides scholarships for disadvantaged students; with Stanford University's Education Program for Gifted Youth, offers Distance Learning Project (DLP), providing at-home computer-guided instruction with tutorial assistance available by e-mail and phone; publishes newsletter *Imagine: Opportunities and Resources for Academically Talented Youth* and other materials, such as *Identifying and Cultivating Talent in Preschool and Elementary School Children, Educational Resources for Academically Talented Adolescents,* and *Program Opportunities for Academically Talented Students.*

Creative Education Foundation (CEF), 716–675–3181. Publishes *Awakening Your Child's Natural Genius: Enhancing Curiosity, Creativity and Learning Ability.* (For full group information, see HELP ON LEARNING AND EDUCATION on page 659.)

ERIC (Educational Resources Information Center) Clearinghouse on Disabilities and Gifted Education, 800–328–0272. (For full group information, see HELP ON LEARNING AND EDUCATION on page 659.)

National Association of Private Schools for Exceptional Children (NAPSEC), 202–408–3338. (For full group information, see HELP FOR SPECIAL CHILDREN on page 689.)

ONLINE RESOURCES

Parents' Information Network (America Online: PIN) Online forums and libraries cover gifted children. (For full information, see GENERAL PARENTING RESOURCES on page 634.)

OTHER RESOURCES

FOR PARENTS

Keys to Parenting the Gifted Child. Sylvia B. Rimm. Barron's, 1994.

Your Gifted Student: A Guide for Parents. Joan F. Smutny and others. Facts on File, 1993.

Diamonds in the Dust: Discover and Develop Your Child's Gifts, 2nd ed. Jackie Mallis. MultiMedia, 1992.

The Joys and Challenges of Raising a Gifted Child. Susan K. Golant. Prentice Hall, 1991.

The Survival Guide for Parents of Gifted Kids: How to Understand, Live with, and Stick Up for Your Gifted Child. Sally Yahnke Walker. Free Spirit, 1991.

Your Gifted Child: How to Recognize and Develop the Special Talents in Your Child from Birth to Age Seven. Joan F. Smutny and others. Ballantine, 1991.

RESOURCE GUIDES

Second Annual Directory of Programs for Gifted Children. Graduate Group, 1994.

Educational Opportunity Guide, 1994: A Directory of Programs for the Gifted. Daniel Trollinger, ed. Duke University, 1994.

Bringing Out the Best: A Resource Guide for Parents of Young Gifted Children, rev. ed. Jacqulyn Saunders and Pamela Espeland. Free Spirit, 1991.

ON LEGAL CONCERNS

Gifted Children and Legal Issues in Education: Parents' Stories of Hope. Frances A. Karnes and Ronald G. Marquardt. Ohio Psychological Press, 1991.

Gifted Children and the Law: Mediation, Due Process and Court Cases. Frances A. Karnes and Ronald G. Marquardt. Ohio Psychological Press, 1991.

FOR CHILDREN

The Gifted Kids Survival Guide (For Ages 10 & Under). Judy Galbraith. Free Spirit Publishing Inc., 1984. Children's version (preschool-grade 5).

Archibald Frisby. Michael Chesworth. Farrar, Straus & Giroux, 1994. Fiction.

Legend of the Nine Talents. Joan Hutson. St. Paul, 1992. Fiction.

The Puzzled Prodigy. Jeffrey A. Nesbit. Victor/SP Publications, 1992. Fiction.

FOR PRETEENS AND TEENS

The Gifted Kids Survival Guide: A Teen Handbook. Judy Galbraith, M.A and Jim Delisle, Ph.D. Free Spirit Publishing Inc., 1996. Teens version (grades 6–12).

Knee Holes. Jerome Brooks. Orchard/Watts, 1992. Fiction.

Maizon at Blue Hill. Jacqueline Woodson. Delacorte, 1992. Fiction.

ON GIFTED CHILDREN GROWN UP

The Gifted Group in Later Maturity. Carole K. Holahan and others. Stanford University Press, 1995.

Genius Revisited: High IQ Children Grown Up. Rena Subotnik, ed. Ablex, 1993.

Terman's Kids: The Groundbreaking Study of How the Gifted Grow Up. Joel N. Shurkin. Little, Brown, 1992.

Gifted Children Growing Up. Joan Freeman. Heinemann, 1991.

BACKGROUND WORKS

Parent Education: Parents As Partners. Dorothy Knopper. Open Space, 1994.

The Drama of the Gifted Child: The Search for True Self, rev. ed. Alice Miller. Basic, 1994. Originally titled: *Prisoners of Childhood.*

Smart Kids: How Academic Talents Are Developed and Nurtured in America. William G. Durden and Arne E. Tangherlini. Hogrefe and Huber, 1993.

Exceptionally Gifted Children. Miraca U. Gross. Routledge, 1993.

Child Prodigies and Exceptional Early Achievement. John Radford. Free Press/Macmillan, 1990.

gingivitis, a mild inflammation of the gums (*gingiva*), in which they become reddish, swollen, tender, and prone to bleed, especially during brushing. Gingivitis normally results from infection due to PLAQUE, which has collected on teeth because of inadequate cleaning. Local irritation from too much brushing or flossing or MALOCCLUSION can also lead to gingivitis, as can some nutritional diseases, such as SCURVY, and some types of medications that cut saliva flow, such as antihistamines. Because of hormonal changes in the body, pregnant women and women taking BIRTH CONTROL PILLS are susceptible to gingivitis. So are people with DIABETES, including perhaps 20 percent of teenagers who developed insulin-dependent diabetes mellitus (IDDM) as children.

Treatment of gingivitis involves regular, careful cleaning of the teeth by the dentist, at least once a year. If gingivitis is untreated, the gums loosen their hold on the teeth and form pockets where plaque collects. Eventually, infection attacks both the bone and tissues surrounding the teeth, resulting in an advanced stage of gingivitis called *periodontitis*, in which teeth are loosened and may be lost. Dentists or specialist PERIODONTISTS may still be able to save some teeth by cutting away diseased gum tissue, a procedure called *gingivectomy*, to see if healthy gum tissue will grow back around the tooth. If that fails, periodontists may attempt to rebuild the tooth support through a combination of bone-like laboratory materials and grafts of healthy gum tissue from elsewhere. Though often associated with adults, gingivitis can also affect adolescents and cause serious damage and premature loss of teeth. (See TEETH AND DENTAL PROBLEMS.)

glucose, a type of sugar that forms the body's main form of energy (also called *dextrose*). People with DIABETES lack the HORMONE *insulin* needed to convert the sugar to usable form; as a result, glucose builds up in the blood, leading to *hyperglycemia* and sometimes a diabetic COMA. People under insulin treatment can sometimes have too little glucose in the blood, a condition called *hypoglycemia* or *insulin shock*. To prevent either of these extremes, many people with diabetes carefully monitor the levels of glucose in their blood, often using a HOME MEDICAL TEST.

Glucose is often stored in the body as the CARBOHYDRATE *glycogen*. Problems in converting glycogen into usable form for energy are involved in the group of GENETIC DISORDERS called GLYCOGEN STORAGE DISEASE. (See GLYCOGEN STORAGE DISEASE; DIABETES, including a description of do-it-yourself blood glucose monitoring.)

gluten, the insoluble PROTEIN that is part of wheat, rye, barley, and some other grains, such as oats. Sensitivity to gluten is a type of FOOD INTOLERANCE called CELIAC SPRUE or *gluten-induced enteropathy*.

glycogen storage disease (GSD), a group of relatively rare GENETIC DISORDERS involving problems with storage of excess glycogen—the CARBOHYDRATE storage form of the sugar GLUCOSE—in the liver. At least a dozen of these metabolic liver diseases have been identified, most of the AUTOSOMAL RECESSIVE type. Retarded growth and CONVULSIONS, resulting from insufficient sugar in the blood (*hypoglycemia*), often result from these disorders, at least two of which can be fatal without a liver TRANSPLANT. Others can be treated with a special diet.

The most common kind of glycogen storage disease in North America and Europe is Type I, called *von Gierke's disease*, which results from lack of *glucose–6-phosphatase*, needed in the final stage of the liver transformation of glycogen into glucose (dextrose). Without treatment, people have extremely low blood sugar, causing large livers, excess fat in the blood, and increased uric acid, which can lead to gout. Another common form is Type III, or *short-chain glycogen storage disease*; symptoms are often similar to those of Type I, though perhaps milder, and muscles may also be affected. Type IV, or *long-chain glycogen storage disease*, causes cirrhosis of the liver (see LIVER AND LIVER PROBLEMS). It is the most serious of the forms affecting the liver; without a liver transplant, children with Type IV GSD often die before age six.

Type II, also called *generalized glycogen storage disease* or *Pompe's disease*, is the best known form of the GSD diseases that affect the muscles. In the infantile form, babies appear normal at birth, but become progressively weaker within a few months and generally die before age two. Forms appearing later progress more slowly and produce symptoms like those of MUSCULAR DYSTROPHY. Other muscle-affecting forms of GSD tend to be milder, with symptoms seem primarily after vigorous EXERCISE.

FOR HELP AND FURTHER INFORMATION

Association for Glycogen Storage Disease
Box 896
Durant, IA 52747
319–785–6038
Hollie Swain, President
Organization concerned with glycogen storage disease; acts as advocate, gathers and disseminates information; publishes various materials, including quarterly newsletter.

National Digestive Disease Information Clearinghouse (NDDIC), 301–654–3810. (For full group information, see DIGESTIVE SYSTEM AND DISORDERS.)

National Institute of Child Health and Human Development (NICHD), 301–496–5133. (For full group information, see PREGNANCY.)

National Organization for Rare Disorders (NORD), 800–999–6673. (For full group information, see RARE DISORDERS.)

(See also METABOLIC DISORDERS.)

Goldman-Fristoe Test of Articulation, an individually administered test designed to assess the speaking skills of children ages two through sixteen or older, focusing on articulation of the major speech sounds in various positions, articulation of sounds in ordinary speech, and articulation of sounds difficult for the child to pronounce. The nonverbal test uses a picture format and so can be used with many children, including those who are highly distractible or have MENTAL RETARDATION. The results are used as a guide to planning REMEDIAL INSTRUCTION. (See TESTS.)

gonads, the sex glands, the parts of the REPRODUCTIVE SYSTEM that produce the cells that can join together to form a fertilized egg at CONCEPTION. The male's gonads, the TESTES, produce the SPERM; the female gonads, the OVARIES, produce the OVUM (egg).

gonorrhea, infection by the bacterium *gonococcus,* a common SEXUALLY TRANSMITTED DISEASE and one of the traditional *venereal diseases,* infecting more than one million people each year in the United States alone, with an estimated million more unreported, generally teenagers and young adults. Initial symptoms are mild and sometimes absent altogether, so gonorrhea can readily be spread unknowingly. Symptoms (if any) generally occur within a month after contact with an infected partner, and include painful or burning urination, discharge from the vagina or PENIS, and in women abdominal pain, nonmenstrual vaginal bleeding, VOMITING, and FEVER. The infection often takes hold in moist, warm parts of the body, such as the VAGINA, CERVIX, urinary tract, mouth, and rectum. Probably the most common serious complication in women is infection of the OVARIES and FALLOPIAN TUBES, resulting in PELVIC INFLAMMATORY DISEASE (PID), a major cause of INFERTILITY and even STERILITY. In men, the reproductive system can also be so badly damaged as to make them sterile. Other serious complications including infection in joints, heart, and brain.

Doctors often use two laboratory tests to make a positive diagnosis of gonorrhea, one of which is a quick office procedure. Gonorrhea is sometimes confused with, and often occurs with, CHLAMYDIA; both are treated with ANTIBIOTICS, though some strains of gonorrhea have developed resistance to certain antibiotics. Anyone who suspects gonorrhea should seek treatment immediately, since any damage done before treatment cannot be undone. The patient's partner should also be checked and treated, and both should avoid sex until the treatment is completed.

The presence of gonorrhea in young children is taken as an indication of possible child sexual abuse. Pregnant women who have gonorrhea can pass the infection on to their children, possibly causing BLINDNESS. To prevent that, many doctors recommend that women be tested for gonorrhea at least once during pregnancy, and many states require that silver nitrate or other medication be put into the eyes of newborns to prevent vision-impairing infection. (For help and further information, including how to avoid infection, see SEXUALLY TRANSMITTED DISEASES.)

Goodenough-Harris Drawing Test, a type of INTELLIGENCE TEST used with children ages three through fifteen, including a Draw-a-Man Test and a Draw-a-Woman Test, and sometimes an optional, experimental Self-Drawing Test, administered either to groups or to individuals. Drawings are scored for a variety of characteristics, with separate NORMS for males and females. The test attempts to measure intelligence without reliance on verbal skills. A different type of DRAW-A-PERSON TEST may be used as a PROJECTIVE TEST. (See TESTS; INTELLIGENCE TESTS.)

governess, a person with educational credentials hired by a family for full- or part-time EDUCATION of children at home; a form of HOME SCHOOLING long used in affluent families, though now less common. When found today, a governess—as the name implies, traditionally a woman—is employed as a teacher only, not for CHILD CARE or domestic work. (See EDUCATION; CHILD CARE.)

graafian follicle, of the egg-producing structures in the OVARIES, the one that produces the lead egg (OVUM) ready for FERTILIZATION.

grade, in EDUCATION, a level of instruction corresponding roughly to age levels (such as KINDERGARTEN—age five, grade 1—age six, grade 2—age seven), with an established CURRICULUM to be covered during a particular school year.

A grade is also a mark (such as a number or letter) given by a teacher to indicate the student's level of performance on a piece of work or on the work for a complete course. If number grades are used (as is common in HIGH SCHOOLS), the PASSING grades usually range from 100 to 70 or 65, with lower numbers indicating FAILING work. If letter grades are used, the range is usually:

- A—excellent, roughly equivalent to 90–100 or 95–100.
- B—above average, 80–90 or 85–94.
- C—average, 70–80 or 75–84.
- D—below average, 65–70 or 65–74.
- F—failure, below 65.

In COLLEGE, letter grades are often converted into GRADE-POINT AVERAGES, to indicate relative academic rank. Some schools have a *dual grading system,* in which teachers give a student two separate grades, one for achievement as compared to others in the class (the usual grade) and one for achievement relative to one's ability, sometimes popularly called "for effort." (See EDUCATION; GRADE-POINT AVERAGE.)

grade-equivalent (grade-level), a score indicating how a student's performance on a TEST ranks in terms of the average performance of students of various grades on the same or similar test. For example, if the NORM for students in the fifth month of seventh grade is a score of 85 on a particular test, and your starting sixth grader gets an 85 on the test, her grade-equivalent score is seventh grade, fifth month, and she may be described as "above grade level" in the subject area of the test. (See TESTS.)

grade-point average (GPA), conversion of letter GRADES into numerical figures, to indicate relative academic rank, usually at the COLLEGE level; generally A = 4.0, B = 3.0, C = 2.0, and D = 1.0. Because courses differ in length and difficulty and are given varying numbers of CREDITS (an organic chemistry course with heavy laboratory work might be five credits, for example, while a course on literature might be three credits), the grade for each course is multiplied by the number of credits the college awards to the course. The resulting grade-point values for all the courses are then totaled and the sum divided by the total number of CREDITS (also called *hours of study*). The result is the student's grade-point average for the period examined—a semester, a year, or a whole college career. If a student received a B (3.0) in the five-credit organic chemistry course and an A (4.0) in a three-credit art course, then, the calculation would work like this:

$[(3 \times 5) + (4 \times 3)] \div 8 = (15 + 12) \div 8 = 27 \div 8 = 3.375$ GPA.

Colleges and universities vary somewhat in the points and credits assigned to letter grades and courses, but most use variations of this approach. Students who receive a grade point average of B or better (in this case, 3.0 or above) are honored by being placed on the school's DEAN'S LIST. An average calculated from a student's entry into a school or college to graduation (or to an interim point) is called a CUMULATIVE AVERAGE.

grading on the curve, an educational policy in which a teacher gives GRADES according to a student's relative performance in a class, rather than on the basis of how well each student met a preestablished standard of skill or knowledge. More specifically, the policy is to assign grades so that the distribution of the grades (if graphed) would roughly resemble the bell-shaped NORMAL DISTRIBUTION curve.

With a difficult TEST, grading on the curve has the advantage of sorting out the actual distinctions of knowledge levels among students, without unduly discouraging students. With an easy test, it keeps everyone from getting A's and B's, which would obscure the real differences in skill levels among them. For example, the grades given out might read this way: three A's, five B's, nine C's, five D's, three F's. But in fact, if the test was very easy, most people would have done well—well enough to have received an A or B, if measured against a preset standard. Conversely, if the test was very hard, perhaps only one or two would have PASSED, according to a preset standard.

Because of the widespread use of statistics, grading on the curve has been common in many schools for decades. However, the practice tends to keep students in the same relative position on tests and so can tend to discourage learning. An alternative is to focus on some form of PASS-FAIL system or MASTERY LEARNING, in which the main effort is to bring all students up to a particular level of skill and knowledge. (See EDUCATION; GRADES; TESTS.)

graduate, a person who has successfully completed the course of study offered at a school, often receiving a CERTIFICATE or DIPLOMA. The term is also used to describe educational programs beyond the level of the BACHELOR'S DEGREE, including programs leading to a MASTER'S DEGREE or DOCTORAL DEGREE.

graduation, in EDUCATION, in general, moving from one level of learning to another, such as from addition to subtraction. Graduation also signifies PROMOTION from one GRADE to another, but more specifically completion of a set course of study, for which a student receives formal recognition. Graduation ceremonies, or exercises, are often held to honor students who have completed study at a school and are ready to move on, to another section of the school system (as from ELEMENTARY SCHOOL to MIDDLE SCHOOL), to another school (as from HIGH SCHOOL to COLLEGE), or out of the school system (as from HIGH SCHOOL to work). When students are ranked academically, the highest-ranked student at a graduation is called the VALEDICTORIAN, who often gives the ceremony's closing speech, with the second ranked student, the SALUTATORIAN, generally giving the opening speech.

grandparents' rights, the legally supported ability for grandparents to have the right to visit their grandchildren, even if the parents have separated or divorced or if grandparents and parents have become estranged. In practice, many parents wish to continue relationships between grandparent and grandchild, but some do not, and their attempt to bar such contact has led to a great deal of lobbying for legal protection of grandparents' VISITATION RIGHTS.

Many states now have laws supporting grandparents' rights, but these vary considerably, and in some cases are being modified by the courts. Georgia's Grandparent Visitation Statute, for example, was voided by that state's Supreme Court. One state, Illinois, has even passed a landmark law guaranteeing grandparents' visitation rights while the parents remain together, regardless of the parents' wishes in the matter. Nebraska's Court of Appeals has upheld grandparent visitations at times separate from those of the parents. In cases of ADOPTION, which involve TERMINATION OF PARENTS' RIGHTS, grandparents often lose their visitation rights, although some states protect them when the adoption is by a stepparent.

FOR HELP AND FURTHER INFORMATION

Grandparents Rights Organization (GRO)
555 South Woodward Avenue, Suite 600
Birmingham, MI 48009
810–646–7191
Fax: 810–646–9722
Richard S. Victor, Founder and Executive Director
Organization concerned with the grandparent-grandchild relationships; acts as advocate for grandparents denied access to their grandchildren; publishes newsletter.

Grandparents Anonymous (GPA)
1924 Beverly
Sylvan Lake, MI 48320
810–682–8384
Luella M. Davison, Founder
Organization of grandparents denied access to their grandchildren after divorce, death of a son or daughter, or other family problem; aids grandparents in regaining legal visitation rights.

Lavender Families Resource Network, 206–325–2643, voice/TT. Publishes article reprint *Grandparents and Psychological Parents: Rights and Remedies.* (For full group information, see HOMOSEXUALITY.)

PACER Center (Parent Advocacy Coalition for Educational Rights), 612–827–2966, voice/TT. Has special Grandparent to Grandparent support program for families of children with disabilities. (For full group information, see HELP FOR SPECIAL CHILDREN on page 689.)

OTHER RESOURCES

Grandparent Power Guide. Arthur Kornhaber. Crown, 1994. By the author of *Between Parents and Grandparents* (1986) and head of Foundation for Grandparenting (see listing in this entry).
Grandmother Time, Anytime. Judy G. Smith. Abingdon, 1994.
Grandparenting: The Agony and the Ecstasy. Jay Kesler. Servant, 1993.
Grandfather. Tom Brown, Jr. Berkley, 1993.
The Grandmother Book. Betty Southard and Jan Stoop. Nelson, 1993.
Grandmothers. Ariel Books Staff. Andrews and McMeel, 1992.
Grandmother's Book. Marcia O. Levin. Random, 1992.
Loving Someone Else's Child. Angela Hunt. Tyndale, 1992. On stepgrandparenting.
The Grandparent Book: A Guide to Changes in Birth and Child Rearing. Linda B. White. Gateway Books, 1990.

FOR PRETEENS AND TEENS

Everything You Need to Know About Moving in with Your Grandparents or Other Relatives. Carolyn Simpson. Rosen, 1995.

BACKGROUND WORKS

Grandmothers As Caregivers: Raising the Children of the Crack Cocaine Epidemic. Meredith Minkler and Kathleen M. Roe. Sage, 1993.
Generation to Generation: Older People As an Educational Resource. Maureen O'Connor. Cassell, 1993.
The New American Grandparent: A Place in the Family, a Life Apart, rev. ed. Andrew J. Cherlin and Frank F. Furstenberg, Jr. Harvard University Press, 1992.

grant, in relation to educational FINANCIAL AID, money that can be applied to the costs of attending a COLLEGE or PRIVATE SCHOOL, but which does not have to be repaid, such as a SCHOLARSHIP or a sum of money for carrying out a specified academic project. Many grants are offered on the basis of special need, including several federal programs, such as the PELL GRANT and the SUPPLEMENTAL EDUCATIONAL OPPORTUNITY GRANT. (See FINANCIAL AID.)

grasping reflex, the automatic response of a baby to clutch any object placed in his or her palm; a type of "primitive" REFLEX found only in babies that disappears during the first few months of life.

gravida, a medical term for a pregnant woman; it is often used with a prefix indicating the number of pregnancies, such as PRIMIGRAVIDA for a first pregnancy or MULTIGRAVIDA for multiple pregnancies.

Gray Oral Reading Tests—Revised (GORT-R), an individually administered TEST of READING skills for children aged seven through seventeen used to evaluate oral reading development and as a DIAGNOSTIC ASSESSMENT TEST to identify reading difficulties. A child reads aloud a series of increasingly difficult passages and orally answers several comprehension questions on each. The results are given in converted SCORES and PERCENTILES. (See TESTS.)

grip age, a summary of the relationship between a child's gripping ability (a key early MOTOR SKILLS) and the statistical average for a child of the same size and sex. If a child of six has gripping power normally seen in a 7-year-old, that child's grip age is seven. (See AGE.)

gross motor skills, the type of MOTOR SKILL that involves the large muscles of the arms, legs, torso, and feet and is used in activities requiring strength and balance, such as WALKING, running, and jumping.

group home, a residential facility providing LONG-TERM CARE in a homelike setting for MINORS or adults who require substantial help or supervision, such as those who have serious DISABILITIES, MENTAL DISORDERS, or MENTAL RETARDATION, or those classed as JUVENILE DELINQUENTS or INCORRIGIBLE CHILDREN. The aim is to place them in the LEAST RESTRICTIVE ENVIRONMENT possible.

Such an approach is sometimes called *community living, community care, assisted living,* or more widely, *inclusion.*

Normally staffed twenty-four hours a day, group homes generally serve fewer than fifty people and provide the kind of supervision a family on its own might not be able to provide. Children in group homes generally attend local public schools, often in special programs. Young children without parents or GUARDIANS, who once would have been placed in large orphanages, are now more likely to be placed in a group home, pending placement in FOSTER CARE or for ADOPTION.

When appropriate services and care are available, group homes can work extremely well, providing more individual attention, privacy, and independence in a homelike atmosphere within the community than in a larger institution. However, it is not necessarily the right approach for everyone; some have disabilities so severe that they require the more specialized care afforded by a larger residential institution. A more serious drawback is that many group homes are not properly staffed and funded, and some are not properly licensed and supervised.

Before a child is moved into a group home, parents or guardians should carefully examine the setting and the people running it, especially in terms of their round-the-clock supervision, training, and HEALTH CARE arrangements. Sometimes placement decisions are made by state or community service organizations, though in most cases family members and guardians are supposed to be consulted. In such cases, parents will need to monitor how well the setting works for the individual and lobby for changes if necessary.

Another problem is that many people resist placement of group homes in their communities, out of ignorance, fear, or other concerns, especially for those that house people with mental illnesses. In some areas, ADVOCACY organizations (see ADVOCACY; also HELP FOR SPECIAL CHILDREN on page 689) have had to go to court, invoking federal laws, notably the Fair Housing Act, to prevent neighborhoods from barring group homes. Partly because of problems in placement of group homes, many states have long waiting lists for community living centers.

FOR HELP AND FURTHER INFORMATION

Child Welfare League of America (CWLA),
202–638–2952. Publishes *Permanence and Family Support: Changing Practice in Group Child Care, Healing the Heart: A Therapeutic Approach to Disturbed Children in Group Care, Choices in Caring: Contemporary Approaches to Child and Youth Care Work,* the novel *In Motion,* about a 15-year-old boy seeking a new home after learning that his group home is closing, and materials for caregivers. (For full group information, see FOSTER CARE.)

growing pains, general aches and pains in the muscles and joints of children's limbs, appearing for unknown causes, often at night. Public health experts note that these are no cause for medical concern unless they are severe or are linked with other symptoms, which may require diagnosis and treatment. "Growing pains" is also a popular phrase referring to the emotional and social trials and tribulations of ADOLESCENCE.

growth and growth disorders, increase in a child's height and weight and associated changes in body parts and their relative proportions. These processes form the physical basis for a child's development and can be adversely affected in a variety of ways. Apart from the enormous growth of the EMBRYO and FETUS (see PREGNANCY for a month-by-month description of fetal development), a child experiences two major growth spurts.

The first is during the first year of life. Infants average about 7½ pounds at birth, though some may weigh a good deal more and some much less. (Those under 5½ pounds are termed LOW BIRTH WEIGHT and have increased risk of various medical problems.) But within a year, most infants have tripled their weight and added about 50 percent to their weight. The head grows markedly in this first year, starting out at about one-quarter of the body's length and ending the year at almost full adult size. By about 18 months, the FONTANELLES (soft spots) disappear as the skull hardens and fuses. The brain it encases will grow more slowly, approaching adult size only after age five. It has only recently been discovered that babies grow in minor growth spurts as well, in infancy sometimes growing as much as an inch a day.

In newborns, the legs account for only about three-eighths of the body's length. In the months and years of early childhood, much of the increase in length takes place in the limbs, more precisely at the ends of the long bones, called *epiphyses* or more popularly *growth plates* or *growth centers.* (In this period, also, enormous development occurs in skills, outlined in the CHART OF NORMAL DEVELOPMENT on page 637.)

The immediate concern in childhood is that the growth be steady. In general, children from age two to puberty grow at a relatively steady rate of 2 to 3 inches a year. If growth suddenly slows down or if the child's growth lags far behind the average, that may indicate a physical disorder that should be diagnosed and treated before long-term damage is done. Another main concern in early childhood is that the epiphyses not be damaged, as can happen in cases of FRACTURES, sometimes even in what appear to be sprained ankles.

The second great growth spurt occurs during PUBERTY. Since puberty normally starts earlier in girls, they sometimes grow temporarily taller than boys, but boys tend to be taller in the long run. In this period, the trunk grows faster than before, while the limbs also continue to grow, reaching their limit of growth only in the late teens, when the growth plates turn completely to bone, forming the adult skeleton. By that time, the legs will account for about one-half of the body's height and the head for only about one-eighth. (Subscribers to the America Online computer service can find a fuller discussion in the Moms

Online Desk Reference section of Moms Online, under "Normal Growth and Development.")

The rate, timing, and overall height of a child depend on many factors. GENETIC INHERITANCE, an important one, is very much affected by environmental factors, including NUTRITION and general physical and mental health. Long-term MALNUTRITION, FAILURE TO THRIVE, or CHRONIC illness (such as ASTHMA or TUBERCULOSIS) can slow growth significantly. Among the many other disorders that can retard growth are ACHONDROPLASIA (in which the growth centers turn to bone prematurely), CYSTIC FIBROSIS, CELIAC SPRUE (gluten intolerance), disorders of the THYROID GLAND, CHROMOSOMAL ABNORMALITIES such as DOWN SYNDROME and TURNER'S SYNDROME, and METABOLIC DISORDERS such as PHENYLKETONURIA. Children treated with chemotherapy (see CANCER) and some other drugs can also have slowed growth. ADOLESCENT PREGNANCY, too, often causes short stature because teenage girls have not completed their own growth when the fetus is calling on vital nutritional resources.

The growth process itself is triggered and regulated largely by several HORMONES, most notably the HUMAN GROWTH HORMONE (hGH), the thyroid hormone, and the sex hormones that bring on puberty and regulate sexual development. Deficiency or excess of any of these hormones can cause a child to be abnormally short or tall.

In particular, too much human growth hormone, as from a TUMOR of the PITUITARY GLAND, can cause excessive height and weight, a condition called *gigantism* (in adults, *acromegaly*). Great height is also associated with some other disorders, such as MARFAN SYNDROME.

On the other hand, too little human growth hormone leads to markedly short stature, in the past often called DWARFISM. The range of "normal" height is a very wide one. But if any other physical disorders have been treated and the child's growth is still extremely slowed, doctors may administer some human growth hormone to bring the child's growth to normal level.

FOR HELP AND FURTHER INFORMATION

Human Growth Foundation (HGF)
7777 Leesburg Pike
Falls Church, VA 22043
800–451–6434
Organization concerned with growth disorders; provides information; supports research; publishes various materials, including monthly *Fourth Friday*, and quarterlies *Outreach for Growth* and *Just for Kids*; books *Good Food to Grow On*, *Understanding Growth Hormone*, and *Growing Up Small*; pamphlets and booklets *Patterns of Growth*, *Growth Hormone Deficiency*, *Intrauterine Growth Retardation*, *Short and OK*, and *Short Stuff* (a child's eye view of growth hormone treatment); and professional materials.

American Academy of Pediatrics (AAP), 800–433–9016. Publishes *Rx for Good Health Growth Chart*.(For full group information, see HEALTH CARE.)

National Digestive Disease Information Clearinghouse (NDDIC), 301–654–3810. (For full group information, see DIGESTIVE SYSTEM AND DISORDERS.)

Short Stature Foundation
17200 Jamboree Road, Suite J
Irvine, CA 92714
714–474–4554; 800–24DWARF [243–8273]
Organization that provides services, information, and advocacy for people of short stature; formerly Little People of America; publishes *Dwarfism: A Family and Professional Guide*.

Shriner's Hospitals for Crippled Children, 800–237–5055. Provides free medical care for children with orthopedic problems. (For full group information, see BONE AND BONE DISORDERS.)

National Organization for Rare Disorders (NORD), 800–999–6673. (For full group information, see RARE DISORDERS.)

OTHER RESOURCES

GENERAL WORKS

The First Twelve Months of Life: Your Baby's Growth Month by Month, rev. ed. Theresa Caplan. Berkley, 1993.
See How They Grow: The Early Childhood Years. Dorothy Dixon. Twenty-Third, 1993.
Parents' Guide to Growth and Nutrition: Birth to Five Years. George S. Sturtz. Hojack, 1992.
Child Growth and Behavior. Joan Wyde and Stanley Fitch. CaT Publishing, 1992.
The Challenges Facing Dwarf Parents: Preparing for a New Baby. Ellen H. Fernandez. Distinctive, 1990.

FOR CHILDREN

Birth and Growth. Anita Ganeri. Raintree Steck-Vaughn, 1994.
See How I Grow. Angela Wilkes. Dorling Kindersley, 1994.
While I Am Little. Heidi Goennel. Tambourine/Morrow, 1993.
I'm Growing! HarperCollins, 1992.
Bigger Than a Baby. Harriet Ziefert. HarperCollins, 1991.

FOR PRETEENS

Discovering the Whole You. Joan Thiry. Chateau Thierry, 1991.

growth spurt, a child's most rapid period of growth after infancy, normally starting shortly before the onset of PUBERTY, specifically before MENARCHE in females and SPERMATOGENESIS in males. Infancy itself is another period of rapid growth, with (it has only recently been discovered) smaller growth spurts in which an infant grows as much as an inch in a single day. (See GROWTH AND GROWTH DISORDERS.)

G6PD deficiency, a type of METABOLIC DISORDER, in which the body's red blood cells produce abnormal molecules of a key enzyme called *glucose-6-phosphate dehydrogenase* (G6PD) that makes the blood cells vulnerable to damage, disease, and destruction, and often results in severe ANEMIA. An X-LINKED GENETIC DISORDER involving a RECESSIVE malfunctioning gene, G6PD deficiency is carried and passed on by women CARRIERS but affects mostly males, and is especially common among Black males. Some Whites of Mediterranean ancestry have a related disorder called *favism*, so-named for their adverse reaction to fava beans. Some types of drugs, such as ANTIBIOTICS, can trigger destruction of red blood cells among people with G6PD deficiency and favism. The G6PD deficiency can be detected by a BLOOD TEST, but the condition cannot be cured, only its effects moderated.

FOR HELP AND FURTHER INFORMATION

National Heart, Lung, and Blood Information Center (NHLBIC), 301–251–1222. (For full group information, see HEART AND HEART PROBLEMS.)

guardian, an adult who has been given temporary or long-term legal responsibility for a MINOR (called a WARD), acting in place of the BIOLOGICAL PARENTS, though not necessarily having day-to-day CUSTODY and care of the child. Foster parents are often appointed guardians of the children in their care (see FOSTER CARE). In some circumstances, as in legal proceedings relating to CHILD ABUSE AND NEGLECT or CUSTODY, the court may appoint a *guardian ad litem (GAL)* to represent the child's interests during the case (see ADVOCACY). A guardian may also be appointed for adults who have been judged legally INCOMPETENT or adults with DISABILITIES so severe that they are unable to care for themselves. In such cases, the guardian is sometimes called a CONSERVATOR. A person may be appointed for more limited purposes to act on the child's behalf during the EDUCATION process in the absence of a parent. In some areas, such a person is called SURROGATE PARENT.

Parents of young children, especially those with disabilities that will require care into adulthood, should designate a guardian in their will. Otherwise, in case of their death, the court will appoint one. Good choices are a close friend or relative, one who is willing and able to serve as guardian—young enough, strong enough, and with a lifestyle compatible with raising children. Discussing the idea, getting the prospective guardian's agreement, and informing other relatives about the choice can also avoid possible unhappiness and even court battles over custody in case of the parents' death.

FOR HELP AND FURTHER INFORMATION

Guardian Association (GA)
P.O. Box 1826
Pinellas Park, FL 34644
813–448–0730
Organization for legal guardians and interested others; offers education to prospective guardians and others, aimed at improving the quality of guardianship; publishes monthly newsletter *The Guardian.*

National Guardianship Association
c/o Office of Conferences and Institutes
Western Michigan University
Kalamazoo, MI 49008–5161
616–387–4171
Fax: 616–387–4189
Joan Gray, Association Manager
Organization seeking to strengthen guardianship and related services; acts as advocate, to shape public policy; publishes newsletter *National Guardian* and membership directory.

Center on Children and the Law, 202–662–1720. Publishes *A Review of Bar Sponsored Child Advocacy Projects* and *Lawyers for Children.* (For full group information, see HELP AGAINST CHILD ABUSE AND NEGLECT on page 680.)

PACER Center (Parent Advocacy Coalition for Educational Rights), 612–827–2966, voice/TT. Publishes *Future Planning: Guardianship and Estate Planning.* (For full group information, see HELP FOR SPECIAL CHILDREN on page 689.)

gynecologist, a physician who specializes in providing medical and surgical care relating to women's REPRODUCTIVE SYSTEM, often working as an OBSTETRICIAN-GYNECOLOGIST.

gynecomastia, abnormal enlargement of the BREASTS of a male, generally resulting from too much of the female sex HORMONE ESTROGEN. Temporary swelling of a male's breasts can occur in newborns (from hormones from his mother) and at PUBERTY, when the body is going through many hormonal changes. Gynecomastia is also common in males who have KLINEFELTER'S SYNDROME, and it can also be a sign of disease in a male, especially a grown man, such as cirrhosis of the liver (see LIVER AND LIVER PROBLEMS) or a TUMOR in the TESTES or breast. It can be treated with hormones or surgery.

FOR HELP AND FURTHER INFORMATION

National Institute of Child Health and Human Development (NICHD), 301–496–5133. (For full group information, see PREGNANCY.)

H

hair, strands of material—actually specialized skin cells—that grow out of the SKIN. Made up largely of the protein *keratin*, each strand grows from a separate site, called a *follicle*; oil (sebaceous) and sweat glands release their secretions at the same sites, lubricating hair.

A silky, down-like hair called *lanugo* covers the body of a FETUS before birth and can sometimes still be seen on newborns and on women with severe ANOREXIA NERVOSA. Short, slow-growing hair called *vibrissae* makes up the eyelashes and eyebrows and grows in the interior of the nose, while *terminal* hair covers the scalp, underarms, and pubic areas. The rest of the body (apart from the palms of the hands and soles of the feet) is covered by often barely noticeable hair called *vellus*. The body and scalp hair of children is generally fine and silky. Then, in response to the hormonal changes of PUBERTY, hair on arms and legs darkens and becomes coarser. At the same time, hair begins to grow under the arms and in the pubic area and among men also on the face (see SECONDARY SEX CHARACTERISTICS).

Scalp hair is the fastest-growing type of hair, with the growth coming in cycles. At any one time 80 to 90 percent of a person's approximately 100,000 scalp hairs are in a two to seven year growing phase, while the rest are in a two to four month "resting" phase. Parents should not be concerned about a newborn being or becoming almost bald; that can occur when the hairs are simply slow to start growing.

The darkness and coarseness of hair is determined by sex and genetic background. Men generally have darker and coarser hair than women. In general, people of Caucasian background have more hair than those of Black African background; people of Asian descent, including Native Americans, have the least body hair. Hair color is also an inherited trait; it depends both on the amount, type, and concentration of pigment in the hair, on the structure of the individual hairs, and so the way they reflect light. Structure also affects the overall appearance of a person's hair. Hair strands that are round (when looked at in a microscopic cross-section) will grow straight; oval strands produce wavy hair; while flattened strands produce kinky hair. Age and inheritance both also affect questions of thinning or loss of hair. This is most common among men, since *male pattern baldness* is an X-LINKED trait carried by women and passed on to men.

If the hair is deprived of necessary nutrients, many hairs at once may stop growing and then fall out two to four months later. This can result from major surgery or severe illness; traumatic experiences such as an accident or the death of a loved one; thyroid disorders; iron-deficiency ANEMIA; and extreme vitamin and mineral deficiencies (see NUTRITION), as may result from anorexia nervosa or BULIMIA. Some medical treatments can also have the same effect, most noticeably the chemotherapy medications used to treat many types of CANCER. In sufficient doses, ionizing radiation can produce permanent baldness, as can some skin-related disorders, such as shingles or ringworm, and some chemicals, if they destroy the hair follicles. Conversely, the HORMONES produced during PREGNANCY or found in BIRTH CONTROL PILLS can extend the growing phase for many of a woman's hairs; afterward, more than the usual number of hairs may go into the resting phase at once, leading to thinning over two to four months, before the hair returns to its previous fullness.

Hair thinning and damage can also be caused by mistreatment, such as constant use of braids, cornrows, tight ponytails, hot combs, curling irons, tight barrettes, and the like that pull or strain the strands, or from too frequent or improper use of chemicals to straighten, curl, or color hair. Excess sun can also make hair dry and brittle.

Hair loss can also result from some other types of disorders. Some people, especially preteen girls, have a nervous habit of yanking hairs from part of their scalp, a disorder called *trichotillomania. Tinea capitis* also involves hair loss in patches; this contagious, possibly infectious, disease is generally seen among children.

In *alopecia areata*, bare patches appear on the scalp and elsewhere when hair follicles slow down growth so much that no hair is visible above the surface for months or years. Why this occurs is unknown, though it is believed to result from a disorder in the IMMUNE SYSTEM; a family history of the problem is common. These sometimes go away by themselves, though with recurring episodes, hair loss in those areas may become permanent. The conditions affects both sexes and all ages, but especially young people. Treatment involves application or injection of medications to attempt to "restart" hair growth.

Sometimes excess body hair is a problem, especially when it grows on a woman in a masculine pattern; this condition is called *hirsutism* or *hypertrichosis*. Where hair grows rapidly or appears in a new area suddenly, excess hair growth may signal a medical problem, such as a tumor of the adrenal glands or of the OVARIES. Excess hair growth also occurs among athletes who take drugs such as anabolic STEROIDS. It can also be associated with BIRTH DEFECTS such as those giving rise to CORNELIA DE LANGE SYNDROME. Unwanted hair can be removed in a variety of ways, such as electrolysis, shaving, or rubbing with pumice, or it can be bleached.

From the start of life, the best protection for hair is to treat it gently, brushing it to remove surface dirt and distribute natural oils; washing it regularly; trimming it every six weeks or so; wearing a hat and/or sunblocking lotion to protect against ultraviolet rays; using a conditioner to prevent tangling; and being especially careful combing hair immediately after washing, when hair can easily be pulled out of the softened scalp.

FOR HELP AND FURTHER INFORMATION

National Alopecia Areata Foundation (NAAF)
P.O. Box 150760
San Rafael, CA 94915–0760
710 C Street, Suite 11
San Rafael, CA 94901
415–456–4644
Fax: 415–456–4274
Vicki Kalabokes, Executive Director
Organization concerned with alopecia areata; provides information; publishes bimonthly newsletter and brochures *Do You Have Alopecia Areata? Help Yourself, What You Should Know About Alopecia Areata,* and *Helping You Cope with Alopecia Areata.*

National Arthritis and Musculoskeletal and Skin Diseases Information Clearinghouse (NAMSIC), 301–495–4484. Publishes information packages *Hair Loss, Hair Loss in Women, Alopecia Areata/Hair Loss* and bibliography *Alopecia.* (For full group information, see ARTHRITIS.)

National Organization for Rare Disorders (NORD), 800–999–6673. (For full group information, see RARE DISORDERS.)

OTHER RESOURCES

GENERAL WORKS

Your Health and Your Hair, 14th ed. Paul C. Bragg and Patricia Bragg. Health Sciences, 1991.
Saving Your Skin: Secrets of Healthy Skin and Hair. Anne E. Hunt. ARE Press, 1991.
How to Cut, Curl and Care for Your Hair. Charles Booth and Sharon Esche. Outlet, 1990.

FOR CHILDREN

Hats off to Hair!. Virginia Kroll. Charlesbridge, 1995.
Hair There and Everywhere. Karin L. Badt. Children's, 1994.
Hair Flair. Dianne Balasco. Troll, 1994.
All about Your Skin, Hair and Teeth. Donna Bailey. Raintree Steck-Vaughn, 1990.

half-brother or half-sister, SIBLINGS who share one, rather than two, parents. With modern complicated patterns of DIVORCE and remarriage, many more children are living in a FAMILY with half-brothers and sisters.

halitosis, medical term for bad breath. It often results from poor dental care (see TEETH AND DENTAL PROBLEMS), as in a teenager who fails to keep up regular toothbrushing, but it can also be a symptom of illness, such as mouth infection or sinusitis.

hallucination, the perception of something that is not, in fact, present (as opposed to an ILLUSION, which is a misinterpretation of something that *is* present); a common symptom of PSYCHOSIS. Hallucinations may be labeled by the main sense involved:

- *Auditory,* as in hearing voices.
- *Visual,* as in seeing objects.
- *Haptic* or *tactile,* as in touching or feeling objects.
- *Olfactory,* as in smelling.
- *Gustatory,* as in tasting.
- *Somatic,* as in perception within the body, such as feeling a current of electricity.

Drugs or chemicals that induce hallucinations are called *hallucinogens.* (See MENTAL DISORDERS; DRUG ABUSE.)

handedness, the tendency of a person to rely most heavily on and to be most easy and proficient at using one hand more than the other; also called *chirality.* The preference for one hand over the other is believed to reflect the DOMINANCE of one side of the brain over the other, but why this occurs is unknown. About two-thirds of the population—with males and females in equal proportions—are right-handed for fine MOTOR SKILLS, with perhaps 90 percent WRITING right-handed. Some people are *ambidextrous,* or able to use both hands equally well. Despite popular notions, no special artistic or intellectual abilities are clearly linked with left-handedness.

Though few parents and teachers any longer force left-handed children to use their right hands for writing and other fine motor activities, social pressure is still great to use the right hand. The equipment in this technological world is generally geared to right-handed people, so many left-handed people come to use their right hands a good deal. Left-handers have a higher proportion of accidents than right-handers—due, many people feel, to the right-handed orientation of the things around them. Parents of left-handed children may well want to select left-handed versions of various tools and equipment, commonly available in special catalogs.

FOR HELP AND FURTHER INFORMATION

Lefthanders International (LHI)
P.O. Box 8249
Topeka, KS 66608
913–234–2177; 800–203–2177
Fax: 913–232–3999
Dean R. Campbell, President
Organization publishing *Lefthander Magazine* and *Lefthander's Catalog,* focusing on products, research, and success stories of special interest to lefthanders.

OTHER RESOURCES

GENERAL WORKS

Living Left-Handed. Diane Paul. Bloomsbury/Trafalgar, 1993.

The Left-Handers Guide and Reference Manual. John Diana. Left-Handed Sol, 1992.
The Left-Hander's Guide to Life. Leigh W. Rutledge and Richard Donley. NAL-Dutton, 1992.

FOR CHILDREN

Left or Right? Karl Rehm and Kay Koike. Houghton Mifflin, 1991.

BACKGROUND WORKS

The Left-Hander Syndrome: The Causes and Consequences of Left-Handedness. Stanley Coren. Free Press, 1991.
Handedness and Developmental Disorder. D. V. Bishop. Cambridge University Press, 1991.

handicapped, an umbrella term referring to a wide range of people with minor or major physical or mental impairments, who have some degree of difficulty in certain activities such as walking, seeing, hearing, speaking, and learning. Often used loosely in the past, the term "handicapped" came to be more precisely defined, regarding children, with the passage of the EDUCATION FOR ALL THE HANDICAPPED ACT. This federal law defines handicapped children as those who are "mentally retarded, hard of hearing, deaf, speech impaired, visually handicapped, seriously emotionally disturbed, orthopedically impaired, other health impaired, blind, multihandicapped, or as having specific learning disabilities" and who require special educational services because of these disabilities. While still in use in some situations, notably where it is written into laws, the term *handicapped* has more generally been phased out in favor of the term DISABILITIES (see separate entry for more information on laws and services available).

hard signs, clear differences in the way a child's CENTRAL NERVOUS SYSTEM functions and responds, as compared to that of the average child; a term NEUROLOGISTS sometimes use when talking about a child with LEARNING DISABILITIES or other DEVELOPMENTAL DISORDERS, referring to inappropriate responses or the absence of appropriate responses. Less clear-cut observations are called *soft signs,* the term SIGNS indicating an objective finding by a physician, rather than a subjective SYMPTOM described by the patient.

hard-to-place children, children who are available for ADOPTION, but for whom it is hard to find adoptive parents. Many unplaced children are less attractive to would-be adopters because they are older; have SIBLINGS who wish to stay together; are of a different religious, ethnic, or racial background than most potential adopters; or have SPECIAL NEEDS, such as those who have physical DISABILITIES or MENTAL RETARDATION or are victims of CHILD ABUSE AND NEGLECT. To encourage adoption of hard-to-place children, the government has developed *adoption subsidies* or *adoption assistance plans* to cover some of the costs incurred by parents. (See ADOPTION.)

Head Start, a federally funded, locally operated program that provides PREKINDERGARTEN educational opportunities, as well as health, social, psychological, and nutritional services, for disadvantaged 3–to–5-year-olds from low-income families, including many children with DISABILITIES, who are given special individualized help. Started in 1965, it is run by the ADMINISTRATION FOR CHILDREN YOUTH AND FAMILIES (ACYF). It survived the many social cuts of the 1980s, because its value was so widely recognized. Its future in the late 1990s is still unclear.

The Head Start program produced a valuable series of books, *Mainstreaming Preschoolers,* about how to recognize young children with disabilities, how those disabilities affect their learning and behavior, and how to help them. Selections from some of these (sometimes modified for wider use by parents) are reproduced in this book under specific topics, such as LEARNING DISABILITIES, EAR AND HEARING PROBLEMS, EYE AND VISION PROBLEMS, MENTAL RETARDATION, CHOKING, ARTIFICIAL RESPIRATION, and ORTHOPEDIC DEVICES, including some Observational Checklists for spotting problems.

Parents should find these materials useful in assessing whether or not their young children have problems of any sort, since early diagnosis and treatment will minimize the effects of any problems and maximize the child's chance to develop normally.

FOR HELP AND FURTHER INFORMATION

National Head Start Association (NHSA)
201 N. Union Street, Suite 320
Alexandria, VA 22314
703–739–0875
Fax: 703–739–0878
E-mail (publishing and marketing):
mkarwowski@national.nhsa.org
Head Start online bulletin board: 703–247–3073
Sarah M. Greene, Executive Director
Organization of parents, Head Start staff, and others concerned with the Head Start program; seeks to expand and enhance Head Start services; publishes various materials including quarterly *NHSA Newsletter.*

OTHER RESOURCES

Project Head Start: Models and Strategies for the Twenty-First Century. Valora Washington and Ura J. Bailey. Garland, 1995.
Head Start: The Inside Story of America's Most Successful Educational Experiment. Edward F. Zigler and Susan Muenchow. Basic, 1992.

(See also PRESCHOOL and EDUCATION.)

health care, provision for a person's medical needs, including prevention. In relation to children, health care in the widest sense can be seen to start even before CONCEPTION, with GENETIC COUNSELING, which can help parents identify and change conditions of their current lives that might be harmful to a possible PREGNANCY (such as work with toxic chemicals or with high exposure to radiation) or might even cause INFERTILITY (such as a man working in high-heat conditions). If parents have trouble conceiving, they turn to various kinds of REPRODUCTIVE TECHNOLOGY.

Once a pregnancy has begun, PRENATAL CARE focuses on identifying and treating any conditions that might harm the health of either mother or child. Various PRENATAL TESTS are used in attempts to identify possible GENETIC DISORDERS or CHROMOSOMAL ABNORMALITIES; this has become increasingly common as scientists have discovered more "genetic markers" that are linked with such disorders. In some cases, if severe abnormalities are found the parents may choose an ABORTION to end the pregnancy. In recent years, doctors have developed techniques for correcting kinds of malformations or defects while the FETUS is still in the UTERUS; these come under the heading of IN UTERO SURGERY.

From the time a child is born, various SCREENING TESTS are performed to identify quickly any possible health problems, beginning with the APGAR SCORE taken immediately after CHILDBIRTH. This is important because some kinds of disorders that can have serious and even life-threatening effects on a developing child can be prevented or at least controlled if identified early. Many of these tests are conducted during a series of WELL-BABY EXAMINATIONS by a PEDIATRICIAN, along with various vaccinations designed for prevention (see IMMUNIZATION).

Once past infancy, health care focuses more on dealing with the diseases and accidents of childhood. But it is still important for children to have annual physical examinations, along with any appropriate "booster shots." Parents should also examine a young child's body periodically to check for any early warning signs of serious problems such as CANCER or disorders that develop in older children.

In decades past, families traditionally had a single family doctor. That is still the case in some rural areas. But in recent decades, it has become much more common for children to be cared for by a PEDIATRICIAN, specializing in child care, then during ADOLESCENCE to switch over to the family doctor. Either way, each member of the family is cared for by a single doctor. The main advantage of this approach is that, ideally, the doctor knows the individual patient well and so can recognize the signs of a medical problem more readily than a stranger. One traditional disadvantage of a single doctor was the lack of a backup, a problem that many doctors solved by joining together in a group, in which doctors rotating duty "on call" on nights and weekends. Groups often include specialists who can be called on at will.

The past few years have seen the start of a revolution in health care, and the shape of the future is unclear. Parents now have to make health care choices their own parents never faced. In this new world of medical care, the traditional pattern of choosing a single doctor or group and paying for medical care directly is called *fee-for-service*, because the patient is charged for each service, often when part or all of the charges being paid by HEALTH INSURANCE. However, in recent years, with rapidly rising medical and insurance costs, various *managed care approaches* have been developed as alternatives to traditional fee-for-service medical care and traditional insurance. These approaches often combine medical care with insurance, but limit the patient's choice of doctors and access to specialized care. (For a fuller discussion, see HEALTH INSURANCE; also WHAT DO YOU NEED TO ASK ABOUT HEALTH INSURANCE AND MANAGED CARE? on page 288.)

Whatever plan is chosen, parents increasingly will find themselves needing to press to get services and care necessary for children, very much including PAIN treatment for children, as well as explanations of diagnoses and treatments. For serious medical conditions, many organizations can help parents assess what information and help they need and how to get it (see specific conditions; also ADVOCACY). Families with substantial medical bills should keep a record of all expenses—not just direct doctor and laboratory fees and prescriptions, but also costs such as transportation, since some of those expenses may be tax deductible, depending on current laws. Families pressed for funds because of heavy medical bills can sometimes negotiate with their doctors for lowered fees; in particular, doctors in such a situation will often accept as "payment in full" the amount paid by the insurance company. Parents can also set up payment plans to pay bills over time, while children continue to receive care.

If families have no health insurance, medical bills can pile up quickly. Even without insurance, they can obtain emergency medical care at a local public HOSPITAL or community health center, and may in some instances quality for public medical expense assistance, as through Medicaid.

Some philanthropic organizations provide free medical care or help with medical expenses, often locally. One national organization that provides free medical care for children with orthopedic problems or burns is the Shrine of North America, which operates a network of Shriners Hospitals, including three burn institutes (for full group information, see BONE AND BONE DISORDERS).

FOR HELP AND FURTHER INFORMATION

American Academy of Pediatrics (AAP)
141 Northwest Point Boulevard
Elk Grove Village, IL 60067
or: P.O. Box 927
Elk Grove Village, IL 60009–0927
708–228–5005; 800–433–9016
Fax: 708–228–5097
Joel Sanders, Director
Professional organization of pediatricians; through The Injury Prevention Program (TIPP), establishes safety guidelines for many areas; publishes numerous materials;

those of interest to parents include magazine *Healthy Kids*, for parents of children from birth to age ten; brochures *Your Child's Growth: Developmental Milestones, You and Your Pediatrician*, and *Effectively Using Your Managed Health Care Plan: Questions and Answers for Families with Children; Child Health Care*, an overview and record book; and book series *Caring for Your Baby and Young Child: Birth to Age 5, Caring for Your School-Age Child: Ages 5 to 12*, and *Caring for Your Adolescent: Ages 12 to 21*.

National Council on Patient Information and Education (NCPIE)
666 Eleventh Street NW, Suite 810
Washington, DC 20001
202–347–6711
Fax: 202–638–0773
Ray Bullman, Executive Director
Organization focusing on patient information, especially concerning prescription medicines; publishes quarterly *The NCPIE News* and brochures *A Parent's Guide to Medicine Use by Children, The Active Consumer: Getting the Most from Your Medicines, A Consumer's Guide to Prescription Medicine Use, Medicine: Before You Take It, Talk About It, Alcohol and Medicines: Ask Before You Mix, Medicines: What Every WOMAN Should Know, Get the Answers*, and *Directory of Prescription Medicine Information and Education Programs, Programs and Services.*

American Medical Association
515 North State Street
Chicago, IL 60610
Answer Center: 312–464–4818; 800–621–8335
Fax: 312–464–4184
Professional organization of physicians; provides information and referrals; publishes *The American Medical Association Encyclopedia of Medicine, The AMA Guide to Your Family's Symptoms*, and numerous professional materials.

National Association of Children's Hospitals and Related Institutions, 703–684–1355. Provides information on managed care, doctors, and hospitals. (For full group information, see HOSPITAL.)

Pediatric Projects, 800–947–0947. Publishes *Maintaining Cultural Integrity in Child Health Care.* (For full group information, see HOSPITAL.)

People's Medical Society
462 Walnut Street
Allentown, PA 18102
610–770–1670; Publications: 800–624–8773
Fax: 610–770–0607
Organization advocating better and less expensive medical treatment, including alternative and preventive health care and self-care; publishes bimonthly newsletter *People's Medical Society Newsletter* and pamphlet *A Parents' Rights Guide.*

Centers for Disease Control and Prevention (CDC)
Public Health Service
U.S. Department of Health and Human Services
1600 Clifton Road NE
Atlanta, GA 30333
For publications: Mail Stop E–52 (at above address)
404–639–3311; Publications: 404–639–8225
Press Office: 404–639–3286
National Immunization Program 404–639–8225
Federal agency charged with investigating, identifying, controlling the spread of, preventing, and if possible eradicating diseases; provides information, such as recommended schedules of vaccinations for children.

Parent Care (PC), 317–872–9913. Publishes *Strategies: A Practical Guide for Dealing with Professionals and Human Service Systems.* (For full group information, see PREMATURE.)

National Black Child Development Institute (NBCDI), 800–556–2234. Publishes newsletters *Child Health Talk* and booklet *Keeping Your Baby Healthy: A Practical Manual for Black Parents.* (For full group information, see HELP ON LEARNING AND EDUCATION on page 659.)

Human Growth Foundation (HGF), 800–451–6434. Publishes *Better Health Care for Less* and *How to Get Quality Care for a Child with Special Needs.* (For full group information, see GROWTH AND GROWTH DISORDERS.)

Accent, 800–787–8444 (for orders). Publishes *What to Do When You Can't Afford Health Care.* (For full group information, see HELP FOR SPECIAL CHILDREN on page 689.)

Children's Defense Fund (CDF), 800–233–1200. Publishes *Managed Care and Children's Health, Decade of Indifference: National Child Health Trends, Improving Health Programs for Low-Income Youths*, and various works on Medicaid programs for children. (For full group information, see ADOLESCENT PREGNANCY.)

Agency for Health Care Policy and Research Clearinghouse, 800–358–9295. Publishes *Health Habits of School-Age Children, Barriers to Medical Care for White, Black, and Hispanic American Children, Low Income Children: The Effect of Expanding Medicaid on Well-Child Visits*, and *Health Status and Access to Care of Rural and Urban Populations.* (For full group information, see HEALTH INSURANCE).

American Council on Science and Health (ACSH), 212–362–7044. Publishes *HMOs: Are They Right for You?* (For full group information, see SAFETY.)

Family Voices, 505–867–2368. Publishes information sheet *Managed Care.* (For full group information, see HELP FOR SPECIAL CHILDREN on page 689.)

National Alliance for the Mentally Ill (NAMI), 800–950–6264. Online forum and libraries include health care reform. (For full group information, see MENTAL DISORDERS.)

National Chronic Pain Outreach Association, Inc. (NCPOA), 301–652–4948. Publishes *How to Get Your Medical Records.* (For full group information, see PAIN AND PAIN TREATMENT.)

Healthy Mothers, Healthy Babies National Coalition (HMHB), 202–863–2458. Publishes resource list *Homelessness and Access to Care.* (For full group information, see PREGNANCY.)

National Easter Seal Society, 800–221–6827. Publishes *Understanding Physical Therapy, Understanding Occupational Therapy,* and *Rehabilitation.* (For full group information, see HELP FOR SPECIAL CHILDREN on page 689.)

National Fathers' Network (NFN), 206–747–4004. Publishes video *Health Care Delivery for African-American Fathers.* (For full group information, see HELP FOR SPECIAL CHILDREN on page 689.)

ON LONG-TERM HEALTH CARE NEEDS

PACER Center (Parent Advocacy Coalition for Educational Rights), 612–827–2966, voice/TT. Publishes books *Speak Up for Health Parent Handbook* and *Thoughts About My Child,* for organizing information about the child; *Family-Centered Health Care for Medically Fragile Children* and *Home Care for the Chronically Ill or Disabled Child*; information handouts *Become Informed About Your Child's Special Health Needs, Learn About Agencies Servicing Young Adults: Division of Rehabilitation Services (DRS) Counselors Can Be Important Team Members, Parents Can Play a Role in Local IEICs (Interagency Early Intervention Committees)* and *Parents and Professionals* (2 articles), *Vocational Rehabilitation Appeal Procedures,* and *Choices* (on self-advocacy, health care, and decision-making skills); *Speak Up for Health: Training Package for Adolescents with Developmental Disabilities*; and video *Young People with Chronic Illness and Disabilities Speak About Independence in Health Care.* (For full group information, see HELP FOR SPECIAL CHILDREN on page 689.)

American Academy of Child and Adolescent Psychiatry (AACAP), 202–966–7300. Publishes information sheet *The Child with a Long-Term Illness.* (For full group information, see MENTAL DISORDERS.)

National Mental Health Association (NMHA), 800–969–6642. Publishes *Understanding and Dealing with a Child's Illness.* (For full group information, see MENTAL DISORDERS.)

National Center for Youth with Disabilities (NCYD), 800–333–6293. Publishes annotated bibliography *Transition from Pediatric to Adult Health Care for Youth with Disabilities* and *Promoting Decision-Making Skills by Youth with Disabiities—Health, Educational, and Vocational Choices.* (For full group information, see HELP FOR SPECIAL CHILDREN on page 689.)

Council for Exceptional Children (CEC), 800–328–0272. Publishes *Special Health Care in the School.* (For full group information, see HELP ON LEARNING AND EDUCATION on page 659.)

Lupus Foundation of America (LFA), 800–558–0121. Publishes *We Are Not Alone: Learning to Live with Chronic Illness* and *Sick and Tired of Feeling Sick and Tired.* (For full group information, see LUPUS.)

ONLINE RESOURCES

Better Health and Medical Forum (America Online: Health, Medicine) Provides discussion areas and libraries with information on diseases and disorders, medications, medical tests, surgeries, and rehabilitation, health news, health insurance, health reform, and patient's rights, alternative medicine, caregiving, human sexuality, mental health, addictions, exercise, environment, safety and accident prevention, stress management, smoking/chemical dependencies, with separate sections focusing on health of men, women, children, and seniors. (Location: Lifestyle: Better Health and Medical Forum)

Internet: National Institutes of Health (NIH). Provides access to NIH resources, including databases and library catalogs, on full range of medical disorders and concerns. telnet://gopher.nih.gov or gopher://gopher.nih.gov or gopher://odie.niaid.nih.gov

Internet: National Institute for Allergy and Infectious Disease (NIAID). Contains wide range of medical resources. gopher://gopher.niaid.nih.gov/1

Internet: The Wellness List. Discussion group and collection of resources on health, nutrition, physical fitness, and related topics. To subscribe, send the message "subscribe wellnesslist" to:
mailto:majordomo@wellnessmart.com

OTHER RESOURCES

ON CHILDREN'S HEALTH CARE

The Pocket Pediatrician: An A-Z Guide to Your Child's Health. David Zigelman. Doubleday, 1995.

The Portable Pediatrician. Laura W. Nathanson. HarperCollins, 1994.

Raising Healthy Kids: A Book of Child Care and Natural Family Health. Michio Kushi and others. Avery, 1994.

Taking Care of Your Child: A Parent's Guide to Complete Medical Care, 4th ed. Robert H. Pantell. Addison-Wesley, 1993.

The Doctors Book of Home Remedies for Children: From Allergies and Animal Bites to Toothache and TV Addiction: Hundreds of Doctor-Proven Techniques and Tips to Care for Your Kid. Prevention Magazine Health Books, eds. Rodale, 1993.

Your Child's Health. Charles B. Clayman, ed. Reader's Digest, 1993.

Complete Book of Children's Everyday Ailments and Emergencies. Martin Edwards. Atrium, 1992.

Childhood Symptoms: Every Parent's Guide to Childhood Illnesses, rev. ed. Edward R. Brace and John P. Pacanaowski. HarperCollins, 1992.

Taking Care of Your Own: Parenthood and the Medical Mind. Perri Klass. Whittle Communications, 1992.

Keys to Childhood Illness. Norman B. Schell. Barron's, 1992.
Take This Book to the Pediatrician with You: The Guide to Your Child's Health. Charles B. Inlander. People's Medical Society, 1992.
Parents Guide to Baby and Child Medical Care, rev. ed. Terril H. Hart, ed. Meadowbrook, 1991.
Your Child's Health: The Parents' Guide to Symptoms, Emergencies, Common Illnesses, Behavior, and School Problems, rev. ed. Barton D. Schmitt. Bantam, 1991.
The New American Encyclopedia of Children's Health. Robert Hoekelman and others. NAL-Dutton, 1991.
The Prevention and First-Aid Treatment of Childhood Injuries. William H. Brady, ed. Medlife Communications, 1991.
Your Healthy Child: A Guide to Natural Health Care for Children. Alice Likowski [Duncan]. Tarcher, 1991.
The Well Baby Book: A Comprehensive Manual of Baby Care, from Conception to Age Four, rev. ed. Mike Samuels and Nancy H. Samuels. Summit, 1991.

On children with special health needs

Your Child and Health Care: A "Dollars & Sense" Guide for Families with Special Needs. Lynn Robinson Rosenfeld. Paul H. Brookes, 1994.
Book of Matthew: What Would You Do If Your Child Was Faced with a Serious Medical Problem? Betty J. Wylie. Shapolsky, 1994.
Why Can't I Eat That?: Helping Kids Obey Medical Diets. John F. Taylor and R. Sharon Latta. R & E Publishers, 1993.
Parenting Plus: Raising Children with Special Health Needs. Peggy Finston. Viking Penguin, 1992.

For children

Mother Mother I Feel Sick Send for the Doctor Quick Quick Quick. Remy Charlip and Burton Supree. Buccaneer Books, 1993.
Who's Sick Today? Lynne Cherry. Puffin, 1993.
The Medibears Guide to the Doctor's Exam: For Children and Parents. John A. Ogden. University Press of Florida, 1991.
Jimmy's Last Wish: A Story about Forever. Rashelle Haines. Glastonbury, 1992. Fiction.
Aa-Choo! Wendy Orr. Firefly, 1992. Fiction.
Lumps, Bumps, and Rashes: A Look at Kids' Diseases, rev. ed. Alan E. Nourse. Watts, 1990.

For preteens and teens

I Am Fifteen: And I Don't Want to Die. Christine Arnothy. Scholastic, 1993.
Medical Dilemmas. Margaret Hyde and Elizabeth Forsyth. Putnam, 1990.

General works

Giving Comfort: What You Can Do When Someone You Love Is Ill. Linda B. Milstein. Viking Penguin, 1994.
When Do I Call the Doctor? Loraine M. Stern. Doubleday, 1993.
The Better Life Institute Family Health Plan. Steven M. Zifferblatt, Ph.D., Patricia M. Zifferblatt, and Norm Chandler Fox. Nelson, 1991.
The New Handbook of Health and Preventive Medicine. Kurt Butler and others. Prometheus, 1990.
Take Care of Yourself: Your Own Master Plan for Maintaining Health and Preventing Illness, 4th ed. James F. Fries and Donald M. Vickery. Addison-Wesley, 1990.
Columbia University College of Physicians and Surgeons Complete Home Medical Guide, rev. ed. Genell Subak-Sharpe, ed. Crown, 1989.
American Medical Association Encyclopedia of Medicine. Charles B. Clayman, ed. Random House, 1989.
American Medical Association Family Medical Guide. Jeffrey R.M. Kunz and Asher J. Finkel. Random, 1987.

On patients' rights, medical choices, and consumer advocacy

Your Medical Rights: How to Become an Empowered Consumer. Charles B. Inlander and Eugene Pavalon. Little, Brown, 1990.
A Doctor's Prescription for Getting the Best Medical Care. Kurt Link. Dembner, 1990.
Medical Choices, Medical Chances: How Patients, Families and Physicians Can Cope with Uncertainty. Harold Bursztain and others. Routledge, 1990.
Choosing the Right Health Care Plan. Henry Berman and Louisa Rose. Consumer Reports, 1989.
Taking Charge of Your Medical Fate. Lawrence Horowitz. Random, 1988. Encourages patients (including parents) to become active in obtaining the best medical treatment; approach credited by Edward Kennedy for saving his son's life.

Background works

The Work of Human Hands: Surgical Wonder at Children's Hospital. G. Wayne Miller. Random, 1993.
Child Health Care and the Working Mother: The Juggling Act. Jenny Hewison and Therese Dowswell. Singular, 1993.
One Children's Place: A Profile of Pediatric Medicine. Lee Gutkin. Grove Weidenfeld, 1990. *One Children's Place: Inside a Children's Hospital.* NAL-Dutton, 1991.

(See also HOSPITAL)

health insurance, a contract under which the insured person pays a premium to a company, which agrees to pay a certain portion of possible future medical expenses. Health insurance plans will not cover *all* expenses, but the idea behind insurance is to spread the risk, so that if major medical expenses are incurred, they will not fall so heavily on the individual family, but will be spread among all the people insured by the company.

Traditional health insurance policies provide various kinds of coverage:

- *Basic coverage plans,* which provide limited coverage, paying a certain proportion of those expenses covered, often much less than the fee actually charged; the higher the premium routinely paid, the higher the proportion of expenses covered. Most commonly covered are the more expensive surgical and medical procedures, either as an inpatient or outpatient, and HOSPITAL room and board. Generally the patient must pay a certain amount, called a *deductible,* such as $250, for each hospital admission, plus a small portion (*co-payment*) of the daily room charge. Preventive care, such as IMMUNIZATION and regular physical examinations, are not covered.
- *Major medical plans,* which provide wider coverage, often to supplement basic plans; they also use deductibles and copayments, commonly requiring the insured person to pay an annual deductible of $100 or more and at least 20 percent of outpatient services. That copayment could be larger if the fee charged is considered higher than the *usual and customary rate* for that geographical area. Major medical plans generally have a lifetime maximum of benefits that will be paid, though that can sometimes be restored, if the insurance company is satisfied that the person is insurable.
- *Excess major medical or catastrophe plans,* which are designed to meet extremely heavy medical expenses, taking over beyond the traditional major medical plans, often with deductibles as high as $20,000 or $25,000. They also have lifetime maximums, which may range up to $1 million or more.

In general, traditional health insurance has been better at covering medical and surgical procedures and some prescription drugs than medical equipment, home health care, and medical and related costs for a CHRONIC ILLNESS or DISABILITY. Partly because of ADVOCACY groups, however, this is changing somewhat, so policies now vary widely and people considering traditional insurance policies need to compare them carefully to see how well they fit their family's needs. This is especially true of families with long-term medical needs.

Many health insurance plans are provided through employers or obtained through other groups, such as a union or a professional organization, with some or all of the premiums paid by the individual. In that case, the basic policy is negotiated between the employer or group and the insurance company. Often an employee can enroll within a certain period after employment or during an "open enrollment" period; otherwise the employee and family members may have to demonstrate their insurability, as through a physical examination. Though small employers may not offer health insurance or may not cover families, sometimes a group of small employers can be formed to obtain group health insurance, which is cheaper than individual policies.

Though employer-provided insurance is generally cheaper than individual policies, it has significant hazards. If the employed parent leaves a job, the family may have a gap in insurance coverage until some months after that parent begins a new job. That is because new health insurance coverage generally does not kick in until the person has been on the job for several months. Even then, the new policy generally does not cover *preexisting conditions,* generally meaning injuries or sicknesses existing for a given period (such as three months or six months) before the insurance began; it includes disorders treated during that period, including taking medication. Sometimes, however, this preexisting condition clause is waived, as when a person is transferring between companies in the Blue Cross network or from one group policy to another.

To avoid the preexisting condition trap, many families carry what is called *secondary coverage* on their own, to at least tide them over any such gap. Where a family has two working parents, and both employers provide health insurance, the second one can provide secondary coverage. Secondary coverage is also important for union employees; when they go on strike, their insurance benefits generally end, if the employer is the group provider.

When a person has been fired or laid off from a company employing 20 or more people, federal law ensures them of the right to convert their former employer's group policy into an individual policy for a limited period of time, though they must pay the full premium themselves. And some companies require an individual policy to be maintained for at least thirty-six months. Premiums on converted policies can be high, however, and their coverage is often more limited, so other alternatives should be explored. A more serious problem is that such insurance ends when a new insurance policy goes into effect—even though pre-existing conditions may leave the family without some coverage for some months

Children are generally covered on the family policy up to age nineteen (though up to twenty-one or even twenty-five, depending on the policy, if a full-time student), and then are dropped from the policy, *often without warning from the company.* Parents must plan ahead for separate coverage for the child, often taking out secondary coverage some months ahead of time to get past the preexisting condition problem. Some colleges and universities offer group insurance; also some states offer student plans, with a September enrollment and no preexisting conditions clauses; these are often programs with limited coverage, however.

Adult children with disabilities who are incapable of supporting themselves may in many states be classed as *dependents* indefinitely and retained on the family health insurance policy. However, the family must request this before the cut-off date of the child's nineteenth birthday; the insurance company will require proof, such as a letter from the child's doctor describing the nature and severity of the disability.

In case of medical problems, families with secondary coverage have more of their expenses covered. However, they are generally prevented from collecting more than 100 percent of their medical costs; in what is called *coordination*

What Do You Need to Ask About Health Insurance and Managed Care?

Before you buy an insurance policy or enroll in a medical plan, be sure to request all available information. You will often have to be persistent to get that information beforehand, since it is generally not included in the promotional brochure, but the questions that follow will help you assess what kinds of information to seek. It is very important to get answers to your questions in writing, as insurance companies or employers may later repudiate verbal assurances as misunderstandings or later-changed policies.

GENERAL QUESTIONS

- What medical services are *not* covered? These *exclusions* vary widely. Many traditional insurance policies do not cover preventive care, such as vaccinations or genetic counseling, for example. Many kinds of policies and managed care approaches limit coverage for MENTAL DISORDERS. Families should examine these aspects very carefully, especially if any family member has special needs, such as speech therapy or physical therapy. Insurance policies often exclude some chronic diseases, though the policy pamphlet given to the public does not indicate that.
- What happens if I die? Will my family continue to be covered? If so, on what basis and for how long?
- What happens to coverage for spouse and family members in case of divorce or legal separation?
- What coverage is provided for treatments still considered experimental?
- What coverage is provided for out-of-state or out-of-country services, if those are the best choice?
- Which family members are covered and until what age? Children are generally covered only until age nineteen, sometimes later if they are full-time students. A child with DISABILITIES who is dependent is usually covered (this coverage always requires the insurance carrier's approval).

ON A TRADITIONAL INSURANCE POLICY

- What deductibles will I be required to pay? These are amounts that the insured must pay per year before benefits start, such as one hundred dollars per individual or three hundred dollars per family.
- Are there annual maximum limits on payments for specific procedures? For example, a policy may pay an annual maximum of fifty dollars for X-rays.
- What proportion of the medical costs will be paid by the insurance company? Under what is called *coinsurance*, the insured must typically pay 20 percent of medical costs up to a certain point.
- At what point does the insurance begin to pay 100 percent of medical expenses? In what is called the *stop-loss*, for example, a company may pay 100 percent of covered expenses above one thousand dollars a year. The lower the stop-loss point, generally the higher the premium. If the stop-loss point is high, families may find it cheaper to buy a secondary or supplementary policy than to pay for a policy with a low stop-loss point.
- Does the policy have a lifetime maximum in benefits? If so, what is it? Parents must carefully examine this. If anyone in the family has a serious disorder, or if there is a family history of medical problems, a relatively low maximum, such as fifty thousand or two hundred and fifty thousand dollars would not be sufficient to cover medical costs. If a policy has a low maximum, parents may want to consider getting a supplementary excess major medical or catastrophe insurance policy, with a high deductible (such as twenty thousand or two hundred and fifty thousand dollars) but a high maximum (such as one million dollars).

ON A COMPANY-RELATED POLICY OR PROGRAM

- When will I be able to enroll in the medical plan? Often a new employee must wait three months or more before being eligible for the company's health insurance plan. Sometimes an employee will be able to enroll at once, but will have to pay the full premium until that probationary period has ended.
- Is there a pre-existing condition clause? If so, what does it cover and under what circumstances

would it be waived? This is often waived between Blue Cross companies or between group policies.

■ If I leave the job, when does my group coverage end? It may end that day or at the end of a quarter or be extended beyond that. Under federal law, individuals employed by firms with twenty or more employees have the right to remain with the group for up to 18 months, though they must pay their own full premium.

Note: If you are considering a new job and have special health needs in the family, be sure to ask for information about the prospective employer's health care program before you accept the job to be sure it will cover your family adequately.

ON SPECIAL MEDICAL SERVICES

■ Are outpatient services covered? Many traditional insurance plans cover hospitalizations well, but have little coverage for care provided in a clinic or a doctor's office. This can be important when a family member has a CHRONIC ILLNESS or DISABILITY that is often monitored and treated on an outpatient basis.

■ Are special medical needs covered? These will vary with the family situation, but parents should check specifically to see that a family member's requirements are covered. For example, some policies do not cover blood or blood products, so if a family member has HEMOPHILIA, you must be sure that the specific medications for blood coagulation are covered. Often the entry level staff at the insurance company will not have that information, and you may need to go above that level to the supervisor. In some cases, you may need to get help from an ADVOCACY group or social worker. In the case of a group policy, generally someone in the personnel department is appointed to find the answers to such questions. Get your answers in writing, as a policy given verbally can be changed.

ON MANAGED CARE

■ Can I choose my own doctor? In most managed care approaches, you must choose your primary care provider from a given list.

■ Can I choose my own specialist if I or a family member needs specialized care? In managed care approaches, visits to a specialist must generally be approved in advance by the primary care provider, and the specialists are drawn from a given list of *affiliated physicians.* In some kinds of managed care, you can go outside that list, but the amount of expenses covered will be significantly less.

Once you have decided on a policy or plan, be sure to get a copy of all the documents (often called a *certificate*) that describe in detail the coverage available to you. Study them carefully, paying special attention to any particular problems your family is likely to encounter. If you have any further questions, ask them *before* you need the answers. Because the certificate may not cover all your questions and specific needs, and as discussed earlier, be sure to get all of the answers to all of your questions in writing.

of benefits, only the amount not paid by the first insurer can usually be billed to the second insurer.

When a family member has severe medical problems, including a chronic condition that becomes acute, some policies offer special *prolonged illness coverage* (PIC) or *catastrophic illness coverage,* which can be activated by a physician's request. People covered under Medicare also have some catastrophic health insurance. Private foundations can also provide help in paying medical and related costs, especially for children with chronic illnesses and disabilities. (Depending on the medical condition, many of the organizations in this book can point families toward help, as can local social service agencies.)

In many states, individuals who have been refused health insurance because of past or current medical problems can obtain insurance in state-operated "risk pools"; though this is more expensive than traditional coverage, premiums cannot be more than 125 percent of the current market rate for similar individual insurance. Some other states instead provide special individual health insurance plans for people considered medically "uninsurable." Families with no health insurance can get emergency medical care at many public hospitals and federally funded community health centers, and may in some instances qualify for public medical expense assistance, as through Medicaid. Low-income families should be aware that they may receive a tax deduction or credit on health insurance premiums paid for one or more children during the tax year, depending on current tax laws.

The long-dominant *fee-for-service* approach—in which the patient is charged for each service, with part or all of the charges being paid by HEALTH INSURANCE—has increasingly come under attack in recent years of rising medical costs. Though the shape of the future health care and health insurance picture is still unclear, various alternatives have become popular, classed as *managed care approaches*, which combine medical and insurance in a single program.

Generally managed care approaches attempt to limit health services to the minimum necessary, including tests, emergency room services, psychiatric services, and access to specialists, all of which must be approved beforehand (except for life-threatening situations) and coordinated by the *primary care provider*, such as a pediatrician, internist, or family practice physician. (Indeed, some traditional health insurance plans also now require prior approval of surgery, except in emergencies.) Managed care plans attempt to hold down costs by using *service coordination* and *case management*, including close monitoring of health services provided under the plan. The patients' choice of doctor is also limited, often to those affiliated with a specific program or network. Some managed care programs operate under federal regulations, others under state laws with various requirements. In general, in exchange for a steady flow of patients, managed care approaches have arranged for physicians to take lower fees; some even offer physicians financial incentives to limit medical services.

The main current managed care approaches include:

- *Health maintenance organization* (HMO), which provides general health care, including hospitalization and surgery, to individuals and families who pay a flat monthly or yearly fee, regardless of the amount or kind of medical services needed. Some cover dental, mental, eye care, and prescription drugs as well, for a supplemental fee. Some HMOs (such as Kaiser-Permanente) double as insurers and medical care providers, while others consist of a network of providers in a region. Some own their own hospitals, while others have contract arrangements with hospitals. In some HMO plans, doctors work on salaries; in others, they are private doctors who bill the HMO. Medical services from outside the plan or unauthorized services within the plan must be paid for by the individual or family.
- *Preferred provider organization* (PPO), which is an organization of independent physicians, hospitals, and pharmacists who work under contract with an employer or insurance company to provide health care to subscribing patients for set fees, usually less than elsewhere. If families obtain their health care services from members of the PPO network, they are generally reimbursed for the full amount paid, minus a small *copayment* (see HEALTH INSURANCE). If they wish, they can go outside the network for services without prior approval, but will be reimbursed at a lower rate.
- *Point-of-service plan* (POS), which combines features of HMOs and PPO. As in a PPO, a POS plan uses a network of health care providers from which the patient selects a physician; if medical care is obtained from providers outside the network, patients will be reimbursed at a lower rate. However, as in an HMO, a primary care provider chosen by the patient coordinates all care, including referral to specialists.

Unlike most traditional health insurance plans, managed care programs often cover preventive services, may cover preexisting conditions, and can offer lower premiums. They have the advantage of holding down medical costs and seeming to eliminate the need for health INSURANCE, but they can limit the patient's choice of doctor, hospital, or both in special situations, such as maternity care and severe CHRONIC ILLNESS. A woman with a high-risk pregnancy or families with long-term medical problems should carefully examine their alternatives to be sure that the plan they choose provides coverage they need, and should periodically review their alternatives in this fast-developing area.

Whether under traditional insurance or managed care, parents will often find they need to be persistent to obtain coverage of particular services. If a claim for payment has been denied by the insurance company, you have the right to know why. Sometimes it has been denied improperly, and getting additional information allows you to provide additional documentation in support of your claim, if necessary. You may need to request a letter from your doctor. If the claim has been refused at least twice, you can contact your state insurance department; if you get no satisfactory response, you can explore legal avenues, either through local legal aid services or your state's Protection and Advocacy Agency (see ADVOCACY). (Lynn Robinson Rosenfeld's *Your Child and Health Care* gives detailed advice, including sample letters, on how to make such approaches; see below.) In any case, you must keep careful records of all your costs and correspondence. Some advocacy organizations even offer recordkeeping books to help you do that.

FOR HELP AND FURTHER INFORMATION

Agency for Health Care Policy and Research Clearinghouse
P.O. Box 8547
Silver Spring, MD 20907–8547
800–358–9295
InstantFAX (24 hours): 301–594–2800 (Call for contents list; press 1 at prompt and follow instructions)
An arm of the Public Health Service, seeking to improve quality and delivery of health care; publishes numerous materials, most for professionals; on health insurance these include: *Checkup on Health Insurance Choices, Choices of Health Insurance and the Two-Worker Household, Insuring the Children: A Decade of Change, Children Without Health Insurance, Children: Effect of Family Characteristics on Health Insurance Coverage,* and *Health Insurance of Minorities in the United States.*

National Insurance Consumer Helpline,
800–942–4242. Information line sponsored primarily by Health Insurance Association of America, American

Council of Life Insurance, and Insurance Information Institute; publishes *The Consumer's Guide to Health Insurance.*

Help Abolish Legal Tyranny (HALT), 202–347–9600. Publishes *Consumer's Legal Guide to Today's Health Care* and *The Smart Consumer: A Legal Guide to Your Rights in the Marketplace.* (For full group information, see CUSTODY.)

PACER Center (Parent Advocacy Coalition for Educational Rights), 612–827–2966, voice/TT. Publishes *Understanding Your Health Insurance Options: A Guide for Families Who Have Children with Special Health Care Needs.* (For full group information, see HELP FOR SPECIAL CHILDREN on page 689.)

National Chronic Pain Outreach Association, Inc. (NCPOA), 301–652–4948 Publishes *Health Insurance for People with Chronic Illness* and *Filing Social Security Disability Claims.* (For full group information, see PAIN AND PAIN TREATMENT.)

American Academy of Child and Adolescent Psychiatry (AACAP), 202–966–7300. Publishes information sheet *Know Your Health Insurance Benefits* and pamphlet *When You Are Choosing Your Health Insurance or HMO.* (For full group information, see MENTAL DISORDERS.)

National Mental Health Consumer Self-Help Clearinghouse, 800–553–4539. Publishes reprint packets on insurance and managed care. (For full group information, see MENTAL DISORDERS.)

Children's Defense Fund (CDF), 800–233–1200. Publishes *The Health Insurance Crisis for America's Children.* (For full group information, see ADOLESCENT PREGNANCY.)

National Ataxia Foundation (NAF), 612–473–7666. Publishes fact sheets *Financial Planning* and *Health Insurance.* (For full group information, see ATAXIA.)

ONLINE RESOURCES

Better Health and Medical Forum (America Online: Health, Medicine) Provides discussion areas and libraries covering health insurance. (For full information, see HEALTH CARE.)

National Alliance for the Mentally Ill (NAMI), 800–950-NAMI. Online forum and libraries include health insurance reform. (For full group information, see MENTAL DISORDERS.)

OTHER RESOURCES

How to Buy the Right Insurance at the Right Price. Bailard, Biehl & Kaier. Irwin, 1995.

Insurance and Alternatives for Uninsurables. Kessinger, 1990.

(See also HEALTH CARE; WHAT DO YOU NEED TO ASK ABOUT HEALTH INSURANCE AND MANAGED CARE? on page 288.)

hearing aid, an electronic aid used by people with certain kinds of hearing impairment to make sounds louder. The effect of a hearing aid depends on the severity and type of the hearing loss. As explained in *Mainstreaming Preschoolers: Children with Hearing Impairment*:

> For some children a hearing aid makes spoken words understandable. For others, it only helps them to hear speech partially. And for still others, it may only help them know that sounds are being made. One problem with a hearing aid is that it makes all sounds louder, not just speech. This means that sounds such as radiators, outside traffic, the crashing of blocks, people walking, and so on will be made louder and will interfere with the child's listening.

Improvements in digital signal processing are lessening those problems somewhat. Most hearing aids today are small devices worn at ear level; these generally consist of five basic parts:

- A microphone to pick up the sound.
- Batteries to provide power to make the sound louder, in a case behind the ear, attached to eyeglasses, or in an earpiece (earmold).
- A receiver that adapts the sound so the ear can use it.
- An earmold that holds the receiver and carries the sound into the ear.
- Wires to connect the system.

In rare cases in which a child is unable to use a standard earmold and receiver (due to a missing ear or ear canal), a small vibrator may be worn on a headband near the ear to act as a receiver. For some profoundly deaf children, *tactile devices* can transmit speech signals in the form of vibrations or codes that are felt, rather than heard. Traditional hearing aids have had only volume control; however, newer models being developed have the capability of being tuned to the specific frequency losses of the individual (which can vary considerably; see HEARING TEST).

Hearing aids are often prescribed by an AUDIOLOGIST or OTOLOGIST after HEARING TESTS have indicated hearing impairment. The sooner a hearing impaired child is properly diagnosed and fitted with a hearing aid the less the negative impact on the child's development in COMMUNICATIONS SKILLS and therefore in many other areas, such as COGNITIVE DEVELOPMENT. Infants and young children need to be taught how to use hearing aids and to listen using them and other such devices. Parents should also check the hearing device, preferably each day, to make sure that it is turned on and that the sound is being transmitted properly—loud and clear, not weak, fuzzy, intermittent, and full of static. Check also for physical condition; the earpiece should be dry, clean, and free of dirt and wax, and wires should have no cuts or breaks. Also change the battery as often as is recommended by the audiologist. The child should wear the hearing aid all day, both at school and at home, since it can only help if it is worn. If parents are concerned about the hearing aid being lost, they can check with the audiologist about possible insurance coverage.

Hearing aids have traditionally been uniform in design, allowing the person only to make sounds louder or softer. However, newer, still-experimental hearing aids are being developed that are designed to be customized to the specific needs of the wearer, tuned to be louder in the higher frequencies, for example, if that is the area of greatest hearing loss. The difference is equivalent to the difference between off-the-rack eyeglasses that provide uniform magnification, and eyeglasses specially ground to fit the needs of the individual's eyes. (For full group information, see also EAR AND HEARING PROBLEMS.)

FOR HELP AND FURTHER INFORMATION

Alexander Graham Bell Association for the Deaf (AGBAD), 202–337–5220, voice/TT. Publishes *Hearing Aids for You and the Zoo* (for young children), *Hearing Aids: Who Needs Them?*, *Hearing Aid Accessory Kit*, video *Getting the Most Out of Your Hearing Aid*, and *Hearing Aid Accessory Kit*. (For full group information, see EAR AND HEARING PROBLEMS.)

Self-Help for Hard of Hearing People (SHHH), 301–657–2248; 301–657–2249, TT. Publishes *Troubleshooting Your Hearing Aid, ABC's of Hearing Aids, A Consumer's Guide for Purchasing a Hearing Aid*, and *How to File a Complaint Regarding Your Hearing Aid Purchase*, and video *Getting the Most Out of Your Hearing Aids*. (For full group information, see EAR AND HEARING PROBLEMS.)

Hear You Are, Inc. (HYAI), 800–278–3277, voice/TT. Publishes *Hearing Aids: Who Needs Them?* and *Hearing Aids: A User's Guide*. (For full group information, see EAR AND HEARING PROBLEMS.)

International Hearing Society (IHS)
20361 Middlebelt
Livonia, MI 48152
810–478–2610; Hearing Aid Helpline:
800–521–5247, U.S. and Canada
Trade association of certified hearing aid dealers; monitors professional standards; provides information and referrals; operates toll-free line; distributes brochure *The World of Sound: Facts About Hearing and Hearing Aids*.

National Information Center on Deafness (NICD), 202–651–5051; 202–651–5052, TT. Publishes *All about the New Generation of Hearing Aids, Hearing Aids and Other Assistive Devices: Where to Get Assistance, Hearing Aids: What Are They?*, and *The New Hearing Aids and You*. (For full group information, see EAR AND HEARING PROBLEMS.)

American Speech-Language-Hearing Association, 800–638–8255, voice/TT. Publishes brochure *How to Buy a Hearing Aid*. (For full group information, see COMMUNICATION SKILLS AND DISORDERS.)

OTHER RESOURCES

Understanding Digitally Programmable Hearing Aids. Robert E. Sandlin, ed. Allyn, 1993.

Hearing Aids—Who Needs Them? What They Can Do for You, Where to Buy Them, How to Use Them. David P. Pascoe. Big Bend Books, 1991.

Now Hear This: A Consumer's Guide to Testing for Hearing Loss, and the Selection and Purchase of a Suitable Hearing Aid. Lindsay L. Pratt and Dominic Quinn. Forum, 1991.

The Hearing-Aid Handbook: User's Guide for Children. Donna S. Wayner. Gallaudet University Press, 1990.

hearing tests, a series of MEDICAL TESTS, normally performed by an AUDIOLOGIST, OTOLOGIST, or OTOLARYNGOLOGIST, designed to screen for possible hearing loss, to assess the amount of hearing loss, and to identify the problem causing the loss.

Basic hearing loss is assessed by a *Pure Tone Test* (*audiometric test* or *sweep-check test*), which measures two things: the *frequency* (high or low pitch) and the *loudness* of tones the child is able to hear. For this test, the audiologist places earphones on a child; a machine called an *audiometer* then sends tones of different pitch and loudness through the earphones, testing one ear at a time. The audiologist asks the child to do something—such as raise a hand or put a toy in a bucket—on hearing the tone. The results—what pitches the child can hear and how loud sounds must be for the child to hear them—are recorded on a chart called an *audiogram*.

The audiometric test measures hearing in a range of 0 to 110 *decibels* (a measure of loudness). People with unimpaired hearing begin to hear sounds at approximately 0 to 10 decibels. People with hearing loss do not begin to hear sounds until higher decibel levels are reached. If, for example, a child cannot begin to hear sounds until they are at least 50 decibels loud, then the child is said to have a 50 decibel hearing loss. These decibel levels serve as the basis for the categories of hearing impairment:

- *Mildly hearing impaired*: loss between 20 and 40 decibels.
- *Moderately hearing impaired*: loss between 40 and 70 decibels.
- *Severely hearing impaired*: loss between 70 and 92 decibels.
- *Profoundly hearing impaired*: loss greater than 92 decibels.

In everyday terms, a faint whisper 3 feet away would be about 10 decibels, average conversation about 60 decibels, an auto horn about 100 decibels, and a propeller airplane revving up 15 feet away about 120 decibels.

In the *auditory brainstem response test* (*auditory evoked response test*), the audiologist attaches electrodes to the child's scalp, to record how the brain responds to sounds. This test is commonly used with infants, children with MENTAL RETARDATION, and others who are unable to respond appropriately in the Pure Tone Test. It is also used to check for possible ACOUSTIC NEUROMA.

Tuning fork tests are generally used to determine the type of hearing loss: conductive (in the ear) or sensori-neural (in the transmission to the brain). In the *Rinne test*, the tuning fork is held at the opening of the outer ear (with sound traveling through air) and against the mastoid bone behind the ear (with sound traveling through bone). The person is asked to say which sounds louder. If there is conductive hearing loss, bone conduction will be greater than or equal to air conduction; air conduction is greater in normal hearing and with sensori-neural loss. In *Weber's test*, the tuning fork is held to the center of the child's forehead, and he or she is asked to tell whether the sound appears louder in one ear than the other. With conductive hearing loss, the sound will appear louder in the ear that is more impaired.

An *impedance audiometry* test may be used in cases of conductive hearing loss to assess the kind of middle-ear problem involved. A probe is tightly fitted into the ear canal and emits a steady sound; air is pumped through the probe and the miniature microphone in the probe records the changes in the sound as it bounces off the eardrum. The results, recorded on a chart called a *tympanogram*, indicate the elasticity of the eardum, the pressure in the middle ear, and the flexibility of the middle-ear bones.

Except for the auditory evoked response test, hearing tests in children can be inaccurate and the degree of hearing loss hard to diagnose, for a variety of reasons, as explained in *Mainstreaming Preschoolers: Children with Hearing Impairment*:

TAKING TESTS IS A LEARNED SKILL

Up to ages three and four, the child may not understand what to do during the test. For example, when Jan was 2½ years old, she was diagnosed as having an average loss of 80 decibels. Later tests showed that Jan had an average loss of 72 decibels. Jan's hearing had not improved, however. She had simply learned how to take the test.

TESTS MAY BE INADEQUATELY ADMINISTERED

Hearing screening tests are often conducted under adverse circumstances. The room may be noisy or the testing may be rushed, so that a child does not do as well as he or she might. In other cases, the screening diagnosis may indicate "normal" hearing, even though the teacher or parent suspects a hearing loss.

As a teacher or parent, you should definitely request a more thorough hearing test if you have any suspicion of hearing loss in a child.

HEARING IMPAIRMENT MAY BE MISDIAGNOSED

One of the most common problems is that a hearing impairment can be diagnosed as another problem. For example, Timothy is a four-year-old with an undiagnosed moderate hearing loss. Because his hearing loss had gone untreated, he had missed out on learning a lot of the words that other four-year-olds know. When he didn't understand questions asked of him on a psychological test, he either guessed or didn't respond. His test score was very low and he was misdiagnosed as mentally retarded.

This kind of mistake doesn't happen often. But it can occur. If your observation of a child tells you something different from the information on diagnostic reports or from what others tell you, follow it up.

Parents can use an observation checklist (see EAR AND HEARING PROBLEMS) to help them assess if their child might have an undiagnosed hearing problem and need to be referred to an audiologist for hearing tests. From the child's point of view, referral is better than nonreferral. If you find out that the child does not have a DISABILITY, no harm has been done. But if you find there is a problem, the sooner special treatment and services begin, the better.

heart and heart problems, the fist-shaped muscular organ that continuously pumps blood throughout the body, and the disorders affecting it. The bulk of the heart is made up of muscle called *myocardium*, which in a healthy, well-nourished body contracts regularly normally about 70 times a minute, providing the heart's pumping action. Inside the heart are four chambers, divided by a vertical wall, called the *septum*; each half has an upper chamber (*atrium*) and a lower one (*ventricle*). The pumping action in the four chambers is timed so as to move the blood along smoothly in the desired direction. One-way "doors" called *valves* are situated at each of the entrances and exits to the chambers, to prevent blood from flowing backward.

From the lungs, blood newly freshened with oxygen pours into the heart's left atrium by way of the *pulmonary veins*. When the valve between two left-side chambers opens, this blood moves into the left ventricle. From there, the blood, bright red and carrying its fresh oxygen, is pumped on through the body's main artery, the *aorta*, and then on into the artery network in the rest of the body. On its return from the body's tissues, having "dropped off" oxygen and picked up waste products, notably carbon dioxide, and in the process having become increasingly darker, the blood gathers into two large veins (the *vena cava*), which empty into the right atrium. After being transferred into the right ventricle, this blood is then pumped through the *pulmonary artery* into the lungs to receive fresh oxygen and start the process all over again.

In the unborn FETUS, the blood circulates differently. Blood-carrying oxygen is received, not from the lungs, but from the mother through the PLACENTA and UMBILICAL CORD to the liver and then into the lower (*inferior*) vena cava and right atrium. It is then forced through a hole in the septum into the left atrium and then into the left ventricle, from which it is pumped to the upper part of the body. This hole in the septum, the *foramen ovale*, normally closes at birth, when the baby begins to use its lungs, but can remain open for a time, especially in some PREMATURE babies.

On its return to the fetus's heart, blood flows into the right atrium through the upper (*superior*) vena cava and then on into the right ventricle. From there it is pumped through the pulmonary artery and into the *ductus arteriosus* (a connection that normally exists only in the fetus) and then into the lower branch of the aorta, to supply the lower part of the body. Having completed its circuit, the blood (now carrying carbon dioxide and other waste products) exits through the umbilical cord to the placenta. The key role of the vena cava in circulating blood during PREGNANCY is the reason why pregnant woman are advised not to sleep or EXERCISE lying on their backs, since the weight of the fetus can press on the vena cava and cut off blood flow.

As such a central organ, the heart is subject to a variety of disorders. Many of them apply to adults, reflecting the wear and strain of years, but some affect young children. In particular, children often have structural or functional abnormalities in the heart at birth. Taken together, these CONGENITAL heart defects are the most common kind of BIRTH DEFECT, occurring in at least 1 out of every 100 live births, and by some estimates a good many more. The causes of most heart defects are unknown, though RUBELLA is one known cause (now preventable by vaccination), and some accompany other birth defects and GENETIC DISORDERS, such as DOWN SYNDROME. Congenital heart defects are not themselves passed on as part of GENETIC INHERITANCE.

Some of these congenital heart defects may disappear on their own, as the infant's body completes its development. On the other hand, some can be so severe that infants die within the first year, especially the first month. Most are not immediately life-threatening, but can severely impair the child's development, since the body is receiving insufficient oxygen. This leaves the child susceptible to infection, especially *endocarditis*, infection of the heart's lining. But with modern medical advances, many more heart defects are correctible by surgical or other techniques, and the life-expectancy of many such children is near normal.

Immediate symptoms of congenital heart problems are breathlessness and CYANOSIS (blueness, especially of the lips and NAILS, from lack of oxygen). In fact, newborns with congenital heart defects are often called *blue babies* for their characteristic cyanosis; they often require emergency aid, sometimes including surgery, to correct the defect. Some defects may not be immediately apparent, but develop as the child gets older; undetected, they may cause slowed growth, thickening (*clubbing*) of fingers and toes, poorly developed muscles, and fatigue from even small amounts of exercise.

Among the main kinds of congenital heart defects are:

- *Ventricular septal defect* (VSD), a hole in the septum, popularly often called a "hole in the heart" (*foramen ovale*; see above), the most common congenital heart defect. If this fails to close on its own, it may need to be repaired surgically, preferably in early childhood. If not detected and corrected, later in life it could lead to the *Eisenmenger complex*, in which the blood vessels of the lungs are damaged and increasingly resist blood flow, eventually reversing the blood flow back across the hole in the septum. When such damage has occurred, life expectancy is shortened to the thirties or forties, though a heart-lung TRANSPLANT offers some hope for survival.
- *Transposition of the great vessels*, in which the pulmonary artery exits from the left (instead of the right) ventricle and the aorta from the right (instead of the left) ventricle. Unless a hole exists in the septum, by which oxygen-rich blood can be exchanged for oxygen-poor blood, a child cannot live with this malformation uncorrected. When possible, however, surgery is performed only after a few months, to give the baby a better chance of survival.
- *Coarctation of the aorta*, in which the aorta is narrowed and so cuts down the flow of blood to the body, normally to the lower part. Surgery is generally performed to prevent complications, such as high BLOOD PRESSURE and *congestive heart failure* (see below).
- *Patent ductus arteriosus* (PDA), in which the ductus arteriosus (see fetal heart circulation above) fails to close at birth, a defect common in PREMATURE babies. Sometimes the artery closes off on its own as the baby develops. If not, surgery will need to be performed.
- *Pulmonary* STENOSIS, in which the pulmonary valve or sometimes the upper right ventricle are abnormally narrow, cutting blood flow to the lungs, a problem that can also occur after birth in connection with other disorders. Surgery may be required in infancy and sometimes also later in childhood.
- *Tetralogy of Fallot*, a common combination of four heart defects, including a hole in the septum, misplaced aorta, pulmonary stenosis, and thickening of the right ventricle. Newborns with this combination of problems often need urgent medical help after birth, but when possible, surgery is postponed until the child is somewhat older.

Once immediate, life-threatening conditions are dealt with, the doctor's main concern is to assure sufficient blood circulation to supply the brain, and so prevent MENTAL RETARDATION, and to allow for normal growth. Various techniques are used to help the infant's body repair defects, including some drugs and sometimes insertion of small inflatable balloons through CATHETERS, which can be used to widen narrow passages.

But sometimes *open-heart surgery* may need to be performed in cases of congenital heart defects, though doctors will often, if possible, delay such an operation until after the child is 6 months old, or perhaps even 3 to 4 years old. In open-heart surgery, a machine is used to maintain blood flow in the child's body, and the heart itself is drained of blood and kept very cool to avoid tissue damage, while surgeons makes appropriate repairs, including implantation of artificial valves where necessary.

Young people sometimes, though more rarely, experience other kinds of heart problems, including:

- *Cardiomyopathy*, in which the heart muscle itself is damaged, reducing pumping ability and causing *atrial fibrillation*, irregular rapid contractions of the heart's upper chambers. In some cases this may be an inherited condition, but more often it is caused by a viral infection, VITAMIN deficiency, ALCOHOL ABUSE, or an AUTOIMMUNE DISORDER. It can be somewhat controlled by drugs, but gradually deterioriates, in severe cases sometimes requiring a heart TRANSPLANT.
- *Myocarditis*, inflammation of the heart muscle, generally as a result of bacterial or viral infection, such as RHEUMATIC FEVER, but sometimes from drugs, radiation therapy (see CANCER), or even parasites. Doctors recommend that exercise be limited until the inflammation subsides.
- *Endocarditis*, inflammation of the heart valves from infection, a common side effect of rheumatic fever, and increasingly likely with some kinds of congenital heart defects.
- *Valvular heart disease*, in which the valves narrow and restrict blood flow or malfunction and allow backflow. This can occur as a congenital heart defect or as a result of some other disorder, such as rheumatic fever. The characteristic abnormal sound of the valve action is called a *heart murmur* or a *cardiac murmur*.
- *Cardiac arrhythmia*, disrupted rhythm of the heartbeat.
- *Heart block*, uncoordinated heartbeat of the heart's chambers.
- *Cor pulmonale*, failure of the right side of the heart, generally in connection with LUNG AND BREATHING PROBLEMS, such as *emphysema*.

If repairs cannot be made, if the heart is damaged before the defect is detected, or if the heart is damaged by some other disorders, *congestive heart failure* (CHF) may develop. This simply means that part of the heart becomes incapable of carrying out its normal functions. If other parts of the heart are still functioning, life may continue, though on a carefully monitored basis with restricted diet and activity. In the long run, however, congestive heart failure places great strain on the heart and circulatory system, often causing enlargement of the heart. The result is generally a somewhat shortened life span. One of the key tests for monitoring heart problems is the ELECTROCARDIOGRAPH.

Pregnant women who have heart problems, either from congenital defects or later damage, need to exercise special care, since theirs will be a HIGH-RISK PREGNANCY. They may well want to consult with their doctors before considering pregnancy, to assess the possible risks to themselves and to a child. If the decision is to go ahead, they may want to allow time to get in the best possible physical condition before CONCEPTION.

NUTRITION is vital to the health of the heart. Lack of proper nutrients can cause the heart to work less effectively, leaving the whole body functioning at a sub-par level. It is also important to avoid harmful substances, such as FATS and especially CHOLESTEROL, which can build up in the body's arteries and lead to heart disease later in life. Recent research has shown that even young children begin to show signs of narrowed arteries from cholesterol buildup, so parents will do their children a favor by avoiding fatty and cholesterol-rich foods in the family's diet.

FOR HELP AND FURTHER INFORMATION

American Heart Association (AHA)
7320 Greenville Avenue
Dallas, TX 75231
214–750–5300 (see telephone directory white pages for local number)
800-AHA-USA1 [242–8721]
Fax: 214–706–1341
Organization concerned with heart disease; provides information; offers services to heart patients; maintains Council on Cardiovascular Disease in the Young and Mended Hearts; publishes newsletter *Heartbeat, Safeguarding Your Heart During Pregnancy, Feeding Infants with Congenital Heart Disease, If Your Child Has a Congenital Heart Defect, If Your Child Needs a Heart Test, Innocent Heart Murmurs, Kawasaki Disease*, and numerous general materials, including *Heart Attack, Heart Attack and Stroke Signals and Action, About Heart Transplants, After a Heart Attack, Controlling Your Risk Factors, Mitral Valve Prolapse*, and *Patient Information Kit.*

National Heart, Lung, and Blood Institute (NHLBI)
31 Center Drive, MSC
Building 31, Room 4A21, 2480
Bethesda, MD 20892–2480
301–496–4236
Fax: 301–402–2405
One of the National Institutes of Health, sponsoring research on heart, lung, and blood disorders and diseases; provides information and publishes various materials, through National Heart, Lung, and Blood Information Center (see next organization listing).

National Heart, Lung, and Blood Information Center (NHLBIC)
P.O. Box 30105
Bethesda, MD 20824–0105
301–251–1222; Information Line on Heart Health (recorded messages): 800–575-WELL [575–9355]
Fax: 301–251–1223
E-mail: nhlbic@dgsys.com
Internet: fido.nhlbi.nih.gov
Federal information clearinghouse, a service of the National Heart, Lung, and Blood Institute (NHLBI; see previous organization listing); answers questions and makes referrals; publishes various materials, including *The Healthy Heart Handbook for Women* (source of numerous fact sheets on heart disease and women), *The Human Heart—A Living Pump, Check Your Healthy Heart I.Q.*; works on heart attacks and emergency response; fact sheets *Angina, Arrhythmias/Rhythm Disorders, Coronary Heart Disease, Heart Failure, Hormone Replacement Therapy, Idiopathic Pulmonary Fibrosis, Mitral Valve Prolapse,* and *Raynaud's Phenomenon*; and professional materials.

March of Dimes Birth Defects Foundation (MDBDF), 914–428–7100. Publishes information sheet *Congenital Heart Defects.* (For full group information, see BIRTH DEFECTS.)

American Council on Science and Health (ACSH), 212–362–7044. Publishes *Coronary Heart Disease: The Facts and Myths.* (For full group information, see SAFETY.)

Agency for Health Care Policy and Research Clearinghouse, 800–358–9295. Publishes *Living with Heart Disease: Is It Heart Failure? Patient and Family Guide, Managing Unstable Angina: Patient and Family Guide, Patient Selection for Heart or Liver Transplantation,* and InstantFAX materials on unstable angina and heart failure. (For full group information, see HEALTH INSURANCE)

Food and Nutrition Information Center (FNIC), 301–504–5414. Publishes resource list *Nutrition and Cardiovascular Disease Nutri-Topics.* (For full group information, see NUTRITION.)

National Organization for Rare Disorders (NORD), 800–999–6673. (For full group information, see RARE DISORDERS.)

OTHER RESOURCES

FOR PARENTS

The Heart of a Child: What Families Need to Know about Heart Disorders in Children. Catherine A. Neill and others. Johns Hopkins, 1993.
A Parent's Guide to Heart Disorders. James H. Moller and others. University of Minnesota Press, 1988.

GENERAL WORKS

Your Heart: A Battery for Life. Joan Wikman-Coffelt. Dorrance, 1994.
The Johns Hopkins Complete Guide for Preventing and Reversing Heart Disease. Peter Kwiterovich. Prima, 1993.
Mayo Clinic Heart Book. Mayo Clinic Staff. Morrow, 1993.
The Black Health Library Guide to Heart Disease. Paul Jones and Angela Mitchell. Holt, 1993.
Your Heart: Questions You Have, Answers You Need. Peoples Medical Society, 1992.
Heart Myths: Setting the Record Straight on Prevention, Diagnosis, and Treatment. Bruce D. Charash. Viking Penguin, 1992.
Yale University School of Medicine Heart Book. Barry L. Zaret and others, eds. Morrow, 1992.

ON HEART SURGERY

Avoiding the Heart Surgery Trap: What Everyone with a Heart Problem Needs to Know to Stay Out of the Hospital. Julian M. Whitaker. Regnery, 1994.
The Heart Surgery Trap: Why Most Invasive Procedures Are Unnecessary and How to Avoid Them. Julian Whitaker. Poseidon/Simon & Schuster, 1992.
To Heal a Heart. Tedi T. Wixom. NW Publishers, 1992. On heart-transplantation.
Taking Heart. A.C. Greene. Simon & Schuster, 1990. On undergoing heart transplant operation.
Going for Heart Surgery: What You Need to Know. Carole A. Gassert. Pritchett and Hull, 1990.
Heart Disease. Leonard Mervyn. Thorsons, 1990.

FOR CHILDREN

Heart Disease. John C. Gold. Crestwood/Macmillan, 1995.
Heart and Lungs. Jane Saunderson. Troll, 1992.

FOR PRETEENS AND TEENS

How Our Blood Circulates. Merce Parramon. Chelsea House, 1994.
Circulatory System. Alvin Silverstein and others. Twenty-First Century Books, 1994.
The Pulse of Life: The Circulatory System. Jenny Bryan. Dillon/Macmillan, 1993.
The Heart and Blood, rev. ed. Steve Parker. Watts, 1991.
Living with Heart Disease. Steve Parker. Watts, 1989.

Heimlich maneuver, a procedure to use in cases of CHOKING, when a person's air passages are obstructed by food or a foreign object; also called the *Heimlich hug.* Standing behind the choking person, the rescuer makes a fist, with thumb side up, but thumb tucked in; wraps the other hand around it; places the fist in the choking person's abdomen, just above the navel and below the rib cage; and makes a quick thrust upward and inward, attempting to use air from below to push the obstruction out of the throat. If the maneuver fails after several tries, an emergency TRACHEOSTOMY may be required to restore breathing before the person suffocates. (See CHOKING; also illustrated guidelines: WHAT IF AN INFANT IS CHOKING? on page 122; WHAT IF A CHILD IS CHOKING? on page 123.)

helpline, a telephone number that can be called for information, counseling, or referrals, often staffed by trained counselors. Unlike HOTLINES, which are more often designed for real emergency situations and are often staffed twenty-four hours a day, helplines generally have more limited hours, such as standard business hours. Many helplines do, however, have toll-free numbers that people can call.

hematoma, a swelling resulting from blood collecting in a restricted space, such as under the skull or skin, often found among victims of CHILD ABUSE AND NEGLECT. A *subdural hematoma* is blood collected between the brain's covering membrane and the spinal cord, which may be caused by accidental injury or by some types of child abuse, including violent shaking or a blow to the head.

hemolytic disease of the newborn, a serious type of ANEMIA that results in a newborn in cases of RH INCOMPATABILITY between the baby and its mother.

hemophilia, a group of disorders in which the blood fails to clot properly, usually because of deficiency or total lack of one or more enzymes, called *coagulation factors*, needed for proper clotting. These are called *bleeding disorders* because the dominant characteristic is that blood fails to clot and so keeps on flowing, not only from external cuts but also internally, with blood often gathering painfully in the knee and elbow joints. The disorder is identified as a result of various BLOOD TESTS, such as *prothrombin time*.

Some types of hemophilia are inherited and are identified by the missing coagulation factor. Classic hemophilia, called *hemophilia A*, is caused by a deficiency in factor VIII or *antihemophiliac globulin* (AHG), while *hemophilia B* (also called *Christmas disease*) is due to a shortage of factor IX or *plasma thromboplastin component*; and *hemophilia* C or *Rosenthal's syndrome* from lack of factor XI or *plasma thromboplastin antecedent*. These are all GENETIC DISORDERS of the X-LINKED type, meaning that they generally affect males. By contrast, *von Willebrand's disease*, also missing factor VIII, is a genetic disorder that affects males and females equally. Prospective parents, women as well as men, with a family history of hemophilia may want to seek GENETIC COUNSELING to assess the risk of having a child with the disorder.

Some other types of hemophilia may result from other causes, including:

- Digestive disorders, especially those that affect absorption of VITAMIN K, important in clotting (see DIGESTIVE SYSTEM AND DISORDERS).

How to Find Hotlines and Helplines: A Quick Guide

Listed throughout this book are many organizations that provide information, support, and resources on a wide range of topics that concern parents. You can locate descriptions of these groups quickly by looking up the topic that concerns you, such as EDUCATION, NUTRITION, or LEARNING DISABILITIES. There you will find a writeup on the topic, followed by a list of organizations (including contact information) and reference works relating to the subject.

But organizations change their names, addresses, and phone numbers with some frequency—as we found when updating the information for this second edition. If you cannot reach the organization you want at the number listed, or if you want information on any other topics of interest, the telephone numbers that follow will give you quick access to whatever you need.

- Federal Information Center, 800–688–9889. This center will refer you to the proper government agency for your question.
- National Institutes of Health, 301–496–4000. Staff at this number will direct you to the government organization dealing with your specific health questions.
- National Health Information Center, 800–336–4797; Fax: 301–984–4256. This organization will give you current contact information on health-related hotlines or helplines around the country.
- Toll-free Number Directory, 800–555–1212. This is the commercial AT&T directory of 800 numbers, the equivalent of general information directories.
- Internet: Government-Sponsored Electronic Bulletin Boards (BBSs). This provides access to the full range of government information currently available to the public, including access to databases. gopher://gopher.ncsu.edu
- Finding Resources on the Internet. Collection of files, utilities, and resources canted toward new users. gopher://proper.com

- Effect of various medications (see DRUG REACTIONS AND INTERACTIONS).
- *Thrombocytopenia,* a deficiency in *platelets* (*thrombocytes*), blood cells important in clotting, which can result from LEUKEMIA.
- Conditions that affect the blood vessels, such as SCURVY (VITAMIN C deficiency).

The underlying cause of hemophilia is treated, when that is possible. Beyond that, the main treatment is to supply the patient with the missing factor or platelets, though this carries the risk of infection, especially with AIDS, as with other BLOOD TRANSFUSIONS.

FOR HELP AND FURTHER INFORMATION

National Hemophilia Foundation (NHF)
Soho Building
110 Greene Street, Suite 406
New York, NY 10012
212–219–8180; 800–42HANDI [424–2634]
Fax for HANDI: 212–431–0906
Alan P. Brownstein, Executive Director
Organization concerned with hemophilia and related bleeding disorders; operates Hemophilia and AIDS/HIV Network for the Dissemination of Information (HANDI); provides information and support; acts as advocate; sponsors research; publishes various materials, including quarterlies *Hemophilia Newsnotes* and *HANDI Quarterly, Raising a Child with Hemophilia, Your Child and Hemophilia, Your Child's Hemophilia: What to Expect During Infancy, Your Child's Hemophilia: What to Expect During the School-Age Years, Hemophilia and Sports, Don't Be Victimized by Hemophilia: How to Be a More Responsible, Effective Parent, Inheritance of Hemophilia, Hemophilia: Current Medical Management, Comprehensive Care for the Person with Hemophilia,* and *The Student with Hemophilia: A Resource for the Educator.*

World Federation of Hemophilia
1310 Green Avenue, Suite 500
Montreal, Quebec H3Z2B2
Canada
514–933–7944
Fax: 514–933–8916
International organization that provides information, including special advice to hemophiliac travelers; publishes *Passport,* a guide to world hemophilia treatment centers.

National Heart, Lung, and Blood Information Center (NHLBIC), 301–251–1222. (For full group information, see HEART AND HEART PROBLEMS.)

National Organization for Rare Disorders (NORD), 800–999–6673. (For full group information, see RARE DISORDERS.)

OTHER RESOURCES

Living with Haemophilia, 3rd ed. Peter Jones. Oxford University Press, 1991.

Go Toward the Light. Chris Oyler and others. Harper & Row, 1988. On children with hemophilia who contracted AIDS.

(See also BLOOD AND BLOOD DISORDERS; BLOOD TRANSFUSIONS.)

hemorrhage, bleeding from the blood vessels, often as the result of an accident or disease, such as HEMOPHILIA, but also an indicator of possible CHILD ABUSE AND NEGLECT. Bleeding under the skin is called a bruise or *intradermal hemorrhage*; very small bruises are called *petechiae,* small ones or groups of petechiae are *purpura,* and a larger bruise (over 1 centimeter) is an *ecchymosis.* Hemorrhage is one of the main hazards facing women after a HIGH-RISK PREGNANCY and a difficult CHILDBIRTH.

hepatologist, a medical PHYSICIAN who specializes in treating the LIVER AND LIVER PROBLEMS.

herpes, infections caused by one of the two forms of *herpes simplex virus* (*HSV*), which produce sores generally on the mouth or in the genital area, the latter being a form of SEXUALLY TRANSMITTED DISEASE. HSV type 1 causes *oral herpes,* resulting in "fever blisters" or "cold sores" around the mouth. But both HSV type 1 and HSV type 2 can also affect the genital area, as well as other parts of the body that might come into contact with the genitals or mouth of an infected person. However, the National Institute of Allergy and Infectious Diseases (NIAID) notes, "It is unlikely that the virus can be spread by contact with an object such as a toilet seat."

Within two to ten days of contact with an infected person, small, red bumps often appear around the nose, mouth, and genitals. Over several days, they develop into blisters or open sores (*lesions*), which then crust over and heal. This *primary episode* lasts about two to three weeks and is sometimes accompanied by flu-like symptoms, such as FEVER, headache, muscle aches, painful urination, and swollen glands. After the infection, the virus lies dormant in the body, and is thought not to be contagious in this state. But occasionally the virus is reactivated (precisely when and why is unclear), affecting the same area as the original sores, but generally in a milder form. Such recurrences are sometimes signaled by tingling in the genitals or pain in the buttocks or legs (medically termed *prodromal symptoms*). During these recurrences, the activated virus can be spread to others.

If genital herpes is active in a woman giving birth, the child can be infected, with extremely severe results including blindness, brain damage, or even death. Many doctors recommend that pregnant women carrying the virus be tested each week in the latter stages of PREGNANCY and that if any question exists as to whether the virus might be active, a CESAREAN SECTION should be used to protect the baby. In addition, a woman who is infected during pregnancy faces increased risk of MISCARRIAGE,

PREMATURE delivery, and infection of the FETUS, possibly with resulting BIRTH DEFECTS. Herpes can also have serious effects in some people with weakened IMMUNE SYSTEMS, such as those with AIDS or LEUKEMIA.

To keep from spreading an active infection, the NIAID recommends:

- Keep the infected area clean and dry, to prevent the development of secondary infections.
- Try to avoid touching the sores directly, and if unavoidable, wash hands afterwards.
- Avoid sexual contact from the first recognized symptoms until the sores are completely healed.

Herpes sores are visible, but doctors need a variety of laboratory tests to tell if they are caused by an HSV or something else. No cure yet exists, but the drug acyclovir is used to treat initial outbreaks and to speed healing and limit the severity of a herpes outbreak. A related virus, *varicella-zoster virus* (VZV), medically termed *herpes zoster*, causes CHICKEN POX and (sometimes later in life) shingles.

FOR HELP AND FURTHER INFORMATION

American Social Health Association (ASHA), National Herpes Hotline: 919–361–8488; Herpes Resource Center: 800–230–6039. Publishes quarterly newsletter *The Helper*; brochures *Herpes: Questions/Answers, When Your Partner Has Herpes, Telling Your Partner About Herpes*; video *Living with Herpes: The Facts and the Feelings*; and books *Managing Herpes: How to Live and Love with a Chronic STD, Understanding Herpes, Herpes Bibliography*, and professional materials. (For full group information, see also SEXUALLY TRANSMITTED DISEASES.)

National Institute of Allergy and Infectious Diseases (NIAID), 301–496–5717. (For full group information, see ALLERGY.)

Planned Parenthood Federation of America (PPFA), 800–230–7526. Operates nationwide network of counseling and health services centers; publishes pamphlet *Herpes: Questions and Answers*. (For full group information, see BIRTH CONTROL.)

National Foundation for Infectious Diseases (NFID), 301–656–0003. Publishes *Turning the Tide On Herpes*. (For full group information, see CHICKEN POX.)

March of Dimes Birth Defects Foundation (MDBDF), 914–428–7100. Publishes information sheet *Genital Herpes*. (For full group information, see BIRTH DEFECTS.)

National Organization for Rare Disorders (NORD), 800–999–6673. (For full group information, see RARE DISORDERS.)

(See also SEXUALLY TRANSMITTED DISEASES; also WHAT CAN YOU (OR YOU CHILD) DO TO AVOID STDS? on page 541.)

Hib disease, a very serious illness caused by a parasitic bacterium (unlike influenza, which is caused by a virus), especially threatening to children younger than 5 years old, more formally known as *Haemophilus influenzae type b*. In the United States, Hib disease strikes approximately 1 in every 200 children under age five, with 70 percent of the cases, and these generally the most serious ones, occurring under the age of eighteen months. Hib disease can cause pneumonia (see LUNG AND BREATHING DISORDERS) and infections of the blood, joints, bones, soft tissues, throat, and worst of all, the covering of the heart and brain. Before the advent of antibiotics, it was almost always fatal, and even now it can develop to life-threatening stages within hours of the first symptoms if the child is unimmunized and untreated. About 12,000 cases of Hib-caused MENINGITIS (inflammation of the membranes covering the brain) occur in the United States each year, causing death in 1 of every 20 affected children, and permanent brain damage in 1 of 4.

Fortunately a VACCINE now exists to protect children from this potentially devastating illness. It is normally given in a series of four injections to children between two months and fifteen months of age, the precise schedule usually varying with the type of vaccine used. The vaccine provides protection for at least one and a half to three years, covering the most dangerous period for this disease in children. Children under age five are recommended to receive the Hib vaccine, if they have not already done so. Those over age five have usually been exposed to the "H flu" bug and have developed immunity to it, so immunization is generally considered unnecessary.

The Hib vaccine is regarded as one of the safest of all vaccines—it cannot cause meningitis. Approximately 1 in every 8 children will have some slight redness or swelling or tenderness in the area where the shot was given. Perhaps 1 in every 140 children will develop a fever higher than 102.2°F. These reactions begin within twenty-four hours after the shot, but usually go away quickly. (See IMMUNIZATION, including a recommended immunization schedule.)

higher education, a program offering academic education beyond the HIGH SCHOOL level, normally referring to programs at two-year or four-year COLLEGES or universities, graduate schools, and professional schools, that is designed to lead to a further degree, such as an ASSOCIATE, BACHELOR'S, MASTER'S, or DOCTORAL DEGREE. The phrase *higher education* does not usually apply to PROPRIETARY SCHOOLS, which focus on occupational and technical fields and do not offer advanced degrees.

high-risk babies, infants who have an increased risk of dying or developing diseases or disorders, especially during the *neonatal period*, the first month of life; also called *special babies*. Among these are babies of LOW BIRTH WEIGHT or low GESTATIONAL AGE, because of PREMATURE delivery, or those considered high-risk because of SIGNS observed by the medical staff or information from POSTNATAL CARE. If medical problems are recognized before mother and child go home, the baby may need to remain in the hospital, often in a NEONATAL INTENSIVE CARE UNIT (NICU), also called a *high-risk nursery*, equipped with the special equipment and trained staff necessary for proper medical care. If the baby is kept at the hospital, parents will need to make special arrangements to stay close to their infant, since BONDING in a child's early life is important (see SPECIAL CARE FOR SPECIAL BABIES on page 336).

FOR HELP AND FURTHER INFORMATION

National Institute of Child Health and Human Development (NICHD), 301–496–5133. (For full group information, see PREGNANCY.)

OTHER RESOURCES

Deciding Who Lives: Fateful Choices in the Intensive-Care Nursery. Renee R. Anspach. University of California Press, 1993.

(See also MORBIDITY; INFANT MORTALITY; DEATH AND DYING.)

high-risk pregnancy, a PREGNANCY in which there is an increased likelihood of complications developing, because of the presence of various RISK FACTORS in the woman or her life situation. Most women with high-risk pregnancies will, with proper PRENATAL CARE, go on to bear healthy, FULL-TERM babies without problems. The label simply means that such women are somewhat more likely than normal to have problems during pregnancy or CHILDBIRTH, and so should exercise due caution. A woman with a high-risk pregnancy will be well advised, for example, to have her child in a well-equipped HOSPITAL (Level II or III), rather than to consider a community hospital, MATERNITY CENTER, or HOME BIRTH. Among the factors that increase risk during a pregnancy are:

- ADOLESCENT PREGNANCY, in which a girl is bearing a child before her own body has fully matured (see separate entry).
- *The mother is over 35 years old*, and so carries a greater risk of having a child with BIRTH DEFECTS, especially CHROMOSOMAL ABNORMALITIES, such as DOWN SYNDROME, and for complications such as hypertension (high BLOOD PRESSURE), DIABETES, and AUTOIMMUNE DISORDERS. Older women also have an increased chance of having twins or triplets, itself a risk factor.
- *Too little time between pregnancies*, especially when conception occurs within three months of a previous delivery, before the woman's body has fully recovered. If the woman is still BREASTFEEDING a previous child, she is generally advised to wean the infant as soon as possible, to see that the developing FETUS gets all necessary NUTRITION.
- *Use of* CONTRACEPTION *at the time of* CONCEPTION, some forms of which may cause birth defects, including an INTRAUTERINE DEVICE (IUD) and possibly SPERMICIDES and BIRTH CONTROL PILLS, though scientific studies are so far unclear on the effects of these methods on the fetus.
- MULTIPLE BIRTHS, both because of highly increased nutrition needs and the strain on the mother's body.
- *Maternal-fetal blood group incompatibility*, especially problems with the RH INCOMPATIBILITY, which can cause severe blood disorders in newborns.
- DES, women whose mothers took the medication *diethylstilbestrol* between 1946 and 1970 during their pregnancies.
- *Previous delivery of a* PREMATURE *baby*, though prenatal care can focus on lowering the risk of premature delivery, by stressing proper nutrition, avoidance of alcohol, SMOKING, and drugs, change of work patterns, and by teaching women to recognize and stop premature contractions if they occur.

Numerous diseases and conditions in the mother can also increase risk in a pregnancy, affecting fetal development or putting the woman herself in poorer medical condition. Among these are hypertension, EPILEPSY, ASTHMA, LUPUS, thrombocytopenia, diabetes, MULTIPLE SCLEROSIS, heart disorders (see HEART AND HEART PROBLEMS), HERPES, and hepatitis (see LIVER AND LIVER PROBLEMS). (See specific topics mentioned above; see also PREGNANCY; CHILDBIRTH.)

high school (secondary school), an institution providing EDUCATION to students after MIDDLE SCHOOL or directly after ELEMENTARY SCHOOL; sometimes used to refer only to grades 9–12, with grades 7–8 considered *junior high school* or *early secondary*. In high school, students generally have a homeroom to which they report at the beginning and ending of each day for ATTENDANCE checking and school announcements. But, unlike in elementary school, they then generally change classrooms and teachers with every subject. During the high school years, most students pass the age of COMPULSORY ATTENDANCE, so the schools have a major challenge in preventing student DROPOUTS.

Americans have traditionally resisted any attempts at formulating a national CURRICULUM for elementary and secondary schools, but in recent decades concern over the decline of some basic educational skills among students has inclined many to view the idea more favorably (see NATIONAL STANDARDS). Though no national agreement yet exists on what specific matter should be covered in the various grades, a widely accepted general curriculum developed by the U.S. Department of Education includes:

- *Four years of English*, emphasizing literary heritage and requiring students to understand, discuss, and write effectively about what they have read.
- *Three years of mathematics*, providing an understanding of algebra, geometry, probability, and statistics, and teaching students to apply math to everyday problems.
- *Three years of science*, covering the major concepts and methods of the physical and biological sciences along with their applications to everyday life.

- *Three years of social studies*, explaining world economic and political systems, the differences between free and repressive societies, and "the broad sweep of ancient and contemporary ideas that have shaped our world."
- *A half year of computer science.*
- *Two years of foreign language study* for all college-bound students.

Many students take a far less demanding set of courses in high school, especially those who are not college-bound.

High schools vary widely, depending on their location—inner city, suburban, or rural, for example—and on their purpose. While most students have traditionally simply attended their neighborhood or district high school, some areas, especially those with heavy populations, are increasingly offering choices to parents and students, including MAGNET SCHOOLS, VOCATIONAL SCHOOLS, or ALTERNATIVE SCHOOLS. The Department of Education has increasingly urged parents and students to exercise choice in education, by choosing schools, not simply by selecting the area in which to live. For their advice to parents on finding the right school for their child, see CHOOSING A SCHOOL FOR YOUR CHILD (on page 659), which includes a checklist for evaluating schools. Specially oriented public schools—any schools beyond the neighborhood public schools—are called SCHOOLS OF CHOICE. Many parents choose to educate their children outside the public school system altogether, as in a PRIVATE SCHOOL or through HOME SCHOOLING.

OTHER RESOURCES

FOR PARENTS

One Hundred One Educational Conversations with Your Ninth Grader. Other series titles cover grades 10–12. Vito Perrone. Chelsea House, 1995.

GENERAL WORKS

College Board Guide to High Schools, 2nd ed. College Board, 1994.
How to Succeed in High School. Barbara Mayer. NTC Publishing, 1992.
Countdown to College: A Student's Guide to Getting the Most Out of High School. Zola Dincin Schneider and Phyllis B. Kalb. College Entrance Examination Board, 1989.

PERSONAL EXPERIENCES

Ask Me If I Care: Voices from an American High School. Nancy Rubin. Ten Speed Press, 1993.
Greetings from High School. Marian Salzman and Teresa Reisgies. Peterson's Guides, 1991.
Small Victories: The Real World of a Teacher, Her Students and Their High School. Samuel G. Freedman. Harper & Row, 1990.

BACKGROUND WORKS

Angry Classrooms, Vacant Minds: What's Happened to Our High Schools? Martin M. Wooster. PRIPP, 1993.
American High School Adolescent Life and Ethos: An Ethnography. Heewon Chang. Taylor and Francis, 1992.

(See also EDUCATION; PRIVATE SCHOOL; also HELP ON LEARNING AND EDUCATION on page 659.)

hip, the ball-and-socket joint between the pelvis and the thigh bone (*femur*), abnormally formed in newborns who have CONGENITAL DISLOCATION OF THE HIP.

histocompatibility testing, a medical technique used in attempting to match organs and tissue for use in TRANSPLANTS; also called *tissue typing.* (See IMMUNE SYSTEM.)

home birth, DELIVERY of a baby in the home, under the care of a midwife, rather than in a HOSPITAL. Partly in reaction to traditional hospital deliveries, criticized as cold, invasive, and impersonal, some people have chosen to have their babies at home, often with a CERTIFIED NURSE-MIDWIFE in attendance. The main hazards here are loss of time in getting to a hospital if complications arise, and the possibility of infection, since the setting is not as germ-free as either a hospital's DELIVERY ROOM or a MATERNITY CENTER'S BIRTHING ROOM would be. People considering home birth should be even more careful than usual about PRENATAL CARE and checkups, since any complication could be disastrous. They should also make very careful arrangements for obtaining backup medical care, should emergencies arise.

FOR HELP AND FURTHER INFORMATION

Association for Childbirth at Home, International (ACHI)
1989 Riverside Drive
Los Angeles, CA 90039
213–663–4996; 818–545–7128
Fax: 213–663–6153
Tonya Brooks, Founder and Director
Organization concerned with home birth; acts as advocate; offers training for parents, midwives, and childbirth educators; publishes various materials, including quarterly newsletter *Birth Notes.*

(See also PREGNANCY; CHILDBIRTH; CERTIFIED NURSE-MIDWIFE.)

homebound student, a school-age child who is confined to home and so must be taught by a VISITING TEACHER or *itinerant teacher.* The child is sometimes linked with a classroom by means of telephone, television, and/or computer. A homebound student is often a child with severe physical DISABILITIES or MENTAL RETARDATION.

home monitor, a general term for electronic devices used in the home to check the breathing and/or heartbeat of a child susceptible to SLEEP APNEA or considered to be AT-RISK for SUDDEN INFANT DEATH SYNDROME (SIDS); most commonly some type of CARDIAC MONITOR or *car-*

diorespiratory monitor. The aim is to alert parents or CARE-GIVERS to problems, so they can attempt to relieve the problems before the brain and other organs are damaged. While home monitors are clearly useful in some situations, as among infants who have already experienced an APPARENT LIFE-THREATENING EVENT (ALTE), evidence is less clear or simply unavailable about their usefulness among other infants.

Home monitors are not wholly reliable, sometimes giving a FALSE POSITIVE (indicating a problem where none exists) or a FALSE NEGATIVE (failing to signal that a problem does exist). The Public Health Service's report on *Infantile Apnea and Home Monitoring* (1986) defined these as the essential features of an infant cardiorespiratory monitor:

> Primary among these [essential criteria] is the ability to recognize central, obstructive, or mixed apneas and/or bradycardia as they occur. Alarms that accurately reflect the predisposing condition must consistently be alert and be understandable to the care giver. In other words, the monitor must be efficacious in recognizing apnea and triggering its alarm for prolonged apnea. In addition, the monitor must be capable of monitoring its own internal essential functions to assure proper operation. It must be noninvasive and easy to use and understand.

Because of the life and death importance of meeting such criteria, the PHS recommends that monitoring devices should not be sold "over the counter" to consumers, but supplied only with professional recommendation, training, supervision, and support. Parents need, for example, to have been taught techniques to use in cases of emergency, such as RESUSCITATION. (See SUDDEN INFANT DEATH SYNDROME.)

home medical tests, simple, generally inexpensive MEDICAL TESTS designed for people to perform themselves in their homes. While most medical tests and procedures require special equipment and training, an increasing number of tests are being developed for home use. In the Food and Drug Administration's *Do-It-Yourself Medical Testing*, Dixie Farley noted that the three main categories of self-testing products were:

- Tests that help diagnose a specific condition or disease in people with symptoms, such as a PREGNANCY TEST kit to be used after a missed menstrual period.
- SCREENING tests that identify indications of disease in people without symptoms.
- Doctor-recommended monitoring devices that provide ongoing checkups on an existing disease or condition—blood glucose monitoring by people with DIABETES, for instance. Many of these tests analyze urine, blood, or other fluid or tissue samples taken from the body.

Self-tests allow people to get a much more detailed picture of their body's functioning. Using a self-test, for example, a woman can pinpoint her time of OVULATION, important information if she is being treated for INFERTILITY. Monitoring of blood glucose is another self-test that has allowed people with diabetes to live much healthier, more normal lives.

It is important, however, to note what self-tests can and *cannot* do. No self-test can tell you definitively that you have a disease or that you are free from the disease. No test is 100 percent accurate and reliable. But more to the point, self-test does not mean *self-diagnosis*. As Farley points out:

> But considering the results of one test to be a diagnosis is risky...The fact is, a diagnosis by a physician involves an evaluation of the patient's medical history, a physical examination, most likely other tests, and sometimes consultation with other medical experts. And even a carefully gathered patient profile is subject to error.

With self-tests, error may be compounded precisely because the test is being performed by people untrained in either testing or interpretation, and in conditions not specifically designed for scientific testing. As Farley continues:

> The inexperienced, untrained user may misinterpret results, a mistake that can be compounded by the fact that no test is 100 percent accurate even under the best conditions and that results can differ from brand to brand.

This is especially true of tests that were originally designed for use only by medical professionals, but which individuals have purchased from medical supply firms. Such tests may indeed be useful, but generally only when used under a doctor's guidance.

An additional concern about self-tests is that individuals may not seek medical advice when advisable—that is, when there are symptoms. For example, if a menstrual period is overdue, taking a home pregnancy test is only a first step. The missed period may be due to a TUMOR or other condition that should be diagnosed and treated quickly, not ignored if the pregnancy test is negative. The greatest value of a pregnancy self-test is that a woman may go to her doctor early in the first TRIMESTER, so she and her baby may get the maximum benefit of PRENATAL CARE.

Home medical tests hold great promise for the future, allowing individuals to have better information and therefore more meaningful control of their own health and that of their children. In the meantime, while self-tests are still relatively new, people using them should keep in mind the advice in the box entitled CAUTIONS IN USING HOME MEDICAL TESTS, on the following page. (See MEDICAL TESTS; DIABETES; PREGANCY; OVULATION; WHAT TO ASK ABOUT A MEDICAL TEST on page 387.)

Cautions in Using Home Medical Tests

For the maximum safety and effectiveness in using a medical self-test, here are some general precautions (all precautions do not necessarily apply to all tests).

- For test kits that contain chemicals, note the expiration date. Beyond that date, chemicals may lose potency and affect results. Don't buy or use a test kit if the date is past.
- Consider whether the product needs protection from heat or cold. If so, don't leave it in the car trunk or by a sunny window on the trip home. At home, follow storage directions.
- Study the package insert. First read it through to get a general idea of what the test is about. Then go back and study the instructions and pictures until you fully understand each step, before using it.
- If something isn't clear, don't guess. Consult a pharmacist or other health professional. Or check the insert for a toll-free "800" number to call.
- Learn what the test is *intended* to do and what its limitations are. Remember: The tests are not 100 percent accurate.
- If color is part of the test and you are color blind, be sure you have someone with you who *can* discern color to interpret the results.
- Note special precautions, such as avoiding physical activity or certain foods and drugs before testing.
- Follow instructions exactly, including the specimen collection process, if that is a part of the test. Sequence is important. Don't skip a step. If a step to validate the test or calibrate an instrument is included, do it.
- When collecting a urine specimen—unless you use a container from a kit—wash the container thoroughly and rinse out all soap traces, preferably with distilled water, which is generally purer than tap or other bottled water.
- When a step is timed, be precise. Use a stopwatch or at least a watch with a second hand.
- Note beforehand what you should do if the results are positive, negative, or unclear.
- Keep accurate records of results.
- As with medications, keep test kits that contain chemicals out of the reach of children. Promptly discard used test materials as directed.

Any malfunction of a self-test should be reported to the manufacturer or to FDA through the agency's reporting system...Another reporting option, especially in an emergency, is to call the nearest FDA district office listed in the telephone directory. Describe the product completely, stating the product name, type, and—as appropriate—serial and lot numbers, dosage strength, and expiration date. Explain all details of the problem, including the date it occurred.

Source: Do-It-Yourself Medical Testing, by Dixie Farley (1989). Prepared for the Public Health Service, Food and Drug Administration.

home school district, the school district serving the area of a student's legal place of residence. In cases in which a student is found to have SPECIAL NEEDS that the home school district cannot meet, the student may be assigned an OUT-OF-DISTRICT PLACEMENT to a school with appropriate services at the cost of the home school district. If, however, parents voluntarily place the child in a school outside the home district, they are responsible for most if not all costs.

home schooling, EDUCATION of children at home, under parental supervision, rather than in a public or PRIVATE SCHOOL. In some cases, parents use materials they prepare themselves, though many use materials prepared by organizations specializing in home-school education. For children in the United States, COMPULSORY ATTENDANCE at school is required, between ages set by various state laws—often six through sixteen. States have different rules about what parents must do to meet compulsory schooling requirements. Some require parents to register as home schoolers, to submit a formal CURRICULUM plan, or to obtain a state teaching certificate. Parents considering home schooling should carefully explore the laws in their state by contacting their state department of education or one of the organizations listed in this entry. They should also read about the subject and talk with others who have been involved in home schooling to get a full appreciation of the substantial commitment required.

Home schooling has been successful in some families, with children achieving educational levels comparable to (and sometimes even higher than) children attending HIGH SCHOOL, even when the parents in the family were not themselves highly educated in formal terms. It can be effective in allowing students to develop considerable independent initiative in learning, under the proper circumstances. However, in some cases, it can also limit and stunt children, by failing to give them the exposure to a wide range of other people and ideas—the "intangible" education from socializing with other students in a school setting—and to trained teachers in specialized areas. And sometimes home schooling can fail children totally, as when parents make little or no pretense to real home-based education and the local school districts fail to require them to do so.

Home schooling is a course adopted by relatively few parents, partly because of the enormous personal commitment involved, if it is to be done well. Perhaps 100,000 to 250,000 students are presently being educated at home. Many parents who choose home schooling for their children do so for reasons of principle, often wishing to have control of their children's education or, conversely, wishing their children to have a freer, more unstructured education. Various organizations (see those listed in this entry) have been formed for home schooling parents and students to share experiences and information on educational materials. For adults or former DROPOUTS enrolled in a correspondence school course and studying at home, the term more commonly used is HOME STUDY.

FOR HELP AND FURTHER INFORMATION

Alliance for Parental Involvement in Education (ALLPIE), 518–392–6900. (For full group information, and more titles, see HELP ON LEARNING AND EDUCATION on page 659). Publishes various materials, including:

- General works: *The Home School Source Book, Should I Teach My Kids at Home? A Workbook for Parents, Taking Charge Through Homeschooling: Personal and Political Empowerment, Family Matters: Why Homeschooling Makes Sense, Homeschooling for Excellence: How to Take Charge of Your Child's Education—And Why You Absolutely Must.*
- On learning in home-schooling: *I Learn Better by Teaching Myself* (about "child-led learning") and *Writing Because We Love to: Homeschoolers at Work.*
- Practical guides: *Write Your Own Curriculum: A Complete Guide to Planning, Organizing and Documenting Homeschool Curriculums, How to Write a Low Cost/No Cost Curriculum for Your Home-School Child, Family Learning Cooperatives: Getting Started* (on group learning for older children), and *For New Homeschoolers* (selections from *Home Education Magazine*).
- By or for children or teens: *The Teenage Liberation Handbook: How to Quit School and Get a Real Life and Education, My Life as a Traveling Homeschooler in the Words of an 11-year-old,* and *Real Lives: Eleven Teenagers Who Don't Go to School.*

Home School Legal Defense Association (HSLDA)
P.O. Box 159
Paeonian Springs, VA 22129
17333 Pickwick Drive
Purcellville, VA 22132
703–338–5600
Fax: 703–338–2733
Michael P. Farris, President
Organization to provide low-cost legal assistance for member parents operating HSLDA-accepted home schools; seeks to shape public policy; publishes various materials, including bimonthly *Home School Court Report, Should Home Schoolers Obey the Law?, Home Schooling in the United States: A Legal Analysis, Where Do I Draw the Line?, A Nationwide Study of Home Education: Family Characteristics, Legal Matters, and Student Achievement, Constitutional Law for Christian Students,* and video *Home Schooling: A Foundation for Excellence.*

National Challenged Homeschoolers Associated Network (NATHHAN)
5383 Alpine Road, SE
Olalla, WA 98359
206–857–4257
Fax: 206–857–7764
Christian-oriented organization of families providing home schooling for children with special needs; publishes quarterly *Nathhan News.*

International Association of Parents and Professionals for Safe Alternatives in Childbirth (NAPSAC), 314–238–2010. Publishes *Home School.* (For full group information, see CHILDBIRTH.)

National Organization on Legal Problems of Education (NOLPE), 913–273–3550. Publishes *The Law of Home Schooling.* (For full group information, see HELP ON LEARNING AND EDUCATION on page 659.)

National Association for Legal Support of Alternative Schools (NALSAS), 505–471–6928. (For full group information, see ALTERNATIVE SCHOOLS.)

ONLINE RESOURCES

Parents' Information Network (America Online: PIN) Online forums and libraries cover home schooling. (For full information, see GENERAL PARENTING RESOURCES on page 634.)

OTHER RESOURCES

Home School, Taking the First Step: A Complete Program Planning Handbook, rev. ed. Borg Hendrickson. Mountain Meadow, 1994.

Homeschooler's Resource Directory, 1995: The Sourcebook of Companies, Products and Services for Home Educators. Kathy Fisher, ed. Brand Cross, 1994.

Kids Who Start Ahead, Stay Ahead: What Actually Happens When Home-Taught Early Learners Go to School. Neil Harvey. Avery, 1994.

The Home School Manual: Plans, Pointers, Reasons, and Resources, 5th ed. Theodore E. Wade, Jr. Gazelle, 1994.

The Home-Schooling Resource Guide and Directory of Organizations. Mary Hood. Ambleside, 1994.

The Relaxed Home School: A Family Production. Mary Hood. Ambleside, 1994.
Write Your Own Curriculum: A Complete Guide to Planning, Organizing and Documenting Homeschool Curriculums. Jenifer O'Leary. Whole Life, 1993.
Family Matters: Why Home Schooling Makes Sense. David Gutterson. Harcourt Brace, 1993.

home study, enrollment in a school that has, instead of classes, sequenced materials for a student to study at home; the student's work is then evaluated and graded by school staff; also called *correspondence courses* and now, more commonly, DISTANCE EDUCATION.

A home study is also an analysis of the family situation of parents wishing to adopt, which by law is generally prepared by a licensed social worker, often from an ADOPTION agency, whether the child is from the U.S. or from abroad. Would-be adopters meet with the social worker in the home or agency setting, over a period of several weeks or months. Some agencies use a group approach, in which parents are evaluated during a parenting preparation course. The social worker who writes the home-study report is attempting to screen out parents who might be unsuitable as adoptive parents, for instance, because of financial or psychological instability.

Would-be adoptive parents also often contribute autobiographies or other personal statements that help social workers understand what they have to offer children. As part of the evaluation process, parents often have to supply many other materials, including personal references and numerous certificates (see ADOPTION PAPERWORK on page 15). The final home-study report is then sent out every time parents make an application for a child. Papers submitted abroad for an international adoption often need to be notarized and authenticated.

homosexuality, sexual attraction to people of the same sex, a pattern of sexual preference that exists in substantial segments of the population. Though reliable, current data is lacking, perhaps 5 percent of the population is estimated to be fully homosexual by preference, while another 15 to 35 percent may be *bisexual,* having both homosexual and heterosexual relationships at various points during their lives. Today, male homosexuals are often called *gay men* and women homosexuals *lesbians.*

Though accepted in some times and places in history, people with same-sex preferences have traditionally been shunned and in the past generally have kept silent about their sexual orientation, an approach that causes enormous emotional stress and isolation among homosexuals. But in recent years, many of them have elected to "come out of the closet," openly showing their sexual preferences. This change has affected the parent-child relationship in a variety of ways.

Some homosexual or bisexual men and women have married and had children, sometimes because they were attempting to conform to the heterosexual lifestyle or did not realize that they were bisexual until after they married. When they later became openly homosexual or bisexual, many of them risked losing CUSTODY of and sometimes even access to their children. In bitter divorce battles, an ex-spouse has often been able to successfully use homosexual activities against a former partner in battles over custody, VISITATION RIGHTS, and financial settlements—or to use threats to expose sexual orientation as a way to obtain unfair DIVORCE settlements (see SEPARATION AGREEMENT).

Homosexual orientation is no longer an absolute bar to a favorable decision in many courts, and in some states, courts are instructed to disregard a parent's sexual orientation unless it affects the person's fitness as a parent or CAREGIVER. However, custody and related questions are still highly subjective and are likely to require anyone who is homosexual to stage a hard fight for a successful ruling. In addition, if a person becomes openly homosexual after receiving a favorable court decision, many courts consider that a CHANGE OF CIRCUMSTANCE sufficient to reopen the question of custody—necessitating another court battle. At the very least, formerly married homosexual parents face the delicate task of explaining their stance to the children.

Some homosexual couples, desiring to form their own families, have arranged for ADOPTION of a child, sometimes one born to a SURROGATE MOTHER, or (in the case of lesbians) for birth by one of the women following ARTIFICIAL INSEMINATION. Such arrangements carry their own hazards. The nontraditional family arrangement can be confusing to young children and can lead to some taunts and discrimination from others, so the parents need to very carefully prepare the children to understand the special family situation. If such couples break up, they can have all the usual battles over custody, VISITATION RIGHTS, and CHILD SUPPORT, but these are made more difficult because they do not come under the usual protection of marital laws. These legal matters are further complicated when one lesbian partner bore the child, since she is considered the biological mother. In many states, the other partner has no legal relationship to the child at all, though in some areas the same-sex COPARENT is allowed also to adopt the child.

The new openness has also changed the situation for parents of children who are—or think they may be—homosexual. In the past, such young people were isolated and alone, especially during the difficult period of ADOLESCENCE, feeling (often rightly) that they could not talk to their parents and feeling bereft of other sources of help. That is still the case for many, but in at least some areas, various groups now openly offer assistance to adolescents in such situations, and some school systems even provide counseling for children uncertain about their sexual orientation. More such young people also feel that they can tell their parents, although in the past they might have spent decades painfully hiding the truth. The situation has been complicated by the advent of AIDS, a SEXUALLY TRANSMITTED DISEASE that can be spread by many kinds of sexual contact, especially some forms of male homosexual intercourse.

In the not-so-distant past, homosexuality was considered a form of MENTAL DISORDER. Though that is no longer true, some related disorders may be treated by psychologists or psychiatrists, including *gender idenity disorder* (see GENDER IDENTITY), in which people's inner sense of gender (male or female) does not match their external SECONDARY SEX CHARACTERISTICS. This may lead to *transsexualism,* in which the person desires to live like one of the opposite sex and sometimes also seeks surgical and hormonal treatment to change his or her sex.

Various organizations (see listings in this entry) have been formed to help homosexual parents and children deal with their special problems.

FOR HELP AND FURTHER INFORMATION

Lavender Families Resource Network
P.O. Box 21567
Seattle, WA 98111
206–325–2643, voice/TT
Nancy Rickerson, Executive Officer
Organization to aid lesbian, gay, bisexual, or transsexual parents, coparents, or grandparents; formerly Lesbian Mothers National Defense Fund (LMNDF); provides information and support on custody issues—its original focus—but also on wider parenting rights, donor insemination, and adoption; acts as an advocate; maintains volunteers to act as child advocates or guardians *ad litem* in custody disputes; has fund to aid low-income parents in related litigation; publishes numerous materials, including quarterly newsletter *Mom's Apple Pie*, pamphlets: *Coming Out to Your Kids: Tips for Lesbian and Gay Parents, Glossary for Lesbian and Gay Families, Introduction to Lesbian Families: A Fact Sheet,* and *National Coming Out Day: Ideas for Lesbian and Gay Families*; and numerous article reprints.

Parents, Families, and Friends of Lesbians and Gays (FLAG)
1101 14th Street NW, Suite 1030
Washington, DC 20005
202–638–4200
Fax: 202–638–0243
E-mail: pflagntl@aol.com (America Online: PFLAGNTL)
Sandra Gillis, President
Network of peer-support groups of parents of homosexuals; seeks to maintain and strengthen parent-child communication; acts as advocate; publishes various materials.

National Federation of Parents and Friends of Gays (NF/PFOG)
8020 Eastern Avenue NW
Washington, DC 20012
202–726–3223
Eugene M. Baker, Executive Secretary
Network of peer-counseling groups, aimed at helping families and friends of homosexuals understand the problems faced by gay men and lesbians; acts as advocate; publishes various materials, including recommended reading list.

Lambda Legal Defense and Education Fund (LLDEF)
666 Broadway
New York, NY 10012
212–995–8585
Fax: 212–995–2306
Kevin Cathcart, Executive Director
Organization that defends homosexuals' civil rights in many areas, including housing, child custody, and AIDS; provides information and referrals; assists in legal preparation; litigates test cases; maintains library of cases affecting homosexual rights; publishes various materials.

Sexuality Information and Education Council of the United States (SIECUS), 212–819–9770. Publishes fact sheet *Sexual Orientation and Identity* and annotated bibliography *Gay Male and Lesbian Sexuality and Issues.* (For full group information, see SEX EDUCATION.)

Custody Action for Lesbian Mothers (CALM), 610–667–7508. (For full group information, see CUSTODY.)

ONLINE RESOURCES

Internet: gaynet Focuses on gay, lesbian, and bisexual issues, especially on college campuses. To subscribe, send this message "SUB gaynet [your first name] [your last name]" to: mailto:majordomo@queernet.org

Internet: Moms Forum for lesbian mothers. To subscribe, send e-mail message to: mailto:moms-request@qiclab.scn.rain.com

OTHER RESOURCES

FOR OR ABOUT GAY AND LESBIAN PARENTS

The Family Next Door. Bimonthly for lesbian and gay parents and friends. Address: Next Door Publishing, P.O. Box 21580, Oakland, CA 94620; phone/fax: 510–482–5778.

Lesbian and Gay Parenting Handbook. April Martin. HarperCollins, 1993.

Preserving and Protecting the Families of Lesbians and Gay Men. Roberta Achtenberg. National Center for Lesbian Rights, 1991.

Different Mothers: Sons and Daughters of Lesbians Talk about Their Lives. Louise Rafkin, ed. Cleis Press, 1990.

ON COMING OUT

Coming Out in College: The Struggle for a Queer Identity. Robert A. Rhoads. Greenwood, 1994.

Coming Out to Parents. Mary V. Bornoh. Pilgrim Press (New York City), 1990.

There's Something I've Been Meaning to Tell You. Loralee Macpike, ed. Naiad Press, 1989. On homosexual or bisexual parents coming out to children; includes review of legal implications.

How Will I Tell My Mother? Jerry Arterburn with his brother Steve. Nelson, 1988.

On legal issues

The Rights of Lesbians and Gay Men: The Basic ACLU Guide to a Gay Person's Rights, 3rd ed. Nan D. Hunter and others. Southern Illinois University Press, 1992.

Sexual Orientation and the Law. Harvard Law Review eds. Harvard University Press, 1990.

A Legal Guide for Lesbian and Gay Couples, 5th ed. Hayden Curry and Denis Clifford. Nolo, 1989.

For or about children

Heather Has Two Mommies. Lesléa Newman. In Other Words, 1990.

For or about teens

Gay and Lesbian Youth. R.C. Williams Savin. Hemisphere, 1990.

Coping with Your Sexual Orientation. Deborah A. Miller and Alex Waigandt. Rosen, 1990.

Jack. A. M. Holmes. Macmillan, 1989. About a teenage boy adjusting to his father's homosexuality.

Background works

Straight Parents, Gay Children: Keeping Families Together. Robert Bernstein. Thunder's Mouth, 1995.

Prayers for Bobby: A Mother's Coming to Terms with the Suicide of Her Gay Son. Leroy Aarons. HarperSanFrancisco, 1995.

Encyclopedia of Homosexuality. Wayne R. Dynes and others, eds. Garland, 1990.

(See also sex education.)

honor roll, a list prepared by a school at the end of each marking period indicating which students achieved an AVERAGE of B or better, or, if number GRADES are used, generally 90 or better; the HIGH SCHOOL equivalent of a college or university's DEAN'S LIST.

hormones, a wide variety of chemicals produced by various organs in the body to help control various body functions, including METABOLISM, growth, development of SECONDARY SEX CHARACTERISTICS, a woman's MENSTRUAL CYCLE, a man's SPERM production, the changes involved in PREGNANCY and LACTATION, and the general circulatory system. Some hormones are produced by body organs such as the kidneys or intestines (and during pregnancy, the PLACENTA), but most are produced by ENDOCRINE GLANDS, among them the HYPOTHALAMUS, PITUITARY GLAND, THYROID GLAND, parathyroid glands, thymus, ADRENAL GLANDS, and the sex organs called GONADS (TESTES in the male and OVARIES in the female). STEROIDS are one key family of sex hormones, including TESTOSTERONE, ESTROGEN, and PROGESTERONE. Among the other main hormones relating to the REPRODUCTIVE SYSTEM are HUMAN CHORIONIC GONADOTROPIN, FOLLICLE-STIMULATING HORMONE, and LUTEINIZING HORMONE.

FOR HELP AND FURTHER INFORMATION

National Institute of Child Health and Human Development (NICHD), 301–496–5133. (For full group information, see PREGNANCY.)

National Digestive Disease Information Clearinghouse (NDDIC), 301–654–3810. (For full group information, see DIGESTIVE SYSTEM AND DISORDERS.)

National Clearinghouse for Alcohol and Drug Abuse Information (NCADI), 301–468–2600. Publishes *Alcohol and Hormones.* (For full group information, see HELP AGAINST SUBSTANCE ABUSE on page 703.)

Other resources

The Good News about Women's Hormones: Complete Information and Proven Solutions for the Most Common Hormonal Problems. Geoffrey P. Redmond. Warner, 1995.

Raging Hormones: Do They Rule Our Lives? Gail Vines. University of California Press, 1994.

What's Wrong with My Hormones?, rev. ed. Gillian Ford. D. Ford, 1992.

hospice, specialized care in a home or home-like setting for people who are dying, focusing on freedom from pain, emotional support, and quality of life for the time remaining. Originally the term referred to a HOSPITAL annex devoted to caring for terminally ill people, and perhaps 10 percent of such care is still provided in a hospice center or nursing home. But most hospice care today is provided in the patient's home. Unlike traditional hospital-based care, which focuses on trying to "beat" the disease, hospice care halts aggressive therapy and focuses on *palliative care*, stressing pain relief and control of symptoms. Of course, if the patient unexpectedly improves or the disease goes into remission, aggressive medical therapy can be resumed. The patient's family also receives support, both during the final illness and often for a year or more after the death of a family member. Many hospices sponsor bereavement support groups for anyone in the community who has experienced a death of a friend or relative. Initially most hospices did not include care for children, but many now do. This lets parents have more control over their child's health care and allows all family members to be involved, rather than isolated from one another.

Under the hospice approach, much of the daily care of the patient is provided by family members. Their efforts are supplemented by hospice staff who come in to provide specialized services, including administration of pain medication, help with personal cleanliness, talking with the patient about feelings, and preparing favorite foods, helping with household chores, and putting financial affairs in order. Trained volunteers also provide

RESPITE CARE, giving family members a break from care. Along with volunteers, the hospice team may include doctors, nurses, social workers, counselors, home health aides, clergy, and a variety of specialist therapists, such as physical and occupational therapists, music or art therapists, massage therapists, and diet counselors, each brought in as needed. Approximately 84 percent of all hospice patients have CANCER; most of the rest have AIDS or heart disease.

By law, the decision to enter a hospice program is the patient's. When MINOR children are involved, parents must make the decision on their behalf. Adults who would wish to have hospice care for themselves, should the need arise, should strongly consider contacting an attorney and drawing up ADVANCE DIRECTIVES, including a living will and durable power of attorney (health care proxy), to make their wishes clear should they be so gravely ill as to be unable to make and express that decision. Hospice care is largely covered by many HEALTH INSURANCE policies and by Medicaid in many states, as well as by Medicare. However, parents should check beforehand to see if their insurance or HEALTH CARE plan covers hospice care, and what portion of the care, if any, they would need to pay. If hospice care is not covered, the hospice will generally seek other coverage, if possible, and otherwise will often cover costs from memorial funds.

If the patient's physician agrees that hospice care is appropriate, the patient or parent will be asked to sign consent and insurance forms, including a *hospice election form*, confirming that they understand the care to be provided is palliative. The hospice provider assesses the situation and arranges to provide the necessary medication, equipment, supplies, and services, providing additional equipment and helpers in the home as needed, as the disease worsens.

FOR HELP AND FURTHER INFORMATION

Children's Hospice International (CHI)
1850 M Street NW, # 900
Washington, DC 20036
703–684–0330; Helpline: 800–2–4-CHILD [242–4453]
Fax: 703–684–0226
Ann Armstrong-Dailey, Founding Director
Organization of people seeking to expand hospice care for children; provides information; publishes various materials, including *Hospice Care for Children, Home Care for Seriously Ill Children: A Manual for Parents, Children's Hospice/Home Care: An Implementation Manual for Nurses,* and *Hospice Approaches to Pediatric Care.*

National Hospice Organization (NHO)
1901 North Moore Street, Suite 901
Arlington, VA 22209
703–243–5900; National Hospice Helpline: 800–658–8898
Fax: 703–525–5762
John J. Mahoney, President
Organization of hospices; provides information, referrals, and advocacy; publishes *NHO Hospice News*; annual directory of hospices; consumer brochures *What's Hospice, About Hospice, About Hospice Under Medicare, Basics of Hospice, How to Get Help with Medicare Expenses, Helping Confused Patients, Be a Volunteer, About Caregiving, About Pain Management, Universal Precautions, Advanced Medical Directives,* and *Timeline Phases of Terminal Care*; books *Hospice Care for Children, Hold Me While I Cry* (by a mother), *Carpe Diem: Enjoying Every Day with a Terminal Illness,* and *The Hospice Handbook*; and many technical assistance publications and works for health professionals.

OTHER RESOURCES

GENERAL WORKS

At Home with Terminal Illness. Michael Appleton and Todd Henschell. Prentice Hall, 1995.
Hospice Care for Children. Ann Armstrong-Dailey and Sarah Z. Goltzer, eds. Oxford University Press, 1993.
The Hospice Handbook: A Complete Guide. Larry Beresford. Little, Brown, 1993.
Hospice Means Hope. Kenneth B. Wentzel. Semaphore, 1991.

BACKGROUND WORKS

In the Light of Dying: Journals of a Hospice Volunteer, 2nd ed. Joan L. Taylor. Crossroad, 1993.
Hospice Movement: Easing Death's Pains. Cathy Siebold. Twayne/Macmillan, 1992.
The Hospice Movement: A Better Way of Caring for the Dying, rev. ed. Sandol Stoddard. Random, 1991.

hospital, an institution providing medical care of a type or level that cannot generally be offered at home. Many hospitals are government institutions, run by federal, state, county, community, or city governments, sometimes at least partly funded by local contributions. Many others are owned and operated by religious groups, and some are linked with university research and teaching programs. Still others are run on a for-profit basis by medical-care corporations. Hospitals are often classed by the level and kind of care they are equipped to provide, such as:

- *The primary-care level (Level I)*, where the care is basic and generally directed toward handling routine medical emergencies, such as a broken arm. Many Level I hospitals are public hospitals or federally funded community health (or mental health) centers. These often provide not only routine emergency care but also include clinics that provide basic maternity care, WELL-BABY EXAMINATIONS, vision and hearing examinations, and dental care, as well as facilities for DELIVERY, often with home-like BIRTHING ROOMS. Families who lack HEALTH INSURANCE often receive care at public centers.

  Level I hospitals are generally geared to handle only routine care, including normal or low-risk pregnancies.

Before Delivery: What to Pack for the Hospital

Approximately two weeks before your delivery date, pack a bag with the personal things you will want to take with you. You will probably want to include:

- Bathrobe.
- Two nightgowns (opening in front if you plan to breastfeed).
- Slippers.
- Two bras (nursing bras if you plan to breastfeed).
- Underpants.
- Self-adhesive sanitary pads.
- Toothbrush and toothpaste.
- Comb, brush, and curlers, if desired.
- Cosmetics, if desired.
- Books or magazines.
- Something to wear home (remember to make it loose fitting; you won't yet have your figure back).
- Any prenatal reports or hospitalization papers.

You should also—ahead of time—pack the clothes you will want to take the baby home in. Remember to tell the person who will be taking you home where they are. If the weather is cool, the baby will need a blanket, sweater, or cap. If it is warm, you need only diapers, safety pins, a shirt, and a receiving blanket.

Also ahead of time, plan on how you will get to the hospital, both during the day and at night. Have telephone numbers in an obvious and handy place so that you can call your husband, friend, mother, or a taxicab when you are ready to go. Have the doctor's phone number on your list also, so that you can call to find out if it is time to go to the hospital or to report that you are going. It is usually an exciting time and it is otherwise easy to forget phone numbers.

Source: Adapted from Prenatal Care (1983). Prepared for the Public Health Service by the Bureau of Health Care Delivery and Assistance, Division of Maternal and Child Health.

HIGH-RISK PREGNANCIES are better handled by more sophisticated facilities; and if complications develop during LABOR OR DELIVERY, the medical staff may stabilize the mother and infant and transport one or both to a higher-level facility. Children with severe CHRONIC ILLNESS OR DISABILITIES may also be referred to a higher-level hospital better equipped to meet their special needs.

- *The secondary-care level (Level II)*, an intermediate level of care, serving a larger area and population than a Level I hospital, and having more sophisticated medical equipment and laboratory facilities, sometimes including a NEONATAL INTENSIVE CARE UNIT (ICU). A Level II hospital would handle normal or moderate-risk pregnancies, referring pregnancies with high risk or complications to a Level III facility.
- *The tertiary-care level (Level III)*, which provides far more sophisticated facilities for diagnosis and treatment, including highly specialized staff and extensive support systems. Level III hospitals are often associated with university research and training facilities, and are then sometimes called UNIVERSITY-AFFILIATED FACILITIES (UAF's). A woman with a high-risk pregnancy will be wise to arrange to have her child in a tertiary care facility or UAF, if possible, where the specialist staff will be best trained and equipped to deal with any complications that may occur. Similarly a child with severe health problems may well be referred to a Level III or UAF facility for diagnosis and extensive or sophisticated treatment, such as BONE MARROW TRANSPLANT OR OPEN-HEART SURGERY. One major concern in choosing between medical plans is whether such special care would be covered (for a full discussion of such questions, see HEALTH INSURANCE; also WHAT DO YOU NEED TO ASK ABOUT HEALTH INSURANCE AND MANAGED CARE? on page 288.)

If a woman decides to give birth in a hospital, she and her partner will want to assess (with the doctor's help) any risk factors in the pregnancy, and also the policies of the hospital regarding such questions as the administration of enemas, FETAL MONITORING, EPISIOTOMIES, intravenous supplements, and the policies regarding BIRTH PARTNERS, including who will or will not be allowed to attend the birth and what training (if any) is required of birth partners. The couple can then assess what level hospital, and which particular facility, will be most appropriate. In fact, the choice of an OBSTETRICIAN-GYNECOLOGIST is intertwined with the choice of a hospital, since doctors are only allowed to admit and treat patients at hospitals to which they have been granted *admitting privileges*. Before delivery, a woman should also plan ahead, packing a bag of items ready to take to the hospital, and another of clothes for the baby to come home in (see box entitled BEFORE DELIVERY: WHAT TO PACK FOR THE HOSPITAL, above).

In addition to specialized medical care, tertiary care facilities or UAFs also generally offer special preparation and support for parents and children facing medical crises.

If possible, children should go to a hospital that specializes in care for children, and so will be geared to help both child and family come to terms with the medical procedures. Some hospitals have made special arrangements for children who spend long periods in hospitals. RECREATIONAL THERAPISTS, sometimes called *child life workers*, attempt to develop recreational programs in homelike quarters. Some hospitals even having social rooms where adolescents can entertain their friends. Parents may also find help from the various self-help and ADVOCACY groups that have been formed by other parents dealing with severe health problems, often linked with hospital facilities. (See entries under the particular type of health problem faced, such as CANCER, LIVER PROBLEMS, or CYSTIC FIBROSIS.) In a hospital at whatever level, parents may find that they need to be persistent to obtain information and clear explanations of their medical choices, including provision of pain medication for children (see PAIN AND PAIN TREATMENT).

FOR HELP AND FURTHER INFORMATION

Pediatric Projects
P.O. Box 571555
Tarzana, CA 91357–1555
818–705–3660
Fax: 800–947–0947
E-mail: medpub@kaiwan.com
Pat Azarnoff, Executive Director
Nonprofit organization concerned with the well-being of children with special needs and their families; consults by phone with parents to provide medically oriented toys, including customized "exceptional animals" such as teddy bears with scars from open-heart surgery or using wheelchairs; publishes various materials, including:

- Bimonthly newsletter *Pediatric Mental Health*, covering support services for parents, therapeutic recreation programs for children, preparation of children for hospitalization, surgery and other medical procedures, and visits to the clinic or doctor.
- On preparation for hospitalization: *Preparing Children for the Stress of Hospitalization, Hospitalized Children: How You Can Lessen the Emotional Impact, Preparing Well Children for Possible Hospitalization, The Need for Teachers to Prepare Children for Hospitalization, Preparing the Pediatric Family, Helping the Hospitalized Child Cope Through Control, Mediating the Trauma of Serious Illness and Hospitalization, Preparation of Children for Hospitalization in U.S. Acute Care Hospitals, Preparation Programs and New Strategies, Centers of Learning in a Pediatric Playroom, Creative Dramatics Programs in Hospitals, Play and the Hospitalized Child, The Preparation Debate and the Importance of a Prepared Patient, Teaching Materials for Pediatric Health Professionals*, and the game *SomeBody: The Human Anatomy Game.*
- For parents: *Questions When Surgery Is Recommended for Your Child, Staying with Your Child Before Surgery, Your Child (Baby) in the Hospital*, and *Plain Talk About Mutual Help Groups.*
- General materials: *Parents and Siblings of Pediatric Patients, Factors in Reducing Children's Anxiety About Clinic Visits, Breathing Management for Reducing Stress with Pediatric Patients, Bringing Bad News to Children, Chronically Ill Hospitalized Children's Concepts of Their Illness, Children's Mental Development in Medical Practice, Children's (Multicultural) Health Fair*, and *Teaching Crisis Counseling Skills to Pediatric Residents.*
- Child-oriented bandages for children who must wear them to cover injection sites and the like, with designs including the Little Mermaid, the Muppets, the Simpsons, Snoopy and Peanuts, Super Mario Bros., Where's Waldo?, various jungle animals, and more.
- Zaadi dolls, anatomically correct female or male dolls that open up to show internal organs and can be used to prepare children or adults for medical procedures, such as setting a broken leg, finding a vein for an intravenous site, inserting a tube for catheterization, or transplanting a kidney.
- Materials for health professionals on the psychosocial aspects of caring for children and youth.

American Academy of Pediatrics (AAP), 800–433–9016. Publishes video *Slim Goodbody's—The Before Tour*, preparing children ages three through eleven for a first visit to a hospital or ambulatory surgery center. (For full group information, see HEALTH CARE.)

National Mental Health Association (NMHA), 800–969–6642. Publishes *Preparing Your Child for the Hospital* and *Understanding and Dealing with a Child's Illness.* (For full group information, see MENTAL DISORDERS.)

Agency for Health Care Policy and Research Clearinghouse, 800–358–9295. Publishes *Rural Health Care: The Future of the Hospital.* (For full group information, see HEALTH INSURANCE).

OTHER RESOURCES

GENERAL WORKS

The Best Hospitals in America, 2nd ed. John W. Wright and Linda Sunshine, eds. Gale, 1995.

Fight Back Guide To: Hospital Care. David Horowitz. Dell, 1993.

And How Are We Feeling Today?: The Impatient Patient's Hospital Survival Guide. Kathryn Hammer. Contemporary, 1993.

Take This Book to the Hospital with You: A Consumer Guide to Surviving Your Hospital Stay, rev. ed. Charles B. Inlander and Ed Weiner. Panthon, 1991.

Waiting Room: Writing by Children and Adult Patients in a Hospital Setting. Todd Beers, ed. Writers and Books, 1991.

FOR OR BY CHILDREN

Going to the Hospital. Random House, 1990.

Once I Had an Operation. Seventeen-minute film produced and directed by Laurie Wagman. Churchill Media,

1991. Introduces children (ages five through nine) to surgical procedures and hospital experiences in general.

Background works

Deciding Who Lives: Fateful Choices in the Intensive-Care Nursery. Renee R. Anspach. University of California Press, 1993.

Compelled Compassion: Government Intervention in the Treatment of Critically Ill Newborns. Arthur L. Caplan, ed. Humana, 1992.

Pickwickian and Other Stories of Intensive Care: Medical and Ethical Challenges in the ICU. Lawrence Martin. Lakeside, 1991.

hospital hold, temporarily retaining in the HOSPITAL a child brought to an emergency room for treatment, often against the wishes of the parent or CAREGIVER, when the medical or social work staff suspect possible CHILD ABUSE OR NEGLECT. Often social workers are quickly called in and the state takes temporary CUSTODY of the child.

hotline, a telephone number that can be called in times of emergency, often staffed twenty-four hours a day by trained counselors. Classic hotlines are special-purpose numbers, as for runaways, drug addicts, people considering SUICIDE, or people reporting CHILD ABUSE AND NEGLECT. Some hotlines are local, but others are toll-free numbers that can be called long distance. Many organizations operate general information lines on a toll-free basis, sometimes for limited hours but occasionally around the clock; these are more properly called HELPLINES.

House-Tree-Person (H-T-P) Projective Technique, a type of individually administered PROJECTIVE TEST for people from age three to adult used to assess personality and especially to highlight any emotional disturbance. The child is asked to make separate drawings of a house, a tree, and a person, and then to interpret each of the drawings, responses to which the administrator then gives SCORES according to the test manual. (See TESTS.)

human chorionic gonadotropin (hCG), a HORMONE produced by the PLACENTA during PREGNANCY that triggers the production of the additional ESTROGEN and PROGESTERONE needed during pregnancy. Excreted in urine, hCG is used in testing to see if pregnancy has occurred. In cases of INFERTILITY, hCG is also sometimes given to stimulate OVULATION in a woman or SPERM production in a man. It may also be administered as a preventive for MISCARRIAGE and as a treatment for some forms of undescended TESTES. (For a description of a HOME MEDICAL TEST using hCG, see PREGNANCY TESTS.)

human growth hormone (hGH), the key HORMONE in regulating growth produced by the PITUITARY GLAND, which is sometimes administered when a child's growth has been extremely slow. Beginning in 1963, this hGH extract was made from human pituitary glands, but in 1985 it was discovered that a few people receiving it had died of a rare slow brain virus (*Creutzfeldt-Jakob disease*), apparently from contaminated pituitary tissue in the extract. Since that time, a synthetic form of hGH has been used that does not carry that risk of contamination and seems to work as well to bring a child's growth into the normal range. (See GROWTH AND GROWTH DISORDERS.)

Huntington's disease (HD or Huntington's chorea), a GENETIC DISORDER that causes the brain to deteriorate, resulting in the quick, jerky movements called CHOREA and—over a period of ten to twenty-five years—gradual mental degeneration and loss of physical control, as in speaking, walking, and swallowing. Recent medications have eased the effects of Huntington's, but no cure is known to stop the disease's progression.

HD is passed on by a single, defective, DOMINANT gene—meaning each child of an HD-affect parent has a 50 percent risk of inheriting the disorder—and appears equally in both sexes, also affecting all races and ethnic groups. Though symptoms can appear as early as age two and as late as eighty, they generally do not appear until between ages thirty and fifty, so people may have children and pass on the disease before realizing that they have it themselves. The 1993 discovery of the HD gene has allowed development of a test to tell whether or not a person carries the disease. It involves taking a blood sample from the person being tested and sometimes from a parent. The samples are then analyzed at special testing centers (for a list, see Huntington's Disease Society of America listing in this entry). Discovery of the gene also holds promise for the future; as genetic researchers continue to study the defective gene, they hope to learn how to postpone its progress and even prevent it, through GENE THERAPY. Prospective parents with Huntington's in their family history will want to seek GENETIC COUNSELING.

FOR HELP AND FURTHER INFORMATION

Huntington's Disease Society of America (HDSA)
140 West 22nd Street, 6th Floor
New York, NY 10011
212–242–1968; 800–345-HDSA [345–4372]
Fax: 212–243–2443
Stephen E. Bajardi, Executive Director
Organization concerned with Huntington's disease; provides information referrals; supports research; operates Brain Donor program, under which families donate tissue vital for research; publishes newsletter *The Marker* and other materials, including:

- Books: *Living with Juvenile Huntington's Disease, Toward a Fuller Life: A Guide to Everyday Living with Huntington's Disease, You Are Not Alone: A Guide to Establishing Huntington's Disease Support Groups,* and *A Physician's Guide to the Management of Huntington's Disease: Pharmacologic and Non-Pharmacologic Interventions.*

- Brochures: *Huntington's Disease: A Disease of Both Mind and Body, So You Got the News: What Happens Now?, Huntington's Disease: Facts at a Glance,* and *The ABC's of Government Disability Programs: SSD & SSI.* On genetic testing: *We've Got the Gene! But What Does It Mean?, Testing for the Huntington's Disease Gene, Guidelines for Genetic Testing for Huntington's Disease.*
- Videos: *Within Reach: Closing in on a Cure* and *Communication Strategies for People with Huntington's Disease.*
- Numerous materials for support groups and for health professionals.

Hereditary Disease Foundation (HDF)
1427 7th Street, #2
Santa Monica, CA 90901
310–458–4183
E-mail: 75051.3604@compron.com or hereditary@earthlink.com
Nancy S. Wexler, President
Organization supporting research into causes, prevention, diagnosis, and treatment of genetic disorders, especially Huntington's disease; provides information.

National Institute of Neurological Disorders and Stroke (NINDS), 800–352–9424. Publishes special report *Huntington's Disease.* (For full group information, see BRAIN AND BRAIN DISORDERS.)

National Organization for Rare Disorders (NORD), 800–999–6673. (For full group information, see RARE DISORDERS.)

hydrocele, an accumulation of fluid (literally a "water sac") in the area around the TESTES and within the SCROTUM, sometimes resulting from inflammation or injury and generally painless. Though often found in middle-aged men, hydroceles sometimes occur in male babies shortly after birth. In the booklet *Infant Care,* the Public Health Service notes:

> One or both of a [newborn] boy's testicles may seem particularly large, and may be surrounded by a water sac or "hydrocele." Seek medical care for any swelling in the groin, and go to the doctor or clinic immediately if there is a red or painful swelling in the groin or testicles. Hydroceles are painless, cause no harm and go away without treatment, usually within a few months.

hydrocephalus, a condition involving excessive amounts of CEREBROSPINAL FLUID circulating in the brain and spinal cord, and sometimes blockage of the normal circulation; popularly called "water on the brain." Hydrocephalus may be present at birth, as the result of a GENETIC DISORDER such as SPINA BIFIDA; it may develop because of a disorder, such as Hurler syndrome or Hunter syndrome (see MUCOPOLYSACCHARIDOSES), or from other causes, such as TRAUMATIC BRAIN INJURY, a BRAIN TUMOR, or infections, such as MENINGITIS or ENCEPHALITIS. Recent studies suggest a link between hydrocephalus and the mother's exposure to general ANESTHESIA during the first three months of PREGNANCY.

With hydrocephalus, the fluid in the brain is generally under increased pressure and expands the fluid-filled cavities (VENTRICLES) in the center of the brain and in the process compresses and damages brain tissue. In infants, whose skulls are still soft and expandable, the skull becomes abnormally large, while in older children and adults, the pressure soon becomes dangerously high.

If unchecked, hydrocephalus can lead to EPILEPSY, severe brain damage, SEIZURES, and sometimes death. The condition can be diagnosed using a variety of MEDICAL TESTS, notably the CT SCAN or MRI. Treatment generally involves draining away excess fluid, as through a SHUNT, and (when possible) dealing with the underlying cause.

FOR HELP AND FURTHER INFORMATION

National Hydrocephalus Foundation (NHF)
400 North Michigan Avenue, Suite 1102
Chicago, IL 60611–4102
312–645–0701; 800–785–6161
Fax: 312–427–9311
James A. Mazzetti, Executive Director
Organization concerned with hydrocephalus; provides information and referrals; rents videos; publishes quarterly newsletter, pamphlet *The Facts About Hydrocephalus,* pamphlets on related fields, and article reprints.

National Institute of Neurological Disorders and Stroke (NINDS), 800–352–9424. (For full group information, see BRAIN AND BRAIN DISORDERS.)

Spina Bifida Association of America (SBAA), 800–621–3141. Publishes *A Guide to Hydrocephalus.* (For full group information, see SPINA BIFIDA.)

National Institute of Child Health and Human Development (NICHD), 301–496–5133. (For full group information, see PREGNANCY.)

Autism Network International, 315–476–2462. (For full group information, see AUTISM.)

hymen, a thin piece of membrane that mostly covers the opening of the VAGINA; it generally has a small opening in the center that is stretched or torn during the first penetration of the area, as in sexual intercourse, use of tampons during MENSTRUATION, or during a medical examination. In some rare cases, a girl's hymen will have no opening, a condition called *imperforate hymen.* This is often discovered at MENARCHE, since menstrual blood cannot be released; it may need to be opened surgically.

hyperactivity (hyperkinetic syndrome), a behavior pattern in which a person is constantly or excessively moving about and making rapid motions, often in a disorganized or disruptive way, or if seated is fidgeting or squirming in such a way as to bother others, among schoolchildren often interfering with learning among other children. Hyperactivity is a general term, used loosely to refer to a wide range of behaviors; in psychiatric parlance, it is no longer generally considered a separate disorder, but part of a wider complex of behaviors called ATTENTION-DEFICIT HYPERACTIVITY DISORDER (ADHD). (See ATTENTION-DEFICIT HYPERACTIVITY DISORDER.)

hyperlipidemias, a group of METABOLIC DISORDERS that involve abnormally high levels of CHOLESTEROL (especially *low-density lipoproteins*, or LDLs) in the bloodstream, increasing the risk of buildup of fatty tissue in the arteries (*atherosclerosis*) and resulting heart disorders (see HEART AND HEART PROBLEMS). Some kinds of hyperlipidemias seem to be GENETIC DISORDERS, so people with a family history of heart disease before age fifty should have their own and their children's blood levels checked. The buildup often starts in childhood and can cause heart problems in early adulthood if not recognized and treated, usually by drugs and low-fat diets to bring down the cholesterol level.

FOR HELP AND FURTHER INFORMATION

National Heart, Lung, and Blood Information Center (NHLBIC), 301–251–1222. (For full group information, see HEART AND HEART PROBLEMS.)

hyphema, a HEMORRHAGE in the front of the eye, often looking like a bloodshot eye. Hyphema can be caused by violent shaking or a blow to the head, as in the SHAKEN CHILD SYNDROME, and is one sign of possible CHILD ABUSE AND NEGLECT.

hypoactive, listless, lethargic, or considerably less active than is normal for a particular age group, seeming almost to move in slow motion, a characteristic found among some children with LEARNING DISABILITIES, MENTAL RETARDATION, or MENTAL DISORDERS; the opposite of HYPERACTIVITY.

hypogenitalism, underdevelopment of the reproductive organs, or GENITALS, as through disorders of the sex glands (GONADS) or wider disorders such as LAURENCE-MOON-BIEDL SYNDROME.

hypoglycemia, abnormally low levels of GLUCOSE (a sugar used in the body for energy) in the blood, common among people with DIABETES who are treating themselves with INSULIN; also called *insulin shock*.

hypogonadism, underactivity of the sex glands (GONADS), the TESTES in the male and the OVARIES in the female. The condition can result from a problem with the PITUITARY GLAND, which triggers production of male and female HORMONES, and by disorders in the gonads themselves, sometimes as a result of wider problems, such as LAURENCE-MOON-BIEDL SYNDROME.

hypospadias, a CONGENITAL defect in which the URETHRA, the tube by which urine and SEMEN pass through the PENIS, is misplaced. In males, the misplaced opening is found on the underside of the penis, rather than on its head, and may be associated with a downward curving of the penis, called *chordee*. Sometimes the urethra's opening is found on the upper surface, a condition called EPISPADIAS, often associated with an upward curving of the penis. Such conditions can be corrected during infancy, with surgical reconstruction of the urethra and penis so that the adult male will be able to direct his urine stream and have normal sexual relations. In rare cases, females may have a urethra opening into the VAGINA.

hypothalamus, a cherry-sized portion of the brain behind the eyes (and under the brain section called *thalamus*, as its name implies), which manages a wide range of functions in the body:

- It controls the *sympathetic nervous system* (part of the AUTONOMIC NERVOUS SYSTEM), which prepares our bodies to meet alarm or excitement, notably by increasing the heart and breathing rates, increasing blood flow to the muscles, and widening the pupils of the eyes.
- Controls our responses to heat and cold, triggering sweating or shivering, as appropriate.
- Responds to information from elsewhere in the body regarding thirst and hunger.
- Coordinates the NERVOUS SYSTEM and the ENDOCRINE SYSTEM that produces the HORMONES that run many other body systems and therefore influences the important PITUITARY GLAND, the sex glands (GONADS), the THYROID GLAND, and the brain (especially the adrenal cortex).

Because of its many functions, problems with the hypothalamus—as with a brain hemorrhage or a BRAIN TUMOR (as in the pituitary)—can have wide-ranging consequences. LAURENCE-MOON-BIEDL SYNDROME is believed to be associated with a malfunction of the hypothalamus.

FOR HELP AND FURTHER INFORMATION

National Institute of Child Health and Human Development (NICHD), 301–496–5133. (For full group information, see PREGNANCY.)

National Digestive Disease Information Clearinghouse (NDDIC), 301–654–3810. (For full group information, see DIGESTIVE SYSTEM AND DISORDERS.)

hypotonia, abnormal limpness of the muscles, when the muscles do not have the "tension" they normally have even in relaxation. Some babies with hypotonia have what is called the FLOPPY INFANT SYNDROME, which is especially common among PREMATURE infants, who develop normal muscle tension as they mature. But hypotonia is also associated with several other kinds of health disorders, such as heart disorders (see HEART AND HEART PROBLEMS); MALNUTRITION or nutritional deficiencies and related diseases such as RICKETS and SCURVY; MUSCULAR DYSTROPHY and some MOTOR NEURON DISEASES, including *Werdnig-Hoffman disease* and *Wohlfart-Kigelberg-Welander disease*; and a variety of other disorders such as severe SLEEP APNEA, CEREBRAL PALSY, and DOWN SYNDROME.

FOR HELP AND FURTHER INFORMATION

National Institute of Neurological Disorders and Stroke (NINDS), 800–352–9424. Publishes fact sheet *Dystonias.* (For full group information, see BRAIN AND BRAIN DISORDERS.)

hypoxia, lack of oxygen vital to the cells of the brain, a condition resulting when blood or the flow of the precious oxygen it carries are cut off, as during CHILDBIRTH, drowning, or CHOKING. Hypoxia during the birth process is regarded as a main cause of CEREBRAL PALSY and a possible cause of LEARNING DISABILITIES.

hysterectomy, a surgical operation to remove a woman's UTERUS, one of the most common operations in the United States today, but one that ends MENSTRUATION and renders a woman incapable of bearing children afterward. Surgically, the procedure is deceptively simple. In a *simple hysterectomy*, the uterus is removed through the abdomen (with an incision much like that in a CESAREAN SECTION), along with the CERVIX, and often the FALLOPIAN TUBES and OVARIES, and sometimes the pelvic lymph nodes in advanced stages of cancer. Alternatively, in a *vaginal hysterectomy*, the uterus and cervix are removed through the vagina. However, a hysterectomy is a major operation, requiring general or spinal ANESTHESIA, and with a death rate of 1 to 2 per 1000 patients and complications for perhaps half.

Hysterectomies are performed for many reasons, some of them controversial. Few would argue against hysterectomies performed for reasons such as CANCER in the uterus, FALLOPIAN TUBES, or OVARIES; severe, chronic PELVIC INFLAMMATORY DISEASE (PID); or HEMORRHAGE from the uterus that is unresponsive to other, less drastic measures. Similarly there is widespread support for hysterectomies when a woman has fibroids (benign growths) so large as to cause pressure or excessive bleeding, or in severe and painful cases of ENDOMETRIOSIS, growth of uterine tissue in abnormal places.

Many hysterectomies are, however, performed for less urgent reasons, and so are controversial. Women who wish to retain the capability to bear children need to examine their alternatives carefully, depending on their individual condition and situation. Among the common conditions and alternatives are:

- *Fibroids causing no symptoms of medical concern*; many doctors today prefer to monitor such fibroids, which usually shrink after MENOPAUSE. Where an operation is indicated, a *myomectomy* is often possible, which involves surgically removing the fibroids, but leaving the uterus intact. However, this works only for small fibroids and is as serious an operation; it also has a higher complication rate and its succes depends more on a high degree of skill and patience in the surgeon. A woman should also be aware that, once the uterus has been exposed, a surgeon may find that a myomectomy is not possible, because of too-large fibroids, hemorrhaging, or cancerous or precancerous growths, and a hysterectomy may have to be performed. Even if the surgery is limited, adhesions may occur and new fibroids may grow, which could still cause INFERTILITY. If a woman does become pregnant, hers would be considered a HIGH-RISK PREGNANCY and will often require a Cesarean delivery. For fibroids inside (rather than outside or in the wall of) the uterus, the least common kind, surgeons can use LAPAROSCOPY and sometimes laser surgery to remove the fibroids. When possible, this is a far safer operation with shorter recovery time and fewer complications. (A procedure called *ablation* can be used to remove the uterine lining, the *endometrium*, but that is called a *functional hysterectomy*, because the uterus will no longer support a pregnancy.) Fibroids affect two to three women in ten after age thirty-five, so many woman who have not borne a child early or who wish to have more children, will face the difficult question of how to deal with fibroids.
- *Uterine prolapse*, in which the uterus sags into the vagina, because of weakened pelvic muscles and ligaments. Alternatives to surgery include pelvic floor or Kegel EXERCISES (see BASIC EXERCISES FOR DURING AND AFTER PREGNANCY on page 634) to strengthen the pelvic muscles and use of a DIAPHRAGM-like device called a *pessary* to hold the uterus in place.
- *Endometrial hyperplasia*, excessive growth of the uterine lining. The condition sometimes reverses itself, and many doctors today prefer to follow the condition, hoping that surgery will be unnecessary.
- *In-situ cervical cancer*, affecting only the outermost layer of the cervix. While many doctors argue that a hysterectomy should be performed, because cancer is life-threatening and can spread, others feel that removal of the affected outer cell layer—by use of a knife, laser, or cryosurgery (extreme cold used to freeze and kill cells)—is effective as a treatment. A woman with this diagnosis who wishes to retain her childbearing capability will need to consult very carefully with her doctor.

In some cases, a woman may prefer to have a hysterectomy. Those who wish to bear no more children, but seek to circumvent religious prohibitions against traditional STERILIZATION or BIRTH CONTROL, have long opted for a hysterectomy, though it is far more dangerous than other forms of sterilization. In addition, where a woman has a family history of uterine CANCER, she may in some cases, after consultation with her doctor, decide to have her uterus removed as preventive surgery.

A woman for whom a hysterectomy has been recommended should by all means get a second opinion and explore all her alternatives. The rate of hysterectomies varies widely—it is twice as high in the South as in the Northeast, and the operations in general occur more often when the doctor is being paid directly (rather than as part of a health plan) and less often when a second opinion is obtained. Some recent studies have suggested that perhaps a third of all hysterectomies in the United States are being performed unnecessarily. In some cases, and under some HEALTH INSURANCE plans, a second opinion is now mandated.

FOR HELP AND FURTHER INFORMATION

Hysterectomy Education Resources and Services (HERS) Foundation
422 Bryn Mawr Avenue
Bala Cynwyd, PA 19004
215–667–7757
Nora Coffey, Founder and President
Organization concerned with hysterectomy; provides information and referrals; publishes quarterly newsletter, conference proceedings, reading lists, article reprints, and audiovisual materials.

American College of Obstetricians and Gynecologists (ACOG), 202–638–5577. Publishes *Uterine Fibroids* and *Dilation and Curettage (D&C)*. (For full group information, see PREGNANCY.)

RESOLVE, Inc., HelpLine: 617–623–0744. Offers adoption services, along with infertility treatments. Publishes fact sheet *Surgery: Who, When and Where?* (For full group information, see INFERTILITY.)

OTHER RESOURCES

Options: A Woman's Guide to Hysterectomy. Adelaide Haas and Susan L. Puretz. Celestial Arts, 1995.

The Hysterectomy Hoax: A Leading Surgeon Explains Why 90 Percent of All Hysterectomies are Unnecessary.... Stanley West and Paula Dranov. Doubleday, 1994.

Hysterectomy: Making a Choice. Martin D. Greenberg. Berkley, 1993.

You Don't Need a Hysterectomy: New and Effective Ways of Avoiding Major Surgery. Ivan K. Strausz. Addison-Wesley, 1993.

Well-Informed Patient's Guide to Hysterectomy. Kathryn Cox. Dell, 1991.

(See also UTERUS.)

hysterosalpingogram, an X-ray of a woman's reproductive organs, a picture enhanced by dyes pumped in through the VAGINA and CERVIX, often during a search for causes of INFERTILITY. The test is aimed at identifying structural problems that might be interfering with CONCEPTION, such as FIBROIDS or TUBAL BLOCKAGE. On occasion the pumping of the dye into the region even clears partially blocked FALLOPIAN TUBES. A hysterosalpingogram is performed during the early part of a woman's MENSTRUAL CYCLE, so no possible PREGNANCY would be exposed to X-rays. The procedure is somewhat painful, especially the dilation of the cervix and the inward flow of the dye. Some doctors will give medications for pain and to aid in relaxation of muscles and sometimes ANTIBIOTICS to minimize risk of infection. A woman should, if at all possible, have someone accompany her to the test who is prepared to drive home, if necessary.

FOR HELP AND FURTHER INFORMATION

RESOLVE, Inc., HelpLine: 617–623–0744. Publishes fact sheet *Hysterosalpingograms.* (For full group information, see INFERTILITY.)

hysteroscopy, a medical procedure in which an ENDOSCOPE, a flexible tube containing a periscopelike viewing device, is introduced into the UTERUS through the VAGINA and CERVIX. The procedure is often performed during a search for causes of INFERTILITY. Most reliably performed at the early part of a woman's MENSTRUAL CYCLE, the hysteroscopy can help physicians detect fibroids (see HYSTERECTOMY), polyps, or other abnormalities that might interfere with CONCEPTION.

FOR HELP AND FURTHER INFORMATION

RESOLVE, Inc., HelpLine: 617–623–0744. Publishes fact sheet *Laparoscopy and Hysteroscopy: What to Expect.* (For full group information, see INFERTILITY.)

American College of Obstetricians and Gynecologists (ACOG), 202–638–5577. Publishes *Hysteroscopy.* (For full group information, see PREGNANCY.)

I

ichthyosis, a condition characterized by dry, thickened, darkened, scaly, "fishlike" skin (the name's literal implication), due to a problem with production of *keratin,* an important protein in skin. Sometimes popularly called the *fish-skin disease,* ichthyosis is inherited, often as part of a disorder such as SJOGREN SYNDROME, appearing soon after birth, especially on the arms, thighs, and back of the hands. Soap and dry air make the condition worse, and the skin easily blisters and sheds, but lubricants, oils, and humid air ease the condition, which moderates through childhood.

FOR HELP AND FURTHER INFORMATION

Foundation for Ichthyosis and Related Skin Types (FIRST)
P.O. Box 20921
Raleigh, NC 27619
919–782–5728; 800–545–3286
Fax: 919–781–0679
E-Mail: 74722.1571@compuserve.com (CompuServe: 74722,1571)
Nicholas Gattuccio, Executive Director
Organization of people concerned with ichthyosis and related skin disorders; gathers and disseminates information; publishes quarterly newsletter *Ichthyosis Focus* and books *Release the Butterfly: Handbook for Parents and Caregivers with Ichthyosis* and *Ichthyosis: A Guide for Teachers.*

National Arthritis and Musculoskeletal and Skin Diseases Information Clearinghouse (NAMSIC), 301–495–4484. Publishes annotated bibliography *Ichthyosis and Related Disorders* (For full group information, see ARTHRITIS.)

National Organization for Rare Disorders (NORD), 800–999–6673. (For full group information, see RARE DISORDERS.)

(See also SKIN DISORDERS.)

identity disorder, a type of MENTAL DISORDER that affects young people, in which the child is unable to mesh the various aspects of self into a coherent and acceptable identity; it is called *borderline personality disorder* if it persists into adulthood. Though many people have uncertainties about such questions as long-term goals, sexual orientation, religious and moral beliefs, and social relations with friends and groups, adolescents with identity disorder are so uncertain as to cause ANXIETY and DEPRESSION. Some become almost immobilized as a result, often harming their everyday functioning at home and school, while others experiment impulsively. (See MENTAL DISORDERS.)

illegitimate, a child whose parents have not been legally married; a term now seldom used. In some states, illegitimate children have no INHERITANCE RIGHTS from their FATHERS, and in some states, if the child dies a WRONGFUL DEATH, an UNWED FATHER cannot file a suit against the party responsible (though mothers and married fathers can do so). But in most states, if the father acknowledges the child as his own, or a PATERNITY SUIT successfully identifies him as the father, an illegitimate child has much the same rights as one born to parents who were married at the time of birth or later.

Illinois Test of Psycholinguistic Abilities (ITPA), a widely used, individually administered DIAGNOSTIC ASSESSMENT TEST that measures the COMMUNICATIONS SKILLS of children ages two to ten, especially to identify any specific problems, such as LEARNING DISABILITIES. Test examiners use a variety of materials, including booklets, picture books, and other objects, in a dozen subtests that together assess VISUAL SKILLS and AUDITORY SKILLS in reception, expression, association, and sequential memory, and other skills. (See TESTS.)

illiteracy, inability to read and write, but more specifically the inability to read and write well enough to operate effectively in our information-packed society—reading signs, filling out forms, calculating figures, and dealing with words and numbers in all their many aspects. Adults who cannot read, write, or calculate beyond eighth-grade level are often considered *functionally illiterate* and are the focus of many adult education or continuing education classes, sometimes attended by parents wishing to gain the skills they need to work with their own children in school. Many functional illiterates received automatic PROMOTION while in school and failed to learn the basic skills, sometimes because they had undiagnosed DISABILITIES, such as LEARNING DISABILITIES or EAR AND HEARING PROBLEMS, that hindered learning.

illusion, a faulty perception or misinterpretation of something perceived, such as hearing a train whistle and interpreting it as a woman's scream; a common symptom of PSYCHOSIS. By contrast, HALLUCINATION is a perception of something that is not, in fact, present. (See MENTAL DISORDERS.)

immersion course, a course in which students focus entirely and intensively on one subject area for a certain period of time, as in a week-long course where students speak only in a foreign language.

immune system, a complex network of specialized cells and organs that work to defend the body against attack from what are perceived as "foreign" invaders. Often these invaders, including bacteria, viruses, fungi, and parasites, are indeed foreign and dangerous, and the immune system continuously saves the body from threatening and potentially lethal attack.

The key to the immune system's operation is the distinction between "self" and "not-self." Normally the body's own cells carry markers that identify them as part of the self. Anything without those markers is perceived as not-self and attacked accordingly. Any substance that is capable of triggering this immune response is called an *antigen*. (It is such antigens that distinguish the different types of blood, such as A, B, or O; see BLOOD AND BLOOD DISORDERS.)

Physically, the heart of the immune system is a network of vessels called the *lymphatic system*. These carry a milky fluid, called *lymph*, containing *lymphocytes* (a type of white BLOOD cell), PROTEINS, and FATS, from near the blood vessels through various filtering mechanisms, including *lymph nodes* in the groin and underarm areas, and in other organs such as the *spleen* in the lower left side of the chest, the TONSILS and ADENOIDS in the neck, even the APPENDIX, a projection off the intestines. There foreign substances, such as bacteria, are trapped and neutralized or destroyed. In case of illness or infection, when much matter is being trapped in these filtering tissues, the area can become swollen, as when someone has "swollen glands." The body can function without some of these organs, such as the tonsils, adenoids, spleen, and appendix, if necessary, but their filtering is an important part of the body's protective defenses, and a ruptured spleen is a life-threatening emergency.

Lymphocytes form the body's defensive army. There are two main types of lymphocytes, B cells and T cells, both originally formed in the BONE MARROW. B cells, which also mature in the bone marrow, work by triggering creation of substances called *antibodies* that connect with and destroy antigens.

If a person has previously been exposed to a disease or has had a vaccination against it (see IMMUNIZATION), antibodies will be present in the body, ready for defense in any later exposure to the disease. The person is then said to have IMMUNITY against that particular disease. Babies are often born with temporary natural immunity from their mothers, which is enhanced during BREASTFEEDING. Antibodies belong to a wider class of immune-system molecules called *immunoglobulins*. In some situations, immunoglobulins may be injected into the body to provide temporary immunity, as when a pregnant woman has been exposed to RUBELLA. It is *immunoglobulin E* (IgE) that is mainly responsible for the reactions in ALLERGIES and ASTHMA.

T cells, which mature in an upper-chest gland called the *thymus*, directly attack cells that have been taken over by foreign organisms, such as viruses, or that become abnormal, as in CANCER. They do this in a variety of ways. Some kinds (*suppressor cells*) turn off or suppress problem cells, while others trigger growth of beneficial cells, destroy problem cells, and encourage *phagocytes* (cell-eaters). Though a key part of the body's defenses, these T-cell activities cause problems in TRANSPLANTS, because tissue from other people (except identical twins) is rejected. To counter this reaction, transplant patients are given *immunosuppressive drugs* (see TRANSPLANTS).

The immune system can also fail to function properly in defending against disease. This *immunodeficiency* can result in a variety of ways:

- *Inherited immunodeficiency*, in which children are born with flawed immune systems, conditions sometimes called *agammaglobulinemia* or *hypogammaglobulinemia*, in which they are highly susceptible to infections. Sometimes these can be treated with injections of immunoglobulin or transplants of thymus tissue. In very rare cases, babies are born totally or mostly lacking immune defenses, resulting in *severe combined immunodeficiency disease* (SCID), in which children must be kept in totally germ-free settings or "bubbles." A few SCID patients have been successfully treated with BONE MARROW TRANSPLANTS; early experiments in treating SCID with GENE THERAPY have showed promise.
- *Acquired immunodeficiency*, which can occur temporarily and partially with some viral infections, such as MEASLES, MONONUCLEOSIS, and influenza, or under other conditions, such as BLOOD TRANSFUSIONS, surgery, MALNUTRITION, or STRESS. It can also occur in a permanent, devastating way in the disease called *acquired immunodeficiency syndrome*, or AIDS, in which a virus destroys helper T cells and is harbored by other immune cells, leaving the body defenseless against infections and cancers.
- *Side effects of anticancer therapy*, such as radiation or chemotherapy (see CANCER).

The immune system itself is sometimes affected by CANCER, such as LEUKEMIA (abnormal proliferation of the white blood cells), *multiple myeloma* (abnormal growth of the cells that produce antibodies), and *lymphomas*, cancers of the lymph organs, including *Hodgkin's disease*.

Sometimes the immune system malfunctions, and mistakenly attacks part of the body itself, as if it were foreign. The result is an AUTOIMMUNE DISORDER, such as rheumatoid ARTHRITIS or LUPUS. In allergies, the body responds in excessive and harmful ways to foreign substances; in this case the antigens are generally termed *allergens*.

FOR HELP AND FURTHER INFORMATION

Immune Deficiency Foundation (IDF)
25 W. Chesapeake Avenue, Suite 206
Towson, MD 21204–4820
410–321–6647; Patient Support Line: 800–296–4433
Fax: 410–321–9165
E-mail: idf@clarknet.com
Marcia Boyle, President
Organization concerned with primary immune deficiency diseases; provides information; supports research; operates Chronic Granulomatous Disease registry; publishes various materials, including *IDF Newsletter.*

National Institute of Allergy and Infectious Diseases (NIAID), 301–496–5717. Publishes *The Immune System: How It Works.* (For full group information, see ALLERGY.)

National Cancer Institute (NCI), 800–422–6237. Publishes *The Immune System—How It Works* (For full group information, see CANCER.)

National Jewish Center for Immunology and Respiratory Medicine, 800–222–5864, U.S. except CO. (For full group information, LUNG AND BREATHING DISORDERS.)

National Organization for Rare Disorders (NORD), 800–999–6673. (For full group information, see RARE DISORDERS.)

National Arthritis and Musculoskeletal and Skin Diseases Information Clearinghouse (NAMSIC), 301–495–4484. (For full group information, see ARTHRITIS.)

OTHER RESOURCES

Defending the Body: Unraveling the Mysteries of Immunology. Joel Davis. Atheneum, 1990.
The Immune System. Edward Edelson. Chelsea House, 1990.

(See also specific disorders mentioned in article.)

immunity, in medicine, the state of being unaffected by or unsusceptible to a disease, because the body's IMMUNE SYSTEM is operating effectively—specifically because ANTIBODIES are present to fight off the disease organisms. Babies are born with *natural immunity* from antibodies they have received from their mother's bloodstream, which wears off during the first year of life. In centuries past, this meant that a child a year old lacked internal defenses against some of the most serious diseases, so INFANT MORTALITY was high. But in this century, VACCINES have been developed to give children an *acquired* or *induced* immunity that allows them to survive attack by various disease organisms. (See IMMUNIZATION.)

immunization, the process of inducing IMMUNITY, or internal resistance to disease, in a person of any age, but especially in children, who are so very vulnerable to diseases—especially after their first year, as the natural immunity they received from their mothers wears off. Immunization can be induced in two main ways. The first, and most familiar, is *active immunization,* in which a VACCINE is introduced into a person's system, either by injection or by mouth, triggering the formation of ANTIBODIES and the develop of immunity for a limited time or a lifetime, depending on the vaccine. In the less common *passive immunization,* antibodies are directly injected into a person's body, supplying a short-term immunity. This approach is sometimes used during PREGNANCY when a woman has been exposed to a dangerous disease or has RH INCOMPATIBILITY.

Vaccines work best when they are given at the recommended time and on a regular schedule, generally in a series of properly spaced doses and shots. Parents should check the following entries for the recommendations as of mid-1996: hepatitis B vaccine (see LIVER AND LIVER PROBLEMS), oral POLIO vaccine (OPV), Hib vaccine (see HIB DISEASE), DTP VACCINE (for DIPHTHERIA, TETANUS, and WHOOPING COUGH, or pertussis), and MEASLES-MUMPS-RUBELLA. Such recommendations change, however, so parents should be sure to check with their doctor or clinic about current immunization guidelines.

Vaccine recommendations are not absolute. For example, two months can be six to ten weeks. Also health recommendations change, as do state legal requirements, so parents should consult their doctor or clinic to find out the current schedule and see that their children receive vaccinations when recommended. As of mid-1996, all currently recommended vaccines can be given simultaneously. If the children have missed early vaccinations, they can make up for them now. If money is a problem, children can get their vaccinations at public health clinics or community health centers.

Despite evidence of the important of immunization, many children are not properly immunized. In the United States, only 45 to 60 percent of all children have received their full set of recommended vaccinations, and in some areas only 20 percent have been vaccinated. Most children are required to have certain basic vaccinations in order to enter school, but many younger children lack adequate protection against childhood diseases. A 1992 Centers for Disease Control survey of nine major cities found that among children younger than age two, the best vaccination rate was 42 percent and the worst was only 10 percent. The lack of vaccinations has caused a resurgence in some preventable childhood diseases, such as whooping cough and measles. Parents should be aware that this is a special problem in nursery schools and day-care centers, which generally have no immunization requirements. Some researchers have been exploring the possibilities of a "super vaccine" that in a single dose would protect children against all major childhood infections, possibly employing some timed-release mechanism within the body.

Among children, some of the most important diseases for which vaccines are commonly given are DIPHTHE-

RIA, TETANUS (lockjaw), WHOOPING COUGH (pertussis), POLIO, MEASLES, RUBELLA (German measles), MUMPS, hepatitis B (see LIVER AND LIVER PROBLEMS), CHICKEN POX, and HIB DISEASE (Haemophilus influenzae type b). Most doctors or clinics will provide parents with an immunization record form, usually an official state record. If they do not, parents are advised to keep their own record of their children's immunizations, showing the specific vaccines given and the dates. The record acts not only as a reminder of timing for remaining immunization and booster doses, but also as a record that the child is protected. The doctor should date and sign the record each time an immunization is given, to keep the record current and correct. The signed document should be kept in a safe, accessible place. In many places state law requires that children who have not yet been properly immunized against specific diseases (with some exceptions) will not be allowed to enter or attend school until started on a course of immunization.

In general, vaccines are safe and effective, protecting against life-threatening diseases, but they can cause side effects. These are usually mild and temporary, such as a slight fever, a sore arm, or a rash, but can sometimes be more serious. If a child gets sick and visits a doctor, HOSPITAL, or clinic during the four weeks after an immunization, parents should report the illness to the doctor's office or the clinic where the vaccine was given.

On occasion, children can have serious side effects and may even die, though death is rare. The risk from disease has been proven far greater than the risk of injury from vaccines, but the risk is still there. Children who experience serious complications and their families may be entitled to compensation from the NATIONAL VACCINE INJURY COMPENSATION PROGRAM, established under the Childhood Vaccine Injury Act of 1986. (For more information on the side effects of the various vaccines, see entries under the names of the individual vaccines, including DTP VACCINE.)

Parents traveling out of the country should also be careful to have themselves and their children vaccinated—and should plan well ahead of time, since most vaccinations take at least some days to take effect. For visits to Central or South America and to Western or Central Africa, for example, a vaccination for yellow fever is obligatory and must be taken at least ten days before departure. Travelers need to carry an international certificate of vaccination. For the same areas, vaccinations for polio, tetanus, typhoid, and gamma globulin are optional but strongly recommended for all or many destinations. For current information on immunization requirements, parents can contact the International Traveler's Hotline, Centers for Disease Control, 1600 Clifton Road, Atlanta, GA 30333; 404–639–2572 or 404–332–4559; or the Traveler's Medical Service, 2141 K Street NW, Suite 48, Washington, DC 20037; 202–466–8109.

Travelers should, of course, contact the family doctor before trips to foreign destinations. The state or local health department also offers information on current recommendations. In early 1992, for example, an outbreak of a type of bacterial meningitis prompted an American recommendation that children ages two through nineteen traveling to Canada should be vaccinated against the disease (this particular vaccine has not been demonstrated as effective in children under age two).

FOR HELP AND FURTHER INFORMATION

American Academy of Pediatrics (AAP), 800–433–9016. Publishes brochures *What Parents Need to Know About Vaccination and Childhood Disease* and *Immunization Protects Children*; video *Before It's Too Late, Vaccinate*; Vaccine Information Sheets (VIS) *DTP, MMR, Polio,* and *Td*; and *Vaccine Administration Record.* (For full group information, see HEALTH CARE.)

National Institute of Allergy and Infectious Diseases (NIAID), 301–496–5717. (For full group information, see ALLERGIES.)

National Institute of Child Health and Human Development (NICHD), 301–496–5133. (For full group information, see PREGNANCY.)

Centers for Disease Control (CDC), 404–639–3311. Publishes recommended immunization schedules. (For full group information, see HEALTH CARE.)

National Vaccine Information Center (NVIC)
c/o Dissatisfied Parents Together (DPT)
512 West Maple Avenue, #206
Vienna, VA 22180
703–938–3783; 800–909-SHOT [909–7468]
On DPT vaccine and problem lot numbers:
900–288–1222
Kathi Williams, Director
Organization concerned with preventing injuries and deaths from vaccines, especially the DPT vaccine; seeks safer vaccines; provides information and referrals; publishes various materials, including newsletter *The Vaccine Reaction, Vaccine Information: A Guide for Parents, Whooping Cough, the DPT Vaccine and Reducing Vaccine Reaction, The Compensation System and How It Works, FDA/VAERS Vaccine Lot Numbers* (cross-listed with reported adverse events), *Law Firm Directory* (of attorneys handling vaccine compensation claims), *State Law* (when available), and videotapes.

National Maternal and Child Health Clearinghouse (NMCHC), 703–821–8955. Publishes *Before It's Too Late, Vaccinate* and *Overcoming Barriers to Immunization.* (For full group information, see PREGNANCY.)

The Arc, 817–261–6003. Publishes *Facts About Childhood Immunizations.* (For full group information, see MENTAL RETARDATION.)

Children's Defense Fund (CDF), 800–233–1200. Publishes *Building a National Immunization System: A Guide to Immunization Services and Resources* and *Medicaid and*

Childhood Immunizations: A National Study. (For full group information, see ADOLESCENT PREGNANCY.)

Healthy Mothers, Healthy Babies National Coalition (HMHB), 202–863–2458. Publishes *Removing Roadblocks to Vaccination* and resource list *Immunization.* (For full group information, see PREGNANCY.)

American Vegan Society (AVS), 609–694–2887. (For full group information, see VEGETARIANISM.)

OTHER RESOURCES

GENERAL WORKS

Vaccinations: Rest of the Story. Mothering Magazine, 1993.

Vaccines—Are They Really Safe and Effective?: A Parent's Guide to Childhood Shots. Neil Z. Miller. New Atlantean, 1992.

What Every Parent Should Know about Childhood Immunization. Jamie Murphy. Earth Healing, 1993.

Immunizations: Building Blocks for Healthy Children. Catholic Health, 1992.

Vaccines—Are They Really Safe and Effective?: A Parent's Guide to Childhood Shots. Neil Z. Miller. New Atlantean, 1992.

The Immunization Decision: A Guide for Parents. Randall Neustaedter. North Atlantic, 1990.

PRECAUTIONARY WORKS

What Price Vaccinations? Simone Delarue. Happiness Press, 1995.

Vaccines Are Dangerous: A Warning to the Black Community. Curtis Cost. A&B Books, 1992.

A Shot in the Dark: Why the P in the DPT Vaccination May Be Hazardous to Your Child's Health. Harris L. Coulter and Barbara L. Fisher. Avery, 1991.

FOR PRETEENS AND TEENS

Vaccines: Preventing Disease. Michael C. Burge. Lucent, 1992.

BACKGROUND WORKS

Adverse Events Associated with Childhood Vaccines: Evidence Bearing on Causality. Institute of Medicine, Vaccine Safety Committee Staff. National Academy Press, 1993.

Adverse Effects of Pertussis and Rubella Vaccines. Christopher P. Howson and others, eds. Institute of Medicine. National Academy Press, 1991.

implantation, the attachment of a fertilized egg to the lining of the UTERUS (*endometrium*) after it has traveled down the FALLOPIAN TUBES. After implantation (if not before), the egg, called an EMBRYO, begins to grow, while some of its cells begin to develop the nourishing PLACENTA. If implantation takes place outside the uterus, such as in the Fallopian tubes, the result is a potentially life-threatening ECTOPIC PREGNANCY. (See PREGNANCY; UTERUS.)

impulse control disorder, a type of MENTAL DISORDER that involves a person failing to resist a drive or temptation to do something harmful. People with the disorder may or may not consciously plan to do harm and may not be conscious of resisting the impulse, but they characteristically feel a sense of tension or arousal beforehand and a sense of release, pleasure, or gratification afterward, often followed by self-reproach, guilt, or regret.

Among the main kinds of impulse control disorders are:

- *Intermittent explosive disorder,* in which the person has episodes—generally self-described as "spells" or "attacks"—during which he or she loses control of aggressive impulses and assaults others or destroys property, often soon expressing regret over the damage done and the inability to maintain control. Between episodes, aggressive impulses are not particularly noticeable. The disorder can appear at any age, but most often in the teens and twenties and especially in males.
- *Kleptomania,* in which a person is unable to resist impulses to steal items, not for their value or use and not because money is lacking to buy them. Often the items are thrown away or given away, returned, or hidden and not used. Kleptomania can begin at any age, including childhood.
- *Pyromania,* in which a person has irresistible impulses to start fires, deliberately and often with considerable planning, rather than accidentally. Pyromania often begins in childhood, but psychiatrists consider it most destructive during ADOLESCENCE and adulthood.
- *Trichotillomania,* in which a person fails to resist the impulse to pull out his or her own HAIR, but not because of any skin problem or delusion, a condition often beginning in childhood and somewhat more common among children with MENTAL RETARDATION. Mostly hair from the scalp is involved, but the person may also pull eyebrows, eyelashes, and less frequently other body hair.
- *Pathological gambling,* in which a person is unable to resist impulses to gamble, regardless of the disruption caused in his or her life, a pattern that often begins in adolescence in males, though somewhat later in females.

Such behaviors may also be associated with other kinds of mental disorders. They may also appear in people without particular disorders, such as children who pull their hair absentmindedly (see COMFORT HABITS), but apparently without the feeling of tension or gratification and release associated with impulse control disorders. (See MENTAL DISORDERS.)

inborn errors of metabolism, a medical phrase referring to the genetic deficiencies behind a group of METABOLIC DISORDERS that cause disruption of the chemical and physical processes by which food is broken down for use in the body.

in camera, a private consultation in a judge's office; literally "in chambers." In a contested CUSTODY case, for example, a judge may interview a child in camera to discover the child's preference, if any, for living with mother or father. The records of such an interview are generally SEALED.

incest, in a strict legal sense, sexual intercourse or marriage between a man and a woman who are so closely related that they cannot legally marry. In a wider sense, sexually oriented activity of any kind, including touching of the GENITALS, exhibition of the genitals, and verbal propositioning, between close relatives.

Incest prohibitions against sexual activity between close blood relations are virtually universal, but the precise relations barred vary. In the United States, state incest laws generally prohibit a person from having sexual relations with a parent, child, brother, sister, half-brother or half-sister (with one parent in common), uncle, aunt, niece, nephew, grandparent, great-grandparent, grandchild, and great-grandchild. Some states may also bar such relations with a first cousin, step-child, step-parent, parent-in-law, child-in-law, brother-in-law, sister-in-law, or a spouse's grandchild or grandparent. Prohibitions based on AFFINITY—that is, created by a marital relationship, such as in-laws—generally end with DIVORCE or the death of the person connecting the two. For example, after the death of a woman, sexual relations or marriage between her second husband and her daughter by a previous husband would no longer be considered incest.

Incest is a criminal offense that may be punished by a prison sentence. However, incest laws are relatively narrow, applying in cases of sexual relations or marriage. When a child under the AGE OF CONSENT (often eighteen) is involved, child sexual abuse laws may be applied instead, because these are broader and include genital touching (see CHILD ABUSE AND NEGLECT). Incest without the consent of one party (usually the female) may also come under RAPE laws. If a child under the age of consent is involved, the charge may be statutory rape, regardless of whether or not the child gave consent or had previously had sexual relations with others.

Because it has been kept hidden from view, it is unclear how common incest is. However, it is clear that an overwhelming amount of child sexual abuse takes place in the home, much of it involving incest. In most cases, the perpetrator is male, in a small proportion of cases—which some researchers estimate as less than 5 percent—a female is an incestuous abuser.

A major controversy relating to incest and child sexual abuse in general is the extent to which memories of childhood abuse can be repressed and resurface in adulthood, often in the course of therapy. (See CHILD ABUSE AND NEGLECT.)

incompetent, in the law, unable, unqualified, or inadequate to act or fulfill responsibilities. MINORS and people with some severe DISABILITIES may be considered legally incompetent and, in some cases, the state may act on their behalf.

incompetent cervix, a condition of PREGNANCY in which the muscles of a woman's CERVIX are too weak to hold the FETUS within the UTERUS for the full period of GESTATION. Normally the cervix widens only just before birth, in preparation for LABOR and DELIVERY, but in a woman with this condition, the cervix begins to gradually widen months earlier, as can be detected with ULTRASOUND scans. When a woman has had previous MISCARRIAGES or is diagnosed as having an incompetent cervix, a stitch may be placed across the end of her cervix to hold it together, generally under an *epidural anesthetic* (see ANESTHESIA) in a HOSPITAL at about the fourteenth week of pregnancy. She is then advised to limit activity for the rest of the pregnancy, when (once the suture is taken out) she should be able to deliver normally. (See PREGNANCY.)

incontinence, inability to control the release of urine from the bladder and of feces from the bowels, sometimes including inability to sense fullness, to empty thoroughly, and to close completely. Incontinence can result for a variety of reasons. Among toilet-trained children (as well as adults), short-term bouts of incontinence can occur as a result of local inflammation in the anus or URETHRA, temporary damage to the muscles in the area (as after CHILDBIRTH or surgery), infection (such as that which causes DIARRHEA), or physical stress, as in heavy athletic activity. In children, long-term or permanent incontinence most often occurs as a result of damage to the NERVOUS SYSTEM or to muscles in the area, as in cases of SPINA BIFIDA or PARAPLEGIA. The procedure of CLEAN, INTERMITTENT CATHETERIZATION helps some such children handle bladder-emptying functions. By contrast, BEDWETTING (*enuresis*) and SOILING (*encopresis*) are not necessarily the result of physical damage alone, though some physical factors may be involved.

FOR HELP AND FURTHER INFORMATION

Spina Bifida Association of America (SBAA), 800–621–3141. Publishes *Achieving Bowel Continence* and *Bowel Continence and Spina Bifida*. (For full group information, see SPINA BIFIDA.)

incorrigible, in family law, a term for JUVENILES who refuse to obey their parents, such as juvenile DELINQUENTS, RUNAWAYS, or chronic TRUANTS. When parents are unable to exercise parental control, the police, social work system, school, or parents may bring the child to court. If found incorrigible, the child may then be made a WARD of the court and either returned home under the SUPERVISION of a PROBATION officer or placed elsewhere, as in FOSTER CARE, a GROUP HOME, or an institution. Incorrigible children are often STATUS OFFENDERS, who would not be brought before the court for their offenses, except that they are MINORS.

incubation period, the time between a person's exposure to an infectious disease and the onset of an illness.

incubator, a special device providing careful control of the environment, including heat, light, oxygen, and humidity. In NEONATAL INTENSIVE CARE UNITS (NICU's), incubators are often used for PREMATURE or LOW BIRTH WEIGHT infants or newborns with health problems. Sometimes these incubators may include tubes that assist in breathing (see VENTILATOR) and feeding (see PARENTERAL NUTRITION). Incubators may have portholes in the sides so that parents and nursing staff can handle the baby, for BONDING and stimulation of the senses.

independent study, a self-directed course of learning in which a student works outside a regular classroom, but under the guidance of a teacher who evaluates the completed work, often for academic credit (depending on the school setting); sometimes also called HOME STUDY. Independent study is used in many ALTERNATIVE SCHOOLS and in some honors classes for "fast track" students in a TRACKING system. (See HOME STUDY; EDUCATION.)

individualized education program (IEP), a written plan outlining the SPECIAL EDUCATION and other services to be provided for a child with DISABILITIES, as specified under the EDUCATION FOR ALL HANDICAPPED CHILDREN ACT (EHC) and its successor, the INDIVIDUALS WITH DISABILITIES EDUCATION ACT (IDEA).

An IEP is required to include:

- The child's present levels of educational performance. This would vary depending on the nature of the child's disabilities, but might include the child's level of ability in areas such as COMMUNICATIONS SKILLS, SOCIAL SKILLS, SELF-HELP SKILLS, MOTOR SKILLS, and academic achievement.
- Annual instructional goals and an outline of individual short-term instructional objectives by which that goal is to be reached.
- The specific educational services to be provided to the child, including the amount of time the child will spend in a regular classroom, the projected date for initiation, and the anticipated duration of special services.
- Appropriate objective criteria and evaluation procedures and schedules for determining, on at least an annual basis, whether instructional objectives are being achieved.

An IEP is to be prepared for every child who has been evaluated and found to have some sort of disability that would hinder learning. The IEP is developed at a meeting involving one or both of the child's parents or a guardian, the child's teacher (if he or she has more than one, the state may specify which should be involved), sometimes the child, another representative of the school or public agency (such as a SPECIAL EDUCATION teacher, LEARNING DISABILITIES specialist, or school principal), and perhaps other people brought by the parents or by a state agency.

To prepare for such a meeting, a parent or guardian may want to visit the child's classes, talk with the child about school, perhaps talk with the teacher, and think realistically about the child's strengths and weaknesses and what the child should reasonably be expected to accomplish in a year. Parents should be as well-informed as possible before the IEP meeting and should be sure to convey to the others their special view of the child. They have the right to see all records relating to their child (see FAMILY EDUCATIONAL RIGHTS AND PRIVACY ACT) and, ideally, should have copies of evaluation reports to review before the meeting; however, they may need to specifically request them. They will also be well advised to bring a partner, friend, or advocate (see ADVOCACY) to the meeting.

No decisions on an IEP can be made without parental permission, except in emergencies. However, parents should not rush to agreement; they have 30 days to decide whether or not to approve an IEP. They are advised, at least, not to accept the IEP at the meeting, but to take a day or two to think it over. If they agree that the plan is a good one, they should accept it promptly, so the child can begin receiving services quickly. Once the plan goes into effect, parents will want to keep in touch with the school and monitor how well the child is progressing with the program; if progress is not being made, the program may need to be modified. It will, in any case, be reviewed periodically.

However, if parents have questions or concerns, they should take the 30 days to address them. Sometimes parents may object to only part of a plan, and the plan can be modified to their satisfaction. If they disagree with the results of the assessment itself, or with the goals and services recommended in the IEP, they may reject the plan altogether. If parents and school are not able to agree on a reasonable program for the child, if the program is not properly implemented, or if it is implemented and found not to work, but the school fails to modify it appropriately, parents have the right to appeal the program suggested by the school. They do this by asking in writing for a DUE PROCESS hearing before an impartial hearing officer appointed by a public agency. For such a hearing, the parents may:

- Have full access to all records.
- Require full explanations of all records.
- Request clarification, explanation, or removal of false or misleading information in the records.
- Have with them people of their choice, including legal counsel, an advocacy group representative, an impartial educator, or independent evaluator; (This is strongly advised; see ADVOCACY.)

- Call and question officials and call other witnesses.
- Obtain an independent educational evaluation (at their own expense).
- Prevent introduction of any document not made available to them at least five days earlier (school officials have the same right).
- Have the child attend, if appropriate.
- Have the hearing closed to the public, if desired.

The hearing officer may accept or reject the school's proposed IEP or may require that the school provide other services not mentioned in the original IEP.

If parents fail to obtain satisfaction at the due process hearing, they can appeal to the state department of education (unless the hearing was handled by that department) and ultimately to civil court, if necessary, though it is, of course, preferable to settle matters informally, when possible. Since 1986 amendments to the Education for All Handicapped Children Act, parents who win at a hearing, appeal, or court proceeding may be awarded reimbursement from the school for "reasonable" legal and evaluative fees. (This was in response to an earlier decision denying payment of legal costs in challenges to EHC decisions, which had the effect of allowing some agencies to blatantly ignore violations of the law.) The U.S. Supreme Court has ruled that in some cases, if the court agrees with the parents that the school's original program for the child was incorrect, parents may be able to collect from the school the costs of private schooling paid for a child.

One area of substantial disagreement has been the initial evaluation of a child. Because many TESTS are geared toward middle-class students speaking standard English, children who speak another language or nonstandard English or who come from a disadvantaged background have sometimes been wrongly diagnosed as mentally retarded or having communications disorders. As a result, the law now specifies that children cannot be placed in special education programs on the basis of only one test, that the tests must be given in the child's language and must take into account his or her disability, and that the evaluation must include observation of the child. Schools are also obliged to communicate with the parents using the family's primary language. Parents who believe their child has been wrongly diagnosed may call for a due process hearing.

Conversely, many parents have found that their children had undiagnosed LEARNING DISABILITIES and have had to use the due process hearing to obtain proper educational services for their children. While such evaluations are in dispute, the child generally stays in whatever program he or she is in. Parents should be aware that even when a child does not qualify for services under an IEP, special assistance may be available under a 504 Accommodation Plan (see SECTION 504).

By the time the child is 16, at the latest, the IEP is also required to include an explicit plan for transition to employment or to postsecondary education (see COLLEGE).

FOR HELP AND FURTHER INFORMATION

PACER Center (Parent Advocacy Coalition for Educational Rights), 612–827–2966, voice/TT. Publishes book *A Guide for Parents to the Individual Education Program Plan* and information handout *New Year's Resolution,* on parents and the IEP process. (For full group information, see HELP FOR SPECIAL CHILDREN on page 689.)

Center for Law and Education, 202–986–3000. Publishes "Information for Parents" brochures *Individualized Education Program, When You Disagree,* and *How to Appeal.* (For full group information, see HELP ON LEARNING AND EDUCATION on page 659.)

National Information Center for Children and Youth with Disabilities (NICHCY), 800–695–0285, voice/TT. Publishes *Individualized Education Programs (IEPs)* and *Transition Services in the IEP.* (For full group information, see HELP FOR SPECIAL CHILDREN on page 689.)

The Arc, 817–261–6003. Publishes fact sheet *Due Process: Procedural Safeguards in P.L. 94–142.* (For full group information, see MENTAL RETARDATION.)

National Organization on Legal Problems of Education (NOLPE), 913–273–3550. Publishes *Due Process for School Officials: A Guide to the Conduct of Administrative Proceedings.* (For full group information, see HELP ON LEARNING AND EDUCATION on page 659.)

Council for Exceptional Children (CEC), 800–328–0272. Publishes *Preparation for Special Education Hearings: A Practical Guide for Lessening the Trauma of Due Process Hearings, Integrating Transition Planning into the IEP Process, Teaching,* and transition-oriented materials, such as the Life-Centered Career Education package, including *Daily Living Skills, Personal-Social Skills,* and *Occupational Guidance and Preparation.* (For full group information, see HELP ON LEARNING AND EDUCATION on page 659.)

Parents Helping Parents (PHP), 408–727–5775. Provides training in working with IEPs; publishes *I.E.P. Manual* and information packet *IEP.* (For full group information, see HELP FOR SPECIAL CHILDREN on page 689.)

Alliance for Parental Involvement in Education (ALLPIE), 518–392–6900. Publishes *How to Write an IEP* and leaflet *How to Participate Effectively in the IEP (Individual Education Plan) Process.* (For full group information, see HELP ON LEARNING AND EDUCATION on page 659).

United Cerebral Palsy Association (UCPA), 800–872–5827. Publishes *Building Integration with the I.E.P.* (For full group information, see CEREBRAL PALSY.)

OTHER RESOURCES

Your Child and Health Care: A "Dollars & Sense" Guide for Families with Special Needs. Lynn Robinson Rosenfeld. Paul H. Brookes, 1994.

Parents' Guidelines to the Evaluation Process

WHY DO SCHOOL OFFICIALS RECOMMEND THAT CHILDREN BE TESTED?

There are many reasons, most of which concern the suitability of the child's placement or program. School officials may recommend testing if a child has difficulty learning or accepting school rules when usual methods of dealing with such problems have not been effective. They hope that educational or psychological tests will provide them with information about the way in which the child learns, the child's strengths and weaknesses, the nature of his or her problems, and the kind of special help he or she may need.

SHOULD I AGREE TO HAVE MY CHILD TESTED?

Public Law 94–142, the Education for All Handicapped Children Act of 1978, states that children attending public school can be given educational and psychological tests only with the approval of their parents or guardians. Your child's teacher, counselor, principal, or other staff member should explain to you the reasons for the request to test, discuss the tests that will be given, and tell you what school people hope to learn from the tests. Based on this, you can decide whether to give permission or not.

MAY I REQUEST TESTING FOR MY CHILD IF SCHOOL OFFICIALS DO NOT?

Yes, Public Law 94–142 gives you the right to a free series of tests to determine whether a handicapping condition exists and the right to have an Individual Educational Program designed for your child if tests confirm the presence of such a condition.

IF I AGREE TO HAVE MY CHILD TESTED, WHAT SHOULD I DO BEFORE TESTING TAKES PLACE?

There are several important steps you can take to insure that the testing will be useful and that your child will profit from it:

- Be sure you know what tests will be used, why these particular tests were selected, and what information these tests may provide that can help in planning a more suitable program for your child. Be sure to ask for definitions and explanations of any terms that are not clear to you and ask school officials to be specific regarding the skills, aptitudes, and/or behaviors they will be testing.

- Discuss and agree upon the child's preparation for the evaluation. Usually the child should be told about the testing and the reasons for it in advance, although there are instances when this may not be the best procedure. If the child is to be informed in advance, you should determine whether he or she will respond better to being told by you or by some member of the school staff. Tests results can be influenced by the child's attitude toward the testing process. Thus, the person who discusses it with him or her should guard against words and actions that may make the child anxious or heighten feelings of inadequacy.

- Be sure that the examiner or the person who schedules the testing is aware of anything which might adversely affect your child's performance. If your son is pitching his first Little League game on Wednesday, he may have more than usual trouble concentrating on that day.

- Find out what the physical setting for the testing will be. Individual tests should be given in a quiet comfortable room. Some evaluations include observations of the child as he or she participates in a variety of daily activities.

WHAT ARE MY RIGHTS AND RESPONSIBILITIES AFTER MY CHILD HAS BEEN TESTED?

P. L. 94–142 clearly guarantees certain important rights, including these:

- The right to receive a copy of the results of all testing and evaluation and to have these results explained.

- The right to be present at all meetings of the team that plans your child's program. Your child's teacher, the testers and evaluators, the learning specialist and others responsible for your child's education are members of this team. They are responsible for studying the results and the interpretations of all the testing and evaluation your child has had and for preparing an Individual Educational Program (IEP) for your child.
continued

- The right to be accompanied by a friend, lawyer, or child advocate at all meetings at which test results are discussed and plans for the child's program and placement are considered.

- The right to request retesting in areas in which test results disagree with your assessment of your child's abilities, achievements, or behavior patterns.

- The right to obtain an outside evaluation if you question the accuracy or fairness of the evaluation completed by school staff. You must be prepared to pay for outside evaluations.

- he right to accept or reject the IEP and to request modifications in the IEP after it has been accepted.

For detailed information about your rights under P.L. 94–142, refer to *The Rights of Parents and the Responsibilities of Schools*, compiled by James G. Meade, Ph. D., and published in paperback by Educators Publishing Services, Inc., 75 Moulton Street, Cambrige, MA 02138.

WHAT KINDS OF PROGRAMS MIGHT THE IEP INCLUDE?

Based on the results of evaluations and the meetings of the team, the IEP may provide for special help in any of several settings. The overriding goal of P.L. 94–142 is to provide the help each child needs in the least restrictive setting. Depending on the extent of your child's needs, the IEP may call for:

- modified program in the regular classroom.

- Regular class placement with supplemental tutoring, remedial instruction, counselling, or therapy.

- Special class placement; or,

- Special school placement.

In addition to the rights guaranteed you by law, you have several important responsibilities to fulfill if your child is to have the best chance to overcome or compensate for his or her handicap. These include:

- Understanding the results of testing and evaluation. Psychological and educational language can be confusing. Never hesitate to ask for clarification of anything you do not understand.

- Being sure that the goals in the IEP are those agreed upon by the team of which you are a member and being sure that these goals are specific and realistic for your child.

- Working to establish and maintain a cooperative rather than an adversarial relationship with members of the team who are responsible for carrying out the IEP.

- Sharing with school personnel information about your child and his or her life outside of school that may affect school performance or behavior.

Source: Orton Dyslexia Society, 800-ABCD–123 [222–3123] (For full group information, see LEARNING DISABILITIES*). Reprinted by permission.*

See also EDUCATION; SPECIAL EDUCATION; ADVOCACY; HELP ON LEARNING AND EDUCATION on page 659; INDIVIDUALS WITH DISABILITIES EDUCATION ACT; also PARENT'S GUIDELINES TO THE EVALUATION PROCESS above; HELP FOR SPECIAL CHILDREN on page 689 and entries on special DISABILITIES, for specific advocacy groups.)

individualized family service plan (IFSP), a plan outlining services that might be needed by the family of a child from birth through the age of two who has DISABILITIES or CHRONIC ILLNESS. Under the EDUCATION FOR ALL HANDICAPPED CHILDREN ACT OF 1975 and its successor, the INDIVIDUALS WITH DISABILITIES EDUCATION ACT (IDEA), states are required to develop an IFSP within forty-five days of a child's initial referral, as part of a comprehensive EARLY INTERVENTION services program. An IFSP includes not only a description of necessary services, but also some other services that might be helpful to the family, such as CHILD CARE or RESPITE CARE.

Under safeguards built into the laws, parents and GUARDIANS are allowed full access to all records and evaluations of the child, the family assessment, and the child's progress under the IFSP. No services are given without parental consent, and records of services provided to child or family are to be kept confidential.

Individuals with Disabilities Education Act (IDEA), a law succeeding and reauthorizing the EDUCATION FOR ALL HANDICAPPED CHILDREN ACT (EHC); more formally, the law is known as the Individuals with Disabilities Education Act Amendments of 1991. This law requires providing EDUCATION and related services to children ages three through twenty-one who have DISABILITIES and CHRONIC ILLNESS. It also provides EARLY INTERVENTION services for infants and toddlers from birth to age two.

If schools fail to comply with this law, they risk losing all federal funding and can also be sued in federal court. (Private and parochial schools, which receive no federal funds, are not affected, except in some cases by emulation.) These laws cover children regardless of where they are living—with their parents, with FOSTER PARENTS, in an institution, in a GROUP HOME, or anywhere else—and affirm the right of children with disabilities to a "free, appropriate [public] education in the least restrictive environment possible."

In keeping with a general usage change, the phrase "handicapped children" was changed under IDEA to "children with disabilities," who were defined as those with:

- Hearing impairment or deafness (see EAR AND HEARING PROBLEMS).
- Speech or language impairment (see COMMUNICATION SKILLS AND DISORDERS).
- Visual impairment or blindness (see EYE AND VISION PROBLEMS).
- Serious emotional disturbance (see MENTAL DISORDERS).
- ORTHOPEDIC DISABILITIES.
- AUTISM.
- TRAUMATIC BRAIN INJURY.
- MENTAL RETARDATION.
- Specific LEARNING DISABILITIES.
- Other health impairments that require children to receive SPECIAL EDUCATION.

For children of PRESCHOOL age (three through five), a state may include those who are experiencing DEVELOPMENTAL DELAYS—as defined by the state and measured by appropriate DEVELOPMENTAL SCREENING TESTS—in the areas of COGNITIVE DEVELOPMENT, physical development, communication development, social and emotional development, or ADAPTIVE BEHAVIOR, if they therefore need SPECIAL EDUCATION or related services.

EHC and IDEA produced a revolution in the provision of education and related services to children with disabilities—estimated to be 1 out of 8 to 10 children—but many parents were daunted by the enormous amount of work often required to arrange for such education and services. As a result, many parents formed advocacy groups to share experiences and information on how best to get compliance from local public school systems. Many such groups are listed throughout this book, under entries on many kinds of physical and mental disabilities. HELP FOR SPECIAL CHILDREN on page 689 lists many other more general groups and reference books—all of which are geared to helping parents and advocacy groups work with local school districts.

In addition, amendments to EHC and IDEA provided for practical help for parents. PARENT TRAINING AND INFORMATION (PTI) CENTERS were established in each state to help parents understand the rights of their children with disabilities. These centers in turn established TECHNICAL ASSISTANCE FOR PARENTS PROGRAM (TAPP) agencies to help families take advantage of the programs for their children. Three clearinghouses were also authorized to provide specialized education information to people with disabilities, their families, and the professionals who work with them: The HEATH Resource Center (National Clearinghouse on Postsecondary Education for Individuals with Disabilities), the National Information Center for Children and Youth with Disabilities (NICHCY) (for information on both, see HELP FOR SPECIAL CHILDREN on page 689), and the National Clearinghouse for Professions in Special Education.

"Appropriate education" has been interpreted to mean not the best or the most expensive programs possible, but specialized programs designed to suit a child's individual needs and to allow the child to make meaningful progress, the overriding goal being to provide the basic skills necessary for self-sufficiency: SELF-HELP, READING, writing, speaking, and arithmetic. Clearly the interpretation of what is required to do this is a main area of contention between parents and school districts and one reason for the emergence of so many advocacy groups.

Among the services that may be provided under the EHC and IDEA are speech and language therapy, medical services for diagnostic or evaluation purposes, physical therapy (see PHYSICAL THERAPIST), occupational therapy (see OCCUPATIONAL THERAPIST), school health services, psychological services, vocational education, educational programs extending year-round or beyond the normal school year, counseling (for student and parent), training for parents, specially trained teachers and teacher's aides, special materials and equipment, special transportation to school and to activities within school, and college placement services.

The laws cover extracurricular activities as well, giving children with disabilities the same rights as their peers to participate in programs and activities such as clubs and other special-interest activities (including music, arts, crafts, homemaking, and industrial arts), meals, recess periods, physical education (with a specially designed *adaptive physical education* program, if necessary), school athletic programs, before-school and after-school CHILD CARE programs, health services, career and educational counseling, employment services, and referrals to agencies providing special aid to people with disabilities.

All school and extracurricular activities are to be provided on a fully integrated basis or similar opportunities are to be provided, because the underlying approach is MAINSTREAMING, bringing children with disabilities into regular and ongoing contact with their peers beginning in early childhood, as preparation for independent living as adults, as far as possible. As a result, the laws emphasize that at school, the child should be in the LEAST RESTRICTIVE ENVIRONMENT, meaning the most natural, most integrated setting possible. The school is barred from shunting children with disabilities into separate buildings and trailers because of ARCHITECTURAL BARRIERS and is obliged to make the regular building accessible, as through building ramps and relocating classes. Any new buildings (from PRESCHOOL to college and postsecondary vocational schools) must be fully accessible.

Only if evaluation and experience indicate that the child's disabilities are so great that the school is unable to provide appropriate education—and even then, only if the parents approve—is a child referred to a separate program in a PRIVATE SCHOOL, day program, or residential program. However, that program must meet federal and state standards and all costs (including educational expenses, room, board, transportation, and nonmedical care) must be paid for by the school district. Such a residential program is also required to be as near to the child's home as possible. If parents on their own place the child in a residential program, the school district does not have to pay, but the child is still eligible for the school district's special education services.

The law places parents at the center of decisions regarding the child. Parents are encouraged to attend any discussions affecting their child, and they have the right to bring with them anyone they choose, such as a lawyer, friend, or other advocate. The school must keep parents fully informed in writing of alternatives discussed and decisions made, with reasons spelled out. School districts need parental approval before they can conduct an evaluation of the child's abilities and educational needs, determine what special educational services may be necessary, or move the child from regular classes into a SPECIAL EDUCATION program. Another federal law, the FAMILY EDUCATIONAL RIGHTS AND PRIVACY ACT, gives parents the right to inspect the child's STUDENT RECORD. If parents disagree with the child's identification, evaluation, and placement—for example, if they feel that a child has been incorrectly classed as mentally retarded because she has limited English-speaking skills—they may call for a DUE PROCESS hearing to review the decision.

An evaluation is recommended whenever someone has reason to suspect that a child has some problem interfering with learning—if the child has trouble understanding, for example, or difficulty speaking. States and local school districts are required to have special programs for identifying children who may need special attention. Approaches vary by state, but among the people who may refer a child for evaluation are parents, teachers, social workers, doctors, agencies, and community services. Except for obvious physical or mental problems likely to be spotted soon after birth by a physician, parents and teachers are the people most likely to sense a possible problem and call for an evaluation. (See PARENT'S GUIDELINES TO THE EVALUATION PROCESS on page 324.)

If there is any question about whether a child has any impairment or disability, parents should have the child evaluated by a physician or other appropriate specialist immediately. In most cases, the earlier the condition is identified the sooner special services can be started to minimize the handicap. That is why so much attention has been placed on EARLY INTERVENTION programs, including EARLY AND PERIODIC SCREENING, DIAGNOSIS, AND TREATMENT (EPSDT) and EARLY EDUCATION PROGRAMS FOR CHILDREN WITH DISABILITIES (EEPCD).

Checklists on what kinds of behavior and other signs might indicate problems in young children are provided in several areas in this book, notably under these headings: EAR AND HEARING PROBLEMS, EYE AND VISION PROBLEMS, LEARNING DISABILITIES, MENTAL RETARDATION, MENTAL DISORDERS, CHRONIC illness, physical disabilities, and COMMUNICATION SKILLS AND DISORDERS. Checklists and other descriptions can help parents assess whether or not to send their child for SCREENING TESTS. The above entries will also provide descriptions of some kinds of tests that might be given to a child to screen for different kinds of problems.

If a child has been evaluated and some sort of disability identified, information from the DEVELOPMENTAL SCREENING and DIAGNOSTIC ASSESSMENT TESTS, along with observations by parents and educational staff, will be used to develop an INDIVIDUALIZED EDUCATION PROGRAM (IEP). This will be modified as the child progresses, but IEP's will form a significant part of the child's education throughout the school years.

Parts of the IDEA were up for reauthorization in 1995. As of this writing, much concern was being expressed over the possibility of cuts and adverse changes in IDEA as part of attacks on federal spending.

FOR HELP AND FURTHER INFORMATION

National Information Center for Children and Youth with Disabilities (NICHCY), 800–695–0285, voice/TT. Publishes *Questions and Answers about the Individuals with Disabilities Education Act.* (For full group information, see HELP FOR SPECIAL CHILDREN on page 689.)

(See also EDUCATION; SPECIAL EDUCATION.)

infant, a very young child, usually one not yet able to walk. In law, the term generally refers to a MINOR, usually meaning a young person under age eighteen, but the BABY DOE STATUTES define *infant* as a child under age one year.

infanticide, the killing of a baby. Historically, many unwanted babies—especially girls, infants of unacknowledged paternity, or babies with BIRTH DEFECTS—were simply abandoned, if not directly killed. Such infanticide and ABANDONMENT is rare in Western cultures today, but is still found in some countries, such as India and China, as a form of after-birth SEX SELECTION that generally involves killing girl children, boys being more highly prized, in what is called *son preference.* The term *infanticide* is sometimes applied to the killing of a FETUS (more properly called *feticide*), as through ABORTION.

infant mortality, the death of an infant during the first year of life. Two-thirds of such infant deaths occur during the first month (called *neonatal mortality*), and are normally expressed as a rate of the number of deaths per specified number of pregnancies. Infant mortality has generally declined in recent years due to a variety of factors, including better PRENATAL CARE, improved NUTRITION, availability of NEONATAL INTENSIVE CARE UNITS (NICU'S), and a wide variety of advancements in medical technology. However, the improvement has not been felt uniformly. In the United States, the infant mortality rate among Blacks is almost twice as high as that for Whites. And in the world, the United States ranked 22nd in 1985, with an overall rate of 10.6 per 1,000 live births, while in some parts of the world the rate is almost 10 times that high.

FOR HELP AND FURTHER INFORMATION

National Institute of Child Health and Human Development (NICHD), 301–496–5133. (For full group information, see PREGNANCY.)

(See also DEATH AND DYING.)

infertility, inability to conceive a baby, also often encompassing the related inability to carry a child, once conceived, to FULL-TERM in a healthy birth. In practice, infertility is often not permanent and absolute (a condition called *sterility*), but temporary or a matter of decreased odds, more properly called *subfertility*. For a couple who have never had a child, the condition is called *primary infertility*; but many couples also experience *secondary infertility*, which is inability to have an additional child.

Among specialists in the field, infertility is often defined as the inability to conceive, after two years of trying, without medical intervention. Sometimes the problem is simply the result of not timing sexual intercourse with OVULATION in such a way as to maximize the chances of CONCEPTION. But a wide variety of problems can lead to temporary or permanent infertility, including:

- *Poor general physical condition*, such as being overweight, underweight, or having ANEMIA.
- *Abuses of the body*, such as ALCOHOL ABUSE, SMOKING, or DRUG ABUSE, which can lower the sperm count.
- *Hostile conditions in the woman's reproductive system*, such as acidic or impenetrable mucus in the VAGINA or CERVIX, but also sometimes a woman's ALLERGY to her partner's sperm and perhaps in both partners the formation of ANTIBODIES that cause sperm to clump together.
- *GENETIC DISORDERS*, such as TURNER SYNDROME (for women), KLINEFELTER SYNDROME (for men), and CYSTIC FIBROSIS (for men).
- *Problems with HORMONES and glands*, such as the PITUITARY, THYROID, or ADRENAL glands.
- *Problems with the OVARIES*, as in not producing eggs, a condition called *anovulation*, or irregularity of ovulation.
- *Problems with the SPERM*, such as a low sperm count, insufficiently active sperm, or too short a life span. Lack of sperm is called *azoospermia*, while too few sperm is termed *oligospermia*.
- *Physical malformations*, such as deformed UTERUS, undescended testicles, undeveloped ovaries or TESTES (as in HYPOGONADISM), lack of essential organs (such as the uterus or Fallopian tubes), or blocked tubes or ducts through which the sperm and egg must pass (sometimes because of infection or injury, as noted below). An INCOMPETENT CERVIX may make it impossible for a child to be held in the uterus for the full term.
- *Problems in getting the sperm into the vagina*, including impotence and problems with EJACULATION.
- *Problems with development of the sperm*, sometimes apparently caused by the testicles being too hot, as in cases of VARICOCELE (swollen vein in a testicle, easily treated surgically).
- *Current infection or damage from previous infection*, affecting various reproductive organs. SEXUALLY TRANSMITTED DISEASES are common culprits, especially in women, including PELVIC INFLAMMATORY DISEASE, CHLAMYDIA, and GONORRHEA.
- *Other abnormalities*, such as ENDOMETRIOSIS, scarring or adhesions in the Fallopian tubes, cervical polyps, or fibroid TUMORS in women and HYDROCELE in men, including scars and damage from previous injuries, as from an INTRAUTERINE DEVICE, or operations, such as for ECTOPIC PREGNANCY.
- *The effects of earlier diseases that might affect fertility*, such as MUMPS, MEASLES, WHOOPING COUGH, DIPHTHERIA, RUBELLA, DIABETES MELLITUS, TUBERCULOSIS, and EPILEPSY.

Among the changes that have led to wider infertility are the rise in sexually transmitted diseases in recent decades, partly linked to multiple sexual partners, use of intrauterine devices, delay of childbearing until later (since a woman's fertility decreases with age), and exposure to various ENVIRONMENTAL HAZARDS, many of the effects of which are unknown. Women are more likely to have infertility problems than men, but in many cases where a couple cannot conceive, both partners have problems that decrease their chances of achieving a pregnancy (such as low sperm count and irregular ovulation). In some cases, perhaps 1 in 10, it proves impossible to identify the cause of the infertility. And in many cases, couples conceive children while they are consulting about infertility, but without any treatment being given.

If a couple decides to seek help with an infertility problem, they are advised to start with a thorough physical examination, including routine URINE TESTS and BLOOD TESTS, with their INTERNIST or FAMILY PRACTICE PHYSICIAN. If no problems are found, the next step would be visits with a GYNECOLOGIST and UROLOGIST, respectively. This is important since general health problems—rather than problems with the reproductive system itself—are often found to be the cause of subfertility. Indeed, fertility problems can be among the first signs of an emerging health problem. Among the common culprits are CHLAMYDIA, mycoplasma, and hepatisis (see LIVER AND LIVER PROBLEMS).

Only if no solution is offered, should the couple then consult a FERTILITY SPECIALIST (*sterologist*), preferably part of a team of specialists, who will then do an *infertility workup*, which is a major medical evaluation, including numerous tests during several office sessions and sometimes a brief hospital stay.

The fertility specialist will generally meet with the couple together on the first visit, beginning to develop a detailed medical and sexual history and explaining the tests that may be involved. Some doctors also arrange separate interviews, to ensure confidentiality for the individuals, as about previous prenancies or SEXUALLY TRANSMITTED DISEASES. The tests will be done over a period of months, because many are done only if previous tests have proved negative and also because some must be done during a certain part of a woman's MENSTRUAL CYCLE. This places special burdens on working women, who must take time off from work and sometimes postpone business trips. Testing for men is much less restrictive. The total cost may range from one thousand to a few thousand dollars. Whether any of the costs will be covered by HEALTH INSURANCE depends on the couple's coverage.

On the first or second visit, the fertility specialist will generally conduct intensive physical examinations, paying special attention to the development of SECONDARY SEX CHARACTERISTICS, such as breast development in the woman and size, position, and condition of the man's PENIS and TESTES, and the amount and location of body HAIR for both. The woman will also be given a pelvic examination to check for the size, position, condition, and shape of the reproductive organs and a pap smear, to check for cervical CANCER. The man will receive a rectal examination to check for the size and condition of the prostate gland and seminal vesicles.

This is then followed by a series of tests—which are given and in what sequence depends on the particulars of the couple's background. These three tests are normally performed first in most cases:

- *Semen analysis,* in which SEMEN produced by MASTURBATION (usually after two days of sexual abstinence) is analyzed in the laboratory. This is the first and most important test for the male partner. Analysts note the number of sperm per volume and their shape and "swimming power." If the specimen has at least 20 million sperm, at least half of which have good shape and movement, this may be the last test for the male.
- *Post-coital test* (*Huhner test*), in which samples of mucus are taken from a woman's CERVIX a specified number of hours after sexual intercourse, to see if sperm are present and active or dead and sluggish.
- *Endometrial biopsy,* in which a sample (BIOPSY) is taken of the endometrium (lining of the UTERUS) late in the MENSTRUAL CYCLE, to check whether OVULATION has in fact occurred. Sometimes this test shows that ovulation *has* occurred, but that a hormonal imbalance prevents the endometrium from being properly developed to receive a fertilized egg.

If the semen analysis test indicates problems, several types of tests may be performed on the male partner. Some of these are additional semen analysis tests, with analysis focusing on different aspects of the sample. These include:

- *Fructose test,* which checks for the sugar *fructose*; its absence may indicate blockage in the EPIDIDYMIS.
- *Infection and antibody tests,* such as the *MAR Test* or *Immunobead Binding Test,* in which semen is examined for bacteria and also antibodies that might cause death or clumping (*agglutination*) of the sperm, a possible indication of an immune problem; a *white blood cell count* in semen might also indicate an infection.
- *Zona free hamster egg test* (*sperm penetration assay*), which tests the sperm's ability to penetrate a hamster egg, similar to a human's, which has a protective outer layer, the ZONA PELLUCIDA.
- *Kreuger test,* which evaluates the shape of the sperm head.
- *Cervical mucus penetration test,* which examines the sperm's ability to navigate through cow (*bovine*) mucus.

If necessary, the fertility specialist may also draw blood samples, to test for the levels of various HORMONES; do a physical examination of the scrotum, to check for a possibly VARICOCELE, which has been linked with fertility problems; or do a rectal ULTRASOUND SCAN to check for prostate and testes for possible cysts. To check for possible blockage of the VAS DEFERENS, a VASOGRAPHY may be performed. If the vas deferens is not blocked, but there are still few or no sperm in the semen, a BIOPSY of the testicles may be performed, generally in a hospital under local or general ANESTHESIA, to see if sperm-producing tissue is present.

For the woman, further evaluation is more complex and time-consuming. These will include various tests to see if OVULATION has actually occurred (see OVULATION; NATURAL FAMILY PLANNING) and a *basal body temperature record,* a temperature chart using a specially calibrated thermometer (see NATURAL FAMILY PLANNING for a fuller description). Other tests may include:

- *Additional blood tests,* some of them involving quite esoteric and expensive laboratory analyses, to monitor the rise and fall of hormones, especially when a woman has no or irregular menstruation and other tests have proved uninformative.
- *Ultrasound scan,* in some special situations, to detect evidence of ovulation.
- *HYSTEROSALPINGOGRAM,* an X-RAY using a contrast dye, to see if the Fallopian tubes are open.
- *Endoscopy,* a variety of minor procedures using a lighted flexible tube (ENDOSCOPE) to examine internal pelvic organs, the tube being inserted through natural body openings or small surgical incisions. In LAPAROSCOPY, the endoscope is inserted through abdominal incisions and is used to examine the ovaries, Fallopian tubes, and outside of the uterus. If adhesions or scar tissue are found, these can sometimes be removed during the procedure. In any case, the doctor can assess whether an operation could correct the condition found. In a *culdoscopy,* the tube is introduced into the abdominal cavity through an incision in the

wall of the vagina. The woman must be in a knee-chest position during this procedure. In a HYSTEROSCOPY, the tube is fed in through the vagina and cervix. Sometimes a biopsy may be taken as well and some obstructive tissue may be removed.

Whatever the tests involved, the couple should be sure that their doctor gives them the results and an explanation of their significance as each test is given. Sometimes the tests are given by different doctors, and communication is incomplete. If that occurs, they should make an appointment with their primary infertility specialist to assess where they are in the testing process and what has been learned—and is yet to be learned.

Treatment of infertility varies according to the results of the tests. Sometimes the problem is simply that the couple is not well-enough attuned to the changes in their bodies to maximize their chances of conception. When ovulation does indeed take place, and other obstructions do not exist, use of natural family planning techniques to identify the woman's most fertile time can lead to successful conception. And sometimes an underlying physical problem needs to be treated, such as a tumor in a pituitary gland or a thyroid disorder. But often other kinds of treatments are indicated, including:

- *Fertility drugs*, which can be used in men to improve a low sperm count, and in women can help correct problems with ovulation, by acting on the glands that produce key hormones. These fertility drugs in women are associated with a significantly higher risk of MULTIPLE BIRTHS than normal, since sometimes more than one egg is produced in response to the drug and becomes fertilized.
- *Surgery*, as to correct a VARICOCELE or to unblock ducts or tubes, when that is technically feasible, or to remove a section of an ovary containing cysts and thickened tissue (a procedure called an *ovarian wedge resection*), in an effort to restart ovulation, though the scar itself can cause problems.
- *Lowering the heat of the man's SCROTUM*; this can involve spending less time in a sauna or hot tub, wearing looser briefs and pants (which allow the testicles to lie further away from the body, and therefore be cooler), and perhaps temporarily changing work that involves long exposure to heat.
- *Modifying the semen*, when it hinders movement of the sperm. Often the sperm are "washed" to separate them out of the semen and are then deposited into the uterus, in ARTIFICIAL INSEMINATION, or used in other techniques (noted below). This approach is often used when the man, woman, or both have developed antibodies to the sperm or when the semen is so thick that it hinders movement of the sperm.

Beyond these are several other techniques (discussed in separate entries), some of them relatively new, that have been breaking the bonds of REPRODUCTIVE TECHNOLOGY and raising a great many social and ethical questions—which are much discussed but unresolved, as medical technology proceeds apace. Some of these techniques are still experimental, are very expensive, often involve MICROMANIPULATION, and have a high failure rate. Yet for couples seeking a child, they offer a promise not available to previous generations. These techniques are new, all stemming from IN VITRO FERTILIZATION (IVF), from which the first child was born only in 1978. Related approaches include GAMETE INTRA-FALLOPIAN TUBE TRANSFER (GIFT) and EMBRYO TRANSFER. When more conventional reproductive technologies have failed, some even newer, but still highly experimental ASSISTED FERTILIZATION approaches have been used to facilitate fertilization by helping sperm penetrate the egg's outer protective layer, the ZONA PELLUCIDA; these include INTRACYTOPLASMIC SPERM INJECTION (ICSI), PARTIAL ZONA DISSECTION (PZD), and SUBZONAL SPERM INSERTION (SZI). In addition, ASSISTED HATCHING techniques focus on helping the embryo shed the zona pellucida, which it normally does before IMPLANTATION in the uterus wall. Beyond these are some more traditional approaches to infertility, including ARTIFICIAL INSEMINATION, SURROGATE PARENTING, and ADOPTION.

FOR HELP AND FURTHER INFORMATION

American Society for Reproductive Medicine (ASRM)
1209 Montgomery Highway
Birmingham, AL 35216–2809
205–978–5000
Fax: 205–978–5005
Alan H. DeCherney, President
Professional organization, formerly the American Fertility Society; maintains affiliate Society for Assisted Reproductive Technology (SART); provides information and referrals; publishes various materials including *A Patient's Guide to the Assisted Reproductive Technologies* and the *SART Report*, statistics on success rates for more than 200 centers.

RESOLVE, Inc.
1310 Broadway
Somerville, MA 02144–1731
HelpLine: 617–623–0744; Business Office: 617–623–1156
Fax: 617–623–0252
E-mail: resolveinc@aol.com (America Online: RESOLVEINC)
Internet Website:
http://www.ihr.com//resolve//index.htm
Diane D. Aronson, Executive Director
Network of mutual-support groups of couples dealing with inferility, counseled by trained professionals; provides information and referrals; acts as advocate; publishes newsletter and other materials, including:

- Starter kits: *Introduction to Infertility: The First Steps, Emotional Aspects of Infertility,* and *Exploring Adoption.*

- Booklets: *Assisted Reproductive Technology Workbook, Infertility Insurance Advisor,* and *Donor Insemination: Facts and Decision-Making.*
- Fact sheets on male infertility: *Collection on Male Perspective, Male Infertility—Medical Management, Semen Analysis, Sperm Antibodies and Immunologic Infertility,* and *Varicocele: Surgical and Medical Treatment.*
- Fact sheets on other specific topics: *Older Women Attempting Pregnancy, Overview of the Infertility Work-up, Secondary Infertility, Unexplained Infertility, Uterine Factors in Infertility, Personal and Medical Viewpoints, What Is an Infertility Specialist?, When to Consider Stopping Medical Treatment, When to Seek Professional Help for the Emotional Aspects of the Infertility Experience, Infertility as a Chronic Illness and Stress Disorder, Meditation and Infertility, Stress of Infertility/How to Cope, Views on Patient Rights, Pregnancy after Infertility, Luteal Phase Defect, Collected Articles on IVF/GIFT, Assisted Reproductive Technologies, Q&A, Overview of the New Technologies,* and *Micromanipulation (SUZI, ICSI, Assisted Hatching), Multi-Fetal Pregnancy Reduction, Alternative Treatments: Naturopathic and Acupuncture, Childfree Decision-Making, Friends and Family: How They Can Help, Holidays, Religious Perspectives and Infertility, Sex and Infertility,* and on specific drugs.

Planned Parenthood Federation of America (PPFA), 800–230–7526. Publishes pamphlets *Infertility: Questions and Answers* and *Ways to Chart Your Fertility Pattern.* (For full group information, see BIRTH CONTROL.)

National Institute of Child Health and Human Development (NICHD) 301–496–5133. (For full group information, see PREGNANCY.)

Couple to Couple League (CCL), 513–471–2000. Publishes brochure *Practical Helps for Seeking Pregnancy.* (For full group information, see NATURAL FAMILY PLANNING.)

Center for Surrogate Parenting and Egg Donation, 213–655–1974. (For full group information, see SURROGATE PARENTING.

Endometriosis Association (EA), 800–992–3636. (For full group information, see ENDOMETRIOSIS.)

OTHER RESOURCES

GENERAL WORKS

The Couple's Guide to Fertility: Updated with the Newest Scientific Techniques That Can Help You Have a Baby, rev. ed. Gary S. Berger and others. Doubleday, 1995.

Wanting Another Child: How to Cope with Secondary Infertility. Harriet F. Simons. Free Press, 1995.

A Woman Doctor's Guide to Infertility: Essential Facts and Up-to-the Minute Information on the Techniques and Treatments to Achieve Pregnancy. Susan Treiser and Robin Levinson. Hyperion, 1994.

Overcoming Infertility Naturally. Karen Bradstreet. Woodland, 1994.

Taking Charge of Infertility. Patricia Irwin Johnston. Perspectives, 1994.

Beyond Infertility: The New Paths to Parenthood. Ellen S. Glazer and Susan L. Cooper. Free Press, 1994.

In Vitro Fertilization. Carl Wood and Robyn Riley. Seven Hills, 1994.

How to Be a Successful Fertility Patient: Your Guide to Getting the Best Possible Medical Help to Have a Baby. Peggy Robin. Morrow, 1993.

Getting Pregnant When You Thought You Couldn't: The Interactive Guide That Helps You Up the Odds. Helene S. Rosenberg and Yakov M. Epstein. Warner, 1993.

In-Vitro Fertilization Clinics: A North American Directory of Programs and Services. Mary Partridge-Brown. McFarland, 1993.

Free Money for Treating Infertility. Laurie Blum. Simon & Schuster, 1993.

Men, Women, and Infertility: Intervention and Treatment Strategies. Aline P. Zoldbrod. Free Press, 1992.

The Fertility Solution: A Revolutionary Approach to Reversing Infertility. A. Toth. Atlantic Monthly, 1992.

The Infertility Book: A Comprehensive Medical and Emotional Guide. Carla Harkness. Celestial Arts, 1992.

Getting Pregnant: What Couples Need to Know Right Now. Niels H. Lauersen and Colette Bouchez. Macmillan, 1991.

Overcoming Infertility: A Practical Strategy for Navigating the Emotional, Medical, and Financial Minefields of Trying to Have a Baby. Robert Nachtigall and Elizabeth Mehren. Doubleday, 1991.

Conquering Infertility: A Guide for Couples, rev. ed. Stephen L. Corson. Prentice Hall, 1991.

A Baby of Your Own: New Ways to Overcome Infertility. William G. Karow. Taylor, 1991.

Missed Conceptions: Overcoming Infertility. Anne Mullens. Shapolsky, 1991.

Overcoming Infertility. Robert Nachtigall. Thorsons, 1991.

What You Can Do about Infertility. Pamela P. Novotny. Dell, 1991.

How to Get Pregnant with the New Technology. Sherman Silber. Warner, 1991.

ON MALE INFERTILITY

Male Sexual Vitality. Michael T. Murray. Prima, 1994.

When a Husband Is Infertile: Options for the Christian Couple. Byron C. Calhoun. Baker, 1994.

Male Infertility: Men Talking. Mary-Claire Mason. Routledge, 1993.

ON EMOTIONAL ASPECTS OF INFERTILITY

Infertility: Emotional Journey. Michelle F. Hanson. Deaconess Press, 1994.

Psychological Aspects of Infertility. Anthony Reading, ed. Wiley, 1994.

Stolen Joy: Healing after Infertility and Infant Loss. Anne Barney. Icarus, 1993.

Longing for a Child: Coping with Infertility. Bobbie Reed. Augsburg Fortress, 1994.
Never to Be a Mother: A Guide for All Women Who Didn't—or Couldn't—Have Children. Linda H. Anton. HarperCollins, 1992.
Give Us a Child: Coping with the Personal Crisis of Infertility. Lynda R. Stephenson. Zondervan, 1992.
Surviving Infertility: A Compassionate Guide Through the Emotional Crisis of Infertility, rev. ed. Linda P. Salzer. HarperCollins, 1991.
For Want of a Child: A Psychologist and His Wife Explore the Emotional Effects and Challenges of Infertility. James McGuirk and Mary McGuirk. Continuum, 1991.
Without Child: A Compassionate Look at Infertility, rev. ed. Martha Stout. Shaw, 1990.
Healing the Infertile Family: Strengthening Your Relationship in the Search for Parenthood. Gaylene Becker. Bantam, 1990.

PERSONAL STORIES

Infertility Miracles Can Happen: Success Stories and the Science Behind Them. Herbert A. Goldfarb. Wiley, 1994.
When You Can't Have a Child: Personal Stories of Living Through Infertility and Childlessness. Susan Powell. Independent Publishers Group/Chicago Review Press, 1993.
Dear Barbara, Dear Lynne: The True Story of Two Women in Search of Motherhood. Barbara Shulgold and Lynne Sipiora. Addison-Wesley, 1992.
Waiting for Baby: One Couple's Journey Through Infertility to Adoption. Mary Earle Chase. McGraw-Hill, 1990.

ON REPRODUCTIVE TECHNOLOGY

Manufacturing Babies and Public Consent: Debating the New Reproductive Technologies. Jose Van Dyck. New York University Press, 1995.
Issues in Reproductive Technology: An Anthology. Helen B. Holmes, ed. New York University Press, 1994.
Babies in Bottles: Twentieth-Century Visions of Reproductive Technology. Susan M. Squier. Rutgers University Press, 1994.
Children of Choice: Freedom and the New Reproductive Technologies. John A. Robertson. Princeton University Press, 1994.
Women as Wombs: Reproductive Technologies and the Battle Over Women's Freedom. Janice G. Raymond. HarperCollins, 1994.
The Stork and the Syringe: A Political History of Reproductive Medicine. Naomi Pfeffer. Blackwell, 1994.
Tough Choices: In Vitro Fertilization and the Reproductive Technologies. Patricia Stephenson and Marsden G. Wagner, eds. Temple University Press, 1993.
Technology of Procreation: Kinship in the Age of Assisted Conception. Jeanette Edwards. St. Martin's, 1993.
Living Laboratories: Women and Reproductive Technology. Robyn Rowland. Indiana University Press, 1992.
The Ethics of Reproductive Technology. Kenneth D. Alpern, ed. Oxford University Press, 1992.

BACKGROUND WORKS

Barren in the Promised Land: Childless Americans and the Pursuit of Happiness. Elaine Tyler May. Basic, 1995.
With Child in Mind: Studies of the Personal Encounter with Infertility. Margarete Sandelowski. University of Pennsylvania Press, 1993.

(See also PREGNANCY; ARTIFICIAL INSEMINATION; IMPLANTATION; IN VITRO FERTILIZATION; SURROGATE MOTHER; and other specific topics mentioned in article.)

inflammatory bowel disease (IBD), an umbrella name for a group of chronic digestive disorders affecting the small and large intestines. These disorders go by many names, some of them simply indicating inflammation of the affected part, such as *ileitis* (ileum, part of the small intestine), *enteritis* (small intestine), *colitis* (colon, or large intestine), *ileocolitis* (ileum and colon), *enterocolitis* (small and large intestines), or *proctitis* (rectum and anus). More often doctors divide IBD into two groups:

- *Ulcerative colitis,* which involves ulcers (raw sores) and inflammation of the lining (*mucosa*) of the colon.
- *Crohn's disease,* which involves inflammation in the deeper layers of the intestinal wall and may also affect not only the colon but the whole digestive tract, including the mouth, esophagus, stomach, duodenum (upper part of the small intestine), and even the appendix, the tiny but troublesome projection off the intestines.

Symptoms of IBD include DIARRHEA, CHRONIC pain in the abdomen, occasional FEVER, and sometimes bleeding from the rectum (especially from ulcerative colitis), which can lead to ANEMIA and weight loss. In children, persistent symptoms can stunt GROWTH, especially affecting the joints, cause DEVELOPMENTAL DELAY, and slow sexual maturation. Ulcerative colitis is relatively easy to diagnose, through visual examinations using a PROCTOSCOPE or SIGMOIDOSCOPE or BARIUM X-RAY EXAMINATIONS. The same examinations are not so helpful with Crohn's disease, because the affected areas are not always so accessible.

No cure is yet available for IBD. Drugs can help suppress cramps and diarrhea. Many people are helped by avoiding foods that trigger symptoms; these may vary from person to person but often include MILK, alcohol, hot spices, and FIBER. The National Institute of Diabetes and Digestive and Kidney Diseases (NIDDK) notes that: "Maintaining good general nutrition and adequate intake is far more important than emphasizing or avoiding any particular food. Also large doses of vitamins are useless and may even produce harmful side effects." Doctors sometimes recommend nutritional supplements, often high-calorie liquid formulas, to growing children. In severe cases, such as when patients need extra nutrition or when their bowels need complete rest or are too inflamed to absorb sufficient nourishment from food, doctors may place patients on PARENTERAL NUTRITION, supplied intravenously.

Among the complications of IBD are the formation of holes (*perforations*) and abnormal openings (*fistulas*), which may spread infection and inflammation to the abdominal cavity, including the potentially dangerous *peritonitis* (inflammation of the *peritoneum*, the abdomen's lining). Ulcerative colitis carries an increased risk of colon or rectal cancer. With Crohn's disease, obstructions or blockages may form and need surgical correction. IBD, which can also have wider effects on the body, is associated with some forms of ARTHRITIS, skin problems, inflammation of the eyes and mouth, kidney stones, gallstones, and some liver problems.

Both main forms of IBD may go into REMISSION for long periods, sometimes years, for unknown reasons, and then recur equally unexpectedly, though sometimes with obvious triggers. In the long run, the NIDDK estimates, perhaps one-third of the people with ulcerative colitis may need to have part or all of the colon removed, sometimes making an artificial opening called an OSTOMY in the abdomen for emptying of the bowels. Likewise, the NIDDK estimates that about 2 out of 3 patients with Crohn's disease will require intestinal surgery at some time during their lives. Unfortunately, removing sections of the intestine does not solve the problem, because the inflammation tends to reappear in the sections near those removed (it does not in ulcerative colitis).

The NIDDK estimates that one to two million people suffer from IBD. Men and women are equally afflicted, as are people of all socioeconomic backgrounds. The disorder appears to be especially common among people from England and the Scandinavian countries and among Jews (though rates are low in Israel), and in general it is more common among Whites than among Blacks, Hispanics, Native Americans, and people of Asian ancestry. In about 1 case in 4, a person with IBD has a BLOOD RELATION, often a SIBLING, who also has the disorder, but researchers are not sure to what extent that connection is genetic and to what extent environmental. Researchers are also exploring the possible role of IMMUNE SYSTEM dysfunction and infection with an as-yet-unrecognized microorganism. SMOKING is linked with a somewhat lower risk of ulcerative colitis, but a much greater risk of getting and having recurring episodes of Crohn's disease. IBD seems to be on the rise around the world, but for unknown reasons. The peak time for onset of the disease is between ages fifteen and twenty-five.

Women with active Crohn's disease may have slightly increased difficulty in conceiving, perhaps because of associated symptoms, such as FEVER and ANEMIA. They also have a higher-than-normal risk of having a STILLBIRTH, MISCARRIAGE (spontaneous ABORTION), or PREMATURE delivery. Because IBD can worsen during PREGNANCY, women should try to bring the disorder under control before attempting conception. They will also wish to consult with their doctors about the effect that any medication may have on the developing FETUS or on the baby, if they choose BREASTFEEDING.

FOR HELP AND FURTHER INFORMATION

National Foundation for Ileitis and Colitis (NFIC)
386 Park Avenue, 17th Floor
New York, NY 10016
212–685–3440; 800–932–2423
Fax: 212–779–4098
Barbara Boyle, Executive Director
Terry Jennings, Director of Communications, Contact
Organization concerned with ileitis and colitis; sponsors research; supports peer-support groups; provides information and referrals; publishes many materials, including quarterly newsletters *IBD News* and *National Newsletter.*

National Digestive Disease Information Clearinghouse (NDDIC), 301–654–3810. (For full group information, see DIGESTIVE SYSTEM AND DISORDERS.)

OTHER RESOURCES

Eating Right for a Bad Gut: The Complete Nutritional Guide to Ileitis, Crohn's Disease and Inflammatory Bowel Syndrome. James Scala. NAL, 1990.

(See also DIGESTIVE SYSTEM AND DISORDERS.)

informal assessment, a method of evaluating student performance by writing evaluations, rather than assigning numerical or letter GRADES; sometimes called *summative evaluation.* Informal assessments are used in some ALTERNATIVE SCHOOLS or other types of experimental institutions, and are common in PRESCHOOL and early PRIMARY SCHOOLS.

informed consent, formal written permission to be obtained from a patient by medical personnel before invasive and possibly risky MEDICAL TESTS or other medical procedures, such as operations, are performed. By law, the doctor is required to tell patients, in language they can understand, the risks as well as the benefits of the test or procedure to be performed and to give patients information about possible alternative tests available to find the same or similar information. Before certain types of procedures, the patient may be asked to sign a document outlining that information in language designed to be understandable to nonprofessionals, often before a witness and generally a specified number of hours or days ahead of time. Because children, as MINORS, are usually not legally able to sign such documents, parents must obtain and analyze the information and give consent for them. (See MEDICAL TESTS.)

inheritance rights, legal rights to inherit a share of the estate of someone who has died. If the person died with a valid will, these rights are spelled out in that document, which must be affirmed as valid by a PROBATE COURT. But if the person died INTESTATE (without a will), the *intestate succession* laws of the particular state will determine precisely who is entitled to what share of the estate, if any. Among those who usually have inheritance rights by state law are BLOOD RELATIONS or KIN, adopted children, ADOPTIVE PARENTS, and a surviving spouse. Questions of inheritance by a child can be extremely complicated, especially with the advent of new REPRODUCTIVE TECHNOLOGY, and to a large extent depend on who is, under current law, considered the child's legal FATHER and MOTHER. Someone who would normally have inheritance rights, but who was deliberately or inadvertently (such as an AFTER-BORN child) left out of the will is termed *disinherited*, or more formally a *pretermitted heir*.

injection, in medicine, the technique of forcing a liquid into the body by means of a *syringe*, a hollow-barreled cylinder with a plunger (or sometimes a rubber bulb) affixed to a needle. Health professionals name types of injections for the different parts of the body into which the fluid is being introduced, common forms being:

- *Intraarterial*, directly into an artery, such as one that supplies a TUMOR.
- *Intradermal*, directly into the skin, specifically the *dermis*.
- *Intramuscular*, directly into the muscle.
- *Intravenous*, directly into a vein, as in a post-operative situation.
- *Intrathecal*, directly through the membrane enclosing the spinal cord and into the CEREBROSPINAL FLUID (CSF).
- *Subcutaneous*, directly into the tissue beneath the skin, such as the upper arm or buttocks, as in most common "shots."

Sometimes nutrients and medications may be introduced into the body by any of various types of injections, bypassing the digestive system; such injections are termed PARENTERAL NUTRITION.

When carefully sterile conditions are maintained, such injections pose little risk, and we have come to accept them as everyday occurrences. But where proper caution is not exercised, injections can introduce infections, since they are INVASIVE procedures, a matter of special concern in the AIDS era.

injunction, a court order to do or *not* to do a specified act. In cases of threatened CHILD ABUSE OR NEGLECT or PARENTAL KIDNAPPING, a judge might first issue a TEMPORARY RESTRAINING ORDER and then an injunction that the threatening parent be barred from the FAMILY HOME or forbidden to take the child out of a specified area, such as a county.

in loco parentis, the legal term for the duties and rights of an organization or GUARDIAN acting as temporary parent to a child, as in a boarding school or camp; from the Latin for "in place of a parent."

insulin, a HORMONE produced by the pancreas, lack of which produces the disease DIABETES. Too much insulin, as during treatment, can cause HYPOGLYCEMIA or *insulin shock*.

integration, in learning theory, ability to use all the available MODALITIES or senses to gain new learning. (See LEARNING STYLE.) More generally, the practice of keeping together people who might otherwise be separated on the basis of one or more characteristics, such as race or the presence of DISABILITIES (see DESEGREGATION; MAINSTREAMING).

intelligence quotient (IQ), the final score on an INTELLIGENCE TEST, derived by means of a formula from a child's score on the TEST, notably the STANFORD-BINET INTELLIGENCE TEST, for which NORMS have been established with other children of the same age; a somewhat outdated concept.

intelligence test, a type of TEST that is intended to measure general mental abilities, dubbed "intelligence." The VALIDITY of such tests has been strongly attacked in recent decades, because it is still unclear what intelligence tests actually measure (a question of *content validity*) and how well the tests estimate future intellectual performance (*predictive validity*). Old-style, strongly verbal intelligence tests, such as the STANFORD-BINET INTELLIGENCE TEST (the original IQ test), have been accused of unfairly discriminating against children who are not from White, comfortably middle-class, two-parent families. The criticism is that, far from measuring innate abilities, the tests are measuring certain kinds of experiences, leaving children without those experiences at a distinct disadvantage.

Some testmakers have attacked the thorny cultural problem by trying to devise tests that are independent of (or at least evenhanded regarding) cultural experience. Such tests are called CULTURE-FAIR or culture-free. Others have developed kinds of tests that do not depend on either verbal ability or cultural background, and as a result also measure different aspects of "intelligence." Examples include the GOODENOUGH-HARRIS DRAWING TEST, KOHS BLOCK DESIGN TEST, MERRILL-PALMER SCALE, and STANDARD PROGRESSIVE MATRICES. In addition, some intelligence tests have been developed for very young, even preverbal children, such as the CATTELL INFANT INTELLIGENCE SCALE. Other intelligence tests in wide use for children today include the WECHSLER INTELLIGENCE SCALE FOR CHILDREN, REVISED (probably the most widely used) and the KAUFMAN ASSESSMENT BATTERY FOR CHILDREN.

OTHER RESOURCES

GENERAL WORKS

The Ultimate IQ Book. Marcel Feenstra and others. Sterling, 1993.

A Question of Intelligence: The IQ Debate in America. Daniel Seligman. Carol, 1992.

Practical guides

Succeed at I. Q. Tests. Gilles Azzopardi. Trans-Atlantic, 1994.

Getting Better at IQ Tests for Ages 11–13. Getting Better at IQ Tests for Ages 14–16. Ken Russell and Philip Carter. Trans-Atlantic, 1994.

Background works

The IQ Mythology: Class, Race, and Inequality. Elaine Mensh and Harry Mensh. Southern Illinois University Press, 1991.

Intelligence: The Psychometric View. Paul Kline. Routledge, 1990.

The IQ Controversy, the Media and Public Policy. Mark Snyderman and Stanley Rothman. Transaction, 1990.

(See also STANFORD-BINET INTELLIGENCE TEST, including the standard "IQ" categories; TESTS.)

intensive care unit (ICU), a division of a HOSPITAL designed to provide continuous monitoring and HEALTH CARE for people with acute, life-threatening conditions, such as severe BURNS, multiple injuries, and certain heart problems. ICUs have far more sophisticated monitoring and treatment equipment than ordinary hospital wards and have specially trained staff. LOW BIRTH WEIGHT, PREMATURE, or seriously ill infants are often placed in an intensive care unit. Some large, sophisticated hospitals (Level III or tertiary care) have separate NEONATAL INTENSIVE CARE UNITS (NICU's).

intermediate school, an alternate term for MIDDLE SCHOOL; the term *intermediate* is sometimes used to refer to the upper elementary grades 4–6.

internist, a PHYSICIAN who specializes in treating diseases affecting the internal organs of adults and in providing primary health care for adults.

intervention, action to identify a problem at an early stage, when it is most effectively treated, as in EARLY INTERVENTION, or to relieve a stressful situation or series of problems threatening someone's health or welfare, as in CRISIS INTERVENTION.

intestate, a legal term for someone who died without a valid will. The estate of a person who died intestate is distributed by the PROBATE COURT under the current *intestate succession* laws of each state, which specify who has what INHERITANCE RIGHTS, if any. These are usually near BLOOD RELATIONS, adopted children, ADOPTIVE PARENTS, and a surviving spouse.

intracytoplasmic sperm injection (ICSI), an ASSISTED FERTILIZATION technique, a variation on IN VITRO FERTILIZATION; a new, still highly experimental form of REPRODUCTIVE TECHNOLOGY to help SPERM and egg (OVUM) join to achieve FERTILIZATION. Using MICROMANIPULATION, the EMBRYOLOGIST uses two tiny needles (*micropipettes*), one (the *holding pipette*) to fix the egg in place, the other (the *injection pipette*) to insert a single sperm underneath the ZONA PELLUCIDA, the protective outer layer of the egg. ICSI is an approach of last resort and can cost as much as ten thousand to fifteen thousand dollars, but it holds promise for the most extreme cases of male-related INFERTILITY, since it can be used with some men who have no active or normally shaped sperm and even with some who have no sperm in their semen, as when their VAS DEFERENS are blocked or when they have previously had a VASECTOMY (previously regarded as effectively irreversible), as long as they have some sperm-producing tissue in their TESTES. (See INFERTILITY; REPRODUCTIVE TECHNOLOGY.)

intrapartal care, medical care for a pregnant woman through the whole of LABOR, from the onset of CONTRACTIONS through the DELIVERY of the baby and expulsion of the PLACENTA (afterbirth); a part of the MATERNITY CYCLE. Care for the baby in the same period is called *newborn intrapartal care.* (See POSTNATAL CARE.)

intrauterine device (IUD), a form of BIRTH CONTROL that involves the insertion of a metal or plastic device into a woman's UTERUS to prevent IMPLANTATION of a fertilized egg. Some IUDs are biochemically neutral, but others contain HORMONES that also aid in CONTRACEPTION; a string hangs down to allow women to check that the IUD is still in place.

The main attraction of IUDs is that the neutral (inert) types can remain in place for up to five years, so the woman has no pills to take, no devices to put in or take out, and no calculations to make. The Food and Drug Administration (FDA) also rates them as 95 to 96 percent effective as contraceptives.

However, some types of IUDs, notably the Dalkon Shield, were linked with increased risk of many serious problems, including infection in the REPRODUCTIVE SYSTEM, septic ABORTION (with severe infection), perforation of the uterus, PELVIC INFLAMMATORY DISEASE, ECTOPIC PREGNANCY (in the FALLOPIAN TUBES), and other causes of INFERTILITY. Other less serious side effects occurred shortly after insertion, including cramping, dizziness, backache, bleeding, and heavy MENSTRUATION. The Dalkon Shield was removed from the market in 1974. The manufacturer later agreed to pay medical costs of women injured by their IUDs. Because of these medical and legal problems, many manufacturers have ceased making IUDs in the United States. Some are still available and being used, however. And IUDs are widely used elsewhere; they are the most widely used form of reversible contraception worldwide.

Long-term experience has been more favorable, notably in Europe, and in 1991 a new American study raised questions about the association between IUDs and increased pelvic infections, though it did not exonerate

Special Care for Special Babies

Each new baby is unique. All newborns need love, attention and care. Some will need medical attention as well.

If your baby is premature (early), very small, or has another medical problem, your infant may need special medical care and you may not be able to bring him or her home from the hospital as soon as you expected. You and your family may be faced with disappointment and worry at a time usually reserved for great joy. It is normal to be upset and confused. Sharing your feelings with your partner, family, or friends may help deal with your and your partner's pain and problems.

The hospital may have a separate nursery for babies who need special care. This nursery may be called a "Neonatal Intensive Care Unit" (NICU) or a "High Risk Nursery." These nurseries have a specially trained health care team to help your baby. They are there to help you and your family through this hard time as well. These tips may help you.

- Ask if there is a social worker to help you and your family with your questions and concerns. This person can be your "contact point" each time you have a question.
- If you don't understand something that is happening or are confused about what you have been told, *ask* your doctor, social worker, nurse, or someone else on the health care team. It might help if you keep a small notebook with you and write down questions when you think of them. When you are at the hospital, you can write down the answers and read them again later.
- Most nurseries will let you visit twenty-four hours a day. You and your partner should be there often to touch and hold your baby. This contact will help your baby and you become a famliy.
- You may still be able to provide your breastmilk for your baby. Be sure to discuss this with your doctor as early as possible.
- There may be meetings of parents like you ("support groups") during which you can discuss your problems and feelings. There may be other sources of help in your community as well. Ask the hospital social worker about resources that may be helpful for you and your partner.
- When you take your baby home, he or she may need special kinds of care. Be sure to get clear written instructions from the hospital staff before you leave. You and your partner or another family member, if possible, should be there, so that you both know what you should do. If you think that you may need help at home caring for your baby, ask the hospital social worker about sources of assistance.

WHAT TO ASK YOUR DOCTOR OR NURSES

Don't be afraid to ask about anything you want to know. Your baby's doctor and the nursing staff are there to help you, and if you don't ask about caring for your baby, they may think you already know. If you forget something they said or don't understand, *ask again.* Keep asking questions until you understand. The kind of advice you get will depend upon how much you tell them you want to understand and learn. Remember:

- Think about all the questions you have about your baby and those things you want to learn.
- Make a list of questions, if you want. You may want to write down the answers, too.
- Ask your doctor or nurse to explain anything you don't understand.
- Ask them to explain any medical terms you don't know.
- If they give you advice that sounds hard to follow, keep asking questions to find out what they really mean, to help you follow their advice.

Source: Infant Care (1989). Prepared for the Public Health Service by the Health and Resources Administration, Bureau of Maternal and Child Health and Resources Development.

the Dalkon Shield. In the United States, the FDA recommends IUDs only for women who have had children and are in a monogamous relationship. IUDs offer no protection against SEXUALLY TRANSMITTED DISEASES, including AIDS. (See BIRTH CONTROL.)

intrauterine growth retardation, slow growth of the FETUS during a PREGNANCY, often resulting in a child labeled SMALL FOR GESTATIONAL AGE. Growth can be slowed when the mother has certain medical conditions, such as PREECLAMPSIA, high BLOOD PRESSURE, or chronic KIDNEY AND UROLOGICAL PROBLEMS, as well as improper NUTRITION, SMOKING, or ALCOHOL ABUSE. Slow growth can also result from failure of the PLACENTA to provide appropriate nutrients, from viral infection caught from the mother, such as RUBELLA (German measles), or from conditions resulting from CHROMOSOMAL ABNORMALITIES, such as DOWN SYNDROME. (See LOW BIRTH WEIGHT; GESTATIONAL AGE; PREGNANCY.)

intraventricular hemorrhage (IVH), severe bleeding into the VENTRICLES of the brain, a problem often associated with PREMATURE babies. (See PREMATURE; BRAIN AND BRAIN DISORDERS.)

in utero surgery, a medical procedure in which a PHYSICIAN, using FETOSCOPY, operates on the FETUS while it is still in the UTERUS, to correct abnormalities; also called *fetal surgery*. One common type of fetal surgery is the insertion of a catheter to bypass a fetus's blocked urinary tract, to prevent kidney damage. Another, newer operation involves correction of a DIAPHRAGMATIC HERNIA. For a fetus suffering from RH INCOMPATIBILITY in the blood, an EXCHANGE TRANSFUSION can also be carried out.

invasive, a general descriptive term for something that intrudes or tends to spread into its surroundings, such as a CANCER or TUMOR. In relation to MEDICAL TESTS, the term *invasive* describes a procedure that involves "breaching the body's defenses." It is generally used to refer to tests in which foreign substances are introduced by a potentially risky procedure, as when a dyed fluid is injected into the body by way of a LUMBAR PUNCTURE in a MYELOGRAM. A simple procedure, such as inserting a needle into a child's arm to take a BLOOD sample, can also be regarded as invasive. In most medical establishments in the United States, where high standards of hygiene obtain and needles are either new and sterile or carefully sterilized, there is little risk from the taking of a blood sample. But when needles are reused without careful sterilization, even the seemingly simple puncture of a needle can lead to serious infection—which can be deadly in the case of AIDS. By contrast, a simple chest X-RAY would be regarded as noninvasive, since nothing is injected or ingested into the body. (For help and more information, see MEDICAL TESTS; CANCER; TUMOR.)

in vitro fertilization (IVF), a treatment for INFERTILITY in which the SPERM and egg (OVUM) are brought together for FERTILIZATION, not in a woman's FALLOPIAN TUBES but in a glass laboratory dish ("in vitro" means literally "in glass"); also called *test-tube fertilization*. The technique was originally developed for situations in which the woman's Fallopian tubes are so damaged or clogged that they cannot be used as a site for fertilization, but the rest of her reproductive organs are functioning normally. However, many centers now use IVF techniques when women have other problems, including ENDOMETRIOSIS and cervical mucus problems, when men have infertility problems, or when the cause of the infertility is undiagnosed. In general, a woman requires at least one accessible ovary, from which eggs are harvested, unless EGG DONATION is used. Many centers test a woman for immunity to RUBELLA. If she is not immune, she is given a vaccination before IVF. She may also be given an HIV test (see AIDS) and a test for blood type.

In the actual procedure, the woman is given fertility drugs during the first week of her MENSTRUAL CYCLE to stimulate the maturation of eggs, which is monitored using ULTRASOUND SCANS, URINE TESTS, and BLOOD TESTS during the next few days. Sometimes other drugs are given to supress unwanted hormonal activity, especially that of LUTEINIZING HORMONE (LH). Some centers have recently reported success in harvesting eggs without stimulating drugs. This is preferable because the fertility drugs have been linked to increased risk of breast or ovarian CANCER. If blood levels of FOLLICLE-STIMULATING HORMONE (FSH) are too high, some centers may cancel attempts during that cycle, since the chances of harvesting good eggs is low.

If all goes well, just before OVULATION, which is sometimes pushed along by injections of HORMONES, doctors remove as many ripe eggs as possible, using a technique such as LAPAROSCOPY or ASPIRATION. A few hours later, the eggs are mixed with the man's sperm (produced at the center or brought in from home) in a glass dish and placed in an incubator. Fertilization, if it occurs, will usually take place within twelve hours, and the fertilized eggs (EMBRYOS) will begin to divide. They are transferred to a growth medium for thirty-eight to forty hours and are examined for normal size and shape. Then the woman returns to the center. At that point, several fertilized eggs are drawn into a CATHETER, which is then inserted through the woman's CERVIX, and the eggs are deposited into the UTERUS. Several eggs are used, because the failure rate is so high. Many eggs fail to implant or spontaneously abort in the weeks that follow, some because of CHROMOSOMAL ABNORMALITIES (as is true of many normally achieved pregnancies). On the other hand, the insertion of multiple fertilized eggs leads to MULTIPLE BIRTHS in as many as 1 out of every 5 cases. Because this can lead to complications, most centers limit the number of embryos used to four or five.

The woman often remains at the center for four to six hours and is then sent home to rest in bed while the EMBRYOS—it is hoped—implant. She is advised to avoid sexual intercourse for a few days and is often given additional PROGESTERONE to build up the uterine lining and increase the likelihood of IMPLANTATION. The woman returns to the center periodically for tests of hormone levels and for a PREGNANCY TEST ten to fourteen days after the transfer. When the FETUS has developed enough so that an ULTRASOUND SCAN reveals heart movement and a fetal sac, the woman is then referred to be OBSTETRICIAN, who will handle the actually pregnancy and DELIVERY, though hers will, of course, be considered a high-risk pregnancy.

Couples should be aware that the "vanishing fetus" is common. Often two or more fetal sacs may be seen on the earliest ultrasound, but one or more will disappear and be absorbed in the first three months of pregnancy. Also ECTOPIC PREGNANCY can occur (in one study in 6 percent of the cases), perhaps because the woman commonly has damaged Fallopian tubes and if the embryo floats to an opening, the tube is unable to propel it back into the uterus. With IVF, a woman is more like to experience bleeding during pregnancy, PREMATURE delivery, and CESAREAN SECTION, though this is partly due to the frequency of multiple births. However, no higher rate of GENETIC DISORDERS or CHROMOSOMAL ABNORMALITIES has been reported.

Unused embryos are often frozen, in a process called *cryopreservation,* for use in a later cycle, if desired. About half to two-thirds of the embryos survive the process of freezing and later thawing. Use of frozen embryos eliminates the need for the woman to take additional hormones and undergo further surgical retrieval. The second attempt succeeds surprisingly often—in one study, in nineteen of sixty-five couples—and studies show that the probability of pregnancy remains fairly constant for at least six cycles, for couples under the age of forty. However, the emotional and financial toll of going through repeated attempts is considerable. If desired, the man's sperm can sometimes be frozen as well. For example, a man who is to undergo CANCER treatment that could make him sterile may choose to store some sperm so that he can later father children.

In general, the recovery rate for mature eggs from ovaries ranges from 90 to 100 percent, and when the sperm is normal, IVF can achieve fertilization in 80 to 90 percent of attempts. However, the average birth rate from IVF in centers that report their statistics (not all do) is 14 to 20 percent, with MISCARRIAGE rates of 20 to 29 percent. The actual birth rate is so much lower for a variety of reasons, many of them unknown, but including improper timing or placement of the transfer, inadequate uterine lining, irritation of the uterus by the actual transfer procedure, and disturbance of the mucus plug in the cervix that normally protects the embryo from developing normally. Considerable research is focused on the reasons for failure and methods for avoiding the problems.

Some centers have been experimenting with alternatives to traditional IVF. These include *intravaginal culture* (IVC) and *natural oocyte retrieval intravaginal fertilization* (NORIF). In these, few drugs or no drugs are used. Eggs are retrieved, immediately mixed with the partner's sperm, then placed in the vagina for 44 to 50 hours, held in place by a cup much like a DIAPHRAGM. After this incubation period, the resulting embryos are transferred to the uterus. This still-new approach is simpler and less expensive than traditional IVF and has a roughly equivalent rate of success.

Some other alternatives include:

- *GAMETE INTRA-FALLOPIAN TUBE TRANSFER* (GIFT), in which sperm and egg are together placed into the woman's Fallopian tube or a related procedure *zygote intrafallopian transfer* (ZIFT) or *pronuclear state transfer* (PROST), in which zygotes (newly fertilized embryos) or preembryos are placed in the Fallopian tube a day after retrieval.
- *Direct intraperitoneal insemination* (DIPI), in which washed sperm are injected into the woman's peritoneal cavity using a needle inserted behind the cervix at the top of the vagina. It is used in cases of cervical mucus problems, poor sperm quality, or unexplained infertility.
- *Tubal embryo stage transfer* (TEST or TET), in which early embryos are placed in the Fallopian tubes two days after retrieval, using LAPAROSCOPY to guide placement. A related approach, *transuterine tubal embryo transfer,* uses ULTRASOUND SCANS and a catheter to perform a similar procedure.
- *EGG DONATION,* using an egg provided by another woman; depending on the policies of the center and the laws of the state, some women may donate some or all of their unused eggs to other women, though many are now choosing to have them frozen for their own possible future use.

In recent years, a number of new, still highly experimental techniques have developed, all of them variations on the basic in vitro fertilization procedures. These include INTRACYTOPLASMIC SPERM INJECTION (ICSI), PARTIAL ZONA DISSECTION (PZD), SUBZONAL SPERM INSERTION (SZI), and ASSISTED HATCHING. Also, EMBRYO BIOPSY has been developed to test embryos for possible GENETIC DEFECTS, so that only those that seem normal can be implanted or frozen.

In vitro fertilization, though dramatic, still has a very low success rate. The procedures are enormously expensive, in 1995 ranging up to eight thousand dollars per cycle, and are only partly covered by HEALTH INSURANCE policies, as well as being emotionally and physically very taxing, involving travel to the clinic, loss of work time, and cost of accommodations for at least two weeks each time the procedure is tried. Fertility experts recommend that IVF should not be entered into lightly and should be the last resort, chosen only after full fertility workups and thorough exploration of other options. IVF clinics also vary widely in their success rates, with some having nearly zero. Parents exploring IVF should certainly question clinics carefully about the actual number of live births that have resulted from their clinic's work.

Questions also abound about the legal status of the fertilized eggs, some of which may be frozen for future use. Some states have even barred the procedure because of ethical questions regarding EMBRYOS created in test-tubes. In addition, the Roman Catholic Church and some others are opposed to in vitro fertilization and related reproductive technology. (See INFERTILITY; REPRODUCTIVE TECHNOLOGY.)

iodine, a MINERAL needed in the body, though only in trace amounts, for the normal functioning of the THYROID GLAND, which through HORMONES control the body's METABOLISM, growth, and development. The best natural source of iodine is seafood, but to ensure that they get enough iodine, many people use iodized salt—table salt with iodine added. Iodine deficiency can lead to various thyroid problems, including a thyroid-related kind of physical and MENTAL RETARDATION in the past sometimes called *cretinism.* Radioactive forms of iodine are sometimes used to treat thyroid problems and as part of some kinds of radioisotope scans. Iodine is also sometimes used as an antiseptic. (See MINERALS; NUTRITION.)

Iowa Tests of Basic Skills (ITBS), a series of group-administered paper-and-pencil tests that attempt to measure basic academic skills, available in various forms for children in grades K–9. The tests cover vocabulary, READING, language, spelling, capitalization, punctuation, usage, work and STUDY SKILLS, visual materials, reference materials, concepts in mathematics, problem-solving, and computation, and sometimes also listening, word analysis, science, and social studies. For older students, in grades 9–12, schools may use the *Iowa Tests of Educational Development (ITED),* which focus on more sophisticated material and skills, such as critical analysis, understanding scientific material, distinguishing between different literary approachs, and using common information tools. Any of these tests may be hand- or computer-scored, and student SCORES are compared with national NORMS. The "Iowas" are used to identify strengths and weaknesses in a student's basic skills, to evaluate the effectiveness of classroom instruction, and to monitor a student's progress year by year. The NORMS for these STANDARDIZED TESTS were developed on the same population of students as those for the COGNITIVE ABILITIES TEST, and the two may be given together to allow comparison of actual and anticipated achievement test scores. (See TESTS.)

IQ, abbreviation for INTELLIGENCE QUOTIENT.

iron, a MINERAL required by the body to work with PROTEIN to make HEMOGLOBIN, the vital blood substance that transports oxygen from the lungs to the cells, and *myoglobin,* which stores oxygen in muscles. Iron is found in many foods, including meat (especially liver), egg yolks, shellfish, green leafy vegetables, dried fruits such as prunes and raisins, apricots, whole-grain and enriched breads and cereals, and beans. Deficiency is uncommon with a balanced diet, but public health officials advise women to take iron supplements during PREGNANCY, LACTATION, or extremely heavy MENSTRUATION. Lack of sufficient iron can lead to iron-deficiency ANEMIA. To avoid this, a pregnant woman's level of iron is often checked as part of PRENATAL CARE. Only small amounts of iron are needed; excess iron should be avoided, since it can build up in the internal organs, causing problems such as cirrhosis of the liver (see LIVER AND LIVER PROBLEMS). (See MINERALS; NUTRITION.)

irritable bowel syndrome (IBS), a CHRONIC digestive disorder of the colon (large intestine) of unknown cause; also sometimes called *mucous colitis, spastic colon, colitis, spastic bowel,* and *functional bowel disease.* The National Institute of Diabetes and Digestive and Kidney Diseases (NIDDK) points out that at least some of these terms are inaccurate, since they wrongly imply the presence of inflammation, as in the quite different disorder INFLAMMATORY BOWEL DISEASE (IBD). Symptoms of IBS include abdominal pain, gas, bloating, CONSTIPATION, DIARRHEA, and sometimes alternating constipation and diarrhea. It seems to stem partly from abnormalities in the movement of the large intestine, which sometimes lead to muscle spasms and resulting cramps.

Because it is hard to identify precisely, physicians need to eliminate other more serious diseases before IBS is diagnosed. Symptoms can be lessened by careful management of diet, especially eating smaller meals and restricting the amount of fats in a meal and by minimizing stress. Dietary FIBER can help, as can reduction of some kinds of dairy products, but people with IBS must be sure that the rest of their diet gives them sufficient CALCIUM. Drugs such as antispasmodic medications, laxatives, and tranquilizers are sometimes used, but doctors tend to prescribe them in moderation, to avoid potential DRUG ABUSE. (See DIGESTIVE SYSTEM AND DISORDERS.)

issue, a legal term for a person's biological descendants—children, grandchildren, and so on—commonly used in reference to wills and INHERITANCE RIGHTS. Before an ADOPTION, parents should make sure to change their life insurance and HEALTH INSURANCE policies and wills to be sure they include not only issue but also adopted children.

Ivy League, a group of COLLEGES and universities that include seven of the oldest such institutions in the United States. The eight members are Brown, Columbia, Cornell, Dartmouth, Harvard, Princeton, University of Pennsylvania, and Yale. The equivalent group of schools for women, though some of them are now coeducational are the Seven Sisters: Mount Holyoke, Smith, Wellesley, Vassar, Radcliffe, Barnard, and Bryn Mawr. While the private institutions that make up the Ivy League and the Seven Sisters have maintained their traditionally high prestige and often high academic standards, in recent decades some public colleges and universities have attained equal or even greater academic excellence, partly because public funding has often allowed for better plant and equipment, salaries, and materials. In recent ratings by American professors, in fact, the top schools in many areas have often been public universities, such as University of California (Berkeley or Los Angeles) or University of Michigan. That may change somewhat in states such as California where public funding has been sharply cut. Parents looking ahead to college for their children may want to explore public colleges, not automatically look to private ones. The difference in cost is enormous. (See COLLEGE.)

J

Jordan Left-Right Reversal Test (JLRRT), a paper-and-pencil TEST used with children ages five through twelve to measure how often a child reverses letters, numbers, or words (see TRANSPOSITIONS). The test asks students to pick out errors (reversed or upside down) among groups of letters and numbers and to identify which words have similar errors. Children with perceptual problems often miss the real transpositions, while mistakenly perceiving others. The JLRRT may be administered to individuals or groups, alone or as part of a series of tests. It is scored by hand, and the SCORES converted into a DEVELOPMENTAL AGE. It is sometimes used as a DEVELOPMENTAL SCREENING TEST, but also as a DIAGNOSTIC ASSESSMENT TEST, especially for children thought to have possible LEARNING DISABILITIES. (See TESTS.)

jurisdiction, a court's legal authority over certain people, types of cases, or geographical regions. For example, a PROBATE COURT has jurisdiction over wills and estates, while a FAMILY LAW COURT may have jurisdiction over DIVORCE, CUSTODY, and CHILD SUPPORT. When the parties to a lawsuit—the DEFENDANT and the PLAINTIFF—live in different states, problems of jurisdiction arise as to which court has the right to handle certain types of cases, such as child support problems. Then various laws, popularly dubbed *long-arm statutes*, may allow a state to claim jurisdiction over someone living in another state, though this is not always so.

juvenile, a young person who is not old enough to be treated as an adult under criminal law. (By contrast, the term MINOR refers to a young person's legal ability to *act* as an adult.) The age limit varies somewhat from state to state; in most jurisdictions, a juvenile is someone under age eighteen. If found to have committed a crime, the young person is usually labeled a *youthful offender* or juvenile DELINQUENT, the latter being a term often applied more loosely and widely to ADOLESCENTS who are disruptive, troublesome, or UNSOCIALIZED. Juveniles are often STATUS OFFENDERS and so may be made WARDS of the court and committed to an institution for acts that, if committed by an adult, would not be considered criminal. A relatively recent major trend in criminal cases is to try youthful offenders as adults.

juvenile court, the type of court that handles most cases involving MINORS. JUVENILES involved in criminal cases generally appear in juvenile court, rather than in CRIMINAL COURT, as do children considered INCORRIGIBLE. In cases of CHILD ABUSE AND NEGLECT or TERMINATION OF PARENTS' RIGHTS, parents may sometimes be called before a JUVENILE COURT, with the minor's interest often represented by a court-appointed *guardian ad litem* (see GUARDIAN) or *court appointed special advocate* (see ADVOCACY). In some states, the role of the juvenile court is taken over by the FAMILY COURT. Judges sometimes appoint referees or commissioners to handle actual hearings in juvenile court.

K

Kaufman Assessment Battery for Children (K-ABC or ABC), an individually administered test designed to act as both INTELLIGENCE TEST and ACHIEVEMENT TEST, used with children from ages 2½ through 12½. Its various subtests focus on mental processing (both sequential and simultaneous—which are scored separately and then together) as well as acquired knowledge, READING, and arithmetic, which yields a SCORE for achievement. The K-ABC is often used as a DIAGNOSTIC ASSESSMENT TEST for preschoolers and older children by those who are attempting to learn more about the strengths and weaknesses of children who may have learning problems, such as those with LEARNING DISABILITIES and MENTAL RETARDATION or those who are exceptional in other ways—for instance, GIFTED CHILDREN and those from minority backgrounds. The test may be given in the child's native language, if it is not English, or using gestures for those with EAR AND HEARING PROBLEMS. Test scores may be converted to comparative rankings, such as national PERCENTILES, AGE-EQUIVALENTS, or GRADE-EQUIVALENTS. (See TESTS.)

Kernig's sign, pain and resistance at flexing the thigh at the hip and extending the leg at the knee, a SIGN that generally indicates the existence of MENINGITIS.

ketoacidosis, a result of unchecked DIABETES, in which the body begins to break down its stores of fat, releasing acids (*ketones*) into the blood. The resulting diabetic ketoacidosis can lead to diabetic COMA and death, if not reversed.

key words, the words most commonly taught to children in the early grades and generally found in materials written for them. Lists of these words, such as the *Dolch Word List*, are used in preparing new materials for children of various AGE and GRADE levels.

kidney and urological disorders, the system that filters unwanted substances from the blood, producing urine, which is excreted from the body, in the process maintaining the proper balance of ELECTROLYTES in the body, and the problems associated with that filtering system. The two bean-shaped kidneys lie on either side of the spinal column, toward the back and above the waistline, with the left one slightly higher than the right.

About one quarter of blood pumped with each heartbeat goes directly to the kidneys, where it is pushed through the delicate *mesangial membrane* into tiny structures called *nephrons*, about 1 million of them in each kidney. Blood passes through a cluster of tiny blood vessels called the *glomerulus*, which filters out larger particles such as blood cells and proteins and sends the smaller particles and fluid through another filtering structure called a *tubule*. Depending on the body's blood chemistry at the time, the tubule will select out certain chemicals and some amounts of water to be returned to the system. The rest will then be sent out of the kidney as urine, pouring down thin tubes called *ureters* into a sac called the *bladder*. There it is stored until the bladder is full, at which point signals of "fullness" are sent to the brain. The person then decides, at an appropriate time and place, to release the urine through the URETHRA, which in women is an opening above the VAGINA and in men is a thin tube that exits through the PENIS.

The kidneys' filtering structures maintain a delicate balance (called the *acid-base balance*) in the body's chemistry by:

- Regulating how much water stays in the blood and how much is removed from the body in urine.
- Regulating the concentration of key substances in the body, such as SODIUM, POTASSIUM, CHLORIDE, bicarbonate, CALCIUM, and PHOSPHORUS, ensuring that the body retains the nutrients it needs for normal functioning, such as building bone, but does not have too much of harmful substances.
- Removing potentially harmful waste products from the blood, primarily urea (also called *blood urea nitrogen*, or BUN), creatinine, and uric acid.

The kidneys also regulate BLOOD PRESSURE, partly by regulating blood volume and partly by producing HORMONES that cause blood vessels to expand or contract, and produce a hormone, *erythropoietin*, that stimulates the BONE MARROW to make red blood cells. That such a complex system works so well so much of the time is actually remarkable. But because of its many and complex functions, the kidney and urological system is subject to a wide variety of problems in children and pregnant women, some of them easily treatable, some life-threatening.

To recognize the abnormal, parents first need to know what is normal. The American Kidney Foundation offers these guidelines:

- Urine is normally clear to medium yellow, though it may be dark yellow in the morning, when a child has had nothing to drink overnight and the urine has become concentrated, and may change color temporarily after a child has eaten certain foods, such as beets. But bloody or tea-colored urine is *never* normal, and a doctor should be consulted if an infant's diapers have red or brown urine stains.
- Urine has a mild odor when passed, becoming strong only after some exposure to air, except after eating foods such as asparagus that impart a strong smell.

Foul-smelling odor in fresh urine can be a sign of infection.

- It is hard to judge what is normal or abnormal frequency of urination, since it depends on the amount of fluid consumed. As a rough guide, parents might expect that in twenty-four hours infants will have twelve to twenty wet diapers, toddlers will urinate six to ten times, and preschoolers to school age children four to seven times. Children will sometimes seem to have more frequent urination, but really have only a dribble, rather than a full urination, each time. If the frequency or amount of urination changes from a previously normal pattern, it is important to see a doctor, as that may be a sign of some sort of problem.
- The stream of urine should be strong and steady, without interruption, fanning, or excessive dribbling, especially for boys. If it is not, check with your doctor to see if there is any abnormality or problem.
- Urination should be painless. If your baby cries when wetting a diaper, or your older child has pain on urinating, it may be a sign of infection, so a doctor's visit is in order.

Because the kidneys play such an important role in the body, any infection, injury, or disorder affecting them can have widespread effects. Among the warning signs of kidney disease, in addition to those noted above, are poor FEEDING; VOMITING; chronic DIARRHEA; slow growth; slow weight gain; persistent abdominal pain; lack of energy; pale, washed-out appearance; frequent severe headaches; lower back pain; unexplained low-grade FEVER; BEDWETTING (*enuresis*) in children over 4 to 5 years old, especially if they have previously been dry through the night; and collection of fluid in the tissues (EDEMA), signaled by swelling or puffiness about the eyes and ankles, especially in the morning, and distension of the belly later in the day. Lack of bladder control (INCONTINENCE) can be a problem for young children and also for pregnant women, since the developing FETUS presses on the bladder.

The main kinds of kidney problems affecting children are:

- *Urinary tract infection (UTI)*: Bacteria readily infect the urethra, bladder, ureters, and kidneys. In infants, such infections can be hard to recognize, but failure to gain weight, vomiting, persistent loose stool, and fussiness when diapers are wet are clues to a possible problem. In a newborn, the problem can be an obstruction somewhere in the system, blocking the normal flow of urine. In adolescents and adults, UTIs are twenty-five times more common among women then men. Pregnant women are especially susceptible, because changes in the body and pressure on the urinary tract increase the risk of infections and also more often lead to further, more serious infections, notably of the bladder (*cystitis*) and kidneys (*pyelonephritis*). As a result, women are routinely checked for UTIs during PRENATAL CARE. UTIs are also more frequent among people who frequently use CATHETERS, such as those with SPINA BIFIDA, and people whose IMMUNE SYSTEMS are suppressed.

  Symptoms of UTIs include pain and a burning sensation during urination; frequent urination of small amounts, often with the feeling that the bladder has not been emptied; a sensation of fullness or pressure, in males near the rectum, in females above the pubic bone; and cloudy or pinkish urine. Chills, fever, nausea, and vomiting can be signs of more serious infection involving the kidneys. If untreated, UTIs can lead to serious illness, possibly involving septicemia (blood poisoning; see BLOOD AND BLOOD DISORDERS), scarring of the kidneys, and even kidney failure.

  UTIs are usually diagnosed by URINALYSIS. Because quick response is important, treatment with an ANTIBIOTIC is often begun even before laboratory results indicate the type of bacteria involved. In severe cases, hospitalization may be needed, to provide fluids and medicines intravenously. In cases of recurring infection, urinalysis may be repeated several times, to be sure the infection has been cleared up.

  To help prevent UTIs, doctors recommend drinking at least eight glasses of water a day, to help "flush" the infection from the body, along with other fluids such as coffee, tea, or soda. Cranberry juice is often recommended because, being acidic, it makes the urine less hospitable to bacteria. Young girls should be taught to wipe their stool from front to backward, rather than forward toward the urethra, which can spread bacteria to the urethral opening. Sexually active girls and women should urinate just before and after sexual intercourse, to lower the risk of bacterial infection. They should also take showers, rather than baths, especially avoiding hot tubs; avoid highly perfumed soaps or feminine hygiene products that can irritate the urethra; wear loose, natural-fiber clothing, especially underwear, since tight, synthetic clothing can trap heat and encourage bacterial proliferation; and change sanitary napkins or tampons frequenting during MENSTRUATION. Women who use a DIAPHRAGM may be more susceptible to UTIs, because the device presses against the neck of the bladder, preventing complete emptying and fostering bacterial growth. For unknown reasons, use of SPERMICIDES, either with diaphragms or CONDOMS, also increases the risk of UTI in women.
- *Nephrosis* (*nephrotic syndrome*): This is actually a group of kidney disorders resulting from damage to the glomerular filter in the nephrons. This causes large protein molecules, which normally remain in the blood, to leak into urine, starving the body of necessary proteins and upsetting the body's chemistry. The result is often edema, paleness, waxy skin, poor appetite but rapid increase in body weight (from fluid retention), stomachache, CONSTIPATION, and susceptibility to infections and skin injuries. The American Kidney Fund notes that nephrotic syndrome is the most common serious kidney disease in children, but that it is usually very responsive and seldom leads to total kidney failure. Treatment often includes medication (commonly prednisone), restriction

of salt in the diet, diuretics (drugs to control edema), and on occasion hospitalization. Children may sometimes have relapses periodically until they have reached full adulthood.

- *Glomerulonephritis*: This is a general term for a result—inflammation of the glomerulus in the nephrons—that can have a variety of causes, most often from infection with *streptococcus*, the bacterium best known for causing STREP THROAT. Urination will often be abundant and more frequent, and may contain blood; children will often have edema, headaches, blurred vision, and general aches and pains. The American Kidney Foundation notes that with careful control of high BLOOD PRESSURE and excess body fluids—hospitalization may be required to manage fluid and food intake—90 percent of the children affected with streptococcus glomerulonephritis will recover completely.

  Glomerulonephritis from other causes is rare but more serious. While some forms may respond, damage may remain and in many the illness becomes PROGRESSIVE, culminating in total kidney failure.
- *Hypertension (high blood pressure)*: Some children have very seriously high blood pressure, because of abnormalities in the kidneys or in the network of blood vessels linked with the kidneys, or abnormalities associated with other diseases or disorders. Because high blood pressure can damage the body's delicate internal organs, it is important to spot it quickly and begin the search for a cause and treatment. This is one of the areas normally checked in a WELL-BABY EXAMINATION. Childhood hypertension stems from different causes than the high blood pressure common in adults, though some teenagers may be subject to the adult form of high blood pressure.

In searching for the cause of various kinds of kidney disorders, UROLOGISTS—physicians specializing in kidney and urological disorders—use a range of KIDNEY FUNCTION TESTS to attempt to determine how well the kidney is operating and what problems it may have.

Some other rarer kidney and urological disorders that affect children are:

- *Congenital abnormalities*: Some kidney and urological abnormalities may be present from birth. Most commonly the two kidneys are joined (called a *horseshoe kidney*), but sometimes a kidney is missing, both kidneys are on one side, a kidney has double ureters, or the kidneys, bladder, and their related structures are otherwise improperly developed. Some of these abnormalities are not serious or are correctible. Sometimes an artificial opening must be created for release of urine from the bladder, a surgical procedure called *urostomy* or *urinary ostomy*. (See OSTOMY.)
- *Polycystic kidney disease (PKD)*: Sometimes numerous cysts (fluid-filled sacs) grow in the kidneys, gradually increasing so as to destroy most of the normal kidney tissue. This condition is often diagnosed by a SCAN such as ULTRASOUND or a CT SCAN. The liver, pancreas, heart, blood vessels, and intestines may also be affected. The adult form of PKD is a GENETIC DISORDER of the AUTOSOMAL DOMINANT type and is relatively common, affecting perhaps half a million Americans.

  The infantile form, sometimes called *childhood polycystic disease (CPD)*, is a rarer genetic disorder, of the AUTOSOMAL DOMINANT type, but is more severe. Most infants born with the disease die in the first few months; in some cases their kidneys fail to develop. However, those in whom the disease initially involves less of the kidney, generally later recognized in childhood, may survive into adolescence.

  Perhaps half of all PKD patients will have kidney failure and will require dialysis and a kidney TRANSPLANT for long-term survival. The 1993 discovery of a gene triggering polycystic kidney disease and later the discovery of a second gene hold promise of finding a cure or treatment, possibly through GENE THERAPY. GENETIC SCREENING can be performed at some specialized medical centers.
- *Cystinosis* (*cystine storage disease*), *Fanconi's syndrome*, and *renal tubular acidosis*: These rare congenital disorders involve loss into the urine of key nutrients and chemicals, such as AMINO ACIDS, CALCIUM and PHOSPHATE, important to growth, sometimes because the body is unable to respond to HORMONES designed to balance these substances. The causes are unclear; some are apparently GENETIC DISORDERS, while others may result from poisons ingested or created within the body.
- *Wilm's tumor* (*nephroblastoma*): This type of MALIGNANT TUMOR often affects children, generally under age five, accounting for 20 percent of the CANCERS in children. It affects boys more than girls. The tumor spreads rapidly and is generally diagnosed by hypertension, a hard mass in the abdomen, pain, and blood in the urine. If caught and treated early by surgery and radiotherapy, many children can survive, but sometimes the cancer spreads too quickly to other parts of the body. (See CANCER.)

When kidney problems are undiagnosed, untreated, or unresponsive to treatment, the kidney can become so diseased or damaged that it can no longer function properly. The result is kidney (*renal*) failure. Sometimes this is ACUTE kidney failure, resulting from a severe, temporary situation, such as surgery, severe infection, BURNS, ALLERGIES to medicines, poisons, or severe DIARRHEA or vomiting. Hospitalization, with careful control of food and fluids, is indicated, and sometimes an artifical machine will be used to take over the kidney's functions temporarily, in a procedure called DIALYSIS. Children suffering acute kidney failure often regain normal kidney function, with little permanent damage, though that may take as long as a year or more.

More serious is *chronic kidney (renal) failure*, in which kidney function is gradually, irreversibly, and permanently lost. This is called *end-stage renal disease* (ESRD), and the life-threatening condition that develops from ESRD is called *uremia* (literally, urine in the blood). As the kidneys fail, every aspect of a child's life will be affected, from growth to ATTENTION SPAN. In addition to control of diet and medication, dialysis treatments will be required on a regular basis. Depending on their state of health otherwise, children suffering from chronic kidney failure are often prime candidates for kidney TRANSPLANTS. Of the over 39,000 people awaiting transplants in 1995, some 28,000 of them—over 70 percent—were awaiting kidney transplants.

FOR HELP AND FURTHER INFORMATION

American Kidney Fund (AKF)
6110 Executive Boulevard, Suite 1010
Rockville, MD 20852
301–881–3052; HELP-LINE: 800–638–8299
Fax: 301–881–0898
Francis J. Soldovere, Executive Director
Organization concerned with patients who have chronic kidney disease; provides information; supports research; supplies financial aid to qualified needy patients with kidney problems, including an emergency fund program and a disaster relief program for ESRD patients in areas struck by natural disasters; operates pediatric camper program, providing financial aid to cover special expenses; operates kidney donor program; publishes various materials including bimonthly *AKF News* and *AKF Responds to Most Frequently Asked Questions.*

National Kidney Foundation (NKF)
30 E. 33 Street, Suite 1100
New York, NY 10016
212–889–2210; 800–622–9010
Fax: 212–689–9261
John Davis, Executive Director
Organization of people concerned with kidney disease; provides information and referrals; offers patient services through local groups; operates an organ donor program; publishes various materials including:

- Quarterly newsletters *Parent Connection, Family Focus, Straight Talk* (for children and teens), and numerous professional bulletins and journals;
- General brochures: *What Everyone Should Know About Kidneys and Kidney Diseases, Warning Signs of Kidney Disease* and *Your Kidneys: Master Chemists of the Body*;
- On childhood disorders: *Practical Suggestions for Parents of Children with Chronic Kidney Disease, Childhood Nephrotic Syndrome, Drug Abuse Can Hurt Your Kidneys, Reflux Disorders in Children, Nutrition for Children with Chronic Kidney Failure,* and video *It's Just Part of My Life: A Kid's View of Dialysis*;
- On specific disorders: *Urinary Tract Infections, Bone Disease in Chronic Kidney Failure, About Kidney Stones, Focal Glomerulosclerosis, Alport Syndrome, Goodpasture's Syndrome, Hemolytic Uremic Syndrome, IgA Nephropathy, Interstitial Cystitis, Urinary Incontinence: Treating Loss of Urine Control,* and *Kidney Cancer*;
- Numerous materials on early intervention, treatment, nutrition, and rehabilitation.

National Kidney and Urologic Disease Information Clearinghouse (NKUDIC)
Box NKUDIC, 3 Information Way
Bethesda, MD 20892–3580
301–654–4415
Organization sponsored by federal government to provide information on kidney and urological problems; publishes various materials for health professionals and general public, including *Understanding Urinary Tract Infections, When Your Kidneys Fail. A Handbook for Patients and Their Families,* and *End-Stage Renal Disease: Choosing a Treatment That's Right for You.*

American Association of Kidney Patients (AAKP)
100 South Ashley Drive, Suite 280
Tampa, FL 33602
813–223–7099; 800–749-AAKP [749–2257]
Fax: 813–223–0001
Kris Robinson, Executive Director
Organization focusing on kidney patients; formerly National Association of Patients on Hemodialysis and Transplantation (NAPHT); provides information; sponsors organ donation program; offers special services, including summer camp for children on dialysis; maintains international directory of dialysis centers; publishes various materials, including *AAKP Bulletin* and *Renalife.*

National Cancer Institute (NCI), 800–422–6237. Publishes "What You Need to Know About" brochures on cancers of the bladder and kidneys. (For full group information, see CANCER.)

American Cancer Society (ACS), 800–227–2345. Publishes materials on cancer of the bladder. (For full group information, see CANCER.)

Polycystic Kidney Research Foundation (PKR)
4901 Main Street, Suite 320
Kansas City, MO 64112
816–931–2600; 800-PKD-CURE [753–2873]
Fax: 816–931–8655
E-mail: 75713.2275@compuserve.com (CompuServe: 75713,2275)
Dan Larson, President
Organization concerned with polycystic kidney disease; supports research; sponsors kidney donation program; publishes various materials, including newsletter *PKR Progress,* book *Q&A on PKD,* and other materials.

Cystinosis Foundation (CF)
1212 Broadway, #830
Oakland, CA 94612
510–834–2270
Fax: 510–834–3741

Jean Hotz, President
Organization concerned with cystinosis; provides support; acts as advocate; supports research; publishes various materials, including quarterly newsletter *Help Us Grow* and information sheets.

National Organization for Rare Disorders (NORD), 800–999–6673. (For full group information, see RARE DISORDERS.)

OTHER RESOURCES

On dealing with urological problems

Urinary Incontinence and How to Overcome It. Gordon Press, 1991.
Overcoming Bladder Disorders: Compassionate, Authoritative Medical and Self Help Solutions for Incontinence, Cystitis, Interstitial Cystitis, Prostate Problems, Bladder Cancer. Rebecca Chalker and Kristene E. Whitmore. HarperCollins, 1990.
Urine Testing, rev. ed. Do It Now, 1990.

(See also BEDWETTING; INCONTINENCE)

On dealing with kidney disorders

Kidney Disorders. Martha Miller. Chelsea House, 1992.
The Kidney Patient's Book: New Treatment, New Hope. Timothy P. Ahlstrom. Great Issues Press, 1991.

(See also TRANSPLANTS; DIALYSIS; ENURESIS.)

kidney function tests, a series of tests analyzing the chemistry of the body, to provide information about how well the kidney and urological system is carrying out its tasks of filtering unwanted substances out of the blood and excreting fluid as urine. The simplest kind of kidney function test is URINALYSIS, which involves testing the urine for the presence of various substances. BLOOD TESTS may also be used to assess kidney function; if substances such as urea (blood urea nitrogen) and creatinine are found concentrated in the blood, it may indicate kidney disease. The kidneys can also be examined by various imaging techniques, including SCANS; in an *intravenous urogram* (or *pyelogram*), a dye is injected into a vein and then, as it passes through the body, outlines the urinary tract and any possible abnormalities, which show up clearly with RADIOGRAPHY. (See KIDNEY AND UROLOGICAL PROBLEMS; MEDICAL TESTS.)

kin, an alternate term for BLOOD RELATIONS. When someone dies INTESTATE (without a will), the PROBATE COURT uses the specific relationships of kin to determine INHERITANCE RIGHTS under the current applicable laws.

kindergarten, full-day or half-day classes for children of about age five offered in the year before the first grade, either in the same building as the ELEMENTARY SCHOOL or in a separate structure; sometimes called *preprimary, junior primary,* or *primary.* Kindergarten classes traditionally focused on play activities and SOCIAL SKILLS, as some PRESCHOOLS and nursery schools still do. Today, in addition, kindergarten educators stress educational skills, especially those that prepare children for READING and WRITING, and many schools give students tests to assess their readiness for school and to identify if they have any learning problems that might require SPECIAL EDUCATION. The Department of Education has also increasingly recommended that parents exercise choice in finding the right school for their child; see CHOOSING A SCHOOL FOR YOUR CHILD (on page 659), which provides a checklist for evaluating schools.

FOR HELP AND FURTHER INFORMATION

National Association for the Education of Young Children (NAEYC), 800–424–2460. Publishes books *Kindergarten Politics: What Is Best for Children?* and *Changing Kindergartens: Four Success Stories*; brochure *Appropriate Education in the Primary Grades*; and works on developmentally appropriate teaching practices for kindergarten. (For full group information, see PRESCHOOL.)

Association for Childhood Education International (ACEI), 800–423–3563. Publishes book *Kindergarten,* position paper *The Child-Centered Kindergarten,* and reprint *When Parents of Kindergartners Ask "Why?"* (For full group information, see HELP ON LEARNING AND EDUCATION on page 659.)

OTHER RESOURCES

Basic Skills Every Kindergarten Student Should Know. Stan Bippus. Applied Resources, 1993.
The Kindergarten Survival Handbook: The Before School Checklist and Guide for Parents, rev. ed. Allana Elovson. Parent Education, 1993.
How to Prepare Your Child for Kindergarten. Florence Karnofsky and Trudy Weiss. Fearon Teacher Aids, 1993.
Kindergarten—It Isn't What It Used to Be: Getting Your Child Ready for the Positive Experience of Education. Susan K. Golant and Mitch Golant. Lowell House, 1991.

For children

Kindergarten Kids. Ellen B. Senisi. Scholastic, 1994.
When You Go to Kindergarten, rev. ed. James Howe. Morrow, 1994.
Kindergarten Carousel. Penina Issaroff. Yellow Brick Road, 1993.
Rachel Parker, Kindergarten Show-Off. Ann Martin. Holiday, 1993.
Born in the Gravy. Denys Cazet. Orchard/Watts, 1993. Mexican-American girl's first day at school.
Cat's Got Your Tongue?: A Story for Children Afraid to Speak. Charles E. Schaefer. Magination Press, 1992. About a timid kindergartener.
Annabelle Swift, Kindergartner. Amy Schwartz. Orchard/Watts, 1991.

My Mom Made Me Go to School. Judy Delton. Delacorte, 1991.

(See also EDUCATION; DEVELOPMENTAL SCREENING TESTS; READINESS TESTS; also HELP ON LEARNING AND EDUCATION on page 659.)

kinesthetic, a general term referring to a person's sense of his or her own body motion, often employed in MULTISENSORY approaches to learning, such as VAKT, for children with LEARNING DISABILITIES.

Klinefelter's syndrome, a CONGENITAL condition resulting from a CHROMOSOMAL ABNORMALITY in which a male has not just the usual two SEX CHROMOSOMES (XY), but also one or more additional X chromosomes. Males with one extra X chromosome (labeled XXY) are often tall and lean, with some tendency to LEARNING DISABILITIES in the verbal area. In many, the syndrome is recognized only during a search for causes of INFERTILITY, since most lack SPERM. Even for those with two or more additional X chromosomes, Klinefelter's syndrome generally shows itself only at PUBERTY, when such males tend to develop enlarged breasts (GYNECOMASTIA) and other SECONDARY SEX CHARACTERISTICS that tend toward the female. These can sometimes be modified surgically or through hormone treatment. The TESTES, however, remain small, giving the syndrome an alternate name, *primary microorchidism.* People with Klinefelter's syndrome are somewhat more likely than most to have some MENTAL RETARDATION and difficulty in social adaptation.

FOR HELP AND FURTHER INFORMATION

National Institute of Child Health and Human Development (NICHD), 301–496–5133. (For full group information, see PREGNANCY.)

National Organization for Rare Disorders (NORD), 800–999–6673. (For full group information, see RARE DISORDERS.)

(See also CHROMOSOMAL ABNORMALITIES.)

knowledge-level thinking, simple recall of previously learned information; one of kinds of thinking or learning processes described by Benjamin Bloom. The other main types are COMPREHENSION-LEVEL, APPLICATION-LEVEL, ANALYSIS-LEVEL, SYNTHESIS-LEVEL, and EVALUATION-LEVEL.

Kohs Block Design Test, a type of INTELLIGENCE TEST for children or adults with a MENTAL AGE of three to nineteen years, especially people with DISABILITIES that affect use of language or hearing, as well as children from disadvantaged or non-English-speaking backgrounds. Though it can be used with groups, it is often individually administered. The child is given a variety of colored blocks and is asked to use them to copy designs shown on a series of cards. The test administrator evaluates not only success in copying the design but also attention to the task, ADAPTIVE BEHAVIOR, and self-criticism. The Kohs Block Design Test is sometimes included in other tests, such as the MERRILL-PALMER SCALES OF MENTAL DEVELOPMENT. (See TESTS.)

kyphosis, excessive curving of the spine that produces a rounded or "humped" upper back, a type of spinal disorder often associated with SCOLIOSIS or LORDOSIS; once popularly called *humpback.* In adults, the condition is often related to OSTEOPOROSIS (bone weakening from CALCIUM loss). In children, kyphosis more often results from injury, a TUMOR on the spine, or a GENETIC DISORDER, such as Hunter syndrome (see MUCOPOLYSACCHARIDOSES). (See SCOLIOSIS; SPINE AND SPINAL DISORDERS.)

L

labeling, tagging a child as good or bad, bright or dull, pretty or plain, and the like. Labeling is a destructive habit, because such labels can damage a child's self-esteem and (since children often live up to adults' expectations for them) may become SELF-FULFILLING PROPHECIES. Child development experts recommend that parents and teachers avoid labels, such as "problem child" or "slow learner," which are sometimes based on a single, possibly unreliable TEST, and that they focus instead on what children can and cannot do, helping them to grow in areas in which their skills are weak.

labia, Folds of flesh in a woman's VULVA; Latin for "lips." Two sets of lips protect the vaginal opening and are part of the female external GENITALS.

The smaller, inner lips—the *labia minora*—cover the VAGINA and urethra; the lips meet at the upper end to form a sort of hood (equivalent to a man's FORESKIN) over the CLITORIS, the main organ of female sexual response. Both the labia minora and the clitoris are covered with moist mucous membrane and are highly sensitive to the touch and sexual arousal.

The larger, outer lips—the *labia majora*—are thicker. Their moist inner surfaces contain many sebaceous (oil) glands and have little or no hair. The outer surfaces are covered with dry SKIN; after PUBERTY, these are covered with HAIR.

The labia change during a woman's lifetime. At birth, they are often enlarged, due to the influence of HORMONES from the mother, but become smaller over the next few weeks. The labia may also be joined together at birth; normally they will separate on their own, without medical intervention. In a young girl, especially a virgin, the labia minora are small and completely hidden by the labia majora, which lie so close together that, when the girl's legs are together, they completely cover the GENITALS underneath. In the form of genital mutilation called FEMALE CIRCUMCISION, these labia majora are sometimes stitched to literally grow together, after removal of the clitoris.

In a sexually active mature woman, the labia majora gape somewhat. After childbearing, the labia minora often grow larger, sometimes extending beyond the labia majora, which shrink somewhat after MENOPAUSE. CANCER of the vulva most often affects the labia. (See GENITALS.)

lability, Emotional instability or mood swings, found in mild form in some children with LEARNING DISABILITIES and in more severe form in some MENTAL DISORDERS such as BIPOLAR DISORDERS and some kinds of SCHIZOPHRENIA.

labor, in PREGNANCY, the events and actions involved in the actual DELIVERY of a baby, from the beginning of the dilation (widening) of the CERVIX to the expulsion of the PLACENTA (afterbirth); also the period in which these activities occur.

Several changes often take place in the previous weeks and days before actual labor starts, including:

- The settling of the baby into its final FETAL PRESENTATION in the mother's pelvis, an action called ENGAGEMENT, a "dropping," or "falling." That may not happen until just before the actual delivery.
- A burst of energy in the days before labor.
- A dull ache in the lower back or pelvis, somewhat like menstrual cramps.
- Appearance of a bloody mucus discharge from the VAGINA. Called *show* or *bloody show*, this is the expulsion of a mucus plug from the cervix before labor.
- Appearance of small or large amounts of watery fluid (AMNIOTIC FLUID) from the vagina. This is the "rupture of the membranes" or "breaking of the bag of waters" that results when the amniotic sac protecting the FETUS breaks, often within about twelve hours of the start of labor. The time of the first fluid release should be reported immediately to the doctor or midwife; since the baby is no longer protected by the amniotic fluid, some health professionals wish to bring the mother into the hospital or birthing center at this time.

Any or all of these signs can (but will not necessarily) indicate that labor will start in a matter of days or hours.

Labor itself generally has three stages:

- *First stage*, which begins with regular, intense contractions, which are a powerful, spasmodic, painful, rhythmic squeezing of the walls of the UTERUS, and ends when the cervix has become fully dilated, to about 4 inches. In a first pregnancy, this stage often takes thirteen hours or longer, but is generally significantly shorter in subsequent pregnancies. The contractions settle into a regular pattern, gradually coming closer together, lasting longer, and intensifying. Meanwhile the cervix *effaces*—that is, shortens, flattens, and merges with the uterus walls—and opens. During the early part of this first stage, the mother should be making her way to where the child will be delivered. In a HOSPITAL, she will generally go into a LABOR ROOM or sometimes a combination LABOR/DELIVERY/RECOVERY (LDR) room. There, the extent of the cervix's dilation will be measured periodically. If it has not occurred earlier, engagement generally takes place at this time. In HIGH-RISK PREGNANCIES, and sometimes routinely, FETAL MONITORING will sometimes be used to detect early signs of FETAL DISTRESS.

- *Second stage*, the actual delivery, which starts when the baby's head reaches the pelvic floor muscles, with contractions and an accompanying urge to push the baby on through the BIRTH CANAL. It is at this stage that the mother can be especially helped by preparation in PREPARED CHILDBIRTH classes. How long this stage of labor takes depends on many factors, including the position of the baby and the size of the baby in relation to the mother's pelvis. As the baby's head begins to appear in the VAGINA, an event called *crowning*, the tissue between the vagina and anus (*perineum*) is stretched very thin. If a woman is in a HOSPITAL's labor room, she will at this point (if not before) be moved to a DELIVERY ROOM. If it appears that the perineum will tear, and sometimes routinely, a doctor may perform an EPISIOTOMY, making a surgical incision to provide more room for the baby.

  Once the head emerges, the doctor or midwife will check to be sure the UMBILICAL CORD is not wrapped around the baby's neck and may use a suction bulb to clear out the nose and mouth so the baby can begin to breathe freely. The baby then normally rotates the head and with it the body somewhat, a process the doctor or midwife will assist. This allows shoulders, angled sideways, to come out more easily, one first, then the other. After that, the rest of the baby comes out relatively easily, along with the remaining AMNIOTIC FLUID.

  The baby may then be placed on the mother's abdomen and lightly massaged. Immediately or within a few minutes, the umbilical cord is clamped and cut. At this point, in many states, silver nitrate or erythromycin ointment is placed in the baby's eyes to prevent damage from possible infection, such as GONORRHEA. The baby may also be given an injection of VITAMIN K, to aid in blood clotting. In a hospital, identification bands will be placed on mother and infant, and the baby's footprint may be taken. The baby may also be briefly placed in a warmer, before being returned to the mother. At one minute and again at five minutes after the birth, an APGAR SCORE will be taken, to see if the baby has any urgent health needs.
- *Third stage*, which is the period between the baby's actual delivery and the delivery of the placenta, literally the *afterbirth*. Contractions starting a few minutes after the birth expel the tissue, though some medical assistance may be necessary if not all the tissue is delivered. Some drugs may be given to help with the expulsion and then to help control the bleeding that often follows. Then, often while the mother holds the baby, the doctor generally cleans the mother's genital area and stitches up any tears or cuts.

In most births, labor follows roughly this pattern, when the child is born normally. But sometimes, for various reasons, labor is difficult and does not proceed normally, as when the cervix fails to dilate enough, the baby's head is too large for the mother's pelvis (*cephalopelvis disproportion*), the baby has an abnormal FETAL PRESENTATION, the mother is hemorrhaging, the mother has ECLAMPSIA, or the mother is having a MULTIPLE BIRTH. Then other forms of delivery may be used, including FORCEPS DELIVERY, VACUUM EXTRACTION, or CESAREAN SECTION.

In certain cases, physicians may decide that labor must be *induced*, that is, brought on by artificial means, as in cases of POSTMATURE babies, RH INCOMPATIBILITY between mother and baby, or PREECLAMPSIA or eclampsia in the mother. If the amniotic fluid has not already been released, the physician may release it by breaking open the amniotic sac, which may in itself bring on labor. Otherwise, various HORMONES can be given, either as vaginal suppositories or intravenous INJECTIONS, to stimulate labor. If they fail to do so, cesarean section may be necessary. However, it is important not to induce labor before the DUE DATE, unless serious medical conditions warrant it, since the baby will then be PREMATURE, and so subject to a variety of other health problems.

Sometimes, for a variety of reasons, many of them unknown, labor starts well before the due date. The result is a premature delivery, though some drugs can halt the process. Sometimes a woman experiences *false labor*, medically called *Braxton-Hicks contractions*, in which contractions occur for an hour or two, not coming more often or intensifying, and then stop. Unlike true labor contractions, these often go away when the woman relaxes. (See CHILDBIRTH.)

laboratory school, an ELEMENTARY SCHOOL or HIGH SCHOOL linked with a teacher's college or university and staffed largely by student teachers working under their professors' direction; also called a *model, demonstration*, or *experimental school*.

labor room, in traditional HOSPITAL births, the room where the woman waits during LABOR until delivery is imminent, at which point she is moved into the DELIVERY ROOM.

labor/delivery/recovery room (LDR), a room in which the mother stays from arrival in a HOSPITAL through CHILDBIRTH, after which she moves to a POSTPARTUM ROOM, generally a regular room in a maternity ward. The aim is to avoid the often-unsettling shift from LABOR ROOM to DELIVERY ROOM. On the model of the BIRTHING ROOM, some hospitals have gone even further, developing the *labor/delivery/recovery/postpartum room (LDRP)*, where a mother stays from arrival at the hospital, through labor and delivery and until discharge.

lactation, the production of milk from the BREASTS of a new mother, used in BREASTFEEDING.

lactation specialists, people who offer advice on BREASTFEEDING, generally with experience and some training, though not necessarily any formal certification. These specialists are often associated with local groups formed especially to advise new mothers.

lacto-ovo-vegetarian, a type of VEGETARIAN diet that eliminates meat, poultry, and fish, but allows eggs, milk, and other dairy products, such as cheese. A *lactovegetarian* diet permits dairy products, but not eggs. (See VEGETARIAN; NUTRITION.)

lactose intolerance, a type of digestive disorder involving inability to break down milk sugar *(lactose)* into forms that can be used by the body, generally because of shortage of the enzyme *lactase*; also called *lactase deficiency*. Sometimes lack of lactase results from some kinds of disorders or injuries affecting the intestinal tract, but in many cases, especially after age two, children's bodies begin to produce less lactase.

Common symptoms of indigestion of lactose are nausea, cramps, bloating, gas, and DIARRHEA, about 30 to 120 minutes after eating foods containing lactose. The problem is especially common among people of Black African, Asian, or Jewish ancestry, and less common among those of Caucasian background from northern Europe. Lactose intolerance is in itself not a danger, but because CALCIUM is so important to growth and repair of bones, especially in the growing years, it is necessary to be sure that children (and adults) get anough calcium from other sources. The National Institute of Diabetes and Digestive and Kidney Diseases (NIDDK) advises:

> Small children born with lactase deficiency should not be fed any foods containing lactose. Most older children and adults need not avoid lactose completely, but they differ in the amounts of lactose they can handle. For example, one person may suffer symptoms after drinking just a small glass of milk, while another can drink one glass but not two. Others with lactase deficiency may be able to manage ice cream and aged cheeses, such as Cheddar and Swiss, but not other dairy products. Dietary control of the problem depends on each person's knowing, through trial and error, *how much* milk sugar and *what forms* of it his or her body can handle.
>
> For those who react to very small amounts of lactose or have trouble limiting their intake of foods that contain lactose, lactase additives are available from drug stores without a prescription.
>
> At somewhat higher cost, shoppers can buy lactose-reduced milk at most supermarkets. It contains all the other nutrients found in milk and remains fresh for about the same time. Some stores also have cottage cheese and ice cream with decreased lactose content.

FOR HELP AND FURTHER INFORMATION

American Celiac Society/Dietary Support Coalition (ACS/DSC), 201–325–8837. (For full group information, see CELIAC SPRUE.)

Lactaid Hotline, 800–LACTAID [522–8243].

(See also DIGESTIVE SYSTEM AND DISORDERS.)

Landau's reflex, the automatic response of an infant 3 to 12 months old when laid face downward to raise the head and arch the back. Absence of this REFLEX can suggest possible problems that affect MOTOR SKILLS, such as CEREBRAL PALSY or MENTAL RETARDATION.

language disorder, difficulty in understanding language or putting words together to make sense, often resulting from some kind of malfunction of the brain.

(See COMMUNICATION SKILLS AND DISORDERS.)

laparoscopy, a surgical procedure in which a physician passes a flexible tube through an incision in the patient's abdomen and then uses a small periscope-like device, called a *laparoscope* or *peritoneoscope*, to view the internal organs. Sometimes a fiber optic CATHETER is fed in through the tube. A gas is generally pumped into the abdomen for better viewing of the pelvic organs. This often presses on the diaphragm and causes referred pain in the shoulder and neck area. Because of the small size and placement of the incision, the procedure is sometimes popularly nicknamed *Band-Aid surgery* or *belly-button surgery*.

Used in a wide range of medical situations, laparoscopy is an important tool in identifying causes of INFERTILITY in women, such as blockage of the FALLOPIAN TUBES, PELVIC INFLAMMATORY DISEASE, or ENDOMETRIOSIS, or other reproductive problems, such as ECTOPIC PREGNANCY. Laparoscopy is also employed in some treatments of infertility, such as IN VITRO FERTILIZATION and GAMETE INTRA-FALLOPIAN TUBE TRANSFER (GIFT); in some female STERILIZATION methods, notably TUBAL LIGATION; and in examining a fetus in the womb, a procedure called FETOSCOPY. The procedure is commonly performed in a HOSPITAL or clinic under general ANESTHESIA, though often on an outpatient basis, and requires one to two days of recuperation.

FOR HELP AND FURTHER INFORMATION

American College of Obstetricians and Gynecologists (ACOG), 202–638–5577. Publishes *Diagnostic Laparoscopy* and *Sterilization by Laparoscopy*. (For full group information, see PREGNANCY.)

RESOLVE, Inc., HelpLine: 617–623–0744. Offers adoption services, along with infertility treatments. Publishes fact sheet *Laparoscopy and Hysteroscopy: What to Expect* and *Laparoscopic Surgery: Laser, Electro.* (For full group information, see INFERTILITY.)

laser surgery, use of a highly concentrated narrow beam of light focused through a microscope to do extremely precise, delicate surgery; a kind of MICROSURGERY. In eye surgery, for example, lasers can be used in treating tears in the retina, retinopaphy, macular degeneration, glaucoma, and in connection with removal of cataracts (see EYE AND VISION PROBLEMS). Laser beams may also be used in a wide variety of other ways, including some kinds of STERILIZATION, removal of small birthmarks (see NEVUS) or scar tissue, and destruction of abnormal or CANCER cells.

latchkey child, a child who returns from school or play to an empty home, so-called because the child must carry a key to enter the house or apartment. With the rise in single parents and working couples, increasing numbers of children—today an estimated eight to ten million—fall into this category, often because of the inadequacy, unavailability, or expense of CHILD CARE. If parents are obliged to leave their children unattended, though certainly not before ages seven or eight and preferably when they are a good deal older than that, they should take great care to prepare the children to meet potential emergencies.

Among the most important areas in which a child needs protection are:

- *Key safety*: The key should be hidden on a chain or pinned inside clothing, so no one is alerted that the child is alone. A spare should be available in a safe place (such as a neighbor's) in case the child's is lost, and the child should understand that it is to be given to no one.
- *Dealing with potentially dangerous people.* Young children need help in recognizing strangers and dangerous people or situations. Role-playing may help the child recognize trouble and learn how to deal with it. (See TIPS FOR PROTECTING CHILDREN AGAINST ABDUCTION on page 408.)
- *Handling traffic*: Apart from teaching children how to cross roads safely at intersections (not between them), parents should map out with the children safe routes and alternative plans if a child misses a bus or car pool.
- *Handling the telephone*: Children need to know how to reach key numbers, such as parents, police, fire, poison control, ambulance, neighbors, and 911. Parents should be sure their children have memorized and know how to give their address and phone number and explain the nature of the emergency. Children also need to know how to respond to telephone calls received, including prank calls, and to beware telling anyone they are at home alone. (The same holds for answering the door.)
- *Handling fire*: Children should know how to handle matches and gas appliances safely, if necessary; what to do if their clothes are on fire; how to put out a small fire; and, most important, how to escape. Parents should stress escape first (not hiding, as from fear of being blamed for the fire), then calling the fire department from a neighbor's.
- *Other household or weather emergencies*: Children need to know how to respond in case of power failure, household breakdowns such as plumbing problems, or a storm that prevents parents from reaching home. Parents may want to prepare a survival kit for children for such emergencies, including flashlight, transister radio, extra batteries, and the like, and also give their child some basic first aid training and supply a first aid kit, with bandages, gauze, IODINE, and so on. (Subscribers to the America Online computer service can find "Are You Ready?: Emergency Preparedness Checklist" in the Moms Online Desk Reference of Moms Online, under "Emergency Checklist.") Firearms should be unloaded and locked up (see SAFETY), and any other dangerous appliances the child should not be using should be unplugged or otherwise disabled.
- *Recreation*: Children alone should be clear about what kinds of activities are safe and allowed and which are dangerous and not allowed. Parents should try to arrange for the child to join community or after-school recreation programs, such as at a local YMCA or YWCA. The main danger occurs around activities such as swimming, bicycling, or playing in unsupervised, dangerous areas, but also in unsupervised use of home gym equipment (see EXERCISE).

Whatever the area of concern, the child should have places to turn and alternative plans to follow in case of emergency. Most important, parents need to help children accept and deal with their natural fears about being alone. This can include seemingly small things such as having the child listen to and identify household noises, so they will not seem strange when the child is home alone.

FOR HELP AND FURTHER INFORMATION

National Safety Council (NSC), 800–621–7615. Publishes booklet *Child Alone.* (For full group information, see SAFETY.)

American Academy of Child and Adolescent Psychiatry (AACAP), 202–966–7300. Publishes information sheet *Home Alone Children.* (For full group information, see MENTAL DISORDERS.)

National Congress of Parents and Teachers (National PTA), 312–670–6782. (For full group information, see HELP ON LEARNING AND EDUCATION on page 659.)

OTHER RESOURCES

FOR PARENTS

Teaching Your Child to Be Home Alone. Earl Grollman. Free Press, 1992.

Latchkey Kids: Their Safety and Care. Marilyn Dreilinger and Ron Kerner. Bureau for At-Risk Youth, 1992.

Latchkey Kid. Elizabeth Greene. Carlton, 1992.

For young children

Being Home Alone: A Kid's Guide to Becoming a Disaster Blaster. Karin Kasdin and Laura Szabo-Cohen. Avon, 1995.

Ellen Is Home Alone. Francine Pascal. Bantam, 1993. Fiction.

Latchkey Children. Judy Monroe. Crestwood, 1990.

Playing It Smart: What To Do When You're On Your Own. Tova Navarra. Barron's, 1989. On how to deal with problems such as fire, accidents, answering phone, fear of dark.

For older children

Being Home Alone: A Kid's Guide to Dealing with Doom, Destruction, and Disaster. Karin Kasdin and Laura Szabo-Cohen. Avon, 1995.

Home Alone Survival Guide. Jane Hammerslough. Dell, 1993.

late bloomer, an informal term for a student seen as an UNDERACHIEVER who, somewhat later than other students, begins to fulfill the expected potential indicated by previous performance on STANDARDIZED TESTS of ability; sometimes called *latent achiever.* (See EDUCATION; TEST.)

laterality, an awareness of the two sides of one's body and which is left and right. Some children with RIGHT-LEFT DISORIENTATION have a poor sense of laterality and frequently confuse left and right. These are often children who lack DOMINANCE of one eye, ear, hand, and foot for most proficient use.

Laurence-Moon-Biedl syndrome, a rare GENETIC DISORDER of the AUTOSOMAL RECESSIVE type, also called *Laurence-Moon-Bardet-Biedel syndrome* or *retinodiencephalic degeneration.* It is characterized by increasing obesity; RETINITIS PIGMENTOSA, which often leads to blindness; mild-to-severe MENTAL RETARDATION; underactive TESTES or OVARIES (HYPOGONADISM); underdeveloped genitals (HYPOGENITALISM); and extra fingers and/or toes (POLYDACTYLY). Although the complex of symptoms seems to be caused by a problem with the HYPOTHALAMUS, which controls HORMONE balance, the precise cause of the syndrome is unknown and no treatment currently exists. Prospective parents with history of the syndrome in their family may want to seek GENETIC COUNSELING.

FOR HELP AND FURTHER INFORMATION

National Institute of Neurological Disorders and Stroke (NINDS), 800–352–9424. (For full group information, see BRAIN AND BRAIN DISORDERS.)

National Organization for Rare Disorders (NORD), 800–999–6673. (For full group information, see RARE DISORDERS.)

(See also GENETIC DISORDERS; AUTOSOMAL RECESSIVE.)

lay midwife, a MIDWIFE with no formal training or certification, though generally with wide practical experience, allowed to practice in only a few states. Most states require formally trained, licensed practitioners called CERTIFIED NURSE-MIDWIVES. (See CERTIFIED NURSE-MIDWIFE.)

lead poisoning, Damage to the body by lead, which builds up in the body, affecting all organs and systems. Because it is often unrecognized and so goes untreated—or, if recognized, is treated only after signs of damage become apparent—lead poisoning has been called the "silent epidemic." A 1991 Department of Health and Human Services Report concluded that lead poisoning is "the most common and societally devastating environmental disease of young children." And for good reason: An estimated 10 percent of all American preschoolers—as many as three million children—are affected by lead poisoning.

In some urban communities, lead poisoning affects more than half the young children, though it is no respecter of classes, affecting children from both rich and poor families. That is because the main source of lead is from chips of the lead-containing paint that, until its 1978 banning, was used in most homes and remains on walls, ceilings, windows, woodwork, and even floors. A 1990 survey showed that, in the United States alone, fifty-seven million private homes built before 1980 have lead-based paint in them, and nearly ten million of them house children under age seven. Of the fifty-seven million homes, 10.7 million had unsafely high lead levels in surface dust. Lead poisoning is also the leading *preventable* disease of childhood, but its dangers have come to be widely recognized only in recent years.

Infants and children, as well as developing fetuses, are especially vulnerable to lead poisoning. At low levels of exposure, lead poisoning affects children's intellectual and physical development. It causes impairment of IQ and of a whole range of reading, writing, math, visual, motor, and language skills, as well as of abstract thinking and concentration. Long-term effects can include MENTAL RETARDATION, LEARNING DISABILITIES, impaired growth, hearing loss (see EAR AND HEARING PROBLEMS), reduced attention span, and behavior problems. Symptoms of high levels of lead in the blood include irritability, insomnia, colic, and ANEMIA. At high levels, it can cause degenerative brain disease, which if untreated can lead to death. In 1990, a homeless Wisconsin child died after living for four months with his family in a building littered with lead-containing paint chips and piles of dust. Young children are especially AT RISK, because so many nonfood objects end up in their mouths. Many researchers now feel that swallowing lead-contaminated dust is even more dangerous than eating chips of leaded paint. Near roadways, another major danger is soil impregnated with lead from decades of exposure to exhaust from cars using leaded gasoline.

Health officials have been rapidly revising their assessments of what amounts of lead in children's blood constitute a danger. As recently as 1985, the federal government's "threshold of concern" was set at 25 micrograms per deciliter of blood. But in their revised recommendations on lead levels and children, the threshold of concern is less than half that figure. The problem is that symptoms generally do not appear until lead has reached dangerous and possibly even deadly levels, leaving the vast majority of cases undiagnosed and untreated. The new recommendations are part of a program urging wider testing of lead levels in children's blood and issuing new guidelines for action to be taken. These new recommendations for children at risk from lead poisoning are:

*Blood Level **	*Children Affected*	*Action*
10 or more	4–6 million	Consider checking levels in high-risk areas.
15 or more	1.2 million	Test children and advise on cleanup or diet changes
20 or more	545,000	Monitor closely and visit homes
25 or more	188,000	Start medical treatment

* measured in micrograms of lead per deciliter of blood

The Wisconsin child who died had a level of 144, so high that the lead had begun to replace calcium in his bones. The HHS estimates that three to four million children aged six or under have lead levels of over 14, noting that this is far greater than the number of children affected by other childhood illnesses. The Centers for Disease Control sees these recommendations as part of a program to phase in universal screening for young children. Because the problem is so widespread and its dimensions still unknown, some health experts have called for yearly testing.

The main treatment for lead poisoning is a process called *chelation therapy*, in which the patient is given drugs that chemically bind with the lead and remove it from the bloodstream. Traditionally such drugs have been given by injections. But the FDA has approved a new chelation drug, called Chemet (succimer), that can be given orally, though its early use has been limited.

Various federal agencies have launched plans to eliminate lead paint in America's houses, calling for testing of houses and apartments and cleaning up those that require it. The least expensive approach involves putting a protective layer of plastic over the lead-based paint, though it is uncertain how long the layer would last under everyday conditions. The most expensive approach involves stripping all the lead-based paint. This has its own hazards, since doing so releases much *more* lead into the air. The Environmental Protection Agency also proposed various rules to lessen lead in the environment and especially in the water supply.

Federal agencies, notably the Food and Drug Administration, have also warned against several other previously little recognized sources of lead poisoning. Among these are leaded crystal which, researchers found, release (leach) lead into liquids stored in them, especially alcoholic or acidic liquids, including fruit juices and even infant formula. The FDA also found that Kombucha mushroom tea (also called Manchurian or Kargasok tea), which is highly acidic, readily leaches lead from ceramic and painted containers, as well as from lead crystal.

Meanwhile, lead continues to be found in many other areas—at home, in imported ceramic ware, houseware decorations, house paint, water pipes, soldered cans, some calcium supplements, and lead-containing wine bottle seals, and in the wider world, in such sources as artist's materials, some older commercial coffee urns, lead-acid batteries, power plant scrubbers, and gasoline. Though many such uses have been ended, lead concentrations remain. Some newly recognized sources can be seemingly innocuous, such as lead-pigmented inks used on plastic wrappers. If these are turned inside out and used to store foods, the contents may become contaminated with lead. (For tips on avoiding lead, see GET THE LEAD OUT! on page 354.)

FOR HELP AND FURTHER INFORMATION

National Lead Information Center
202–833–1071; Hotline, to receive information by mail: 800-LEAD-FYI [532–3394]; to reach an information specialist: 800–424–5323
Fax: 202–659–1192
Clearinghouse operated by the National Safety Council, funded by the Environmental Protection Agency, the Centers for Disease Control and Prevention, and the Department of Housing and Urban Development; provides information; publishes materials such as *Lead Poisoning and Your Children, Home Repairs and Renovations: What You Should Know About Lead-Based Paint,* and *Home Test Kits for Lead in Paint, Soil, and Dust.*

American Academy of Pediatrics (AAP),
800–433–9016. Publishes video-and-booklet set *Poison in Disguise: The Dangers of Lead-Based Paint.* (For full group information, see HEALTH CARE.)

Alliance to End Childhood Lead Poisoning (AECLP)
227 Massachusetts Avenue NE, Suite 200
Washington, DC 20002
202–543–1147
Fax: 202–543–4466
E-mail: aeclp@aeclp.permanet.org
Don Ryan, Executive Director
Organization concerned with lead poisoning; seeks to educate public and shape policy; publishes bimonthly newsletter *Alliance Alert, Childhood Lead Poisoning* (3 vol. prevention strategies handbook), *Guide to Medicaid for Childhood Lead Poisoning Prevention Programs and Other Public Health Providers, Making the Most of Medicaid: State Process in Childhood Lead*

Get the Lead Out!

In line with recent understandings about lead hazards (see LEAD POISONING), parents are advised to:

- Make sure children's hands are clean before they eat.
- If you use leaded crystal ware for drinking, do not use it on a daily basis; do not store beverages or foods in it, especially alcoholic beverages and other products with a high acid content (such as fruit juice, tomato sauce, vinegar, or wine); do not use it while pregnant or of child-bearing age; and do not feed infants and children from leaded crystal baby bottles or glasses.
- Since some imported foods are still packed in lead-soldered cans, limit consumption of imported canned foods, unless your grocer can assure you that a particular product is not packed in a lead-soldered can. The U.S. food processing industry reported to the FDA that, from mid–1991, lead soldering was not being used in domestically produced foods. It has for some time not been used for baby foods (which are usually packed in glass containers) and juices.
- Get a water analysis to test for lead. Generally, two samples are taken: one of water that has been standing in the plumbing lines overnight, preferably for eight hours or longer, and another after letting the water run several minutes to flush the lines. (Contact your local health department or the Environmental Protection Agency's Safe Drinking Water Hotline: 800–426–4791 for information and referrals on water analysis.)
- If you know, or suspect, that your household water contains elevated lead levels before the morning's first use, let water run for at least thirty seconds or until it runs cool, to flush the lines. Use cold water for drinking or cooking, since lead leaches more readily into hot water.
- Contact your local water supplier to find out if your home or apartment has lead water service connections. If so and you own the lines, ask for a contractor who can change them. If the supplier owns lead connections, pressure for them to be changed.
- Never use lead solder to repair plumbing.
- If you use older or imported ceramic products, avoid storing acidic foods in them. Better yet, the FDA recommends testing them and, if high lead content is found, disposing of them or using them for decorative purposes only.
- Keep painted surfaces in good shape, so older layers of paint are not exposed, chipping, or peeling. Be sure children do not eat paint chips.
- Before you disturb a surface with old paint on it, have your home tested for lead-based paint. Your local health department may do it. If not, employees there can refer you to someone who can, or you can use a home test kit, available at hardware stores.
- If you find lead-based paints, avoid doing any work that might produce paint dust or chips, including scraping, sanding, using a heat gun before repainting, making holes in the walls, tearing out walls, and the like. People can poison themselves by burning or scraping off layers of paint. Also, lead dust is generated and, if not properly contained, becomes dispersed in the air and sticks to household surfaces, affecting all of the house's occupants.
- If repairs or renovations are necessary, have the work done by a professional contractor who is trained in how to protect the family and home from undue exposure to lead dust and chips.
- If you *must* do the repairs yourself, move children and pregnant women to another apartment or house until the work is complete and the area if fully cleaned. Keep exposed areas covered with plastic to seal off entrances and ducts and to protect furniture, carpets, rugs, and floors from paint dust and chips. Dispose of the plastic carefully. Before working, wet painted surfaces, to keep dust down.
- Avoid sweeping or vacuuming the work area, which spreads dust around. Clean up dust and chips with *wet* mops or rags soaked in a solution of trisodium phosphate (TSP) or phosphate-containing powdered dishwasher detergent and warm water, wearing gloves to protect your hands. Use two buckets—one for wash water and one for rinse water—and always wring dirty water into the wash water bucket. After each use, wash mops and rags thoroughly, to prevent recontamination of cleaned surfaces. If this is not possible, or if you have already used the mops

and rags several times, place them in plastic bags and dispose of them carefully.

- If repairs or renovations have occurred before you suspected the presence of lead-based paint, keep children away from paint dust and chips. Clean up all dust and chips with wet mops and rags, as described above, with special attention to floors, window sills, and window wells.
- If work is going on nearby that may produce lead dust, close your windows. Use wet mops and rags to clean up any dust that has gotten into your home.
- Test your child's blood-lead levels, especially children under 6 years old, through your doctor or local health department. Testing is recommended starting at six months of age, and again at twelve and twenty-four months, and beyond that based on previous test results, the child's risk of lead exposure, and your state's lead screening requirements.

Source: Adapted from materials from the Food and Drug Administration and the National Lead Information Center.

Poisoning Prevention, National Action Plan for Preventing Childhood Lead Poisoning, Would Your Child Be Covered? Lessons for Health Reform from Private Health Insurance Lead Poisoning Coverage, International Action Plan for Preventing Lead Poisoning, Directory of State and Local Lead Poisoning Prevention advocates, and various technical reports.

Center for Safety in the Arts (CSA), 212–227–6220. Publishes fact sheet *Lead Hazards.* (For full group information, see ENVIRONMENTAL HAZARDS.)

American Academy of Child and Adolescent Psychiatry (AACAP), 202–966–7300. Publishes information sheet *Lead Exposure.* (For full group information, see MENTAL DISORDERS.)

National Safety Council (NSC), 800–621–7615. Publishes *Stop Lead Poisoning.* (For full group information, see SAFETY.)

American Heart Association (AHA). Publishes *Chelation Therapy.* (For full group information, see HEART AND HEART PROBLEMS.)

National Maternal and Child Health Clearinghouse (NMCHC), 703–821–8955. Publishes *Childhood Lead Poisoning: Current Perspectives—Proceedings, Manual for the Identification and Abatement of Environmental Lead Hazards,* and *Nutrition and Childhood Lead Poisoning Prevention: A Quick Reference Guide for Health Providers—Nutrition and Lead Bibliography.* (For full group information, see PREGNANCY.)

The Arc, 817–261–6003. Publishes *Childhood Lead Poisoning Prevention.* (For full group information, see MENTAL RETARDATION.)

National Organization for Rare Disorders (NORD), 800–999–6673. (For full group information, see RARE DISORDERS.)

learning block, a general term for anything that might hinder a student's gaining of new knowledge and skills, including DISABILITIES of various kinds and lack of the necessary PREREQUISITE skills, such as READING.

learning disabilities (LD), an umbrella term for a wide range of educational problems that involve continuing difficulties in speaking, listening, READING, writing, interpreting, understanding, and remembering, but that are not due to any other kind of DISABILITY, unfamiliarity with the culture and its language, or failure of instructional methods, though they may involve uneven development or DEVELOPMENTAL DELAY in certain areas. The kinds of problems and the ways in which they show themselves vary widely from person to person, but in general learning disabilities involve difficulties in four major areas:

- *Input,* the process of receiving and registering information in the brain. People with LD often have trouble seeing and hearing accurately, though their ears and eyes function normally; they have problems DECODING, or extracting meaning from symbols, such as written, spoken, or signed words or numbers. They often confuse letters or words, frequently making REVERSALS (transpositions), and so may misunderstand directions and be easily distracted. Input problems also affect EYE-HAND COORDINATION and other VISUAL and MOTOR SKILLS.
- *Integration,* the process of putting information together in a meaningful sequence and understanding it. Partly because of input problems, people with LD often have difficulty in putting letters, words, gestures, and ideas in correct order. They may have trouble recalling the order of events in a story or steps in a group of instructions.
- *Memory,* the process of storing information in the brain and retrieving it as desired. People with LD may have trouble with short-term memory, as in being unable to remember instructions long enough to carry them out. Part of the problem may be that input and integration problems cause information to be "scrambled" in storage. They may also have trouble with long-term mem-

ory or "permanent" storage, as in remembering their address and phone number.
- *Output*, the process of carrying out commands given by the brain, such as communicating (writing, signing, or speaking) or doing physical things that require muscular coordination, in gross motor skills (such as jumping) or fine motor skills (as in the physical act of writing). People with LD have problems with ENCODING, or converting spoken or signed words or numbers into written symbols, and often grope for or misuse words.

Children with LD often have associated problems, including a short ATTENTION SPAN and HYPERACTIVITY, as in ATTENTION DEFICIT HYPERACTIVITY DISORDER; DISTRACTIBILITY problems with socializing, partly due to poor communication skills; and general frustration at having trouble over learning tasks that seem easy to most, which can in turn lead to behavioral problems.

Many other people have learning problems, too, but if these are people with physical DISABILITIES, MENTAL RETARDATION, MENTAL DISORDERS, or socioeconomic disadvantages, they are not considered to be learning disabled. By contrast, people with LD have average or above average intelligence, but some malfunction bars them from being able to learn as effectively as their mental ability would seem to indicate. They are also not simply UNDERACHIEVERS, though some so-called underachievers may have undiagnosed learning disabilities.

The causes of learning disabilities are so far obscure. At the heart of the problem seems to be some disorder in the brain and nervous system. Among the causes that may be linked with such neurological problems are:

- Injuries at or during birth, or in early childhood.
- PREMATURE birth.
- Serious illness in infancy or early childhood.
- GENETIC INHERITANCE, since learning disabilities tend to run in families.
- Gender, since boys are five times more likely than girls to have LD. Their problems are compounded because boys tend to mature more slowly, as well.

The erratic spelling and form of the English language and modern society's increasing dependence on floods of words and numbers, on paper and on screens, exacerbate these problems.

Because learning disabilities are various and often subtle, they can be hard to diagnose, especially in young children. Although learning problems may be recognized early, some experts do not feel it possible to diagnose these as learning disabilities in PRESCHOOL children, because the problems may result from other causes, such as unfamiliarity with structured learning, cultural differences, language differences (as when a language other than English is spoken in the home), or simply widely different rates of development. But the important thing is for learning problems to be identified as soon as possible and for special training or services to be provided if necessary.

In brief, the Foundation for Children with Learning Disabilities outlines several warning signs for learning disabilities:

- *In spoken language*: delays, disorders, and deviations in listening and speaking.
- *In written language*: difficulties with reading, writing, and spelling.
- *In arithmetic*: difficulties in performing mathematical operations or in understanding basic mathematical concepts.
- *In reasoning*: difficulties in organizing and integrating thoughts.
- *In memory*: difficulties in remembering information and instructions.

Parents can use the OBSERVATION CHECKLIST FOR POSSIBLE LEARNING DISABILITIES IN PRESCHOOLERS on page 359 to help them assess (with the help of the child's PRESCHOOL teacher or CHILD CARE provider, if appropriate) whether or not their child needs professional evaluation. (Subscribers to the America Online computer service can find general advice on teaching and specific activities for helping young children with learning disabilities, in the Moms Online Desk Reference section of Moms Online, under "Teaching Young Children.")

Learning disabilities are increasingly being recognized as a common problem—but how common is still not yet known, because experts believe that many people with LD have not been diagnosed (including both children and adults). Some experts believe that learning disabilities are behind many behavioral problems in schools and that many people who are underachievers, DROPOUTS, or DELINQUENTS have undiagnosed (and therefore untreated) learning disabilities. Government and educational organizations have been making increasingly stronger efforts to identify people who suffer from LD and to get them the special educational and other services they need, focusing especially on preschool and ELEMENTARY SCHOOL age children.

One problem with identification of learning disabilities is that people define LD in different ways for different purposes, often using different names and terms. The set of problems known as learning disabilities has in the past been given dozens of names, including PERCEPTUAL HANDICAPS, *minimal brain dysfunction (MBD)*, *perceptual disturbances*, *minimal cerebral dysfunction*, or *minimal neurological dysfunction*, and some professionals still use these names. And the term *learning disabilities* as it is used today often includes a number of specific kinds of disabilities, such as:

- DYSLEXIA—difficulty with reading and understanding written words.
- DYSCALCULIA—difficulty with numbers and mathematical calculations.
- DYSGRAPHIA—difficulty in producing readable handwriting.

- DYSARTHRIA—difficulty in producing readily understandable speech.

The result is a thicket of definitions and descriptions that many parents must be prepared to cut through if their child may have learning disabilities. As the people of the HEAD START program point out in their booklet series, *Mainstreaming Preschoolers*:

> It is usually more helpful to describe what children with learning problems are like rather than to classify them. This is partly because different diagnosticians use different definitions of learning disabilities, and follow different theories in labeling problems. This means that three children for whom you have the same diagnostic information could be classified or categorized in three different ways, depending on the diagnostician or diagnostic team. On the other hand, just because two children are both diagnosed as learning disabled doesn't mean that they will behave in the same way. The only way to understand a child's problem is to consider what he or she currently can and cannot do.
>
> Classifying can, however, serve several purposes. Current special education laws require that a diagnostic category be assigned to each handicapped child, in order to provide that child with special education services and so that he or she can receive necessary state and federal reimbursement. So, for that purpose, categories are required. Also, when there is a need for common understanding, categories can be a useful shortcut. You will want to be familiar with certain terms and categories that may appear in medical reports. They may guide you in asking further questions about a child's strengths and weaknesses.

Various definitions may determine whether or not a child is eligible for certain kinds of aid and special services, so parents whose children may have learning disabilities will need to "decode" them as preparation for helping their children. The federal EDUCATION FOR ALL HANDICAPPED CHILDREN ACT (Public Law 94–142) defines learning disabilities this way:

> Specific learning disability means a disorder in one or more of the basic psychological processes involved in understanding or in using language, spoken or written, which may manifest itself in an imperfect inability to listen, think, speak, read, write, spell, or to do mathematical calculations. The term includes such conditions as perceptual handicaps, brain injury, minimal brain dysfunction, dyslexia, and developmental aphasia. The term does not include children who have learning problems that are primarily the result of visual, hearing, or motor handicaps, of mental retardation, of emotional disturbance, or of environmental, cultural, or economic disadvantage.

This definition is widely used because PUBLIC SCHOOLS must comply with the law and its successor, the INDIVIDUALS WITH DISABILITIES EDUCATION ACT (IDEA). But state laws vary, as do interpretations. As a result, there are wide variations in the number of people diagnosed as being learning disabled. The Foundation for Children with Learning Disabilities reports, for example, that (as of 1980) 5.7 percent of students in Maryland were diagnosed as having learning disabilities, while in Massachusetts the figure was only 1.5 percent. Overall, the U.S. Department of Education estimates that about 4.4 percent (about 1,750,000) of American school children are classed as learning disabled. More recent estimates have ranged as high as 15 percent.

The problem has been further complicated by some recent studies that have thrown into questions previous assumptions about LD.

Dyslexia has long been thought to have a biological basis, and to be a permanent disability. But a major 1992 study suggested that dyslexia may not be permanent, but instead may change during a child's development. Following 414 children in a Connecticut school from kindergarten through eighth grade, a Yale-based team found some surprising results, notably that:

- Children classed as borderline dyslexics moved in and out of the dyslexic group over the years.
- Most children who were diagnosed as dyslexic in the early grades were not classed so in later years. Specifically, fewer than one in three labeled dyslexic in the first grade remained so in the third grade; by sixth grade the ratio was one in six.
- Other children who were not considered dyslexic in the early years came to be considered so later on.

The meaning and implication of these findings are just beginning to be explored.

Certainly the study raised further questions about what dyslexia is and how it is identified. Children are generally given various tests, assessing their ability to receive information accurately (input), transmit it accurately (output), put pieces of information together (integration), as in matching sounds with the written word, and remember pieces of information (memory). These tests focus on areas that characteristically cause trouble, such as reversing letters (for example, b and d) or transposing letters (*was* for *saw*). Children who score low on such tests are considered dyslexic. But students are sometimes classed as dyslexic or learning disabled if their IQ scores are substantially higher than their reading achievement scores.

Among the questions raised by the new study are:

- Can we distinguish between children with dyslexia and those who, for a variety of other reasons, are poor readers? Some people have suggested that, even if dyslexia has a biological basis, the term has been too broadly and imprecisely defined, becoming a catch-all. The Yale study suggests the possibility that some students, though they seem able to read normally, actually have dyslexia, which may become apparent only later. Dyslexia may be like high blood pressure or obesity, in that the severity of the condition varies and children move in and out of the "abnormal" group.
- Are we able to identify dyslexia and learning disabilities in very young children? Many experts have long felt that dyslexia and other learning disabilities could not be identified in preschool children, because early reading and learning problems may result from other causes, such as unfamiliarity with structured learning, cultural differences, social or emotional problems (as when a family is homeless or in the process of breaking up), or language differences (as when a language other than English is spoken in the home). More important, children develop at widely different rates, so it is possible that those labeled as dyslexic early in school are simply developing more slowly than average.
- More generally, are children being properly identified as dyslexic or learning disabled? Some people have suggested that both parents and schools have too readily applied the notion of dyslexia and learning disabilities, regarding these categories as a convenient, socially acceptable explanation of educational problems—and one that may relieve parents and teachers from feeling responsible for a child's failure to learn. Others believe that dyslexia and learning disabilities are to some extent "socially created" categories, reflecting the priorities of a high-pressure society, as well as the lower status accorded to nonacademic skills, such as woodworking or dancing. In addition, some people have charged that, because learning disabilities qualify for special aid under federal laws, schools have more readily classed children as learning disabled, not always for proper cause.
- Do dyslexia and learning disabilities have a biological basis? Educators, psychologists, neurologists, and other experts have long assumed that such disabilities are permanent and so have sought specific biological defects common among dyslexic children. In 1991, a study scanned the brains of twenty-one people with dyslexia and twenty-nine normal readers and reported significant differences in one area of the left half of the brain. Such results are yet to be confirmed, however, and their implications explored.
- Can children "outgrow" dyslexia or learning disabilities? The Yale study suggests that we need to know much more about how children with dyslexia fare over time. Can they, for example, learn how to overcome their disabilities, so they can read and learn normally? Or might some parts of the brain develop in such a way as to compensate for the original problem, as was suggested by some findings in the 1991 Miami study? Or were many people mislabeled as dyslexic, having only a slower-than-normal development in some areas?
- Do specific treatments and therapies help children with dyslexia and learning disabilities? Indeed, does treatment explain the children who moved out of the "dyslexic" category during the study? In the past, any child who was able to move out of a reading disability group was regarded as a success for whatever teaching or therapy approach was being employed. But if, as the Yale study showed, children move in and out of the dyslexic group for other, as yet unknown reasons, treatments and therapies will need to be generally reevaluated.
- Are the study's results caused by a fluke? What we do not yet know is whether or not there were some special circumstances in the school and community used in the Yale study that would have caused the results obtained. It remains for other researchers to confirm, expand on, modify, or contradict the results of this single study.

In a different study, a team of brain researchers reported finding a physical basis for dyslexia; specifically, they found indications that dyslexia was not purely a language problem, but may result from unsynchronized timing in the visual system's circuits, where information is not received in the proper sequence for processing by the brain. The visual system involves two major pathways: one for seeing motion, depth perception, stereoscopic vision, low contrast, and spatial orientation; the other for seeing color, detailed forms, high contrast, and stationary images. The study found that, in people with dyslexia, the first system worked "sluggishly," and that in autopsies on brains of dyslexics, the first system seemed to be more disorganized and to involve smaller cells. This 1991 study involved only a small group of subjects, but, if confirmed, offers the possibility of identifying dyslexia in very young children, even infants, and of providing help early, when it presumably would do the most good. One of the authors stressed that such slightly sluggish visual systems should not be viewed as disorders, but may in fact be part of the normal variation of the human brain, often in people otherwise highly gifted.

Observers note that the findings gave support to one approach to treating dyslexia, which involves using colored filters in reading, and may suggest new ways to help people with dyslexia. Other studies suggest that hearing and touch may be involved in a similar way. Also, researchers have found that animals can form antibodies that destroy proteins found only in the first visual pathway and suggest the possibility that dyslexia may be an AUTOIMMUNE DISORDER (in which the body mistakenly attacks and damages part of itself) that is acquired or triggered before or shortly after birth.

Observation Checklist for Possible Learning Disabilities in Preschoolers

Note: This checklist is from materials prepared for teachers and parents of Head Start preschoolers, to help them decide whether or not screening is advisable for possible learning disabilities.

Children with learning problems generally exhibit certain behaviors that can be observed by the child's teachers and parents. [Note: At preschool age, they may be hard to diagnose as learning disabilities.] The checklist of behaviors that follows can alert you to undiagnosed learning problems, and help you know when to refer a child for professional evaluation. This checklist is intended to help you carry out systematic observations, which you can then share with others who might, if necessary, diagnose your child.

USING THE CHECKLIST

The "red flag." The checklist is only one of several observational devices that you can use to learn more about your child. Its main purpose is to help you to identify needs that have not been identified before. It should be considered only the first step in an overall program of systematic observation and assessment of a child's performance over time. It acts as a red flag because it can call your attention to behaviors that require much more careful observation and ongoing assessment. It can send you a signal that something may be wrong.

Knowing when to refer a child. Some behaviors may require urgent attention, while others can wait while you observe them more carefully over time. For instance, if a child complains of an earache, he or she requires immediate medical attention. It is important to find out whether the earache is a symptom of an infection, because untreated ear infections may result in hearing loss. Similarly, in case of dizziness, feverish forehead, and other possible signs of illness, the child should be taken to a doctor or clinic right away.

But other behaviors need to be watched carefully over time. For example, if your initial observations tell you that Jack really does have two tantrums a day, then that is the red flag that alerts you to continue, in a systematic way, to observe and assess these tantrums. You need to have time to examine these behaviors to find whether something happening in the home or classroom is causing them—something that can be changed to reduce or stop the tantrums. If, after all of your efforts to modify and adjust your home or classroom situation and teaching techniques, you find that Jack's tantrums continue and are highly disruptive to the family or other children, it is time to seek additional services.

If Tina is not using at least two- and three-word phrases to ask for what she wants, you need time to find out why. Is Tina not using phrases because she really cannot do so, or because she has simply never needed to use them or been expected to do so? Perhaps she has always gotten what she wanted just by pointing to the object or by saying only one word. She may need some prompting from you, the teachers in her class, and her friends and classmates to get her to use words to ask for what she wants. However, if you try for some time and have no success, Tina should be referred to an appropriate professional or team of professionals for help.

Parents and teachers are the best judges of when they have watched long enough to decide whether diagnostic services outside the classroom are necessary.

How often should this checklist be used? This observational checklist is a part of the first step in identifying problems and seeking help for them. But observation, like assessment or evaluation, should be a continuous process. This is because behavior is always changing, and some behavior changes may signal a problem. In addition, some children have secondary or associated problems that are very slow to develop and hard to detect—but that need to be identified and helped. It is not possible to give a surefire rule or formula for how often to use this observation form. But once you become familiar with the behaviors listed and the questions asked, you will

(*continued*)

(continued)

probably find that these questions occur to you naturally as you watch your child and other children. The checklist form should help you to organize the information that you collect.

USING CHECKLIST RESULTS

It is important to remember that any child may exhibit one of the behaviors described under a particular skill area. This does not mean that the child is learning-disabled. Learning-disabled children will exhibit several of the behaviors described in one or several of the skill areas. There are many different combinations of behaviors that learning-disabled children display.

If your answers fall in the gray boxes on a number of observational questions in one or more skill areas, this may indicate potential problems and the need for extra help in those areas.

If you observe the same behaviors frequently in a child, you should concentrate on helping the child acquire skills in the areas you have checked. If your efforts are unsuccessful, and if the specific problems interfere with the child's general success in learning, you may need to refer the child for an evaluation.

COMMUNICATION SKILLS	YES	NO	SOMETIMES
1. Does the child use at least two- and three- word phrases to ask for what he or she wants? (For example, "more juice" or "more juice please.")	☐	☐	☐
2. Does the child use complete sentences to tell you what has happened? (For example, "My doggie ran away" versus "doggie gone.")	☐	☐	☐
3. When the child is asked to describe something, does he or she use at least two sentences to talk about it?[1]	☐	☐	☐
4. Does the child ask questions? (For example, "Where is Juan?")	☐	☐	☐
5. Does the child seem to have difficulty following directions?	☐	☐	☐
6. Does the child respond to questions with an appropriate answer?	☐	☐	☐
7. Does the child seem to talk too softly or too loudly?	☐	☐	☐
8. Are you able to understand the child?	☐	☐	☐
9. Does the child have difficulty paying attention to group activities for more than five minutes at a time?	☐	☐	☐

MOTOR SKILLS	YES	NO	SOMETIMES
1. Does the child stumble often, or appear awkward when he or she moves?	☐	☐	☐
2. Does the child seem afraid of or unable to use stairs, climbing equipment, or tricycles?	☐	☐	☐
3. When the child walks or runs, does one side of his or her body seem to move differently than the other side? For instance, does the child seem to have better control of the leg and arm on one side than on the other?	☐	☐	☐
4. Can the child hop on one foot?	☐	☐	☐
5. Is the child capable of dressing him- or herself except for tying shoes?[2]	☐	☐	☐
6. Does the child hold a pencil or a crayon appropriately with the thumb, index, and middle fingers?	☐	☐	☐
7. Does the child continually switch a crayon from one hand to the other when coloring?	☐	☐	☐
8. Do the child's hands appear clumsy or shaky when he or she is using them?	☐	☐	☐

(continued)

(continued)

MOTOR SKILLS	YES	NO	SOMETIMES
9. When the child is coloring with a crayon, does the hand that he or she is *not* using appear tense? (For example, clenched into a fist.)	☐	☐	☐
10. Can the child color inside a circumscribed area with any accuracy?	☐	☐	☐
11. Can the child cut with a pair of scissors?	☐	☐	☐

SOCIAL SKILLS	YES	NO	SOMETIMES
1. Does the child engage in at least two disruptive behaviors a day? (For example, tantrums, fighting, screaming.)	☐	☐	☐
2. Does the child appear withdrawn from the outside world? (For example, fiddling with pieces of string, staring into space, rocking his or her body, banging his or her head, talking to him- or herself.)	☐	☐	☐
3. Does the child appear extremely shy in group activities? (For example, does the child avoid volunteering answers or answering direct questions, even when you think he or she knows the answers?)	☐	☐	☐
4. Does the child play alone and seldom talk to the other children?	☐	☐	☐
5. Does the child spend most of the time trying to get attention from the adults?	☐	☐	☐
6. Does the child have toileting problems (wet or soiled) at least once a week?	☐	☐	☐

VISION OR HEARING SKILLS	YES	NO	SOMETIMES
1. Do the child's eye movements appear jerky or uncoordinated?	☐	☐	☐
2. Does the child seem to have difficulty seeing objects?	☐	☐	☐
... tilt his or her head to look at things?	☐	☐	☐
... hold objects close to his or her eyes?	☐	☐	☐
... squint?	☐	☐	☐
... show sensitivity to bright lights?	☐	☐	☐
... have uncontrolled eye-rolling?	☐	☐	☐
... complain that his or her eyes hurt?	☐	☐	☐
... bump into things constantly?	☐	☐	☐
3. Does the child appear awkward in tasks requiring eye-hand coordination? (For example, pegs, puzzles, coloring.)	☐	☐	☐
4. Does the child seem to have difficulty hearing?	☐	☐	☐
... consistently favor one ear by turning the same side of his or her head in the direction of the sound?	☐	☐	☐
... ignore, confuse, or not follow directions?	☐	☐	☐
... rub or pull on his or her ear frequently, or complain of earache?	☐	☐	☐
... complain of head noises or dizziness?	☐	☐	☐
... have a high, low, or monotonous tone of voice?	☐	☐	☐
... respond to your voice when he or she is not looking at you?	☐	☐	☐
... ask "what?" excessively?	☐	☐	☐
... have speech that is very difficult for you to understand?	☐	☐	☐
5. Does the child seem to have an excessive number of colds?	☐	☐	☐

(continued)

(continued)

GENERAL HEALTH	YES	NO	SOMETIMES
1. Does the child have frequent absences because of illness?	☐	☐	☐
2. Do the child's eyes water?	☐	☐	☐
3. Does the child have a discharge from his or her eyes?	☐	☐	☐
...his or her ears?	☐	☐	☐
4. Does the child have periods of unusual movements (such as rapid eye blinking) or "blank spells" that seem to appear and disappear without relationship to the social situation?	☐	☐	☐
5. Does the child have hives or rashes?	☐	☐	☐
6. Does the child have a persistent cough?	☐	☐	☐
7. Is the child excessively thirsty?	☐	☐	☐
...ravenously hungry?	☐	☐	☐
8. Have you noticed any of the following conditions?			
...constant fatigue	☐	☐	☐
...irritability	☐	☐	☐
...restlessness	☐	☐	☐
...tenseness	☐	☐	☐
...feverish cheeks or forehead	☐	☐	☐
9. Is the child overweight?	☐	☐	☐
10. Is the child physically or mentally sluggish?	☐	☐	☐
11. Has the child lost weight without being on a diet?	☐	☐	☐

[1] Question applies if child is four years or older.
[2] Question applies if child is four years or older.

Source: Mainstreaming Preschoolers: Children with Learning Disabilities: A Guide for Teachers, Parents, and Others Who Work with Learning Disabled Preschoolers, by Alice H. Hayden et al. The checklist was adapted from materials prepared by the OCD/BEH Collaborative Project with Head Start, Model Preschool Center for Handicapped Children, Experimental Education Unit, Child Development and Mental Retardation Center, University of Washington.

Meanwhile, parents of children who have reading difficulties—whether or not they have been labeled as "dyslexic" or "learning disabled"—must make practical day-to-day decisions on how to give and get help. In general, experts recommend that parents in this situation keep in mind several guidelines:

- Try to clear aside any anger at the school or at yourself as having somehow "failed;" such judgments are generally counterproductive and often damaging to the child.
- Encourage and support your child, rather than driving the child to succeed and placing disproportionate emphasis on academic performance.
- Focus on what the child does well, not on failures.
- Understand that your child has, not an *in*ability, but a *dis*ability, making learning more difficult, not impossible.
- Recognize that there are various ways of learning, and be alert and open to ways of learning that may be easier for your child.
- Communicate your love and acceptance of the child, and your understanding of his or her frustration at having to work so hard at some things.

As the prevalence of learning disabilities has become recognized, numerous organizations (see listings in this entry) have emerged to explore and coordinate research into the causes of LD and the best ways to help children overcome learning problems. They may also help parents obtain proper diagnoses for their children's learning disabilities and then arrange for special educational services.

Many children can be helped by a variety of special programs, often using more than one SENSORY MODE to reinforce learning. Among approaches that have had some success are:

- Using recorded material to supplement printed matter, such as textbooks.
- Using a typewriter or tape recorder, instead of writing by hand.
- Having students make outlines and run through drills before testing.
- Supplying outlines of classroom presentations.
- Focusing on PHONICS in reading or on highly structured multisensory reading approaches (such as VAKT), rather than on learning whole words.

(See LEARNING STYLES for suggestions on how to use different sensory modes in learning.)

When learning disabilities are severe or parents are unable to obtain proper services for their child, special schools are available (see organizations listed). Increasing numbers of camps and college programs are tailored to the needs of learning disabled students, and special arrangements can be made for LD students in some testing situations, as with the SCHOLASTIC APTITUDE TEST or the ACT (American College Testing Program); see SPECIAL HELP FOR SPECIAL COLLEGE STUDENTS on page 366. Some vocational and on-the-job training programs are also now being modified to help learning disabled people, including people who only learn as adults that their educational difficulties were caused by learning disabilities.

FOR HELP AND FURTHER INFORMATION

Orton Dyslexia Society (ODS)
Chester Building, Suite 382
8600 LaSalle Road
Baltimore, MD 21286–2044
410–296–0232; 800-ABCD–123 [222–3123]
Fax: 410–321–5069
E-mail: laubache@pie.org
Steve Laubacher, Executive Director
Organization concerned with dyslexia; provides information; publishes various materials, including quarterly *Perspectives on Dyslexia*; annual journal *Annals of Dyslexia*; books such as *The Many Faces of Dyslexia, Understanding Learning Disabilities: A Parent Guide and Workbook, Language and the Developing Child, Basic Facts About Dyslexia: What Everyone Ought to Know, The Other 16 Hours: The Social and Emotional Problems of Dyslexia,* and *Doctors Ask Questions About Dyslexia: A Review of Medical Research*; booklets and pamphlets such as *The Dyslexic Child, What Is Dyslexia?,* and *Dys-lex-i-a: Defining the Problem,* and reprints.

Learning Disabilities Association of America (LDA)
4156 Library Road
Pittsburgh, PA 15234
412–341–1515
Fax: 412–344–0224
Jean Petersen, Executive Director
Organization concerned with learning disabilities; formerly Association for Children and Adults with Learning Disabilities (ACLD); acts as advocate; provides information and referrals, as on special schools and camps; publishes *Newsbriefs* and distributes many publications.

National Center for Learning Disabilities (NCLD)
381 Park Avenue South, Suite 1420
New York, NY 10016
212–545–7510
Fax: 212–545–9665
Shirley Cramer, Executive Director
Organization concerned with learning disabilities; provides information and referrals; seeks to educate public; publishes annual magazine *Their World,* quarterly newsletter *NCLD News,* periodic *NewsAlerts,* and *NCLD Learning Disabilities Resource Guide,* indispensable guide to state-by-state programs, schools, services, and organizations for learning disabled children and adults, including overview, warning signals, rights of LD children, moving into adulthood and work, bibliography, and glossary of terms.

Council for Exceptional Children (CEC), 800–328–0272. Includes Division for Learning Disabilities (DLD), which publishes triannual *DLD Times,* quarterly *Learning Disabilities Research and Practice,* and other materials; CEC also publishes brochure *Inclusion: What Does It Mean for Students with Learning Disabilities?* and numerous special-topic reports such as *Learning Disabilities, Gifted But Learning Disabled: A Puzzling Paradox, Learning Disabilities Glossary of Some Important Terms, College Planning for Students with Learning Disabilities, Reading About Children and Youth with Learning Disabilities,* and *Stress Management for the Learning Disabled.* (For full group information, see HELP ON LEARNING AND EDUCATION on page 659.)

American Academy of Pediatrics (AAP), 800–433–9016. Publishes brochures *Learning Disabilities and Children: What Parents Need to Know* and *Learning Disabilities and Young Adults.* (For full group information, see HEALTH CARE.)

Learning Disabilities Network
72 Sharp Street, Suite A–2
Hingham, MA 02043
617–340–5605
Fax: 617–340–5603
Carolyn Cowen and Maria Bacigalupo, Co-Executive Directors
Organization focusing on learning disabilities; provides information and referrals; publishes semiannual magazine *The Network Exchange* and materials for educational therapists.

HEATH Resource Center, National Clearinghouse on Postsecondary Education for Individuals with Disabilities, 800–544–3284, voice/TT. Publishes *Young Adults with Learning Disabilities and Other Special Needs, Getting Ready for College: Advising Students with Learning Disabilities, Summer Pre-College Programs for Students with LD, Learning Disabilities Among High Achieving Students, Foreign Language for Students with LD, Learning Disabled Adults in Postsecondary Education,* and *National Resources for Adults with Learning Disabilities.* (For full group information, see HELP FOR SPECIAL CHILDREN on page 689.)

National Institute of Child Health and Human Development (NICHD), 301–496–5133. Publishes *Facts About Dyslexia* and research reports *Learning Disabilities, Advocacy, Science and the Future of the Field,* and *Learning Disabilities: A Report to the U.S. Congress.* (For full group information, see PREGNANCY.)

American Academy of Child and Adolescent Psychiatry (AACAP), 202–966–7300. Publishes information sheet *Learning Disabilities.* (For full group information, see MENTAL DISORDERS.)

National Neurofibromatosis Foundation (NNF), 800–323–7938. Publishes *Achieving in Spite of . . . A Booklet on Learning Disabilities* and *"LD" Does NOT Mean Learning Dumd,* and *Mainstreaming Children with Learning Disabilities.* (For full group information, see NEUROFIBROMATOSIS.)

Council for Learning Disabilties (CLD)
P.O. Box 40303
Overland Park, KS 66204
913–492–8755
Fax: 913–492–2546
Kirsten McBride, Executive Secretary
Organization for professionals in learning disabilities and remedial education; publishes periodicals *Learning Disability Quarterly* and *LD Forum, Preventing School Failure, Intervention in School and Clinic,* and professional journals and other materials.

National Institute of Neurological Disorders and Stroke (NINDS), 800–352–9424. (For full group information, see BRAIN AND BRAIN DISORDERS.)

National Institute of Mental Health (NIMH), 301–443–4513. Publishes *Learning Disabilities.* (For full group information, see MENTAL DISORDER.)

National Easter Seal Society, 800–221–6827. Publishes *Understanding Learning Disabilities.* (For full group information, see HELP FOR SPECIAL CHILDREN on page 689.)

National Information Center for Children and Youth with Disabilities (NICHCY), 800–695–0285, voice/TT. Publishes *Learning Disabilities, Reading and Learning Disabilities Resource Guide.* (For full group information, see HELP FOR SPECIAL CHILDREN on page 689.)

National Library Services for the Blind and Physically Handicapped, Library of Congress, 800–424–8567, U.S. except DC. Publishes *Learning Disabilities: National Information and Advocacy Organizations* and brochure *Facts: Talking Books and Reading Disabilities.* (For full group information, see HELP FOR SPECIAL CHILDREN on page 689.)

Parents Helping Parents (PHP), 408–727–5775. Has division focusing on learning disabilities; publishes information packet *Learning Disabilities.* (For full group information, see HELP FOR SPECIAL CHILDREN on page 689.)

Alliance for Parental Involvement in Education (ALLPIE), 518–392–6900. Publishes *Everyone Is Able: Exploding the Myth of Learning Disabilities.* (For full group information, see HELP ON LEARNING AND EDUCATION on page 689.)

American Association of University Affiliated Programs for Persons with Developmental Disabilities (AAUAP), 301–588–8252. (For full group information, see HELP FOR SPECIAL CHILDREN.)

Co-ADD (Coalition for the Education and Support of Attention Deficit Disorder), 612–425–0423. (For full group information, see ATTENTION DEFICIT HYPERACTIVITY DISORDER.)

National Association of Private Schools for Exceptional Children (NAPSEC), 202–408–3338. (For full group information, see HELP FOR SPECIAL CHILDREN on page 689.)

National Organization for Rare Disorders (NORD), 800–999–6673. (For full group information, see RARE DISORDERS.)

OTHER RESOURCES

For parents

Parenting a Child with a Learning Disability: A Practical, Empathetic Guide. Cheryl G. Tuttle and Penny Paquette. Lowell House, 1993.

Crossover Children: A Source Book for Helping the Learning Disabled—Gifted Child. Marlene Bireley. Greyden, 1993.

The Misunderstood Child: A Guide for Parents of Learning Disabled Children, rev. ed. Larry B. Silver. TAB-McGraw-Hill, 1992.

Learning Disabilities: What To Do after Diagnosis: Vol. 1: A Survival Guide Kindergarten Through Third Grade. Vol. 2: A Survival Guide Fourth Through Sixth Grade. Vol. 3: A Survival Guide Seventh Through Twelfth Grade. Vol. 4: A Survival Guide—College and the Workplace. Jill Smith and Howard Diller. Apodixis, 1991.

Parent's Guide to Learning Disabilities. Stephen B. McCarney and Angela M. Bauer. Hawthorne Educational Services, 1991.

Can Anyone Help My Child?: Therapies and Treatment for Attention Deficit and Other Learning and Behavioral Disorders in Children, Adolescents, and Adults, rev. ed. Guy D. Ogan. Faith Publications & Media, 1991.

Beyond the Rainbow: A Guide for Parents of Children with Dyslexia and Other Learning Disabilities. Patricia Dodds and others. Educational Intervention, 1991.

Why Is My Child Having Trouble at School?: A Parent's Guide to Learning Disabilities. Barbara Novick and Maureen Arnold. Villard/Random, 1991.

Understanding Dyslexia: A Practical Handbook for Parents and Teachers. Anne M. Huston. Madison Books, 1991.

Help Me To Help My Child: A Sourcebook for Parents of Learning Disabled Children. Jill Bloom. Little, Brown, 1990.

General works

Not Lazy, Crazy, or Dumb: Performance Breakthroughs for Adolescents and Young Adults with Learning Difficulties.

Geraldine Markel and Judith Greenbaum. Research Press, 1994.

Square Peg in a Round Hole: Coping with Learning Differences at Home, in School and at Work. Jimmie Shreve. Square Peg, 1993.

Dyslexia and Other Learning Difficulties. Mark Selikowitz. Oxford University Press, 1993.

Understanding Learning Disabilities. Jane C. Sacknowitz. Bureau for At-Risk Youth, 1992.

Help ??? Help !!!: Solving Learning Problems (Even Dyslexia). David Conway. Academic Reading, 1992.

Succeeding Against the Odds: How the Learning Disabled Can Realize Their Promise. Sally L. Smith. Putnam, 1992.

Succeeding Against the Odds: Strategies and Insights from the Learning-Disabled. Sally L. Smith. Tarcher, 1992. By the founder of Washington, D.C.'s Lab School, on her experiences with learning-disabled students.

Smart in Everything...Except School. G. N. Getman. VisionExtension, 1992.

The Learning Disabled Child. Sylvia Farnham-Diggory. Harvard University Press, 1992.

Attention Deficits, Learning Disabilities, and Ritalin: A Practical Guide, 2nd ed. Robert B. Johnston. Singular, 1991.

Upside-down Kids. Harold N. Levinson. M. Evans, 1991.

Living with a Learning Disability, rev. ed. Barbara Cordoni. Southern Illinois University Press, 1990.

For children

Trouble with School: A Family Story about Learning Disabilities. Kathryn B. Dunn and Allison B. Dunn. Woodbine House, 1993.

Brain Train: Ready-to-Use Tapes and Activities to Develop Confidence and Competence in Children with Learning Difficulties. Janna Spark. Center for Applied Resources, 1993.

Learning Disabilities. Paul Almonte and Theresa Desmond. Crestwood, 1992.

The School Survival Guide for Kids with LD (Learning Differences): Ways to Make Learning Easier and More Fun. Rhoda Cummings and Gary Fisher. Free Spirit, 1991. With optional audiocassette.

What Do You Mean I Have a Learning Disability? Kathleen M. Dwyer. Walker, 1991.

Dyslexia. Elaine Landau. Watts, 1991.

For preteens and teens

Feeling Different, Feeling Fine: Kids Talk about Their Learning Problems. Cynthia Roby. A. Whitman, 1993.

Learning Disabilities. Jean McBee Knox. Chelsea House, 1989.

Personal experiences

Something's Not Right: One Family's Struggle with Learning Disabilities. Nancy Lelewer. VanderWyk and Burnham, 1994.

The Success of Failures: A True Story of a Learning Disabled Student. Brian Wilson. Mar Co Prods., 1993.

An Autobiography of a Dyslexic. Abraham Schmitt as told to Mary Lou Hartzler Clemens. Good Books, 1992.

Reversals: A Personal Account of Victory over Dyslexia. Eileen Simpson. Farrar, Straus, & Giroux, 1991.

Mothers Talk about Learning Disabilities: Personal Feelings, Practical Advice. Elizabeth Weiss. Prentice-Hall, 1991.

Speaking for Themselves: Ethnographic Interviews with Adults with Learning Disabilities. Paul J. Gerber and Henry B. Reiff. University of Michigan Press, 1991.

Directories and guides

Directory for Exceptional Children. Porter Sargent, annual.

The Complete Learning Disabilities Directory, 1995/1996. Grey House, 1995.

A National Directory of Four Year Colleges, Two Year Colleges, and Post High School Training Programs for Young People with Learning Disabilities, 7th ed. P.M. Fielding and John R. Moss, eds. Partners In Publishing, 1994.

Directory of Facilities and Services for the Learning Disabled, 1993–94. Academic Therapy, 1993.

Colleges with Programs for Students with Learning Disabilities, 3rd ed. Charles T. Mangrum II and Stephen S. Strichart, eds. Peterson's, 1992.

The K & W Guide to Colleges for the Learning Disabled. Marybeth Kravets and Imy F. Wax, eds. HarperCollins, 1992.

On college for kids with LD

Swimming Upstream: A Complete Guide to the College Application Process for the Learning Disabled Student. Diane W. Howard. Hunt House, 1994.

Survival Guide for College Students with ADD or LD. Kathleen G. Nadeau. Magination Press, 1994.

(See also Apodixis series, under "For parents.")

Background works

The Gift of Dyslexia: Why Some of the Smartest People Can't Read and How They Can Learn. Ronald D. Davis. Ability Workshop, 1994. With audiocassette.

Learning Disabilities Spectrum: ADD, ADHD, and LD. Arnold J. Capute and others, eds. York, 1994.

Learning Disabilities and the Law. Peter S. Latham and Patricia H. Latham. JKL Communications, 1993.

Attention Deficit Disorder and Learning Disabilities: Reality, Myths, and Controversial Treatments. Barbara D. Ingersoll and Sam Goldstein. Doubleday, 1993.

The Schoolsearch Guide to Colleges with Programs or Services for Students with Learning Disabilities. Midge Lipkin. Schoolsearch, 1993.

Dyslexia and Other Learning Difficulties. Mark Selikowitz. Oxford University Press, 1993.

Better Understanding Learning Disabilities: New Views from Research and Their Implications for Education and Public Policies. G. Reid Lyon and others, eds. P. H. Brookes, 1993.

Special Help for Special College Students

Students with learning disabilities, attention deficit disorder, or other disabilities that affect learning can get special help during their college years, if they and their families plan ahead. Many colleges still know or care little about learning problems, but an increasing number of colleges are both knowledgeable and supportive. Such schools often have special programs under headings such as Learning Support Services, Student Disability Services, or Special Services.

Students and their families should gather all appropriate documents relating to the student's disabilities, including diagnoses and results of tests and evaluations by physicians, psychologists, and educators, including copies of INDIVIDUALIZED EDUCATION PROGRAMS (IEPs), which some colleges require as a prerequisite for providing special services. Students should also outline the kinds of special services they think they need. Among the possibilities are:

- Priority scheduling, often allowing special students to select their courses before the main registration, to allow for more control of timing, spacing, and length of class.
- Reduced course loads, allowing special students to take fewer courses than usual to maximize the time they can spend on those selected. A reduced course load, however, can affect FINANCIAL AID, depending on the school, and can require increasing the time spent in college, either through summer school or additional semesters.
- Special test arrangements, such as allowing special students to take examinations in smaller test areas, with fewer distractions; providing scribes for students with difficulty in writing; and offering untimed tests.
- Note-takers and tutors, people who can assist special students in taking notes during classes, preparing assignments, and studying and reviewing.
- Single rooms, arranging for special students to live singly, rather than with a roommate, which reduces distraction, though it may have the unwanted effect of being somewhat isolating.

In addition, many schools offer special classes, such as developmental math or English, time management, and study skills, as well as orientation programs specifically designed for students with disabilities, counseling centers, additional diagnostic testing, and campus advocates to explain problems to faculty members.

Special students can sometimes, formally or informally, arrange for other accommodations, such as sitting in the front of the room, using a calculator, using a laptop computer for note-taking and coursework, having drafts of papers evaluated by a professor or editor before completion, recording lectures for later relistening, ordering textbooks on tape from Recordings for the Blind (which requires considerable advance planning; see EYE AND VISION PROBLEMS), arranging for more time in completing assignments or taking exams, or taking exams in short segments.

Language-Related Learning Disabilities: Their Nature and Treatment. Adele Gerber. P. H. Brookes, 1992.

Learning about Learning Disabilities. Bernice Y. Wong, ed. Academic Press, 1991.

The Reading Brain: The Biological Basis of Dyslexia. Drake D. Duane and David B. Gray, eds. York Press, 1991.

(See also BRAIN AND BRAIN DISORDERS; COMMUNICATION SKILLS AND DISORDERS; ATTENTION DEFICIT HYPERACTIVITY DISORDER; READING.)

learning readiness skill, an alternate term for PREREQUISITE, in the sense of a simpler skill that is regarded as fundamental to the mastering of a more complex, higher-level skill. Such skills are sometimes measured on various READINESS TESTS.

learning style, the way a child most readily receives and processes new information. Learning style is a general term used in many different ways, depending on how educators and psychologists themselves approach the question; it is also called *cognitive style.*

A child who tends to first grasp a concept and then focus on the parts or supporting details may be classified as an *analytic learner*; at the opposite pole would be a *synthetic learner,* who learns best when presented with various aspects or parts of a skill or concept, and then moves on to the general.

Sometimes discussions of learning style focus on the SENSORY MODES OR MODALITIES a child uses to receive and process information most efficiently and easily. An acronym often used for these modes is VAKT, for *visual, auditory, kinesthetic,* and *tactile.* Sometimes the term *haptic*

Learning Styles

Sometimes the term "learning styles" refers to the way in which material is taught or presented and is used as a synonym for *educational approach*. If a parent or teacher lectures while a child sits and listens, what results is *passive learning*. By contrast, when a child is doing something, such as building a model or conducting an experiment and in the process is using a variety of sensory modes, the result is *activity learning*. If the parent or teacher presents a general rule and then has students learn to recognize or work with that rule in specific situations, the result is *expository learning* or *deductive learning*. Conversely, if the child is given information or materials on a number of specific situations and is asked to draw general conclusions, the result is *discovery learning, inductive learning,* sometimes *experiential learning,* or (if the emphasis is on independent problem-solving) *heuristic learning*.

When the student primarily memorizes material, without necessarily understanding it in context, it is called *rote learning*. But when the focus is on relating new information to prior knowledge, the result is *associative learning*. When the information is carefully structured with ever-more-difficult tasks building on earlier material, it is called *sequential learning*.

Concepts and skills acquired in daily life without specific instruction result from what is called *trial-and-error learning* or (if the focus is on learning from the experience of others) *vicarious learning*. Conscious use of these skills, expecting that a child will imitate the teacher, is sometimes called *modeling*.

CLUES

VISUAL

- Needs to see it to know it.
- Strong sense of color.
- May have artistic ability.
- Difficulty with spoken directions.
- Overreaction to sounds.
- Trouble following lectures.
- Misinterpretation of words.

AUDITORY

- Prefers to get information by listening — needs to hear it to know it.
- Difficulty following written directions.
- Difficulty with reading.
- Problems with writing.

LEARNING TIPS

- Use of graphics to reinforce learning— films, slides, illustrations, diagrams, doodles.
- Color coding to organize notes and possessions.
- Written directions.
- Use of flow charts and diagrams for note-taking.
- Visualizing spelling of words or facts to be memorized.
- Inability to read body language and facial expressions.
- Use of tapes for reading and for class and lecture notes.
- Learning by interviewing or by participating in discussions.
- Having test questions or directions read aloud or put on tape.

HAPTIC

- Prefers hands-on learning.
- Can assemble parts without reading directions.
- Difficulty sitting still.
- Learns better when physical activity is involved.
- May be very well coordinated and has athletic ability.
- Experiential learning (making models, doing lab work, and role playing).
- Frequent breaks in study periods.
- Tracing letters and words to learn spelling and remember facts.
- Use of computer to reinforce learning through sense of touch.
- Memorizing or drilling while walking or exercising.
- Expressing abilities through dance, drama, or gymnastics.

is used to refer to physical, hands-on learning, in a sense combining kinesthetic and tactile. Children (and adults) can use various of these modes for learning, a process often called *integration.* But some kinds of learning focus on some modes more than others, and children with DISABILITIES, including LEARNING DISABILITIES, may not be able to use some modes as well as others. LEARNING STYLES (on page 367) describes some of the main characteristics of these styles of learning, and offers some tips for helping children learn more easily. The MONTESSORI METHOD uses materials designed to increase the child's use of all the sensory modes, in what is called *sensory education.*

FOR HELP AND FURTHER INFORMATION

Alliance for Parental Involvement in Education (ALLPIE), 518–392–6900. Publishes *In Their Own Way: Discovering and Encouraging Your Child's Personal Learning Style, You Are Your Child's First Teacher.* (For full group information, see HELP ON LEARNING AND EDUCATION on page 659).

OTHER RESOURCES

Teaching Young Children Through Their Individual Learning Styles: Practical Approaches for Grades K–2. Rita S. Dunn and others. Allyn, 1994.

You Are Smarter Than You Think: A Practical Guide to Academic Success Using Your Personal Learning Style. Renee Mollan-Masters. Reality Productions, 1992.

(See also EDUCATION; Subscribers to the America Online computer service can find general advice on teaching and specific activities for helping young children with learning problems, in the Moms Online Desk Reference section of Moms Online, under "Teaching Young Children.")

least restrictive environment (LRE), specification that children with DISABILITIES should be educated in the most natural, most integrated, least inhibiting school setting possible and that they should to the extent possible be educated in the same settings as children without disabilities, as mandated by in the EDUCATION FOR ALL HANDICAPPED CHILDREN ACT and its successor, the INDIVIDUALS WITH DISABILITIES ACT. LRE is a key concept in MAINSTREAMING, designed to maximize the social and cultural contacts of children with disabilities, as well as their growth and independence.

lefthanded, a type of HANDEDNESS in which a person relies more heavily on and is more easy and proficient at using the left hand than the right.

Lesch-Nyhan syndrome, a rare GENETIC DISORDER of the X-LINKED, RECESSIVE type, only recognized in the early 1960s, involving a deficiency of HGPRT enzyme (*hypoxanthine-guanine-phosphoribosyltransferase*). Lacking this enzyme, the body is unable to break down and use a group of compounds called *purines,* some of which are produced naturally in the body, while others result as a byproduct of the digestion of PROTEINS. In a mild form, the syndrome might produce gout. But in its most severe form, it is characterized by MENTAL RETARDATION, impaired kidney (renal) function, abnormal physical development, CHOREA (jerky, fidgeting movements), ATHETOSIS (slow, writhing movements), SPASTICITY (increasing rigidity of the muscles), and most strikingly, SELF-MUTILATION, in which the child compulsively bites away lips and fingers. No treatment is yet known, and most children with the syndrome die before PUBERTY.

FOR HELP AND FURTHER INFORMATION

National Arthritis and Musculoskeletal and Skin Diseases Information Clearinghouse (NAMSIC), 301–495–4484. (For full group information, see ARTHRITIS.)

National Institute of Neurological Disorders and Stroke (NINDS), 800–352–9424. (For full group information, see BRAIN AND BRAIN DISORDERS.)

National Institute of Mental Health (NIMH), 301–443–4513. (For full group information, see MENTAL DISORDERS.)

National Organization for Rare Disorders (NORD), 800–999–6673. (For full group information, see RARE DISORDERS.)

(See also GENETIC DISORDERS; X-LINKED; RECESSIVE.)

lesion, a general term for an abnormality anywhere in or on the body, due to injury or disease, including a wound, an injury, a TUMOR, a change in body tissue, a sore, or a rash.

leukemia, a form of CANCER that involves unchecked production of white blood cells in the BONE MARROW. These gradually crowd out the red blood cells and platelets required for health, leading to severe ANEMIA and hemorrhages (see BLOOD AND BLOOD DISORDERS). Leukemia is the most common cause of cancer deaths in children ages one through fourteen, accounting for one-third of all such deaths in the United States. Childhood leukemia often develops rapidly and, if untreated, can cause death within weeks or months. But a variety of drugs are used to try to halt the process, producing REMISSIONS and sometimes full cures.

If relapses occur, physicians may consider a BONE MARROW TRANSPLANT, though the operation is risky and finding a donor with matching bone marrow is difficult. As with cancer in general, the causes of leukemia are obscure, though some forms may be triggered by a virus or by ENVIRONMENTAL HAZARDS such as radiation or individual cancer-causing chemicals (*carcinogens*). People with some GENETIC DISORDERS or CHROMOSOMAL ABNORMALITIES, such as DOWN SYNDROME, are at increased risk for leukemia.

FOR HELP AND FURTHER INFORMATION

Leukemia Society of America
600 Third Avenue, 4th Floor
New York, NY 10016
212–573–8484; 800–955–4LSA [955–4572]
Fax: 212–856–9686
Jerry Valez, Executive Director
Organization concerned with leukemia, lymphomas, and multiple myelomas; provides financial aid, transportation, and other services; acts as advocate; provides information; publishes various materials, including bimonthly *Society News* and *What it is that I have, don't want, didn't ask for, can't give back, and how I feel about it* (for teens on handling feelings).

Children's Leukemia Research Association
585 Steward Avenue, Suite 536
Garden City, NY 11530
516–222–1944
Fax: 516–222–0457
Organization that seeks to combat leukemia, formerly the National Leukemia Association; funds research; supplies financial aid to needy families to meet heavy expenses of leukemia treatment; applications should be send to Patient Aid Director with letter of diagnosis from attending physician.

American Cancer Society (ACS), 800–227–2345. Publishes *Facts about Leukemia* and *Why, Charlie Brown, Why?* for children. (For full group information, see CANCER.)

National Cancer Institute (NCI), 800–422–6237. (For full group information, see CANCER.)

National Organization for Rare Disorders (NORD), 800–999–6673. (For full group information, see RARE DISORDERS.)

OTHER RESOURCES

General works

Childhood Leukaemia: The Facts. John S. Lilleyman. Oxford University Press, 1994.
Young People with Cancer: A Handbook for Parents. Diane, 1992.
Fight the Good Fight. Philip Bedsworth and Joyce Bedsworth. Herald, 1991.
Understanding Leukemia. Cynthia P. Margolies and Kenneth B. McCredie. Macmillan, 1990.

For children

Leukemia. Dorothy S. Siegel and David E. Newton. Watts, 1994.
One Day at a Time: Children Living with Leukemia. Thomas Bergman. Gareth Stevens, 1990.

For preteens and teens

Leukemia. Judy Monroe. Crestwood/Macmillan, 1990.

Personal experiences

Life's Blood: A Story of Medical Science and Human Courage. Madeline Marget. Simon & Schuster, 1992. On her sister's fight against leukemia.
Looking Down from the Mountain Top: The Story of One Woman's Fight Against All Odds. Christine Michael. Spirit of Success, 1992.
Borrowed Blood: Victory over Leukemia. Shawn S. Riley. Lion Press and Vid, 1991.
Not Today, God. Mary F. Hinson. Vantage, 1990.
Eric. Doris Lund. Dell, 1976. Mother's story of son with leukemia.

(See also CANCER, including information on chemotherapy; BLOOD AND BLOOD DISORDERS; BONE MARROW; BONE MARROW TRANSPLANT; HOSPITAL; HOSPICE; DEATH AND DYING; also HELP FOR SPECIAL CHILDREN, on page 689, under "On wishes for terminally or chronically ill children.")

liberal arts, traditionally, the courses that made up the classical CURRICULUM, such as literature, art, philosophy, history, music, and foreign languages, usually referring to COLLEGE level education. Today the term is more widely used to refer to a broad, general, "liberal" education, including study of the humanities, the social sciences, and the sciences, as opposed to a narrowly specialized, vocationally oriented education.

lice, small, parasitic insects that feed on blood, causing an infestation called *pediculosis.* In humans, there are three main kinds of infestations:

- Affecting the head: *pediculosis capitis,* or infestation with the head lice *Pediculus humanus capitis.*
- Affecting the body: *pediculosis corporus,* or infestation with the body lice Pediculus humanus corporus.
- Affecting the pubic area: *pediculosis pubis,* or infestation with the pubic lice *Phthirus pubis,* a condition commonly called crabs.

Lice (singular: louse) are found in all parts of the world, including in every social strata of the United States, but most commonly in areas where people are crowded together. Lice infestation does not necessarily imply poor hygiene; rather it results from direct contact with other people or things infested with lice, which crawl (not jump or fly) from one place to another. In northerly areas of North America, infestation occurs seasonally, peaking around September, but in the South and West it occurs year-round, peaking around November. For unknown reasons, African-Americans are less likely than others to be affected, and girls are somewhat more likely to get lice than boys, perhaps because they often have longer hair, giving them more exposure.

The main effect of having lice is itching (*pruritis*), which increases as the lice rapidly multiply, laying as many as 300 eggs (*nits*) a month, which themselves hatch in seven to ten days. The intense itching makes people feel "lousy," a word drawn from the condition, and can result also in secondary bacterial infection. In crowded areas, especially in wartime or in poor populations, body lice can spread serious diseases such as typhus and plague. Some people have suggested the possibility that lice could carry AIDS, but there is no evidence of such transmission. In fact, for many children today, lice—however unattractive—may not be as dangerous as some treatments used to kill them.

Among children, head lice are most common, and if a school or other gathering place is infested, they are hard to avoid. But it is worth trying, since lice can be picked up and spread widely before they are recognized. In general, parents should warn children not to borrow or exchange any personal gear, especially combs, brushes, hair ribbons, barrettes, hats, and scarves, and not sit so close to others that their heads touch, especially during "lice alerts." If possible, they should hang their hats and coats separately from those of others; it is worth checking in a nursery, school, or meeting place to see if a separate hook or locker is available for each child, rather than having clothes of several children hung atop one another. If separate storage places are not available, children should hang their coats on the backs of their chairs, with hats and scarves stored in the sleeves. Children should not wear clothing retrieved from a lost-and-found area until it has been washed and should not try on clothing of unknown history, such as a scarf picked up on the street or a hat tried on in a store. Helmets and other sporting equipment should either be assigned to individuals and stored separately or washed between uses. The same is true of earphones or headphones, including those in music stores. Children should not share pillows, blankets, or sleeping bags; at preschools or elementary schools, where young children take naps, their individual mats and other items should be stored separately, not piled together. Also to be avoided are sharing of wigs, costumes, and stuffed animals that might harbor lice.

Many schools routinely check for lice at the start of the school year and periodically thereafter. Generally, any child found to have lice is sent home for treatment. (Subscribers to the America Online computer service can find "What to Do If You Suspect Your Child Has Head Lice" in the Moms Online Desk Reference section of Moms Online, under "lice.") If lice infestation is widespread, a school may close for the day, during which all children will be treated at home, whether or not they are known to have lice, while the school itself is thoroughly cleaned and deinfested. Unfortunately, that takes a high degree of cooperation among all involved. Recognition of a lice infestation is also complicated because many people are ill-informed about both identification and treatment. It is important that administration and parents not become panicky or hysterical and not treat the children as "guilty" in some way, but rather deal calmly with the problem, respecting the children's feelings.

Pubic hair is also commonly infested with lice, a condition popularly called *crabs.* Pubic lice are generally spread by sexual contact, and so are considered a SEXUALLY TRANSMITTED DISEASE, though they can also be spread by contact with infested clothing or bedding. The main symptoms are itching; scratching should be avoided, if possible, since that may spread lice elsewhere on the body. The lice and their tiny white eggs (*nits*) can be diagnosed by sight under a microscope. Various lotions and shampoos are available to kill pubic lice; however, pregnant women should use no such products without consulting a doctor. Itching may persist for a time afterward, until the SKIN heals. Any clothing or bedding that has been in contact with an infected person should be dry cleaned or washed in very hot water (125°F). Once off the body, pubic lice die within 24 hours, but eggs can live for up to 6 days. (See SEXUALLY TRANSMITTED DISEASES; also WHAT CAN YOU (OR YOUR CHILD) DO TO AVOID SEXUALLY TRANSMITTED DISEASES? on page 541.)

FOR HELP AND FURTHER INFORMATION

National Pediculosis Association (NPA)
P.O. Box 149
Newton, Massachusetts 02161
617–449-NITS [449–6487]
Organization concerned with lice infestation; publishes newsletter *Progress.*

OTHER RESOURCES

The Lice-Buster Book: What to Do When Your Child Comes Home with Head Lice. Lennie Copeland. Authentic Pictures, 1995.

Barney Barks about Head Lice. Video produced by Smith Kline Beecham. Modern Talking Picture Service.

lie, in PREGNANCY, a general term for whether the FETUS is *longitudinal* (up-and-down) or transverse (horizontal) in the UTERUS. (See FETAL PRESENTATION.)

lien, a legal claim on someone's property to prevent sale or transfer until a debt is satisfied. In certain cases, for example, to satisfy unpaid CHILD SUPPORT, the property may be sold to pay off the debt.

Lincoln-Oseretsky Motor Development Scale, a type of individually administered TEST to assess the development of MOTOR SKILLS in children and adolescents, more specifically fine and gross motor skills, finger dexterity and speed, and EYE-HAND COORDINATION. The test's thirty-six tasks include such activities as walking backwards, catching a ball, winding a thread, tapping with feet and fingers, and balancing on tiptoe while opening and closing hands. NORMS for test results are given for both sexes for ages six through fourteen, with PERCENTILES. (See TESTS.)

linea nigra, a dark streak that sometimes develops between a woman's NAVEL and pubic area during PREGNANCY, later fading away.

lipid storage diseases (lipidoses), a group of METABOLIC DISORDERS in which abnormal amounts of FATS, or *lipids*, are stored in the body. Fats are found in almost all of the body's cells. When these cells are ready to be routinely replaced, certain substances called *enzymes* normally help break down the worn-out cells, with each enzyme acting on a different part of the lipid molecule. But in some people, an inherited defect keeps the body from producing any or enough of a particular enzyme, so lipids that are normally broken down instead accumulate in various of the body's tissues, causing PROGRESSIVE damage, sometimes including MENTAL RETARDATION, enlarged SPLEEN and liver, bone degeneration, and even death.

The abnormal fat accumulation is often named for the missing deficient enzyme; in Gaucher's disease, for example, the defective enzyme is *glucocerebrosidase*, and the fat that accumulates is called *glucocerebroside*. Some forms of lipid storage disease show themselves in infancy, but others do not appear until later childhood or adulthood.

Lipid storage diseases are generally rare, but among the more common ones so far been identified are:

- *Gaucher's disease* (*glucosyl cerebroside lipidosis*), the most common of the lipid storage diseases; the adult form affects perhaps 20,000 people in the United States. The main symptoms are enlarged spleen and liver, eroded bones, and mental retardation or MENTAL DISORDERS, as fats are stored in the brain. The most common form, Type I, does not have mental or neurological involvement. The most severe form (Type II or the *acute infantile neuronopathic form*) strikes in infancy, producing major neurological damage and an enlarged spleen, and usually brings death within one to two years. Type III, the *juvenile form*, generally strikes later in childhood, progresses more slowly, and involves less neurological damage. Children with Gaucher's who survive to adolescence may live for many years. The most common and least severe form of Gaucher's disease is Type III, the *adult chronic nonneuronopathic form*, which produces enlarged spleen and liver and eroded bones, but does not involve neurological damage.
- *Fabry's disease* (*angiokeratoma corporis diffusum universale* or *alpha-galactosidase deficiency*), which affects about 2,000 people in the United States, mostly males. Symptoms include skin abnormalities (*angiokeratomas*), opacity of the cornea, episodes of FEVER, and burning pain in the extremities.
- *Tay-Sachs disease* (*GM2 gangliosidosis*), which strikes infants, usually around the age of six months, bringing physical and mental retardation, PARALYSIS, blindness, DEMENTIA, and generally death by ages three or four, as fats (*gangliosides*) accumulate in the brain. Because of public education and PRENATAL TESTS, the rate of Tay-Sachs disease has been much reduced. Only recently, a new form of late-onset Tay-Sachs has been discovered in older children or adolescents; common symptoms are ATAXIA, DYSARTHRIA, night leg muscle cramps, and muscle atrophy, so it has often been misdiagnosed as a muscular or neurological disorder. A related variant of Tay-Sachs is *Sandhoff's disease*.
- *Generalized (GM2) gangliosidosis*, in which the gangliosides accumulate in the NERVOUS SYSTEM, often bringing death by age two.
- *Niemann-Pick disease* (*sphingomyelin lipidosis*), in which sphingomyelin accumulates in the BONE MARROW, spleen, and lymph nodes. The disorder may appear at different ages and with varying severity, involving an enlarged spleen and liver and some mental retardation, but often brings death within a few years.
- *Krabbe's disease* (*globoid leukodystrophy*), involving a deficiency of *galactocerebroside ß-galactosidase*, which leads to progressive physical and mental retardation, paralysis, blindness, deafness, and death in infancy.
- *Metachromatic leukodystrophy* (*sulfatide lipidosis*), in which a deficiency of the enzyme *cerebroside sulfatase* causes accumulation of fats in the CENTRAL NERVOUS SYSTEM, kidney, and spleen. Apparent by about age two, it generally brings progressive paralysis and dementia until death by about age ten.

Among other rare lipid storage diseases are *fucosidosis*, *Farber's disease*, *Wolman's disease* (*acid cholesteryl ester hydrolase deficiency*), *cholesteryl ester storage disease*, *cerebrotendinous xanthomatosis* (*van Bogaert's disease*), *ß-sitosterolemia and xanthomatosis*, and *Refsum's syndrome* (*phytanic acid storage disease*).

Lipid storage diseases are GENETIC DISORDERS, almost all of them so far identified being of the AUTOSOMAL RECESSIVE type, in which an affected child inherits a defective gene from both parents, who may be unaffected CARRIERS. Of the known lipid storage diseases, Fabry's disease is the exception, being an X-LINKED disorder, passed on to a son by a carrier mother.

Most lipid storage diseases first appear in infancy and show themselves in retarded physical and mental skills. Diagnosis is often confirmed by a BLOOD TEST that measures the enzymes active in the white blood cells and by a CULTURE of the skin cells, in which the enzyme activity can be measured. These techniques can also be used as GENETIC SCREENING tests to detect carriers. Parents with any family history of lipid storage diseases should seek GENETIC COUNSELING, especially those whose ancestry is Ashkenazi Jewish, from Central and Eastern Europe, since several of the lipid storage diseases are found predominantly among people of this background. The same people may also want to consider prenatal tests, such as AMNIOCENTESIS or CHORIONIC VILLUS SAMPLING, to see if a FETUS has a lipid storage defect. Tests and screening have sharply reduced the number of children born with lipid storage diseases, especially Tay-Sachs disease.

For the children and adults already living with lipid storage diseases, often no therapy exists, other than attempting to minimize pain and other symptoms. Several promising approaches are being explored, however. One is *enzyme replacement therapy*, in which healthy enzymes taken from the PLACENTA of newborns are injected into the bloodstream to replace or supplement the person's defective enzymes. But problems exist with obtaining enough purified enzymes and directing them to the places where they are needed. Another approach is BONE MARROW TRANSPLANT, a risky, expensive form of treatment. Genetic engineering researchers are also attempting to find ways to create and insert healthy replacement genes, to create the missing enzymes, but considerable work remains to be done on this experimental *gene therapy.*

FOR HELP AND FURTHER INFORMATION

National Institute of Neurological Disorders and Stroke (NINDS), 800–352–9424. Publishes fact sheet *Lipid Storage Diseases.* (For full group information, see BRAIN AND BRAIN DISORDERS.)

National Tay-Sachs and Allied Diseases Association (NTSAD)
2001 Beacon Street
Brookline, MA 02146
617–277–4463; 800–90-NTSAD [906–8723]
Fax: 617–277–0134
Organization concerned with Tay-Sachs or related diseases, including Gaucher disease, Krabbe disease, Niemann-Pick disease, and Sandhoff disease; sponsors mutual-support groups; provides information and referrals; publishes various materials, including newsletter *Breakthrough, What Every Family Should Know, Services to Families, Tay Sachs Is...,* and *One Day at a Time.*

National Digestive Disease Information Clearinghouse (NDDIC), 301–654–3810. (For full group information, see DIGESTIVE SYSTEM AND DISORDERS.)

National Maternal and Child Health Clearinghouse (NMCHC), 703–821–8955. (For full group information, see PREGNANCY.)

National Foundation for Jewish Genetic Diseases (NFJGD), 212–371–1030. (For full group information, see GENETIC DISORDERS.)

March of Dimes Birth Defects Foundation (MDBDF), 914–428–7100. Publishes information sheet *Tay-Sachs.* (For full group information, see BIRTH DEFECTS.)

National Organization for Rare Disorders (NORD), 800–999–6673. (For full group information, see RARE DISORDERS.)

(See also GENETIC DISORDERS; GENETIC COUNSELING.)

literacy, the ability to read and write, but more specifically the ability to read, write, and calculate at above an eighth-grade level, which is considered the minimum for an adult to operate effectively in modern society. Someone who is unable to do so is termed *functionally illiterate.* In recent years, the term has been extended to new fields. People who can readily work with computers, for instance, are called *computer literate*—a term that applies to many young children, although sometimes their parents are *computer illiterates.* (See ILLITERACY; READING; WRITING.)

liver and liver problems, an internal organ in the upper right abdomen and the problems affecting it. The liver has hundreds of functions, mainly to produce key PROTEINS and other chemicals, to regulate the chemistry of the blood, to store the sugar GLUCOSE as glycogen until needed, and to clear drugs, poisons, and other unwanted substances from the blood. The liver receives one-quarter of the blood pumped at each beat of the heart, an indication of its central role and position in the body. Blood also flows in from the intestines and spleen, carrying nutrients such as glucose and FATS, which are used by and stored in the liver. The liver also produces a liquid called *bile* that flows through tubes called *bile ducts* into the *hepatic duct* and on into the *gallbladder,* a smaller sac-like organ below the liver; this bile is concentrated and released into the intestines to aid in digestion. Both blood and bile carry away waste products and other substances.

Among the waste products carried by bile is *bilirubin,* a yellowish pigment, the remains of "retired" red blood cells. If the liver is malfunctioning, an excess amount of bilirubin builds up in the blood, a condition called *hyperbilirubinemia.* By the time bilirubin has reached double the normal amount, it normally shows in a pattern of symptoms called *jaundice,* a yellowish discoloration of the skin, mucus membrane, and whites of the eyes. Jaundice is a common early sign of liver disease or problems with associated bile ducts; diagnostic tests to determine the cause of the problem are important, because the consequences can be extremely serious.

In *hemolytic jaundice,* the liver is unable to handle the amount of bilirubin produced by the body, as in cases of hemolytic ANEMIA. Newborns often have this kind of jaundice, which gradually clears up as the body matures. Traditionally, babies have been treated with lights (*phototherapy*) to reduce their bilirubin levels; however these require the baby to be undressed and to wear eye patches (to protect against the bright light) and can be difficult to administer at home. A more recent approach is the *bili blanket,* which uses fiber optic technology to deliver light to the baby. The bili blanket is wrapped around the baby's body, which is then wrapped in a normal blanket, leaving the baby free from eye patches and able to be held and fed without hindrance. Jaundice also occurs in some infants temporarily during BREASTFEEDING, in a condition called *breast milk jaundice.*

Unchecked bilirubin buildup can have serious effects in the body. In a condition called *kernicterus,* large excess amounts can accumulate, causing widespread damage to the brain and other parts of the body, including MENTAL RETARDATION, CEREBRAL PALSY, EAR AND HEARING PROBLEMS, some EYE AND VISION PROBLEMS, and sometimes death. Because of this, it is important to identify the cause of the buildup of bilirubin as soon as possible.

Jaundice can also indicate blockage that keeps bile from exiting the liver, in what is called *obstructive jaundice.* Some infants are born with a condition called *biliary atresia,* which involves absence or malformation of the bile ducts. Causes for the disorder are unclear, but some bile duct damage may be caused by viral infection near birth. Symptoms generally appear two to six weeks after birth, and include jaundice and a swollen abdomen. The actual diagnosis may be made by ULTRASOUND, X-RAYS, and other radioactive scanning devices, along with BLOOD TESTS, URINE TESTS, and LIVER FUNCTION TESTS. These help distinguish biliary atresia from a case of *hepatitis,* or inflammation of the liver (see discussion below). About half of the cases of biliary atresia are treatable by surgery. The *Kasai procedure,* or *hepatoportoenterostomy,* involves removing damaged bile ducts and creating artificial bypass ducts from the baby's intestine. For other children with biliary atresia, however, such as those whose damaged ducts are inside the liver, a liver TRANSPLANT at present offers the only hope for long-term survival. More than half the children awaiting liver transplants have biliary atresia.

In *hepatocellular jaundice,* buildup of bilirubin results from inflammation of the liver, as in severe cases of *hepatitis* or more generalized failure of the liver. Whatever the condition causing the jaundice, if it goes unchecked, it will destroy the liver and eventually cause death.

Among the main results of unchecked liver problems is *cirrhosis of the liver,* which is scarring of the liver, as fibrous tissue replaces damaged liver cells. This gradually blocks blood flow within the liver and causes liver cells to die. Most people think of cirrhosis in connection with ALCOHOL ABUSE or DRUG ABUSE, problems rare in young children, though found among some adolescents. But cirrhosis can also result from many other causes, including infectious diseases such as hepatitis, inherited METABOLIC DISORDERS, such as ALPHA 1-ANTITRYPSIN DEFICIENCY and GALACTOSEMIA, and other disorders such as CYSTIC FIBROSIS and HEART PROBLEMS, as well as some medications and ENVIRONMENTAL HAZARDS. If such causes are identified and treated early, the scarring process can be arrested.

Early warning signs of cirrhosis include mild jaundice, EDEMA (collection of fluid in body tissues), and VOMITING of blood. Routine blood tests or liver function tests may sometimes suggest cirrhosis, a diagnosis that can be confirmed by a liver BIOPSY, a painful and risky procedure. More recently, new blood tests have been developed to detect and monitor the amount of liver scarring, though their long-term RELIABILITY remains to be seen. If cirrhosis is not recognized early enough or if the scarring process cannot be halted, the result is a series of ever-more-serious complications, including massive hemorrhaging, damage to other organs, notably the kidneys, and eventually COMA and death, if a liver transplant is not available or a transplant fails.

Among the main causes of cirrhosis is infection in the liver, or *hepatitis,* often signaled by jaundice. The infection can be either ACUTE—short and limited, though perhaps severe—or CHRONIC, then leading to cirrhosis and liver failure. Hepatitis is often caused by a one of several viruses, the two most common being types A and B.

Hepatitis A—also called *infectious* or *epidemic hepatitis* or *Type A viral hepatitis*—can affect people of any age, but is most common among children between five and fourteen years of age. It is often a relatively mild infection, though it can be severe, even leading to COMA and death, especially in older people. Common symptoms include fatigue, nausea, VOMITING, dark urine, light-colored stool, and pain in the liver, although children under age two may have few or no symptoms. Approximately half the patients have fever; many older children have DIARRHEA; many adults develop jaundice. LIVER FUNCTION TESTS are generally elevated. Hepatitis A infection is largely preventable by good hygiene, since it is passed mainly through direct contact with infected people or contaminated food and water, as in CHILD CARE facilities, household or sexual contact with an infected person, or exposure in areas of poor sanitation. Young people who contract hepatitis A generally recover fully and are thereafter immune. A new vaccine for Hepatitis A approved in 1995 was tested primarily on children, given in an initial dose and a booster six to twelve months later. Its long-term effectiveness remains to be seen.

Hepatitis B—*type B viral hepatitis* or *serum hepatitis*—is generally more serious, often becoming chronic, and is linked with a 200-fold increased risk of liver CANCER. In severe cases, cirrhosis and eventual liver failure occur. Sometimes the initial symptoms are not severe, and the disease is not recognized until the liver has already been damaged. The type B hepatitis virus is spread by contact with infected blood, saliva, semen, and other body fluids, as through blood transfusions, shared intravenous drug or ear-piercing needles, and sex, and as such is regarded as a type of SEXUALLY TRANSMITTED DISEASE. Not everyone exposed to the type B virus contracts hepatitis and many unaffected people are unknowing CARRIERS. Some 300,000 people are infected annually in the United States alone, most of them people in their teens and twenties. Because of the danger from hepatitis B, a vaccine against it (given in three shots) is strongly recommended for anyone who is exposed to body fluids, such as health care workers or substance abusers, and for anyone who is sexually active with multiple partners. Centers for Disease Control guidelines have for some years recommended the vaccine for all young adults, among whom infection is most widespread. More recently, it has been recommended for younger children, as well, starting in infancy. The 1995 guidelines call for a series of three injections: at birth, at one to two months, and at six months; or at one to two months, four months, and six to eighteen months (see IMMUNIZATION). Experimental research with a drug that stops the hepatitis B virus from reproducing has shown promising results.

Babies can catch hepatitis B if their mothers are carriers. While mostly protected in the UTERUS, they are exposed to the virus during CHILDBIRTH and through later contact, especially BREASTFEEDING. Many such cases of *neonatal hepatitis* can be prevented by administration of hepatitis B immune globulin and hepatitis B vaccine immediately after birth. Pregnant women at high risk for exposure to the virus, such as health care workers, are advised to have screening for the type B virus. Hepatitis B patients who require a liver transplant may also be given immune globulin, to lessen the likelihood that the new liver will be affected.

A vaccine has also recently been developed against hepatitis C, formerly called non-A, non-B hepatitis. In early use, the drug interferon has also been found effective in treating this previously untreatable disease, and also in treating hepatitis B. Interferon produces cures in a small proportion of patients, reduces severity of the infection, and produces remissions in perhaps half of those treated.

Children or adults may also experience *cholangitis*, inflammation of the bile duct. The most common form is *acute ascending cholangitis*, which generally involves bacterial infection in the bile duct, often because of blockage, as by a gallstone, TUMOR, or worm infestation. Mild cases can be treated with ANTIBIOTICS, but serious cases may require surgery, as they can lead to severe, even life-threatening liver problems, kidney problems (see KIDNEY AND UROLOGICAL PROBLEMS), and blood poisoning, or septicemia (see BLOOD AND BLOOD DISORDERS). A rarer form, *sclerosing chiolangitis*, involves narrowing of the bile ducts and progressive liver damage. So far no treatment has been developed for this condition, except for a liver transplant. Doctors may use liver function tests, an ultrasound scan, or ENDOSCOPY to help diagnose cholangitis.

Children may experience various other kinds of problems with the liver. Inherited abnormalities may cause the liver to malfunction, as in GLYCOGEN STORAGE DISEASES and WILSON'S DISEASE, as can disorders in the body's IMMUNE SYSTEM. Ailments of even more complicated or obscure origin may also affect the liver, including REYE SYNDROME. Acute or chronic hepatitis can also result from damage to the liver by some drugs, chemicals, or poisons.

Many people are awaiting transplants, and some may die because of a shortage of organ donations. For these and others with progressive liver damage, some hope is offered in experiments being done on transplanting livers of other mammals, notably baboons, into humans. Researchers have also developed an artificial liver grown from clones of human liver cells, which is in the early stages of testing. In some cases, also, a person may be saved by donation of only part of a liver. In one highly publicized recent case, a mother saved her young child by donating a section of her liver, which then grew.

FOR HELP AND FURTHER INFORMATION

American Liver Foundation (ALF)
1425 Pompton Avenue
Cedar Grove, NJ 07009–1000
201–256–2550; 800–223–0179
Fax: 201–256–3214
Alan P Brownstein, Chief Executive Officer
Organization concerned with liver diseases; encourages formation of support groups; acts as advocate; supports research; provides information and referrals; operates Gift of Life Organ Donor Program; publishes quarterly newsletter *Progress.*

Children's Liver Foundation (CLF)
76 South Orange Avenue, Suite 202
South Orange, NJ 07079
201–761–1111
Maxine Turon, President
Organization concerned with liver disease in children; provides support for children and their families; seeks to educate public and acts as advocate for children with liver disease; fosters research; publishes various materials, including quarterly newsletter *CLF Lifeline, Your Child Has Been Diagnosed as Having a Liver Disorder: How Do You Cope?, What Common Liver Deficiency Spares Some Children, Dooms Many Others? Alpha–1 Antitrypsin (a1AT), What Kills Children at Higher Rate Than Childhood Leukemia?,* and *What Liver-Destroying Illness in Children May Respond Well to Bold Drug Therapy?*

American Academy of Pediatrics (AAP), 800–433–9016. Publishes brochure *Hepatitis B: What Parents Need to Know, Hepatitis B Fact Sheet.* (For full group information, see HEALTH CARE.)

National Digestive Disease Information Clearinghouse (NDDIC), 301–654–3810. (For full group information, see DIGESTIVE SYSTEM AND DISORDERS.)

National Clearinghouse for Alcohol and Drug Abuse Information (NCADI), 301–468–2600. Publishes *Alcohol and the Liver.* (For full group information, see HELP AGAINST SUBSTANCE ABUSE on page 703).

National Cancer Institute (NCI), 800–422–6237. Publishes *In Answer to Your Questions About Liver Cancer.* (For full group information, see CANCER.)

Biliary Atresia and Liver Transplant Network
3835 Richmond Avenue, Box 190
Staten Island, NY 10312
Network offering support and information to families of children with biliary atresia.

National Foundation for Infectious Diseases (NFID), 301–656–0003. Publishes *Hepatitis A: Q & A.* (For full group information, see CHICKEN POX.)

American Social Health Association (ASHA), 800–227–8922. Publishes *Hepatitis B: The Sexually Transmitted Disease with No Cure.* (For full group information, see SEXUALLY TRANSMITTED DISEASES.)

National Organization for Rare Disorders (NORD), 800–999–6673. (For full group information, see RARE DISORDERS.)

The Arc, 817–261–6003. Publishes *Facts About Hepatitis B.* (For full group information, see MENTAL RETARDATION.)

Agency for Health Care Policy and Research Clearinghouse, 800–358–9295. Publishes *Patient Selection for Heart or Liver Transplantation.* (For full group information, see HEALTH INSURANCE).

(See LIVER FUNCTION TESTS; also SEXUALLY TRANSMITTED DISEASES, including how to avoid them.)

liver function tests, a series of BLOOD TESTS that seek to determine, from analyzing the chemistry of the body, how well the liver is carrying out its various tasks, including METABOLISM (breaking down substances from food for use in the body), storage, filtering out unwanted substances, and excreting them from the body. Among the common liver function tests are:

- *Alkaline phosphatase test,* checking the level of the enzyme *alkaline phosphatase* in the blood. High levels are found in some kinds of liver problems, such as hepatitis and blockage of the flow of bile (see LIVER AND LIVER PROBLEMS), and also in some disorders of the bones and gall bladder.
- *Prothrombin time (PT),* checking the time it takes for blood to clot (somewhat differently than THROMBIN TIME), a slow clotting time being an indication of various liver disorders, as well as deficiency in VITAMIN K. The test is often used to check how well anticoagulant medicine (designed to slow clotting in heart disease) is working.
- *Bilirubin test,* checking the amount of *bilirubin,* a yellowish substance formed by the breakdown of "retired" red blood cells. High levels of bilirubin in the blood can indicate liver malfunction or obstruction of ducts in the liver.
- *Aminotransferases (transaminases) test,* checking the amount of the enzyme *aminotransferase* (*transaminase*) in the blood. It is normally present in heart and liver tissues, so high amounts in the blood could signal damage to those organs.

(See LIVER AND LIVER PROBLEMS; MEDICAL TESTS.)

locational skills, a set of READING skills necessary for a child to be able to find information in printed sources. These are PREREQUISITE skills, such as understanding how to find an item in an alphabetized dictionary or index, how to find material using the page numbers in a table of contents, or how to find a book in the library.

long-arm statute, a law that allows the court of one state to have legal authority, or JURISDICTION, over people living in another state, as in cases of CHILD SUPPORT enforcement.

long-term care, medical, social, and personal care for people with CHRONIC illness or MENTAL DISORDERS, often in a large institution, but increasingly (when appropriate) in a GROUP HOME or private home. Such care often includes treatment of symptoms, maintenance of physical and mental stability, and rehabilitation.

lordosis (hyperlordosis), excessive curving of the lower spine, a type of spinal disorder often associated with SCOLIOSIS and/or KYPHOSIS; sometimes popularly called *swayback.* In adults often related to OSTEOPOROSIS (bone weakening from CALCIUM loss), in children kyphosis more often results from injury, a TUMOR on the spine, or a GENETIC DISORDER, and can be exaggerated by poor posture. (See SCOLIOSIS; SPINE AND SPINAL DISORDER.)

low birth weight (LBW), a term referring to a baby who is under 5.5 lb (2,500 g) when born; those under 3.3 lb (1,500 g) are called *very low birth weight* (VLBW) infants. Infants of low birth weight are considered to be AT-RISK, because LBW is associated with higher rates of illness (MORBIDITY) and death (INFANT MORTALITY) than are infants of higher weight. Indeed, the Surgeon General has reported that low birth weight is the most important factor in America's relatively high infant mortality rate. The lower the birth weight, the greater an infant's risk of illness and death. Low birth weight babies frequently experience FETAL DISTRESS during LABOR, especially from lack of oxygen (HYPOXIA).

This does not mean that every LBW infant has medical problems. Many have quite normal development, outgrowing any temporary problems. Some PREMATURE babies have low birth weight because they have not sufficiently developed and may—when they have reached the full forty weeks that would have completed their GESTATION—develop normally.

However, LBW infants are at significantly increased risk for BIRTH DEFECTS, developmental DISABILITIES, MENTAL RETARDATION, respiratory or other infectious diseases, behavior problems, and complications during medical treatment. Some 6 to 7 percent of infants are classed as low birth weight, but they account for two-thirds of all infant deaths in the first month, and approximately 60 percent of infant deaths overall.

Low birth weight can result from many causes, but is found especially often in cases of ADOLESCENT PREGNANCY, DRUG ABUSE during pregnancy, or INTRAUTERINE GROWTH RETARDATION; when problems with the PLACENTA prevent the FETUS from receiving sufficient nutrients; when the mother had a CHRONIC illness, such as DIABETES or hypertension (high BLOOD PRESSURE), ANEMIA, ECLAMPSIA, or PREECLAMPSIA; when the mother was too thin at conception or had had too many recent pregnancies; when the mother had experienced major stress during pregnancy; or when the mother had poor NUTRITION and inadequate weight gain during pregnancy. Socioeconomic factors that the U.S. Surgeon General has linked with LBW are low socioeconomic status, low educational level, minority race, single marital status, adolescence, inadequate PRENATAL

CARE, SMOKING, and use of drugs and alcohol, concluding: "Evidence indicates that the more of these risk factors present, the greater the risk to mother and child."

FOR HELP AND FURTHER INFORMATION

National Maternal and Child Health Clearinghouse (NMCHC), 703–821–8955. Publishes *Neonatal Intensive Care for Low Birthweight Infants: Costs and Effectiveness.* (For full group information, see PREGNANCY.)

March of Dimes Birth Defects Foundation (MDBDF), 914–428–7100. Publishes information sheet *Low Birthweight.* (For full group information, see BIRTH DEFECTS.)

National Institute of Child Health and Human Development (NICHD), 301–496–5133. (For full group information, see PREGNANCY.)

lumbar puncture (spinal tap), a medical procedure involving insertion of a hollow needle (*aspiration needle*) into the base of the spine to withdraw CEREBROSPINAL FLUID for analysis, generally to test for such conditions as infections, brain hemorrhage, or TUMORS. Though often done under local ANESTHESIA, the procedure is uncomfortable. Serious side effects are relatively rare, but include possible introduction of infection and the risk of damaging the *arachnoid membrane* that surrounds the spinal cord. Lumbar puncture is also used as part of some other medical procedures, such as a MYELOGRAM. An alternative or complement to the lumbar puncture is the *cisternal puncture*, in which a small amount of fluid is removed from the base of the brain. (See MEDICAL TESTS.)

lung and breathing disorders, Problems involving the *respiratory system*, including the lungs and associated network of air passages, which takes in air, removes oxygen from it, passes the oxygen on to the bloodstream, and then expells unwanted carbon dioxide. From the mouth, air passes through the windpipe (*trachea*) and the large bronchial tubes (*bronchi*) and narrower *bronchioles* into the lungs, more precisely into the tiny air sacs called *alveoli* that line the lungs. From the alveoli, oxygen from the air is passed into the blood, in exchange for waste carbon dioxide brought to the lungs from elsewhere in the body, which is then expelled from the body in exhaled breath. A special muscle called the *diaphragm* divides the chest from the abdomen and helps move air in and out of the lungs.

The respiratory system can be threatened in a number of ways, leading to lung and breathing disorders:

- *Infection*, disease caused by bacteria, viruses, and fungi, which can all infect the air passages. This can produce sometimes life-threatening inflammation, including *tracheitis* (inflammation of the trachea), *bronchitis* (inflammation of the bronchial tubes), *bronchiolitis* (inflammation of the bronchi), *bronchiectasis* (swelling of the bronchi), and *pneumonia* (inflammation of one or both lungs). Such infections are often associated with other diseases, such as TUBERCULOSIS, WHOOPING COUGH, or MEASLES, and some can become CHRONIC (recurrent). Many forms (though not all) can be treated with ANTIBIOTICS.
- ALLERGY, reactions to foreign irritants in the body, including ASTHMA and allergic *alveolitis* (inflammation of the alveoli).
- TUMORS, abnormal growths, sometimes CANCERS, often associated with SMOKING.
- *Injury*, penetration of the respiratory area, as in an accident, which can cause collapse of the lung.
- *Toxic substances*, inhalation of poisonous gases or dusts can injure the delicate lungs and can sometimes (as in the case of inhalation of silica or asbestos) cause the lungs to become scarred and fibrous, impairing ability to breathe.
- *Foreign substances*, which can be drawn into the lungs through inhalation (*aspiration*). Children can sometimes draw foreign objects into their lungs directly or indirectly from vomit, and newborns sometimes inhale MECONIUM, possibly causing pneumonia.
- *Blockage of air passages*, often by bodily substances produced in abnormal amounts that hinder breathing, as in CYSTIC FIBROSIS. If congenital, chronic, or PROGRESSIVE conditions tend increasingly to block air passages and decrease breathing capacity, the condition is often called *chronic obstructive lung disease* (COLD), *chronic obstructive pulmonary disease* (COPD), or *chronic obstructive respiratory disease* (CORD).
- *Impaired blood and oxygen supply*, which can result from a variety of causes. A blood clot may block an artery feeding the lungs. Heart problems may cause *edema* (collection of fluid) in the lungs. In *emphysema*, which is often associated with chronic bronchitis and asthma, the walls of the alveoli are damaged, cutting down their ability to exchange oxygen. Some infants are born with *congenital lobar emphysema*. In newborns, RESPIRATORY DISTRESS SYNDROME (*hyaline membrane disease*) can cut down on the vital oxygen supply, as can PERSISTENT FETAL CIRCULATION (PFC). Even before birth, a DIAPHRAGMATIC HERNIA may constrict the development of the lungs so much that a newborn dies soon after birth, unable to breathe independently. This condition can now be repaired through IN UTERO SURGERY.

Young children are especially vulnerable to lung and breathing diseases. In PREMATURE babies, the lungs are not yet as fully developed as they should be at birth. Even full-term babies have no more than one-tenth of the alveoli they will have as adults, and the lungs do not reach full maturity until ADOLESCENCE, so damage in this period (especially before age eight) can have compound effects. Children's air passages are also much narrower and more subject to blockage than an adults. The American Lung Association estimates that of all the infants who die in their first year, approximately one-third die of respiratory disorders. Breathing problems are also involved in SLEEP APNEA and have been implicated in SUDDEN INFANT DEATH SYNDROME.

It is important to the overall health of a baby that a steady flow of oxygen be provided to the lungs. If breathing is difficult, or for some reason, is not supplying sufficient oxygen to the body, the child may be placed in a VENTILATOR to assist breathing, often with electronic monitoring of pulse, respiration, and heartbeat. Lung and breathing disorders are diagnosed using a variety of MEDICAL TESTS, including X-RAYS of the chest, PULMONARY FUNCTION TESTS, SPUTUM ANALYSIS, BLOOD TESTS, and BIOPSY.

FOR HELP AND FURTHER INFORMATION

American Lung Association (ALA)
National Headquarters
1740 Broadway
New York, NY 10019
212–315–8700; 800-LUNG-USA [586–4872]
Fax: 212–265–5642
John R. Garrison, Executive Director
Organization concerned about lung diseases and related conditions; acts as advocate; provides information; publishes various materials.

National Heart, Lung, and Blood Information Center (NHLBIC), 301–251–1222. Publishes booklets *Do I Have a Chronic Cough?*, *Chronic Obstructive Pulmonary Disease*, and *Sarcoidosis*, and professional materials. (For full group information, see HEART AND HEART PROBLEMS.)

National Jewish Center for Immunology and Respiratory Medicine
1400 Jackson Street
Denver, CO 80206
303–398–1571
LUNG LINE Information Service (8 A.M.–5 P.M. MT, M-F; staffed by specialist nurses): 800–222-LUNG [222–5864], U.S. except CO; 303–355-LUNG [355–5864], CO
LUNG FACTS™ (24 hours): 800–552-LUNG [552–5964], recorded information on lung, immune, and allergy-related topics
Nonsectarian, nonprofit hospital and research center for treatment of chronic respiratory, allergic, and immunologic disease in children and adults, including asthma, tuberculosis, chronic sinus disease, allergies, juvenile rheumatoid arthritis, lupus, immunodeficiencies, and other lung diseases. Operates COPE (Comprehensive Out-Patient Evaluation) program, including pediatric clinic; provides information and referrals.

National Institute of Allergy and Infectious Diseases (NIAID), 301–496–5717. (For full group information, see ALLERGY.)

National Cancer Institute (NCI), 800–422–6237. Publishes "What You Need to Know About" brochures on oral cancers and cancers of the larynx and lung. (For full group information, see CANCER.)

American Cancer Society (ACS), 800–227–2345. Publishes materials on oral cancer and cancer of the larynx and lungs. (For full group information, see CANCER.)

National Organization for Rare Disorders (NORD), 800–999–6673. (For full group information, see RARE DISORDERS.)

OTHER RESOURCES

Living Well with Chronic Asthma, Bronchitis, and Emphysema: A Complete Guide to Coping with Chronic Lung Disease. Consumer Reports Books Editors and others. Consumer Reports, 1991.

The Chronic Bronchitis and Emphysema Handbook. Francois Haas and Sheila Sperber Haas. Wiley, 1990.

The Breath Connection: How to Reduce Psychosomatic and Stress-Related Disorders with Easy-To-Do Breathing Exercises. Robert Fried. Plenum, 1990.

The Lungs and Breathing, rev. ed. Steve Parker. Watts, 1989. For children.

(See also ASTHMA; ALLERGY; TUBERCULOSIS; CHRONIC ILLNESS.)

lupus, an AUTOIMMUNE DISORDER, in which the body mistakenly attacks the connective tissue in the body, more formally called *lupus erythematosus* or *systemic lupus erythematosus* (SLE). It is most common in women of childbearing years, affecting women nine times more often than men and African-American women three times more often than those of European ancestry, but it can also affect children as well. The causes of lupus are unclear, but seem to result from a combination of genetic, environmental, and hormonal factors, often triggered by a virus or sometimes a drug.

SLE may start suddenly with a high fever or may develop slowly and intermittently over months or even years, with only occasional mild bouts of fever and fatigue. It is difficult to diagnose in its early stages, often being confused with other disorders, such as rheumatoid arthritis. Generally, doctors use BLOOD TESTS and BIOPSY to check for characteristic ANTIBODIES. Common symptoms include a reddish butterfly-shaped patch on the cheeks and nose, ARTHRITIS, ANEMIA, and *pleurisy* (inflammation of the lining of the lungs). The disease can affect many parts of the body, including the skin, joints, kidneys, lungs, heart, CENTRAL NERVOUS SYSTEM, and blood vessels, with kidney disease the most common serious complication. The effects of lupus range from mild to life-threatening, if vital parts of the body are affected. However, with early diagnosis, close monitoring, and treatment of related conditions, the MORTALITY RATE for severe cases of lupus has been sharply cut. Drugs are used to try to control inflammation, and often patients are advised to avoid the sun, which can worsen the condition. A mild form of lupus, called *discoid lupus erythematosus* (DLE), primarily affects the skin.

Women with lupus may decide to have children, if their heart and kidneys are not badly affected, but have an increased likelihood of MISCARRIAGE and flareups of the disease after DELIVERY (see HIGH-RISK PREGNANCY). In some studies, miscarriages that occurred for unknown reasons have occasionally been linked to the mother's undiagnosed lupus.

FOR HELP AND FURTHER INFORMATION

Lupus Foundation of America (LFA)
4 Research Place, Suite 180
Rockville, MD 20850–3226
301–670–9292; 800–558–0121
Fax: 301–670–9486
Glenda K. Amon, President
Organization concerned with lupus; sponsors peer-support groups; provides information; supports research; publishes various materials, including *Lupus News, Facts About Lupus* (series of twenty-one brochures), *Social Security Disability Package* (three publications), *When Mom Gets Sick* (by a 9-year-old), and books *Coping with Lupus, Understanding Lupus,* and *Lupus Erythematosus: A Handbook for Physicians, Patients and their Families.*

American Lupus Society
260 Maple Court, #123
Ventura, CA 93003
805–339–0443; 800–331–1802
Joan Lavelle, Executive Director
Organization fighting lupus; provides information, support, and referrals; acts as advocate; sponsors research; publishes various materials including *Lupus Erythematosus: A Patient's Guide to Lupus, Lupus—A Guide for Patients, So Now You Have Lupus, What Black Women Should Know About Lupus, SLE in Children and Adolescents, Tell Me About Lupus—A Booklet for Young People, The Heart in SLE,* and *The Lungs in SLE.*

National Arthritis and Musculoskeletal and Skin Diseases Information Clearinghouse (NAMSIC), 301–495–4484. Publishes information package *Lupus,* patient education booklet *What Black Women Should Know About Lupus,* annotated bibliography *Lupus* (patient and professional), and research report *Arthritis, Rheumatic Diseases, and Related Disorders.* (For full group information, see ARTHRITIS.)

American Juvenile Arthritis Organization (AJAO), Arthritis Foundation, 800–283–7800. Publishes *Meeting the Challenge: A Young Person's Guide to Living with Lupus.* (For full group information, see ARTHRITIS).

National Kidney Foundation (NKF),
800–622–9010. Publishes *Lupus and Kidney Disease.* (For full group information, see KIDNEY AND UROLOGICAL DISORDERS.)

Resources for Rehabilitation, 617–862–6455. Publishes book *A Woman's Guide to Coping with Disability,* with section on lupus. (For full group information, see EYE AND VISION PROBLEMS.)

National Organization for Rare Disorders (NORD), 800–999–6673. (For full group information, see RARE DISORDERS.)

OTHER RESOURCES

GENERAL WORKS

Living with Lupus: A Comprehensive Guide to Understanding and Controlling Lupus While Enjoying Your Life. Mark Horowitz and Marietta Abrams-Brill. NAL-Dutton, 1994.

Living with Lupus: All the Knowledge You Need to Help Yourself. Sheldon P. Blau. Addison-Wesley, 1993.

Red Butterfly: Lupus Patients Can Survive, 2nd ed. Linda R. Bell. Branden, 1993.

Coping with Lupus: A Guide to Living with Lupus for You and Your Family, 2nd ed. Robert H. Phillips. Avery, 1991.

Living with It: Why You Don't Have to Be Healthy to Be Happy. Suzy Szasz. Prometheus, 1991.

Heartsearch: Toward Healing Lupus. Donna H. Talman. North Atlantic, 1990.

PERSONAL EXPERIENCES

Pumpkin—a Young Woman's Struggle with Lupus. Patricia M. Fagan. Branden, 1994.

Lupus: My Search for a Diagnosis. Eileen Radziunas. Hunter House, 1990.

Embracing the Wolf: A Lupus Victim and Her Family Learn to Live with Chronic Disease. Joanna Baumer Permut. Cherokee, 1989.

luteinizing hormone (LH), a kind of HORMONE produced by the PITUITARY GLAND that stimulates the production of other hormones from the OVARIES and the TESTES, among them FOLLICLE-STIMULATING HORMONE (FSH), ESTROGEN, and PROGESTERONE. High levels of LH, triggered in turn by ESTROGEN, stimulate OVULATION, so levels of LH are used in some HOME MEDICAL TESTS to indicate ovulation.

Lyme disease, a bacterial disease that can cause serious ARTHRITIS, neurological disorders, and heart problems, if not recognized and treated quickly. The bacteria, *Borrelia burgdorferi,* is spread by poppy-seed-sized ticks (*Ixodes dammini*) carried by several woodland animals, including deer and mice. Within a few days of a bite by an infected tick, various symptoms appear, including most characteristically, a red "bull's eye" rash at the site; swollen, aching joints and muscles; fever, fatigue, weakness, and dizziness; and other generalized symptoms.

But sometimes the symptoms are absent—the rash is found only about 75 percent of the time—or are indistinct, often being mistaken for influenza, especially since people may be unaware that they were bitten. In that case, the infection goes unrecognized and untreated and so is able to remain in the body and damage the joints, heart, and NERVOUS SYSTEM, while the early symptoms gradually decline, sometimes flaring up in cycles. Even when suspected by doctors, Lyme disease is often hard to diagnose. Various MEDICAL TESTS exist, but they are of varying reliability, and in many cases, the bacteria's presence is effectively masked.

When recognized and treated quickly, Lyme disease responds to antibiotics in most cases. If unresponsive or recognized weeks, months, or years after the initial infection, intravenous antibiotic treatments, along with anti-inflammatory drugs and other treatments, are often needed to combat the infection. Long-term experience is limited, however, since the bacteria responsible was discovered only in 1982, so it is unclear whether or how much permanent damage may remain.

Originally discovered in Connecticut, after a mother noticed an unusual incidence of arthritis in young people in her heavily wooded Old Lyme neighborhood (hence the early name, *Lyme arthritis*), the disease was at first concentrated on the East Coast. Now Lyme disease is spreading rapidly across North America. (In Europe, its effects have been known from the nineteenth century, although it was not recognized as a distinct disease.) Parents can best protect themselves and their children by dressing in long clothing, with pants tucked into socks, in wooded or grassy areas; by checking themselves for ticks after an outdoor excursion; by checking pets as well, since they both carry and can be infected by the ticks; and by being alert to possible symptoms and seeing a doctor promptly.

A related tick-borne disease has been discovered only in the mid–1990s. Called *erlichiosis,* it is apparently more rare but more dangerous, sometimes quickly producing high FEVER and occasionally fatal complications, unlike Lyme disease, which has been associated with virtually no deaths.

FOR HELP AND FURTHER INFORMATION

National Arthritis and Musculoskeletal and Skin Diseases Information Clearinghouse (NAMSIC), 301–495–4484. Publishes patient education booklet *Lyme Disease: The Facts, The Challenge,* annotated bibliography *Lyme Disease,* and *Arthritis, Rheumatic Diseases, and Related Disorders.* (For full group information, see ARTHRITIS.)

National Institute of Allergy and Infectious Diseases (NIAID), 301–496–5717. Publishes *Lyme Disease: The Facts, the Challenges* (For full group information, see ALLERGY.)

National Organization for Rare Disorders (NORD), 800–999–6673. (For full group information, see RARE DISORDERS.)

American Council on Science and Health (ACSH), 212–362–7044. Publishes *Lyme Disease.* (For full group information, see SAFETY.)

OTHER RESOURCES

Ticks and What You Can Do About Them. Roger Drummond. Wilderness Press, 1990.

For children

Lyme Disease. Elaine Landau. Watts, 1990.

For preteens and teens

Lyme Disease and Other Pest-Borne Illnesses. Sean P. Mactire. Watts, 1991.

Lyme Disease, the Great Imitator: How to Prevent and Cure It. Alvin Silverstein and others. Avstar, 1990.

lymphatic system, the network of vessels and organs through which the body's IMMUNE SYSTEM operates.

M

macronutrient, any element or compound, notably a VITAMIN or MINERAL, that is necessary for proper health and functioning of the body in relatively large amounts, as opposed to MICRONUTRIENTS. Examples include oxygen, carbon, hydrogen, nitrogen, CALCIUM, PHOSPHORUS, MAGNESIUM, POTASSIUM, SULFUR, SODIUM, and CHLORIDE.

magical thinking, the idea or belief that one's thoughts or feelings influence people or the environment nearby and can trigger events. Such thinking is common in children under age five and may also occur among some uneducated adults or among people with some kinds of MENTAL DISORDERS, such as PARANOIA.

magnesium, a MINERAL vital to the formation of bones and TEETH, the proper functioning of nerves and muscles, and the work of enzymes (substances promoting biochemical reactions in the body). It is abundant in green leafy vegetables, nuts, whole grain products, and soy beans; it is also found in various antacids and laxatives. Lack of magnesium can lead to muscle weakness; severe deficiency is sometimes associated with DIARRHEA, DIABETES, ALCOHOL ABUSE, and KIDNEY AND UROLOGICAL PROBLEMS, and is sometimes found in infants fed on cow's milk or FORMULA containing insufficient magnesium. Too much magnesium, as when someone is overusing antacids and laxatives, can cause nausea, disruption of normal heart function, and confusion. (See MINERALS; NUTRITION.)

magnet school, a school that attracts students from many different neighborhoods or backgrounds, because of special interests, needs, or approaches; a type of ALTERNATIVE SCHOOL or SCHOOL OF CHOICE, usually found in a heavily populated area. A HIGH SCHOOL that focuses on music and art, science, or foreign languages, for example, might be considered a magnet school, as might a school with an intensive COLLEGE-oriented program, a vocationally oriented CURRICULUM, a nontraditional educational approach, or a "second chance" program for former DROPOUTS. Some magnet schools have been developed as part of voluntary DESEGREGATION plans, which attempt to draw a mix of students, rather than rely on involuntary BUSING. The term *magnet school* is also sometimes used to apply to a school district's centralized special services for children with DISABILITIES. (See CHOOSING A SCHOOL FOR YOUR CHILD on page 659, for a useful checklist for evaluating schools.)

mainstreaming, an approach to EDUCATION that involves integrating children with DISABILITIES as much as possible into a school's regular classes and activities; also called *inclusion*. The aim is to help the child to develop to the fullest extent possible, in contrast to the previous pattern of routinely segregating children with mental or physical disabilities from other children, and so markedly limiting their opportunities and possibilities. The EDUCATION FOR ALL HANDICAPPED CHILDREN ACT and its successor, the INDIVIDUALS WITH DISABILITIES EDUCATION ACT (IDEA), have been extremely important in making mainstreaming a widespread approach, requiring that public schools provide a "free, appropriate education" in the LEAST RESTRICTIVE SETTING to children of ages three to twenty-one. It has helped to make mainstreaming work by providing programs for identifying disabilities in early childhood—in the PRESCHOOL years or even in infancy—and services to help children overcome these disabilities to the greatest extent possible before the school years. Special services are supposed to be delivered to them in the classroom (see SPECIAL EDUCATION).

Mainstreaming has problems, however. In many classrooms, the teachers are not given the training they need in already overcrowded classes, lessening their ability to teach all their students effectively, and mandated special services may be indifferently delivered. In such cases, some children with minimal disabilities may still bloom, but many others may wither or fail to grow, without more specific help and support, and sometimes fewer distractions than a regular classroom provides. For these children, a more traditional special education approach may be more appropriate. Some ADVOCACY organizations, such as Voice of the Retarded (see MENTAL RETARDATION), urge that the full continuum of educational approaches be maintained, and the child placed in the setting most appropriate for his or her individual needs. Parents should monitor their children's progress and seek changes as appropriate.

FOR HELP AND FURTHER INFORMATION

Center on Human Policy (CHP), 315–443–3851. (For full group information, see HELP FOR SPECIAL CHILDREN on page 832.)

Alexander Graham Bell Association for the Deaf (AGBAD), 202–337–5220, voice/TT. Publishes *The Possible Dream: Mainstream Experiences of Hearing-Impaired Students, They Do Belong: Mainstreaming the Hearing-Impaired,* and *Hearing-Impaired Children in the Mainstream.* (For full group information, see EAR AND HEARING PROBLEMS.)

National Federation of the Blind (NFB), 410–659–9314. Publishes *Problems of Placement and Responsibility: Mainstreaming Revisited.* (For full group information, see EYE AND VISION PROBLEMS.)

National Information Center on Deafness (NICD), 202–651–5051; 202–651–5052, TT. Publishes *Mainstreaming Deaf and Hard of Hearing Students: Questions and Answers—Research, Readings, and Resources,* and *Mainstreaming Deaf and Hard of Hearing Students: Further Readings.* (For full group information, see EAR AND HEARING PROBLEMS.)

(See also EDUCATION FOR ALL HANDICAPPED CHILDREN ACT; DISABILITIES; EDUCATION; SEGREGATION.)

majority, in family law, adulthood. The AGE of majority is the age at which a child is no longer considered a MINOR and can be legally treated as an adult; set by state law, but usually around eighteen.

malignant, in medicine, a general term for a PROGRESSIVE condition, especially a TUMOR, that is expected to worsen and may cause death. By contrast, a BENIGN condition is a mild one, not expected to be life-threatening.

malignant hyperthermia (MH), a GENETIC DISORDER of the AUTOSOMAL DOMINANT type in which a person has an often-fatal reaction to certain anesthetics and muscle relaxants. In those affected, the temperature rises dangerously (sometimes to 110°F or more), metabolism is speeded up, and the muscles become rigid. Death can result from cardiac arrest, brain damage, internal HEMORRHAGE, or failure of various body systems. Before the condition was recognized (in 1960), the MORTALITY RATE was nearly 80 percent; it is now nearer 10 percent, though some survivors may experience brain damage, kidney failure, or damage to other major organs. Treatment involves administration of an antidote, bringing down body temperature, and restoration of chemical imbalances.

If there is any history of MH in the family, every family member must be considered at risk—even if they have previously undergone surgery with ANESTHESIA, since deaths have sometimes occurred in people who have undergone prior surgery. All health personnel, including dentists, should be informed, so they can use only those anesthetics that do not trigger the reaction. A diagnostic test, the *halothane-caffeine contracture test* (CHCT), can tell if a person is susceptible to MH, but it is expensive, involves taking a muscle biopsy, and is performed only at a few centers, so it is generally reserved only for people with a family history of the disorder or a previous suspicious reaction to anesthesia. People affected by MH should carry a warning card and wear a warning tag, such as that from MEDIC ALERT; when traveling, they should carry literature about MH translated into the host country's language to present to medical personnel, and possibly even a supply of an antidote, if it is not readily available in the country being visited.

FOR HELP AND FURTHER INFORMATION

Malignant Hyperthermia Association of the United States (MHAUS)
32 South Main Street
P.O. Box 1069
Sherburne, NY 13460
607–674–7901; 800–98–MHAUS [986–4287]
MHAUS/Medic Alert Hotline: 209–634–4917
Fax: 607–674–7910
Richard A. Hillman, Executive Director
Organization concerned with malignant hyperthermia; provides information; acts as advocate; supports research; publishes newsletter *The Communicator*; pamphlets *What Is Malignant Hyperthermia?*, *Traveling with MH*, and *Testing for Susceptibility to MH*, *What Is MHAUS?*; and materials for medical professionals.

(See also ANESTHESIA.)

malnutrition, the condition of having an improper amount and balance of nutrients to maintain proper body functioning. Malnutrition is most often thought of as referring to deficiencies in the diet, such as insufficient PROTEIN, VITAMINS, and MINERALS, which can lead to DEFICIENCY DISEASES. But malnutrition also can stem from excessive amounts of food or vitamin and mineral supplements, and from a wide variety of disorders that hinder the body from properly absorbing and using the nutrients found in foods. In Western countries, various government programs are available to help combat nutrient deficiency; apart from poor and homeless families not reached by such programs, general nutrient deficiency is most often associated with ALCOHOL ABUSE, DRUG ABUSE, or eating disorders such as ANOREXIA NERVOSA and BULIMIA. (See NUTRITION; MINERALS; VITAMINS.)

malocclusion, the dental term for a bad bite, in which the teeth meet unevenly. Ideally, the upper front teeth should be slightly forward of the lower front teeth, and the rear teeth should meet evenly, but most people have some slight malocclusion.

If the jaw and upper front teeth project too far forward, the result is *overbite* or *buck teeth*, which dentists call *retrognathism.* The reverse, with the lower jaw and front teeth in front of the upper ones, is called *underbite*, or *prognathism.* Even when the two jaws meet each other properly, malocclusion can result when teeth are badly spaced or twisted out of normal position. Too many teeth or teeth too large for the size of the jaw can lead to overcrowding. Malocclusion can lead to pain in the joint of the jaw from an awkward bite, BRUXISM (teeth-grinding), and tooth decay and loss, especially where teeth do not meet and so are not used in chewing.

Most cases of malocclusion result from GENETIC INHERITANCE. However, some bite problems can be caused or exaggerated by behavioral habits, such as pressing at the teeth with the tongue, fingers, or lower lip, or continual sucking on a thumb or pacifier in the years beyond infancy.

Dentists can often deal with slight malocclusion by smoothing off uneven surfaces of teeth or building up teeth with a *dental onlay*. More serious cases may require treatment by a specialist called an *orthodontist*, who often uses orthodontic braces to bring teeth into proper position.

Braces are generally worn for 12 to 36 months, applying persistent pressure to move teeth into proper position; bone in the jaw fills in spaces left by tooth movement, so eventually teeth will be set in their proper place. Braces may be fixed, worn for a year or more, then replaced by a removable retainer plate, or they may removable from the start. Fixed braces require more careful fitting, and so are more expensive; they also tend to trap plaque, making teeth harder to clean. However, they interfere less with speaking. Removable braces are more cumbersome, and sometimes interfere with speech so much that children stop wearing them.

A major advance in recent years is the use of plastics and ceramics in braces on the front teeth, with just a thin metal wire holding them; these produce almost invisible braces. These are, however, more expensive than traditional stainless steel braces. (Metal bands are still used on the back teeth, which are harder to move.) Newer alloys are also being used to make braces; some of these are promising because they hold their shape better, requiring fewer replacements and visits to the orthodontist.

Another alternative is *lingual braces*, which fit completely out of sight on the inside of the teeth. However, these can cause problems with speaking, because the tongue hits them, and they are harder to adjust. Since they are not as strong as front-of-the-teeth braces, they must also be worn longer. Elastic hooks, rubber bands, and even small magnets may also be used to pull teeth into position, along with various other appliances, including headgear, which fits around the head or neck to ease jaws into a new position, and mouth guards, to help align jaws and chewing muscles.

For all types of braces, a major problem is keeping the teeth clean, so children may have more dental cavities than they would otherwise have had. Sticky, hard, crunchy, and sweet foods are all best avoided, since they can damage the braces or increase tooth decay. Careful brushing and flossing are vital. Children must also keep track of removable braces, retainers, and other gear, if they've taken them off at school or in a restaurant. In the end, the success of the braces depends on the child's willingness to wear the braces or other gear, to keep the teeth clean, and to avoid damaging foods.

In cases of overcrowding, one or more teeth must sometimes be extracted to make room for the remaining teeth. In severe cases, the jaw may need to be reshaped or repositioned. This requires a procedure called ORTHOGNATHIC SURGERY, normally performed by an ORAL SURGEON in a hospital.

Work to correct malocclusion is best carried out during childhood and ADOLESCENCE, when young bones are still growing, but can be done later if necessary. (See TEETH AND DENTAL PROBLEMS.)

manual communication, use of expressive gestures of hands, face, and body to communicate with others, whether as part of a "private language," FINGER SPELLING, or a widely taught and used language such as AMERICAN SIGN LANGUAGE. Some people believe that children with EAR AND HEARING PROBLEMS should not be allowed to use any form of manual communication, but should instead be trained to use and understand oral speech, especially through SPEECHREADING. Others stress a TOTAL COMMUNICATION approach, which believes that deaf children should be taught to use any communication skills at their disposal. (See EAR AND HEARING PROBLEMS; COMMUNICATION SKILLS AND DISORDERS.)

marasmus, extreme MALNUTRITION and resulting emaciation, resulting from insufficient CALORIES and PROTEIN for growth. Most often found in regions where starvation or semistarvation are common, marasmus can also result when children have been fed solely on breast MILK for too long, or were given a nutritionally inadequate diet when introduced to SOLID FOODS. Marasmus can also be found in children who exhibit FAILURE TO THRIVE, for physical, social, or emotional reasons. (See NUTRITION; GROWTH AND GROWTH DISORDERS.)

Marfan syndrome, a rare GENETIC DISORDER of the body's connective tissue, affecting the heart and circulatory system, lungs, eyes, and skeletal system. Common symptoms include long fingers (the traditional name, *arachnodactyly*, means "spider fingers"), long, thin skeleton, SCOLIOSIS (sidewise curvature of the spine), dislocated lens in the eye, and outsized valves and aorta in the heart. Though the disorder is sometimes recognizable nearly from birth, people occasionally grow to adulthood not knowing they have the syndrome, until their lungs collapse or heart suddenly fails. Recent research has identified genetic markers for Marfan syndrome, promising a means of earlier and more accurate diagnosis in the future. Women with Marfan syndrome are especially prone to HEART PROBLEMS during pregnancy. Because it is passed on by a single AUTOSOMAL DOMINANT gene, people with a family history of Marfan syndrome may want to seek GENETIC COUNSELING when considering pregnancy. Treatment involves careful monitoring of the skeletal system, eyes, and heart, through annual echocardiograms; and avoidance of strenuous exercise to limit strain on the heart. Medications may also be given to control BLOOD PRESSURE and to limit risk of infection.

FOR HELP AND FURTHER INFORMATION

National Marfan Foundation (NMF)
382 Main Street
Port Washington, NY 11050
516–883–8712; 800–8-MARFAN [862–7326]
Priscilla Ciccariello, Executive Director

Organization concerned with Marfan syndrome; fosters support groups; sponsors research; provides information; publishes quarterly newsletter *Connective Issues*, book *The Marfan Syndrome, The Marfan Syndrome: A Booklet for Teenagers, How John Was Unique* (for children), *Marfan Syndrome: Physical Education and Activity Guidelines, Do You Know Marfan?* (video); and materials for educators and health professionals.

National Arthritis and Musculoskeletal and Skin Diseases Information Clearinghouse (NAMSIC), 301–495–4484. Publishes information package *Marfan Syndrome*. (For full group information, see ARTHRITIS.)

March of Dimes Birth Defects Foundation (MDBDF), 914–428–7100. Publishes information sheet *Marfan Syndrome*. (For full group information, see BIRTH DEFECTS.)

American Heart Association (AHA), 800–242–8721. Publishes *Marfan Syndrome*. (For full group information, see HEART AND HEART PROBLEMS.)

National Organization for Rare Disorders (NORD), 800–999–6673. (For full group information, see RARE DISORDERS.)

master's degree, a DEGREE awarded to a COLLEGE student who has successfully completed a course of study beyond the BACHELOR'S DEGREE level, normally after a one- or two-year course of full-time enrollment; the first degree awarded for most GRADUATE work, sometimes later followed by a DOCTORAL DEGREE.

mastery learning, an educational approach that emphasizes teaching every student to meet preset instructional objectives, such as learning skills, acquiring knowledge, or solving certain types of problems; the basic philosophy is to have all students meet at least a minimum standard level. In mastery learning, students are allowed varying amounts of time—as much time as each needs—to meet the objectives, as opposed to the traditional approach of giving PASSING grades to those who can learn material within a limited time, and FAILING the rest. (See EDUCATION.)

masturbation, stimulation of one's genitals, in young children often general stimulation, but in adolescents and adults usually massaging of the PENIS or CLITORIS to ORGASM. Though for centuries believed to cause physical or psychological damage, masturbation is now thought to cause no harm, though parents can sometimes mistake orgasmic convulsions in their children for SEIZURES.

maternal and child health (MCH) services, facilities and programs that focus on medical and social care for mothers and children, especially PRENATAL CARE, POSTNATAL CARE, BIRTH CONTROL advice, and infant care.

maternal and fetal specialists, OBSTETRICIAN-GYNECOLOGISTS who specialize in the care of mother and FETUS in HIGH-RISK PREGNANCIES.

maternal deprivation syndrome, a pattern of retarded growth and development, or FAILURE TO THRIVE, that occurs mainly in infants who have experienced physical and emotional deprivation. Sometimes the normal BONDING failed to take place between parent and child, as in cases when the mother has MENTAL DISORDERS, insecurity or lack of knowledge about caring for a baby, or disappointment in the child (based on unrealistic expectations, or health problems in the child). Sometimes family poverty makes the parents unable to provide for the child's physical or emotional needs. An infant kept in a HOSPITAL without sufficient stimulation, warmth, and human contact, especially from a parent, may also experience maternal deprivation syndrome.

Symptoms include slow growth, low weight (for the child's age), MALNUTRITION, withdrawal, irritability, unusual stiffness in posture and movements, and slow reactions to others. If the syndrome is not recognized and the situation changed—by educating the parents or helping them better understand the child, or having parents or volunteers visit babies in hospital—permanent physical, social, and emotional damage may result. However, in cases of failure to thrive, physical causes should be explored, since not all cases of failure to thrive result from maternal deprivation syndrome. (See FAILURE TO THRIVE.)

maternal mortality, the death of a MOTHER that is immediately related to a PREGNANCY, including CHILDBIRTH, MISCARRIAGE, or ABORTION, or to a condition significantly worsened by these events. Maternal mortality, normally expressed as a rate of the number of deaths per specified number of pregnancies, has declined greatly in recent years, to approximately 8 per 100,000. Among the factors involved in this reduction are better PRENATAL CARE, better NUTRITION, ANTIBIOTICS, ready access to BLOOD TRANSFUSIONS, and availability of CONTRACEPTION, which allows women to limit and better space pregnancies. Women who are relatively poor, are not well educated, and lack proper prenatal care have a higher than average risk of mortality; so do women under age twenty and over thirty, and those having their first pregnancy, or their fifth or more. Among the conditions that can cause maternal death are hypertension (high BLOOD PRESSURE), ECLAMPSIA, abortion, miscarriage, CESAREAN SECTION, ECTOPIC PREGNANCY, and HEMORRHAGE before or after birth (*antepartum* or *postpartum*). Other conditions that increase a woman's risk of mortality are heart problems, ANEMIA, thyroid problems, DIABETES, and CANCER.

maternity center, a freestanding institution—one not directly attached to a HOSPITAL—where women come to give birth, often attended by CERTIFIED NURSE-MIDWIVES; also called *alternative birthing centers* or simply *birthing centers.* Maternity centers have been developed with the resurgent midwife movement, partly in response to what was seen as the cold, invasive, impersonal nature of traditional hospital delivery. Maternity centers encourage a more relaxed, personal approach to CHILDBIRTH, with birth taking place in a relatively homelike atmosphere, and with BIRTH PARTNERS and sometimes also other family members in attendance.

Maternity centers are only for women with low-risk, normal pregnancies. Other women are generally referred to doctors and hospitals that can give them the more sophisticated medical care they may need. And, if complications develop during delivery, the mother and infant are stabilized and transferred to a hospital for emergency care. Therein lies the main hazard, the loss of time in what may be an emergency situation, along with the slightly increased risk of infection, since birthing rooms cannot necessarily be made as germ-free a setting for the birth. Parents considering alternative birthing centers should carefully investigate the emergency medical arrangements, including how transport is arranged.

FOR HELP AND FURTHER INFORMATION

National Association of Childbearing Centers (NACC)
3123 Gottschall Road
Perkiomenville, PA 18074
215–234–8068
Fax: 215–234–8829
Kate Ernst, Director
Organization of birth centers; provides information and referrals; publishes quarterly newsletter, brochure *The Birth Center, Birth Center Information Packet, NACC Fact Folder, Standards for Freestanding Birth Centers, Sample Birth Center Policies and Procedures, Quality Assurance/Risk Management Manual,* video *The Birth Center.*

Maternity Center Association (MCA)
48 East 92 Street
New York, NY 10128
212–369–7300
Fax: 212–369–8747
Ruth Watson Lubic, Director
Organization concerned with family-centered maternity and infant care; provides information, referrals, counseling, and training; publishes quarterly newsletter *Special Delivery* and other materials.

(See also PREGNANCY; CHILDBIRTH; CERTIFIED NURSE-MIDWIFE.)

maternity cycle, the period from CONCEPTION to about six weeks after CHILDBIRTH. In terms of medical care, the cycle is divided into three periods: PRENATAL or antepartal (before the birth), INTRAPARTAL (during LABOR), and POSTNATAL or postpartal (after the birth). Care offered in the 28 days after the birth may also be termed PERINATAL.

maternity leave, unpaid time off for a MOTHER before and after CHILDBIRTH, ideally without prejudice to the mother's returning on the same level and promotion track; today more widely considered part of FAMILY AND MEDICAL LEAVE, and in the United States covered by the Family and Medical Leave Act of 1993. In many large corporations, maternity leave (often of about three months) and related fringe benefits have long been routinely provided to pregnant women. But in many others, especially small firms, which are not covered by federal laws in these areas, such leave and benefits are not guaranteed and indeed the announcement of PREGNANCY can lead to a woman being summarily firing (see PREGNANCY DISCRIMINATION ACT). Even in those companies where maternity leave and benefits are offered, many women who return to work after maternity leave find that they have been shunted onto a slower promotion track, the so-called *mommy track.*

maturity, a general term referring to a child's relative stage of development, in areas such as growth, SOCIAL SKILLS, and COMMUNICATION SKILLS, as compared to the development of other children of the same AGE. Various TESTS (such as the GESELL PRESCHOOL TEST) may be used to help estimate a child's maturity, with the results sometimes being converted to AGE-EQUIVALENT scores, indicating whether a child's development stands at, above, or below the AVERAGE for children of his or her age.

McCarthy Scales of Children's Abilities, an individually administered TEST designed to assess the MOTOR SKILLS and COGNITIVE DEVELOPMENT of children aged 2½ to 8½. Using a wide variety of puzzles, toy-like materials, and game-like tasks, the test focuses on five areas: verbal ability, numerical ability, and perceptual performance (which together are scaled to give a General Cognitive Index), plus short-term memory and motor coordination. One-third of the lower-level tasks are sometimes used as a DEVELOPMENTAL SCREENING TEST for the early grades, called the *McCarthy Screening Test.* (See TESTS.)

means test, an evaluation of a person's financial resources to judge eligibility for a benefit. Assistance programs such as Medicaid, food stamps, and AID TO FAMILIES WITH DEPENDENT CHILDREN (AFDC), for example, are only available to those who do not have the means to pay for them otherwise. The same is true of some, but not all, kinds of SCHOLARSHIPS. Some other programs, such as SOCIAL SECURITY and ADOPTION assistance to people who adopt children with SPECIAL NEEDS, apply no means test.

measles (rubeola), a serious, highly contagious disease caused by a virus passed from infected people to others in droplets from coughs, sneezes, or while just talking. In most cases, measles causes a widespread rash, high FEVER, cough, runny nose, and watery eyes, and runs its course in one to two weeks, without serious result. But in some cases, and in people of all ages, it can be far more severe. One out of every 10 children with measles develops an ear infection or pneumonia (see LUNG AND BREATHING DISORDERS), and about 1 in every 1000 develops ENCEPHALITIS (inflammation of the brain), which can lead to CONVULSIONS, EAR AND HEARING PROBLEMS, and MENTAL RETARDATION. Young children age one to four are especially vulnerable to respiratory problems, because they have small airways; they can also develop life-threatening DEHYDRATION. Perhaps the most vulnerable are children who were born prematurely and so lack the full complement of ANTIBODIES from their mother, and especially those who spent some time on VENTILATORS. Measles causes death in approximately 2 children in every 10,000. The disease can also be very serious in adults, leaving them vulnerable to dangerous and sometimes life-threatening bacterial infections, and sometimes causing death; among pregnant women, it can cause MISCARRIAGE or premature birth.

Before the development of a measles vaccine, almost every child caught measles before age fifteen, and more than 400 died from it every year. Today, measles is largely preventable, though some epidemics occur because of laxness in immunization. The measles vaccine is normally given in a combination injection of the MEASLES-MUMPS-RUBELLA (MMR) VACCINE at about age fifteen months. Parents should keep careful records of immunization or evidence of their child's having measles, since many states in the U.S. require one or the other before admitting a child into school.

Earlier forms of the measles vaccine were not as effective at immunization, so some adults (such as couples considering PREGNANCY) who have not had measles, but who were immunized before 1967, may need to be reimmunized. Parents who have not themselves had measles should check with their own doctors, to see that they are properly protected against the disease. A pregnant woman who has never had measles or was immunized before 1967, and is exposed to someone with measles, is advised to get an injection of IMMUNOGLOBULIN within five days, to provide so-called PASSIVE IMMUNIZATION.

FOR HELP AND FURTHER INFORMATION

National Institute of Allergy and Infectious Diseases (NIAID), 301–496–5717. (For full group information, see ALLERGIES.)

National Institute of Child Health and Human Development (NICHD), 301–496–5133. (For full group information, see PREGNANCY.)

Centers for Disease Control (CDC), 404–639–3311. (For full group information, see IMMUNIZATION.)

National Organization for Rare Disorders (NORD), 800–999–6673. (For full group information, see RARE DISORDERS.)

(See also MEASLES-MUMPS-RUBELLA VACCINE; IMMUNIZATION.)

measles-mumps-rubella (MMR) vaccine, a combination VACCINE normally given to children at age twelve to fifteen months, and again at four to six years, to provide IMMUNIZATION against several serious childhood diseases: MEASLES (rubeola), MUMPS, and RUBELLA (German measles). Sometimes the child may be given the measles vaccine alone, or just measles and rubella (MR) vaccine. The CHICKEN POX vaccine may also be given at the same time.

The current measles vaccine provides lifelong immunization in most people. However, some adults (such as couples considering PREGNANCY) who have not had measles, but who were immunized before 1967, may need to be reimmunized, since the earlier type of vaccine was less effective. All fifty states in the U.S. require that a child must either show immunization to measles or evidence (such as a doctor's statement) of having had the disease, before being allowed to enter and attend school.

In areas of measles outbreaks, some local public health authorities may recommend additional and earlier shots for infants, sometimes at six months, twelve months, and then again before entering school. Unfortunately, the earlier measles shots are given, the less reliable they are, since the antibodies the child receives from the mother counteract the effect of the vaccination.

As with measles, the current mumps vaccine provides lifelong immunization in most people. About two-thirds of the states in the U.S. require that a child must either show immunization to mumps or evidence of having had the disease (such as a doctor's statement), before being allowed to enter and attend school. The mumps vaccine alone can be given by age twelve months, but is normally given at twelve to fifteen months as part of the MMR vaccine.

The rubella vaccine also gives lifelong protection to most people, and can be given from age twelve to fifteen months. Though the disease is not serious among children, rubella can cause devastating BIRTH DEFECTS in the FETUS in a pregnant women. So any adult who has not previously had rubella itself, or immunization to the disease, is recommended to take the vaccine; a woman should take the vaccine at least three months before beginning a PREGNANCY. If desired, a BLOOD TEST can tell if they are already immune, but reimmunization is safe, if any doubt exists. The rubella virus cannot be spread from one person to another from the vaccine, so it is considered safe for a child to be immunized even if a pregnant woman lives in the household.

Adverse reactions to these vaccines are generally mild. Perhaps one in every five children will develop a rash or slight-to-moderate fever starting one to two weeks after receiving the measles vaccine and lasting a few days. On rare occasions, the mumps vaccine produces a mild brief fever one to two weeks after the injection, and sometimes some swelling of the salivary glands. Serious reactions are considered extremely rare.

After receiving the rubella vaccine, approximately one in every seven children will develop a rash or swelling in the lymph glands within one to two weeks and lasting one to two days. Perhaps one in twenty, and as many as four in ten adults, experience some mild pain and stiffness in the joints one to three weeks after immunization and lasting two to three days. Other temporary side effects are uncommon, but include pain, numbness, or tingling in the hands and feet.

A 1991 report by the National Academy of Science's Institute of Medicine found that, in a small minority of children, the rubella vaccine triggered acute and sometimes long-term arthritis. However, it found "little or no evidence that would connect [the rubella vaccine] with adverse effects such as LEARNING DISABILITIES, HYPERACTIVITY, ANEMIA, or chronic nerve damage" and "insufficient evidence linking the rubella vaccine to nerve disorders (such as radiculoneuritis) or low blood platelet cell counts," suggesting further study.

Some researchers have suggested that, on rare occasions, children who receive the combination MMR vaccine experience a more serious reaction, such as ENCEPHALITIS, or inflammation of the brain. Medical authorities believe the benefits of immunization far outweigh the risks. However, parents may want to discuss this concern with their doctor. (See IMMUNIZATION, including a recommended immunization schedule; see NATIONAL VACCINE INJURY COMPENSATION PROGRAM.)

meconium, a dark, thick, sticky material that collects in the intestines of a FETUS and makes up the first bowel movement of the newborn. Sometimes the meconium is released into the AMNIOTIC FLUID, generally a sign of FETAL DISTRESS. The material can then be inhaled and taken into the lungs (a process called *meconium aspiration*), causing pneumonia. (See LUNG AND BREATHING DISORDERS.)

mediation, a procedure under which two parties submit their dispute for resolution to a neutral third party, an increasingly popular alternative to a court suit. Like ARBITRATION, mediation is a way to avoid the cost, delay, and hard feelings that often attend court cases. However, unlike arbitration, in mediation the neutral party has no power to impose a solution, instead attempting to help the disputants reach a solution themselves. In some states, such as California, mediation is mandatory in cases of disputes over CUSTODY and VISITATION RIGHTS, and counseling services often act as court-associated mediators in DIVORCE and other family law situations. The result is a written agreement, sometimes called a *parenting plan.*

Mediation is not a cure-all, however. In cases of domestic VIOLENCE, the battered party, generally a woman, may be too fearful to speak up strongly on their own behalf, as is required in mediation, since the third party is designed to be neutral. Many people in that situation are so anxious to end a relationship that mediation can result in a disadvantageous agreement. For that reasons many ADVOCACY organizations and many mediators as well urge that the parties have the agreement reviewed by their lawyers before signing it—keeping in mind that, although the mediator may be a lawyer, he or she is not looking out for individual interests.

Even where mediation is mandated, the parties should remember that, if they do not believe the proposed plan is in their or their children's best interests, they retain the option to go to court for settlement of their disputes. If the mediated settlement is acceptable, however, they should have the agreement approved by the court; only that way will it have the status of an enforceable court order, which may be important in case of future disputes.

FOR HELP AND FURTHER INFORMATION

National Center for Women and Family Law, 212–674–8200. Publishes *Mediation and You* and legal materials. (For full group information, see CUSTODY.)

Association of Family and Conciliation Courts (AFCC), 608–251–4001. Publishes pamphlet *Is Mediation For Us?* and legal materials. (For full group information, see DIVORCE.)

Lavender Families Resource Network, 206–325–2643, voice/TT. Publishes article reprint *Mediation for Lesbian and Gay Families.* (For full group information, see HOMOSEXUALITY.)

Academy of Family Mediators (AFM), 617–674–2663. (For full group information, see CUSTODY.)

(See also CUSTODY.)

medical tests, a wide variety of procedures that help health professionals diagnose ailments and disorders. Some medical tests are entirely BENIGN, noninvasive, and risk-free, such as—at the simplest level—the placing of a stethoscope on a child's chest or collecting a urine sample for testing. By contrast, some tests are INVASIVE—that is, they involve intrusions into the body, as with an INJECTION of dyed fluid—and entail at least some pain or risk, and so should not be used unless the information sought is of sufficient importance to warrant their use.

Before subjecting their children (or themselves) to any TEST, parents should be sure they understand what the procedure involves. By law, medical personnel are required to give patients the information they need about tests and procedures—about the risks, as well as the benefits—and to obtain INFORMED CONSENT before the test or procedure is carried out. Since a child is not legally able to make such decisions, parents must obtain and weigh medical information and give informed consent on their child's behalf. (See WHAT TO ASK ABOUT A MEDICAL TEST on page 387.)

A key question to be considered is the test's RELIABILITY. No test is 100 percent accurate. Any test will result in a certain number of false readings—either FALSE POSITIVES, indicating that you have a disorder, when in fact you do

What to Ask About a Medical Test

- *What is the test designed to show?* Is the test to rule out possible diseases, to narrow down the field for diagnosis, for example? Is it to confirm a diagnosis already tentatively made? Is it to screen for possible signs of a disorder?
- *How accurate is the test?* What is the probability that the test will give a false negative or false positive?
- *How definitive is the test?* Will the test give an answer reliable enough to act on, if necessary? Or is it a preliminary test that will probably need to be followed by more sophisticated tests, if a positive result is obtained?
- *What kind of side effects are likely, and how long might they last?* Side effects may range from a pinprick to active discomfort to severe pain to disability for some hours or longer; that depends on the test, including the kind of anesthesia, if any, and the patient's initial physical condition. You need as much information as possible to prepare yourself and your child to deal with possible side effects. (See HOSPITAL for preparation; also PAIN AND PAIN TREATMENT.)
- *What are the risks of taking the test?* If few or none, excellent. But you need to know if there are substantial risks. Is there, for example, risk of infection, injury to internal organs, allergic reaction to foreign substances introduced into the body, paralysis, or even death from the test itself? Such risks are different from side effects, which are simply temporary discomforts.
- *Does the test pose any special risks for pregnant women or children?* Tests that might be reasonably safe for others can prove unacceptably risky if a woman is—or suspects she may be—pregnant. And children, whose bodies are still growing and developing, may respond differently to a test than would a fully mature adult.
- *What are the risks of not taking the test?* Nothing in life is risk-free, and sometimes inaction can be more dangerous than action. If a physician suggests that your child may have a brain tumor, for example, taking a test would allow such a tumor to be diagnosed and possibly treated, while not taking the test might mean an undiagnosed tumor could be growing. Many situations are not so clear-cut, but you need to weigh the risks, side effects, and costs against the danger of leaving a disorder undiagnosed and untreated.
- *Where will it be done?* Will the test be performed in the doctor's office, in the hospital on an outpatient basis, or in a hospital as an inpatient? If there are alternatives, what is the balance between safety and cost among them, including insurance coverage?
- *How much will it cost?* In particular, are there separate charges for the attending physician, anesthetist (if necessary), nurse, laboratory work, and hospital quarters, or are all charges included in one fee?
- *Is the test covered by your insurance or medical care plan?* Depending on your health insurance or health care plan, you may need to obtain rather precise information about a test and often prior permission for it to be covered. Also, it may only be covered if performed in a hospital, sometimes a specific hospital or group or hospital, and sometimes only if performed by certain doctors.
- *What is necessary to prepare for the test?* You or the child may, for example, need to stop taking all medication some days or hours before the test, and may need to avoid certain kinds of foods. Many tests require that the patient not eat or drink for a specified number of hours beforehand; some may also require an enema. Because tests may be highly sensitive to changes in the body, the patient may need to get a good rest before the test, in order not to throw off the results.
- *What does the test result mean?* After a test has been taken, what does the result actually indicate—that a disorder exists, that it does not exist, or that it may exist? If the result is a numerical value, what is the "normal" value and how does your result compare to it? Are the results clear-cut or ambiguous? Do they indicate action now, retesting, or a "wait-and-see" attitude?

not, or FALSE NEGATIVES, indicating that you are free from a disorder, when in fact you have it. If a test is considered 80 percent accurate, that means that 1 out of every 5 times, it gives a false reading. That would seem far too much for a test carrying any risk, but in fact, many tests are far less accurate than that. Ideally, for a diagnostic test (as opposed to a SCREENING TEST) to be useful, it should be reliable enough so that, in most cases, another test will not be necessary to confirm the results of the first test.

But even when they are relatively reliable, medical tests rarely give definitive answers. Some tests are "disease-specific," so that a positive (abnormal) result strongly suggests that the patient has the disease, but in most tests, a positive result could be produced by a range of disorders. Where serious questions hang on the results of a test, it may well be appropriate to have a second test, of the same or different type, to confirm the results. For example, if a test showed that your child had a BRAIN TUMOR, and the doctor suggested an operation, you should certainly seek a second opinion, and possibly a second test or a second kind of test, to confirm that the operation is necessary.

Similarly, you should not embark on a major course of treatment, as for DIABETES, on the basis of a single test result. Tests can give inaccurate results for many reasons. A sample may be kept at the wrong temperature, or be confused with someone else's; a machine may be set improperly, or a technician may misread a test; a test may be thrown off by the patient's lack of rest or by something unusual in the patient's blood or chemical makeup, such as other medications (see DRUG REACTIONS AND INTERACTIONS). Results from health fairs have been found especially unreliable—though, as recent highly publicized cases have shown, some widely used laboratories have grossly mishandled many medical tests. But the converse is also true: If a test shows up negative, and symptoms continue, you should have further testing done. In their *Patient's Guide to Medical Tests,* Cathey Pinckney and Edward Pinckney put it bluntly:

> Never, under any circumstances, rely upon the good or bad results of a single medical test. Any medical test report that could change your life must be repeated at least twice—and in different settings, such as another laboratory or another doctor's office—before it can be considered a valid part of your medical record.

This advice applies especially to tests that can be performed in the home. (See HOME MEDICAL TESTING; also CAUTIONS IN USING HOME MEDICAL TESTS on page 303.)

In addition to giving informed consent *before* a test or procedure, patients have the right to expect full, understandable explanations of test results. In some states this "consumer" right has been given legal force, with laws that allow patients to review their medical records and obtain copies of them on request (though sometimes only with a court order; for help, see ADVOCACY). In such states, if you fail to get the information you require from your doctor, you can go to court to obtain access to the documents. If your doctor is not giving you the information you require, however, a new doctor would seem advisable, with your old records being transferred to the new doctor.

Various health books (see HEALTH CARE) discuss medical tests, what they involve, the risks they entail, and their reliability, often in the context of the various diseases and disorders they are designed to identify. Among the general types of medical tests briefly described in this book are:

- SPECIMEN TESTS, such as a BIOPSY, BLOOD TEST, or URINE TEST.
- RADIOGRAPHY, such as FLUOROSCOPY or X-RAYS.
- SCANS, such as a CT SCAN, ULTRASOUND, MRI, including NUCLEAR SCANS, such as PET SCAN.
- PRENATAL TESTS such as AMNIOCENTESIS, CHORIONIC VILLUS SAMPLING, ALPHA FETOPROTEIN,
- Medical tests that can be performed at home, such as blood glucose monitoring (see DIABETES), OVULATION monitoring, and PREGNANCY TESTS.
- Other types of tests, such as ELECTROCARDIOGRAM (ECG or EKG), ELECTROENCEPHALOGRAPH (EEG), ELECTROMYOGRAM (EMG), MYELOGRAM, LUMBAR PUNCTURE (spinal tap), CISTERNAL PUNCTURE, and ANGIOGRAM (arteriogram).

In these days of rising medical costs, another consideration relates to coverage of the costs of testing. In comparing HEALTH CARE plans, parents should evaluate how well the plans they are considering cover medical tests. *Where* the test is given sometimes affects HEALTH INSURANCE; for example, tests given in a hospital may be covered, but not the same test given in a doctor's office.

FOR HELP AND FURTHER INFORMATION

Food and Drug Administration (FDA),
301–443–3170. (See DRUG REACTIONS AND INTERACTIONS.)

The Arc, 817–261–6003. Publishes *Newborn Screening to Prevent Mental Retardation.* (For full group information, see MENTAL RETARDATION.)

ONLINE RESOURCES

Better Health and Medical Forum (America Online: Health, Medicine), Provides discussion areas and libraries covering medical tests. (For full information, see HEALTH CARE.)

(See also HEALTH CARE.)

Meeting Street School Screening Test, a type of individually administered DEVELOPMENTAL SCREENING TEST that is used to help identify possible LEARNING DISABILITIES in kindergarteners and first-graders, ages five to seven and a half. Subtests focus on three main areas, MOTOR SKILLS (including SPATIAL RELATIONS), VISUAL SKILLS, and LANGUAGE SKILLS. Tests are scored from a behavior rating scale and book of NORMS at half-year intervals (based on 1966 testing). (See TESTS.)

megadoses, amounts of VITAMINS or MINERALS that are greatly in excess of the RECOMMENDED DAILY ALLOWANCE of VITAMINS, which can sometimes lead to serious health problems.

menarche, the onset of the first MENSTRUATION, which marks the beginning of the regular MENSTRUAL CYCLES that signal a woman's sexual maturity and FERTILITY; also called *pubarche.*

meningitis, infection and inflammation of the *meninges,* the membranes that cover the brain and spinal cord. Although meningitis can occur at any age, it is especially a disease of children under five. The most common types of meningitis are caused by viruses; these are generally relatively mild, clearing up in a short period with little or no damage, though some rare forms can be more serious. Some YEASTS can also cause meningitis, but these are rare.

The most dangerous type of meningitis is caused by bacteria, which often reach the brain from infection elsewhere in the body, though sometimes may be introduced through a TRAUMATIC BRAIN INJURY. In the days before ANTIBIOTICS, bacterial meningitis caused death in nearly all afflicted with it. Even today, unless the disease is diagnosed, treated, and responds quickly, the disease still can cause death or serious brain damage in many children. The Public Health Service estimates that "in about 8 percent of the patients (particularly those with *meningococcal meningitis*) the disease progresses so rapidly that death occurs during the first 48 hours, despite early treatment with antibiotics."

The most common forms of bacterial meningitis are:

- *Neonatal meningitis,* which affects as many as 40–50 of every 100,000 newborns, is particularly dangerous. The Public Health Service estimates that if the disease occurs during the first week of life, as many as half will die, and half of the survivors will have some neurological damage. Babies often get the infection during DELIVERY, as from their mothers or the birthing staff or equipment, which is one of the reasons that germ-free delivery rooms are so important. PREMATURE or LOW BIRTH WEIGHT infants are especially at risk because their IMMUNE SYSTEMS are as yet insufficiently developed to protect them from infection. The main culprits are *Streptococcus group B* and *Escherichia coli.*
- *Haemophilus meningitis* has traditionally been the most common type of meningitis in children up to age ten. In recent years, however, a vaccine has been developed which protects children from the HIB DISEASE caused by the *Haemophilus influenzae type B* bacteria. Parents should be sure to include this vaccine on their IMMUNIZATION schedule.
- *Meningococcal meningitis,* caused by *Neisseria meningitidis,* is more common in older children and young adults. It is slightly less severe, with somewhat less lasting damage, but still causes a significant proportion of deaths. A vaccine is available against some forms of this bacteria, and is used sometimes in epidemic situations.
- *Pneumococcal meningitis,* caused by *Streptococcus pneumoniae,* is less common but perhaps the most dangerous, with a death rate estimated at over 30 percent and with considerable lasting damage. Found in infants as well as older children and adults, it usually follows a respiratory infection or TRAUMATIC BRAIN INJURY.

The key to preventing death and damage from meningitis is to get help quickly. Suspicious symptoms (see SIGNS OF BACTERIAL MENINGITIS below) should be

Signs of Bacterial Meningitis

Meningococcal and pneumococcal meningitis usually begin suddenly, with high fever, lack of energy, headache, and vomiting. There may also be stiffness of the neck, shoulders, and other joints. In about half the meningococcal cases there is a rash—consisting of small red spots or irregular bruise-like lesions—scattered over the whole body. Young children are likely to be irritable and restless during the early stages of the disease.

Within twenty-four to forty-eight hours, the patient usually becomes drowsy and mentally confused and may slip into a coma. There may also be convulsions.

The symptoms of haemophilus meningitis are similar, but the onset of the disease may be more gradual, with fever and lack of energy lasting for several days before the other symptoms appear.

With neonatal meningitis, the picture is very different because the infant may show no signs of disease or infection other than general irritability, poor feeding, and unstable temperature. Since such symptoms are common to a number of disorders, any unexplained fever or other sign of infection should be regarded with extreme suspicion, particularly in infants who may be at special risk for meningitis.

Source: Bacterial Meningitis. 1984. Public Health Service.

reported as quickly as possible. Often diagnosis will involve a LUMBAR PUNCTURE to remove some of the CEREBROSPINAL FLUID for analysis; this is important because doctors must identify which bacteria is involved in order to tell which antibiotics to prescribe.

Among the most common kinds of problems resulting from meningitis are MENTAL RETARDATION, EAR AND HEARING PROBLEMS, EPILEPSY, HYDROCEPHALUS, various LEARNING DISABILITIES, and sometimes problems with movement or coordination. Because damage is not always apparent until later, children who have had meningitis, especially neonatal meningitis, should be checked by a NEUROLOGIST periodically over the following two years, to identify any damage quickly and undertake therapy as necessary.

FOR HELP AND FURTHER INFORMATION

National Institute of Allergy and Infectious Diseases (NIAID), 301–496–5717. (For full group information, see ALLERGY.)

National Institute of Neurological Disorders and Stroke (NINDS), 800–352–9424. (For full group information, see BRAIN AND BRAIN DISORDERS.)

National Organization for Rare Disorders (NORD), 800–999–6673. (For full group information, see RARE DISORDERS.)

menopause, cessation of the regular cycle of MENSTRUATION, either gradually or suddenly, marking the natural end of a woman's ability to bear children, generally occurring between ages forty-five and fifty-five. During menopause, the eggs (see OVUM) stop being produced and the body makes less of the HORMONE called ESTROGEN. Women approaching menopause generally do not conceive as readily as they would earlier in their lives for a variety of reasons, not least of which is that fewer follicles (egg-forming cells) are available to produce eggs suitable for possible FERTILIZATION. Some surgical procedures, such as HYSTERECTOMY (removal of the UTERUS), or physiological problems can bring on *premature menopause*, ending early a woman's ability to reproduce.

menstrual cycle (reproductive cycle), the regular growth of the *endometrium* (lining of the UTERUS) to prepare for a possible fertilized egg (OVUM) and, if no PREGNANCY occurs, the expulsion of the unused lining in a bloody fluid at the end of the cycle, in the process called MENSTRUATION. The cycle itself is managed by various HORMONES and goes through a sequence of phases:

- *Proliferative or follicular phase*: In response to ESTROGEN hormones, the endometrium begins to thicken in the uterus. (If the woman becomes pregnant during the cycle, this endometrium will continue to grow and supply nourishment for the fertilized egg, after IMPLANTATION.)
- *Secretory or luteal phase*: OVULATION (release of an egg, or ovum) occurs roughly midway through the cycle (measured from the beginning of the previous menstrual period). At the same time the body begins to produce the hormone PROGESTERONE, which causes swelling and thickening of the endometrium, to further prepare the uterus to accept a fertilized egg. It is during this period that a woman is able to become pregnant.
- *Menstruation*: If no PREGNANCY occurs, the production of estrogen and progesterone declines, the unfertilized egg and unused lining are gradually expelled by contractions of the uterus, after which the process begins again.

Except during pregnancies, the cycle will normally repeat, sometimes with breaks and irregularities, from its onset (MENARCHE) during PUBERTY through to its final cessation (MENOPAUSE). (See MENSTRUATION; CONCEPTION.)

menstrual extraction, a type of ABORTION performed early in a PREGNANCY, using a procedure called VACUUM EXTRACTION.

menstruation, the periodic drainage of a bloody fluid through the VAGINA of a woman who is not pregnant; the fluid contains the unused *endometrium* (lining of the UTERUS) and the unfertilized egg (OVUM). On the average, menstruation occurs approximately once every four weeks, generally every 24 to 35 days, and lasts four to five days, though sometimes as short as one and as long as eight days. For most girls, *menarche*, the onset of the first menstruation, occurs as part of PUBERTY between ages ten and sixteen. It can occur much earlier, as part of what is termed *precocious puberty*. It can also arrive somewhat later; however, if a girl has not begun menstruating by age sixteen, parents should probably consult a doctor, to check for any underlying physical problem (see below). Girls who are overweight tend to begin their periods earlier, while those who are very thin, are involved in strenuous physical EXERCISE (such as ballet and some SPORTS), or have CHRONIC illness may begin to menstruate later. In recent decades, perhaps partly because of improved NUTRITION, menstruation has tended to start ever earlier.

The establishment of a regular MENSTRUAL CYCLE is a sign of sexual maturity and fertility, and its cessation (MENOPAUSE) later in life, either gradually or all at once, marks the end of a woman's fertile life. Parents will want to be alert to signs of puberty in a girl and prepare her for the coming of menstrual periods before they occur; many schools also have SEX EDUCATION courses that cover such matters, but parents may not wish to leave such matters in the hands of others. (Some of the books below may help parents in talking with their daughters about menstruation.)

In the complicated and delicate process of menstruation, various kinds of disorders can occur, including:

- *Dysmenorrhea,* painful menstruation, usually resulting from contractions of the UTERUS and slight dilation of the CERVIX, and can be accompanied by nausea, VOMITING, and intestinal cramps. Why dysmenorrhea occurs is not entirely clear, but perhaps 1 woman in 10 has menstrual periods so painful that they cause partial or complete disability for a few hours to a few days. BIRTH CONTROL PILLS can provide some relief, as can some painkillers (*analgesics*). Dysmenorrhea can also accompany other kinds of disorders, such as abnormalities of the pelvis, ENDOMETRIOSIS, fibroid TUMORS (see HYSTERECTOMY), or PELVIC INFLAMMATORY DISEASE. Where possible, the cause is treated, as by surgery.
- *Amenorrhea,* absence of menstruation. When a girl has failed to begin menstruating by age sixteen, it is called *primary amenorrhea,* which can result from a variety of causes, most of them very rare, including hormonal disorder, TURNER'S SYNDROME, CONGENITAL absence of reproductive organs, or lack of perforation in the HYMEN to allow blood to escape. By contrast, *secondary amenorrhea* is the halting of the menstrual cycle after establishment of regular periods, as during periods of stress or starvation (as in ANOREXIA NERVOSA), or in cases of hormonal imbalance. This can be caused by a tumor in the reproductive system, by hormonal disorders, or by surgical removal of the uterus. The most common causes for secondary amenorrhea are, of course, PREGNANCY and MENOPAUSE.
- *Polymenorrhea,* periods that come in a cycle of less than 22 days.
- *Oligomenorrhea,* periods that occur infrequently or with very small loss of blood.
- *Menorrhagia,* excessive bleeding during periods, which can also result from hormonal imbalance, from fibroid tumors or polyps, or an INTRAUTERINE DEVICE (IUD).
- *Metrorrhagia,* bleeding at extremely irregular intervals; this is often not menstrual periods at all, but bleeding associated with abnormalities such as CANCER.
- *Premenstrual syndrome* (PMS), a series of physical and emotional symptoms that occur in the week or two between OVULATION and the onset of menstruation, presumably triggered by cyclical hormonal changes. Symptoms of PMS include BREAST soreness, EDEMA (fluid buildup), headache, aches in the back and lower abdomen, DEPRESSION, fatigue, tension, and irritability, in some cases mild, in others severe enough to disrupt a woman's personal life. Treatments that have been tried with varied success include diuretic drugs to counter fluid buildup, hormonal supplements or birth control pills to smooth out hormonal swings, and elimination of foods that can cause fluid retention or headaches, such as salt, caffeine, and chocolate.

In a woman who is attempting to conceive a child, many of these menstrual disorders can make pregnancy more difficult, if not impossible, and so would need careful exploration and treatment to maximize the chance of becoming pregnant.

FOR HELP AND FUR

American College of Ob gists (ACOG), 202–638–
(For full group information,

Planned Parenthood Fede
800–230–7526. Publishes p
(For full group information, se

OTHER RESOURCES

GENERAL WORKS

The Period: Humorous, Light Hearted Look at Woman's Oldest Dilemma. Danna J. Krause. Red Hot Press, 1994.
Menstrual Cramps: A Self-Help Program. Susan M. Lark. National Nursing, 1993.
Periods: From Menarche to Menopause. Sharon Golub. Sage, 1992.

FOR PRETEENS AND TEENS

Getting Your Period. Jean Marzollo. Puffin, 1993.
Period. JoAnn Gardner-Loulan and others. Volcano Press, 1990.
Getting Your Period: A Book about Menstruation. Jean Marzollo. Dial, 1990.

(See also INFERTILITY.)

mental age (MA), a numerical summary reflecting a child's comparative performance on a mental ability or INTELLIGENCE TEST, notably the STANFORD-BINET INTELLIGENCE TEST, which relates a child's score to NORMS for others of the same age. Mental age is a somewhat outdated concept. (See also AGE.)

mental disorder, a pattern or SYNDROME of behavior that causes distress, disability, increased risk of pain or death, or grossly impaired functioning in a person to such an extent that it becomes a clinical problem. Individuals may have conflicts with society, and they may have personal behavior that is nonstandard, in areas relating to political, religious, or sexual norms. Many such conflicts and behavior were once regarded as signs of "mental illness." But under the American Psychiatric Association's widely accepted current classification of mental disorders (see *Diagnostic and Statistical Manual of Mental Disorders,* below), they would not be considered mental disorders unless they involved severe personal DYSFUNCTION.

Many mental disorders primarily affect adults, but some appear first during childhood, or have their roots in childhood trauma. Under the EDUCATION FOR ALL HANDICAPPED CHILDREN ACT, and its successor the INDIVIDUALS WITH DISABILITIES EDUCATION ACT, states are charged with identifying children with *emotional disturbances* as early as possible, through such programs as CHILDFIND, so that they can receive treatment. The aim of such programs is to put children in the best possible position to benefit from public EDUCATION, with special services provided needs it. For reporting purposes, programs AD START use the following definition:

> A child shall be considered seriously emotionally disturbed who is identified by professionally qualified personnel (psychologist or psychiatrist) as requiring special services. This definition would include but not be limited to the following conditions: dangerously aggressive towards others, self-destructive, severely withdrawn and non-communicative, hyperactive to the extent that it affects adaptive behavior, severely anxious, depressed or phobic, psychotic or autistic.

A child thought to have possible emotional disturbance will be referred for screening (as with a DEVELOPMENTAL SCREENING TEST) and possibly then evaluation (often using a DIAGNOSTIC ASSESSMENT TEST) by a PSYCHOLOGIST or PSYCHIATRIST. The evaluation generally outlines the child's development—both strengths and weaknesses—and explains what special services the child should receive in the schools. Sometimes, however, evaluations say only that the child is emotionally disturbed or give the name of a particular disturbance. Though useful as shorthand among professionals, since a single word can convey a whole range of related behaviors, such labels can sometimes get in the way of seeing the child as an individual, as noted in Head Start's *Mainstreaming Preschoolers: Children with Emotional Disturbance*:

> Classifying a child usually limits rather than extends our understanding, and often produces negative and inaccurate expectations for that child. The use of these names doesn't allow us to think of the range of skills and behaviors a child may demonstrate. It doesn't describe the severity of the child's problem with a particular skill or set of skills. For example, the term "disturbed" cannot possibly tell you whether a child has problems with sharing. One disturbed child may have problems sharing a certain toy with certain people, while another disturbed child may have trouble sharing anything with anyone. Still another disturbed child may have no special difficulty sharing. A word or phrase cannot possibly describe all of the possibilities to [teachers and parents]. Describing children in terms of strengths and weaknesses is much more valuable to [them] than being able to fit them into a category.
>
> Another real disadvantage of classifying is that the terms tend to stick with a child for a long time, regardless of whether the handicapping condition is still present. This can lead to social isolation and incorrect assumptions about a child's ability. Young children change and grow so rapidly that some children with handicaps may overcome their disabilities before entering public school. Names acquired in preschool are likely to follow children into public schools, and may be used as a basis for excluding them from the regular school program. It is hard to outlive or live down how you have been classified.

Parents should try their best to see that teachers get to know the whole child, and do not focus on simply a label. They also need to be sure that the diagnosis is a correct one; they should be sure that all possible physical causes of seeming emotional problems are thoroughly checked, so that a child is not misdiagnosed and severely disadvantaged. For example, a child who has an undiagnosed problem with hearing or vision may be thoroughly frustrated in his or her attempts to communicate with others, which can show itself in severe aggression, withdrawal, or other kinds of problems; if the child is then diagnosed as emotionally disturbed, the underlying EYE AND VISION PROBLEMS or EAR AND HEARING PROBLEMS may go undetected for a considerable time.

Similarly, parents need to be sure that cultural or language differences at home do not make the child seem emotionally disturbed in the new and alien setting of a classroom; when any evaluation is being done, it is important that the evaluator be fully aware of the child's home background. As the Head Start program comments:

> Some children are "street wise" at an early age: they know how to fight for their rights and take care of themselves. This behavior might include using physical force and yelling to settle problems, rather than talking things out. These children may be very assertive in this way because it is how they have learned to respond and, perhaps, because this way is acceptable to other people around them. They may in fact not be disturbed at all.

All that being said, however, parents may need to know something about the kinds of mental disorders that can affect children. Among those that normally appear during infancy, childhood, or adolescence are:

- MENTAL RETARDATION.
- AUTISM, classified by psychiatrists as a *pervasive developmental disorder*.
- LEARNING DISABILITIES and communication disorders (see COMMUNICATION SKILLS AND DISORDERS), classified by psychiatrists as *specific developmental disorders*.
- ATTENTION-DEFICIT HYPERACTIVITY DISORDER (ADHD) and CONDUCT DISORDER, classified by psychiatrists as *disruptive behavior disorders*.
- *Anxiety disorders* (see ANXIETY), including SEPARATION ANXIETY DISORDER, AVOIDANT DISORDER, and OVERANXIOUS DISORDER.
- ANOREXIA NERVOSA, BULIMIA NERVOSA, PICA, and RUMINATION DISORDER OF INFANCY, classified by psychiatrists as *eating disorders*, as well as BINGE EATING DISORDER.
- GENDER IDENTITY DISORDERS.

- TOURETTE SYNDROME, classified by psychiatrists as a *tic disorder.*
- SOILING (*encopresis*), classified by psychiatrists as an *elimination disorder.*
- IDENTITY DISORDER.
- REACTIVE ATTACHMENT DISORDER.
- *Stereotypy/habit disorder* (see COMFORT HABITS).

In addition, some other disorders may appear at any age and affect children and adults in many of the same ways, including:

- ORGANIC MENTAL DISORDERS, resulting from physical problems in the brain.
- MOOD DISORDERS, including DEPRESSION and BIPOLAR DISORDERS (manic-depression).
- Other anxiety disorders, including PANIC DISORDERS, *phobic disorders* (see PHOBIA), and OBSESSIVE COMPULSIVE DISORDER.
- DISSOCIATIVE DISORDERS, including MULTIPLE PERSONALITY DISORDER.
- IMPULSE CONTROL DISORDERS, including INTERMITTENT EXPLOSIVE DISORDER, PYROMANIA, and *trichotillomania* (see COMFORT HABITS; HAIR).
- ADJUSTMENT DISORDERS.
- PERSONALITY DISORDERS, including DEPENDENT PERSONALITY DISORDER, PARANOID PERSONALITY DISORDER, PASSIVE AGGRESSIVE PERSONALITY DISORDER.

FOR HELP AND FURTHER INFORMATION

ORGANIZATIONS FOCUSING ON CHILDREN

PACER Center (Parent Advocacy Coalition for Educational Rights), 612–827–2966, voice/TT. Publishes newsletter *Children's Mental Health Update*; books *A Guidebook for Parents of Children with Emotional or Behavioral Disorders* and *Honorable Intentions: A Parent's Guide to Educational Planning for Children with Emotional or Behavioral Disorders*; booklet *Why Is My Child Hurting? Positive Approaches to Dealing with Difficult Behavior*; information handout *Recommended Readings for Parents of Children with Emotional or Behavioral Disorders*; and video *Parent Perspectives: Raising Children with Emotional Disorders.* (For full group information, see HELP FOR SPECIAL CHILDREN on page 689.)

Council for Exceptional Children (CEC), 800–328–0272. Includes Council for Children with Behavioral Disorders (CCBD), which publishes quarterlies *CCBD Newsletter* and *Behavioral Disorders*; triannual magazine *Beyond Behavior*; and other materials. CEC also publishes special report *Emotional Disturbances* and numerous materials on education. (For full group information, see HELP ON LEARNING AND EDUCATION on page 659.)

Federation of Families for Children's Mental Health
1021 Prince Street
Alexandria, VA 22314–2971
703–684–7710
Jane Walker, President
Organization concerned with children who have mental, emotional, or behavioral problems; provides information, referrals, and support; advises on parent advocacy; publishes quarterly newsletter *Claiming Children, Fact Sheet on Childhood Disorders, Finding Help—Finding Hope: A Guide Book to School Services for Families With a Child Who Has Emotional, Behavioral, or Mental Disorders*, and *All Systems Failure: An Examination of the Results of Neglecting the Needs of Children with Serious Emotional Disturbance*, and provides information on materials from many other sources.

American Academy of Child and Adolescent Psychiatry (AACAP)
3615 Wisconsin Avenue NW
Washington, DC 20016–3007
202–966–7300
Fax: 202–966–2891
E-mail: 74003.264@compuserve.com (CompuServe: 74003.264)
Professional organization of child and adolescent psychiatrists; fosters research; provides information; acts as advocate; publishes various materials, including:

- Quarterly *Newsletter*, triannual *Child and Adolescent Research Notes*, and bimonthly *Journal of the American Academy of Child and Adolescent Psychiatry.*
- "Facts for Families" information sheets: *Children Who Steal, Psychiatric Medication for Children, Normality, Know When to Seek Help for Your Child, Know Where to Seek Help for Your Child, Children's Major Psychiatric Disorders, 11 Questions to Ask Before Psychiatric Hospital Treatment of Children and Adolescents, Conduct Disorders, Helping Children After a Disaster, Manic-Depressive Illness in Teens, Children of Parents with Mental Illness, The Continuum of Care, Children and Lying, The Anxious Child, Schizophrenia in Children, Panic Disorder in Children, Questions to Ask About Psychiatric Medications for Children and Adolescents, Comprehensive Psychiatric Evaluation*, and *What Is Psychotherapy for Children and Adolescents.*
- *Questions and Answers About Child Psychiatry* and *Glossary of Mental Illnesses Affecting Teenagers.*
- Numerous professional materials.

American Association of Psychiatric Services for Children (AAPSC)
c/o Sidney Koret
1200C Scottsville Road, Suite 225
Rochester, NY 14624
716–235–6910
Organization concerned about psychiatric and related services for children; encourages coordinated efforts between psychiatrists, psychologists, and social workers; provides information and referrals; publishes newsletters.

Division of Child and Youth Services, American Psychological Association (APA)
750 First St. NE
Washington, DC 20002–4242
202–336–6013

Raymond Powles, Executive Officer
Organization of professionals devoted to studying, preventing, and treating emotional disturbances in children; acts as advocate; provides information; publishes *Psychological Testing of Language Minority and Culturally Different Children* and other materials.

C. Henry Kempe National Center for the Prevention and Treatment of Child Abuse and Neglect, 303–321–3963. Publishes *Playing for Their Lives: Helping Troubled Children Through Play Therapy.* (For full group information, see HELP AGAINST CHILD ABUSE AND NEGLECT on page 680.)

National Association of Psychiatric Treatment Centers for Children (NAPTCC)
2000 L Street NW
Washington, DC 20036
202–955–3828
Organization of accredited residential centers treating emotionally disturbed children.

Pediatric Projects, 800–947–0947. Publishes bimonthly newsletter *Pediatric Mental Health* on caring for seriously ill children. (For full group information, see HOSPITAL.)

National Information Center for Children and Youth with Disabilities (NICHCY), 800–695–0285, voice/TT. Publishes *Emotional Disturbance* and bibliographies *Mental Health/Mental Illness* and *Behavior Management.* (For full group information, see HELP FOR SPECIAL CHILDREN on page 689.)

HEATH Resource Center, National Clearinghouse on Postsecondary Education for Individuals with Disabilities, 800–544–3284, voice/TT. Publishes *Adults with Psychiatric Disabilities on Campus.* (For full group information, see HELP FOR SPECIAL CHILDREN on page 689.)

National Institute of Child Health and Human Development (NICHD), 301–496–5133. Publishes *Treatment of Destructive Behaviors in Persons with Developmental Disabilities* (For full group information, see PREGNANCY.)

GENERAL ORGANIZATIONS

National Mental Health Association (NMHA)
1021 Prince Street
Alexandria, VA 22314–2971
703–684–7722; Information Center: 800–969-NMHA [969–6642]
John Horner, Executive Director
Organization acting as advocate for people with mental illness; provides information; sponsors support groups; seeks to educate public and influence public policy; publishes quarterly newsletter *Focus,* monthly newsletter *The BULLETIN,* quarterly *Prevention Update,* and other materials, including:

- For parents: *What Every Child Needs for Good Mental Health, Building Your Child's Self-Confidence, Troubled and Troubling Children: A Guide for Parents Seeking Help for Their Children with Emotional Disturbance,* and the "Feelings and Your Child" pamphlet series, such as *How to Deal with Destructive Behavior, How to Deal with Lying and Stealing, Learning to Enjoy Eating,* and *Nervous Mannerisms and What's Behind Then.*
- "Coping With" pamphlets: such as *Everyday Problems, Family Life, Mental Illness in the Family,* and *Getting Help When You Need It.*
- General pamphlets: *Mental Health Is 1–2–3, What You Learn About Mental Illness Could Change a Life: A Message of Hope, Teenager's Guide to Surviving Stress, How to Deal With Your Tensions,* and *Stigma: A Lack of Awareness and Understanding.*
- Program and resource materials.

National Alliance for the Mentally Ill (NAMI)
200 North Glebe Road, Suite 1015
Arlington, VA 22203–3754
703–524–7600; NAMI Helpline: 800–950-NAMI [950–6264]
Fax: 703–524–9094
E-mail: namiofc@aol.com (America Online: NAMI)
Laurie M. Flynn, Executive Director
Organization focusing on mental illness and treatments; acts as advocate; provides information; publishes or distributes various materials, including:

- Brochures: *Families Just Like Yours...An Introduction to NAMI, Mental Illness Is Everybody's Business, Mental Illness Information for Writings* (on avoiding stigmatizing language), *Dual Diagnosis: Substance Abuse and Mental Illness, Mood Disorders, Tardive Dyskinesia, Panic Disorder,* and *Benzodiazepines;*
- Books and booklets: *Coping with Mental Illness in the Family: A Family Guide, Understanding Low Motivation in Mental Illness, Neurobiological Disorders in Children and Adolescents, When Someone You Love Has a Mental Illness, Patient Confidentiality and You, Surviving Mental Illness,* and *A Guide to Mental Illness and the Criminal Justice System.*
- Personal accounts: *My Sister's Keeper: Learning to Cope with a Sibling's Mental Illness* and *Tell Me I'm Here* (about a son's illness).
- Videos: *Straight Talk About Mental Illness* and *NAMI—An Oral History.*
- Works on counseling, treatment, medication, reform, and advocacy.

National Institute of Mental Health (NIMH)
Information Resources and Inquiries Branch (IRIB)
Parklawn Building, 7C–02
5600 Fishers Lane
Rockville, MD 20857
301–443–4513; Depression: 800–421–4211; Panic Disorder: 80064–PANIC [647–2642]
Fax: 301–443–0008
Rex William Cowdry, Acting Director
One of the National Institutes of Health; provides infor-

mation; sponsors research; publishes numerous materials, including:

- General materials: *A Consumer's Guide to Mental Health Services, Plain Talk About Dealing with the Angry Child, Handling Stress, Medications, Lithium, You Are Not Alone, Useful Information on Paranoia, Bipolar Disorder,* and *Alzheimer's Disease.*
- On anxiety: *Anxiety Disorders. Panic Disorder, Understanding Panic Disorder, Panic Disorder Fact Sheet, Panic Disorder Referral List, Panic Disorder Resource List, Getting Treatment for Panic Disorder,* and video *Panic Disorder: Stories of Hope.*
- Numerous publications for professionals.

Hazelden Foundation (HF), 800–262–5010. Publishes *Embracing the Fear: Learning to Manage Anxiety and Panic Attacks* and materials on dual disorders: substance abuse and mental illness. (For full group information, see HELP AGAINST SUBSTANCE ABUSE on page 703.)

National Mental Health Consumer Self-Help Clearinghouse
1211 Chestnut Street, Suite 1000
Philadelphia, PA 19107
215–751–1810; 215–751–9655, TT;
800–553–4KEY [553–4539]
Fax: 215–636–6310
E-mail: thekey@delphi.com (Delphi: THEKEY)
Joseph A. Rogers, Director
Organization providing information, technical assistance, and referrals on mental health self-help groups nationwide; publishes newsletter *The Key*:

- Pamphlets: *Fighting Stigma, Jobs, Jobs, Jobs!,* and *Who's Who in the Mental Health System.*
- Book: *Crisis and Support Manual: When Crisis Occurs: The Least Restrictive Intervention Options.*
- Reprint packets: on specific disorders, including anxiety/panic disorder, borderline personality disorder, chronic fatigue syndrome, multiple personality disorder, obsessive compulsive disorder, phobias, post-traumatic stress disorder, and schizophrenia; and many general topics, such as choosing a therapist, children and mental health, dual diagnosis, family and mental health, legal assistance, and patients' rights and involuntary treatment.

Anxiety Disorders Association of America (ADAA)
6000 Executive Boulevard, Suite 513
Rockville, MD 20852
301–231–9350
Jerilyn Ross, President
Organization focusing on anxiety disorders; acts as information clearinghouse; publishes quarterly *ADAA Reporter* and other materials, including:

- Pamphlets: *Consumer's Guide to Treatment, Panic and Agoraphobia, Post-Traumatic Stress Disorder, Social Phobia, Obsessive-Compulsive Disorder, Generalized Anxiety Disorder, Breaking the Panic Cycle,* and *Anxiety Disorders: Helping a Family Member.*
- Books: *Anxiety Disorders in Children and Adolescents, The Essential Guide to Psychiatric Drugs, Breaking the Panic Cycle: Self-Help for People with Phobias, Triumph Over Fear: A Book of Help and Hope for People with Anxiety, Anxiety, Phobias and Panic, The Anxiety and Phobia Workbook, Dying of Embarrassment, Panic Disorder and Agoraphobia: A Guide, The Fearful Flyers Resource Guide, Fly Without Fear, Help Yourself: A Guide to Organizing a Phobia Self-Help Group, Panic Attacks, and Phobias, Obsessive Compulsive Disorder: A Guide, Stop Obsessing, When Once Is Not Enough,* and works for health professionals.
- National directories and conference reports.

National Clearinghouse for Alcohol and Drug Abuse Information (NCADI), 301–468–2600. Publishes *Prevention of Mental Disorders, Alcohol and Other Drug Use in Children and Adolescents* and *Family-Centered Treatment of Adolescents with Alcohol, Drug Abuse, and Mental Health Problems.* (For full group information, see HELP AGAINST SUBSTANCE ABUSE on page 703).

National Information Center on Deafness (NICD), 202–651–5051; 202–651–5052, TT. Publishes *Residential Programs for Deaf/Emotionally Disturbed Children and Adolescents.* (For full group information, see EAR AND HEARING PROBLEMS.)

National Association for the Dually Diagnosed (NADD), 914–331–4336. (For full group information, see MENTAL RETARDATION.)

American Psychiatric Association (APA)
1400 K Street NW
Washington, DC 20005
202–682–6000; For orders: 800–368–5777
Fax: 202–789–2648
Melvin Sabshin, Medical Director
Professional organization of psychiatrists, including special council on children, adolescents, and their families; publishes various materials.

Thresholds Psychiatric Rehabilitation Center
2700 North Lakeview Avenue
Chicago, IL 60614
312–281–3800; 312–989–8991, TT
Fax: 312–281–8790
Center serving people with severe and persistent mental disorders, with model program focusing on education, social skills, avoidance of rehospitalization, physical health, independent living, and vocation; publishes *Supported Competitive Employment Newsletter* and materials for parents on postsecondary education and employment.

Mental Disability Legal Resource Center (MDLRC)
American Bar Association
740 15th Street NW, 9th Floor
Washington, DC 20005
202–662–1570
202-662-0132
E-mail: cmpdl@attmail.com

Internet website: http://www.abanet.org
John Parry, Director
Organization that monitors court decisions, legislation, and administrative rulings relating to people with mental or physical disabilities, including civil commitment, rights of the disabled, education of children with disabilities, discrimination against the disabled, and environmental barriers; publishes various materials, including bimonthly *Mental and Physical Disability Law Reporter.*

Judge David L. Bazelon Center for Mental Health Law
1101 Fifteenth Street NW, Suite 1212
Washington, DC 20005–5002
202–467–5730; 202–467–4232, TT
Fax: 202–223–0409
Organization acting as advocate for legal rights of people with mental disabilities; formerly Mental Health Law Project; provides training and assistance; publishes various materials.

The Arc, 817–261–6003. Publishes fact sheet *Mental Illness in Persons with Mental Retardation.* (For full group information, see MENTAL RETARDATION.)

Center for Psychiatric Rehabilitation
Psychiatric Rehabilitation Services Center
Boston University
730 Commonwealth Avenue
Boston, MA 02215
617–353–3550; 617–353–7701, TT
Fax: 617–353–7700
Research and training center in mental health, focusing on quality of life for people with psychiatric disabilities; conducts research; provides information; publishes various materials.

National Organization for Rare Disorders (NORD), 800–999–6673. (For full group information, see RARE DISORDERS.)

Resource Center on Substance Abuse Prevention and Disability, 202–628–8442. Publishes *A Look at Alcohol and Other Drug Abuse Prevention and Mental Illness.* (For full group information, see HELP FOR SPECIAL CHILDREN on page 689.)

SELF-HELP GROUPS FOR THE MENTALLY ILL

Emotions Anonymous (EA)
P.O. Box 4245
St. Paul, MN 55104
612–647–9712
Fax: 612–647–1593
Network of support groups for people recovering from emotional illness; modeled on Alcoholics Anonymous; publishes magazine *Carrying the EA Message*; *EA World Directory*; books *Emotions Anonymous* and *My EA Workbook*; pamphlets *Introduction to Children's EA, Introduction to Youth EA, Loner's Emotions Anonymous* (for those unable to attend meetings), *Depression, Self-Esteem, Fear, Resentments, Anger, Indecision, Perfectionism,* and *Love*; and other materials on recovery and on forming groups.

Depression and Related Affective Disorders Association (DRADA), 410–955–4647. Publishes pamphlet *What You Need to Know About Psychiatric Medications* and books *Selected Readings on Mood Disorders* and *Manual for Affective Disorder Support Groups.* (For full group information, see DEPRESSION.)

ONLINE RESOURCES

Issues in Mental Health (America Online: IMH). Provides forum for discussion and exchange of information on mental health questions, for public and professionals; also provides online library; major topics covered include parenting, daily living, divorce and separation, relationships, teen forum, attention deficit disorder, general self-help information, and current issues. (Location: Lifestyles and Interests: Issues in Mental Health)

Internet: Panic. Mailing list providing online discussion and support group for people who have panic disorders. To subscribe, send e-mail message to: mailto:panic-request@guu.ai.mit.edu

Internet: altconspiracy. Usenet newsgroup focusing on paranoia. Subscribe through newsreader: news:alt.conspiracy

OTHER RESOURCES

FOR PARENTS AND OTHER ADULTS

Family Encyclopedia of Child Psychology and Development: An Easy-to-Understand Parent's Guide. Frank J. Bruno. Wiley, 1992.
When Your Child Needs Help: A Parent's Guide to Therapy for Children. Norma Doft with Barbara Aria. Harmony, 1992.
Children and Adolescents with Mental Illness: A Parents' Guide. E. McElroy. Woodbine House, 1988.

ON ANXIETIES IN GENERAL

All I Did Was Entertain a Little Anxiety: A Children's Book for Adults. Sheila Dickinson. P. B. Publishing, 1994.
When Anxiety Attacks: What the Health Care Community Does Not Know about Anxiety Attacks. Stan H. Looper and others. Swan, 1993.
Answers to Anxiety. John R. Mumaw. Christian Light, 1993.
Manic-Depressive Illness. Frederick K. Goodwin and Kay Redfield Jamison. Oxford University Press, 1990.
Childhood Anxiety Disorders. Siegel and Brown. W. Gladden, 1991.
Anxiety. Bonnie Timmons. Fawcett, 1991.
Anxiety Attacks. Karen Randau. Rapha, 1991.

(See also PHOBIA.)

ON TREATMENT AND RECOVERY

Managing Your Anxiety: Regaining Control When You Feel Stressed, Helpless, and Alone. Christopher J. McCullough and Robert W. Mann. Berkley, 1994.
Learning to Tell Myself the Truth: A 12-Week Guide to Freedom from Anger, Anxiety, Depression. William Backus. Bethany House, 1994.
Triumph over Fear. Jerilyn Ross. Bantam, 1994. By the founder of the Anxiety Disorder Association of America.
Surviving Mental Illness: Stress, Coping, and Adaptation. A.B. Hatfield and H.P. Lefley. Guilford, 1993.
What You Need to Know About Psychiatric Medications. S.C. Yukofsky and others. Ballantine, 1992.
Anxiety Disorders: A Practical Guide. Paul M. Emmelkamp and others. Wiley, 1992.
Overcoming Panic Attacks: Strategies to Free Yourself from the Anxiety Trap. Shirley Babior and Carol Goldman. Whole Person, 1991.
You Have Choices: Recovering from Anxiety, Panic and Phobia. William N. Penzer and Bonnie Goodman. Esperance, 1991. Original title: *Overcoming Anxiety, Panic, Phobias Through a Support Group.*

FOR CHILDREN

A Child's First Book About Play Therapy. Marc Nemiroff and Jane Annunziata. American Psychological Association, 1991.

FOR PRETEENS AND TEENS

Straight Talk about Anxiety and Depression. Michael Maloney and Rachel Kranz. Facts on File, 1991.
Don't Be S.A.D.: A Teenage Guide to Handling Stress, Anxiety and Depression. Susan Newman. Messner/Simon & Schuster, 1991.
Diagnosing and Treating Mental Illness. Alan Lundy. Chelsea House, 1990.

PERSONAL EXPERIENCES

What of the Night?: A Journey Through Depression and Anxiety. Jeffrey J. Knowles. Herald Press, 1993.
A Child Like That. Rikva Walburg. Philipp Feldheim, 1992. About a young mother's struggle to come to terms with her child's mental disability.
A Brilliant Madness: Living with Manic-Depressive Illness. Patty Duke and Gloria Hochman. Bantam, 1992.
Ghost Girl: The Story of a Child Who Refused to Talk. Torrey L. Hayden. Little, Brown, 1991. Teacher attempts to help a severely disturbed, emotionally neglected, sexually abused child.
Rickie. Frederick F. Flach. Ballantine, 1990. Psychiatrist's account of adolescent daughter's ten years of mental illness.
Prisoner of Fear: My Long Road to Freedom from Anxiety Disease, Panic Attacks and Agoraphobia. Richard Maro. Hickory Grove, 1990.
Dibs: In Search of Self. Virginia Axline. Ballantine, 1976.
I Never Promised You a Rose Garden. Hannah Green. New American Library, 1964.

BACKGROUND WORKS

How Therapists Diagnose: Seeing Through the Psychiatric Eye. B. Hamstra. St. Martin's Press, 1994.
Touched with Fire: Manic-Depressive Illness and the Artistic Temperament. Norman E. Rosenthal. Guilford, 1993.
Portrait of the Artist as a Young Patient: Psychodynamic Studies of the Creative Personality. Gerald Alper. Plenum, 1992.
Manic-Depressive Illness. F.K. Goodwin and K.R. Jamison. Oxford University Press, 1990.
The Untouched Key: Tracing Childhood Trauma in Creativity and Destructiveness. Alice Miller. Doubleday, 1990.

(See also DEPRESSION; SUICIDE; AUTISM; CHILD ABUSE AND NEGLECT; various specific disorders listed above; also HELP FOR SPECIAL CHILDREN on page 689.)

mental retardation, significantly lower-than-normal capacity for learning and COGNITIVE DEVELOPMENT. As the name implies, the condition shows itself by clear delays in reaching DEVELOPMENTAL MILESTONES (see CHART OF NORMAL DEVELOPMENT on page 637). But where children of normal mental capacity may overcome initial DEVELOPMENTAL DELAY from various causes, mentally retarded children develop only to a certain plateau, at which their learning levels off. Traditionally they have been classed by their mental ability, as measured by standard INTELLIGENCE TESTS, the usual classifications being:

- *Mild:* IQ 50–55 to 70, formerly termed *educable.*
- *Moderate:* IQ 35–40 to 50–55, formerly termed *trainable.*
- *Severe:* IQ 20–25 to 35–40.
- *Profound:* IQ under 20–25.

In psychology and education, these categories are now somewhat outmoded, but they are still widely used, if only because they are written into many laws relating to mental retardation.

Today, however, parents, educators, and others focus much more on what the individual child can and cannot do, especially on ADAPTIVE BEHAVIOR. A widely adopted 1992 definition from the American Association on Mental Retardation describes an individual as having mental retardation if:

- IQ is below 70–75;
- The person has significant limitations in two or more adaptive skills, defined as communication, self-care, home living, social skills, leisure, health and safety, self-direction, functional academics, community use, and work; and
- The condition has been present from childhood.

The aim is to provide an in-depth evaluation of the person's individual strengths and weaknesses, and to focus on enhancing skills and independence as much as possible.

Observational Checklist for Possible Mental Retardation

INFORMATION COMING FROM THE ENVIRONMENT

	OFTEN OR ALWAYS	RARELY OR NEVER
The child doesn't understand directions, reacts slowly to them, or waits to see what the other children are doing first.	☐	☐
The child seems confused and doesn't do what other children are doing along with them.	☐	☐
The child doesn't know what to do with materials and toys, or uses them for the wrong purposes.	☐	☐
Loud sounds disturb the child.	☐	☐
A lot of unorganized moving around in the classroom confuses the child.	☐	☐
The child has trouble noticing fine details.	☐	☐
The child doesn't answer to his or her name.	☐	☐
The child can't carry out a one-step direction.	☐	☐
The child can't concentrate on one thing for very long, and is easily distracted.	☐	☐
The child doesn't show interest in classroom surroundings.	☐	☐

PROCESSING THE INFORMATION

	OFTEN OR ALWAYS	RARELY OR NEVER
The child has trouble remembering what he or she has seen or heard, or what has happened.	☐	☐
The child can't match colors and shapes.	☐	☐
The child can't sort colors and shapes.	☐	☐
The child can't answer simple questions (such as "What's your name?") or gives answers that make no sense.	☐	☐
The child doesn't know things that other children in the class know.	☐	☐
The child does things in the wrong order (such as drying the pan before it has been washed).	☐	☐
The child can't predict dangerous consequences of actions before he or she does them.	☐	☐
The child can't hear small differences in words (such as boy/toy, Fred/red).	☐	☐
The child can't retell a simple story.	☐	☐
The child has trouble following two or more directions in the right order.	☐	☐
The child doesn't understand common environmental sounds (for example, can't tell you "a car" upon hearing the beep of a car horn).	☐	☐
The child doesn't remember the classroom routine.	☐	☐
The child forgets what he or she is doing in the middle of it.	☐	☐
The child has trouble inventing stories and actions in pretend play.	☐	☐

PROCESSING THE INFORMATION *(continued)*

	OFTEN OR ALWAYS	RARELY OR NEVER
The child doesn't understand basic concepts such as relationships, time, space, and quantity as well as other children do.	☐	☐

USING THE INFORMATION

	OFTEN OR ALWAYS	RARELY OR NEVER
Verbal Responses: Talking		
The child doesn't talk at all.	☐	☐
You can't understand the child's speech.	☐	☐
The child can't communicate using words and gestures, either alone or together.	☐	☐
The child can't name or describe familiar objects.	☐	☐
Motor Responses: Moving the Body		
The child trembles or shakes.	☐	☐
The child falls down or bumps into things a lot.	☐	☐
The child walks unevenly, or limps.	☐	☐
The child has poor eye-hand coordination (for example, knocks things over a lot).	☐	☐
The child can't pull simple clothing on or off.	☐	☐
The child has trouble using toys such as blocks and puzzles.	☐	☐
The child can't copy simple forms, such as a line, circle, square.	☐	☐

THE CHILD'S BEHAVIOR IN THE CLASSROOM

	OFTEN OR ALWAYS	RARELY OR NEVER
The child resists change and variety in activities by crying, throwing tantrums, or refusing to participate.	☐	☐
The child cannot make choices about what to do or select activities independently.	☐	☐
The child imitates the games of other children rather than inventing his or her own games.	☐	☐
The child withdraws from participating in most or all of the activities.	☐	☐
The child is constantly disrupting the class.	☐	☐

Source: Mainstreaming Preschoolers: Children with Mental Retardation: A Guide for Teachers, Parents, and Others Who Work with Mentally Retarded Preschoolers, by Eleanor Whiteside Lynch et al. (1978). Prepared for the Head Start Bureau of the U.S. Administration for Children, Youth, and Families.

Though its precise causes are unknown, mental retardation is associated with a variety of other problems, including genetic disorders, chromosomal abnormalities, and difficulties relating to pregnancy and childbirth. The three most common known causes of mental retardation are Down syndrome, fetal alcohol syndrome, and fragile X syndrome. By definition, it appears in children during development, though similar retardation can result from later problems, such as traumatic brain injury, malnutrition, or severe fever and illness, such as that resulting in meningitis or encephalitis. Where associated with a specific disorder, such as Down syndrome or phenylketonuria (PKU), mental retardation often appears with other characteristics. If not, it can be hard to diagnose properly, especially in young children, since they develop at varying rates and may have other problems.

The incidence of mental retardation has been lessened in recent decades by advances in treatment, as of PKU; by immunization, as for measles, chicken pox,

WHOOPING COUGH, and HIB DISEASE; by other preventive therapies, as for RH INCOMPATIBILITY; and by new treatments for brain injury, ASPHYXIA during childbirth, and infections affecting the brain (see BRAIN AND BRAIN DISORDERS). Even so, as of the 1990 census, an estimated 6.2–7.5 million people were found to have mental retardation. Previous studies had suggested that mental retardation affects 2.5–3 percent of the population, directly affecting an estimated one family in ten. By far the largest group, perhaps 87 percent, show only mild retardation, and many cases are not diagnosed until the child enters school.

Parents who are concerned that their preschool child might be mentally retarded may want to use the OBSERVATION CHECKLIST FOR POSSIBLE MENTAL RETARDATION IN PRESCHOOLERS (on page 398). That checklist should be used only as a guideline in judging when to refer a child for evaluation. It is important for parents to realize that slow mental development is not necessarily mental retardation. Medical and educational files abound with cases of children misdiagnosed as mentally retarded. Many of these had normal intelligence, but had other problems that interfered with learning and led to apparent retardation, including EAR AND HEARING PROBLEMS, EYE AND VISION PROBLEMS, LEARNING DISABILITIES, communication problems (see COMMUNICATION SKILLS AND DISORDERS), and sometimes lack of stimulation and learning opportunities at home, different cultural background, and inability to use English fluently, from lack of experience in speaking, hearing, or reading it. Parents who suspect possible mental retardation should have their child evaluated promptly, but they should be sure that these other areas are also checked, so that *any* problems are properly diagnosed and treated.

In the past, the outlook for many children with mental retardation was grim, as they were often shunted aside or institutionalized in notoriously unresponsive and often abusive settings. But since the EDUCATION OF ALL THE HANDICAPPED ACT and its successor, the INDIVIDUALS WITH DISABILITIES EDUCATION ACT, much more concerted attention has been paid toward reaching each child's highest potential, with special preschool and school programs made available.

Children with mental retardation learn basic skills more slowly, but those with mild retardation can learn skills up to about the sixth-grade level. They do best if skills or tasks are simple and presented in small, concrete steps. Those with moderate retardation (about 10 percent) can learn skills up to about the second-grade level.

As adults, many of those with mild and moderate retardation are able to work and live with some measure of independence, often prepared for the transition through VOCATIONAL REHABILITATION SERVICES, and living independently in the community, with some supportive services, sometimes working in SUPPORTED EMPLOYMENT. Others can perform some kinds of unskilled or semi-skilled work under close supervision, but need more support and guidance, often living in supervised apartments or GROUP HOMES.

Children with severe mental retardation (3–4 percent) have poor MOTOR SKILLS and communication skills are limited in early childhood, though during the usual school-age period they may respond to TOILET TRAINING and learn to talk, and may be able to learn some "survival" words like "stop" or "men" and "women." Those with profound retardation (1–2 percent) have extremely limited capacity for skill development, and require continuous supervision and help in a carefully structured environment. As adults, many of these would formerly have been institutionalized, but now more often live in group homes or remain at home with their families, with some supportive services from the community.

As a child with mental retardation grows into adulthood, professionals ideally monitor progress in key areas of functioning, tailoring educational programs and vocational rehabilitation services to the individual's needs. A basic part of the analysis is to determine what level of support is, and is likely to be, needed:

- *Intermittent:* occasional support on an as-needed basis, such as help in finding a new job, if a previous one is lost.
- *Limited:* support for a finite period of time, such as during a transition from school to work or during training for a new job.
- *Extensive:* assistance of some sort (though not necessarily in all areas of functioning) on a daily basis, probably throughout life, but certainly without foreseeable limit.
- *Pervasive:* constant support in virtually all areas of functioning on a daily basis for a lifetime, perhaps including life-sustaining support.

Parents with mentally retarded children will need to make long-term plans for their welfare and care. Many parents choose to keep such children in the home environment as long as possible, moving them into group homes only later. With severe or profound retardation, however, some parents find the enormous amount of care and supervision required to be beyond their capacities. Many social and educational services are available, but parents often need to fight to get such services for their children (see ADVOCACY). Parents also need to make special arrangements for the care of a mentally retarded child or adult, often appointing a GUARDIAN to look out for the child's interests, should something happen to them. Organizations and reference works such as those below and those in HELP FOR SPECIAL CHILDREN (on page 689) can help by providing experience from those who have faced similar problems and are keeping up-to-date on new approaches.

FOR HELP AND FURTHER INFORMATION

The Arc
500 East Border Street, Suite 300
Arlington, TX 76010

817–261–6003; 800–433–5255
Fax: 817-277-3491
E-mail: thearc@metronet.com
Alan Abeson, Executive Director
Organization concerned with mental retardation; formerly Association for Retarded Citizens (ARC); acts as advocate; provides information; helps find employment for adults with mental retardation; publishes *Introduction to the Arc*, semimonthly *Government Report*, newsletter *Advocates Voice*, quarterly newspaper *The Arc Today*, and various other materials including:

- For parents: *If You Are the Parent of a Child with Special Needs, To Our Future—and Theirs, Family Support: A Check for Quality, The Arc's Family Book, How to Provide for Their Future* and *A Family Handbook on Future Planning, Meeting the Needs and Challenges of At-Risk Two-Generation Elderly Families* (about elderly parents caring for an adult with mental retardation in the home), and fact sheets *Family Support, Social Security and SSI Benefits for Children with Disabilities,* and *Appealing a Social Security Disability Benefits Decision.*
- General works: *Developmental Checklist, Mental Retardation: Think About It* (video), and fact sheets *Introduction to Mental Retardation, Parents with Mental Retardation, Healthy People 2000 and Mental Retardation,* and *Members of Minority Groups and Mental Retardation.*
- On independent living: *10 Steps to Independence: Promoting Self-Determination in the Home, A Home of One's Own,* and fact sheets *How to Evaluate and Select Assistive Technology Devices, Assistive Technology for People with Mental Retardation, Residential Options for People with Mental Retardation, Facts on Transition from School to Work and Community Life, The Importance of Friendships Between People With and Without Mental Retardation,* and materials on voting.
- Many materials to ease integration into communities, on employment of people with mental retardation, and for professionals and organizations serving people with disabilities.

American Association on Mental Retardation (AAMR)
444 N. Capitol Street NW, Suite 846
Washington, DC 20001
202–387–1968; 800–424–3688
Fax: 202–387–2193
M. Doreen Croser, Executive Director
Organization concerned with mental retardation; sponsors research, training, and program development; sets standards for services; acts as advocate; publishes quarterly *AAMR News & Notes*, bimonthly journal *Mental Retardation, The American Journal on Mental Retardation, Parent Involvement in Vocational Education of Special Needs Youth, Parent Training and Developmental Disabilities, Recognizing Choices in Community Settings by People with Significant Disabilities, Pathways to Success: Training for Independent Living, Life Course Perspectives on Adulthood and Old Age,* and numerous analyses, monographs, and professional reports.

Voice of the Retarded (VOR)
5005 Newport Drive, Suite 108
Rolling Meadows, IL 60008
708–253–6020
Fax: 708–253–6054
Polly Spare, President
Organization serving as advocate for people with mental retardation; urges maintaining continuum of approaches in education and support services; publishes quarterly newsletter.

Council for Exceptional Children (CEC), 800–328–0272. Includes Division on Mental Retardation and Developmental Disabilities (MRDD), which publishes triannual newsletter *MRDD Express*; quarterly *Education and Training in Mental Retardation and Developmental Disabilities*; special report *Mental Retardation*; and other materials. (For full group information, see HELP ON LEARNING AND EDUCATION on page 659.)

National Association for the Dually Diagnosed (NADD) Mental Illness/Mental Retardation
110 Prince Street
Kingston, NY 12401
914–331–4336; 800–331–5362
Fax: 914–331–4569
Robert J. Fletcher, Founder and Executive Director
Organization concerned with people diagnosed with both mental illness and mental retardation; maintains computer database; provides information and referrals; publishes *The NADD Newsletter*, a membership directory, and a catalog of educational and training materials.

National Information Center for Children and Youth with Disabilities (NICHCY), 800–695–0285, voice/TT. Publishes *Mental Retardation.* (For full group information, see HELP FOR SPECIAL CHILDREN on page 689.)

Special Olympics International, 202–628–3630. Publishes fact sheet *Mental Retardation.* (For full group information, see SPORTS.)

American Academy of Child and Adolescent Psychiatry (AACAP), 202–966–7300. Publishes information sheet *Mental Retardation.* (For full group information, see MENTAL DISORDERS.)

Agency for Health Care Policy and Research Clearinghouse, 800–358–9295. Publishes *Characteristics of Facilities for the Mentally Retarded.* (For full group information, see HEALTH INSURANCE).

Resource Center on Substance Abuse Prevention and Disability, 202–628–8442. Publishes *A Look at Alcohol and Other Drug Abuse Prevention and Mental Retardation.* (For full group information, see HELP FOR SPECIAL CHILDREN on page 689.)

People First International (PFI), 503–362–0336. (For full group information, see HELP FOR SPECIAL CHILDREN on page 689.)

National Institute of Child Health and Development (NICHD), 301–496–5133. (For full group information, see PREGNANCY.)

OTHER RESOURCES

For Parents and Other Adults

We Have Been There: Families Share the Joy and Struggles of Living with Mental Retardation. T. Cougan and L. Isbell. Abingdon, 1983.

For or by Children

We Laugh, We Love, We Cry: Children Living with Mental Retardation. Thomas Bergman. Gareth Stevens, 1990.

More Time to Grow: Explaining Mental Retardation to Children: A Story. Sharon Hya Grollmen and Robert Perske. Beacon Press, 1977. Story about a young girl with a retarded brother; includes a guide for working with retarded children.

Background Works

Dictionary of Mental Handicaps. Mary P. Lindsey. Routledge, 1989.

Transitions to Adult Life for People with Mental Retardation—Principles and Practices. B. Ludlow and others. Paul H. Brookes, 1988.

(See also HELP FOR SPECIAL CHILDREN on page 689.)

mental status examination, an organized attempt by a PHYSICIAN or PSYCHOLOGIST to assess a person's orientation to time and place and general level of intellectual, emotional, and social functioning, as when a person has been through a trauma or had a TRAUMATIC BRAIN INJURY. The examiner observes general appearance, attitudes, and behavior, and attempts to assess orientation by asking questions such as "What is your name?" or "What day is today?" and mental grasp by asking the person to complete some basic mental tasks, such as interpreting a common saying or counting backwards and forwards.

Merrill-Palmer Scale, a type of INTELLIGENCE TEST used with young children, age eighteen months to four years. Items, such as pegboards, formboards, cubes, buttons, scissors, sticks, strings, and Kohs blocks (see KOHS BLOCK DESIGN TEST), are used in nineteen subtests, designed to indicate development in LANGUAGE SKILLS, MOTOR SKILLS, manual dexterity, and matching. The test administrator evaluates the child's performance by reference to a manual, and the child's final SCORE is converted into various forms, including a MENTAL AGE and PERCENTILE. (See TESTS.)

metabolic disorders, a group of GENETIC DISORDERS that cause disruption of the chemical and physical processes by which food is broken down for use in the body (see DIGESTIVE SYSTEM AND DISORDERS). Dozens of such disorders are known, but they are individually quite rare. Each is caused by a defect in the production of a single enzyme or protein. Many are classed as STORAGE DISORDERS because the deficiency leads to abnormal and damaging accumulation of certain compounds in the body tissues, often especially affecting the brain. Among the diseases regarded as metabolic disorders are PHENYLKETONURIA, GALACTOSEMIA, various MUCOPOLYSACCHARIDOSES (including *Hurler syndrome, Hunter syndrome,* and *Morquio syndrome*), MUCOLIPIDOSES, LIPID STORAGE DISEASES (including *Tay-Sachs disease* and *Gaucher's disease*), LESCH-NYHAN SYNDROME, and GLYCOGEN STORAGE DISEASES.

Diagnoses of such disorders are often made on the basis of the SIGNS and SYMPTOMS linked with that particular disorder, often followed by LIVER FUNCTIONS TESTS and KIDNEY FUNCTION TESTS. Some metabolic disorders can now be diagnosed using various kinds of GENETIC SCREENING tests, such as AMNIOCENTESIS or CHORIONIC VILLUS SAMPLING. Sometimes treatment involves avoidance of particular types of foods or other things to which the body is sensitive; taking enzymes orally or by INJECTION can, in some metabolic disorders, help make up the deficiency. Researchers have also shown some early, experimental success in GENE THERAPY, transplanting healthy cells to replace deficient ones in some disorders, though therapy by manipulation of genes is still some way in the future.

FOR HELP AND FURTHER INFORMATION

National Digestive Disease Information Clearinghouse (NDDIC), 301–654–3810. (For full group information, see DIGESTIVE SYSTEM AND DISORDERS.)

National Tay-Sachs and Allied Diseases Association (NTSAD), 800-90-NTSAD [9096-8723]. (For full group information, see LIPID STORAGE DISEASES.)

National Maternal and Child Health Clearinghouse (NMCHC), 703–821–8955. Publishes *Dental Health in Children with Phenylketonuria (PKU) and Other Inborn Errors of Amino Acid Metabolism Managed by Diet* and *National Survey of Treatment Programs for PKU and Selected Other Inherited Metabolic Diseases.* (For full group information, see PREGNANCY.)

(See also specific types of disorders, such as MUCOPOLYSACCHARIDOSES.)

metabolism, a general term for all of the biochemical processes that take place in the body, including two main types of processes:

- *Catabolism,* conversion of foods to energy, in which complex substances are broken down to simpler ones, in the process often releasing energy for the body's use, such as breaking down GLUCOSE (a sugar); some of the resulting compounds are stored for later use.
- *Anabolism,* building complex substances out of simpler ones, usually using energy, as in making PROTEINS out of AMINO ACIDS.

Any activities, such as EXERCISE, fighting infection, or intellectual effort, increase the *metabolic rate*, which is the amount of calories needed to supply necessary energy. The amount needed when the body is healthy and completely at rest is called the *basal metabolic rate* (BMR). Abnormalities in or absence of various kinds of *enzymes*, substances that trigger metabolic activities, can lead to a wide variety of serious medical disorders, called METABOLIC DISORDERS or INBORN ERRORS OF METABOLISM, such as PHENYLKETONURIA (PKU). Many VITAMINS are necessary for the basic metabolic processes to occur, and MALNUTRITION can also cause metabolic problems. (See METABOLIC DISORDERS; NUTRITION.)

metastasis, a medical term for a condition in which a TUMOR or CANCER is spreading beyond its original site.

metatarsus valgus, (duck walk or toeing out) a common abnormality in which the foot and toes point somewhat outward, because of rotation of the leg or foot. It is generally left to correct itself, but in severe cases may need to be corrected surgically. (See WALKING.)

metatarsus varus, (pigeon toes or toeing in) a common abnormality in which the foot and toes point somewhat inward, because of rotation of the leg or foot. It is generally left to correct itself, but in severe cases may need to be corrected surgically. (See WALKING.)

Metropolitan Achievement Tests, a series of group-administered ACHIEVEMENT TESTS for grades K–12, paper-and-pencil tests geared to measure acquisition of general language and arithmetic skills and READING comprehension at various graded levels. Additional material is covered in a fuller series of tests (BATTERY). The results are often recorded as GRADE-EQUIVALENTS. (See TESTS.)

Metropolitan Readiness Tests, a series of READINESS TESTS used for children grades prekindergarten to first grade, assessing development of skills necessary for early learning. The two levels, one for early kindergarten and the other for first grade, partly overlap, and each may be given either individually or in group. Among the areas in the subtests (called *composites*) of Level I are Letter Recognition, Visual Matching, School Language and Listening, Quantitative Language, Auditory Memory, and Rhyming. Level II also includes Visual Matching and School Language and Listening, but then adds Beginning Consonants, Sound-Letter Correspondences, Finding Patterns, Quantitative Concepts, and Quantitative Operations, some parts of which are optional. These are paper-and-pencil tests that can be computer scored. A child's result is shown as a raw SCORE, a national performance rating, and a PERCENTILE (and STANINE) ranking. The Metropolitan Readiness Tests are not generally used as ADMISSIONS TESTS, but rather as aids to class placement according to levels of skills in READING, language, and mathematics, and also sometimes to aid in making a decision about PROMOTION to first or second grade. (See TESTS.)

microcephaly, an abnormally small head, a common BIRTH DEFECT, as from exposure to ACCUTANE.

micromanipulation, use of a microscope connected with remote-controlled tiny robotic arms, developed initially for use by embryologists in various new reproductive techniques. Microtools, some no larger than the head of a sperm, are attached to the robot-arms, and are manipulated by the embryologist in a manner akin to playing a video game, using pedals and joysticks, while the SPERM, eggs (see OVUM), and EMBRYOS being manipulated are magnified 400 to 1000 times or more on a television monitor. Among the new techniques using micromanipulation, many still highly experimental (and all described in separate entries), are INTRACYTOPLASMIC SPERM INJECTION (ICSI), PARTIAL ZONA DISSECTION (PZD), SUBZONAL SPERM INSERTION (SZI), ASSISTED HATCHING, and EMBRYO BIOPSY for diagnosing GENETIC DISORDERS.

micromelia, a type of BIRTH DEFECT in which someone has abnormally short arms or limbs, as in such disorders as CORNELIA DE LANGE SYNDROME.

micronutrient, a general term for any element or compound, notably VITAMINS or MINERALS, that is necessary for proper health and functioning of the body, though only in small amounts (as opposed to MACRONUTRIENTS). Examples include *trace elements* such as IRON, COPPER, IODINE, ZINC, and FLUORIDE.

microsurgery, highly complex, precise, and delicate type of surgery in which the surgeon works through a special operating microscope, often employing LASER SURGERY. Microsurgery is used in a wide variety of areas, including eye surgery (as for cataracts or a cornea TRANSPLANT), ear surgery, unblocking a woman's FALLOPIAN TUBES, attempted reversal of a VASECTOMY, or reconnecting a severed body part. Related work, performed on EMBRYOS in the laboratory, is MICROMANIPULATION.

middle school, an institution providing education to students between ELEMENTARY SCHOOL and HIGH SCHOOL; sometimes called *junior high school* or *intermediate school.* If commonly refers to the middle grades—for example, grades 5–8, 6–8, or 7–8—when they are taught in a separate set of buildings. Some school districts have only elementary and high school buildings, with no distinct middle school.

School districts vary widely in their handling of middle schools. In some, students continue to spend much of their time with a single teacher in a single classroom, as in elementary school; in others, students follow the high school model, going to a different teacher and classroom for most subjects; some middle schools try a different approach, organizing students and teachers into smaller units, or teams. No national agreement yet exists on what subjects should be covered in the various grades, though there has been increasing discussion of establishing NATIONAL STANDARDS, including a CURRICULUM and TESTS. The Department of Education has increasingly recommended that parents exercise choice in finding the right school for their child; see CHOOSING A SCHOOL FOR YOUR CHILD on page 659, which provides a checklist for evaluating schools. (See EDUCATION.)

midwife, a person, usually a woman, who assists a woman during PREGNANCY and CHILDBIRTH. Most often today, the term refers to a CERTIFIED NURSE-MIDWIFE (CNM), who meets training and licensing requirements set by various states. Midwives without formal training or certification, though they may have extensive practical experience, are called *lay midwives,* and are allowed to practice in only a few states. (See CERTIFIED NURSE-MIDWIFE.)

milk, the nutritious fluid secreted by the mammary glands of mammals, BREASTS in humans and udders in many other mammals, such as cows or goats. Milk is made up of various nutrients, including PROTEIN, FATS, CARBOHYDRATES (primarily LACTOSE), and various VITAMINS and MINERALS. The proportion and kind of these nutrients varies somewhat between human milk and milk from other mammals. Human milk itself varies from person to person, and even in the same person at different times of the day and stages of nursing, or with varied diets. Human milk also has important ANTIBODIES to provide early IMMUNIZATION to infants during BREASTFEEDING and other anti-infection factors that protect against gastrointestinal infections. In addition, it rarely causes allergic responses and is quite digestible by most newborns, even those who a few months later will show signs of LACTOSE INTOLERANCE, or inability to digest and absorb milk's nutrients.

For infants in the first few months of life, a mother's milk generally provides all the NUTRITION necessary. However, that assumes that the mother's diet is such that the milk contains the proper proportion of nutrients. Mothers with special health problems that might hinder their own ability to absorb nutrients from food, or those who are on some kinds of VEGETARIAN diets, must consult closely with their doctors or clinics to be sure that the infant is experiencing no nutritional deficiency, especially in IRON, FOLIC ACID, and VITAMINS B_{12}, D, and K.

Milks other than mother's milk often lack the right amount and balance of nutrients the newborn needs, and can put a strain on the infant's immature gastrointestinal system and kidneys, sometimes causing intestinal bleeding, KIDNEY PROBLEMS, MALNUTRITION, and other health problems. Cow's milk, for example, is too low in iron and too high in protein, among other things, and there is some suggestion of a link between Type 1 DIABETES and early exposure to cow's milk proteins. It is to overcome just such problems that infant FORMULAS were developed, for feeding infants whose mothers choose not to or are unable to breastfeed. The most common formulas are based on cow's milk, modified and diluted to be more easily digestible and more properly balanced for newborns' systems to handle, and heated to be more digestible, assuming it is properly prepared. If a child proves unable to digest this properly, soy-based or other formulas are also available to simulate human milk. The actual composition of commercially prepared formulas is set by the Food and Drug Administration to ensure that they include the proper amount and balance of nutrients (though they cannot, of course, reproduce the immunization that a mother's milk gives). Parents should not try to develop their own formula or to use imitation milks, which are inadequate in calories and nutrients; malnutrition and its consequent problems have been observed in babies fed on nondairy creamer or on a formula made of barley water, corn syrup, and whole milk.

In the past, cow's milk was often eased into the baby's diet after age six months, along with SOLID FOODS. However, since 1992 various authorities, including the American Academy of Pediatrics, have recommended that babies not be given unmodified cow's milk (whole, 2 percent, or skimmed) at all during their first year. After that, however, cow's milk and dairy products made from it become an extremely important part of a child's diet, a major source of CALCIUM, vital for proper bone growth and prevention of diseases such as OSTEOPOROSIS. Public health experts recommend that 1-year-olds should be fed whole milk, not skimmed milk, which provides insufficient nutrition. For older children and adults, low-fat and skimmed milk are recommended. However, experts currently disagree about when to switch children to lower-fat dairy products, so parents should discuss this with their doctor or clinic.

Some individuals have expressed concern about excess vitamin D in fortified milk and possible contaminants in the milk, including residues of drugs used to treat dairy cows. However, the American Council on Science and Health report *Much Ado About Milk* reports that a nationwide milk quality program provides for testing loads of milk for such residues and rejecting any loads containing them. In rare cases, milk has been either over-fortified or under-fortified with vitamin D, routinely added to help prevent RICKETS, but these too are isolated cases. Some individuals still drink "raw" or unpasteurized milk, believing it to be more "healthful"; in fact, the opposite is true, since pasteurization kills disease-causing microorganisms. Parents and children are advised never to drink raw milk. (See BREASTFEEDING; VITAMINS; MINERALS.)

minerals, elements that must be in the diet for the proper health and functioning of the body. At least thirteen of them have been identified as necessary. Those needed in relatively large amounts are called *macrominerals* or MACRONUTRIENTS, including CALCIUM, POTASSIUM, MAGNESIUM, SODIUM, CHLORIDE, PHOSPHORUS, and SULFUR. Those needed in relatively small amounts are called *microminerals* or MICRONUTRIENTS, including IRON, COPPER, IODINE, ZINC, and FLUORIDE.

While these elements are vital to the body, excess amounts can cause severe health problems, even death, for in concentration some of these minerals are dangerous poisons and others can cause disruption or failure of vital body organs, such as the heart, kidneys, and liver. Public health officials advise parents not to give their children any mineral supplements without first consulting their doctor or clinic. The Food and Drug Administration has established RECOMMENDED DAILY ALLOWANCES (RDAs) for key minerals, which include increased amounts for women during PREGNANCY, especially of IRON, and for infants and young children. (See NUTRITION.)

minimal (or minimum) brain dysfunction (MBD), minor delay or disorder in the development of MOTOR SKILLS and ability to use the senses appropriately; a general term that has often been used (though mostly in the past) to describe the disorders now more often called LEARNING DISABILITIES and ATTENTION DEFICIT HYPERACTIVITY DISORDER (ADHD).

minimum competency testing, use of a testing program to ensure that no students will be promoted from one grade to the next, or graduated from HIGH SCHOOL, without demonstrating that they have acquired certain minimum skills and knowledge; also called *minimal competency testing*. The aim is to ensure that students will not receive automatic PROMOTION and thereby graduate functionally ILLITERATE. But use of ACHIEVEMENT TESTS for minimum competency testing has been criticized because it may cause a lowering of general educational standards, as teachers focus on preparation for the minimum test. Even so, as part of a BACK-TO-BASICS move, many states have adopted some form of minimum competency testing, often locally optional; most test not each year but every second or third year. If adopted widely, NATIONAL STANDARDS would involve such testing on a countrywide scale. A similar approach, designed to assure that teachers meet basic standards, is called *teacher competency testing*.

FOR HELP AND FURTHER INFORMATION

Center for Law and Education, 202–986–3000.
Publishes *Minimum Competency Testing*. (For full group information, see HELP ON LEARNING AND EDUCATION on page 659.)

Minnesota Multiphasic Personality Inventory (MMPI), a test widely used to gather information on personality, mental condition, and attitudes in people age sixteen or older. Existing in various forms, for administration to groups or individuals, the test consists of hundreds of true–false items designed to highlight aspects of personality, including those that may be related to MENTAL DISORDERS. The results are graphed on a personality profile sheet. (See TESTS.)

minor, a person under the legally defined age of adulthood (MAJORITY), and therefore normally required to be in the CUSTODY of a parent or GUARDIAN, in FOSTER CARE, or under other legally responsible supervision; in legal terms, a minor is a CHILD or INFANT, unable to act as an adult in many respects, as in signing a contract. The age defining a minor varies by state, but in the federal 1974 Child Abuse Prevention and Treatment Act "child" is specified as someone under eighteen. In some states, an adult with certain DISABILITIES may be classified as a minor for legal purposes. Minors who have been freed from parental control and care, as by marriage or military service, are called EMANCIPATED MINORS. The term *minor* refers to legal ability to act as an adult; by contrast a JUVENILE is someone who is not yet old enough to be treated as an adult under criminal law.

mirror sign, standing in front of a mirror or other shining surface for an unusually long time; a SIGN that is generally associated with MENTAL DISORDERS such as SCHIZOPHRENIA.

miscarriage, the loss of a FETUS before the 28th week of GESTATION; an involuntary termination of a PREGNANCY, often medically called a *spontaneous abortion*. (Death of a fetus at a later stage is called a STILLBIRTH.) Miscarriage is extremely common, affecting at least 10 percent of all pregnancies, and perhaps as many as 30 percent or even more, since many occur in the first ten weeks, often without the woman even being aware that she is pregnant.

Most miscarriages result from CHROMOSOMAL ABNORMALITIES and GENETIC DISORDERS so severe that they are incompatible with life, though exposure to ENVIRONMENTAL HAZARDS, such as poisons and radiation, severe illness of the mother, and AUTOIMMUNE DISORDERS in the mother may also trigger loss of the fetus. Later in the pregnancy, miscarriage can also be caused by an INCOMPETENT CERVIX, fibroid TUMORS in the UTERUS, and structural abnormalities, but public health experts say it is very rarely caused by injury or overactivity.

Warning signs of miscarriage are bleeding, cramping, and dizziness. Sometimes bed rest can save the pregnancy. But often the spontaneous abortion, once started, cannot be stopped. Bleeding becomes heavier, the CERVIX dilates, the AMNIOTIC FLUID spills out, and the fetus and its associated tissues, such as the PLACENTA and amniotic sac, are expelled. This would be termed a *complete abortion*. Sometimes the fetus dies but is not expelled, though the associated tissues die, the uterus returns to its normal size, and the symptoms of pregnancy cease. This is called a *missed abortion*; in this case, the dead fetus and tissue must be removed to avoid infection and other disorders in the mother. In most cases of miscarriage, doctors will perform an operation called a *dilation and curettage* (D & C), in which they remove the dead tissue.

Though one miscarriage may not signal future trouble, any later pregnancy would medically be treated as a HIGH-RISK PREGNANCY for the safety of mother and baby. Before attempting another conception, however, doctors advise couples to let themselves recover physically and emotionally for a few months after a miscarriage, while they go through the grieving process.

FOR HELP AND FURTHER INFORMATION

Pregnancy and Infant Loss Center (PILC), 612–473–9372. Publishes *Miscarriage: A Book for Parents Experiencing Fetal Death, Miscarriage: A Shattered Dream,* and *Preventing Miscarriage: The Good News* (on a pregnancy after a loss). (For full group information, see DEATH AND DYING.)

RESOLVE, Inc., 617–623–0744. Publishes fact sheet *Medical Causes of Miscarriage (Including Immune Factors)* and *Emotional Aspects of Miscarriage.* (For full group information, see INFERTILITY.)

OTHER RESOURCES

General works

LIFELINE, A Journal for Parents Grieving a Miscarriage, Stillbirth or Early Infant Death. Joanie Reid. Pineapple, 1994.

Miscarriage—Women Sharing from the Heart. Marie Allen and Shelly Marks. Wiley, 1993.

Surviving Pregnancy Loss: A Complete Sourcebook for Women and Their Families, rev. ed. Rochelle Friedman and Bonnie Gradstein. Little, Brown, 1992.

When a Baby Dies: The Experience of Late Miscarriage, Stillbirth, and Neonatal Death. Nancy Kohner. HarperCollins, 1992.

Hidden Loss: Miscarriage and Ectopic Pregnancy. Valerie Hey. Quartet, 1990.

Preventing Miscarriage: The Good News. Jonathan Scher and Carol Dix. Harper & Row, 1990.

(See also DEATH AND DYING, under "On pregnancy and infant loss"; INFERTILITY; ABORTION; PREGNANCY.)

missing children, children who have disappeared from the home of the parent(s) who legally have CUSTODY of them. Because disappearance of children, temporary or permanent, causes enormous anguish, a great deal of furor has surrounded the issue in recent years. More heat than light was often shed, however, until 1990 when a three-year study on missing children, under the auspices of the Congress and Justice Department, clarified the nature of the problem.

The results were surprising. Although many parents' greatest fear is that a child will be kidnapped by a stranger, such abductions in fact accounted for only a very small proportion of missing children, about 200–300 a year, while another 3200–4600 children a year were temporarily abducted by someone outside the family, often for purposes of sexual assault.

These figures were dwarfed by the more than 350,000 kidnappings by parents or other family members, often in dissatisfaction over CUSTODY arrangements. Many of these children were taken to undisclosed locations, often out of state, though in most family abductions the children were returned within a week.

Beyond even that are the 450,000 children who run away from home each year, many of them with no secure place to stay, and the 125,000 children who are thrown out of the home by their parents, with no other arrangements made for their care. Many of these so-called *runaways* and *thrownaways*, some of whom later return home, are victims of CHILD ABUSE AND NEGLECT. In addition, over 430,000 children at some point during each year become lost (generally for less than a day), injured and unable to return home, or are otherwise missing.

These numbers are truly staggering, and reflect enormous disruption and dislocation in the lives of the children involved. They also suggest that social emphasis has been somewhat misplaced. Certainly parents and children's organizations are right to be concerned about possible kidnapping or abuse by strangers or others outside the family, and to prepare their children to deal with such eventualities. (For help on that, see the list of organizations that follows; also LATCHKEY CHILD; CHILD ABUSE AND NEGLECT; also TIPS FOR PROTECTING CHILDREN AGAINST ABDUCTION on page 408.)

But for prevention, as the figures make clear, it is perhaps more important for divorced or separated parents to work out any differences between them, putting the best interests of the children ahead of any custody or related parental dispute they may have; to keep lines of communication open with their children during the difficult period of ADOLESCENCE, rather than allowing conflict to result in teenagers leaving home; and to be alert to possible child abuse within the home situation that might cause a child to run away.

Parents considering kidnapping their children over a custody dispute should realize that, under both the UNIFORM CHILD CUSTODY JURISDICTION ACT and the more general CLEAN HANDS DOCTRINE, they may be risking any possibility of later gaining more favorable custody arrangements. Under a federal law labeled Title 18, Section 1201A, parents are, however, exempt from kidnapping charges regarding their children under eighteen, a state of affairs many custodial parents who have had their children kidnapped are trying to change.

For families with missing children, the focus is very different—on finding, identifying, making contact with, helping, and obtaining the return of their children. In this many of the organizations listed later in this entry can help. Some are geared to help families find children who are lost or kidnapped. Because young children change so much as they develop, some parents prepare fingerprints, footprints, identification bracelets or buttons, and even stored samples of DNA so that, if missing children are found years later, they can be identified with certainty. Other organizations provide a contact point between runaways and their families, serving to reopen a dialogue, while shielding the runaway's location, if desired, and to provide needed services, as for health care or DRUG ABUSE treatment.

FOR HELP AND FURTHER INFORMATION

On missing children in general

National Center for Missing and Exploited Children (NCMEC)
2101 Wilson Boulevard, Suite 550
Arlington, VA 22201
703–235–3900; Hotline: 800–843–5678;
800–826–7653, TT
Fax: 703–235–4067
E-mail: 74431.177@compuserve.com (CompuServe: 74431,177)
Ernest Allen, President
Organization that acts as clearinghouse for parents and agencies searching for missing children; seeks to influence legislation and public policy; helps individuals arrange for return of the children, once found; publishes various print and video materials, including handbook on parental kidnappings and material on searching techniques.

Missing Children Help Center (MCHC)
410 Ware Boulevard, Suite 400
Tampa, Florida 33619
813–623–5437; Hotline 800-USA-KIDS [872–5437]
Fax: 813–664–0705
Ivana DiNova, Executive Director
Organization serving as contact point for missing children, parents, private and public agencies, and others; collects data on missing children and on child search agencies; acts as advocate.

Missing Children of America (MCA)
P.O. Box 949
Chugiak, AK 99567
907–248–7300
Dolly Whaley, Executive Director
Organization that helps locate missing children; advises parents on preparing identification packages and obtaining media coverage; maintains computer files; acts as advocate; publishes various materials.

Child Find of America (CFA)
P.O. Box 277
New Paltz, NY 12561
914–255–1848; 800-I-AM-LOST [426–5678]
Fax: 914–255–5706
Cheryl Kane, Executive Director
Network that provides a contact point for separated children and parents, working with other organizations to pool information in a missing children registry; publishes newsletter and annual directory with physical descriptions and photographs.

Find the Children
11811 West Olympic Boulevard
Los Angeles, CA 90064
310–477–6721
Fax: 310–477–7166
Judi Sadowsky, Executive Director
Organization focusing on prevention of child abduction and recovery of missing children; acts as liaison between parents and legal and law enforcement systems; provides information and referrals; maintains register of children and computerized database of missing children.

National Center for Women and Family Law, 212–674–8200. Publishes *Defending a Battered Woman Accused of Parental Abduction, Interstate Child Custody and Parental Kidnapping Resource Packet,* and *Domestic Violence as a Statutory Defense to Custodial Interference or Kidnapping.* (For full group information, see CUSTODY.)

National Legal Resource Center for Child Advocacy and Protection, 202–331–2200. (For full group information, see HELP AGAINST CHILD ABUSE AND NEGLECT on page 680.)

National Woman's Christian Temperance Union (WCTU), 800–755–1321. Publishes booklets *Missing Children* and *About Runaways.* (For full group information, see HELP AGAINST SUBSTANCE ABUSE on page 703.)

National Clearinghouse on Child Abuse and Neglect Information (NCCAN), 800–394–3366. Publishes annotated bibliography *Runaway, Throwaway, and Homeless Children.* (For full group information, see HELP AGAINST CHILD ABUSE AND NEGLECT on page 680.)

On kidnapping prevention programs

American Academy of Pediatrics (AAP), 800–433–9016. Publishes video and family guide *Child Lures: Think First and Stay Safe*; also lesson plans for school program. (For full group information, see HEALTH CARE.)

Hug-A-Tree and Survive (HAT)
6465 Lance Way
San Diego, CA 92120
619–286–7536
Jacqueline Heet, Executive Officer
Program for training young children on what to do if they are lost—that is, hug a tree until they are rescued; produces slide show for training children.

For runaway children

National Runaway Switchboard (NRS)
3080 North Lincoln
Chicago, IL 60657
800–621–4000

Tips for Protecting Your Children Against Abduction

- Teach children *early* about the possibility of abduction, but also teach them coping skills, such as those that follow, which will help replace fear with confidence.
- Never leave young children alone in a car or inside or outside a store or other public place.
- Carefully vet all child care facilities, preschools, and babysitters. Check all references thoroughly. Instruct the staff not to release your child to anyone without your specific prior permission.
- Teach your children their full names, addresses, and telephone numbers, including area code and long-distance dialing information, as early as possible. If children are old enough, also teach them your work numbers and the number of a trusted relative or friend. Consider an automatic dialing device, such as Phone Home™, which allows children to phone home, even if they have no money and don't know the number—and even if they're so young (or disabled) that they don't know how to use a telephone.
- Establish a family password. Teach your children never to go anywhere with anyone who does not know the password, and never to tell *anyone* else the secret word. Explain that, if an adult volunteers the password, that means you have sent them and it is safe to go with them. Explain that possible abductors may tell them lies, and that they should never believe it if someone tells them that their family doesn't want them any more or that their other parent is dead.
- Teach children that, if they suspect someone is following them, they should not try to hide but instead should go to a place where there are other people, such as a store, or to a trusted neighbor's or relative's home. Establish emergency routines for such situations with your children; consider using role-playing to show children how to react in emergencies.
- Tell children to scream "Help!" or otherwise try to attract attention if threatened by a stranger. Consider getting an alarm device for children to carry with them.
- Do not put your children's name on the outside of personal items such as clothing, lunchboxes, backpacks, to help prevent strangers from calling them by name.
- Have children immediately report to you—or to a designated emergency person—any threats by a stranger or any other suspicious incidents.
- Instruct babysitters and children home alone not to open the door to strangers, and not to tell anyone at the door or over the telephone that they are alone. Instead, tell them to say you are at home but cannot come to the door or phone.
- Post emergency numbers near the telephone; along with parents' work numbers and the traditional fire and police numbers; also include numbers for parents and trusted neighbors, relatives, or friends. If possible, program the numbers into the telephone, to make them easy to dial in an emergency.
- Obtain passports for your children and hold them in a safe place, so they cannot be taken out of the country by someone else without your permission. In case of abduction, contact the Office of Citizenship Appeals and Legal Assistance, Passport Services, Department of State, to block use of the passport or issuance of a new one.
- Have your children fingerprinted and keep accurate dental records; some parents also take footprints, and even store DNA samples. Keep this information private and safe, as in a safe deposit box, and plan to destroy it when the children are older.
- Maintain current photos of your children, having them taken twice yearly for children under seven and annually for older children. Also videotape children, if possible.
- When children are old enough to be out on their own, establish with them safe routes to and from school, avoiding empty lots, fields, and parks. Encourage them to use a "buddy system."
- Know your children's friends and activities.
- Listen to what your children say and take their fears and concerns seriously. If they say they don't want to be with or are fearful of someone, explore the reasons why.
- Warn your children not to give their address or phone number to anyone they "meet" online (on computer), not to make any appointments to meet them, and to alert you if anyone tries to get them to do either.

■ Keep lines of communication open as your children enter adolescence.
■ Be alert to the possibility of abuse (see CHILD ABUSE AND NEGLECT; INCEST) in the family situation, such with a stepparent or older sibling, that might cause the child to run away or be tempted away by a possible abductor.
■ Make sure older children know the number of the National Runaway Switchboard 800–621–4000 (see MISSING CHILDREN).

IF PARENTAL ABDUCTION IS A POSSIBILITY

■ If you are concerned about possible abduction by a noncustodial parent after a divorce, be sure to have custody papers in order and properly filed with the court. Terms of visitation should be as specific as possible. File copies of the custody papers with the children's school, preschool, or child care provider, and specifically tell them who is allowed to pick up the child.
■ Do not interfere with your ex-spouse's legal visitation rights, except in emergencies, and maintain a civil relationship for the sake of the children.
■ If a password was established before a divorce, teach the child a new password. You may also want to establish new emergency numbers and procedures.
■ Take seriously any threats of parental abduction, and be alert for sharp changes in the behavior or life-style of an ex-spouse.
■ If you have had to obtain restraining orders against an ex-spouse over violation of custody and visitation rights, be sure copies of those are on file with the local police.
■ Keep a file containing vital information on an ex-spouse, including Social Security number, birthdate, driver's license number, automobile license number and description, employer, credit cards, and other financial records. Also keep information about your ex-spouse's close relatives and friends, and keep on good terms with them, if possible; some of them may help in case of parental abduction.

IF YOUR CHILD HAS BEEN ABDUCTED

■ Contact the police and also ask for help from the local District Attorney's office. If child-stealing or concealment is a felony in your state, ask for a felony warrant to be issued.
■ If you can prove that your child has been taken out of the state, ask the FBI to issue a UFAP (Unlawful Flight to Avoid Prosecution) warrant.
■ Be sure your child is listed in the National Crime Information Center (NCIC) computer.
■ Contact the National Center for Missing and Exploited Children at 800–843–5678 (see MISSING CHILDREN). Register your child with the key organization in your area for dealing with missing children.
■ Contact state and federal Parent Locator Services (see CHILD SUPPORT).
■ If you suspect a friend or relative may be in touch with the abductor, ask the police to issue search warrants for telephone records and a mail cover.
■ Have your child's school records, birth certificate, and medical records, and ask to be informed if anyone requests a copy.
■ Be persistent and use any information and resources at your disposal.

Source: Adapted in part from various materials of the organization Find the Children, and from What's New for Parents, by Irene Franck and David Brownstone.

Laura Thomas, Executive Director
Confidential switchboard service for runaways, allowing them to pass messages to their families without revealing their location; operates twenty-four-hour, seven-day-a-week toll-free hotline; provides referral to social services, including medical and legal help, transportation, drug treatment centers, shelter, and other hotlines.

Mothers Without Custody (MWOC), 713–840–1622. (For full group information, see CUSTODY.)

Defense for Children International-United States of America (DCI-USA), 212–228–4773. (For full group information, see HELP AGAINST CHILD ABUSE AND NEGLECT on page 680.)

OTHER RESOURCES

FOR PARENTS

When Parents Kidnap: The Families Behind the Headlines. Geoffrey L. Greif and Rebecca Heger. Free Press, 1992.

Missing Children: Rhetoric and Reality. Martin L. Forst and Martha-Elin Blomquist. Free Press, 1991.

Personal experiences

Understanding Survivors of Abuse: Stories of Homeless and Runaway Adolescents. Jane Levine Powers and Barbara Weiss Jaklitsch. Lexington, 1989.

A Cry of Absence: The True Story of a Father's Search for His Kidnapped Children. Andrew Ward. Viking, 1988.

Missing: A Family's Triumph in the Tragedy No Parent Ever Wants to Face. Fay Overly. Accent, 1985.

Have You Seen My Son? Jack Olsen. Atheneum, 1982. Novel about parental kidnapping.

For preteens and teens

Missing Children. JoAnn Bren Guernsey. Crestwood, 1990.

Runaways: In Their Own Words Kids Talking About Living on the Streets. Jeffrey Artenstein. Tor, 1990.

mixed dominance (cross dominance), a condition in which DOMINANCE in hands, feet, and eyes is not clearly established on one side of the body or the other.

modalities, a general term referring to the senses by which a child takes in information for learning, the *preferred modality* being the sense that a child uses most easily and efficiently. These modalities are often described as VAKT (for *visual, auditory, kinesthetic,* and *tactile*); but sometimes the term HAPTIC is used to refer to physical, hands-on learning, in a sense combining kinesthetic and tactile. (See LEARNING STYLE; SENSORY MODES.)

modeling, a type of LEARNING STYLE that involves teaching by example, expecting that children will imitate the teacher. (Subscribers to the America Online computer service can find a fuller discussion of modeling and examples of how to use it in teaching, in the Moms Online Desk Reference section of Moms Online, under "Teaching Young Children.")

Mongolian spot, a large area of skin colored pale blue, found in some dark-skinned infants, generally on the buttocks or lower spine; a BENIGN kind of skin disorder that usually disappears or becomes less obvious as the child grows older. Parents must be sure that others do not mistake the area for a large bruise, and a sign of possible CHILD ABUSE AND NEGLECT. (See SKIN AND SKIN DISORDERS.)

mononucleosis (infectious mononucleosis or "mono"), an ACUTE infection generally caused by the *Epstein-Barr virus* (EBV), which is related to the HERPES simplex virus and (like herpes) remains in the body for life. The virus reproduces in the salivary glands and is probably spread through saliva, as during kissing (hence its nickname, the "kissing disease") or sharing drinks, but is not highly contagious. Much is unknown about mononucleosis, including how long a person remains infectious and why infections are often extremely mild or even symptomless in young children, but are severe and long-lasting in people between ages fifteen and thirty, where perhaps 70–80 percent of the cases are found.

Symptoms start slowly, characteristically including FEVER, sore throat, and swollen glands (actually lymphatic tissue acting as filters in the IMMUNE SYSTEM) in the neck, but also under the arms and in the groin. Often the SPLEEN is enlarged, and sometimes the liver as well; secondary bacterial infections may also result, especially since immune system activity is somewhat depressed. In itself, mononucleosis is not generally a severe disease, but the Public Health Service reports:

> There are rare cases of death from the [mononucleosis] infection, following airway obstruction, rupture of the spleen, inflammation of the heart or tissues surrounding the heart, or central nervous system involvement. Steroid drugs are used to treat these complications. If the spleen should rupture, surgery to remove it, and transfusions and other therapy for shock, must be initiated immediately.

Mononucleosis is difficult to diagnose at first, because its symptoms are vague and resemble those of other ailments. The main concern is often to distinguish mononucleosis from the generally more serious hepatitis (see LIVER AND LIVER PROBLEMS), which can be done through a BLOOD TEST to detect ANTIBODIES to the EB virus. Only the symptoms of mononucleosis can be treated, the disease itself cannot, though associated infections may respond to ANTIBIOTICS. In years past, the standard treatment was bed rest for four to six weeks and limited activity for three months after symptoms disappeared. Today, however, doctors in general recommend that activity levels be limited on the basis of the individual's symptoms, with the proviso that strenuous EXERCISE should be avoided, since it can damage an enlarged spleen. Researchers are exploring the possibility that the Epstein-Barr virus may trigger SJOGREN'S SYNDROME.

FOR HELP AND FURTHER INFORMATION

National Institute of Allergy and Infectious Diseases (NIAID), 301–496–5717. (For full group information, see ALLERGY.)

Montessori method, an approach to the education of PRESCHOOL-age children developed by Italian physician-educator Maria Montessori, featuring special materials for teaching numbers, letters, and abstract ideas. The materials are designed to foster independent thinking and creativity and to enhance a child's use of the various SENSORY MODES or MODALITIES for learning, in what is called *sensory education.* From Italy, the Montessori approach spread worldwide, with small Montessori schools springing up locally in many countries, many following her original methods, while those in the United States were somewhat modified.

FOR HELP AND FURTHER INFORMATION

American Montessori Society (AMS)
150 Fifth Avenue, Suite 203
New York, NY 10011–4384
212–924–3209
Fax: 212–727–2254
Michael Eames, Executive Director
Organization of people and schools interested in the Montessori methods of teaching young children; sets standards and offers accreditation; advises new and existing schools; provides information and referrals; publishes quarterly *Montessori Life Magazine*, annual *School Directory*, pamphlet *Montessori Education: Questions and Answers*, and Montessori materials.

Alliance for Parental Involvement in Education (ALLPIE), 518–392–6900. Publishes leaflets *Purpose of Montessori Education, Montessori or Traditional Kindergarten?* (For full group information, see HELP ON LEARNING AND EDUCATION on page 000.)

OTHER RESOURCES

Montessori at Home: A Complete Guide to Teaching Your Preschooler at Home Using the Montessori Method, rev. and exp. ed. *Modern Montessori at Home: A Creative Teaching Guide for Parents of Children 6 through 9 Years of Age. Modern Montessori at Home, No. II: A Creative Teaching Guide for Parents of Children 10 through 12 Years of Age.* Heidi A. Spietz. American Montessori Consulting (Rossmoor, CA), 1991.

Michael Olaf's Essential Montessori: A Guide and Catalogue for Montessori Education from Birth—at Home and at School. Susan Stephenson and Jim Stephenson, ed. M. Olaf, 1990.

Modern Montessori at Home: A Creative Teaching Guide for Parents of Children Six through Nine Years of Age. American Montessori Consulting (Rossmoor, CA), 1989.

mood disorders, a general classification of MENTAL DISORDERS that involve prolonged disturbance of mood, coloring the person's outlook, such as DEPRESSION and BIPOLAR DISORDERS (popularly called manic-depression); formerly called *affective disorders.* Mood disorders sometimes occur in connection with other mental or physical disorders. (See MENTAL DISORDERS.)

morbidity, the condition of having a disease or disorder. In medicine, the morbidity ratio is the number of people with a particular disease or disorder (such as CEREBRAL PALSY, DOWN SYNDROME, or MEASLES) as compared to the total number of people in a group (such as all babies, only LOW BIRTH WEIGHT babies, or all female babies).

morning after pill, a drug taken after sexual intercourse that is designed to block a PREGNANCY, as by preventing a fertilized egg (OVUM) from implanting in the UTERUS or by expelling the contents of the uterus. In years past, doctors have sometimes tried giving high doses of ESTROGEN and other sex hormones to women seeking to block a possible pregnancy, with limited success; one such drug used on college campuses as late as 1980 was DES, despite knowledge of its adverse and long-term side effects. Though much sought after, no such fully tested safe, effective drug is available as a morning after pill, though a 1992 Scottish study showed that RU-486—the so-called ABORTION pill—had potential in this regard. A 1995 study indicated promise for a two-drug approach to early abortion, using the already widely available prescription drugs *methotrexate* and *misoprostol*, administered during the first eight weeks of pregnancy. If further studies find this approach safe for frequent and long-term use, and if it were effective early enough in a pregnancy, it could operate as a "morning after" pill (see ABORTION).

morning sickness, nausea and VOMITING that often accompany the early months of PREGNANCY. (See VOMITING.)

Moro reflex (startle reflex), the automatic response of a baby, on hearing a loud noise or when the head is left momentarily unsupported, to swing arms outward and then together, as if embracing something, to flex the legs, and often to cry; a type of "primitive" REFLEX found only babies and disappearing in three to four months.

mortality rate, the number of people who die, on the average, in a specified group of a certain number, such as 1 per 1000 newborns. (See INFANT MORTALITY; MATERNAL MORTALITY; DEATH AND DYING.)

mother, the woman who has PARENTS' RIGHTS and PARENTS' RESPONSIBILITIES toward a child, especially a MINOR. The woman whose GENETIC INHERITANCE contributed directly to the child, and who is one of the child's nearest BLOOD RELATIONS, is the child's BIOLOGICAL MOTHER, also called *natural mother* or *birth mother.* If the biological mother gives up her rights and allows her child to be placed for ADOPTION, a female who adopts the child is called the *adoptive mother*; if the placement is temporary or pending final adoption, the woman may be called the *foster mother.* If a woman marries a man with children, she is their *stepmother.* However, though she may have informal authority over them in the home, she is not their legal mother unless she formally adopts the children.

If a woman agrees to become pregnant with the SPERM from another woman's husband and bear the child for that couple, she is called a SURROGATE MOTHER. Newer REPRODUCTIVE TECHNOLOGY can produce complications, however. In *in vitro fertilization/embryo implant* (see IN VITRO FERTILIZATION), the egg and sperm come from a husband and his wife, who can produce eggs, but is unable to carry a child; the fertilized egg is then implanted in a *host surro-*

gate mother, who carries it to term. In this situation, the host surrogate mother is the birth mother, but the infertile wife is the biological mother. The Center for Surrogate Parenting (see INFERTILITY) reports that it has successfully petitioned in some courts to enter the biological mother's name, rather than the birth mother's name, on the birth certificate. (The husband is already the biological FATHER.)

If a woman has an unplanned, unwanted PREGNANCY, she can choose to carry the child full-term or to have an ABORTION, without consent from her husband or the *unwed father* (if she is unmarried). However, governments have attempted to place various restrictions on her reproductive rights. Depending on the state law, a pregnant adolescent under the AGE OF CONSENT may be required to notify or to obtain the consent of her parents, or of the court, before having an abortion. In addition, going beyond the role of educating women about proper PRENATAL CARE and persuading them to care for themselves and their baby, the state has attempted in various ways to hold women legally responsible for the health of the FETUS they are carrying. Some women have even been charged in criminal court for failing to heed medical advice that their activities, such as DRUG ABUSE, could harm or kill the fetus. Such issues have just begun to be addressed in the courts in recent years, however, and are far from resolution.

Immediately after the birth, in most cases, the mother and newborn begin to form a specially close attachment called BONDING. Where this does not occur, for whatever reason, lack of a warm and stimulating relationship between mother and child (or another older person and the child) can lead to MATERNAL-DEPRIVATION SYNDROME, a complex of symptoms including general physical and MENTAL RETARDATION, a condition sometimes called FAILURE TO THRIVE.

Traditionally, motherhood has, along with the flag and apple pie, been almost a sacred status in the eyes of many, and it was long assumed that the rightful place of a mother was at home caring for her child. Many women still do stay at home while raising their children, especially in the early years, but social conditions have changed. Many others choose to return to work soon after a child's birth. And many other mothers, including some who might wish to stay home, find themselves forced by economics to go to work, because the family economy requires two incomes to stay afloat, or because they find themselves relatively impoverished single parents, often after a DIVORCE.

As a result, the role of the mother and the relationship between child and mother is in a considerable state of flux. The mother still tends to be the PSYCHOLOGICAL PARENT, the one closest to the child's aspirations and fears; however, much of the child's waking, growing, and learning hours are spent in the care of others, whether BABYSITTERS, NANNIES, or CHILD CARE workers. Both mothers and fathers, then, have to carefully think through what kind of approach they want others to take toward the child, so that the child is presented with a relatively consistent, and consistently loving and stimulating, view of the world.

FOR HELP AND FURTHER INFORMATION

Single Mothers by Choice (SMC)
P.O. Box 1642, Gracie Square Station
New York, NY 10028
212-988-0993
Jane Mattes, Founder and Director
Organization for single women who are, or may be, adopting a child or bearing a child outside marriage (not for widows or divorcees); provides information; offers workshops; publishes quarterly newsletter and resource packets on donor insemination, adoption, and single motherhood.

Mothers at Home (MAH)
8310A Old Courthouse Road
Vienna, VA 22182
703-827-5903; For publication orders: 800-783-4-MOM [783-4666]
Fax: 703-790-8587
E-mail: mah@netrail.net
Tammy De Martino, Executive Director
Organization of and for mothers who choose to stay at home to raise their children; seeks to raise morale and image of mothers at home; provides information; publishes monthly *Welcome Home,* and books *What's a Smart Woman Like You Doing at Home?* and *Discovering Motherhood.*

FEMALE (Formerly Employed Mothers at the Leading Edge)
P.O. Box 31
Elmhurst, IL 60126
708-941-3553
Organization supporting mothers who have taken time out from work to raise their children at home; seeks to educate public; publishes monthly newsletter *FEMALE Forum.*

Mothers' Home Business Network
P.O. Box 423
East Meadow, NY 11554
516-997-7394
Georganne Fiumara, Founder
Organization of mothers running businesses from home; provides information; publishes quarterly newsletter *Homeworking Mothers,* semiannual *Kids and Careers: New Ideas and Options for Mothers, Mothers' Moneymaking Manual, Mothers' Home Business Pages: A Resource Guide for Homeworking Mothers, Mothering and Managing a Typing Service at Home, Mothering and Managing a Mail-Order Business at Home,* and fact sheets on business concerns.

OTHER RESOURCES

For mothers

A New Mother's Home Companion. Paula Elbirt-Bender and Linda L. Small. Dell, 1995.

Working from the Margins: Voices of Mothers in Poverty. Virginia E. Schein. ILR, 1995.

Your 30-Day Journey to Being a World-Class Mother. C.W. Neal. Thomas Nelson, 1992.

Mothering Heights: Reclaiming Motherhood from the Experts. Sonia Taitz. Morrow, 1992.

Motherhood and Representation. E. Ann Kaplan. Routledge, 1992.

Life after Birth: Every Woman's Guide to the First Year of Motherhood. Wendy Blumfield. Element, 1992.

Mothers Talk Back. Susan Swan and others, eds. Coach House/InBook, 1992.

Managing Motherhood: Support and Survival Techniques for Mothers of Very Young Children. Marianne P. Seidenstricker. KMS Productions, 1991.

Terrible Angel: Surviving the First Five Years of Motherhood. Patricia H. Clifford. Paulist Press, 1991.

Mothering: The Complete Guide to Mothers of All Ages. Grace Ketterman. Thomas Nelson, 1991.

The Unofficial Mother's Handbook. Art Peterson and Norma Peterson. NAL-Dutton, 1991.

One Thousand Mother's Questions Answered: All You Need to Know about Child Care From Conception to School. Davina Lloyd and Ann Rushton. Thorsons, 1991.

It's a Mom's Life. David Sipress. NAL-Dutton, 1991.

The Stay-at-Home Mom: For Women at Home and Those Who Want to Be. Donna Otto. Harvest House, 1991.

I Wish Someone Had Told Me. Nina Barrett. Simon & Schuster, 1990. Interviews on first year of motherhood.

Motherhood. Running Press, 1990.

For working mothers

Women's Two Roles: A Contemporary Dilemma. Phyllis Moen. Auburn House/Greenwood, 1992.

The Best Jobs in America for Parents Who Want Careers and Time for Children Too. Susan B. Dynerman and Lynn O. Hayes. Macmillan, 1991.

Sock Hunting and Other Pursuits of the Working Mother. Pam Raven. Aglow Publications, 1991.

Making It Work: Finding the Time and Energy for Your Career, Marriage, Children, and Self. Victoria Houston. Contemporary, 1990.

Working Parent/Happy Child: You Can Balance Job and Family. Caryl Waller Krueger. Abingdon, 1990.

Answers to the Mommy Track: How Wives and Mothers in Business Reach the Top and Balance Their Lives. Trudi Ferguson. New Horizon, 1990.

For children, on mothers

We're Very Good Friends, My Mother and I. P.K. Hallinan. Ideals, 1990.

Heather Has Two Mommies. Lesléa Newman. In Other Words, 1990.

(See also General Parenting Resources on page 634.)

motion sickness, nausea, dizziness, and vomiting during travel, whether by automobile, train, plane, or boat. This can affect people of any age, but it is most common in children, especially under age twelve. Paleness, yawning, and restlessness can be warning signs that motion sickness is developing. The main trigger for this queasiness is excess stimulation of the fluid-filled canals of the inner ears (see ear and hearing problems), which control the body's sense of balance. Motion sickness sometimes can result from an infection, often in the middle ear. If that has been medically ruled out, parents may—after advice from a doctor—treat the problem with over-the-counter medications. These are generally forms of antihistamines, drugs used to treat allergies and colds. But parents should be very aware of age restrictions on these; some are not to be used by children under age twelve, some not by those under age six, and others not by those under two. (See Tips for Avoiding Motion Sickness below.)

motor neuron diseases, a general term for a group of diseases involving damage to the nerves that supply communication between muscles and nerves, and resulting in weakness and wasting (*atrophy*) of the muscles. The group includes *amyotrophic lateral sclerosis* (ALS or *Lou Gehrig's disease*), which appears during middle age, and *spinal muscular atrophies*, which mostly affect children.

The most common of the spinal muscular atrophies is labeled "Type 1," also called *infantile spinal muscular atro-*

Tips for Avoiding Motion Sickness

- Don't read while traveling.
- Sit so your line of vision is straight ahead, as much as possible.
- Eat lightly before and during travel. On short trips, avoid all food and drink.
- Place yourself where you will feel the motion least, such as in the front seat of a car, near the wings of an airplane, or amidships on a boat, preferably on deck in the fresh air, weather permitting.
- Avoid tobacco smoke and strong odors, especially from food.

(Source: Adapted from "Taming Tummy Turmoil," Dixie Farley, FDA Consumer, June 1995.)

phy, or *Werdnig-Hoffman disease.* This condition involves HYPOTONIA (floppiness), PARALYSIS, and deformities appearing in the first few months of life, often apparent at birth. Infants have difficulty sucking, swallowing (DYSPHAGIA), and breathing; they generally die in early childhood, often from respiratory illnesses, though some survive with severe DISABILITIES into their teens. Infantile spinal muscular atrophy is a GENETIC DISORDER, of an AUTOSOMAL RECESSIVE type.

Other forms that appear less often or somewhat later are *Type 2 or intermediate spinal muscular atrophy; Type 3, juvenile spinal muscular atrophy, or Kugelberg-Welander disease;* and *benign congenital hypotonia (Aran-Duchenne type).* (See MUSCULAR DYSTROPHY.)

FOR HELP AND FURTHER INFORMATION

Amyotrophic Lateral Sclerosis Association (ALSA)
21021 Ventura Boulevard, Suite 321
Woodland Hills, CA 91364
818–340–2060; 800–782–4747
Michael Havlicek, President
Organization concerned with ALS; supports research; provides information and referrals; publishes various materials, including newsletter.

Families of S.M.A. (FSMA)
P.O. Box 1465
Highland Park, IL 60035–7465
Phone and fax: 708–432–5551; 800–886–1762
Marilyn Naiditch, Secretary
Organization concerned with spinal muscular atrophy, including adult progressive S.M.A. (Aran-Duchenne type), juvenile S.M.A. (Kugelberg-Welander disease), benign congenital hypotonia, and Werdnig-Hoffman disease; acts as advocate; supports research; publishes various materials, including quarterly newsletter *Direction.*

Muscular Dystrophy Association, 520–529–2000. (For full group information, see MUSCULAR DYSTROPHY.)

National Organization for Rare Disorders (NORD), 800–999–6673. (For full group information, see RARE DISORDERS.)

OTHER RESOURCES

Charlie's Victory: An Autobiography. Charlie Wedemeyer and others. Zondervan, 1993.

motor skills, skills relating to motion, involving both the muscles that carry out the motion and the brain and nervous system that direct the activity.

Gross motor skills involve the large muscles of the arms, legs, torso, and feet. For a growing child, many of the major DEVELOPMENTAL MILESTONES, such as crawling, sitting up, and WALKING, are gross motor skills. So are the even more complex skills of body control and rhythm, as in jumping, hopping, skipping, moving rhythmically to music, throwing, kicking, pushing, pulling, and lifting things; *bilateral movement,* or using both arms and hands at the same time; *cross-lateral movement,* or using opposite arms and legs at the same time; *crossing the midline,* as in using a right hand to pick up a toy placed at the left side; and balance. The CHART OF NORMAL DEVELOPMENT (on page 637) lists the age at which each milestone is reached, *on the average,* in each of various skill areas.

Closely related to the gross motor skills are SPATIAL ORIENTATION and SPATIAL RELATIONS. Children who have LEARNING DISABILITIES and some other DEVELOPMENTAL DISORDERS may show problems in gross motor skills by reaching developmental milestones later than most, by jerky or uncoordinated movements, and by clumsiness, as with tripping, bumping into things, or dropping things. Some may also require help from ORTHOPEDIC DEVICES to gain the strength and balance to move about.

Fine motor skills are those that use the small muscles of the fingers, toes, wrists, lips, and tongue. Among the developmental milestones involving fine motor skills are grasping an object and putting it in the mouth, picking up an object with thumb and one finger, transferring an object from one hand to another, building a tower, putting rings on sticks or pegs into pegboards, scribbling, turning knobs, throwing a small ball, and painting with sweeping strokes. Children who have learning disabilities and some other developmental disorders may have trouble handling small objects, such as buttons and snaps, tying and untying ties, using scissors smoothly, holding pencils and crayons securely, gripping or picking up small things between thumb and index finger, copying vertical or horizontal lines or circles, using rhythm instruments, or stringing beads. They may also lack the fine motor coordination between lips and tongue needed for clear speech, and so may sometimes be reluctant to talk. The inability to produce in sequence the movements necessary to draw shapes and figures or copy words and letters is called *apraxia.*

Closely related to the fine motor skills are the VISUAL SKILLS, especially those sometimes called the *perceptual motor skills,* involving hand-eye, body-eye, or visual-motor coordination. Among the other kinds of skills crucial in the development of the child are AUDITORY SKILLS, COGNITIVE SKILLS, SELF-HELP SKILLS, SOCIAL SKILLS, and communication skills (see COMMUNICATION SKILLS AND DISORDERS). Children develop at individual and varying paces, but every child can benefit from activities designed to enhance their natural development. (Subscribers to the America Online computer service can find activities designed to develop children's skills in the Moms Online Desk Reference section of Moms Online, under "Teaching Young Children.")

FOR HELP AND FURTHER INFORMATION

Association for Children with Down Syndrome (ACDS), 516–221–4700. Publishes *Movement and Dance Curriculum.* (For full group information, see DOWN SYNDROME.)

Blind Children's Center, 800–222–3566. Publishes *Move with Me* and *Reaching, Crawling, Walking. . .Let's Get*

Moving. (For full group information, see EYE AND VISION PROBLEMS.)

OTHER RESOURCES

Movement Activities for Early Childhood. Carol T. Hammett. Human Kinetics, 1992.
Perceptuo-Motor Difficulties: Theory and Strategies to Help Children, Adolescents, and Adults. Dorothy E. Penso. Singular, 1992.

FOR CHILDREN

I Touch, 2nd ed. Helen Oxenbury. Candlewick, 1995. Baby board book.
I Can Tell by Touching. Carolyn Otto. HarperCollins, 1994.
Moving. Anita Ganeri. Raintree Steck-Vaughn, 1994.
Touch. Mandy Suhr. Carolrhoda/Lerner, 1994.
Touching. Lillian Wright. Raintree Steck-Vaughn, 1994.
Keeping Your Balance. Julian Rowe and Molly Perham. Childrens, 1993.
Feel and Touch. Julian Rowe. Childrens, 1993.
Your Balance Sense. Jane Koomar and Barbara Friedman. American Occupational Therapy, 1992.
Your Muscle Senses. Jane Koomar and Barbara Friedman. American Occupational Therapy, 1992.
Feeling Things. Allan Fowler. Childrens, 1991.
Touch... What Do You Feel? Nicholas Wood. Troll, 1991.

(See also EXERCISE.)

MRI (Magnetic Resonance Imaging), a type of MEDICAL TEST similar to a CT SCAN in its use of computers to give physicians three-dimensional pictures of the inside of the body, but different in using measurement of the natural magnetism in the atoms within the body; formerly called *nuclear magnetic resonance (NMR).* It is not an INVASIVE procedure, and has no known adverse effects, but for safety, women who are pregnant are advised not to have MRI. Since the patient must lie in a narrow tunnel-like tube, people with claustrophobia sometimes are unable to complete the test, or do so only under sedation.

mucopolysaccharidoses (MPS), a family of STORAGE DISORDERS or METABOLIC DISORDERS, in which the body tissues accumulate abnormal and damaging amounts of certain compounds, called *mucopolysaccharides,* due to lack of enzymes needed to break them down. The various MPS disorders each have an MPS number and a name; related storage disorders, each also with several variant forms, are *mucolipidoses* (ML), in which compounds called *mucolipids* accumulate, and LIPID STORAGE DISEASES (*lipidoses*).

MPS and ML are GENETIC DISORDERS; of the known types, all are of the AUTOSOMAL RECESSIVE; the exception is Hunter syndrome (see below), which is X-LINKED, being carried by the mother and affecting only boys. The main types can be detected before birth with PRENATAL TESTING, as through AMNIOCENTESIS or CHORIONIC VILLUS SAMPLING. After birth, the disorders are often diagnosed through URINE TESTS and X-RAY analysis of skeletal development.

Children with MPS or ML have a shortened life expectancy, often dying in childhood or adolescence, though some with a mild form may live a relatively normal life. Among the characteristics shared by many are MENTAL RETARDATION, skeletal deformity (especially of the face), retarded GROWTH often resulting in DWARFISM, cloudy corneas, stiff joints, speech and hearing impairments, hyperactivity, and chronic runny nose. Many will require physical therapy to help drain mucus from their chest. Other characteristics are specific to the individual type of disorder.

The best-known types of MPS disorders are:

- *Hurler syndrome (MPS I)*; in addition to the above, it is characterized by a group of defects called GARGOYLISM (a now-outdated name for the disorder), including large head with protruding tongue and prominent brows, thick arms, legs, hands, and ribs along with various other skeletal deformities, enlarged liver and spleen. Features also often include mental retardation, short, stubby hands, enlarged tonsils, a constricted chest, breathing difficulties, some degree of deafness, abdominal hernias, bowel problems, thickened skin, KYPHOSIS (excessive curvature of the spine), abdominal hernias, often heart disease, and sometimes accumulated fluid in the brain (HYDROCEPHALUS), which may require the insertion of a thin tube (*shunt*) to drain the excess fluid. The disorder is identifiable at about six to twelve months of age. Babies are often quite large at birth and grow fast initially, but their growth slows by around age three, and few grow taller than four feet. Most children with Hurler's syndrome die before they reach age twenty-two. Some children with a mild form of MPS I, called *Scheie syndrome,* generally have normal intelligence and live into adulthood. Some others with normal or near-normal intelligence but more severe physical symptoms are said to have *Hurler/Scheie syndrome.*
- *Hunter syndrome (MPS II),* which affects only males; in addition to the general features, it is characterized by gargoylism, kyphosis (excessive curvature of the spine), EAR AND HEARING PROBLEMS, abdominal hernias, thickened skin, and breathing problems; both liver and spleen become enlarged, hydrocephalus sometimes occurs; bowel problems may lead to frequent bouts of DIARRHEA. Short, stubby hands gradually become curved and can cause problems with fine MOTOR SKILLS. Some children have a painful *carpal tunnel syndrome,* involving pressure of ligaments passing through wrist bones called *carpals,* which can be eased by surgery. Feet have high arches, and toes may also be curved; some children have a tight Achilles tendon, causing them to walk on their toes. Children most severely affected are likely to die by their midteens. They also have varying degrees of mental retardation, some severe; they reach a plateau of learning in early life and then regress. However, some

with milder forms can life a full life span, if their heart and lung problems are not too severe—one person with Hunter is recorded to have lived to age eighty-seven—and their intelligence can be normal or near normal. Children with Hunter reach PUBERTY two or three years later than their peers; some can do very well in school and even go to college. Some men with Hunter have married and had children; their children would not have the syndrome unless the mother was a carrier, but any daughters would be carriers.

- *Morquio syndrome (MPS IV)*: it is characterized by retarded GROWTH often resulting in DWARFISM and abnormal muscular and skeletal development (*chondrodysplasia*) leading to kyphosis or SCOLIOSIS (sideways curvature of the spine), enlarged breastbone (*sternum*), fused or missing vertebrae, and knock-knees. The syndrome is often first diagnosed when the child is learning to walk, by the unusual waddling gait. Children with Morquio grow normally at first, slow down by around 18 months; the most severely affected stop growing by around age eight, reaching a final height of three to four feet, while others grow into their teens, reaching five feet. Heart problems are common, but generally do not cause problems until later in life; some form of hearing problem is also common. Problems in the cervical portion of the spine can leave the spinal cord with inadequate protection; this is sometimes corrected with an operation called *cervical fusion.* Intelligence is usually not affected. In the past, people with severe Morquio syndrome generally died by their thirties, though those more mildly affected could live into their sixties; recent medical advances have increased life expectancy. People with Morquio have somewhat delayed puberty and can marry; their children would be not have the disorder unless the other parent was a carrier. However, women with severe Morquio are advised against pregnancy because of the risks to their health.

BONE MARROW TRANSPLANTS have been tried in some cases, where a child has a family member who is a proper match to be a donor. This has relieved some symptoms of Hurler and Hunter syndrome (though it has had little effect on Morquio), but the operation is both painful and extremely risky, and it is not yet clear whether the transplant can prevent long-term damage to the brain. Some have tried dietary approaches to relieve symptoms, which may help individual children; parents will need to consult carefully with the family doctor about any special diets.

Other forms of MPS, some so rare and so recently described that not much is known about them in the long term, include:

- *Sanfilippo syndrome,* in which children initially develop normally, but during the preschool years begin to lag and lose much of what they have learned. Otherwise they have few notable external physical characteristics, though they may have more thick, bushy HAIR than normal. Life expectancy averages into the teens, but in rare cases people with mild forms have lived into their 40s.
- *Maroteaux-Lamy syndrome,* in which children generally grow to three-and-a-half to four-and-a-half feet, with a variety of physical problems; intelligence is not affected. Puberty is delayed and people with the syndrome can marry and have children, who will be carriers, though women with severe forms are advised against pregnancy. Life expectancy is unknown.

Characteristics of children affected with mucolipidoses vary widely among various forms of the disorder. Some have normal intelligence; others have LEARNING DISABILITIES. Some have distinctive physical appearances, others have few distinguishing characteristics. Heart problems, some amount of deafness, and chest and ear infections are common. Many children with the *I-cell* form will die young, though some may survive into their preteens. However, people with other forms, such as *ML-III,* go through puberty, often delayed, and live into adulthood, though women are advised against having children for their own health. Life expectancy is unknown.

Any child with MPS or ML is at special risk if given ANESTHESIA because of respiratory difficulties. Parents should be sure that school, CHILD CARE workers, and all health professionals are aware of the child's special problems, and should seek an anesthetist experienced in dealing with them.

FOR HELP AND FURTHER INFORMATION

National MPS Society
17 Kraemer Street
Hicksville, NY 11801
516–931–6338
Fax: 516–822–2041
Marie Capobianco, President
Organization concerned with mucopolysaccharidoses or mucolipidoses; maintains national registry; provides support, information, and referrals; sponsors research; publishes newsletter *Courage* and various brochures.

Zain Hansen M.P.S. Foundation
1200 Fernwood Drive
P.O. Box 4768
Arcata, CA 95521
707–822–5421
Carl Zichella, President
LeAnna Carson-Hansen, Contact
Organization concerned with mucopolysaccharidoses and related disorders; offers some financial and other aid; supports research; provides information; operates medical equipment exchange bank; publishes various materials, including quarterly newsletter.

National Tay-Sachs and Allied Diseases Association (NTSAD), 800–906–8723. (For full group information, see LIPID STORAGE DISEASES.)

National Digestive Disease Information Clearinghouse (NDDIC), 301–654–3810. (For full group information, see DIGESTIVE SYSTEM AND DISORDERS.)

National Organization for Rare Disorders (NORD), 800–999–6673. (For full group information, see RARE DISORDERS.)

(See also GENETIC DISORDER; METABOLIC DISORDERS.)

multifactorial disorder, a pattern of GENETIC INHERITANCE that involves several factors—some genetic, some environmental—for the disorder to be expressed. Among the characteristics of multifactorial disorders are that:

- They seem to occur in a given family with no discernible pattern (unlike an AUTOSOMAL DOMINANT, AUTOSOMAL RECESSIVE, or X-LINKED disorder).
- Conditions often vary in severity.
- Frequency may vary with race and sex.
- The risk of a particular disorder occurring in a particular person is assessed on the basis of statistical data.

Examples of multifactorial disorders are CLEFT LIP AND PALATE, CLUBFOOT, ASTHMA, SPINA BIFIDA, EPILEPSY, DIABETES, ARTHRITIS, certain heart disorders (see HEART AND HEART PROBLEMS), CONGENITAL DISLOCATION OF THE HIP, and some forms of CANCER.

multigravida, a medical designation for a woman who has been pregnant more than once.

multipara, a medical designation for a woman who has given birth to more than one live baby.

multiparent family, a type of FAMILY in which adults living in a collective household or commune share the rearing of children in the house.

multiple birth, two or more babies developing during a single PREGNANCY. Multiple births occur naturally in every 1 out of 88–90 births. About one-third of these develop from a single ZYGOTE (fertilized egg), which divides after conception; these twins (or other multiples) are called *identical, monozygotic*, or *monovular*. Because they have the same genetic material, they are of the same sex and look alike, though one is generally larger than the other at birth. Identical twins also share the same PLACENTA and CHORION in the UTERUS, though with individual UMBILICAL CORDS and generally separate sacs of AMNIOTIC FLUID. About 1 out of 4 pairs of identical twins are *mirror twins*, meaning that they have the same features, but on opposite sides, sometimes even including internal organs, such as the heart. If division of the single egg is not fully complete, the two may be joined in some part of the body, often the chest, and need to be separated surgically after birth, where possible; these so-called *Siamese twins* occur about once in every 50,000 births.

But two out of three cases of multiple births involve fertilization of separate eggs (see OVUM) by separate SPERM, and are called *fraternal, nonidentical, dizygotic*, or *binovular*. They are genetically distinct beings, and may look quite different and be of the same or different sexes. Each has its own PLACENTA, but because these may be placed near each other, laboratory tests are sometimes needed to determine whether twins are identical or fraternal. Fraternal twins are more likely to occur in women who are older or have borne several children previously and those who have a personal or family history of multiple births. People of Black African descent have a somewhat higher than normal likelihood of having fraternal twins, while people of Asian background have a lower rate.

With pregnancies of three or more babies, all may be identical or all fraternal, or they may be a mixture of the two forms. Births of such *supertwins* are far more rare—triplets in every 1 per 8000–9000 births, and quadruplets far less, at perhaps 1 in 73,000 births.

Use of fertility drugs has made multiple births more common, as have various techniques to counter INFERTILITY, some of which (such as IN VITRO FERTILIZATION) deliberately implant multiple eggs to increase the chances of achieving pregnancy. BIRTH CONTROL PILLS are also associated with somewhat higher rate of twinning.

Because of such increased likelihood, doctors are more alerted to the possibility of twins than in the past, when perhaps half of the cases of multiple births were not recognized until the seventh month, and a quarter not until the actual DELIVERY. Multiple pregnancy is generally identified by a larger than usual abdomen for the woman's time of GESTATION, and by the doctor's hearing more than one fetal heartbeat. An ULTRASOUND scan is often used to confirm the diagnosis of multiple pregnancy.

Multiple births are, almost by definition, HIGH-RISK PREGNANCIES. Two or more beings are competing for space and nourishment normally meant for a *singleton*, and one fetus is normally larger and better nourished than the other(s), though both or all may have relatively LOW BIRTH WEIGHT (on the average, a little over 5 pounds). LABOR often starts two to four weeks early, resulting in PREMATURE DELIVERY, with its attendant risks and problems. During the birth of the first baby, the remaining multiple babies are likely to suffer some mild to severe ANOXIA, and so may have some DEVELOPMENTAL DELAY or other problems in later GROWTH. To lessen FETAL DISTRESS, especially since MALPRESENTATION is common, doctors perform more CESAREAN SECTIONS with multiple than with single pregnancies. Even so, there is an increased risk of losing one or more babies (see DEATH AND DYING). For mothers, multiple pregnancy is also associated with increased risk of high BLOOD PRESSURE (*hypertension*), excess amniotic fluid (HYDRAMNIOS), and postpartum HEMORRHAGE.

Twins and other multiples are generally extremely close from birth, with their own special BONDING. One of the major decisions parents must make during twins' development is when and how much to separate them. In the past it was the fashion to dress twins alike. Today many parents and child development experts believe it more important to dress twins differently and emphasize their individuality, often sending them to different schools (either at the start or at some point during grade school) and directing them toward different kinds of activities, especially since one is often somewhat better coordinated and quicker than the other, presumably because of influences in the womb. Various organizations and studies can help parents make such decisions about raising their multiples.

FOR HELP AND FURTHER INFORMATION

National Organization of Mothers of Twins Clubs (NOMOTC)
P.O. Box 23188
Albuquerque, NM 87192
505–275–0955
Lois Gallmeyer, Executive Secretary
Network of clubs for parents of multiple births; provides information; acts as advocate; supports research; publishes *MOTC's Notebook.*

Twins Foundation
P.O. Box 6043
Providence, RI 02940–6043
401–729–1000
Paul R. Campbell, President
Organization concerned with multiple birth; maintains National Twin Registry; provides information and referrals; publishes quarterly *The Twins Letter* and *Research Update, Should Twins Be Separated in School?, Twins and Language Problems,* and *Source Directory.*

Twin Services
P.O. Box 10066
Berkeley, CA 94709
TWINLINE: 510–524–0863
Fax: 510–524–0894
Patricia Malmstrom, Executive Director
Organization interested in multiple births; provides information and referrals; publishes various information handouts (packaged into kits for new and expectant parents, and for parents of toddlers), including:

- General issues: *Twinshock: Twins Are a Hard Happiness, Identical or Fraternal?, Staying Sane Under Twin Stress, Good Reading for Parents, The Social World of Young Twins, Twins and Competition, Twins Learning to Talk, When Twins Grow Up, Supertwin Management: Triplets and More, Single Parents of Twins, Fathers of Twins Need Help Too,* and *Surviving Toddler Twins.*
- On preparing and caring for newborns: *Layette List for Twins, Survival Suggestions for New Parents,* and *Getting Help.*
- On practical questions: *Transporting Twins, Equipment for Twins, Dressing Twins, When Twins Bite, Twin Games: A Delicate Balancing Act,* and *Is Your Home Twinproof?*

Triplet Connection (TC)
P.O. Box 99571
Stockton, CA 95209
209–474–0885
Fax: 209–474–2233
Janet Bleyl, President
Organization for families of multiple babies; helps parents prepare for high-risk birth; publishes quarterly newsletter and information packets.

C/SEC (Cesareans/Support, Education, and Concern), 508–877–8266. Publishes *Having Twins.* (For full group information, see CESAREAN SECTION.)

OTHER RESOURCES

For parents

Multiple Blessings: From Pregnancy Through Childhood, a Guide for Parents of Twins, Triplets, or More. Betty Rothbart. Hearst, 1994.

The Twinship Sourcebook: Your Guide to Understanding Multiples. TWINS Magazine Editors; Barbara C. Unell, ed. TWINS Magazine, 1993.

Mothering Twins: From Hearing the News to Beyond the Terrible Twos. Linda Albi and others. Simon & Schuster, 1993.

Twins, Triplets, and More: From Pre-Birth Through High School—What Every Parent Needs to Know When Raising Two or More. Elizabeth Bryan. St. Martin's, 1992.

Keys to Parenting Twins. Karen Kerkhoff. Barron's, 1992.

Understanding Twins. Miram P. Braunstein. Sigo Press, 1991.

Having Twins: A Parent's Guide to Pregnancy, Birth, and Early Childhood, 2nd ed. Elizabeth Noble. Houghton Mifflin, 1990.

The Parents Guide to Raising Twins, 2nd ed. Elizabeth Griedrich and Cherry Rowland. St. Martin's, 1990.

Twins. Roxanne Pulitzer. Villard Books, 1990.

Periodicals

Double Talk. Quarterly. Karen Kerkhoff Gromada, Box 412, Department ND, Amelia, OH 45102; 513–231–8946.

Twins Magazine. Twins Customer Service, P.O. Box 12045, Overland Park, KS 66282–2045; 913–722–1090; 800–821–5533.

For children, fiction on twins

One Up, One Down. Carol Snyder. Atheneum/Macmillan, 1995. About twin brother and sister.

Egg-Drop Blues. Jacqueline T. Banks. Houghton Mifflin, 1995. African-American twin brother and sister.

A Week with Zeke and Zach. Lindsay L. Johnson and Holly Kowitt. Dutton, 1993.

Twins, Two by Two. Catherine Anholt. Candlewick, 1992.

Mac and Zach from Hackensack. George L. Rogers. Acorn, 1992.

Twins in Trouble. Amu Djoleto. Chelsea House, 1992. African-American twins.
Twins. Monica Colli. Child's Play, 1992.

FOR CHILDREN, FICTION ON TRIPLETS

Rosalie, Sylvia and Melanie. Felix Pirani. Childs World, 1992.
Triplets. Felix Pirani. Viking, 1991.

FICTION FOR PRETEENS AND TEENS

Karen's Twin. Ann M. Martin. Scholastic, 1994.
New One. Jacqueline T. Banks. Houghton Mifflin, 1994. About African-American twins.
My Sister Is Driving Me Crazy. Mary E. Ryan. Simon & Schuster, 1991.

PERSONAL EXPERIENCES

Growing up Different: The Diaries of Twin Boys. Gary Hutchison. G.F. Hutchison, 1994.
We are Twins: But Who Am I? Betty J. Case. Tibbutt, 1991. Also the author of *Living Without Your Twin* (1994).

multiple disabilities, the presence of more than one kind of disability in a child, such as both vision and hearing problems (see DEAF-BLIND) or MENTAL RETARDATION and ORTHOPEDIC DISABILITIES. (See DISABILITIES.)

multiple sclerosis (MS), a disorder in which *myelin*, the fatty substance protecting nerve cells in the brain and spinal cord, is damaged or partly destroyed and replaced by scar tissue (*sclerosis*), the whole process disrupting communications in the NERVOUS SYSTEM. Symptoms vary widely, depending on what parts of the body are most affected, and how severely, but can include tingling sensations, numbness, muscle weakness (PARESIS), muscle cramps, lack of coordination, PARALYSIS, blurred or double vision, abnormal fatigue, confusion, forgetfulness, INCONTINENCE (difficulty in controlling bladder and bowels), and impaired sexual function. The disorder is also highly variable. Some people may have a single attack, with no recurrence afterward. Some other people have periods when the disease is active, called EXACERBATIONS, and times when they are free of symptoms, called REMISSIONS. In still others, the disease is CHRONIC and PROGRESSIVE, becoming increasingly severe.

The cause of the disease is unknown. It is not a GENETIC DISORDER, nor is it thought to be contagious, though it is possible that some families may be more susceptible to it, either because of hereditary predisposition or by sharing the same environment. It most often strikes in young adulthood, affecting women somewhat more than men, and Whites more often than Blacks or Asians. It is also more common in the world's temperate zones than in tropical climates, and the area in which a child spends the first fifteen years of life affects future risk of contracting MS. It is unclear why all this is so, but many speculate that a virus picked up early in life triggers an AUTOIMMUNE DISORDER, in which the body mistakenly attacks its own tissue.

Recent animal studies indicate that some kinds of ANTIBODIES in the IMMUNE SYSTEM can help repair myelin, and may help both to explain the disease's unusual remission cycles and to offer promise of a treatment or even a cure in the future, if these antibodies can be boosted in the body. At present, however, no cure exists, though some drugs and therapy can help alleviate symptoms.

Because the symptoms of the disease are so variable, and are similar to those of many other disorders, MS is often hard to diagnose. Doctors may need to perform a variety of MEDICAL TESTS, including LUMBAR PUNCTURE, CT SCANS, and MRI SCANS. Multiple sclerosis does not affect life expectancy and most people with MS can live relatively normal lives. Though in the past it was thought that PREGNANCY could cause the disease to worsen, more recent studies have, according to the National Multiple Sclerosis Society, "not shown there to be any effects of pregnancy on the long-term course of multiple sclerosis. In general pregnancy is no longer held to be necessarily detrimental." They caution, however, that a woman with MS may not have the physical stamina to care for a baby and active child, and needs to consider carefully whether she will have the resources to help her do so.

FOR HELP AND FURTHER INFORMATION

National Multiple Sclerosis Society (NMSS)
733 Third Avenue
New York, NY 100173288
212–986–3240; Information Line: 800-FIGHT-MS [344–4867]
Online service forums: America Online: NMSS
Prodigy: Multiple Sclerosis Forum
Michael J. Dugan, President and Chief Executive Officer
Organization concerned with multiple sclerosis; provides information and referrals; offers services such as counseling, training programs for caregivers, swimming programs, vocational rehabilitation, and medical equipment on loan; publishes quarterly *Inside MS* and other materials, including:

- For families: *What Is Multiple Sclerosis?, Plain Talk: A Book about Multiple Sclerosis for Families, Someone You Know Has MS: A Book for Families* (for children ages 8–15), *When a Parent Has MS: A Teenager's Guide, Taking Care: A Guide for Well Partners,* and *Check Your MS Facts.*
- For patients: *Things I Wish Someone Had Told Me: Practical Thoughts for People Newly Diagnosed with Multiple Sclerosis, Living with MS, Moving with MS: An Exercise Manual for People with Multiple Sclerosis, Multiple Sclerosis and Your Emotions, Coping with Stress, The Rehab Outlook: Preventing Disabilities or Impairments from Becoming Handicaps, Sexual Dysfunction in Multiple Sclerosis—Dare We Discuss It?, ADA and People with MS: A Guarantee of Full Participation in American Society, Understanding Bladder*

Dysfunction in Multiple Sclerosis, and other materials on research and employment.

National Institute of Neurological Disorders and Stroke (NINDS), 800–352–9424. Publishes brochure *Multiple Sclerosis: Hope Through Research* and special report *Multiple Sclerosis.* (For full group information, see BRAIN AND BRAIN DISORDERS.)

Accent, 800–787–8444. Publishes *Multiple Sclerosis: A Rehabilitative Approach to Management.* (For full group information, see HELP FOR SPECIAL CHILDREN on page 689.)

Resources for Rehabilitation, 617–862–6455. Publishes books *Resources for People with Disabilities and Chronic Conditions* and *A Woman's Guide to Coping with Disability,* both including sections on multiple sclerosis. (For full group information, see EYE AND VISION PROBLEMS.)

OTHER RESOURCES

GENERAL WORKS

Multiple Sclerosis, the Unseen Enemy, rev. ed. Arline Dean. Carlton, 1994.

Multiple Sclerosis, 3rd ed. Bryan Matthews. Oxford University Press, 1993.

Living Well with Multiple Sclerosis: A Guide for Patient, Caregiver, and Family. David L. Carroll and Jon Dorman. HarperCollins, 1993.

MS'ing in Action. Martin Rimm. Carnegie, 1993.

Multiple Sclerosis and the Family. Rosalind C. Kalb and Labe Scheinberg. Demos, 1992.

Multiple Sclerosis. Louis J. Rosner and Shelley Ross. Simon & Schuster, 1992.

FOR PRETEENS AND TEENS

Coping When a Parent Has Multiple Sclerosis. Barbara Cristall. Rosen, 1992.

BACKGROUND WORKS

Multiple Sclerosis: A Neuropsychiatric Disorder. Uriel Halbreich, ed. American Psychiatric Press, 1993.

(See also HELP FOR SPECIAL CHILDREN on page 689.)

multisensory, employing all or most of the senses, including *auditory* (hearing), *visual* (seeing), *tactile* (touch), *olfactory* (smell), *gustatory* (taste), and *kinesthetic* (body motion). Some approaches for teaching children with LEARNING DISABILITIES or others kinds of learning difficulties employ various of the senses to enhance success at learning, as in the VAKT approach to teaching READING.

mumps, a highly contagious disease caused by a virus that is passed from person to person in droplets from coughing, sneezing, or just talking; also called *epidemic parotitis* or *infectious parotitis.* Common symptoms of the disease are FEVER, headache, and inflammation of the salivary glands, causing the cheeks to swell. In some cases, however, mumps can cause more severe complications. Approximately 1 affected child in 10 has MENINGITIS (inflammation of the membranes covering the brain and spinal cord) or the even more serious ENCEPHALITIS (inflammation of the brain itself); this sometimes disappears without damage, but mumps can cause deafness (see EAR AND HEARING PROBLEMS). Mumps also poses a threat to adolescent or adult males; 1 in 4 affected males experience painful inflammation and swelling of one or occasionally both of the TESTES, a condition called *orchitis,* in some instances causing STERILITY.

Fortunately since 1967 a mumps VACCINE has existed, often given to children at about 15 months of age as part of a combination MEASLES-MUMPS-RUBELLA (MMR) VACCINE. Older adults who have never had mumps and have not been immunized can also take the vaccine. Parents should keep careful records of either IMMUNIZATION or evidence of their child's having had the disease, since many states in the U.S. require one or the other before admitting a child into school.

FOR HELP AND FURTHER INFORMATION

National Institute of Allergy and Infectious Diseases (NIAID), 301–496–5717. (For full group information, see ALLERGIES.)

National Institute of Child Health and Human Development (NICHD), 301–496–5133. (For full group information, see PREGNANCY.)

(See also MEASLES-MUMPS-RUBELLA VACCINE.)

muscular dystrophy (MD), not a single disease, but a group of relatively rare diseases, mostly appearing during childhood and ADOLESCENCE, that result from muscle destruction or degeneration, with fatty tissue often replacing the wasted (*atrophied*) muscle. MD is a group of GENETIC DISORDERS apparently resulting from abnormality in production of a key protein. It can be diagnosed by tests for certain substances released from damaged muscle cells; by an ELECTROMYOGRAM, which detects electrical activity in muscles; or by a BIOPSY (tissue sample). The forms of MD vary in their GENETIC INHERITANCE pattern, AGE of onset, muscles initially affected, and rate of progression.

The main types of muscular dystrophy affecting young people are:

- *Duchenne muscular dystrophy* or *pseudohypertrophic MD,* the most common form of MD, affecting 1–2 in 10,000 boys and accounting for 50 percent of MD cases. Duchenne normally appears between ages two and five, often first affecting the muscles of the pelvic girdle, then progressing rapidly to nearby muscles. Affected children are slow to sit up and walk, have trouble climbing stairs, and often have LORDOSIS (swayback). By age twelve, most children with Duchenne MD are confined to a wheelchair, and are experiencing progressively worsening heart and lung problems, as those muscles are attacked. This form of MD generally brings death by the late teens, often from sudden heart failure. Duchenne may arise spontaneously, but usually is an X-LINKED RECESSIVE trait passed on to male children by unaffected mothers who are CARRIERS.

- *Becker's muscular dystrophy* or *benign pseudohypertropic muscular dystrophy*, a less common form of MD, appearing between ages two and twenty and progressing more slowly and with less life-threatening results, with affected people often reaching age fifty. Like Duchenne's, it has an X-linked recessive hereditary pattern.
- *Myotonic dystrophy*, a form of MD that can appear at any age, though generally ages twenty to forty, involving weakness or "floppiness" and MYOTONIA, or inability to readily relax muscles after use. Myotonic dystrophy often affects hands, feet, face, and neck first, and may be associated with abnormalities in the heart, endocrine, and CENTRAL NERVOUS SYSTEMS, sometimes including MENTAL RETARDATION. It has an AUTOSOMAL DOMINANT inheritance pattern, and can be passed on by either mother or father.
- *Limb-girdle muscular dystrophy*, form of MD that may actually be several disorders, appearing in late childhood to early adulthood, differing greatly in severity and rate of progression, and characteristically affecting the shoulder or pelvic area. Limb-girdle MD is an autosomal recessive trait, which both parents must pass on.
- *Facioscapulonumeral muscular dystrophy* or *Landouzy-Dejerine muscular dystrophy*, a form of MD that primarily affects the face and shoulder regions, and sometimes also the pelvic region, appearing between infancy and early adulthood, but often in adolescence. Like myotonic dystrophy, it is passed as an autosomal dominant trait, but its progression is slow and does not generally cause severe DISABILITY.
- *Congenital muscular dystrophy*, a form of MD present at birth and not usually PROGRESSIVE, causing weakness in muscles of the limbs, trunk, and face, as well as overall limpness. Its inheritance progression is not fully clear, but it is probably autosomal recessive, like limb-girdle dystrophy.
- *Distal muscular dystrophy*, a form of MD that may actually be several disorders, which appears at various ages and first affects the muscles of the hands and feet, perhaps progressing to hips and shoulders. Its inheritance pattern is unclear, but some forms seem to be autosomal dominant, like myotonic dystrophy.

Other, rarer muscular dystrophies also exist.

No successful treatment currently exists for muscular dystrophy, though the recent discovery of some *genetic markers* linked to some forms of MD, and promising experiments in GENE THERAPY offer hope for the future. Researchers are following various other lines, including some drugs that may slow the progression of muscle-wasting. Meanwhile the main options are supportive measures. PHYSICAL THERAPISTS help MD patients keep the unaffected muscles in working condition for as long as possible and ORTHOPEDIC DEVICES can help prevent deformity.

Prospective parents with a personal or family history of muscular dystrophy may well want to seek GENETIC COUNSELING. Prepregnancy tests can detect whether a parent carries a defective gene. During PREGNANCY, some kinds of MD can be detected through GENETIC SCREENING tests such as CHORIONIC VILLUS SAMPLING and AMNIOCENTESIS.

Research and helping organizations (see the resource list that follows this entry), both public and private, that focus on muscular dystrophy generally also encompass several other kinds of muscular diseases, including:

- MOTOR NEURON DISEASES, a group of diseases involving damage to the nerves that supply communication between muscles and nerves, and resulting in weakness and wasting of the muscles. The group includes *amytrophic lateral sclerosis* (ALS or *Lou Gehrig's disease*) and *spinal muscular atrophies*, including *Type 1*, *infantile*, or *Werdnig-Hoffman disease*; *Type 2*, *intermediate*; *Type 3*, *juvenile*, or *Kugelberg-Welander disease*; or *Aran-Duchenne type*.
- *Myotonias*, inherited disorders in which the muscles do not readily relax after use, but remain bulging and stiff, as in MYOTONIA CONGENITA (*Thomsen's disease*) and *paramyotonia congenita*.
- *Diseases of neuromuscular junction*, in which voluntary muscles cannot contract normally, leaving the person very weak, such as MYASTHENIA GRAVIS and *Eaton-Lambert syndrome*.
- *Diseases of the peripheral nerve*, such as PERONEAL MUSCULAR ATROPHY (*Charcot-Marie-Tooth disease*), Friedreich's ATAXIA, and *Dejerine-Sottas disease*.
- *Inflammatory myopathies*, such as *polymyositis*, *dermatomyositis*, and *myositis ossificans*, in which the muscles become inflamed and weak.
- METABOLIC DISORDERS that affect muscles, such as GLYCOGEN STORAGE DISEASE and periodic PARALYSIS.
- *Myopathies due to endocrine abnormalities*, such as *hyperthyroid myopathy* and *hypothyroid myopathy*, which result from THYROID GLAND problems.

Other rare muscle disorders, or *myopathies*, also exist.

FOR HELP AND FURTHER INFORMATION

Muscular Dystrophy Association (MDA)
3300 East Sunrise Drive
Tucson, AZ 85718
520–529–2000
Fax: 520–529–5300
Robert Ross, Executive Director
Organization concerned with muscular dystrophy and related neuromuscular diseases; operates network of diagnostic, research, and treatment clinics, offering social service and genetic counseling, free care to families not covered by health insurance, and special services such as assistance for transportation costs and repair of orthopedic aids; operates children's summer camps; acts as advo-

cate; publishes quarterly newsmagazine and numerous other materials.

National Institute of Neurological Disorders and Stroke (NINDS), 800–352–9424. Publishes fact sheet *Dystonias.* (For full group information, see BRAIN AND BRAIN DISORDERS.)

National Arthritis and Musculoskeletal and Skin Diseases Information Clearinghouse (NAMSIC), 301–495–4484. (For full group information, see ARTHRITIS.)

National Organization for Rare Disorders (NORD), 800–999–6673. (For full group information, see RARE DISORDERS.)

Gazette International Networking Institute (GINI), 314–534–0475. Publishes *Ventilators and Muscular Dystrophy.* (For full group information, see HELP FOR SPECIAL CHILDREN on page 000.)

OTHER RESOURCES

Muscular Dystrophy: The Facts. Alan E. Emery. Oxford University Press, 1994.

Muscular Dystrophy and Other Neuromuscular Diseases: Psychosocial Issues. Leon I. Charash and others. Haworth, 1991.

For children

Muscular Dystrophy. Gail L. Burnett. Crestwood/Macmillan, 1995.

The Will to Live: The Battle of a Young Boy Against Muscular Dystrophy. A. J. Mills. Humor Books, 1992.

(See also ATAXIA; MOTOR NEURON DISEASES; MYASTHENIA GRAVIS; MOTOR SKILLS; EXERCISE; SPORTS; also HELP FOR SPECIAL CHILDREN on page 689.)

mutation, a change in the coding for the DNA in the genes and chromosomes that form a being's GENETIC INHERITANCE. Sometimes mutations can be beneficial, or at least neutral. But most mutations are dangerous and possibly life-threatening, giving rise to GENETIC DISORDERS and CHROMOSOMAL ABNORMALITIES. Some mutations occur spontaneously, as mistakes in the duplication of DNA in the cells, which are then duplicated in the normal process of reproduction. If the mutation occurs in the "sex cells" from which the SPERM and egg (OVUM) are formed, it may be passed on to any children. But if the mutation occurs in other parts of the body, it will not be heritable, though its effects may be deadly, as a cancerous TUMOR. Some mutations are, at least partly, triggered by ENVIRONMENTAL HAZARDS, such as radiation or cancer-triggering substances (*carcinogens*). (See GENETIC DISORDERS.)

mute, a state of silence, or being without speech, for whatever reason. Some children have APHASIA and are unable to speak, because of damage to the speech apparatus or the connections to the brain. Some are almost totally unresponsive, except perhaps for a whispered "yes" or "no," for physical reasons such as BRAIN TUMORS or HYDROCEPHALUS; this is called *akinetic mutism.* But some children, who are both physically able to speak and understand language, choose not to speak, communicating instead mostly by gestures or nods. This *elective mutism* is often found in young children, usually under age five, and is sometimes associated with shyness or SEPARATION ANXIETY, though the possibility of MENTAL RETARDATION or speech problems should always be explored. In somewhat older children, elective mutism may be linked with SCHOOL PHOBIA, or a response to a change of school. Mutism may also be a symptom of some kinds of MENTAL DISORDERS. (See COMMUNICATIONS SKILL AND DISORDERS and other specific topics.)

myasthenia gravis (MG), a rare AUTOIMMUNE DISORDER, a disease affecting the joinder of nerves and muscles, in which voluntary muscles cannot contract normally, leaving the person very weak. Eye movements, facial expression, chewing, swallowing, and breathing, and later arm and leg muscles are often first affected. This rare disorder can appear at any age, but most commonly in young women and older men.

A rare inherited disorder that is sometimes misdiagnosed as myasthenia gravis is *congenital disorders of neuromuscular transmission* (CDNT), which also results from problems with the connection between nerves and muscles. It is important that the two be properly distinguished at the onset, since the treatments for MG, including immunosuppressive drugs, will not be beneficial and may be harmful to people with CDNT.

FOR HELP AND FURTHER INFORMATION

Myasthenia Gravis Foundation (MG)
222 South Riverside Plaza, Suite 1540
Chicago, Illinois 60606
312–258–0522; 800–541–5454
Fax: 312–427–8437
Anna El-Qudsi, Executive Director
Organization of patients with myasthenia gravis, their friends and families, and health professionals; sponsors research and treatment centers; operates a national patient registry; provides information and referrals; operates discount "drug banks"; publishes various materials, including *Myasthenia Gravis Survival Guide: A Guide to Patient Directed Health Management, Practical Guide to MG, Facts on Myasthenia Gravis,* and flyers on medications such as *Mestinon, Prednisone,* and *Imuran.*

National Organization for Rare Disorders (NORD), 800–999–6673. (For full group information, see RARE DISORDERS.)

(See also MUSCULAR DYSTROPHY.)

myelogram, an X-RAY examination of the spinal cord and brain to see if there is evidence of a TUMOR, SPINAL CORD INJURY, or dislocated disk, which might show up in narrowing or obstruction of the spaces where the CEREBROSPINAL FLUID flows. Using a procedure called a LUMBAR PUNCTURE (spinal tap), a small amount of cerebrospinal fluid is removed and replaced with a fluid that will show up with contrast on the X-ray. The patient is tilted on a table while a series of X-rays are taken at different angles, and then most or all of the contrast fluid is removed. The procedure is uncomfortable; common side effects include nausea, VOMITING, flushing, pressure, headaches, and some PAIN, especially as fluid is removed. Serious side effects are relatively rare, but involve possible introduction of infection and ALLERGY to the contrasting fluid. (See MEDICAL TESTS.)

myotonia, inability of a muscle to relax readily after use, a symptom seen in diseases such as *myotonic dystrophy*, a form of MUSCULAR DYSTROPHY, and MYOTONIA CONGENITA.

myotonia congenita (Thomsen's disease), a rare inherited disorder in which muscles do not readily relax after use, but remain bulging and stiff, especially when the person is tired and has been inactive; a mild, nonprogressive muscular disorder. A related disorder brought on by exposure to cold is *paramyotonia congenita.* (See MUSCULAR DYSTROPHY.)

N

nails, the hard material that grows atop the ends of fingers and toes, made of specialized skin cells, mostly the protein *keratin.* The nail tissue on the surface is made up of dead cells, but under the *cuticle* (the crescent-shaped, skin-covered area), the nail is alive and sensitive, with a rich blood supply. In general, it takes about six to nine months for a nail to grow out, from the edge of the cuticle to the tip of the finger.

Because of their long growing time, nails are actually a window on a person's well-being. Health problems of various kinds are reflected in lines, ridges, pits, spots, and other marks or changes in shape, which can speak volumes to a physician. ANEMIA, for example, may show itself in spoon-shaped nails; traumatic events, including a serious infection or an operation—may be reflected on the nails. Parents should check their children's nails periodically to see if they show any change that might be an early warning sign of health problems. Healthy nails should be smooth, shiny, and evenly show the color of the skin beneath them. Severe injury to the fingertip may cause the nail to be lost, but it will generally grow back normally, unless the nail "bed" has been badly damaged.

Common nail problems include:

- *Fungal infections,* which may need to be treated medically for some months, until the diseased nail has been replaced by healthy growth.
- *Bacterial infections,* when bacteria invade through cuts, hangnails, or other openings, a condition called *paronychia.* These are treated with soaking, and sometimes lancing and antibiotics.
- *Ingrown toenails,* a condition common when people wear shoes so tight that they force distorted growth of the nail. Caught early, the problem can be gradually eased by inserting a cotton swab under the problem corner of the nail and lifting it slightly so it can grow normally. If severe, and if infection has set in, medical treatment may be necessary. The problem can be prevented by cutting nails straight across, rather than on a curve, and by wearing shoes with sufficient toe room.

Manicuring or pedicuring too often can cause splitting of the nails, as can poor NUTRITION and reactions to substances such as detergents, nail polish, or nail-hardening agents. Softening creams can help decrease splitting of the cuticles or the likelihood of hangnails. Girls or women who paint their nails should be sure not to push the cuticle back too far, and so expose live tissue to the nail polish.

FOR HELP AND FURTHER INFORMATION

The Nail File. Leo Palladino and June Hunt. Scholium, 1992.

Great Nails for Girls. Jamie Kyle. Checkerboard, 1993.

nanny, a person employed to take care of a young child, living in or out of the home, but generally having full responsibility for CHILD CARE and domestic tasks related to the child during a work week of forty to sixty hours. Nannies may or may not have had formal training, but generally have considerable experience in caring for children. Minimum standards set by the International Nanny Association (INA) call for nannies to be at least 18 years old, have a high school diploma, be in good health, with up-to-date IMMUNIZATIONS, including a negative test or chest X-ray for TUBERCULOSIS, where required.

A 1993 survey of INA members found that nearly all were women (99.3 percent) and more than 82 percent had a bachelor's or master's degree, often in early childhood or elementary education, most of them caring for children under 5 years old. Just under 60 percent lived in the employer's home; two-thirds of them were placed in their jobs by an agency; their median income was $280 a week, but some earned as much as $600 a week.

Though their primary responsibility is child care, some nannies also do light housekeeping; that is a question to be settled between nanny and employer; both parties should be clear beforehand about what is, and is not, expected in terms of tasks and hours. The demand for nannies often allows them to weigh such matters before accepting a position, along with other factors such as paid vacations and holidays, health insurance, use of a car, and, for live-in nannies, room and board, usually including private room and private bath.

In Britain, specially trained nannies receive instruction in child care subjects and practice over a two-year period, leading to certification as a *nursery nurse.* However, such nannies—and indeed most trained nannies from abroad—are seldom allowed to work in the United States legally, under current American immigration laws. Those who do work in the United States on tourist visas do so illegally, and are subject to deportation, and their employers subject to fines. However, AU PAIRS from abroad may work for up to a year in the United States, while gaining experience of American life.

FOR HELP AND FURTHER INFORMATION

International Nanny Association (INA)
125 South Fourth Street
Norfolk, NE 68701–5200
402–691–9628
Wendy Sachs, President

212–496–1213
Organization of nannies, employment agencies, and nanny training schools; sets professional standards; publishes directory of training programs, placement agencies, and special services; membership directory; and *A Nanny for Your Family*.

OTHER RESOURCES

Nannies, Maids and More: The Complete Guide for Hiring Household Help. Linda F. Radke. Five Star Publications, 1995.
Nannies: How I Went Through Eighteen Nannies for One Little Boy Before I Found Perfection in a Former Marine Sargeant Named Margaret. Elizabeth Fuller. Fine, 1993.
How to Hire a Nanny: A Step by Step Guide for Parents. Elaine S. Pelletier. Andre and Lanier, 1992.
Is There a Nanny in the House? Wanda Draper. Macedon, 1992.
Today's Nanny and In-Home Child Care. J. Lukas. Delmar, 1992.

(See also CHILD CARE; also CHECKLIST FOR CHOOSING CHILD CARE on page 114.)

national standards, in EDUCATION, a proposed set of CURRICULUM standards—core knowledge and skills each student should be expected to have—that would be applied nationwide, and possibly national tests to see how well those standards are met. Given the highly publicized flaws and shortcomings of the current educational system, particularly its variability in curriculum and resources, this approach has been much discussed.

Supporters of national standards say that this is only way to produce across-the-board educational reforms and bring all students up to clearly defined high standards. They point out that national standards would help parents to know how their children compare with other children all across the country, not just in a locality; would allow localities to properly evaluate their teachers and school systems; and would make postsecondary schools and employers better able to assess the meaning and value of a student's record and DIPLOMA.

Critics charge that it would end up penalizing students from poor schools and depriving local communities of control over their children's learning, while also diverting attention *away from* basic educational reform. They stress that there is no evidence that a national curriculum and TESTS will lead to better instruction, and note that American students are already overtested, more than in any other country in the world, an emphasis that sometimes seems to have turned schools into test-coaching centers, and that what students really need is better teaching, and better funded schools.

Many people are also concerned that, as in some parts of Europe and in Japan, national testing would result in a kind of TRACKING system, determining who will be in line for elite careers, with tests used as barriers, not gateways, for poorer students. Ironically, this comes at a time when traditional tracking has come under widespread attack. Many people are also concerned that national tests would be biased against minorities, as most standardized tests are, since many questions draw largely on the content of experiences of the *majority*.

Supporters of national testing would ideally like not more standardized, multiple-choice tests, but instead open-ended questions, forcing students to think, and often related to the kinds of tasks they will need to perform once they leave school and enter the workforce. They also propose that ways be found for regions to be able to devise their own tests, and still have the results be compared with national standards. However, such testing is far more sophisticated than standardized testing and requires more teacher training, and therefore is more expensive, in a time when school funding is hard-pressed. Some people are concerned that such performance-oriented nationwide testing may reflect a vision of education tailored to the commercial world, which may not reflect what the entire community wants from its schools, and especially that it may undercut traditional emphasis on the humanities or liberal arts.

Even the standards themselves do not exist, and would probably take far longer to develop than most politicians recognize, even if it were clear that Americans wanted and could agree on what skills and knowledge students should have in all academic subjects. While that would be relatively easy in mathematics, considerable controversy exists over content and approaches to history and aspects of science, such as evolution.

More than that, simply mandating national standards—without providing poorer schools with the funds necessary to meet those standards—would make the promise of educational reform a cruel hoax. The ambivalence of concerned educators and policy-makers toward the national testing proposals was made clear in 1991 in comments by Phyllis McClure of the NAACP Legal Defense and Education Fund:

> One of the worst things about American schooling now for poor and disadvantaged kids is that they are held to few and sometimes no standards at all. The thing that attracts me about this proposal is that it establishes a common, high standard for all kids. But how do you expect high standards of kids who go to the worst possible schools? There's got to be some kind of leverage to force the system to provide the resources that these kids need.

Proponents say that national standards for students are needed if America is to keep up with its international competitors, noting that the United States is the only industrialized country without minimum standards for what children should know at various grade levels, in core subjects such as mathematics, science, history, and geography. Critics point out, however, that none of these competing countries has a national examination system of the sort proposed; most have no government-mandated testing in the higher grades, nor do they use tests to hold schools accountable. (see EDUCATION.)

National Vaccine Injury Compensation Program (VICP), a program established under the 1986 federal Childhood Vaccine Injury Act, which provides compensation for injuries to a child, including death, related to IMMUNIZATION, specifically to the DTP VACCINE (diphtheria-tetanus-pertussis), MEASLES-MUMPS-RUBELLA VACCINE (MMR), and POLIO vaccines. By offering a "no-fault" system of compensation, it has aimed to help the families of affected children gain proper compensation without costly and burdensome litigation, while also offering doctors and vaccine manufacturers relief from lawsuits—which had caused many companies to stop making vaccines, threatening the country's vaccine supply system.

The VICP program provides claim forms and guidelines specifying what is covered, timetables for onset of various types of symptoms, the time period for filing, and the type and amount of awards. To be eligible, someone must have incurred over $1000 in expenses as a result of a child's vaccine-related injury or death. Claims must be filed within three years of the first symptoms, with effects having continued for at least six months, and within 24 months of death and 48 months of the onset of the vaccine-related injury leading to death. As described in the September 1990 *FDA Consumer*, if the court rules favorably on the claim, the person is eligible for up to $250,000:

> for present and future pain and suffering. This includes past and future unreimbursed medical expenses, residential and custodial care and rehabilitation costs, and projected lost earnings from age eighteen. Attorney's fees may also be awarded, even if the petition is denied.... $250,000 is awarded in the event of death.

A vaccine injury table is used to establish legal links between administration of a vaccine and injury or death. As the *FDA Consumer* notes:

> For example, to show that a child's seizure disorder was caused by the DTP vaccine, the child's first seizure must have occurred within three days of vaccination. To show that the MMR vaccine caused encephalitis, the injury must have occurred within 15 days of receiving the MMR vaccine. To establish that either the DTP or MMR vaccine caused a severe anaphylactic reaction or shock, the reaction must have taken place within twenty-four hours of immunization.

If the court's judgment is favorable, the person can either accept it—thereby giving up the right to take any legal action against the doctor of manufacturer—or reject it, keeping the right to bring a lawsuit. (See also IMMUNIZATION; DTP VACCINE; MEASLES-MUMPS-RUBELLA VACCINE, and POLIO.)

FOR HELP AND FURTHER INFORMATION

National Vaccine Injury Compensation Program (NVICP)
Parklawn Building, Room 8A–35
5600 Fishers Lane
Rockville, MD 20857
301–443–6593; 800–338–2382
Fax: 301–443–8196
Thomas E. Balbier, Director
Federal arm that oversees implementation of the Childhood Vaccine Injury Act; provides information packet.

National Vaccine Information Center (NVIC), 800–909–7468. Publishes *The Compensation System and How It Works* and *FDA/VAERS Vaccine Lot Numbers* (cross-listed with reported adverse events). (For full group information, see IMMUNIZATION.)

(See also IMMUNIZATION; DTP VACCINE; MEASLES-MUMPS-RUBELLA VACCINE; ORAL POLIO VACCINE.)

natural childbirth, a general term for an approach to LABOR and DELIVERY that attempts to minimize medical intervention during CHILDBIRTH; an alternate term for PREPARED CHILDBIRTH. (See CHILDBIRTH; PREGNANCY.)

natural family planning (NFP), an approach to BIRTH CONTROL that avoids the use of artificial or mechanical means. The various NFP approaches use natural signs and changes in the woman's body to identify the time of OVULATION, when she has produced an egg (OVUM) available to be fertilized.

If the aim is to avoid CONCEPTION, the couple may abstain from sexual intercourse from the time of ovulation to the beginning of the woman's period (see MENSTRUATION). This approach is also called *periodic abstinence.* If the aim is to achieve conception, as where INFERTILITY is a concern, the couple will plan to have sexual intercourse in the period of maximum fertility; this would also be the prime time for ARTIFICIAL INSEMINATION or extracting an egg for IN VITRO FERTILIZATION.

There are three main NFP approaches:

- *Calendar (rhythm) method*, which involves tracking the successive dates of a woman's menstrual cycle, and calculating the most likely date for ovulation. The effectiveness of this method depends on the woman having a regular menstrual cycle, and on the assumption that—whatever the length of the cycle—ovulation occurs about 14 days before the beginning of the next period. As a birth control method, this traditional approach is highly unreliable, though it becomes somewhat more effective in conjunction with one or both of the methods below.

- *Basal body temperature method*, in which a woman takes her temperature every morning, using a basal thermometer specially calibrated to measure very small temperature changes. The *basal body temperature*—the temperature of the body at rest—is taken at about the same time each day, before rising. When the temperature rises one-half to one degree and remains elevated for three days, ovulation is assumed to be taking place.
- *Cervical (vaginal) mucus method* or *Billings method*, which involves observing and charting changes in the color and texture of the mucus in the VAGINA, secreted by the CERVIX. At around the time of ovulation, the cervical mucus changes from thick and opaque to clear and slippery, much like raw egg white, allowing easier passage for SPERM. The most fertile period is from the time the mucus changes until at least three days afterward. For contraception, couples are advised to avoid intercourse during this time, while for couples wishing to conceive, this is the target period. Women must receive training, from doctors or NFP groups (see below), in what to look for. Some use a supplemental home MEDICAL TEST, based on the knowledge that, at ovulation, the mucus has more sugar; these fertility kits show, from cervical mucus smeared on it, whether glucose is elevated.

When couples use all three, or the latter two, methods together, the Public Health Service reports that the effectiveness rate for preventing conception "can approach 76–98 percent"; this is called the *symptothermal method.* A related approach is the *ovulation method,* in which a woman uses a home medical test to monitor her urine for levels of LUTEINIZING HORMONE (LH). Since LH triggers ovulation, an LH surge suggests that ovulation will probably occur in twenty-four to thirty-six hours. (See OVULATION.)

Another common approach to natural family planning is the *withdrawal method,* also called *coitus interruptus* or *coitus incompletus,* in which the male withdraws his penis from his partner's VAGINA before EJACULATION. In use at least since biblical times, withdrawal requires no supplies or medical visits—but it does require enormous self-control and motivation on the part of the male. But even with a maximum of good will and experience, it is an unreliable method, since some semen is released into the vagina even before ejaculation. Conception can also be avoided by varieties of sexual activity that do not require vaginal penetration, such as oral sex. Another traditional though unreliable form of natural contraception is prolonged BREASTFEEDING.

FOR HELP AND FURTHER INFORMATION

Couple to Couple League (CCL)
P.O. Box 111184
Cincinnati, OH 45211
513–471–2000
Frederick Haas, Jr., Public Information Director
Organization focusing on natural birth control methods; helps train CCL teaching couples who teach techniques through local teaching groups; supports premarital chastity; publishes numerous materials, including:

- Brochures on NFP: *The Case for Natural Family Planning, Creative Continence* (on handling the period of abstinence), *Dear Father* (for Catholic priests), *Dear Pastor* (for Protestant clergy), *The Effectiveness of Natural Family Planning, Fruit of the Spirit, Fruit of NFP, NFP: Safe, Healthy, Effective, A Physician's Reference to Natural Family Planning, The Sympto-Thermal Method and the Ovulation Method, Until Death Do Us Part* (on the permanence of marriage), *What Can the Couple to Couple League Do for My Community?, What Others Are Saying About NFP and CCL*
- General brochures and booklets: *Marital Sexuality: Moral Considerations, Catholic Sexual Ethics, Human Reproduction: Three Issues for the Moral Theologian,* and *Natural Family Planning—Why It Succeeds.*
- Books from various publishers offered through the CCL catalog.

Family of the Americas Foundation (FAF)
P.O. Box 219, 1150 Lovers Lane
Mandeville, LA 70488
504–626–7724
Mercedes Wilson, Executive Director
Organization fostering the Billings Ovulation Method; trains workshop teachers; provides sex education to teenagers; helps parents teach their own children about sex; provides information and referrals; publishes various materials, including films and charting kits.

Human Life International (HLI), 800–549–5433. (For full group information, see BIRTH CONTROL.)

Food and Drug Administration (FDA), 301–443–3170. (For full group information, see DRUG REACTIONS AND INTERACTIONS.)

OTHER RESOURCES

The Ovulation Method of Natural Family Planning: An Introductory Booklet for New Users, rev. ed. Thomas W. Hilgers. Pope Paul Sixth, 1993.

Fertility: A Comprehensive Guide to Natural Family Planning. Elizabeth Clubb and Jane Knight. Sterling, 1992.

The Billings Method. Evelyn Billings and Ann Westmore. Ballantine, 1989.

(See also BIRTH CONTROL.)

navel (umbilicus), the scar left on the outside of the abdomen after the cut end UMBILICAL CORD falls off, some days after birth. During the first week after birth, while the scar is healing, public health experts recommend that the baby not be immersed in water, but rather washed with cloth and warm water. Often the abdominal wall will be pushed out somewhat because of weakness near the navel, in boys somewhat more often than girls, a condition called an *umbilical hernia;*

that should be no cause for concern (see CARE OF THE BABY'S NAVEL below). Umbilical hernias can also sometimes occur in women after CHILDBIRTH.

neck righting reflex, a type of REFLEX normally found in newborns in which, if the head is turned toward one side while the INFANT is lying face upward, the baby will turn the shoulders and trunk in the same direction. If this reflex is absent in newborns, or if it persists beyond infancy, physicians may suspect and test for damage to the CENTRAL NERVOUS SYSTEM.

neonatal, the first four weeks after birth, during which the newborn, or *neonate*, especially a HIGH-RISK or PREMATURE BABY, is often cared for by a NEONATALOGIST.

neonatal intensive care unit (NICU), a type of INTENSIVE CARE UNIT that specializes in the care of LOW BIRTH WEIGHT, PREMATURE, or seriously ill newborns; sometimes called a *high-risk nursery*.

neonatal screening tests, tests routinely given to many newborns, often involving analysis of blood samples taken from the baby's heel a day or so after delivery. Though the precise tests vary from region to region, the aim of all is to identify possible BIRTH DEFECTS and medical problems, especially METABOLIC DISORDERS that can cause MENTAL RETARDATION and sometimes death unless detected and treated in the first few months of life. Among the disorders commonly screened for are PHENYLKETONURIA, GALACTOSEMIA, and certain THYROID GLAND problems. Couples who have their baby outside a hospital should be sure to have such tests done soon after the birth, to prevent unnecessary damage to the baby's development. (See MEDICAL TESTS; METABOLIC DISORDERS.)

neonatalogist, a physician who specializes in care for newborns, generally for the first four weeks of life, but sometimes longer, as when an infant is PREMATURE or is a LOW BIRTH WEIGHT baby. The neonatalogist is often the doctor who gives the major first SCREENING TESTS for BIRTH DEFECTS, including GENETIC DISORDERS, and manages early treatment of infant health problems. After 28 days, a PEDIATRICIAN normally takes over an infant's care, with other medical specialists called in, as necessary.

nervous system, the network of connections that receives and registers information from within and outside the body, interprets it, and transmits information that causes the body to take actions. In terms of the body's anatomy, the "command center" is the CENTRAL NERVOUS SYSTEM (CNS), made up of the brain and spinal cord; transmitting information between the CNS and the outlying parts of the body is a network of nerves called the PERIPHERAL NERVOUS SYSTEM (PNS).

In terms of the body's functioning, the nervous system is divided differently. The *autonomic nervous system* controls the actions that the body makes "automatically" or "involuntarily," such as heartbeat, breathing, production of substances by various glands, and the like. The autonomic nervous system is itself made up of two complementary systems. The *sympathetic nervous system* (controlled by the HYPOTHALAMUS) responds to situations such as danger or EXERCISE by speeding up heartbeat and breathing and raising BLOOD PRESSURE, while the *parasympathetic nervous system* slows heartbeat and breathing, causing a general relaxation, as when danger has passed or

Care of the Baby's Navel

The end of the umbilical cord, attached to the baby's navel cut at birth, usually falls off within days. You can keep the umbilical cord clean and dry until it falls off by dabbing it with rubbing alcohol on a cotton ball. Then, the navel may slightly bleed or ooze for a few days. If it does, clean it once or twice a day with alcohol. If it looks red and irritated or continues to bleed or ooze for more than two or three days after the cord falls off, you should call your doctor or clinic.

About one-fourth of all babies develop a bulging at the navel. This gets larger for several months, then grows gradually with the baby for several months, then gets smaller and disappears. Large bulges (or "umbilical hernias") may not go away until the child is 4 to 6 years old. The bulge often gets tight or tense when the baby cries or coughs.

Since these bulgings almost always go away if they are left alone for long enough, there is usually no reason to have them repaired by surgery. They almost never cause any kind of trouble or pain. Occasionally a 4- to 6-year-old may be embarrassed by a particularly large hernia, and it can be repaired at that time. By waiting, you will probably save your baby an unpleasant and unnecessary operation. If you have concerns, discuss them with your doctor or clinic staff.

Source: Infant Care (1989). Prepared for the Public Health Service by the Bureau of Maternal and Child Health and Resources Development.

during sleep. Parallel with the autonomic nervous system is the *somatic nervous system,* which responds to and provides the brain with information about voluntary movements of the body, as in walking or moving an arm.

neurofibromatosis (NF), a rare GENETIC DISORDER, of the AUTOSOMAL DOMINANT type, which involves the growth of many TUMORS of nerve cells under the skin (or deeper); also called *Von Recklinghausen's disease* or *Elephant Man disease.* Though BENIGN (not cancerous), these tumors can be disfiguring (as in the case of the so-called Elephant Man) and may grow in sensitive areas, such as the nerves serving the eyes or ears, which could cause deafness and blindness. In most cases, however, the number and size of the tumors is less severe, and the person can lead a relatively normal life. Early signs of neurofibromatosis, often present at birth, are large tan spots called *café au lait spots* (French for "coffee with milk"), which darken and become more numerous over the years, especially during PUBERTY, PREGNANCY, and other times when the body's HORMONES are unbalanced. Neurofibromatosis is often associated with SCOLIOSIS and LEARNING DISABILITIES.

If tumors are painful or very disfiguring, and sometimes if they are near eye or ear nerves, they can be removed by surgery, but the hazard is that they will grow back in greater numbers. Though NF cannot currently be detected by PRENATAL TESTING, prospective parents with NF in their family history may want to seek GENETIC COUNSELING. The recent discovery of a *genetic marker* linked with NF holds promise for future prenatal tests and possibly also for GENE THERAPY.

FOR HELP AND FURTHER INFORMATION

National Neurofibromatosis Foundation (NNF)
95 Pine Street, 16th Floor
New York, NY 10005
212–344-NNFF [344–6633]; 800–323–7938
Fax: 212–747–0004
E-mail: nnff@aol.com (America Online: NNFF)
Peter R. W. Bellerman, President
Organization concerned with neurofibromatosis; provides information and referrals; publishes various materials, including quarterlies *National Neurofibromatosis Foundation Newsletter* and *Research Newsletter*; pamphlets *The Child with Neurofibromatosis Type 1, Facing Neurofibromatosis: A Guide for Teens, Neurofibromatosis Type 2: Information for Patients and Families, Information for Patients and Families, Questions and Answers*; *Neurofibromatosis: Handbook for Patients, Families, and Healthcare Professionals*; and materials for professionals.

National Institute of Neurological Disorders and Stroke (NINDS), 800–352–9424. Publishes fact sheet *Neurofibromatosis.* (For full group information, see BRAIN AND BRAIN DISORDERS.)

March of Dimes Birth Defects Foundation (MDBDF), 914–428–7100. Publishes information sheet *Neurofibromatosis.* (For full group information, see BIRTH DEFECTS.)

National Organization for Rare Disorders (NORD), 800–999–6673. (For full group information, see RARE DISORDERS.)

(See also GENETIC COUNSELING.)

neurologist, a PHYSICIAN who specializes in diagnosing and treating disorders of the brain and nervous system, and also performs surgery in those areas. If a child has abnormal behavior, a neurologist will seek to find whether that is caused by a brain or nervous system problem. The neurologist performs a variety of physical examinations and MEDICAL TESTS—such as an ELECTROENCEPHALOGRAM (EEG) or LUMBAR PUNCTURE—aimed at seeing how the body gains information from the sense organs and how it uses the muscles to perform MOTOR SKILLS.

neuromuscular development, the growth of a child's control over fine and gross MOTOR SKILLS, especially in the early childhood and preschool years; a term often used by child psychologists.

neuro-otologist, a PHYSICIAN who focuses on the subspecialty of EAR AND HEARING PROBLEMS involving the acoustic nerve.

neurosurgeon, a PHYSICIAN who specializes in performing surgery of the NERVOUS SYSTEM.

nevus, a general name for a variety of blemishes on the skin. One main kind of nevus (plural: nevi) is caused by abnormal production of skin cells producing the pigment *melanin,* popularly called *moles.* Among the most common pigmented nevi are *freckles* and *café au lait* spots (the color of coffee with milk). Most pigmented nevi are harmless, but some nevi, such as the large, multicolored, perhaps hairy mole called the *giant hairy nevus,* can be or become MALIGNANT.

The other main type of nevi is formed by abnormal collections of blood vessels, medically termed *vascular nevi* or *hemangiomas*; these appear on newborn infants, and so are more popularly called *birthmarks*:

- *Stork bites,* small, flat marks on the back of the neck and sometimes elsewhere as well. These marks generally disappear harmlessly in early childhood; they are a localized form of TELANGIECTASIA.
- *Strawberry mark,* raised, bright red mark (but sometimes blue, if fed by a vein) that is essentially a BENIGN blood-filled TUMOR, sometimes called a *capillary hemangioma.* It grows quickly in the first few months of life and often disappears on its own by the time the child is school age. It normally requires attention only in cases of trauma and bleeding.
- *Port-wine stain,* large, flat, purplish-red marks, though sometimes pale red, often on the back of the head but also elsewhere on the body, that are present at

birth and permanent; also called *nevus flammeus.* No technique has yet been successful in removing such "stains," but some hold future promise. In rare occasions, the port-wine stain on the face is associated with STURGE-WEBER SYNDROME, which involves brain abnormalities, including MENTAL RETARDATION.

Though most nevi are not dangerous, for safety parents should closely examine and take notes on the size, location, and color of any markings on the skin of a young child, and then check them periodically. Some doctors take periodic photographs of moles, to serve as a basis for comparison; parents may want to do the same. Any changes or problems, such as darkening, growing, bleeding, or appearance of new marks, should be noted and reported to the doctor immediately, to be sure no CANCER is developing.

FOR HELP AND FURTHER INFORMATION

National Cancer Institute (NCI), 800–422–6237. Publishes *What You Need to Know About Moles and Dysplastic Nevi.* (For full group information, see CANCER.)

(See also SKIN AND SKIN DISORDERS.)

newborn intrapartal care, medical care for the baby through the whole of LABOR, from the onset of CONTRACTIONS through the actual DELIVERY of the baby and expulsion of the PLACENTA (afterbirth); care of the mother in the same period is called INTRAPARTAL CARE.

next friend (prochein ami), in the law, a person who acts on behalf of a MINOR or someone who is legally INCOMPETENT, when that party's parent or legal GUARDIAN is not available. Someone appointed to act for a minor only in a specific lawsuit is called a *guardian ad litem* (see GUARDIAN; ADVOCACY).

next of kin, a person's closest BLOOD RELATIONS; more precisely, in its legal origin and as defined by current laws, those people who have INHERITANCE RIGHTS and would receive a share of the estate of a person who died INTESTATE, or without a will.

niacin (nicotinamide or nicotinic acid), a VITAMIN that is important to the health of tissue and nerve cells, and to normal appetite and digestion, including the use of CARBOHYDRATES and FATS, and to the manufacture of sex HORMONES; part of a group of vitamins known as the vitamin B complex. Niacin is found in poultry, fish, and meat, especially liver, as well as whole-grain or fortified grain products, peas, and beans. Deficiencies may result from long-term heavy alcohol consumption and from digestive disorders affecting intestinal absorption of nutrients. Severe deficiency of niacin causes *pellagra,* once a common DEFICIENCY DISEASE, which involves mouth sores, rough skin, DIARRHEA, and MENTAL DISORDERS. Less severe symptoms of deficiency include weakness and dizziness, changes in the skin and intestinal lining, loss of appetite, and irritability. Overconsumption of some forms of niacin can lead to headache, cramps, and nausea. (See RECOMMENDED DAILY ALLOWANCES; VITAMINS.)

nocturnal emission, an EJACULATION that occurs during sleep, often among adolescent males; also called a *wet dream.*

noncustodial parent, a parent whose ex-partner has been awarded sole legal CUSTODY of a child, as in a DIVORCE case without shared custody. Noncustodial parents normally retain VISITATION RIGHTS.

nondextrous, unskilled in both hands, as opposed to AMBIDEXTROUS, or skilled with both hands. This condition often occurs in young children where HANDEDNESS or lateral DOMINANCE is not yet established.

nonresident student, a student whose legal place of residence is not in the district served by a school, and who therefore is not necessarily eligible for services or TUITION breaks, as opposed to a RESIDENT STUDENT; at the ELEMENTARY or SECONDARY level, often called an *out-of-district student.*

normal distribution, a bell-shaped curve that graphically represents statistical data called NORMS, such as test scores; an ideal form that tends to result when large numbers of data are depicted on a graph. This form, like an upside-down tulip-shaped bowl, with most scores falling in the middle, and far fewer scores at the top and bottom ranges, is also used by teachers in GRADING ON THE CURVE. A curve that does not have the standard shape, but instead has scores clustered at either the high or low end of the graph, is called a *skewed distribution.*

norm-referenced test, a type of TEST in which a student's performance is measured not against a set standard (such as 75 out of 100 correct), but against the performance of a large group, as in the case of STANDARDIZED TESTS. The range of scores on the test are often published in tables, with the average scores for a particular group (such as all fifth-graders) being called the NORM for that group. The particular student's result may then be compared with the norm, giving an ACHIEVEMENT AGE or a DEVELOPMENTAL AGE. (See TESTS.)

norms, in testing, usually the average scores of groups of people who have taken a particular STANDARDIZED TEST, which are then used as a basis for comparison for people taking the test later. A child's test score is compared with the norm, and the comparison is sometimes expressed as a GRADE-EQUIVALENT score or AGE-EQUIVALENT score. Most widely used numerically scored tests are developed and standardized on large populations, and the scores tend to be distributed evenly along a *normal distribution* or *bell curve,* like a bottom-up tulip-shaped bowl, with most scores falling in the middle, and far fewer scores at the top and bottom ranges.

More generally, norms may also refer to social expectations about behavior and to the "average" behavior seen in a group. Some kinds of tests, such as the GESELL PRESCHOOL TEST, use the term "norm" more in this sense, a norm being a behavior observed in over half of the children of a particular age group. Confusion results when many who use the test, however, wrongly treat the Gesell norms as if they were standardized norms with a heavy statistical basis. (For help and further reference, see TESTS.)

Norplant, a form of BIRTH CONTROL that involves implanting in a woman's arm capsules containing *progestin,* a synthetic form of PROGESTERONE, which is also used in BIRTH CONTROL PILLS. In pill or implant form, progestin inhibits OVULATION, and also thickens the mucus of the CERVIX, making it more hostile to SPERM; it may also have other contraceptive actions, but they are not proven.

Norplant consists of six matchstick-sized silicone-rubber capsules, arrayed like a small fan. These are implanted under a woman's skin, normally on the inside of the upper arm, where they can be felt, though not seen. For up to five years, these release small amounts of progestin into the bloodstream. The main advantage is that, once in the implant is in place, the woman need not be concerned about birth control for nearly five years. If she wishes to become pregnant before then, the implants can be removed at any time; her fertility will be restored within a short time—blood levels of progestin become undetectable within 5 to 14 days.

Norplant is inserted during an outpatient procedure requiring approximately 10 to 15 minutes. After using local ANESTHESIA to numb the upper-arm area of insertion, the doctor makes a small incision, about one-eighth inch long and uses a special instrument to insert the six capsules under the skin. The area is then covered with gauze and a bandage; no stitches are needed. After the anesthetic wears off, the woman may experience tenderness or itching in the area, as well as possible discoloration, bruising, and swelling, all temporary. Norplant becomes effective within twenty-four hours. Occasionally the area becomes infected, and the woman will need to consult her doctor.

Removal is slightly more complicated, and generally takes longer. Sometimes it requires two visits, with the second perhaps a week later; that is because the area puffs up with anesthetic, and the doctor may therefore have difficulty locating and removing all the capsules in one visit. A new set of capsules can be inserted at the same time, if desired, either in the same site, or elsewhere on either arm. Implantation is covered by Medicaid and some states also subsidize costs to make the procedure more widely available.

In development and experimental use since the late 1960s, Norplant has been used in Finland since 1983, and was approved for use in the United States in 1990. Studies have shown Norplant to be more than 99 percent effective in preventing PREGNANCY; a 1991 report by the Alan Guttmacher Institute rated it the most effective form of birth control, with a pregnancy rate of 0.05–0.5 percent, compared to permanent STERILIZATION, at 0.2–0.5 percent. Early reports indicated that, after two years of use, Norplant was slightly less effective in women who weighed over 150 pounds, but as capsules have since been made softer, that may no longer be so.

Among the side effects experienced by women using Norplant the most common, affecting approximately 45 percent of women studied, is irregular menstrual bleeding (see MENSTRUATION); another 10 percent had periods three to four months apart. Other common side effects are headache, DEPRESSION, nervousness, dizziness, nausea, skin rash or ACNE, change of appetite, tenderness of the BREASTS, weight gain, enlargement of the OVARIES, and excessive growth of body or facial HAIR. Some other women have experienced discharge from the breasts or VAGINA, inflammation of the CERVIX, abdominal discomfort, and muscle and skeletal pain, but it was unclear whether these symptoms were linked to Norplant, since they are such common experiences.

Norplant is not recommended for women with unexplained vaginal bleeding, BREAST CANCER, blood clots (especially in the legs, lungs, or eyes), acute liver disease, or liver tumors, whether malignant or benign. In addition—even though most of the adverse side effects of BIRTH CONTROL PILLS are believed to result from ESTROGEN, not progesterone—the Food and Drug Administration (FDA) advises physicians to "consider the possible increased risks associated with oral contraceptives, including elevated blood pressure, thromboembolic disorders [blood clots obstructing blood vessels], and other vascular problems that might occur with use of the contraceptive implant." Women and their doctors will also want to closely monitor the site for possibly adverse reactions to the silicone, implicated in adverse effects linked to breast implants.

In general, Norplant is most attractive to women who want long-term contraception, without the permanence of STERILIZATION, and are unhappy with other forms of contraception, including those who cannot use estrogen. It will be less attractive to women who want to have a birth control method that they can stop at any time, without the necessity of one or more visits for removal.

Although designed for voluntary birth control, some judges and legislators have sought to use Norplant as an instrument of social control. In the United States, for example, some people have proposed measures that would pay women on welfare if they agreed to use Norplant, or would require insertion of Norplant in women convicted of certain drug offenses, though most such proposals died quickly and the fate of others remains to be determined by the judicial system. (See BIRTH CONTROL.)

nuclear family, a type of FAMILY that includes basically two generations, parents and children.

nuclear medicine, a medical specialty that involves the use of radioactive materials in diagnosis and therapy, in techniques such as NUCLEAR SCANS.

nuclear scan, a type of MEDICAL TEST similar to a CT SCAN, but involving the use of slightly and temporarily radioactive materials to show certain aspects of the body's organs more clearly; also called *radioisotope scanning* or *radionuclide imaging*. These are INVASIVE PROCEDURES, in which the radioactive materials are introduced into the body, as by INJECTION or inhalation. The principle behind nuclear scanning is that various kinds of substances tend to be absorbed or concentrated in specific body organs; the material introduced will depend on which organ is to be studied, and its concentration in that organ can indicate if there is any abnormality, such as a problem in liver functioning or a TUMOR. In a PET SCAN, for example, radioactive glucose helps indicate the functioning of the circulatory system. (See MEDICAL TESTS.)

nullipara, the medical designation for a woman who has never given birth to a live baby, often noted on a hospital medical chart as "para 0."

number facts, basic information about how the digits 1–10 are added, subtracted, multiplied, and divided, often referred to separately as *addition facts, subtraction facts*, and so on. The number facts are basic to later number work, and so are considered important PREREQUISITE skills for children to learn.

nurse practitioner, a nurse with special training (often including a MASTER'S DEGREE) and experience in a particular area of nursing. WELL-BABY EXAMINATIONS are sometimes given by a *pediatric nurse practitioner* (PNP), working alone or as part of a doctor/nurse team; a *family nurse practitioner* (FNP) often works in collaboration with PRIMARY HEALTH CARE PROVIDERS to help families who have continuing long-term medical needs, such as a child with SPINA BIFIDA.

nursery school, a separate school for children of PREKINDERGARTEN age, from ages two or three to five; a type of PRESCHOOL educational program. Many nursery schools are cooperative, local affairs, in which parents donate some of their time to serve as teacher's aides, in such areas as dressing or undressing children (and teaching them to do both themselves) and serving as extra adults on field trips. Because of parents' help, *cooperative nursery schools* generally have lower fees. Some are staffed, managed, and financed entirely by parents. Nursery schools follow various approaches to teaching and play for children, such as the MONTESSORI METHOD. (See PRESCHOOL; EDUCATION.)

nursing bottle syndrome, the rapid decay of a baby's TEETH when the infant is allowed to go to sleep with a bottle containing anything other than water. During sleep, little saliva is available to wash away sugars from liquids such as MILK, sugar, or FORMULA, so bacteria quickly attacks the tooth enamel, especially on the front teeth. The same is true if the baby falls asleep during BREASTFEEDING. Many dentists recommend that parents clean the infant's teeth with gauze or a damp washcloth after feeding, to prevent nursing bottle syndrome.

nurturance, support for a child's basic psychological growth and development, and responsiveness to the child's needs, hopes, fears, and aspirations. For the child to develop normally, at least one person in his or her life—often, but not necessarily, a parent—must supply that nurturance, a process that usually starts with BONDING. Failure to supply that support constitutes a real, though rarely provable, form of CHILD ABUSE AND NEGLECT, and can lead to MATERNAL DEPRIVATION SYNDROME or FAILURE TO THRIVE.

nutrition, the provision of food substances in sufficient amounts and variety so that the body functions in a normal, healthy way; also the study of how the body uses foods and the proper amounts for daily consumption. Quantity alone is insufficient without quality and balance. The diet must every day contain several necessary elements: PROTEINS, CARBOHYDRATES, FAT, FIBER, VITAMINS, MINERALS, and water.

The old "four food groups" image used in nutrition education since the 1950s has, since 1992, been replaced by a new approach: the Food Guide Pyramid. The pyramid is made up of five food groups—fruits and vegetables are now considered separately—with recommendations on the number of servings a person should have each day. "Serving" does not mean the normal amount a person might eat at one sitting, nor is it arbitrarily set by the manufacturer (as in the past), but is defined by the FDA according to the food group. The basic recommendations are:

- Grains (bread, cereal, rice, and pasta), 6–11 servings (such as one slice of bread or one ounce of cereal)
- Vegetables, 3–5 servings (such as one cup of raw leafy greens or one-half cup of other vegetables)
- Fruits, 2–4 servings (such as one medium banana, orange, or apple)
- Dairy products (milk, yogurt, and cheese), 2–3 servings (such as one cup of milk or 1.5 ounces of cheese)
- Meat, poultry, fish, eggs, nuts, and dry beans, 2–3 servings (such as 2–3 ounces of cooked lean beef or chicken)

At the top of the pyramid is a small category of fats, oils, and added sugars, with the recommendation to "use sparingly," as part of more general guidelines on reducing fat in the diet. In past decades, dieters passed up bread while eating a hamburger, but modern nutrition advice calls for having grain products provide a substantial part of a healthy daily diet, while avoiding high-fat meats. To aid consumers in making food purchases, the federal government has required more useful information on food packages (see FOOD LABELS), including what is considered an appropriate serving size for the particular food. Pregnant women will need to modify their diet somewhat, on advice from their doctor, to be sure they are getting the right amount and balance of nutrients for their own and their baby's health.

Many people take vitamin and mineral supplements to be sure they meet the RDAs for vital nutrients. Nutrition experts say it is best to get vitamins and minerals from the foods you eat. When you select an adequate diet, you usually won't need other vitamin and mineral supplements. For pregnant women, iron and folic acid are exceptions. Because of increased needs during pregnancy, it is difficult to obtain adequate iron and folic acid from food alone, so some doctors prescribe iron and folic acid supplements. Such pills do not, however, supply all the other essential nutrients such as protein, carbohydrate, fat, and some vitamins and minerals, so eating balanced meals is still important. The same holds for supplying nutrition to growing children, though some doctors suggest that vitamin and mineral supplements may be useful for those days when parents know their child has not eaten well-balanced meals.

In addition, our bodies need water and other fluids. For pregnant women, the recommendation is for 6 to 8 glasses of water or other liquids each day. Fruit and vegetable juices and milk, as well as water, count as fluids, though some doctors recommend that pregnant women should only sparingly drink (or eat) foods containing caffeine. Fluids are especially important for infants (see DEHYDRATION).

The diet described above is in the traditional mainstream of nutrition. But, for a variety of reasons, some people choose to have more restricted diets, such as the VEGETARIAN or the even more restricted VEGAN diet. If such a diet eliminates meat and fish, but retains milk and eggs, the nutritional balance is thought to be adequate, even during pregnancy. However, people on a diet that also eliminates milk and eggs will probably get properly balanced nutrition only with very careful planning and vitamin and mineral supplements, because protein from animal sources is easier for the body to use than that from plant sources. They should check carefully with a doctor and nutritionist, especially when planning a pregnancy or providing a diet for growing children.

Many other people are on restricted diets for medical reasons, such as ALLERGY to or intolerance of certain kinds of foods, such as milk (see LACTOSE INTOLERANCE). They, too, will need careful counseling to be sure they and their children are getting all the nutrients necessary. Various eating disorders can also disrupt nutrition; see separate entries on ANOREXIA NERVOSA, BULIMIA, OBESITY, PICA, and BINGE EATING DISORDER.

For people with any kind of digestive disorder, and for pregnant women, the Public Health Service recommends eating smaller meals, saving some food to snack on a couple of hours later. They also recommend raw vegetables and fruits, juices, milk, breads, and cereals for between-meal snacks; these are especially good to have available for children and adolescents, as alternatives to junk food, which is of little or no nutritional value and contains excess fat, to encourage habits of good nutrition from their early years.

Some people have inadequate nutrition because of poverty. For these, various federal, state, and local programs exist, including WIC (Supplemental Food Program for Women, Infants and Children), which provides selected foods for pregnant or BREASTFEEDING mothers and PRESCHOOL children. Focus on these groups reflects the widespread recognition that inadequate nutrition leads to a wide variety of health problems, such as LOW BIRTH WEIGHT and many associated disorders. The Food Stamp program can also help stretch food budgets. People in need should contact their local clinic or health department for help.

In selecting food for themselves and their families, parents also need to be concerned about FOOD ADDITIVES, some of which can have harmful effects on health, naturally occurring contaminants such as AFLATOXIN or *Salmonella*, and other kinds of contaminants that can affect food (see DIGESTIVE SYSTEM AND DISORDERS; ENVIRONMENTAL HAZARDS; also TIPS FOR AVOIDING FOODBORNE ILLNESS on page 178). Parents may well want to subscribe to some periodicals that give them frequent updates on new information about hazards to food and nutrition; one excellent one available from the U.S. government is the Food and Drug Administration's *FDA Consumer* (see the resource list that follows this entry).

With the new FOOD LABELS, parents can also get important information from the packages of products they buy, not only about nutrition, but also about substances they may want to avoid, especially in the case of ALLERGIES. Other good sources of nutrition information (in addition to those listed below) are local branches of the Public Health Service and County Extension Departments.

FOR HELP AND FURTHER INFORMATION

Food and Drug Administration (FDA),
301–443–3170. Publishes *FDA Consumer.* (For full group information, see DRUG REACTIONS AND INTERACTIONS.)

Food and Nutrition Information Center (FNIC)

National Agricultural Library, Room 304

10301 Baltimore Boulevard
Beltsville, MD 20705–2351
301–504–5414
Fax: 301–504–6409

E-mail: fnic@nalusda.gov
Sandra L. Facinoli, Coordinator, Foodborne Illness Education Information Center
E-mail: croberts@nalusda.gov
Internet website: http://www.nalusda.gov/fnic.html
Federal center providing pamphlets on nutrition and related topics, as well as books and audiovisual materials on loan; publishes resource lists (in print, on disk, or online), including *Food Fun and Food Facts for Children, Sensible Nutrition Nutri-Topics,* and *Food Composition Nutri-Topics.*

American Academy of Pediatrics (AAP), 800–433–9016. Publishes brochures *Healthy Start…Food to Grow On, Right From the Start: ABCs of Good Nutrition for Young Children, What's to Eat? Healthy Foods for Hungry Children, Feeding Kids Right Isn't Always Easy: Tips for Preventing Food Hassles,* and *Growing Up Healthy—Fat, Cholesterol, and More.* (For full group information, see HEALTH CARE.)

American Institute for Cancer Research (AICR), 800–843–8114. Publishes numerous works on nutrition, including *Infant Nutrition: Sound Eating Habits Start Early, Sound Nutrition for Your Pregnancy, Billy Buck Hightrail's Secret Mysterious Magical Garden* (for children), *Dietary Guidelines to Lower Cancer Risk, Nutrition of the Cancer Patient, Diet and Cancer: What's the Link?, Ten Tips to Change Your Diet and Lower Cancer Risk, Get Fit, Trim Down, Diet, Nutrition and Prostate Cancer, All About Fat and Cancer Risk, Dietary Fiber to Lower Cancer Risk, The Facts About Fat, The Facts About Fiber;* and cookbooks and shopping guides. (For full group information, see CANCER.)

Food and Consumer Services
3101 Park Center Drive
Alexandria, VA 22302
703–305–2281
Fax: 703–305–1117
Organization that administers food assistance programs for the U.S. Department of Agriculture, including the Food Stamp Program, Special Supplemental Nutrition Program for Women, Infants, and Children (WIC), National School Lunch Program, School Breakfast Program, Summer Food Service Program, The Emergency Food Assistance Program (TEFAP), the Child and Adult Care Food Program, the Special Milk Program, and other; provides information about the programs.

American Council on Science and Health (ACSH), 212–362–7044. Publishes special reports *Much Ado About Milk, Holiday Dinner Menu, Beef Controversy,* and *Nutrition Accuracy in Popular Magazine (1990–1992);* and booklets *Eating Safely: Avoiding Foodborne Illness, Facts About Fats, Food and Life: A Nutrition Primer, Irradiated Foods, Low-Calorie Sweeteners, Microwave Ovens, Natural Carcinogens in American Food,* and *Pesticides and Food Safety.* (For full group information, see SAFETY.)

American Cancer Society (ACS), 800–227–2345. Publishes *Taking Control* and educational kit *Changing the Course* for children. (For full group information, see CANCER.)

National Institute of Child Health and Human Development (NICHD), 301–496–5133. Publishes *Nutrition.* (For full group information, see PREGNANCY.)

National Maternal and Child Health Clearinghouse (NMCHC), 703–821–8955. Publishes *Healthy Foods, Healthy Baby, Nutrition Resources for Early Childhood—A Resource Guide, Call to Action: Better Nutrition for Mothers, Children, and Families, Celebrating Diversity: Approaching Families Through Their Food.* (For full group information, see PREGNANCY.)

American Heart Association (AHA), 800–242–8721. Publishes *American Heart Association Diet, An Eating Plan for Healthy Americans, Dining Out: A Guide to Restaurant Dining, Eat Well, But Wisely, How to Read the New Food Label, Nutrition for the Fitness Challenge, Nutritious Nibbles: A Guide to Healthy Snacking,* and *How to Choose a Nutrition Counselor for Cardiovascular Health: A Consumer Guide.* (For full group information, see HEART AND HEART PROBLEMS.)

March of Dimes Birth Defects Foundation (MDBDF), 914–428–7100. Publishes pamphlet *Eating for Two: Nutrition During Pregnancy,* and information sheet and video *Eating for Two.* (For full group information, see BIRTH DEFECTS.)

Twin Services, TWINLINE: 510–524–0863. Publishes *Nutrition in Multiple Pregnancy.* (For full group information, see MULTIPLE BIRTH.)

National Clearinghouse for Alcohol and Drug Abuse Information (NCADI), 301–468–2600. Publishes *Alcohol and Nutrition.* (For full group information, see HELP AGAINST SUBSTANCE ABUSE on page 703.)

Food and Drug Administration (FDA), 301–443–3170. (For full group information, see DRUG REACTIONS AND INTERACTIONS.)

Center for Science in the Public Interest (CSPI)
1875 Connecticut Avenue NW, Suite 300
Washington, DC 20009
202–332–9110; 800–237–4874
Fax: 202–265–4954
E-mail (for *Nutrition Action Healthletter*): nah@essential.org
Michael Jacobsen, Executive Director
Organization of health professionals and others of many backgrounds concerned about the adverse effects of science and technology, especially on food safety and nutrition; seeks to educate public and influence government policy, especially in testing, labeling, and advertising; publishes various materials, including *Nutrition Action Healthletter,* books *Safe Food: Eating Widely in a Risky World, Fast-Food Guide, Kitchen Fun for Kids,* and *Cooking with the Stars;* and software *Dine Healthy* and *Chemical Cuisine;* oper-

Eating Patterns in Children

Preschool children are a nutritionally vulnerable group. Their growth rate is slower than it was in infancy and their nutritional needs in relation to body size proportionately reduced. Thus, they often want and eat relatively little food. Food intake can be reduced even further by the increasing independence (expressed as refusals to eat) and immature feeding skills that are characteristic of very young children. Despite these problems, surveys have indicated that, with the exception of a small subgroup, American preschool children are in relatively good nutritional health. Children of lower socioeconomic status are at higher risk of inadequate nutrient intakes (especially iron deficiency) and poorer growth. Although parents have the main responsibility for providing adequate and appropriate food for preschool children, day-care providers supply an increasing proportion of the food that children consume.

Parents continue to be the main influence on the food intake of school-aged children, although an increasing proportion of the diet is consumed in schools, day-care centers, and fast food restaurants. Between the ages of four and six, children increase the varieties of foods they are willing to eat. Snacks become an important source of calories and nutrients and may contribute as much as one-third of calories and fat, one-fifth of the protein, and nearly one-half of the carbohydrate 10-year-old children consume. These patterns emphasize the need for parents and schools to provide appropriate meals and snacks and guidance in food choices. Of special concern is the need to encourage appropriate levels of daily physical activity and choice of nutritious snacks that do not promote tooth decay.

The growth spurt of adolescence demands significant increases in calories and nutrient intake to support the rapid growth rate and increased body size. In early adolescence, children still depend on their parents for food, but by the end of adolescence they are largely independent. Irregular eating patterns are common in adolescence, reflecting this growing independence from the family and the teenager's increasingly busy social life and athletic, academic, and vocational activities. Breakfast and lunch are often skipped or eaten on the run. Snacking is characteristic of this age group and contributes significantly to nutrient intake; these snack foods are often higher in calories, fat, and sugar—and lower in vitamins, minerals, and fiber—than foods consumed at family meals. Because lifetime dietary patterns are established during these years, adolescents should be encouraged to choose nutritious foods, to develop good eating habits, and to maintain appropriate levels of physical activity.

Source: The Surgeon General's Report on Nutrition and Health. Rocklin, CA: Prima, 1988.

ates Americans for Safe Food project, which publishes quarterly newsletter *Safe Food Action.*

American Dietetic Association
216 West Jackson Boulevard, Suite 800
Chicago, IL 60606–6995
312–899–0040; 800–877–1600
Fax: 312–899–1739
Beverly Bajus, Chief Operating Officer
Organization of professional dietitians; operates National Center for Nutrition and Dietetics, for educating the public; provides referrals and information, such as guidelines for using infant formula; publishes various materials.

National Association for the Education of Young Children (NAEYC), 800–424–2460. Publishes book *More Than Graham Crackers: Nutrition Education and Food Preparation with Young Children.* (For full group information, see PRESCHOOL.)

Blind Children's Center, 800–222–3566. Publishes *Let's Eat: Feeding a Child with a Visual Impairment.* (For full group information, see EYE AND VISION PROBLEMS.)

National Center for Youth with Disabilities (NCYD), 800–333–6293. Publishes annotated bibliography *Issues in Nutrition for Adolescents with Chronic Illnesses and Disabilities.* (For full group information, see HELP FOR SPECIAL CHILDREN on page 689.)

American Allergy Association (AAA), 415–322–1663. Publishes *The New Food Labels* and *Food Families.* (For full group information, see ALLERGY.)

ONLINE RESOURCES

Internet: International Food and Nutrition (INFAN) Database. Collection of information on nutrition, food, and general health, including food safety, diet, and eating patterns. telnet://penpages@psupen.psu.edu

OTHER RESOURCES

For parents and other adults

The Well-Fed Baby. O. Robin Sweet and Thomas A. Bloom. Macmillan, 1994.
Food, Nutrition, and the Young Child, 4th ed. Jeanette Endres and Robert E. Rockwell. Macmillan, 1993.
Parents' Guide to Growth and Nutrition: Birth to Five Years. George S. Sturtz. Hojack, 1992.
Child of Mine: Feeding with Love and Good Sense. Ellyn Satter. Bull, 1991.
Feeding Your Baby: From Conception to Age Two. Jean Meyer. Surrey, 1991.
How to Feed the Baby to Make It Healthy and Happy. C. E. Page. Gordon Press, 1991.
Keys to Children's Nutrition. Carolyn E. Moore and others. Barron's, 1991.

General works

Food for Recovery: The Next Step. Joseph D. Beasley and Susan Knightly. Crown, 1994.
Common Sense Guide to Growth and Nutrition. George S. Sturtz and Susan S. Zabriskie. Hojack, 1991.
Everywoman's Guide to Nutrition. Judith E. Brown. University of Minnesota Press, 1990.
The Nutrition Desk Reference, rev. ed. Robert H. Garrison, Jr., and Elizabeth Somer. Keats, 1990.
The Tufts University Guide to Total Nutrition. Stanley Gershoff with Catherine Whitney. Harper & Row, 1990.
What's In My Food? A Book of Nutrients. Xandria Williams. Avery, 1990.

On nutrition during pregnancy and breastfeeding

Nutrition Pregnancy. Elizabeth Somer. Holt, 1995.
The Nine Month Cookbook: Healthy Gourmet Eating for Pregnant Women. Fred Plotkin and Dana Cernea. Crown, 1994.
The Quick and Easy Nutrition Counter for Pregnancy. Lynn Sonberg. Avon, 1994.
Alive and Well in the Fast Lane!. Pamela Smith and Carolyn Coats. Nelson, 1994.
A Guide to Eating Right During Pregnancy. Susan K. Podell. Doubleday, 1993.
Eating Expectantly: The Essential Eating Guide and Cookbook for Pregnancy. Bridget Swinney and Tracey Anderson. Fall River, 1993.
Eat Well, Lose Weight While Breastfeeding: The Complete Nutrition Book for Nursing Mothers. Eileen Behan. Random, 1992.
Doctor Discusses Nutrition During Pregnancy and Breast Feeding. Bonnie Worthington and Lynda Taylor. Budlong, 1992.
Eating for Two: The Complete Guide to Nutrition During Pregnancy. Mary Anne Hess and Anne Hunt. MacMillan, 1992.
What To Eat When You're Expecting. Arlene Eisenberg and others. Workman, 1986.

On cancer-fighting nutrition

Antioxidant Pocket Counter: A Guide to the Essential Nutrients That Can Help Fight Cancer. Gail Becker. Random, 1994.
Beating Cancer with Nutrition. Patrick Quillin. Nutrition Times, 1993.
Apricots and Oncogenes: On Vegetables and Cancer Prevention. Eileen Jennings. McGuire and Beckley, 1993.
The Conquest of Cancer: Vaccines and Diet. Virginia Livingston-Wheeler and Edmond G. Addeo. Waterside, 1993.
Eating Hints: Recipes and Tips for Better Nutrition During Cancer Treatment. Yale-New Haven Medical Center Staff, ed. Diane, 1992.
Cancer and Nutrition: A Ten-Point Plan to Reduce Your Risk of Getting Cancer, rev. ed. Charles Simone. Avery, 1992.

On vitamins and minerals

The Vitamin and Mineral Encyclopedia. Sheldon Saul Hendler. Simon & Schuster, 1990.
Good Health with Vitamins and Minerals: A Complete Guide to a Lifetime of Safe and Effective Use. John Gallagher. Summit, 1990.
Drugs, Vitamins, Minerals in Pregnancy. Ann Karen Henry and Jill Feldhausen. Fisher Books, 1990.

For teenagers

Looking Good, Eating Right: A Sensible Guide to Proper Nutrition and Weight Loss for Teens. Charles A. Salter. Millbrook Press, 1991.
New Theories on Diet and Nutrition. Sally Lee. Watts, 1990.

(See also FEEDING; SOLID FOODS; VITAMINS; MINERALS; IRON; PROTEIN; also EATING PATTERNS IN CHILDREN on page 435.)

nutritionist, a health professional who specializes in the study and application of principles of NUTRITION. Nutritionists evaluate the healthfulness of eating habits, and advise on changes in diet, both for normal diets or for people who require therapeutic diets with special health problems. They may also advise people with DISABILITIES on mechanical aids and techniques that will allow them to feed themselves independently.

O

obesity, the condition of being 20 percent or more over the maximum weight considered ideal for a person's height and age. Put simply, obesity results from eating more calories in food than the body requires for its energy needs; the excess is stored in fat cells (*adipose tissue*). The American diet—plentiful food, rich in FATS—plus a more sedentary, TV-dominated life-style has led to an epidemic of obesity. By the late 1980s, some studies estimate, nearly 1 out of 4 children were so overweight as to be considered obese.

Though some obese people eat far more than normal, many obese people eat no more than their leaner counterparts. Recent studies have confirmed what many researchers have long suspected: that obesity has genetic and biochemical components. Considerable research has been focused on genes possibly connected with obesity, at least one of which seems to follow the AUTOSOMAL RECESSIVE pattern. But many other genes also seem to be involved, including those affecting appetite and metabolism—the biochemical reactions that provide energy for the body. Researchers have also found that obese people have a tendency to store extra calories as fat, where leaner people tend to burn up extra calories or convert them into muscle, and that when dieting the bodies of obese people produce an enzyme that tend to make weight *gain* easier.

Several studies have also indicated that many people become obese not because they eat too much, but because their bodies burn calories too slowly, storing as fat any unused food energy. Whether in infants or adults, in general, people with the slowest metabolisms are more likely to become overweight; and this low metabolic rate seems to run in families. Worse, when many overweight or obese people diet, their bodies slow their metabolism even more, making it even harder to lose fat.

These results point up the difficulty of losing weight. But the excess weight came originally from excess fat in the diet, and it is there that parents can best help themselves and their children: by feeding them a balanced diet with fats controlled, after age two (see NUTRITION and FATS). Beyond that, if parents or children are obese, EXERCISE may be employed in the difficult process of taking the weight down. In past decades, doctors sometimes advised obese women not to gain any weight during PREGNANCY, but medical opinion now is that they should gain weight as in any other pregnancy, though in a controlled way.

Some obese children later develop eating disorders that require clinical treatment. Surprisingly, however, many adolescents with ANOREXIA NERVOSA and BULIMIA, which involve obsessions with food coupled with compulsions to diet and purge, are not obese but more often only slightly overweight and, especially in the case of anorexia, often actually thin.

FOR HELP AND FURTHER INFORMATION

National Digestive Disease Information Clearinghouse (NDDIC), 301–654–3810. (For full group information, see DIGESTIVE SYSTEM AND DISORDERS.)

American Heart Association (AHA), 800–242–8721. Publishes *A Guide to Losing Weight, Taking It Off,* and diet manuals. (For full group information, see HEART AND HEART PROBLEMS.)

National Heart, Lung, and Blood Information Center (NHLBIC), 301–251–1222. Publishes *Check Your Weight and Heart Disease I.Q.* and professional materials. (For full group information, see HEART AND HEART PROBLEMS.)

Food and Nutrition Information Center (FNIC), 301–504–5414. Publishes resource list *Weight Control and Obesity Nutri-Topics.* (For full group information, see NUTRITION.)

OTHER RESOURCES

FOR PARENTS AND OTHER ADULTS

A Parent's Guide to Eating Disorders and Obesity. Martha Jablow. Delacorte, 1992.

Overweight Children: Helping Your Child Achieve Lifetime Weight Control. Michael D. LeBow. Plenum, 1991.

Beyond Baby Fat: Weight-Loss Plans for Children and Teenagers. Frances S. Goulart. Berkley, 1991.

Helping Obese Children: Weight Control Groups That Really Work. Roselyn Marin. Learning, 1990.

Big Kids: A Parent's Guide to Weight Control for Children. Gregory Archer. New Harbinger, 1989.

GENERAL WORKS

Rational Weight Control: A Revolutionary Approach to Training Your Appetite. Lois Trimpey and Jack Trimpey. Delacorte, 1995.

How to Win at Weight Loss, rev. ed. Stephen E. Langer and James F. Scheer. Instant Improvement, 1994.

Diets and Weight Loss. Larry A. Richardson. L. A. Richardson, 1993.

The Black Health Library Guide to Obesity. Kirth Johnson. Holt, 1993.

Solving the Riddle of Losing Weight: How to Restore Your Body Chemistry, Overcome Fatigue and Lose Weight. . . . Gordon, 1992.

Living Without Dieting. John P. Foreyt and G. Ken Goodrick. Harrison, 1992.

For preteens and teens

Weight: A Teenage Concern. Elaine Landau. Lodestar, 1991.
So You Think You're Fat. Alvin Silverstein and Sylvia Silverstein. HarperCollins, 1991.

Background works

Encyclopedia of Obesity and Eating Disorders. Dana K. Cassell. Facts on File, 1994.
Is Your Family Making You Fat?: How Your Family Makes You Fat and What You Can Do about It. Don Martin and others. Sulzburger and Graham, 1994.
The Forbidden Body: Why Being Fat Is Not a Sin. Shelley Bovey. HarperCollins, 1994.
The Fat Girl Companion (1993). *Fat Girl: One Woman's Way Out,* Irene O'Garden. HarperCollins, 1994.
Obesity and Anorexia Nervosa: A Question of Shape. Peter Dally and Joan Gomez. Faber and Faber, 1991.

(See also BULIMIA; BINGE EATING DISORDER; ANOREXIA.)

objective test, a type of TEST that is designed to be presented equally to all, regardless of who administers the test. The administrator follows a "script" in introducing the test and presenting the specific questions. Scoring does not depend on the administrator's discretion, and may even be done by machine, often requiring only counting up the number of correct "boxes" checked or checking answers against a key. Examples of objective tests include the WECHSLER PRESCHOOL AND PRIMARY SCALE OF INTELLIGENCE (WPPSI), the WECHSLER INTELLIGENCE SCALE FOR CHILDREN, REVISED (WISC-R), METROPOLITAN ACHIEVEMENT TESTS, SCHOLASTIC APTITUDE TESTS, and ACT TESTS, as well as classroom tests that have clear right and wrong answers, and unambiguous answer keys, as opposed to SUBJECTIVE TESTS.

object permanence, the understanding that an object continues to exist, even though one does not have immediate knowledge of the object through the senses, such as touch, sight, or smell. This is a key concept that children develop in the sensory motor stage of COGNITIVE DEVELOPMENT, according to Jean Piaget.

obligated parent, the parent who has been ordered by a court to pay CHILD SUPPORT, as a NONCUSTODIAL PARENT pays to help support the child in the CUSTODY of the CUSTODIAL PARENT; also called the *responsible parent.*

obsessive compulsive disorder (OCD), a type of MENTAL DISORDER, classed by psychiatrists as an *anxiety disorder,* in which a person focuses persistently on certain unpleasant thoughts and repetitive behaviors, to the extent that the person's normal working and living routine is affected, significant amounts of time are consumed, social activities or relationships are affected, or the person feels intense distress. Common obsessions—thoughts, ideas, impulses, or images—center around violence, contamination (such as fear of being infected from shaking someone's hand), and doubt about whether something has been done (such as a light turned off) or something has happened (such as an accident). Common compulsions—repeated, ritualistic behaviors, often performed in a stereotyped way and related to obsessive thoughts—involve hand-washing, counting, touching, pulling of HAIR (*trichotillomania*), and checking, as to see that something has been done or happened. People with OCD often build up great tension in trying to resist their obsessions and compulsions, with release of tension on yielding to them.

Obsessive compulsive disorder often begins in ADOLESCENCE or early adulthood, but can appear in childhood, and is often associated with or complicated by ANXIETY, DEPRESSION, TOURETTE SYNDROME, DRUG ABUSE, and ALCOHOL ABUSE. It is thought to affect approximately 3 percent, or some 5 million people, in the United States. Its causes are unknown, but biochemical imbalance is suspected, with psychological factors, including stress, exaggerating symptoms. The most useful treatment so far has been a combination of BEHAVIORAL THERAPY, which involves learning to confront obsessive fears and stopping or reducing repetitive behaviors (see BEHAVIOR MODIFICATION), and medications affecting chemical balance within the brain.

FOR HELP AND FURTHER INFORMATION

Obsessive Compulsive (OC) Foundation
P.O. Box 70
Milford, CT 06460–0070
203–878–5669; Recorded message on OCD developments: 203- 874–3843
Fax: 203–874–2826

Organization of and for people with obsessive compulsive disorder and their families; publishes numerous materials, including brochures and booklets *OCD Questions and Answers, Obsessive Compulsive Disorder in Children and Adolescents—A Guide, Obsessive Compulsive Disorder—A Guide, Obsessive Compulsive Disorders: A Survival Guide for Family and Friends, Trichotillomania, Learning to Live with OCD—For Family Members,* and *School Personnel: A Critical Link in the Identification, Treatment, and Management of OCD in Children and Adolescents,* and numerous newsletter and article reprints, audiotapes, videotapes, and books.

National Institute of Mental Health (NIMH), 301–443–4513. Publishes *Obsessive-Compulsive Disorder.* (For full group information, see MENTAL DISORDERS.)

National Alliance for the Mentally Ill (NAMI), 800–950–6264. Publishes brochure *Obsessive/Compulsive Disorder,* online forum and libraries cover OCD. (For full group information, see MENTAL DISORDERS.)

National Organization for Rare Disorders (NORD), 800–999–6673. (For full group information, see RARE DISORDERS.)

OTHER RESOURCES

General Works

Obsessive Compulsive Disorder: A Survival Guide for Family and Friends. Obsessive-Compulsive Anonymous, 1993.
Obsessive-Compulsive Disorder: The Facts. Padmal De Silva and Stanley J. Rachman. Oxford University Press, 1992.
Obsessive-Compulsive Related Disorders. Eric Hollander, ed. American Psychiatric Press, 1992.
Over and Over: A Survival Manual for Understanding OCD. Jose A. Fugen and others. Free Press, 1991.
Getting Control: Overcoming Your Obsessions and Compulsions. Lee Baer. Little, Brown, 1991.
Children with Obsessive-Compulsive Disorder. Siegel and Brown. W. Gladden, 1991.

Personal Experiences

Polly's Magic Games: A Child's View of Obsessive-Compulsive Disorder. Constance H. Foster. Dilligaf, 1994.
Alone in the Crowd: One Man's Struggle with Obsessive Compulsive Disorder. Joe H. Vaughan. J. Vaughan Assocs., 1993.
Emotional Overload. Joseph Redden. Winston-Derek, 1992.
The Boy Who Couldn't Stop Washing: The Experience and Treatment of Obsessive-Compulsive Disorder. Judith L. Rappaport. NAL, 1990.

obstetrician-gynecologist (OB-GYN), a physician who specializes in providing medical and surgical care related to women's REPRODUCTIVE SYSTEM, throughout their adult lives, including during PREGNANCY. Some obstetricians specialize only in care of women during pregnancy, while some gynecologists specialize only in women's reproductive system care apart from pregnancy, but most carry out both activities. Obstetricians who specialize in caring for women having HIGH-RISK PREGNANCIES are called FETAL AND MATERNAL SPECIALISTS or PERINATALOGISTS.

occupational therapist, a health professional who evaluates, treats, and counsels people whose physical activity has been limited by illness, injury, DEVELOPMENTAL DISORDERS, LEARNING DISABILITIES, or other causes. Their aim is to help such people maximize independence and maintain health. For example, occupational therapists may help people learn or relearn the physical control and coordination necessary to perform independently such everyday tasks as dressing, eating, washing, and going to the toilet, and to be able eventually to work at some form of meaningful employment. Working with children, they may also focus on developing PERCEPTUAL-MOTOR SKILLS and the ability to play or carry out school-related activities, such as sitting, walking, handling physical objects, drawing and other paper-and-pencil activities, cutting, pasting, and general hand-eye and body-eye coordination. Occupational therapists often work at HOSPITALS and outpatient clinics, but may also work in the person's home.

oligospermia, a condition of low SPERM count, an INFERTILITY problem.

oncologist, a PHYSICIAN who specializes in the treatment of TUMORS and CANCER.

open-book test, a TEST in which a student can consult any materials desired. Sometimes that simply means that a child can look up information in a textbook during a classroom exam. But often, especially in college, the student can take the examination questions home overnight and look into any sources available for information. Open-book tests are designed to focus not on the student's ability to memorize information, but on the ability to use reference sources relating to the particular topic in an intelligent, knowledgeable way.

Open University, a type of EXTERNAL DEGREE PROGRAM that allows people to gain college CREDIT with little or no attendance at regular courses on a college campus, often offering a combination of CORRESPONDENCE STUDY and learning via radio and television broadcasts, and sometimes computer networks as well.

ophthalmologist, a PHYSICIAN who specializes in diagnosing and treating disorders of the eyes, as from disease, injury, or BIRTH DEFECTS, including performing surgery on the eyes. Ophthalmologists often work with other physicians, because eye problems frequently result from other medical problems, such as DIABETES, BRAIN TUMOR, or various birth defects. With children, they may use lights, simple pictures, or special instruments to examine the eyes to see if vision needs correction, as with glasses (though these may be prescribed by an OPTOMETRIST), or if an eye condition needs medication. In some cases, an ophthalmologist may recommend that special materials or seating arrangements be used for the child in school. (See EYE AND VISION PROBLEMS.)

ophthalmoscope, basic equipment used to explore the interior of the eye in an eye examination. (See EYE AND VISION PROBLEMS.)

optician, a health professional who specializes in grinding and fitting eyeglasses or contact lenses, according to prescriptions given by an OPTOMETRIST or OPHTHALMOLOGIST.

optometrist, a health professional who specializes in screening for and diagnosing vision problems, and may prescribe glasses or contact lenses, as needed. The lenses themselves are generally ground and fitted by an OPTICIAN. Not physicians, optometrists refer to OPHTHALMOLOGISTS any eye problems that may need to be treated with drugs or surgery.

oral surgeon, a dental-medical professional who specializes in performing surgery on the mouth, face, teeth, or jaw. An oral surgeon must be a trained dentist with an additional specialty in oral and maxillofacial (upper face) surgery, and is often trained as a physician as well. Oral surgeons perform ORTHOGNATHIC SURGERY in severe cases of MALOCCLUSION, fix broken jaws, remove some BENIGN TUMORS from the mouth, repair CLEFT LIP AND PALATE, and do some other forms of craniofacial surgery. (See TEETH AND DENTAL PROBLEMS.)

orchioectomy, an operation to remove one or both TESTES. In infants or young boys, orchioectomy may be done to remove a testicle that has failed to develop normally, or in cases of irreparable damage due to TORSION OF THE TESTES. Removal of one testicle does not affect the other one, or the male's later ability to have children and to have a normal sex life. In adults an orchioectomy is often performed in cases of CANCER of the testicles.

orchiopexy, a surgical operation to bring one or both undescended TESTES down into the SCROTUM, when they have failed to descend on their own, as they normally do before or after birth. Usually performed in a HOSPITAL under general ANESTHESIA when the boy is between ages one and five, orchiopexy involves making a small incision in the groin and, through that, maneuvering the testicles into proper position and sometimes fixing them there with sutures.

orchitis, inflammation of one or both TESTES, often with the MUMPS virus but sometimes with a bacterial infection, as in EPIDIDYMO-ORCHITIS. Treatment often involves cold packs to reduce swelling, painkillers (*analgesics*), support for the SCROTUM, and ANTIBIOTICS. Orchitis is sometimes followed by shrinking of the testes, but rarely results in INFERTILITY.

order, in law, a formal, written directive from a judge, administrative officer, or other judicial officer, as in a case involving CHILD SUPPORT or CUSTODY.

order to show cause hearing, an order issued by a judge for a person to tell in court why a judge should not take a specified action. In a case of threatened CHILD ABUSE AND NEGLECT, for example, the judge may issue a TEMPORARY RESTRAINING ORDER against the abusive parent, and then call for an order to show cause hearing to hear the accused parent's side of the story. Someone who does not appear in court in response to an OCS may be held in CONTEMPT OF COURT.

organic brain syndrome, a general medical term for MENTAL DISORDERS that have no precisely known physical cause, but which are presumed to result from disorders in the chemistry of the brain.

organic mental disorder, MENTAL DISORDERS that result from physical causes in or affecting the brain, such as infection, TRAUMATIC BRAIN INJURY, BRAIN TUMOR, DRUG ABUSE, ALCOHOL ABUSE, or METABOLIC DISORDERS; when the cause is known, it is sometimes called *organic mental syndrome.* A wide variety of disorders can result, including DEMENTIA, DELIRIUM, HALLUCINATIONS, DELUSIONS, and MOOD DISORDERS. (See MENTAL DISORDERS.)

organismic age, a summary of a whole range of age comparisons—including educational, mental, dental, carpal (wrist), height, weight, and social—as compared to established norms. (See AGE.)

organ of Corti, the organ of hearing in the inner ear, a minute duct filled with microscopic hair cells that take incoming sound vibrations and transform them into electrical signals, which are then transmitted to the brain. Damage to the organ of Corti causes significant EAR AND HEARING PROBLEMS.

orgasm, powerful, climactic sensations involving involuntary muscular contractions in the GENITALS, following rhythmic sexual activity and excitement. While orgasm brings intense pleasure to both men and women, it plays a role in reproduction only in men, by triggering the EJACULATION of the SEMEN that carries the SPERM.

orientation and mobility instructors (peripatologists), specialists who help children with vision disabilities to learn the concepts and skills they need to understand where they are and to move about safely and easily. (See EYE AND VISION PROBLEMS.)

orphan, a child who has no parents, and often no GUARDIAN. Such a child would once have routinely been placed in a large institutional orphanage, but is now more likely to be placed in a GROUP HOME and then in FOSTER CARE, until arrangements can be made for the child's ADOPTION.

Under immigration law, for purposes of adoption, an orphan is defined as a child under age sixteen at the date on which a visa application is filed, whose parents are dead, have disappeared, or have abandoned the child, or whose surviving parent is unable to provide proper care and has formally consented to the emigration and adoption.

orphan drug, a medication that pharmaceutical companies often do not produce because it is for treatment of a RARE DISORDER, one affecting relatively few people, in the United States generally considered to be under 200,000 people. This is so especially if the patent has run out on the drug, so that competitors might enter the field at any time if they wished (see DRUG REACTIONS AND INTERACTIONS). In 1983, the federal government passed the Orphan Drug Act, which offers financial inducements to encourage the development, testing (including testing of drugs developed in other countries), and distribution of such drugs to the people who need them, such as medication for TOURETTE SYNDROME. (See RARE DISORDERS.)

orthodontic braces, devices used by dentists to correct poor positioning of teeth. (See MALOCCLUSION.)

orthodontist, a dentist who specializes in treating people whose teeth are not in proper position. (See MALOCCLUSION.)

orthognathic surgery, an operation to reshape or reposition the jaws, as to correct severe cases of MALOCCLUSION, in which the teeth do not meet evenly. Such surgery is normally performed by an ORAL SURGEON in a hospital. (See TEETH AND DENTAL PROBLEMS.)

orthopedic devices, a variety of mechanical aids and equipment developed to help people with ORTHOPEDIC DISABILITIES, especially in the areas of sitting, standing, walking, and using their hands, as well as maintaining balance and protecting the body from harm. These are, more widely, considered forms of ASSISTIVE TECHNOLOGY, aimed at the greatest extent of independent living.

Orthopedic devices are basic necessities for some children, if they are to develop other skills to the fullest. Among the most common kinds of orthopedic devices are:

- *Wheelchairs*, which for children should always be equipped with seat belts, used whenever the child is in the chair. Parents may need to learn some basic techniques for maneuvering a wheelchair, and for helping a child into and out of one; the child's doctor, physical therapist, or teacher may have some useful experience to pass along. One newly recognized problem is that radio waves, such as those from a two-way radio, television station, cellular phone, CB radio, or paging transmitter, can interfere with the action of powered wheelchairs, causing them to move erratically, and sometimes damaging both the chair and the occupant. Some wheelchairs are constructed so the person is able to stand, using armpit-high arm rests as needed.
- *Walkers*, which help children move about independently. Of the several types available, some have four wheels and are quite easy for children to push. Some, often called *chariots*, have two parallel railings and an enclosed front, offering support on three sides.
- *Carts* or *boards*, low-to-the-ground, hand-propelled devices with four wheels that allow a child to lie on his or her stomach and push around the room using hands and arms. (If these are not available locally, parents should contact the Easter Seal Society.)
- *Canes* and *crutches*, traditional items, built child-size. Some canes are tripods, with three feet on the floor, offering more support than a single cane. In addition to the crutches that fit under the armpits, children may use shorter *Canadian crutches* (or *elbow crutches*), which have bands around the arm, above or below the elbow, with handles at waist height. Some children put their crutches ahead of them, then swing their bodies behind, while others use a four-point "crutch-foot-crutch-foot" type of walking pattern. Parents should check with the doctor or physical therapist to see the best way for the child's particular condition.
- *Braces*, mechanical devices of metal bars and bands designed to provide support, to hold part of the body in place, to protect it from further deformation, or to prevent deformities. Ankle braces fit into the sole of the child's shoe and limit movement. Some children have braces that run the length of the leg, sometimes extending to the pelvis, with locks at the knees and joints. These lock joints have sliding catches, which the child releases to bend at the knees and hips, and then relocks for walking. These tasks become routine for children, though they (and parents) may need help at first.
- *Grab bars*, devices installed in bathrooms, dressing areas, and other places where the person will be transferring to or from a wheelchair or other device.
- *Helmets*, lightweight protective gear (like bicycling helmets) to protect children from TRAUMATIC BRAIN INJURY, especially those with poor balance or those who have had surgery, as for a BRAIN TUMOR. (For information on bicycle helmets, see SAFETY.)
- *Artificial limbs*, or *prostheses*, which replace a lost limb or a limb absent at birth. The limb helps the child maintain balance and normal development, allows for easier activity, and in all makes for a more normal life. Artificial legs often take more activity, because they are used in walking. Children who have had amputations will need special training in walking, at first often using canes or crutches. An artificial hand may simply be two hooks that open and close together, but can allow a child to develop many important MOTOR SKILLS. Children will need training in using it, and occasionally some adjustment. PHYSICAL THERAPISTS stress that it is important that the child wear the artificial limbs all day (unless medical advice is otherwise), so it becomes accepted as part of the body.

In making a home setting convenient for children with orthopedic disabilities, parents might also use bolsters, rolls, and slanting wedges to allow children to be supported while they play on the floor, and sometimes an old chair, with high back and arms, but with the legs cut off, on the floor for sitting, with seat belts, pillow, or sandbags for added support. If tables are too low for the wheelchair's arms, blocks can be used to raise the table, or trays placed over the wheelchair's arms for playing, working, and eating. Frames can be added to tricycles to give vertical support to the body, and doll carriages can be weighted to help provide balance.

The main objective should be to allow the child the maximum scope for exploration and development, while providing for the child's safety and comfort. In school settings, this is called the LEAST RESTRICTIVE ENVIRONMENT. (For help and further information, see HELP FOR SPECIAL CHILDREN on page 689; see also organizations related to the child's particular physical problems.)

In a long-term way, children and adults who use orthopedic devices must be careful not to overstrain the parts of the body on which they rely. The wrists, shoulders, and elbows of those who use wheelchairs and crutches take great strain, and people are advised to be alert for pain, redness, swelling in the joints, avoiding unnecessary use until signs of stress have disappeared. As with any athletic activity, they should warm up with stretching, be careful of their posture, ease into any new physical activity, and in general remain as fit as possible, exercising the active muscle groups evenly. Other common problems are *decubitus ulcers* or *pressure ulcers*, where the skin breaks down under friction and pressure, for the bedridden commonly known as "bed sores," and OSTEOPOROSIS, increasing weakness and brittleness of bones from inactivity.

orthopedic disabilities, in education, a general term for child who has a physical condition that adversely affects mobility and development of normal motor skills; also called *physical disabilities.* In the HEAD START PRESCHOOL programs, for example, one classic definition reads:

> A child shall be reported as crippled or with an orthopedic handicap who has a condition which prohibits or impedes normal development of gross or fine motor abilities. Such functioning is impaired as a result of conditions associated with congenital anomalies, accidents, or diseases; these conditions include, for example, spina bifida, loss of or deformed limbs, burns which cause contractures, and cerebral palsy.

If children meet the definitions that apply in their school and state, they will be entitled to SPECIAL EDUCATION services under the EDUCATION FOR ALL HANDICAPPED CHILDREN ACT and its successor, the INDIVIDUALS WITH DISABILITIES EDUCATION ACT. (See also specific types of physical disabilities; also HELP FOR SPECIAL CHILDREN on page 689.)

orthopedist, a PHYSICIAN who specializes in diagnosing and treating diseases and injuries of bones and joints, and associated muscles, tendons, cartilage, and ligaments. Orthopedists set and put casts on FRACTURES as needed; perform surgery, as to repair BIRTH DEFECTS or remove TUMORS, including ARTHROSCOPIC SURGERY; and may also replace joints, as in a knee, hip, or finger. SPORTS injuries are often treated by orthopedists, and some specialize in sports medicine.

osteogenesis imperfecta (OI), a type of GENETIC DISORDER involving defective development of the normally hard bones of the body, resulting in abnormally brittle, fragile bones, and so sometimes called the *brittle bone disease.* Some cases are so severe that infants are born with multiple fractures, a soft skull, and often deformities; most of these die shortly after birth, or survive with growth retardation. Milder cases may not be so obvious, and may not be detected until ADOLESCENCE or later. These children have multiple fractures from minimal traumas, and are sometimes mistaken as victims of CHILD ABUSE AND NEGLECT. Many have related EAR AND HEARING PROBLEMS, especially because of *otosclerosis,* or deformities of the bones in the middle ear. They are especially susceptible to skull fractures, which may readily cause brain damage or death. Among other signs of this bone disorder are blue sclera (normally the white part of the eye), loose joints, poor teeth, and excessive sweating. Research continues on the precise defect that causes OI, but no cure presently exists.

FOR HELP AND FURTHER INFORMATION

Osteogenesis Imperfecta Foundation (OIF)
5005 W. Laurel St., Suite 210
Tampa, FL 33607
813–282–1161; 800–981–2663
Fax: 813–287–8214
E-mail: bonelink@aol.com (America Online: BONELINK)
Joe Antolini, President
Organization concerned with osteogenesis imperfecta; provides information; sponsors conferences; supports research; publishes quarterly newsletter *Breakthrough* and other materials, including:

- Books: *Living with Osteogenesis Imperfecta: A Guidebook for Families* and *Adaptive Equipment Reference Manual.*
- Pamphlets, booklets, and reprints: *Care of a Baby and Child with Osteogenesis Imperfecta, Education of a Child with Osteogenesis Imperfecta, Decide For Yourself Is This an Abused Child?, We're Growing Stronger, Genetics Questions Answered on OI, An Explanation of Rodding Surgery, I Have Osteogenesis Imperfecta and Can, One Family's Experience with Public Schools and Special Education, Available Resources,* and *Bed Card,* to hang over the bed of a hospitalized child.
- Conference transcripts, such as *Parenting a Child with OI: Ages 6–12, Medical Panel for Parents of Children with OI, Making Educated Surgical Decisions, OI—The Basics, Psychological Aspects of OI, Taking a Bite Out of OI—Dentinogenesis Imperfecta,* and *Living with a Disability;*
- Videos (for rental), such as *The OI Newborn A Loving Look at the Future, Look How Far We've Come, We're Growin' Stronger, Within Reach* (on independent living).

Shriners' Hospitals for Crippled Children, 800–237–5055. Provides free medical care for children with orthopedic problems. (For full group information, see BONE AND BONE DISORDERS.)

National Arthritis and Musculoskeletal and Skin Diseases Information Clearinghouse (NAMSIC), 301–495–4484. (For full group information, see ARTHRITIS.)

Paget Foundation for Paget's Disease of Bone and Related Disorders (PFPDBRD), 800–237–2438. (For full group information, see OSTEOPETROSIS.)

National Organization for Rare Disorders (NORD), 800–999–6673. (For full group information, see RARE DISORDERS.)

(See also BONE AND BONE DISORDERS.)

osteomyelitis, infection of the bone and BONE MARROW, often by bacteria, as in some cases of compound FRACTURES or TUBERCULOSIS. In children, the infection generally involves the long bones of the arms and legs and the vertebrae of the spine. If promptly diagnosed, as by a bone SCAN, culture of the infectious organism, or X-RAY, the disease can often be successfully treated with ANTIBIOTICS; if not, an operation may be needed to clean out infected tissue and bone.

In neglected or unresponsive cases, pain, deformity, and stunted growth can occur as osteomyelitis becomes CHRONIC. Sometimes whole sections of the bone may need to be removed and replaced with bone grafts from elsewhere in the body. Among populations with good NUTRITION, high resistance, and accessible HEALTH CARE, osteomyelitis is seen less often than it once was, but it is still a risk for children who have a compound fracture, which allows infectious organisms to come into contact with bone.

FOR HELP AND FURTHER INFORMATION

National Arthritis and Musculoskeletal and Skin Diseases Information Clearinghouse (NAMSIC), 301–495–4484. Publishes information package *Osteomyelitis.* (For full group information, see ARTHRITIS.)

National Organization for Rare Disorders (NORD), 800–999–6673. (For full group information, see RARE DISORDERS.)

National Institute of Allergy and Infectious Diseases (NIAID), 301–496–5717. (For full group information, see ALLERGIES.)

(See also BONE AND BONE DISORDERS.)

osteopathic physician, a health professional with the degree of Doctor of Osteopathy, or D.O., who has trained in and is licensed to perform general medicine and surgery, including use of drugs, but who works within the system of osteopathic medicine, which sees the body's nerve-muscle-skeletal network as key to health functioning and uses various manipulative techniques as part of therapy to restore what are seen as imbalances in the system.

osteopetrosis, a GENETIC DISORDER in which the bones become abnormally hard and dense ("petr" = rock), causing excess bone creation because of disruption in the normal breaking down and rebuilding of the bone; also called *Albers-Schönberg disease, marble bones,* or *osteosclerosis fragilis.* People with severe osteopetrosis often have a high susceptibility to FRACTURES, severe ANEMIA as bone fills in cavities for the blood-making BONE MARROW, and growth deformities, especially in the skull. Resulting pressure on nerves often leads to EAR AND HEARING PROBLEMS, EYE AND VISION PROBLEMS, PARALYSIS of the face, and early death. The severe form of osteopetrosis is passed on from parents to child as an AUTOSOMAL RECESSIVE trait. A milder form, passed on as an AUTOSOMAL DOMINANT trait, generally involves short stature, easily fractured bones, and a tendency toward OSTEOMYELITIS, or infection in the bone.

FOR HELP AND FURTHER INFORMATION

Paget Foundation for Paget's Disease of Bone and Related Disorders (PFPDBRD)
200 Varick Street, Suite 1004
New York, NY 10014–4810
212–229–1582; 800–23-PAGET [237–2438]
Fax 212–229–1502
Charlene Waldman, Executive Director
Organization concerned with various bone disorders, including osteopetrosis, osteogenesis imperfecta, Paget's disease, and fibrous dysplasia (in children, McKune-Albright syndrome); formerly Paget's Disease Foundation (PDF); encourages research; provides information and referrals; publishes various materials, including newsletter and brochures *Questions and Answers on Osteopetrosis* and *Questions and Answers about Fibrous Dysplasia.*

National Arthritis and Musculoskeletal and Skin Diseases Information Clearinghouse (NAMSIC), 301–495–4484. (For full group information, see ARTHRITIS.)

(See also BONE AND BONE DISORDERS; GROWTH AND GROWTH DISORDERS.)

osteoporosis, weakening and fracturing of the bone, due to decrease in the density of bone, resulting in pain, injury, and sometimes deformities; literally "porous bone." This condition is generally seen in older people, especially women after MENOPAUSE or hysterectomy (since CALCIUM loss from the bones speeds up with decline in the production of ESTROGEN). But it is a condition that young couples should keep in mind for themselves and their children, because bone mass is built primarily in youth, a good reason to see that children eat a proper amount of

MILK and other dairy products; later on bone mass cannot easily be replaced, only the loss of bone slowed.

Osteoporosis is also associated with some HORMONE disorders, such as CUSHING'S SYNDROME; with some LUNG AND BREATHING DISORDERS, such as BRONCHITIS and EMPHYSEMA; with lack of EXERCISE; with SMOKING and ALCOHOL ABUSE; with use of STEROIDS; and with some ethnic backgrounds and body types, particularly tall, thin, northern Europeans. Young women who exercise at such an extreme level that they stop MENSTRUATION are also at risk for bone loss. Pregnant and nursing women should be sure to take extra calcium, especially if they are under age twenty.

FOR HELP AND FURTHER INFORMATION

National Osteoporosis Foundation (NOF)
1150 17th Street NW, Suite 500
Washington, DC 20036
202–223–2226
Fax: 202–223–2237
Sandra C. Raymond, Executive Director
Organization of people concerned about osteoporosis; seeks to education public and professionals and to influence social policy; provides information and referrals; supports research; publishes various materials, including quarterly newsletter *The Osteoporosis Report*; booklets such as *Stand Up to Osteoporosis, Boning Up on Osteoporosis, Are You at Risk?, Talking with Your Doctor About Osteoporosis, Osteoporosis: A Woman's Guide, Osteoporosis and Women: A Major Public Health Problem, Facts About Osteoporosis, Arthritis and Osteoarthritis, Testing Your Bone Health, Medications and Bone Loss,* and *How Strong Are Your Bones?*; and professional resources.

National Arthritis and Musculoskeletal and Skin Diseases Information Clearinghouse (NAMSIC), 301–495–4484. Publishes *Osteoporosis.* (For full group information, see ARTHRITIS.)

American College of Obstetricians and Gynecologists (ACOG), 202–638–5577. Publishes *Preventing Osteoporosis.* (For full group information, see PREGNANCY.)

American Academy of Orthopaedic Surgeons (AAOS), 800–346–2267. Publishes brochure *Osteoporosis.* (For full group information, see BONE AND BONE DISORDERS.)

National Organization for Rare Disorders (NORD), 800–999–6673. (For full group information, see RARE DISORDERS.)

American Council on Science and Health (ACSH), 212–362–7044. Publishes *Osteoporosis.* (For full group information, see SAFETY.)

Resources for Rehabilitation, 617–862–6455. Publishes book *A Woman's Guide to Coping with Disability*, including section on osteoporosis. (For full group information, see EYE AND VISION PROBLEMS.)

OTHER RESOURCES

GENERAL WORKS

A Woman Doctor's Guide to Osteoporosis: Essential Facts and Up-to-the-Minute Information on the Prevention, Treatment and Reversal of Bone Loss. Yvonne Sherrer and Robin K. Levinson. Hyperion, 1995.

The Osteoporosis Handbook: Every Woman's Guide to Prevention and Treatment. Sydney L. Bonnick. Taylor, 1994.

What You Can Do about Osteoporosis. Judith Sachs. Dell, 1993.

Special Report: Osteoporosis: How to Stop It, How to Prevent It, How to Reverse It. Elizabeth Vierck. Prentice Hall, 1993.

One Hundred-Fifty Most-Asked Questions about Osteoporosis: What Women Really Want to Know. Ruth S. Jacobowitz. Hearst, 1993.

Winning with Osteoporosis, 2nd ed. Harris H. McIlwain and others. Wiley, 1993.

Osteoporosis—Questions and Answers. John Stevenson and Michael C. Ellerington. Merit Communications, 1993.

Preventing and Reversing Osteoporosis: Every Woman's Essential Guide. Alan Gaby. Prima, 1993.

Understanding Osteoporosis. G. Birdwood. Parthenon, 1993.

Keys to Understanding Osteoporosis. Jan Rozek. Barron's, 1992.

Healthy Bones: What You Should Know About Osteoporosis. Nancy Appleton. Avery, 1991.

(See also BONE AND BONE DISORDERS.)

ostomy, a surgical procedure in which an artificial opening is created on the body's surface, generally referring to an opening in the abdomen for the release of stool or urine. An *ileostomy* is one performed on the *ileum* (small intestine), often because of INFLAMMATORY BOWEL DISEASE (ulcerative colitis and Crohn's disease). A *colostomy* is performed on the *colon* (large intestine), most often because of CANCER. A *urinary ostomy* provides a new outlet for the bladder. Among the other causes for ostomies are BIRTH DEFECTS, obstructions, inflammations, injury, and nerve damage. If the air passages in the throat are blocked, an emergency TRACHEOSTOMY, or hole in the trachea, may be performed.

People with ostomies can become parents, if their REPRODUCTIVE SYSTEMS are not directly affected. Perhaps 1 or 2 in 10 men who have an ileostomy suffer some impairment of sexual function, though this is often temporary; even where it is not, some new forms of REPRODUCTIVE TECHNOLOGY allow a male to father a child, as long as his sperm-producing capabilities are not impaired. Urinary ostomies can also cause impotence and sometimes sterility. Women who have ostomies are able to bear children; however, the condition that necessitated the ostomy may sometimes require a HYSTERECTOMY as well, which would end the ability to bear a child.

FOR HELP AND FURTHER INFORMATION

United Ostomy Association (UOA)
36 Executive Park, Suite 120
Irvine, CA 92714
714–660–8624; 800–826–0826
Fax: 714–660–9262
Darlene Smith, Executive Director
Organization concerned with colostomy, ileostomy, or urostomy; encourages patient-to-patient support; provides information and referrals; publishes various materials, including *Ostomy Quarterly*, booklets such as *My Child Has an Ostomy, Chris Has an Ostomy* (coloring book for children), *Anatomy of Ostomy, Colostomies: A Guide*, and *Ileostomy: A Guide.*

National Digestive Disease Information Clearinghouse (NDDIC), 301–654–3810. (For full group information, see DIGESTIVE SYSTEM AND DISORDERS.)

National Foundation for Ileitis and Colitis (NFIC), 800–932–2423. (For full group information, see INFLAMMATORY BOWEL DISEASE.)

OTHER RESOURCES

Ostomy Book: Living Comfortably with Colostomies, Ileostomies, and Urostomies, 2nd ed. Barbara D. Mullen and Kerry A. McGinn. Bull, 1991.

(See also CHOKING; DIGESTIVE SYSTEM AND DISORDERS; KIDNEY AND UROLOGICAL PROBLEMS.)

otolaryngologist (otorhinolaryngologist, ear-nose-throat doctor, or ENT), a PHYSICIAN who specializes in identifying and treating ear, nose, and throat disorders, including performing surgery in these areas. A doctor who specializes exclusively in ear disorders is called an *otologist.*

otologist, a health professional who specializes in the diagnosis and treatment of EAR AND HEARING PROBLEMS; a subspecialist who focuses on treatment of disorders involving the acoustic nerve is called a *neuro-otologist.* PHYSICIANS who specialize in treating ear, nose, and throat together are called OTOLARYNGOLOGISTS.

out of control children, children who refuse to obey their parents and are therefore labeled INCORRIGIBLE and can be made WARDS of the court.

out-of-district placement, assignment of a student to a school outside his or her HOME SCHOOL DISTRICT, the one serving the area of the student's legal residence. Such a NONRESIDENT STUDENT may be assigned by a court order, or be placed in a school providing special services under the EDUCATION FOR ALL HANDICAPPED CHILDREN ACT and its successor, the INDIVIDUALS WITH DISABILITIES EDUCATION ACT, in which case the home school district must bear the cost. Parents may also choose to place their child in an out-of-district school, but if it is a voluntary placement, they (not the home school) would bear most if not all of the cost.

ovaries, the pair of small, oval-shaped sex glands (GONADS) in a woman, which produce the key female sex HORMONES, ESTROGEN and PROGESTERONE, and also the eggs (*ova*; singular OVUM). The ovaries are on either side of the UTERUS in the lower abdomen, each lying under one of the FALLOPIAN TUBES. At birth, a baby girl's ovaries each contain about 1 million *follicles*, egg-producing structures that remain immature until PUBERTY.

When a girl becomes sexually mature, FOLLICLE-STIMULATING HORMONE (FSH), produced by the PITUITARY GLAND, begins periodically to signal the ovaries to ripen some of these immature eggs. At the beginning of the MENSTRUAL CYCLE, on the first day of bleeding, FSH signals the ovaries to mature a group of eggs, which also produce the hormone estrogen. At this point each egg cell, which carries 46 chromosomes in 23 pairs, subdivides into two identical cells, each with 23 chromosomes, to prepare for possible FERTILIZATION. (A man's SPERM also undergoes this division process, called *meiosis*, unlike other cells in the body.) The duplicate cell, called a *polar body*, shrivels up and disappears. Gradually, one of the egg cells becomes dominant, while the others also disappear. This dominant egg cell, called the *graafian follicle*, develops a 4-layered protective coating and prepares to burst out of its growth site in the ovaries.

At about 14 days into the menstrual cycle, the pituitary gland sends out a surge of LUTEINIZING HORMONE (LH), which breaks down the outer wall of the graafian follicle, releasing the single mature egg, still enclosed in two outer layers, called the ZONA PELLUCIDA. This event is OVULATION. The third and fourth layers shed by the egg, called the *corpus luteum*, remain behind in the ovary and trigger release of progesterone; that causes the *endometrium* (the lining of the UTERUS) to thicken, in preparation for a possible fertilized egg. (This is the *proliferative phase* of the MENSTRUAL CYCLE.) Meanwhile, the egg released from the uterus gradually is drawn into the Fallopian tube suspended above the ovary, where fertilization, if it occurs, will take place.

This same process takes place month after month from sexual maturity until MENOPAUSE, but each time with a diminishing number of potential eggs, one reason why a woman's chances of conception decline as she grows older. Of the approximately 2 million potential eggs in the two ovaries, only a few hundred will ever mature and be available for possible fertilization.

A number of problems can interfere with the workings of this complicated, delicate egg-developing system in the ovaries, including:

- *Oophoritis,* inflammation of the ovaries, sometimes as a result of infections such as MUMPS, GONORRHEA, or PELVIC INFLAMMATORY DISEASE.
- *Ovarian cysts,* fluid-filled or semisolid sacs that form in the ovaries, mostly BENIGN, sometimes so many as to be called *polycystic syndrome.* Aside from hindering the normal workings of the ovaries themselves, these cysts can trigger production of male sex hormones, which can lead to *amenorrhea* (lack of MENSTRUATION) and INFERTILITY.
- *Ovarian failure,* in which for unknown reasons MENOPAUSE comes abnormally early, when the ovaries cease to function.
- *Abnormality in or absence of ovaries,* a rare defect associated with some CHROMOSOMAL ABNORMALITIES, such as TURNER'S SYNDROME.
- *Ovarian cancer,* form of CANCER generally found in women over 50.
- *Anovulation,* failure of the ovaries to produce, ripen, and release eggs. This happens during PREGNANCY and LACTATION (which acts as a natural form of CONTRACEPTION) and also may occur during PUBERTY and approaching menopause, and sometimes because of hormonal imbalance, illness, stress, or drugs. BIRTH CONTROL PILLS using hormones act by suppressing ovulation.

Any of these things and more can cause problems in conception; some of them are susceptible to treatment, but many are not.

FOR HELP AND FURTHER INFORMATION

RESOLVE, Inc., HelpLine: 617–623–0744. Offers adoption services, along with infertility treatments. Publishes fact sheet *Ovulation, Pinpointing Polycystic Ovarian Disease,* and *Premature Ovarian Failure.* (For full group information, see INFERTILITY.)

National Cancer Institute (NCI), 800–422–6237. Publishes "What You Need to Know About" brochures on cancer of the ovaries. (For full group information, see CANCER.)

American Cancer Society (ACS), 800–227–2345. Publishes materials on cancer of the ovaries. (For full group information, see CANCER.)

(See also INFERTILITY; PREGNANCY.)

overachiever, a student whose academic performance is well above educators' estimates of his or her potential. The term refers especially a student whose scores on INTELLIGENCE TESTS are consistently lower than those on ACHIEVEMENT TESTS. Outperforming expectations may result when a student has strong motivation to succeed and the ability to focus effort, sometimes with a specific long-term goal in mind.

overanxious disorder, a type of ANXIETY DISORDER in which children worry excessively and needlessly about future events, past behavior, and personal characteristics and competence, and are self-conscious and require constant reassurance, as about social or academic achievement, though the child is often seen as at least average and often superior. Persistent ANXIETY and associated tension bring with them physical complaints. The disorder affects boys and girls equally, seems to be found often among elder or only children in affluent families concerned about academic and social achievement, and in severe cases, can be incapacitating. (See MENTAL DISORDERS.)

overflow behavior, in individual testing, such as DEVELOPMENTAL SCREENING TESTS, any of a child's actions or interplay that are not directly related to the test items, including innocuous small talk and attempts to distract the examiner from continuing with a test item that seems difficult.

overplacement, a child who may be chronologically old enough to be in a particular grade in school, but whose DEVELOPMENTAL AGE is considered too young for that grade. Some experts in child development believe that overplacement is a major cause of failure at school, and as a result some parents have held their children back to have them be the oldest, and presumably therefore the most developed, in the class. This can boomerang, however, when the child grows older, especially during ADOLESCENCE, and is far more mature than the rest of the class, and perhaps bored in class as well as restless and socially isolated.

ovulation, the release of a mature egg (OVUM) from a woman's OVARIES into the FALLOPIAN TUBES, where FERTILIZATION may take place. Ovulation generally occurs monthly, as a key part of the MENSTRUAL CYCLE, but regular MENSTRUATION does not necessarily mean a woman is ovulating. Especially during PUBERTY and approaching MENOPAUSE, but also at some other times, a woman may have *anovulatory* (without ovulation) periods. If a couple and their doctor are exploring possible INFERTILITY, one of the earliest questions to determine is whether or not ovulation is actually taking place.

At about the time of ovulation, the body's temperature rises slightly, the nature of the mucus at the CERVIX changes, and the woman sometimes experiences slight abdominal pain (called *Mittelschmerz*). These signs are used in a NATURAL FAMILY PLANNING form of BIRTH CONTROL, which involves monitoring various changes in the body, to identify when OVULATION has occurred. Couples who do not wish to have a child can then avoid sexual intercourse at that time, while those attempting to conceive can time their intercourse or ARTIFICIAL INSEMINATION to maximize their chances.

Among the other changes at the time of ovulation is a surge of LUTEINIZING HORMONE (LH), triggering the actual release of the egg, which occurs twenty-four to thirty-six hours later. The amount of LH in the blood can be measured by using an ovulation monitoring home medical test. For a week in the middle of the menstrual cycle, the woman takes urine specimens, dipping a chemically treated strip into each specimen and comparing the color to a guide. When the color changes to indicate an LH surge, ovulation is generally expected within twenty-four to thirty-six hours. Women are advised to keep their liquid intake relative stable, since excess liquids may dilute the specimen, causing the test not to detect the hormone. They are also advised to consult a doctor immediately if tests show an LH surge of more than four days in a row, since that could indicate a possible PREGNANCY, ovarian failure, early MENOPAUSE, ENDOMETRIOSIS, or other conditions, including a response to medication (see DRUG REACTIONS AND INTERACTIONS).

ovum, the egg cell (plural: ova) produced by a female, one of over a million ova in each of the two OVARIES at birth. Normally only a few ova mature and only one of these is released each month, in the process called OVULATION. If a SPERM (male sex cell) unites with the ovum, FERTILIZATION or CONCEPTION results. Then, if all goes normally, the fertilized egg travels to the UTERUS, to develop into an EMBRYO. Before and for a week or so after fertilization, the egg is protected by an outer layer called the ZONA PELLUCIDA, which is shed before the embryo implants itself in the uterine wall.

P

pacifier, a device for babies to suck on, if parents would prefer that they not suck on thumbs and fingers. Though widely used, pacifiers can cause severe problems, such as CHOKING, and can also be a source of infection, especially if they end up on the floor and are put back into the mouth without being cleaned. (See SUCKING.)

pain and pain treatment, an unpleasant sensation, ranging from irritating to agonizing, as a result of an injury, disease, or medical procedure, and the use of medications or other therapies to reduce those sensations.

For centuries, pain was the lot of women in CHILDBIRTH. For women, that began to change in the late nineteenth century, with the introduction of ANESTHESIA to ease the pain of labor and delivery. Anesthesia came to be widely used (see ANESTHESIA for a discussion of different approaches), to the extent that the pendulum has now swung in the other direction, toward natural delivery (see CHILDBIRTH), which relies largely on the body's own systems to lessen and deal with the pain.

In most other areas of medicine, pain has been badly managed and generally undertreated. Physicians receive little training in the treatment of pain; they generally focus on the course of the disease, rather than on the nature or intensity of pain. Health professionals in general have also been much concerned about possible addiction to narcotic drugs used as pain medicines; as a result, they often underprescribe pain medications. Even where prescribed, the doctor's indication is often "as needed," leaving the patient to the highly variable interpretation of the nursing staff. And even when dosages and timings are indicated, nurses may administer less medication less often than prescribed, or sometimes none at all.

This continues despite studies of recent decades showing that, when used legitimately to treat pain, narcotic drugs rarely result in addiction (recent studies have shown that fewer than .04 percent of people become addicted to pain medications through HOSPITAL use). The practice also continues in cases of dying patients, where the question of addiction no longer has any real meaning. It even persists in the face of recent studies showing that poor pain control at an ACUTE stage can lead to damage in the CENTRAL NERVOUS SYSTEM, resulting in CHRONIC pain, and that pain has other pronounced negative effects on the body, including stress and depression of the IMMUNE SYSTEM. In fact, studies have shown that aggressive treatment of pain at the start is best, since pain is harder to handle once it has become established. It is partly the mismanagement of pain that has led to the popularity of the HOSPICE movement. Some families have even gone to court over the question of pain; in 1990, a family won a case against a North Carolina hospital that had failed to give prescribed pain medicine to an elderly man dying of excruciatingly painful bone cancer.

The mismanagement of pain is worst for infants and young children. Many doctors practicing today were trained in the centuries-old mistaken belief that babies and young children felt no pain, the assumption being that their CENTRAL NERVOUS SYSTEMS were not sufficiently developed. That mistaken belief was disproved by at least the early 1970s, but even into the late 1980s surgery was often performed on infants without anesthesia, and the picture is changing only slowly in the 1990s. However, recent studies have shown that operations performed on infants who had received anesthesia and sedation had fewer postoperative complications, while infants who underwent surgery with "minimal" anesthesia had more postoperative complications and a higher death rate. Even where anesthesia is used during surgery, pain in infants and young children is often not treated after surgery. Doctors have been concerned about depressing respiration; but recent studies have not supported the belief that painkillers depress breathing in infants. In its 1992 guidelines on pain management, the federal Agency for Health Care Policy and Research specifically included newborn infants among those who require special pain treatment, for medical and ethical reasons.

Even on the rather minor level of needles and other pinpricks of medical diagnostic procedures, failure to use topical and local anesthetics to relieve the pain is at the very least counterproductive. Some put it more strongly: Neil Schechter, Director of Development Pediatrics at Hartford, Connecticut's St. Francis Hospital and a pioneer in pain research in children, says that not to adequately treat infant and child pain caused by diagnostic, medical, or surgical procedures or disease is "now known to be medically unsound as well as barbaric." In his classic 1974 study of pain treatment in 25 hospitalized children ages four to eight, Schechter found that 13 children received *no pain medication*, despite having operations such as amputation of a foot, removal of a neck mass, and repair of a heart defect.

The pain-management picture is slowly changing, however. One major advance in recent years is *patient-controlled analgesis* (PCA), in which pain medications are administered to the patient through an intravenous (IV) line, with a button allowing the patient to control the delivery of medication. This allows for more even pain relief, without the "hills and valleys" of pain involved in widely spaced medications, and with a steadier low level of relief, which often allows patients to sleep through the night. Even children can learn to use PCA. As one doctor put it: "If a child can play Nintendo, they can operate PCA," as long as they have the mental acuity to understand how to use the device and the physical ability to push the button.

Pain is an area where children desperately need parents as strong advocates (see ADVOCACY). As part of their evaluation of any doctor, parents should discuss attitudes and approaches to pain, and be sure that they are in agreement. If parents find that a doctor does not recognize and deal with a child's pain and fear of unknown procedures, they should seek another doctor. This is especially true if the doctor proposes to use physical restraint to hold a child down bodily during a procedure, a practice that not only cruelly and unnecessarily increases the child's trauma but also increases the likelihood of complications and slows recovery.

Where time permits, as for non-emergency surgery, parents should consider having procedures performed in a children's hospital, where staff is attuned to the needs of children and have experience with administering pain medications to them. They also need to talk with the hospital staff to ensure that their child gets the pain relief required to minimize the trauma of surgery and hospitalization. Beyond that, such hospitals often have staff experienced in helping children overcome pain and the fear of pain through a variety of techniques that prepare, soothe, and distract the child.

FOR HELP AND FURTHER INFORMATION

Children's Hospice International (CHI), 800–242–4453. Publishes *Palliative Pain and Symptom Management for Children and Adolescents.* (For full group information, see HOSPICE.)

National Chronic Pain Outreach Association, Inc. (NCPOA)
7979 Old Georgetown Road, Suite 100
Bethesda, MD 20814–2429
301–652–4948
Fax: 301–907–0745
Laura S. Hitchcock, Executive Director
Organization focusing on chronic pain and its management; provides information; maintains computerized registry of support groups; publishes quarterly newsletter *Lifeline* and other materials, including:

- General materials: *Pain Management Strategies, Flare-Up Coping Tips, Choosing a Pain Clinic or Specialist, Communication: Getting the Most from Your Doctor-Patient Relationship, Myths and Conceptions About Chronic Pain, Resources: Getting More Information about Chronic Pain, Taking Charge of Your Chronic Pain, The Stigma of Chronic Pain, Sex and Chronic Pain: The Healing Touch, Chronic Pain and the Family, Adapting a Dream: Traveling Despite Chronic Pain, TMJ Disorders: An Overview,* and *What Is Stress?*
- On pain management: *Implantable Pain Management: An Overview; Using Antidepressant Drugs to Treat Chronic Pain;* "for pain management" pamphlets *Heat, Cold, or Both, Distraction, Humor, Breathing,* and *Touch and Simple Massage;* and other works on specific problems.
- On support groups: *Support Group Discussion Topics, Keeping Support Groups Going,* and *How I Started a Pain Support Group.*
- Audiocassettes on self-hypnosis, relaxation, and pain management.

National Institute of Neurological Disorders and Stroke (NINDS), 800–352–9424. Publishes *Chronic Pain: Hope Through Research.* (For full group information, see BRAIN AND BRAIN DISORDERS.)

Cancer Care, Inc. and the National Cancer Care Foundation, 800–813–4673. Publishes *Cancer Care's Pain Resource Center.* (For full group information, see CANCER.)

Brain Injury Association, 800–444–6443. Publishes *Living with Chronic Pain.* (For full group information, see TRAUMATIC BRAIN INJURY.)

National Cancer Institute (NCI), 800–422–6237. Publishes *Get Relief from Cancer Pain, Patient Guide: Managing Cancer Pain, Questions and Answers About Pain Control: A Guide for People with Cancer and Their Families.* (For full group information, see CANCER.)

National Institute of Child Health and Human Development (NICHD), 301–496–5133. Publishes *Chronic Pain Management: Treatment System for People with Disabilities.* (For full group information, see PREGNANCY.)

OTHER RESOURCES

Pain Relief: How to Say No to Acute, Chronic, and Cancer Pain!. Jane Cowles. Mastermedia, 1993. Includes thorough discussion of pain in children.

palilalia, a rare condition in which a person repeats a phrase over and over with increasing rapidity, often resulting from a brain dysfunction or disease, such as ENCEPHALITIS, or a condition such as TOURETTE SYNDROME.

panic attack, a brief abrupt period of intense apprehension, fear, or terror, often with accompanying physical symptoms such as difficult breathing, heart palpitations, chest pain, sensations of CHOKING, trembling or shaking, nausea, and fear of losing control, going crazy, or dying. It is a key characteristic of PANIC DISORDERS, but also found in other MENTAL DISORDERS, such as SCHIZOPHRENIA or DEPRESSION.

panic disorders, a group of MENTAL DISORDERS, classed as ANXIETY DISORDERS, in which a person experiences sudden, unexpected PANIC ATTACKS, often without obvious triggers; sometimes associated with PROLAPSE of the mitral valve (see HEART AND HEART PROBLEMS). (See MENTAL DISORDERS; PHOBIA; ANXIETY DISORDERS.)

pantothenic acid, a VITAMIN that is important in the body's growth, maintenance, and energy METABOLISM; part of a group of vitamins known as the vitamin B complex. Pantothenic acid is found in many foods, including meats (especially liver and kidneys), milk, egg yolks, whole grains (especially wheat), peanuts, peas, white and sweet potatoes, and most other vegetables. Deficiencies are rare, but can occur from digestive disorders affecting intestinal absorption of nutrients; long-term heavy alcohol use; or severe illness, injury, or surgery. Symptoms of deficiency include headache, fatigue, poor muscle coordination, nausea, and cramps. Symptoms of excess are unknown, since it is water-soluble and excess is normally excreted in urine. (For help and further information, see RECOMMENDED DAILY ALLOWANCES; VITAMINS.)

Pap smear, a test to detect abnormal cells (*cervical dysplasias)* in the CERVIX, which are warning signs of possible CANCER formation; named after its developer, George Papanicolaou, it is also called a *cervical smear.* In this simple test, some cells and mucus are painlessly scraped off the end of the cervix and analyzed in the laboratory for possible abnormalities; if found, the usual follow-up would be a BIOPSY of tissue, and then treatment as indicated, possibly delayed if the woman is pregnant. Women (including sexually active teenagers) are advised to have Pap tests regularly starting a few months after beginning sexual activity, and thereafter, once a year, especially if they have many sex partners; otherwise, every two to three years, as their doctor or family planning clinic recommends. (For help and further information, see CERVIX; CANCER.)

paralysis, complete or partial loss of the ability to move one or more muscles at will in a controlled way, often accompanied by loss of feeling as well; sometimes called *palsy.* Paralysis does not necessarily imply total immobility, as is sometimes assumed. Muscles can be rigid, a condition termed *spastic,* but they may also be weak and "floppy," lacking the tension that muscles normally have, even at rest. Weakness alone is sometimes called *paresis.*

Paralysis can be permanent (at least at the present stage of medical technology), as when a spinal cord is severed, or temporary, as in response to something pressing on a nerve. It may affect only one small muscle, such as a muscle in the face, or a major network of muscles, as in severe SPINAL CORD INJURY.

Paralysis affecting all four limbs and the trunk, as from a neck injury, is termed *quadriplegia.* Paralysis affecting the legs and part of the trunk, as with an injury to the lower back, is called *paraplegia.* Paralysis affecting one half of the body, as from a BRAIN TUMOR or sometimes CEREBRAL PALSY, is called *hemiplegia.* Paralysis of like parts on both sides of the body, such as both legs or both sides of the face, is called *diplegia.* Some young people suffer from PERIODIC PARALYSIS, a rare GENETIC DISORDER characterized by brief periods of paralysis, lasting from a few minutes to two days, and recurring every few weeks. (See SPINAL CORD INJURY; also HELP FOR SPECIAL CHILDREN on page 689.)

para 1, a medical designation for a woman who has given birth to one live baby, standing for PRIMIPARA. A woman who has never borne a live infant is designated NULLIPARA, or *para 0.*

paraphimosis, a condition in which a retracted FORESKIN is too tight and acts like a tourniquet on a PENIS, an extremely painful condition, especially during an erection. Avoidance of it is one of the medical reasons traditionally advanced for CIRCUMCISION, since it may need to be treated surgically.

parental liability, a parent's obligation for damage caused by a MINOR child, whether through criminal acts, intention, or negligence. State laws vary as to the extent and nature of parental liability. Most states hold parents responsible for willful or malicious property damage caused by their children; more than half hold parents liable for willful or malicious personal injuries caused by children. Most states do, however, limit the dollar amount of parental liability, and do not hold parents liable for actions of children under 8 or so, except in cases where the parent was grossly negligent, as in giving a loaded gun to a young child. Under the FAMILY CAR DOCTRINE, the parent may also be liable for actions caused by a child driving a car owned by the parent.

parenteral nutrition, nutrients and medications introduced to a patient's body by various forms of INJECTION, bypassing the digestive system. Parenteral nutrition is often administered to PREMATURE newborns in NEONATAL INTENSIVE CASE UNITS and to patients generally after surgery or in other special situations, as in cases of SHOCK, COMA, MALNUTRITION, or failure of the kidneys or liver. Among the nutrients contained in parenteral fluids are often saline (salt) solution, GLUCOSE, AMINO ACIDS, VITAMINS, and ELECTROLYTES, the aim being not to supply full NUTRITION but to stabilize the electrolyte balance in the patient's system.

Parent Locator Service (PLS), a service of the Office of Child Support Enforcement, an arm of the U.S. Department of Health and Human Services, designed to help locate ABSENT PARENTS, generally to obtain CHILD SUPPORT payments, but also in cases of PARENTAL KIDNAPPING. The Federal PLS (FPLS) uses computer searches through income tax records, SOCIAL SECURITY earnings and benefit records, and the like, while state PLSs scan voter registration, motor vehicle, driver's license, welfare, prison, Worker's Compensation, and similar records.

parent's helper (mother's helper), a person, usually young and relatively inexperienced, who is employed to assist in CHILD CARE and light housework where at least one parent is at home most of the time. This is a typical holiday or summer job for HIGH SCHOOL or COLLEGE students. Parent's helpers do not necessarily have any formal training, though many have experience as BABYSITTERS and may have full responsibility for a child for brief periods. (See CHILD CARE; also CHECKLIST FOR CHOOSING CHILD CARE on page 114.)

parents' night, an evening or weekend day when parents are invited to visit their child's school, meet the teachers, and see work of the students, such as art displays or plays. Most schools hold parents' nights at least once a year, some more often. They are not, however, an effective substitute for a PARENT-TEACHER CONFERENCE.

parents' responsibilities, the legal duty of parents to take care of their MINOR children, a duty running alongside their PARENTS' RIGHTS; part of a wider (though in the law less clear) concept of people's responsibilities to take care of family members, including adults with DISABILITIES. Parents are responsible for providing the basic necessities of life—food, clothing, shelter, and medical treatment—as well as EDUCATION and DISCIPLINE. If a parent fails to provide proper care, SUPERVISION, and control (or attempts at control), charges of CHILD ABUSE AND NEGLECT may be brought; these can, in some cases, lead to temporary or permanent TERMINATION OF PARENTS' RIGHTS. If parents are unable to exercise control of their JUVENILE children, as in cases of juvenile DELINQUENTS, chronic TRUANTS, or runaways, the children may be legally labeled INCORRIGIBLE, put under court supervision, and placed in FOSTER CARE, or in a GROUP HOME or institution.

parents' rights, the legal rights of parents, in the United States protected under the Constitution, to have CUSTODY and SUPERVISION of their own MINOR children, including making decisions about their HEALTH CARE. Running along with these rights are PARENTS' RESPONSIBILITIES, legal duties to care for minors and some adult children with DISABILITIES. Parents can lose these rights under certain circumstances, as in some cases of ABANDONMENT and CHILD ABUSE AND NEGLECT. Legal proceedings to negate parents' claims on their child are called TERMINATION OF PARENTAL RIGHTS (TPR). In some cases, as when a child is judged INCORRIGIBLE, the parents may voluntarily transfer their rights to the state. In cases of DIVORCE or separation, when custody of a child is awarded to the one parent, the other parent—called the NONCUSTODIAL PARENT—may lose some parental rights, but generally retains VISITATION RIGHTS. Parents whose views—often their religious views—bar them from obtaining some kinds of medical care for their children, have sometimes come into conflict with the state's obligation to protect the rights of children, generating a whole body of law and many landmark Supreme Court cases.

parent-teacher conference, a meeting between a child's teacher and parent or parents, to discuss the child's educational progress. This provides an opportunity for parents and teacher to get to know each other, ask questions and share experiences about the child's situation, and discuss ways that each might enhance the child's performance. At such conferences, parents also have a chance to ask questions about classroom approaches, DISCIPLINE policies, teaching styles, CURRICULUM, GRADING, and other policies that may affect the child.

Many schools schedule regular parent-teacher conferences in October or November, after the child has settled into the school year, but soon enough so that any problems that have emerged can be dealt with expeditiously. Some schools hold conferences several times a year, after report cards are issued. If the school does not initiate such conferences, parents can do so. They should certainly do so at any time if the child seems unhappy or anxious about school, or if they have any concerns about the child's academic progress or social and emotional development. If the child has SPECIAL NEEDS or problems, or if anything in the child's health or family situations has changed or presents problems that may affect the child's performance at school—for example, if there has been a death, serious illness, or DIVORCE in the family—the parent may want to schedule a conference at the beginning of the school year, to inform the teacher.

If the child lives with both parents, it is best if both parents meet with the teacher, to avoid or minimize confusion or misinterpretation later on, as in the recollection or retelling. If that is not possible, or if the child has a single parent, a friend or relative might go along to take notes on important points raised in the conference, for later reference, if necessary. If parents cannot meet at school during the day, because of a job or family situation, many teachers will make arrangements to meet early in the morning or in the evening; and if parents do not speak English, they can request that an interpreter for their language be present at the conference.

Where possible, parents should try to give the conference a cooperative tone, stressing both parents' and teacher's desires to help a child do well. If appropriate, parents should take the time to note the positive things occurring with the child, and to express thanks for the teacher's part in them, rather than focusing solely on complaints or problems.

Parents who expect a difficult, confrontational meeting, however, should try to have an impartial third party join in, along with possibly another school official (such as a principal, assistant principal, or guidance counselor)

Tips for Parent-Teacher Conferences

Your preparation for the parent-teacher conference should include a review of the materials you file at home—including report cards, progress reports, and any papers brought home from school—*and* the child's school records. If the school provides a parent handbook, curriculum materials, or other information, review them beforehand. Talk with your child about his or her experiences, especially about which subjects he or she likes and which he or she dislikes. Explore how your child feels about all classes and teachers, and be sure to cover those in the checklist below. But remember that time is limited, so focus on those areas of special concern to your child's educational progress.

CHECKLIST FOR PARENT-TEACHER CONFERENCE	Yes	No	Need More Info
Have I received satisfactory answers to the following questions?	☐	☐	☐
Is my child performing at, above, or below grade level in basic skills, such as math and reading?	☐	☐	☐
Has my child taken achievement, intelligence, or aptitude tests in the past year? What do the scores mean?	☐	☐	☐
Does my child have strengths and weaknesses in major subject areas?	☐	☐	☐
Can we go over some examples of my child's classwork together?	☐	☐	☐
Does my child need special help in any academic subject?	☐	☐	☐
If so, what help and special services are available?	☐	☐	☐
Does my child need special help in social adjustment?	☐	☐	☐
Would you recommend referral to other school specialists?	☐	☐	☐
Has my child regularly completed homework you assigned?	☐	☐	☐
Has my child attended class regularly?	☐	☐	☐
Does my child participate in class?	☐	☐	☐
How are my child's work habits and attitude?	☐	☐	☐
Does my child get along well with classmates?	☐	☐	☐
Have you observed any changes in learning progress during the year? Has learning improved or declined dramatically?	☐	☐	☐
Have you noticed any changes in behavior, such as squinting, extreme fatigue, or irritability, which may be signals of medical problems?	☐	☐	☐
How do teachers keep parents informed about their children's progress or problems?	☐	☐	☐
Are there specific ways I can help my child at home?	☐	☐	☐

Keep in touch with the teacher, by phone, by written notes, or through additional conferences. In any case, it would be wise to schedule an end-of-the-year conference to review your child's progress. At this meeting you might ask if the teacher has suggestions for summer activities such as summer school, remedial help, or home learning activities. The child's class, grade, and teacher assignment for next year may also be discussed at this time.

If your conference results in strong disagreements between you and the teacher, set up another meeting, including the school principal, to try to resolve them. If you are still dissatisfied, you can appeal to the superintendent, possibly the school board, and sometimes a state or federal agency. But appeal procedures are long, difficult, and often unsatisfactory and are best avoided if at all possible.

Source: National Committee for Citizens in Education (now dissolved; see Center for Law and Education).

and an advocate to act as advisor (see ADVOCACY). But even where problems are serious, it is important to emphasize the need to work together to solve them, rather than blaming anyone for them. If parents think the teacher is incorrect about something, they should explain carefully why they think so; if the teacher disagrees, they should ask for specific examples to support their opinion. The key point is not to let the discussion become personally critical and argumentative, but to keep the focus on joint efforts to improve the child's situation. (Parents may find helpful TIPS FOR PARENT-TEACHER CONFERENCES on page 452.)

FOR HELP AND FURTHER INFORMATION

Center for Law and Education, 202–986–3000. Publishes "Information for Parents" brochure *Parent/Teacher Conference.* (For full group information, see HELP ON LEARNING AND EDUCATION on page 659.)

(See also EDUCATION.)

Parent Training and Information Centers (PTIs), a network of centers established in each state, originally under the EDUCATION FOR ALL HANDICAPPED CHILDREN ACT, then under the INDIVIDUALS WITH DISABILITIES EDUCATION ACT (IDEA), to help parents understand the rights of children with DISABILITIES or CHRONIC illnesses, and to prepare them to act on the child's behalf in planning for the child's EDUCATION, especially in developing INDIVIDUALIZED EDUCATION PLANS. These in turn operate TECHNICAL ASSISTANCE FOR PARENTS PROGRAM (TAPP) agencies, to help families take full advantage of these programs. (For help and further information, see Federation of Children with Special Needs under HELP FOR SPECIAL CHILDREN on page 689.)

parochial school, a church-related PRIVATE SCHOOL, generally referring to schools affiliated with the Roman Catholic Church, but also sometimes referring to schools of other religious denominations, such as Baptist, Quaker, Methodist, or Jewish schools.

partial zona dissection (PZD), an ASSISTED FERTILIZATION technique, a variation on IN VITRO FERTILIZATION; a new, still highly experimental form of REPRODUCTIVE TECHNOLOGY to help SPERM and egg (OVUM) join to achieve FERTILIZATION. Using MICROMANIPULATION, the EMBRYOLOGIST creates a partial opening in the ZONA PELLUCIDA, the protective outer layer of the egg; sperm are then mixed with the egg, with the hope that sperm will be able to penetrate the zona. One main problem with PZD is that it often allows multiple sperm to enter, making the resulting fertilized egg unviable. It also requires a relatively large number of active sperm for success. An alternative approach is SUBZONAL SPERM INSERTION (SZI). (For help and further information, see INFERTILITY; REPRODUCTIVE TECHNOLOGY.)

pass, in EDUCATION, to be graded as having a level of performance that is considered evidence of satisfactory learning, whether for a specific test or piece or work, or for a whole course, in which case a teacher will award the student CREDIT (formal or informal) for the course. Sometimes the passing level is a preset GRADE, such as a D average or a numerical average above 65 or 70. Sometimes no grade or ranking is assigned, and the "pass" label only distinguishes those who received credit for the course from those who FAIL and so receive no credit, in a PASS-FAIL SYSTEM.

pass-fail, a grading system in which students receive no letter or numerical GRADES or other kinds of assessment to indicate differences in level of performance or relative ranking within a class, but are only given one of two evaluations: PASS, for which credit is granted, or FAIL, with no credit allowed. This grading system is sometimes called *credit-no credit.*

passive abuser, someone who, while not actively abusive, fails to intervene to stop CHILD ABUSE OR NEGLECT by another person, in the home or other institution.

passive immunization, a type of IMMUNIZATION in which ANTIBODIES are directly injected into a person's body, supplying a short-term immunity; as opposed to the more common ACTIVE IMMUNIZATION.

passive vocabulary, words that a person can recognize or understand in context in READING matter, as opposed to the ACTIVE VOCABULARY that can be used independently in speaking or writing. Because children, like adults, always understand much more than they can express, their passive vocabulary is much larger than their active one.

Patau's syndrome (trisomy 13), a CONGENITAL condition resulting from a CHROMOSOMAL ABNORMALITY in which a child has three copies (*trisomy*) of chromosome 13. Infants with Patau's syndrome have severe MENTAL RETARDATION and often numerous defects, including MYELOMENINGOCELE, CLEFT LIP AND PALATE, and brain deformities, such as failure of the brain to divide properly. Fewer than one in five survive the first year.

FOR HELP AND FURTHER INFORMATION:

Support Organization for Trisomy 18, 13 and Related Disorders (SOFT), 716–594–4621. Publishes *Trisomy 13: A Guidebook for Families, Care of the Child and Infant with Trisomy 18 and Trisomy 13,* and brochure *Trisomy 13.* (For full group information, see EDWARDS' SYNDROME.)

National Organization for Rare Disorders (NORD), 800–999–6673. (For full group information, see RARE DISORDERS.)

(See also GENETIC DISORDERS.)

paternity suit, a legal action to identify the FATHER of a child, especially one born outside of marriage; also called a *parentage action*. Often brought in order to require the father to provide CHILD SUPPORT, many paternity suits are filed by MOTHERS under the AID TO FAMILIES WITH DEPENDENT CHILDREN (AFDC) program, who otherwise risk losing welfare money. A successful paternity action also generally involves granting VISITATION RIGHTS to the father, if he desires them. MEDICAL TESTS can show (or rule out) paternity with great accuracy, using analysis of DNA showing the child's GENETIC INHERITANCE, as compared to that of the presumed father.

pathologist, a PHYSICIAN who specializes in studying the nature, cause, development, and effects of disease, both in general and in specific cases, often working in laboratories, HOSPITALS, medical schools, or research institutes. Apart from their own research, they are often consultants to other physicians, using their expert knowledge of how disease changes the tissues and fluids of the body to help in diagnosing disorders, as in analyzing material from SPECIMEN TESTS. Some specialize in doing autopsies, attempting to learn for the future from detailed analysis of the effects of a disease in someone who has died.

Peabody Picture Vocabulary Test (PPVT), an individually administered DIAGNOSTIC ASSESSMENT TEST used to measure the LANGUAGE SKILLS, and by extension the academic aptitude, of people from age two and a half through adulthood. The examiner says a word, and the child is asked to point to which of four pictures depicts the word; the 175 words and four-picture sets become increasingly complex, but the test is continued only to the limit of the child's ability. Because the test focuses on RECEPTIVE LANGUAGE—that is, the ability to understand language, as opposed to speaking or reading it—is it widely used with children for whom English is a second language and those who may have MENTAL RETARDATION, as well as GIFTED CHILDREN. The PPVT is a NORM-REFERENCED TEST, and the result of the test is a PERCENTILE (and STANINE) and AGE EQUIVALENT (EDUCATIONAL AGE). (For help and further information, see TESTS.)

pediatrician, a physician who specializes in treating children and their disorders from birth through ADOLESCENCE. (If the newborn has special medical problems, such as being PREMATURE or LOW BIRTH WEIGHT, a specialist called a NEONATALOGIST may care for the baby during the first month of life, as in a NEONATAL INTENSIVE CARE UNIT.) Pediatricians advise on infant care, conduct WELL-BABY EXAMINATIONS, give VACCINATIONS, treat childhood disorders and diseases, and screen for any possible health problems, among them EAR AND HEARING PROBLEMS, EYE AND VISION PROBLEMS, DEVELOPMENTAL DISORDERS, and NUTRITION problems. If specific health problems are found, the pediatrician will either treat them directly or refer the child to a specialist. If the child has long-term DISABILITY, the pediatrician will assess the kind of activity the child is capable of handling and will recommend, for example, whether or not a child is able to spend a full day in the classroom. (See SELECTING A DOCTOR OR CLINIC, on page 455.)

pedigree, a carefully constructed family tree showing the pattern of GENETIC INHERITANCE of traits and disorders, for purposes of research and often for GENETIC COUNSELING for prospective parents, especially those who are concerned about passing GENETIC DISORDERS on to their children; sometimes more generally called a *genealogy*. Such information is not always easy to come by, given the prevalence of immigration, DIVORCE, separation, and ADOPTION, but various government departments can help in gathering genealogical data for reconstruction of meaningful family ancestry information.

In a pedigree, males are represented by squares, females by circles, and members of each generation appear on the same line. Siblings are attached to the line by "branch bars," in order by birth, where possible, with information about deceased siblings, stillbirths, miscarriages, and spontaneous abortions being vitally important. Symbols and rules for charting are not universally standard, but the most common ones are given in COMMON PEDIGREE SYMBOLS AND SAMPLE OF A PEDIGREE on page 456.

OTHER RESOURCES

GENERAL WORKS

How Healthy is Your Family Tree?: A Complete Guide to Creating a Medical and Behavioral Family Tree. Carol Krause. Macmillan, 1995.

(See also GENETIC COUNSELING; GENETIC DISORDERS; GENETIC INHERITANCE; also GENERAL PARENTING RESOURCES on page 634, under "On family history.")

peer tutoring (student tutoring), the use of students to help teach skills to other students, especially those who need extra help, often in a HETEROGENEOUS GROUP containing students of varying abilities, but sometimes as part of a formal program in which older students tutor students in lower grades. With peer tutoring, students get extra help when they need it, the peer tutors have their own skills reinforced while teaching others, and both learn valuable social skills. Because children vary in their skills, peer tutoring is not always one-way. A student might coach another in math, and herself be coached by a peer in hitting a softball. Many people also encourage peer tutoring among SIBLINGS.

FOR HELP AND FURTHER INFORMATION:

Council for Exceptional Children (CEC),
800–328–0272. Publishes *Peer Tutoring: When Working Together Is Better Than Working Alone* and *Peer Tutoring and*

Selecting a Doctor or Clinic

A good time to select your baby's doctor (such as a pediatrician or family physician) is before your baby is born. You may also choose a doctor/nurse practitioner team, or a pediatric nurse practitioner to take care of your baby. It is better to make this decision while you have the time to carefully choose who will advise you about your baby's health over the years. You may ask your own doctor or a nurse at the clinic for a recommendation; your friends or family members who have children of their own are good sources, too. If you have other children, you will probably find it easier to use the same care provider for all of your children. Once you have located a potential care provider, make an appointment to meet him or her if you can. Think about these questions as you decide whether this person is the one for you:

- What have been the experiences of friends (or family) with this care provider?
- Do you feel comfortable with and trust him or her?
- Do you feel that he or she will take the time to answer your questions or help you deal with new situations?
- How does he or she feel about issues of importance to you (such as breastfeeding or toilet training)?
- Is the office in a convenient location, so that you and your baby can get there easily?
- Will he or she be available by telephone if you need advice?
- What are the office hours, telephone hours, and fees?
- How can he or she be reached in an emergency?
- What hospital does the doctor work at?
- Does this care provider have any special training?

Remember, your doctor, nurse, or clinic staff will be your partner in looking after your baby's health and development. You can get a head start on developing that partnership by choosing a care provider before your baby is born.

Source: Infant Care (1989). Prepared for the Public Health Service by the Bureau of Maternal and Child Health and Resources.

Small-Group Instruction for Students with Autism and Developmental Delays. (For full group information, see HELP ON LEARNING AND EDUCATION on page 000.)

Johnson Institute, 800–231–5165, U.S. except MN. Publishes *Peer Helping Skills: A Program for Training Peer Helpers and Peer Tutors for Middle and High School.* (For full group information, see HELP AGAINST SUBSTANCE ABUSE on page 000.)

OTHER RESOURCES

Mindful of Others: Teaching Children to Teach. Suzanne Brady and Suzie Jacobs. Heinemann, 1994.

Tutoring and Mentoring: Starting a Peer-Helping Program in Your Elementary School. Nancy Keim and Cindy Tolliver. Resource Publications, 1993.

Tutoring: Learning by Helping: A Student Handbook for Training Peer and Cross Age Tutors, rev. ed. Elizabeth S. Foster. Educational Media, 1992.

Children Helping Children: Teaching Students to Become Friendly Helpers. Robert D. Myrick and Robert P. Bowman. Educational Media, 1991.

(See also EDUCATION.)

Pell Grant, a type of GRANT in FINANCIAL AID that helps undergraduate students meet the expenses of attending COLLEGE. The amount of grants depends on the program funding, with the money being paid either directly to the student or credited to the school account. Pell Grant recipients have priority in receiving SUPPLEMENTAL EDUCATIONAL OPPORTUNITY GRANTS. As one of the conditions of receiving a Pell Grant, a student must sign a statement certifying that he or she will not make, distribute, dispense, possess, or use drugs during the period covered by the grant; the grant may be suspended or terminated by a court if the student is convicted of possessing or distributing drugs. (For help and further information, see FINANCIAL AID.)

pelvic inflammatory disease (PID), infection of the upper genital tract in woman, including the UTERUS, OVARIES, FALLOPIAN TUBES, and other parts of the reproductive system; a SEXUALLY TRANSMITTED DISEASE that is a major cause of INFERTILITY and ECTOPIC PREGNANCY, with other dangerous complications. The National Institute of Allergy and Infectious Diseases (NIAID) estimates that PID affects 1 million American women annually, nearly 200,000 of them teenagers. Of these, up to 75 percent experience no symptoms before complications

Common Pedigree Symbols and Sample of a Pedigree

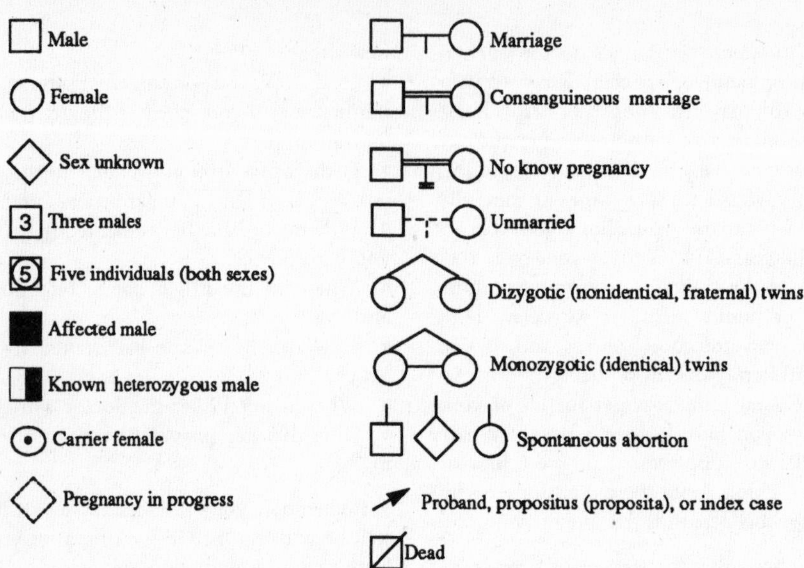

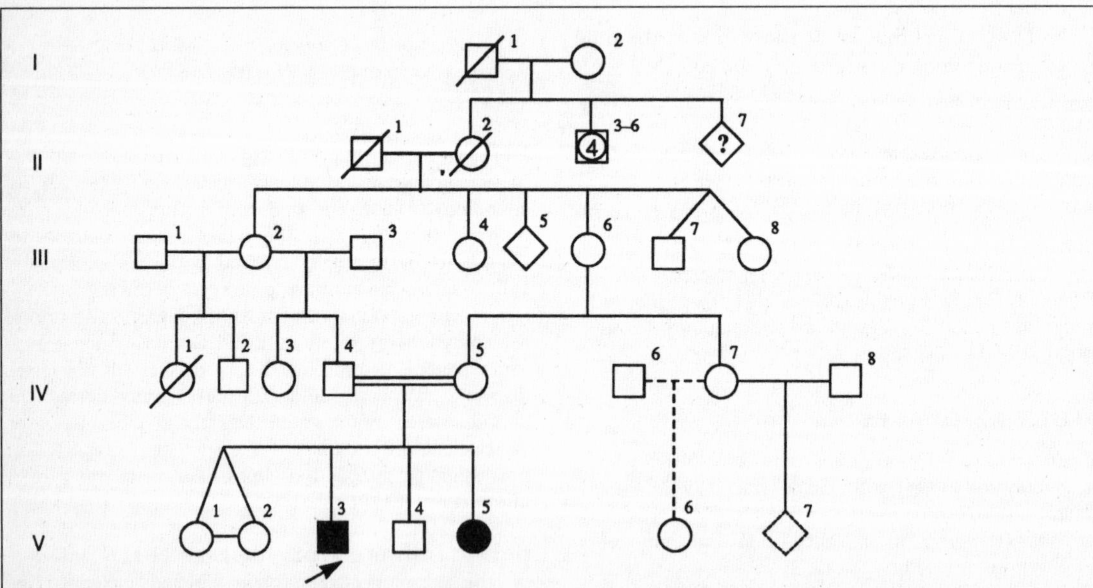

Siblings are indicated by arabic numerals from left to right in order of birth. Generations are represented by roman numerals, the earliest at the top.

Source: Genetic Family History: An Aid to Better Health in Adoptive Children (1984). Published by the National Center for Education in Maternal and Child Health (NCEMCH) for the Public Health Service's Genetic Diseases Service Branch, Division of Maternal and Child Health, from materials from a conference sponsored by Wisconsin Clinical Genetics Center and Waisman Center on Mental Retardation and Human Development, University of Wisconsin-Madison.

set in; some 10 percent become infertile, while tens of thousands experience potentially life-threatening ectopic pregnancies.

Pelvic inflammatory disease can be caused by many kinds of organisms, including some normally present in the VAGINA and CERVIX, but most often results from GONORRHEA or CHLAMYDIA; women seem to be most vulnerable to infection during MENSTRUATION. The disease-causing organisms apparently travel up into the Fallopian tubes, possibly by attaching themselves to SPERM, where they penetrate and destroy the lining of the tubes, producing pus, which spreads the infection elsewhere. The infection leaves behind scarred tissue, which blocks the normal passage of the egg to the uterus. As a result, a fertilized egg can plant itself and start to grow in the tubes, which can threaten the life of both mother and FETUS. Women who have had PID (even if they had no recognizable symptoms) are 6 to 10 times more likely to have an ectopic pregnancy, risks that rise with the woman's age, the severity of the infection, and the number of episodes of PID.

PID may produce only mild symptoms in the early stages, so serious damage can sometimes be done before the disease is recognized. Symptoms include pain in the lower abdomen, discharge from the VAGINA, and FEVER. Diagnosis is generally made using laboratory tests and confirmed by a LAPAROSCOPY, visual examination of the region through a slit in the abdomen. Once the condition and the infectious organisms causing it have been identified, it is generally treated with some form of ANTIBIOTICS. Serious ACUTE cases, as where ectopic pregnancy or APPENDICITIS have resulted, may require emergency surgery. Less severe CHRONIC cases can cause long-term chronic pelvic pain. (For help and further information, including how to avoid infection, see SEXUALLY TRANSMITTED DISEASES.)

penis, the male organ of sexual reproduction, made up largely of spongy tissue, which on stimulation fills with blood and becomes erect; running through the penis is the URETHRA, the passageway for both urine and SEMEN, exiting through an opening at the head of the penis, called the *glans*. A loose fold of skin over the glans is called the *foreskin* or *prepuce*, which is often removed in an operation called CIRCUMCISION.

The penis is relatively large at birth, but becomes slightly smaller over the next few weeks and remains small through childhood, then grows significantly larger with PUBERTY, as part of the development of SECONDARY SEXUAL CHARACTERISTICS. If the boy is not circumcised, the foreskin and glans remain connected by a common membrane, which gradually dissolves. Parents should not try to pull back the skin of an infant's penis, which will cause pain, irritation, and possible damage and infection. As the child grows, the foreskin will gradually loosen, until it can be pulled back. Usually by age eighteen, the foreskin opening is wide enough so that it can be fully retracted.

The penis needs no special care, though parents may want to teach the boy to slip the foreskin back, rinse the glans and inside of the foreskin with warm water, then slip the foreskin back into place. Occasionally white lumps may form under the foreskin; these are made up of old cells that collect in pockets between the glans and the gradually loosening foreskin, and will work their way to the tip where they will be wiped away normally.

Among the disorders that may affect a child's penis are BALANITIS, CHORDEE, EPISPADIAS, HYPOSPADIAS, PARAPHIMOSIS, and PHIMOSIS.

percentile, one of 100 divisions into which a group of SCORES is ranked, such as children's scores from a STANDARDIZED TEST; the particular division into which the child's actual score falls often is the reported "score" for the test. The percentile indicates the percent of people doing less well on the test, rather than the actual number or percent of questions answered correctly. If a child scores in the 79th percentile, for example, that means that she did better than 79 percent of all the students who took the test during its development and standardizing. The *decile* operates on the same principle, but has divisions from 1 to 10, while a *stanine* runs from 1 to 9 and a *quartile* from 1 to 4 (often simply called *quarters*). Among the many children's tests that commonly use percentiles are the WECHSLER PRESCHOOL AND PRIMARY SCALE OF INTELLIGENCE (WPPSI), the WECHSLER INTELLIGENCE SCALE FOR CHILDREN, REVISED (WISC-R), and METROPOLITAN ACHIEVEMENT TESTS.

perceptual disability, inability to interpret stimuli received through the senses, even though the sense organs themselves—eyes, ears, and so on—are in normal functioning order. This is a disorder of the sensory skills, including VISUAL SKILLS, AUDITORY SKILLS, and COGNITIVE SKILLS.

perceptual-motor skills, a type of VISUAL SKILL requiring hand-eye and body-eye coordination; closely related to MOTOR SKILLS.

perinatal, a general term for the period around the time of CHILDBIRTH.

perinatal asphyxia, a severe kind of HYPOXIA (lack of oxygen) affecting a baby in the period just before, during, and after DELIVERY. For physiological reasons not fully understood, babies can generally survive temporary loss of oxygen better than an older child or adult; that allows them to survive the usually brief period between the time the PLACENTA separates from the UTERUS wall and the time the newborn infant begins to breathe independently. Even so, perinatal asphyxia is a leading cause of death both in the FETUS and in newborns.

Babies may be AT RISK for perinatal asphyxia when LABOR is long and difficult, when FETAL PRESENTATION (position at birth) is abnormal, when the placenta separates prematurely, with RH INCOMPATIBILITY between the blood types of the mother and fetus, with long-standing high BLOOD PRESSURE in the mother, and with MULTIPLE BIRTHS. Obstetricians check fetal position and heartbeat, as with FETAL MONITORS, looking for early warning signs of perinatal asphyxia.

Infants with this oxygen starvation often gasp for breath or do not breathe at all (*apnea*) and have slow heartbeat (*bradycardia*), limited activity, low body temperature, pale color or blueness (CYANOSIS), and abnormally high levels of hydrogen in the body (*acidosis*). An asphyxiated infant receives immediate RESUSCITATION, often including pure oxygen poured into the air passages through a tube, cardiac massage, and various medications, depending on the analysis of blood samples from the infant.

One of the main reasons for women with HIGH-RISK pregnancies to give birth at high-level HOSPITALS, such as regional medical centers, is because they are best equipped to deal with asphyxia. Even with the best treatment, however, many babies who survive may have serious complications affecting one or more of the main systems of the body. (For help and further information, see DELIVERY; LUNG AND BREATHING DISORDERS.)

perinatal care, medical care offered in the first 28 days after CHILDBIRTH, especially immediately afterward. Often suction is used to clear mucus from the infant's air passages and silver nitrate or other ointment is put in the child's eyes. An APGAR SCORE is performed in the minutes after DELIVERY, to assess quickly whether any special medical intervention is needed to aid the child. In the days just after childbirth, if the parents have chosen it and the child has no special medical problems, CIRCUMCISION may also be performed. Some of these procedures have sparked considerable controversy, with some groups supporting actions seen as ensuring continuing good health in a baby, while others criticize those actions as invasive. Perinatal care overlaps with POSTNATAL CARE, which extends for the first six weeks after delivery.

FOR HELP AND FURTHER INFORMATION

National Perinatal Information Center
One State Street, Suite 102
Providence, RI 02908
401–274–0650
Fax: 401–455–0377
David Gagnon, Executive Director
Organization that provides public and professionals with information on perinatal care.

National Association of Postpartum Care Services (NAPCS)
326 Shields Street
San Francisco, CA 94132–2734
800–45-DOULA [453–6852]
Organization of professional postpartum doulas, trained to provide practical, in-home, nonmedical, education and emotional support services in the post-delivery period; provides accreditation and certification; publishes *NAPCS Newsletter*, *NAPCS Archives* (a collection of articles), directory of members, *Cooking: After the Baby Comes*, and tapes from conferences.

Certified Perinatal Educators Association (CPEA)
4 David Court
Novato, CA 94947
415–893–0439
Claudia Lowe, President
Organization affiliated with National Association of Childbirth Assistants (see CHILDBIRTH); conducts training programs; publishes quarterly newsletter *BSP International* and *The Childbirth Companion Directory*.

National Perinatal Association (NPA)
3500 East Fletcher Avenue, Suite 209
Tampa, FL 33613
813–971–1008
Fax: 813–971–9306
E-mail: npaonline@aol.com (America Online: NPAONLINE)
Julie Leachman, Executive Director
Organization of professionals in perinatal health care; provide referrals; publishes quarterly newsletter *The Bulletin*, occasional newsletter *The Network*, and bimonthly *Journal of Perinatalogy*.

Newborn Rights Society (NRS), 610–323–6061.
(For full group information, see CIRCUMCISION.)

(See CIRCUMCISION; POSTNATAL CARE; DELIVERY; PREGNANCY.)

perinatalogist, an OBSTETRICIAN-GYNECOLOGIST who specializes in caring for women with HIGH-RISK PREGNANCIES, including ADOLESCENTS, women over age thirty-five, those with medical problems such as DIABETES, hypertension (high BLOOD PRESSURE), and SEXUALLY TRANSMITTED DISEASES, women with a personal or immediate family history of GENETIC DISORDERS, and women who have had problems during a previous PREGNANCY.

periodic paralysis, a rare GENETIC DISORDER affecting young people and characterized by brief periods of PARALYSIS, lasting from a few minutes to two days, and recurring every few weeks. The cause of the paralysis is unclear, but seems to be associated with a drop in POTASSIUM (a MINERAL vital for muscle functioning) as a result of eating too much CARBOHYDRATES. Restriction of carbohydrates, taking potassium, and modest EXERCISE at onset may moderate the effects of the condition, which generally disappears by about age thirty. (For help and further information, see MUSCULAR DYSTROPHY.)

periodontist, a dental specialist who treats advanced cases of GINGIVITIS, or gum inflammation.

peripheral nervous system (PNS), the network of nerves that transmits information to and from the CENTRAL NERVOUS SYSTEM (CNS). Damage to the PNS tends to be local and can sometimes be repaired surgically, unlike damage to the CNS, which tends to affect wide areas of the body in the long term.

Perkins Loans, a federally SUBSIDIZED LOAN program under which the school lends money to undergraduate and graduate COLLEGE students; formerly called the *National Direct Student Loan Program.* The amounts available are (as of 1990) a maximum of $4500 for vocational programs or the first two years of a college program leading to a BACHELOR'S DEGREE; up to $9000 after two years in a bachelor's program; and up to $18,000 for graduate or professional study (this would include amounts borrowed under the program for undergraduate study). The student signs a promissory note and money is either paid to the student directly or credited to the school account. Interest charged is only 5 percent and the repayment period is up to ten years. Repayments of at least thirty dollars a month do not begin until nine months after the student either leaves school or drops below half-time, though payments may be further delayed under certain circumstances. (For help and further information, see SUBSIDIZED LOAN.)

peroneal muscular atrophy (Charcot-Marie-Tooth disease), a rare GENETIC DISORDER that involves weakness and wasting (ATROPHY) of the muscles in the lower limbs and sometimes the upper limbs as well, as a result of damage to the peripheral nerves. The disorder generally appears in late childhood or adolescence, more often in boys than girls, and progresses slowly, sometimes stopping altogether. Life expectancy is not generally affected, but people with the disorder may need ORTHOPEDIC DEVICES.

FOR HELP AND FURTHER INFORMATION

National Ataxia Foundation (NAF), 612–473–7666. (For full group information, see ATAXIA.)

(See also MUSCULAR DYSTROPHY.)

perseveration, a tendency to repeat tasks, motions, or spoken words over and over, often long after the occasion for them has passed, a pattern of activity found in some children with LEARNING DISABILITIES, MENTAL RETARDATION, or MENTAL DISORDERS.

persistent fetal circulation (PFC), a condition in which a newborn has not made the appropriate transition from a fluid-filled environment (as in the UTERUS) to an air-dependent one. Blood flow temporarily fails to effectively exchange carbon dioxide for the needed oxygen, resulting in insufficient oxygen in the blood. In these cases the baby may turn blue (CYANOSIS), breathe rapidly (*tachypnea*), and seem to have RESPIRATORY DISTRESS SYNDROME. (For help and further information, see CHILDBIRTH; LUNG AND BREATHING DISORDERS; HEART AND HEART PROBLEMS.)

personality disorder, a type of MENTAL DISORDER in which affected people have a view of themselves and their social and personal environment that is so rigid and ill-suited as to cause them distress and to significantly impair their ability to function in society. Among the various personality disorders found among children and adolescents (and treated in separate entries) are CONDUCT DISORDER (in adults called *antisocial personality disorder*), AVOIDANT DISORDER OF CHILDHOOD OR ADOLESCENCE (in adults called *avoidant personality disorder*), IDENTITY DISORDER (in adults called *borderline personality disorder*), and OBSESSIVE COMPULSIVE DISORDER.

In addition to those noted above, personality disorders include:

- *Paranoid personality disorder*, in which a person has a characteristic tendency, from at least early adulthood, to see others as threatening or hateful, and act accordingly suspicious and excessively vigilant of personal rights, being extremely sensitive to perceived insults or attacks.
- *Schizoid personality disorder*, in which a person feels perpetually divided (the literal meaning of "schizoid") from other people, being indifferent to most or all social relationships and having an extremely limited range of emotions, as both felt and expressed (see AFFECT).
- *Schizotypal personality disorder*, in which a person has disturbances in thought, self-perception, and behavior, but not so severe as to be classified as schizophrenic.
- *Histrionic personality disorder*, in which a person is excessively emotional and dramatic in continually drawing attention to themselves, exaggerating personal roles, such as "victim."
- *Narcissistic personality disorder*, in which a person has a grandiose sense of self, and his or her abilities and "specialness," and unreasonably expects attention, admiration, and favorable treatment.
- *Dependent personality disorder*, in which a person relies excessively on others for advice and reassurance, being unable to make everyday decisions without massive support.
- *Passive aggressive personality disorder*, in which a person characteristically resists personal and social demands indirectly, as by procrastinating, working slowly or ineffectively, protesting "unreasonable demands," or claiming to have forgotten them.

Many of the characteristics of personality disorders overlap with those of other kinds of mental disorders, including DEPRESSION and SCHIZOPHRENIA. (See MENTAL DISORDERS.)

PET scan (positron emission transaxial tomography or PETT), a type of NUCLEAR SCANNING similar to a CT SCAN, but using slightly radioactive

GLUCOSE introduced into the body, as by inhalation or INJECTION. The PET scan is especially useful in examining the activity of internal organs, including the brain, the heart, and the circulatory system in general, and in diagnosing and studying CANCER. (For help and further information, see MEDICAL TESTS.)

phenylketonuria (PKU), a GENETIC DISORDER in which children have a defect in the liver enzyme that normally converts the PROTEIN *phenylalanine* into a useful form. In children with PKU, the phenylalanine (sometimes abbreviated *phe*) builds up in the blood stream, blocking normal development of the brain. The defect affects at least 1 baby in every 16,000, most commonly those of northern European background, less often those of Jewish, Asian, or Black African descent.

Undetected, PKU can cause MENTAL RETARDATION by the time a child is 1 year old; if detected, but not properly treated or responsive to treatment, PKU can lead to behavioral disturbances and LEARNING DISABILITIES. To prevent this, the *Guthrie (PKU) test* is routinely given (often by law) to newborns; a few drops of blood taken from the baby's heel will show if there is excess phenylalanine in the blood.

Treatment involves a diet low on foods that contain large amounts of phenylalanine, such as cow's MILK, meat, regular FORMULA, and other protein-rich foods, with regular monitoring of the blood's phenylalanine level. Infants may be given a special formula containing no phenylalanine; later the child is advised to follow a low-protein, largely VEGETARIAN diet. (The BABYSITTER'S GUIDE TO PKU, on page 461, will help parents instruct CHILD CARE workers.) Most but not all cases of PKU respond to such a diet, but how long the diet should be maintained is controversial. In practice, many children go off the special diet on reaching their teens.

Women who have PKU must be extremely careful to maintain a low-protein diet during pregnancy—or when there is a possibility that they may become pregnant—because the buildup of phenylalanine can cause irreparable brain damage to the FETUS in the UTERUS. This is a special problem because some women were never told that they had PKU and may not remember being on a special diet when young.

FOR HELP AND FURTHER INFORMATION

Children's PKU Network (CPN)
8388 Vickers Street, Suite 113
San Diego, CA 92111
619–569–9881
Fax: 619–292–6231
Suzanne Ervine, Administrative Assistant
Organization concerned with children who have PKU; provides support and exchange of experiences for parents; acts as advocate; offers numerous reprints from information clearinghouse, on topics such as Aspartame, maternal PKU, paternal PKU, adult PKU, newborn screening, breastfeeding, diet management, genetics, life-style and PKU, current research (on and off special diets), and explaining PKU to others, such as babysitters or teachers, as well as materials geared to children with PKU.

March of Dimes Birth Defects Foundation (MDBDF), 914–428–7100. Publishes information sheet *PKU.* (For full group information, see BIRTH DEFECTS.)

National Institute of Child Health and Human Development (NICHD), 301–496–5133. Publishes research report *Education of Students with Phenylketonuria (PKU).* (For full group information, see PREGNANCY.)

National Maternal and Child Health Clearinghouse (NMCHC), 703–821–8955. Publishes *Dental Health in Children with Phenylketonuria (PKU) and Other Inborn Errors of Amino Acid Metabolism Managed by Diet* and *National Survey of Treatment Programs for PKU and Selected Other Inherited Metabolic Diseases.* (For full group information, see PREGNANCY.)

National Organization for Rare Disorders (NORD), 800–999–6673. (For full group information, see RARE DISORDERS.)

(See also LIVER AND LIVER PROBLEMS.)

phimosis, a condition in which a too-tight FORESKIN cannot be fully drawn back over the head, or glans, of the PENIS, and so impedes free urination. Avoidance of phimosis is one of the medical reasons traditionally advanced for CIRCUMCISION, since it may need to be treated surgically.

phobia, a powerful, persistent fear of an object or situation, where in fact no danger or threat exists; sometimes thought to be a kind of DEFENSE MECHANISM called DISPLACEMENT, in which unconscious fears are attached to an external object. Phobia is a key characteristic of *phobic disorders* (see below), but is also a symptom of other MENTAL DISORDERS, such as PANIC DISORDERS and other anxiety disorders (see ANXIETY). A much milder problem, SCHOOL PHOBIA, is more often a form of SEPARATION ANXIETY or reflects other kinds of social or academic problems.

Phobic disorders are a type of anxiety disorder characterized by phobia, an irrational fear of an object or setting, a fear so strong it brings on anxiety and a PANIC ATTACK if the person is confronted with it, and so leads to AVOIDANCE BEHAVIOR; also called *phobic neuroses.* The most common kind of phobia, especially among children, is *simple phobia*, involving fear of a specific thing. Phobias about dogs, cats, snakes, mice, or bugs often begin in childhood.

However, other phobias, such as about blood, cuts, closed spaces (*claustrophobia*), heights (*acrophobia*), and air travel, more often begin in ADOLESCENCE or early adulthood. *Social phobia*, or fear of social situations, often

Babysitter's Guide to PKU

PKU

You are babysitting a child and there is a special restriction. The child has PKU and you have never before heard of that. PKU stands for "phenylketonuria." This child's body cannot use protein foods which contain phenylalanine or "phe" the same way other children do. Sometimes we say this child is "allergic" to foods containing protein and phe, or we say this child is on a "special diet."

This child grows like other children of the same age, acts like other children of the same age, and looks like other children of the same age. The only difference is the foods this child can and cannot eat. This special diet is *very* important to keep this little individual growing well both physically and mentally.

WHAT IS A SPECIAL DIET?

Because this child cannot use protein and phe like you do, the diet strictly limits the amounts of foods that have protein and phe. Many foods besides meat, eggs, milk, and milk products have protein and phe, and must be eaten in limited amounts. All foods must be carefully measured.

This child has a special milk called *Lofenalac*©. It is very important for this child to drink the special milk in the amount the nutritionist has told Mom and Dad. *Phenylfree*© is another special milk for older children with PKU.

If you are babysitting during mealtime, Mom or Dad will have written out a menu of foods to offer this child and how to prepare them. Write down how much food you offered and how much was eaten, for example:

Foods to Offer	Foods Child Ate
8 oz. Lofenalac	8 oz. Lofenalac
1 peach	½ peach
2 tablespoons Rice Chex	2 tablespoons Rice Chex

Important: Give the child only the foods and amounts you were told to give.

WHAT IF THE CHILD IS EXTRA HUNGRY?

There are foods this child can eat that contain very little or no protein and phe. They are called "free foods" and may be used as needed to satisfy hunger. Some free foods are: apples, apple juice, chewing gum (except that made with Nutrasweet—read the label), and candy such as lollipops, gumdrops, jelly beans, or life savers. Popsicles (without ice cream, pudding, or gelatin) are also okay, and so is KoolAid (regular—not with Nutrasweet).

FOOD SURPRISES YOU CAN MAKE

Make Tang, KoolAid, Hawaiian Punch and freeze it into popsicles. Or cut apple wedges into different shapes. Describe the different shapes and sizes and colors of apples. Count jelly beans and name the colors of the beans. (Be sure to tell Mom or Dad how much food the child ate during the games.)

YOUR RESPONSIBILITY IN FEEDING THIS CHILD

1. Remember, even small amounts or "just a taste" of certain foods contain more protein and phe than this child should eat all day. So offer only foods okayed by Mom or Dad.
2. Tell Mom or Dad if the child refused to eat a certain food so that the diet can be adjusted for the rest of the day.
3. If the child's playmates question the child's food, explain that the child is "allergic" to certain foods.
4. Most important: Remember this is a normal child who can do all of the things other children can do.

Source: A Babysitter's Guide to PKU, by Christine M. Trahms and Carla Cox (1987). Prepared for the Child Development and Mental Retardation Center, University of Washington, Seattle, WA 98195.

begins during ADOLESCENCE, when children fear they will be humiliated or embarrassed, and so may drastically curtail their activities.

Perhaps most severe is *agoraphobia*, or fear of open, exposed places, in which the person fears the situation may trigger incapacitating symptoms such as a panic attack, but also temporary loss of identity, VOMITING, or INCONTINENCE. To avoid such possible symptoms (or their recurrence), many people with agoraphobia stay at home, venturing out only rarely with a trusted companion. Such a restricted life may lead them to seek professional help, with therapy often involving BEHAVIOR MODIFICATION and DESENSITIZATION.

FOR HELP AND FURTHER INFORMATION

National Institute of Mental Health (NIMH),
301–443–4513. (For full group information, see MENTAL DISORDERS.)

CALL (Concerned Agoraphobics Learning to Live)
380 Tolosa Way
San Luis Obispo, CA 93405
805–543–3764
Daryl Woods, Contact
Mutual-support, self-help group of and for agoraphobics; maintains telephone and mail contacts nationwide with housebound sufferers.

OTHER RESOURCES

For parents and other adults

Monsters Under the Bed and Other Childhood Fears: Helping Your Child Overcome Anxieties, Fears, and Phobias. Stephen W. Garber and others. Random House, 1993.

Anxiety, Phobias and Panic: A Step-by-Step Program for Regaining Control of Your Life. Reneau Z. Peurifoy. Warner, 1995. Previously: *Anxiety, Phobias and Panic: Taking Charge and Conquering Fear*, 2nd ed. Life Skills, 1992.

From Panic to Peace of Mind: Overcoming Panic and Agoraphobia. C. B. Scrignar. Bruno, 1991.

The Anxiety and Phobia Workbook. Ed Bourne. New Harbinger, 1990.

Panic and Anxiety Attacks: Warning of a Physical Problem. Glenn M. Alger. Glendor, 1990.

Good News about Panic Anxiety and Phobias. Mark S. Gold. Bantam, 1990.

Coping with Panic: A Drug-Free Approach to Dealing with Anxiety Attacks. George A. Clum. Brooks-Cole, 1990.

The Encyclopedia of Phobias, Fears and Anxieties. Ronald M. Doctor and Ada P. Kahn. Facts on File, 1989.

On social anxiety and phobias

Beyond Shyness: How to Conquer Social Anxieties. Jonathan Berent. Simon & Schuster, 1993.

Dying of Embarrassment: Help for Social Anxiety and Social Phobia. Barbara Markway and others. New Harbinger, 1992.

Always at Ease: Overcoming Anxiety and Shyness in Every Situation. Christopher J. McCullough. Tarcher, 1990.

For children

Fears and Phobias. Renardo Barden. Crestwood, 1990.

For preteens and teens

Anxiety and Phobias. Don Nardo. Chelsea House, 1992.

(See also MENTAL DISORDERS.)

phocomelia, a BIRTH DEFECT in which a child has nearly nonexistent limbs, with hands or feet attached almost directly to the body; also called *seal limbs.* Phocomelia is associated with some other disorders, notably CORNELIA DE LANGE SYNDROME and with certain drugs, such as thalidomide, but occasionally occurs with no known triggering event.

phonics method, a traditional method of teaching READING by having the child sound out the letters and learn how they fit together to form words, one of the key WORD-ATTACK SKILLS; also called the *phonetics, alphabet,* or *ABC method.* Some children, such as those with LEARNING DISABILITIES, may need extra help in effectively learning the connections between sounds and written letters, especially if they are being taught by the WHOLE WORD METHOD; for them phonics methods may be needed such as the highly structured HEGGE-KIRK-KIRK method or VAKT, which takes a MULTISENSORY approach, having students write letters while sounding them out and reading them. (See READING.)

phosphorus, a MINERAL that works with CALCIUM to build strong bones and teeth, and helps in the body's METABOLISM. Some significant sources of phosphorus are milk, cheese, meats, egg yolks, fish, poultry, whole-grain products, beans, and nuts. Lack of sufficient phosphorus can cause weakness, bone pain, and abnormal growth. Too much phosphorus can hinder the body's use of calcium. More than that, phosphorus as an element used in pesticides and industrial uses can be a dangerous poison, in cases of CHRONIC exposure causing ANEMIA, cirrhosis of the liver (see LIVER AND LIVER PROBLEMS), and KIDNEY AND UROLOGICAL PROBLEMS. ACUTE phosphorus poisoning can cause VOMITING, bloody DIARRHEA, failure of the heart, kidney, or liver, DELIRIUM, SEIZURES, and death. (For help and further information, see MINERALS; NUTRITION; POISONS.)

phototherapy, medical treatment of diseases with light, in any of a variety of forms, including sunlight, ultraviolet light, and visible blue light (as in fluorescent bulbs), and sometimes also lasers. Newborns who are affected with jaundice or hyperbilirubinemia (see LIVER AND LIVER PROBLEMS) are often exposed nude to fluorescent lights, the blue range of which speeds decomposition of the bilirubin that gives a yellowish cast to the skin. Some skin disorders, such as VITILIGO and severe forms of PSORIASIS, may be treated with light plus drugs, a type of phototherapy nicknamed PUVA (for the drug psoralen plus ultraviolet A).

OTHER RESOURCES

Light: Medicine of the Future: How We Can Use It to Heal Ourselves NOW. Jacob Liberman. Bear, 1991.
The Light Book: How Natural and Artificial Light Affect our Health, Mood and Behavior. Jane Wegscheider Hyman. Tarcher, 1990.

physical therapist (physiotherapist), a health professional who uses various physical techniques and therapies to help a patient gain or regain mobility, strength, and control over joints and muscles damaged by disease, disorder, or injury, and to reduce pain, inflammation, and muscle spasms. Physical therapists may give a child various muscle tests, to assess strength and mobility, and decide what methods or treatments to use, including EXERCISE, massage, heat treatment, ULTRASOUND treatment, ice packs, HYDROTHERAPY, and PHOTOTHERAPY. Physical therapists also help people learn to use ORTHOPEDIC DEVICES, as necessary, such as wheelchairs, braces, and crutches, the aim being to help the patient to be self-sufficient in the gross MOTOR SKILLS, such as WALKING and shifting position, and beyond that to hopping, skipping, and going up and down stairs. Physical therapists may prescribe exercises to be done at home. (See ORTHOPEDIC DEVICES for help and further information on mechanical aids.)

physician, a health professional who has the degree of Doctor of Medicine, or M.D. The term may also refer to an OSTEOPATHIC PHYSICIAN, a health professional who has the degree of Doctor of Osteopathy, or D.O. Many physicians are *general practitioners* (GPs), today more often called *family practice physicians,* who provide medical care to people of all ages and either sex, treating all aspects of a patient's care. They are PRIMARY HEALTH CARE PROVIDERS, who act as a patient's "first port of call." If the condition warrants it, a patient will be referred to a *specialist,* a physician with advanced training and experience in certain areas of medical care, such as a PEDIATRICIAN who specializes in treating children or a NEONATALOGIST who specializes in treating newborns. (See SELECTING A DOCTOR OR CLINIC on page 455.)

pica, a craving or compulsive desire to eat substances that are not food, such as dirt, clay, paint, laundry starch, chalk, wood, glue, HAIR, or ice; a kind of eating disorder that often stems from a nutritional deficiency, especially of IRON. It also sometimes occurs during PREGNANCY and may also be associated with some forms of MENTAL DISORDERS.

Pierre Robin syndrome, a CONGENITAL disorder of unknown origin, which involves various craniofacial abnormalities; also called *Pierre Robin malformation sequence, Pierre Robin sequence,* or *Robin triad.* Common characteristics include cleft palate (see CLEFT LIP AND PALATE), an abnormally small lower jaw (*micrognathia*), and malformation of the tongue (*glossoptosis*), which is too large for the mouth and tends to fall backward toward the throat, blocking air passages and making feeding difficult. Because of this, children with Pierre Robin sequence should not be placed on their back to sleep. In severe cases, a physician will suture the tongue to the lower lip for a few months, to allow room for the jaw to grow. Children with Pierre Robin sequence are more likely to have defects of the eyes, ears, and heart, and sometimes MENTAL RETARDATION, and so their development should be monitored carefully, especially for fluid buildup behind the eardrum. PLASTIC SURGEONS, SPEECH AND LANGUAGE THERAPISTS, ORTHODONTISTS, and other medical specialists often must work together to treat COMMUNICATION DISORDERS and respiratory disorders.

FOR HELP AND FURTHER INFORMATION

Cleft Palate Foundation, 800–242–5338. Publishes *Information About Pierre Robin Malformation Sequence.* (For full group information, see CLEFT LIP AND PALATE.)

National Institute of Dental Research (NIDR), 301–496–4261. (For full group information, see TEETH AND DENTAL PROBLEMS.)

National Institute of Child Health and Human Development (NICHD), 301–496–5133. (For full group information, see PREGNANCY.)

National Organization for Rare Disorders (NORD), 800–999–6673. (For full group information, see RARE DISORDERS.)

pituitary gland, one of the key organs that produce HORMONES, a tiny gland attached to the HYPOTHALAMUS in the brain. It is sometimes called the master gland because it regulates the activities of so many other glands and organs in the body. The pituitary secretes a number of key hormones:

- HUMAN GROWTH HORMONE (hGH), which stimulates the growth of the body.
- *Thyroid-stimulating hormone* (TSH), which stimulates the THYROID GLAND.
- *Prolactin,* which stimulates the development of a woman's BREASTS and LACTATION during BREASTFEEDING.
- LUTEINIZING HORMONE (LH), which stimulates production of other hormones by the OVARIES and TESTES.
- FOLLICLE-STIMULATING HORMONE (FSH), which stimulates maturation of eggs (see OVUM) in the OVARIES.
- *Melanocyte-stimulating hormone* (MSH), which regulates the pigmentation of the skin.
- *Adrenocorticotropic hormone* (ACTH), which stimulates the ADRENAL GLANDS.

- *Antidiuretic hormone* (ADH), which stimulates the kidneys to decrease the amount of water sent to form urine.
- *Oxytocin*, which stimulates contractions of the UTERUS during CHILDBIRTH, and also affects milk released from the breasts.

Because of its wide range of functions, any abnormality in the pituitary, which causes excess or deficiency in production of these hormones, can seriously affect the rest of the body.

Among the pituitary disorders that can affect children are:

- *Growth disorders*, resulting from GENETIC DISORDERS, other CONGENITAL disorders (such as from injury during CHILDBIRTH), or later TRAUMATIC BRAIN INJURY that affected the pituitary (see GROWTH AND GROWTH DISORDER).
- TUMORS, usually benign in themselves, but possibly causing substantial problems because of a malfunctioning pituitary (see BRAIN TUMORS).
- *Loss of blood supply*, as from a tumor or HEMORRHAGE; in a woman with massive hemorrhaging during childbirth, this can lead to SHEEHAN'S SYNDROME.
- *Underactivity of the pituitary* as a result of radiation (see ENVIRONMENTAL HAZARDS) or radiation therapy (see CANCER).
- Disorders of the pituitary are investigated using a variety of MEDICAL TESTS, including X-RAYS, CT SCANS, MRI, and ANGIOGRAMS.

FOR HELP AND FURTHER INFORMATION

National Digestive Disease Information Clearinghouse (NDDIC), 301–654–3810. (For full group information, see DIGESTIVE SYSTEM AND DISORDERS.)

Human Growth Foundation (HGF), 301–656–7540. (See GROWTH AND GROWTH DISORDERS.)

placenta, an organ that develops in the UTERUS and acts as the site of the exchange of nutrients and oxygen from the mother's blood for waste products from the baby's blood. The placenta grows from the outer layer of the fertilized egg (OVUM) implanted in the lining of the uterus and is connected to the baby by the UMBILICAL CORD. The placenta also produces HORMONES—ESTROGEN, PROGESTERONE, and HUMAN CHORIONIC GONADOTROPIN (hCG)—which are detectable in a woman's urine and are the basis of many PREGNANCY TESTS. The placenta normally remains in place until after the child has been delivered, when it is expelled as the *afterbirth*.

In some cases, the placenta begins to separate from the uterus wall prematurely, a condition called *abruptio placentae*, sometimes signaled by bleeding from the VAGINA during pregnancy. The separation may be only partial, as indicated on an ULTRASOUND scan and by only small amounts of bleeding. In that case the pregnancy may continue, if the mother has bed rest for the balance of the pregnancy. But if the separation is severe, and heavy bleeding ensues, the baby may need to be delivered immediately, either by induced labor, if possible, or CESAREAN SECTION. Increased risk of abruptio placentae occurs with PREECLAMPSIA, hypertension (high BLOOD PRESSURE), ANEMIA, SMOKING, and sometimes trauma, such as an automobile accident.

The placenta may sometimes be placed abnormally low in the uterus, so that it covers the opening of the CERVIX, a condition called *placenta previa*. Bleeding often results, with possible risk of severe HEMORRHAGE, which can cause life-threatening SHOCK. The woman will often be hospitalized and confined to complete bed rest for as long as possible; the baby is often delivered by cesarean section, especially when the cervix is completely covered. (For help and further information, see PREGNANCY; CHILDBIRTH.)

plantar response, in children and adults, the normal REFLEX of curling the toes, when the foot is firmly stroked on the outside of the sole. In newborns, the normal response is, instead, a flexing upward of the big toe and fanning of the other toes, called BABINSKI'S REFLEX; if this occurs in children and adults, it can indicate brain or spinal cord disorders.

plaque, a mixture of bacteria, saliva, and leftover food that forms a deposit on teeth and eats into the enamel, causing tooth decay, or *caries*. If plaque is not cleaned off routinely, it hardens into a mineral deposit called *calculus* or *tartar*, which the dentist must remove by SCALING. (See TEETH AND DENTAL PROBLEMS; GINGIVITIS.)

plastic surgeon, a PHYSICIAN who specializes in reconstructive or cosmetic surgery to correct damage and defects or to alter appearance. (See PLASTIC SURGERY.)

plastic surgery, surgical operations performed to reconstruct, repair, or alter skin and underlying tissue and bone. When the area has been damaged by injury or disease, such as BURNS or CANCER, it is called *reconstructive surgery*. However, if the work is being done not for medical reasons, but to alter the look and shape of an otherwise normal area, it is called *cosmetic surgery*. Many children are born with CONGENITAL disorders requiring plastic surgery, such as CLEFT LIP AND PALATE, or HYPOSPADIAS. Automobile and other kinds of accidents are also common reasons for plastic surgery on children.

In general, plastic surgeons remove or reshape excess skin, tissue, and cartilage, where appropriate adding skin grafts, using skin drawn from elsewhere on the patient's body, or implants; the cuts are then stitched together in new contours. The aim in general is to give the person as natural and normal a look as possible. Where the deformity is substantial, the surgeon may also need to work on the bony structure underneath, as in cases of *craniofacial* (skull and face) or *maxillofacial* (upper jaw, nose, and cheek) deformities. Traditionally surgeons have worked with the knife, or scalpel; high-intensity light beams called *lasers* are increasingly used in some kinds of surgery, but these must be used with extreme care because they can cause deep, serious damage if misdirected. Implants may be fashioned from the patient's own cartilage or bone, especially in the chin or cheekbones, in cases where the facial skeleton must be reshaped. Some scarring will result, though in some cases the work can be done largely from the inside, as on the nose or cheeks.

Two cosmetic procedures commonly performed on children are:

- *Rhinoplasty*, in which the nasal cartilage, bone, and skin are reshaped, such as to give a smaller, straighter nose, or a differently angled tip.
- *Otoplasty*, in which skin and sometimes cartilage is cut from the back of the ear, generally to make the ears lie flatter to the head. Where a child is born with a missing or malformed outer ear, plastic surgery can create one.

Another common kind of cosmetic surgery, which can affect women in their role as mothers, is breast surgery of various kinds, including:

- *Breast enlargement* (*augmentation mammoplasty*), which involves insertion of implants—sacs filled with a gel or liquid—into the breast. This has traditionally been among the most common types of cosmetic surgery for women, but in recent years health concerns have been raised about the implants. Of greatest concern are those filled with silicone gel, which can rupture and leak the silicone into the body. Many women have charged that they experienced health problems from receiving silicone-gel implants, especially autoimmune disorders (see IMMUNE SYSTEM); research and law suits are pending, and many manufacturers have halted production of implants. A woman considering implants should explore the decision thoroughly with her doctor. The question is not only her own health but possible adverse effects on a child during a future PREGNANCY or BREASTFEEDING. Implants filled with saline solution cause less concern, since saline solution is not harmful to the body, but the implant "envelope" is made of silicone, again with uncertain effects on the body. Also a concern is whether such implants make mammograms ineffective in showing possible cancerous tissue (see BREASTS).
- *Breast reduction* (*reduction mammoplasty*), which involves removing some fat and glandular tissue to lessen the size of uncomfortably large breasts, with the nipple and areola being moved higher. This long and complex procedure leaves scars and may cause loss of sensation in the nipples or wider areas of the breasts; it also bars the possibility of BREASTFEEDING in the future.
- *Breast reconstruction*, which involves rebuilding the breast after a mastectomy (see BREAST CANCER), either using implants or tissue from elsewhere in the woman's own body.
- *Breast lift* (*mastoplexy*), which involves cutting excess skin to reduce sagging, an operation commonly performed after PREGNANCY, when the breast tissue shrinks within its skin "envelope." However, it should be noted that the operation has only temporary effects, especially if a woman is planning another pregnancy.

When approaching plastic surgery, it is wise to keep expectations realistic. No matter how skillful the surgeon, all such surgery will involve some pain and disfigurement (such as swelling or bruises) during the healing process and will result in some permanent scars. Not all surgery is successful, and sometimes further surgery is required, as when an implant shifts out of position. There is also a certain hazard associated with the use of ANESTHESIA. Medical problems can also result, including infection, bleeding, blood clots, nerve damage, fluid accumulation, and loss of feeling in the affected area. Some patients may also develop abnormal scarring, called *keloids*, or capsules of scar tissue may form around implants, in *capsular contracture*. For themselves and their children, parents will need to consider carefully whether the desired changes are sufficiently strong to outweigh the possible risks. They can minimize those risks by having the operation performed by a surgeon who specializes in the procedure (*any* license doctor can perform such surgery, even if not specially trained), and at a HOSPITAL that is geared to handle the type of case involved.

In particular, parents should talk with both surgeon and doctor about how pain will handled (see PAIN AND PAIN TREATMENT); children in particular, but frequently also adults, are often unconscionably undermedicated following surgery (and in the case of children, even *during* surgery). They should also discuss reasonable expectations about the recuperation period and the probable end result, and should avoid any kind of experimental procedure. An informed consent form is generally required, in the case of a minor to be signed by a parent.

FOR HELP AND FURTHER INFORMATION

American Society of Plastic and Reconstructive Surgeons (ASPRS)
444 East Algonquin Road
Arlington Heights, IL 60005
708–228–9900; Plastic Surgery Information Service: 800–635–0635
Fax: 708–228–9131
Dave Fellers, Executive Director
Professional society for plastic surgeons, affiliated with the Plastic Surgery Educational Foundation; provides information and referrals.

FACES—The National Association for the Craniofacially Handicapped
P.O. Box 11082
Chattanooga, TN 37401
615–266–1632
Organization concerned with people who have a face, neck, or face disorder, many of them children; acts as clearinghouse; fosters support groups; provides informa-

tion and referrals to specialized craniofacial centers; offers some financial aid; publishes quarterly newsletter *FACES.*

OTHER RESOURCES

GENERAL WORKS

Reshaping the Female Body: The Dilemma of Cosmetic Surgery. Kathy Davis. Routledge, 1994.

The Work of Human Hands: Surgical Wonder at Children's Hospital. G. Wayne Miller. Random, 1993.

A Complete Guide to Cosmetic Facial Surgery, rev. ed. John A. McCurdy. Lifetime, 1993.

The American Society of Plastic and Reconstructive Surgeons' Guide to Cosmetic Surgery. Josleen Wilson. Simon & Schuster, 1992.

ON BREAST SURGERY AND IMPLANTS

Breast Implants: Everything You Need to Know, 2nd ed. Nancy Bruning. Hunter House, 1995.

You Decide: Every Woman's Guide to Reconstruction, Cosmetic Breast Surgery, and Implants. Neil Handel. Shapolsky, 1994.

The Truth about Breast Implants. Randolph H. Guthrie. Wiley, 1994.

A Woman's Decision: Breast Care, Treatment, and Reconstruction, 2nd ed. Karen Berger and John Bostwick, III. Quality Medical, 1994.

Silicone Breast Implant Controversy: What Women Need to Know Now. Frank B. Vasey and others. Crossing Press, 1993.

Breast Implants: Making Safe Choices. Kathlyn Gay. Macmillan, 1993.

play group, a circle of PRESCHOOL-age children who are gathered together (by their parents or CAREGIVERS) on a fairly regular basis at the home of one child or another, often in rotation, the idea being to help children learn to develop SOCIAL SKILLS by playing with others and to give them the stimulation of new people and activities. Such experience is especially important for children who are otherwise relatively isolated from other children of their age, whether far out in the country, in a suburban home, or a high-rise apartment, including an only child or one with much older SIBLINGS.

Children who have no experience of a play group or preschool program—or the rough-and-tumble of brothers and sisters—before they enter KINDERGARTEN may be at a distinct disadvantage in being able to learn how to be with others and do cooperative activities. On entering school, such children have to deal with normal SEPARATION ANXIETY, rather than at a play group or preschool; that shocking transition may, at least initially, interfere with learning. But children who have siblings at home and others their age nearby may not need any regularly established play group.

Parents are well advised not to push their children into a group if they are made unhappy by it, but to wait for some time to pass and more development to occur. What is "too much too soon" for a child of 2 might be just right for a 3-year-old. (Subscribers to the America Online computer service can find tips for organizing play activities for preschoolers in the Moms Online Desk Reference section of Moms Online, under "Teaching Young Children.")

FOR HELP AND FURTHER INFORMATION

National Association for the Education of Young Children (NAEYC), 800–424–2460. Publishes books *Helping Young Children Develop Through Play: A Practical Guide for Parents, Caregivers, and Teachers, Play in the Lives of Children, Let's Play Outdoors, The Significance of the Young Child's Motor Development, The Block Book, Woodworking for Young Children,* and *Group Games in Early Education: Implications of Piaget's Theory;* brochures *Play Is FUNdamental* and *Toys: Tools for Learning;* and videos *Block Play: Constructing Realities* and *A Classroom with Blocks.* (For full group information, see PRESCHOOL.)

Association for Childhood Education International (ACEI), 800–423–3563. Publishes book *Play: Working Partner of Growth* and position paper *Play: A Necessity for All Children.* (For full group information, see HELP ON LEARNING AND EDUCATION on page 659.)

Pediatric Projects, 800–947–0947. Distributes medically oriented toys, including customized "exceptional animals" such as teddy bears that have scars from open-heart surgery or use wheel chairs; publishes reprints on play: *The Value of Play, Centers of Learning in a Pediatric Playroom, Creative Dramatics Programs in Hospitals, Games and Toys for Children by Age, No Play Permitted: Indicator of Psychological Abuse, Play and the Hospitalized Child, Profoundly Disabled Children Learn by Touch, The Theory Behind Stuffed Animals and Dolls That Have Disabilities, and Ideas on Using Them with Children.* (For full group information, see HOSPITAL.)

Institute for Childhood Resources (INICR), 415–864–1169. Publishes *The Toy Chest: A Sourcebook of Toys for Children* and audiotapes *Tips on Toys.* (For full group information, see CHILD CARE.)

The Children's Foundation (TCF), 202–347–3300. Publishes *Checklist of Toys, Books, and Materials,* guidelines for choosing appropriate materials. (For full group information, see CHILD CARE.)

Parents Helping Parents (PHP), 408–727–5775. Publishes *Where Do I Begin? Integrated Neighborhood Playgroups,* on children with special needs. (For full group information, see HELP FOR SPECIAL CHILDREN on page 689.)

National Mental Health Association (NMHA), 800–969–6642. Publishes pamphlet *Learning Through Play.* (For full group information, see MENTAL DISORDERS.)

Blind Children's Center, 800–222–3566. Publishes *First Steps: A Handbook for Teaching Young Children Who Are*

Visually Impaired and *Learning to Play* and *Dancing Cheek to Cheek*, on early social, play, and language interactions. (For full group information, see EYE AND VISION PROBLEMS.)

National Federation of the Blind (NFB), 410–659–9314. Publishes *Games*. (For full group information, see EYE AND VISION PROBLEMS.)

OTHER RESOURCES

Playing Around: Activities and Exercises for Social and Cooperative Learning. Susan Rose and Susan Humphries. Forbes, 1994.
Playful Parenting: Turning the Dilemma of Discipline into Fun and Games. Denise Chapman Weston and Mark S. Weston. Tarcher, 1993.
The House of Make-Believe: Children's Play and the Developing Imagination. Dorothy G. Singer and Jerome L. Singer. Harvard University Press, 1992.
Children, Play, and Development. Fergus P. Hughes. Allyn, 1991.

BACKGROUND WORKS

Toys, Play, and Child Development. Jeffrey H. Goldstein, ed. Cambridge University Press, 1994.
Children's Play in Diverse Cultures. Jaipaul L. Roopnarine and others, eds. State University of New York Press, 1994.
The Development of Play. David Cohen. Routledge, 1993.
Parent-Child Play: Descriptions and Implications. Kevin MacDonald, ed. State University of New York Press, 1993.

(See also PRESCHOOL.)

PLUS Loans/Supplemental Loans for Students (SLS), a federally SUBSIDIZED LOAN program under which banks, credit unions, or other financial institutions lend parents or students money for educational expenses, in addition to other loans, such as STAFFORD LOANS. PLUS Loans are taken out and meant to be repaid by parents, while SLS loans are taken out and meant to be repaid by students. Borrowers sign promissory notes; PLUS loan amounts are paid directly to parents, while SLS loans are paid either directly to the student, or to both student and school, sometimes in installments. Amounts available are up to $4000 a year, to a total of $20,000, in addition to Stafford Loans. However, in no case can this be more than the actual cost of the education, minus any other FINANCIAL AID the student receives. Interest varies yearly, and an insurance premium of up to 3 percent may be charged. Payments begin within 60 days after the last installment of the loan was paid, but principal payments may be deferred in certain circumstances. (For further information, see SUBSIDIZED LOAN.)

pneumothorax or pneumomediastinum, leakage of air into the chest area around the lungs. While small air leaks are common and not of great concern, severe air leaks can be life-threatening, exposing the lungs to infection. Such leaks are often associated with treatment for RESPIRATORY DISTRESS SYNDROME.

polio, a severe, highly contagious disease, more formally called *poliomyelitis*; it is caused by a virus that inhabits the nose, throat, and intestinal tract, and is spread from person to person, sometimes by affected people, but sometimes by unaffected CARRIERS. In mild cases, which might last only a few days, people with polio have fever, sore throat, nausea, HEADACHE, stomach ache, and often pain and stiffness in the neck, back, and legs. More severe cases, called *paralytic polio*, start the same way, but often involve severe muscle pain and PARALYSIS as soon as the first week. About half of the people with paralytic polio recover with only mild—sometimes no—DISABILITIES, but the rest may suffer permanent paralysis and occasionally even death.

Adults who remember the days before the 1954 discovery of the first polio VACCINE by Jonas Salk recall the fear among parents of young children, as epidemics of polio swept many regions, leaving many children disabled and dependent on ORTHOPEDIC DEVICES for mobility, and often RESPIRATORS ("iron lungs") for breathing. The Salk vaccine is also called the *inactivated polio vaccine* (IPV), because it is made from killed polio viruses; it is given as a series of injections to children between ages 2 months and 6 years. It is not known to produce any side effects other than minor local pain and redness.

However, the most commonly used polio vaccine today is the *oral polio vaccine* (OPV), or *Sabin vaccine*. which is made from live polio viruses. It is preferred because it is easier to store and administer, generally given by mouth in several doses, currently recommended at two months, four months, fifteen months, and four to six years. It also is more effective in the intestinal tract (where infection first occurs) and in preventing the spread of the polio virus, conferring lifelong immunity on more than 90 percent of those receiving the OPV vaccine.

On extremely rare occasions, the live viruses used in the Sabin vaccine can induce polio (in an estimated 1 person in every 7.8 million doses), especially after the first dose, and especially among people with abnormally low resistance to infections, and in adults. The live viruses can also spread from the immunized person to others (estimated at once in every 5.5 million doses) and actually produce polio. Even though the risk is very small, where a child or family member has low resistance to serious infection, the Salk vaccine may be given instead. The American Academy of Pediatrics (AAP) has also recommended that doctors administer the IPV when parents have a strong preference for that form of the vaccine.

Fortunately, use of these vaccines have made cases of polio extremely rare in those parts of the world, such as the United States, where immunization is widespread. Polio immunization is required by all 50 states in the U.S. for children entering or attending school.

FOR HELP AND FURTHER INFORMATION

National Institute of Allergy and Infectious Diseases (NIAID), 301–496–5717. (For full group information, see ALLERGIES.)

National Institute of Child Health and Human Development (NICHD), 301–496–5133. (For full group information, see PREGNANCY.)

March of Dimes Birth Defects Foundation (MDBDF), 914–428–7100. Publishes information sheets *Polio* and *Post Polio.* (For full group information, see BIRTH DEFECTS.)

National Easter Seal Society, 800–221–6827. Publishes *Understanding Post Polio Syndrome.* (For full group information, see HELP FOR SPECIAL CHILDREN on page 689.)

Gazette International Networking Institute (GINI), 314–534–0475. Publishes quarterly *Polio Network News,* annual *Post-Polio Directory,* and *Handbook on the Late Effects of Poliomyelitis for Physicians and Survivors.* (For full group information, see HELP FOR SPECIAL CHILDREN on page 689.)

Accent, 800–787–8444. Publishes *Post Polio.* (For full group information, see HELP FOR SPECIAL CHILDREN on page 689.)

National Organization for Rare Disorders (NORD), 800–999–6673. (For full group information, see RARE DISORDERS.)

(See also HELP FOR SPECIAL CHILDREN on page 689.)

polydactyly (polydactylism, polydactylia, or hyperdactly), a BIRTH DEFECT in which a baby is born with extra fingers and/or toes, either fully formed digits or small stumps. The condition, which in the United States affects approximately 1 baby in every 2000 births, is often corrected by surgery soon after birth. Polydactyly is often a GENETIC DISORDER, of the AUTOSOMAL DOMINANT type, but it may also be associated with LAURENCE-MOON-BIEDEL SYNDROME.

FOR HELP AND FURTHER INFORMATION

National Institute of Child Health and Human Development (NICHD), 301–496–5133. (For full group information, see PREGNANCY.)

postsecondary education, any formal education beyond HIGH SCHOOL (secondary school), usually referring to undergraduate and postgraduate college programs, but sometimes also including a wide range of nondegree programs for continuing education adults, including special programs for people with DISABILITIES.

postmature, referring to an infant born at 42 weeks or more—that is, two or more weeks after the DUE DATE, normally calculated as 40 weeks from the beginning of the woman's last MENSTRUATION. Postmaturity is a problem because the PLACENTA, which nourishes the developing FETUS, no longer does its job as efficiently late in the PREGNANCY, after about the 30th week. The child may be larger boned than average and have less moldable bones because of the longer development. Indeed largeness itself is sometimes a cause of postmaturity, since the baby's head may be too big to descend properly. All of these factors can make DELIVERY difficult, with a greater possibility of attendant damage; the risk of STILLBIRTH is much increased by the forty-third and forty-fourth weeks of pregnancy. To avoid this, doctors often act by the 42nd week to either induce LABOR (if appropriate) or to perform a CESAREAN SECTION. The baby itself will often look gaunt, since FAT has been lost from the body, and have wrinkled, peeling skin and long fingernails. There is often considerable imbalance in the key MINERALS in the blood, notably CALCIUM and POTASSIUM, which need correction, to prevent SEIZURES and possible neurological damage. (For help and further information, see PREGNANCY.)

postnatal care (postpartal care), medical care of mother and newborn in the first few days to six weeks after birth. In a normal birth, this is the period in which BONDING takes place between infant and MOTHER (and FATHER), starting immediately after CHILDBIRTH. After one or more days, the baby usually is able to go home with the parents. However, if the baby was PREMATURE, was of LOW BIRTH WEIGHT, or has special medical problems, he or she may need to be placed in a NEONATAL INTENSIVE CARE UNIT (NICU). Then parents may need to make special arrangements to go to the hospital to be with the child, for bonding and stimulation of the child. For the mother, the main medical hazards in the postpartal period are possible infection or HEMORRHAGE, along with possible POSTPARTUM DEPRESSION. The baby's health and development are monitored by a series of WELL-BABY EXAMINATIONS. Care offered in the first 28 days after the birth may also be called PERINATAL CARE.

In many parts of the country, HEALTH CARE plans and HEALTH INSURANCE plans, seeking to keep down medical costs, have been covering only one day's hospital stay for the woman after the birth, sometimes sending her home within just a few hours. Many doctors and hospitals have protested this practice, saying that it gives mothers too little time to recover and to receive counseling on BREASTFEEDING and early infant care, and that it gives hospitals too little time to assess mothers and infants for possible health problems. Several states have passed laws mandating that health plans cover at least two days in hospital after childbirth, and at least one hospital has made a policy to provide two days of post-pregnancy care, whether or not the woman's health plan covers it. (For help and further information, see PERINATAL CARE; PREMATURE BABIES.)

FOR HELP AND FURTHER INFORMATION

American College of Obstetricians and Gynecologists (ACOG), 202–638–5577. Publishes *You and Your Baby: Prenatal Care, Labor and Delivery, and Postpartum Care.* (For full group information, see PREGNANCY.)

National Institute of Child Health and Human Development (NICHD), 301–496–5133. Publishes *Neonatal Intensive Care: A History of Excellence.* (For full group information, see PREGNANCY.)

New Parents' Network, 520–327–1451. Offers information (through telecommunications services) on early childhood parenting. (For full group information, see GENERAL PARENTING RESOURCES on page 634.)

OTHER RESOURCES

A Doctor Discusses Your Life After the Baby Is Born. Paul Neimark and others. Budlong, 1991.
After the Baby Is Born: A Complete Postpartum Guide for New Parents. Carl Jones. Holt, 1990.
After the Baby's Birth: A Woman's Way to Wellness. Robin Lim. Celestial Arts, 1990.

(See also GENERAL PARENTING RESOURCES on page 634.)

postpartum depression, a form of DEPRESSION common among women after CHILDBIRTH. Among women who have just given birth, perhaps two or three of every four experience some form of "baby blues" and feeling of letdown some days after delivery; generally this is a mild, short-lived condition, involving mood swings, crying, impatience, restlessness, anxiety, irritability, and just plain feeling miserable, It is apparently triggered by the great hormonal changes that occur in the body after PREGNANCY, as well as broken sleep and stress at dealing with the massive lifestyle changes that accompany a new child.

For approximately 1 woman in 10, the blues are sufficiently severe or persistent to be called *postpartum depression,* and may occur soon after delivery or up to a year later. Additional symptoms include confusion, poor concentration, memory loss, panic, uncontrollable crying, excess fatigue or exhaustion, more exaggerated mood swings, insomnia, feelings of inadequacy or worthlessness, lack of interest in—or conversely overconcern for—the baby, and lack of interest in sex. In the most severe cases, occurring in perhaps one woman in a thousand, and usually appearing suddenly and shortly after birth, symptoms become so severe—sometimes involving hallucinations, bizarre behavior, and fears of committing SUICIDE or harming the baby—that they constitute what is called *postpartum psychosis* or *puerperal psychosis.*

Whatever the severity, postpartum depressions can be treated with drugs, counseling, and therapy; sometimes temporary hospitalization may be required. Many women find support and relief by talking with family and friends, or by sharing their experiences with others in SELF-HELP GROUPS, such as those below.

Women AT RISK for experiencing postpartum depression are those with a family or personal history of depression or other mental disorders; those who experienced CHILD ABUSE AND NEGLECT as a child; those in difficult or unsupportive marriages; and those who have had a difficult or somehow unusual CHILDBIRTH. Some evidence also suggests a connection between postpartum depression and low activity of the THYROID GLAND. (See also DEPRESSION.)

FOR HELP AND FURTHER INFORMATION

Depression after Delivery (DAD)
P.O. Box 1282
Morrisville, PA 19067
215–295–3994; 800–944–4PPD [944–4773]
Nancy Berchtold, Founder
Organization concerned with postpartum depression (PPD); provides information and referrals; publishes newsletter *Heart-Strings*; book *The New Mother Syndrome*; brochure *Feelings after Birth: Postpartum Adjustment*; information packets for new mothers and fathers, attorneys, health professionals, and people wishing to start a PPD support group; and transcripts such as *Having Another Child After Postpartum Illness.*

Postpartum Support International (PSI)
927 North Kellogg Avenue
Santa Barbara, CA 93111
805–967–7636
Fax: 805–967–0608
Jane Honikman, Executive Director
Organization concerned with mental health of women after childbearing; fosters support groups; maintains lending library; publishes quarterly *PSI News* and *Postpartum Mood and Anxiety Disorder: A Research Guide and International Bibliography.*

American College of Obstetricians and Gynecologists (ACOG), 202–638–5577. Publishes *Postpartum Depression.* (For full group information, see PREGNANCY.)

OTHER RESOURCES

This Isn't What I Expected: Recognizing and Recovering from Depression and Anxiety after Childbirth. Karen R. Kleima and Valerie D. Raskin. Bantam, 1994.
Banish the Post-Baby Blues: All the Advice, Support and Encouragement You Need to Cope with Post-Natal Depression. Anne-Marie Sapsted. Thorsons, 1990.

(See also DEPRESSION; MENTAL DISORDERS.)

post-traumatic stress disorder (PTSD), a pattern of ANXIETY-related symptoms found in people who have had frightening or stressful experiences, such as RAPE, CHILD ABUSE AND NEGLECT, military combat, concentration camps, earthquakes, or other mass disasters. Symptoms commonly include reliving the experiences in daydreams or nightmares, other sleep disorders, a sense of separation and lack of responsiveness to others, DEPRESSION, disorders in memory and concentration, and exaggerated startle responses. If many or most others died in the experience, the disorder is often called *survivor syndrome,* and involves strong guilt at having survived. Children (and adults) who have survived a car crash, fire, or airplane accident in which many or most others died are often given special counseling to help them deal with the questions of death and their own survival. If PTSD stems from military situations, it is sometimes called *battle fatigue* or *shell shock.* With emotional support and counseling, many people are able to recover their "sense of balance," but in some people the experience can last for months, years, or a lifetime, sometimes being retriggered by reminders of the event.

FOR HELP AND FURTHER INFORMATION

National Institute of Mental Health (NIMH), 301–443–4513. (For full group information, see MENTAL DISORDERS.)

OTHER RESOURCES

Unchained Memories: True Stories of Traumatic Memory Loss. Lenore Terr. Basic Books, 1994.
The Trauma Response: Treatment for Emotional Injury. Diane S. Everstine and Louis Everstine. Norton, 1993.
Trauma and Recovery: The Aftermath of Violence—From Domestic Abuse to Political Terror. Judith L. Herman. Basic Books, 1992.
Post-Traumatic Stress Disorder: The Victim's Guide to Healing and Recovery. Raymond B. Flannery, Jr. Crossroad, 1992.
Prisoners of the Past: Overcoming Post-Traumatic Stress Disorder. Howard *Levine.* PIA Press, 1992.
Too Scared to Cry: Psychic Trauma in Childhood. Lenore Terr. Harper & Row, 1990.

(See also CHILD ABUSE AND NEGLECT.)

postural drainage, a physical therapy technique used for patients with CYSTIC FIBROSIS and other kinds of disorders that obstruct the air passages. The patient's chest is "pounded" to dislodge mucus and the body is positioned so that gravity will help the mucus drain from the body.

potassium, a MINERAL that is vital to maintaining the body's normal heart rhythm, water balance, and functioning of nerves and muscles, often working in combination with SODIUM and CALCIUM. Potassium is found in many foods, but especially good sources are orange juice, bananas, dried fruits, peanut butter, and potatoes. Too little potassium (*hypokalemia*) can cause muscle weakness and irregular heartbeat; it is associated with loss of body fluids through VOMITING and DIARRHEA, and is especially common in children, with DIABETES and Cushing's syndrome (see ADRENAL GLANDS). Too much (*hyperkalemia*), as from taking excess potassium supplements or from KIDNEY AND UROLOGICAL PROBLEMS, can also cause heart irregularities and even cardiac arrest. (For help and further information, see MINERALS; NUTRITION.)

power of attorney, a formal written document, also called a *letter of attorney,* in which one person (the *principal*) gives another (the *attorney in fact*) the power to act in place of the principal. It can cover a single named situation, as in a specific property transfer; or certain kinds of specified situations, as in named kinds of financial transactions or medical situations; or be more general, covering an unlimited range of business and personal decisions. It can cover a range of times, from a brief specified time period to a lifetime, or could come into effect only after a specified occurrence, such as legal incapacity.

A *durable* power of attorney continues in effect even after the principal has become incapacitated (see ADVANCE DIRECTIVE). Parents of children who are no longer MINORS but are unable to care for themselves (such as adults with MENTAL RETARDATION or other severe DISABILITIES) may wish to draw up a durable power of attorney, giving the person of their choice power to act in case the parents become incapacitated, as through illness. Without such a power of attorney, the court would appoint a CONSERVATOR to act. (For help and further information, see ADVANCE DIRECTIVE.)

precollege program, a program that specifically prepares a student for COLLEGE, often a student who has some DISABILITIES or educational deficiencies that require some special training to reach college entry level; sometimes a general term referring to any formal education below college level.

preeclampsia, a condition affecting women late in PREGNANCY, generally after the 20th week, in about 5–7 percent of all pregnancies. Symptoms include *hypertension* (high BLOOD PRESSURE), EDEMA (fluid buildup), and PROTEIN in the urine (*proteinuria*), as well as more general symptoms such as headache, nausea, VOMITING, abdominal pain, and blurred vision. If unchecked, however, preeclampsia can cause severe disorders in both mother and child, especially separation of the PLACENTA (*abruptio placentae*), which cuts off nourishment to the fetus, and ECLAMPSIA, which can threaten the life of both. (Preeclampsia and eclampsia are sometimes considered a mild and more severe form of a disorder called *toxemia of pregnancy.*)

Preeclampsia is most common in first pregnancies, in women under twenty and over forty, and in those with personal or family history of related disorders, including DIABETES or KIDNEY AND UROLOGICAL PROBLEMS. Good

NUTRITION, rest, and regular EXERCISE lessen the risk of the disorder. PRENATAL CARE includes regular screening for signs of preeclampsia, which is normally treated with bed rest and drugs to bring down blood pressure. In severe cases, hospitalization and intravenous blood pressure medication may be advised; and once the mother's condition has been stabilized, emergency delivery may be necessary, as through induction of LABOR or CESAREAN SECTION. Causes of preeclampsia are unknown; its effects diminish after the pregnancy ends, though some damage may have been done. (For help and further information, see PREGNANCY.)

pregnancy, the growth of a new being in a woman's body, and the changes the body makes in order to carry out its reproductive functions, from the moment of FERTILIZATION—the union of a woman's egg (OVUM) and a man's SPERM—to the baby's emergence, normally some nine months later, as a fully formed individual. In size, the new being will grow from a speck smaller than the dot on this letter "i" to a baby approximately 20 inches long and weighing 7 to 8 pounds.

Growth takes an average of 266 days, a period known as GESTATION or *full term.* However, because the precise date of fertilization is generally unknown or uncertain, doctors traditionally calculate the *due date* or *delivery date* from the woman's *last menstrual period* (LMP). This is often two weeks before fertilization, so gestation is generally considered to be 9⅓ months, 40 weeks, or 280 days. Changes occur daily, but in general the term of pregnancy is divided into three periods of three months each, called *trimesters.* (For an overview of what occurs when, see WHAT HAPPENS DURING PREGNANCY on page 472.)

Fertilization normally takes place in the woman's FALLOPIAN TUBES, with the resulting ZYGOTE then traveling into the UTERUS (womb) for IMPLANTATION, where it grows. After implantation the developing being is called an EMBRYO and, after approximately eight weeks, a FETUS. If implantation takes place outside the uterus, it is called an ECTOPIC PREGNANCY, and is a potentially life-threatening condition. Usually the sperm and egg come together as a result of sexual intercourse, but where a couple has INFERTILITY problems, a variety of REPRODUCTIVE TECHNOLOGY methods might be used to achieve conception, including ARTIFICIAL INSEMINATION, IN VITRO FERTILIZATION, GAMETE INTRAFALLOPIAN TRANSFER (GIFT), EGG DONATION, EMBRYO TRANSFER, surrogate births (see SURROGATE MOTHER), and newer ASSISTED FERTILIZATION approaches, including INTRACYTOPLASMIC SPERM INJECTION (ICSI), PARTIAL ZONA DISSECTION (PZD), and SUBZONAL SPERM INSERTION (SZI), as well as ASSISTED HATCHING.

The first sign of possible pregnancy is often a missed menstrual period, though MENSTRUATION can temporarily cease for other reasons, and some menstrual bleeding can occur early in pregnancy. Sore or tender BREASTS, nausea, VOMITING, heartburn, reflux of stomach acids, frequent urination, fatigue, weight gain, swelling of the abdomen, and EDEMA (fluid buildup) are also common signs in early pregnancy. A woman who is using the *basal body temperature method* as part of NATURAL FAMILY PLANNING will notice that her temperature remains high, if she is pregnant.

The most reliable signs of pregnancy, however, are the presence of certain HORMONES in the blood or urine; these are used as the basis of PREGNANCY TESTS, either done in a medical laboratory through a doctor or clinic, or with a HOME MEDICAL TEST. Most home tests involve urine testing, but blood testing done by doctors is generally considered more reliable, especially for older women. In the publication *Prenatal Care,* the Public Health Service recommends: "It is important to have a pregnancy test as soon as possible after you miss your first period or as soon as you think you might be pregnant. Some tests can be done as early as a few days after a single missed period." The PHS also recommends that, if you use a do-it-yourself test, you see your doctor *whatever* the result, if the missed period does not arrive, since that can signal health problems, some of them quite serious, such as ectopic pregnancy.

Early testing is important because the first two to three months of the baby's development are crucial. The sooner a woman knows she is pregnant, the sooner she can take steps to maximize her chances of having a healthy baby and to minimize risks to herself (see PRENATAL CARE). Among other things, she will want to:

- Stop any activities that could damage the fetus, such as SMOKING, drinking alcohol, taking drugs (medical or "recreational") that might cause BIRTH DEFECTS, exposure to ENVIRONMENTAL HAZARDS such as radiation or poisons, and potentially dangerous EXERCISES or SPORTS activities such as ski-jumping.
- Modify her diet so that she provides sufficient NUTRITION for herself and her baby. (See NUTRITION for a recommended diet during pregnancy.)
- Identify and take steps to treat any health problems that might affect the pregnancy, such as high BLOOD PRESSURE; DIABETES; SEXUALLY TRANSMITTED DISEASES such as GONORRHEA, SYPHILIS, and HERPES; blood disorders such as ANEMIA or RH INCOMPATIBILITY; PREECLAMPSIA; and lack of immunity to RUBELLA (German measles).

As part of prenatal care, physicians will also check the woman's general health and advise on how to prepare for the pregnancy.

Prenatal care concerns itself not only with the baby's healthy development but also with the mother's long-term health, because pregnancy is not risk-free (see MATERNAL MORTALITY for a discussion of the hazards to pregnant women). Beyond mortality risk, pregnancy takes a toll on the body. The old saw "For every baby, a woman loses a tooth" is not true, but a woman can increase the likelihood of long-term health problems, such as OSTEOPOROSIS, if she has too many children too close together, has irreversible damage from pregnancy-related illnesses, or fails to have adequate nutrition, since the body will deplete her

What Happens During Pregnancy

At the start, the fertilized egg formed by the union of egg (OVUM) and SPERM is no larger than the dot over this letter "i." This new being will normally grow for about nine months, a period known as GESTATION. Changes take place every day, but traditionally gestation is divided into three periods of three months, called *trimesters.*

FIRST TRIMESTER

This is the most critical period of a pregnancy. During this first three months, the new being will grow to about three inches long and one ounce in weight, and will develop all major organs, though these will not be usable for independent functioning for many months yet. Alcohol and drugs (see alcohol abuse; drug abuse), smoking, medications (including birth control pills and spermicides), environmental hazards such as radiation or toxic chemicals, poor nutrition, untreated illnesses and diseases—these and many other influences can harm a baby for life. That is why a woman should avoid such influences if she even suspects a pregnancy, and should quickly schedule pregnancy tests and, if positive, prenatal care. In case of birth defects or genetic disorders so severe as to be incompatible with life, a pregnancy may end spontaneously shortly after it begins, often without a woman even knowing it. The new being's genetic inheritance is determined at the point of fertilization.

During the first trimester, the mother will begin to experience the early signs of pregnancy. These include MORNING SICKNESS or nausea; tenderness and heaviness in the BREASTS, as glands develop for their milk-producing function; darkening and sensitivity of the nipples; frequent urination, partly triggered by hormonal changes; a weight gain of 3 to 4 pounds, usually around the waist, as the body begins to build up reserves; and lethargy and tiredness, partly due to sleeplessness from the hormonal changes, and partly from the HORMONES themselves.

FIRST MONTH

As soon as FERTILIZATION takes place, the fertilized egg begins to grow through division of its cells, slowly moving down the Fallopian tubes and into the UTERUS. There, within roughly a week, it implants itself in the uterine wall and begins to grow. Many health professionals regard that pregnancy only starts at the point of implantation, and that so-called "morning after" pills act as neither CONTRACEPTION nor ABORTION, but as "interception." During implantation, some blood may be released, which can be mistaken for a period. Hormonal changes triggered by implantation are assessed in many early pregnancy tests.

Shortly after implantation, the AMNIOTIC SAC begins to form around the developing being, now generally called an EMBRYO. This sac gradually fills with amniotic fluid, which cushions the embryo from injury and pressure. This first trimester also sees the development of the special tissue called the PLACENTA, which supplies nourishment to the embryo, and the UMBILICAL CORD, which carries nourishment to and waste products away from the embryo. It is samples of fluid or tissue from these organs that are examined in PRENATAL TESTS such as AMNIOCENTESIS and CHORIONIC VILLUS SAMPLING. By the end of this first month, the head (including nose, mouth, and wide-apart fish-like eyes), heart, lungs, brain, spinal column, and GENITALS are beginning to develop, and the tiny heart is beating.

SECOND MONTH

During this month, the embryo comes to be known as a FETUS, a word meaning "young one" or "offspring." Arms and legs are developing from "limb buds," forming tiny hands, fingers, elbows, knees, ankles, and toes. Internal organs such as the stomach and liver are developing. The head is growing very large, compared to the rest of the body, and is developing tiny ears and the beginnings of hair on the head.

THIRD MONTH

Fingernails and toenails are developing, as are external signs of the new being's sex. Movements of the hands, legs, and head, including opening and closing of the mouth, can be seen on ULTRASOUND, though not yet felt by the mother.

The mother will generally feel warmer than usual, since the heart will have increased its cir-

(continued)

(continued)

culation by about one-third, to supply the uterus and fetus; her heart and metabolic rate are also higher. Her clothes will feel a little tight, as fat reserves are laid down, not only in the midsection but also in the arms and thighs.

SECOND TRIMESTER

During these three months, many of the minor discomforts of pregnancy will disappear, and pregnant women often feel very good physically. They will often gain 3 to 4 pounds during each of these months, and during the fourth month they will usually begin to "show" and to feel more comfortable in maternity clothes, including a maternity bra. The fetus's heartbeat can be heard through a special instrument called a fetoscope (see fetoscopy). If she has not done so already, the mother will want to make her final decisions as to various childbirth options during this trimester.

Fourth Month

Growing fast, the fetus weighs about six ounces and reaches about eight to ten inches long by the end of the month, and is beginning to develop sucking and swallowing reflexes. The umbilical cord continues to develop, to provide enough blood and nourishment. During this month, the mother usually feels a slight fluttering or "bubbling" sensation in the lower abdomen; this is the first felt movement of the baby, called *quickening*. The mother should write down the date she first feels this movement, as it helps the doctor to determine the due date.

Fifth Month

By the end of this month, the fetus will weigh about a pound and be about a foot long. The heartbeat can be strongly heard, and movements are more definitely felt. Nipples grow darker and wider, as breasts prepare to make milk. Many women will begin to breathe more deeply and more frequently during this period.

Sixth Month

By the end of this sixth month, the second trimester, the fetus is a fully formed baby, about 1½ pounds and 14 inches long. It needs much more growth and development, but if born prematurely has a chance to survive with special care. Skin is red and wrinkled, with virtually no fat underneath the skin. Movements can be felt more regularly, and the baby can be seen to suck its thumb. The mother may develop a backache from the weight gain and pressure of the pregnancy. Low-heeled shoes provide balance and comfort; exercises can also help. (See Basic Exercises for During and After Pregnancy on page 634.)

THIRD TRIMESTER

This is the time during which the baby completes its growth and the development of its internal systems, such as the heart and circulatory system and the respiratory system. With the growth, the mother will generally experience discomfort from pressure on the stomach and bladder. Smaller meals and more frequent urination can ease symptoms. She herself will be gaining another 3 to 4 pounds a month. During this period, if not before, the mother should be making final preparations for the arrival of the baby. She will need to decide whether she will be breastfeeding or bottlefeeding, and provide the necessaries for each; she will also want to gather together the things she will want to take with her to delivery (see Before Delivery: What to Pack for the Hospital on page 309).

Seventh Month

The baby grows to about 2 to 2½ pounds and 15 inches long, and may suck its thumb, cry, and respond to external stimuli. The volume of fluid in the amniotic sac begins to decline, as does the nourishing function of the placenta. The baby becomes stronger and more active, as it kicks, stretches, and changes position, with movements that can sometimes even be seen on the abdomen. If born during this month, the baby has a relatively good chance of surviving. Women will often experience some swelling of the ankles from fluid retention, which can be eased by propping the feet up during the day or lying down.

Eighth Month

With its eyes now open, the baby has grown to about 4 to 5 pounds and 16 to 18 inches long. Most organs and systems are well-developed, except for the lungs; this can cause problems

(continued)

(continued)

with premature birth, but a baby born now has an excellent chance of surviving. During most of the pregnancy, the fetus is in a head-up position in the uterus, but often during this month, the baby changes to a head-down position in preparation for birth, though some do not adopt an ideal position (see FETAL PRESENTATION). If she has not done so already, the mother will want to stop any heavy lifting or other work that causes strain, and may want to take rest periods during the day, if possible.

NINTH MONTH

As birth approaches, the baby settles further down in the mother's pelvis, the action being described as the baby "dropping" (see LABOR). Once this takes place, the mother will often feel more comfortable, and especially be able to breathe easier, though pressure on the bladder may increase the need for frequent urination and can cause INCONTINENCE. A baby born in the ninth month—that is, 36 to 40 weeks from the mother's last menstrual period (LMP)—is considered to be a "full-term" baby, generally 19 to 20 inches long and weighing 6 to 9 pounds.

A baby born before the ninth month is described as *premature.* Why early birth occurs is unclear, but the risk of premature delivery is increased in adolescent pregnancies, with poor NUTRITION, and with SMOKING, ALCOHOL ABUSE, and DRUG ABUSE. Sometimes drugs may be administered to try to stop premature labor. On the other hand labor may sometimes be induced prematurely because the health of infant or mother is endangered, as in cases of PREECLAMPSIA or DIABETES. Because their organs are small and not fully developed, premature babies have various health problems and in the past many died; however, with modern medical technology, approximately four out of five babies born after 28 weeks of development can be saved, and even some babies born after 23 weeks and weighing under two pounds have survived.

A baby born after 42 weeks or more is called *postmature.* Because the placenta works less efficiently late in pregnancy, the baby will generally look gaunt, and have wrinkled, peeling skin since much fat has been lost from the body. The baby may also have serious chemical imbalances in the blood, especially of the minerals calcium and potassium, which require immediate treatment, to prevent neurological damage. A postmature birth is more difficult and damaging for the mother, because the child is larger and its bones less moldable than normal. Risk of STILLBIRTH is increased. To avoid such problems, doctors will often induce labor or perform a CESAREAN SECTION by the 42nd week of gestation.

After the birth, the woman's blood and fluid volume returns to normal prepregnancy levels. The uterus also returns to normal size, although the breasts remain enlarged as long as the woman is lactating, which will continue until she stops breastfeeding. The stores of body fat accumulated during pregnancy also are gradually used up; this takes place most readily if the woman is breastfeeding, and can be complete by the time the nursing infant is six months old.

own reserves to provide for the baby. These are special concerns for teenage women, who have not yet completed their own physical growth, which may be limited by the drain on the body's reserves during pregnancy.

Because many of these questions are so important, couples who are planning a pregnancy in advance are well advised to take many of the above steps some weeks or months ahead of the planned time of conception, so that both mother and father are in top physical condition, and the baby is not exposed to dangers before a woman even realizes she is pregnant. A woman may want to start getting physically fit before conceiving, for example, because doctors recommend against starting any new exercise regimen once pregnancy has been confirmed. (See EXERCISE for general advice on exercise during pregnancy; see also BASIC EXERCISES FOR DURING AND AFTER PREGNANCY on page 634.) Similarly, if the prospective mother or father are normally exposed to radiation (as pilots or flight attendants, for example) or chemicals, they may want to move to different work temporarily before conceiving.

Another area that couples will want to explore, either as soon as pregnancy is confirmed or suspected, or even better beforehand, is whether they or anyone in their families has any history of GENETIC DISORDERS, CHROMOSOMAL ABNORMALITIES, or difficulties with pregnancy, such as MISCARRIAGES or STILLBIRTHS. If so, they may want to seek GENETIC COUNSELING (see separate entry) to assess the risk of their having similar problems in a pregnancy.

Once a pregnancy is confirmed, couples may want to consider various kinds of PRENATAL TESTS or GENETIC SCREENING tests to see if the fetus has any identifiable health problems. Among these tests are AMNIOCENTESIS, ALPHA FETO-PROTEIN, CHORIONIC VILLUS SAMPLING, and ULTRASOUND scans. Some kinds of problems can now be corrected in the womb, as through IN UTERO SURGERY. With other kinds of problems, couples may be faced with difficult choices if a child is diagnosed as having a serious genetic disorder. Some will decide to bear the child, in which case the test will have given them time to prepare for the child's SPECIAL NEEDS. Others may choose to have an elective ABORTION. If abortion is being considered, the sooner such testing is done the better, within the optimum time recommended for each test.

Not all pregnancies are planned, or even wanted, of course. Because ADOLESCENT PREGNANCY is so common today—in the United States, involving 1 in 8 pregnancies—many people think of unexpected pregnancies primarily in terms of young, unmarried women, but they can occur in women of any age or marital status. Unplanned does not necessarily mean unwanted, but it does mean that the woman, or the couple, is going to have a major, unexpected life-style change. There can be many situations in which the woman or couple feels unable to cope with having a child, such as when the woman herself is still a teenager, still growing, without job skills, and often unmarried and still dependent on parents; when she or they have not yet completed HIGH SCHOOL or COLLEGE education; when the family has experienced abuse and she fears to bring into the world another child who may be abused; when the pregnancy is the result of sexual abuse (see RAPE; INCEST; CHILD ABUSE AND NEGLECT); when she or they already have more children they can feed and provide for; when a woman is not making enough money at her job to provide for a baby, as a single parent, without going on welfare; or when she fears that a pregnancy will break into and limit her career. In some cases of unwanted or crisis pregnancy, the couple or the mother alone decides not to keep the baby, and then faces the difficult choice of having an ABORTION or placing the child for ADOPTION, both of which can be traumatic in their way. Various organizations exist to help women in such difficult situations, often working confidentially (see ABORTION; ADOPTION).

But where the mother is going to bear the child, a number of decisions have to be made. First, and most basic, who will be the basic health care provider during the pregnancy, such as an OBSTETRICIAN-GYNECOLOGIST, FAMILY PRACTICE PRACTITIONER, CERTIFIED NURSE-MIDWIFE, or a clinic. Who is chosen depends partly on personal attitudes and partly on medical concerns. If the mother is under age twenty or above thirty to thirty-five, if she or the fetus has any medical problems, if too little time has elapsed since a previous pregnancy, or if this is a MULTIPLE BIRTH, for example, hers would be considered a HIGH-RISK PREGNANCY. In that case, she is generally advised to be under the care of a MATERNAL AND FETAL SPECIALIST, who specializes in handling high-risk births, and plan to deliver in a relatively sophisticated (Level II or III) HOSPITAL.

Women who do not fall into the high-risk group have other options. They may choose to have their child in a community hospital, at a MATERNITY CENTER, or even in a HOME BIRTH. Closely connected with these choices is the kind of delivery the parents envision, which may range from a high-tech birth in a hospital, using all the painkillers (*analgesics*), ANESTHESIA, and sophisticated equipment available, to a kind of PREPARED CHILDBIRTH, which tries to avoid medical intervention unless absolutely necessary, in favor of a more natural approach.

When investigating possible health-care providers and hospitals, parents will want to find those who agree with them on issues they feel strongly about, such as prepared childbirth, BREASTFEEDING or BOTTLEFEEDING, CIRCUMCISION or not, the father's presence or participation in the DELIVERY ROOM, ROOMING-IN, and prenatal classes. Among the questions the Public Health Service recommends couples consider in choosing health-care providers are:

- Their reputation with other patients and physicians.
- Their office hours and location of the office and the hospital.
- Their fees.
- The couple's feelings of well-being during the first few visits.

The couple will want to explore their options carefully and make their decisions early, so they have consistent follow-through from whichever health-care provider they choose and can, if desired, plan to take prepared childbirth classes, especially if the father is going to be the BIRTH PARTNER. Parents will also want to explore their health plan or insurance coverage for after childbirth (see POSTNATAL CARE).

Other plans and decisions must also be made. If the woman is still in school, she will need to think through the timing of her leaving, and more generally plan how she will complete her education or obtain needed job skills. If she is employed, she will need to consider privately her own long-term desires regarding employment, before discussing the pregnancy with anyone at work. In particular, she will need to decide whether she plans (assuming the birth proceeds normally) to return to work immediately, to take a longer term leave, to continue in the labor force but in more flexible work (see MOTHER for some organizations to support that decision), or to leave the labor force and stay at home indefinitely. Once she has decided what she wants, she should explore how her firm or institution has handled other pregnancies, to see the likelihood that her desires will be honored. Many companies have liberal FAMILY AND MEDICAL LEAVE policies (broader versions of the more traditional MATERNITY

LEAVE) and flexible work arrangements for new mothers, while other employers may summarily fire or demote a woman who announces that she is pregnant, despite the fact that, in many areas, such a response is against the law (see PREGNANCY DISCRIMINATION ACT).

Women who plan to continue out-of-the-home employment will also have to make arrangements for CHILD CARE, which itself can take some months to put into place. Beyond that, a woman will need to prepare herself for a new role as a mother, understanding that today, even if she is married at the time of her children's births, she may very well later become a single parent at some point in her children's lives.

FOR HELP AND FURTHER INFORMATION

ABOUT PREGNANCY AND CHILDBIRTH IN GENERAL

National Center for Education in Maternal and Child Health (NCEMCH)
2000 15th Street North, Suite 701
Arlington, VA 22201–2617
703–524–7802
Fax: 703–524–9335
E-mail: ncemch01@gumedlib.dml.georgetown.ed
Federally funded organization concerned with maternal and child health, including human genetics; provides information through National Maternal and Child Health Clearinghouse (see later in this list).

National Maternal and Child Health Clearinghouse (NMCHC)
8201 Greensboro Drive, Suite 600
McLean, VA 22102–3843
703–821–8955, ext. 254
Fax: 703–821–2098
E-mail: lcramer@dgs.dgsys.com
Internet gopher site: gopher://mchnet.ichp.ufl.edu
Linda Cramer, Project Director
Federally funded organization, sponsored by the National Center for Education in Maternal and Child Health (see earlier in this list), supplying education and information on maternal and child health, including human genetics; makes referrals to appropriate hotlines; publishes many materials, including *Reaching Out: A Directory of National Organizations Related to Maternal and Child Health—1994, The Health of America's Youth, Home Visiting: Opening Doors for America's Pregnant Women and Children, Bright Futures: Guidelines for Health Supervision of Infants, Children, and Adolescents, The Forgotten Child in Health Care: Children in the Juvenile Justice System,* and *Hard Time, Healing Hands: Developing Primary Health Care Services for Incarcerated Youth*; and materials for professionals.

National Institute of Child Health and Human Development (NICHD)
Building 31, Room 2A32
31 Center Drive
NSC–2420
Bethesda, MD 20892
301–496–5133
For information on sleep positions and sudden infant death syndrome:
P.O. Box 29111
Washington, DC 20040
800–505-CRIB [505–2742]
One of the U.S. National Institutes of Health; sponsoring research; provides information; publishes technical reports for medical specialists and the government, such as *Pregnancy, Birth and the Infant,* and numerous general brochures.

American College of Obstetricians and Gynecologists (ACOG)
409 12th Street SW
Washington, DC 20024–2188
202–638–5577
Fax: 202–484–5107
Ralph W. Hale, Executive Director
Professional organization of obstetricians and gynecologists; establishes guidelines for exercises during pregnancy; publishes various materials, many of them pamphlets to be distributed by health professionals, including *ACOG Guide to Planning for Pregnancy, Birth, and Beyond, Drugs and Pregnancy: Alcohol, Tobacco, and Other Drugs, Group b Streptococcus and Pregnancy, Especially for Fathers, Working During Your Pregnancy,* and *Later Childbearing.*

Healthy Mothers, Healthy Babies National Coalition (HMHB)
409 12th Street, SW
Washington, DC 20024
202–863–2458
Fax: 202–554–4346
Lori Cooper, Executive Director
Network of national and local organizations concerned with maternal and child health. Acts as information clearinghouse; seeks to educate public on perinatal health issues; publishes various materials, including quarterly newsletters, *Unity Through Diversity: A Report on Healthy Mothers, Healthy Babies Communities of Color Leadership Roundtable,* and resource lists on various topics, including *Cultural Diversity.*

March of Dimes Birth Defects Foundation (MDBDF), 914–428–7100. Some local chapters have available certified midwives; publishes pamphlets *How Your Baby Grows, Be Good to Your Baby Before It Is Born*; information sheets *Stress and Pregnancy* and *Pregnancy After Age 30*; and videos *Journey to Birth.* (For full group information, see BIRTH DEFECTS.)

New Parents' Network, 520–327–1451. Offers information (through telecommunications services) on pregnancy and childbirth. (For full group information, see GENERAL PARENTING RESOURCES on page 634.)

Agency for Health Care Policy and Research Clearinghouse, 800–358–9295. Publishes *Women's Health: Hospital Statistics Raise Questions About Obstetrical Care* and

Home Uterine Monitoring. (For full group information, see HEALTH INSURANCE.)

International Childbirth Education Association (ICEA), 612–854–8660. (For full group information, see CHILDBIRTH.)

National Association of Childbirth Education (NACE), 714–686–0422. (For full group information, see CHILDBIRTH.)

Childbirth Education Foundation (CEF), 215–357–2792. (For full group information, see CHILDBIRTH.)

Positive Pregnancy and Parenting Fitness
R.R. #1, Box 172, Glenview Road
Waitsfield, VT 05673
802-496-4944; 800–433–5523
Fax: 802-496-5222
Sylvia Klein Olkin, Executive Director
Organization providing support to pregnant women and new mothers; trains people to teach pregnancy and parenting fitness classes, including exercises with the baby; offers "Be Healthy" mail-order catalogs; publishes newsletter.

National Organization of Adolescent Pregnancy and Parenting (NOAPP), 703–435–3948. (For full group information, see ADOLESCENT PREGNANCY.)

DES Action, 800–337–9288. Publishes *Fertility and Pregnancy Guide for DES Daughters and Sons* and *Natural Remedies for Pregnancy Discomforts.* (For full group information, see DES.)

United Cerebral Palsy Association (UCPA), 800–872–5827. Publishes *Mother to Be: A Guide to Pregnancy and Birth for Women with Disabilities.* (For full group information, see CEREBRAL PALSY.)

The Arc, 800–433–5255. Publishes fact sheet *Take Care of Yourself, You and Your Baby, Think Before You Drink,* and fact sheet *Prevention of Neural Tube Defects.* (For full group information, see MENTAL RETARDATION.)

Twin Services, TWINLINE: 510–524–0863. Publishes *Symptoms of Plural Pregnancy* and *Bedrest: What Are the Options.* (For full group information, see MULTIPLE BIRTH.)

Planned Parenthood Federation of America (PPFA), 800–230–7526. Publishes pamphlet *What if I'm Pregnant?* (For full group information, see BIRTH CONTROL.)

Pregnancy and Infant Loss Center (PILC), 612–473–9372. Publishes *Affirmations for Your Healthy Pregnancy, Preventing Miscarriage: The Good News, Still to Be Born, Pregnancy After a Loss;* and video *The Journey of the Next Pregnancy.* (For full group information, see DEATH AND DYING.)

National Woman's Christian Temperance Union (WCTU), 800–755–1321. Publishes booklet *About Pregnancy and Drugs* and leaflet *Marijuana and Pregnancy.* (For full group information, see HELP AGAINST SUBSTANCE ABUSE on page 703.)

On crisis pregnancies

The Nurturing Network (TNN)
910 Main Street, Suite 360
P.O. Box 2050
Boise, ID 83701
208–344–7200; 800-TNN–4MOM [866–4666]
Fax: 208–344–7200
Mary Cunningham Agee, Executive Director and Founder
Organization that helps women of all ages and backgrounds faced with an unplanned, unwanted, life-disrupting crisis pregnancy; provides a "professional, medical, counseling, and residential network" to enable a woman to avoid abortion without sacrificing her own educational or career goals; arranges adoptions; publishes newsletter *Heart to Heart.*

National Adoption Information Clearinghouse (NAIC), 301–231–6512. Provides referrals to adoption agencies and crisis pregnancy centers; publishes *Are You Pregnant and Thinking About Adoption?* (For full group information, see ADOPTION.)

ONLINE RESOURCES

Internet: Bethany Christian Services. Includes information on pregnancy and pregnancy counseling. gopher://gopher.bethany.org/11 (For full information, see ADOPTION.)

OTHER RESOURCES

General works

You're Pregnant: A Guide for the Longest Nine Months of Your Life. Kathryn Hammer. Contemporary, 1995.
Pregnancy Pure and Simple. Tracie Hotchner. Avon, 1995.
What You Didn't Think to Ask Your Obstetrician: Answers to 1000 Questions about Your Pregnancy. Raymond I. Poliakin. Contemporary, 1994.
Perfectly Pregnant!. Pamela Smith and Carolyn Coats. Nelson, 1994.
The Pregnancy Sourcebook: Everything You Need to Know. M. Sara Rosenthal. Lowell House, 1994.
Ward Lock Family Health Guide: Pregnancy. Julia Goodwin. Sterling, 1994.
When Baby Makes Two. Helen C. Keen. Larksdale, 1994.
Year of Birth: A Month by Month Companion to Pregnancy, Birth and the First Three Months of Infancy. Robbie Snow and John Milder. Crystal, 1991.
When Men Are Pregnant: Needs and Concerns of Expectant Fathers. Jerold Lee Shapiro. Dell, 1993.
Doctor Discusses Pregnancy. William G. Birch and Dona Z. Meilach. Budlong, 1993.
What Happens If You Have a Baby? Ann Redpath. Capstone Press, 1992.
The Illustrated Book of Pregnancy and Childbirth. Margaret Martin. Facts on File, 1991.

Three Hundred Questions New Parents Ask: Answers about Pregnancy, Childbirth, and Infant and Child Care. William Sears and Martha Sears. NAL-Dutton, 1991.
Natural Pregnancy. Janet Balaskas. Interlink, 1990.
Pregnancy Day by Day. Sheila Kitzinger. Random, 1990.
The Illustrated Dictionary of Pregnancy and Childbirth. Carl Jones. Meadowbrook, 1990.
Welcoming Your Second Baby. Vicki Lansky. Book Peddlers, 1990.

General guides

Mothercare's New Guide to Pregnancy and Childcare: An Illustrated Guide to Caring for Your Child from Pregnancy through Age Five. Penny Stanway, ed. Simon & Schuster, 1994.
Mayo Clinic Book of Pregnancy and Baby's First Year. Mayo Foundation for Medical Education and Research. Morrow, 1994.
Planning for Pregnancy, Birth, and Beyond: Gynecologists. American College of Obstetricians and Gynecologists Staff. NAL-Dutton, 1994.
Pregnancy and Your Baby's First Year. Lawrence Kutner. Morrow, 1993
Choices: A Pregnancy Guide. N. Bryne. State Mutual, 1993.
The A-to-Z of Pregnancy and Childbirth: A Concise Encyclopedia. Nancy Evans. Hunter House, 1993.
The Pregnancy Book for Today's Woman, 2nd ed. Harold I. Shapiro. HarperCollins, 1993.
Pregnancy, Birth and Bonding: A Guide for the Mother-to-Be. Longmeadow Press Staff. Longmeadow, 1993.
Baby and Me: The Essential Guide to Pregnancy. Deborah D. Stewart. Willapa Bay, 1993.
Pride and Pregnancy: The Guide to Being a Mother-to-Be. Jennifer Rogers. Simon & Schuster, 1993.
Complete Pregnancy and Baby Book. Consumer Guide Editors; Vicki Lansky. Consumer Reports, 1993.
Be'sha'ah Tovah: The Complete Clinical and Halachic Guide to Pregnancy and Childbirth. Baruch Finkelstein and Michal Finkelstein. Feldheim, 1993.
Sharpe's Guide to a Fit Pregnancy. Liz Brody and others. Weider Health, 1993.
Conception, Pregnancy, and Birth. Miriam Stoppard. Dorling Kindersley, 1993. Perhaps the first popular guide to pregnancy and childbirth to qualify as a coffee-table book.
Great Expectations: An Illustrated Guide to Your Pregnancy, Your Birth, Your Baby. Antonia Van der Meer. Dell, 1993.
The Pregnancy Planner: The Flexible Loose-Leaf Journal That Will Help You Organize All You Need to Do Til You're Due. Barbara Binswanger. Delacorte, 1993.
A New Life: Pregnancy, Birth, and Your Child's First Year—A Comprehensive Guide, 2nd ed. John T. Queenan and Carrie N. Queenan, eds. Little, Brown, 1992.
The Miracle Year: An Expectant Parents' Guide to the Miraculous Six Months Before—and after—the Birth of Their First Baby. Lanie Carter and Lauren S. Ostrow. Pocket Books, 1992.
Planning for Pregnancy, Birth, and Beyond. American College of Obstetricians and Gynecologists Staff. NAL-Dutton, 1992.
Pregnancy, Birth, and the Early Months, 2nd ed. Richard I. Feinbloom. Addison-Wesley, 1992.
What to Expect When You're Expecting, 2nd ed. Arlene Eisenberg and others. Workman, 1991. (See also the parody *Expect the Unexpected When You're Expecting.* Eunice Glick. HarperCollins, 1995.)
Pregnancy, Childbirth and the Newborn: The Complete Guide, rev. ed. Penny Simkin and others. Meadowbrook, 1991.
From Here to Maternity: Your Guide for the Nine-Month Journey Toward Motherhood. Connie C. Marshall. Prima, 1991. *The Mother's Guide to a Healthier Pregnancy and Easier Birth.* Jeanine L. LaBaw and Mary M. Lepley. Lifesounds, 1991.
Labor of Love: The Perfect Pregnancy Planner. Janet Bartlett and Barbara McHale. Heart-Bound, 1991.
Guide to Pregnancy and Childbirth. William G. Birch. Budlong, 1991.

On planning for pregnancy

Do You Want to Have a Baby: Conception and Natural Prenatal Care. Linda Rector-Page. Healthy Healing, 1993. *Preconception: A Woman's Guide to Pregnancy and Parenthood.* Brenda E. Aikey-Keller. John Muir, 1990.
Getting Pregnant: How Couples Can Protect Their Reproductive Powers Throughout Their Childbearing Years. Niels H. Lauersen and Colette Bouchez. Rawson, 1990.

On unplanned pregnancy

Wake up Little Susie: Single Pregnancy and Race Before Roe versus Wade. Rickie Solinger. Routledge, 1994.
Bitter Fruit: Women's Experiences of Unplanned Pregnancy, Abortion, and Adoption. Ann Perkins and Rita Townsend. Hunter House, 1992.
Having Your Baby When Others Say No: Overcoming the Fears about Having Your Baby. Madeline Nugent. Avery, 1991.
Coping with An Unplanned Pregnancy, rev. ed. Carolyn Simpson. Rosen, 1990.
Pregnant and Single: Help for the Tough Choices. Carolyn Owens and Linda M. Roggow. Pyranee/Zondervan, 1990.
Pregnant by Mistake: The Stories of Seventeen Women, rev. ed. Katrina Maxtone-Graham. Remi Books, 1990.
More Than Kindness: A Compassionate Approach to Crisis Childbearing. Susan Olasky and Marvin Olasky. Crossway, 1990.

On fetal development

A Child Is Born, rev. ed. Lennart Nilsson, photographer. Delacorte, 1990. Color photos of life before birth, from conception.
How Your Baby Grows in Pregnancy. Glade B. Curtis. Fisher Books, 1989.

(See PRENATAL CARE for dangers to the fetus.)

For children

How Was I Born? Lennart Nilsson and Lena K. Swanberg. Delacorte, 1994.
How You Were Born, rev. ed. Joanna Cole. Morrow, 1994.
Baby. Nicole Taylor. Creative Education, 1993.
How I Was Born. Marie Wabbes. Morrow, 1991.

On problems during pregnancy

When Pregnancy Isn't Perfect: A Layperson's Guide to Complications in Pregnancy. Laurie A. Rich. NAL-Dutton, 1993.
Getting Pregnant and Staying Pregnant: Overcoming Infertility and Managing Your High-Risk Pregnancy, 2nd ed. Diana Raab. Hunter House, 1991.
Intensive Caring: New Hope for High-Risk Pregnancy. Dianne Hales and Timothy R.B. Johnson. Brown, 1990.
Pregnancy Bedrest: A Guide for the Pregnant Woman and Her Family. Susan H. Johnston. Holt, 1990.
Past Due: A Story of Disability, Pregnancy and Birth. Anne Finger. Seal Press Feminist, 1990.

On the pregnancy experience

Excited, Exhausted, Expecting: The Emotional Life of Expectant Mothers. Arlene M. Matthews. Putnam, 1995.
A Mother is Born: Preparing for Motherhood During Pregnancy. Merete Leonhardt-Lupa. Bergin & Garvey/Greenwood, 1995.
Letters for Tomorrow: A Journal for Expectant Moms and Dads. Robin F. Bernstein and Cathy Moore. Doubleday, 1995.
The Dream Worlds of Pregnancy: How Understanding Your Dreams Can Help You Bond with Your Baby and Become a Better Parent with Your Mate. Eileen Stukane. Station Hill, 1994.
The Wish, the Wait, the Wonder: A Book of Wisdom for Expectant Mothers. Gail P. Johnston. HarperCollins, 1994.
Before and After Your New Baby. Victoria Brown. St. Martin's, 1994.
Hard Labor: Hilarious, Real-Life Stories about the Things Men and Women Do During Pregnancy—from Conception to That First Dirty Diaper!. Brian Krueger and Jack York. Armchair, 1994.
Seasons of Change: Growing Through Pregnancy and Birth. Suzanne Arms. Kivaki, 1993.
Before Baby Arrives. Joan Miller. Atrium, 1993.
Pregnancy: The Psychological Experience. Libby L. Colman. Noonday/Farrar, Straus & Giroux, 1991.
Psychological Processes of Childbearing. Joan Raphael-Leff. Chapman and Hall, 1990.
Stress and Pregnancy. John J. Sullivan and Joyce C. Foster. AMS Press, 1990.
Making Love During Pregnancy. Elisabeth Bing and Libby Colman. Farrar, Straus, & Giroux, 1989.

On pregnancy for women over thirty

Birth over Thirty-Five. Sheila Kitzinger. Viking-Penguin, 1995.
Pregnancy over Thirty-Five. Kathryn Schrotenboer-Cox and Joan Weiss. Ballantine, 1989.
Having a Baby After 30. Elisabeth Bing and Libby Colman. Farrar, Straus & Giroux, 1989.

Background books

At Women's Expense: State Power and the Politics of Fetal Rights. Cynthia R. Daniels. Harvard University Press, 1993.
Fetal Protection in the Workplace: Women's Rights, Business Interests, and the Unborn. Robert H. Blank. Columbia University Press, 1993.
Disembodying Women: Perspectives on Pregnancy and the Unborn. Barbara Duden. Harvard University Press, 1993.
Mother with Child: Transformation Through Children. Kathryn Allen Rabuzzi. Indiana University Press, 1993.
The Stork Is Coming: Myths and Superstitions from Around the World about Having a Baby. Sue Reynolds. Paragon House, 1993.
Postponing Parenthood: The Effect of Age on Reproductive Potential. G.A. Sloan. Plenum, 1993.

(See also ABORTION; ADOLESCENT PREGNANCY; BIRTH CONTROL; BIRTH DEFECTS; BREASTFEEDING; CHILDBIRTH; CIRCUMCISION; DEATH AND DYING; DELIVERY; DES; ENVIRONMENTAL HAZARDS; EXERCISE; FAMILY AND MEDICAL LEAVE; GENETIC DISORDERS; HIGH-RISK PREGNANCY; LABOR; MISCARRIAGE; PERINATAL CARE; PREMATURE; PRENATAL CARE; POSTMATURE; POSTNATAL CARE; PREGNANCY DISCRIMINATION ACT; REPRODUCTIVE TECHNOLOGY; STILLBIRTH; and other specific topics noted in article.)

Pregnancy Discrimination Act (PDA), a U.S. federal law barring discrimination against a woman because of PREGNANCY, CHILDBIRTH, or related medical conditions; it is an amendment to TITLE VII OF THE CIVIL RIGHTS ACT OF 1964, extending to women who work in firms with more than 15 employees the same civil rights protection as people with "other" disabilities.

The PDA bars firms of 15 or more employees from discriminating against a woman because she is pregnant, specifically from refusing to hire, firing, demoting, or penalizing her. However, it does not guarantee any particular benefits, only specifying that employers' benefit plans may not discriminate against women—that is, if HEALTH INSURANCE, DISABILITY leave, and fringes such as vacations, seniority, and raises are available to the firm's disabled employees, then they must be made available to pregnant women as well. In some states, laws do mandate specific kinds of benefits or protections for pregnant women, although these vary widely; attempts to secure similar laws at the federal level have so far generally failed, except for FAMILY AND MEDICAL LEAVE. How the existing laws are interpreted by the courts is still very much open to question, and at times employers have tried to use them to *limit* the rights of women, under the cloak of protection. In practice, individual women have great difficulty bringing a pregnancy discrimination case to court and winning. As a result, many women still find themselves harassed or fired during their pregnancy, either immediately, as the pregnancy develops, or later while out on leave.

When contemplating a pregnancy or before announcing one, a working woman would be wise to review her state's pregnancy discrimination laws, perhaps contacting one of the groups (such as those below) that are active in seeking stronger protection for pregnant women in the workplace. They may also want to discreetly explore how other pregnant women in their firm have fared, seeking to learn from their experience and prepare for possible problems. More personally, they will want to think through their own plans and desires, regarding the length of desired maternity leave, CHILD CARE arrangements, BREASTFEEDING VS. BOTTLEFEEDING, and future intentions regarding work—whether to return to work full time or part time (and if so, how quickly), to work at home (for the same firm or another), or to leave employment and stay at home with the child. Having the answers to these questions before any announcement of a pregnancy will put a woman in the strongest possible position to protect her own interests. In corporate settings, some observers recommend that women lay out their plans and requests in writing, to present to their managers.

FOR HELP AND FURTHER INFORMATION

9 to 5, National Association of Working Women
614 Superior Avenue NW, Room 852
Cleveland, OH 44113–9990
216–566–9308; 9 to 5 Office Survival Hotline
800–522–0925; Media: 414–274–0926
Organization of people concerned with the rights of working women; offers counseling; publishes *The 9 to 5 Newsline, 9 to 5 Profile of Working Women, Wage Replacement for Family Leave: Is It Feasible?, The 9 to 5 Guide to Combating Sexual Harassment,* and other work-related materials.

Women's Legal Defense Fund, 202–986–2600. Publishes *What the Pregnancy Discrimination Act Means to You.* (For full group information, see FAMILY AND MEDICAL LEAVE.)

National Organization for Women (NOW)
1000 16th Street NW, Suite 700
Washington, DC 20036
202–331–0066
Fax: 202–785–8576
E-mail: now@now.org
Patricia Ireland, President
Organization active in support of women's rights in many areas; seeks to educate public and influence legislation.

OTHER RESOURCES

Everything A Working Mother Needs to Know about Pregnancy Rights, Maternity Leave, and Making Her Career Work for Her. Anne Cicero Weisberg and Carol A. Buckler. Doubleday, 1994.

pregnancy tests, MEDICAL TESTS designed to tell if a woman is pregnant or not, generally by measuring the level of HUMAN CHORIONIC GONADOTROPIN (hCG), a hormone produced by the PLACENTA during PREGNANCY, in the blood or urine. Urine tests are most common, especially in home pregnancy tests. In these, a woman places a urine specimen in a small test tube and mixes in the chemicals provided. If the result is positive, that will be signaled in various ways, depending on the brand, such as by the presence or absence of a ring formation, or by color changes in the solution or on a dipstick. Though some urine tests can detect a pregnancy within a few days of a missed menstrual period, not all women produce hCG at the same rate and the level measured by tests varies. A pregnancy will be more likely to show as positive if the test is delayed until at least seven to nine days after the due date of the period.

If that result is negative, but a period still does not arrive, the test should be performed again after a week, since the woman may still be pregnant. If this second test is also negative, but menstruation has not occurred, a woman should see her doctor immediately, since that may indicate a medical problem. Of particular concern is a possible ECTOPIC PREGNANCY, or pregnancy outside the uterus, which can cause life-threatening hemorrhaging; the hCG level stays slow and may not be picked up by the test. Infections, ovarian cysts, excess protein in the urine, and some medications can also cause false readings, as can keeping the test in sunlight or on a vibrating surface (such as a refrigerator), or allowing it to incubate—that is, to grow or develop, as with a culture, or to undergo a chemical reaction.

prekindergarten, an organized school-affiliated class for children in the year (or two) before KINDERGARTEN, taught by a professional educator, and physically held either in an ELEMENTARY SCHOOL as a separate GRADE or in a NURSERY SCHOOL housed elsewhere.

Preliminary Scholastic Aptitude Test/National Merit Scholarship Qualifying Test (PSAT/NMSQT), a test similar to the SCHOLASTIC APTITUDE TEST, but offered to high school juniors for test experience, and also used as a qualifying test for National Merit Scholarships. (See SCHOLASTIC APTITUDE TEST.)

premature, in PREGNANCY, referring to an infant born well before DUE DATE, especially before the 37th week of GESTATION, either because LABOR began prematurely or because a physician induced labor, as when the mother's or infant's health is endangered or when the infant is mistakenly thought to be POSTMATURE.

Various medical conditions can cause triggering of premature labor and DELIVERY, including PREECLAMPSIA, hypertension (high BLOOD PRESSURE), KIDNEY AND UROLOGICAL PROBLEMS, DIABETES, heart disorders (see HEART

AND HEART PROBLEMS), HEMORRHAGE (often as a result of problems with the PLACENTA), excess AMNIOTIC FLUID, and MULTIPLE BIRTHS. Premature infants are often common among ADOLESCENT PREGNANCIES, women with poor NUTRITION, women who smoke, drink alcohol, or use drugs, or who have a previous history of childbearing problems. More recently, research has indicated that mothers who experienced major stress during the pregnancy were more likely to have a premature baby. But in many cases, it is unclear why labor started prematurely. In some cases, a doctor may administer a drug to try to halt premature or *preterm* labor.

Premature babies—perhaps 1 in 10 of all babies born in the United States—are small and their organs not fully developed, so at birth many of them are not yet capable of fully independent life. Often, for example, they are unable to suck effectively, to maintain body temperature, and to fight off infection. As a result, many premature babies must be placed in an INCUBATOR and carefully monitored for some days or weeks, often until they reach 5 pounds. (For advice to parents on how to handle this difficult period, see SPECIAL CARE FOR SPECIAL BABIES on page 336.) In some poor regions of the world, where incubators are unavailable, premature infants may be kept alive through what is called "kangaroo care," involving keeping the infants in skin-to-skin contact in an upright position, to supply both warmth and support; this approach has been adopted in some NEONATAL INTENSIVE CARE UNITS as part of a parent bonding with the premature baby.

Premature babies are generally of LOW BIRTH WEIGHT and so are subject to all the problems associated with LBW. They are at special risk for RESPIRATORY DISTRESS SYNDROME, HYPOGLYCEMIA, hemorrhage in the VENTRICLES of the brain (*intraventricular hemorrhage* or IVH), and jaundice and other liver disorders (see LIVER AND LIVER PROBLEMS).

In the past, the INFANT MORTALITY associated with premature infants was extremely high, but advances in medical technology have allowed many more to survive. Even some born weighing under two pounds or with a GESTATION AGE (dating from FERTILIZATION) of under 23 weeks have survived, though that is rare. Of those born at 28 weeks gestation age, approximately 4 of 5 survive today, and that ratio is rising. (For help and further information, see PREGNANCY; HIGH-RISK PREGNANCY.)

FOR HELP AND FURTHER INFORMATION

Parent Care (PC)
9041 Colgate Street
Indianapolis, IN 46268–1210
317–872–9913
Fax: 317–872–0795
Frank Andrews, President
Organization concerned with premature or critically ill infants requiring neonatal intensive care; fosters local support groups; provides information and referrals; seeks to educate public and shape policy; publishes quarterly *News Brief*, bimonthly *The Network*, *Bringing Your Baby Home*, *The Premie Calendar: The First Year*, *Guiding Your Child Through Preterm Development*, and *Briefly Speaking;* monographs on various issues.

IVH Parents (IVHP)
P.O. Box 56–1111
Miami, FL 33256–1111
305–232–0381
Fax: 305–232–9890
Ronnie Londner, Executive Director
Organization supporting parents of children with bleeding in the brain, from intraventricular hemorrhage (IVH), common in very premature babies; offers information and counseling; publishes newsletter.

Pediatric Projects, 800–947–0947. Publishes reprints *Coping in Infants and Toddlers* and *Your Child (Baby) in the Hospital.* (For full group information, see HOSPITAL.)

American Academy of Pediatrics (AAP), 800–433–9016. Publishes video and booklet set *Special Delivery: Safe Transportation of Premature and Small Infants.* (For full group information, see HEALTH CARE.)

National Institute of Child Health and Human Development (NICHD), 301–496–5133. (For full group information, see PREGNANCY.)

March of Dimes Birth Defects Foundation (MDBDF), 914–428–7100. Publishes booklet *Premature Labor: A Teaching Guide for Pregnant Women.* (For full group information, see BIRTH DEFECTS.)

National Institute of Mental Health (NIMH), 301–443–4513. Publishes *Pre-Term Babies.* (For full group information, see MENTAL DISORDER.)

DES Action, 800–337–9288. Publishes *Preventing Preterm Birth: A Parents' Guide.* (For full group information, see DES.)

Parents Helping Parents (PHP), 408–727–5775. Has division focusing on intensive care nursery infants; publishes information packet *Premature Babies.* (For full group information, see HELP FOR SPECIAL CHILDREN on page 689.)

Twin Services, TWINLINE: 510–524–0863. Publishes *Preventing Premature Multiple Birth* and *When Twins Are Premature.* (For full group information, see MULTIPLE BIRTH.)

La Leche League International (LLLI), 800–525–3243. (For full group information, see BREASTFEEDING.)

American Association on Mental Retardation (AAMR), 800–424–3688. Publishes *Before Their Time: Fetuses and Infants at Risk.* (For full group information, see MENTAL RETARDATION.)

OTHER RESOURCES

GENERAL WORKS

Kangaroo Care: The Best You Can Do to Help Your Preterm Infant. Susan M. Ludington-Hoe and Susan K. Golant. Bantam, 1993.

Early Beginnings: Development in Children Born Preterm. Barton MacArthur. Oxford University Press, 1993.

Your Premature Baby: Everything You Need to Know about the Childbirth Treatment and Parenting of Premature Infants. Frank P. Manginello and Theresa F. Digeronimo. Wiley, 1991.

Your Premature Baby: Everything You Need to Know about the Problems, Treatment, and Parenting. Frank P. Manginello. Doubleday, 1990.

Parenting Your Premature Baby. Janine Jason. Doubleday, 1990.

PERSONAL EXPERIENCES

Born Too Soon: The Story of a Mother and a Very Small Baby. Elizabeth Mehren. Doubleday, 1991. On a premature baby's struggle to survive.

prenatal care, medical care of a pregnant woman and the FETUS she is carrying during the whole period of PREGNANCY, the aim being to ensure the health and ease of both; also called *antepartal care.* In medical terms, prenatal care is the long early part of the MATERNITY CYCLE. With much heavier stress on prenatal care in recent decades, it has become clear that the earlier a woman begins prenatal care, the better for herself and her baby. A woman is advised to see her doctor or clinic as soon as she suspects she might be pregnant. The doctor or clinic staff will perform PREGNANCY TESTS to confirm the pregnancy; will explore the woman and her family's medical history, to be alerted to any likely problems; and will give a variety of MEDICAL TESTS, to identify any problems that might threaten the health or continuance of the pregnancy. At this time, also, the doctor or clinic staff will advise the mother on what she should and should not do during the pregnancy, in such areas as NUTRITION, EXERCISE, and avoiding SMOKING, alcohol, and drugs (unless the doctor confirms that specific medications are known not to harm a fetus).

The first prenatal visit will be lengthy and extensive, as described in PRENATAL VISITS: WHAT TO EXPECT (see page 483). The medical and social history, and the various tests, will allow health care providers to assess whether the pregnancy should be classed as a normal or HIGH-RISK PREGNANCY. This classification will affect CHILDBIRTH options, since alternatives such as HOME BIRTH, birth at a MATERNITY CENTER, or even delivery in a community HOSPITAL will generally be open only to those with no RISK FACTORS. Women with high-risk pregnancies are advised to plan on delivery in a relatively sophisticated hospital (see HOSPITAL for levels of care). Similarly, a woman with a high-risk pregnancy is wise to be under the care of a MATERNAL AND FETAL SPECIALIST; other women may choose to have prenatal care and delivery in the hands of an OBSTETRICIAN/GYNECOLOGIST, FAMILY PRACTICE PHYSICIAN, or CERTIFIED NURSE-MIDWIFE.

Later prenatal visits will be briefer, generally monthly for the first six months, then every two weeks through the eighth month, and then weekly, though visits may be spaced more closely if problems exist. On these later visits, once the results of earlier tests are known, other tests may be performed, among them GENETIC SCREENING TESTS, such as AMNIOCENTESIS, CHORIONIC VILLUS SAMPLING, FETOSCOPY, and ULTRASOUND scanning, as well as follow-up tests to see that the woman is not developing any health problems as a result of the pregnancy, such as DIABETES or PREECLAMPSIA. In high-risk pregnancies, hospitalization may be required for diagnosis or treatment at some period during the pregnancy.

FOR HELP AND FURTHER INFORMATION

National Maternal and Child Health Clearinghouse (NMCHC), 703–821–8955. Publishes *Baby on the Way Basics, Health Diary: Myself—My Baby, Nutrition During Pregnancy and Lactation, Every Child Deserves a Healthy Start, Prevent Infant Mortality: A Resource Directory,* and *Caring for Our Future: The Content of Prenatal Care.* (For full group information, see PREGNANCY.)

American College of Obstetricians and Gynecologists (ACOG), 202–638–5577. Publishes *You and Your Baby: Prenatal Care, Labor and Delivery, and Postpartum Care.* (For full group information, see PREGNANCY.)

National Institute of Child Health and Human Development (NICHD), 301–496–5133. Publishes research report *Caring for Our Future: The Content of Prenatal Care.* (For full group information, see PREGNANCY.)

National Clearinghouse for Alcohol and Drug Abuse Information (NCADI), 301–468–2600. Publishes *How to Take Care of Your Baby Before Birth, Drug Abuse and Pregnancy, Healthy Delivery, Pregnancy and Exposure to Alcohol and Other Drug Use, Confidentiality of Patient Records for Alcohol and Other Drug Treatment, Pregnant, Substance-Using Women, Maternal Substance Use Assessment Methods Reference Manual,* and *Maternal Drug Abuse and Drug Exposed Children: Compendium of HHS Activities.* (For full group information, see HELP AGAINST SUBSTANCE ABUSE on page 703.)

Children's Defense Fund (CDF), 800–233–1200. Publishes *Mounting a Prenatal Care Campaign in Your Community.* (For full group information, see ADOLESCENT PREGNANCY.)

OTHER RESOURCES

GENERAL WORKS

Healthy Moms and Healthy Babies: Your Role in the Prenatal Care Initiative. Diane, 1994.

Life Before Life. Sarah Hinze. CFI, 1993.

Prenatal Visits: What to Expect

YOUR FIRST VISIT

Your first visit will probably take more time than later appointments. In addition to a physical examination, you will need to give information about yourself and your pregnancy.

First there will be questions about you:

- About your previous pregnancies, miscarriages, or abortions.
- About your periods—when they started, what they are like.
- About your medical history—illnesses you have had, illnesses the father has had, illnesses in members of either family.
- About your diet and lifestyle.

Then there will be a physical examination. This will include:

- The measurement of your height and weight and blood pressure.
- An examination of your eyes, ears, nose, throat, and teeth.
- An examination of your heart, lungs, breasts, and abdomen.
- An internal examination (pelvic examination) of the growth of your uterus and the amount of room in your pelvis for the baby.

In addition, several laboratory tests will be performed:

- A Pap smear to detect any signs of cervical cancer.
- A pregnancy test (even if you have done a home test).
- A culture of the cervix to check for gonorrhea.
- Blood tests:
  To see if you are anemic.
  To learn your blood type and Rh factor.
  To check for syphilis.
  To check if you have had rubella (German measles).
- Urine tests:
  For diabetes.
  For kidney function and toxemia.
  To check for the possibility of infection.

It is very important that you ask the doctor or nurse any questions you have about your pregnancy, your general health, or your examination and tests. If you don't ask, they may assume you understand. Remember, there is no such thing as a foolish question.

Tell your doctor if you have any physical problems, if you are under stress, or if you have any other special concerns. It is important for your doctor to understand how your pregnancy is affecting you and your family. In some instances the doctor or nurse may refer you to someone else for help with certain problems.

LATER VISITS

Usually you will return about once a month during the first six months of pregnancy. During the seventh and eighth months, you will make visits every two weeks, and after that, every week until delivery. During these visits, your weight, blood pressure, and urine will be checked. Your abdomen may be measured to see how the baby is growing. These examinations help insure that your pregnancy is progressing normally. Internal (pelvic) examinations and blood tests are not performed on every routine visit. If you have questions or concerns between visits, write them down and bring them to your next appointment.

Remember, it's important for your doctor to know about any medical problems you or your family may have had, particularly such chronic conditions as diabetes, kidney disorders, thyroid problems, heart conditions, and respiratory illnesses. Once the doctor knows about them, the necessary steps can be taken to reduce any risk to you or to the baby.

Source: Prenatal Care (1989). Prepared for the Public Health Service by the Health Resources and Services Administration, Bureau of Health Care Delivery and Assistance, Division of Maternal and Child Health.

Do You Want to Have a Baby: Conception and Natural Prenatal Care. Linda Rector-Page. Healthy Healing, 1993.
Before You Were Born…A Prenatal Journal. Monica J. Davis. Homestyle, 1992.
Caring For Your Unborn Child. Roy Ridgway. Thorsons, 1990.
Loving Your Preborn Baby. Carol Van Klompenburg and Elizabeth Siitari. Shaw, 1990.

On prenatal dangers

Born Hooked: Poisoned in the Womb, rev. ed. Gary E. McCuen, ed. G.E.M., 1994.
When the Bough Breaks: Pregnancy and the Legacy of Addiction. Kira Corser and Frances P. Adler. NewSage, 1993.
Drug Safety in Pregnancy. P.I. Folb. Elsevier, 1991.
Everyday Drugs and Pregnancy: Alcohol, Tobacco, and Caffeine, rev. ed. Do It Now, 1991.
Alcohol, Tobacco, and Other Drugs May Harm the Unborn. Paddy S. Cook and Tineke Haase. U.S. Government Printing Office, 1990.
Drugs, Alcohol and Pregnancy, rev. ed. Do it Now, 1990.

On prenatal influences

Remembering Your Life Before Birth: How Your Womb Memories Have Shaped Your Life—and How to Heal Them, rev. ed. Michael Gabriel. Aslan, 1995.
Primal Connections. Elizabeth Noble. Simon & Schuster, 1993.

On social and legal concerns

Mother and Fetus: Changing Notions of Maternal Responsibility. Robert H. Blank. Greenwood, 1992.
Preventing Prenatal Harm: Should the State Intervene? Deborah Mathieu. Kluwer, 1991.

(See also GENETIC COUNSELING; PRENATAL TEST; PREGNANCY; CHILDBIRTH; and specific topics noted in article.)

prenatal test, a type of MEDICAL TEST performed on a woman during PREGNANCY but before CHILDBIRTH, generally focusing on the health and condition of the FETUS. Many such tests are given to identify GENETIC DISORDERS before birth, often at a stage when ABORTION or IN UTERO SURGERY can be performed, if appropriate. Among the common prenatal tests are AMNIOCENTESIS, ALPHA FETOPROTEIN (AFP), CORDOCENTESUS, and CHORIONIC VILLUS SAMPLING (CVS).

FOR HELP AND FURTHER INFORMATION

March of Dimes Birth Defects Foundation (MDBDF), 914–428–7100. Some local chapters have available certified midwives for prenatal services; publishes information sheets *Alpha-Fetoprotein, Amniocentesis, Chorionic Villus Sampling, Ultrasound,* and *Newborn Screening Tests.* (For full group information, see BIRTH DEFECTS.)

DES Action, 800–337–9288. Publishes *Every Woman's Guide to Tests During Pregnancy.* (For full group information, see DES.)

Pregnancy and Infant Loss Center (PILC), 612–473–9372. Publishes *Difficult Decisions* and *A Time to Decide, A Time to Heal: For Parents Making Difficult Decisions About Babies They Love*, both on prenatal diagnosis of a serious medical problems. (For full group information, see DEATH AND DYING.)

(See also specific tests; also PRENATAL CARE; MEDICAL TESTS; GENETIC COUNSELING; GENETIC DISORDERS; GENETIC SCREENING; REPRODUCTIVE TECHNOLOGY; also PRENATAL VISITS: WHAT TO EXPECT on page 483.)

preparatory school, a type of PRIVATE SCHOOL, generally a boarding school. "Prep" schools provide intensive secondary education aimed at putting their students on a "fast track" to prestigious COLLEGES and universities, such as the IVY LEAGUE schools.

prepared childbirth, an approach to CHILDBIRTH that emphasizes educational programs for pregnant women and their BIRTH PARTNERS, focusing on relaxation techniques for dealing with LABOR pains, with the aim of minimizing medical intervention in the childbirth process; in general, a synonym for NATURAL CHILDBIRTH, also called *psychoprophylaxis* or *psychophysical preparation for childbirth.* (For help and further information, see CHILDBIRTH; PREGNANCY.)

prerequisites, learning that must be accomplished successfully before more advanced learning can be started. A prerequisite is often a course that a student is required to take before taking another (algebra before calculus, for example). A prerequisite is also a skill that is felt necessary before a high-level skill can be learned, in this sense also called a PRECURSOR SKILL or learning READINESS skill. For example, a young child must learn to distinguish between an apple and a pear before she can begin to learn their names, so telling the two fruits apart is a prerequisite or precursor skill. WORD-ATTACK SKILLS are regarded as prerequisites for effective, independent READING, and reading is itself a prerequisite for most other academic learning.

preschool, a general term for a range of programs for prekindergarten children, generally from ages two or three to five; sometimes used synonymously with EARLY CHILDHOOD EDUCATION. Although the term does not cover informal PLAY GROUPS, *preschool* refers to any group or class organized to provide educational experience for children before they enter ELEMENTARY SCHOOL (either in

KINDERGARTEN or first grade). That includes NURSERY SCHOOLS, schools following the MONTESSORI METHOD, HEAD START programs, and similar schools that are not established as part of an organized, graded system.

Preschool programs vary widely in their approach and in their relative emphasis on play and EDUCATION. But it is widely accepted that preschool programs give students a literal "head start" on learning, helping them develop the PREREQUISITE skills basic to more advanced skills—in essence, developing learning READINESS. Children need not attend preschool programs to do well in school, of course, but if they do not, they do need to have available to them in the home the kind of stimulation and range of experiences that a preschool provides.

The preschool years are extremely important in the child's overall development. The CHART OF NORMAL DEVELOPMENT (on page 637) indicates when between birth and age six children first *on the average* begin to develop the key skills: MOTOR SKILLS (gross and fine), communication skills (understanding and speaking language), COGNITIVE SKILLS, SELF-HELP SKILLS, and SOCIAL SKILLS. If the home is stimulating and active, with adults, other children, and new experiences, and if the child gets sufficient attention and teaching, the child may develop these skills in the normal course of everyday life. But many parents feel that approach is too haphazard, and prefer to place their child in some kind of preschool program that is specially designed to help the child develop these skills.

Preschool programs have special value for children who have or may have DISABILITIES. There the children are under the eyes of trained observers, who may recognize early warning signs of problems that the parents do not—or that parents have seen but not wanted to acknowledge. Observational Checklists for spotting signs of learning problems or disabilities in preschool-age children are given in this book under these headings: LEARNING DISABILITIES, EAR AND HEARING PROBLEMS, EYE AND VISION PROBLEMS, MENTAL RETARDATION, and COMMUNICATION SKILLS AND DISORDERS. These can be useful if parents think their child may have a problem that could interfere with learning; if they have any serious questions, they should have the child professionally evaluated at once.

The earlier children's learning problems are diagnosed, the sooner special services can be provided—under the EDUCATION FOR ALL HANDICAPPED CHILDREN ACT, and its successor, the INDIVIDUALS WITH DISABILITIES EDUCATION ACT—and the less trouble the children are likely to have later on when they actually start school. Studies have generally shown that when AT-RISK children have preschool programs, including diagnosis and treatment of any special problems, they are more likely to graduate from HIGH SCHOOL, less likely to have to REPEAT A GRADE, less likely to need special services later on in school, more likely to be able to get and hold a job after high school, and less likely to become DELINQUENTS. Families benefit from such EARLY INTERVENTION, too, generally feeling less stress and isolation because services are being provided.

Most children do not have learning problems of any significance. But children develop at individual and varying paces, and every child can benefit from activities designed to enhance their natural development. (Subscribers to the America Online computer service can find activities designed to develop various kinds of skills for preschoolers, as well as general guidelines for teaching that apply to children of any age, in the Moms Online Desk Reference section of Moms Online, under "Teaching Young Children." These may be useful at home, or may be shared with CHILD CARE workers or in preschool situations, especially if the program is parent-run or parent-assisted.)

Because preschool programs vary widely in approach, parents will want to visit those available locally to see the schools in action and assess which program seems most appropriate for their child. Since preschools are generally local and privately run, the question of evaluation is even more important than with many other schools. The National Association for the Education of Young Children (see below) suggests that parents ask the following questions in evaluating preschools:

- Are the children in the program generally comfortable, relaxed, and happy, and involved in play and other activities?
- Are there sufficient numbers of adults with specialized training in early childhood development and education?
- Do adult expectations vary appropriately for children of differing ages and interests?
- Are all areas of a child's development stressed equally, with time and attention being devoted to cognitive development, social and emotional development, and physical development?
- Do the staff meet regularly to plan and evaluate the program?
- Are parents welcome to observe, discuss policies, make suggestions, and participate in the work of the program?
- Are staff alert to the health and safety of young children and of themselves?

Questions such as these are part of NAEYC's ACCREDITATION criteria for early childhood programs; if possible, parents should seek a preschool program that has been accredited as meeting basic professional standards. The U.S. Department of Education's booklet CHOOSING A SCHOOL FOR YOUR CHILD (on page 659), while intended for evaluating ELEMENTARY SCHOOLS and HIGH SCHOOLS, may also be usefully applied to preschools.

In some highly selective preschools, the shoe is somewhat on the other foot, with children being given various kinds of DEVELOPMENTAL SCREENING TESTS as ADMISSIONS TESTS for preschool, even when the tests were not originally developed for that purpose. Parents should be wary of pushing their children into too-competitive situations, and of the possible negative effects of LABELING, if a student does poorly on a particular TEST. Above all, they should be sure to recognize—and be sure the school is aware—that children vary widely in their rates of development.

FOR HELP AND FURTHER INFORMATION

National Association for the Education of Young Children (NAEYC)
1509 16th Street NW
Washington, DC 20036–1426
202–232–8777; 800–424–2460
Fax: 202–328–1846
Online service forum: Prodigy: America Tomorrow (center for online subscribers)
Organization of people concerned with child care and school programs for young children through age eight; encourages professional development; provides accreditation through National Academy of Early Childhood Programs; provides information and referrals; publishes bimonthly journal *Young Children* and *Early Childhood Research Quarterly;* and other materials, including:

- General materials: brochures *Off to a Sound Start: Your Baby's First Year* and *Teaching Young Children to Resist Bias: What Parents Can Do*; videos *Young Children—Our Hope for the Future* and *Mister Rogers Talks with Parents*; and books *How Young Children Learn to Think, Images of the Young Child: Collected Essays on Development and Education, Young and Old Together* (on bringing older generations into the classroom), *The Case for Mixed-Age Grouping in Early Education, Parent Involvement in Early Childhood Education,* and *Teacher-Parent Relationships, Families and Early Childhood Programs, Listen to the Children,* and *How to Generate Values in Young Children: Integrity, Honesty, Individuality, Self-Confidence, and Wisdom.*
- On creativity: books *Art: Basic for Young Children, Feeling Strong, Feeling Free: Movement Exploration for Young Children,* and *Music in Our Lives: The Early Years*; and videos *Music Across the Curriculum* and *Learning Can Be Fun,* on using music to promote learning.
- On science, math, and technology: books *Young Children: Active Learning in a Technological Age, Science with Young Children,* and *Mud, Sand, and Water*; brochure *More Than 1, 2, 3: The Real Basics of Mathematics*; videos *Computers and Young Children, Sharing Nature with Young Children,* and *The Adventure Begins: Preschool and Technology.*
- Videos *Partnerships with Parents, Education of the Young Child—Past, Present, and Future* and *Culture and Education of Young Children.*
- Numerous works on teaching and curriculum, on developmentally appropriate teaching practices through the early primary grades, and on running early childhood programs.

High-Scope Educational Research Foundation
600 North River Street
Ypsilanti, MI 48198–2898
313–485–2000. For orders only: 800–40-PRESS [407–7377]
Fax: 313–485–0704; For fax orders only: 800–442–4FAX [442–4329]
David P. Weikart, President
Organization concerned with research and curriculum development on education of children, especially preschoolers, incorporating Piaget's ideas of cognitive development; develops training materials, including some for home teaching of infants; maintains laboratory school; offers parent and teacher programs in infant education and development; publishes bimonthly newsletter *Extensions,* quarterly *High/Scope ReSource,* and numerous other materials for educators on curriculum and activities, including computers and rhythmic movement; those of particular interest to parents include *Round the Circle: Key Experiences in Movement for Children, Movement in Steady Beat, Movement Plus Music, Movement Plus Rhymes, Songs & Singing Games, Rhythmically Moving* (record, cassettes, or compact discs; for grades 1–9), and *High/Scope Buyer's Guide to Children's Software.*

ERIC (Educational Resources Information Center) Clearinghouse on Elementary and Early Childhood Education, 800–583–4135. (For full group information, see HELP ON LEARNING AND EDUCATION on page 659.)

Association for Childhood Education International (ACEI), 800–423–3563. Publishes *Mudpies to Magnets: A Preschool Science Curriculum* and Kelly Bear educational series. (For full group information, see HELP ON LEARNING AND EDUCATION on page 659.)

Parent Cooperative Pre-Schools International (PCPI)
P.O. Box 90410
Indianapolis, IN 46290
317–842–0730; 800–721-PCPI [721–7274]
Fax: 317–842–0731
Kathy Mensel, Executive Secretary
Organization concerned with parent-run cooperative nursery schools; provides information and advice; sets standards for cooperative programs; publishes *Cooperatively Speaking,* annual *PCPI Directory,* and other materials.

Mothers of Preschoolers (MOPS) International
1311 South Clarkson
Denver, CO 80210
303–733–5353
Fax: 303–733–5770
Elisa Morgan, President
Christian-oriented ministry and support network for mothers; publishes newsletter *Mom Sense* and *What Every Mom Needs.*

Families and Work Institute (FWI), 212–465–2044. Publishes *The Preschool Years, Education Before School: Investing in Quality Child Care,* and *The Cost of Not Providing Quality Early Childhood Programs.* (For full group information, see GENERAL PARENTING RESOURCES on page 634.)

National Head Start Association (NHSA), 703–739–0875. (For full group information, see HEAD START.)

American Montessori Society (AMS), 212–924–3209 (For full group information, see MONTESSORI METHOD.)

Institute for Childhood Resources (INICR), 415–864–1169. (For full group information, see CHILD CARE.)

Children's Defense Fund (CDF), 800–233–1200. Publishes *First Steps, Promising Futures: State Prekindergarten Initiatives in the Early 1990s* and *State Investments in Child Care and Early Education.* (For full group information, see ADOLESCENT PREGNANCY.)

ON CHILDREN WITH SPECIAL NEEDS

National Information Center for Children and Youth with Disabilities (NICHCY), 800–695–0285, voice/TT. Publishes *Accessing Programs for Infants, Toddlers, Preschoolers with Disabilities* (ages 0–5). (For full group information, see HELP FOR SPECIAL CHILDREN on page 689.)

PACER Center (Parent Advocacy Coalition for Educational Rights), 612–827–2966, voice/TT. Publishes newsletter *Early Childhood Connection, Parents Can Play a Role in Local IEICs (Interagency Early Intervention Committees)* and *Parents and Professionals* (2 articles). (For full group information, see HELP FOR SPECIAL CHILDREN on page 689.)

Association for Children with Down Syndrome (ACDS), 516–221–4700. Publishes *ACDS Infant, Toddler and Preschool Curriculum for Children with Down Syndrome.* (For full group information, see DOWN SYNDROME.)

National Library Services for the Blind and Physically Handicapped, Library of Congress, 800–424–8567, U.S. except DC. Publishes *Parents' Guide to the Development of Preschool Children with Disabilities: Resources and Services.* (For full group information, see HELP FOR SPECIAL CHILDREN on page 689.)

National Federation of the Blind (NFB), 410–659–9314. Publishes *The Blind Child in the Regular Preschool Program.* (For full group information, see EYE AND VISION PROBLEMS.)

Parents Helping Parents (PHP), 408–727–5775. Publishes information packet on preschoolers with special needs. (For full group information, see HELP FOR SPECIAL CHILDREN on page 689.)

OTHER RESOURCES

GENERAL WORKS

How to Choose a Nursery School: A Parents' Guide to Preschool Education. Ada Anbar. Pacific Books, 1994.

Your Child's First School: A Handbook for Parents. Diana Townsend-Butterworth. Walker, 1992.

Guiding Your Catholic Preschooler. Kathy Pierce and Lori Rowland. Pierce, 1992.

Getting Your Child Ready for School... and the School Ready for Your Child. Kristen Amundson. American Association of School Administrators, 1992.

What's Best for Kids: A Guide to Developmentally Appropriate Practices for Teachers and Parents of Children Age 4–8. Anthony Coletta. Modern Learning Press, 1991. Includes checklists for assessing readiness for kindergarten and evaluating learning.

The Preschool Handbook: Making the Most of Your Child's Education. Barbara Brenner. Pantheon, 1990.

ON SCHOOL-PREPARATION ACTIVITIES

Helping Your Child Get Ready for School: With Activities for Children from Birth Through Age 5. Nancy Paulu. Diane, 1993.

Your Home Is a Learning Place. Pamela Weinberg. New Readers, 1993.

One-Two-Three Reading and Writing: Pre-Reading and Pre-Writing Opportunities for Young Children. Jean Warren. Warner, 1992.

Help Your Child Excel in Math: Easy, Practical Methods That Make Learning Fun. Margaret Berge and Philip Gibins. Lifetime Books, 1992.

The Ready-to-Read, Ready-to-Count Handbook: A School Readiness Guide for Parents and Preschoolers. Teresa Savage. Newmarket Press, 1991.

Prepping Your Preschooler: A Sourcebook for Helping Your Child Succeed in School. Patsy Lord and Margaret Sebern. McGraw-Hill, 1990.

Kindergarten Ain't What It Used to Be: Getting Your Child Ready for the Positive Experience of Education. Susan Golant and Mitch Golant. Lowell House/Contemporary, 1990.

Teach Your Baby Math, rev. ed. Glenn Doman. M. Evans, 1990.

(See also READING; PLAY GROUP; also GENERAL PARENTING RESOURCES on page 634.)

FOR PRESCHOOLERS

My First Day at Preschool. Edwina Riddell. Barron's, 1992.

Nathan's Day at Preschool. Susan Conlin and Susan Friedman. Parenting Press, 1991.

(See also education; play group; kindergarten; Montessori method; Gesell Preschool Test; readiness tests; tests.)

primary-care level hospital (Level I), a medical facility such as a community HOSPITAL primarily directed to handle routine medical emergencies.

primary health-care provider, the health professional who is a patient's first "port of call" in dealing with a disease or disorder, and who refers the patient to an appropriate medical specialist as necessary. Primary HEALTH CARE providers may be PHYSICIANS, specially trained NURSE PRACTITIONERS, or clinics. They often also provide advice on general health and disease prevention.

primary sex characteristics, those reproductive organs and structures that are present at birth and determine an infant's sex. In a female, these include the VULVA (including the CLITORIS and LABIA), VAGINA, CERVIX, UTERUS, FALLOPIAN TUBES, and OVARIES, all key elements of the female REPRODUCTIVE SYSTEM. In males, primary sex characteristics include possession of a PENIS and TESTES. By contrast, SECONDARY SEX CHARACTERISTICS are those that develop at PUBERTY, such as pubic hair or development of the breasts or penis to adult form. Sometimes primary sex characteristics can be ambiguous, with a person lacking some primary organs, having undeveloped organs, or having organs from both sexes (see SEXUAL IDENTITY).

primary school, an alternate term for ELEMENTARY SCHOOL; the term *primary* is also used to refer to the lower elementary grades 1 to 3, sometimes including KINDERGARTEN.

primary teeth, the set of 20 TEETH that push through the gums in an infant's mouth in the first 25 to 33 months of life; also called *baby, milk,* or *deciduous teeth.*

primigravida, a medical designation for a woman who is pregnant for the first time.

primipara, a medical designation for a woman who has given birth to one live infant, often noted on the hospital medical chart as "para 1."

primitive reflexes, a group of REFLEXES—involuntary, automatic movements in reaction to particular stimuli, or events—that are found only in newborns, and normally disappear in the first few months. Among them are the GRASP REFLEX, TONIC NECK REFLEX, MORO'S REFLEX (STARTLE REFLEX), WALKING REFLEX, and ROOTING REFLEX. In some children, such as some of those with CEREBRAL PALSY, such *sensori-motor* reactions are retained later, and can interfere with the ability to learn voluntary control of movement.

private school, a school that is under the control of a person, board, or agency not responsible to the public, and is not primarily supported by federal funds; sometimes a SCHOOL OF CHOICE that is an alternative to a PUBLIC SCHOOL. Parents send their children to private schools for a wide variety of reasons. Many want their children to be taught in a religious context, as in a Catholic parochial school, a Protestant Christian-oriented school, or a school for Jews, Muslims, Buddhists, or other groups. Some wish to have the child taught in a more tightly disciplined, structured setting, while others conversely want the child to be freer to develop with individualized or independent learning, as might be provided in an ALTERNATIVE SCHOOL. Some parents are simply dissatisfied with the quality of the EDUCATION offered in their local schools, and so opt out to private schools, or they are unhappy with BUSING and DESEGREGATION plans. Some parents choose private schools primarily for the prestige, notably PREPARATORY SCHOOLS, and some to meet special needs of students, such as those with severe LEARNING DISABILITIES.

In recent years, since passage of the EDUCATION FOR ALL HANDICAPPED CHILDREN ACT and then the INDIVIDUALS WITH DISABILITIES EDUCATION ACT, many parents have had some legal support in pushing public schools to provide the kind of special instruction needed for their children, especially those with DISABILITIES. Others have turned to private schools. Parents should not consider private schools a cure-all, however. Some are well funded and well staffed, offering a high quality education; others are poorly funded, equipped, and staffed, and lack any kind of ACCREDITATION. Parents must carefully evaluate any private school before entering their children. The U.S. Department of Education's CHOOSING A SCHOOL FOR YOUR CHILD (on page 659) includes a checklist for evaluating schools.

Clearly private schools continue to meet felt needs in the community. In the mid–1990s approximately 12 percent of all school-age children were being educated in a private school. Of the approximately 110,000 schools in the United States, nearly 23 percent are private schools, more than half of them small schools, with fewer than 150 students. More than 80 percent of them have a religious affiliation, over one-third of these with the Catholic Church.

FOR HELP AND FURTHER INFORMATION

Council for American Private Education (CAPE)
1726 M Street NW, Suite 703
Washington, DC 20036
202–659–0016
Fax: 202–659–0018
E-mail: cape@connectinc.com
Joyce G. McCray, Executive Director
Organization concerned with private school education; seeks to shape public policy; publishes monthly newsletter *CAPE Outlook, Facts about Private School in America,* and directory *Private Schools of the United States.*

Advisory Service on Private Schools and Camps
501 East Boston Post Road
Mamaroneck, NY 10543–3740
914–381–8096
Paul Johnston, Director
Organization of private schools and summer camps, affiliated with National Association of Independent Schools (NAIS); provides free information, catalogues, and guidance in choosing a private school or camp.

National Organization on Legal Problems of Education (NOLPE), 913–273–3550. Publishes *Legal Problems of Religious and Private Schools.* (For full group information, see HELP ON LEARNING AND EDUCATION on page 659.)

National Coalition of Alternative Community Schools (NCACS), 615–964–3670. (For full group information, see ALTERNATIVE SCHOOLS.)

OTHER RESOURCES

Handbook of Private Schools. Porter Sargent, annual.
How to Pick a Perfect Private School. Harlow G. Unger. Facts on File, 1993.
Free Money for Private Schools. Laurie Blum. Simon & Schuster, 1992.
The College Board Guide to High Schools. The College Board, 1990. Directory of over 25,000 public and private high schools.
Peterson's Independent Secondary Schools 1989–1990. Peterson's, 1989.
Keeping Them Out of the Hands of Satan: Evangelical Schooling in America. Susan D. Rose. Routledge, 1990.
The Boarding School Guide. Kiliaen V.R. Townsend. Agee Publishers, 1992.

(See also ALTERNATIVE SCHOOLS; EDUCATION.)

privileged communication, conversations that are legally regarded as confidential, and cannot be disclosed in court, if the persons involved object. In general, a person's conversations with a lawyer or a priest are seen as privileged communications. Doctors and psychologists generally consider conversations with their patients as private, under their professional code of CONFIDENTIALITY, but whether or not they are legally considered privileged communications depends on the current law. If the state law allows it, these and other professionals such as social workers may be required to testify in court in certain circumstances, such as cases involving CHILD ABUSE OR NEGLECT.

proband, the person about whom medical and genetic information is being gathered for the construction of a family PEDIGREE during GENETIC COUNSELING; also called *propositus* (female: *proposita*) or *index case.*

probate court, the type of court that handles questions regarding the estates of people who have died, either affirming the validity of an existing will or overseeing distribution of assets if the person died INTESTATE (without a will), under the state's INHERITANCE RIGHTS laws. Probate courts may also handle some questions relating to ADOPTION and GUARDIANS. In some states, the role of the probate court has been partly taken over by the FAMILY COURT.

probation, in the law, suspending a sentence imposed by a court, on certain conditions, often including good behavior, some kind of treatment, and supervision by a court-appointed professional probate officer. A JUVENILE convicted of a crime, especially a first offense, may be made a WARD of the court and put on probation; parents convicted of CHILD ABUSE AND NEGLECT may also be placed on probation. Violation of the set conditions may cause the probation to be withdrawn and the original sentence to be imposed; in the case of abusive parents, that can mean TERMINATION OF PARENTS' RIGHTS.

probationary promotion, passing a student on to a higher grade even when academic performance has not been fully satisfactory, on the understanding that the PROMOTION will become permanent only if the student shows ability to handle the more advanced work.

problem child, a child who exhibits disruptive behavior, often one who has some kind of MENTAL DISORDER. Many such children have undiagnosed or untreated DISABILITIES that interfere with learning and so lead to frustration and emotional disturbance.

proctologist, a PHYSICIAN who specializes in treating disorders of the anus and rectum, the final parts of the digestive system.

proctoscope, a type of ENDOSCOPE used by doctors in visually examining the anus and rectum, the last parts of the digestive system. (For help and further information, see DIGESTIVE SYSTEM AND DISORDERS.)

prodigy, an unusually talented individual, a term generally used in referring to a CHILD PRODIGY.

Proficiency Examination Program (PEP), a program run by the American College Testing Program (ACT), in which students are able to earn college CREDIT if they take and pass a set examination, having studied on their own, in a special course, or through INDEPENDENT STUDY.

progesterone, a key female HORMONE produced in the OVARIES that works with the hormone ESTROGEN to regulate the MENSTRUAL CYCLE, and is important to the development of the PLACENTA and the FETUS during PREGNANCY. A drop in the amount of progesterone in the body helps bring on LABOR.

projective test, a test designed so that the responses given will stem from the person's underlying mental condition, personality, and mood, rather than from the test material itself. The best-known example is the RORSCHACH PSYCHODIAGNOSTIC TEST, in which the person is asked to interpret a series of inkblots. Other projective tests commonly used with children include the HOUSE-TREE-PERSON PROJECTIVE TECHNIQUE, DRAW-A-PERSON TEST, BLACKY PICTURES, THEMATIC APPERCEPTION TEST, and CHILDREN'S APPERCEPTION TEST.

prolapse, a condition in which an organ has fallen or slid out of its normal position in the body. That sometimes happens to the UTERUS after CHILDBIRTH or to a long UMBILICAL CORD during LABOR; the term may also refer to INTUSSUSCEPTION, or telescoping of the bowel.

promotion, in EDUCATION, the advancement of a student from one GRADE to another, or in an UNGRADED CLASS from one instructional level to another. Promotion implies that the student has developed the skills, learned the material, and met the academic standards of the grade, and is therefore academically ready to move on to the next grade.

The corollary assumption is that any student who has *not* fulfilled those requirements will be retained in the class until he or she does so. But no one—parents, students, or school officials—is happy about RETENTION, so in practice, many students have been given *automatic promotion*, being passed on from grade to grade, regardless of performance. This is sometimes called *social promotion*, being based on social, rather than educational, reasons. In this way, some students have been graduated from HIGH SCHOOL, even though they remained functionally ILLITERATE. This creates significant personal and social problems, because these students lack the basic skills needed to operate within society. Public recognition of that fact, not least from the highly publicized cases of sports figures who have later returned to ELEMENTARY SCHOOL to learn to read, or adults who have sued the school system for failing to teach them to read, has led schools to focus more on the development of basic skills as a basis for promotion.

Sometimes a student may be given *probationary promotion*; if he or she is able to satisfactorily handle the work in the higher grade, the promotion will be considered permanent. Since students have variable levels of skills, students may sometimes REPEAT course material in one subject area, while being promoted to the next level in other areas. More to the point should be an examination of why and how the student failed, and especially whether the student has any undiagnosed DISABILITIES, such as LEARNING DISABILITIES or EAR AND HEARING PROBLEMS, that prevented learning.

proprietary school, a nonpublic or PRIVATE SCHOOL providing EDUCATION primarily as a business for profit. The term most often refers to postsecondary schools that teach non-COLLEGE subjects such as cosmetology or secretarial skills, or provide coaching for college-related examinations, such as the SCHOLASTIC APTITUDE TEST.

pro se, a legal term for a person acting in court without representation by a lawyer; literally, Latin for "for himself," sometimes called *pro per*. Some people feel that family issues are best not dealt with by lawyers, who are by definition advocates, accustomed to adversarial stances (ADVOCACY), rather than conciliators, and so may exaggerate divisions within a family, rather than attempting to resolve them reasonably. However, if one party in a family dispute has retained a lawyer, other members may be in a weakened position if they adopt a *pro se* approach.

FOR HELP AND FURTHER INFORMATION

Help Abolish Legal Tyranny (HALT),
202–347–9600. (For full group information, see CUSTODY.)

prostate gland, an oval organ in males that secretes fluid that mixes with SPERM to form SEMEN. The prostate gland sits just under the bladder, and the URETHRA passes through it. Tiny at birth, the prostate begins to grow at PUBERTY, triggered by male sex HORMONES, reaching adult size by the end of the teens. In older men the prostate becomes further enlarged, which can cause painful urination, and is sometimes cancerous. In younger men, the main prostate problem is bacterial infection, often from SEXUALLY TRANSMITTED DISEASES.

prostheses, medical name for artificial limbs, a common type of ORTHOPEDIC DEVICE.

proteins, complex chemical compounds, made up of AMINO ACIDS, which are vital to the body's functioning, not only forming the structure of many parts of the body but also promoting many of the most basic biochemical reactions in the body. Common sources of protein are meat, poultry, fish, eggs, milk, and cheese; these are called *complete proteins* because they contain all the essential amino acids. Other sources of protein that contain some, but not all, essential amino acids are nuts, beans, and peas.

In the digestive system, proteins are broken down into usable components, which are then reformed to make up basic body tissues, HORMONES, and vital parts of the blood; the basic building blocks of life, DNA, are codes for proteins. Protein deficiency in children leads to MARASMUS, or FAILURE TO THRIVE, and more seriously (as starving children) the life-threatening stunting and malfunctioning called *kwashiorkor*. In adults, lack of protein leads to weakness, DEPRESSION, lack of resistance, and slow recovery from illness or injury.

During PREGNANCY women need to eat more protein than nonpregnant women; however, in most cases this is not a problem, because the American diet includes large amounts of protein. Indeed some studies have shown a somewhat higher risk of PREMATURE birth and neonatal mortality among pregnant women whose diets have 20 percent of total calories protein, instead of the recommended 13–14 percent. (For help and further information, see NUTRITION; DIGESTIVE SYSTEM AND DISORDERS.)

prothrombin time (PT), a kind of BLOOD TEST, often considered one of the LIVER FUNCTION TESTS, which can also indicate VITAMIN K DEFICIENCY and help physicians monitor use of anticoagulant (anti-blood-clotting) medicine.

psoriasis, a common SKIN DISORDER that involves thickened, reddened skin, often covered by silvery scales, as a result of excessive formation of skin cells, and in severe cases, formation of pus-filled blisters. The parts of the body affected vary, especially with different forms of the disease. A CHRONIC condition, psoriasis may go into REMISSION and then erupt again, as in response to illness, stress, or injury to the skin; some researchers believe it to be a type of AUTOIMMUNE DISORDER. One mild form, characterized by formation of small red bumps on the skin, commonly occurs in children following a throat infection. It generally eases during summer warmth, but worsens as cold comes on. Mild forms are generally treated with ointments and creams, including STEROID creams. Some cases are also treated with ultraviolet light (see PHOTOTHERAPY), though that carries the risk of SKIN CANCER and cataracts. Whatever the form of treatment, parents should be sure the child understands the purpose of the treatment, and should be alert for any possible adverse reactions to it.

More severe forms, sometimes linked with ARTHRITIS, are often treated with powerful drugs related to VITAMIN A and ACCUTANE. Such drugs are known to cause BIRTH DEFECTS and even death of the FETUS. Couples are advised to avoid PREGNANCY for at least three months after the male has taken such drugs, and at least one MENSTRUAL CYCLE for the woman. However, how long a woman should wait for safety is unclear, since the drug continues to circulate in the body for at least three years after intake has ended.

Though the cause of the disease and its pattern of inheritance are unknown, psoriasis is apparently a GENETIC DISORDER, affecting both sexes and appearing at any age, sometimes even in infancy, but generally in the teens or twenties. The American Academy of Dermatology notes that 30 percent of those afflicted have a family history of the disorder, and if both parents have psoriasis, their child has a fifty-fifty chance of getting it. It is most common among people of European ancestry, less so among those of African or Asian descent, and rare among Native Americans. Recent studies suggest that people who come down with psoriasis before age forty are likely to have a family history of the disorder and to have a more severe case.

FOR HELP AND FURTHER INFORMATION

National Psoriasis Foundation (NPF)
6600 SW 92nd Avenue, Suite 300
Portland, OR 97223–7195
503–244–7404; 800–723–9166
Fax: 503–245–0626
E-mail: 76135.2746@compuserve.com (CompuServe: 76135,2746)
Organization concerned with psoriasis; provides information, referrals, and telephone counseling; encourages support groups and person-to-person contact as through Pen Pal Club for children; offers mail-order discount drugs; publishes various materials, including bimonthly *Bulletin* and *Pharmacy News*; booklets *Young People and Psoriasis, My Child Has Psoriasis, Cosmetic Cover-Ups, Genital Psoriasis, Home UVB, Mild Psoriasis, Nutrition and Psoriasis, Psoriatic Arthritis, Psoriasis: How It Makes You Feel, Psoriasis Research, Psoriasis On Special Skin Sites, PUVA, Rare Forms of Psoriasis, Steroids, Tar, Tegison, Methotrexate (MTX)*, and *UVB*; audiotapes *Youth and Young Adult Symposium* and *Psoriatic Arthritis*; and three videotapes, one for general audiences, one for elementary school-age children, and one on emotional aspects of psoriasis.

National Organization for Rare Disorders (NORD), 800–999–6673. (For full group information, see RARE DISORDERS.)

OTHER RESOURCES

Managing Your Psoriasis. Nicholas J. Lowe. MasterMedia, 1993.
Beat Psoriasis. Gibbons. Thorsons, 1992.
Healing Psoriasis: The Natural Alternative. John O. Pagano. Pagano, 1991.

(See also SKIN DISORDERS.)

psychiatrist, a physician who specializes in diagnosing, preventing, and treating people with MENTAL DISORDERS and other psychological, emotional, behavioral, and developmental problems. All psychiatrists are able to prescribe medications, but they vary widely in their orientation. Some focus on genetic and biochemical causes of mental problems, while others (such as PSYCHOANALYSTS) stress environmental and personal experience. Some psychiatrists specialize in treating children or adolescents with behavioral or developmental problems. A psychiatrist does not generally do formal testing (normally done by a PSYCHOLOGIST), but talks with, plays with, and observes the child, both alone and with others, looking for underlying physical problems that may produce mental problems, and then carries out or supervises treatment.

psychoanalyst, a health professional who treats mental, emotional, and behavioral problems using a therapeutic technique based on FREUDIAN THEORY or related approaches; a kind of PSYCHOTHERAPIST. Often medically trained as PSYCHIATRISTS, psychoanalysts offer deep exploratory therapy, sometimes over a period of years, especially probing the patient's unconscious and early childhood experiences. Some psychoanalysts, such as followers of Melanie Klein, specialize in psychoanalysis of children and adolescents.

Psychoeducational Profile (PEP), an individually administered DIAGNOSTIC ASSESSMENT TEST used to assess the learning abilities and behavior of children with AUTISM or related developmental disorders, previously seen as untestable. The multiple-item task-performance test is used to develop a profile of the child's individual characteristics, and used in developing an INDIVIDUALIZED EDUCATION PLAN. (For help and further information, see TESTS.)

psychological parent, the person who has the strongest emotional ties with the child and is closest to the child's day-to-day activities, hopes, and fears. That is usually the child's MOTHER, FATHER, or GUARDIAN, but can sometimes be a neighbor or other relative with no legal responsibility for the child, such as a stepparent or aunt, or a NANNY or other CHILD CARE worker. If it appears that breaking such a relationship would be harmful to the child, on some occasions courts may grant such a psychological parent VISITATION RIGHTS.

psychologist, a health professional who specializes in diagnosing and treating people with social, emotional, psychological, behavioral, and developmental problems. *Clinical psychologists*—who treat patients, rather than focusing on the general study of human behavior—often offering testing and counseling services, among them PSYCHOTHERAPY. Not trained as physicians, most psychologists cannot prescribe medications (though in some areas that is changing).

Children who may have problems, such as possible LEARNING DISABILITIES, will often be referred either to a *child psychologist* or a *school psychologist* for assessment. The psychologist will meet and talk with the child and often the parents, and will observe the child at play and with the parents; depending on the potential problem, the psychologist may also administer INTELLIGENCE TESTS, PROJECTIVE TESTS (personality tests), DEVELOPMENTAL SCREENING TESTS, and DIAGNOSTIC ASSESSMENT TESTS. The psychologist will then suggest a course of therapy, perhaps including recommendations about educational programs and activities best suited to enhancing the child's skills.

psychomotor domain, one of three key categories of instructional content and learning objectives described by Benjamin Bloom, referring to the physical and muscular functioning of an individual. (See DOMAIN.)

psychosis, a general mental condition in which the person has gross misperceptions of reality, including creation of a "new" reality, as in DELUSIONS or HALLUCINATIONS; used loosely, also a synonym for MENTAL DISORDERS. Psychosis may be part of various other mental disturbances, such as DEPRESSION and SCHIZOPHRENIA. (For help and further information, see MENTAL DISORDERS.)

psychotherapist, a health professional who treats mental, emotional, and behavioral problems, using an approach in which a patient talks about problems in a regular therapeutic relationship. The aim is for patients to learn more about themselves, both their deep personal thoughts and feelings and their relationship with others, and to change some aspects of their behavior. Psychotherapists vary widely in their orientation and background. Some are PSYCHOLOGISTS with advanced, though not medical, training, who offer relatively short-term counseling services; others, especially PSYCHOANALYSTS, may have medical training as PSYCHIATRISTS and offer deeply exploratory therapy that can last for years. Psychiatric SOCIAL WORKERS and others with special training may also work as psychotherapists. Some psychotherapists specialize in treating children and adolescents.

puberty, the series of physical changes that occur during the development of sexual maturity, usually starting in girls between ages ten and twelve, and in boys between ages twelve and thirteen. Puberty results from a series of hormonal changes. The brain begins to secrete a HORMONE called *luteinizing hormone-releasing hormone* (LHRH) in periodic bursts; this triggers the PITUITARY GLAND to produce hormones called GONADOTROPINS, which in turn stimulate the GONADS (OVARIES in girls and TESTES in boys) to make sex hormones, primarily ESTROGEN for girls and TESTOSTERONE for boys.

These hormones begin to produce the outward physical changes—the SECONDARY SEX CHARACTERISTICS—by which young people signal that they are approaching sexual maturity. In girls, BREASTS and LABIA develop, HAIR grows in the underarm and pubic area, the hips widen, fat is deposited in the adult female distribution, the UTERUS enlarges, and MENSTRUATION and OVULATION begin. In boys, the PENIS and testes develop, hair appears on the face, underarms, and pubic area, shoulders widen, the voice deepens, SPERM are produced, and spontaneous erections begin to occur. The hormones also trigger a GROWTH SPURT, of perhaps four to six inches a year, until full height is reached in the late teens. Then the ends of the skeletal bones, where the growth takes place, close off and growth ends.

The changes of puberty are the physical part of the massive changes that take place in ADOLESCENCE. These changes are made more difficult for children—perhaps 1 out of 10,000, including more girls than boys—who experience puberty abnormally early. *Precocious puberty* generally refers to puberty that begins in girls before age nine and in boys before age ten. What triggers precocious puberty is unclear, though in some cases it seems to be a BENIGN TUMOR in the part of the brain that releases LHRH (see BRAIN TUMORS). Other causes include disorders of the CENTRAL NERVOUS SYSTEM, such as NEUROFIBROMATOSIS, disorders of the ADRENAL GLANDS, and rare disorders such as *McCune-Albright syndrome.* Some forms of precocious puberty are apparently inherited, especially in males (sometimes by way of unaffected female CARRIERS). Though in precocious puberty, sex hormones speed up growth initially, growth stops sooner than usual, so these children often end up shorter than normal, with many females under 5 feet and many males under 5 feet 2 inches.

Early therapies to halt or slow precocious puberty have had little success. But therapy that involves desensitizing the pituitary gland to the effects of LHRH has not only stopped maturation but reversed it in some cases. Long-term effects of this therapy are unknown, however.

FOR HELP AND FURTHER INFORMATION

National Institute of Child Health and Human Development (NICHD), 301–496–5133. Publishes *Facts About Precocious Puberty.* (For full group information, see PREGNANCY.)

(See also SEX EDUCATION.)

public school, a school funded and controlled mainly by community and government, under the direction of a school board or publicly elected or appointed officials, as opposed to a PRIVATE SCHOOL controlled and funded mostly by individuals not responsible to the public. (For help and further information, see EDUCATION.)

pudendum, an alternate name for a woman's VULVA, a region sometimes anesthetized during CHILDBIRTH using a *pudendal block.* (See ANESTHESIA.)

puerperal sepsis, an infection of the UTERUS following CHILDBIRTH; once a major cause of death following childbirth, and still sometimes a cause of MATERNAL MORTALITY.

puerperium, a medical term for the six or so weeks after a woman gives birth, during which the body begins to normalize after its massive anatomical and physiological changes, and the woman begins to adjust to the changed family life involving the new infant.

pulmonary function tests, a group of MEDICAL TESTS to test how well a person's lungs are operating, sometimes to help in diagnosing or monitoring a LUNG AND BREATHING DISORDER, sometimes to assess a person's condition before an operation. Among the assessments performed are:

- *Spirometry,* in which the patient exhales air through a tube into a machine, which measures the volume exhaled and the speed of the exhalation. Children with ASTHMA cannot exhale as fast as normal.
- *Peak flow meter,* a device that measures how fast air can be expelled from the lungs, as a person exhales into the meter's mouthpiece. In children with asthma, the rate is slower than normal because the air passages are constricted; this test is sometimes used to assess their response to various treatments, and may be used as a daily monitor.
- *Blood gases,* a test that measures the acidity or alkalinity of the blood, using just a few drops, an emergency procedure to assess the acidity or alkalinity of the blood and to see the amount of oxygen, carbon dioxide, and hydrogen in the blood; this is useful in monitoring cases of possible respiratory failure.
- *Diffusing capacity,* a test that indicates how efficient the lungs are at transferring oxygen into the blood.

(See also LUNG AND BREATHING DISORDERS; MEDICAL TESTS.)

Pure Tone Test (audiometric test), a type of HEARING TEST that measures the frequency and loudness of sounds that a person is able to hear, a common test in assessing EAR AND HEARING PROBLEMS.

putative father, a legal term for the presumed biological FATHER, if a child's parents are not married and paternity has not been acknowledged or established. A PATERNITY SUIT may be brought against the alleged father in some situations.

Q

quarter, a fourth. In EDUCATION, the school year is sometimes divided into four equal quarters, instead of two SEMESTERS or three TRIMESTERS. Quarter is also an alternate term for *quartile*, a way of ranking test scores, on the same principle as a PERCENTILE, only from 1 to 4.

quickening, the baby's first felt movements in the UTERUS, generally perceived by mothers during the 18th to 20th weeks of the PREGNANCY, but sometimes as early as the 16th, especially in second and subsequent pregnancies. It often starts as a flutter, but later the woman should be able to feel—and sometimes even see on her abdomen—distinct kicks.

quinmester, an educational schedule that divides the school year into five 45-day units, plus one 30-day vacation unit. Students are expected to attend at least four, and if they wish all five, of the units. (See YEAR-ROUND EDUCATION.)

quinsy, inflammation and often infection of one or both TONSILS and surrounding tissues.

R

rabies, a life-threatening disease caused by a virus, transmitted from saliva of an infected animal through a bite or other break in the skin. The virus travels through the NERVOUS SYSTEM to the brain, where it incubates, causing at first generalized symptoms, such as FEVER and restlessness, then inflammation (ENCEPHALITIS), intense thirst but inability to drink due to violent muscle spasms in the throat (source of the alternate name *hydrophobia*), sometimes PARALYSIS of the face and eye muscles, and COMA. Once symptoms have appeared (usually in four to eight weeks, but as early as nine days), rabies is almost always fatal, though some people have survived with special treatment in INTENSIVE CARE UNITS.

If a child or adult has been bitten by or otherwise exposed to a rabid animal, the break, wound, or general area should be cleaned thoroughly and medical treatment should be sought immediately. The physician will normally begin a course of injections of *immunoglobulin*, ANTIBODIES that provide passive IMMUNIZATION against the virus during the period of hazard. While these injections have some side effects, they are no longer the painful injections in the stomach of earlier decades. If started promptly (within two days of the exposure) this treatment almost always prevents development of the disease.

Beyond that, the main focus is on preventing the spread of the disease among wild or domestic animals. If possible, the biting animal is captured, killed, and examined for signs of rabies; if none are found, the injection series may be ended. Because of prevention measures, especially vaccinating dogs, rabies is no longer common. However, in recent years it has begun to spread more widely among wild animals, such as raccoons and bats. Parents who live in areas where rabies is known to exist should be alert to the possibility if a child is bitten or has contact with a questionable animal.

FOR HELP AND FURTHER INFORMATION

National Institute of Allergy and Infectious Diseases (NIAID), 301–496–5717. Publishes brochure *Rabies*. (For full group information, see ALLERGY.)

National Organization for Rare Disorders (NORD), 800–999–6673. (For full group information, see RARE DISORDERS.)

radiography, a general medical term for the use of X-RAYS, either in still pictures, as in a chest x-ray, or in moving images, as in FLUOROSCOPY, to give a picture of the internal workings of the body. Some kinds of radiography are regarded as INVASIVE PROCEDURES, meaning that they involve INJECTION or ingestion of foreign substances into the body, such as the dyed fluid in a MYELOGRAM. Most X-rays are considered noninvasive, but because they can damage a FETUS, women who are or suspect they may be pregnant are advised not to have such a test. (For help and further information, see MEDICAL TESTS.)

rank, a relative standing within a group, in EDUCATION generally referring to the numerical order in which students rank by their GRADE-POINT AVERAGES. In a graduating class, the highest ranking student is the VALEDICTORIAN, the second highest is the SALUTATORIAN, with other students listed in numerical order (third, fourth, fifth, etc.). In addition to GRADE average and scores on certain STANDARDIZED TESTS, class rank is one of the key criteria considered by COLLEGES evaluating students for possible ADMISSION. However, a student who was twentieth in the graduating class of a highly competitive science-oriented school might be considered more favorably than someone who was tenth graduating from a small rural central school, though in practice college admissions teams would look at a variety of measures in assessing a student.

rape, the act of forcing someone to perform sexual acts, unknowingly or unwillingly, under threat of VIOLENCE. What actually constitutes rape varies. Traditional definitions of rape have generally involved references to "carnal knowledge." In some states, that has been narrowly defined as involving actual or attempted vaginal sexual intercourse. Other states have a wider definition, including vaginal penetration by objects, including fingers; oral or anal sex; and also rape of men, not just women, though females continue to be the main victims. Some states consider rape to have occurred if the woman was unconscious or otherwise incapable of giving or withholding consent, as if she was under the heavy influence of drugs or was mentally retarded, or if she was faced with the *threat* of irresistible force.

Rape does not always require force. Sexual intercourse with a child under the AGE OF CONSENT is labeled *statutory rape*, literally because the child is regarded by law as unable to give consent. That law is less often applied today between consenting adolescents, but may still be applied when an adult (especially one in a position of trust or authority) has relations with a significantly younger adolescent. For young children, being compelled to perform sexual acts generally comes under the heading of child sexual abuse (see CHILD ABUSE AND NEGLECT) or INCEST, and may be chargeable under the relevant state laws.

While children, like adults, may be at risk of being raped in many times and places in their lives, they are most at risk among the people they know—their families, neighbors, coworkers, and fellow students. A 1990 National Crime Survey estimated that of the known rapes against women, 58 percent were committed by someone she knew, including a husband or boyfriend, and 35 percent took place in her own home. Commonly called *date rape, acquaintance rape,* or *marital rape,* these kinds of attacks are especially damaging because they come not from the stereotypical crazed sadist roaming the streets, but from someone known and trusted, who had been freely admitted into their "private space." Sometimes the attack comes out of the blue, in what had seemed a perfectly normal relationship, but in others, the trust may have been partly or completely gone before the attack, as with an ex-lover.

Indeed, because date rape fails to fit the stereotype of rape, many women have not even considered their experiences of forced sex as fitting the definition of "rape." A 1980s *Ms.* magazine study reported that, of 3000 college women, 1 in 4 had been the victim of rape or attempted rape and 84 percent knew their intended attacker; however, only 27 percent of these women realized that the sexual assault they experienced met the legal definition of rape. Many women who tried to tell others of their experiences of date rape—or of *gang rapes* by groups such as fraternities—were met with disbelief. That has changed somewhat in recent years, as HIGH SCHOOLS and COLLEGES have become more aware of the problem. Some have instituted programs to educate students of both sexes about what constitutes consent in sexual relations; some have also added self-defense classes for women. The question of consent has also come to the fore because the threat of AIDS has required CONDOMS to be worn for protection during sex, a decision often pressed by the woman.

Children as well as adults are also at risk for *custodial rape,* committed by those in positions of power, such as police officers, doctors, soldiers, prison officers, priests, and hostel staff. This is a widespread problem all over the world, though it is only in recent years that it has been acknowledged.

Treatment of rape cases has traditionally been abysmal, with a woman often experiencing a "second rape" from abusive treatment by police and courts, in which she was commonly assumed to be wanting it, "asking for it," and meaning "yes" when she said "no." Rape victims were routinely sent for psychiatric examinations, since it was assumed that many were making false accusations. If a case went to trial, the woman found her name and reputation smeared. Not surprisingly, few cases were reported, fewer went to trial, and only a very few resulted in conviction.

In recent years, that picture has changed somewhat. Rape crisis centers offer support and counseling for dealing with *rape trauma syndrome,* a kind of POST-TRAUMATIC SHOCK. Police departments often have teams specially trained to deal with rape cases; district attorney's offices have sometimes added witness support services; and some court procedures have been changed for less biased treatment. Many states have enacted *rape shield laws,* which keep the victim's name confidential and limit inquiry into her past sexual history. Even so, only a small percentage of rape cases actually go to trial.

Parents can best protect their children by teaching them how to prevent sexual assault, especially to avoid being in places and situations where they are targets. For young children, see TIPS FOR PROTECTING YOUR CHILDREN AGAINST ABDUCTION on page 408. Older children, who are going on dates and may be on their own, call for different kinds of counsel. With dates or acquaintances, unless they know a man *very* well, they should be advised not to:

- Go to the man's home, even if he says others are there; many men take this as an implicit assent to have sex.
- Go in the car with him to an isolated area.
- Depend solely on him for a ride home; arrange for other alternatives, such as a cab.
- Become intoxicated and so seem more vulnerable; alcohol can also loosen the man's inhibitions.
- Bring a man home to an apartment or dorm room, even if other adults are there.

They should also be alert to signs of excessive control, inappropriate anger, or extreme possessiveness, and seek advice or help from parents or other trusted adults.

FOR HELP AND FURTHER INFORMATION

C. Henry Kempe National Center for the Prevention and Treatment of Child Abuse and Neglect, 303–321–3963. Publishes *Man-to-Man: When Your Partner Says No, Pressured Sex, and Date Rape.* (For full group information, see HELP AGAINST CHILD ABUSE AND NEGLECT on page 680.)

People Against Rape (PAR), 800–877–3252. (For full group information, see HELP AGAINST CHILD ABUSE AND NEGLECT on page 680.)

National Center for Women and Family Law, 212–674–8200. Publishes *Stalking Statutes* and *Marital Rape Laws and Litigation* (For full group information, see CUSTODY.)

OTHER RESOURCES

GENERAL GUIDES

If You Are Raped, 2nd abridged ed. Kathryn M. Johnson. Learning Publications, 1992.

Rape: What Would You Do If?, rev. ed. Dianne D. Booher. Simon & Schuster, 1991.

Acquaintance Rape: The Hidden Crime. Andrea Parrot and Laurie Bechhofer, eds. Wiley, 1991.

FOR PRETEENS AND TEENS

Everything You Need to Know about Date Rape, rev. ed. Frances Shuker-Haines. Rosen, 1992.

Rape. JoAnn B. Guernsey. Crestwood/Macmillan, 1990.
Rape in Marriage, rev. ed. Diana E. Russell. Indiana University Press, 1990.

On recovery

Quest for Respect: A Healing Guide for Survivors of Rape. Linda Braswell. Pathfinder (CA), 1990.
New Beginnings, rev. ed. Beth Haseltine and Lynn Peterson. Rape Abuse Crisis, 1990.

Personal experiences

It Happened to Nancy: A True Story from the Diary of a Teenager. Beatrice Sparks, ed. Avon, 1994. A teenage girl who contracts AIDS after being raped, presented by the editor of *Go Ask Alice.*
The Voices of Rape. Janet Bode. Watts, 1990.

Background works

Rape, Incest and Child Sexual Abuse: Consequences and Recovery. Pat Gilmartin. Garland, 1994.
The Second Rape: Society's Continued Betrayal of the Victim. Lee Madigan, Lee and Nancy Gamble. Free Press, 1991.

(See also CHILD ABUSE AND NEGLECT.)

rapprochement, the third stage of a baby's SEPARATION-INDIVIDUATION process.

rare disorders, disorders that appear in relatively few people, including GENETIC DISORDERS, CHROMOSOMAL ABNORMALITIES, unusual infectious diseases, and other health problems of unknown origin. A rare disorder is considered to be one that affects fewer than 200,000 people in the United States, though the National Organization for Rare Disorders (see the list of organizations following this entry) estimates that there are more than 5000 orphan diseases, together affecting perhaps one person in twelve, or some 20 million Americans. The 1983 Orphan Drug Act began subsidies to pharmaceutical companies so that they would produce drugs needed by people suffering from rare disorders (see ORPHAN DRUG). This book contains information on many specific rare disorders; for those not covered, parents may want to contact the organizations listed, as well as checking with local self-help clearinghouses to see if support groups exist.

FOR HELP AND FURTHER INFORMATION

National Organization for Rare Disorders (NORD)
P.O. Box 8923
New Fairfield, CT 06812–8923
203–746–6927, TT; 800–999–6673; 800–937-NORD [937–6673]
Fax: 203–746–6896
E-mail: 76703.3014@compuserve.com (CompuServe: 76703, 3014)
Abbey S. Meyers, President

Organization concerned with rare disorders, its members including over 135 nonprofit health organizations; operates information clearinghouse; makes referrals; sponsors Networking Program and Medication Assistance Program; monitors availability of medicines for rare disorders under the Orphan Drug Act; publishes quarterly *Orphan Disease Update, Physicians' Guide to Rare Diseases*, and reprints from its Rare Disease Database on specific disorders, including both rare diseases and others of high interest.

Parents Helping Parents (PHP), 408–727–5775. Publishes information packet *Rare Conditions.* (For full group information, see HELP FOR SPECIAL CHILDREN on page 689.)

(See also HEALTH CARE; also HOW TO FIND HOTLINES AND HELPLINES: A QUICK GUIDE on page 297.)

rash, a general term for reddish spots or reddish, inflamed skin, sometimes associated with itching or FEVER. Many rashes, especially in babies, are associated with local irritation. Diaper rash results from exposure to urine and feces, and to ammonia produced by bacteria working on them, and is one of the most common problems experienced by babies (see BABIES AND RASHES on page 498.) A more general type of rash, common in hot weather in people of all ages, is *heat rash* or *prickly heat*, resulting from local irritation from perspiration. It is best treated by wearing loose clothing, keeping as dry as possible, and exposing the area to air.

These are but two common examples of what is perhaps the most common skin disorder: *contact dermatitis*, in which the skin reacts either to direct damage by an irritating substance, or because the body has been sensitized to a substance, such as tomatoes. If the skin is sensitive or the irritating substance strong, rashes go beyond a mild reddening to blisters or ulcers and even to chronic thickening, drying, cracking, and hardening of the skin, or *eczema.* In the case of something like poison ivy, the cause is clear, but often it is not, especially when the reaction is mild and builds up over time. Then parents (and their doctor) may need to do some detective work to locate the source of the problem. Sometimes the location of the rash can be useful. A line of redness around a wrist or neck, for example, might point to jewelry containing nickel, a common irritant. In such cases, removing the offending item from contact with skin may solve the problem. In other cases, parents may need to consult a *dermatologist* specializing in such disorders. to identify the source of the problem and prescribe a treatment.

Parents of children with sensitive skin can take a number of steps to prevent or lessen contact dermatitis:

- Read labels on all substances used on the skin, which are by law required to be listed on the label in descending order of predominance. If a particular substance, such as a cosmetic, causes a problem, note its

Babies and Rashes

Almost every baby develops a fine pink or red rash when the skin is irritated by rubbing on bed covers, by spitting up, or by very hot weather. Almost all of these fine pink rashes will go away promptly if the skin is bathed with clean water whenever it is dirty, and washed with mild soap once a day.

When should you worry about a baby's skin? Any pimple or rash that gets bright red and enlarges, or that develops blisters or pus, may be the beginning of an infection that will need medical care. You can soak such a rash with a washcloth or towel wrung out in warm water, and keep it clean by washing with mild soap and water twice a day. If it gets worse, or if it doesn't get better in twenty-four hours, you should call your doctor or clinic.

Any rash that looks like bleeding or bruising in the skin *should be seen by a doctor promptly.*

PREVENTING DIAPER RASHES

Parents can prevent diaper rash in their infants by:

- Changing diapers frequently,
- Rinsing the baby's diaper area with clean water at each diaper change,
- Rinsing cotton diapers thoroughly before washing them,
- Avoiding "super-absorbent" disposable diapers,
- Leaving off plastic pants whenever possible,
- Applying a layer of zinc oxide paste or diaper rash ointment to any irritated area.

If your baby gets a diaper rash in spite of this, you should:

- Leave off plastic pants (or plastic covered disposable diapers) except when absolutely necessary. Using two or more cloth diapers together at nap time and at night will make this less messy.
- Leave the baby's diaper area completely uncovered for a few hours each day (nap time or early evening is most convenient). Be sure to place a couple of diapers under the baby to prevent soiling.
- Apply a thin layer of zinc oxide paste or diaper rash ointment to any irritated area after cleansing at each diaper change.

If the problem persists, the doctor or clinic staff may recommend another medication. Be sure to wash your hands with soap and water after diapering to avoid passing infection.

Source: Infant Care (1989). Prepared by the Bureau of Maternal and Child Health and Resources Development, Public Health Service.

ingredients and avoid similarly formulated substances. Fragrances and preservatives are common culprits; specific fragrance components are not listed, but you can switch to fragrance-free products.

- Wash new clothing and bed linens several times before first using them to rid them of chemicals and dyes used in finishing the fabrics.
- Stick with natural fibers, such as cotton, linen, and silk (wool, though natural, can be an irritant). Avoid polyester blends and other fabrics labeled "permanent press" and "wrinkle-resistant."
- If soaps or detergents seem to be a problem, stick with those formulated for babies' wash, double-rinse the wash, and avoid fabric softeners and antistatic products.
- Be sure you and your children can recognize the three-leaved poison ivy and poison oak, and the oval-leaved poison sumac. If exposed to them, wash hands and skin thoroughly. Have available before needed an over-the-counter poison ivy medication. You may want to avoid those containing zirconium, benzocaine, and diphenhydramine hydrochloride; though these work fine for most people, those with sensitive skin may react to them, resulting in another dermatitis on top of the poison ivy rash.
- If you or your children get rashes from handling other plants, note which ones and stay clear of them, or handle them only with long gloves on. Among the common problem vegetables are parsnips, garlic, onions, tomatoes, carrots, and ginger.
- Wear gloves—some recommend heavy-duty vinyl gloves with cotton liners, if possible—before coming into contact with abrasive soaps, harsh cleansers, or other chemicals at home or work.
- Keep hands and skin well-moisturized with a fragrance-free cream or lotion.

If you are self-treating dermatitis in yourself or your children, do not do so beyond a week or ten days. If it is not better by then, or if it becomes worse, see your doctor. Rashes can be caused by superficial fungal or bacterial infections, or they can be symptoms of others kinds of problems, including SCABIES, a mite infestation, or Hodgkin's disease (see IMMUNE SYSTEM). Rashes are also associated with numerous disorders common in children, such as CHICKEN POX and SCARLET FEVER, as well as in some less common diseases such as ROCKY MOUNTAIN SPOTTED FEVER, some AUTOIMMUNE DISORDERS such as LUPUS, and some kinds of VITAMIN deficiency. Some kinds of SEXUALLY TRANSMITTED DISEASES (STDs) show themselves partly by sores and blisters on the skin, notably HERPES. Treatment depends on the cause, and the type of spots distinguished by a physician. Sometimes the tendency of skin to turn red or form crusty patches can be turned to advantage in MEDICAL TESTS, such as the TUBERCULIN SKIN TEST. (For help and further information, see SKIN AND SKIN DISORDERS.)

reactive attachment disorder, a type of MENTAL DISORDER affecting infants and children under five, in which they have disturbances in their social interactions. Infants, for example, often have poor VISUAL SKILLS and communication skills (see COMMUNICATION SKILLS AND DISORDERS), and lack the reciprocal visual contact and playfulness to develop the skills. Slightly older children with the disorder are often apathetic, incurious, and lack social interest; however, in some cases they may be sociable, though indiscriminately, as with strangers. Some of the above symptoms are similar to those in AUTISM, but this disorder is termed *reactive* because it is generally a response to lack of BONDING between child and CAREGIVER, to CHILD ABUSE AND NEGLECT, or to absence of stable family attachments, as when a child has been moved from one home to another in FOSTER CARE. Reactive attachment disorder is often the psychosocial accompaniment to FAILURE TO THRIVE or MATERNAL DEPRIVATION SYNDROME. (For help and further information, see MENTAL DISORDERS.)

readiness, possession of the PREREQUISITE skills and MATURITY necessary to learn new skills, sometimes used generally to apply to any area of EDUCATION, but often used specifically in relation to young children and READING. Without such readiness, a child may quickly fall behind the rest of the class academically, because so much other learning depends on the ability to read. As a result, educators use various READING READINESS TESTS to help them in trying to assess whether or not a child is ready to learn to read, in addition to other READINESS TESTS relating to other kinds of skills.

readiness class, a school class for children who are AGE-ELIGIBLE—that is, eligible and perhaps even required to enter school, as measured by CHRONOLOGICAL AGE—but whose DEVELOPMENTAL AGE is considered too low, based on various READINESS TESTS or DEVELOPMENTAL SCREENING TESTS.

readiness tests, a range of tests used to assess whether a child has the necessary skills and development to benefit fully from instruction, as in READING READINESS TESTS. Where DEVELOPMENTAL SCREENING TESTS focus on a child's ability to learn, readiness tests focus more precisely on whether the child has acquired the PREREQUISITE skills necessary for more advanced learning. A low score on a readiness test may indicate a child's lack of basic experience or teaching at home, and does not necessarily indicate a learning problem (which is what developmental screening tests are supposed to identify). Examples of widely used readiness tests are the CALIFORNIA ACHIEVEMENT TEST, METROPOLITAN READINESS TEST, BOEHM TEST OF BASIC CONCEPTS, and BRIGANCE® INVENTORY OF EARLY DEVELOPMENT. Such tests are widely used for class placement and CURRICULUM planning for children—even though current research indicates that tests for young children are notorious for having very poor RELIABILITY and VALIDITY, because children change so fast and grow at such individual and varying rates.

FOR HELP AND FURTHER INFORMATION

National Association for the Education of Young Children (NAEYC), 800–424–2460. Publishes brochure *Ready or Not: What Parents Should Know About School Readiness.* (For full group information, see PRESCHOOL.)

OTHER RESOURCES

Accepting the Readiness Idea. Linda D. Pass. Programs for Education, 1992.
Ready for School? Jim Grant. Programs for Education, 1992.
Some More Things That Affect School Readiness. James K. Uphoff. Programs for Education, 1992.
Ready for What?: Constructing Meanings of Readiness for Kindergarten. M. Elizabeth Graue. State University of New York Press, 1992.

(See READINESS; TESTS; also PRESCHOOL for works on preparing children for preschool.)

reading, the process of perceiving and recognizing written symbols and translating them into words that individually and together convey meaning. Though many of us take reading for granted, it is in fact a highly complex process, and many people have difficulty with one or another stage of the process (see WHAT IS READING? on page 500).

Most notably, some people with DYSLEXIA, sometimes called *word blindness,* or other kinds of LEARNING DISABILITIES have difficulty in transmitting an accurate picture of letters and words to the brain; these are often scrambled, with REVERSALS such as *saw* for *was,* or *word test* for *test word.* Some people have problems with their short-term memory, so that they cannot remember letters and words they have read long enough to be able to put them

What Is Reading?

Many people believe that reading is just the process of turning printed words into their spoken equivalents. However, this view of reading represents only part of the picture. Years of research have shown reading to be far more than just knowing how sounds correspond to letters and words.

Skilled readers do much more than just turn printed words into spoken ones. They use their knowledge of the world, of how information is organized on a page, and their awareness of whether something makes sense to guide their efforts to construct meaning. For example, children faced with the sentence, "Mommy and Daddy gave the waiter a tip." might be able to say the words in the sentence. But if those children had only eaten at a fast food restaurant and had never seen a waiter or observed their parents leaving money on the table, they may completely fail to understand the meaning of the sentence.

Consequently, for all readers, beginning or skilled, the capacity to understand a written message or text depends as much on experience with the world (including books) outside of school as on the formal education provided by the school. Hence the fundamental importance of home-based experiences.

Reflecting this expanded idea of reading, in *Becoming a Nation of Readers*, the U.S. Department of Education's Commission on Reading defined reading as: "the process of constructing meaning from written texts. It is a complex skill requiring the coordination of a number of interrelated sources of information."

The report went on to describe skilled reading in five ways:

- Reading is a *constructive process.* Since no piece of written matter can possibly tell readers everything they need to know, readers must "fill in the blanks" from their experience.
- Reading must be *fluent.* Readers must be able to recognize words quickly and accurately, so that the process of constructing meaning from the text takes place fluidly.
- Reading must be *strategic.* Readers vary *how* they read according to the complexity of the material, their familiarity with the topic, and their purpose in reading it. For example, they might read difficult materials slowly and with care, skim an advertisement, and whiz through an exciting story.
- Reading requires *motivation,* which stems from the recognition that reading can be interesting and informative.
- Skilled reading is a *lifelong pursuit.* Like playing a musical instrument, it is not something that is mastered once and for all, but a skill that continues to improve through practice.

Because reading is a complex skill that develops over a lifetime, teachers alone are not enough. Learning to read begins when you talk with and listen to your children, especially when you read with them, and let them see you reading for your own enjoyment. In doing just those few things, you teach your children the most important lessons about reading.

Source: Adapted from Becoming a Nation of Readers: What Parents Can Do, *prepared by Marilyn R. Binkley, and others. Published by D.C. Heath and Company in cooperation with the Office of Educational Research and Improvement of the U.S. Department of Education, 1988.*

together in a meaningful way. The general term for an error that a person makes in READING (such as dropping a word, adding a word, or substituting one word for another) is a *miscue.* The difficulty of reading has been pointed out with some poignancy in recent years by many adults (including some well-known professional athletes) publicly acknowledging that, although they are graduates of high school and sometimes even COLLEGE, they are functionally ILLITERATE.

Such problems point up some of the complexities that young children face in learning how to read. Because reading is such an important skill (sometimes called a PRECURSOR or PREREQUISITE skill), much attention is placed on evaluating whether or not a child has the skills and maturity—what educators call READINESS—to learn how to read effectively. To assess these, educators employ various READING READINESS TESTS.

Traditionally reading was taught primarily using the PHONICS METHOD, by which the child learned to associate letters with sounds and "sounded out" words, later applying that method to new words. But in recent decades, many educators have preferred some variation of the

WHOLE WORD METHOD (also called the *word-recognition, sight method,* or more generally the *whole language approach*), in which children learn words as whole units, only later breaking them down into parts and learning how to put them together in new words. The whole word approach has the advantage of focusing on meaning and context. However, children who have PERCEPTUAL HANDICAPS that cause reading difficulty often seem to fare better with strong use of the phonics approach, usually highly structured methods (see VAKT).

Beginning readers often practice *oral reading,* in which they speak the words out loud; later they move to *silent reading,* though sometimes with *subvocalization,* in which words are formed by the lips or even whispered while reading. Subvocalization can significantly slow their reading speed, but may be useful for students with reading difficulties, such as DYSLEXIA. In *controlled reading,* the student's reading speed, and the level and the content of the material, are carefully paced to maximize learning.

Because reading is a skill basic to many other kinds of learning, much attention is paid to evaluating how well a student has progressed. Among the aspects of reading that educators assess are:

- *Reading comprehension,* or the ability to understand and recall data from material just read.
- *Speed* or rate of reading.
- *Scanning,* or running the eye down a page to find information, as in an index or catalog (a kind of LOCATIONAL SKILL).
- *Skimming,* a type of speeded-up reading in which a person gets a general idea of a selection's content, without reading it word for word.
- WORD-ATTACK SKILLS, the skills a child needs to deal with new or unfamiliar words.
- *Passive vocabulary,* words that a child can recognize or understand in context, but cannot use independently.
- *Active vocabulary,* words that a child can use independently in his or her own speaking or writing; this is always more limited than the passive vocabulary, because children (like adults) understand more than they can independently express.
- *Sight vocabulary,* words that a student can read and understand without looking them up, as in a dictionary.
- *Sight word,* words that a student recognizes and understands in a READING selection without needing to sound them out.

Often a student's scores on STANDARDIZED TESTS assessing various aspects of reading ability are compared with the average test scores for students on such tests, the result being expressed as a reading AGE or GRADE-EQUIVALENT.

Reading researchers have developed numerous ways to measure the difficulty of reading passages. Various kinds of formulas (named for their developers, such as Lorge, Dale-Chall, Flesch, Washburne-Vogel, or Yoakam), measure *readability,* taking into account the number of syllables per word and the average number of words per sentence. The numerical results are related to typical levels of reading matter for certain age or grade levels, and are used to judge whether reading matter is appropriate for given students or grades. The ability of a student to comprehend reading matter of a certain level of difficulty is sometimes expressed as *reading power,* and may be measured by a test called *Degrees of Reading Power.*

Reading experts have also formulated lists of *key words* (such as the Dolch Word List). These are words targeted for teaching in the early grades; they are most common in material written for children, and new material for these grades may be restricted to using primarily words on that list. In preparing textbooks for young readers, educators often take into account both the readability of the work and the specific vocabulary included in it.

Parents are often the key to the child's reading ability. In *Becoming a Nation of Readers,* the U.S. Department of Education's Commission on Reading made a number of suggestions for how parents can help their children not only learn to read but *want* to read, recognizing it as an opening to the whole world and time, most importantly:

- *Parents should read to preschool children and informally teach them about reading and writing.* Reading to young children, discussing stories and experiences with them, and—with a light touch—helping them learn letters and words are practices that are consistently associated with eventual success in reading.
- *Parents should support school-aged children's continued growth as readers.* Parents of children who become successful readers monitor their children's progress in school, become involved in school programs, support homework, buy their children books or take them to libraries, encourage reading as a free time activity, and place reasonable limits on such activities as TV viewing.

Parents will find information about some of the best books for children in the resource list that follows this entry. Also, throughout the A-Z portion of this book, parents will also find books for children under specific topics, such as ASTHMA or DIVORCE, as well as in the Special Help Section, including HELP ON LEARNING AND EDUCATION on page 659; HELP AGAINST SUBSTANCE ABUSE on page 703; and HELP AGAINST CHILD ABUSE AND NEGLECT on page 680. Books on some family situations may also be found in GENERAL PARENTING RESOURCES on page 634.

FOR HELP AND FURTHER INFORMATION

National Association for the Education of Young Children (NAEYC), 800–424–2460. Publishes books *Emerging Literacy: Young Children Learn to Read and Write,*

Language in Early Childhood Education, Young Children and Picture Books: Literature From Infancy to Six, and *More Than the ABCs: The Early Stages of Reading and Writing;* brochures *Helping Children Learn About Reading* and *African American Literature for Young Children;* and videos *Reading and Young Children* and *Whole Language Learning.* (For full group information, see PRESCHOOL.)

Alliance for Parental Involvement in Education (ALLPIE), 518–392–6900. Publishes leaflets *Encouraging Soon-to-Be-Readers—How to Excite Preschoolers About Books, Children Who Can Read, But Don't—How to Help Reluctant Readers Ages 9–13 Discover the Fun of Reading, Upbeat and Offbeat Activities to Encourage Reading, T.V. and Reading, Choosing Good Books for Your Children, Infancy to Age 12, You Can Help Your Child in Reading by Using the Newspaper,* and *You Can Help Your Child Connect Reading to Writing;* and journal *Books I Have Read.* (For full group information, see HELP ON LEARNING AND EDUCATION on page 659).

Association for Childhood Education International (ACEI), 800–423–3563. Publishes *Whole Language Course Packet,* reprints *Censorship in Children's Literature: What Every Educator Should Know, Communicating with Parents About Beginning Reading Instruction, The Parent's Role in Literacy Development: Fostering Reading Strategies at Home,* and *Writing in Kindergarten: Helping Parents Understand the Process;* audiotape *Constructivism and Whole Language;* and *Bibliography of Books for Children.* (For full group information, see HELP ON LEARNING AND EDUCATION on page 659.)

National Black Child Development Institute (NBCDI), 800–556–2234. Publishes *African American Family Reading List.* (For full group information, see HELP ON LEARNING AND EDUCATION on page 659.)

ERIC (Educational Resources Information Center) Clearinghouse on Reading, English, and Communication, 800–759–4723. (For full group information, see HELP ON LEARNING AND EDUCATION on page 659.)

ON READING IN GENERAL

Reading Is Fundamental (RIF)
600 Maryland Avenue SW, Suite 500
Washington, DC 20024
202–287–3220
Fax: 202–287–3196
Rut Graves, President
Network of local reading motivation programs, supported by corporate, foundation, private, and government funding; aims to stimulate reading in children from preschool through high school; publishes various materials, including:

- General works: *The RIF Guide to Encouraging Young Readers, Reading Is Fun!, Family Facts Brochure* (booklet for recording information about children), and *Family of Readers Activity Book.*
- On RIF groups: *The Fun and Fundamentals of Running a RIF Program* and *Shared Beginnings Leader's Guide and Idea Book.*
- Parent guide brochures: *Building a Family Library, Reading Aloud to Your Children, Encouraging Soon-to-Be Readers, Encouraging Young Writers, Family Storytelling, Magazines and Family Reading, Children Who Can Read, But Don't…, Choosing Good Books for Children, Reading: What's in It for Teenagers?/Teenagers and Reading* (half for parents, half for teens), *Summertime Reading,* and *Upbeat and Offbeat Activities to Encourage Reading.*

International Reading Association
P.O. Box 8139
800 Barksdale Road
Newark, DE 19714–8139
302–731–1600; Membership: 800–336-READ [336–7323]; For application brochures: 800–628–8508
Fax: 302–731–1057
Organization of educators and parents concerned with reading; provides information; operates a book club; publishes various materials, including:

- Bimonthly newsletter *Reading Today* and three professional journals.
- Brochures for parents: *Your Home Is Your Child's First School, You Can Encourage Your Child to Read, Good Books Make Reading Fun for Your Child, Summer Reading Is Important, You Can Use Television to Stimulate Your Child's Reading Habits, Studying: A Key to Success—Ways Parents Can Help, You Can Help Your Child in Reading Using the Newspaper, Eating Well Can Help Your Child Learn Better, You Can Prepare Your Child for Reading Tests, Reading and Your Adolescent,* and *You Can Help Your Child Connect Reading to Writing.*
- Booklets for parents: *How Can I Prepare My Young Child for Reading?, Beginning Literacy and Your Child, Creating Readers and Writers, Helping Your Child Become a Reader, You Can Help Your Young Child with Writing, Encouraging Your Junior High Student to Read, You Can Encourage Your High School Student to Read, Your Child's Vision Is Important.*
- Booklist: *Children's Choices, Young Adults' Choices, Teens' Favorite Books: Young Adults' Choices 1987–1992, Teachers' Choices,* and annual *Favorite Paperbacks* list.
- Books: *Comics to Classics: A Parent's Guide to Books for Teens and Preteens, Emerging Literacy: Young Children Learn to Read and Write. The Language of Learning: How Children Talk, Write, Dance, Draw, and Sing Their Understanding of the World, Hey! Listen to This: Stories to Read Aloud, Fostering the Love of Reading, Celebrate Diversity!, Teaching Reading Skills Through the Newspaper, Citizens Together: You and Your Newspaper, Censorship: A Threat to Reading, Learning, Thinking, More Kids' Favorite Books, A Survey of Family Literacy, Reading in the Middle School, Responses to Literature, Grades K–8, Developing a Whole Language Program for a Whole School,* and numerous professional materials.

- Videos: *Read to Me, Reading and Young Children: A Practical Guide for Childcare Providers, Whole Language: A New Zealand Approach,* and others for professionals.

AVKO Educational Research Foundation (AVKO-ERF)
3084 West Willard Road
Clio, MI 48420–7801
810–686–9283
Fax: 810–686–1101
E-mail: donmccabe@.aol.com (America Online: DONMCCABE)
Don McCabe, Research Director
Organization of people interested in audio, visual, kinetic, and oral (AVKO) techniques for teaching reading and spelling, especially for people with dyslexia or other learning disabilities; operates reading and spelling center; provides information training for adult tutors; publishes various materials, including the quarterly *AVKO Newsletter, The SQ3R Reading Formula Really Works, Underlining—Cuing the Computer Brain, A Practical Use for Miscue Analysis: Building Egos/Self-Esteem, Index of Phonic Patterns by Vowel Types, AVKO Spelling "Difficulty" Dictionary, The Patterns of English Spelling, The Mechanics of English Spelling,* and a full range of books and exams for their Sequential Spelling approach.

National Institute of Child Health and Human Development (NICHD), 301–496–5133. Publishes research reports *Getting Ready to Read.* (For full group information, see PREGNANCY.)

On selecting books and stories

Parents Choice Foundation
P.O. Box 185
Waban, MA 02168
617–965–5913
Fax: 617–965–4516
Diana H. Green, President
Organization providing information about books, movies, television, toys, games, records, videos, and computer software for children; publishes quarterly *Parents' Choice.*

American Library Association
Young Adult Services Division (YASD)
50 East Huron Street
Chicago, IL 60611
312–944–6780
Evelyn Shaevel, Executive Director
Division of American Library Association that evaluates books and other library materials for young adult readers; publishes various materials, including *Best Books for Young Adults, Outstanding Books for the College Bound,* brochure *Building a Home Library,* and an annual "best books" list (often available from your local library).

Great Books Foundation (GBF)
35 E. Wacker Drive, Suite 2300
Chicago, IL 60601–2298
312–332–5870; 800–222–5870
Alice Letvin, President
Organization encouraging reading of classic books among children and adults; offers programs and reading aids for discussion groups; trains teachers and volunteer discussion leaders; publishes various materials, including paperback versions of Great Books and Junior Great Books.

The Children's Foundation (TCF), 202–347–3300. Publishes *Recommended Starter List of Anti-Bias, Multicultural Children's Books to Enhance Your Existing Library* and *Checklist of Toys, Books, and Materials,* guidelines for choosing appropriate materials. (For full group information, see CHILD CARE.)

National Information Center for Children and Youth with Disabilities (NICHCY), 800–695–0285, voice/TT. Publishes bibliography *Children's Literature.* (For full group information, see HELP FOR SPECIAL CHILDREN on page 000.)

National Federation of the Blind (NFB), 410–659–9314. Publishes *Braille Storybook Resources, Reading by Touch,* and *Literacy for the Blind at School and Work: A Panel Discussion.* (For full group information, see EYE AND VISION PROBLEMS.)

National Information Center on Deafness (NICD), 202–651–5051; 202–651–5052, TT. Publishes *Books for Parents of Deaf and Hard of Hearing Children, Have You Ever Wondered About Hearing Loss and Deafness?: An Annotated Bibliography of Children's Books About Hearing Loss, Deafness, and Deaf and Hard of Hearing People.* (For full group information, see EAR AND HEARING PROBLEMS.)

On combating illiteracy

National Center for Family Literacy (NCFL)
Waterfront Plaza, Suite 200
325 West Main Street
Louisville, KY 40202–4251
502–584–1133
Fax: 502–584–0712
Organization concerned with family literacy; offers programs for adult education, preschool education, and parental support; publishes books *Generation to Generation: Realizing the Promise of Family Literacy, Family Literacy: The Need and the Promise, The Power of Family Literacy, Using Computers in Family Literacy Programs, Family Portfolios: Documenting Change in Parent/Child Relationships,* and *A Guide for Funding Sources for Family Literacy;* videos *The Power of Family Literacy* and *A Success Story;* and video-and-manual sets *Empowering People: Parent Groups* and *The Power of Parenting: Parent and Child Interaction.*

Laubach Literacy International
Box 131, 1320 Jamesville Avenue
Syracuse, NY 13210
315–422–9121
New Readers Press: 800–448–8878

Signal Hill Press: 800–506–7323
Center for Workforce Education: 800–221–6676
Peter Waite, Executive Director
Organization serving other volunteer literacy programs for adolescents or adults, including those for whom English is a second language; provides training for tutors, trainers, and program leaders; provides information; certifies literacy volunteers; counsels on development of literacy materials; publishes various materials, including quarterly *Literacy Advance* and annual directory; runs New Readers Press, with books for adolescent or adult beginning readers.

CETA Services
Contact Literacy Center
P.O. Box 81826
Lincoln, NE 68501
Literacy Hotline: 800–228–8813
Fax: 402–464–5931
Referral service for people wishing to learn how to read, in English or Spanish.

OTHER RESOURCES

For parents and other adults

Gifts of Love and Literacy: Begin the Magical Pathways to Literacy with Warm Cuddles, Rocking Chairs and Books. Barbara Keller and Ray Keller. Eagles, 1994.
How to Teach Your Baby to Read, 4th ed. Glenn Doman. Avery, 1994.
Parents and Teachers: Helping Children Learn to Read and Write. Timothy V. Rasinski. Harcourt Brace, 1994.
The Child's View of Reading: Understandings for Teachers and Parents. Pamela A. Michel. Allyn, 1994.
Read For the Fun of It. Caroline Feller Bauer. H.W. Wilson, 1992.
Nurturing Your Child's Natural Literacy. William Cole Cliett and H. Thomas Filmer. Maupin House, 1992.
Journey into Literacy: A Workbook for Parents and Teachers of Young Children. Barbara E. Swaby. Swaby, 1992.
Get Ready to Read: A Practical Guide to Teaching Young Children at Home and in School. Toni S. Gould. Walker, 1991.
Literacy at Home and School: A Guide for Parents. Vivienne Nicoll. Heinemann, 1991.
Readers, Writers and Parents Learning Together. Vince Dundas and George Strong. R. Owen, 1991.

(See also PRESCHOOL for school-preparation activities.)

On computers and reading

From Curiosity to Confidence: Help to Build Self-Esteem through Early Reading by Using Home Computers. Roger Young. Ten Speed/Celestial Arts, 1992.
Literacy Online: The Promise (and Peril) of Reading and Writing with Computers. Myron C. Tuman, ed. University of Pittsburgh Press, 1992.

Children on literacy

Children Talking about Books. Sarah G. Borders and Alice P. Naylor. Oryx Press, 1993.
Listening In: Children Talk about Books (and Other Things). Thomas McLure and Patricia Newkirk. Heinemann, 1993.
Children's Voices: Children Talk about Literacy. Sally Hudson-Ross and others, eds. Heinemann, 1992.

On multicultural literacy

Our Family, Our Friends, Our World: An Annotated Guide to Significant Multicultural Books for Children and Teenagers. Lyn Miller-Lachmann. Bowker, 1991.
Cross Cultural Literacy. Fraida Dubin and Natalie Kuhlman. Prentice Hall, 1992.
Multicultural Folktales: Stories to Tell Young Children. Judy Siera and Robert Kaminski. Oryx, 1991.
Language Issues in Literacy and Bilingual—Multicultural Education. Masahiko Minami and Bruce P. Kennedy, eds. Harvard Education, 1991.

On whole language approaches

Fun with Whole Language: Activity Ideas for Parents and Teachers of Young Children, Ages 2–6. Moira D. Green. GoodYearBooks, 1994.
Write to Read and Spell: Teaching the Basics Through a Whole-Language Journal Program. Laura Rose. Zephyr, 1993.
Joyful Learning: A Whole Language Kindergarten. Bobbi Fisher. Heinemann, 1991.
The Whole Language Kindergarten. Shirley C. Raines and Robert J. Canady. Teachers College, 1990.

Guides to books for young children

The Latest and Greatest Read-Alouds. Sharron L. McElmeel. Libraries Unlimited, 1994.
Hooray for Heroes!: Books and Activities Kids Want to Share with Their Parents and Teachers. Dennis Denenberg and Lorraine Roscoe. Scarecrow, 1994.
Picture Book Storytelling: Literature Activities for Young Children. Janice J. Beaty. Harcourt Brace, 1993.
The ALA Best of the Best for Children. American Library Association. Random House, 1992.
Children's Book Awards International: A Directory of Awards and Winners, from Inception through 1990. Laura Smith. McFarland, 1992.
Classics to Read Aloud to Your Children. William F. Russell. Crown, 1992.
Children's Catalog, 16th ed. H.W. Wilson, 1991. A basic librarians' guide to "the best new and established fiction and non-fiction titles written for children from pre-school through the sixth grade."
Alleyside Book of Flannelboard Stories: 20 Read-to-Tell Flannelboard Stories with Easy Patterns. Jeannette Graham Bay. Freline/Alleyside Press, 1991.
Play, Learn, and Grow: An Annotated Guide to the Best Books and Materials for Very Young Children. James L. Thomas. Bowker, 1991.

Books, Babies, and Libraries: Serving Infants, Toddlers, Their Parents, and Caregivers. Ellin Greene. American Library Association, 1991. Includes lists of useful books, magazines, films, and videotapes for parents and their children.

The Best in Children's Books: The University of Chicago Guide to Children's Literature, 1985–1990. Zena Sutherland and others. University of Chicago Press, 1991. Sutherland also edited previous "Best in Children's Books" covering 1966–72, 1976, 1973–78, 1980, 1979–84, and 1986.

Best Books for Children: Preschool through Grade 6, 4th ed. John T. Gillespie and Corinne J. Naden. Bowker, 1990.

Picture Books for Children, 3rd ed. Patricia J. Cianciolo. American Library Association, 1990.

Books Kids Will Sit Still For: The Complete Read-Aloud Guide, 2nd ed. Judy Freeman. Bowker, 1990.

GUIDES TO BOOKS FOR PRETEENS AND TEENS

Read for Your Life: Turning Teens into Readers. Gladys Hunt and Barbara Hampton. Zondervan, 1992.

Your Reading: A Booklist for Junior High and Middle School Students, 8th ed. Alleen Pace Nilsen, ed. National Council of Teachers of English, 1991.

Storytelling for Young Adults: Techniques and Treasury. Gail de Vos. Libraries Unlimited, 1991.

ON ILLITERACY

Illiteracy. Sean M. Grady. Lucent, 1994.

Coping with an Illiterate Parent. Nancy N. Rue. Rosen, 1990. On how to deal with a parent's reading problems.

BACKGROUND WORKS

Family Literacy. Lesley M. Morrow, ed. International Reading, 1995.

No Quick Fix: Rethinking Literacy Programs in America's Elementary Schools. Richard Allington and Sean Walmsley, ed. Teachers College, 1995.

Mikey and Mary Are Illiterate: And Nobody Cares. Mary C. Ericson. Excellent Education, 1994.

Adolescent Literacy: What Works and Why, 2nd ed. Judith Davidson and David Koppenhaver. Garland, 1993.

From A to Z with Books and Me. Imogene Forte. Incentive, 1991.

Literacy in the Television Age. Susan B. Neuman. Ablex, 1991.

Unfulfilled Expectations: Home and School Influences on Literacy. Catherine E. Snow and others. Harvard University Press, 1991.

Early Literacy. Joan Brooks McLane and Gillian Dowley McNamee. Harvard University Press, 1990.

The Reading Crisis: Why Poor Children Fall Behind. Jeanne S. Chall et al. Harvard University Press, 1990.

(See also WHOLE WORD METHOD; PHONICS METHOD; LEARNING DISABILITIES; ILLITERACY; EDUCATION; READING READINESS TESTS.)

reading age, a numerical summary reflecting a child's ability on READING tests, as compared to established NORMS. (See AGE; TESTS.)

reading power, the ability of a student to comprehend READING matter of a certain level of difficulty, sometimes measured by a test called *Degrees of Reading Power.*

reading readiness test, a type of READINESS TEST employed to help educators assess whether or not a child has the PREREQUISITE skills necessary for learning to read. This is a key question because, if not, a child will quickly fall behind the rest of the class academically, since so much other learning depends on reading ability. Among the areas measured by such a test are the child's maturity in using language (listening and speaking), perceptual maturity (ability to distinguish between different line drawings, for example), attention and responsiveness to storytelling, and general background and experience. (For help and further information, see READING.)

rebus approach, method of teaching READING by using sentences that combine words with pictures and symbols (such as a drawing of a pig or the symbol "4"), which help the beginning reader by introducing new or unfamiliar words in context.

recessive, in GENETIC INHERITANCE, a gene that produces its effects only when its paired gene is identical, or when it is unpaired on an X SEX CHROMOSOME; a recessive gene will not be expressed in the presence of a DOMINANT gene. If a mother contributes to her child a recessive gene for blue eyes, for example, the child will have blue eyes only if the father also contributes a gene for blue eyes. If both parents carry a recessive gene for a GENETIC DISORDER, any child of theirs has a 25 percent chance of inheriting the disorder, and a 50 percent chance of being a healthy CARRIER, someone who carries a defective gene, but is unaffected by it and may not even know it (see AUTOSOMAL RECESSIVE). A recessive defective gene whose effects are blocked by a dominant gene is said to be *masked.* Prospective parents whose family history includes genetic disorders are well advised to consider GENETIC COUNSELING when planning a pregnancy and GENETIC SCREENING during a pregnancy. Among the most common recessive disorders are CYSTIC FIBROSIS, PHENYLKETONURIA, sickle cell ANEMIA, GALACTOSEMIA, Friedreich's ATAXIA, *Hurler syndrome* (see MUCOPOLYSACCHARIDOSES), and LIPID STORAGE DISEASES, such as *Tay-Sachs disease* and *Gaucher disease.* (For help and further information, see GENETIC DISORDERS.)

recommended daily allowances (RDAs), the amounts of certain essential substances, such as VITAMINS and MINERALS, that a person should ingest daily to maintain normal body functioning. The amounts are set on recommendations by the Food and Nutrition Board of the National Academy of Sciences. Because research on human nutritional requirements is often incomplete or inconsistent, these are only estimates and are updated every five to ten years on the basis of new research. They are also deliberately set higher than the actual requirement for that nutrient in most individuals, so they will exceed the nutrient requirements of most people. RDAs for men are generally higher than for women, except for women who are pregnant or BREASTFEEDING. The recommendations are designed to "be adequate to meet the known nutritional needs of practically all healthy persons." They are averages, however, and must be modified for individual circumstances, as the *Surgeon General's Report on Nutrition and Health* notes:

> The fact that most RDA's are intentionally established to exceed the nutrient requirements of most people means that a dietary intake below the RDA is not necessarily inadequate for an individual whose requirement for a nutrient is average or even above average. It also means that the small percent of persons who have unusually high nutrient requirements may not meet nutritional needs even when they consume nutrients at RDA levels. The RDA's are estimates of the nutrient requirements for populations rather than for individuals. In addition, RDA's may need to be modified for people who are ill or injured.

Bottles of vitamins and mineral supplements and many foods carry information about the amount of the RDA provided for the key substances it contains. In some cases, where research has been so limited that no RDAs have been established, a range has been proposed that is believed to be "safe and adequate." **Caution**: The *Surgeon General's Report* also notes that: "the toxic level for many TRACE ELEMENTS may be only several times usual intake, [so] the upper levels for the trace elements given in this table should not be habitually exceeded." This is especially important for infants and children, whose bodies are even less able to handle excess amounts of vitamins and minerals than adults are, and so are subject to poisoning. (For help and further information, see VITAMINS; MINERALS; NUTRITION; FOOD LABELS.)

recovery room (RR), a room near a HOSPITAL's DELIVERY ROOM or operating room, to which patients are taken while they are still under ANESTHESIA. There trained staff monitor the patient's return to consciousness and maintenance of vital signs, with special equipment available should complications occur. From there, patients are taken to their regular hospital room, after childbirth sometimes called a POSTPARTUM ROOM. To avoid unsettling room shifts before, during, and after CHILDBIRTH, some hospitals have developed all-in-one LABOR/DELIVERY/RECOVERY ROOMS.

reflex, an involuntary, automatic movement in reaction to a particular event (*stimulus*) that triggers a response from the body's NERVOUS SYSTEM, such as the knee-jerk that follows a sharp tap below the kneecap. Some such *sensori-motor* reactions are found only in newborns, and disappear in the first few months. Among these so-called *primitive reflexes* are the GRASP REFLEX, TONIC NECK REFLEX, MORO'S REFLEX (startle reflex), WALKING REFLEX, and ROOTING REFLEX. Physicians use various reflexes as SIGNS to help indicate the health or illness of a patient. Primitive reflexes are especially important in the judging the early health and development of a baby. Absence or disturbance of one of these reflexes can indicate a problem in the nervous system, as LANDAU'S REFLEX can suggest possible CEREBRAL PALSY or MENTAL RETARDATION.

regurgitation, the back-flow of fluid, generally referring to the bringing up of food, drink, and perhaps some digestive acids from the stomach to the mouth. The term can also refer to the back-flow of blood in the heart, if a valve is defective (see HEART AND HEART PROBLEMS). Regurgitation from the stomach or esophagus is a less forcible action than VOMITING, and in relation to babies is often simply called "spitting up" (see SPITTING UP IN BABIES, on page 507). A rare related eating disorder is RUMINATION DISORDER OF INFANCY.

rehydration, restoration of the fluids and essential substances (ELECTROLYTES) normally dissolved in body fluids, to replace those lost during DEHYDRATION.

rejection, in relation to a TRANSPLANT, the attack of the body's IMMUNE SYSTEM on a donated organ or tissue. More widely, the term may refer to instances where one or both parents fail to fully accept their role as parent of a child, often leading to lack of BONDING and MATERNAL DEPRIVATION SYNDROME or FAILURE TO THRIVE.

reliability, in relation to TESTS, the degree to which a particular test consistently gives the same scores or readings. For an INTELLIGENCE TEST, reliability would concern whether or not a student got approximately the same score on a different form of the test given at a different time (this is *test-retest reliability*); sometimes conditions in the testing situation, variability in the tests, or change in the person giving the test (*interobserver reliability*) can produce widely varying results. For a MEDICAL TEST, reliability primarily concerns how often a test gives accurate results, as opposed to FALSE POSITIVES (suggesting a problem where none exists) or FALSE NEGATIVES (showing no problem, when one does exist).

Spitting Up in Babies

Most babies spit up some or even a lot of milk after a feeding. The milk seems to overflow from the baby's mouth. It is often curdled from normal stomach action. This is really not a problem—it is just messy. Babies who spit up grow as fast and as strong as those who do not.

There are several tricks to reduce the amount of spitting up. None of them works all the time, and most babies will continue some spitting up even when all the tricks are tried:

- Burp the baby carefully midway through the feeding, at the end of the feeding, and a few minutes after the feeding.
- Place the baby so that his or her head is higher than the stomach for ten or fifteen minutes after each feeding. This can be done by placing the baby in an infant seat or propping up the head of a cradle or bassinet.

Source: Infant Care (1989). Prepared by the Bureau of Maternal and Child Health and Resources Development for the Public Health Service.

remedial instruction, extra teaching, often tailored to individual needs, aimed at helping students to make up deficiencies in knowledge or skills, especially those needed for developing more advanced skills. It generally refers to short-term additional instruction for students who are otherwise expected to be able to handle coursework in regular classes, as opposed to SPECIAL EDUCATION, which is for students with DISABILITIES who are expected to need longer term help. Remedial instruction overlaps with COMPENSATORY EDUCATION, which attempts to make up deficiencies caused by a student's special circumstances, such as being socioeconomically disadvantaged or having English as a second language.

remedial school, a school, often UNGRADED, designed to help students make up for previous academic deficiencies, such as a school for former DROPOUTS returning to school; also called *tutoring school* or *catch-up school.*

remission, the lessening or disappearance of the SYMPTOMS and SIGNS of a disease considered CHRONIC, such as PSORIASIS, or PROGRESSIVE, such as MULTIPLE SCLEROSIS. Remission is the aim of many kinds of medical treatments, such as the radiation therapy used to treat CANCER. But remissions also occur spontaneously and for unknown reasons, even in cancers, and they are even characteristic of some diseases, such as multiple sclerosis. If the remission lasts long enough (the length depending on medical experience with the disease), the disease is considered to be *cured.*

repeat, in EDUCATION, to take over again a course that a student has failed to complete satisfactorily, whether through inability to develop the required knowledge and skills, inattention to course work, or other reasons.

Report of Student Answers (ROSA), a personalized scoring sheet for students, which reports scores for the student's responses on the SCHOLASTIC APTITUDE TEST.

reproductive system, the sexual organs, or GENITALS, that allow men and women to produce the eggs (see OVUM) and SPERM required for a new being, with a unique GENETIC INHERITANCE; and in the woman to develop the growing FETUS and give birth.

The main parts of the woman's reproductive system (discussed more fully in separate entries) are:

- The OVARIES, which produce the egg (ovum) required for FERTILIZATION (CONCEPTION).
- The FALLOPIAN TUBES, narrow ducts through which the egg and sperm normally travel and meet.
- The UTERUS, into which the Fallopian tubes open. The sperm pass through the uterus on the way to the egg. If the egg is fertilized, it is implanted in the lining of the uterus and grows; if not, the lining prepared monthly in advance is shed in periodic MENSTRUATION.
- The CERVIX, the narrow entry at the lower end of the uterus, through which the sperm pass on the way to the uterus. Biochemical changes occur around the time of maximum fertility (see NATURAL FAMILY PLANNING). If a pregnancy occurs, the cervix also helps hold the growing FETUS in place, until it widens at the end of GESTATION for CHILDBIRTH.
- The VAGINA, through which the sperm pass; the vagina and the widened cervix form the birth canal for the baby's passage to independent life.

These parts of the reproductive system also play various roles in the pleasures of sexual intercourse, in the process enhancing the process of reproduction, as do the external genitals, in women known as the VULVA, and including the CLITORIS, LABIA, and Bartholin's glands. In addition, various HORMONES control the stages of the reproductive cycle, which includes menstruation.

The male reproductive system includes:

- The TESTES, the pair of sex glands (GONADS) where SPERM are actually manufactured, and which also produce various hormones. The testes are normally suspended outside the body in a protective SKIN sac called the *scrotum*, which hangs between the anus and the PENIS.

- The *epididymis*, two long, coiled tubes, one behind each testicle; actually a holding area into which immature sperm pass, by way of small tubes called *vasa efferentia*, and where they mature.
- The *seminal vesicles*, structures that produce the fluid that makes up most of SEMEN, the sperm-containing fluid released at EJACULATION during ORGASM.
- The *prostate gland*, a chestnut-sized organ that produces secretions forming part of the semen; it is situated under the bladder and in front of the rectum. It grows to adult size during PUBERTY, and enlarges further in older men, sometimes causing urinary problems.
- The *vas deferens*, one of a pair of tubes through which mature sperm pass on their way from the epididymis; the two loop up out of the scrotum in a kind of open-ended "figure 8" to the base of the bladder. It is these two tubes (the *vasa deferentia*) that are cut during the type of male STERILIZATION called VASECTOMY.
- The *ejaculatory duct*, a short tube in which—shortly before ejaculation—sperm from the vas deferens and fluids from the seminal vesicles and prostate gland mix to form semen. This duct actually passes through the prostate gland.
- The PENIS, the main male organ of sexual response, through which semen passes. During sexual intercourse, the *urethra* through which urine normally flows becomes a passageway for semen, which is ejaculated as part of the male orgasm; some semen may leak out before ejaculation, so natural family planning techniques that rely on withdrawal of the penis before ejaculation are relatively unreliable.

In a newborn male, the penis and testes are relatively large, due to the effect of hormones from the mother; they soon grow smaller, and then during PUBERTY gradually grow to their adult size.

reproductive technology, a general term for laboratory approaches to achieving FERTILIZATION in cases of INFERTILITY. Among the main approaches are IN VITRO FERTILIZATION (IVF), EMBRYO TRANSFER, and GAMETE INTRA-FALLOPIAN TUBE TRANSFER (GIFT). Newer, still highly experimental ASSISTED FERTILIZATION approaches—which are all variations on in vitro fertilization—include INTRACYTOPLASMIC SPERM INJECTION (ICSI), PARTIAL ZONA DISSECTION (PZD), and SUBZONAL SPERM INSERTION (SZI), as well as ASSISTED HATCHING. Reproductive technology has been highly controversial, sparking widespread discussion of what limits can and should be placed on intervention into the creation of new human beings. However, for all the talk, the trend has been for every new technology to be put into practical application, to help fill the human hunger for babies.

FOR HELP AND FURTHER INFORMATION

Birth-Tech: Tests and Technology in Pregnancy and Birth. Ann Charlish and Linda H. Holt. Facts on File, 1990.

Science and the Unborn: Choosing Human Futures. Clifford Grobstein, Basic Books, 1990.

Science and Babies: Private Decisions, Public Dilemmas. National Academy Press, 1990.

(See also INFERTILITY; PRENATAL TESTS.)

required course, a course a student must take to fulfill the requirements of a school and eventually to GRADUATE, as opposed to optional courses, or ELECTIVES.

resection, a medical term for surgery in which something is removed; in the case of telescoping (INTUSSUSCEPTION), for example, a section of a child's bowel may be cut out to remove an obstruction.

residency requirement, in EDUCATION, a COLLEGE or university's requirement that a student must be enrolled in the institution for a specified number of years (generally one or two) before being eligible to receive a DEGREE; that requirement is waived in EXTERNAL DEGREE PROGRAMS. In a looser sense, the term *residency requirement* sometimes refers to a public COLLEGE or university's requirement that a student must have lived in the state for a specified period of time (often one year) to be eligible for the lower TUITION offered to state residents.

resident student, a student whose legal place of residence is in the district served by a school, such as the school district of a local PUBLIC SCHOOL or the state for a state-supported COLLEGE. NONRESIDENT STUDENTS must make special arrangements to attend a school that does not serve their neighborhood; at the college level, they are not eligible for the lower TUITION offered to state residents.

respiratory distress syndrome (RDS), a disorder in which lungs' air sacs (*alveoli*) tend to collapse after each breath, due to lack of a substance called *surfactant*, which normally prevents that; also called *hyaline membrane disease* (HMD). The disease is most often seen in PREMATURE babies, born after 28 weeks or less of PREGNANCY, and affects boys more severely than girls. A child also has a higher risk of RDS if the MOTHER has DIABETES, if the delivery was by CESAREAN SECTION, or if the mother was poor and had little or no PRENATAL CARE. Among the signs of respiratory distress are rapid breathing (*tachypnea*), blueness (CYANOSIS), abnormally rapid heartbeat (*tachycardia*), grunting and straining of the chest and neck muscles with the effort of breathing, and sometimes lack of breathing altogether (see APNEA OF PREMATURITY). Some other disorders, such as MENINGITIS or low blood sugar (HYPOGLYCEMIA), can present similar symptoms, but RDS is generally diagnosed by chest X-RAYS and BLOOD TESTS.

An RDS baby is often administered oxygen, as through a mask, hood, or tubes; may be given ANTIBIOTICS and fluids intravenously (PARENTERAL NUTRITION); and is often placed in a VENTILATOR (respirator) to assist breathing, with electronic monitoring of pulse, respiration, and heartbeat. Among the newer treatments employed in NEONATAL INTENSIVE CARE UNITS (NICUs) are:

- *Surfactant replacement therapy*, in which surfactant is given to babies through an endotracheal tube (ETT). This has had significant success in lessening the days a baby needs to spend on a ventilator, and in lowering MORTALITY from RDS, though it does not work for all babies.
- *High frequency oscillatory ventilation* (HFOV), which supplies oxygen at a respiratory rate of 300 to 900 breaths per minute—a rate that literally shakes the baby—rather than the 40 to 120 breaths of normal ventilators. This has had some success in saving seriously ill babies who have not responded to other therapies.

Many RDS babies improve over two to three days, but others do not respond to treatment or may develop a variety of related problems, some of which can be fatal, such as malformation of the lungs (*bronchopulmonary dysplasia* or BPD) or air leak into the chest area around the lungs (*pneumothorax* or *pneumomediastinum*; see LUNG AND BREATHING PROBLEMS). Babies with BPD sometimes have difficulty in being "weaned" from the ventilator; STEROIDS are sometimes administered to help this process, but only where the benefits outweigh its negative side effects, notably increased BLOOD PRESSURE and risk of infections in general.

Among babies who survive using these and other therapies, some will require supplemental oxygen for weeks or months in the hospital and even later after discharge to the home. RDS survivors may also have other associated disorders, such as MENTAL RETARDATION, HYDROCEPHALUS, and sometimes EAR AND HEARING PROBLEMS and EYE AND VISION PROBLEMS.

Pregnant women who are at risk for having an RDS baby may wish to consider PRENATAL TESTING, such as an ULTRASOUND scan to assess the maturity of the fetus or AMNIOCENTESIS to check the level of surfactant, especially in cases of possible elective CESAREAN SECTION, when a low level would suggest letting the fetus mature for longer. Some doctors have been giving steroids to mothers before delivery of a premature baby, in attempts to reduce the severity of likely respiratory distress syndrome. (For help and further information, see LUNG AND BREATHING DISORDERS.)

respiratory system, the system that takes oxygen from the air and passes it into the bloodstream; it can be subject to a variety of LUNG AND BREATHING DISORDERS.

respite care, custodial and medical assistance provided for a person with DISABILITIES, to allow the normal CAREGIVER time off to ease the strain. As many more children with severe DISABILITIES or illnesses live at home and attend regular schools, where once they might have spent most of their time in HOSPITALS or other institutions, their families have had much increased responsibilities and considerable stress. With the rise of the HOSPICE movement, many people are now choosing to die in their homes, with the main care falling on well family members. To help relieve the stress of such care, some public and private organizations have made arrangements to provide occasional respite care.

FOR HELP AND FURTHER INFORMATION

National Information Center for Children and Youth with Disabilities (NICHCY), 800–695–0285, voice/TT. Publishes *Respite Care: A Gift of Time.* (For full group information, see HELP FOR SPECIAL CHILDREN on page 689.)

National Adoption Information Clearinghouse (NAIC), 301–231–6512. Publishes *Respite Care: A Guide for Parents.* (For full group information, see ADOPTION.)

United Cerebral Palsy Association (UCPA), 800–872–5827. Publishes manual *Respitality.* (For full group information, see CEREBRAL PALSY.)

Epilepsy Foundation of America (EFA), 800–332–1000. Publishes book *Respite Care: Time Out for Families.* (For full group information, see EPILEPSY.)

The Arc, 817–261–6003. Publishes fact sheet *Respite Care.* (For full group information, see MENTAL RETARDATION.)

Rural Institute on Disabilities, 800–732–0323, voice/TT. Publishes reprints on respite care. (For full group information, see HELP FOR SPECIAL CHILDREN on page 689.)

resuscitation, the attempt to restore heartbeat and breathing in a person who has stopped breathing. (See ARTIFICIAL RESPIRATION for a description of procedures.)

retention, in EDUCATION, requiring a student to stay in the same GRADE for another school year (especially in ELEMENTARY SCHOOL), because of failure to develop the skills, learn the material, and meet the academic standards required of that grade. Because parents, students, and school officials are all—for various reasons—unhappy with retention, many students receive automatic PROMOTION, regardless of their academic performance. That causes serious personal and social problems, when students are graduated without necessary skills, some of them being functionally ILLITERATE. In some, perhaps many, cases, the problems have been caused by undiagnosed DISABILITIES, such as LEARNING DISABILITIES or EAR AND HEARING PROBLEMS, which prevented learning.

OTHER RESOURCES

On the Success of Failure: A Reassessment of the Effects of Retention in the Primary Grades. Karl L. Alexander and others. Cambridge University Press, 1992.

reversal (transposition), a type of common perceptual mistake involving confusion or shifting of letters and words, often because of RIGHT-LEFT DISORIENTATION or lack of SPATIAL ORIENTATION. Children with LEARNING DISABILITIES, for example, may mistake *tap* for *pat,* or *pat* for *bat,* and may transpose letters within a word, as in *fist* for *sift.*

Reye syndrome, a severe, sometimes fatal, disorder of unknown origin that affects all organs of the body, but most seriously causes swelling of the brain and accumulation of fats in the liver. It affects primarily children and teenagers, almost always as they are recovering from a viral infection, such as influenza, CHICKEN POX (varicella), or EPSTEIN-BARR VIRUS, frequently after they have taken aspirin or aspirin-related medication. It is most common January through March, at the height of the flu season, though it may occur any time of the year.

Early signs of Reye syndrome, often about a week into a viral illness, include persistent VOMITING, listlessness, and lethargy. These may be followed by disorientation or confusion, slurred speech, sensitivity to touch, and personality change, including irritability and combativeness, and then by COMA, SEIZURES, disruption of heart rhythm, and cessation of breathing. Reye syndrome is often misdiagnosed as ENCEPHALITIS, MENINGITIS, DIABETES, SUDDEN INFANT DEATH SYNDROME, drug overdose, poisoning, or MENTAL DISORDER. Early diagnosis is vital because with prompt treatment victims have a 90 percent chance of recovery; otherwise death can occur within just a few days, with a 15 percent recovery rate for cases diagnosed late. A parent who suspects Reye syndrome should contact a doctor immediately.

The cause of the syndrome is unknown, but it is not considered contagious, though some clusters of cases have occurred. It is frequently, though not always, associated with the taking of aspirin, so parents are advised *never* to give children aspirin or anti-nausea medicine when they are suffering from any kind of illness that may be viral; indeed, they are advised to consult with their doctor before giving their child any medication in cases of flu or chicken pox. That widely publicized caution has caused a drop in the number of cases of Reye syndrome. However the number of cases in adolescents is rising, perhaps because many teens are unaware of the danger, or do not recognize aspirin products under another name. Parents should be sure their teens do not self-medicate with any product containing acetylsalicylate, acetylsalivylic acid, salicylic acid, or salicylate, as well as aspirin.

Reye syndrome is often diagnosed by LIVER FUNCTION TESTS and other confirming tests. No specific treatment exists, but intensive nursing care—involving STEROID drugs to reduce brain swelling, BLOOD TRANSFUSIONS and DIALYSIS to correct problems in body chemistry, and a VENTILATOR to aid breathing—will increase the chance of survival, though survivors of serious cases may still suffer brain damage. Parents are advised to have their child transferred to a HOSPITAL where the staff is experienced in treating Reye syndrome or, if that is not possible, to be sure the hospital staff consults immediately with an experienced treatment center on specialized care for the condition. Even with more widespread knowledge of Reye syndrome, the overall MORTALITY RATE is still approximately 50 percent, and it is a leading cause of death among children beyond infancy.

FOR HELP AND FURTHER INFORMATION

National Reye's Syndrome Foundation (NRSF)
426 North Lewis
P.O. Box 829S
Bryan, OH 43506
419–636–2679; Hotline: 800–233–7393
John Freudenberger, President
Organization concerned with Reye's syndrome; gathers and disseminates information; provides information and counseling; sponsors research; publishes brochure *Reye's Syndrome: Cause and Cure: Unknown* and list of aspirin-containing compounds.

National Institute of Neurological Disorders and Stroke (NINDS), 800–352–9424. (For full group information, see BRAIN AND BRAIN DISORDERS.)

American Allergy Association (AAA), 415–322–1663. Publishes *Protect Your Child from Reye Syndrome.* (For full group information, see ALLERGY.)

National Institute of Diabetes and Digestive and Kidney Diseases (NIDDK), 301–496–3583. (For full group information, see DIGESTIVE SYSTEM AND DISORDERS.)

National Organization for Rare Disorders (NORD), 800–999–6673. (For full group information, see RARE DISORDERS.)

American Liver Foundation (ALF), 800–223–0179. (For full group information, see LIVER AND LIVER PROBLEMS.)

rheumatic fever, a once very common childhood disease that causes inflammation in many of the body's tissues and joints, and often causes permanent damage to the heart, which is sometimes apparent only later. It can also affect the NERVOUS SYSTEM, causing Sydenham's CHOREA, and in severe cases sometimes causing death. Rheumatic fever is associated with infection by *streptococcus* bacteria (as in STREP THROAT), which seems to trigger a kind of AUTOIMMUNE DISORDER, in which ANTIBODIES to the strep mistakenly attack the body itself (see IMMUNE SYSTEM). Since the development of ANTIBIOTICS, rheumatic fever has been far less common in developed countries, though it is still widespread elsewhere. But in the United States, rheumatic fever is on the increase again, possibly because a more virulent, antibiotic-resistant strain of strep bacteria has developed. No IMMUNIZATION is available, nor do any specific tests exist to diagnose rheumatic fever.

If a child has a sore throat or fever for more than a day or two, especially if previously exposed to strep, public health experts advise that the child be examined by a doctor for the presence of strep. Mild cases may pass in three to four weeks with little effect, but severe cases can last for two to three months, with long-term effects, and may recur. In cases of heart damage, surgery may later be needed.

FOR HELP AND FURTHER INFORMATION

National Heart, Lung, and Blood Information Center (NHLBIC), 301–251–1222. (For full group information, see HEART AND HEART PROBLEMS.)

National Institute of Allergy and Infectious Diseases (NIAID), 301–496–5717. (For full group information, see ALLERGY.)

National Institute of Child Health and Human Development (NICHD), 301–496–5133. (For full group information, see PREGNANCY.)

National Organization for Rare Disorders (NORD), 800–999–6673. (For full group information, see RARE DISORDERS.)

Rh incompatibility, a mismatch between blood types, in which the blood of one person carries an Rh factor on the red blood cells (Rh positive) and blood from the other person does not (RH negative). About 85 percent of the population is Rh positive. Problems occur when the two types of blood are mixed, because the incompatibility causes many of the red blood cells to self-destruct, a process called *hemolysis*. As a result, blood to be used for BLOOD TRANSFUSIONS must be carefully labeled by type and only given to people of a compatible type; even so, it is generally tested on a blood sample beforehand to make sure.

Special problems occur during PREGNANCY, when a mother and a father have incompatible blood. If the mother's blood is Rh negative and the baby's is Rh positive (from the father), the first pregnancy is generally untroubled by incompatibility. But that first baby may sensitize the mother to Rh positive blood, so she develops ANTIBODIES to it. Then, in later pregnancies, these antibodies may attack and kill the FETUS of any Rh positive baby, a condition called *erythroblastosis fetalis.* Or the baby may survive, but be born with *hemolytic disease of the newborn,* involving destruction of large numbers of red blood cells, which results in buildup of the waste product *bilirubin* in the blood (see LIVER AND LIVER PROBLEMS) and possible brain damage. Rh incompatibility occurs in approximately 10 percent of all births.

In recent decades, physicians have been able to reduce the incidence of sensitization by giving the mother injections of *immunoglobulin* (see IMMUNE SYSTEM) two to three days before DELIVERY, and after MISCARRIAGE, ABORTION, AMNIOCENTESIS, or other such procedures in which fetal blood cells might come into direct contact with the mother's blood cells. Where the mother has already been sensitized, the condition of the child is carefully monitored for signs of damage, such as high bilirubin levels. If GESTATION has proceeded far enough, LABOR may be induced to keep the baby from being too severely affected. But if the fetus is too PREMATURE for safe delivery, fetal blood transfusions may be required.

After birth, the newborn will be carefully monitored and may require special care to counteract the effects of the incompatibility. In severe cases, an *exchange transfusion*—a BLOOD TRANSFUSION that completely replaces the baby's blood—may be required. Rh compatibility is routinely checked during PRENATAL CARE, so incidence of these problems has declined sharply.

In 1995, a new drug was introduced designed to suppress Rh sensitization in Rh negative pregnant women. Given by injection, it produces only mild adverse reactions, including soreness at the site of the injection, FEVER, chills, and headache. Its long-term effectiveness remained to be tested.

FOR HELP AND FURTHER INFORMATION

National Heart, Lung, and Blood Information Center (NHLBIC), 301–251–1222. (For full group information, see HEART AND HEART PROBLEMS.)

March of Dimes Birth Defects Foundation (MDBDF), 914–428–7100. Publishes information sheet *Rh Disease.* (For full group information, see BIRTH DEFECTS.)

National Organization for Rare Disorders (NORD), 800–999–6673. (For full group information, see RARE DISORDERS.)

rickets, a DEFICIENCY DISEASE, in which lack of sufficient CALCIUM and PHOSPHATE results in deformation of a growing child's bones, especially bowing of the legs, flattening of the soft skull and feet, and deformation of the spine, giving a "pot belly" appearance; in adults, the same deficiency is called *osteomalacia*. Often associated with rickets are other bone disorders, such as SCOLIOSIS and KYPHOSIS, and a tendency to FRACTURES, as well as DEVELOPMENTAL DELAY, as in the MOTOR SKILLS of crawling and WALKING.

Rickets is most often caused by lack of VITAMIN D, which is necessary for calcium to be transported to and made into bone, and it is generally found among children in underdeveloped countries, who have both an unbalanced diet and too little sunlight (a main nonfood source of vitamin D). But rickets can occur in other children as well. PREMATURE babies are vulnerable to rickets, as are children whose families have a restricted diet, such as a VEGETARIAN diet that has not adequately provided for vitamin D. Mothers who are BREASTFEEDING may be advised to give the baby a vitamin D supplement, as breast milk alone is an inadequate source of vitamin D; however, that should be done only under a doctor's direction, since too much can result in excess calcium, or *hypercalcemia*. ACHONDROPLASIA, a mostly hereditary bone disorder, is sometimes called *fetal rickets*, but its origins are not the same. From age one, children receive vitamin D in fortified MILK.

FOR HELP AND FURTHER INFORMATION

Shriner's Hospitals for Crippled Children, 800–237–5055. Provides free medical care for children with orthopedic problems. (For full group information, see BONE AND BONE DISORDERS.)

National Digestive Disease Information Clearinghouse (NDDIC), 301–654–3810. (For full group information, see DIGESTIVE SYSTEM AND DISORDERS.)

National Arthritis and Musculoskeletal and Skin Diseases Information Clearinghouse (NAMSIC), 301–495–4484. (For full group information, see ARTHRITIS.)

National Organization for Rare Disorders (NORD), 800–999–6673. (For full group information, see RARE DISORDERS.)

(See also VITAMINS; NUTRITION; BONE AND BONE DISORDERS.)

right-left disorientation, inability to consistently distinguish right from left, a perceptual confusion often found in children with LEARNING DISABILITIES, especially those in which DOMINANCE of hand, eye, and foot has not been clearly established. Right-left disorientation can cause great difficulty in READING and working with numbers.

right-handed, a type of HANDEDNESS in which a person relies more heavily on and is easier and more proficient at using the right hand than the left.

risk factors, those characteristics or habits that increase the likelihood that a person will develop a certain disease or condition, as SMOKING is a risk factor for CANCER. In relation to PREGNANCY, a woman who has one or more risk factors is said to have a HIGH-RISK PREGNANCY, or to be AT RISK of developing complications. Similarly, a child from a family with a history of CHILD ABUSE AND NEGLECT may be termed *at risk* or a *high-risk child*.

Rocky Mountain spotted fever, an acute disease caused by infection with a bacteria-like microorganism, *Rickettsia rickettsii*, which is transmitted from small woodland animals to humans through the bites of ticks. Originally recognized in the Rocky Mountains (hence the name), it is now found in much of North America, especially along the East Coast. Symptoms generally appear three to twelve days after a bite by an infected tick, often including abrupt and severe fever, chills, headache, muscle pains, coughing, and (about four days after the early symptoms) a rash starting on the wrists, palms, ankles, soles, and forearms, and then spreading elsewhere in the body. In more serious cases, complications such as ENCEPHALITIS and pneumonia (see LUNG AND BREATHING PROBLEMS) may develop, in some cases leading to DELIRIUM, COMA, damage to the brain and heart, and death. Before the discovery of antibiotics, 1 out of every 5 cases resulted in death; the MORTALITY RATE is still 7 percent, though that is generally because treatment is not started quickly enough.

Parents can best protect themselves and their children by dressing in long clothing, with trousers tucked into socks, when in tick-infested areas, such as woods and meadows; by checking themselves on returning from such areas; by checking pets, which can carry ticks into the house; by learning how to properly deal with the type of ticks found in the area; by being aware of the symptoms; and by seeking treatment quickly if Rocky Mountain spotted fever is suspected.

FOR HELP AND FURTHER INFORMATION

National Institute of Allergy and Infectious Diseases (NIAID), 301–496–5717. Publishes brochure *Rocky Mountain Spotted Fever* (For full group information, see ALLERGY.)

National Organization for Rare Disorders (NORD), 800–999–6673. (For full group information, see RARE DISORDERS.)

OTHER RESOURCES

Rocky Mountain Spotted Fever: History of a Twentieth-Century Disease. Victoria A. Harden. Johns Hopkins, 1990.

Ticks and What You Can Do About Them. Roger Drummond. Wilderness Press, 1990.

Romberg sign, swaying of the patient when standing with feet together and eyes closed; a SIGN that often indicates the existence of ATAXIA.

rooming-in, in HOSPITALS, the practice of allowing MOTHER and newborn (and sometimes the FATHER as well) to stay in the same room, instead of placing the baby in a NURSERY; sometimes the baby remains in the room only during daytime hours, but is placed in the nursery at night to give the mother more time to recover from the birth. This allows BREASTFEEDING to take place at any time and is valuable for the early BONDING of parent and child. Parents making choices about delivery may want to examine hospital options and rules in this area.

root canal therapy, a dental procedure to clean out infected pulp from a tooth, fill it temporarily until the infection has been cleared up, and then fill the cavity, or root canal, with a neutral filling. The procedure can often save teeth that would otherwise have to be pulled. After root canal therapy, a tooth may turn grayish, but the tooth can be bleached by a DENTIST or covered by a CROWN. Root canal therapy is often performed by general dentists, but those who specialize in root canal therapy are called ENDODONTISTS. (For help or further information, see TEETH.)

rooting reflex, the automatic response of a baby, when the cheek is touched or stroked, as with a finger, to turn the head to that side and start sucking; a type of "primitive" REFLEX found only in babies and disappearing generally in three to four months, but sometimes as late as twelve months. It is this type of reflex that allows the baby to find the nipple in BREASTFEEDING.

Rorschach Psychodiagnostic Test, one of the best known types of PROJECTIVE TESTS, in which a person is given a series of ten inkblots, one at a time, and is asked to interpret them. It is an individually administered test used in evaluations of personality for people age three and up. The administrator scores it according to an elaborate system. Variations on this classic inkblot test are also sometimes used. (For help and further information, see TESTS.)

roseola infantum, an infectious, probably viral, disease common in young children, especially those under two years old, involving an abruptly arriving high FEVER, as high as 105°F, which lasts for four to five days, then drops back to normal. At that time a pink rash spreads over the body, especially the trunk, neck, and thighs, generally lasting for a few hours up to two days. Accompanying symptoms may be sore throat, swollen lymph nodes in neck, and sometimes CONVULSIONS or SEIZURES. In the absence of a specific therapy, the main treatment is generally to bring the body temperature down, as by giving a sponge bath with lukewarm water or giving acetaminophen (not ASPIRIN because of its link to REYE SYNDROME).

Roswell Chall Auditory Blending Test, an individually administered TEST to assess ability to blend sounds heard orally into recognizable whole words. The test is given to children in grades 2 to 6 when problems in AUDITORY SKILLS are suspected, and attempts to identify children who are or may have trouble with the PHONICS approach to learning READING. (For help and further information, see TESTS.)

rote learning, memorization of materials, with no guarantee that any understanding or linking with other knowledge is taking place. (See LEARNING STYLE.)

rubella (German measles), a highly contagious disease caused by the rubella virus, which is spread in droplets through coughing, sneezing, and just talking. In young children, rubella generally causes only slight discomfort and mild, temporary symptoms, a low fever for a day or so, and a rash on the face and neck for two to three days, hence its alternate name: *three-day measles*. Teenagers may also get swollen glands in the back of the neck and experience temporary ARTHRITIS, or pain and stiffness in the joints.

But in an unimmunized pregnant woman rubella can cause devastating BIRTH DEFECTS; perhaps 1 in 4 or 5 affected pregnant women has babies with deformities, while many others have MISCARRIAGES. The last major rubella epidemic, in 1964, left some 20,000 babies with severe birth defects, including blindness and other EYE AND VISION PROBLEMS, deafness and other EAR AND HEARING PROBLEMS, abnormally small brains, and MENTAL RETARDATION. Since 1969 a rubella VACCINE has been in use, generally given in a combination MEASLES-MUMPS-RUBELLA VACCINE, to infants at about 15 months old. Teenage and adult women who have never had rubella and have not been immunized should take the vaccine at least three months before considering pregnancy. And, to prevent the further spread of rubella, so should any child or adult.

FOR HELP AND FURTHER INFORMATION

March of Dimes Birth Defects Foundation (MDBDF), 914–428–7100. Publishes information sheet *Rubella*. (For full group information, see BIRTH DEFECTS.)

National Institute of Allergy and Infectious Diseases (NIAID), 301–496–5717. (For full group information, see ALLERGIES.)

National Institute of Child Health and Human Development (NICHD), 301–496–5133. (For full group information, see PREGNANCY.)

National Organization for Rare Disorders (NORD), 800–999–6673. (For full group information, see RARE DISORDERS.)

(See MEASLES-MUMPS-RUBELLA VACCINE.)

RU-486, a drug used to induce ABORTION; also called *mifepristone* or *mifegyne.* Because it acts to prevent GESTATION, or growth of an EMBRYO in the UTERUS, its developer, Etienne-Emile Baulieu (of the French pharmaceutical company Roussel-Uclaf), calls it a *contragestive*; however, is more popularly called the "abortion pill."

RU-486 has been lauded and reviled by people on opposite sides of the abortion controversy, with many pro-choice activists hailing it as a breakthrough, an alternative to a long-sought MORNING AFTER PILL. However, though the pill has been used by at least 175,000 women in Europe, it is still being tested in the United States. More to the point, it is neither as easy to use nor as totally free of possible side effects as has been popularly thought. Also, its long-term effects on women's health are still unclear; even some pro-choice observers have urged caution, noting that DES was widely used, but was later found to produce significant adverse effects that were passed on to the next generation.

RU-486 works by blocking the action of PROGESTERONE, which is vital for maintaining a PREGNANCY; the lining of the uterus breaks down, preventing or weakening implantation, and is then sloughed off. The result is an induced MISCARRIAGE or MENSTRUATION. RU-486 is effective only during the first seven weeks of pregnancy, at which state the embryo is no larger than a pea. RU-486 alone is effective only 80 percent of the time, but it is 95 percent effective when used in combination with the drug *prostaglandin,* which causes uterine contractions and helps ensure complete expulsion.

Not a simple "pill-popping," use of RU-486 is a several-stage process. In France, where it was originally approved in 1988, a woman goes to a BIRTH CONTROL center for a pregnancy test and a GYNECOLOGICAL EXAMINATION, registers her decision to have an abortion, and signs a form agreeing to have a surgical abortion if RU-486 fails, required because of concerns that the drug might cause BIRTH DEFECTS in the FETUS if the pregnancy were then taken to term. A week later, she returns and is given an oral dose of RU-486. Two days later she returns again for a dose of prostaglandin, either as an injection or a vaginal suppository. She stays in the clinic for approximately four hours, while doctors monitor and treat side effects from the prostaglandin, including pain, nausea, VOMITING, and DIARRHEA. In three out of four women, bleeding begins while they are in the clinic; in most others, it does not start until their return home. It can last from a few days to over a month. A week later, the woman returns to the clinic to be sure the abortion is complete. In approximately 1 out of 20 women, the abortion does not occur or is incomplete; in that case, the woman is then scheduled to have a surgical abortion, to avoid possibly life-threatening infections from matter remaining in the uterus, and to prevent her carrying to term a baby with drug-induced birth defects.

At this point also, doctors check the amount of bleeding; in about 1 to 2 women out of every 1000, bleeding is so heavy as to require a BLOOD TRANSFUSION. In 1991, a 31-year-old French woman, a smoker, died of cardiovascular shock, due to a life-threatening drop in BLOOD PRESSURE. As a result, France issued new guidelines for RU-486, barring its use in women who smoke (see SMOKING) or are over age thirty-four. RU-486 is also not recommended for women who have had a recent CESAREAN SECTION or certain health problems, including circulatory problems or high blood pressure, fibroids (see UTERUS; HYSTERECTOMY), ASTHMA, glaucoma (see EYE AND VISION PROBLEMS), ulcers or colitis (see DIGESTIVE SYSTEM AND DISORDERS), ANEMIA, gynecological infections (see SEXUALLY TRANSMITTED DISEASES), or problems with the ADRENAL GLANDS.

While RU-486 can be prescribed and administered anonymously in a doctor's office, and so (unlike abortion clinics) would not make the women or her doctor the target of anti-abortion protesters, it still requires several visits to the doctor. That poses special problems for women who are young or poor, live in rural areas, or have young children and inadequate CHILD CARE. RU-486 may also be more expensive—and in 5 percent of the cases may need to be followed by a surgical abortion as well.

Another limit is that RU-486 is effective only in the first seven weeks of pregnancy, or up to five weeks after a missed period. However, many women barely know they are pregnant by this time, and even if they do, most are not prepared to make a decision on abortion so quickly. This is especially true of young women, who tend to make such decisions later, and are more likely to have a second trimester abortion.

A 1992 Scottish study suggested that RU-486 might be effective as a MORNING AFTER PILL, though questions about long-term effects are still to be answered. It has also shown promise for other uses, such as slowing development of BREAST CANCER and brain tumors, and relaxing the CERVIX during difficult deliveries, to lessen CESAREAN SECTIONS, especially in STILLBIRTHS.

OTHER RESOURCES

The Quick and the Dead: RU-486 and the New Chemical Warfare Against Your Family. George Grant. Good News, 1992.

A Woman's Book of Choices: Abortion, Menstrual Extraction, RU–486. Rebecca Chalker and Carol Downer. Four Walls Eight Windows, 1992.

RU-486: The Pill That Could End the Abortion Wars and Why American Women Don't Have It. Lawrence Lader. Addison-Wesley, 1991.

The Abortion Pill: The Most Controversial Medical Discovery of Our Time—the French Unpregnancy Pill—As Described by the Scientist Who Created It. Etienne-Emile Baulieu and Mort Rosenblum. Simon & Schuster, 1991.

RU-486: Myths, Misconceptions and Morals. Janice G. Raymond and others. Institute for Women's Technology, 1991.

rumination disorder of infancy, a rare type of eating disorder, usually affecting children under age one, that involves REGURGITATION of food from the stomach without the usual involuntary spasms or nausea. The main problems associated with it are FAILURE TO THRIVE and MALNUTRITION, leading to retarded growth and development.

S

safety, freedom from injury, danger, or risk, a key concern for parents, one of whose main responsibilities is protecting their children from harm. This responsibility lasts for many years, in some respects for a lifetime, but its nature varies widely as the child grows, changes, learns, and becomes more independent.

In the early years, the child is almost totally dependent on parents and other caregivers, and safety concerns reign supreme. Even in the first year, however, the type of dangers faced by the child vary greatly with the child's stage of growth. As suggested by YOUR BABY'S FIRST YEAR: A SAFETY CHECKLIST on page 520, the main dangers faced by infants are drowning, burning, choking or strangling, poisoning, and automobile accidents. Parents should make sure they have emergency numbers handy for quick reference. (Subscribers to the America Online computer service can find "Are You Ready?: Emergency Preparedness Checklist" in the Moms Online Desk reference section of Moms Online, under "Emergency Checklist.") They should also have basic first aid kits and guides available, and may also want to get some special first aid training, such as treating burns, giving ARTIFICIAL RESPIRATION (see IF YOUR INFANT IS NOT BREATHING on page 48), or using the Heimlich maneuver (see WHAT IF AN INFANT IS CHOKING on page 122 and What IF A CHILD IS CHOKING on page 123).

Many of the safety suggestions from the first year—such as not giving plastic bags or balloons to young children—continue throughout childhood, though the nature of the dangers faced varies as children grow. Parents should have accessible in the home only toys and other items that are safe for the *youngest* child in the family; other items should be placed safely out of reach.

From age 1 through the teens, the leading cause of death among children is accidental injuries, including automobile accidents. Among children aged one to four, falls are still a widespread danger, and parental vigilance is extremely important. But crawlers, toddlers, and early walkers, being mobile, face additional hazards not faced by a baby. Gates should be used at the bottom and top of stairways until the child is able to walk up and down the stairs safely. At home or elsewhere, parents should always scan the environment for potential dangers (see CHILDPROOFING); in particular, they should:

- Keep windows and screens in good repair, but do not rely on a screen alone to keep a child from falling out of a window.
- Install window guards to prevent children from opening windows more than a few inches—even five inches can pose a danger to children under age ten.
- Keep furniture, including beds, away from windows.
- Place step ladders and stools stored away in a place inaccessible to children.
- Keep doors to decks, balconies, fire escapes, and hallways closed and locked.
- See that all slides, swings, and climbing equipment have mats or energy-absorbent material (such as sand or woodchips) packed under and around them, in case of a fall.

For older children, if parents decide to use bunk beds, they should carefully examine the construction of the beds and caution children about using them safely.

Car injuries continue to be a major concern for young children. Because safety seats have shown their ability to save children's lives, many states require them for children. Many hospitals even provide loaner car seats, for new parents who do not have them. It is important that parents know and follow the specifications for any car safety seats they purchase, and use them only in the prescribed ways and for children of the right ages and sizes for the particular seat. Otherwise, they may cause severe internal or spinal injuries during accidents, instead of protecting their children from danger.

Children under 28 inches tall, under 20 pounds, and under 1 year old should always be placed in a rear-facing infant seat (either a special infant seat or a convertible one), since an infant's neck and spine are not developed enough to support the weight of the head in case of a collision. Children between 20 and 40 pounds, approximately up to age four, may use a safety seat specifically designed for them, or one that converts from the rear-facing one used for infants. (Some Chrysler Corporation models have built-in child safety seats.)

For children from 40 to 60 pounds, a booster seat is recommended. It should be made especially for car use and be designed to bring the child's ears to a level higher than an automobile seat; this is important because the seat belt must be positioned properly across the shoulder and pelvis, not the neck and abdomen, where the belts themselves can cause injury in case of accidents. In looking for a booster seat, parents should select one that is easy to use, light and portable, easy to clean, allows the child to see, provides shoulder and head support so the child can rest or sleep, and is comfortable for the child—all important so that safety becomes the norm, not a battle.

As of this writing, a major controversy exists over whether children on airplanes should be placed in safety seats, and if so, of what type. Various safety organizations have differing recommendations, and so do various airlines, some requiring them, others barring them, or barring some types, over concern that children in some safety seats may be *more,* not less, vulnerable. Parents should watch this developing story for guidance. Children are, as of now, not required to have their own seats, but that is because the cost is seen as a hardship for parents. Where money is not a factor, children are probably safest seat-belted in their own seat (with or without a safety seat), since the force of any crash would cause the child to be ripped away from a parent's arms.

Equally important throughout childhood is that the parent always use seat belts, so that when the child finally outgrows the car seat, using seat belts will be virtually automatic, as passengers, and in their late teens as drivers themselves. Children should never be allowed to ride in the open bed of a pickup truck, since this is extremely dangerous, not only leading to injuries but also to possible carbon monoxide poisoning. Once children are in their teens, warn them never to "park" in a car with the motor running, since this also causes carbon monoxide poisoning, which can cause death.

Many childhood injuries also involve bicycles. Parents are in general not advised to take infants under one year old on a bicycle or in an infant backpack while bike riding. If they later take the child in a bicycle child carrier, racing stroller, or other wheeled child cart designed for parents to use while exercising outdoors, they should walk, run, or ride "defensively," attempting to avoid danger from other vehicles to the stroller, cart, or trailer in which the child is sitting. They should keep the carrier attached to their wrist by a safety strap to see that it does not roll away and attach a flag on a stick to the cart, so drivers and other cyclists can clearly see the child's cart.

From the time that children are old enough to be taken for a ride in a bicycle child carrier or cart for roadside use, they should always wear a bicycle helmet—as they should from the moment they begin riding tricycles or *any other riding toy.* Bicycle helmets have been found to reduce the risk of head injury by 85 percent and TRAUMATIC BRAIN INJURY by almost 90 percent. Fit is important, since the helmet must stay level on the head, touching all around, and must stay in place firmly once strapped, in order to provide maximum protection. The Bicycle Helmet Safety Institute (see the list of resources following this entry) reports that the three main types of helmets—hard shell, soft shell, and no-shell (all foam)—all offer good impact protection, though the shelled ones may offer better protection in a high-speed crash on a rough surface. As with seat belts, parents can get best cooperation from their children and more safety for themselves if they wear safety helmets also. Any helmet worn in a crash should be replaced, since the impact crushes some of the foam, lessening its cushioning power. Helmets should, in any case, be replaced at least every five years, depending on wear. Helmets are best vented, since foam tends to hold heat in. For extra safety, any cycle carrying a child—even a tricycle—should be made more visible by attaching a flag pole.

In general, children should not move to two-wheeled bicycles until after age five. They should only ride bikes of a proper size for them, as improperly sized bikes make them more vulnerable. They should never ride their bicycles at dusk or after dark, which are extremely dangerous times for riders. And they should be warned against carrying passengers.

Safety helmets should also be used for protection while sledding, which injures some 33,000 people each year in the United States alone. The *American Journal of Diseases of Children* (October 1990) suggested the following checklist for sledding safety:

S: Snow packed, not icy.
L: Long, flat runoff at bottom.
E: Examine area for hazards and traffic.
D: Dress with helmet, boots, and gloves.
D: Don't ride in prone position (head first).
I: Incline not too steep or long.
N: Non-reckless behavior.
G: Good condition of sled.

Drowning is another major safety concern with young children, and the greatest danger is right in the backyard. Perhaps 90 percent of all drowning deaths among children ages one to three occur in home swimming pools. If the family has a pool, it should be fenced in and kept locked; a soft pool cover should not be used, since these can trap young children. Parents who wish to install a pool should wait until their children are over age five. Hot tubs should be locked or drained after each use. Even young children who have been taught to swim from infancy may be in danger, since they may not be able to swim in all situations, especially in emergencies. Rafts and flotation devices should not be used, since they give children—and parents—a false sense of security, and may even *cause* drowning, rather than prevent it. On boats, all children and adults should wear life vests.

Older children can easily overestimate their swimming ability and underestimate water depth. They should be taught never to dive into unknown bodies of water, but to jump feet-first to avoid head injury on a shallow bottom. They should also not swim alone, and if swimming in a group, to have a "buddy," and should never push or jump on others. Children should not be allowed to swim without an adult present, and should never swim during storms or lightning.

Among children ages five to nine, pedestrian injuries are the most common cause of accidental death, as children begin to navigate streets on their own. Parents must carefully teach children to always look left, right, then left again before crossing, and to continue looking while crossing. They should not count on safety in a crosswalk, because drivers do not always stop and sometimes do not even see walkers, especially small children. Where there are traffic lights, children should be taught the meaning of red and green, but parents should emphasize that vehicles do not always obey the lights strictly, so they should check before starting to cross.

As children grow older, they also face hazards from

power tools and other machinery, especially tractors, mowers, and other powered gardening equipment. Nearly 10,000 children under age fifteen are injured each year in lawn mover accidents alone in the United States. Parents are advised not to let children under twelve operate powered walk-behind mowers, and to limit ride-on mowers to children fourteen or over, in both cases only after they have been instructed in how to use them safely. Parents should lock garden equipment away from the reach of young children. Farm children are at special risk because they work on farms with much heavy equipment; they should be taught very early what equipment they must avoid, and how to safely use and work around other equipment.

Beyond these, of course, are numerous other safety issues, many of them taken up elsewhere in this book, in separate articles such as: ADOLESCENT PREGNANCY; ALCOHOL ABUSE; CHILD ABUSE AND NEGLECT; DRUG ABUSE; ENVIRONMENTAL HAZARDS; EXERCISE; FOOD ADDITIVES; IMMUNIZATION; LATCHKEY CHILD; LEAD POISONING; MISSING CHILDREN; NUTRITION; SEXUALLY TRANSMITTED DISEASES; SMOKING; SPORTS; SUICIDE; TIPS FOR AVOIDING FOODBORNE ILLNESS on page 178; TIPS FOR PROTECTING YOUR CHILD AGAINST ABDUCTION on page 408; as well as numerous specific diseases and disorders.

FOR HELP AND FURTHER INFORMATION

American Academy of Pediatrics (AAP),
800–433–9016. Publishes First Aid Chart, Choking Prevention and First Aid for Infants and Children, Toy Safety, Playground Safety, and other materials, including:

- On car safety: quarterly newsletter *Safe Ride News*; brochures *Family Guide to Car Seats, Don't Risk Your Child's Life* (on car seats), *Are You Using Your Car Seat Correctly?, Children and Car Safety: Making Friends with a Safety Seat, Enforcement Strategies: For Child Passenger Safety Laws*, and *Teens Who Drink and Drive: Reducing the Death Toll*; and video Special *Delivery: Safe Transportation of Premature and Small Infants.*
- Videos: *Baby Alive* (with booklet, on safety from birth to five years), *Home Safe, Baby Proof Home, Bicycle Safety Camp, Child Safety Outdoors*, and *Swim Lessons for Kids* (with booklet).
- TIPP (The Injury Prevention Program) materials:
  - Age-Related Safety Sheets (for birth to 6 months, 6–12 months, 1–2 years, 2–4 years, 5 years, 6 years, 8 years, and 10 years); Safety Surveys (for first year of life; 1–4 years, in two parts; 5–9 years; 10–12 years).
  - Child Safety Slips: Infant Furniture: Cribs, Safety Tips for Home Playground Equipment, Protect Your Child...Prevent Poisoning, Safe Driving...A Parental Responsibility, Protect Your Home Against Fire...Planning Saves Lives, Water Safety for Your School-Aged Child, Lawn Mower Safety, Home Water Hazards for Young Children, Pool Safety for Children, and Life Jackets and Life Preservers.
  - Bicycle Safety Sheets: About Bicycle Helmets, Bicycle Safety: Myths and Facts, Tips for Getting Your Kids to Wear Helmets, Choosing the Right Size Bicycle for Your Child, Safe Bicycling Starts Early, and The Child as Passenger on an Adult's Bicycle.

(For full group information, see HEALTH CARE.)

National Safety Council (NSC)
1121 Spring Lake Drive
Itasca, IL 60143–3201
800–621–7615
Organization promoting safety in all areas of life; provides training; maintains library; publishes numerous materials, including quarterly *Family Safety and Health, First Aid Guide, The Pocket Emergency Handbook, Your Home Safety Checklist, Ride 'Em Safely* (on child restraints and infant carriers), *Preschool Pedestrian Safety Program, Handling Stress, Holiday Safety, Surviving Hotel Fires, Picture Perfect Vacation* (film/video), and materials for educational programs.

National Association for the Education of Young Children (NAEYC), 800–424–2460. Publishes brochures *Playgrounds: Safe and Sound* and *Merrily We Roll Along*, on keeping children busy in safety seats; curriculum kits *We Love You—Buckle Up!, Walk in Traffic Safely (WITS)*, and *Children Riding on Sidewalks Safely (CROSS)*; and video *Building Quality Child Care: Health and Safety.* (For full group information, see PRESCHOOL.)

American Council on Science and Health (ACSH)
1995 Broadway, 2nd Floor
New York, NY 10023–5860
212–362–7044
Fax: 212–362–4919
Elizabeth M. Whelan, President
Consumer-education consortium that seeks to provide sound, scientifically based analyses of public health issues; publishes numerous materials, including quarterly magazine *Priorities: For Long Life and Good Health*; booklets *Priorities in Caring for Your Children: A Primer for Parents* (on the main health and safety issues for children of different ages), *Automobile Occupant Restraint Systems, Aspirin and Health, Fluoridation*, and *Alzheimer's Disease*; and special reports *America's Health: A Century of Progress, The Unhealthy Alliance: Crusaders for "Health Freedom,"* and *Quackery and the Elderly.*

American Medical Association, 800–621–8335. Publishes *The AMA First Aid Guide* and *The AMA Handbook of First Aid and Emergency Care.* (For full group information, see HEALTH CARE.)

American Academy of Orthopaedic Surgeons (AAOS), 800–346–2267. Publishes brochure *Live It Safe.* (For full group information, see BONE AND BONE DISORDERS.)

Prevent Blindness America, 800–221–3004. Publishes *Home Eye Safety Guide, Play It Safe* (on eye safety for very young children); and video *Play It Safe with*

Your Eyes (for children preschool through grade 2). (For full group information, see EYE AND VISION PROBLEMS.)

Center for Safety in the Arts (CSA), 212–227–6220. Publishes fact sheets *Health and Safety Resources for the Arts, Introduction to Theater Hazards, Occupational Hazards in Music, Theater Health and Safety Self-Evaluation Checklist, Fire Prevention,* and *Flammable/Combustible Liquids Safety Checklist*; and videos *Art Safety: Hazards and Precautions, Play It Safe: Introduction to Theatre Safety,* and *Firearm Safety Onstage.* (For full group information, see ENVIRONMENTAL HAZARDS.)

New Parents' Network, 520–327–1451. Offers information (through telecommunications services) on child safety. (For full group information, see GENERAL PARENTING RESOURCES on page 634.)

Alliance for Parental Involvement in Education (ALLPIE), 518–392–6900. Publishes *Kids to the Rescue: First Aid Techniques for Kids.* (For full group information, see HELP ON LEARNING AND EDUCATION on page 659.)

Association for Childhood Education International (ACEI), 800–423–3563. Publishes *Creating Safer Environments for Children in the Home, School and Community;* and videotape *Playground Safety.* (For full group information, see HELP ON LEARNING AND EDUCATION on page 659.)

National Maternal and Child Health Clearinghouse (NMCHC), 703–821–8955. Publishes *Injury Prevention Professionals: A National Directory, Child and Adolescent Fatal Injury Data Book—November 1994.* (For full group information, see PREGNANCY.)

Consumer Product Safety Commission
Office of Information and Public Affairs
Washington, DC 20207
301–504–0990; Safety Hotline: 800–638-CPSC [638–2772]
Fax-on-demand: 301–504–0051
Internet site: gopher://cpsc.gov
Federal agency that oversees safety in a wide range of products; collects and disseminates information on product-related injuries; publishes numerous safety-related materials, including booklets such as *For Kids Sake: Think Toy Safety* and *Bicycle Safety: Sprocket Men,* and others on topics such as fire safety, pool safety, safety in the nursery, and poison prevention.

Bicycle Helmet Safety Institute (BHSI)
4611 Seventh Street South
Arlington, VA 22204–1419
Phone, fax, and fax-on-demand: 703–486–0100
E-mail: helmets@bhsi.org
Internet website: http://www.bhsi.org
Randy Swart, Director
Organization promoting the use of bicycle helmets, a program of the Washington Area Bicyclist Association; acts as advocate; provides information; publishes semiannual newsletter *Helmet Update*; pamphlets *Consumer's Guide to Bicycle Helmets* and *Must I Buy a Bicycle Helmet for My Child?*; technical reports *Helmet Standard Comparison* and *Helmet Workshop,* on new developments; collections of crash stories and helmet legislation; and annotated bibliography.

Danny Foundation
3158 Danville Boulevard
P.O. Box 680
Alamo, CA 94507
800–83-DANNY [833–2669]
Jack Walsh, Executive Director
Organization concerned with safety in cribs and other nursery equipment; publishes brochure *Is Your Crib Safe?;* and newsletter *Cribnotes.*

Brain Injury Association, 800–444–6443. Publishes *Community Guide* (on establishing a bicycle safety program), *Head Smart™ Activity Book* (for children), *Barriers to Bicycle Helmet Use Among Children: Results of Focus Groups with 4th, 5th, and 6th Graders, A Case-Control Study of the Effectiveness of Bicycle Safety Helmets, Safety Belts in School Buses,* and *Air Bags: Reducing the Toll of Brain Trauma.* (For full group information, see TRAUMATIC BRAIN INJURY.)

Twin Services, TWINLINE: 510–524–0863. (For full group information, see MULTIPLE BIRTH.)

National Clearinghouse for Alcohol and Drug Abuse Information (NCADI), 301–468–2600. Publishes fact sheet *Impaired Driving, Injury and Trauma and Alcohol and Other Drugs* and Prevention Resource Guides *Impaired Driving* and *Injury Control.* (For full group information, see HELP AGAINST SUBSTANCE ABUSE on page 703.)

National Easter Seal Society, 800–221–6827. Publishes *A Safe Home Is No Accident.* (For full group information, see HELP FOR SPECIAL CHILDREN on page 689.)

National Water Safety Congress
96 Shela Drive
Oxford, MS 38655
601–234–1828
Gene Gathright, Business Manager
Organization of water safety councils and people managing natural water areas; promotes safety in swimming, boating, and scuba diving; publishes quarterly *Water Safety Journal* and safety guidelines for beaches and marinas.

ONLINE RESOURCES

Better Health and Medical Forum (America Online: Health, Medicine) Provides discussion areas and libraries covering safety. (For full information, see HEALTH CARE.)

OTHER RESOURCES

GENERAL WORKS

Are You Really Safe?: Protecting Yourself in America Today. Larry Talley. Longstreet, 1994.

Your Baby's First Year: A Safety Checklist

Babies born healthy are more likely to get hurt or die from accidents than from illness. Accidental injuries can cause severe disabilities. You can prevent almost all accidents by knowing what your baby is able to do and making sure it is done in a safe way. Use the following checklists to be sure your home is safe.

FOR BABIES FROM BIRTH TO FOUR MONTHS

WHAT BABIES CAN DO

- Eat, sleep, cry, play, smile
- Roll off a flat surface, wiggle a lot.

Babies at this age need complete protection all of the time.

SAFETY CHECKLISTS

In the bath

- Turn the thermostat on your hot water heater down to below 120°F.
- Check bath water temperature with your hand to avoid burns.
- Keep one hand on your baby at all times in the bath. Never leave your baby alone in the bath.

To avoid falls

- Never turn your back on your baby on a table, bed, chair, or other surface.
- Always keep crib sides up, even when turning away for just a *moment.*
- If interrupted, put your baby in the crib, under your arm, or on the floor.
- Do not leave your baby in an infant seat on a table or counter unattended.

To avoid burns

- Put screens around hot radiators, floor furnaces, stoves, or kerosene heaters.
- Do not let caregivers smoke when they are caring for your baby.
- Do not hold your baby when you are drinking a hot beverage.
- Do not leave a filled coffee or tea cup on a placemat or near a table edge where it could be pulled down.
- Be sure that foods, bottles, and bath water are not too hot. Test before using.
- Avoid heating baby food or formula in a microwave oven—it can get "hot spots."

In the crib, bassinet, carriage, or playpen

- Be sure the bars are close enough so that your baby cannot slide through or get stuck (2½ inches at most). (Especially check old ones, made before the 1976 standard setting 2⅜ inches as the maximum slat interval.) Be sure also that the vertical posts on porches or stairway railings are not wider apart; if so, arrange to have the spaces covered with mesh, so children cannot get caught between them.
- Be sure the mattress fits the crib snugly so your baby cannot slip between the mattress and the sides of the crib.
- Do not use a pillow, soft mattress, or soft bedding, which can smother the baby. Avoid swaddling the baby in sheets or blanket and overheating the room where the baby sleeps. [See SLEEP AND SLEEPING DISORDERS for more tips on safety for sleeping babies.]
- Never use plastic material, such as trash bags and dry cleaning bags, as mattress covers, which can also smother.
- Select toys that are too large to swallow and too tough to break, with no small breakable parts and no sharp points or edges.
- Keep pins, buttons, coins, and plastic bags out of reach.
- Never put anything but things a baby can eat or drink in a baby bottle, baby-food jar, or baby's dish. Someone might feed it to the baby by mistake.
- Do not use a harness or straps in the crib.
- Toys and mobiles that hang by a string should be out of your baby's reach and should never be strung across the crib.

In motor vehicles

- Always use your car safety seat in the infant position (semireclining and facing rearward) for your baby when traveling in a motor vehicle.
- The safest place for an infant is in the rear seat of a car, correctly secured into a car safety seat.
- Adults cannot hold on to a baby in even a minor crash. The child is torn from the adult's arms, even if the adult is buckled up.
- Not all models of car safety seats fit all cars. Use a seat that is convenient for you to install;

(continued)

(continued)

install it in the car according to the instructions; and use it each and every time your child rides in the car.

- Safety seats must *always* be anchored to the car with the car's manual lap belt *exactly* as specified by the manufacturer.
- Automatic safety belts are not designed, and should not be used, to install safety seats in a car. For cars without manual lap belts in the front, the safety seat must be installed in the rear.
- Whenever a child safety seat is involved in a crash it must be replaced.
- For the best protection, use the seat only for the length of one child's growth through childhood.
- Never use plastic feeder stands, car beds, pillows, or cushions that are not certified for use in cars.

Other tips

- Never put a loop of ribbon or cord around your baby's neck to hold a pacifier or for any other reason.
- Do not put necklaces, rings, or bracelets on babies.
- Take all toys and small objects out of the crib or playpen when your baby is asleep or unsupervised. If you have older children, they must be taught how to put their toys away safely.

On supervision

- Do not leave your baby alone with young children or with pets.
- Have the telephone numbers of your physician, the rescue squad, and the poison control center posted near your telephone. In case of poisoning, call the center for treatment advice before taking any other actions (apart from stopping further ingestion).

Household tips

- Teach your older children how and when to call "911," the emergency telephone number.
- Install smoke detectors if you do not already have them. Keep a small fire extinguisher out of children's reach in the kitchen.

(Subscribers to the America Online computer service can find "Are You Ready?: Emergency Preparedness Checklist" in the Moms Online Desk Reference section of Moms Online, under "Emergency Checklist.")

FOR BABIES FROM FOUR TO SEVEN MONTHS

WHAT BABIES CAN DO

- Move around quickly.
- Put things into their mouth.
- Grasp and pull things

Babies at this age will need more time out of the crib.

SAFETY CHECKLISTS

- Recheck the Birth to Four Months list.
- Never leave your baby on the floor or bed or in the yard without watching constantly.
- Fence all stairways, top and bottom, with mesh gates. Do not use accordion-style expandable gates that can strangle babies.
- Do not tie toys to crib or playpen rails—a baby can strangle in the tapes or string.
- If you have installed a crib gym, remove by the time the baby is five months old or is able to push onto hands and knees.
- Keep your baby's crib away from drapery or venetian blind cords that can strangle.
- Never use a mesh playpen or crib that has holes in the mesh—your baby's head can get caught.
- Baby-proof all rooms where the child will play by removing matches, cigarette lighters, cigarette butts, other small objects, breakable objects, sharp objects, or tables or lamps that can be pulled over.
- Cover all unused electrical outlets with safety caps or tape.
- Keep all electric cords out of reach. Also check them periodically and replace damaged or frayed cords.
- Keep high chairs, playpens, and infant seats away from stoves, work counters, radiators, furnaces, kerosene heaters, electrical outlets, electric cords, draperies, and venetian blind cords.
- Remove furniture that is hard or has sharp edges, or cover them with cushioning guards as the baby begins to explore.
- Always use restraining straps on a high chair, stroller, shopping cart, or other wheeled cart. Do not leave your baby unattended in one. Especially for outside use, parents should have a safety strap between their wrist and cart, to be sure the cart does not roll away—with the baby strapped inside.

(continued)

(continued)

- Keep cans, bottles, spray cans, and boxes of all cleansers, detergents, pesticides, bleaches, liquor, and cosmetics out of reach.
- Never put a poisonous household product into a food jar, bottle, or soft drink can. Someone may swallow it or feed it to the baby by mistake.
- Do not use old paint that might have been made before February 1978—it could contain lead. If a toy or crib is old and needs repainting, remove the old paint completely (with a chemical—do not sand) and paint it with safe lead-free household paint (check the label). Let it dry thoroughly to avoid fumes.
- If your house is old and has any chipping paint or plaster, repair it (do not sand it) and cover it with wallpaper or safe, new paint. If there is chipped paint or plaster in halls or other places you can't repair, have it tested for lead by the health department. If it contains lead, cover it with wallpaper or fabric, or put furniture in front of it to keep it out of reach.

FOR BABIES FROM EIGHT TO TWELVE MONTHS

What babies can do

- Move fast
- Climb on chairs and stairs
- Open drawers and cupboards
- Open bottles and packages

At this point, your baby needs more opportunity to explore *while you are watching.*

Safety Checklists

- Recheck the Birth to Four Months List.
- Recheck the Four to Seven Months List.
- If you use a toy chest or trunk, make sure it has a safety hinge (one that holds the lid open) or remove the lid.
- Baby-proof all cupboards and drawers that can possibly be reached and opened. Remove all small objects and sharp objects, breakables, household products that might poison, plastic bags, and foods that might cause choking (small foods such as nuts, raisins, popcorn, hard candy, hot dogs, or carrots).
- Keep hot foods and beverages and hot pots and pans out of your baby's reach. Turn pot or pan handles toward the back of the stove, and use an inside or back burner, where possible.
- Don't use a dangling tablecloth; it can be pulled and everything on it can crash onto your baby and the floor.
- Keep medicines and household products (such as bleach, oven and drain cleaners, paint solvents, polishes, and waxes) that might poison in a *locked* cabinet, not only in the house, but also in basement, garage, or other outbuildings.
- Try to buy items in child-*resistant* containers (remembering that does not mean child-*proof*).
- Never leave your baby alone in the bathtub or wading pool. Babies can drown in only a few inches of water. Do not rely on bathtub bathing rings. Young children can also turn on the faucet and scald themselves; parents may want to consider installing an anti-scald device at the spigots.
- Keep young children out of the bathroom unless you are watching; close bathroom doors and toilet lids, which can also be locked with a special device. Young children can drown in a few inches of water (including the toilet or buckets filled with water.)
- Be very careful when you or someone else in the family is sick. Medicines are likely to be out of their usual safe place, and your baby may want to imitate you by eating them.
- Keep medicines separate from household products and household products separate from food.
- Never give medicine in the dark. Turn on the light and read the label—EVERY TIME.
- Avoid overexposure to the sun, which can lead to sunburn. Use sunscreens on advice from your doctor or clinic staff.
- Keep diaper pails tightly closed and out of reach.
- Keep a bottle of Ipecac syrup on the medicine shelf to treat poisoning, using as directed. Keep another in the car glove compartment or to pack when you travel. Check dates periodically and replace when outdated.
- Keep a close watch for moving machinery when your baby is outdoors (such as lawnmowers or cars backing up) or indoors (such as exercise equipment).
- The car safety seat can be used in the toddler position with the child sitting up and facing forward when your baby is about 20 pounds at about nine months of age, either in the front seat with a driving adult (though never in a front seat with a passenger-side airbag) or in the back seat with another adult, or with older children seated at the sides of the car.

(continued)

(continued)

- Never leave your baby alone in a child safety seat in a car.
- During hot weather, if your car is parked in the hot sun, cover your child's safety seat with a towel to avoid burning your child.
- Do not give toddlers balloons; if they are deflated or popped, they can be swallowed and are extremely difficult to extract from the child's air passages.
- Avoid infant walkers, since children can injure themselves, even falling downstairs.
- Check your yard for poisonous plants (such as rhododendron, lily of the valley, or foxglove) and remove them or install fencing to keep toddlers away from them.
- Be alert for possible poisoning or other dangers when visiting homes that have not been childproofed, such as grandparents or other homes without young children.

Source: Adapted from Infant Care (1989). Prepared for the Public Health Service by the Health Resources and Services Administration, Bureau of Maternal and Child Health and Resources Development, and other materials.

Safe in the City: A Streetwise Guide to Avoid Being Robbed, Raped, Ripped off, Or Run Over. Marc MacYoung and Chris Pfouts. Paladin, 1994.
American Red Cross Community First Aid and Safety. Mosby, 1993.
Lightning and Boats: A Manual of Safety and Prevention. Michael Huck. Seaworthy, 1993.
The Human Side of Safety. Eugene F. McKenna and Ian Glendon. Chapman and Hall, 1993.
Wellness: Safety and Accident Prevention. David Lawson. Dushkin, 1992.
Child Safety Is No Accident. Jay M. Arena and Miriam B. Settle. Berkley, 1991.
Street-Smart Survival: A Nineties Guide to Staying Alive and Living Well. Victor Santoro. Paladin, 1991.
The Gun Safety Handbook. Marty Hayes. Special Child, 1990.

ON SAFETY FOR INFANTS AND TODDLERS

Keeping Your Baby Safe: A Guidebook for You to Protect Your Child. June Dyche. Tri-Oak, 1994.
Is It Safe?: Injury Prevention for Young Children. Becky J. Smith. ETR Assocs., 1994.
A Parent's Guide to Making a Home Safe and Suitable for an Infant or Toddler. Michael K. Meyerhoff. W. Gladden, 1992.
The Baby and Child Emergency First-Aid Handbook. Mitchell Einzig, ed. Meadowbrook, 1992.
Infant and Toddler Safety: What You Don't Know Can Hurt Your Child!. Eric Wallin. LiteWorks, 1992.

ON GENERAL CHILD SAFETY

On the Safe Side: Teach Your Child To Be Safe, Strong, and Street Smart. Paula Statman. HarperCollins, 1995.
Be Street Smart—Be Safe: Raising Safety Minded Children. Nily Glaser. Gan, 1994.
One Hundred One Ways to Make Your Home Toddler-Friendly. Joy M. Johnson. Spirit Dance, 1993.
Raising Safety-Smart Kids. S.R. McDill, Jr. Nelson, 1993.
Keys to Child Safety and Care of Minor Childhood Injuries. Robert J. Vinci. Barron's. 1992.
Safety Is No Accident: Children's Activities in Injury Prevention. William M. Kane and Kathleen E. Herrera. ETR Assoc., 1992.
Fifty Ways to Keep Your Child Safe: Physically, Emotionally, Medically, Environmentally. Susan K. Golant. Lowell House, 1992.
Are the Children Safe? Dan Cates. Aegina, 1991.
Safe Kids: A Complete Child Safety Handbook and Resource Guide for Parents. Vivian K. Fancher. Wiley, 1991.
Household Safety. Ellen Jackson. Horizon, 1991.
Home Safe Home. William J. Kelly. Avon, 1991.
Family Safety Handbook. Karl J. Hiller. Jackson, 1991.
Parents Book of Child Safety. David Laskin. Ballantine, 1991.
Fireproof Children Education Kit. Hendrik De Leeuw and others. National Fire Service Support Systems, 1990. Includes activities for elementary school children on the consequences of fireplay.

FOR CHILDREN

Let's Be Safe: Containing Such Useful Information As the Avoidance of Strangers and Their Candy, How Not to Be Run Over by a Car, and How Generally Not to Cut Oneself Open. Benjamin Darling. Chronicle, 1994.
In Water. In the Outdoors. Kyle Carter. Rourke, 1994.
The Preschoolers' Be Careful Book. Alida Allison. Price Stern, 1994.
Adrift!: Boating Safety for Children. Joan Neudecker and Colleen Politano. ICS Books, 1994.
With Fire. Kyle Carter. Rourke, 1994.
What Every Child Should Know and Do...for Surviving in the 90's: A Small Picture Book. Judy A. Hall. Personal Productions, 1992.
Bicycles Are Fun. Dorothy Chlad. Children's, 1992.
I Am Safe: A Child's Book of Personal Safety. Kate Soucheray. Wakefield, 1992. With study guide.
Know and Tell: A Work Book for Parents and Children. Yvette K. Lehman. Artmans, 1991.
The Aware Bears. Mac Hovec. Oceana Education, 1991.
Stay Safe, Play Safe. Barbara Seuling. Western, 1991.
Carefulness. Janet Reihecky. Child's World, 1990.

Safe and Sound Safety Program for Kids. Susan Erling and E. Gordon Franks. Safe and Sound, 1990.

For preteens and teens

Safety-Wise, rev. ed. Girl Scouts USA, 1993.
The Encyclopedia of Danger, 10 vols. Michel Peissel and Missy Allen. Chelsea House, 1993.
Fire in the Night. Sandra D. Bricker. Group, 1991.

salutatorian, in a graduating class, the student with the second highest academic rank, generally as measured by GRADE-POINT AVERAGE, so-called because he or she is often asked to give the opening speech, or *salutation,* at GRADUATION ceremonies. The highest-ranked student is the VALEDICTORIAN.

sarcoma, a general term for a kind of MALIGNANT TUMOR, or CANCER, in soft or connective tissues, bone, or muscles, including fibrous body organs, blood vessels, the lymph system, the *meninges* (membrane covering the BRAIN), and cartilage, sometimes associated with radiation or BURN scars. Small sarcomas can be cut out and the area treated with radiation therapy (see CANCER), but large sarcomas in the limbs may require amputation.

savant syndrome, a rare disorder in which a person has MENTAL RETARDATION or MENTAL DISORDERS (in centuries past lumped together as "idiocy") linked with extraordinary ability in certain distinct areas, usually relating to memory feats or artistic ability. The combination gave the condition its earlier name *idiot savant* (French for "learned idiot"). In a classic 1929 description, W.A. White in his *Outlines of Psychiatry* described the syndrome:

> These are rare cases, who, although idiots, still have some special faculty wonderfully developed. It may be music, calculation, memory for some certain variety of facts, etc.
>
> The calculators can name the answer to mathematical problems almost instantly; the musical prodigies often play well and even improvise; one of my cases could instantly name the day of the week for any date for years back.

In the movie *Rain Man,* Dustin Hoffman played a man with savant syndrome.

OTHER RESOURCES

Extraordinary People: Redefining the "Idiot Savant." Darold A. Treffert. Harper & Row, 1989.
Extraordinary People: Understanding Savant Syndrome. Ballantine, 1990.
Fragments of Genius: Investigating the Strange Feats of Idiots Savants. Michael J. Howe. Routledge, 1989.

(See also MENTAL RETARDATION; MENTAL DISORDERS; HELP FOR SPECIAL CHILDREN on page 689.)

scabies, infestation of the skin by tiny mites (*Sarcoptes scabiei*). Because these are often spread by sexual contact, scabies is considered a SEXUALLY TRANSMITTED DISEASE, but it may also be spread by contact with other infested materials, such as clothing or furniture, or by nonsexual contact with infested skin. Symptoms include intense itching in the affected areas, most commonly the hands (especially between the fingers), wrists, elbows, lower abdomen, and GENITALS. The female scabies mite burrows into the skin to lay eggs; after a month or more, these will show up as small red bumps or lines on the skin. But in the meantime, a person can unknowingly transmit the infestation to others. Irritation on the skin can be mistaken for the kind that results from poison ivy (see RASH), but infestation can be diagnosed from a microscopic examination of skin scrapings.

Scabies can be treated by various creams and lotions. Sex partners and family members should also be treated, and any clothing or bedding that has been in contact with any of them should be dry cleaned, washed in very hot water, dried at a high setting, and ironed—or boiled—to get rid of mites. (See also SEXUALLY TRANSMITTED DISEASES; also WHAT YOU (OR YOUR CHILD) CAN DO TO AVOID SEXUALLY TRANSMITTED DISEASES on page 541.)

scan, in medicine, one of various techniques to give a picture of the body's internal organs. Some kinds of scans, such as a CT SCAN, ULTRASOUND, and MRI, are not INVASIVE, requiring no INJECTIONS or other intrusions to prepare the body for the test. Many other scans are invasive, requiring the injection of foreign materials into the body to show up on the screen, such as dyed fluid in ANGIOGRAPHY or slightly radioactive material in NUCLEAR SCANS. (See MEDICAL TESTS.)

In reading, scanning is also a rapid READING technique for finding a piece of information in a larger work, such as an index, telephone book, or catalog; a basic LOCATIONAL SKILL.

scarlet fever (scarlatina), a disease caused by infection with the streptococcus bacteria, spread by droplets in the air; its name comes from the common symptoms of a reddish flush and rash, along with a sore throat and high fever. Once a common and dangerous childhood disease, scarlet fever (like STREP THROAT) can still cause RHEUMATIC FEVER and other serious complications, if not recognized and properly treated. But since the development of antibiotics, scarlet fever is relatively rare and usually easily treatable, if medication is started promptly.

FOR HELP AND FURTHER INFORMATION

National Institute of Allergy and Infectious Diseases (NIAID), 301–496–5717. (For full group information, see ALLERGY.)

schizophrenia, a group of MENTAL DISORDERS that have in common pervasive disturbances in thinking, behavior, and emotional reactions, especially lack of relation or connection between thoughts and feelings. It is this split that gives the disorder its popular name: *split personality.* (That term may also be applied to MULTIPLE PERSONALITY DISORDER, but there the split is between different personalities.) Often young people with schizophrenia are so disoriented as to be unable to function on a day-to-day basis; they often need supervision to ensure that the daily necessities of life are met and that they do not come to, or cause, harm.

Schizophrenia is a common form of mental illness that generally appears in ADOLESCENCE or early adulthood, possibly triggered by the massive hormonal changes of that period. The causes of the various kinds of schizophrenic disorders are unclear. Some genetic component seems to be involved, since the disorder "runs in families," but other factors must play a part, because the disorder sometimes appears in one identical twin but not the other. Some researchers think it may be triggered by a viral infection early in life or from mild brain damage during CHILDBIRTH. Schizophrenia affects both sexes, but slightly more males than females. Recent studies have shown that at least some forms of schizophrenia involve some actual physical changes in the brain, notably enlarged VENTRICLES, though how and why they occur is unknown.

Various drugs are used to treat schizophrenia, though some of them have dangerous, even life-threatening side effects and must be used in great caution. Parents whose children have schizophrenia face a difficult period, as the disease may last for years, even decades. A substantial portion of young people with schizophrenia recover to a considerable extent by their early thirties. According to recent studies, by ten years after diagnosis approximately one-fourth of all people diagnosed with schizophrenia have completely recovered; another fourth have shown considerable improvement, and another fourth modest improvement. Approximately 15 percent have shown no improvement, and perhaps 10 percent have died, usually by SUICIDE or accident. Early diagnosis, treatment, and support are vital for all. Parents face special difficulties in paying for psychiatric care, since many HEALTH CARE or HEALTH INSURANCE plans have sharply limited coverage for such care.

FOR HELP AND FURTHER INFORMATION

American Schizophrenia Association (ASA)
900 North Federal Highway, #330
Boca Raton, FL 33432
407–393–6167
Mary Roddy Haggerty, Executive Director
Organization of health professionals concerned with schizophrenia, seeing it as biochemical disorder, probably inherited; supports research; seeks to educate public; encourages formation of local self-help groups, called Schizophrenics Anonymous (SA), for people diagnosed as schizophrenics, guided by volunteer professional.

National Institute of Mental Health (NIMH), 301–443–4513. Publishes *Schizophrenia: Questions and Answers* and *Medication for the Treatment of Schizophrenia: Questions and Answers.* (For full group information, see MENTAL DISORDER.)

National Mental Health Association (NMHA), 800–969–6642. Publishes *Schizophrenia.* (For full group information, see MENTAL DISORDERS.)

National Alliance for the Mentally Ill (NAMI), 800–950–6264. Publishes brochures *Understanding Schizophrenia* and *Schizophrenia*; booklets *What Is Schizophrenia?* and *Schizophrenia and Genetic Risks: A Guide to Genetic Counseling*; and book *Surviving with Schizophrenia: A Guide for Families*; online forum and libraries cover schizophrenia. (For full group information, see MENTAL DISORDERS.)

OTHER RESOURCES

For parents and other adults

Understanding and Helping the Schizophrenic: A Guide for Family and Friends. Silvano Arieti. Karnac/Brunner-Mazel, 1994.
Coping with Schizophrenia: A Guide for Families. Kim T. Mueser and Susan Gingerich. New Harbinger, 1994.
Understanding Schizophrenia: A Guide to the New Research on Causes and Treatment. Richard S. Keefe and Philip D. Harvey. Free Press, 1994.
Schizophrenia: Straight Talk for Family and Friends. Maryellen Walsh. Morrow, 1993.

On dealing with schizophrenia

Recovery from Schizophrenia, 2nd ed. Richard Wagner. Routledge, 1994.
How to Live with Schizophrenia, rev. ed. Abram Hoffer and Humphry Osmon. Citadel/Carol, 1992.
Living and Working with Schizophrenia, rev. ed. J.J. Jeffries and others. University of Toronto Press, 1990.

For preteens and teens

Schizophrenia. Douglas W. Smith. Watts, 1993.

Personal experiences

The Family Face of Schizophrenia: True Stories of Mental Illness with Practical Counsel from America's Leading Experts. Patricia Backlar. Tarcher/Putnam, 1994.
Tell Me I'm Here: One Family's Experience of Schizophrenia. Anne Deveson. Viking Penguin, 1992.
The Dinosaur Man: Tales of Madness and Enchantment from the Back Ward. Susan Baur. HarperCollins, 1991. On work with schizophrenic patients.
Rickie. Frederic Flach and Rickie F. Hartman. Fawcett, 1990. On a teenage girl's battle with schizophrenia.

(See also MENTAL DISORDERS.)

scholarship, a type of FINANCIAL AID given to a student for use in meeting the costs of attending a COLLEGE or PRIVATE SCHOOL; also, more generally, excellence in academic studies. An *open scholarship* is one for which anyone may apply, while a *closed scholarship* is restricted to certain kinds of applicants, such as those living in a certain state or those whose last name is Brown. Unlike loans, scholarships are a type of GRANT that do not have to be repaid.

Scholarships may be awarded on the basis of scholastic excellence alone, or for other reasons, as with an ATHLETIC SCHOLARSHIP to an outstanding player or an award to a minority student by a school that wants a more balanced student body. The dollar amount of the scholarship may depend totally on merit, with the largest amount going to the one with the highest ranking, or primarily on need, as indicated by a MEANS TEST. Scholarships are often contingent, remaining in effect only as long as the student continues to meet a preset standard, such as a B average in college. Some scholarships may also be voided in other circumstances; for example, some may be suspended or terminated if a student is convicted of possessing or distributing drugs. (See FINANCIAL AID.)

Scholastic Aptitude Test (SAT), a series of group-administered ADMISSIONS TESTS required of most HIGH SCHOOL seniors who are applying to COLLEGES and universities, prepared by the EDUCATIONAL TESTING SERVICE (ETS) for the COLLEGE ENTRANCE EXAMINATION BOARD. This dreaded precollege hurdle—the "gatekeeper" exam that largely makes or breaks college entrance and scholarship offerings for most students—is a six-section, three-hour STANDARDIZED, OBJECTIVE TEST, offered at locations around the country on various dates. Traditionally the SAT—the test as taken in the past by most of today's parents—covered these main areas:

- *Verbal*, in two test sections, with questions involving analogies, reading comprehension, antonyms, and sentence completions.
- *Math*, also in two sections, with questions covering arithmetic, algebra, geometry, and quantitative comparisons.
- *Test of Standard Written English* (TSWE), with questions covering usage and sentence corrections, more specifically grammar, sentence structure, and word choice. This section is supposedly used only for class placement, but (contrary to stated intent) is widely used in college admissions.
- *Experimental*, questions being tried out by the ETS and a way of evaluating whether or not the SAT questions are at the same level of difficulty as in the past. This section is not scored, except for ETS's internal use.

While these same areas are covered in the current tests, the SAT has undergone some changes and more are in store. One major set of changes took place in 1993–94; these included:

- Increased emphasis on reading, including longer reading passages.
- Elimination of verbal questions involving antonyms (word opposites, such as "scarce" and "plentiful"). Such questions have been frequently criticized because the material is not directly taught in high schools, though it does result from general reading.
- More emphasis on problem-solving ability in the mathematics section, with 20 percent of the multiple choice questions being replaced by questions calling for students to work out their solutions with pencil on paper for submission to the examiners.
- Allowing the optional use of hand-held calculators. Some are concerned that low-income students, who have less access to and so may be unfamiliar with using calculators, will be at a disadvantage.
- Addition of a separate, optional twenty-minute writing exam. Various groups, including some civil rights activists and politicians from heavily immigrant areas, had fought against the inclusion of a writing exam in the SAT itself, as posing an undue hardship for recent immigrants for whom English is a second language. Others say that making the writing exam optional sends the wrong message—that writing is a skill of peripheral importance—when decline in writing skills is a major and widespread concern.
- The addition of language proficiency exams in Japanese and Chinese.
- Provision of an English exam for people for whom English is a second language.

Some educators have hailed the changes as the most sweeping in decades, and as likely to encourage schools to focus less on teaching toward multiple-choice tests, and more on building thinking, analysis, writing, and problem-solving techniques. Critics have charged that the changes are merely superficial, and that they will not improve the SAT's long-questioned ability to predict student success in college—the purported aim of the test. The SAT and related tests have been widely criticized on the basis of both RELIABILITY and VALIDITY. So have colleges and universities, for placing undue emphasis on SAT scores, especially when they are used as CUTOFF SCORES without reference to a student's wider abilities and accomplishments.

The verbal and math sections of the SAT are scored separately, with the raw SCORE for each (the number of questions answered correctly) being converted to a figure on a scale ranging from 200 to 800, in jumps of 10; the scores are also shown as PERCENTILES. The TSWE is scored on a scale from 20 to 60+, with the top score possible even if a few questions are missed. Several weeks after the test, scores are sent to the schools and scholarship programs a student indicates. In another major change, in 1995, the SAT scores were "recentered;" that is, all scores were shifted upwards, meaning that a student could get the top score of 800 without answering 100 percent of the questions correctly.

The related *Preliminary Scholastic Aptitude Test (PSAT)/National Merit Scholarship Qualifying Test (NMSQT)* is offered to high school juniors. Originally it was designed to give high school juniors experience in taking an SAT-like examination (and incidentally giving the test designers a chance to try different formats), but since 1971 the PSAT itself has been a qualifying test for students seeking a National Merit Scholarship. The PSAT/NMSQT contains only two fifty-minute sections, math and verbal, with questions often being taken from previous SATs. The final converted scores range between 20 and 80.

The SAT program also includes a range of ACHIEVEMENT TESTS on specific subjects, as well as tests for college students applying to graduate school. Scores are sent to the schools and scholarship programs indicated. Among the changes planned for the not too distant future are offering the SAT on computer, and not just a transfer of the test to the screen but an interactive type of test that will vary with the test-taker's answers (see ADAPTIVE TEST).

Ideally, the SAT and similar tests are meant to provide colleges and universities with a useful standard of comparison among students coming from widely different backgrounds and schools, and graded on very different bases. On a very practical level, they also give students and their parents and counselors some gauge of where they stand among other students in the country, which can help in the process of deciding what colleges students should apply to.

Traditionally, students were told that there was no way they could prepare for the SAT because it was an APTITUDE TEST, not an ACHIEVEMENT TEST. In practice, students have for decades bought books to help them prepare (see below), and many have also enrolled in costly commercial preparation courses, which favored those who could afford them. Schools were long reluctant to "teach to the test," but they, too, have felt increasing pressure on the question of test scores. In this era of school choice, parents deciding which school their child should attend often base their judgments to a large extent on how well the school's students have been doing on such exams.

As a result, many school systems have established SAT review classes to help students prepare for the exams, openly acknowledging what has long been clear: that students who prepare intensively for the SAT do better than those who do not (as even the College Entrance Examination Board has finally acknowledged in recent years). Such SAT preparation and review programs vary widely. Some are offered for a low fee as a series of Saturday, late-afternoon or evening classes; some are informal lunchtime tutoring sessions; some are free, semester-long courses, often for credit; some are courses offered on a cable television channel (sometimes for a fee, sometimes not); and some are centered on computer programs or self-help videotapes, often made available through the school. Some schools even routinely offer practice SATs as "warm-ups" in English and mathematics classes.

A student may, for example, take a course in "developmental reading," in which the textbook is an SAT preparation guide, and the course includes instruction on how to approach SAT questions, as by narrowing choices on the multiple-choice exam. Another student may spend a certain part of weekly class time studying vocabulary such as "propitious" or "querulous," drawn directly from previous SAT exams. The object is not only to prepare students on the content and approach, but also to make them so familiar with the SAT format as to blunt the test-phobia that has hindered so many SAT-takers in the past.

For years, students have been preparing themselves for the SAT in a different way: by taking the PSAT/NMSQT in their freshman or sophomore years. But now the SAT itself is being taken by many far younger students. By the early 1990s, over 100,000 of the students taking the SAT were seventh- and eighth-graders, making up a surprising 6 percent of the students taking the exam annually. In addition to early preparation, many are taking the SATs as entrance exams for college-based special summer programs for academically GIFTED CHILDREN, such as the Johns Hopkins University's Center for Talented Youth program, started in 1972, and others modeled on it.

Many parents and educators sharply criticize the giving of SATs to children who have not even been taught the algebra and geometry that form much of the content of the mathematical portion. Critics are also concerned that the stress of taking such exams further diminishes the years of childhood. Educators who run programs for the gifted generally acknowledge such problems, but say they have no better way to evaluate prospective entrants. They also note that many bright young people are able to solve mathematical problems or understand words they have never seen before by using their general knowledge and intelligence. The College Entrance Examination Board does not encourage use of the test with such young students, but has not attempted to bar it. Recognizing the need, however, an advisory panel has recommended that the College Board develop new tests of college potential to be used with seventh- and eighth-graders—though many people object to yet *another* standardized test for America's already overtested students.

Many people have also challenged the questions themselves, and the ETS/College Board's choice as to the single "correct answer." In New York (and later elsewhere), the TRUTH IN TESTING law forced the College Board to make available to students their answers and a copy of the questions and officially correct answers. Responding still further, the College Board now provides a Report of Student Answers (ROSA), giving personalized scoring sheets informing students of how points for their scores were calculated, and Summary of Answers for the PSAT/NMSQT, giving high school officials a question-by-question analysis of how their students answered questions, and how those responses compare to other students around the country.

Despite criticism, the SAT and similar tests are a fact of life, and parents who want to help their children will certainly want to at least get books of sample tests (available from the College Board) and one or more "review" or "strategies" books, and explore local availability of review courses. For those with computers, some SAT tests and study materials are available on CD-ROM and other electronic forms.

Some students do not do well on any traditional tests, SATs or otherwise. They may want to explore colleges that have alternative entrance policies or programs, for students who do not meet the usual admissions standards for high school grades and test scores, for whatever reason, but can in other ways demonstrate the potential to succeed in college. (See especially Stacy Needle's *Other Routes into College: Alternative Admission* under COLLEGE.)

Special arrangements can be made for children with DISABILITIES, such as LEARNING DISABILITIES, motor disabilities, EAR AND HEARING PROBLEMS, and EYE AND VISION PROBLEMS, including those who are DEAF-BLIND; these may include untimed testing or use of a scribe. Students may be eligible for these if they have on file at their school a current INDIVIDUALIZED EDUCATION PROGRAM (IEP), indicating the nature of the disability and the need for modification of test arrangements. Alternatively, a student must have signed test results, from two separate parties (a physician, psychologist, child-study team, or specialist in LEARNING DISABILITIES), describing the disability, the tests used to diagnose it, and the need for modification; the disability must meet state certification guidelines, where they exist. (See SPECIAL HELP FOR SPECIAL COLLEGE STUDENTS on page 366; see also HELP FOR SPECIAL CHILDREN on page 689.)

As for the future, a computerized version of the SAT is in preparation, and may be introduced before the year 2000. Early computer-given tests introduced for some graduate school examinations in the early 1990s were essentially the old paper-and-pencil tests transferred to computer. However, versions under development are ADAPTIVE TESTS, in which the questions presented vary depending on the student's previous answers. (See TESTS.)

School and College Ability Tests (SCAT), a set of group-administered TESTS that attempt to measure basic verbal and mathematical abilities for children from grades 3 to 12, available in three levels (grades 3–6; 6–9; and 9–12). The pen-and-pencil test uses analogies in the verbal portion of the test, and in the quantitative part, comparisons demonstrating grasp of basic number skills. Scored by the test administrator or computer, the test yields SCORES for the subtests and an overall score, which can be converted in various ways, including PERCENTILES and STANINES. (See TESTS.)

school of choice, any school other than the neighborhood public school, but generally still in the public school system, such as MAGNET SCHOOLS or ALTERNATIVE SCHOOLS, to which parents might send their child. It can also refer to a public school in a different district, to which parents choose to send their children, perhaps one with a more attractive CURRICULUM, focus, or approach. Sometimes the term is used more widely, then also including church-affiliated or other PRIVATE SCHOOLS, including schools for children with SPECIAL NEEDS. The U.S. Department of Education has been recommending that parents be able to exercise choice in schooling for their children; their CHOOSING A SCHOOL FOR YOUR CHILD (on page 659) includes a checklist for evaluating schools.

Among the advantages cited for school choice is that it:

- Offers diversity to suit a wide range of children (not just those from high-income families).
- Decentralizes education and gives more power to parents and teachers.
- Strengthens schools by fostering competition for students among them and so making them accountable to the people they serve.
- Will force the closure of poor schools unable to attract students.
- Allows parents to have their children in a school near their place of work, if desired, rather than near the home.
- However, critics argue that:
  - The benefits of choice will accrue only to those families motivated enough and probably sufficiently well educated to learn about the options available and select the one best for their children.
  - The poorest, most disadvantaged children will be left in the least popular, least effective schools.
  - The program breaks up the security and convenience of neighborhood schools.
  - The money might better be spent on more meaningful reforms.

Over the last few decades, one main reason that many parents have "chosen" private schools is to maintain segregation in education, in the face of orders for mandatory DESEGREGATION and BUSING. But in recent years, choice among public schools has been increasingly used as a tool for voluntary desegregation. Indeed, several states experimenting with school choice have, by law, barred programs that would tend toward segregation; such plans are sometimes called *controlled choice*, because they have certain kinds of brakes built in. For example, before enrolling their children in school, parents may visit a volunteer-staffed information center to find out about the kinds of programs and approaches offered in each of thirteen schools. On the basis of this, parents make a first, second, and third choice of school for their child. The final assignment of schools is made by district administrators, keeping racial and ethnic balance in mind. Where this approach

If Your School District Is Considering Schools of Choice

The National Coalition of Chapter 1/Title I Parents recommends that, if their school district is considering a school choice plan, parents ask these questions:

- Is free transportation provided?
- In the final school assignment process, do all students have equal chance to be placed in their first choice school, regardless of their previous academic or behavioral record?
- Is the enrollment process simple and are there arrangements to explain them adequately to all parents? More specifically, is there a parent information center in the neighborhood staffed by multilingual counselors?
- Are there enough classroom places for all students who want to exercise choice?
- Do neighborhood schools have the same funding and facilities as magnet schools and other schools with special programs?
- Are parents consulted and their preferences considered in designing school programs?

has been used, most families get into one of their first three choices.

Early indications are that student achievement levels are higher in school choice programs, especially when inner-city students go to magnet schools; but the long-term effects, especially on students in the "last-choice" schools, are yet to be seen. Families in districts offering choice may want to look at IF YOUR SCHOOL DISTRICT IS CONSIDERING SCHOOLS OF CHOICE (above).

FOR HELP AND FURTHER INFORMATION

The Case for School Choice. David R. Henderson. Hoover Institute, 1993.

The School-Choice Controversy: What Is Constitutional? James W. Skillen. Baker, 1993.

School Choice: Why We Need It, How We Get It. James B. Van Treese, ed. Ingram, 1993.

School Choice Programs: What's Happening in the States. Angela Hulsey. Heritage Foundation, 1993.

The Exhausted School: The First National Grassroots Speakout on the Right to School Choice. John T. Gatto. Oxford Village, 1993.

Choice in Public Education. Timothy Young and Evans Clinchy. Teachers College, 1992.

The Choice Controversy. Peter W. Cookson, Jr., ed. Corwin, 1992.

Opting Out: Choice and the Future of Schools. Martin Rogers. Lawrence and Wishart/Humanities, 1992.

(See also VOUCHER SYSTEM; CHAPTER 1; PRIVATE SCHOOL; EDUCATION; also HELP ON LEARNING AND EDUCATION on page 659.)

school phobia, a general term for the occasional reluctance or refusal of a child to attend school, accompanied often by ANXIETY, nausea, abdominal pain, and headache; also called *school refusal syndrome.* A child may also express resistance to school by electing to be MUTE. Not really a PHOBIA, in many cases school phobia may simply be a form of SEPARATION ANXIETY, and unwillingness to leave home and parents, though in severe cases it may result from SEPARATION ANXIETY DISORDER.

School phobia may also reflect academic or social problems that the child does not want to face, such as bullying by other students or abuse by a teacher. Parents will want to explore carefully the origins of the resistance, and help the child deal with whatever problems exist, while seeing that the child returns to school quickly.

OTHER RESOURCES

School Phobia and Other Anxieties in Youth. Ron Kerner. Bureau for At-Risk Youth, 1992.

scoliosis, abnormal sideways curvature of the spine, in excessive cases becoming almost S-shaped, a type of SPINAL DISORDER commonly associated with LORDOSIS and/or KYPHOSIS. Most people have some amount of irregular curvature in the spine; perhaps 1 in 10 has a curvature of at least 10 degrees. Curvature of 10 to 20 degrees is labeled mild, less than that, simply "postural variation." According to the National Scoliosis Foundation, for over half the people diagnosed, the condition does not get progressively worse, and indeed the majority never require treatment. In the others, however, the condition gradually worsens, in some cases significantly, and if unrecognized and untreated, may progress to severe and painful deformity, and cause increasing pulmonary problems as the lungs are restricted. Scoliosis often appears in childhood or ADOLESCENCE, in infancy in more boys than girls, but by school age in both sexes. It becomes increasingly obvious as growth occurs, both to the eye and on X-RAYS.

Scoliosis can result from unequal leg length, which

causes tilting of the body; from TUMORS or injuries; or from diseases such as MUSCULAR DYSTROPHY or POLIO; but is often a GENETIC DISORDER. If detected early, scoliosis can be treated simply by exercises or ORTHOPEDIC DEVICES, such as shoe lifts to even the leg lengths. Where curvature is between 25 and 40 degrees, braces are often prescribed in an attempt to halt progression of the curvature, especially during the growth years of adolescence, which is successful in nearly 80 percent of patients in recent studies. Various types of braces are used, depending on the location and severity of the curvature; some are worn full time, others only at night. In young children, in what is called *early onset scoliosis,* a plaster cast may be used to help keep the curvature from progressing, this being more comfortable, since it is molded to the body, and easier for parents to deal with than braces; the plaster cast will need to be changed every three to four months, depending on the child's growth rate. Plaster casts are regarded as successful over 90 percent of the time. Serious or worsening cases may require surgery, in which bone grafts are used to help force and fuse the spinal vertebrae into a straight line. Good posture and exercise such as swimming, especially the sidestroke and the backstroke, can ease the pain associated with scoliosis, though it will not stop progression. People with the condition should avoid being sedentary and overweight, as that may aggravate the condition. Electrical stimulation was for some years tried as a treatment, but studies showed no beneficial effect.

Children should be checked for scoliosis from early childhood, and if it is detected, the degree of curvature should be checked annually to see that measures being taken are keeping the condition from worsening. This is especially important for preteens and teens, since curves often markedly worsen during periods of rapid growth, in young girls especially in the year or two before their first menstrual period.

FOR HELP AND FURTHER INFORMATION

National Scoliosis Foundation (NSF)
72 Mt. Auburn Street
Watertown, MA 02172
617–926–0397
Fax: 617–926–0398
E-Mail: scoliosis@aol.com (America Online: SCOLIOSIS)
Joseph P. O'Brien, President
Organization concerned with scoliosis, kyphosis, and lordosis; seeks to educate public and influence legislation; aids in setting up local screening programs; publishes various materials, including semiannual newsletter *The Spinal Connection*; books *Stopping Scoliosis* and *Getting Ready, Getting Well* (on anticipating surgery); audiovisual materials *Growing Straighter and Stronger* and *School Screening with Dr. Robert Keller;* brochures *1 in Every 10 Persons Has Scoliosis* and *When the Spine Curves*; medical updates (from newsletter); resource lists; and papers for medical professionals.

Scoliosis Association (SA)
P.O. Box 811705
Boca Raton, FL 33481–1705
Crystal Corporate Center
2500 North Military Trail
Boca Raton, FL 33431
407–994–4435; 800–800–0669
Janice T. Sacks, President
Organization concerned with scoliosis and related conditions; provides information; encourages screening programs in school; sponsors research; publishes quarterly newsletter *Backtalk*, fact sheet, bibliography, article reprints, and videos, including *Scoliosis: An Adult Perspective.*

Shriner's Hospitals for Crippled Children, 800–237–5055. Provides free medical care for children with scoliosis. (For full group information, see BONE AND BONE DISORDERS.)

American Academy of Orthopaedic Surgeons (AAOS), 800–346–2267. Publishes brochure *Scoliosis.* (For full group information, see BONE AND BONE DISORDERS.)

National Arthritis and Musculoskeletal and Skin Diseases Information Clearinghouse (NAMSIC), 301–495–4484. Publishes information packages *Scoliosis in Children* and *Scoliosis in Adults.* (For full group information, see ARTHRITIS.)

OTHER RESOURCES

Stopping Scoliosis: The Complete Guide to Diagnosis and Treatment. Nancy Schommer. Avery, 1991.

(See also SPINAL CORD AND SPINAL DISORDERS.)

score, in educational testing, a grade or mark indicating the number of correct answers or the number of points awarded for acceptable work. On many OBJECTIVE TESTS, especially STANDARDIZED TESTS, the *raw score* is the actual number of correct answers. Often, however, this is converted into a different kind of score for reporting purposes, such as a PERCENTILE, GRADE-EQUIVALENT, or AGE-EQUIVALENT (EDUCATIONAL AGE). These *converted scores* (sometimes called *scaled scores*) attempt to put the raw score into comparative perspective with the scores of a large number of other students who have taken the test. In the case of ADMISSIONS TESTS, students are sometimes required to score above a certain point, called a CUTOFF SCORE. Scores derived from the results of two or more tests are called *composite scores.*

screening tests, tests given to see if a person has certain characteristics, especially problems. Among the common types are GENETIC SCREENING or PRENATAL SCREENING TESTS, seeking to identify possible BIRTH DEFECTS or other health problems before or during PREGNANCY; NEONATAL SCREENING TESTS, which try to identify medical problems so they can be treated before doing harm to the developing infant; and DEVELOPMENTAL SCREENING TESTS, used in preschool and early school years to identify problems that may adversely affect learning. (See MEDICAL TESTS; TESTS; and the specific types of tests above.)

sealed records, documents kept confidential by the court, and not available for open inspection. In cases of traditional ADOPTION, records have generally been open only to the court and the adoption agency. However, some recent laws and other forms of adoption have allowed the records to be somewhat more accessible, such as to the adopted child (on reaching adulthood). Records from JUVENILE COURT are also not made public, and are generally restricted if not actually sealed, and sometimes later EXPUNGED.

secondary-care level hospital (Level II), an intermediate-care medical facility offering more sophisticated equipment and laboratories, and often more specialized staff, than in a community HOSPITAL, but less than a *tertiary-care (Level III)* facility, such as a UNIVERSITY-AFFILIATED FACILITY (UAF). (See HOSPITAL.)

Secondary School Admission Tests (SSAT), an ADMISSIONS TEST for children in grades 5 to 10, widely used by selective PRIVATE SCHOOLS in deciding whether or not to admit students. Existing in two forms (grades 5–7 and 8–10), the tests are paper-and-pencil, multiple-choice tests focusing on verbal and mathematical abilities and reading comprehension. Tests are scored by hand or by computer, and the subtest and overall SCORES are compared with NORMS for the student's grade level, and converted in various ways, including into PERCENTILES. Reports of the scores and a booklet on interpreting them are provided by the publisher, the Educational Testing Service, which also provides a booklet called *Preparing for the SSAT* for students studying ahead of time. Special testing arrangements can be made for students with some DISABILITIES. (See TESTS.)

secondary sex characteristics, the physical changes that take place in a boy and girl during PUBERTY, in response to various HORMONES, such as ESTROGEN in females and TESTOSTERONE in males; more generally, the external signs of sexual maturity. Among the secondary sex characteristics in women are the development of BREASTS and LABIA; the growth of HAIR in an adult pattern, notably in the pubic area and under the arms; and the laying down of fat deposits in various parts of the body to give the characteristic figure of an adult woman. The corresponding secondary sex characteristics in men including development of PENIS and TESTES; hair in the pubic and underarm areas and on the face; and general bodily development to adult form.

Section 504, that portion of the Civil Rights Act for Handicapped Persons—more formally, Section 504 of the Rehabilitation Act of 1973, or Public Law (P.L. 93–112)—which bars any organization or institution receiving federal funds from discriminating in any way against qualified people with DISABILITIES, at the risk of losing those funds. Enforced by the U.S. Department of Justice, this expansion of the civil rights of people with DISABILITIES applied also to schools and laid the groundwork for the EDUCATION FOR ALL HANDICAPPED CHILDREN ACT (EHC), which guaranteed public educational services for handicapped children, and for the AMERICANS WITH DISABILITIES ACT (ADA), which expanded requirements of access to wider areas of life, notably to state and local governments and to private employers of 15 or more people. Indeed, the Rehabilitation Act was amended in 1992 to integrate its provisions with those of the ADA.

Section 504 also helped shape those later laws by establishing a functional definition of disability, defining a person with a disability as someone with "a substantial limitation of a major life activity or with a record of disability or someone who is regarded as having a disability," a broad definition including most individuals with a disability or CHRONIC ILLNESS. It proclaims that "no handicapped child can be excluded from an appropriate public education solely because of a mental or physical handicap in a school system receiving federal funds of any kind."

A child who has a disability or chronic illness, but does not require SPECIAL EDUCATION and an INDIVIDUALIZED EDUCATION PLAN, may still be able to get special assistance under a *504 Accommodation Plan.* The plan may cover such things as an extra set of books to be left at home, a locker on all levels of a school, classes arranged close together, and minor medical services, such as catheterization (see CATHETER).

FOR HELP AND FURTHER INFORMATION

Your Child and Health Care: A "Dollars & Sense" Guide for Families with Special Needs. Lynn Robinson Rosenfeld. Paul H. Brookes, 1994.

Access to Education for the Disabled: A Guide to Compliance with Section 504 of the Rehabilitation Act of 1973. Salome M. Heyward. McFarland, 1992.

(See HELP FOR SPECIAL CHILDREN on page 000; also specific disabilities.)

segregation, in general, separation of people into groups on the basis of certain characteristics, such as White from Black, male from female, or those with DISABILITIES from those without. In the past, much segregation was open, deliberate, and formal, written into law and so called DE JURE (by law). In the schools such legislated segregation was struck down by the landmark 1954 Supreme Court case *Brown* v. *Board of Education*; subsequent federal civil rights legislation outlawed other kinds of formal discrimination, including some relating to women and to people with disabilities. Separation continued, however, as a result of informal social pressures; the result was DE FACTO (in fact) segregation, which has similarly been attacked by the courts. In education, one court-mandated approach to segregation has been controversial BUSING; more recently, many school districts have tried to establish voluntary DESEGREGATION programs, such as those involving SCHOOLS OF CHOICE and MAGNET SCHOOLS.

seizure, a sudden period of involuntary, uncontrolled electrical activity in the brain, often accompanied by violent muscular contractions called CONVULSIONS. Most widely known are the wide range of recurrent seizures that result from long-term conditions; these generally fall under the umbrella name of EPILEPSY. (For discussion of the main types of epileptic seizures, see EPILEPSY; see also WHAT SHOULD YOU DO IF SOMEONE HAS A SEIZURE? on page 225.)

Seizures can also be caused by short-term conditions, such as a reaction to a particular medication or an abrupt high FEVER in a young child. Many children have a seizure at some time in their lives, as from infections such as MENINGITIS or OTITIS MEDIA. The child may lose consciousness and twitch for a few minutes, during which time dangerous objects should be cleared away from the vicinity. To prevent recurrence, parents should attempt to reduce the child's body temperature (see FEVER).

In the past some children who had experienced febrile (fever) seizures were given anti-seizure medications to help prevent the development of recurring seizures, or EPILEPSY. But in the 1980s the National Institutes of Health recommended that such preventive (*prophylactic)* treatment was not necessary unless there was a history of epilepsy in the family, signs of impairment of the NERVOUS SYSTEM, or some special complications in the nature of seizures that might suggest other problems.

self-fulfilling prophecy, an event or result caused at least partly by one's belief that it will occur. In relation to children, that often means that they tend to live up to the expectations that others, especially adults in authority, have of them; sometimes called the PYGMALION EFFECT. In EDUCATION, researchers have clearly established that a teacher's expectations of a child's potential influence how well the child will perform in class; most notably, in experiments where children chosen at random were labeled LATE BLOOMERS, and their names given to their teachers, those children showed marked improvement.

self-help skills (self-care skills), skills that allow a person to take care of his or her own needs, such as feeding, bathing or hygiene, dressing, grooming, and going to the toilet, skills that children learn gradually as they develop independence. In the first year, for example, infants generally learn to eat crackers by themselves, hold a cup with two hands and drink from it with help, and hold out their arms and legs when being dressed; in the next year, they usually progress to using a spoon, holding a cup with one hand and drinking from it without help, chewing food, and removing their outer clothes. The CHART OF NORMAL DEVELOPMENT (on page 637) indicates when between birth and age six children first *on the average* begin to exhibit the main self-help skills. (Subscribers to the America Online computer service can find activities designed to develop children's skills in various areas, including self-help, in the Moms Online Desk Reference section of Moms Online, under "Teaching Young Children.")

Children with MENTAL RETARDATION and some other DEVELOPMENTAL DISORDERS will develop self-help skills at a slower pace. Some children with mental retardation, CHRONIC illness, MENTAL DISORDERS, or severe physical DISABILITIES may never be able to care for themselves without some help. Under current laws, medical and social agencies are assigned to reevaluate their skills periodically through ADOLESCENCE and (if necessary) through adulthood, the aim being to provide therapy and rehabilitation as seems appropriate to help disabled people maximize their independent self-help skills.

An individual will often function independently on one skill, but not another; self-care skills are often graded from 0 (for fully independent functioning) to 4 (for complete dependence). For example, someone might need help in getting to the toilet, and removing and then replacing the necessary clothes, but might be able to feed herself food brought in on a tray. For people with severe medical problems, self-help skills also include the ability to carry out various necessary procedures, such as giving an INSULIN injection or inserting a CATHETER for CLEAN, INTERMITTENT CATHETERIZATION.

FOR HELP AND FURTHER INFORMATION

Association for Children with Down Syndrome (ACDS), 516–221–4700. Publishes *A Self-Help Curriculum*, on teaching young children self-help skills. (For full group information, see DOWN SYNDROME.)

(See also HELP FOR SPECIAL CHILDREN on page 689.)

self-mutilation syndrome, a pattern of behavior that involves willful infliction of pain or injury to one's own body, but not necessarily intending to commit SUICIDE (though that may result); also known by several other names, including *autoaggression, deliberate self-harm syndrome, symbolic wounding,* and *attempted suicide.* Self-mutilation takes a wide variety of forms, including wrist-cutting, amputation (as of ear or tongue), mutilating GENITALS (including castration or insertion of foreign objects), biting (as of lips or fingers), pulling out HAIR, gouging out one's eyes, burning, banging one's head against a wall, swallowing harmful substances or objects, and jumping from heights. The syndrome often begins in late ADOLESCENCE and is associated with BORDERLINE PERSONALITY DISORDER or SCHIZOPHRENIA. Self-mutilation also occurs as part of LESCH-NYHAN SYNDROME, in which a child compulsively bites away his lips and fingers.

FOR HELP AND FURTHER INFORMATION

National Institute of Mental Health (NIMH), 301–443–4513. (For full group information, see MENTAL DISORDERS.)

semen, the fluid forcefully ejected from the PENIS during EJACULATION, at the point of ORGASM, which carries the SPERM required for FERTILIZATION. In volume, the fluid is largely secretions from structures called *seminal vesicles,* but it also contains secretions from the *prostate gland;* with the sperm, these are mixed together in a short tube called the *ejaculatory duct* (see REPRODUCTIVE SYSTEM; TESTES; SPERM).

semester, originally a period of six months, but in EDUCATION today, two equal periods that often make up the school year, each far short of six months; common alternatives are TRIMESTERS (three equal periods) or QUARTERS (four equal periods).

sensory education, in the MONTESSORI METHOD, use of materials designed to enhance a child's use of the various SENSORY MODES or MODALITIES for learning.

sensory modes (modalities), any of the five avenues by which someone receives information: seeing (*visual*), hearing (*auditory*), touching (*tactile*), smelling (*olfactory*), and tasting (*gustatory*), plus the sense of the body's motion (*kinesthetic,* sometimes called *haptic*). According to Jean Piaget's theory, the first stage of a child's COGNITIVE DEVELOPMENT is the *sensory motor* (or *sensori-motor*) *stage,* during which children gain an awareness of their sense perceptions and use this knowledge in developing MOTOR SKILLS.

Parents, other family members, and caregivers can help their children learn about themselves and the world from infancy by exploring the senses. (Subscribers to the America Online computer service can find "Stimulating Your Baby's Senses" in the Moms Online Desk Reference section of Moms Online, under "sensory modes.") Babies who have, for whatever reasons, had too little stimulation of the senses may develop a syndrome called FAILURE TO THRIVE, involving physical and MENTAL RETARDATION. When the sense organs are functioning normally, but the person is unable to interpret the information received, that person is said to have a PERCEPTUAL HANDICAP, a common problem among children with LEARNING DISABILITIES or other DEVELOPMENTAL DISORDERS.

OTHER RESOURCES

For children

Exploring Our Senses, 5 vols. Touching. Tasting. Smelling. Seeing. Hearing. Henry Pluckrose. Gareth Stevens, 1995.
My Five Senses Activity Book. Gloria Truitt. Concordia, 1994.
You Can't Smell a Flower with Your Ear!: All about Your 5 Senses. Joanna Cole. Grossett and Dunlap/Putnam, 1994.
My Five Senses. Margaret Miller. Simon & Schuster, 1994.
Touching. Smelling and Tasting. Seeing. Hearing. Lillian Wright. Raintree Steck-Vaughn, 1994.
Touch. Smell. (1994) *Taste. Sight. Hearing.* (1993) Mandy Suhr. Carolrhoda/Lerner.
The Sensible Book: A Celebration of Your Five Senses, rev. ed. Barbara K. Polland. Celestial Arts, 1993.
Experiment with Senses. Monica Byles. Lerner, 1993.
That Tickles! The Disney Book of Senses. Cindy West. Disney, 1993.
The Senses. Angela Royston. Barron's, 1993.
Professor I. Q. Explores the Senses. Seymour Simon. Boyds Mills, 1993.
See, Hear, Touch, Taste, Smell. Melvin Berger. Newbridge, 1993.
Science Book of the Senses. Neil Ardley. Harcourt Brace, 1992.
Looking at Senses. David Suzuki and Barbara Hehner. Wiley, 1991.
Tasting and Smelling. Nigel Snell. Trafalgar, 1991.
Tasting Things. Smelling Things. Seeing Things. Hearing Things. Feeling Things. Allan Fowler. Childrens, 1991.
All about Your Senses. Donna Bailey. Raintree Steck-Vaughn, 1990.

For preteens and teens

Sound and Vision. Smell, Taste and Touch. Jenny Bryan. Silver Burdett, 1994.
How Our Senses Work. Jamie Ripoll. Chelsea House, 1994.
Senses. Marshall Cavendish. 1991.
The Senses. Mary Talbot. Chelsea House, 1990.
Nerves to Senses: Projects with Biology. Steve Parker. Watts, 1991.

separation agreement, a document that marks the ending of a relationship—of marriage or cohabitation—and specifies the legal rights and obligations that the two people will carry into their new life, a process especially difficult where children are involved. A separation agreement is the basic document that underlies the final divorce, but couples who have never married and also same-sex couples may also draw up a separation agreement.

Once a couple has agreed to split, the separation agreement should be written as soon as possible, even before the actual separation if possible. Ideally, the two should decide between themselves matters such as CUSTODY of any children, CHILD SUPPORT, alimony, division of marital property, and possible inheritance rights, or possible share in each other's estate in case of death—keeping in mind that, if they fail to do so, the court may make decisions for them. Since it may affect the rest of their—and their children's—lives, the actual legal agreement should be drawn up by lawyers who are not personally involved in the decisions. The two should have separate lawyers, since their interests are different.

Among the many areas that may be covered in a separation agreement are:

- CHILD SUPPORT, payments to provide for continuing support for children of the marriage. Child support should be clearly distinguished from alimony (see later in this list), and both should continue year-round, even during periods when the child is living with the paying parent, since these payments go not only to support the child but also to help maintain the child's home.
- CUSTODY, the main rights and responsibilities regarding children and their care. If parents are unable to agree on custody, the court may mandate custodial arrangements.
- VISITATION RIGHTS, arrangements for a noncustodial parent to see a child. The arrangements should be as specific as possible, including everything from travel costs to out-of-state trips to safety concerns.
- *Alimony,* also called *maintenance* or *spousal support,* payments to provide for the continuing support of a spouse, today usually for limited periods. Traditionally made by a husband to a wife, payments may also be made by a wealthy or high-earning wife to a husband. But today alimony is far less common than in earlier times, and is most often awarded to women who are primarily homemakers. Alimony should be kept separate from child support, which is normally treated differently for tax purposes.
- *Division of marital property,* an equitable distribution of marital assets between the partners, taking into account also the past and present contributions of each, the length of the marriage, the background and employment prospects of a nonemployed spouse, the present and future needs of the children, and sometimes questions of fault. This is one of the most complicated, contentious, and difficult areas covered by a separation agreement. In regions that have *community property* laws, assets are equally divided between the partners; but this in itself can cause problems, because often the major asset is the family home, which must be sold, causing further disruption for the family, very much including the children. In other areas, if the couple cannot decide between them on division of assets, the court will divide them on the basis of *equitable distribution,* following guidelines that vary around the country, but take into account such matters as the parties' ages, health, economic circumstances, and future earning capacities; the ages of children; who has custody of the children, and whether it is desirable for that person to work outside the home; the length of the marriage; and the contributions and sacrifices made in the marriage by each, including the homemaker's services.
- CHILD CARE costs, where the custodial parent is a working parent, since child care costs may not be covered by child support payments.
- EDUCATION costs, especially the cost of a COLLEGE education. This, too, is not covered by child support. Judges cannot mandate that a parent contribute to a child's college education, and in a surprising number of cases, noncustodial parents—generally fathers—stop paying child support when the child reaches eighteen and fail to contribute at all to college expenses. This leaves the child disadvantaged, and places the whole burden on the custodial parent.
- HEALTH CARE costs, including HEALTH INSURANCE coverage, and also routine medical care, including eye exams and glasses, dental work and orthodontia, psychological counseling, and the like.
- *Life insurance costs,* to provide for the children. Some experts recommend that the policy on the noncustodial parent (usually the father) be owned by the custodial parent, who also maintains the responsibility for making premium payments, in trust for the children.
- *Family debts,* covering who shall be responsible for which debts.
- *Income-tax deduction,* indicating who shall take a deduction for the children as dependents.
- *Attorney fees,* covering who shall pay for the attorneys.
- *Warranty of full disclosure of all income and assets,* so that both parties are assuring that all property has been included.
- *Mutual covenant to execute documents,* to put the terms of the separation agreement into effect, such as assigning insurance benefits or changing property deeds.
- *Mutual waiver of inheritance rights,* if not otherwise covered in the agreement.
- *A provision that reconciliation will not negate the agreement.* However, if the parties reconcile after a time of separation, a *reconciliation agreement* should replace the separation agreement and lay out the terms of the new relationship. And should another separation occur, a new separation agreement should be made.

Both parties should also sign a statement that they understand the agreement and are not under duress to sign it. Many people also include a clause specifying that MEDIATION and ARBITRATION may be used to settle disputes arising from the agreement; some states, notably California, mandate mediation in cases involving custody and visitation. (See DIVORCE; CUSTODY; CHILD SUPPORT.)

separation anxiety, fear of being divided from home and MOTHER—or whoever is the primary CAREGIVER who bonded with the infant. Whether the threat is real or imagined, separation anxiety is normal among young children, with their cries often causing great anguish to parents. For most, the crying is a means of communication, saying "Don't go!" In many CHILD CARE situations, however, such cries often dry up once the parent has gone. To ease the process, psychologists recommend that parents prepare children beforehand for transitions, familiarizing the child with the place and people with whom she will be staying; equally important is to give the child a good dose of one-to-one personal attention on the return. Separation anxiety may also be linked to SCHOOL PHOBIA. In some children, ANXIETY grows so great as to constitute SEPARATION ANXIETY DISORDER.

FOR HELP AND FURTHER INFORMATION

National Association for the Education of Young Children (NAEYC), 800–424–2460. Publishes book *Separation: Strategies for Helping Two to Four Year Olds*; and brochure *So Many Goodbyes: Ways to Ease the Transition Between Home and Groups for Young Children.* (For full group information, see PRESCHOOL.)

OTHER RESOURCES

Mommy's Coming Back. Madeleine Yates. Abingdon, 1988.

(See also BONDING; SEPARATION-INDIVIDUATION.)

separation anxiety disorder, a type of MENTAL DISORDER in children or adolescents in which normal SEPARATION ANXIETY becomes elevated to a level of panic (see PANIC ATTACKS), so that children fear to leave the house or other familiar areas. Even at home, they may cling persistently to family members, to avoid being alone, especially at bedtime. Nightmares (see SLEEP AND SLEEP DISORDERS) and physical and emotional signs of distress are common, as is associated SCHOOL PHOBIA.

separation-individuation, the stage during which a child begins to recognize the self as distinct from the MOTHER (or other primary CAREGIVER); it follows the SYMBIOTIC STAGE in which the child sees mother and self as one (as in early BONDING). Separation-individuation, once considered to begin around 18 months, when the child usually begins to walk, is now thought to start as early as seven months. Some psychologists believe that it progresses through four phases:

- *Differentiation,* or beginning of recognition of separateness of mother and child.
- *Practicing,* in which the baby is somewhat oblivious to the mother.
- *Rapprochement,* in which the baby once again approaches the mother actively.
- *Separation-individuation,* in which the baby becomes fully aware of his or her discrete individuality and identity.

Some psychologists believe that some MENTAL DISORDERS that spring from early childhood, such as IDENTITY DISORDER, SEPARATION ANXIETY DISORDER, PERSONALITY DISORDERS, or borderline PSYCHOSIS, are related to failure of the child to satisfactorily complete the separation-individuation process. (See MENTAL DISORDERS.)

Sequential Tests of Educational Progress (STEP), a series of group-administered ACHIEVEMENT TESTS, offered at ten different levels, for children from prekindergarten through grade 12. The Preprimary and Primary Levels (from prekindergarten through midgrade 3) cover prereading, reading, mathematics, and listening skills, with writing skills added in grade 2, and study skills, social studies, and science skills in grade 3. For older children, end-of-course tests are also provided for algebra, geometry, biology, chemistry, and physics. The tests, which can be hand- or computer-scored, are used to assess individual mastery, and are used in some programs to help identify GIFTED CHILDREN, and also to evaluate group progress and assess the effectiveness of educational programs. (See TESTS.)

service dogs, dogs specially trained to aid people with DISABILITIES, to allow independent living to the greatest extent possible. Most service dogs are assigned to work with adults, or people from their late teens, but some are available for children as well. Many of these dogs are rescued from shelters, though some are specially raised for the purpose, and all are given extensive training to fit them for the particular situations in which they will be used. Generally dogs are taken from a shelter, or puppies are raised by a "foster family," and then are given general obedience training and training in specific tasks at the training center. Then the person who will be receiving the dog is generally brought in, so the two can be taught how best to work together.

Perhaps the best known service dogs are the *guide dogs,* or *seeing-eye dogs,* which help people with vision impairment to move about in the community with considerable independence, helping them navigate through crowded streets and traffic. *Hearing dogs*—or, by analogy, *hearing-ear dogs*—aid people who have hearing loss; they are trained to respond to sounds such as a telephone, door bell, door knock, name being called, oven buzzer, or baby crying, leading the person to the sound or, in the case of a smoke alarm, to an exit. Certified guide and hearing dogs can legally accompany their humans to places where normal pets are not allowed, including stores, restaurants, and public transportation. *Specialty dogs* are trained to help people with two or more disabilities, such as someone who is deaf and also uses a wheelchair.

Working companion dogs, or more generally simply *service dogs,* help adults or children who use wheelchairs, picking up dropped items, retrieving things from high shelves, turning lights on and off, carrying items in a special pack, and even pulling the wheelchair; these are often dogs used only in the home.

Social-therapy dogs or *social dogs* are trained to provide companionship and social contact for others who have mental or physical disabilities, from children to the elderly. These are often dogs that have received obedience training but, for whatever reason, not advanced training.

FOR HELP AND FURTHER INFORMATION

PRAISE Guide Dog Center for the Blind, Inc.
30050 Dracaea Avenue
Moreno Valley, CA 92555
909–486–9874; 800–598–8240
Steven Southard, Founder and Executive Director
Organization providing guide dogs for people with visual

or other physical disabilities, the "first and only" to provide such dogs for teenagers; publishes newsletter *Paws with a Cause Center Fold.*

The Seeing Eye
P.O. Box 375
Morristown, NJ 07963–0375
201–539–4425
Fax: 201–539–0922
Organization that breeds, raises, and trains dogs (the original "Seeing Eye®" dogs) for people with vision loss from their late teens and older; publishes quarterly newsletter *The Seeing Eye Guide,* brochure *The Seeing Eye,* and videos *Partners: Life with a Seeing Eye Dog, Harnessing Freedom, Seeing Eye Puppy-Raisers: People Like You,* and *Choices: Living with Vision Loss* for newly blind people and their families.

National Education for Assistance Dog Services (NEADS)
P.O. Box 213
West Boylston, MA 01583
508–835–3304
Fax: 508–835–2526
Sheila O'Brien, Executive Director
Organization that trains hearing dogs for people who are hearing-impaired, service dogs for those who use wheelchairs, and specialty dogs to aid people with two or more disabilities; formerly New England Assistance Dog Service; publishes quarterly newsletter.

Canine Companions for Independence (CCI)
P.O. Box 446
Santa Rosa, CA 95402–0446
707–528–0830; 800–572–2275
Fax: 707–528–0146
Corey Hudson, Executive Director
Organization that provides dogs to qualified individuals with disabilities, to help them live more independently, as by helping them up after a fall or opening doors; publishes newsletter.

Support Dogs for the Handicapped, Inc.
301 Sovereign Court, Suite 113
St. Louis, MO 60311
314–394–6163
Organization that trains and places services dogs for people with disabilities who are 17 or older; for young children with disabilities, TOUCH dogs visit the home weekly or biweekly for companionship.

Dogs for the Deaf (DD)
10175 Wheeler Road
Central Point, OR 97502
503–826–9220, voice/TT
Fax: 503–826–6696
Robin Dickson, Director
Organization that trains and provides listening dogs for people who are deaf or hard of hearing; publishes newsletter *Canine Listener.*

International Hearing Dog, Inc. (IHDI)
5901 East 89th Avenue
Henderson, CO 80640
303–287-EARS [287–3277], voice/TT
Fax: 303–287–3425
Martha Foss, President
Organization that trains hearing dogs from animal shelters and supplies them cost-free in the United States and Canada, normally for people with significant hearing impairment living in homes without hearing people and able to care for and continue to train the dog; publishes quarterly newsletter *Paws for Silence.*

National Information Center on Deafness (NICD), 202–651–5051; 202–651–5052, TT. Publishes *Hearing Ear Dogs.* (For full group information, see EAR AND HEARING PROBLEMS.)

National Federation of the Blind (NFB), 410–659–9314. Publishes *Of Dog Guides and White Canes.* (For full group information, see EYE AND VISION PROBLEMS.)

Self-Help for Hard of Hearing People (SHHH), 301–657–2248; 301–657–2249, TT. Publishes *Hearing Dogs.* (For full group information, see EAR AND HEARING PROBLEMS.)

National Center for Law and the Deaf, 202–651–5373, voice/TT. Provides help with legal problems relating to hearing ear dogs. (For full group information, see EAR AND HEARING PROBLEMS.)

American Council of the Blind (ACB). 800–424–8666, U.S. except DC. Has affiliate **Guide Dog Users**. (For full group information, see EYE AND VISION PROBLEMS.)

OTHER RESOURCES

A Service Dog Goes to School: The Story of a Dog Trained to Help the Disabled. Elizabeth Simpson Smith. Morrow, 1988. For children.

severe combined immunodeficiency disease (SCID), a condition in which a child is born lacking all or most defenses of the IMMUNE SYSTEM, and so must live in germ-free settings or "bubbles."

sex chromosomes, the pair of CHROMOSOMES that determines the sex of an individual, normally with two X chromosomes for a female and an X and a Y chromosome for a male. Traits or disorders associated with genes carried on the X chromosome are called X-LINKED, sex-linked, or sex-limited; among them are COLOR BLINDNESS, HEMOPHILIA, MUSCULAR DYSTROPHY (Duchenne), and G6PD DEFICIENCY. The smaller Y chromosome carries little genetic information beyond those directly related to male sexual development. Among the CHROMOSOMAL ABNOR-

MALITIES linked with the sex chromosomes are TURNER'S SYNDROME, KLINEFELTER'S SYNDROME, and FRAGILE X SYNDROME. (See X-LINKED; GENETIC DISORDERS.)

sex education, teaching children about their own sexuality, its joys and hazards and its place in human life. Traditionally children picked up information about sexuality in bits and pieces, not in any formal way, and only on rare occasions from their parents or any knowledgeable person; in fact, as often as not, what they got was misinformation. In many families and communities, this state of affairs still exists. But the events of these past few decades—the revolution in sexual habits, the enormous increase in ADOLESCENT PREGNANCY, and the spread of SEXUALLY TRANSMITTED DISEASES, most notably the deadly threat of AIDS—have made that state of affairs dangerously outmoded.

Some communities have responded by establishing sex education programs, frequently called FAMILY LIFE EDUCATION, *life skills*, or *health education.* Some families have responded, too, by taking responsibility for teaching their children vital knowledge about their own beings. But in many cases, parents still resist any personal involvement in sexual education. Some of these also protest school and community attempts to fill the gap, as by providing BIRTH CONTROL information and sometimes devices, such as CONDOMS.

Sex education experts advise that parents who wish to help their children develop responsible attitudes toward their sexuality should respond openly to their questions from early childhood, helping them to understand the role of sexuality in an adult life, and in the process helping them develop the wisdom to make the difficult, sometimes life-or-death sexual decisions that young people now have to make.

FOR HELP AND FURTHER INFORMATION

Sexuality Information and Education Council of the United States (SIECUS)
130 West 42 Street, Suite 350
New York, NY 10036
212–819–9770
Fax: 212–819–9776
E-mail: siecusinc@aol.com (America Online: SIECUSINC)
Debra Haffner, President
Organization concerned with sexuality and HIV/AIDS education and sexual rights; acts as advocate; serves as information clearinghouse; publishes various materials, including:

- Bimonthly *SIECUS Report* and *SIECUS Position Statements.*
- Booklets: *Oh No! What Do I Do Now! Messages About Sexuality: How to Give Yours to Your Child, Teens Talk About Sex: Adolescent Sexuality in the 90's,* and reports on community education programs.
- Fact sheets: *Sexuality Education and the Schools: Issues and Answers, Sexual Orientation and Identity, Adolescents and Abstinence, The Far Right and Fear-based Abstinence-only Programs, Guidelines for Comprehensive Sexuality Education: K–12,* and *The National Coalition to Support Sexuality Education (NCSSE).*
- Annotated bibliographies: T*alking with Your Child About Sexuality and Other Important Issues, Growing Up* (on sexuality for children and adolescents), *Current Books on Sexuality, Current Religious Perspectives on Sexuality, Sexuality Education Resources for Religious Denominations, Comprehensive Sexuality Education,* and *Global Sexuality.*
- Reprint packets: *Health Adolescent Sexual Development.*
- Directory *Sexual Dysfunction Clinics.*

Planned Parenthood Federation of America (PPFA), 800–230–7526. Operates nationwide network of counseling and health services centers; publishes pamphlets *How to Talk with Your Child About Sexuality: A Parent's Guide, Human Sexuality: What Children Should Know and When They Should Know It, How to Talk with Your Teen About the Facts of Life, Feeling Good About Growing Up, Teensex? It's OK to Say: No Way!, A Woman's Guide to Sexuality,* and *A Man's Guide to Sexuality*; and video *Facing the Facts.* (For full group information, see BIRTH CONTROL.)

American College of Obstetricians and Gynecologists (ACOG), 202–638–5577. Publishes *Teaching Your Children About Sexuality, Growing Up* (for ages 9–14), *Being a Teenager: You and Your Sexuality* (for ages 11–19), *Practicing Safe Sex,* and *Sexuality in Women.* (For full group information, see PREGNANCY.)

American Academy of Pediatrics (AAP), 800–433–9016. Publishes brochures *Making the Right Choice: Facts Young People Need to Know About Avoiding Pregnancy* and *Deciding to Wait: What You Need to Know*; and training materials on sex education. (For full group information, see HEALTH CARE.)

Couple to Couple League (CCL), 513–471–2000. Publishes brochures *Not in the Public Interest: The Planned Parenthood Version of Sex Education* and numerous materials promoting chastity, such as *The Best Birth Control for Teens, Practical Reasons for Chastity, Dating Guide for Guys 'n Girls, First Aid for AIDS,* and *Gone All the Way—Now Where?* (For full group information, see NATURAL FAMILY PLANNING.)

National Woman's Christian Temperance Union (WCTU), 800–755–1321. Publishes leaflets *Say No to Premarital Sex, The Beautiful Gift of Sex* (on chastity), and *Why Wait Until Marriage?* (For full group information, see HELP AGAINST SUBSTANCE ABUSE on page 703.)

Human Life International (HLI), 800–549–5433. Publishes pamphlet *The "Alternative" to Secular Sex Education.* (For full group information, see BIRTH CONTROL.)

Educational Equity Concepts (EEC), 212–725–1803. Publishes video *Mixed Messages: Teens Talk About Sex, Romance, Education, and Work.* (For full group information, see HELP ON LEARNING AND EDUCATION on page 659.)

March of Dimes Birth Defects Foundation (MDBDF), 914–428–7100. Publishes pamphlet *Teens Talk Sex.* (For full group information, see BIRTH DEFECTS.)

American Association of Sex Educators, Counselors, and Therapists (AASECT)
P.O. Box 238
Mt. Vernon, IO 52314
319–895–8407
Fax: 319–895–6203
E-mail (Linda Newhart Lotz, Contact):
102105.2075@compuserve.com (CompuServe: 102105,2075)
Online Service Forum: CompuServe: AASECT Online, under HSX100 of the Human Sexuality Forum; room 21 of library includes national list of certified members.
Howard Ruppel, Executive Director
Organization of professional sex educators, counselors, and therapists; provides information and referrals; certifies professionals; publishes various monthly newsletter *Contemporary Sexuality* and quarterly *Journal of Sex Education and Therapy.*

National Congress of Parents and Teachers (National PTA), 312–670–6782. Publishes materials on teenage sexuality. (For full group information, see HELP ON LEARNING AND EDUCATION on page 659.)

National Information Center for Children and Youth with Disabilities (NICHCY), 800–695–0285, voice/TT. Publishes *Sexuality Education for Children and Youth with Disabilities.* (For full group information, see HELP FOR SPECIAL CHILDREN on page 689.)

National Center for Youth with Disabilities (NCYD), 800–333–6293. Publishes annotated bibliography *Issues in Sexuality for Adolescents with Chronic Illnesses and Disabilities.* (For full group information, see HELP FOR SPECIAL CHILDREN on page 689.)

Autism Society of America (ASA), 800–328–8476. Publishes *Sex Education: Issues for the Person with Autism.* (For full group information, see AUTISM.)

ONLINE RESOURCES

Better Health and Medical Forum (America Online: Health, Medicine) Provides discussion areas and libraries covering sex education. (For full information, see HEALTH CARE.)

OTHER RESOURCES

FOR PARENTS AND OTHER ADULTS

How to Talk Confidently with Your Children about Sex. Lenore Buth. Concordia, 1995.

How to Get Your Kid Out of School... Without AIDS, a Disease, or a Baby. Carole Marsh. Gallopade, 1994.

Rite of Passage: How to Teach Your Son about Sex and Manhood. E. James Wilder. Vine/Servant, 1994. Originally titled: *Just Between Father and Son.*

What Shall We Tell the Children: Talking with Your Children about Sex. Nancy Kohner. Parkwest, 1994.

The Sex Education Handbook. Richard N. Diggs. Progressive, 1994.

Sex Is Not a Four-Letter Word!: Talking Sex with Children Made Easier. Patricia F. Miller. Crossroad, 1994.

Talking with Your Kids about Love, Sex, and Dating. Barry St. Clair and Carol St. Clair. SP Publications, 1993.

Everybody's Doing It!: How to Survive Your Teenagers' Sex Life and Help Them Survive It, Too. Andrea Warren and Jay Wiedenkeller. Viking Penguin, 1993.

Parents, Children and the Facts of Life: A Text on Sex Education for Christian Parents and for Those Concerned with Helping Parents. Henry V. Sattler. TAN Books, 1993.

The Sexual Dictionary: Terms and Expressions for Teens and Parents. Kathryn T. Johnson and Mary-Lynne J. Balczon. Larksdale, 1993.

From Trauma to Understanding: A Guide for Parents of Children with Sexual Behavior Problems. William Pithers and others. Safer Society, 1993.

Five Hundred Questions Kids Ask about Sex and Some of the Answers: Sex Education for Parents, Teachers and Young People Themselves. Frances Younger. C. C. Thomas, 1992.

Love and Family: How to Teach Your Children Sexuality in the Context of Family and Morality. Mercedes A. Wilson. Family of the Americas Foundation, 1992.

Sex Facts for the Family. Clifford Penner and Joyce Penner. Word, 1992.

How to Talk to Children about Sex. Jane C. Sacknowitz. Bureau for At-Risk Youth, 1992.

Sex Stuff for Parents: The Painless, Foolproof, "Really Works!" Way to Teach 7–17-Year-Olds about Sex So They Won't Get AIDS, a Disease or a Baby and You Won't Get Embarrassed! Carole Marsh. Gallopade, 1990.

Raising Sexually Healthy Children. Lynn Leight. Avon, 1990.

Talking to Your Children About Love and Sex. Leon Somers and Barbara Somers. NAL-Dutton, 1990.

Sex Education for Toddlers to Young Adults: A Guide for Parents. James Kenny. St. Anthony Messenger Press, 1990.

Sex Respect: The Option of True Sexual Freedom: A Public Health Guide for Parents, rev. ed. Coleen K. Mast. Respect, 1990.

Boys' Puberty: An Illustrated Manual for Parents and Sons. Alain Chirinian. St. Martin's, 1990.

GENERAL WORKS

Sex Information, May I Help You? Isadora Alman. Down There Press, 1992. Originally titled: *Aural Sex and Verbal Intercourse.*

Ask Me Anything: A Sex Therapist Answers the Most Important Questions for the '90s. Marty Klein. Simon & Schuster, 1992.

Mom's a Bird, Dad's a Bee: Developing a Healthy Outlook on the Facts of Life. Maryann Mayo. Harvest House, 1991.

Questions You've Asked about Sexuality. Alberta Mazat. Pacific Press, 1991.

What Do You Know about Sex? Diane Zahler. Prentice-Hall, 1991.

FOR CHILDREN

Why Boys and Girls Are Different. Carol Greene. Concordia, 1995.
Where Do Babies Come From? Ruth Hummel. Concordia, 1995.
How You Are Changing. Jane Graver. Concordia, 1995.
Growing up Feeling Good. Ellen Rosenberg. Puffin, 1995.
Growing up Now. Jack Wingfield and Angela Wingfield. Lion USA, 1992.
Susie's Babies: A Clear and Simple Explanation of the Everyday Miracle of Birth. Margaret Clarkson. Eerdmans, 1992.
Mommy Laid an Egg. Babette Cole. Chronicle Books, 1992.
Girls Are Girls and Boys Are Boys: So What's the Difference? Sol Gordon. Prometheus, 1991.
In the Beginning: Teaching Your Children about Sex—Ages 4–7 and *God's Good Gift: Teaching Your Kids about Sex—Ages 8 to 11.* Mary A. Mayo. Zondervan, 1991.
The Birds and the Bees. Sue Baker. Childs Play, 1991.
Bellybuttons Are Navels. Mark Schoen. Prometheus, 1990. On naming body parts and accepting the body.

(See also PREGNANCY for photographic books on fetal development.)

FOR PRETEENS AND TEENS

The Preteen's First Book about Love, Sex and AIDS. Michelle Harrison. American Psychiatric Press, 1995.
Changes in You and Me: A Book about Puberty, Mostly for Boys. Changes in You and Me: A Book about Puberty, Mostly for Girls. Paulette Bourgeois and Martin Wolfish. Andrews and McMeel, 1994.
Sex Stuff for Boys: Sperm, Squirm and Other Squiggly Stuff. Sex Stuff for Girls: A Period Is More Than a Punctuation Mark. Sex Stuff for Kids 7–17: A Book of Practical Information and Ideas for Kids and Their Teachers and Parents. My Lifetime of Sex and How to Handle It. Like a Virgin: How You Can Convince Your Child to Abstain from Sex. Choose-Your-Own-Ending Sex Ed Adventures. AIDS-Zits: A "Sextionary" for Kids. Abstinence Makes the Heart Grow Fonder. Carole Marsh. Gallopade, 1994.
How Sex Works: A Clear, Comprehensive Guide for Teenagers to Emotional, Physical and Sexual Maturity. Elizabeth Fenwick and Richard Walker. Dorling Kindersley, 1994.
Dear Larissa: Sexuality Education for Girls Ages 10–17. Cynthia G. Akagi. Gylantic, 1994.
It's Perfectly Normal: Changing Bodies, Sex, and Sexual Health. Robie H. Harris. Candlewick, 1994.
Teenage Sexuality. Michele Lee. Marshall Cavendish, 1994.
Teenage Sexuality: Opposing Viewpoints. Karin L. Swisher and others, eds. Greenhaven, 1994.
My Feelings, My Self: Lynda Madaras' Growing-Up Guide for Girls. Lynda Madaras and Area Madaras. Newmarket, 1993. Originally titled: *Lynda Madaras' Growing-Up Guide for Girls.* By the author of *The What's Happening To My Body?* Book.
You're in Charge: A Teenage Girl's Guide to Sex and Her Body. Niels H. Lauersen and Eileen Stukane. Fawcett, 1993.
Your Body, Yourself: A Guide to Your Changing Body. Alison Bell and Lisa Rooney. Lowell House, 1993.
Sex and Sense: A Contemporary Guide for Teenagers. Gary F. Kelly. Barron's, 1993.
Dear Judy, Did You Ever Like a Boy Who Didn't Like You? Judy Baer. Bethany House, 1993.
Time We Talk: The Pre-Teen Years. Joyce C. Canterbury. Hoffman, 1993.
Dr. Ruth Talks to Kids: Where You Came from, How Your Body Changes, and What Sex Is All About. Ruth Westheimer. Simon & Schuster, 1993.
Let's Talk about Sex: Facts, Statistics and Information Which May Help You Avoid...Screwin' up Your Life!. Richard N. Diggs. Progressive, 1992.
The New Teenage Body Book, rev. ed. Kathy McCoy and Charles Wibbelsman. Berkley, 1992.
The Changing Me. David Edens. Broadman, 1991.
Kerry's Thirteenth Birthday: Everything Your Parents and Their Friends Know about Sex but Are Too Polite to Talk about. Mary J. Rachner. Oxner Institute, 1991.
Tell It Like It Is: Straight Talk About Sex. Annamaria Formichella and others. Avon, 1991.
Boys and Sex, 3rd ed. Wardell B. Pomeroy. Doubleday/Dell, 1991.
Sex Is Not a Four-Letter Word. James N. Watkins. Tyndale, 1991.

ON PERSONAL DECISIONS, FOR PRETEENS AND TEENS

God's Will for My Body: Guidance for Adolescents. John Coblentz. Christian Light, 1992.
Let's Talk to Teens about Chastity. Center for Learning Network, 1992.
Chastity: The Only Choice: Looking at Life. Center for Learning Network, 1992.
Love in Your Life: A Jewish View of Teenage Sexuality. Roland B. Gittelsohn. UAHC, 1991.
The Dating Dilemma: Handling Sexual Pressures. Bob Stone and Bob Palmer. Baker Books, 1990.
Sex and the Teenager: Choices and Decisions. Kieran Sawyer. Ave Maria, 1990.
Love and Sex and Growing Up. Eric W. Johnson. Bantam, 1990.

(See also HOMOSEXUALITY.)

ON SEX FOR PEOPLE WITH DISABILITIES

Sexuality and People with Intellectual Disability. Lydia Fegan and Anne Rauch. P. H. Brookes, 1993.
Enabling Romance: A Guide to Love, Sex, and Relationships for the Disabled (and the People Who Care about Them). Erica Klein and others. Harmony/Crown, 1992.

BACKGROUND WORKS

Sex Education and Successful Parenting. Ann Murphy and John Murphy. Pauline Books, 1994.

Living Smart: Understanding Sexuality in the Teen Years. Pennie Core-Gebhart and others. University of Arkansas Press, 1991.

What's Wrong with Sex Education?: Preteen and Teenage Sexual Development and Environmental Influences. Melvin Anchell. Hoffman Center, 1991.

Healthy Sex Education in Your Schools: A Parent's Handbook. Anne Newman. Focus on the Family, 1990.

Has Sex Education Failed Our Teenagers?: A Research Report. Dinah Richard. Focus on the Family, 1990.

Family Values and Sex Education. Terrance D. Olson and Christopher M. Wallace. Focus on the Family, 1990.

sex selection, use of any of several procedures aimed at controlling or influencing the sex of child in PREGNANCY, whether before or after FERTILIZATION.

Before CONCEPTION, one of the main techniques used is called *sperm-splitting.* A man's SPERM determines the sex of offspring; if the sperm carries an X chromosome, the offspring will be a girl (XX); if it carries a Y chromosome, a boy (XY). Where desired, some of the Y-bearing or X-bearing chromosomes are separated out of the sperm, increasing the likelihood of the sex desired. The sperm is then used for fertilization in techniques such as ARTIFICIAL INSEMINATION or IN VITRO FERTILIZATION.

Some people try to use DOUCHING to influence sex selection. Since Y-bearing sperm are more vulnerable to acid, the idea is that a mildly acidic douche (such as two tablespoons of vinegar in a quart of warm water) would increase the likelihood of having a girl, while a somewhat alkaline douche (such as two tablespoons of baking soda in a quart of warm water), might make a boy more likely. Also, if the woman has an orgasm near the time of insemination, her vagina becomes more alkaline.

None of these techniques is very successful, though they may increase the chances of having a child of the desired sex. New, still-experimental techniques allow doctors to determine the sex of an EMBRYO before insertion into a woman's body, in *in vitro fertilization.*

In general, X-bearing sperm seem to live slightly longer, and some people suggest, therefore, that having sexual intercourse one to two days *before* ovulation may increase chances of having a girl. However, the factors involved are extremely complex, and some researchers have come to an opposite conclusion.

Post-conception sex selection relies on the results of various PRENATAL TESTS, such as AMNIOCENTESIS, ULTRASOUND, or CHORIONIC VILLUS SAMPLING (CVS). Many such tests show the sex of a FETUS, in addition to desired information on GENETIC DISORDERS or CHROMOSOMAL ABNORMALITIES. Sometimes a woman or couple will choose an ABORTION if the fetus is not of the desired sex; in many parts of the world, most notably India and China, female fetuses are aborted, given a strong preference for male children, called *son preference.* In such countries, "sex selection" may take place after birth, in the form of *female infanticide* or ABANDONMENT. (See FERTILIZATION.)

sexual identity, the labeling of a person as either male or female, based on the individual's biological attributes; by contrast, a person's inner feeling of sexual identification is called GENDER IDENTITY.

In most children, the external GENITALS are obviously either male or female (see REPRODUCTIVE SYSTEM), so their sexual identity is obvious. However, in some children, sexual identity is not clear. A child may have both male and female sex organs, which can occur in some cases with CHROMOSOMAL ABNORMALITIES or some HORMONE disorders. Such a child is called a *hermaphrodite,* or more popularly *bisexual.* For purposes of rearing, dressing, and training, the child is often "assigned" to one sex or the other, but may still later show ambivalence regarding gender identity.

Some children are born with *ambiguous genitalia,* genitals that are not clearly one sex or the other, a condition called *pseudohermaphroditism.* Such a child may, for example, have female chromosomes but a CLITORIS so large that it resembles a PENIS, or LABIA that are fused and resemble the male SCROTUM; or a child with male chromosomes may have an opening similar to a VAGINA behind the penis. In some cases, children have been raised as one sex, but were shown to be the other sex, when SECONDARY SEX CHARACTERISTICS developed at PUBERTY. If the condition is properly recognized, the parents and doctor will generally assign the child to the sex indicated by the chromosomes, raising the child with that sexual identity. Ambiguous genitals can be corrected surgically, and hormone treatments can be given to support the sexual identity assignment.

FOR HELP AND FURTHER INFORMATION

Ambiguous Genitalia Support Network (AGSN)
428 East Elm Street, #4-D
Lodi, CA 95240
209–369–0414
Cherie Sintes, Coordinator
Organization concerned with ambiguous sexual identity from infancy; encourages parent-to-parent contact; provides information and support.

National Organization for Rare Disorders (NORD), 800–999–6673. (For full group information, see RARE DISORDERS.)

OTHER RESOURCES

Sex Errors of the Body and Related Syndromes: A Guide to Counseling Children, Adolescents, and Their Families, 2nd ed. John Money. P.H. Brookes, 1994.

sexually transmitted diseases (STDs), a group of diseases passed between people during vaginal or anal sexual intercourse; by hand or mouth contact with the genitals of an infected person; through other contact with body fluids, such as SEMEN, blood, or vaginal secretions; or from mother to child during PREGNANCY or

CHILDBIRTH. In decades past, it was thought that only a few sexually transmitted diseases existed, such as SYPHILIS and GONORRHEA, which were then called *venereal diseases.* But it is now known that more than 25 diseases are passed through sexual activity, some relatively benign, some deadly; collectively, these are all now called *sexually transmitted diseases.*

STDs affect people of all ages, sexes, sexual orientations, and socioeconomic backgrounds. No one is immune, and you cannot tell from looking at someone that they are free of infection. In the United States, one in every four adults has an STD, with approximately 12 million new cases annually. They are most common, however, among teenagers and young adults, who make up nearly a third of all cases of STDs. The incidence of STDs has been rising in recent decades, partly because people have become sexually active earlier in their lives and are more likely to have multiple sex partners. Any sexually active person has a risk of developing an STD. Except for those infected at birth or through blood transfusions (in the case of AIDS), few young children have STDs; the presence of an STD in a young child is a likely indicator of sexual abuse (see CHILD ABUSE AND NEGLECT; INCEST).

Many STDs initially cause no symptoms and, whenever they develop, the symptoms are easily confused with those of other non-STD diseases. That means an infected person can unknowingly spread the infection to a sex partner, which is why doctors recommend periodic testing (at least every six months) for people who have more than one sex partner. It also means that the infection may damage various parts of the body before the person is aware of being infected.

Some kinds of viral infections—most notably AIDS, a fatal viral infection of the IMMUNE SYSTEM—are not curable. Most other STDs *are* curable, though some organisms have become resistant to drugs traditionally used to treat them, and require higher doses or newer ANTIBIOTICS. However, *nothing can undo damage done before treatment began.* That can include blindness, CANCER, heart disease, and neurological problems, and can be fatal. In both men and

What Can You (or Your Child) Do to Avoid STDs?

Although there is no sure way for a sexually active person to avoid exposure to STDs, there are many things that he or she can do to reduce the risk.

A person who has decided to begin a sexual relationship should take the following steps to reduce the risk of developing an STD:

- Be direct and frank about asking a new sex partner whether he or she has an STD, has been exposed to one, or has any unexplained physical symptoms.
- Learn to recognize the physical signs of STDs and inspect a sex partner's body, especially the genital area, for sores, rashes, or discharges.
- Use a condom (rubber) during sexual intercourse and learn to use it correctly. Diaphragms or spermicides (particularly those containing nonoxynol–9), alone or in combination, also may reduce the risk of transmission of some STDs.

Anyone who is sexually active with someone other than a long-term monogamous partner should:

- Have regular checkups for STDs even in the absence of symptoms. These tests can be done during a routine visit to the doctor's office.
- Learn the common symptoms of STDs. Seek medical help immediately if any suspicious symptoms develop, even if they are mild.

Anyone diagnosed as having an STD should:

1. Notify all recent sex partners and urge them to get a checkup.
2. Follow the doctor's orders and complete the full course of medication prescribed. A follow-up test to ensure that the infection has been cured is often an important final step in treatment.
3. Avoid all sexual activity while being treated for an STD.

Sometimes people are too embarrassed or frightened to ask for help or information. Most STDs are readily treated, and the earlier a person seeks treatment and warns sex partners about the disease, the less the likely that the disease will do irreparable physical damage, be spread to others or, in the case of a woman, be passed on to a newborn baby.

Private doctors, local health departments, and family planning clinics have information about STDs. In addition, the American Social Health Association (ASHA) provides free information and keeps lists of clinics and private doctors who provide treatment for people with STDs.

Source: An Introduction to Sexually Transmitted Diseases (1987). Prepared by the National Institute of Allergy and Infectious Diseases, for the Public Health Service.

women, the REPRODUCTIVE SYSTEM may be so damaged as to make them infertile. This is especially so for women, whose reproductive systems are extremely vulnerable to infection. An estimated 100,000 to 150,000 women become infertile each year in the United States alone because of an STD infection (see INFERTILITY); such infections frequently lead to PELVIC INFLAMMATORY DISEASE (PID) or ECTOPIC PREGNANCY, which is a major cause of MATERNAL MORTALITY. A mother can also pass an STD on to her baby before, during, or after birth; while some such CONGENITAL infections can be readily cured, others may cause permanent DISABILITY or even death of the infant.

The most common STDs are HERPES, affecting an estimated 40 million people, with 500,000 new cases annually; CHLAMYDIA, affecting 4 million Americans; trichomoniasis, affecting 3 million; GONORRHEA, affecting over 1 million; GENITAL WARTS, affecting 750,000; SYPHILIS, affecting 120,000; and hepatitis B (see LIVER AND LIVER PROBLEMS), affecting 100,000 to 120,000. The skin infestation SCABIES and CYTOMEGALOVIRUS INFECTION can also be spread by sexual contact.

Common warning signs of possible infection include sore, bumps, or blisters around the GENITALS, rectum, or mouth; burning or pain on urinating; swelling or redness in the throat; swelling in the genital area; pus or discharge from the PENIS or VAGINA; in men, pain in the TESTICLES; in women, burning or itching around the vagina, pain in the lower abdomen or (during sex) deep in the vagina, or nonmenstrual vaginal bleeding.

STDs can only be avoided absolutely by complete sexual abstinence, or by both sexual partners having sex only with each other from the start of sexual activity, at whatever age (and, in the case of AIDS and some other viruses, also avoiding exchange of bodily fluids, such as blood, semen, or vaginal secretions). But there are steps parents and their sexually active children can take to cut down the risk of contracting an STD (see WHAT CAN YOU (OR YOU CHILD) DO TO AVOID STDS? on page 541).

FOR HELP AND FURTHER INFORMATION

National Institute of Allergy and Infectious Diseases (NIAID), 301–496–5717. Publishes *Sexually Transmitted Diseases Fact Sheets.* (For full group information, see ALLERGY.)

American Social Health Association (ASHA)
P.O. Box 13827
Research Triangle Park, NC 27709
919–361–8400
National AIDS Hotline (24 hours): 800–342-AIDS [342–2437]; 800–344–7432, Spanish; 800-AIDS-TTY [243–7889], TT; Fax: 919–361–4855
National Sexually Transmitted Diseases Hotline: 800–227–8922
National Herpes Hotline: 919–361–8488
Herpes Resource Center: 800–230–6039
Women's Health Initiative: 800–972–8500
Fax: 919–361–8425
Peggy Clarke, President
Organization concerned with sexually transmitted diseases; provides information and referrals; publishes quarterlies *STD News, The Helper* (on herpes), *HPV News* (on the virus that causes genital warts); video *Playing It Safe*; and other materials, including:

- Books: *Straight Talk with Your Gynecologist, Finding the Words: How to Comunicate About Sexual Health,* and various works for professionals.
- General brochures: *Protect Yourself and Your Baby from STD, STD (VD): Questions and Answers, Becoming an Askable Parent, For Teens: Some Questions and Answers, Some Questions and Answers About PID, Better Sex, Healthy Sex, Sex Talk,* and *My Health Matters: How to Talk to Your Doctor About Sexual Health.*
- On specific STDs: *Stopping Gonorrhea, Some Questions and Answers About HPV and Genital Warts, Some Questions and Answers about Chlamydia,* and *NGU (Nongonoccocal Urethritis): Questions/Answers.*
- Information sheets: *Young People and STDs, Women and STDs,* and *STD Fact Sheet.*

American College of Obstetricians and Gynecologists (ACOG), 202–638–5577. Publishes *How to Prevent Sexually Transmitted Diseases, Human Papillomavirus (HPV) Infection,* and *Practicing Safe Sex.* (For full group information, see PREGNANCY.)

Planned Parenthood Federation of America (PPFA), 800–230–7526. Operates nationwide network of counseling and health services centers; publishes pamphlets *Sexually Transmitted Infections: The Facts, Sex—Safer and Satisfying, HPV and Genital Warts: Questions and Answers, Herpes: Questions and Answers,* and *Chlamydia: Questions and Answers.* (For full group information, see BIRTH CONTROL.)

National Woman's Christian Temperance Union (WCTU), 800–755–1321. Publishes booklet *Sexually Transmitted Diseases—Courting Disaster.* (For full group information, see HELP AGAINST SUBSTANCE ABUSE on page 703.)

National Organization for Rare Disorders (NORD), 800–999–6673. (For full group information, see RARE DISORDERS.)

OTHER RESOURCES

GENERAL WORKS

Sexually Transmitted Diseases. David Plummer and others. Seven Hills, 1995.

Sexually Transmitted Diseases: You May Have One but Don't Know It. Antonio N. Feliciano and Antonio E. Feliciano. Vantage, 1992.

How to Avoid Catching Venereal Diseases. Gordon Press, 1991.
What Women Should Know about Chronic Infections and Sexually Transmitted Diseases. Pamela P. Novotny. Dell, 1991.
Sexually Transmitted Diseases. Derek Llewellyn-Jones. Faber and Faber, 1991.
Sexuality and Sexually Transmitted Diseases: A Doctor Confronts the Myth of "Safe" Sex. Joe S. McIlhaney, Jr. Baker Books, 1990.
VD Blues, rev. ed. Do It Now, 1990.

For children

Sexually Transmitted Diseases. Mark McCauslin. Crestwood, 1992.

For preteens and teens

The Truth and Consequences of Sexually Transmitted Diseases. Carole Marsh. Gallopade, 1994.
Your Sexual Health: What Every Teen Should Know about Sex. Jenny McCloskey. Halo Books, 1993.
Sexually Transmitted Diseases. Alan E. Nourse. Watts, 1991.
Sexually Transmitted Diseases. Marjorie Little. Chelsea House, 1991.
Coping with Health Risks and Risky Behavior. Alan R. Bleich. Rosen, 1990.

(See also AIDS; CONDOMS; HERPES; SEX EDUCATION.)

shaken child syndrome, the pattern of injuries resulting from violent shaking of a child, including HEMORRHAGES (including HYPHEMA, or hemorrhage in the eye) and swelling of the brain. Also called *whiplash-shaken infant syndrome,* it is common in cases of CHILD ABUSE AND NEGLECT.

shock, a condition in which blood flow to the body's tissues is so dramatically reduced that blood-starved tissues can be severely damaged, possibly leading to collapse, fainting, COMA, and death. Symptoms of shock include clammy, cold skin; paleness; rapid, weak breathing and pulse; dizziness; and weakness. Emergency medical help should be summoned immediately. Until help arrives, the victim should be wrapped in blankets (with hot water bottles, if possible) to maintain the body temperature, laid prone on his or her back with feet slightly elevated, and calmly comforted and reassured. Bleeding should be stopped if possible and the breathing passages kept open. No food, drink, or drugs should be given. In a HOSPITAL, patients in shock are often given blood, fluids, and medications intravenously, as well as oxygen, while the underlying problem is being treated.

A danger in any severe injury or illness, shock can result from a variety of causes, including SPINAL CORD INJURY, injury involving great loss of blood, heart problems blocking the flow of blood or causing extremely low BLOOD PRESSURE (see HEART AND HEART PROBLEMS), BURNS, DEHYDRATION (as from persistent DIARRHEA or VOMITING), or poisons. Severe bacterial infection can result in *septic shock syndrome,* such as TOXIC SHOCK SYNDROME. A severe allergic reaction to an injected substance, such as penicillin or a bee's venom, is called *anaphylactic shock* (see ALLERGIES).

FOR HELP AND FURTHER INFORMATION

National Heart, Lung, and Blood Information Center (NHLBIC), 301–251–1222. (For full group information, see HEART AND HEART PROBLEMS.)

shunt, a medical technique that involves insertion of a bypass tube, or *shunt,* to allow fluid to flow freely past an obstruction or narrowing. If a child has HYDROCEPHALUS, or excess fluid in the BRAIN (as when a BRAIN TUMOR blocks the flow of fluid), a shunt may be used to relieve possibly dangerous pressure. The procedure carries some risk of introducing infection, causing MENINGITIS or *ventriculitis* (infection of the VENTRICLES, the cavities in the brain where the fluid flows). As a child grows, a new shunt may need to be inserted. A CT SCAN may be used to assess whether the shunt is working properly or needs replacement. One sign that a shunt is malfunctioning can be noisy, difficult breathing called STRIDOR. (See BRAIN TUMOR; HYDROCEPHALUS.)

siblings, a general term for brothers or sisters who share the same two parents, through birth or ADOPTION. Siblings who share only one parent are called HALF BROTHERS and HALF SISTERS; by contrast, STEPBROTHERS and STEPSISTERS are those who have no relation through biology or adoption except that a parent of one is married to a parent of the other. Such FAMILY relationships have complicated even further the traditional rivalry between siblings, on questions of parental attention, power over each other, individual identity, sex differences, jealousy or envy, or any of the myriad other reasons that children find to fight with each other.

Though sibling rivalry is the bane of many families, child development experts suggest that the fights can be useful preparation for dealing with others in the wider world. Parents can even turn them to positive advantage if they do not take sides and force a win-or-lose situation, but instead help the children learn to resolve the conflict themselves, by stating clearly with them the cause of the conflict, then having the children propose possible solutions and settle on a solution themselves. Beyond that, parents will, of course, want to assure that no children come to physical harm, and may want to try some preventive tactics, such as separation, private space, scheduling separate time with each child, and the like.

When a new baby is expected, parents will have to plan when and how to tell their older children and prepare them for the impending arrival, including the fact that mother will not be so readily available. Relationships between siblings can become complicated, at birth or later, if one child has DISABILITIES and so requires an inordinate amount of attention. Numerous organizations (see below) relating to disabilities have been concerned about this kind of family stress and offer advice and help to parents on how to ease the strain.

FOR HELP AND FURTHER INFORMATION

National Adoption Information Clearinghouse (NAIC), 301–231–6512. Publishes *The Sibling Bond: Its Importance in Foster Care and Adoptive Placement.* (For full group information, see ADOPTION.)

Twin Services, TWINLINE: 510–524–0863. Publishes *Helping Siblings Adjust to Twins.* (For full group information, see MULTIPLE BIRTH.)

ON SIBLINGS OF CHILDREN WITH DISABILITIES

Sibling Information Network, 203–486–3783. (For full group information, see HELP FOR SPECIAL CHILDREN on page 689.)

Siblings for Significant Change (SSC), 212–420–0776. (For full group information, see HELP FOR SPECIAL CHILDREN on page 689.)

PACER Center (Parent Advocacy Coalition for Educational Rights), 612–827–2966, voice/TT. Publishes book *Brothers and Sisters Talk with PACER* and information handout *Siblings Resources.* (For full group information, see HELP FOR SPECIAL CHILDREN on page 689.)

National Information Center for Children and Youth with Disabilities (NICHCY), 800–695–0285, voice/TT. Publishes *Children with Disabilities: Understanding Sibling Issues.* (For full group information, see HELP FOR SPECIAL CHILDREN on page 689.)

The Arc, 817–261–6003. Publishes *Sisters and Brothers;* and fact sheet *Siblings: Brothers and Sisters of People Who Have Mental Retardation.* (For full group information, see MENTAL RETARDATION.)

Alexander Graham Bell Association for the Deaf (AGBAD), 202–337–5220, voice/TT. Publishes *It's Not Fair! Siblings of Children with Disabilities.* (For full group information, see EAR AND HEARING PROBLEMS.)

OTHER RESOURCES

FOR PARENTS

From One Child to Two. Judy Dunn. Fawcett, 1995.
Sibling Rivalry: Managing Conflict Between Your Children. Reynold Bean. Price Stern, 1994.
Cheering for the Home Team: Encouraging Team Work in the Family. Dan Quello. Harvest House, 1992.

GENERAL WORKS

Surviving Sibling Rivalry. Lee Canter. Lee Canter and Associates, 1993.
I Didn't Ask to Be in This Family: Sibling Relationships and How They Shape Adult Behavior and Dependencies. Abraham J. Twerski. World Almanac, 1992.
About Sibling Rivalry: Understanding the Legacy of Childhood. Jane Greer with Edward Myers. Crown, 1992.
Brothers and Sisters: How They Shape Our Lives. Jane Mersky Leder. St. Martin's, 1991.

FOR CHILDREN, ON ADJUSTING TO A NEW BABY

This Week I Got a Sister. Myrtle Kirksey. Cool Hand Communications, 1995.
One Hundred One Things to Do with a Baby. Jan Ormerod. Morrow, 1994.
All about Baby! Good Morning, Baby! Baby and Friends. Good Night, Baby! Dorling Kindersley, 1994.
Little Lessons for Little Learners: The New Baby. Patricia R. Mattozzi. Gibson, 1994.
Who's My Baby? Dorling Kindersley, 1994.
Welcoming Babies. Margy Burns Knight. Tilbury House, 1994.
The Baby's Book of Babies. Kathy Henderson. Puffin, 1993.
Here Come the Babies. Catherine Anholt and Laurence Anholt. Candlewick, 1993.
My Baby Brother. Harriet Hains. Dorling Kindersley, 1992.
Will There Be a Lap for Me? Dorothy Corey. Albert Whitman, 1992.
How to Deal with Babies. Richard Powell. Troll, 1992.
Baby. Dorling Kindersley, 1992.
Bigger Than a Baby. Harriet Ziefert. HarperCollins, 1991. About early childhood development; may help children adjust to new siblings.
Don't Wake the Baby. Jonathan Franklin. Farrar, Straus & Giroux, 1991.
The Book of Babies: A First Picture Book of All the Things That Babies Do. Jo Foord, Photographer. Random House, 1991.
The Trouble with Babies. Angie Sage and Chris Sage. Viking Kestrel, 1990.
A New Baby for Us: Sibling Preparation and Activity Book for Big Brothers and Sisters. Lisa Kugler. Glover, 1990.
Our New Baby. Pleasant T. Rowland. Pleasant, 1990. (Two versions: for White family and Black family)

FOR PRETEENS AND TEENS

Sibling Rivalry: Brothers and Sisters at Odds. Elaine Landau. Millbrook, 1994.
Getting Along with Brothers and Sisters. William L. Coleman. Augsburg Fortress, 1994.
Truce: Ending the Sibling War. Janet Bode. Watts, 1991.
Sharing. Nanette Newman. Doubleday, 1990.

(See also BIRTH ORDER.)

sight vocabulary, words that a student can read and understand in a READING selection without looking them up, as in a dictionary. A *sight word* is one that a student recognizes and understands in a READING selection without needing to sound it out.

sigmoidoscope, a type of ENDOSCOPE used by doctors in visually examining the lower parts of the digestive system. (See DIGESTIVE SYSTEM DISORDERS.)

sign, in medicine, an indication of a disease or disorder that is observable or detectable by a PHYSICIAN; this is regarded as an objective finding, as opposed to a SYMPTOM, which is a subjective indication noticed by a patient. An observable skin RASH or a measurable FEVER is a sign, for example, while the feeling of itching or heat is a symptom. If indications are clear-cut and obvious, they are called HARD SIGNS, but if subtle and not so clear-cut, SOFT SIGNS, as in relation to diagnosing LEARNING DISABILITIES or SCHIZOPHRENIA. On occasion, a sign can also be an observation that fairly conclusively indicates the presence of a particular condition, as BRUDZINSKI'S SIGN generally indicates MENINGITIS. *Sign* is also sometimes used as synonymous with REFLEX.

sign language, formalized patterns of expressive gestures and movements of the hands, face, and body that are used to communicate words and concepts. Developed to allow communication with and among people who have EAR OR HEARING PROBLEMS or who are DEAF-BLIND, sign language is a key part of the TOTAL COMMUNICATION approach, but is shunned by people who believe that deaf children should not use any form of MANUAL COMMUNICATION. Though sign language can be translated into English for hearing people who do not know sign language, it actually has its own vocabulary and grammar. Various sign language systems are used, including American Sign Language (ASL or Ameslan), Signed English, Seeing Essential English (SEE), and Signing Exact English (See II). (For help and further information, including books on sign language, see EAR AND HEARING PROBLEMS.)

Sjogren's syndrome, a GENETIC DISORDER, of the AUTOSOMAL RECESSIVE type, characterized by MENTAL RETARDATION, ICHTHYOSIS (dry, thickened, darkened, scaly, "fish-like" skin), and SPASTIC PARALYSIS (involuntary contraction of the muscles, resulting in loss of muscle function). Various EYE AND VISION PROBLEMS and COMMUNICATIONS DISORDERS are sometimes associated with the syndrome, which was first recognized only in the mid–1950s. Also called Sjogren-Lahrsson syndrome, it is an AUTOIMMUNE DISORDER in which the body mistakenly attacks itself, and is often linked with other autoimmune disorders, such as rheumatoid ARTHRITIS and systemic LUPUS ERTYHEMATOSUS. The syndrome affects people of all racial and ethnic backgrounds, but most Sjogren's patients are women. Symptoms generally emerge during adulthood, though the disorder sometimes makes its appearance during childhood. Researchers are exploring the possibility that the disease may be triggered by a virus such as the Epstein-Barr virus that causes MONONUCLEOSIS.

FOR HELP AND FURTHER INFORMATION

National Arthritis and Musculoskeletal and Skin Diseases Information Clearinghouse (NAMSIC), 301–495–4484. Publishes information package Sjogren's and annotated bibliographies. (For full group information, see ARTHRITIS.)

Sjogren's Syndrome Foundation (SSF)
333 North Broadway
Jericho, NY 11753
516–933–6365; 800–475–64736
Fax: 516–933–6368
Jean S. Kahan, President
Organization concerned with Sjogren's syndrome; provides information; fosters research; sponsors support groups; publishes monthly *The Moisture Seekers® Newsletter* and *The Sjogren's Syndrome Handbook.*

National Organization for Rare Disorders (NORD), 800–999–6673. (For full group information, see RARE DISORDERS.)

(See also IMMUNE SYSTEM.)

skeletal survey, a series of X-RAYS of all a person's bones to find evidence of old, as well as new, FRACTURES, commonly done in cases of suspected CHILD ABUSE AND NEGLECT.

skin and skin disorders, the outer covering of the body—sometimes described as the body's largest organ—and problems associated with it. The skin is a protective shield with many functions, among them:

- Protecting the body against dirt, chemicals, and disease-causing organisms, as well as water, which mostly runs off.
- Cushioning the body against injury.
- Recognizing "foreign" substances that attempt to pierce its defenses, and stimulating production of defensive cells, as in a poison ivy rash.
- Producing *melanin,* a pigment that protects against the sun's ultraviolet rays, the result being *tanning.*
- Containing sense receptors for heat, cold, touch, and pain.
- Producing VITAMIN D in the presence of sunlight, keeping teeth and bones strong.
- Helping to regulate body temperature, by producing sweat that evaporates to cool the body, or by constricting surface blood vessels to maintain body heat.

- Maintaining shape as the body inside it moves and changes angles and orientation.

The skin can also repair itself, after cuts, BURNS, or other such injuries, and—using a natural elastic substance called *collagen*—is able to resume its original shape after being stretched in different directions as the body inside it changes orientation.

The skin is actually a multilayered structure made up of the *epidermis*, the thin outer layer; *dermis*, the thick inner layer; and *subcutaneous tissue*, which contains mostly fat but also some muscles, such as those used in changing facial expression. Growing through these layers are HAIR and NAILS, which are actually formed from special kinds of epidermal cells. Several types of structures originate in the dermis but grow through the epidermis, including hair follicles, sweat glands, blood vessels, nerve endings, muscles, and sebaceous glands, which produce oil (*sebum*) to keep the skin and hair moist and soft. The dermis also anchors the epidermis to the underlying subcutaneous tissue, the fatty tissue that is important in conserving body heat and also cushioning the body. The tissue is relatively thin in areas such as the shins or scalp, but thick in others, such as in the buttocks or in a mature woman's BREASTS.

Skin color depends on a person's GENETIC INHERITANCE, with darker skin resulting from more and larger melanin particles. But skin color can also vary for an individual. Most people have small clumps of melanin particles, called *freckles*, or larger ones, called *moles* (see NEVUS). With exposure to the sun, these can become larger and more numerous, and, like skin color overall, darker. Variations in skin color can also result from birthmarks, which are actually collections of blood vessels near the skin's surface (see NEVUS).

Some women may also produce excess amounts of melanin during the hormonal changes of PREGNANCY or when taking BIRTH CONTROL PILLS. The result is brownish patches of skin, often on the face, which can be further darkened by the sun, called *chloasma, melasma gravidarum, mask of pregnancy*, or more generally *hyperpigmentation*. Such hyperpigmentation can also result from Addison's disease (see ADRENAL GLANDS).

In rare instances, the body produces little or no melanin, a condition called *hypopigmentation*, which leaves people vulnerable to skin damage from the sun. This usually results from a type of GENETIC DISORDER, such as ALBINISM, in which cells fail to produce melanin, or VITILIGO, in which melanin-producing cells are absent.

Skin is a protective covering, but it can also be quite sensitive. If it becomes irritated, a RASH—reddish spots or reddish, inflamed skin—may result, as in the common diaper rash. However, many substances encountered in everyday life can irritate sensitive skin.

Among other skin disorders of concern to parents—some harmless, some quite dangerous—are ACNE; ALOPECIA; CRADLE CAP; EPIDERMOLYSIS BULLOSA; MONGOLIAN SPOTS; PSORIASIS; and SKIN CANCER. (See also BABIES AND RASHES on page 498.)

FOR HELP AND FURTHER INFORMATION

National Arthritis and Musculoskeletal and Skin Diseases Information Clearinghouse (NAMSIC), 301–495–4484. Publishes information packages *Sun and Skin, Eczema, Scleroderma*, and *Psoriasis*; report *Sunlight, Ultraviolet Radiation, and the Skin*; and annotated bibliography *Scleroderma*. (For full group information, see arthritis.)

American Academy of Pediatrics (AAP), 800–433–9016. Publishes brochure *Diaper Rash*. (For full group information, see HEALTH CARE.)

National Organization for Rare Disorders (NORD), 800–999–6673. (For full group information, see RARE DISORDERS.)

American Allergy Association (AAA), 415–322–1663. Publishes *Cosmetics, Allergy Alerts*, and multivolume *Allergy Products Directory*, including Vol. 4: *Protecting Your Skin*. (For full group information, see ALLERGY.)

Agency for Health Care Policy and Research Clearinghouse, 800–358–9295. Publishes *Preventing Pressure Ulcers: A Patient's Guide, Treating Pressure Sores: Consumer Guide*, and InstantFAX materials on pressure ulcers. (For full group information, see HEALTH INSURANCE).

Accent, 800–787–8444. Publishes *Pressure Sores*. (For full group information, see HELP FOR SPECIAL CHILDREN on page 689.)

OTHER RESOURCES

GENERAL WORKS

Baby Skin: A Leading Dermatologist's Guide to Infant and Childhood Skin Care. Nelson L. Novick. Crown, 1991.

Skin Healthy: Everyone's Guide to Great Skin. Norman Levine. Taylor, 1995.

Young Skin for Life: Your Guide to Smoother, Clearer, More Beautiful Skin-at Any Age. Julie Davis and Prevention Magazine Editors. Rodale, 1995.

Healthy Skin, Healthy Mind, Body and Spirit—A Holistic Approach to Natural Beauty and Well-Being: The Ultimate Care and Treatment of the Body's Largest Organ—The Skin and the Person Inside It. Ted Emanuel. Diane, 1994.

Healthy Skin: The Facts: Good Skin Care Throughout Life. Rona M. MacKie. Oxford University Press, 1992.

Shedding a Little Light on Your Skin. Richard G. Mora. Aegina Press, 1992.

Don't Go to the Cosmetic Counters Without Me. Paula Begoun. Beginning Press, 1991

Saving Your Skin: Secrets of Healthy Skin and Hair. Anne E. Hunt. ARE Press, 1991.

ON SKIN PROBLEMS

The Skin and Its Troubles. Mokelumne, 1994.
What You Can Do about Chronic Skin Problems. Dell Medical Library Staff and Peggy J. Donahue. Dell, 1992.
Skin Disorders. Lynn Lamberg. Chelsea House, 1990.

FOR CHILDREN AND PRETEENS

Everything You Need to Know about Skin Care. Jane Hammerslough. Rosen, 1994.
All the Colors We Are: The Story of How We Get Our Skin Color. Katie Kissinger and Prisma International Staff editors. Redleaf, 1994.
Why Do People Come in Different Colors? Isaac Asimov and Carrie Dierks. Gareth Stevens, 1993.
Outstanding Outsides. Hana Machotka. Morrow, 1993.
Nose to Toes. JoAnne Nelson. Comprehensive Health Education, 1993.
All about Your Skin, Hair and Teeth. Donna Bailey. Raintree Steck-Vaughn, 1990.

(See also PLASTIC SURGERY.)

skin cancer, a variety of CANCER affecting the outer protective layer of the body. Because such cancers are primarily triggered by exposure to the sun, they are most often found in adults, though sometimes in children. But since children are estimated to receive half of their exposure to sun before age eighteen, and since skin cancers that once appeared only after age forty are now common in the twenties, parents will want to take steps to prevent damage to their children during youth.

There are three main types of skin cancer:

- *Basal cell carcinoma*, the most common form, strongly linked with sunlight exposure and so generally found in the face, hands, and other parts most often exposed to the sun. It develops slowly, often as a white or flesh-colored lump, or as a patch of flaky red skin, which may scab over or ooze blood, but never fully heals.
- *Squamous cell carcinoma*, an irregularly shaped clump of cancerous cells, all strongly linked with sunlight exposure.
- *Malignant melanoma*, a fast-spreading tumor, often arising from a pigmented spot on the skin, such as a freckle or mole (see NEVUS). Unless caught very quickly, it can be fatal, because it spreads (*metastasizes*) so fast.

According to the American Cancer Society, basal cell or squamous cell cancer are highly likely to be cured if detected and treated early. Malignant melanoma is also described as highly curable, if detected and treated in its earliest stages. About 4 out of 5 melanomas are diagnosed at the local stage, and for them the ACS estimates a five-year survival rate of 90 percent. If the melanoma cancer has spread to nearby regions, the survival rate drops to 50 percent and to distant parts 14 percent.

Because melanomas are so dangerous, parents should scan the bodies of their children (and themselves) for any changes, especially darkening or other color change, and especially checking freckles and moles. Of particular concern are growth beyond previously established "borders" to form irregular edges, and oozing or bleeding. Any new mole after PUBERTY bears very careful watching. As a rule of thumb, some doctors summarize the warning signs of melanoma with the ABCD rule:

- *A is for asymmetry.* One half of the mole does not match the other half.
- *B is for border irregularity.* The edges are ragged, notched, or blurred.
- *C is for color.* The pigmentation is not uniform.
- *D is for diameter greater than 6 millimeters.* Any sudden or progressive increase in size should be of special concern.

Any suspicious change calls for an immediate visit to the doctor, so the possible cancer can be identified and removed before it spreads and becomes lethal.

Among the sun's rays, the most dangerous are the ultraviolet (UV) rays, from the purple end of the spectrum, or rainbow, which disables the p53 gene that normally governs cell growth; unchecked growth, along with mutations and other damage, produces what we know as cancer. There are actually three types of UV light, all damaging to the skin:

- Type C (UVC), the most powerful and most damaging. While humans have inhabited Earth, life has been possible because the ozone layer in Earth's upper atmosphere has largely absorbed UVC before it reaches the ground. But progressive thinning of the ozone layer is causing concerns about increasing UVC danger to human and other life.
- Type B (UVB), a high-energy form that passes right through the Earth's atmosphere. This is the type of radiation that produces sunburn and most tanning, as well much skin cancer, especially melanoma.
- Type A (UVA), a lower-energy form that also penetrates the Earth's atmosphere. This type of radiation produces some tanning and causes two types of skin cancer, though apparently not melanoma.

As skin experts describe it, tanning is actually the body's way of trying to prevent skin damage from the sun's rays; tanned skin is damaged skin, and the deeper the color—that is the more *melanin* produced in attempts to block out ultraviolet rays—the more extensive the damage. People who are very fair-skinned do not have many of the type of cells that produce melanin, and so will not get tanned, no matter how much damage they cause to their skin. As a result, they are at special risk from sunlight damage. People who have very dark skin have more melanin, but are still subject to damage from sun exposure. Sunburn results when the skin has been damaged so much that it is painful to return to the sun. Tanning devices produce the same kinds of UVA and UVB rays, deliberately

When Do Kids Need Protection from the Sun?

The answer is: *Much* more often than they get it. Though sunlight is essential for all life, doctors are learning more and more about the dangers for humans of long-term daily exposure to the sun, including sunburns, damage to the retina in the eye, cataracts, and skin cancer. With the continuing passion for tanning and outdoor activities, and probably also because of the progressive thinning of the ozone layer in the Earth's upper atmosphere, and its lessened ability to block out ultraviolet (UV) rays, skin cancer rates are rising. (For information on the three main types of ultraviolet rays that cause skin damage, see SKIN CANCER.)

Sunscreens are designed to offer some protection from ultraviolet rays. Most block out only UVB radiation, and are rated by their ability to do just that. They are given a *sun protection factor* (SPF) indicating how long a person can remain in the sun without burning; if a person would normally get a sunburn after ten minutes unprotected, application of a sunscreen with an SPF of 15 would mean the person could stay in the sun for 150 minutes before burning. Sunscreens as high as 50 are on the market, and federal experts feel that they may be valuable, especially for people who have very fair skin—and for children—though the FDA has not been able to develop procedures for determining the effectiveness of SPFs above 15.

Most sunscreens do not block out UVAs, however. Even for the relatively few sunscreens that do, none blocks *all* UVAs, and no rating systems yet exists for evaluating UVA protection, though some experts estimate that their SPF is equivalent to 3–4. Despite advertising claims to the contrary, no sunscreens are sunblocks. Only totally opaque substances, such as zinc oxide or titanium dioxide, totally block ultraviolet rays. These are usually practical to use only on areas most exposed and vulnerable, such as nose or lips.

Ironically, the advent of UVB sunscreens may be causing more UVA damage, for when people are protected from burning, they have the illusion of safety and stay in the sun longer, unprotected from UVA radiation. The same is true on cool, breezy, or overcast days, when—because ultraviolet rays carry no warmth—people are unaware that they are still at risk from ultraviolet radiation. (Clouds block out the heat-producing infrared rays, but ultraviolet rays pass right through.) Shade often offers little protection, for ultraviolet rays bounce off bright surfaces, such as sand, water, snow, and white concrete. The UVA rays even penetrate several feet underwater, and through glass.

How are parents to best protect their children (and themselves)? Federal agencies and medical organizations make the following recommendations:

- Infants under six months old (some say up to a year) should be kept out of the sun altogether, or as much as possible. Their eyes are particularly vulnerable to sunlight, and sunscreens are not recommended, because they irritate sensitive baby skin.
- Children and parents going out in the sun should wear a hat and tightly woven clothing, fully covering arms and legs. Loosely woven, gauzy, or wet clothes offer little protection.
- Children and parents should avoid being out in the midday sun for any prolonged period of time, in all regions (though especially near the equator and in higher altitudes, where the atmosphere is thinner) and all parts of the year (though especially in the warmer months, when the rays are more direct). Some experts have suggested that schools, child-care centers, and camps reschedule their outdoor play times for early morning and late afternoon, rather than between 10 A.M. and 2 to 3 P.M.
- Parents should see that their children routinely wear sunscreen with an SPF of 15 or more. A waterproof sunscreen is recommended for children, who sweat more heavily and dash in and out of water more frequently than most adults. (Active adults, especially swimmers, should also use a waterproof sunscreen.) For adults or children, sunscreen is recommended even for casual exposure, such as driving a car, walking to the store, or taking an outdoor lunch break, since all contribute to cumulative damage.
- Before using a new sunscreen, test it on a small area of skin (such as the under part of the forearm). Apply some, cover it with a bandage for twenty-four hours, then expose it to sunlight for fifteen minutes; if the skin is sensitive to the ingredients in the sunscreen, the patch will be red and swollen the next day. Many people are sensitive to the widely used substance PABA

(para-aminobenzoic acid), which can also stain clothing. Many newer sunscreens are labeled as greaseless, hypoallergenic, or PABA-free; allergies to non-PABA sunscreens have been less common. Where sensitivity exists, however, higher SPF strengths can cause increased irritation. Parents should also check with their doctor or pharmacist about any medications that can increase sensitivity to sunscreen ingredients, such as certain antibiotics (notably tetracycline given for acne), antihistamines, birth control pills, diuretics, sulfa drugs, and antidepressants.

- Apply sunscreen liberally. Recent studies have found that most people use only half as much as they should, the result being that they may get only an SPF 7 protection from an SPF 15 sunscreen. Actual amounts vary with the brand and the form, but for one application at the beach, an adult might use an ounce or two per application, with accordingly less for children.
- Put sunscreen on every exposed areas, including ears, feet, and the part in the hair. For protection in places with snow, water, sand, white concrete, or other light, bright surfaces that reflect ultraviolet rays, do not neglect areas susceptible to light reflecting upward, such as under the chin, the area under the nose, and the upper lip.
- Put on the sunscreen thirty minutes before going outdoors, to give the skin time to soak it up.
- Put on more sunscreen every two hours, and immediately after being in the water (unless the sunscreen is waterproof).

Eyes also need protection from ultraviolet radiation. For extended outdoor use, especially in snow, on water, or at the beach, sunglasses that filter out all UVA and UVB light are recommended for everyone. Large lenses or wraparound styles are preferred, since they lessen the amount of light entering from the side, around the frames. Some experts recommend that regular glasses for indoor or short-term outdoor wear also have an ultraviolet coating; however, others say that such coatings will not hurt, but are unnecessary, since people who wear glasses with plastic lenses—which is most eyeglass-wearers today—already have 95 percent of the UV rays blocked, and so do not need any extra protective coating.

Families who are installing sun rooms, greenhouses, skylights, or extra large windows and doors are also advised to get low-emissivity (low-e) glass to cut down on ultraviolet radiation. Ordinary clear glass allows most of the sun's rays, including UV and heat, to pass through into the house; they can be made tinted or reflective to block UV and many other rays, but that produces darker rooms and hinders growth of houseplants. By contrast, low-e glass is coated with metal oxides to block ultraviolet rays and heat from outdoors, while still allowing visible light to pass through; low-e also retains indoor heat, for energy efficiency. Even more effective in blocking UV radiation are low-e films; one type is placed between double-paned glass for nearly complete ultraviolet blockage. Many hardware stores now sell low-e film, which homeowners can be applied to ordinary windows.

As far as is known, there are no significant indoor sources of ultraviolet radiation. Though many people are sold coatings to block out UV from computers, impartial experts note that computers and television screens emit less UV radiation than do fluorescent lights, at 1/10,000th of the level believed to cause problems. Scientists have, however, found that tungsten-halogen lamps emit possibly harmful UV rays, and so should not be used near people, as at a desk, unless a UV filter is installed.

Mercury vapor lamps can also emit intense ultraviolet radiation, which has caused various injuries and burns, including burns to the cornea of the eye. Such lamps are normally protected by filters, and most injuries occur when this outer envelope is broken, generally through activities in school gymnasiums. Since 1980, the Food and Drug Administration has recommended that mercury vapor lamps used in proximity to people be of a self-extinguishing type, which shuts off within fifteen minutes. But non-self-extinguishing lamps are still widely found. The FDA recommends that such lamps be checked regularly (with the lamp off) for missing, broken, or punctured outer envelopes; that broken lamps should be turned off, and replaced only while the lamps are off; that broken lamps should be turned off immediately (and people nearby should leave or protect their eyes and skin from UV exposure, as by putting on coats or sweaters and sunglasses); and that people exposed to UV rays from broken lamps see a doctor if they have any symptoms of skin burns or eye irritation.

causing skin damage. To find out how to best protect children from the sun's damage, see WHEN DO KIDS NEED PROTECTION FROM THE SUN? (on page 548).

FOR HELP AND FURTHER INFORMATION

National Cancer Institute (NCI), 800–422–6237. Publishes *Fry Now; Pay Later;* video *Winners in the Sun;* and "What You Need to Know About" brochures on skin cancer and melanoma. (For full group information, see CANCER.)

Skin Cancer Foundation
475 Park Avenue South
New York, NY 10016
212–725–5176; 800-SKIN490 [754–6490]
Fax: 212–725–5751
Mitzi Moulds, Executive Director
Organization for people concerned with skin cancer; publishes various materials, including quarterly newsletter and other materials.

American Cancer Society (ACS), 800–227–2345. Publishes educational kit *Children's Guide to Sun Protection* and other materials on skin cancer. (For full group information, see CANCER.)

American Institute for Cancer Research (AICR), 800–843–8114. Publishes *Reducing Your Risk of Skin Cancer.* (For full group information, see CANCER.)

American Council on Science and Health (ACSH), 212–362–7044. Publishes *Malignant Melanoma.* (For full group information, see SAFETY.)

OTHER RESOURCES

Saving Your Skin: Early Detection, Treatment and Prevention of Melanoma and Other Skin Cancers. Barney Kenet and Patricia Lawler-Kenet. FWEW, 1994.
Protect Your Life in the Sun: How to Minimize Your Exposure to Ultraviolet Sunlight and Prevent Skin Cancer and Eye Disorders. Paul L. Gourley and Gail M. Gourley. High Light, 1993.
The Truth about Sunscreens. Julia M. Busch. Anti-Aging Press, 1992.
Safe in the Sun: Your Skin Survival Guide for the 1990s. Mary E. Siegel. Walker, 1990.

(See also CANCER.)

sleep apnea, brief periods during sleep when breathing ceases, until the brain is alerted to restart breathing. Most often sleep apnea occurs when the breathing passages are obstructed by relaxation of the soft tissues in the mouth, causing snoring with partial blockage and silence with complete blockage; this is called *obstructive apnea.* While such apnea can occur in people of any age, it is especially common in overweight people; in children it is called the CHUBBY PUFFER SYNDROME. Sleep apnea can also occur with the air passages open, if the chest and diaphragm muscles cease to work, presumably because of an irregularity in the brain; this is called *central apnea.* Sometimes the two types of apnea occur together, in *mixed apnea.*

Apnea of up to fifteen seconds occurs normally in all ages, but cessation of breathing for over seconds seconds is called *pathologic apnea,* and can result in BRAIN damage and other problems. Pathologic apnea may be marked by slowed heartbeat (*bradycardia*), color change (pallor, *cyanosis* or blueness, or sometimes *erythematosis* or redness), and muscular limpness (HYPOTONIA), and sometimes choking or gagging. If these symptoms are marked, they are sometimes labeled an APPARENT LIFE-THREATENING EVENT (ALTE).

Apnea of prematurity (AOP) is very common among PREMATURE babies, occurring among nearly 90 percent of newborns with a GESTATIONAL AGE of under 29 weeks. Premature babies who have not had AOP, or who have "grown out of it," are sometimes called *asymptomatic premature infants.* Infants who have a gestational age of more than 37 weeks are said to show *apnea of infancy (AOI).* Sleep apnea is often associated with other health disorders, such as RESPIRATORY DISTRESS SYNDROME or PNEUMONIA, and is thought to be involved in at least some cases of SUDDEN INFANT DEATH SYNDROME.

CARDIAC MONITORS and cardiorespiratory (heart rate and breathing) monitors are often used on HIGH-RISK newborns in NEONATAL INTENSIVE CARE UNITS and later at home, to alert parents or other CAREGIVERS that breathing has ceased. The Public Health Service's report on *Infantile Apnea and Home Monitoring* (see HOME MONITORS) stresses the importance of training and instruction of caregivers so they will know how to act in cases of apnea, such as how to attempt RESUSCITATION.

In adults, sleep apnea is most common in middle-aged men and overweight people; it can cause daytime sleepiness and diminished memory and concentration, and is also linked with increased risk of high BLOOD PRESSURE, heart attacks, and STROKE. It is sometimes treated with a Continuous Positive Airway Pressure (CPAP) device, a small compressor to hold open the airway overnight, or dental appliances to reposition jaw or tongue in milder cases.

FOR HELP AND FURTHER INFORMATION

National Sudden Infant Death Syndrome Clearinghouse, 800–221–7437. Publishes *Facts About Apnea* and *Infantile Apnea and SIDS.* (For full group information, see SUDDEN INFANT DEATH SYNDROME.)

Sudden Infant Death Syndrome Alliance (SIDS Alliance), 800–221–7437. Publishes *Facts About Apnea and Other Apparent Life Threatening Events, At Home with a Monitor: A Guide for Parents,* and *A Manual for Home Monitoring.* (For full group information, see SUDDEN INFANT DEATH SYNDROME.)

Parents Helping Parents (PHP), 408–727–5775. Publishes information packet *Apnea Monitor.* (For full group information, see HELP FOR SPECIAL CHILDREN on page 689.)

OTHER RESOURCES

Phantom of the Night: Overcome Sleep Apnea Syndrome and Snoring—Win Your Hidden Struggle to Breathe, Sleep and Live, rev. ed. T. Scott Johnson and Jerry Halberstadt. New Technology, 1994.

Snoring and Sleep Apnea: Personal and Family Guide to Diagnosis and Treatment. Ralph A. Pascualy and Sally W. Soest. Scope, 1993.

(See also SLEEP AND SLEEP DISORDERS.)

sleep and sleep disorders, a state of lessened consciousness, reduced METABOLISM, and limited activity of the skeletal muscles, and the problems and disruptions associated with it. Not a single, uniform state, sleep goes through stages, which can be recognized on ENCEPHALOGRAMS (EEGs). The two main, alternating stages are named for their main characteristics: NREM (nonrapid eye movement) and REM (rapid eye movement), during which normal dreaming occurs. Adults generally start with a period of NREM sleep, which then alternates with short periods of REM sleep throughout the night. Infants, on the other hand, tend to start with REM sleep.

A major controversy in recent years has involved how to put babies to sleep. For decades, Western parents were urged to put their babies to sleep on their stomachs; the idea was that that would best keep the respiratory passages clear, in case of VOMITING or spitting up. However, recent studies in Scandinavia, Australia, and New Zealand have found that infants who slept on their stomachs had a high incidence of SUDDEN INFANT DEATH SYNDROME (SIDS). The results were so compelling that numerous American organizations launched a "Back to Sleep" campaign, urging parents to place babies on their backs to sleep. The exceptions are where the child has respiratory, gastrointestinal, or other problems that make the face-up (supine or prone) position unwise, a question to be decided in consultation with a PEDIATRICIAN. In some parts of the world, including England, it has been traditional to place babies to sleep on their sides. However, that has been linked with higher risk of spine curvature (see SCOLIOSIS), "molding" of the head, and hip dislocation (see CONGENITAL DISLOCATION OF THE HIP).

Some American researchers question the studies that sparked the "Back to Sleep" campaign, suggesting that the results were not applicable in the United States because the cultures studied used heavier bedding materials, such as sheep's wool, in which a baby could more easily smother itself. Whether or not that is so, parents should certainly be very much aware of the nature of bedding for infants. In the late 1980s at least 35 infants died after being put to sleep face down on beanbag cushions; these molded around their bodies, trapping them to breathe in their own exhaled carbon dioxide, and so to suffocate. All or most of the infants were under three months old, and so were too young to raise their heads, or to roll over or away from the cushions. These particular cushions were voluntarily recalled in 1990, but many remain in homes.

Parents should also be very careful about placing infants to sleep on beds intended for older children or adults. In the decade between 1985 and 1995, several hundred children died lying on adult or youth beds. Many smothered in bedclothes, were trapped between the mattress and part of the bed or a wall, or sank into the mattress or water bed while lying face down. Some also died sleeping in their parents' bed, when an adult rolled over and smothered them. The Consumer Product Safety Commission (see SAFETY) has issued a warning to parents and caregivers about the danger to infants in all these situations.

In general, parents should keep babies on a firm surface; anything that conforms to the child's body or that can trap a child lying face down—including adult beds, pillows, cushions, or rugs—is potentially deadly. Newborns are especially vulnerable, since for the first few weeks they breathe only through their nostrils, and the nose with its soft, compressible cartilage is readily obstructed.

Whether parents decide to allow older children to sleep with them is very much a personal question. Many parents laud the feeling of family togetherness that comes from parents and children sleeping all or part of the night in the same bed. Others decry the loss of sleep and lack of parental privacy.

Individual sleeping patterns vary widely, but in general the need for sleep decreases gradually with age. A newborn may sleep as many as twenty hours out of twenty-four; by age one that will have dropped to more like fourteen hours, by age five to about twelve hours, by adulthood seven to eight hours, and in some people, especially in their later years, to as little as six or less.

Given the amount of our lives spent in sleep, and its importance in "knitting up the raveled sleeve of care," it is not surprising that a wide variety of sleep disorders exist. In general, these concern:

- Difficulty with going to sleep and staying so, or *insomnia.*
- Problems with staying awake, such as *narcolepsy* (see later in this entry).
- Problems with establishing a consistent sleeping/waking schedule, as with jet lag or working rotating shifts.
- Disruptions of sleep patterns, the area in which most childhood sleep disorders fall.

One common sleep disorder found among children is *night terrors* (*pavor nocturnus*), in which a child suddenly sits up in bed exhibiting the behaviors associated with intense fear—screaming, looking terrified, breathing heavily, sweating profusely, and fighting to escape the dreamed

Sleeping Babies

Many new parents worry, at first, if their babies are out of their sight. For your peace of mind, you may want to sleep near the crib for the first few nights. But everyone will get more rest if your baby does not sleep in your bedroom. Especially in the first weeks, frequent snorts, gurgles, sneezes, coughs and irregular breathing will keep you awake wondering what the baby will do next. If you are really needed, your baby will cry loud enough to be heard from nearly everywhere in the house! Even in the smallest apartment, a crib or makeshift crib can be moved to the living room, kitchen or bathroom when you go to bed for the night.

Try not to let your baby sleep with you. It is almost certain your baby will want to become your constant bedfellow! Neither you nor your partner would want to put up with a wiggling, wet baby for very long.

Your baby shouldn't sleep in a strong draft or breeze. He or she doesn't always need open windows. Air that is fresh enough to breathe during the day is fresh enough to sleep in.

Most babies sleep from twelve to twenty hours during the twenty-four-hour day. Your baby will decide how much to sleep. You won't be able to make your baby sleep any more or less than he or she wants. However, you can arrange to keep your infant awake during the times of the day that are most convenient for you, so that he or she will be more likely to sleep during the night and during morning or afternoon naps. Here are a few other ways, suggested by moms and dads, to try to get baby's sleeping schedule to fit with your own:

- Make sure that baby's bed is warm and in a quiet place.
- Taking your baby outside for fresh air may make him or her tired and sleepy.
- A humidifier may make the air in baby's room more comfortable, and the noise is comforting. Be sure to change the water in the humidifier daily.
- Watch for signs of sleepiness (rubbing his or her nose or eyes, yawning) and put the baby to bed.
- When all else fails, a car ride may help your baby go to sleep.

Sometimes the baby will cry when put down for sleep. Crying may persist. If there is no other reason for crying (such as hunger, wetness, illness), be patient. Go out of the room, and the baby will usually stop crying after a while.

Source: Infant Care (1989). Prepared by the Bureau of Maternal and Child Health and Resources Development for the Public Health Service.

phantom. Sometimes the reaction is so severe that it can cause injury to the child or others. The child will generally not remember the brief episode, which (unlike most dreams) takes place during NREM sleep. Parents are advised to offer comfort, warmth, and support, and not to try to make the child stand up, as that may lead to sleepwalking (which accompanies night terrors in many cases; see later in this entry). Night terrors generally occur between ages four and twelve, involving boys more often than girls, and gradually disappear as the child grows older. They are not thought to signal any kind of personality disorder. They are sometimes accompanied by sleep talking, ranging from gibberish to understandable speech, often not remembered; sleep talking alone can occur at any age, often brought on by STRESS or illness.

By contrast, frightening sleep episodes called *nightmares* occur during REM sleep and are often remembered afterward with some vividness, if not in all their details. Nightmares can occur at any age, and recent studies have shown that they are far more common in ADOLESCENCE than was once thought. Scientific evidence has not (so far at least) supported the popular link between nightmares and "creativity" or "genius," nor does the frequency of nightmares seem to signal personality problems; rather, recent research suggests, problems with nightmares may more often be linked to the ANXIETY with which a person responds to the nightmare when awake, than to the nightmare itself.

Sleepwalking or *somnambulism* is also a common sleep disorder among children, affecting perhaps 15 percent of all children between ages five and twelve, the Public Health Service estimates. It tends to run in families. Some may, however, sleepwalk only once or twice in their lives, and most outgrow the disorder. Typically sleepwalkers sit up, get out of bed, and move around, often in an uncoordinated way. Sometimes they may even dress, go outdoors, eat, and go to the bathroom; they can, in the process, often hurt themselves, stumbling over furniture, falling down stairs, going out windows, and the like. Parents need to arrange the environment so as to protect a sleepwalking child, as by locking windows and doors (unless that will cause fire SAFETY hazard), placing a child's bedroom away from a stairway, or placing a barrier across a stairway or window. In severe cases, doctors can prescribe drugs to help, but sleepwalking is not thought to indicate personality disturbance in children.

Another sleep disorder sometimes puts in an appearance between PUBERTY and the midtwenties: *narcolepsy*, characterized by virtually irresistible sleep attacks, in which a person may suddenly drop into sleep while talking, working, or even driving, for periods ranging from a few seconds to more than thirty minutes. Sometimes associated with narcolepsy is a sudden loss of muscle control, called *cataplexy*; an inability to speak or move during the transition between sleeping and waking, called *sleep paralysis*; or vivid dreams, called *hypnagogic hallucinations*. Narcolepsy may develop over time, the earliest symptom being excessive daytime sleepiness. As they fight sleep, people with narcolepsy can sometimes continue to do routine tasks, in what is called *automatic behavior*. Narcolepsy runs in families and may have a genetic component. No cure is yet known, but medications and lifestyle modifications can bring symptoms under control.

Two other common disorders that disrupt sleep are SLEEP APNEA and BEDWETTING (see separate entries).

Parents who have their own sleeping disorders sometimes take sleeping pills, but women should not do so while pregnant, except under a doctor's guidance, as many of them can cause BIRTH DEFECTS. For parents, one of the main problems associated with sleep is getting their child to sleep through the night (see SLEEPING BABIES on page 552).

FOR HELP AND FURTHER INFORMATION

American Academy of Pediatrics (AAP), 800–433–9016. Publishes brochures *Sleep Problems in Children* and *Infant Sleep Positioning* and SIDS Fact Sheet. (For full group information, see HEALTH CARE.)

American Academy of Child and Adolescent Psychiatry (AACAP), 202–966–7300. Publishes information sheet *Children's Sleep Problems*. (For full group information, see MENTAL DISORDERS

National Institute of Mental Health (NIMH), 301–443–4513. Publishes *Useful Information on Sleep Disorders*. (For full group information, see MENTAL DISORDER.)

National Sleep Foundation
1367 Connecticut Avenue NW, Suite 200
Washington, DC 20036
Organization concerned with sleep disorders and sleep deprivation; sponsors research; responds to written requests for information; publishes brochures *The Nature of Sleep*, *When You Can't Sleep: ABCs of ZZZs*, and *Understanding Narcolepsy*.

National Maternal and Child Health Clearinghouse (NMCHC), 703–821–8955. Publishes *Back to Sleep*. (For full group information, see PREGNANCY.)

Sudden Infant Death Syndrome Alliance (SIDS Alliance), 800–221–7437. Publishes *A Message from the SIDS Alliance on Infant Sleep Position*. (For full group information, see SUDDEN INFANT DEATH SYNDROME.)

National Heart, Lung, and Blood Information Center (NHLBIC), 301–251–1222. Publishes booklet *Breathing Disorders During Sleep;* and professional materials. (For full group information, see HEART AND HEART PROBLEMS.)

National Alliance for the Mentally Ill (NAMI), 800–950–6264. Publishes brochure *Sleep Disorders*; has online forum and libraries. (For full group information, see MENTAL DISORDERS.)

National Organization for Rare Disorders (NORD), 800–999–6673. (For full group information, see RARE DISORDERS.)

Twin Services, 510–524–0863. Publishes *Sleep Through the Night*. (For full group information, see MULTIPLE BIRTH.)

OTHER RESOURCES

For parents

The World of Children's Sleep: Parent's Guide. Alexander Z. Golbin. Michaelis Medical Publishing, 1995.
Keys to Children's Sleep Problems. Susan E. Gottlieb. Barron's, 1993.
Winning Bedtime Battles: How to Help Your Child Develop Good Sleep Habits. Charles E. Schaefer and Theresa F. DiGeronimo. Citadel/Carol, 1992.
Hush-a-Bye Know-How: A Parent's Guide to Sleeptime. Robert Datz. Times to Treasure, 1992.
Crying Baby, Sleepless Nights, rev. ed. Sandy Jones. Harvard Common Press, 1992. Originally titled: *Why Your Baby Is Crying and What You Can Do About It*.
Three in a Bed. Deborah Jackson. Avon, 1992.
The Sleep Book for Tired Parents: A Practical Guide to Solving Children's Sleep Problems. Rebecca Huntley. Parenting Press, 1991.
Getting Your Child to Sleep—and Back to Sleep. Vicki Lansky. Book Peddlers, 1991.

General works

Sleep. J. Allan Hobson. W. H. Freeman, 1995.
The Good Sleep Guide. Michael Van Straten. Trafalgar, 1994.
How to Get a Great Night's Sleep: Step-by-Step Practical Advice for Everyone Who Needs to Sleep Better. H. Vafi and Pamela Vafi. Adams, 1994.
The Sleep Rx: 75 Proven Ways to Get a Good Night's Sleep. Norman D. Ford. Prentice Hall, 1994.
Sleep Management Plan. Dale H. Bourke. HarperCollins, 1992.
Bedtime. Moira Kemp and Mathew Kemp. Random, 1992.
Getting to Sleep. Ellen M. Catalano and others. New Harbinger, 1990.

Everybody's Guide to Natural Sleep. Philip Goldberg and Daniel Kaufman. Tarcher, 1990.

On insomnia

Wide Awake at Three A.M.: By Choice or by Chance. Richard M. Coleman. W. H. Freeman, 1995.
Restful Sleep: The Complete Mind-Body Program for Overcoming Insomnia. Deepak Chopra. Crown, 1994.
Conquering Insomnia: An Illustrated Guide to Understanding and Overcoming Sleep Disruption. Colin H. Shapiro and others. Login, 1994.
Goodbye Insomnia, Hello Sleep. Samuel Dunkell. Birch Lane/Carol, 1994.
Sleep Right in Five Nights: A Clear and Effective Guide for Conquering Insomnia. James Perl. Morrow, 1993.
Natural Sleep: Beat Insomnia Without Drugs. Anthea Courtenay. Thorsons, 1991.
Overcoming Insomnia. Donald R. Sweeney. Bantam, 1991.
No More Sleepless Nights. Peter J. Hauri and Shirley M. Linde. Wiley, 1990.

On other sleep disorders

Narcolepsy: A Funny Disorder That's No Laughing Matter. Marguerite J. Utley. M. J. Utley, 1995.
Relief from Sleep Disorders. Barbara Becker. Dell, 1993.
Sleep Disorders: America's Hidden Nightmare. Roger Fritz. National Sleep Alert, 1993.

For children

Sleep on It!. Kevin Kelly and Erin Jaeb. Childrens, 1995.
I Can't Sleep. Kimberlee Graves. Creative Teaching Press, 1994.
Why Do We Need Sleep? Isaac Asimov and Carrie Dierks. Gareth Stevens, 1993.
Where Does the Sun Sleep?: First Questions and Answers about Bedtime. Time Life Inc. Editors and Neil Kagan, ed. Time-Life, 1993.
"I'm Not Sleepy". Denys Cazet. Orchard/Jackson, 1992. A patient father devises a tale to lull his son to sleep.
Animals Don't Wear Pajamas: A Book about Sleeping. Eve B. Feldman. Holt, 1992.
My Getting-Ready-for-Bed Book. Harriet Ziefert. Harper, 1990.

For children, about dreams

How Do We Dream?: And Other Questions about Your Body. Jack Myers. Boyds Mills, 1992.
Dreaming in the Night: How You Rest, Sleep and Dream. Steve Parker. Watts, 1991.
How to Get Rid of Bad Dreams. Nancy Hazbry and Roy Condy. Scholastic, 1990.
Jessica and the Wolf: A Story for Children Who Have Bad Dreams. Theodore Lobby. Magination Press, 1990.

For preteens and teens

Drugs and Sleeping Disorders. Gina Strzzabosco-Hayn. Rosen, 1995.
Coping with Sleep Disorders. Carolyn Simpson. Rosen, 1995.
Sleep. Edward Edelson. Chelsea House, 1992.

Background works

Encyclopedia of Sleep and Dreaming. Mary Carskadon, ed. Macmillan, 1993.
Sleep, Dreaming, and Sleep Disorders: An Introduction, 2nd ed. William H. Moorcroft. University Press of America, 1993.
The Encyclopedia of Sleep and Sleep Disorders. Michael Thorpy and Jan Yager. Facts on File, 1990.

(See SLEEP APNEA.)

Slingerland Screening Tests for Identifying Children with Specific Learning Disabilities, a range of DIAGNOSTIC ASSESSMENT TESTS used to measure the LANGUAGE SKILLS of children in grades 1 to 6, existing in four forms. It is a group-administered, paper-and-pencil test, though some optional parts may be administered individually. The Slingerland tests are widely used to identify children with possible LEARNING DISABILITIES, so they can receive SPECIAL EDUCATION. The main areas covered are visual-motor coordination, visual memory as linked with motor coordination, auditory-visual discrimination, and auditory memory as linked to motor ability, and in some forms also SPATIAL ORIENTATION and ECHOLALIA. (See TESTS; AUDITORY SKILLS; VISUAL SKILLS.)

small gestational age (SGA), a term referring to an infant who is small and of LOW BIRTH WEIGHT, not because of being PREMATURE, but instead because of slow growth in the fetus. By contrast, an infant whose size and stage of development is appropriate to his or her stage of GESTATION, meaning the number of weeks since CONCEPTION is sometimes referred to as *appropriate for gestational age* (AGA). (See GESTATIONAL AGE.)

smoking, inhalation of the fumes of burning tobacco leaves. Long thought soothing and fashionable, smoking has in recent decades been increasingly recognized as a major health hazard. Were it not that tobacco-smoking has been part of American history from its earliest days, smoking might well be considered simply another form of DRUG ABUSE. Like other abused substances, tobacco causes changes in the body; its nicotine produces addiction, with withdrawal symptoms if use ends.

The best-known adverse effect of smoking is increased risk of CANCER, especially of the lungs, but also of the mouth, throat, and esophagus, as well as many internal organs such as the bladder, pancreas, and kidney. Various kinds of LUNG AND BREATHING DISORDERS are also linked with smoking, notably emphysema and bronchitis. Tobacco smoke, in addition to carrying cancer-triggering substances (*carcinogens*), lessens the body's ability to obtain and use oxygen, and is linked with serious heart disease.

Smoking during PREGNANCY poses special risks, with increased likelihood of MISCARRIAGE, PREMATURE DELIVERY, LOW BIRTH WEIGHT, STILLBIRTH, and INFANT MORTALITY. Children of smokers are also more susceptible to ASTHMA and other respiratory diseases. In recent years, studies have indicated that breathing the smoke from someone else's cigarette—called *passive smoking*—causes many of the same kinds of damage as smoking itself.

Despite this, health warnings on cigarette packages, and the ban on television advertising of smoking, many young people continue to regard smoking as attractive and "grown-up." Indeed, in recent years, many tobacco companies seem to have been targeting young people in their advertising, with considerable success. Some parents and community groups are attempting to make sale of cigarettes to young people more difficult, as well as illegal, on the model of alcohol. Once started smoking, both young people and adults often have difficulty breaking the habit. Once smoking ends, the body begins to regenerate itself in many ways, though some damage can never be undone.

FOR HELP AND FURTHER INFORMATION

Office on Smoking and Health
U.S. Department of Health and Human Services
Centers for Disease Control
Mail Stop K–50
4770 Buford Highway NE
Atlanta, GA 30341–3724
404–488–5705
Fax: 404–488–5939; Fax directory of tobacco, smoking, and health information: 404–332–2552
Federal agency that gathers and summarizes scientific evidence on effects of cigarette smoking; provides information and makes public policy; publishes various materials, including:

- General information: *Smoking, Tobacco, and Health: A Fact Book, Smokeless Tobacco or Health: An International Perspective,* and reports on smoking by youth.
- For children and teens: *SGR 4 Kids Magazine* (with Leader's Guide) and *Spit Tobacco and Youth.*
- On smoking and pregnancy: *Is Your Baby Smoking?* and *Pregnant? That's Two Good Reasons to Quit Smoking.*
- On environmental tobacco smoke: *It's Time to Stop Being a Passive Victim, Reducing the Health Risks of Secondhand Smoke,* and *Respiratory Health Effects of Passive Smoking: A Fact Sheet.*
- On quitting: *Health Benefits of Smoking Cessation: At a Glance, Out of the Ashes,* and *Clearing the Air.*
- Numerous technical and professional materials, including *Smoking and Health Database* on CD-ROM.

American Cancer Society (ACS), 800–227–2345. Publishes numerous materials, including:

- General materials: *Why Start Life Under a Cloud?, The American Cancer Society vs. Mr. Butts, The Decision Is Yours!,* and *The Most Often Asked Questions About Smoking, Tobacco and Health, Tick, Tick, Tick;* and videos *Confessions of a Simple Surgeon* and *Death in the West.*
- For preschool and early elementary children: videos *Dusty the Dragon and Dr. Margie Hogan Talk About Tobacco, The Huffless Puffless Dragon,* and *Smoking: The Choice Is Yours;* and educational kits *Changing the Course, Smokebusters,* and *Starting Free: Good Air for Me.*
- For preteens and teens: videos *I Am Joe's Lung, Breathing Easy, Diary of a Teenage Smoker, Secondhand Smoke, Dirty Business, Tobacco and You: Straight Talk, The Wizard of No, The Big Dipper* (on smokeless tobacco), *The Feminine Mistake: The Next Generation, Let's Call It Quits, Smart Move, Smoke Gets in Your Eyes, Tobacco: The Pushers and Their Victims, Who's in Charge Here?* (on physiological effects), *Coach's Final Lesson* (a coach with lung cancer), *Why Quit Quiz,* and *The Ridiculous History of Tobacco.*

(For full group information, see CANCER.)

National Clearinghouse for Alcohol and Drug Abuse Information (NCADI), 301–468–2600. Publishes *Smoking* ("Tips for Teens" brochure); fact sheet *Alcohol, Tobacco, and Other Drugs and the College Experience,* NIDA Capsule *Cigarette Smoking, Healthy Women/Healthy Lifestyles: Here's What You Should Know About Alcohol, Tobacco, and Other Drugs;* and numerous materials on prevention. (For full group information, see HELP AGAINST SUBSTANCE ABUSE on page 703.)

National Woman's Christian Temperance Union (WCTU), 800–755–1321. Publishes booklets *What Parents Should Know About Teens and Smoking, ABCs of Smoking, How to Quit Smoking, Dangers of Smoking, Smokeless But Not Harmless, Smoking and Its Effects, Up in Smoke, What Everyone Should Know About Smokeless Tobacco, Smoking and Your Heart, Smokeless Tobacco—Chemical Time Bomb,* and *Twelve Steps for Tobacco Users;* and numerous anti-smoking leaflets. (For full group information, see HELP AGAINST SUBSTANCE ABUSE on page 703.)

American Heart Association (AHA), 800–242–8721. Publishes *Children and Smoking: A Message to Parents, Calling It Quits, Smoking and Heart Disease,* and *Cigarette Smoking and Cardiovascular Disease.* (For full group information, see HEART AND HEART PROBLEMS.)

American Council on Science and Health (ACSH), 212–362–7044. Publishes *Issues in Tobacco, Smoking or Health: It's Your Choice,* and reports on tobacco industry marketing. (For full group information, see SAFETY.)

American Academy of Pediatrics (AAP), 800–433–9016. Publishes brochure *Environmental Tobacco Smoke, For Today's Teens—A Message From Your Pediatrician, The Risks of Tobacco Use: A Message to Parents and Teens,* and *Smoking: Straight Talk for Teens.* (For full group information, see HEALTH CARE.)

March of Dimes Birth Defects Foundation (MDBDF), 914–428–7100. Publishes pamphlet *Give Your Baby a Healthy Start: Stop Smoking;* and video *Smoking, Drinking and Drugs.* (For full group information, see BIRTH DEFECTS.)

American Lung Association (ALA), 800–586–4872. Publishes *Freedom From Smoking® in 20 Days, A Lifetime of Freedom From Smoking®, Help A Friend Stop Smoking, Stop Smoking/Stay Trim*; and videocassette *In Control: A Home Video Freedom From Smoking® Program.* (For full group information, see LUNG AND BREATHING DISORDERS.)

National Cancer Institute (NCI), 800–422–6237. Publishes *Clearing the Air: A Guide to Quitting Smoking, I Mind Very Much If You Smoke, Smoking Facts and Quitting Tips, Why Do You Smoke,* and for teens *Chew or Snuff Is Real Bad Stuff.* (For full group information, see CANCER.)

Hazelden Foundation (HF), 800–262–5010. Publishes *Quit and Stay Quit: A Personal Program to Stop Smoking, If Only I Could Quit: Recovering from Nicotine Addiction,* and *Breathing Easy* (4 booklets). (For full group information, see HELP AGAINST SUBSTANCE ABUSE on page 703.)

Narcotic Educational Foundation of America (NEFA), 213–663–5171. Publishes *Tobacco Dangers.* (For full group information, see HELP AGAINST SUBSTANCE ABUSE on page 703.)

National Heart, Lung, and Blood Information Center (NHLBIC), 301–251–1222. (For full group information, see HEART AND HEART PROBLEMS.)

Planned Parenthood Federation of America (PPFA), 800–230–7526. Publishes pamphlet *Smoking and the Pill.* (For full group information, see BIRTH CONTROL.)

American College of Obstetricians and Gynecologists (ACOG), 202–638–5577. Publishes *Smoking and Women.* (For full group information, see PREGNANCY.)

American Council for Drug Education (ACDE), 800–488–3784. Publishes pamphlets *Tobacco* and *Tobacco and Marijuana.* (For full group information, see HELP AGAINST SUBSTANCE ABUSE on page 703.)

Stop Teenage Addiction to Tobacco (STAT)
511 E. Columbus Avenue
Springfield, MA 01105
413–732-STAT [732–7828]
Fax: 413–732–4219
John Slade, President
Organization against youth smoking; provides information; sponsors educational programs; publishes quarterly *Tobacco-Free Youth Reporter, Community Organizers Resource Manual, The STAT Speaker Guide and Slide Collection;* video *Say No to Joe*; and periodic news bulletins and action alerts.

National Women's Resource Center for the Prevention of Alcohol, Tobacco, Other Drug Abuse and Mental Illness, 800–354–8824. (For full group information, see HELP AGAINST SUBSTANCE ABUSE on page 703.)

Narcotic Educational Foundation of America (NEFA), 213–663–5171. Publishes *Tobacco Dangers.* (For full group information, see HELP AGAINST SUBSTANCE ABUSE on page 703.)

National Jewish Center for Immunology and Respiratory Medicine, 800–222-LUNG, US except CO. (For full group information, LUNG AND BREATHING DISORDERS.)

National Families in Action, 404–934–6364. Publishes *You Have the Right to Know* training curriculum on tobacco.

ONLINE RESOURCES

Better Health and Medical Forum (America Online: Health, Medicine) Provides discussion areas and libraries covering smoking. (For full information, see HEALTH CARE.)

OTHER RESOURCES

GENERAL WORKS

Smoking: At Issue. Karin L. Swisher, ed. Greenhaven, 1995.
Let's Ban Smoking Outright!. Patrick Griffin. Ten Speed, 1995.
Smoking: To Be or Not to Be. Robert Horning. Portage, 1993.
Smokeless Tobacco, rev. ed. Do It Now, 1993.
Smoking: The Artificial Passion. David Krogh. W. H. Freeman, 1991.
Dying for a Smoke. David A. Rives. Moon River, 1991.
Smoking: Distinguishing Between Fact and Opinion. Bonnie Szumski. Greenhaven, 1990.

GUIDES TO QUITTING SMOKING

Yes! You Can Stop Smoking: Even If You Don't Want To, rev. ed. David C. Jones. Dolphin, 1995.
A Woman's Way: The Stop Smoking Book for Women. Mary Embree. WRS Group, 1995.
How Women Can Finally Stop Smoking. Robert Klesges and Margaret DeBon. Hunter House, 1994.
No If's, And's, or Butts: A Smoker's Guide to Quitting. Harlan Krumholz and Robert H. Phillips. Avery, 1993.
Stop Smoking Without Putting on Weight. Penny Ross. Thorsons, 1994.
Help Someone You Love Quit Smoking. Katina Z. Jones. Berkley, 1993.
Stop Smoking. Ben Wicks. Longmeadow Press, 1992.
Stop Smoking Forever!: The Easy Way. Arthur A. Hawkins. Information Research Laboratory, 1992.
Butt Out: A Guide to Helping a Loved One or Friend Kick the Smoking Habit; Part. 2: A Guide to Helping Yourself Kick the Smoking Habit. David O. Antonuccio. R & E Publishers, 1992.

The Unhooked Celebration: How to Stop Smoking and Start Living. Ed Golden. Dorrance, 1992.
Out of the Ashes: Help for People Who Have Stopped Smoking. Peter Holmes and Peggy Holmes. Fairview Press, 1992.

ON STAYING SMOKE-FREE

Non-Smoker for Life. Mary J. Stevens and Harry Alexander. Carlton, 1995.
Eat, Drink and Sleep Smoke-Free. Catherine Mooney, ed. Seven Hills, 1995.
Growing up Tobacco Free: Preventing Nicotine Addiction in Children and Youths. Barbara S. Lynch and Richard J. Bonnie, eds. National Academy Press, 1994.

FOR CHILDREN

The Gladden Book about Tobacco. Marnie Starbuck. W. Gladden, 1994.
No Smoking: Do You Mind If I Don't Smoke? Toni Goffe. Child's Play, 1992.
Focus on Nicotine and Caffeine. Robert Perry. Twenty-First Century Books, 1991.

FOR PRETEENS AND TEENS

Everything You Need to Know about Smoking, rev. ed. Elizabeth Keyishian, Rosen, 1995.
Caffeine and Nicotine. Richard S. Lee and Mary P. Lee. Rosen, 1994.
Nicotine. Judy Monroe. Enslow, 1994.
Tobacco. Philip Cohen. Raintree Steck-Vaughn, 1991.
Know About Smoking, rev. ed. Margaret O. Hyde. Walker, 1990.

BACKGROUND WORKS

Smoking: The Artificial Passion. David Krogh. W. H. Freeman, 1995.
The Facts about Smoking. Consumer Reports, 1991.

(See also CANCER; HEART AND HEART PROBLEMS.)

social age, a kind of converted AGE-EQUIVALENT SCORE that results from the VINELAND SOCIAL MATURITY SCALE.

Social Security, a wide range of social service and health programs operated by the federal agency formally called the Social Security Administration (SSA). The programs include Medicare, Medicaid, the SUPPLEMENTAL SECURITY INCOME (SSI) PROGRAM, and various maternal and child health services, such as the Children's Special Health Care Needs (CSHCN) Program.

Traditionally most people obtained a Social Security card in their teens or later, enrolling them in the payment-and-pension system established in the 1930s. But since 1991, parents have needed to obtain a Social Security number for every child at birth, if they wish to be able to receive the deduction allowed for dependents on their income tax. Parents can do this by visiting their local Social Security Administration or Internal Revenue Service (IRS) office, bringing with them the child's birth certificate (the original, with raised seal, not a photocopy) and another piece of identification. At the office, they should ask for the Application for a Social Security Number (Form SS–5); to get the form ahead of time, they can call their local Social Security Office. Processing of the application takes about two weeks. Parents will be given an application receipt; if the infant's Social Security number does not arrive before the parents' tax return needs to be filed, a copy of the receipt should be attached with the notation "applied for" on the return. Note: Some parents have received official-looking mail offers to obtain an infant's Social Security number for a $15 "administration fee." This is totally unofficial and unnecessary.

Low-income families—with income below the amount specified by current law—also need Social Security numbers for their children, so they can receive Earned Income Credits from the Internal Revenue Service (IRS) when they file their tax returns. If money is owed on the tax return, these credits may be subtracted from the amount due; but if no taxes are owed, parents may receive these credits as payments. Credits may also be available for a child born during that tax year. Details of such programs vary from year to year.

social skills, skills regarded as necessary for normal interaction with others; in infants, this involves first attending to, responding to, and imitating others, and then gradually playing and sharing with others. A CHART OF NORMAL DEVELOPMENT (on page 000) indicates when between birth and age six children first *on the average* begin to develop the main social skills.

Children with MENTAL DISORDERS, LEARNING DISABILITIES, and some other DEVELOPMENTAL DISORDERS, sometimes have problems with social skills, ranging from aggressiveness to withdrawal. They may have difficulty making friends, get easily overexcited, cling excessively, and have strong mood swings. Some may be easily distracted, moving from one place to another without becoming involved in any activity, while others may focus on one activity, refusing to let others join them. Difficulty with social skills often go hand-in-hand with problems in other areas, such as VISUAL SKILLS, AUDITORY SKILLS, and communication skills (see COMMUNICATION SKILLS AND DISORDERS).

Children develop at individual and varying paces, but every child can benefit from activities designed to enhance their natural development, as in imitating speech and body language. (Subscribers to the America Online computer service can find activities designed to develop children's skills in various areas, including social and communication skills, in the Moms Online Desk Reference section of Moms Online, under "Teaching Young Children.")

OTHER RESOURCES

Wanna Be My Friend?: How to Strengthen Your Child's Social Skills. Leanne Domash and Judith Sachs. Hearst, 1994.

Getting Kids to Mix. Len Woods. SP Publications, 1993.

A Parents' Guide to Promoting Social Skill Development During Infancy and Toddlerhood. Michael K. Meyerhoff. W. Gladden, 1992.

social worker, a professional working with a public or private agency, charged with helping people cope with personal, emotional, or social problems, or the effects of medical problems, and seeing that people get the social and other services available to them, often acting as advocate for individuals or families in working with government agencies, schools, clinics, preschool programs, and the like (see ADVOCACY). *Psychiatric social workers* specialize in working with people with MENTAL DISORDERS, and some are trained to work as PSYCHOTHERAPISTS. *Medical social workers* counsel people in a HOSPITAL setting, helping them deal with problems posed by severe illness or DISABILITY. Social workers often make up part of the team reviewing reports of suspected CHILD ABUSE AND NEGLECT.

sodium, a MINERAL that is extremely important in maintaining water and ELECTROLYTE balance in the body and proper functioning of the nerves and muscles. In the kitchen, sodium is usually found as sodium chloride (table salt, today often with IODINE added) or sodium bicarbonate (baking soda). Most foods contain some sodium, but it is especially abundant in processed foods, ham, cheese, breads and cereals, and meats, fish, and vegetables that have been smoked, pickled, or cured, as well as in water treated with water softener.

Salt deficiency is rare in Western countries, except in abnormal circumstances, as with excessive use of diuretic drugs, persistent DIARRHEA or VOMITING, or certain disorders such as CYSTIC FIBROSIS, ADRENAL GLAND problems, or kidney disorders (see KIDNEY AND UROLOGICAL PROBLEMS), since the kidney controls the level of sodium in the blood. Too little sodium can cause muscle cramps, weakness, and headache, and severe deficiency can lead to low BLOOD PRESSURE, confusion, and fainting. In the West, excess sodium is far more common, and most dietitians urge restraint adding sodium to foods, and stress that people should check manufactured foods for their level of sodium. Too much sodium can lead to *hypertension* (high BLOOD PRESSURE), EDEMA (water buildup), kidney damage, and heart disease (see HEART AND HEART PROBLEMS). (See MINERALS; NUTRITION.)

soft signs, observations that less clearly indicate CENTRAL NERVOUS SYSTEM malfunctions than do HARD SIGNS; a term NEUROLOGISTS sometimes use when talking about a child with LEARNING DISABILITIES or other DEVELOPMENTAL DISORDERS.

soiling, inability to control bowel movements fully, deliberate holding in of feces, or defecation somewhere other than in a toilet; medically called *encopresis.* Encopresis generally refers to otherwise physically normal children who have passed the usual age by which bowel control is normally achieved; by contrast, inability to control bowel movements by children with physical DISABILITIES is called INCONTINENCE.

Since bowel movements are generally easier for young children to control than urination, encopresis is much rarer than BEDWETTING (*enuresis*). An occasional "accident," especially when a child has DIARRHEA, may occur in a child who normally has bowel control, and many young children go through a brief period of resisting use of the toilet for defecation. However, encopresis refers to persistent problems involving defecation in diapers, underpants, in "private places" such as corners—in short, at times and places other than adults wish.

Unlike bedwetting, which many children outgrow, encopresis often seems to stem from emotional problems and parent-child battles that center around TOILET TRAINING. It may require deliberate changing of parental tactics and parent-child dynamics, often with the help of health professionals, if the child is not to develop a distorted self-image and become socially isolated. Parents need to be supportive and to try to defuse any parent-child conflict—anger and scorn are counter-productive here—but help and therapy are important. Chronic "holding-in" of feces can also cause CONSTIPATION and other physical problems. Soiling can sometimes occur in older children who have previously shown bowel control, and may signal digestive disorders or emotional disturbance. Psychiatrists class enuresis and encopresis as *elimination disorders.*

FOR HELP AND FURTHER INFORMATION

American Academy of Child and Adolescent Psychiatry (AACAP), 202–966–7300. Publishes information sheet *Problems with Soiling and Bowel Control.* (For full group information, see MENTAL DISORDERS.)

OTHER RESOURCES

Childhood Encopresis and Enuresis: Causes and Therapy. Charles E. Schaefer. Aronson, 1993.

(See also TOILET TRAINING; INCONTINENCE; DIGESTIVE SYSTEM AND DISORDERS; MENTAL DISORDERS.)

solid foods, nutritious substances other than fluids, which are generally introduced as supplements to infants after four to six months. By this time babies have usually matured enough be able to sit up with some help and have some control over the head and neck, including tongue and lips. They can also indicate when they do and do not want to eat.

The first solid foods given to infants are hardly "solid" at all, being generally cooked cereals and pureed

Starting on Solid Foods

Whenever you decide to start "solids" or spoon foods, here are a few guidelines that will help you:

- *After six months, your baby needs more than breastmilk or formula.* About 6 to 8 breastfeedings or 25 to 32 ounces of formula a day provide enough milk for your baby at this age. Let your baby fill up on other foods.
- *Start slowly:* A few spoonfuls once or twice a day of the same food is enough at first. This food should be very thin (liquid) and smooth. The baby's main nutrition should still come from breastmilk or formula, but spoon-feeding semi-solid foods and sips of water and juice from a cup gives both parents and baby a good opportunity to learn about each other. Fathers should try to share in this baby-feeding time.
- *Try just one new food at a time:* Feed the new food every day for several days. Start with simple, pure foods. For example, use pure rice cereal, not mixed cereal; applesauce, not fruit dessert; chicken or turkey, not meat dinner. Some new foods may cause vomiting, diarrhea, or skin rash in a few infants. By starting only one new food every four or five days, and by using simple, single foods, you will know which food is the cause. Once your baby has eaten a food for three or four days without any ill effects, you can use it in the future without worrying.
- *Choose new foods from each of these food groups:*

  Fruits, fruit juices.
  Vegetables (including at least 1 serving of a pureed leafy green vegetable).
  Meat, fish, poultry, egg yolk, cheese.
  Bread, cereal, rice, crackers, pasta (wheat products are usually not recommended before eight or nine months of age).

- *Feed your baby a variety of foods.* Once you know which foods your baby can eat, the best way to be sure that baby gets what he or she needs is to be sure you satisfy your baby's appetite for a wide variety of foods. In any two to three day period, in addition to breastmilk or formula, a baby should have several servings (mashed or pureed) from each of the above food groups.
- *Don't feed your baby honey until he or she is one year old,* to avoid the possibility of botulism.
- *Do not give your baby candy, cookies, sugar, sweet desserts, and soft drinks.* They don't provide the nutrients your baby needs, they may spoil baby's appetite for healthier foods, and they are bad for your baby's teeth.
- *You can tell if a food is not being digested properly if it comes through in bowel movements.* If it does, chop it finer or use other foods.
- *When feeding your baby "table food" (that you prepare for the entire family), be sure it doesn't contain chunks or stringy, fibrous parts that can choke a baby.* Don't give your baby small foods such as raisins, grapes, cut-up hot dogs, peanuts, or popcorn, hard foods such as raw vegetables, or sticky foods such as peanut butter—which can cause choking. Watch out for strings on celery and green beans.
- *Encourage your baby to feed him- or herself.* Babies enjoy using their fingers to feed themselves foods such as crackers, bits of bread or toast, bits of cheese or meat, small bits of soft fruits or vegetables.
- *Let your baby try drinking from a cup at five or six months.* Put just a little liquid (even breastmilk) in the bottom of the cup at first. Then increase the amount as your baby learns to drink out of it.
- *Let your baby help you handle the spoon.* One parent should sit behind the baby so that he or she can hold onto the spoon or the parent's hand and learn the movements needed to eat without help. This may slow you down and make a mess, but your baby will learn to eat without your help sooner. Heavy plastic bibs and washable plastic or newspapers under the high chair will help control the mess.
- *By one year, your baby will probably be able to eat most of what the rest of the family eats.* Someone will still have to mash up some of the vegetables and cut meat, chicken, or fish into tiny bites. You should still avoid the small foods (such as raisins, grapes, chopped hot dogs, peanuts, popcorn) until your child is 3 or 4 years old and able to chew and swallow these foods without fear of choking.

Source: Infant Care (1989). Prepared by the Bureau of Maternal and Child Health and Resources Development for the Public Health Service.

fruits, vegetables, and meats, also called *spoon foods.* The Public Health Service notes: "There is nothing special about the foods that are sold as baby foods except that they are finely strained and convenient," adding that they are "especially expensive for their limited food value." They note that, with a blender or masher (even just a fork), parents can make their own baby foods out of most plain, simple foods prepared for the rest of the family, with the addition of a little water. *The Surgeon General's Report on Nutrition and Health* agrees, noting: "If properly prepared and stored, pureed foods made at home are nutritionally equivalent to those prepared commercially." They add some cautions, however:

- Do not add salt, butter, FAT, sugar, other seasonings, or sauces.
- Use or refrigerate home-prepared baby food immediately (except spinach, beets, and carrots, which should not be stored).
- If you plan to store it for more than twenty-four hours, try storing it in individual portions (as in an ice cube tray).
- Use only fruits and vegetables from cans especially made for infants; others may contain too much salt, sugar, or possible LEAD.
- Do not heat food (or baby bottles) for your baby in a microwave oven. They heat food unevenly, making some parts cold, some warm, and some hot enough to burn the baby.

Ready-cooked iron-fortified infant cereals are also easy to prepare and should be part of the baby's diet every day until about 18 months of age. By the time the baby is a year old, solid foods should provide more than 50 percent of their energy intake.

The whole process of gradually substituting solid foods for BREASTFEEDING or BOTTLEFEEDING is called *weaning.* Though it generally starts during the middle of the first year and is often complete by the end of the first year, some parents and children continue to have breast or bottle as part of the emotional picture well beyond that, though they play a decreasing role nutritionally.

Later the types of foods offered and eaten will follow a more widely varied pattern, depending on family life style and individual preferences, though working within the guidelines of basic NUTRITION needs and some overall general patterns, related to age level and growth. (See EATING PATTERNS IN CHILDREN on page 435.) A child's appetite, for example, will decrease sharply between ages two and four, as growth needs diminish. However, loss of appetite, medically called *anorexia,* can be a sign of a disease, so the parents should watch for any such changes and, if appropriate, see the doctor or clinic.

If the child seems healthy and normal, apart from lack of appetite, some doctors advise parents not to try to keep up the child's caloric intake, which can develop into a running battle with the child, but to concentrate on seeing that the child has at least some protein, fruit, and, if possible, vegetables to meet basic needs for nutrients. Parents should also recognize that some kinds of food dislikes are based on as-yet-unrecognized mild ALLERGIES or FOOD INTOLERANCES, and so (within reason) they should respect a child's desire to avoid certain foods, and should be on the lookout for possible ill effects following specific types of foods (see STARTING ON SOLID FOODS on page 559). Where children are old enough to communicate verbally, they should listen carefully to what children say about how they feel after eating certain kinds of foods.

Children can also develop, anywhere from early in childhood to late in their teens, a variety of digestive disorders (see DIGESTIVE SYSTEM AND DISORDERS), METABOLIC DISORDERS (involving inability to break down certain kinds of nutrients in the body), and eating disorders, such as ANOREXIA NERVOSA, BULIMIA, and BINGE EATING DISORDER. Children with certain kinds of CHRONIC illnesses, such as DIABETES, may also have eating patterns forced on them by the need to follow special diets.

FOR HELP AND FURTHER INFORMATION

Poor Eaters: Helping Children Who Refuse to Eat. Joel Macht. Plenum, 1990.

Solving Your Child's Eating Problems. Jane Hirschmann and Lela Zaphiropoulos. Fawcett/Columbine, 1990. Formerly titled *Are You Hungry?*

(See also NUTRITION; and other specific topics noted above.)

solvent abuse, inhalation of intoxicating fumes of certain volatile liquids or aerosol sprays, which produces an effect similar to an alcohol- or drug-induced "high." Some of the solvents used are toxic and can harm the air passages, kidneys, liver, and NERVOUS SYSTEM. Of more immediate danger, they can cause COMA and death, either directly by physical effects on the heart or indirectly, as by injuries from a fall or suffocation from lack of oxygen in the plastic bag often used during inhalation. (For an overview of the effects and signs of solvent and other substance abuse, plus organizations, reference works, and recommendations for parents, see HELP AGAINST SUBSTANCE ABUSE on page 703.)

sound-symbol association, the ability to recognize sounds and their origins, and to recognize that sounds go with letters, a key PREREQUISITE skill for READING.

spatial orientation, the ability to understand one's position in space, and the relationship between the self and objects nearby; one aspect of this is FORM CONSTANCY, the ability to recognize an object or shape, regardless of what position or angle it is viewed from. A child with LEARNING DISABILITIES or some other kinds of DEVELOPMENTAL DISORDERS may demonstrate problems of spatial orientation in being unable to recognize a toy or shape when it is placed in a different position, such as upside down, or fail to recognize a familiar object when it appears in a picture, rather than in three-dimensional form. Spatial orientation is closely linked to both MOTOR SKILLS and VISUAL SKILLS.

spatial relations, the ability to judge the relationship of objects to each other and to oneself; closely linked to both MOTOR SKILLS and VISUAL SKILLS. Children with LEARNING DISABILITIES or other DEVELOPMENTAL DISORDERS may have difficulty in judging when they need to duck or crawl under a rope or table, for example, or may consistently try to put an object into too small a box. Children with spatial relations problems often have trouble putting on clothes, going up and down stairs, fitting lids on boxes, putting keys in locks, riding a tricycle, or coordinating arm movements to throw a ball in the desired direction. Problems in such areas can lead to fear of heights, hesitation of movement, and difficulty in assessing the extent and direction of a movement needed to carry out a task.

special education, the training and teaching of children with SPECIAL NEEDS, those who have mental or physical needs and characteristics requiring attention beyond that given to most children. This includes children with MENTAL RETARDATION or MENTAL DISORDERS, GIFTED CHILDREN, those with physical DISABILITIES, including LEARNING DISABILITIES, and those whose cultural background (such as a different family language or socioeconomic disadvantage) requires COMPENSATORY EDUCATION.

Materials and methods of instruction in special education programs are adapted to the child's individual needs. For those children covered under the EDUCATION FOR ALL THE HANDICAPPED CHILDREN ACT and its successor, the INDIVIDUALS WITH DISABILITIES EDUCATION ACT (IDEA), the school in cooperation with parents makes up INDIVIDUALIZED EDUCATION PROGRAMS (IEPs). Special education teachers, sometimes called VISITING TEACHERS (*itinerant* or *resource teachers*), are often employed by school districts or regions to serve several schools, helping to plan long-term and short-term IEPs for each child, working directly with the children, and advising the rest of the school staff, as well as the parents.

Under SECTION 504 of the 1973 Rehabilitation Act, children with disabilities are supposed to be educated in regular classes wherever possible, an approach called MAINSTREAMING or more widely, *inclusion.* Where that is not possible, special students are to be grouped in separate classes, either separately by the type of disability (such as learning disabilities or blindness) or all grouped together as children with exceptional needs.

Whether placement is in separate classes or integrated into regular classrooms, parents will have to carefully monitor their child's progress. Some students will benefit greatly from mainstreaming, especially if there are sufficient and appropriate support services, while others fail to learn and grow properly in an integrated setting. (See HELP FOR SPECIAL CHILDREN, on page 689; see also EDUCATION.)

special needs, in EDUCATION, a term describing the requirements of children who cannot be well served by regular school programs and need SPECIAL EDUCATION or ADAPTED EDUCATION to develop their fullest potential. Children with special needs include GIFTED CHILDREN, who have unusual and superior talents, and children with various DISABILITIES, including LEARNING DISABILITIES, MENTAL RETARDATION, and MENTAL DISORDERS, as well as cultural or socioeconomic disadvantages that require COMPENSATORY EDUCATION. (See HELP FOR SPECIAL CHILDREN on page 689.)

Special Supplemental Food Program for Women, Infants, and Children (WIC), a program operated under the U.S. Department of Agriculture that is intended to help poor women and children who might otherwise not have sufficient NUTRITION to maintain proper health and functioning.

specific developmental disorder, a psychiatric classification for LEARNING DISABILITIES and communication disorders (see COMMUNICATION SKILLS AND COMMUNICATIONS DISORDERS).

Specific Language Disability Tests, a series of tests used as DEVELOPMENTAL SCREENING TESTS for LEARNING DISABILITIES in the area of language; also called the *Malcomesius Test.* Given individually or in groups, the various subtests attempt to highlight problems in LANGUAGE SKILLS, VISUAL SKILLS, AUDITORY SKILLS, and comprehension. Widely used in schools, the Malcomesius Test is used to screen for children who may need further DIAGNOSTIC ASSESSMENT TESTS or might benefit from REMEDIAL INSTRUCTION. (See TESTS.)

specific learning disability, a kind of LEARNING DISABILITY that affects just one area or kind of skills, but not other areas; sometimes called *specific developmental disorders.* For example, a child may have DYSCALCULIA, difficulty in working with mathematical symbols, but have no difficulties in other areas of learning.

specimen test, a general type of MEDICAL TEST which involves taking samples of urine, blood, saliva, stool, and other fluids, waste, and tissue from the body for analysis. The characteristics of normal body substances are well known, so laboratory analysis can indicate whether the patient's sample is markedly different from the norm, and if so, by what measure. If a needle is inserted into a vein and blood withdrawn into a syringe or a CATHETER, the procedure is called *venipuncture.* If a fluid sample is taken from the body using a hollow *aspiration needle,* it is called *centesis,* as in the PRENATAL TEST AMNIOCENTESIS. If a tissue sample is taken from the body using a similar hollow needle, the procedure is called a BIOPSY. (See MEDICAL TESTS.)

speech disorders, difficulties in actually producing the sounds of the language, often because of malfunctioning in the brain or inability to properly control the muscles needed to produce the sounds. (See COMMUNICATION SKILLS AND DISORDERS.)

speech-language pathologist, a specialist who diagnoses and treats communication disorders in children or adults, often working in schools with children referred by AUDIOLOGISTS, teachers, or other professionals; also called a *speech therapist* or *speech clinician.* After obtaining a full history from parents and teachers, the speech-language pathologist generally meets with a child, frequently in a play setting, to informally observe the child, and then gives a variety of tests to assess the child's ability to understand and produce speech. During SCREENING TESTS, the speech-language pathologist may ask the child to draw pictures, say words, manipulate and name objects, describe pictures, repeat sentences, answer questions, or tell a story. On the basis of the results, the speech-language pathologist will design a program of therapy, which may involve special training programs; referral to another specialist, such as an audiologist, PSYCHOLOGIST, or OTOLARYNGOLOGIST; guidance for parents; and suggestions for teachers of the child. (See COMMUNICATION SKILLS AND DISORDERS.)

speechreading (lipreading), a method of understanding spoken language through visual clues, such as the position of the jaw, lips, and tongue. Commonly used by people who have EAR AND HEARING PROBLEMS, speechreading requires considerable training to learn and even then has limited effectiveness alone, because less than half of the common words in spoken English can be interpreted by lip movements alone. However, speechreading can help enormously to supplement a person's residual hearing. Its value is enhanced when speakers use CUED SPEECH, exaggerating their lip movements and using finger signs for particular sounds that are otherwise easily confused, such as "p" and "b."

sperm, the male sex cell which unites with the female egg (OVUM), normally in the FALLOPIAN TUBES, in the process of FERTILIZATION, to form a fertilized egg, or ZYGOTE. More formally called spermatozoa (singular: spermatozoon), sperm are manufactured in the TESTES and matured in the EPIDIDYMIS (a "holding area" behind the testes). Sperm production is the key sign of male sexual maturity, beginning in PUBERTY.

Normally released by the millions into a woman's VAGINA in SEMEN during EJACULATION as part of sexual intercourse, the sperm must make their way through a formidable series of obstacles:

- *The vagina,* where most are killed by acidic secretions.
- *The* CERVIX, which secretes a hostile mucus, though around the time of OVULATION it is somewhat more hospitable to the sperm's entry; many sperm also become entrapped in the walls of the cervix.
- *The* UTERUS, a relatively vast expanse to cross, compared to the size of the microscopic sperm.
- *The Fallopian tubes,* where yet more mucus-covered walls wait to entrap sperm.
- *The egg,* guarded by two tough outer layers that must be penetrated.

The sperm are equipped with some tools to make their way through this obstacle course. While the vital genetic material is packed into the sperm's head, each sperm develops a tadpole-like tail, to help it "swim upstream" to the egg. Also, under a protective screen, the sperm carry a load of chemicals that, on arrival at the egg, help it to make its way through the egg's protective layers.

The whole journey takes one to a few hours, if all goes well, though the sperm can remain alive and active in the Fallopian tube for up to forty-eight hours. In the end, only a few thousand sperm of the many millions ejaculated survive even to reach the egg. Then one, and only one, can successfully fertilize the egg.

In some cases, the number of sperm in a man's semen (*sperm count*) is too low or the sperm lack sufficient propulsion to make their way through to the egg. Various studies give evidence of a decline in sperm concentration in otherwise healthy fertile men in recent years; suggestions of causes include exposure to ESTROGEN or related compounds in the womb or environmental pollution. The acidity of a woman's reproductive organs can also defeat the sperm. In such instances of reduced fertility or INFERTILITY, other alternatives for FERTILIZATION may be tried, such as IN VITRO FERTILIZATION and ARTIFICIAL INSEMINATION. (See PREGNANCY; INFERTILITY.)

spermatocele, a sperm-filled swelling in the EPIDIDYMIS, the SPERM "holding area" behind the TESTES. If the spermatocele grows large and painful, surgery may be indicated, though the result may be INFERTILITY on the side operated on.

sperm bank, a privately run organization that collects SPERM from donors, sometimes for a fee, and sells it to women or doctors for use in ARTIFICIAL INSEMINATION. Such banks generally gather full medical histories from the donors, in case the mother then or later wish such information, but the donor's identity is usually kept confidential, except where both the donee requests and the donor agrees to reveal it. (See ARTIFICIAL INSEMINATION.)

spermicide, a form of BIRTH CONTROL using various substances—including contraceptive foams, creams, jellies, gels, and suppositories—that contain ingredients designed to kill SPERM, notably *nonoxynol–9* or *octoxynol.* The Food and Drug Administration (FDA) rates that spermicides used alone are only 70–80 percent effective as contraceptives; however, they are generally used with a DIAPHRAGM,

CERVICAL CAP, CONDOM, or contraceptive SPONGE, for a far more effective combination. Spermicides also somewhat reduce the risk of contracting SEXUALLY TRANSMITTED DISEASES, though they should not be considered protection against AIDS.

The spermicide needs to be placed in the woman's VAGINA no more than an hour before sexual intercourse, forming a chemical and something of a physical barrier to sperm, and must be left in place (without DOUCHING) for at least six hours after intercourse.

Spermicides can cause allergic reactions in the woman or her sex partner. They are also alleged to cause BIRTH DEFECTS if a woman continues using them after becoming pregnant (generally before she realizes it). In one such case, a woman brought a court suit against a spermicide manufacturer for birth defects in her child. The judge ruled in favor of the woman and her child. However, the FDA said it had not found scientific data to support an association between spermicides and birth defects, though it continued to monitor the situation. Parents considering use of spermicides for themselves or their children should check with their doctor or clinic for the most current information. (See also BIRTH CONTROL.)

spina bifida, a general name for a group of CONGENITAL abnormalities that result when the membrane-and-tissue-covered "tube" housing the CENTRAL NERVOUS SYSTEM fails to close completely during an EMBRYO's development; literally "cleft spine." Medically, this group of disorders is often called *neural tube defects.* Defects can occur anywhere along the spine, but are most common in the lower back. The precise causes of spina bifida are unclear, but both genetic inheritance and environmental influences seem to be involved.

Genetic connections are suggested by the facts that a parent who has one child with spina bifida has an increased risk of having another with the same problem; that more female than male babies are born with the disorders; that rates of spina bifida are lower among some groups (notably Blacks, Asians, and Ashkenazi Jews) than in others (notably White and Egyptians). Environmental connections are suggested by the widely different rates of spina bifida in various geographical areas. In the United States, 1–2 newborns out of 1000 have spina bifida, with rates being higher in the eastern and southern states than in the West; but in western Great Britain and Ireland, the rate is twice that, and some decades ago the rate was 8 out of every 1000. Inadequate maternal NUTRITION has long been suspected, especially because spina bifida is most common among families living in POVERTY and in babies conceived in winter and early spring, when fresh foods are less available. Indeed, studies have shown that women who took the B vitamin FOLIC ACID before conception and during part of PREGNANCY had ⅓ the rate of spina bifida compared to women who did not. That has led to widespread recommendations that women take folic acid (see NUTRITION). Other environmental influences may also be at work, such as deficiencies of other VITAMINS or MINERALS, notably zinc, and chemicals or drugs that decrease the availability of folic acid in the body, notably valproic acid, an anticonvulsant drug taken by people with EPILEPSY.

The main types of spina bifida, from the mildest to the most serious, are:

- *Spina bifida occulta,* which involves a small incomplete closure, but without damage to the spinal cord, occurring in approximately 5 percent or more of the population. The defect is so minor that many people do not know they have it (hence the name *occulta,* or hidden). Externally the site of the defect may be marked by a dimple, tuft of hair, or TELANGIECTASIA (redness from expanded blood vessels). Sometimes it produces urinary or bowel problems, and weakness and poor circulation in the legs.
- *Meningocele,* in which the MENINGES, the membrane covering the spinal cord, pushes out through an abnormal opening in the vertebrae. This forms a sac (*-cele*), which appears externally as a bulge, but the spinal cord itself is not damaged and skin covers the sac. Usually meningocele can be easily repaired by surgery, often during the first few days of life.
- *Myelomeningocele,* in which nerve and tissue from the spinal cord itself protrudes into the sac, which may or may not be covered externally with skin. This most severe form is what many people call simply *spina bifida.* To physicians, the meningocele and myelomeningocele together are sometimes called *spina bifida manifesta,* since signs of it are externally obvious. Among the effects of myelomeningocele may be muscle weakness, loss of sensation, or PARALYSIS below the defect, loss of bladder and bowel control (INCONTINENCE), and buildup of the CEREBROSPINAL FLUID that normally circulates within the spinal cord and brain. This fluid buildup often leads to a condition called HYDROCEPHALUS ("water on the brain"), which may need to be relieved by a SHUNT, to avoid possible neurological damage, including blindness, deafness, SEIZURES, and LEARNING DISABILITIES.

Two related neural tube defects include:

- ENCEPHALOCELE, the bulging of part of the brain through a defect in the skull, causing at least severe brain damage and exposure to infection.
- ANENCEPHALY, the absence of a brain or spinal cord, in which the skull does not close and only a groove appears where the spine should be, a condition from which the child soon dies.

As part of GENETIC SCREENING, various PRENATAL TESTS can be used to try to assess whether a FETUS has neural tube defects, including ALPHA FETO-PROTEIN, ULTRASOUND, and AMNIOCENTESIS. Prospective parents may want to seek GENETIC COUNSELING, especially those with any history of such defects in their families.

In the past, most children with myelomeningocele died soon after birth, but now surgery performed in the first few days after birth allows many of them to survive. They generally require a series of operations during their growing years, however, and often need ORTHOPEDIC DEVICES to aid their mobility. In their brochure, *Spina Bifida: Hope Through Research*, the National Institute of Neurological Diseases and Stroke (NINDS) suggests:

> Physicians recommend that a child with spina bifida be encouraged to progress as normally as possible with the development of motor skills. Between six months and one year, all children should sit; by 12 to 18 months, they should begin to crawl and explore their surroundings. Around age one and a half children should be encouraged to stand—even those with high thoracic [chest] damage who will eventually have to use a wheelchair. Standing reduces osteoporosis (a thinning of the bones that results from inactivity and increases the risk of fractures), improves bladder and bowel function, and strengthens the heart and upper body. Parents should also encourage 18-month-olds to walk.

There are a variety of devices to help spina bifida patients attain these developmental milestones. A wheeled device called a chariot, which moves when the sitting child rolls wheels by hand, helps patients who have trouble crawling. Standing appliances provide total body support so a child can be upright without crutches. The swivel-walker allows a child to shift weight from side to side in a movement that propels the patient forward. A recently developed long-leg brace helps children walk by propelling their legs forward. Mobility varies according to the level of the child's defect.

Many children with myelomeningocele also need special training to learn to manage their bowels and bladder, to prevent possibly serious bladder infections and kidney deteriorations. This special training sometimes involves children, from an early age, learning to insert into their own urethras CATHETERS, or tubes to allow passage of urine (for more information, see CLEAN, INTERMITTENT CATHETERIZATION). Courts in various states have ruled that such children should be able to perform such catheterization (or if they are too young, have it performed by the school nurse) in their schools in order to take advantage of SPECIAL EDUCATION services. In older children, where CIC has proved ineffective, an artifical device is sometimes implanted within the body to control urination. Bowel functions are controlled with more difficulty, often by a combination of special diets and schedules, medication, and enemas, which carry the additional hazard of possible ALLERGY to latex used in the tips of enema bottles.

Children with spina bifida also often lack sensation, leaving them vulnerable to cuts, BURNS, and resulting infections, and sometimes pressure sores that become ulcers. Many also develop spinal disorders such as SCOLIOSIS or KYPHOSIS, and sometimes EYE AND VISION PROBLEMS, such as *strabismus* (potentially serious crossed eyes). Many children gain excess weight, because of decreased mobility, and have some difficulty with fine MOTOR SKILLS. NINDS estimates that 70 percent of the children with spina bifida have normal IQ; the rest have some MENTAL RETARDATION, often caused by hydrocephalus, MENINGITIS, or ventriculitis (infection of the VENTRICLES in the brain). Many have some kinds of LEARNING DISABILITIES, such as poor VISUAL-MOTOR INTEGRATION.

Today, children with myelomeningocele usually attend regular schools. They are generally covered under the EDUCATION FOR ALL HANDICAPPED CHILDREN ACT (EHC) and its successor the INDIVIDUAL WITH DISABILITIES EDUCATION ACT (IDEA), which provides that they should have access to educational services in the LEAST RESTRICTIVE ENVIRONMENT they are able to function in.

Apart from these problems, children with spina bifida develop as normal children do, going through the normal sexual changes of PUBERTY, dealing with the trials of ADOLESCENCE, and preparing for adulthood. Many are able to function as sexual adults, though some (especially males) experience problems because of nerve damage. A woman with spina bifida can bear children, though with some difficulty. The NINDS estimates, however, that she has a 4–5 percent chance of bearing a child with the same defect. Parents of children with spina bifida will require a good deal of information and support, much of it being provided by organizations such as those listed below or under HELP FOR SPECIAL CHILDREN on page 689.

FOR HELP AND FURTHER INFORMATION

Spina Bifida Association of America (SBAA)
4590 MacArthur Boulevard NW, Suite 250
Washington, DC 20007
202–944–3285; 800–621–3141
Fax: 202–944–3295
E-mail: spinabifda@aol.com (America Online: SPINABIFDA)
Lawrence C. Pencak, Executive Director
Organization concerned with spina bifida; sponsors research; acts as advocate; publishes bimonthly newsletter *Insights*, brochure *A Simple Vitamin Can Help Avoid Birth Defects, Friends in the Park* (for children), and other materials, including:

- Books: *An Introduction to Spina Bifida, Answering Your Questions About Spina Bifida, Sexuality and the Person with Spina Bifida, Healthcare Guidelines 1995, Confronting the Challenges of Spina Bifida, Taking Charge: Teenagers Talk About Life and Physical Disabilities,* and *Social Development and the Person with Spina Bifida.*
- Spotlights: *Genetics of Neural Tube Defects, Hip Function and Ambulation, Latex (Natural Rubber) Allergy in Spina Bifida Patients, Sexual Issues in Spina Bifida, Urologic Care of the Child with Spina Bifida,* and *The Chiari Malformation.*
- Videos: *The Challenge*; and conference proceedings.

Shriner's Hospitals for Crippled Children, 800–237–5055. Provides free medical care for children with orthopedic problems. (For full group information, see BONE AND BONE DISORDERS.)

National Information Center for Children and Youth with Disabilities (NICHCY), 800–695–0285, voice/TT. Publishes *Spina Bifida.* (For full group information, see HELP FOR SPECIAL CHILDREN on page 689.)

National Institute of Neurological Disorders and Stroke (NINDS), 800–352–9424. Publishes brochure *Spina Bifida: Hope Through Research.* (For full group information, see BRAIN AND BRAIN DISORDERS.)

March of Dimes Birth Defects Foundation (MDBDF), 914–428–7100. Publishes information sheet *Spina Bifida.* (For full group information, see BIRTH DEFECTS.)

National Easter Seal Society, 800–221–6827. Publishes *Understanding Spina Bifida.* (For full group information, see HELP FOR SPECIAL CHILDREN on page 000.)

National Spinal Cord Injury Association (NSCIA), 800–962–9629 (For full group information, see SPINAL CORD INJURY.)

National Maternal and Child Health Clearinghouse (NMCHC), 703–821–8955 (For full group information, see PREGNANCY.)

National Organization for Rare Disorders (NORD), 800–999–6673. (For full group information, see RARE DISORDERS.)

The Arc, 817–261–6003. Publishes fact sheet *Prevention of Neural Tube Defects.* (For full group information, see MENTAL RETARDATION.)

OTHER RESOURCES

Missed Blessings. Sue S. Nickel. Crossover, 1993. On raising a daughter with spina bifida.

Giant Steps. Gilbert Gaul. St. Martin's, 1992. On raising a son with spina bifida.

Teaching the Student with Spina Bifida. Fern L. Rowley-Kelly and Donald H. Reigel, eds. P. H. Brookes, 1992.

A Parent's Guide to Spina Bifida. Beth-Ann Bloom and Edward Seljeskog. University of Minnesota Press, 1988.

spinal cord injury, damage to the spine, the column of small circular bones (*vertebrae*) running up the trunk to the neck, and to the spinal cord, the column of nerve tissue that transmits signals to and from the BRAIN, which is housed and usually protected within the spine.

The spine is susceptible to injury from various kinds of applied force, mainly:

- *Longitudinal compression*, in which vertebrae are crushed together, as in a fall or dive from some height
- *Hinging*, sharp, sudden, extreme bending, as in the "whiplash" a passenger might get in an automobile accident
- *Shearing*, a combination of hinging and sharp twisting of the spinal column, as when someone is hit and spun around in an automobile accident.

As a result of such injuries, vertebrae may be dislocated, fractured, or torn away from the ligaments that bind them together. In severe cases, blood clots or accumulated fluid from swelling may press on the spinal cord, or the spinal cord itself may be damaged or destroyed.

Roughly 44 percent of all spinal cord injuries result from automobile accidents, 24 percent from acts of VIOLENCE, 22 percent from falls, and 8 percent from sports accidents, two-thirds of them from diving. Some 60 percent of the injuries occur between ages sixteen and thirty, with nineteen the common age for a paralysis-inducing injury.

Someone with a possible spinal cord injury should not be moved unless absolutely necessary until a trained health professional has been able to assess the severity of the injury and the probable danger of further damage. This is especially important in so-called *unstable* cases, in which movement may cause the vertebrae to shift and damage or cut the spinal cord. Then the first order of business is to try to ensure that no further damage is caused, by stabilizing the bones, as through traction or surgical wiring, and minimizing effects such as swelling that can further damage the spinal cord.

Only then can efforts be turned toward rehabilitation. A patient with spinal cord injury will work closely with PHYSICAL and OCCUPATIONAL THERAPISTS, using carefully tailored EXERCISES to keep the muscles and joints from being badly affected by immobility, while the body slowly tries to heal itself. If some disability remains after rehabilitation, the person may rely on one or more ORTHOPEDIC DEVICES.

Below the point of the injury, nerves—and therefore feeling and movement—will be affected. In the worst case, when the spinal cord has been completely severed, PARALYSIS results, and all ability to feel and move will be lost. Such patients will be almost totally dependent, and will require special help (such as use of CATHETERS and enemas) to handle their bodily functions. Where the spinal cord has been damaged, but not severed, some feeling and motion may remain, or may return slowly over a year or so after the accident; in this case the person may feel partial paralysis or weakness (*paresis*).

When the injury is to the neck, paralysis or weakness affects all four limbs and the trunk; this is termed *quadriplegia.* When the injury is below the neck, weakness and paralysis affects the legs and part of the trunk; that condition is called *paraplegia.* Where some sensation remains, patients may feel considerable pain as well.

In recent years, new techniques have been developed to hold down swelling and diminish the initial damage, the first eight hours being the most important in limiting the effects of the injury. In general, doctors can offer little hope for recovery beyond a year or so after the initial accident. But that may be changing. One promising experimental approach uses computers and electrodes to transmit signals to and from the brain, bypassing the point of the initial injury, allowing some people with spinal cord injuries to walk in limited settings; the process is called *functional electrical stimulation* (FES). Promising much for the future, scientists have been able to coax spinal tissue to grow in the laboratory and to regrow after injury, in animals, and some hope to use genetic engineering to transplant cells into the spinal cord for repair and growth. As a result, some patients with spinal cord injuries may in the future be able to make unexpected progress.

Both men and women with spinal cord injuries can have a sexual life, though whether they will experience a full orgasm depends on the nature and extent of the injury. They may need to make some special preparation, such as emptying bowels and bladder before sex, and for women using a water-based lubricant for vaginal lubrication. Women can become pregnant and so should use BIRTH CONTROL devices, such as CONDOMS. BIRTH CONTROL PILLS are not recommended because they can lead to blood clot formation with decreased mobility. DIAPHRAGMS, CERVICAL SPONGE, and CERVICAL CAPS are effective, though they may be difficult to insert with lack of mobility and sensation.

Women with spinal cord injuries who do become pregnant need to take special precautions, such as renting a wider wheelchair to avoid friction-induced ulcers from pressure on skin. They will also want to track the DUE DATE extremely carefully, since they may not sense the onset of LABOR. Theirs would be a HIGH-RISK PREGNANCY, requiring special attention to systemic problems such as elevated BLOOD PRESSURE, but vaginal delivery is appropriate in many cases. Women will also need to plan ahead of time to have available whatever the baby might need, and to have personal assistance for themselves as required.

FOR HELP AND FURTHER INFORMATION

National Spinal Cord Injury Association (NSCIA)
545 Concord Ave., Suite 29
Cambridge, MA 02138
617–441–8500; Member hotline: 800–962–9629
Fax: 617–441–3449
E-Mail: nscia2@aol.com (America Online: NSCIA2)
Thom DeLilla, President
Organization concerned with spinal cord injuries and conditions that produce similar effects, such as spina bifida and Friedreich's ataxia; operates National Spinal Cord Injury Resource Center (NSCIRC) and In Touch with Kids network for children and adolescents with spinal cord injuries; makes referrals; provides special services such as counseling and drugs at discount; publishes quarterly magazine *SCI Life, Options: Spinal Cord Injury and the Future, National Resource Directory,* and other materials, including:

- Fact sheets: *What Is Spinal Cord Injury?, Sexuality After Spinal Cord Injury, Choosing a Spinal Cord Injury Rehabilitation Program, Reading Resources About Youth with Disabilities, Fun and Games, Travel After Spinal Cord Injury;* and materials on statistics, research, and medical updates.
- Information packets: *Fertility Issues in Men After SCI, Reproductive Issues in Women After SCI, Sexuality After SCI,* and *Severe Spasticity and Teaching Spasticity Management.*
- Audiotapes and workbooks for legal and health professionals.

Shriner's Hospitals for Crippled Children, 800–237–5055. Provides free medical care for children with spinal cord injuries. (For full group information, see BONE AND BONE DISORDERS.)

American Paralysis Association
500 Morris Avenue
Springfield, NJ 07081
201–379–2690; 800–225–0292
Mitchell R. Stoller, President and CEO
Organization concerned with paralysis from spinal cord injury, head injury, stroke, or other causes; supports research; publishes newsletters *Progress in Research* and *Walking Tomorrow*; fact sheets; and an annual review.

National Spinal Cord Injury Hotline, 800–526–3456. Sponsored by the American Association of Paralyzed Veterans.

Spinal Cord Society (SCS)
Wendell Road
Fergus Falls, MN 56537
218–739–5252
Fax: 218–739–5262
Charles E. Carson, President
Organization concerned with spinal cord injuries; supports research; maintains data bank; seeks to educate public; publishes monthly *National Newsletter.*

National Institute of Neurological Disorders and Stroke (NINDS), 800–352–9424. Publishes brochure *Spinal Cord Injury: Hope Through Research* and special report *Spinal Cord Injuries.* (For full group information, see BRAIN AND BRAIN DISORDERS.)

Accent, 800–787–8444. Publishes *How to Live with a Spinal Cord Injury* and *Sexual Adjustment: A Guide for the Spinal Cord Injured.* (For full group information, see HELP FOR SPECIAL CHILDREN on page 689.)

National Rehabilitation Information Center (NARIC), 800–346–2742, voice/TT. Publishes resource guide on spinal cord injury.

Resources for Rehabilitation, 617–862–6455. Publishes books *Resources for People with Disabilities and Chronic Conditions* and *A Woman's Guide to Coping with Disability,* both including sections on spinal cord injury. (For full group information, see EYE AND VISION PROBLEMS.)

Resource Center on Substance Abuse Prevention and Disability, 202–628–8442. Publishes *A Look at Alcohol and Other Drug Abuse Prevention and Spinal Cord Injury.* (For full group information, see HELP FOR SPECIAL CHILDREN on page 689.)

OTHER RESOURCES

The Quest for Cure: Restoring Function after Spinal Cord Injury. Sam Maddox. Paralyzed Veterans, 1993.
Spinal Center. David W. Felder. Felder Books, 1995.
Yes, You Can!: A Guide to Self-Care for Persons with Spinal Cord Injury, 2nd ed. Marget C. Hammond and others, eds. Paralyzed Veterans, 1993.

(See also SPINE AND SPINAL DISORDERS.)

spine and spinal disorders, the column of small, generally cylindrical bones (*vertebrae*) and cartilage that runs from the head to the pelvis, which supports the head and trunk, and also houses and protects the column of nerve tissue (*spinal cord*) that transmits signals to and from the BRAIN; and the problems associated with it. The spinal cord (which, with the brain, makes up the CENTRAL NERVOUS SYSTEM) is enclosed by three levels of membrane, collectively called the *meninges* (the *dura mater, arachnoid,* and *pia mater*).

The top seven bones in the spinal column, supporting the head, are the *cervical vertebrae*; the twelve below that are the *thoracic vertebrae*, to which the ribs are attached; the five below that are the *lumbar vertebrae,* which take most of the strain of lifting; the five fused vertebrae below that make up the *sacrum*; and the four fused vertebrae at the bottom are called the *coccyx*.

In young people, the spine may be subject to a number of disorders, among them SPINA BIFIDA, in which part of the spinal cord is exposed; OSTEOMYELITIS, in which the bone and BONE MARROW become infected, as in TUBERCULOSIS; SCOLIOSIS, KYPHOSIS, and LORDOSIS, all involving abnormal curvature of the spine; and SPINAL CORD INJURY. (See entries on separate disorders.)

spitting up, popular term for the backflow of food and fluids from a baby's stomach. (See REGURGITATION.)

spleen, a central organ in the *lymphatic system,* the network of vessels and organs that function as filters in the body's IMMUNE SYSTEM, to protect against disease.

sports, recreational pursuits involving physical activities and skills, often in competition with others, either as individuals or as part of ad hoc or formalized teams. Sports are very much a part of modern life, with sports stars being idols to many children and models—for good or ill—for their own future activities. However, younger and younger children are moving into competitive sports, often pushed by social and parental pressures. The result can be physical and emotional damage, if the child moves into the wrong sport, at the wrong time, and at the wrong pace. In its book, *The Pediatric Athlete,* the American Academy of Orthopaedic Surgeons (see the listing that follows this entry) provides guidelines for children and parents, to try to prevent such damage.

The AAOS stresses that children are not miniature adults, but rather are still developing physiologically, so their bodies react to athletic activity quite differently from an adult's. For example, children's bodies burn more calories, tire faster, have less power for their size (because they use glycogen less efficiently), adjust less quickly to changes in heat and humidity, produce more heat and lose it more slowly (so being at increased risk for heat-related illnesses), breathe faster (and so make take in more polluted air), and recover faster from strenuous activity. The AAOS cautions that children should not undertake training programs intended for adults, noting that excessive training can lead to early "burnout."

The AAOS also stresses the importance of annual medical evaluations of children, generally before each school year, and the selection of sports and other athletic activities to suit a child's age and stage of development, both to increase the child's chances of success and to minimize the risk of injury. Noncontact sports such as baseball, tennis, swimming, and skating may be most appropriate for children ages six to eight, while those ages eight to ten might try contact sports such as basketball, soccer, and wrestling, and older children might try collision sports such as football and hockey. The AAOS also stresses that parents and other adults should keep in mind a child's particular skills or deficits, suggesting that a child with poor eye-hand coordination might be steered into an individual sport such as swimming or running.

More and more parents are becoming involved in their children's sports activities, either as coaches or volunteer assistants. This trend will only increase, as communities across the country feel the pinch of hard times and cut back funding of organized youth sports leagues, while sponsorship from local businesses is also drying up. But while youth leagues in sports such as softball, baseball, soccer, football, basketball, and lacrosse rely increasingly on parents and other volunteers for both funding and coaching, the trend has not all been a happy one.

Indeed, one problem embarrassing to almost everyone, but especially to children, is that of excessively zealous parents in youth sports leagues. Many hard-driving parents, carrying their adult competitive attitudes into their children's lives, totally distort youth sports activities with their anger and verbal violence, which sometimes even escalate into physical violence. Because of that, many communities have instituted clinics for coaches, not just in coaching but also in sensitivity training and many other related activities, including emergency first aid, SAFETY, NUTRITION, and antidrug programs.

A leader in this movement is the National Youth Sports Coaches Association (NYSCA; see resource list that follows this entry), which alone has trained and certified more than 100,000 adults for youth sports coaching. In addition to developing codes of ethics for coaches and parents, the NYSCA has developed numerous training materials, all emphasizing the psychology of coaching children and teaching how to organize interesting and enjoyable practices, and develop children's athletic skills. They stress that while a *professional* coach's goals might be winning games, earning money, and providing entertainment, the youth coach's goals are quite different: teaching effectively, caring about the child's well-being, developing the child's potential, and making the sports experience enjoyable and affirmative, rather than negative and emotionally abusive. The aim is for youth coaches to keep their perspective and to focus on helping children learn how to play the game, while helping spectator-parents—directly and as role models—draw back from the win-at-all-costs attitude that is so damaging to everyone involved. In some communities, where possible, parents are not allowed to coach their own children, and sometimes not those of their friends and neighbors either, to relieve the pressures on all. Sometimes the youngest children play in an "instructional league," in which everybody gets to play, under special rules.

Safety is also a prime concern for parents and coaches of young children involved in sports. Football is the most dangerous of the organized sports, with possible SPINAL CORD INJURY a major concern, and skateboarding, roller-skating, and in-line skating account for tens of thousands of child injuries per year, but virtually all sports carry some risk. These can be reduced by the use of proper protective equipment, including all helmets, knee, elbow, and chin guards, padded gloves, protective batting vests, and mouth gear appropriate for the sport, as well as "tear-away" bases in baseball; by following the rules designed to protect players from harm; and by adhering to other basic safety guidelines under adult supervision. In one sport, boxing, the risk of TRAUMATIC BRAIN INJURY is so high that parents are urged not to let their children participate.

However, no amount of protective equipment can totally insure a child's safety. That was proved once again by a 1995 incident in which a young boy died after being hit in the chest by a pitched ball, even though he was wearing a protective batting vest. Indeed some safety experts have suggested that the vest gives children an illusion of safety, so they fail to move away to avoid being hit by a pitched or hit ball; they urge parents and coaches to teach children to act to protect themselves from injury.

Parents also need to be sure that those people who are working directly with the children are of unimpeachable background. Questions of child abuse, including sexual abuse, are of such concern today that in some communities potential coaches are fingerprinted and undergo a background check with the FBI and local police before they are cleared for coaching or similar work. Conversely, those who work in direct contact with children are now charged with being alert to signs that the child is being abused, at home, at school, in sports activities, or elsewhere (see INDICATORS OF CHILD ABUSE AND NEGLECT on page 106). One recent work, Rebecca Cowan Johnson's *For Their Sake: Recognizing, Responding to, and Reporting Child Abuse* (see HELP AGAINST CHILD ABUSE AND NEGLECT on page 680) is actually a manual for identifying signs of child abuse, understanding its causes, and working with its victims, including a list of reporting laws in various states; it was written for camp counselors, recreational staff, child-care workers, leaders of children's organizations, teachers, and others in regular contact with children.

FOR HELP AND FURTHER INFORMATION

National Alliance for Youth Sports
2050 Vista Parkway
West Palm Beach, Florida 33411
407–684–1141; 800–727–2057
Fax: 407–684–2546
Organization concerned with all aspects of youth sports; formerly National Association for Youth Sports Coaches; operates National Clearinghouse for Youth Sports Information (NCYSI); publishes numerous materials, including *Moms & Dads, Kids & Sports, Youth, Sports & Self Esteem, Positive Coaching*; video *Coaching Children with Disabilities*; and numerous books and videos on coaching in baseball, basketball, football, soccer, softball, hockey, tennis, and golf, and on officiating in baseball and basketball.

Direction Sports
600 Wilshire Boulevard, Suite 320
Los Angeles, CA 90017
213–627–9861
Tulley N. Brown, Executive Director
Organization combining education and sports programs to foster self-esteem and growth in inner-city youth; promotes peer-run team activities.

American Academy of Orthopaedic Surgeons (AAOS), 800–346–2267. Publishes book *The Pediatric Athlete*; brochure *Play It Safe*, on playground injuries; patient education newsletter *Sports Medicine Today*. (For full group information, see BONE AND BONE DISORDERS.)

American Academy of Pediatrics (AAP), 800–433–9016. Publishes brochures *Sports and Your Child* and *Playground Safety*; and professional books *Sports Medicine: Health Care for Young Athletes* and *Preparticipation Physical Evaluation*, on guidelines for clearance of young athletes for play. (For full group information, see HEALTH CARE.)

National Arthritis and Musculoskeletal and Skin Diseases Information Clearinghouse (NAMSIC), 301–495–4484. Publishes conference reports on sports injuries in youth. (For full group information, see ARTHRITIS.)

Prevent Blindness America, 800–221–3004. Publishes *Don't Play Games With Your Eyes* and *Sports Eye Injuries.* (For full group information, see EYE AND VISION PROBLEMS.)

Association for Childhood Education International (ACEI), 800–423–3563. Publishes *A Program for Kids: Success-Oriented Physical Education.* (For full group information, see HELP ON LEARNING AND EDUCATION on page 659.)

National Organization on Legal Problems of Education (NOLPE), 913–273–3550. Publishes *Sport Law.* (For full group information, see HELP ON LEARNING AND EDUCATION on page 659.)

National Safety Council (NSC), 800–621–7615. Publishes *Cruisin' Rules* (for preteens), *Bicycling Skills, The Millers Beat the Heat! The National Safety Council's Summer Activities Guide, Back Tips for All Activities*; and videos *Just a Few Seconds* (on young children drowning in residential swimming pools) and *Water Ski Driver—You're in Charge.* (For full group information, see SAFETY.)

American Academy of Pediatrics (AAP), 800–433–9016. Publishes *Sports and Your Child.* (For full group information, see HEALTH CARE.)

Food and Nutrition Information Center (FNIC), 301–504–5414. Publishes resource list *Sports Nutrition Nutri-Topics.* (For full group information, see NUTRITION.)

National Clearinghouse for Alcohol and Drug Abuse Information (NCADI), 800–729–6686. Publishes video *Downfall: Sports and Drugs.* (For full group information, see HELP AGAINST SUBSTANCE ABUSE on page 703.)

OTHER RESOURCES

GENERAL SPORTS GUIDES FOR PARENTS

Youth, Sports and Self Esteem: A Guide for Parents. Darrell J. Burnett. Masters Press, 1993.

Sports Without Pressure: A Guide for Parents, Coaches and Athletes. Eric Margenau. Gardner Press, 1991.

Sportswise: An Essential Guide for Young Athletes, Parents, and Coaches. Lyle J. Micheli. Houghton Mifflin, 1990. By a past president of the American College of Sports Medicine.

COACHING GUIDES FOR PARENTS

Rookie Coaches Softball Guide (1992), *Rookie Coaches Basketball Guide* (1991), *Rookie Coaches Soccer Guide* (1991), *Rookie Coaches Tennis Guide* (1991), and *Rookie Coaches Wrestling Guide* (1991). American Coaching Effectiveness Program (ACEP). Leisure Press. Series for parent or community volunteer coaches.

Soccer Coach's Guide to Practices, Drills and Skills Training. Butch Lauffer and Sandy Davie. Sterling, 1992.

The Complete Book of Coaching Youth Soccer. Simon Whitehead. Contemporary, 1991

Youth Soccer: A Complete Handbook for Coaches and Parents. Vern Seefeldt, ed. William C. Brown, 1991.

A Parent's Guide to Coaching Football. John P. McCarthy. Betterway, 1991.

Youth League Football Coaching and Playing. Jack Bicknell. Athletic Institute, 1991.

A Parent's Guide to Coaching Tennis. Pierce Kelley. Betterway, 1991. By the president of the Youth Tennis Foundation of Florida.

The Junior Tennis Handbook: A Complete Guide to Tennis for Juniors, Parents, and Coaches. Skip Singleton. Betterway, 1991.

Pass the Biscuit: Spirited Practices for Youth Hockey Coaches and Players. Gary Wright. Ashworth Press, 1991.

A Parent's Guide to Coaching Soccer. John P. McCarthy. Betterway, 1990.

Little League's Official How-to-Play Baseball Book. Peter Kreutzer and Ted Kerley. Doubleday, 1990.

The Parent's Guide to Coaching Tennis, rev. ed. Pierce Kelley. Betterway, 1990.

ON SAFETY

Everything You Need to Know About Sports Injuries. Lawrence Clayton. Rosen, 1995.

Youth Sports Injuries: A Medical Handbook for Parents and Coaches. John Duff. Macmillan, 1992.

Keeping Young Athletes Healthy: What Every Parent and Volunteer Coach Should Know. Alan R. Figelman. Simon & Schuster, 1991.

ON DRUGS AND SPORTS

Adolescents Worlds: Drug Use and Athletic Activity. M. F. Stuck. Praeger/Greenwood, 1990.

Dying to Win: The Athlete's Guide to Safe and Unsafe Drugs in Sports. Michael J. Asken. Acropolis, 1988.

FOR PRETEENS AND TEENS

Violence and Sports. Gilda Berger. Watts, 1990.

ON ATHLETIC SCHOLARSHIPS

Peterson's Sports Scholarships and College Athletic Programs. Kitty Colton and Michele Fetterolf, eds. Peterson's, 1993.

Athletic Scholarships: Thousands of Grants and Over 200 Million Dollars for College-Bound Athletes, 3rd ed. Andy Clark. Facts on File, 1993. Originally titled: *The Directory of Athletic Scholarships.*

College Admissions for the High School Athlete. Jack DiSalvo and Theresa F. DiGeronimo. Facts on File, 1993.

ON COLLEGE AND CAREER ATHLETICS

ABCs of Eligibility for College-Bound Student Athletes, rev. ed. College Board, 1994. Video.

Winning Edge, 1994–95: The Student Athlete's Guide to College Sports, 3rd ed. Frances Killpatrick. Octameron, 1993.

Rethinking College Athletics. Judith Andre. Temple University Press, 1992.

Going the Distance—How to Excel as an Athlete in College—and Graduate. Stephen Figler and Howard Figler. Peterson's, 1990.

Personal experiences

Vicarious Thrill: Reflections on a Championship Season of High School Basketball. Paul E. Bates. Southern Illinois University Press, 1995.

Little League Confidential: A Father, a Son and a Daughter Playing Ball. William Geist. Macmillan, 1992.

My Season on the Brink: A Father's Seven Weeks as a Little League Manager. Paul B. Brown. St. Martin's, 1992. On coaching an "instructional league."

Dreams of Glory: A Mother's Season With Her Son's High School Football Team. Judy Oppenheimer. Summit, 1991.

Background works

Little Girls in Pretty Boxes: The Making and Breaking of Elite Gymnasts and Figure Skaters. Joan Ryan. Doubleday, 1995.

The Importance of School Sports in American Education and Socialization. Ronald M. Jeziorski. University Press of America, 1994.

Lessons of the Locker Room: The Myth of School Sports. Andrew W. Miracle, Jr., and C. Roger Rees. Prometheus, 1994.

And Lead Us Not into Temptation: Educators and Interscholastic Football. J.C. Bennett. Mencken Memorial Press, 1993.

The High School Athlete: Her Personal Journal. Bobbie Schultz, ed. American Alliance for Health, Physical Education, Recreation, and Dance, 1993.

Student Athletes: Shattering the Myths and Sharing the Realities. Sarah V. Kirk and Wyatt D. Kirk, eds. American Counseling Assn., 1992.

The Quality of Effort: Integrity in Sport and Life for Student-Athletes, Parents, and Coaches. Reggie Marra. From the Heart Press, 1991.

(See also EXERCISE; also "On sports and recreation programs," under HELP FOR SPECIAL CHILDREN on page 689.)

sputum analysis, a laboratory analysis of the mucous material in the air passages, called *sputum* or *phlegm*, which is increased by infection, ALLERGIES, and ASTHMA. The amount, color, and makeup of sputum is an aid to diagnosis of LUNG AND BREATHING DISORDERS, such as TUBERCULOSIS or pneumonia.

SRA Achievement Series, widely used set of ACHIEVEMENT TESTS for children in grades K–12, used in schools to monitor general academic achievement year by year. As NORM-REFERENCED TESTS, the SRA series allows student SCORES to be compared with national standards. The pencil-and-paper tests cover READING, mathematics, language, science, social studies, and sometimes educational ability and reference materials. Various forms at various levels are available, and the tests may be hand- or computer-scored. (See TESTS.)

Stafford Loans, a federally SUBSIDIZED LOAN program under which banks, credit unions, other financial institutions, and sometimes schools lend money to undergraduate and graduate COLLEGE students who have had no previous federally subsidized loans; formerly called *Guaranteed Student Loans (GSL)*. Amounts available (as of 1990) vary from up to $2625 a year for the first two years of undergraduate study; up to $4000 a year after two years in a bachelor's degree program; and up to $7500 a year for graduate study; but the maximum available for undergraduate study altogether is $17,250 and for undergraduate and graduate study together is $54,750, though in no case can this be more than the actual cost of the education, minus any other FINANCIAL AID the student receives.

The student signs a promissory note, and the funds will be lent to the school, and then paid either directly to the student or into the school's credit account, less a 5 percent origination fee and up to 3 percent insurance premium. Interest charged is only 7–9 percent and the repayment period is at least five but up to ten years. Repayments of at least fifty dollars a month do not begin until six to twelve months after the student either leaves school or drops below half-time, though payments may be further delayed under certain circumstances. (See SUBSIDIZED LOAN.)

standardized tests, tests that have been developed through use on large groups, with the resulting scores being used to establish NORMS for students of specific ages or grades, the main purpose being to establish a basis of comparison between a particular student's performance and the average performance of others. For example, if most students in the fourth grade score 75 on a particular ACHIEVEMENT TEST, the norm for fourth-graders is 75. If a third-grader later takes the test and scores 75, her score is better than the average for her grade, and she is said to have an EDUCATIONAL AGE of fourth grade, a comparison called a GRADE EQUIVALENT.

Most widely used numerically scored tests, such as ACHIEVEMENT TESTS, are developed and standardized on large populations, and the scores tend to be distributed evenly along a *normal distribution* or *bell curve*, like a bottom-up tulip-shaped bowl, with most scores falling in the middle, and far fewer scores at the top and bottom ranges. Such tests generally have written instructions for use. Among professionals, standardized tests are often evaluated on the basis of their RELIABILITY (consistency) and VALIDITY (accuracy in measuring what is intended). (See TESTS.)

Standard Progressive Matrices (SPM or Raven's Coloured Progressive Matrices), a type of INTELLIGENCE TEST used with people ages eight to sixty-five, which attempts to assess mental ability without relying on verbal skills, offered either by group or individually. The person is given a series of sixty problems, each a pattern or figure with a missing part, and is asked to complete the pattern or figure choosing one of six possible alternatives presented. (See TESTS.)

Stanford Achievement Tests, a widely used series of group-administered ACHIEVEMENT TESTS used with children in grades mid–1 through 9, available in six grade levels, linked with national NORMS. The two earliest tests (Primary 1 and 2) focus on word study skills, word reading, READING and listening comprehension, spelling, concepts of number, computation, and environment. The next three (Primary 3 and Intermediate 1 and 2) add more language, mathematics applications, science, and social science, and drop word reading and environment. The highest level, Advanced, includes all areas except word study skills. Before midfirst grade, and after late ninth grade, schools can use the *Stanford Early School Achievement Tests (SESAT)* and the *Stanford Test of Academic Skills*, respectively, to allow for monitoring of educational progress through the school years. (See TESTS.)

Stanford-Binet Intelligence Test, a widely used, individually administered INTELLIGENCE TEST for people from age two through adult; developed from the "original" intelligence test, which set the standards in the field. Existing in two forms, giving somewhat different levels of SCORES, the Stanford-Binet tests a wide variety of verbal and nonverbal skills, using tasks similar to those used in the WECHSLER INTELLIGENCE SCALE FOR CHILDREN and GESELL PRESCHOOL TEST, but organizing the tasks by age levels rather than by type of task. The examiner first finds the *basal age*, the age level at which the child can answer all items correctly, and continues to the *ceiling age*, at which all items are answered incorrectly.

Unlike the Gesell tests, the Stanford-Binet focuses on the test result itself, not on the child's behavior and attitude, though these are noted for the record. And unlike the Wechsler Intelligence Scale for Children, the Stanford-Binet does not have subdivisions, with separate scores. Instead, it results in a single raw SCORE, which is converted to a child's *mental age* (MA), which is the age, in years and months, of the average person achieving that raw score on the test. That is then converted, by means of a formula, into an INTELLIGENCE QUOTIENT (IQ). If a child's CHRONOLOGICAL AGE and mental age are the same, the IQ will be 100; but if the child's mental age is higher, then the IQ will be over 100. Traditionally IQs have been classified as:

Gifted	140 and above
Very Superior	130–139
Superior	120–129
Above Average	110–119
Average	90–109
Below Average	80–89
Borderline	70–79
Mild Mental Retardation	60–69
Moderate/Severe Mental Retardation	59 and under

These classifications are still in popular use (and, indeed, are written into some laws), but the concepts of mental age, intelligence quotients, and intelligence tests in general have come under heavy attack. In fact, the above categories are now somewhat outdated, and test professionals more often use statistical measures. But the Stanford-Binet test itself is still widely used, especially as a DIAGNOSTIC ASSESSMENT TEST, to identify children who may need SPECIAL EDUCATION. (See INTELLIGENCE TESTS; TESTS.)

stanine, a way of ranking test scores, on the same principle as a PERCENTILE, but with nine divisions.

status offense, an act that is "criminal" only because it is committed by someone having a particular status, such as a MINOR, and breaks a law applying only to such people. An adolescent who runs away from home or is TRUANT from school is a status offender. An act that would be labeled as criminal if committed by an adult is, for a JUVENILE, often labeled as DELINQUENT.

statutory rape, a criminal charge against someone for having sexual intercourse with a person under the AGE OF CONSENT, regardless of whether the parties knew each other's ages, the previous sexual experience of the underage person, or who initiated the contact. Statutory rape is so called because it stems from statutes, or laws, and does not necessarily involve force or threats of VIOLENCE, as generally involved in other forms of RAPE.

stenosis, abnormal narrowing of a passageway in the body, as between two organs in the digestive system, often requiring surgery. (See DIGESTIVE SYSTEM AND DISORDERS.)

stepbrother or stepsister, SIBLINGS who are not directly related through biology or ADOPTION, except that a parent of one is married to a parent of the other. With modern complicated patterns of divorce and remarriage, many more children are living in FAMILIES with stepbrothers and stepsisters.

stepfamily, a FAMILY that includes children who share one parent, not two.

stereotypy/habit disorder, a psychiatric term for COMFORT HABITS which are so pervasive or extreme that they become a clinical problem; a type of MENTAL DISORDER.

sterility, the absolute, permanent, and irreversible inability to have a baby, sometimes occurring for unknown reasons (such as exposure to some ENVIRONMENTAL HAZARDS); sometimes by choice, as in STERILIZATION. This is actually a relatively rare condition; much more common is temporary infertility or impaired fertility (*subfertility*), which is a decreased likelihood of being able to conceive and carry to term a healthy child, because of temporary, treatable, or reversible conditions (see INFERTILITY).

sterilization, in a general sense, the process of making something unreproductive or incapable of supporting life; more specifically, a permanent form of BIRTH CONTROL (see later in this entry).

Special settings such as operating and delivery rooms and tools such as medical instruments are generally sterilized to prevent growth of disease-causing microorganisms; this can be done in a variety of ways, as by use of antiseptics, disinfectants, boiling, steaming (if under high pressure, called *autoclaving*), or radiation, including x-rays and ultraviolet radiation. One of the main medical advantages of hospital-based CHILDBIRTH is precisely that it takes place in a setting that should—if all procedures have been properly followed—be disease-free.

Some women object that the setting is, in *personal* terms "too sterile," and prefer less hospital-like settings, even with somewhat higher risk of disease. But some are also concerned that in HOSPITALS women and their babies may be exposed to diseases not present in their homes. Their fears were given some support by a 1992 study showing that a sizable proportion of doctors and nurses failed to cleanse their hands with antiseptic between examination of one patient and another. Individual women should look hard and skeptically at the cleanliness of their doctor's office, clinic, or hospital, as part of making their choice about where and how to deliver their child.

Sterilization is also a permanent form of birth control, referring to any medical or surgical procedure intended to prevent a person from ever reproducing, specifically by blocking normal passage of the woman's egg (OVUM) and the man's SPERM. For women, this usually involves TUBAL LIGATION, literally tying or clamping of the FALLOPIAN TUBES; for men, the main choice is VASECTOMY, the severing of the *vas deferens*, the tubes that normally carry sperm to the penis, a more minor operation. Both surgical procedures are rated as more than 99 percent effective in preventing PREGNANCY. Some other operations may have sterilization as a side effect, such as HYSTERECTOMY.

Sterilization has traditionally been regarded as a permanent procedure; though some kinds can be reversed, the success rate of such operations is very low. However, with some new REPRODUCTIVE TECHNOLOGY techniques, notably INTRACYTOPLASMIC SPERM INJECTION, men who have undergone vasectomy have a chance of becoming fathers, as long as their bodies have continued to make SPERM.

Sterilization today is generally a voluntary choice. At some times and places, governments have used involuntary sterilization to prevent some people—notably those with physical DISABILITIES, MENTAL RETARDATION, or MENTAL DISORDERS—from bearing children. That is less common today, being widely regarded as infringements on individual rights, though the impulse to social control of reproduction remains (see NORPLANT). Indeed, as late as the 1970s, the U.S. Department of Health and Human Services (HHS) had to issue regulations to curb abuses, such as social services departments threatening to end pregnancy benefits or deny payment for PRENATAL CARE or DELIVERY to women who would not agree to be sterilized.

HHS guidelines require that sterilization be barred for anyone under 21 years old; that the procedure, its risks, and its permanence must be described in the person's native language; that the person *not* give written consent just before, during, or after an ABORTION or LABOR, or while under the influence of drugs and alcohol; and that a 30-day waiting period be mandatory after written consent. The guidelines call for fines or imprisonment as punishment for any threats to terminate benefits. These are primarily an ideal, however, since such guidelines are necessarily difficult to enforce. (See BIRTH CONTROL; TUBAL LIGATION; VASECTOMY.)

steroids, a family of HORMONES that are formed from cholesterol, including *corticosteroids*, produced by the cortex of the adrenal glands, and the male and female sex hormones, including TESTOSTERONE, ESTROGEN, and PROGESTERONE. Many steroids are used legitimately for medical purposes. Various combinations of sex hormones are used in BIRTH CONTROL PILLS and in RU–486. Corticosteroids may be used to ease joint inflammation from ARTHRITIS, and other steroids to treat babies with RESPIRATORY DISTRESS SYNDROME, for example.

However, steroids—especially *anabolic steroids*, synthetic versions of testosterone—are also widely *abused* to enhance athletic performance or physical appearance. Such uses are not medically approved, and can lead to severe health problems, including liver, heart, and kidney disease, high CHOLESTEROL, a depressed IMMUNE SYSTEM, personality changes, stunted growth, sterility, and even death. For women, effects may also include development of HAIR on the face, ACNE, diminishing of the BREASTS, deepening of the voice, enlarging of the CLITORIS, and irregularities in MENSTRUATION. Anabolic steroids have been confirmed to be addictive, most people experiencing withdrawal symptoms on ceasing use, along with a variety of other symptoms of dependence. Since 1991, anabolic steroids have been controlled substances under federal law, in the same category as cocaine, heroin, LSD, and other habit-forming drugs.

Other related substances have since been sold to former steroid users in places such as body-building gyms, fitness centers, health-food stores, and mail-order outlets. One is *gamma hydroxybutyrate* (GHB), also known as *gamma hydroxybutyric acid*, *sodium oxybate*, or *gamma hydroxybutyrate sodium*, sometimes marketed as *Somatomax PM*. GHB has been marketed as reducing fat, building muscle, inducing sleep, and giving a "high," but it is actually poisonous and potentially lethal, causing such symptoms as stomach and intestinal cramps, breathing difficulty, uncontrollable SEIZURE-like movements, and COMA.

Another illicit drug marketed as a "steroid alternative" is *clenbuterol*, a drug not approved for any use in the

United States, though it is used by veterinarians in some countries. Little is known about the effects of clenbuterol, but dozens of people in Spain became ill after eating beef liver that contained residues of the drug.

Parents of teenagers, especially those interested in athletics, will want to be sure their children are aware of the dangers of using any anabolic steroids or substitutes. They should also be aware that no one buying illegal drugs, produced in uninspected, uncontrolled, unapproved settings, can be sure just *what* kind of drug they are getting.

FOR HELP AND FURTHER INFORMATION

National Clearinghouse for Alcohol and Drug Abuse Information (NCADI), 301–468–2600. Publishes *If You Use Steroids, These Aren't the Only Things Stacked Against You, Anabolic Steroids,* and *Anabolic Steroids: A Threat to Body and Mind.* (For full group information, see HELP AGAINST SUBSTANCE ABUSE on page 703.)

National Woman's Christian Temperance Union (WCTU), 800–755–1321. Publishes booklets *Bulk, Biceps and Brutality* and *Pumping Trouble,* and leaflet *Anabolic Steroids.* (For full group information, see HELP AGAINST SUBSTANCE ABUSE on page 703.)

Narcotic Educational Foundation of America (NEFA), 213–663–5171. Publishes *Anabolic Steroids.* (For full group information, see HELP AGAINST SUBSTANCE ABUSE on page 703.)

American Council for Drug Education (ACDE), 800–488–3784. Publishes pamphlet *Steroids.* (For full group information, see HELP AGAINST SUBSTANCE ABUSE on page 703.)

OTHER RESOURCES

FOR CHILDREN

Steroids. Sarah Stevens. Crestwood, 1991.
Focus on Steroids. Katherine Talmadge. Twenty-First Century Books, 1991.
For preteens and teens
Steroids. Hank Nuwer. Watts, 1990.
Drugs in Sports, rev. ed. Edward F. Dolan. Watts, 1992. On the hazardous effects of steroids and other substances used by some athletes.

(See also HELP AGAINST SUBSTANCE ABUSE on page 703.)

stillbirth, the DELIVERY of a FETUS that died before or during CHILDBIRTH, referring to a baby whose GESTATIONAL AGE would have made it expected to live, often beyond the 28th week of PREGNANCY and weighing 2.2 pounds (1000 grams); also called *late fetal death.* The death of a fetus at an earlier stage is called MISCARRIAGE, or *spontaneous abortion.*

In some cases, the cause of death is obvious, such as lack of oxygen because the UMBILICAL CORD is wrapped around the baby's neck or the PLACENTA malfunctioned; severe malformations or damage to the NERVOUS SYSTEM, such as ANENCEPHALY, SPINA BIFIDA, or HYDROCEPHALUS; RH INCOMPATIBILITY between mother and child; or extremely LOW BIRTH WEIGHT or PREMATURE delivery. In other cases, disorders affecting the mother are recognized as responsible, diseases such as DIABETES, RUBELLA, MEASLES, CHICKEN POX, TOXOPLASMOSIS, HERPES, SYPHILIS, CYTOMEGALOVIRUS, and influenza. But in perhaps a third of the cases of stillbirth, the cause of death is unknown, although—after detecting lack of a heartbeat and delivering the child—doctors are required to examine the child and report cause of death, if known, on a death certificate.

FOR HELP AND FURTHER INFORMATION

Pregnancy and Infant Loss Center (PILC), 612–473–9372. Publishes *Stillborn: The Invisible Death.* (For full group information, see DEATH AND DYING.)

OTHER RESOURCES

LIFELINE, A Journal for Parents Grieving a Miscarriage, Stillbirth or Early Infant Death. Joanie Reid. Pineapple, 1994.
When a Baby Dies: The Experience of Late Miscarriage, Stillbirth, and Neonatal Death. Nancy Kohner. HarperCollins, 1992.
Quietus: A Story of a Stillbirth. Jean Gunderson and Donna Harris. Centering Corp., 1990.

(See also CHILDBIRTH; "On pregnancy and infant loss," under DEATH AND DYING.)

storage disorders, a general type of GENETIC DISORDER, classed as a METABOLIC DISORDER, in which the body lacks certain enzymes necessary to break down compounds in the body. The result is abnormal and damaging accumulations of various substances in body tissues, often seriously affecting the brain. Examples include MUCOPOLYSACCHARIDOSES, LIPID STORAGE DISEASES (lipidoses), and *mucolipidoses.*

stranger anxiety, a popular name for a young child's shrinking from contact with unfamiliar people. This is a normal response in a child under age two to two and a half, but when it develops in older children and becomes disabling shyness, it may be classified by psychiatrists as AVOIDANT DISORDER OF CHILDHOOD OR ADOLESCENCE.

strep throat, infection of the throat, tonsils, and sometimes the skin with the bacterium called *streptococcus,* the same organism that causes *glomerulonephritis,* a severe kind of KIDNEY AND UROLOGICAL PROBLEM, and SCARLET FEVER. Streptococcus is today treatable by ANTIBIOTICS, but if the infection is not fully cleared up, RHEUMATIC FEVER may result.

stretch marks, darkened streaks on a woman's abdomen, BREASTS, and thighs. They often result from the body's enlargement during PREGNANCY, in which case they are called *striae gravidarum,* but sometimes also appear during the GROWTH SPURT associated with PUBERTY. The marks later fade, but do not disappear completely. They are also sometimes associated with HORMONE DISORDERS.

stridor, an abnormal high-pitched sound that accompanies breathing, usually on intake of breath, because of narrowing or obstruction of the breathing passages, as in CROUP, throat infections, or TUMORS in the throat. Stridor can also result when a child has swallowed an object that has lodged in the throat, or as a side effect of a malfunctioning SHUNT, a device placed in a child's head to treat HYDROCEPHALUS. In extreme or emergency cases, a TRACHEOSTOMY may need to be performed, an operation in which a breathing pipe is inserted into the windpipe externally.

student record (school record), the cumulative file detailing a student's progress through a school, including basic identifying information, comments about student and family, some kinds of physical and health information, comments about behavior, notes about DISCIPLINE or counseling given, ATTENDANCE data, scores from various STANDARDIZED TESTS, and courses or classes taken and grades received. When a student transfers to another school or applies for ADMISSION to a college, the latter information is summarized for the new school in the form of a TRANSCRIPT. The student record cumulates and is generally kept in the school or system office for immediate reference while the student is enrolled; afterward most of it is maintained as part of the permanent student record. (Some kinds of special confidential reports are kept separately from the main student record.)

Once student records were totally under the control of the school, but that changed with passage of the FAMILY EDUCATIONAL RIGHTS AND PRIVACY ACT (FERPA) of 1974, sometimes called the *Buckley Amendment.* Under FERPA, schools risk loss of federal funds if they fail to give parents access to the record of students under eighteen, and the school can by law release the student record to others outside the school only with the parent's authorization; over age eighteen, the student has control over access to the record and must authorize any access, including that by parents. The law also provides that parents can request modifications, clarifications, corrections, or deletions in the file and allows for an appeals procedure if that request is denied. It is important to review the record and attempt to correct it, if necessary, because—long after the people who wrote comments in the record are gone—other people will refer to that permanent record in writing recommendations and reports, such as those requested by colleges or employers. (See FAMILY EDUCATIONAL RIGHTS AND PRIVACY ACT; EDUCATION.)

student-teacher ratio, the number of students in a school divided by the number of teachers, the result generally being the average size of the classes in the school. A school with 100 students and 4 teachers, for example, has a student-teacher ratio of 100 to 4, more generally expressed as 25 to 1, and its average class size is 25. The lower the student-teacher ratio, the more time and attention teachers have for each student; that time is increased if the school also has aides and assistants working with the teacher. Parents evaluating a school for their child should surely check this key ratio.

study skills, a set of PREREQUISITE skills important in a child's being able to learn effectively from a course, including knowing how and when to take notes, being able to organize material, knowing how to approach TESTS, and having the basic LOCATIONAL SKILLS to find the information they need in printed sources. (See "On study skills," under HELP ON LEARNING AND EDUCATION on page 659.)

Sturge-Weber syndrome, a rare CONGENITAL disorder involving a port-wine stain (see NEVUS) on the face, often on just one side, associated with malformation of blood vessels and CALCIUM deposits in nearby structures, and resulting conditions such as MENTAL RETARDATION, EYE AND VISION PROBLEMS, and EPILEPSY; also called *Dmitri's disease* or *encephalotrigeminal angiomatosis.* No cure is yet available, though medications can provide some relief from symptoms.

FOR HELP AND FURTHER INFORMATION

National Institute of Neurological Disorders and Stroke (NINDS), 800–352–9424. (For full group information, see BRAIN AND BRAIN DISORDERS.)

National Organization for Rare Disorders (NORD), 800–999–6673. (For full group information, see RARE DISORDERS.)

subjective test, a type of TEST in which the administrator's handling of the test, observations, discretion, and rapport with the child very much affect the test score. Often there are no "right" and "wrong" answers, and the test is designed to draw out information about the individual's thinking, knowledge, and functioning. Examples include individual DEVELOPMENTAL SCREENING TESTS such as the GESELL PRESCHOOL TEST or a student's essay for an English class.

subpoena, a legal document requiring that a person appear at court at a specified time to testify as a witness. If the person is required to supply certain documents (such as income records in a CHILD SUPPORT case) to the court or to a specified party, the document is sometimes called *subpoena duces tecum* ("bring with you"). A person who fails to honor a subpoena may be considered in CONTEMPT OF COURT.

subsidized loan, in EDUCATION, a type of FINANCIAL AID in which a student is given money to help meet the expenses of attending COLLEGE or PRIVATE SCHOOL; unlike SCHOLARSHIPS, loans must be repaid, but federal and other subsidies reduce the interest rate, making these loans very attractive. If taken out in the student's name, such loans often require no repayment until some months after the student leaves school (at graduation or before). If taken out in the parent's name, payments generally start almost immediately.

To continue receiving financial aid, the student must maintain satisfactory progress, as defined by applicable school and federal guidelines. The loans may also be voided in some circumstances; for example, some types of federally subsidized financial aid will be suspended or terminated if a student is convicted of possessing or distributing drugs.

Among the major federal loan programs are PERKINS LOANS, STAFFORD LOANS, and PLUS LOANS/LOANS FOR STUDENTS. Repayments on these loans may be deferred under certain circumstances. If students have previous loans that are in default—that is, on which payments were not made when due, as when a student has left school for a time and wants to return—they will be usually ineligible for further loans. (See FINANCIAL AID.)

substance abuse, a general term encompassing ALCOHOL ABUSE, DRUG ABUSE, and SOLVENT ABUSE. (For an overview of the effects and signs of substance abuse, plus organizations, reference works, and recommendations for parents, see HELP AGAINST SUBSTANCE ABUSE on page 703.)

subvocalization, the act of forming words with the lips or even whispering them during silent READING, a practice that can significantly slow a student's reading speed, but may be useful for those with reading difficulties, such as DYSLEXIA.

subzonal sperm insertion (SZI), an ASSISTED FERTILIZATION technique, a variation on IN VITRO FERTILIZATION; a new, still highly experimental form of REPRODUCTIVE TECHNOLOGY to help SPERM and egg (OVUM) join to achieve FERTILIZATION. Using MICROMANIPULATION, the EMBRYOLOGIST uses a tiny needle to place one or a few sperm underneath the ZONA PELLUCIDA, the protective outer layer of the egg. Unlike PARTIAL ZONA DISSECTION (PZD), SZI requires only a few sperm, making it suitable for severe cases of male-related INFERTILITY. It also reduces the likelihood of multiple sperm penetration, a main problem with PZD. (See INFERTILITY; REPRODUCTIVE TECHNOLOGY.)

sucking, an outgrowth of the ROOTING REFLEX, a desire that tends to last beyond such a reflex, sometimes being satisfied by a thumb or finger, or by a PACIFIER; a kind of COMFORT HABIT. For many children sucking seems to be both part of the process of exploring their bodies and also a habit that offers comfort, relaxation, and pleasure. (See SUCKING AND PACIFIERS, on page 576.)

Traditionally it was thought that children sucked their thumbs because they were taken off the breast or bottle too soon, but researchers have found that some children suck their thumbs while still on the breast or bottle, and sometimes give up both at once, often around age two, though it can be a good deal later. The consensus seems to be that there is little good—and potential damage to the parent-child relationship—in forcibly trying to stop the thumb-sucking habit. It is now generally thought to do no great harm, unless carried on to age five or six, when (apart from the social stigma) sucking of thumbs or pacifiers can begin to affect the growth of teeth.

sudden infant death syndrome (SIDS), the abrupt and unexpected death of an infant for which no adequate explanation can be found, even after an autopsy, an examination of the scene of death, and a review of the child's medical history; also called *crib death, cot death,* or *sudden unexplained death syndrome (SUDS).* SIDS is the leading cause of death among infants aged one to twelve months, responsible for approximately 7000 deaths annually, or about 18 percent of INFANT MORTALITY.

By definition, the causes of SIDS are obscure. There is some evidence that SIDS is associated with SLEEP APNEA (temporary cessation of breathing during sleep) and PREMATURE birth; certainly a child who has previously had an APPARENT LIFE-THREATENING EVENT (ALTE) is at much elevated risk of SIDS, even when HOME MONITORS are used with the infant during sleep. SIDS is more common in the winter, when children are most exposed to viruses and other infections, with the risk twice as high in January as in July. Infants are most vulnerable between one and four months old, and Black infants are at somewhat higher risk than White infants, though SIDS crosses racial and socioeconomic barriers. Many children lost to SIDS are later found to have had some respiratory symptoms (such as a cold in the nose) before death, or to have had some other unexplained symptoms, such as weight loss. Parents will want to watch the baby carefully during any minor illness. Some of these deaths may be due to powerful respiratory infections, and others to undetected BIRTH DEFECTS, especially relating to METABOLISM. An infant is at greater risk of SIDS if there were medical complications during pregnancy or delivery, especially if there were multiple births, or if the infant has had to be resuscitated at any time for any reason.

Researchers are continuing to explore links of SIDS with other factors, including SMOKING by the parents; LOW BIRTH WEIGHT; BOTTLEFEEDING (as opposed to BREASTFEEDING, which provides the infant with some immunity in the early months); ADOLESCENT PREGNANCY; DRUG ABUSE or ALCOHOL ABUSE by the mother; ANEMIA in

Sucking and Pacifiers

Most babies get their thumbs and fingers in their mouths and suck on them. Many seem to find it very enjoyable and do it often. It causes no harm and can be ignored.

Some parents don't like the looks of thumb and finger sucking and substitute a pacifier for the thumb. This is also fine. However, do not use a homemade pacifier (such as the nipple from a baby bottle), one without ventilation holes, or an old pacifier that has cracks, tears, stickiness, or separation. These factors can cause choking. Stop giving the baby the pacifier toward the end of the first year, if you can. Never leave the pacifier on a cord around the baby's neck; the baby can be strangled by the cord. And don't substitute the pacifier for the attention, food, or diaper changes that your baby wants and needs when he or she is crying!

Don't use a bottle of formula or juice as a pacifier—your baby's developing teeth can decay from the sugar they contain. (See NURSING BOTTLE SYNDROME.)

Source: Infant Care (1989). Prepared by the Bureau of Maternal and Child Health and Resources Development for the Public Health Service.

the mother; socioeconomic disadvantage; and previous loss of a sibling to SIDS. Whatever the underlying causes, the immediate problem seems to be some interruption of normal heart and breathing rhythms, or a lack of *surfactant,* a substance that normally keeps the air sacs of the lungs from collapsing.

Recent studies in other countries have suggested that at least some cases of SIDS may be caused by infants suffocating in soft bedding. Newborns are especially vulnerable, since for the first few weeks they breathe only through their nostrils, and the nose with its soft, compressible cartilage is readily obstructed. And infants under three months old are too young to raise their heads or roll over and away from cushions or crumpled bedding. In a major recent change, many doctors and medical organizations now recommend that infants be put to sleep on their backs to help avoid such hazards. (For a fuller discussion and safety suggestions, see SLEEP AND SLEEP DISORDERS.)

In some situations, a NEONATALOGIST or PEDIATRICIAN may recommend use of a home monitor, to alert parents if the child stops breathing. Home monitors are not wholly reliable, however, sometimes giving a FALSE POSITIVE (indicating a problem where none exists) or a FALSE NEGATIVE (failing to signal that a problem does exist). The Public Health Service recommends that parents receive training in infant CPR (cardiopulmonary RESUSCITATION), so they can attempt to revive their infant in case of emergency.

FOR HELP AND FURTHER INFORMATION

Sudden Infant Death Syndrome Alliance (SIDS Alliance)
1314 Bedford Avenue, Suite 210
Baltimore, MD 21208
410–653–8226; 24-hour hotline 800–221-SIDS [221–7437]
Fax: 410–653–8709
Judith S. Jacobson, Executive Vice President
Organization concerned with SIDS; provides information and support; publishes various materials, including *What Every Parent Should Know: Facts About Sudden Infant Death Syndrome and Reducing the Risks for SIDS,* and *The Subsequent Child.*

National Sudden Infant Death Syndrome Clearinghouse (NSIDSC)
8201 Greensboro Drive, Suite 600
McLean, VA 22102–3810
703–821–8955, ext. 474 or 249
Fax: 703–821–2098
Olivia Cowdrill, Project Director
Information service, affiliated with the National Center for Education in Maternal and Child Health (see PREGNANCY), providing information on SIDS; publishes various materials including newsletter *Information Exchange, What Is SIDS?, Infant Positioning and SIDS, Sudden Infant Death Syndrome: Trying to Understand The Mystery, Facts About Apnea and Other Apparent Life-Threatening Events, When Sudden Infant Death Syndrome (SIDS) Occurs in Childcare Settings, Nationwide Survey of Sudden Infant Death Syndrome (SIDS) Services,* works on grieving (see DEATH AND DYING), bibliographies, and materials for health professionals.

National Institute of Child Health and Human Development (NICHD), 301–496–5133. Publishes *Reducing the Risk of Sudden Infant Death Syndrome: What You Can Do.* (For full group information, see PREGNANCY.)

American Academy of Pediatrics (AAP), 800–433–9016. Publishes brochures *Reducing the Risk of SIDS: What You Can Do* and *Infant Sleep Positioning and SIDS Fact Sheet.* (For full group information, see HEALTH CARE.)

Pregnancy and Infant Loss Center (PILC), 612–473–9372. Publishes *The Chance to Say Goodbye: Infant Death Through SIDS* and *When the Bough Breaks.* (For full group information, see DEATH AND DYING.)

National Maternal and Child Health Clearinghouse (NMCHC), 703–821–8955. (For full group information, see PREGNANCY.)

National Organization for Rare Disorders (NORD), 800–999–6673. (For full group information, see RARE DISORDERS.)

OTHER RESOURCES

SIDS: A Parent's Guide to Understanding and Preventing Sudden Infant Death Syndrome. William Sears. Little, Brown, 1995.

The SIDS Survival Guide: Information and Comfort for Grieving Family and Friends and Professionals Who Seek to Help Them. Joani N. Horchler and Robin D. Morris. SIDS Educational Services, 1994.

Sudden Infant Death: Enduring the Loss, 2nd ed. John DeFrain and others. Free Press, 1991.

Sudden Infant Death Syndrome: Who Can Help and How. Charles Corr and others, eds. Springer, 1991.

(See also DEATH AND DYING; HIGH-RISK BABIES; SLEEP AND SLEEP DISORDERS.)

suicide, the deliberate killing of oneself, a problem affecting all ages, but most dramatically adolescents and young adults. With the suicide rate more than tripling since the 1950s, suicide has become the fourth leading cause of death for children ages ten to fourteen years (following unintentional injuries, cancer, and homicide), and for ages fifteen to nineteen the third leading cause, behind accidents and homicide. Another major change is that guns are now used in approximately 60 percent of all teenage suicides. Some have suggested that this fact may account for much of the rise in the suicide rate, since 91 percent of suicide attempts with guns succeed, as compared to 23 percent with poisons and 4 percent with knives. Simply reducing availability of guns in the home might have some effect in lowering the suicide rate (see VIOLENCE).

But more to the point is to try to identify and help those people who are contemplating suicide. According to a 1991 national survey of children ages twelve to fourteen, 1 in every 11 girls and 1 in every 25 boys had had "significant suicidal thoughts." Among teenagers altogether, perhaps 25 to 50 attempt suicide for every person who succeeds in the attempt, as compared to eight to ten attempts per each actual suicide in the population as a whole. Uncounted others also have times of *suicide crisis,* when they are obsessed with thoughts of killing themselves, often to the extent of planning a suicide to the tiniest detail, but stop themselves short of an actual attempt. Suicides are less common among children aged five to fourteen; even so, deliberate self-destructive acts (sometimes leading to death) cause as many as 12,000 children a year to be hospitalized.

A large proportion of people who commit suicide—some estimate as high as 90 percent—have some form of MENTAL DISORDER, such as DEPRESSION or SCHIZOPHRENIA, often coupled with ALCOHOL ABUSE or DRUG ABUSE. Beyond that, there are many theories and little solid evidence for why people commit suicide. Many researchers have focused on family history and biochemical imbalances. Among other RISK FACTORS linked with increased likelihood of suicide are CHILD ABUSE AND NEGLECT, personal and social losses, such as a death in the family, serious physical illness, and general social isolation; added to these in older adults are unemployment, financial problems, and problems of dependence and illness related to aging. Especially among young people, suicides can come in "clusters," where one suicide leads to several more in one small community. This happens often enough that many schools and communities have established crisis prevention and intervention programs, attempting to identify those who may be suicidal.

Parents concerned about possible suicide among family or friends should not delude themselves with the popular notion that "people who talk about suicide don't actually kill themselves." In fact, the Public Health Service points out, somewhere between 20 percent and 50 percent of the people who commit suicide have made attempts before. Though there are no surefire ways to identify a potentially suicidal person, they note several warning signs, including:

- Previous suicide attempts.
- Talk about suicide, often oblique, such as "They won't have to worry about me much longer."
- Making arrangements, such as giving away prize possessions or preparing as if for a trip.
- Changes in behavior or personality, often seen through withdrawal from usual activities and reflected feelings of hopelessness or worthlessness.
- General depression, often including loss of appetite or weight, change in sleeping patterns, uncommunicativeness, and slowness of speed in speaking, moving, thinking, and acting.

If parents think a family member or friend may be considering suicide, the Public Health Service recommends the following approaches:

- Listen without judging, giving the person an understanding forum in which to try to talk things through.
- Talk specifically about suicidal thoughts, such as: Does he or she have a plan? Bought a gun? Where is it? Stock-piled pills? Where are they? They note that, "contrary to popular belief, such candor will not give a person dangerous ideas or encourage a suicidal act."
- Evaluate the situation, trying to distinguish between general upset and more serious danger, as when suicide plans *have* been made. If the crisis is acute, *do not leave the person alone.*
- Be supportive, letting the person know you care and trying to break down their feelings of isolation.
- Take charge in finding help, without concern about invading the person's privacy. Do not try to handle the

problem alone, but get professional help immediately. (The groups listed later in this entry may be sources of help, as may the family doctor, local hospital, mental health clinic, suicide prevention or crisis intervention center, clergy, or police station.)

- Make the environment safe, removing from the premises (not just hiding) weapons such as guns, razors, or scissors, medication, and other potentially dangerous household items.
- Do not keep suicide talk or threats secret; these are calls for help and call for immediate action.
- Do not challenge, dare, or use verbal shock treatment. They can have tragic effects.
- Make a contract with the person, getting a promise or commitment, preferably in writing, not to make any suicidal attempt until you have talked further.
- Beware of elevated moods and seemingly quick recoveries; sometimes they are illusory, reflecting the relief of finally deciding to commit suicide, or reflecting the temporary release of talking to someone, though the underlying problems have not been resolved.

Where warning signs have gone unrecognized or help has been insufficient to prevent a suicide, the aftermath is extremely difficult and painful for everyone involved, not only immediate family but friends. Groups such as those in the list that follows can help people deal with the grief and pain that can result, including children getting over loss of a parent or friend, and parents getting over loss of children or partner. They can also help the survivors learn how to prevent further suicides, which sometimes (especially among young people) come in clusters.

FOR HELP AND FURTHER INFORMATION

American Association of Suicidology
4201 Connecticut Avenue NW, Suite 310
Washington, DC 20008
202–237–2280
Fax: 202–237–2282
Alan Berman, Chief Executive Officer
Organization for professionals and others concerned with suicide and life-threatening behavior; operates information clearinghouse; sponsors survivor support groups; publishes various materials, including newsletters *Newslink* and *Surviving Suicide* (for suicide survivors); *Directory of Suicide Prevention and Crisis Intervention Agencies in the U.S.* and *Directory of Survivor of Suicide Support Groups*; booklets *The Tender Leaves of Hope and Survivors of Suicide*; pamphlets *Suicide in Youth and What You Can Do About It—A Guide for Students and Suicide of Older Men and Women*; and suicide prevention notebooks for professionals.

American Academy of Pediatrics (AAP), 800–433–9016. Publishes brochure *Surviving: Coping with Adolescent Depression and Suicide.* (For full group information, see HEALTH CARE.)

National Institute of Mental Health (NIMH), 301–443–4513. Publishes *Suicide Facts.* (For full group information, see MENTAL DISORDER.)

Johnson Institute, 800–231–5165, U.S. except MN. Publishes *Suicide and Homicide Among Adolescents* and *Adolescent Suicide: A School-Based Approach to Assessment and Intervention.* (For full group information, see HELP AGAINST SUBSTANCE ABUSE on page 703.)

American Academy of Child and Adolescent Psychiatry (AACAP), 202–966–7300. Publishes information sheet *Teen Suicide.* (For full group information, see MENTAL DISORDERS.)

National Alliance for the Mentally Ill (NAMI), 800–950–6264. Publishes books *Suicide: Why?*; has online forums and libraries. (For full group information, see MENTAL DISORDERS.)

National Runaway Switchboard, which also functions as Adolescent Suicide Hotline, 800–621–4000.

PACER Center (Parent Advocacy Coalition for Educational Rights), 612–827–2966, voice/TT. Publishes *No One Saw My Pain: Why Teens Kill Themselves.* (For full group information, see HELP FOR SPECIAL CHILDREN on page 689.)

Council for Exceptional Children (CEC), 800–328–0272. Publishes *Depression and Suicide: Special Education Students At Risk* and special report *Suicide and the Exceptional Child.* (For full group information, see HELP ON LEARNING AND EDUCATION on page 659.)

National Mental Health Consumer Self-Help Clearinghouse, 800–553–4539. Publishes reprint packet on suicide. (For full group information, see MENTAL DISORDERS.)

The Compassionate Friends (TCF), 708–990–0010. (For full group information, see DEATH AND DYING.)

National Right to Life Committee (NRLC), 202–626–8800. Publishes *Active Euthanasia and Assisted Suicide.* (For full group information, see ABORTION.)

OTHER RESOURCES

ON SUICIDE OF A CHILD OR TEEN

No One Saw My Pain: Why Teens Kill Themselves. Andrew Slaby and Lili Frank Garfinkel. Norton, 1994.

Surviving Suicide: Young People Speak Up. Susan Kuklin. Putnam, 1994. Conversations with people who survived a teen suicide attempt.

Teen Suicide: Too Young To Die. Cynthia Copeland Lewis. Enslow, 1994.

The Cruelest Death: The Enigma of Adolescent Suicide. David Lester. Charles, 1993.

Suicide of a Child, rev. ed. Adina Wrobleski. Centering Corp., 1993.

Andrew, You Died too Soon: A Family Experience of Grieving and Living Again. E. Corinne Chilstrom. Augsburg Fortress, 1993.

Teenage Suicide. Sandra Gardner and Gary Rosenberg. Simon & Schuster, 1991.

On suicide prevention

Teens at Risk: How to Recognize and Prevent Adolescent Suicide. Kevin Leehey. PIA Press, 1991.

I Want to Kill Myself: Helping Your Child Cope with Depression and Suicidal Thoughts. T.K. Shamoo. Lexington, 1990.

Suicide Prevention in Schools. A. Leenaars and S. Wenckstern, eds. Hemisphere, 1990.

On the effects of suicides or suicide attempts

Prayers for Bobby: A Mother's Coming to Terms with the Suicide of Her Gay Son. Leroy Aarons. HarperSanFrancisco, 1995.

After a Suicide. 12-minute video. Filmmakers Library, 1995.

Healing after the Suicide of a Loved One. Ann Smolin and John Guinan. Simon & Schuster, 1993.

Words I Never Thought to Speak: Stories of Life in the Wake of Suicide. Victoria G. Alexander. Free Press, 1991.

A Special Scar: The Experiences of People Bereaved by Suicide. Allison Wertheimer. Routledge, 1991.

The Other Victims of Suicide. Sharon Craft. Hearthstone, 1991.

Stronger Than Death. S. Chance. Norton, 1992. A psychiatrist writes about the suicide of her son.

For preteens and teens

Teen Suicide: Is It Too Painful to Grow Up? Eleanor Ayer. Twenty-First Century Books, 1995.

Drugs in Society: Are They Our Suicide Pill? John Salak. Twenty-First Century Books, 1995.

Suicide. Margaret Hyde and Elizabeth Forsythe. Watts, 1991.

Straight Talk About Teenage Suicide. Bernard Frankel and Rachel Kranz. Facts On File, 1991.

Teenagers Talk About...Suicide. Marian Crook. NC Press, 1988. Interviews with young people who have considered or tried suicide.

Background works

When Is It Right to Die?: Suicide, Euthanasia, Suffering, Mercy. Joni E. Tada. Zondervan, 1992.

The Encyclopedia of Suicide. Glen Evans and Norman L. Farberow. Facts on File, 1988.

(See also DEATH AND DYING; DEPRESSION.)

sulfur, a MINERAL used in several key AMINO ACIDS, and therefore vital to the building and maintenance functions of the body, especially in bones, tendons, and connective tissue. Among the main sources of sulfur are wheat germ, dried beans, beef, and clams. Before the advent of PENICILLIN and later ANTIBIOTICS, drugs containing sulfur (*sulfa drugs* or *sulfonamides)* were often used to treat infections; they are still used for some kinds of infections, such as urinary tract infections, and in ointments to treat some SKIN DISORDERS. (See MINERALS; NUTRITION.)

supervision, in relation to families, the duty of parents or GUARDIANS to protect and guide the children who are in their CUSTODY and care. Supervision is part of a PARENT'S RESPONSIBILITIES, running along with a PARENT'S RIGHTS to make basic and important decisions for a child. A parent's failure to provide for proper supervision, as defined by social work agencies and the courts, may lead to charges of CHILD ABUSE AND NEGLECT and, in serious cases, to TERMINATION OF PARENTS' RIGHTS and the assumption by the state of the task of supervising the child, often until FOSTER CARE or ADOPTION can be arranged. Parents and their advocates (see ADVOCACY) have every right to contest allegations of "improper supervision" as unfounded, as when they reflect narrow moralizing on the part of others, rather than a real concern for the welfare of children; as a matter of principle and sound practice, the family comes first.

JUVENILES convicted of DELINQUENT acts or STATUS OFFENSES (such as RUNAWAYS, TRUANTS, or INCORRIGIBLE children), who are thought to require more supervision than previously provided by parents or guardians, may sometimes be placed under court supervision. This may involve PROBATION, or the court may transfer CUSTODY to a relative or social agency. Such delinquents are variously called *Children in Need of Supervision* (CHINS), *Juveniles in Need of Supervision* (JINS), *Minors in Need of Supervision* (MINS), or *Persons in Need of Supervision* (PINS).

Supplemental Educational Opportunity Grant (SEOG), a type of GRANT in FINANCIAL AID to help undergraduate students meet the expenses of attending COLLEGE. Grants up to $4000, though depending on the funds available at each school, are offered to students with exceptional financial need; priority is given to those who have PELL GRANTS. Money is paid directly to the student or credited to the school account. (See FINANCIAL AID.)

Supplemental Security Income (SSI) Program, a federal program providing cash assistance to the elderly and to individuals of any age who have DISABILITIES. Individuals can receive as much as several hundred dollars a month; the amount is uniform nationwide because (unlike many federally mandated programs), SSI is federally funded as well. In addition all but a few states supplement these monthly SSI benefits—though all such payments are under sharp attack politically in this period. People who receive SSI payments are automatically eligible for Medicaid, which also makes them eligible for other programs, such as EARLY AND PERIODIC SCREENING, DIAGNOSIS, AND TREATMENT (EPSDT).

Initially SSI benefits were extremely restrictive, barring benefits to many children; however, a key 1990 Supreme Court decision, *Sullivan v. Zebley* (a decision made retroactive to 1980), opened the SSI Program to many children previously denied assistance, including those with CHRONIC illness, providing their family's income and resources are below the allowed limit. For qualifying families, children with certain disabilities are usually accepted into the SSI program immediately (though their medical claims would need to be confirmed), including loss of two limbs; loss of a leg at the hip; total blindness (see EYE AND VISION PROBLEMS); total deafness (see EAR AND HEARING PROBLEMS); immobility or confinement from a long-standing condition; STROKE or TRAUMATIC BRAIN INJURY with obvious difficulty in WALKING or using hand or arm after more than three months; CEREBRAL PALSY, MUSCULAR DYSTROPHY, or muscular atrophy, with obvious difficulty in walking, talking, or hand or arm coordination; DIABETES, with loss of at least one foot; DOWN'S SYNDROME, severe MENTAL RETARDATION in a child over age seven; kidney disease requiring regular DIALYSIS (see KIDNEY AND UROLOGICAL DISORDERS), and infection with HIV (see AIDS.) Children with other conditions would receive no payments until evaluated and approved individually. (See HELP FOR SPECIAL CHILDREN on page 689.)

supported employment, rehabilitation programs for people with DISABILITIES that match their skills and interests with the needs of potential employers. Such programs aim to find jobs appropriate to the person's skills, providing additional training as necessary, including on-site training and coaching during the initial employment period. After the transition period, the program staff generally consults with the employer to monitor the progress and performance of the workers. In recent years, supported employment has allowed many people with disabilities to work and develop self-esteem, who might otherwise have been dependent. It is a key part of the modern trend toward independent living, and the wider move toward integration of people with disabilities into the community, as legislated under the AMERICANS WITH DISABILITIES ACT (ADA). Many of the VOCATIONAL REHABILITATION (VR) services provided for teens with disabilities, especially during their TRANSITION to full adulthood, are aimed at providing them with the skills to work in supported employment—though many, of course, will be able to work with full independence, without special support. (See HELP FOR SPECIAL CHILDREN on page 689.)

surrogate family, a FAMILY-like network of people chosen as close friends and supporters, often people with shared work, culture, interests, and neighborhoods.

surrogate mother, a woman who agrees to bear a child for a couple who are unable to have one themselves, usually for a fee and by contract, an arrangement sometimes termed *noncoital collaborative reproduction.* The approach is generally tried when the husband is fertile but his wife is unable to bear children herself, often because she is infertile, is too ill to have a child, or carries a GENETIC DISORDER that would be passed on to her children. The surrogate mother is inseminated with SPERM from the man, generally through ARTIFICIAL INSEMINATION; gives birth; and then releases the child for ADOPTION to the couple.

Though physically very simple, surrogate parenting is fraught with legal, emotional, and social pitfalls, including uncertain legal status of the child; the legal status of the adults in relation to the child (see MOTHER; FATHER); social pressures for and against the procedure from various quarters; and feelings of confusion, sadness, and guilt, especially on the part of the surrogate mother. Laws regarding surrogate arrangements vary widely, and the legal status of agreements among the parties is unclear.

Some surrogacy arrangements have worked out satisfactorily for all involved, with many surrogate mothers stressing their pleasure at bringing a child to a childless couple. However, the risks are great, the major one being that the surrogate mother will decide not to give the child up for adoption. This was classically illustrated in the "Baby M" case, in which surrogate mother Mary Beth Whitehead refused to give up "Baby M," attempting to retain her PARENTS' RIGHTS; after a long court battle, CUSTODY was awarded to William and Elizabeth Stern, the other parties to the contract, with Whitehead retaining VISITATION RIGHTS, though the New Jersey court ruled that commercial surrogate mother contracts were illegal and that Whitehead was the child's legal MOTHER.

In an alternative surrogacy approach, the wife's egg and the husband's SPERM are mixed together in a laboratory dish (see IN VITRO FERTILIZATION); the resulting fertilized egg or eggs are then implanted into a *host surrogate mother*, who bears the child. In this situation, the host surrogate mother is the birth mother, but the infertile wife is the biological mother. Because the child's genetic inheritance comes from the husband and wife, at least some courts have allowed the name of the wife (the biological mother) to be entered on the child's birth certificate, rather than that of the host or surrogate mother. (The husband is already the biological FATHER.)

Though it is seemingly a simple solution to a situation when a woman is infertile but her husband or partner is not, parents considering surrogacy should explore the ramifications very carefully before making any decision. In particular, they should explore the current status of surrogacy contracts in a fast-developing area of the law, and consider how they would respond to a broken contract.

FOR HELP AND FURTHER INFORMATION

Center for Surrogate Parenting and Egg Donation, Inc.
8383 Wilshire Boulevard, Suite 750
Beverly Hills, CA 90211

213–655–1974
Fax: 213–852–1310
E-mail: centersp@netcom.com
William Handle and Karen Snyesiou, Codirectors
Organization concerned with surrogate parenting and egg donation; provides information, as to lawyers handling surrogate parent cases; acts as advocate; publishes various materials.

National Coalition Against Surrogacy (NCAS)
c/o Sharon Huddle
2625 Fair Oaks Boulevard, Suite 5
Sacramento, CA 95864
916–487–3700
Fax: 916–487–3747
Organization of people opposed to surrogate parenting; offers support to women unhappy as surrogate mothers; seeks to influence public policy and legislation against surrogate maternity contracts.

RESOLVE, Inc., HelpLine: 617–623–0744. Offers adoption services, along with infertility treatments; publishes fact sheets *Overview* and *Surrogating: What Do You Think?* (For full group information, see INFERTILITY.)

Concerned United Birthparents (CUB), 515–263–9558. Publishes *Surrogate and Other Nontraditional Reproduction.* (For full group information, see ADOPTION.)

OTHER RESOURCES

GENERAL WORKS

Surrogate Motherhood: Conception in the Heart. Helena Ragone. Westview, 1994.
Alternatives to Infertility: Is Surrogacy the Answer? Lita L. Schwartz. Brunner-Mazel, 1991.
Birth Power: The Case for Surrogacy. Carmel Shalev. Yale University Press, 1989.
Surrogate Motherhood. Martha A. Field. Harvard University Press, 1988.

PERSONAL EXPERIENCES

Love Child: Our Surrogate Baby. Rona Walker. Trafalgar, 1991.
A Mother's Story. Mary Beth Whitehead. St. Martin's, 1989.
The Case of Baby M: And the Facts of Life. Rochelle Sharpe. Prentice Hall, 1989.

BACKGROUND WORKS

Surrogate Motherhood: A Worldwide View of the Issues. Deiderika Pretorius. C.C. Thomas, 1994.
The Ethics of Commercial Surrogate Motherhood: Brave New Families? Scott B. Rae. Praeger/Greenwood, 1993.
Surrogate Motherhood: Politics and Privacy. Larry Gostin, ed. Indiana University Press, 1990.

surrogate parent, a person appointed to act in the interests of a child with DISABILITIES during the EDUCATION process, to see that the child receives an appropriate education and necessary services if that child has no parent to act as advocate (see ADVOCACY). In some areas, notably Minnesota, parents are recruited, trained, and appointed by the local school districts. More generally, a surrogate parent is an adult in a child's life who plays a quasi-parental role, such as a beloved teacher or neighbor. (See also SURROGATE MOTHER.)

survival skills, those skills a person needs to function effectively in an environment. Used popularly, these sometimes refer to the skills needed if one were stranded on a desert island or mountainous wilderness, but in education, these generally refer to FUNCTIONAL SKILLS necessary for everyday life.

suspension, in EDUCATION, an order for a student to leave a school temporarily, generally for misbehavior. In-school suspension refers to a student being ordered to leave classes, but kept in school elsewhere, as outside a principal's office. Unlike EXPULSION, which is long term or permanent, suspension is normally lifted in a short time, sometimes after consultation with the student's parents. Various Supreme Court rulings have affected the legal rights of students and schools in cases of suspension and expulsion.

FOR HELP AND FURTHER INFORMATION

Center for Law and Education, 202–986–3000. Publishes "Information for Parents" brochure Suspension and Due Process, Procedural Due Process Rights in Student Discipline, and Disciplinary Exclusion of Students with Disabilities Under Federal Law: An Overview. (For full group information, see HELP ON LEARNING AND EDUCATION on page 659.)

PACER Center (Parent Advocacy Coalition for Educational Rights), 612–827–2966, voice/TT. Publishes *Ma, They Suspended Me Again.* (For full group information, see HELP FOR SPECIAL CHILDREN on page 689.)

National Organization on Legal Problems of Education (NOLPE), 913–273–3550. Publishes *The Law of Student Expulsions and Suspensions.* (For full group information, see HELP ON LEARNING AND EDUCATION on page 659.)

sweat test, a MEDICAL TEST that measures concentrations of salt in sweat, abnormally high concentrations of SODIUM and CHLORIDE being a common indicator of CYSTIC FIBROSIS.

Sydenham's chorea, a pattern of involuntary, quick, jerky movements, called CHOREA, often found in children who have RHEUMATIC FEVER, apparently resulting from streptococcus infection in the brain (see STREP THROAT). It generally passes after some weeks, though it may recur in some situations. Sydenham's is relatively rare since the advent of ANTIBIOTICS.

syllabus, an outline of a course offered in a school, often on the COLLEGE level, describing the main topics to be covered, sometimes accompanied by a schedule, and listing the works to be assigned or suggested as additional reading.

symbiotic stage, the early close relationship established between a MOTHER (or other primary CAREGIVER) and child as a result of the BONDING process. In this state, the baby sees the mother as part of self, and the mother acts as a need-satisfying object to the child. Traditionally the symbiotic stage was thought to extend from age three to eighteen months, to roughly around the time that a child begins to walk, but more recent work suggests that the child begins to see the self and mother as separate entities earlier, perhaps by about seven months, beginning the succeeding stage, called SEPARATION-INDIVIDUATION.

symptom, in medicine, a subjective indication of illness observed by a patient, as opposed to an objective indication, or SIGN, of disease or disorder observed or detected by a physician. An observable skin RASH or a measurable FEVER is a sign, for example, while the patient's feeling of itching or heat is a symptom.

syndactyly (syndactylism or syndactylia), a BIRTH DEFECT in which two or more fingers or (more commonly) toes are joined together; these are sometimes joined by the skin only, but sometimes have bones and skin fused and a single nail. Many forms of syndactyly are inherited and affect boys more than girls, but some may be caused by constriction of the FETUS within the UTERUS.

syndrome, a group of signs or symptoms that, when they appear together, indicate the presence of a known condition or disease; literally meaning "running together." Not all syndromes are so-called, such as *Tay-Sachs disease* (see LIPID STORAGE DISEASES) or APPARENT LIFE-THREATENING EVENT (ALTE), but many syndromes are tagged as such. Among the many covered in this book are *acquired immune deficiency syndrome* (AIDS); BATTERED CHILD SYNDROME; CHUBBY PUFFER SYNDROME; COCKAYNE'S SYNDROME; *congenital varicella syndrome* (see CHICKEN POX); CORNELIA DE LANGE SYNDROME; CRI DU CHAT (CRY OF THE CAT) SYNDROME; *Cushing's syndrome* (see ADRENAL GLANDS); DISPLACED CHILD SYNDROME; DOWN SYNDROME; EDWARDS' SYNDROME; FEAR TENSION PAIN SYNDROME; FETAL ALCOHOL SYNDROME; FETAL HYDANTOIN SYNDROME; FLOPPY INFANT SYNDROME; FRAGILE X SYNDROME; *Hurler syndrome, Hunter syndrome, Morquio syndrome, Sanfilippo syndrome* and *Maroteaux-Lamy syndrome* (see MUCOPOLYSACCHARIDOSES); IRRITABLE BOWEL SYNDROME; KLINEFELTER'S SYNDROME; LAURENCE-MOON-BIEDL SYNDROME; LESCH-NYHAN SYNDROME; *Louis-Bar syndrome* (see ATAXIA); MARFAN SYNDROME; MATERNAL DEPRIVATION SYNDROME; *Menke's syndrome* (see WILSON'S DISEASE); NURSING BOTTLE SYNDROME; ORGANIC BRAIN SYNDROME; PATAU'S SYNDROME; PIERRE ROBIN SYNDROME; *premenstrual syndrome* (see MENSTRUATION); *Refsum's syndrome* (see LIPID STORAGE DISEASES); RESPIRATORY DISTRESS SYNDROME; REYE SYNDROME; *Rosenthal's syndrome* (see HEMOPHILIA); SAVANT SYNDROME; SELF-MUTILATION SYNDROME; SHAKEN CHILD SYNDROME; SHEEHAN'S SYNDROME; SJOGREN'S SYNDROME; STURGE-WEBER SYNDROME; SUDDEN INFANT DEATH SYNDROME (SIDS); *survivor syndrome* (see POST-TRAUMATIC STRESS DISORDER); TOURETTE SYNDROME; TOXIC SHOCK SYNDROME; TURNER'S SYNDROME (and *Noonan's syndrome*); and VULNERABLE CHILD SYNDROME.

synthesis-level thinking, the practice of combining knowledge of several pieces of previously learned information to create ideas new to the thinker; from Benjamin Bloom's description of the various kinds of thinking or learning processes, the other main types being KNOWLEDGE-LEVEL, COMPREHENSION-LEVEL, APPLICATION-LEVEL, ANALYSIS-LEVEL, and EVALUATION-LEVEL.

syphilis, a serious PROGRESSIVE disease that, if untreated, can cause MENTAL DISORDERS, BLINDNESS, and death; specifically, infection with the corkscrew-shaped bacterium *Treponema pallidum,* a common SEXUALLY TRANSMITTED DISEASE and one of the traditional *venereal diseases.* A scourge of humanity for centuries, syphilis is today readily treatable by ANTIBIOTICS, but cases have recently been on the rise, perhaps partly because the success of the treatment has left many people unaware of the disease's dangers. The U.S. Public Health Service reports approximately 70,000 new cases annually.

The infection is passed through direct contact with an infected person, often through the genital area, mouth, or anus, but also through a break in the skin anywhere on the body. A pregnant woman with syphilis can (at least after the fourth month of pregnancy) pass the disease to the FETUS, causing serious BIRTH DEFECTS, such as MENTAL RETARDATION, MENINGITIS, and various deformities; they also have increased risk of MISCARRIAGE and SYPHILIS. The National Institute of Allergy and Infectious Disease (NIAID) reports, however: "The syphilis bacterium is very fragile, and the infection is rarely, if ever, spread by contact with objects such as toilet seats or towels."

Early symptoms, which occur ten days to three months from exposure, are often very mild—so mild that people might not seek treatment, and meanwhile can pass the infection on to others. The main symptom of the first stage of syphilis (medically called *primary syphilis*) is a usually painless open sore, a *chancre* (pronounced *SHANK-er*), often in the genital area, but sometimes around the mouth or fingertips; this disappears within a few weeks.

In the second stage, or *secondary syphilis,* about two to twelve weeks after the chancre disappears, a skin rash appears, sometimes only in localized areas, such as the palms or soles of the feet, but sometimes over the whole body. The rash is often accompanied by flu-like symptoms, such as low-grade FEVER, headache, fatigue, sore throat, swollen lymph glands, and sometimes hair loss. These symptoms may come and go for one to two years, during which time the person is actively contagious.

After that, the diseases enters a so-called *latent* stage. NIAID reports:

Many people who are not treated will suffer no further consequences of the disease. However, from 15 to 40 percent of those infected go on to develop the complications of late, or *tertiary,* syphilis, in which the bacteria damage the heart, eyes, brain, nervous system, bones, joints, or almost any other part of the body. This stage can last for years, or even for decades. Late syphilis, the final stage, can lead to mental illness, blindness, heart disease, and death.

Syphilis can be diagnosed by its symptoms (though many are similar to other STDs), by BLOOD TESTS, and by laboratory identification of the bacteria responsible. Treatment at any stage of the disease, NIAID reports, will cure the disease, and within twenty-four hours of beginning treatment, the patient is no longer contagious. But treatment cannot reverse damage already done to the body, or to the fetus within a pregnant woman. Many doctors recommend that pregnant women be tested for syphilis as a routine part of PRENATAL CARE. (For information on how to avoid infection, see SEXUALLY TRANSMITTED DISEASES.)

T

target child, a child who has unusual talents, deficiencies, socioeconomic disadvantage, troubled home situation, or some other special characteristics outlined by a program designed to help children, such as HEAD START, a CHILD ABUSE AND NEGLECT prevention program, or screening for programs under the EDUCATION FOR ALL HANDICAPPED CHILDREN ACT, the INDIVIDUALS WITH DISABILITIES EDUCATION ACT, or the GIFTED AND TALENTED CHILDREN'S ACT.

target schools, schools selected for special programs, notably to receive federal moneys under CHAPTER 1.

task-appropriate, a general term describing behavior considered well chosen for completion of the task set for a child; a common descriptive phrase used in reports of DEVELOPMENTAL SCREENING TESTS. If the task is drawing a picture, for example, sitting down quietly with crayon and paper would be considered task-appropriate, while walking around the table would not.

Td vaccine, the name of the booster vaccine recommended to be given every ten years to maintain IMMUNIZATION against TETANUS and DIPHTHERIA. The original vaccine is generally given as part of the DTP VACCINE.

Technical Assistance for Parents Program (TAPP), a network of agencies, operated by nationwide PARENT TRAINING AND INFORMATION CENTERS (PTIs), established in each state, originally under the EDUCATION FOR ALL HANDICAPPED CHILDREN ACT OF 1975, then under the INDIVIDUALS WITH DISABILITIES EDUCATION ACT (IDEA). TAPPs were originally designed to aid parents of children with DISABILITIES or CHRONIC ILLNESS from minority or other disadvantaged environments, who have traditionally not gained the full benefit of public programs. But TAPP programs have since widened to provide technical aid and peer support to all families of children in need. (See Federation of Children with Special Needs under HELP FOR SPECIAL CHILDREN on page 689.)

teacher competency testing, an approach attempt to ensure that teachers meet basic standards, similar to the approach for students in MINIMUM COMPETENCY TESTING.

teeth and dental problems, the bony structures used for chewing, which are rooted in the jaw and cushioned by the gums, and the disorders relating to them. Each tooth has a coating of enamel and then dentin surrounding living pulp, which includes nerves and blood vessels. Humans get two sets of teeth, the *primary teeth* (also called *baby, milk,* or *deciduous teeth*) that begin appearing in infancy, and the *permanent teeth* that start arriving around age six or seven. There are four main types of teeth:

- *Incisors*—the shovel-shaped front teeth.
- *Canines, cuspids,* or *eye teeth*—the long-rooted, pointed teeth on either side of the incisors.
- *Bicuspids* or *premolars*—the largely flat-topped but two-pointed teeth between canines and molars in adults; children have no bicuspids.
- *Molars*—the large, flat-topped, grinding teeth in the back of the mouth; the third molars, which appear only in adults, are called the WISDOM TEETH.

TEETH—AND WHEN THEY NORMALLY APPEAR (on page 585) shows the location of the various types of teeth and when they generally appear, or *erupt.* GENETIC INHERITANCE may alter this schedule, and certain conditions, such as RICKETS or too little production from the THYROID GLAND or PITUITARY GLAND may slow it down.

During *teething,* the period when the primary teeth appear, the gums over the erupting teeth may become swollen and red. Infants generally become irritable and restless when cutting teeth, and often like to chew on pacifiers or rubber rings. Doctors warn against using teething lotions, liquor, or paregoric on gums, for they can be dangerous to the child. Some doctors suggest rubbing a bit of aspirin on the gums to relieve the pain, but that should not be done if the child seems to have any viral illness, since aspirin may trigger some cases of REYE SYNDROME. Teething does not in itself cause fever and illness, so parents should not assume that signs of illness are caused by teething. Children do often get the viral illness ROSEOLA during the teething period, but the link between the two is unclear.

Most teeth erupt normally, but some are blocked, because the jaw is already overcrowded. Such a blocked tooth is called an IMPACTED TOOTH. This problem mostly affects the last of the permanent teeth to appear: the upper canines and especially the wisdom teeth. Impacted wisdom teeth can often become painful and infected, and may need to be extracted. Teeth blocked from eruption by bone or other tissue are sometimes said to be *imbedded.* Impacted canines can emerge twisted and out of position, and require the attention of an ORTHODONTIST, often with corrective orthodontic braces (see MALOCCLUSION).

The most common dental problem is *caries,* or tooth decay, popularly called *cavities.* Bacteria in the mouth mix with saliva and leftover food to form a deposit on teeth, called *plaque;* as the bacteria break down the food, acid forms, eating away at the enamel and dentin, literally forming indentations or cavities. If the cavity is not cleaned out

Teeth—And When They Normally Appear

PRIMARY (BABY) TEETH

Upper Teeth	
Central incisors	8–12 months
Lateral (side) incisors	9–13 months
Cuspids (canines)	16–22 months
First molars	13–19 months
Second molars	25–33 months

Lower Teeth	
Central incisors	6–10 months
Lateral (side) incisors	10–16 months
Cuspids	17–23 months
First molars	14–18 months
Second molars	23–31 months

PERMANENT TEETH

Upper Teeth	
Central incisors	7–8 years
Lateral (side) incisors	8–9 years
Cuspids (canines)	11–12 years
First bicuspids	10–11 years
Second bicuspids	10–12 years
First molars	6–7 years
Second molars	12–13 years
Third molars	17–21 years

Lower Teeth	
Central incisors	6–7 years
Lateral (side) incisors	7–8 years
Cuspids (canines)	9–10 years
First bicuspids	10–12 years
Second bicuspids	11–12 years
First molars	6–7 years
Second molars	11–12 years
Third molars	17–21 years

and filled with a neutral substance, the acid will eventually eat through to the pulp, causing pain and often infection, and gradually killing the tooth. If the pulp becomes infected, or if an *abscess* (a pocket of infection) forms, ROOT CANAL THERAPY may be necessary; if all else fails, the tooth will need to be extracted. Teenagers with BULIMIA have great problems with tooth decay, because the stomach acid from frequent vomiting attacks the teeth.

Dental caries can start as soon as teeth appear. Though baby teeth will be replaced, it is still important to prevent tooth decay, for the health of the permanent teeth to come. To do this, many dentists recommend that parents:

- Limit the amount of sugar in their children's food, and not allow infants to fall asleep with a bottle, which can lead to NURSING BOTTLE SYNDROME.
- Clean infants' teeth with gauze or a clean, damp washcloth after feeding, or at least once a day, and later switch to toothbrushing twice a day, especially at bedtime.
- Feed their children a well-balanced diet strong in CALCIUM.
- Start flossing when children's teeth fit closely together, around age two or three.
- Once children start brushing their own teeth (perhaps in their second year, though some dentists say not until age seven), use DISCLOSING TABLETS to highlight areas missed in brushing.
- Get a new toothbrush every three or four months.
- Be sure that their children are getting sufficient fluoride, if not from the water supply, then from drops or tablets (later from toothpaste or mouthwash).

FLUORIDATION helps prevent tooth decay by strengthening the enamel coating of the tooth, and reducing the amount of acid formed by bacteria in the mouth. In recent decades, it is credited with helping cut the amount of tooth decay dramatically.

Other common dental problems include GINGIVITIS, or gum inflammation, and BRUXISM, or tooth grinding. Among the specialists treating dental problems, in addition to the dentist, are the ORTHODONTIST, ENDODONTIST, PERIODONTIST, and ORAL SURGEON.

The National Institute of Dental Research recommends that parents start taking children to the dentist around their second birthday, and visit the dentist regularly every six months. Modern dentists focus heavily on prevention, and stress that the sooner they are able to identify dental problems, such as MALOCCLUSION, or bad bite, the better their chances of treating them successfully. They may also detect some inherited GENETIC DISORDERS such as AMELOGENESIS IMPERFECTA.

Cavities in primary teeth must be spotted and filled, to avoid pain for the child and possible loss of the tooth. Lost teeth can cause problems with feeding and speaking. Parents should look for a dentist who is comfortable with and geared to working with very young patients. Pediatric dentists recommend that you prepare young children for a first visit to the dentist by reading a book (see the list of resources that follows this entry), and stress that the visit should be treated as routine, not on occasion for fear or concern. Indeed, there is an ongoing "revolution" in dental care, from a fearful experience to a largely preventive stance. Today's parents may, in fact, need reeducation in this area, for modern dentistry is increasingly focused on painless prevention, as opposed to painful procedures.

Once permanent teeth start arriving, some dentists recommend using a protective sealant to coat the cavity-prone back teeth. If permanent teeth are lost or broken, they should be repaired, as with a CROWN, which replaces the whole top of the tooth, or replaced with a false tooth. Otherwise the remaining teeth may be affected; if a tooth is lost, for example, the opposite tooth may grow abnormally long, or nearby teeth may drift into the empty space, creating malocclusion.

In recent decades, dentists have developed a variety of approaches to restoring discolored or damaged teeth. *Bleaching* several times with a warm peroxide solution can be used to remove some stains, though not the stains caused in children's teeth by the ANTIBIOTIC tetracycline. *Bonding* is a coating "painted" on teeth, which covers stains and may also be used to build up damaged teeth or teeth that are too wide apart. A *laminate veneer* is a layer of material stuck onto a tooth, which may last somewhat longer than bonding. These new treatments offer alternatives to the use of crowns, but are still relatively new and their long-term durability is unknown.

FOR HELP AND FURTHER INFORMATION

National Institute of Dental Research (NIDR)
Building 31, Room 2C35
31 Center Drive, MSC 2290
Bethesda, MD 20892–2290
or: P.O. Box 54793
Washington, DC 20032
301–496–4261
Fax: 301–496–9988
One of the National Institutes of Health; provides information; operates National Oral Health Information Clearinghouse (see below); publishes various materials, including *A Healthy Mouth for Your Baby, Snack Smart for Health Teeth!* (for children), *A Healthy Start—Fluoride Tablets for Children in Preschool Programs, Seal Out Dental Decay, Rx for Sound Teeth, Fluoride to Protect the Teeth of Adults, What You Need to Know About Periodontal (Gum) Diseases, Fever Blisters and Canker Sores*; and materials for health professionals.

National Oral Health Information Clearinghouse (NOHIC)
1 NOHIC Way
Bethesda, MD 20892–3500
301–402–7364
Fax: 301–907–8830
E-mail: nidr@aerie.com
Clearinghouse operated by the National Institute of Dental Research (see above); provides information to public and professionals; publishes various materials, including *OH Notes, Special Care in Oral Health Fact Sheet, NOHIC: A Resource for Special Care Patients, Temporomandibular Disorders: Information for Patients,* and *Dry Mouth (Xerostomia).* (For more titles, see CANCER; DIABETES.)

American Dental Association (ADA)
211 East Chicago Avenue
Chicago, IL 60611
312–440–2500
John S. Zapp, Executive Director
Organization of dental professionals; sponsors research; accredits dental schools; publishes dental health education materials and professional materials, including *Dentist's Desk Reference.*

American Society of Dentistry for Children (ASDC)
John Hancock Center
875 North Michigan Avenue, Suite 4040
Chicago, IL 60611
312–943–1244
Fax: 312–943–5341
Norman Olsen, Executive Director
Organization of dental professionals specialized in treating children; sponsors research; publishes various materials, including bimonthly *Journal of Dentistry for Children* and newsletter.

American Academy of Pediatrics (AAP), 800–433–9016. Publishes brochure *A Guide to Children's Dental Health.* (For full group information, see HEALTH CARE.)

American Heart Association (AHA), 800–242–8721. Publishes *Dental Care for Children with Heart Disease.* (For full group information, see HEART AND HEART PROBLEMS.)

National Diabetes Information Clearinghouse (NDIC), 301–654–3327. Publishes *Dental Tips for Diabetics* and *Periodontal Disease and Diabetes: A Guide for Patients.* (For full group information, see DIABETES.)

National Foundation of Dentistry for the Handicapped (NFDH), 301–496–4261. (For full group information, see HELP FOR SPECIAL CHILDREN on page 689.)

National Maternal and Child Health Clearinghouse (NMCHC), 703–821–8955. Publishes *Protect Your Child's Teeth—Put Your Baby to Bed with Love, Not a Bottle.* (For full group information, see PREGNANCY.)

OTHER RESOURCES

GENERAL WORKS

Protecting Our Children's Teeth: A Guide to Quality Dental Care from Infancy through Age Twelve. Malcolm S. Foster. Plenum, 1992.

The Mount Sinai Medical Center Family Guide to Dental Health. Jack Klatell and others. Macmillan, 1992.

Trust, AIDS and Your Dentist: Key Questions to Ask Your Dentist about Infection Control, HIV and Sterilization. Randall P. Westman. Sweettooth, 1993.

For children

Brush Them Bright. Patricia Quinlan. Hyperion, 1992.
All about Your Skin, Hair and Teeth. Donna Bailey. Raintree Steck-Vaughn, 1990.
Taryn Goes to the Dentist. Jill Krementz. Crown, 1986.

telangiectasia, increased size and number of blood vessels in the skin, causing redness, especially on the ears and face, sometimes (in hereditary forms) readily susceptible to bleeding. Telangiectasias sometimes occur simply from too much sunlight, but are often associated with ALCOHOL ABUSE and with disorders such as a hereditary form of ATAXIA and LUPUS. Some kinds of birthmarks (see NEVUS) are localized forms of telangiectasia.

temporary restraining order (TRO), a court order requiring a person to not carry out threatened acts, such as CHILD ABUSE AND NEGLECT or PARENTAL KIDNAPPING. A TRO is often issued after an EX PARTE hearing, in which one party only appears before the judge. After the TRO is in effect, the judge generally calls for an ORDER TO SHOW CAUSE HEARING to get the other party's side of the question, and will then either remove the TRO or make a permanent INJUNCTION against action. While a TRO in itself will often not stop a potentially violent person, it generally makes the police more likely to intervene.

tender-years doctrine, a popular phrase for the courts' common assumption, from the early twentieth century, that the BEST INTERESTS OF CHILDREN are best served when CUSTODY is awarded to the mother, in case of dispute between the parents.

teratologist, a medical specialist in the study of BIRTH DEFECTS; from the Greek *teras* meaning monster.

term, alternate name for FULL-TERM, referring to a baby born generally on schedule, rather than PREMATURE. In EDUCATION, term generally refers to each of the major divisions of a school year, during which a course is normally completed, such as a SEMESTER or QUARTER.

termination of parental rights (TPR), a legal proceeding, often in JUVENILE COURT, that seeks to end PARENTS' RIGHTS to CUSTODY and SUPERVISION of their child, as in some cases of ABANDONMENT or CHILD ABUSE AND NEGLECT. If a TPR proceeding is successful, the child may be placed for ADOPTION without formal consent from the parents. A BIRTH PARENT who is placing a child for adoption agrees to termination of parental rights, though some forms of adoption modify that somewhat. Sometimes after termination of parental rights, the child may be placed in FOSTER CARE temporarily until the parent demonstrates to the satisfaction of the court fitness to resume parental rights, as by completing a drug rehabilitation program. Parents facing a termination of parental rights proceeding, which can result in family breakup, should be represented by a lawyer, to protect their family rights and those of their children.

tertiary-care facility, a medical designation for those HOSPITALS with the most sophisticated equipment and specially trained staff, sometimes called *Level III* facilities, including many *University-Affiliated Facilities* (UAFs) with special research and teaching connections. (See HOSPITALS.)

test, a systematic form or procedure designed to measure or assess some ability, skill, aspect, or characteristic of a person, such as MEDICAL TESTS (see separate entry) and various educational and psychological tests. Tests come in a sometimes bewildering variety of shapes and forms, and can be described and categorized in many ways.

Many tests for children (as well as adults), especially in EDUCATION, come two main types:

- CRITERION-REFERENCED TESTS, for which a child either does or does not meet a preset standard, such as being able to complete a given puzzle or finishing a typing test with fewer than 5 errors.
- NORM-REFERENCED TESTS, in which a child's performance is compared with the average performance of many other children who have taken the test, with the result sometimes converted into GRADE-EQUIVALENT or AGE EQUIVALENT scores.

But many other types of tests have no "right" or "wrong" answers, instead being designed to show something about how a child thinks, feels, and functions. Among these are some psychological tests, such as PROJECTIVE TESTS seeking information on personality and mental condition; *psychomotor tests* that assess the coordination of brain and hands; and MENTAL STATUS EXAMINATIONS, assessing a person's current orientation and mental condition, which merge into the medical area.

Some are *group tests*, designed to be given to a number of children at the same time, with the test administrator not necessarily being specially trained. Other *individual tests* are meant to be administered to a single child, often by a PSYCHOLOGIST, teacher, or other trained person.

Many are OBJECTIVE TESTS, where scoring does not depend on the administrator's discretion, and is often done by use of a key or even by computer. By contrast, others are SUBJECTIVE TESTS, in which the administrator's handling of the test, observations, and discretion can strongly affect the test score.

Many educational tests are STANDARDIZED TESTS, developed using uniform (standard) procedures on a large population, whose AVERAGE scores become NORMS, to which an individual child's score is compared. Others are developed locally, such as a classroom test, tailored to the needs of a particular group, but without the statistically supported VALIDITY and RELIABILITY of standardized tests.

Some are *paper-and-pencil tests,* requiring at least the ability to read and write; others are *oral tests,* requiring the student to respond verbally to spoken questions; some are questionnaires called *inventories,* designed to discover information about a child's personality, interests, or attitudes; still others try to circumvent writing, reading, and speaking as much as possible, focusing on the doing of particular tasks, such as *performance tests* that require a student to put together a puzzle; some call simply for observing a child's routine behavior, often at play. Tests may, like some INTELLIGENCE TESTS, employ a variety of such approaches.

A test may be given at one sitting, or in several sittings over two days or longer; a number of tests (a BATTERY) may be given over several days; or a series of tests may be given on completion of various parts of a program, called *phased testing* or *progress testing.* Sometimes tests are paired, with one given before instruction (the *pretest*) and the other after (the *posttest*), the attempt being to measure the amount of learning that has taken place.

In a *timed test,* the questions must be completed within a given period; in a *speed test,* the premium is on completing the greatest number of questions in a given amount of time (often set so that few children, if any, will finish the whole test). In some special situations, especially psychological evaluations, observations are made at stated intervals (such as every 10 minutes), a process called *time sampling.*

Traditionally, tests have been given in standard forms, the same to each student. However, the advent of computers has opened the practical possibility of offering ADAPTIVE TESTS, in which the questions presented depend on the student's answers to previous questions.

Though today's parents probably saw an enormous amount of testing in their own lives, their children are seeing even more, and starting much earlier. In both medicine and education, researchers have found that the earlier problem conditions are found, the more easily they can be treated. So children today are undergoing a wide range of tests from infancy, whenever any question arises about the normality of a child's development. This is even enshrined into law as, under the EDUCATION FOR ALL HANDICAPPED CHILDREN ACT and its successor, the INDIVIDUALS WITH DISABILITIES EDUCATION ACT (IDEA), states are required to try to identify (through programs such as CHILDFIND) any children who might have LEARNING DISABILITIES or other DISABILITIES that might affect their learning. The aim is to find and help these children in the PRESCHOOL years, to give them the SPECIAL EDUCATION and medical services they need so that they will be ready for school.

The whole question of readiness, having the necessary skills, abilities, and maturity, to benefit from learning, has spawned other major groups of tests. At the preschool, KINDERGARTEN, and first-grade levels, READINESS TESTS of all kinds are used to help school officials assess whether a child should be admitted to the school (or advised to wait a year before entering) and if so in what class and with what special help, if any. Highly selective PRESCHOOLS and PRIVATE SCHOOLS use such readiness tests as the GESELL PRESCHOOL TEST more in the nature of an ADMISSIONS TEST.

In addition, under the above education laws, schools give periodic DEVELOPMENTAL SCREENING TESTS, sometimes to all students, but sometimes only to those who show some signs of problems. If the tests indicate that problems do exist, the child will generally be given DIAGNOSTIC ASSESSMENT TESTS, which will more precisely pinpoint the areas of difficulties, and be used to plan the child's INDIVIDUALIZED EDUCATION PLAN.

Beyond that, children continue to be barraged by tests of all kinds throughout their school years. In addition to classroom tests, they are periodically given general ACHIEVEMENT TESTS, sometimes called *basic skills tests.* These help schools monitor not only the child's performance, but also the effectiveness of their own instructional programs, by comparing school scores against national NORMS. Schools have, in fact, been so harshly criticized for giving automatic PROMOTIONS to students and graduating some who are functionally ILLITERATE, that schools in some areas now use graded tests of basic skills that a student must pass to be promoted, an approach called MINIMUM COMPETENCY TESTING.

And in the late high school years, a child who is planning to go on to COLLEGE faces various college admissions tests, such as the SCHOLASTIC APTITUDE TEST, ACT TESTS, and the SCHOOL AND COLLEGE ABILITY TESTS. There are also other testing programs that allow students to get advanced college credit, such as the ADVANCED PLACEMENT PROGRAM, PROFICIENCY EXAMINATION PROGRAM, and COLLEGE-LEVEL EXAMINATION PROGRAM.

In this welter of tests, children who are "natural" test-takers have an enormous advantage. So do children who have had a great deal of stimulation and varied experiences at home, especially those from White middle-class, English-speaking, two-parent families. Parents who want to help their children survive in a test-glutted world are advised to help their children from a very young age by encouraging the development of their skills and abilities. Some parents and teachers focus on preparing children specifically for testing, and sometimes for specific tests, an approach sometimes called *hothousing,* for the analogy to the forcing of flower buds. Others focus on more general stimulation, using a wide variety of activities to encourage development of children's skills. (Subscribers to the America Online computer service can find activities designed to develop children's skills in various areas, as well as general guidelines for teaching young children, in the Moms Online Desk Reference section of Moms Online, under "Teaching Young Children.") Some children will inevitably resist testing or become anxious about it, but the best way to avoid that is to forestall it by building the child's skills and confidence in the early years.

FOR HELP AND FURTHER INFORMATION

National Association for the Education of Young Children (NAEYC), 800–424–2460. Publishes books *Achievement Testing in the Early Grades: The Games Grown-Ups Play, Developmental Screening in Early Childhood: A Guide*, and *Reaching Potentials: Appropriate Curriculum and Assessment for Young Children*, Vol. 1; brochure *Testing of Young Children: Concerns and Cautions*; and video *Testing and Tracking*. (For full group information, see PRESCHOOL.)

Alliance for Parental Involvement in Education (ALLPIE), 518–392–6900. Publishes *Standardized Tests and Our Children: A Guide to Testing Reform.* (For full group information, see HELP ON LEARNING AND EDUCATION on page 659).

PACER Center (Parent Advocacy Coalition for Educational Rights), 612–827–2966, voice/TT. Publishes book *Assessment: Special Education Tests, Cultural Competence in Screening and Assessment: Implications for Services to Young Children with Special Needs*; and information handouts *Assessment: What Does It Mean for Your Child?* and *What Is a "Functional Assessment"?* (For full group information, see HELP FOR SPECIAL CHILDREN on page 689.)

National Association for Gifted Children (NAGC), 202–785–4268. Publishes *The Performance of High-Ability Students in the United States on National and International Tests* and *The Use of Published Instruments in the Identification of Gifted and Talented Students.* (For full group information, see GIFTED CHILD.)

Association for Childhood Education International (ACEI), 800–423–3563. Publishes position paper *On Standardized Testing.* (For full group information, see HELP ON LEARNING AND EDUCATION on page 659.)

National Information Center for Children and Youth with Disabilities (NICHCY), 800–695–0285, voice/TT. Publishes *Assessing Children for the Presence of a Disability.* (For full group information, see HELP FOR SPECIAL CHILDREN on page 689.)

Council for Exceptional Children (CEC), 800–328–0272. Publishes *The School Psychologist and the Exceptional Child*; includes Council for Educational Diagnostic Services (CEDS), which publishes quarterlies *CEDS Communique* and *Diagnostique*, and other materials. (For full group information, see HELP ON LEARNING AND EDUCATION on page 659.)

ERIC (Educational Resources Information Center) Clearinghouse on Assessment and Evaluation, 800–464–3742. (For full group information, see HELP ON LEARNING AND EDUCATION on page 659.)

Division of Child and Youth Services c/o American Psychological Association (APA), 202–336–6013. Publishes *Psychological Testing of Language Minority and Culturally Different Children.* (For full group information, see MENTAL DISORDER.)

OTHER RESOURCES

FOR PARENTS

When Your Child Needs Testing: What Parents, Teachers, and Other Helpers Need to Know about Psychological Testing. Milton Shore. Crossroad, 1992.

Testing and Your Child: What You Should Know about 150 of the Most Common Medical, Educational, and Psychological Tests. Virginia E. McCullough. NAL-Dutton, 1992.

BACKGROUND WORKS

A Consumer's Guide to Tests in Print, 2nd ed. Donald D. Hammill and others. PRO-ED, 1992.

Teaching Test Taking Skills: Helping Students Show What They Know. Thomas Scruggs and Margo Mastropieri. Brookline, 1992.

Testing in American Schools: Asking the Right Questions. Diane, 1992.

testes, the pair of male sexual glands (GONADS) that manufacture the SPERM necessary for reproduction; also called *testicles* (singular, *testis*). In a male FETUS, the testes are held inside the abdomen, but by the time of birth, the testes have normally descended into a protective sac, called the *scrotum,* suspended outside the body. The testes are further protected by a fibrous covering called the *tunica albuginea* and nourished by way of the *spermatic cord.* This cord includes arteries, veins, nerves, and other structures, suspended from the abdomen through an opening called the *inguinal ring.* The testes (like the penis) are usually relatively large at birth, but soon grow smaller; during PUBERTY they gradually enlarge to adult size.

Within each testicle are hundreds of coiled, thread-like structures called *seminiferous tubules,* which contain special sperm-generating cells called *spermatogonia.* During puberty, in response to HORMONES from the PITUITARY GLAND, these spermatogonia begin generating sperm, millions each day. Other structures in the testes produce the male hormone TESTOSTERONE.

The spermatogonia actually first produce new cells called spermatocytes. In preparation for possible FERTILIZATION of an egg, each spermatocyte must reduce its genetic contents from 46 chromosomes to 23 strands of DNA, which is done during two divisions called *meiosis.* But while, in the female, duplicate copies of the egg die off, in the male the two divisions produce four sperm, called *spermatids.* It is in these divisions that some CHROMOSOMAL ABNORMALITIES can occur, with errors in dividing. It is also here that each sperm is left with the coded SEX CHROMOSOME that will determine the sex of any child

Testicular Self-Examination

As women make breast self-examinations, from puberty on men should regularly examine their testes for any changes that might signal possible cancer. That is the only way to catch a tumor early enough to be assured of a cure. Perhaps once a month, men should feel their testes over their entire surface, looking for any lump, swelling, or tenderness. The skin of the testes moves freely enough to make self-examination easy. Testicular cancers are often firm and painless lumps, but there may sometimes be pain and inflammation as well. Any lump must be considered a possible cancer, unless testing proves otherwise. If they find any abnormality, they should immediately bring it to their doctor's attention.

that might result from that particular sperm. The woman's egg (OVUM) carries an X sex chromosome. If the sperm also carries an X sex chromosome, then the child will be XX, or female. But if the sperm carries a Y sex chromosome, then the child will be XY, or male. The sperm-generating cells keep on generating sperm daily throughout the man's lifetime, unlike the egg-producing cells in a woman that each produce eggs only once, with eggs maturing only once a month.

The spermatids are then sent through small tubes called *vasa efferentia* into a long, coiled tube called the *epididymis,* a "holding area" that lies along the back of the testicles, where they mature. When ready for use, the sperm are moved out of the epididymis into a long tube called the *vas deferens* (part of the spermatic cord) into the PENIS.

A variety of problems can disrupt this complex, sensitive process, including:

- *Undescended testicles (cryptorchidism)*: Sometimes one or both of the testicles fails to drop from inside the abdomen into the scrotum before birth, for several reasons, including hormonal imbalance, fibrous obstruction of the route of descent, or tubes too short to allow full descent. Undescended testicles is a common problem, especially among PREMATURE babies. Sometimes the testicle descends on its own during the boy's first year; if not, doctors may try HORMONE therapy or a surgical operation called an ORCHIOPEXY, to lower the testicle into the scrotum, generally before school-age. A testicle that remains in the body will not develop normally and will not be able to produce sperm, since the body temperature is too high; it is also associated with an increased risk of CANCER. If both testicles are undescended, the result will be INFERTILITY, though not necessarily impotency. Related problems include:
  - *Ectopic testicles,* in which testicles descend into the groin or base of the penis, rather than into the scrotum; this can be corrected by orchiopexy;
  - *Failure of one testicle to develop normally,* in which case it may be removed, in an ORCHIECTOMY, though the other testicle may be normal.
- *Inflammation of the testes* (ORCHITIS) or *inflammation of the testes and epididymis* (EPIDIDYMO-ORCHITIS): Orchitis most often results from infection with the MUMPS virus, but both the testes and epididymis may become infected by bacteria, often accompanying infection in the PROSTATE GLAND or urinary tract, especially with SEXUALLY TRANSMITTED DISEASES, such as CHLAMYDIA and GONORRHEA.
- *Swelling or fluid collection in the tissues around the testes*: This can result from a variety of problems, including HYDROCELE (a "water sac" in the scrotum), VARICOCELE (swollen veins in the scrotum), or SPERMATOCELE (sperm-filled swelling in the epididymis).
- *Torsion (twisting) of the testis*: The spermatic cord can become twisted, cutting off the blood supply, causing great pain and swelling, a condition that more often affects the left side; it occurs most commonly during PUBERTY or in the first year of life. Complete recovery is normal with prompt diagnosis, often confirmed by ULTRASOUND, and surgical intervention to untwist the cord. But if the condition is not diagnosed and treated within a few hours, loss of blood supply can cause irreparable damage in the testis (and to its future sperm production), including ATROPHY and gangrene (death of tissue). If that occurs, the affected testis is normally removed, an operation called an ORCHIECTOMY, and the other testis sutured to the scrotum to prevent torsion.
- CANCER of the testicles: Malignancies of the testes are relative rare, but they are becoming more common, and indeed have become the most common cancer in American males ages 15–35. The condition is found mostly in males from PUBERTY to middle years, rarely before puberty and in old age. Males who had undescended testicles are at somewhat increased risk; some studies also suggest increased risk for men whose mothers were given estrogen during pregnancy, leading to questions about the ENVIRONMENTAL HAZARDS posed by estrogen-mimicking pollutants. Testicular cancer is often treated by *orchiectomy* (removal of the affected testicle), radiation therapy (see CANCER), and sometimes anti-cancer drugs. Young males should be taught to

make regular self-examinations from puberty (see TESTICULAR SELF-EXAMINATION, on page 590).

Several of these conditions can diminish fertility or cause infertility, and so require prompt and careful treatment.

FOR HELP AND FURTHER INFORMATION

American Cancer Society (ACS), 800–227–2345. Publishes *Testicular Cancer and How to do TSE (A Self Exam)*; video *Testicular Self-Exam*; and other materials on cancers of the testes and prostate. (For full group information, see CANCER.)

National Cancer Institute (NCI), 800–422–6237. Publishes *Testicular Self-Examination* and "What You Need to Know About" brochure on cancers of the testes and prostate. (For full group information, see CANCER.)

American Institute for Cancer Research (AICR), 800–843–8114. Publishes *Testicular Cancer*. (For full group information, see CANCER.)

(See also INFERTILITY; PREGNANCY.)

Test of Adolescent Language (TOAL), an individually administered test of the LANGUAGE SKILLS of children ages twelve through eighteen, often those suspected of having LEARNING DISABILITIES. It is designed to identify areas where additional help is needed. Tasks include both paper-and-pencil and oral responses to questions designed to uncover problems in the areas of vocabulary and grammar (syntax), using listening, speaking, READING, and writing, including both receptive and expressive language. SCORES for the various subtests are combined to give an Adolescent Language Quotient (ALQ). Easier items are included so that the test can also be used with children who have MENTAL RETARDATION, language disorders (see COMMUNICATION SKILLS AND DISORDERS), or other learning problems. (See TESTS.)

Test of Language Development (TOLD), an individually administered, oral-response test designed to measure the LANGUAGE SKILLS of children; the primary test covers children aged four through eight, and the intermediate one ages eight through twelve. The test includes seven areas: picture vocabulary, oral vocabulary, grammatical understanding, sentence imitation, grammatical completion, word articulation, and word discrimination. The tests are sometimes used as language ACHIEVEMENT TESTS, but are much more often used to identify children with language problems, including those with LEARNING DISABILITIES, MENTAL RETARDATION, DEVELOPMENTAL DELAY, and problems with communication (see COMMUNICATIONS SKILLS AND DISORDERS). (See TESTS.)

testosterone, one of the key male sex HORMONES, produced by the TESTES (and, in tiny amounts, also by a woman's OVARIES); one of the family of STEROIDS. Testosterone helps stimulate bone and muscle development, and also triggers the appearance of SECONDARY SEX CHARACTERISTICS. Synthetic or animal forms of the hormone are used to treat some kinds of INFERTILITY. As a form of steroid, testosterone is sometimes used by athletes to stimulate growth and development; in women that can also lead to development of male characteristics, such as hair growth and voice deepening. More serious effects of testosterone therapy can include liver damage and exacerbation of CANCER in the male reproductive system.

Tests of Achievement and Proficiency™ (TAP), a series of paper-and-pencil, multiple-choice, group-administered ACHIEVEMENT TESTS for adolescents, grades 9 to 12. Different tests are given for each grade level, geared to the normal subject matter covered in those grades, and students in each grade can be given either of two forms: the Basic Battery, which covers reading comprehension, mathematics, written expression, and using sources of information, and the Complete Battery, which adds social studies and science. Different forms of the tests are also available for each grade level, some of which include optional Listening and Writing supplements. The TAP tests are designed to measure what students have learned to that point, in comparison to other students in their grade level, and to point out areas of strength and weakness. Scores are also grouped to give a Minimum Competency score, covering reading and mathematics skills, and an Applied Proficiency Skills score, covering practical skills. The student also fills out a TAP Questionnaire about personal interests and plans. These various scores and the questionnaire are used in helping students plan for college or career. The NORMS for these STANDARDIZED TESTS were developed from testing with the same population of students as those for the COGNITIVE ABILITIES TEST, and the two may be given together, to allow comparison of actual and anticipated achievement test scores. (See TESTS.)

Tests of General Educational Development, a series of tests to be passed by someone seeking a GENERAL EQUIVALENCY DIPLOMA (GED).

tetanus (lockjaw), a severe disease caused by a bacterium widely present in the environment, which enters the body through a break in the skin, especially a deep puncture with a piece of metal. Once in the body, the tetanus bacteria produce a powerful toxin (poison) that attacks the body's NERVOUS SYSTEM. From the first symptoms of headache, irritability, and stiffness in the neck and jaw, the disease progresses to spasms that completely immobilize the jaw, neck, and limbs; produce rigidity in the abdominal muscles; and cause painful convulsions; often associated with tetanus are pneumonia (see LUNG AND BREATHING PROBLEMS), FRACTURES, and exhaustion from the muscle spasms. Once tetanus takes hold, doctors can only use TRANQUILIZERS and anti-spasmodic drugs to treat some of the symptoms, but there is no current treatment for the underlying disease, which kills 4 out of 10 people who contract it. Fortunately, a VACCINE exists that is normally given to children as part of a combination DTP VACCINE, in a series of five injections between ages two months and six years, with booster shots of TD VACCINE given every ten years thereafter. (See DTP VACCINE; IMMUNIZATION.)

tetanus vaccine, a type of VACCINE that is normally given first in a combination DTP VACCINE, covering DIPHTHERIA, TETANUS (lockjaw), and WHOOPING COUGH (*pertussis*), and later in booster shots of TD VACCINE.

tetany, spasms, cramps, or twitching in the muscles, especially the hands and feet, sometimes with STRIDOR (noisy breathing) as well. Tetany generally results from too little CALCIUM in the body (*hypocalcemia*), often linked with lack of VITAMIN D. In newborns, tetany can result from imbalance in the parathyroid hormone or imbalance in FORMULA, and is more common in LOW BIRTH WEIGHT babies.

Thematic Apperception Test (TAT), a type of PROJECTIVE TEST, individually administered to people aged fourteen to forty by a trained examiner. The person being tested is shown a series of pictures and asked to make up a story about each. The stories are later analyzed for information about the person's personality and maturity. (See TESTS.)

thyroid gland, a two-lobed gland in the front of the neck, which produces several key thyroid HORMONES. These help regulate METABOLISM (the body's biochemical processes), growth and physical development, and levels of CALCIUM in the body, often working with hormones from other glands, such as the HYPOTHALAMUS, PITUITARY GLAND, and parathyroid gland.

Too little thyroid production leads to a condition known as *hypothyroidism* (or *myxedema*), which in children can cause extremely short stature. Symptoms of hypothyroidism include weight gain, dry skin, HAIR loss, CONSTIPATION, cold sensitivity, and fatigue. By contrast, too much thyroid hormone, or *hyperthyroidism*, can cause weight loss, DIARRHEA, sweating, heat intolerance, and fatigue.

The thyroid gland is subject to a variety of disorders, including:

- *Goiter*, or enlargement of the gland, as from lack of IODINE, hormonal changes during PUBERTY or PREGNANCY, GENETIC DISORDERS, or an unknown cause.
- *Absence, abnormal placement, or malfunction*, often CONGENITAL defects that can lead to severe MENTAL RETARDATION combined with DWARFISM (a condition called *cretinism*).
- *Tumors*, which can be BENIGN or MALIGNANT, but generally need to be surgically treated.
- AUTOIMMUNE DISORDERS, where the body mistakenly attacks its own tissues, including *Graves' disease* and *Hashimoto's thyroiditis*.

Thyroid problems are often diagnosed using BLOOD TESTS that check for the level of hormones, SCANS of the glands, or BIOPSY.

FOR HELP AND FURTHER INFORMATION

National Institute of Diabetes and Digestive and Kidney Diseases (NIDDK), 301–496–3583. (For full group information, see DIGESTIVE SYSTEM AND DISORDERS.)

National Organization for Rare Disorders (NORD), 800–999–6673. (For full group information, see RARE DISORDERS.)

National Cancer Institute (NCI), 800–422–6237. Publishes *In Answer to Your Questions About Thyroid Cancer.* (For full group information, see CANCER.)

tissue typing, a medical technique used in attempting to match organs and tissue for use in TRANSPLANTS; also called *histocompatability testing.* (See IMMUNE SYSTEM.)

Title I of the Elementary and Secondary Education Act, the 1965 law that established the federal program funding educational programs for students from low-income families, now generally called CHAPTER 1.

toilet training, helping a child learn to control urination and bowel movements. In infants, these activities are not controllable, but occur involuntarily. Before children can be toilet trained, they must first be able to recognize urine and feces as coming from them, and also to link these events with the physical signals preceding and accompanying them. Children's muscles and nerves must also develop to the point where it is physically possible for them to control these functions, which normally does not happen until they are approximately 18 to 20 months old. Also, the bladder and bowels must grow large enough so that they can store waste for a time, which usually does not occur until about 30 months. In addition, children must have the general communication skills and MOTOR SKILLS to be able to understand and respond to the toilet training process.

All of these are part of READINESS for toilet training—and here, experts agree, readiness is all. Children may demonstrate this readiness in a variety of ways. They may, for example, have fewer, more regular bowel movements, sometimes asking to be changed afterward. They may keep their diapers dry for several hours at a time. They may leave the room to urinate or have a bowel movement (in the diaper) privately. They may show an interest in the bathroom and imitate actions of others there.

Parents should be extremely wary of pushing a child into toilet training prematurely, since frustration and resentment are the likely results. Certainly parents have many pressures to toilet train early. Quite apart from the obvious chore of changing diapers, many CHILD CARE centers and PRESCHOOLS will accept children only if they are toilet trained, or will charge extra if a child needs diaper-changing. But for the long-term good of the child and the parent-child relationship, such pressures need to be resisted—and in no way communicated to the child. Rather toilet training is best presented as a positive step, as part of the child's natural growing-up process. Indeed, some children in child care centers are toilet trained more easily, because they see others using toilets. Similarly, children who are able to see family members (especially of their own sex) using the toilet also seem to learn more readily, by imitation.

Parents will need to decide beforehand whether to use a separate "potty chair" or a special child-sized insert into the toilet; a shield is used in front for boys, who will urinate sitting down at first, learning the stand-up style only later. Parents will also want to plan how to go about toilet training, making sure that they agree between themselves and with the approach taken by child care workers, because inconsistency (as in the language used or the type of response to an "accident") can breed problems. (The books listed at the end of this entry may help.)

It is often effective to introduce the child to the toilet and its functions (especially flushing, which may intrigue or scare a child) before actually expecting the child to use it. Experts recommend that the start of toilet training be scheduled for a calm period, when the family is not undergoing any particular upheaval (such as a relocation or arrival of a SIBLING) and when one parent can be with the child full-time for a few days.

Parents should also understand that toilet training does not occur in a day, but rather is a long-term, gradual process that will generally take weeks or months. Bowel movements are usually controlled before urination, and full control of daytime urination occurs long before control at night. Accidents will happen, but parents can help in several ways:

- By dressing the child in easy-to-undo clothes, preferably with elastic or Velcro instead of buttons, belts, straps, scarves, and the like.
- By using training pants, especially in the early stages of the process.
- By planning ahead, so a child will not be placed in an impossible position without access to a bathroom, for example, by using diapers on expeditions where no bathrooms are available, or teaching children how to urinate outdoors where appropriate (as in the woods or by the side of a road).
- By being alert, when outside the home, to where toilets are and responding immediately to a child's request to use one, since—with a child's limited storage capacity and muscular control—seconds count.
- By being supportive of the child's efforts and not treating accidents as tragedies or failures.

With a positive approach at the right time, most children are toilet trained without great problems, though some children may not develop full nighttime control for years. Usually this is a form of DEVELOPMENTAL DELAY, and children are clean and dry by the time they enter school. Some school-age children, however, have long-term persistent problems with control of urination, leading to BEDWETTING (*enuresis*), or with control of defecation, leading to SOILING (*encopresis*). Because of physical or emotional DISABILITIES, some children never gain full control over their bodily functions; they need special techniques to handle the resulting INCONTINENCE.

FOR HELP AND FURTHER INFORMATION

American Academy of Pediatrics (AAP), 800–433–9016. Publishes brochure *Toilet Training: A Parent's Guide*. (For full group information, see HEALTH CARE.)

Twin Services, 510–524–0863. Publishes *Toilet Training Twins*. (For full group information, see MULTIPLE BIRTH.)

The Arc, 817–261–6003. Publishes *Toilet Training for Children with Mental Retardation*. (For full group information, see MENTAL RETARDATION.)

OTHER RESOURCES

For adults

Potty Training Your Baby: A Practical Guide for Easier Toilet Training. Kathy Van Pelt. Avery, 1988.
Toilet Training and Bed Wetting: A Practical Guide for Today's Parents. Heather Welford. Harper and Row, 1988.

For training young children

Annie's Potty. Judith Caseley. Greenwillow, 1990.
Your New Potty. Joanna Cole. Morrow, 1989.
Once Upon a Potty. Alona Frankel. Barron's, 1980. Comes in "His" and "Hers" versions, as does the Spanish version, *Mi Bacinica y Yo* (1987).

For training children with disabilities

Manual for Functional Training, 3rd ed. Lynn M. Palmer and Janice E. Toms. Davis, 1992.

(See also BEDWETTING; SOILING; INCONTINENCE; KIDNEY AND UROLOGICAL DISORDERS; DIGESTIVE SYSTEM AND DISORDERS.)

tonic neck reflex, the automatic response of a baby on turning the head to one side to stretch out the arm and leg on the same side, and to bend the arm and leg on the opposite side. This is a type of "primitive" REFLEX found only in babies, which normally disappears in the first few months of life.

tonsils, two small organs at the back of the throat that act as filters in the *lymphatic system*, which is the network through which the body's IMMUNE SYSTEM operates. As an infant grows, so do the tonsils, reaching maximum size by about age seven, then gradually shrinking. In decades past, tonsils were routinely removed in many children, but today they are generally left in place, unless the child has severe, recurring attacks of *tonsillitis* or *quinsy* (inflammation of the tonsils due to infection), or where a tonsil contains abnormal growths, such as CANCER. The operation itself—the *tonsillectomy*—is simple and recovery from it brief; ADENOIDS are often removed at the same time. It is not risk-free, however. On rare occasions, children have died from HEMORRHAGES several days to as much as a week or more after the operation. If parents have questions or concerns about a child's condition after a tonsillectomy, they should consult their doctor; if concerns persist, so should they, acting as advocates for their child.

FOR HELP AND FURTHER INFORMATION

American Academy of Pediatrics (AAP),
800–433–9016. Publishes brochure *Tonsils and Adenoids.*
(For full group information, see HEALTH CARE.)

torsion of the testis, twisting of the spermatic cord, cutting off blood supply to the testis. This can cause irreparable damage and possibly INFERTILITY, if not diagnosed and treated within just a few hours. (See TESTES.)

total communication, an approach in which children with EAR AND HEARING PROBLEMS are taught to use any communications skills (see COMMUNICATION SKILLS AND DISORDERS) at their disposal, and are not barred from employing MANUAL COMMUNICATION, such as FINGER SPELLING and AMERICAN SIGN LANGUAGE.

Tourette syndrome, a neurological disorder that begins in childhood, generally between ages two and fifteen; it affects both sexes, but more males by a ratio of 3 to 1. A type of STEREOTYPED MOVEMENT DISORDER, also called *Gilles de la Tourette syndrome* or *maladie des tics,* it is relatively rare in its full-blown form, affecting some 100,000 people in the United States; however, many more people are believed to have milder forms.

Tourette syndrome is characterized by tics—sudden, rapid, involuntary, repeated movements or vocalizations—that occur in bouts, sometimes many times a day, sometimes intermittently, even disappearing for weeks or months on occasion. Common motor tics range from eye blinking, head jerking, shoulder shrugging, mouth twitching, and other facial grimacing to more complex behaviors such as jumping, compulsive touching of people or things, twirling about, sniffing, and occasional self-injurious actions such as hitting or biting the self. Common vocal tics range from throat clearing, yelping, making guttural noises, and tongue clicking to more complex utterances of words and phrases, including compulsive use of foul language (COPROLALIA), repetition of meaningless phrases (ECHOLALIA), and increasingly rapid repetition of selected phrases (PALILALIA). Though the person can temporarily suppress tics, they are experienced as irresistible, in the nature of a sneeze that can sometimes be postponed but must eventually be expressed.

Early diagnosis is extremely important, because the behavior is otherwise frightening, disruptive, frustrating, and maddening to family, neighbors, friends, educators, and—most importantly—to the child, who is often shunned, mocked, and excluded by those who do not understand the causes of the behavior. Stories abound of children who became isolated and psychologically damaged because no one realized the nature of their problem. Once the disorder is diagnosed, the child can understand what is happening and can explain it to others—or have the family do so.

Most people with Tourette syndrome are not significantly disabled by the symptoms, but where symptoms do interfere with functioning, medications are available to help control them, some of them ORPHAN DRUGS. These are controversial and not to be used lightly, however, because they have various unwanted side effects, ranging from weight gain, muscular rigidity, and fatigue to DEPRESSION and impairment of cognitive thinking. If medications are prescribed, parents should carefully monitor their child, and ask for modification of dosage or a switch of medication if side effects are a problem. Therapy cannot rid a person of tics, but can sometimes help a person substitute one tic for another less disruptive one. Relaxation techniques and biofeedback training can also be used to lessen stress that can increase severity of the tics.

The origin and causes of Tourette syndrome are obscure, but it is believed to have a strong genetic basis. Recent research suggests that it may stem from abnormal METABOLISM of some brain chemicals called *neurotransmitters,* such as dopamine.

Many children with Tourette syndrome also have other types of problems, notably ATTENTION DEFICIT HYPERACTIVITY DISORDER, LEARNING DISABILITIES, OBSESSIVE-COMPULSIVE DISORDER, other MENTAL DISORDERS, and sleep problems (see SLEEP AND SLEEPING DISORDERS). With or without these additional problems, some require SPECIAL EDUCATION assistance, such as INDIVIDUALIZED EDUCATION PLANS and sometimes special test arrangements, such as untimed examinations or examinations given in a private room, as when vocal tics may be disruptive.

FOR HELP AND FURTHER INFORMATION

Tourette Syndrome Association (TSA)
42–40 Bell Boulevard
Bayside, NY 11361
718–224–2999; 800–237–0717
Fax: 718–279–9596
Steven M. Friedlander, Executive Director
Organization concerned with Tourette syndrome; fosters research; offers information, referrals, and counseling; acts as advocate; arranges for discount medications; publishes quarterly newsletter, annual *Medical Letter,* and other materials, including:

- General brochures: *Tourette Syndrome—Questions and Answers, Facts You Should Know About the Genetics of TS, Health Insurance and Tourette Syndrome,* and *TS Medications and Pregnancy.*

- For families: *Coping with TS: A Parent's Viewpoint, Discipline and the TS Child: A Guide of Parents and Teachers, Matthew and the Tics* (for children), and *Coping with TS in Early Adulthood.*
- Personal experiences: *A Tourette Autobiography, Jim Eisenreich: Back to the Dream, The Need to Know,* and *A Neurologist's Notebook: A Surgeon's Life* (by Oliver Sacks).
- Videos and films: *I'm a Person Too, Stop It! I Can't, Tourette Syndrome: The Parent's Perspective—Diplomacy in Action, Talking about Tourette Syndrome,* and *A Regular Kid, That's Me* (for educators).
- Materials for health professionals and educators, such as *An Educator's Guide to Tourette Syndrome, Educational Rights for Students with TS,* and *Helpful Techniques to Aid the TS Student.*

National Institute of Neurological Disorders and Stroke (NINDS), 800–352–9424. Publishes fact sheet *Tourette Syndrome.* (For full group information, see BRAIN AND BRAIN DISORDERS.)

American Academy of Child and Adolescent Psychiatry (AACAP), 202–966–7300. Publishes information sheet *Tic Disorders.* (For full group information, see MENTAL DISORDERS.)

National Institute of Mental Health (NIMH), 301–443–4513. (For full group information, see MENTAL DISORDERS.)

Autism Network International, 315–476–2462. (For full group information, see AUTISM.)

ONLINE RESOURCES

ADD Forum (CompuServe). Maintains discussions and online libraries about Tourette syndrome. (For full group information, see ATTENTION DEFICIT HYPERACTIVITY DISORDER.)

OTHER RESOURCES

Children with Tourette Syndrome: A Parents' Guide. Tracy Haerle, ed. Woodbine House, 1992.

A Mind of Its Own: Tourette's Syndrome, a Story and a Guide. Ruth D. Bruun and Bertel Bruun. Oxford University Press, 1994.

Tourette Syndrome and Human Behavior. David E. Comings. Hope Press, 1990.

For children

Hi, I'm Adam: A Child's Book of Tourette Syndrome. Adam Buehrens. Hope Press, 1991.

Personal experiences

The Unwelcome Companion: An Insider's View of Tourette Syndrome. Rick Fowler. Silver Run, 1995.

Don't Think about Monkeys: Extraordinary Stories by People with Tourette Syndrome. Adam W. Seligman and John S. Hilkevich eds. Hope Press, 1992.

Echolalia: An Adult's Story of Tourette Syndrome. Adam W. Seligman. Hope Press, 1991.

Ryan: A Mother's Story of Her Hyperactive/Tourette Syndrome Child. Susan Hughes. Hope Press, 1990.

Background materials

Teaching the Tiger: A Handbook for Individuals Involved in the Education of Students with Attention Deficit Disorders, Tourette Syndrome or Obsessive-Compulsive Disorders. Marilyn P. Dornbush and Sheryl K. Pruitt. Hope Press, 1995.

Understanding Tourette Syndrome, Obsessive-Compulsive Disorder and Related Problems: A Developmental and Catastrophe Theory Perspective. John M. Berecz. Springer, 1992.

(See also TEST; EDUCATION; also HELP FOR SPECIAL CHILDREN on page 689.)

toxic shock syndrome, a serious, potentially life-threatening condition that results from infection by the *staphylococcus aureus* bacteria, which produces a toxin (poison) in the body. Initial symptoms include high FEVER and skin RASH, followed by SHOCK, a condition in which blood flow is so drastically reduced that blood-starved tissues can be severely damaged. Symptoms of shock include cold, clammy skin; paleness; rapid, weak pulse and breathing; dizziness; and weakness. Emergency medical help should be summoned immediately. If unchecked, the infection and shock can cause collapse, fainting, COMA, liver and kidney failure, and death. Toxic shock syndrome is treated with antibiotics and intravenous therapy; even so, a small percentage of people with TSS may die.

TSS can affect men, children, and menopausal women, since the infection can enter the body in various ways, but it is most common in women during their menstrual years. The disease was first widely recognized in the 1970s, when it was linked with use of super-absorbent tampons; when these were removed from the shelves, the incidence of the disease dropped sharply. However, TSS is still linked to use of tampons and contraceptive devices, such as CERVICAL CAPS, SPONGES, and DIAPHRAGMS. If mothers or their daughters use any of these devices, they should be sure not to leave them in the body for longer than necessary. To lessen the risk of infection, tampons should be changed frequently, and ideally alternated during the day with sanitary napkins.

FOR HELP AND FURTHER INFORMATION

National Institute of Allergy and Infectious Diseases (NIAID), 301–496–5717. (For full group information, see ALLERGY.)

National Institute of Child Health and Human Development (NICHD), 301–496–5133. (For full group information, see PREGNANCY.)

Centers for Disease Control (CDC), 404–639–3311. (For full group information, see IMMUNIZATION.)

toxoplasmosis, a disease caused by infection with the protozoa *toxoplasma gondii*, which is common in many animals and is often passed to humans in undercooked meat and from handling cats and their feces. The human body generally fights off the infection with little difficulty, with two major exceptions.

A person who has a weakened IMMUNE SYSTEM, such as someone with AIDS or *severe combined immunodeficiency* (SCID), has trouble fighting the infection, which results in an illness much like INFECTIOUS MONONUCLEOSIS. It can sometimes cause severe complications, such as inflammation of various sensitive parts of the eye, ENCEPHALITIS, and damage to the heart and lungs.

Even more seriously, a pregnant woman who contracts toxoplasmosis, especially early in pregnancy, has an increased risk of MISCARRIAGE or STILLBIRTH. Her baby may, after birth, experience various serious problems, such as enlargement of liver and spleen, HYDROCEPHALUS, EYE AND VISION PROBLEMS, EAR AND HEARING PROBLEMS, and MENTAL RETARDATION, and is at increased risk of dying in infancy. Women who are or may be pregnant should be especially careful to eat only fully cooked meat and, if they have cats, to wash their hands carefully when dealing with their cat and its feces.

FOR HELP AND FURTHER INFORMATION

March of Dimes Birth Defects Foundation (MDBDF), 914–428–7100. Publishes information sheet *Toxoplasmosis*. (For full group information, see BIRTH DEFECTS.)

National Institute of Allergy and Infectious Diseases (NIAID), 301–496–5717. (For full group information, see ALLERGY.)

National Organization for Rare Disorders (NORD), 800–999–6673. (For full group information, see RARE DISORDERS.)

tracheostomy, a surgical operation to make an artificial opening in the windpipe (*trachea*), which is then kept open by insertion of a tube. Tracheostomy may be performed as a temporary emergency procedure, as in severe cases of CROUP or CHOKING, or it can be a planned semipermanent or permanent procedure, as when someone is on a VENTILATOR (respirator).

tracking, the grouping of students into classes based on assessments of their ability and past performance. In YEAR-ROUND EDUCATION, one of several rotating or alternating school-vacation segments is also called a *track*.

In many schools, children have routinely been divided into groups based on their presumed ability and previous GRADES. In an ELEMENTARY SCHOOL or SECONDARY SCHOOL, for example, the result of tracking might be an honors or "fast track" class, a series of middle-range classes for students of descending ability (the number depending on the size of the school), and a "slow learner" class. Tracking goes under a variety of names, including *ability grouping, streaming, banding,* and *homogeneous grouping*. The main current alternative, in which all students are grouped together no matter how wide their range of achievement or ability, as in early schoolhouse style, is called *heterogeneous grouping*.

The main arguments for tracking are that it allows teachers to tailor instruction to the student's needs and abilities, giving extra time and attention to slow learners, providing extra stimulation and challenges to the most academically able students, and avoiding the frustration of the students who are unable to keep up with the academic pace set in a heterogeneous group.

Key criticisms of tracking are that it results in LABELING and locks students into a track. Once placed in such a "track," however, children are often unable to move out of it, being labeled as "fast," "slow," or "average" by their teachers and increasingly by themselves, with low expectations leading to SELF-FULFILLING PROPHECIES. A major concern is that teachers make insufficient efforts to help children shed earlier expectations and grow in new ways. Critics also point out that the world itself is a heterogeneous place and that all students benefit by working together; in particular, use of PEER TEACHING can benefit all students.

Many parents and educators have come to feel that the damage posed by tracking far outweighs its supposed benefits. No less an organization than the National Educational Association has called for an end to tracking; in a notable 1990 report, the NEA called for a gradual end of tracking and proposed that teachers and schools work together to develop more effective strategies for class groupings. The report also found that tracking—whether deliberately or accidentally—often segregates students into racially identifiable groups. In particular, they found that minorities have been underrepresented in "gatekeeper courses," such as algebra and geometry, which must be completed before students can enter more advanced courses. Many other organizations have called for an end to tracking, but its fate remains to be seen.

FOR HELP AND FURTHER INFORMATION

Ability Grouping and Cooperative Learning, rev. ed. Johns Hopkins University Center for Talented Youth, 1994.

Crossing the Tracks: How Untracking Can Save America's Schools. Anne Wheelock. New Press, 1993.

Keeping Track: How Schools Structure Inequality. Jeannie Oakes. Yale University Press, 1986.

(See also EDUCATION.)

transcript, the official record of a student's performance at a school, including classes or courses completed, the final GRADE or evaluation received for each, any DIPLOMAS awarded, perhaps comments on the student as a person, and appropriate related information, such as an explanation of the school's grading system. If a student transfers from one school to another, or applies for admission to a COLLEGE, the transcript must be supplied to the new institution. The information included on a transcript is drawn from the STUDENT RECORD.

transition, the period during which an adolescent prepares for work, independent living, and adulthood, for various legal purposes, generally considered to be the years between fourteen and twenty-two. The years of transition to adulthood have traditionally been difficult ones, with the teen's needs met with varying degrees of success by family and community.

Transition to independence has been especially difficult for people with DISABILITIES. However, laws such as SECTION 504 of the Rehabilitation Act of 1973 and the AMERICANS WITH DISABILITIES ACT (ADA) of 1990 now bar discrimination against them. In addition, these laws have provided various VOCATIONAL REHABILITATION (VR) SERVICES to help people with disabilities make the transition from school to work and independence, whether after HIGH SCHOOL or COLLEGE. In addition, as increasing numbers of children have been raised in FOSTER CARE, various social organizations have been attempting to help them make the transition to independent adulthood, in the absence of family help. (See ADOLESCENCE; SUPPORTED EMPLOYMENT; also HELP FOR SPECIAL CHILDREN on page 689.)

transitional comfort object, in psychology, an object adopted by a young child as a symbol of comfort, safety, and security, often around the first birthday; a kind of COMFORT HABIT, also called *cuddlies*. Like the traditional teddy bear or Linus's "security blanket" in the cartoon *Peanuts*, comfort objects are often soft, old, worn, intensely beloved, and taken everywhere by the child, and of special importance around sleeptime, during illness, stress, or upset, or when the child is being left with a BABYSITTER or going to a HOSPITAL.

transplant, the surgical implant of a healthy human organ or tissue to replace one that has failed, or is about to fail. The organ is often taken from the body of a person who has died, when the family agrees to make such organs available for transplants, sometimes following the express wish of the person when alive. Organs such as the heart and liver are often removed after a determination of BRAIN DEATH, but while the donor's heart is still functioning, since it is essential that blood supply be maintained to these organs. Sometimes the transplant tissue, such as skin or bone marrow, can come from elsewhere in the patient's own body. And with more recent techniques, the donation can involve just a portion of an organ, notably the liver, lung, or pancreas. At the present time, the list of organs that can be donated includes kidneys, heart, liver, lungs, and pancreas, while the tissues that can be donated include corneas, skin, bone, middle-ear, bone marrow, connective tissues, and blood vessels.

In the case of some kinds of transplants, such as kidneys, the organ may be from a living close relative, such as a SIBLING or BIOLOGICAL PARENT. This kind of donation poses a risk for the relative, who then has only one of the important organs left, but can be a life-saving gift within a family. One area of concern within families is the extent to which parents have the right to donate the organ of one child to save another. On occasion, parents have deliberately conceived a child for the primary purpose of providing organ or tissue that might be suitable to save an older child. But often terribly difficult decisions are involved; in one case, a mother went to court to prevent her ex-husband from forcing their child to donate an organ to save the life of a half sibling, a child of the husband and another woman. Older children can make such a decision themselves, but only with the consent of their parent or legal GUARDIAN; and questions of the amount, kind, and legitimacy of pressure applied by other family members remains.

The number of people needing transplants far outnumbers the number of organs available, even though most donors give multiple organs. People who require a transplant are placed on a national waiting list. As organs become available, the organ procurement organization serving that region searches its computerized listing and identifies the most appropriate potential recipient. The factors considered in this search include medical compatibility between donor and recipient on tissue type (see below), blood type, weight, and age; the length of time on the waiting list; and the urgency of the recipient's need. The latter is indicated by a formal classification: those classed as Status 1 are already in a hospital intensive care unit and have a life expectancy of less than seven days without a transplant; Status 2 patients have been continuously hospitalized for at least five days; Status 3 patients require continuous medical care; Status 4 patients are at home and functioning normally.

Other things being equal, preference is given to recipients in the same geographical area as the donor, since timing is crucial. Hearts can only be preserved for up to six hours, livers twenty-four hours, and kidneys seventy-two hours. While the donated organ is being surgically removed, preserved, and transported to the appropriate transplant center, the recipient is brought in to the center and prepared for surgery. The failing or diseased organ is removed, and replaced by the donated one.

Despite this system, which has replaced the pattern of desperate parents going on television to plead for donors, many people still wait for months or more on the list, and some die before receiving a life-giving transplant. As of March 1995, in the United States alone, over

39,000 people were included on the national waiting list, more than 700 of them children; the great majority—over 28,000—were waiting for kidney transplants. Many states have made organ donor option cards available with driver's license applications, in attempts to ease the shortage, but a person's next-of-kin must still give permission for the donation. HOSPITALS are, by law, required to have procedures in place for asking a family's permission for organ donation. However, in the mid1990s, organs were donated for use in only a quarter of the cases where donation was medically possible.

People who wish to make donations should sign a donor card, have their attorney put their wishes in writing, and be sure the family knows their wishes. Where a child dies, a parent may be asked to approve a donation. They should be assured that the donation does not leave the body disfigured; organs are removed as a surgical procedure in an operating room. The donor family bears no cost for the organ donation (though they remain responsible for the hospital expenses incurred in trying to save the life), and sale of organs is specific prohibited by the National Organ Transplant Act. According to the Division of Organ Transplantation (see the resource list following this entry), most transplant operations are covered by private HEALTH INSURANCE and by Medicare and Medicaid; however, where a family member requires a transplant, parents should check ahead of time to be sure their insurance plan covers the operation, especially with a managed care program (see HEALTH CARE).

Apart from the shortage, the main difficulty with transplants is that the body will often reject the transplanted organ. The rejection response is caused when the IMMUNE SYSTEM recognizes the transplant as foreign and attacks it. Only corneal transplants, somewhat sheltered from attack, are less subject to rejection.

One way to thwart the rejection response, at least somewhat, is to match transplant tissues, so they are as much alike as possible, using techniques called *tissue typing* or *histocompatability*. In the white blood cells (*leukocytes*) used for matching, various markers, called *antigens*, exist in six major forms, and as many as twenty varieties, so the number of possible types is near 10,000. If two or more of the major antigens are alike, the organ donor and recipient are regarded as a "good match." The best matches, of course, are identical twins, though good matches may be made between blood-related family members.

The other main way to counter the rejection response is with *immunosuppressive drugs*, such as cyclosporine, which suppresses the action of the immune system. At the present stage of medical technology, a transplant patient must plan on taking such drugs for the rest of his or her life. And because suppression of the immune system leaves the body open to attack by various disease organisms, the patient will also need careful medical monitoring for life. In addition, transplant patients have been found to be at increased risk for developing certain CANCERS, such as *lymphomas*. But whatever the risks, transplantation has allowed thousands of lives to be saved.

FOR HELP AND FURTHER INFORMATION

Division of Organ Transplantation (DOT)
Department of Health and Human Services
5600 Fishers Lane, Room 7–18
Rockville, MD 20857
301–443–7577
Fax: 301–594–6095
Venus Walker, Secretary, Education Branch
Federal arm charged with overseeing procurement of organs for transplants; provides information; maintains transplant registry; publishes brochures *Questions and Answers about Organ Transplantation* and *Did You Know?*; fact sheets *"Did You Know" Facts About Transplantation in the United States, Organ Donation, Procurement and Transplantation: A Success Story, Organ Transplantation: Matching Donors and Recipients, What Can Be Transplanted?, Minorities, Donation, and Transplantation,* and *History of the National Organ Procurement and Transplantation Network*; and numerous materials for health professionals.

Living Bank
P.O. Box 6725
Houston, TX 77265
800–528–2971
Fax: 713–961–0979
Bruce B. Conway, President
Organization acting as organ and tissue donor registry; seeks to encourage filing of donor forms; publishes various brochures.

National Kidney Foundation (NKF), 800–622–9010. Publishes quarterlies *Transplant Chronicles* and *For Those Who Give and Grieve* (for donor families); book and video *Kidney Transplant: A New Lease on Life;* and brochures *Nutrition and Transplantation, About Organ and Tissue Donation,* and *Controversies in Organ Donation.* (For full group information, see KIDNEY AND UROLOGICAL DISORDERS.)

National Institute of Allergy and Infectious Diseases (NIAID), 301–496–5717. (For full group information, see ALLERGY.)

National Institute of Diabetes and Digestive and Kidney Diseases (NIDDK), 301–496–3583. (For full group information, see DIGESTIVE SYSTEM AND DISORDERS.)

National Heart, Lung, and Blood Information Center (NHLBIC), 301–251–1222. (For full group information, see HEART AND HEART PROBLEMS.)

American Association of Kidney Patients (AAKP), 800–223–7099. (For full group information, see KIDNEY AND UROLOGICAL DISORDERS.)

OTHER RESOURCES

Organ Transplants: A Patient's Guide. Massachusetts General Hospital Organ Transplant Team; H. F. Pizer. Harvard University Press, 1991.

For preteens and teens

Organ Transplants. Deanne Durrett. Lucent, 1993.
Transplants. Laurie Beckelman. Silver Burdett, 1990.

Personal experiences

Transplants: Unwrapping the Second Gift of Life—The Inside Story of Organ Transplants As Told by Recipients and Their Families, Donor Families, and Health Professionals. Pat S. Helmberger. Chronimed, 1992.
Rebirth: My Transplant Experience. Nancy Cassell. Altan, 1993.
Transplant: A Heart Surgeon's Account of the Life-and-Death Dramas of the New Medicine. William Frist and William H. Frist. Grove-Atlantic, 1990.

Background works

The Most Useful Gift: Altruism and the Public Policy of Organ Transplants. Jeffrey Prottas. Jossey-Bass, 1994.
Defying the Gods: Inside the New Frontiers of Organ Transplants. Scott McCartney. Macmillan, 1994.
The Gift of Life: Organ and Tissue Transplantation—An Introduction to Issues and Information Sources. Cecilia Schmitz, ed. Pierian, 1993.
Spare Parts: Organ Replacement in American Society. Renee C. Fox and Judith P. Swazey. Oxford University Press, 1992.

(See also BONE MARROW TRANSPLANT; IMMUNE SYSTEM; and specific types of problems, for example HEART AND HEART PROBLEMS.)

traumatic brain injury (TBI), damage to the brain due to a fall or other accident, assault, or wound affecting the head, or due to loss of oxygen (*anoxia*), as because of a stroke, cardiac arrest, or near drowning.

The brain is protected by a bony skull (see BRAIN AND BRAIN DISORDERS), and sometimes even if the skull itself is fractured, damage may still be superficial. On the other hand, sometimes the brain can be damaged by injuries that leave little or no external sign, as in the SHAKEN CHILD SYNDROME common in child abuse. Such injuries are invisible, and often go undetected in what some have termed a "silent epidemic."

The Brain Injury Association (see the resource list that follows this entry) reports that TBI is among the top five causes of death in children and young adults. Those at highest risk are males between the ages of fourteen and twenty-four. Infants are also at particular risk, one reason for widespread mandated use of safety seats (see SAFETY). So are toddlers, who so readily may climb out of a crib or shopping cart and fall. Among children, after-school hours are the most dangerous times, with over 40 percent of TBIs occurring from injuries on the road, over 34 percent at home, and over 6 percent in recreation areas. The increasing use of helmets in bicycle riding and SPORTS and the call for seat belts in school buses are attempts to limit TBIs.

Medically, traumatic brain injuries are classified into two types: An open head injury (OHI) results from an assault, such as a gunshot wound, and generally affects a specific site in the brain. A closed head injury (CHI) results from the brain being whipped back and forth within the skull, as during the rapid acceleration or deceleration of a car crash. A CHI often has more generalized effects, especially on the brain stem, through which all the body's messages pass between the spinal cord and the brain.

Though most minor "bumps" to the head will not cause permanent problems, even mild head injuries commonly produce HEADACHES and, if repeated, may cause serious damage and increase the likelihood for further injuries. Brain injuries may involve unconsciousness, some amnesia, and in severe cases COMA. Associated symptoms may include PARALYSIS, sometimes with muscle weakness and loss of feeling; persistent VOMITING; EYE AND VISION PROBLEMS, such as double vision or pupils of unequal size; impairment of other senses, including hearing and speech; DEPRESSION and mood swings; loss or deterioration in clarity, memory, concentration, attention, perception, organization, muscle coordination, and communication skills. TBI can also trigger seizures and EPILEPSY.

Any head injury should be referred to a physician; if a child lost consciousness, even briefly, the doctor may want to take X-RAYS of the skull to check for skull fracture or a CAT SCAN to check for hemorrhage or clots in the brain, and may well suggest that the child be hospitalized for observation. In cases of severe injuries, early treatment at an experienced rehabilitation facility will maximize the chance for a complete recovery, which may take five to ten years. Mild or severe, the child should be carefully monitored for some months for possible longer term symptoms.

FOR HELP AND FURTHER INFORMATION

Brain Injury Association
1776 Massachusetts Avenue NW, Suite 100
Washington, DC 20036
202–296–6443; Family Helpline: 800–444-NHIF [444–6443]
Fax: 202–296–8850
George Zitnay, President and Chief Executive Office
Organization of people concerned with head injuries; formerly the National Head Injury Foundation; encourages formation of support groups; acts as information clearinghouse; seeks to educate public and foster prevention; publishes *Family News and Views, Head Injury Update,* quarterly *TBI Challenge!,* and other materials, including:

- General materials: *Traumatic Brain Injury* fact sheet; *Traumatic Head Injury: Cause, Consequence, and Challenge, Basic Questions About Head Injury and Disability*, and *What Is Anoxic Brain Injury?*
- On injuries to children: *Head Injury in Children, Minor Head Injury in Children: Out of Sight But Not Out of Mind, When Your Child Is Seriously Injured: The Emotional Impact on Families, Informed Consent and the Minor Child, When Your Child Goes to School After an Injury*, and *Educational Concerns for the Traumatically Head Injured High School and College Student.*
- For families: *Head Injury: A Guide for Families, The Unseen Injury: Minor Head Trauma: An Introduction for Patients and Families, Living with Head Injury: A Guide for Families, What Does It Feel Like to be Brain Damaged?, A Stroke Manual for Families, Susan's Dad: A Child's Story of Head Injury, Brain Damage Is a Family Affair.*
- On planning for care: *Life Care Planning for the Brain Damaged Baby: A Step-By-Step Guide, Life Care Planning for the Head Injured: A Step-By-Step Guide, Planning for the Future: Providing a Meaningful Life for a Child with a Disability after Your Death, A Family Guide to Evaluating Transitional Living Programs for Head Injured Adults*; and information packet *Legal and Financial Issues for Families.*
- Information packets: *Minor Head Injury, For Children and Parents, Pediatrics, Prevention, Special Education, Cognitive Rehabilitation and Memory, Behavior, Introductory Information for Families*, and *Introduction to Rehabilitation Issues for the Family.*
- Numerous works on treatment, rehabilitation, education, research, prevention, advocacy, and legal issues, and reference materials such as *Catalog of Education Materials*, book list, journal list, and *NHIF National Directory of Head Injury Rehabilitation Services.*

(For more titles, see COMA; COMMUNICATION SKILLS AND DISORDERS; EAR AND HEARING PROBLEMS; EPILEPSY; PAIN AND PAIN TREATMENT; SAFETY.)

National Information Center for Children and Youth with Disabilities (NICHCY), 800–695–0285, voice/TT. Publishes *Traumatic Brain Injury.* (For full group information, see HELP FOR SPECIAL CHILDREN on page 689.)

National Maternal and Child Health Clearinghouse (NMCHC), 703–821–8955. Publishes *Mild Head Injury: Care of the Child at Home* and *Pediatric Head Injury: Nursing Guidelines to Facilitate Hospital Transfer for Rehabilitation.* (For full group information, see PREGNANCY.)

National Institute of Neurological Disorders and Stroke (NINDS), 800–352–9424. Publishes *CNS Trauma, Preventing Stroke*, and *Stroke.* (For full group information, see BRAIN AND BRAIN DISORDERS.)

American Heart Association (AHA), 800–242–8721. Publishes *Stroke: A Guide for the Family, Facts About Stroke, How Stroke Affects Behavior, Recovering from a Stroke, Six Hopeful Facts About Stroke*, and *Caring for the Person with Aphasia.* (For full group information, see HEART AND HEART PROBLEMS.)

National Easter Seal Society, 800–221–6827. Publishes *Understanding Stroke.* (For full group information, see HELP FOR SPECIAL CHILDREN on page 689.)

National Rehabilitation Information Center (NARIC), 800–346–2742, voice/TT. Publishes resource guide on head injury and stroke.

HEATH Resource Center, National Clearinghouse on Postsecondary Education for Individuals with Disabilities, 800–544–3284, voice/TT. Publishes *Head Injury Survivor on Campus: Issues and Resources.* (For full group information, see HELP FOR SPECIAL CHILDREN on page 689.)

Resources for Rehabilitation, 617–862–6455. Publishes brochure *After a Stroke.* (For full group information, see EYE AND VISION PROBLEMS.)

Resource Center on Substance Abuse Prevention and Disability, 202–628–8442. Publishes *A Look at Alcohol and Other Drug Abuse Prevention and Traumatic Brain Injury.* (For full group information, see HELP FOR SPECIAL CHILDREN on page 689.)

Agency for Health Care Policy and Research Clearinghouse, 800–358–9295. Publishes *Recovering After a Stroke: Patient and Family Guide*; and InstantFAX materials on post-stroke rehabilitation. (For full group information, see HEALTH INSURANCE.)

OTHER RESOURCES

GENERAL WORKS

What to Do about Your Brain-Injured Child, 3rd ed. Glenn Doman. Avery, 1994.
One Split Second. Suzan B. Hoppe. R. Dean Press, 1993.
In Search of Wings: A Journey Back from Traumatic Brain Injury. Beverley Bryant. Wings, 1992.

ON REHABILITATION AND EDUCATION

The Shortest Distance: The Pursuit of Independence for Person with Acquired Brain Injury. Brian T. McMahon and Randall W. Evans, eds. GR Press, 1994.
Traumatic Brain Injury Activities: Back into Life. Andrew K. Gruen and Lynn S. Gruen. Thinking Publications, 1994.
Brain Storms: Recovery from Traumatic Brain Injury. John Cassidy. PIA Press, 1992.
Sexuality and the Person with Traumatic Brain Injury: A Guide for Families. Ernest R. Griffith and Sally Lemberg. Davis, 1992.

(See also BRAIN AND BRAIN DISORDERS.)

trial of labor, a medical term for allowing a woman to at least attempt normal vaginal birth after a previous cesarean (VBAC). (See CESAREAN SECTION.)

trimester, a period of three months. The nine months of PREGNANCY are divided into three trimesters, the first being the most crucial in the development of the child, when exposure to ENVIRONMENTAL HAZARDS or lack (or excess) of essential VITAMINS and MINERALS leads to many of the grossest BIRTH DEFECTS. (See WHAT HAPPENS DURING PREGNANCY on page 472, for an outline of development by trimesters.)

In EDUCATION, especially at the COLLEGE level, the trimester generally refers to three equal parts making up a school year, instead of two SEMESTERS.

trisomy, a type of CHROMOSOMAL ABNORMALITY in which a person has three copies of a chromosome, instead of the normal two. Among the most common types are trisomy 21 or DOWN SYNDROME, trisomy 13 or PATAU'S SYNDROME, and trisomy 18 or EDWARDS' SYNDROME.

truant, a student who is out of school without a valid excuse on a day when school is considered in session. Such a student is officially regarded as violating laws of COMPULSORY ATTENDANCE, and chronic truants may be contacted by the school's attendance or truant officer. In some places, local governments have taken various kinds of actions, such as withholding welfare payments, to press parents to see that their children attend school as required. The long-term legal fate and effect of such actions remains to be seen.

truth in testing, a New York State law that requires that testing agencies offering STANDARDIZED TESTS for COLLEGE ADMISSIONS must later provide students with copies of their answer sheets, along with a copy of the test and identification of the correct answers. Once provided in New York State, they were then provided across the country. On some occasions, though rarely, students have successfully made a case for ambiguity in question or answer, and effective invalidation of a particular test item.

tubal ligation, a surgical procedure for a woman who wishes to have no more children; a permanent form of BIRTH CONTROL, or STERILIZATION. The procedure involves the tying (*ligation*) of a woman's FALLOPIAN TUBES so that no egg can pass from the OVARIES into the UTERUS. The National Center for Health Statistics reports that, in the United States, tubal ligation is the most common single type of CONTRACEPTION used by women over thirty, and that of all women who use birth control, 41 percent have their "tubes tied" by age thirty-nine.

Tubal ligation is usually performed under general ANESTHESIA, using one of several different procedures:

- *laparotomy*, which involves a three- to five-inch incision in the abdomen, takes about 30 minutes, and requires a hospital of several days and home recovery of about four weeks. This is the oldest form of tubal ligation, today rarely used, except in women who have already had some type of abdominal surgery or immediately after CHILDBIRTH.
- *Minilaparotomy*, which involves a shorter one-inch incision and takes 20 to 30 minutes, with a shorter recovery time.
- LAPAROSCOPY, which involves a half-inch incision near the navel, and so is popularly called *Band-Aid* or *belly-button surgery*. A special needle and a thin, rigid, lighted, tube-and-lens device, called a *laparoscope*, are introduced through the incision. Through the needle, the doctor pumps an inert gas to push the intestines away from the UTERUS and Fallopian tubes, and uses the laparoscope to see the operating site. Using instruments inserted at the same site, or at a second small incision at the pubic hairline, the doctor then seals off the fallopian tubes. Often done on an outpatient basis, though under general anesthesia, the procedures takes about an hour and requires one to two days' recovery.
- *Vaginal tubal ligation*, which involves incisions through the vagina. This has a higher risk of infection and bleeding, as well as a higher failure rate, so it is less commonly performed today.

Whatever the type of procedure, the end result is that the tubes are sealed. Today they are not actually tied but are generally clipped, clamped, or burned with electrocauterization, though that carries the risk of burning abdominal organs, such as the intestines and bladder, and destroying the blood supply to the OVARIES. One alternative is a *fimbrectomy*, in which the petal-like ends of the Fallopian tubes are removed, so they cannot draw eggs into the tubes.

Women generally experience some pain and discomfort after all of these operations. The complication rate is 1–15.3 percent, depending on the surgeon and the type of procedure. Some unconfirmed studies suggest that women who have had tubal ligation with electrocauterization later have higher rates of HYSTERECTOMY, as well as premenstrual syndrome (PMS), heavy menstrual bleeding, and irregular bleeding (see MENSTRUATION).

Attempts to surgically reopen tubes after ligation have had little success (see TUBOPLASTY), so tubal ligation should be regarded as permanent. However, researchers are exploring various approaches not only to lessen risk of complications but also to make the operation more readily reversible. One possible approach involves insertion of silicone plugs into the Fallopian tubes, which could later be removed, if a woman decided she wanted children. (See STERILIZATION; BIRTH CONTROL.)

FOR HELP AND FURTHER INFORMATION

American College of Obstetricians and Gynecologists (ACOG), 202–638–5577. Publishes *Sterilization for Women and Men*, *Sterilization by Laparoscopy*, and *Postpartum Sterilization*. (For full group information, see PREGNANCY.)

Planned Parenthood Federation of America (PPFA), 800–230–7526. Publishes pamphlet *All About Tubal Sterilization.* (For full group information, see BIRTH CONTROL.)

Association for Voluntary Surgical Contraception (AVSC), (212–351–2500). (For full group information, see VASECTOMY.)

RESOLVE, Inc., HelpLine: 617–623–0744. Publishes fact sheet *Microsurgical and Laser Techniques for Tubal Repair.* (For full group information, see INFERTILITY.)

Couple to Couple League (CCL), 513–471–2000. Publishes brochure *Sexual Sterilization: Some Facts for an Informed Choice.* (For full group information, see NATURAL FAMILY PLANNING.)

tuberculin skin test, a type of MEDICAL TEST used to see if a person has IMMUNITY to TUBERCULOSIS. An extract taken from the tuberculosis bacteria is injected into the skin by various methods; if a few days later, the skin shows no change, this is a *negative* result, indicating lack of immunity. However, if a circle of skin becomes red, hard, and raised, the test is said to be *positive*, indicating that the person has immunity, either because they have previously been infected with the disease, or because they have been effectively immunized by a BCG VACCINE. (See MEDICAL TESTS; TUBERCULOSIS.)

tuberculosis (TB), an infectious bacterial disease that was once a major killer of both children and adults, and is still an active threat in many parts of the world, as in inner-city areas with poor NUTRITION and sanitary conditions, or among people who have diseases that lower their resistance, such as DIABETES or AIDS. The United States still has some 20,000 new cases of tuberculosis a year, and children who have contact with anyone who has the infection are especially at risk, especially from family members, since the infection is spread by airborne droplets from sneezes or coughs. Such children are often given a BCG (*bacille Calmette-Guérin*) vaccine and sometimes preventive ANTIBIOTICS as well.

Active cases of tuberculosis (or shadows of scars from healed tuberculosis infections) show up on chest X-RAYS, and the bacteria responsible can also be found in the sputum a person coughs up. A TUBERCULIN SKIN TEST may also be used; if positive, it indicates that the person has an active case—or that the BCG vaccine has produced IMMUNIZATION. Though tuberculosis generally attacks the lungs first, it can (especially if untreated or unresponsive) spread to various parts of the body. In bone and BONE MARROW it produces OSTEOMYELITIS. A major concern is that some strains of tuberculosis are becoming resistant to current antibiotics, leading to fears of a resurgence of this dread disease.

FOR HELP AND FURTHER INFORMATION

National Jewish Center for Immunology and Respiratory Medicine, 800–222–5864, U.S. except CO. (For full group information, LUNG AND BREATHING DISORDERS.)

National Institute of Allergy and Infectious Diseases (NIAID), 301–496–5717. Publishes *HIV-Related TB* and *Tuberculosis: What Health Care Workers Should Know.* (For full group information, see ALLERGIES.)

Centers for Disease Control (CDC), 404–639–3311. (For full group information, see IMMUNIZATION.)

National Organization for Rare Disorders (NORD), 800–999–6673. (For full group information, see RARE DISORDERS.)

tuboplasty, a surgical operation to open and sometimes rebuild a woman's FALLOPIAN TUBES, where blockage has prevented CONCEPTION; also called *tuberoplasty.* Where the blockage results from scar tissue, microsurgery or laser surgery may be used to try to remove damaged tissue. Where the blockage is near the petal-like ends (*fimbriae*) of the tubes, lying just above the OVARIES, sometimes the scar tissue is removed and a small plastic hood inserted to keep the ends open; the hoods are removed later in a second operation several months later.

Microsurgery may also be used to reopen tubes after TUBAL LIGATION. If the tubes were burned in the original operation, the chances of successfully reopening them are only about 1 in 10; if the fimbriae were removed, near zero. Chances are somewhat better if some other techniques are used, though much still depends on the skill of the surgeon. Sometimes a narrow tube is inserted to keep the Fallopian tubes open, or the end of the tube is pulled into the uterus, with the fimbriae outside. Even if FERTILIZATION takes place, however, a woman still has a relatively high risk of possibly life-threatening ECTOPIC PREGNANCY, with implantation taking place in the tube, instead of the uterus. (See INFERTILITY; TUBAL LIGATION.)

tuition, money paid for instruction, generally at a school or COLLEGE. This normally does not include related expenses such as room and board, books, registration, on-campus HEALTH CARE, and fees for other activities. Schools may reduce or waive tuition for some students, as because of academic excellence, economic need, or minority status; such FINANCIAL AID may be in the form of a SCHOLARSHIP or a GRANT.

tumor, any abnormal mass in the body that results from excessive multiplication of cells; also called a *neoplasm.* The term *tumor* is sometimes applied in a very general way to any swelling or enlargement due to inflammation.

A tumor is labeled BENIGN if it is not expected to progress to the point of being life-threatening, although even a benign tumor can be life-threatening if it affects a vital structure, such as a key part of the BRAIN. Benign tumors grow more slowly and are generally confined, not spreading; a person may have multiple benign tumors, but each would tend to be distinct. Tumors so confined as to seem surrounded, like a capsule, are called *encapsulated.*

By contrast, a MALIGNANT tumor is PROGRESSIVE, meaning that it is expected to worsen and, if untreated or unresponsive to treatment, cause death. Malignant tumors grow rapidly, often reach out into other tissues, and may spread (*metastasize*) to other parts of the body, as through the blood or lymphatic systems (see IMMUNE SYSTEM). A *primary tumor* is one that arises where it was found; a *secondary* or *metastatic tumor* is one that arose from malignant cells that migrated from elsewhere in the body. Even benign tumors need to be monitored, since they can later become malignant.

Tumors are graded according to their severity, especially by their growth rate and their dissimilarity to normal cells. Tumors of grade I or II are either benign or mildly malignant, and grow slowly. Grades III and IV are fully and dangerously malignant. Tumors are given various names, depending on where they originate, whether they are benign or malignant, and their pattern of growth. Among the common general types of tumors are:

- *Adenoma,* a tumor that arises from a gland, usually benign but capable of causing various diseases when they cause overproduction of certain HORMONES.
- *Carcinoma,* a malignant tumor, or CANCER, that arises from the outer skin, or from skin covering or lining organs (notably the liver and kidneys) or systems (such as the digestive, respiratory, urological, and reproductive systems). Cancers of the BREAST, lungs, stomach, skin, and CERVIX, are carcinomas.
- *Sarcoma,* a malignant tumor, or cancer, in soft or connective tissues, bone, or muscles, including fibrous body organs, blood vessels, the lymphatic system, the *meninges* (the membrane covering the BRAIN), and cartilage, sometimes associated with radiation or BURN scars. Small sarcomas can be cut out and the area treated with radiation therapy, but large sarcomas in the limbs may require amputation.
- *Glioma,* a tumor arising from within the brain tissue, generally malignant.

The various therapies used in treating tumors are discussed under CANCER. (For help and further information, see BRAIN TUMORS; CANCER; SKIN CANCER; LEUKEMIA.)

Turner's syndrome, a CONGENITAL condition resulting from a CHROMOSOMAL ABNORMALITY, in which a female has only one, rather than the normal two, SEX CHROMOSOMES (XX). For people with Turner's syndrome, sexual development and MENSTRUATION come late, if at all. Though with hormone treatment they may develop SECONDARY SEX CHARACTERISTICS, they are unable to bear children. People with Turner's syndrome are generally short, are likely to have EAR AND HEARING PROBLEMS and heart problems, and have a characteristic webbing of the skin on the neck. They frequently have problems with SPATIAL ORIENTATION often leading to LEARNING DISABILITIES in mathematics, but have strength in verbal areas; some have MENTAL RETARDATION. Some females (and also some males) with apparently normal sex chromosomes have the characteristics of Turner's syndrome; their condition is called *Noonan's syndrome.*

FOR HELP AND FURTHER INFORMATION

Turner's Syndrome Society
7777 Keele St., Floor 2
Concord, Ontario L4K 1Y7, Canada
905–660–7766; 800–465–6744
Fax: 905–660–7450
Sandi Hofbauer, Executive Director
Organization concerned with Turner's syndrome; provides support and information; publishes various materials, including quarterly newsletter.

National Institute of Child Health and Human Development (NICHD), 301–496–5133. (For full group information, see PREGNANCY.)

Human Growth Foundation (HGF), 800–451–6434. Publishes pamphlet *Turner's Syndrome.* (For full group information, see GROWTH AND GROWTH DISORDERS.)

National Organization for Rare Disorders (NORD), 800–999–6673. (For full group information, see RARE DISORDERS.)

(See also GENETIC DISORDERS.)

21st-century school, a proposed education system that includes before- and after-school CHILD CARE, as well as parenting education, centered on the local public school; the plan was originally put forth by Edward Zigler of Yale University's Bush Center in Child Development and Social Policy. The school, according to Zigler, should coordinate the now highly variable child care system (including family day-care), providing training to caregivers.

Under this proposal, 3- and 4-year-olds would be cared for in the school setting by trained early-childhood professionals, with a play-oriented CURRICULUM. School-age children up to age fourteen would be given before- and after-school care, as needed, and the school itself would operate year-round, a real bonus for working parents. The school would also become a family resource center, providing classes in PRENATAL CARE, parenting skills, and child development.

Supporters cite the crisis in reliable child care and the damage to children who have bad child-care experiences, or (as in the case of LATCHKEY CHILDREN) those who are left unsupervised for substantial periods. Critics say the cost of instituting the 21st-century school proposals nationwide would be prohibitive and that the present patchwork child care network has the virtue of meeting a wide range of parental needs and desires. They fear a monopoly on child care by a school system that is itself in crisis and has not been notably successful at its main objective: EDUCATION.

tympanostomy, a procedure to solve EAR AND HEARING PROBLEMS that involve chronic buildup of fluid in the middle ear, in which a surgeon inserts a tiny drainage tube in the eardrum.

U

ultrasound, pulses of high-frequency sound waves used in medicine to create a moving image, or *sonogram*, of body tissues on a television monitor; a type of SCAN. During PREGNANCY, ultrasound is often employed to check the progress of fetal development, identify multiple pregnancy, perhaps learn the fetus's sex, identify the position of the FETUS and PLACENTA (should prebirth intervention be necessary), and check for abnormalities, such as ANENCEPHALY or ECTOPIC PREGNANCY, especially if the fetus size is inappropriate for the presumed stage of pregnancy or if family history warrants.

Ultrasound scanning is also used as a guide to physicians in some other GENETIC SCREENING procedures, such as AMNIOCENTESIS and CHORIONIC VILLUS SAMPLING. In newborns, it is sometimes used to peer through gaps in the skull, called FONTANELLES, for brain abnormalities, such as HYDROCEPHALUS or BRAIN TUMORS. In patients of all ages, ultrasound examination can help physicians check for abnormalities in internal tissues, such as the liver and gall bladder, with special ultrasound examination of the heart being called *echocardiography.* Ultrasound can also help physicians identify possible structural causes of INFERTILITY.

Ultrasound carries little or no *known* risk to mother or fetus, but for safety's sake, the Food and Drug Administration and others recommend that parents not have ultrasound scans for nonmedical reasons, such as to have a video to show the family.

FOR HELP AND FURTHER INFORMATION

American College of Obstetricians and Gynecologists (ACOG), 202–638–5577. Publishes *Ultrasound Exams in Ob-Gyn.* (For full group information, see PREGNANCY.)

(See also GENETIC DISORDERS; GENETIC SCREENING; and specific disorders.)

umbilical cord, the hollow, rope-like structure, roughly 18 to 24 inches long, that connects the FETUS to the PLACENTA, developing by about the fifth week of PREGNANCY. It supplies oxygen and NUTRITION, and takes away waste products, by way of two arteries and a vein. During PREGNANCY the umbilical cord normally develops numerous twists and turns, sometimes even becoming wrapped around the fetus. In some cases this can cause serious problems, as when it becomes wrapped around the fetus's neck; if that happens during delivery, it can often be slipped free. Sometimes a long cord will slip down (*prolapse*) into the mother's CERVIX during LABOR; since that can endanger the flow of oxygen-containing blood, causing HYPOXIA or ANOXIA, a CESAREAN SECTION or sometimes a FORCEPS DELIVERY may be indicated. If the umbilical cord has only one artery, instead of two, the fetus may get insufficient oxygen and nutrition, possibly leading to BIRTH DEFECTS.

Shortly after DELIVERY, the umbilical cord is clamped and then cut to about an inch. Within days the stump falls off; the remaining scar is called the NAVEL, *umbilicus*, or *belly button* (see CARE OF THE BABY'S NAVEL on page 428). In some cases, the abdominal wall is pushed out because of weakness near the navel; this condition, common among infants, is called an *umbilical hernia*; it also sometimes occurs in women after CHILDBIRTH. (See NAVEL; CHILDBIRTH; FETUS.)

underachiever, a student whose academic performance is generally well below educators' estimates of his or her potential, especially a student whose scores on INTELLIGENCE TESTS are consistently higher than those on ACHIEVEMENT TESTS. Students fail to work up to expected potential for a variety of reasons. A very bright student may be bored and unchallenged by regular schoolwork, in which case ENRICHMENT may be in order. Or a student may have specific LEARNING DISABILITIES that hamper learning in one or more ways, despite high general abilities. Students may also "underachieve" because their family or cultural expectations do not tally with those of the school, because of personal or family problems, or because of problems with one or more teachers or aspects of the school situation, such as CORPORAL PUNISHMENT. Those called underachievers may also simply be LATE BLOOMERS, sometimes termed *latent achievers.*

underage person, a child who is a MINOR, and therefore under the age to be treated legally as an adult. More widely, the term "underage" may be applied to any person younger than the age specified in a law or regulation, such as a legal drinking age, a legal cigarette-buying age, a legal sexual consent age, or a legal age to marry without parental or court permission (see AGE OF CONSENT).

undescended testicle, a condition in which one or both testicles fails to drop from inside the abdomen into the *scrotum*, the protective skin sac outside the male's body, before birth; also called *cryptorchidism.* (See TESTES.)

unfit parent, a description sometimes applied to a parent regarded by the court as having a lifestyle or personal history (such as a record of violence or sexual abuse) so harmful to the child that the court may bar all contact, including VISITATION RIGHTS, as in cases of severe CHILD ABUSE AND NEGLECT or ABANDONMENT.

ungraded class, a class in which students are not grouped according to GRADES (such as first, second, or third), but instead by their level of skill, or by their category (such as all children with DISABILITIES who require special services); also called a *nongraded class*. Many SPECIAL EDUCATION classes are ungraded, as are many adult or continuing education classes.

Occasionally whole schools are run on an ungraded basis, with students being evaluated and frequently reclassified according to their individual progress. In such ALTERNATIVE SCHOOLS, students often pursue INDEPENDENT STUDY and research on projects and courses all or partly of their own selection. Ungraded schools are also particularly attractive for teaching older students, such as former DROPOUTS, who are trying to make up academic deficiencies, as in so-called *remedial*, *tutoring*, or *catch-up schools*.

Uniform Child Custody Jurisdiction Act (UCCJA), a statute under which many states have agreed on consistent ways to handle CUSTODY cases. The uniform law was developed to resolve the many custody dilemmas created when parents and children move from state to state, especially in cases where parents attempt to move from one state to another, seeking a more favorable ruling. It contains rules for deciding which court has jurisdiction and provides that, once a decision has been made, other courts will enforce it, or in some cases modify it, rather than making a new and perhaps different decision. In cases of outright PARENTAL KIDNAPPING, the UCCJA specifies that the offending parent will be denied custody, except in very special circumstances.

Uniform Parentage Act, a law enacted in some states that attempts to provide common court procedures, definitions, and standards for issues of parentage, especially those involved in establishing the legal FATHER in a PATERNITY SUIT.

Uniform Reciprocal Enforcement of Support Act (URESA), a law enacted in some states that provides the legal basis for enforcing CHILD SUPPORT payment orders and related actions between parents living in two different states; the revised form of the statute is often called RURESA (Revised Uniform Reciprocal Enforcement of Support Act).

universal birth number, a unique identification number assigned to a newborn by a state's bureau of vital statistics; the digits of the number include the year of birth, the area code of the birth site, and a birth registration number.

university, an academic institution that offers post-HIGH SCHOOL educational programs and is made up of one or more COLLEGES, GRADUATE schools, and professional schools grouped together, often with a substantial focus on research, in addition to teaching.

university-affiliated facilities (UAFs), HOSPITALS associated with university research and training facilities, which provide highly sophisticated equipment, laboratories, and staff for diagnosis, treatment, and support. Parents with special problems related to PREGNANCY or INFERTILITY, or whose children have serious health problems, are often referred to appropriate UAFs by their PRIMARY HEALTH CARE PROVIDERS.

unsocialized, a term used, especially in social work and psychology, to describe someone (often a JUVENILE DELINQUENT) whose behavior is disruptive and troublesome, especially flaunting authority.

unwed father, the presumed biological FATHER, if a child's parents are not married and paternity has not been formally acknowledged or established. In some situations (as for establishment of CHILD SUPPORT responsibility), a PATERNITY SUIT may be brought against the unwed father, sometimes called in the law the PUTATIVE FATHER.

unwed mother, a MOTHER who is not married at the time she gives birth to a child. Unlike the unwed father, she retains PARENTS' RIGHTS and PARENTS' RESPONSIBILITIES, unless she chooses to give them up.

urethra, the tube by which urine is carried from the bladder to be excreted. In females, the urethra is only about 1½ inches long, exiting just above the VAGINA. However, in males, the urethra is about nine inches long, passing from the bladder through the prostate gland and through the length of the PENIS; it is also used to carry SEMEN.

The urethra is quite vulnerable to injury or to inflammation (*urethritis*), as from untreated GONORRHEA, BALANITIS, or other infections. In males, if scarring results, the urethra can become constricted, leading to painful urination, increased likelihood of infections, and possible damage to bladder or kidneys, as well as painful ejaculation during sex. Such constriction may need to be corrected, through dilation (widening) by a tube inserted through the urethral opening or sometimes by total surgical reconstruction. CONGENITAL defects involving the urethra in the male include HYPOSPADIAS and EPISPADIAS. In females, the urethra is somewhat less vulnerable, but more readily carries infection to the bladder and kidneys. (See KIDNEY AND UROLOGICAL DISORDERS.)

urine tests (urinalysis), a series of tests run on a sample of urine; often considered a kind of KIDNEY FUNCTION TEST, but testing also for a wide variety of other problems and disorders. The urine is first examined for its general characteristics, including color, acidity (pH), clarity or cloudiness, and concentration. Technicians then use a centrifuge to spin the urine, separating out various substances for analysis, including:

- *Blood*, a possible indication of infection, TUMORS, or kidney stones.
- *Pus, bacteria,* or *white blood cells*, which are signs of infection (these may often be further examined in CULTURES).
- *Protein* or *protein fragments* called *casts*, which are signs of possible kidney disease or injury.
- *Bile*, a sign of possible liver disease (see LIVER AND LIVER PROBLEMS).
- *Crystals*, which are signs of possible METABOLIC DISORDERS.
- GLUCOSE or *ketones*, which are signs of possible DIABETES.
- HUMAN CHORIONIC GONADOTROPIN (hCG), a sign of possible PREGNANCY.
- *Worm eggs*, which are signs of possible parasitic infestation.

(See MEDICAL TESTS.)

urologist, a PHYSICIAN who specializes in diagnosis and treatment of disorders of the urinary tract, including the kidney and bladder, in both males and females, and of the male GENITALS.

uterus, a muscular, hollow organ in a woman's lower abdomen, above and behind the bladder, shaped roughly like an upside-down pear, with the FALLOPIAN TUBES lying above and to the right and left. On the bottom of the uterus, the CERVIX, which is actually the neck of the uterus, leads into the VAGINA. The uterus is the center of the REPRODUCTIVE SYSTEM; here the fertilized egg (OVUM) implants itself to grow into a FETUS. And here the monthly MENSTRUAL CYCLE centers, with the uterine lining (the *endometrium*) gradually growing in preparation for a fertilized egg, and being shed in a menstrual period if none appears.

In infant girls, the uterus is tipped backward (*retroverted*), but as a female matures the uterus normally becomes tipped forward about a quarter-turn from the VAGINA. Usually weighing only a few ounces, the uterus grows dramatically during PREGNANCY. Some of the growth comes as the endometrium thickens and develops more blood vessels to supply nourishment to the fetus through the PLACENTA, and some comes from development of powerful muscles that will, at CHILDBIRTH, push the baby through the birth canal (the widened cervix and vagina).

Various kinds of disorders of the uterus can affect a woman's ability to reproduce, including:

- *Inflammation of the endometrium (endometritis)*: This often results from an infection originating elsewhere, such as the cervix or Fallopian tubes; it can also be a complication of childbirth, as after a MISCARRIAGE or when not all of the PLACENTA has been expelled after birth.
- TUMORS: A variety of growths can affect the uterus, including many BENIGN tumors, such as polyps and fibroid tumors; MALIGNANT tumors of the endometrium; or either benign or malignant growths in the placenta. In an operation called a HYSTERECTOMY, the whole uterus may be removed in case of tumors, which would end the possibility of childbearing; however, various alternatives are possible that can allow removal of tumors without loss of the uterus (see HYSTERECTOMY). Women at increased risk of having endometrial cancer are those with long-term high ESTROGEN levels, OBESITY, failure to ovulate, and few or no children; use of the BIRTH CONTROL PILL lowers that risk.
- *Injury*: These mostly result from external causes, such as a badly performed ABORTION or an INTRAUTERINE DEVICE (IUD) that has damaged the uterus.
- *Mispositioning (prolapse)*: Sometimes the uterus can slip out of its normal position, especially when its support ligaments have been stretched and weakened from previous childbirth, though it can also occur in childless women, especially those who are obese. In extreme cases, the uterus slips down so far that it can be seen at the opening of the vagina. The bladder and urethra can also be affected. Pelvic floor or Kegel EXERCISES help strengthen the muscles needed to prevent prolapse after childbirth (see BASIC EXERCISES FOR DURING AND AFTER PREGNANCY on page 634). In severe cases, the uterus may need to be removed (see HYSTERECTOMY), or a plastic ring called a *pessary* may be inserted to hold the uterus in place.
- CONGENITAL malformation: Sometimes a uterus develops not in the usual shape, which can predispose a woman to have MALPRESENTATION (abnormal birth position of the fetus) or other problems during DELIVERY. On rare occasions, a uterus is absent altogether, or a woman has two each of the uterus, cervix, and vagina. In some such cases, surgical correction is possible; in others, a normal pregnancy is not possible.

Also associated with the uterus are various problems involving MENSTRUATION.

FOR HELP AND FURTHER INFORMATION

National Cancer Institute (NCI), 800–422–6237. Publishes "What You Need to Know About" brochure on cancer of the uterus. (For full group information, see CANCER.)

American Cancer Society (ACS), 800–227–2345. Publishes materials on cancers of the uterus. (For full group information, see CANCER.)

(See also PREGNANCY; OVULATION; HYSTERECTOMY; HYSTEROSCOPY; HYSTEROSALPINGOGRAM.)

V

vaccine, a preparation used in IMMUNIZATION, which includes weakened, killed, or partial matter from disease organisms, designed to trigger the person's body to manufacture ANTIBODIES, that will be ready to fight off the actual disease should the person later be exposed to it. The vaccine is usually administered by an injection or taken through the mouth, and the protection it offers may last for a limited time, or a lifetime, depending on the vaccine. One problem with vaccines is to see that they do not unintentionally give the person the disease itself, as can happen on rare occasions with the oral POLIO vaccine. But vaccines have been one of the major successes in modern medicine, responsible for the absolute elimination of one of humanity's greatest enemies throughout history: the dreaded smallpox. (See IMMUNIZATION, or entries on specific vaccines.)

vacuum extraction, in CHILDBIRTH, use of a suction cup placed on a baby's head and attached to a machine called a *vacuum extractor* or *ventouse*, with the suction timed to the contractions of the UTERUS, to help ease DELIVERY. Vacuum extraction may be used in cases of FETAL DISTRESS, especially early in the delivery, or when the mother is unable to push out the baby on her own, as an alternative to FORCEPS DELIVERY. The baby generally has temporary swelling on the scalp following birth. (See CHILDBIRTH.)

The same kind of machine is also used to perform some kinds of ABORTION. In that case, the process is called *menstrual extraction.* (See ABORTION.)

vagina, the muscular, expandable canal between a woman's outer GENITALS and the CERVIX that leads to the UTERUS. The vagina is where, during sexual intercourse, the PENIS deposits SPERM for possible FERTILIZATION; it is also the avenue used for the outflow of blood during MENSTRUATION. During CHILDBIRTH, the vagina and the widened cervix become the BIRTH CANAL.

In a young girl, the vagina is mostly covered by a membrane called a HYMEN, with an opening in the center, which is stretched or torn at the first penetration of the vagina. Partial or complete absence of the vagina (*vaginal atresia*) is a rare CONGENITAL abnormality. Apart from occasional infections, such as from SEXUALLY TRANSMITTED DISEASES, which may involve vaginal discharge or itching, few young people have disorders involving the vagina.

FOR HELP AND FURTHER INFORMATION

American Social Health Association (ASHA), 800–227–8922. Publishes brochure *Vaginitis: What Every Woman Should Know.* (For full group information, see SEXUALLY TRANSMITTED DISEASES.)

American College of Obstetricians and Gynecologists (ACOG), 202–638–5577. Publishes *Vaginitis: Causes and Treatments.* (For full group information, see PREGNANCY.)

Planned Parenthood Federation of America (PPFA), 800–230–7526. Publishes pamphlet *Vaginitis: Questions and Answers.* (For full group information, see BIRTH CONTROL.)

National Institute of Child Health and Human Development (NICHD), 301–496–5133. Publishes *Vaginitis: Questions and Answers.* (For full group information, see PREGNANCY.)

vaginal birth after cesarean (VBAC), a movement to give women the option of delivering a child in the normal manner, when medically possible, after a previous child was delivered by CESAREAN SECTION.

vaginal pouch, a form of BIRTH CONTROL that combines some aspects of the traditional male CONDOM and the DIAPHRAGM; sometimes called a *female condom.* It is a soft, loose-fitting, seven-inch-long, pre-lubricated polyurethane sheath designed to fit inside a woman's VAGINA, where it acts as a physical barrier against a man's SPERM and other fluids. Attached to the sheath are two flexible polyurethane rings; the one inside the closed end of the sheath fits over the CERVIX like a diaphragm, while the outer ring at the open end lies outside the body, anchoring the sheath in place over the LABIA.

Like the condom, the vaginal pouch can be bought over-the-counter, requires no special fitting or prescription, is easy to use, is disposable, and can be used with a SPERMICIDE. Also like a condom, it acts as a barrier against SEXUALLY TRANSMITTED DISEASES, although no birth control device can offer 100 percent protection against AIDS. In Europe, the pouch is marketed under the name *Femidom*; in the United States and Canada, as *Reality*™.

The main advantages of the vaginal pouch are that the woman is in control of her own birth control and sexual health, and that it is less disruptive of sexual activity than a condom, since it can be put into place before arousal. Clinical trials show that the pouch is as effective as the diaphragm or CERVICAL SPONGE in preventing PREGNANCY; it is rated at approximately 85 percent effective for contraception, making it more effective than condoms. It also seems to be more effective than condoms in preventing AIDS and other sexually transmitted diseases, since pouches are significantly less likely to tear, break, or slip during use, with a tear rate of 1 percent (as opposed to 1–14 percent for condoms), and a rate of exposure to SEMEN through either breakage or slippage of 3 percent (as compared to 11 percent for condoms).

In early use, the pouch has not been associated with allergic reactions (see ALLERGIES), or with increased risk of vaginal or URINARY TRACT infections (see VAGINA). Some women, however, found the device cumbersome, or disliked the appearance of the ring outside the vagina. As with condoms and diaphragms, women must be careful of sharp nails and rings during handling or insertion, and should use only water-based lubricants, if additional lubrication is desired.

Under development are other variations on this theme. The *Woman's Choice Female Condomme* is a heavier latex pouch, with an umbrella-like cap, inserted with a plastic applicator. The *Unisex Condom Garment*, or *Bikini Condom*, is a pair of polyurethane bikini-style pants with an attached sheath, which works as either a condom or vaginal pouch, depending on whether the person wearing it is a man or a woman. (See BIRTH CONTROL.)

VAKT, a highly structured multisensory approach to teaching READING, named for the four main senses used: *visual* (seeing), *auditory* (hearing), *kinesthetic* (body motion), and *tactile* (touch). With the VAKT approach, a child traces a written letter or word while reading it, which reinforces learning from the various senses. VAKT approaches are widely used to teach children with LEARNING DISABILITIES, especially DYSLEXIA.

With the *Gillingham (Orton-Gillingham) method*, the child learns the sounds of individual letters, and is then taught to blend them together into words, using tracing throughout, in a series of lessons occurring five times a week over at least two years. In the *Fernald method*, the child learns to read and spell whole words, first by tracing hand-printed words and learning to reproduce them without referring to the original, then by using the word in a sentence or story, then by reading the word in print. The word is then filed in a "word bank," and the child goes on to learning new words, gradually eliminating the tracing, but often speaking and writing the word to "set" it, and eventually learning new words by their similarities to words previously learned. (See READING.)

valedictorian, in a graduating class, the student with the highest academic rank, generally as measured by GRADE-POINT AVERAGE; so-called because he or she is often asked to give a farewell speech, or *valedictory*, at GRADUATION ceremonies. The second-ranked student is the SALUTATORIAN.

validity, in relation to TESTS, the extent to which a test actually measures what it sets out to measure, and so the extent to which test results are actually useful or meaningful. In educational testing, this is of special concern to parents, and a highly controversial question. In INTELLIGENCE TESTS, for example, it is unclear precisely what is being tested, for no one knows for sure what intelligence is and whether and how it would be possible to test it. Professionals often distinguish between different types of validity, including:

- *Content validity*, which concerns how well the content of the test relates to the test's purpose. To be useful, an ACHIEVEMENT TEST for a particular grade needs to reflect approximately what is actually taught in that grade.
- *Predictive validity*, which concerns how well the test scores relate to the future performance they are meant to predict. For example, the SCHOLASTIC ACHIEVEMENT TEST (SAT) is used to predict student success in COLLEGE, and whether or not it succeeds in doing so (a point much at issue) is a question of predictive validity. A test's predictive validity may be measured by analysis of the *correlation* between two sets of figures, such as SAT scores and college GRADE-POINT AVERAGES; this is generally expressed statistically as a decimal number somewhere between 0 correlation (if SAT correctly predicted GPA scores in no cases) to an ideally perfect 1 (if SAT correctly predicted GPA in every case).

Two related concerns are *sensitivity*, the ability of the test to correctly identify a person with a problem, and *specificity*, a test's ability to correctly indicate which people are not AT RISK for a problem. (See TESTS; STANDARDIZED TESTS.)

varicocele, swollen (varicose) veins around the TESTES, most often the left testicle. If painful, the condition can be relieved by wearing an athletic supporter or tight briefs, but this can affect fertility. Where pain is great or INFERTILITY is at issue, surgery may be performed to tie off defective veins.

vas deferens, one of the two tubes by which SPERM leave the EPIDIDYMIS, which is the "holding area" behind each of the two TESTES where the sperm matured; on passing through the vas deferens, the sperm mixes with SEMEN and may be released through the EJACULATORY DUCT in ORGASM. The vasa deferentia (plural of vas deferens) are cut during VASECTOMY, a surgical form of STERILIZATION performed on males.

vasectomy, a surgical procedure for a man who wants to father no more children; a permanent form of BIRTH CONTROL, or STERILIZATION. The operation is often performed in a doctor's office under local ANESTHESIA, and is rated at more than 99 percent effective in preventing PREGNANCY. The brief procedure involves making two cuts, one on either side of the SCROTUM, and then cutting or clamping both of the long tubes called the VAS DEFER-

ENS, so no SPERM can pass through them. Some temporary pain and swelling follow the procedure, and sometimes infection can set in. The Public Health Service reports that human males show no cardiovascular problems, though animal studies showed adverse effects on the cardiovascular system. However, approximately one man in twenty reports having psychological problems related to a vasectomy.

Vasectomy has traditionally been regarded as permanent, since attempts to reverse the procedure have had little success. However, some new and still highly experimental REPRODUCTIVE TECHNOLOGY techniques—notably INTRACYTOPLASMIC SPERM INJECTION (ICSI) and SUBZONAL SPERM INSERTION (SZI)—offer men who have previously had a vasectomy the possibility of fathering a child.

FOR HELP AND FURTHER INFORMATION

Association for Voluntary Surgical Contraception (AVSC), (212–351–2500). (For full group information, see BIRTH CONTROL.)

Planned Parenthood Federation of America (PPFA), 800–230–7526. Publishes pamphlet *All About Vasectomy.* (For full group information, see BIRTH CONTROL.)

American Society for Reproductive Medicine (ASRM), 205–978–5000. (For full group information, see INFERTILITY.)

American College of Obstetricians and Gynecologists (ACOG), 202–638–5577. Publishes *Sterilization for Women and Men.* (For full group information, see PREGNANCY.)

Couple to Couple League (CCL), 513–471–2000. Publishes brochure *Sexual Sterilization: Some Facts for an Informed Choice.* (For full group information, see NATURAL FAMILY PLANNING.)

RESOLVE, Inc., HelpLine: 617–623–0744. Publishes fact sheet *Microsurgery, Vas Blockage/Vasectomy Reversal.* (For full group information, see INFERTILITY.)

OTHER RESOURCES

Is Vasectomy Worth the Risk?: A Physician's Case Against Vasectomania. H. J. Roberts. Sunshine Sentinel, 1993.

(See also STERILIZATION.)

vas efferens, one of the two tubes (plural: *vasa efferentia*) by which SPERM leave the testes for the EPIDIDYMIS, the "holding area" where they mature.

vasography, a MEDICAL TEST sometimes performed as part of an INFERTILITY workup. A special dye is injected into the VAS DEFERENS, through which sperm must pass, and a series of X-RAYS is then taken. This test is performed only if blockage of the vas deferens is suspected, to try to identify the area of the blockage.

vegetarian, a type of diet that excludes at least meat, poultry, and fish, and sometimes also eggs and dairy products. Many peoples of the world follow a largely vegetarian diet, many because of personal poverty and limited regional food resources, but some also because of religious or philosophical conviction. In the West, some people have also adopted a vegetarian approach to NUTRITION in response to concern about misuse of the world's resources, and because of a desire to live what is felt to be a more natural, healthy existence.

There are several different types of vegetarian diets, notably:

- *Semivegetarian*, which excludes meat, but allows some poultry and fish, plus all other kinds of foods.
- *Lacto-ovo vegetarian*, which excludes meat, poultry, and fish, but allows eggs, milk, and other dairy products, including cheese.
- *Lacto vegetarian*, which excludes all animal products except milk and other dairy products, including cheese.
- *Vegan*, also called *strict* or *pure vegetarian*, which excludes animal products in any form (including butter and milk for cooking). Some also avoid vaccines, which are often made with animal matter, such as eggs.
- *Fruitarian*, which includes only plant products that fall off naturally and do not require destruction of the plant for harvesting, including nuts, beans, peas, corn, cucumbers, tomatoes, berries, and fruits such as apples, pears, and peaches.

Except when most protein is gained from high-FAT dairy products and high-CHOLESTEROL eggs, a well-balanced, high-fiber vegetarian diet may lower the risk of a number of diseases, including hypertension (high BLOOD PRESSURE), OBESITY, DIABETES, OSTEOPOROSIS, and digestive disorders (see DIGESTIVE SYSTEM AND DISORDERS), including CANCER of the intestines.

The main concern with a vegetarian diet is to get the proper amount and type of PROTEIN, MINERALS, and VITAMINS. Most animal sources of protein contain all the necessary AMINO ACIDS, but many plant sources contain only some. Because of this, people following a vegan or fruitarian diet, especially, must become very familiar with the nutritional content of plant foods and must plan to eat them in the proper combinations (such as rice and beans) to get the full range of proteins needed. People following a vegan diet, especially pregnant women, may want to take a vitamin supplement, especially including VITAMINS B_{12}, C, and D, on their doctor's advice. (See NUTRITION.)

FOR HELP AND FURTHER INFORMATION

North American Vegetarian Society (NAVS)
P.O. Box 72
Dolgeville, NY 13329
518–568–7970
Brian Graff and Sharon Graff, Codirectors
Organization concerned with vegetarianism; publishes

various materials, including quarterly *Vegetarian Voice, Vegetarianism: Answers to the Most Commonly Asked Questions, Good Nutrition: A Look at Vegetarian Basics, Vegetarianism: A Diet for Life, Vegetarian Express Fast Food Campaign*, and *The Care and Feeding of Vegetarians.*

Vegetarian Information Service (VIS)
P.O. Box 5888
Bethesda, MD 20814
301–530–1737; 800–632–8688
Fax: 301–530–5747
E-mail: farm@clark.net
Alex Hershaft, President
Organization focusing on vegetarianism and its health, social, economic, environmental, and ethical advantages; publishes various materials.

American Vegan Society (AVS)
501 Old Harding Highway
P.O. Box H
Malaga, NJ 08328–0908
Phone and Fax: 609–694–2887
H. Jay Dinshah, President
Organization focusing on veganism; publishes quarterly *Ahimsa*; pamphlets *Now Try Veganism* and *Out of the Jungle*, and philosophical works and cookbooks.

Food and Nutrition Information Center (FNIC), 301–504–5414. Publishes resource list *Vegetarian Nutrition-Topics.* (For full group information, see NUTRITION.).

ONLINE RESOURCES

Internet: rec.food.veg Usenet newsgroup. Subscribe through newsreader: news.rec.food.veg

Internet: veggie (Vegetarian Issues Discussion List) Discussion area. To subscribe, send this message: "SUB veggie [your first name] [your last name]" to: mailto:listserv@gibbs.oit.uus.edu

Internet: veglife Forum for exploring vegetarian lifestyle (formerly called Granola). To subscribe, send this message "SUB veglife [your first name] [your last name]" to: mailto:listserv@vtvml.cc.vt.edu

OTHER RESOURCES

Vegetarian Pregnancy: The Definitive Nutritional Guide to Having a Healthy Baby. Sharon K. Yntema. McBooks, 1994.
The Vegetarian Teen: A Teen Nutrition Book. Charles A. Salter. Millbrook, 1991.

venereal diseases (VD), a group of diseases passed between people during sexual intercourse, today often called SEXUALLY TRANSMITTED DISEASES (STDs).

venipuncture, a type of SPECIMEN TEST in which blood is removed by inserting a needle into a vein and withdrawing it into a syringe or a CATHETER; a somewhat INVASIVE kind of MEDICAL TEST, but generally with little risk.

ventilator, a machine to assist or totally take over breathing, when a person has difficulty or inability in breathing unassisted, as after a TRAUMATIC BRAIN INJURY; often called a *respirator* or *life-support machine.* Such machines are generally used in INTENSIVE-CARE UNITS of hospitals, often in tandem with electronic monitoring of pulse, respiration, and heartbeat. In cases of BRAIN DEATH, parents may sometimes be called upon to make difficult decisions about use of a ventilator with a child or family member. (See LUNG AND BREATHING PROBLEMS; DEATH AND DYING; ADVANCE DIRECTIVE.)

ventricles, cavities of chambers in the body, which are generally filled with fluid. In the brain, the two halves of the cerebrum each surround a ventricle, with two smaller ventricles near the brain stem (see BRAIN AND BRAIN DISORDERS). Enlargement of the ventricles is found in certain diseases and disorders, such as HYDROCEPHALUS and HUNTINGTON'S CHOREA. In cases of hydrocephalus, a SHUNT is sometimes inserted into the head to bypass a blockage or to remove excess CEREBROSPINAL FLUID; that can sometimes cause infection in the ventricles (*ventriculitis*). PREMATURE infants are more than usually susceptible to abnormal, excessive bleeding in the brain ventricles (see INTRAVENTRICULAR HEMORRHAGE).

The name *ventricles* is also applied to the heart's two lower chambers, which pump the blood they receive from the upper chambers, called *atria.* It is the pumping of the ventricles that we hear as a "heartbeat" and that are graphed by an ELECTROCARDIOGRAPH, when physicians are assessing whether the heart or heartbeat is abnormal (see HEART AND HEART PROBLEMS).

Very Low Birth Weight (VLBW), a LOW BIRTH WEIGHT baby weighing under 3.3 pounds (1500 grams) at birth, with sharply increased risk of illnesses and death.

viable, a medical term for an infant who is considered capable of living, growing, and developing independently. Normally the term is applied to an infant weighing at least 2.2. pounds (1000 grams) at birth or having a GESTATION AGE of at least 28 weeks, meaning that the fetus developed in the UTERUS for at least 28 weeks (the normal number of weeks for GESTATION being 40). A child so PREMATURE would, however, probably need a great deal of special care in the first weeks and months of its life, and probably would be placed in a NEONATAL INTENSIVE CARE UNIT (NICU).

Vineland Adaptive Behavior Scales, a TEST that attempts to assess the development of various SOCIAL SKILLS, SELF-HELP SKILLS, and ADAPTIVE BEHAVIOR, for children from infancy to adulthood, especially those who have MENTAL RETARDATION or other DISABILITIES; existing in three forms, this is a revised version of the earlier Vineland Social Maturity Scale. In the Interview Edition, Survey Form, a parent, close relative, or other knowledgeable CAREGIVER is interviewed by a trained examiner about the child's abilities in various areas, such as eating, dressing, communication, movement, and self-direction, with information recorded in a structured record book. The Expanded Form of the Interview Edition is similar, but covers a wider range of behaviors. A Classroom Edition, used for children ages three through twelve, consists of a questionnaire completed by the child's teacher.

The results are scaled by trained examiners according to a standard manual and are converted to an AGE-EQUIVALENT, sometimes called a *social age.* The scores and the profiles are used in planning what activities should be included in the person's educational program, as in INDIVIDUALIZED EDUCATION PLAN, and also in reporting to parents the child's strengths and weaknesses. (See TESTS.)

violence, physical force that hurts, violates, or abuses; the term may also be applied to emotional or psychological force used to the same ends. Violence of many types has risen sharply in the past few decades and has become a major concern of parents, for themselves and even more for their children.

Unfortunately, much violence begins at home, and it is there that many children have their earliest main experiences of violence. For many, the violence is directed specifically at them, as in cases of physical or sexual abuse (see CHILD ABUSE AND NEGLECT; INCEST; RAPE). Often a batterer abuses all or virtually all members in a family, but even where children are exempted, many are daily witnesses to violence visited on a sibling, parent, or other relative. As the American Medical Association put it in 1992, domestic violence was "a public health problem that has reached epidemic proportions." It is an experience that cuts across all lines—age, racial, ethnic, regional, educational, and socioeconomic, primarily affecting women, though some men are victims of battering. The AMA noted that nearly 1 in every 4 women experiences physical abuse by a husband or partner at some time in their lives. For them, as U.S. Surgeon General Dr. Antonia Novello put it in 1991, "The home is actually a more dangerous place for American women than the city streets." Many of these women are trapped in a cycle of threats, low self-esteem, and self-blame; without marketable skills and resources that would allow them to leave the abusive situation; and fearful of leaving, since that may provoke increased violence—as it often does—and lead to loss of CUSTODY.

As the dimensions of the domestic violence problem have become clear, a network of battered women's shelters have sprung up around the country. Their services vary, but most offer basic shelter and food, a safe environment, twenty-four-hour crisis intervention and support, counseling services, transportation assistance, legal assistance and referral, financial assistance, victim advocacy services, information, and medical assistance. Some also offer child care and food and shelter for children as well, but many do not take children. Shelters also advise women who are still in abusive situations, and sometimes counseling for batterers. Mothers seeking to take their children out of an abusive home should plan ahead for their mutual protection. In particular, they are advised to:

- Locate a battered women's shelter that takes children.
- Get expert advice about how to leave the home safely, from that shelter or by calling the National Domestic Violence Hotline (see the list that follows this entry).
- Engage legal support, getting referrals from the shelter.
- Prepare friends and family for your leaving, and seek their moral support for a smooth transition.
- Have an emergency plan—hide away some extra money, car keys, the police number, and addresses and phone numbers for places to go, such as a shelter or trusted relative.
- If you wish to keep custody of the children, take them with you, if at all possible; if you cannot to that, maintain close contact, with continuing care and support, as much as possible in the situation.
- Keep all your important personal papers in a safe place *outside the home*; if possible, include copies of income tax statements, insurance policies, pension plans, property appraisals, receipts for mortgage or rent payments, medical and dental care receipts, and other financial documents that may be needed if DIVORCE is contemplated.
- Open a private mail box, at a post office or mail drop, for personal mail, and a private safe deposit box for your personal valuables and papers, if it seems necessary or advisable.
- Open your own bank account and put into it as much money as you can.
- Open a credit card solely in your own name, if that is possible.
- Consider who, among your family, friends, or banks, might be willing to provide loans, if needed.
- Seek medical attention, since some internal injuries may be serious but not apparent.
- Take photographs of the injuries to yourself or your children, in case you decide to press legal charges at any time.
- Seek support from local groups, therapists, and other resources.

Another major danger in the home comes from firearms. Many American households contain guns, and despite safety warnings to the contrary, more than half of these guns are left loaded, at least some of the time, and are not locked up. Approximately 30 percent of all unintentional shootings are by children under age six, killing themselves or others while playing with a gun found in their own or another's home. A federal report found that almost all of these shootings could have been prevented by a childproofing device: trigger lock. However, neither that nor another safety device, a loading indicator, is required by law, though some groups are attempting to pass legislation requiring them. Each year, hundreds of children die of unintentional gunshot wounds; at least five times as many have nonfatal injuries, many resulting in permanent DISABILITIES, such as PARALYSIS, blindness (see EYE AND VISION PROBLEMS), or loss of limbs. Boys are more at risk than girls for unintentional shootings, and at the greatest risk from ages fifteen to nineteen. Parents who have guns in their homes should see that they are safely locked away, unloaded, and that their older children, if desired, are trained to handle guns properly.

Of much greater danger to children today are intentional shootings, which are rising at an alarming rate. Young Black males ages fifteen to nineteen are most at risk; since 1969, gun homicide has been the leading cause of death among that group, far exceeding the likely death rate from all natural causes combined. This has much to do with the prevailing social climate, including the drug culture, gangs on the street, and the easy availability of handguns, even to children not old enough to get a driver's license.

Guns are also increasingly used in incidents of self-inflicted violence; approximately 60 percent of all SUICIDES by teens involve guns. Because those who commit suicide with a gun are far more likely to succeed in killing themselves, some researchers feel that at least some of the rise in the teen suicide rate in recent decades stems from the availability of handguns.

This spread of guns and violence has spilled over into schools, at all grade levels, including elementary schools. Many students who carry guns say they do so for protection on their way to or from school. Some schools have responded by installing metal detectors, though the long-term effectiveness of this approach remains to be seen. In some affluent areas, elaborate security arrangements are being made; a Dallas education complex housing several schools, which opened in 1995, sports 37 surveillance cameras, six metal detectors, five full-time police officers, and an architectural design based on that for prisons. In other areas, parents must try to guard their children's safety as best they can, through community pressure on schools and law enforcement. Some communities have moved to separate out from the student body those students who are most disruptive and violent.

Overall, for both sexes, all age groups, and for any means of killing, homicide is the fourth leading cause of death among children ages one to nine, and third leading cause of death for ages ten to fourteen, and the second leading cause for ages fifteen to nineteen, second only to unintentional injuries.

With the images and reality of violence all around them, many children need to be specifically taught how to deal with conflict in a nonviolent way. That is the focus of numerous programs around the country today (see resource list below), many of them in schools, but also in religious and other community organizations. These attempt to show children how to deal with anger, frustration, and other such feelings, attempting to teach a kind of "emotional literacy." Some use role-playing in structured, supervised situations to help violent children explore new ways of dealing with conflict.

Many parents have also been concerned about the effect on developing young children of widespread depictions of violence in the media. The American Psychological Association, among others, has concluded that a "great majority of research studies have found a relationship between televised violence and behaving aggressively," and that "viewing televised violence may lead to increases in aggressive attitudes, values, and behavior, particularly in children," and has called on the television industry to reduce "direct imitatable violence" on children's programming, including cartoons, and to produce more programming to mitigate the effects of television violence. More to the point, voluntary programs having proved of little value in the past, the APA has urged parents to monitor and control television viewing by children. A movie rating system has been in place for some years, but that primarily offers guidance to parents on sexual content, not on the level of violence. Parents are also advised to divert children away from war toys and games that foster images and patterns of violence.

In communities with very high levels of violence, some psychiatrists have found that children develop a kind of POST-TRAUMATIC STRESS DISORDER, comparable to having been in a battle zone. Nor is this simply in response to threats or depictions of violence. Many have actually witnessed shootings and killings, or have lost friends or family members. A National Institute of Mental Health researcher, studying a "moderately violent" neighborhood in Washington, D.C., found that 6 percent of students in the fifth and sixth grades had themselves been shot at, and 11 percent had seen someone else shot. Many of these children had also seen violence at home: 13 percent of these children's mothers had resolved arguments at home by threatening to use a gun or knife, and in half the cases had actually done so. Clearly such children need considerable support, education, and often therapy to overcome such difficult backgrounds.

FOR HELP AND FURTHER INFORMATION

National Coalition Against Domestic Violence (NCADV)
P.O. Box 18749
Denver, CO 80218–0749
303–839–1852
Fax: 303–831–9251
Organization concerned with violence in families; provides information and referrals to community-based shelters and support services; acts as advocate; publishes various materials, including quarterlies *NCADV Update* and *NCADV Voice*; fact sheets on domestic violence, children and violence, and lesbian battering; *National Directory of Domestic Violence Programs—A Guide to Community Shelter, Safe Home and Service Programs*; reports *A Current Analysis of the Battered Women's Movement* and *Rural Task Force Resource Packet—Reflections on Rural Realities*; and video *Rough Love*.

Johnson Institute, 800–231–5165, U.S. except MN. Publishes numerous materials, including:

- For parents: *Safe at School: Awareness and Action for Parents of Kids Grades K–12* and *Kids and Gangs: What Parents and Educators Need to Know.*
- For children: *Tulip Doesn't Feel Safe* and *Della the Dinosaur Talks About Violence and Anger Management.*
- For teens: book *How to Control Your Anger (Before It Controls You): A Guide for Teenagers*; and videos *Anger: Handle It Before It Handles You, Conflict: Think About. Talk About It. Try to Work It Out,* and *Double Bind* (on safety and survival skills for unsafe situations).
- General books: *Suicide and Homicide Among Adolescents, Violence in Schools: The Enabling Factor, Preventing Gang Violence in Your School,* and *Solving Violence Problems in Your School: Why a Systematic Approach is Necessary.*
- Numerous violence prevention programs.

(For full group information, see HELP AGAINST SUBSTANCE ABUSE on page 703.)

National Association for the Education of Young Children (NAEYC), 800–424–2460. Publishes books *Character Development: Encouraging Self-Esteem and Self-Discipline in Infants, Helping Young Children Understand Peace, War, and the Nuclear Threat,* and *Early Violence Prevention: Tools for Teachers of Young Children*; brochures *Media Violence and Children: A Guide for Parents* and *The NAEYC Position Statement on Violence in the Lives of Children*; and video *Confronting the Epidemic of Violence—A Community Strategy.* (For full group information, see PRESCHOOL.)

Center for Law and Education, 202–986–3000. Publishes *Responding to Violence in Schools: Legal and Policy Implications to Students and Their Advocates.* (For full group information, see HELP ON LEARNING AND EDUCATION on page 659.)

American Academy of Child and Adolescent Psychiatry (AACAP), 202–966–7300. Publishes information sheets *Children and TV Violence, Children and Firearms* and *The Influence of Music and Rock Videos.* (For full group information, see MENTAL DISORDERS.)

American Academy of Pediatrics (AAP), 800–433–9016. Publishes brochure *Keep Your Family Safe from Firearm Injury.* (For full group information, see HEALTH CARE.)

C. Henry Kempe National Center for the Prevention and Treatment of Child Abuse and Neglect, 303–321–3963. Publishes *Aggression and Violence Through the Life Span.* (For full group information, see HELP AGAINST CHILD ABUSE AND NEGLECT on page 680.)

National Organization on Legal Problems of Education (NOLPE), 913–273–3550. Publishes *Legal Issues Surrounding Safe Schools* and *Violence and School Safety.* (For full group information, see HELP ON LEARNING AND EDUCATION on page 659.)

Committee for Children (CFC), 800–634–4449. Publishes violence prevention materials.

Zero to Three National Center for Clinical Infant Programs, 703–528–4300. Publishes *Caring for Infants and Toddlers in Violent Environments: Hurt, Healing and Hope.* (For full group information, see CHILD CARE.)

Association for Childhood Education International (ACEI), 800–423–3563. Publishes position paper *Children and War;* videotape *The Media and Our Children;* and Kelly Bear education series for teaching appropriate behavior. (For full group information, see HELP ON LEARNING AND EDUCATION on page 659.)

Council for Exceptional Children (CEC), 800–328–0272. Publishes *Programming for Aggressive and Violent Students.* (For full group information, see HELP ON LEARNING AND EDUCATION on page 659.)

National Maternal and Child Health Clearinghouse (NMCHC), 703–821–8955. Publishes *Not Even One: A Report of the Carter Center Consultation on the Crisis of Children and Firearms, Violence as a Public Health Problem: Developing Culturally Appropriate Prevention Strategies for Adolescents and Children—Full Report, Violence: The Impact of Community Violence on African American Children and Families, Firearm Facts: Information on Gun Violence and Its Prevention, Biblio Alert! New Resources for Preventing Injury and Violence* [Vol. 1, No. 1—*Focus on Firearms*; Vol. 1, No. 2—*Focus on Alcohol and Injury*], and *Children's Safety Network: A Resource for Child and Adolescent Injury and Violence Prevention.* (For full group information, see PREGNANCY.)

National Center for Women and Family Law, 212–674–8200. Publishes *The Effect of Woman Abuse on Children, Battered Women: The Facts, Battered Women and Custody, Battering: A Major Cause of Homelessness, State Custody Laws with Respect to Domestic Abuse, Defending a Battered Woman Accused of Parental Abduction,* and *Guide to Interstate Custody: A Manual for Domestic Violence Advocates.* (For full group information, see CUSTODY.)

Association of Family and Conciliation Courts (AFCC), 608–251–4001. Publishes books *Domestic Violence and Empowerment in Custody and Visitation Cases, Domestic Violence Visitation Risk Assessment,* and *Mediation and Domestic Violence—Current Policies and Practices*; and two-part video *Domestic Violence: The Crime That Tears Families* and *Mediation: The Crucial Factor.* (For full group information, see DIVORCE.)

Healthy Mothers, Healthy Babies National Coalition (HMHB), 202–863–2458. Publishes *Domestic Violence.* (For full group information, see PREGNANCY.)

Center on Children and the Law, 202–662–1720. Publishes *The Impact of Domestic Violence on Children.* (For full group information, see HELP AGAINST CHILD ABUSE AND NEGLECT on page 680.)

National Clearinghouse for Alcohol and Drug Abuse Information (NCADI), 800–729–6686. Publishes fact sheets *Domestic Violence and Alcohol and Other Drugs* and *Violence and Crime and Alcohol and Other Drugs*, and Prevention Resource Guide *Violence*. (For full group information, see HELP AGAINST SUBSTANCE ABUSE on page 703.)

Character Education Institute (CEI), 800–284–0499. Publishes antiviolence curriculum. (For full group information, see HELP ON LEARNING AND EDUCATION on page 659.)

National Council on Child Abuse and Family Violence (NCCAFV), 800–222–2000. Publishes "Facts About" booklets *Family Violence, Domestic Violence*, and *Elder Abuse*. (For full group information, see HELP AGAINST CHILD ABUSE AND NEGLECT on page 680.)

National Mental Health Consumer Self-Help Clearinghouse, 800–553–4539. Publishes reprint packet on jail, police, violence, and mental health. (For full group information, see MENTAL DISORDERS.)

National Alliance for the Mentally Ill (NAMI), 800–950–6264. Publishes book *Coping with Aggressive Behavior*; has online forum and libraries. (For full group information, see MENTAL DISORDERS.)

International Association of Parents and Professionals for Safe Alternatives in Childbirth (NAPSAC), 314–238–2010 (phone and fax). Publishes *Childrearing, Peace and Violence*. (For full group information, see CHILDBIRTH.)

American College of Obstetricians and Gynecologists (ACOG), 202–638–5577. Publishes *The Abused Woman*. (For full group information, see PREGNANCY.)

OTHER RESOURCES

FOR PARENTS AND OTHER ADULTS

Taming the Dragon in Your Child: Solutions for Breaking the Cycle of Family Anger. Meg Eastman and Sydney C. Rozen. Wiley, 1994.
Bully-Proofing Your School: A Comprehensive Approach for Elementary Schools. Carla Garrity and others. Sopris, 1994.
Tackling Bullying in Your School: A Practical Handbook for Teachers. Peter K. Smith and Sonia Sharp, eds. Routledge, 1994.
Teaching Young Children in Violent Times: Building a Peaceable Classroom Environment. Diane E. Levin. New Society, 1994.
Helping Kids Handle Anger: Teaching Self-Control, 3rd ed. Pat Huggins. Sopris, 1993.
Coping with Bullying in Schools. Brendan Byrne. Twenty-Third, 1993.

GENERAL WORKS

End the Pain: Solutions for Stopping Domestic Violence. Lynn Hawker. Barclay House, 1994.
Violence in the Lives of Adolescents. Martha B. Straus, ed. Norton, 1994.
Every Eighteen Seconds: A Journey Through Domestic Violence, rev. ed. Nancy Kilgore. Volcano Press, 1993.
Understanding Domestic Violence: A Recovery Resource for Battered Women and Those Who Work with Them. Barbara Corry and others. Care Program, 1993.
Domestic Violence—Battered Women: How and Where to Find Facts and Get Help. Robert D. Reed and Danek S. Kaus. R & E Publishers, 1993.
It Could Happen to Anyone: Why Battered Women Stay. Ola W. Barnett and Alyce D. LaViolette. Sage, 1993.
Breaking Free from Partner Abuse: Voices of Battered Women Caught in the Cycle of Domestic Violence, rev. ed. Mary Marecek. Morning Glory, 1993. (Original title: *Say "No!" to Violence*)
Domestic Violence: No Longer Behind the Curtains. Alison Landes, ed. Information Plus, 1993.
Boys Will Be Boys: Breaking the Link Between Masculinity and Violence. Myriam Miedzian. Doubleday, 1992.
Kids Who Kill. Charles P. Ewing. Avon, 1992.
Family Violence and the Chemical Connection. Sally A. Baker. Health Communications, 1991.
What Causes Teen Violence? Greenhaven Staff, ed. Greenhaven, 1990.

ON ANTIVIOLENCE AND CONFLICT RESOLUTION PROGRAMS

Playing with Fire: Creative Conflict Resolution for Young Adults. Fiona Macbeth and Nic Fine. New Society, 1994.
I Can Solve My Own Problems: A Child Centered Conflict Resolution Program. Harold Fox and Jan Osier. R & E Publishers, 1994.

FOR CHILDREN

Family Abuse: Why Do People Hurt Each Other? Keith Greenberg. Twenty-First Century Books, 1995.
Violence and Drugs. Gilda Berger. Watts, 1990.
Gangs. Renardo Barden. Crestwood, 1990.
Bullying. Angela Grunsell. Gloucester, 1990.
Teenage Violence. Elaine Landau. Messner, 1990.

FOR PRETEENS AND TEENS

Everything You Need to Know About School Violence. Anna Kreiner. Rosen, 1995.
Family Violence. Debra Goldentyer. Raintree Steck-Vaughn, 1995.
Domestic Violence. Keith Greenberg. Millbrook, 1995.
Crime at College: The Student Guide to Personal Safety. Curtis Ostrander and Joseph Schwartz. New Strategist, 1994.
Battered Women: Living with Enemy. Ann Kosof. Watts, 1994.
Domestic Violence. Linda Ribaudo and Darlyne Walker. New Readers, 1994.
Growing up with Family Violence. Rona D. Schenkerman. Bureau for At-Risk Youth, 1993.

Everything You Need to Know about Family Violence, rev. ed. Evan Stark. Rosen, 1993.
Family Violence: Coping with Modern Issues. Janie E. Rench. Lerner, 1991.
Violence and the Family. Gilda Berger. Watts, 1990.

BACKGROUND WORKS

Fist Stick Knife Gun: A Personal History of Violence. Geoffrey Canada. Beacon, 1995.
Suicide and Homicide among Adolescents. Paul C. Holinger and others. Guilford, 1994.
The Prevention of Youth Violence: A Framework for Community Action. Mary A. Fenley. Diane, 1994.
School Bullying: Insights and Perspectives. Peter K. Smith and Sonia Sharp. Routledge, 1994.
Stony Ground: One Teacher's Fight Against Juvenile Crime. Linda W. Post. Sunbelt Media, 1994.
Understanding Black Adolescent Male Violence: Its Remediation and Prevention. Amos N. Wilson. African World, 1992.
Violence in America's Schools. Ronald E. Sharp and Waln K. Brown. W. Gladden, 1992.
Battered Husbands: The Battle of the Sexes Is Running Amuck. Howard Gregory. H. Gregory, 1991.
Youth and Exploitation: A Process Leading to Running Away, Violence, Substance Abuse and Suicide. Alan McEvoy and Edsel Erickson. Learning Publications, 1990.

visitation rights, the right of a separated, divorced, or otherwise absent parent living outside the FAMILY HOME to see his or her children on some agreed-upon basis; some NONCUSTODIAL PARENTS dislike the implication that they are "visitors" and prefer the term *parental access.* The ability to visit one's children is one of the basic PARENTS' RIGHTS; the father of a child born to an unmarried mother, if he acknowledges the child as his own or if a PATERNITY SUIT is successful against him, gains visitation rights, though he is not obligated to exercise them. Some states also legally protect GRANDPARENTS' RIGHTS to visit grandchildren, regardless of possible estrangement in the family, and grandparents' organizations have been conducting intensive lobbying to extend recognition of such rights. In some special cases, a person who has no legal responsibility for the child, but who is considered the PSYCHOLOGICAL PARENT, may also be granted visitation rights.

If a child is placed for ADOPTION, parents generally lose visitation rights, except when the child is being adopted by another family member, such as a stepfather or aunt, or in some forms of *open adoption.* In cases of adoption, grandparents also generally lose visitation rights, though some states protect those rights in special situations, as in adoption by another relative.

Parents can lose visitation rights in some other special situations, as when a parent's lifestyle is considered so harmful to a child as to make the court bar any parent-child contact, or when ABANDONMENT or CHILD ABUSE AND NEGLECT leads to TERMINATION OF PARENTAL RIGHTS. But the court does not usually lightly terminate such rights, and more often sets certain conditions on visitation. For example, in cases where a parent has been violent or abusive in the past, the court may require *supervised visitation,* under which the parent and child can meet only with a court-appointed third party present at all times. If the CUSTODIAL PARENT objects to the child visiting overnight with the noncustodial parent and an unmarried partner, the court may sometimes order the child to visit only during the day. If petitioned by one of the parents, the court can also change visitation arrangements, as when a parent begins drinking heavily or decides to openly acknowledge HOMOSEXUALITY; how the court responds to such petitions varies from state to state.

Parents who are separated or divorced but have joint CUSTODY of the child do not—in strict legal terms—have visitation *rights,* because both have custody. But they, like others, have to face the difficult task of arranging visitation schedules. Where separated parents have agreed on the terms of custody, they are generally free to arrange visitation schedules between themselves—though even with the best of wills it is often very difficult to accommodate the needs of both parents and children. But where custody has been contested and feelings run high, the court sometimes becomes involved in custody and visitation arrangements, and sets visitation schedules with the BEST INTERESTS OF THE CHILD in mind, such as every other weekend and part of the summer.

Where shuttling between parents can pose an undue hardship on a child, or the custodial parent seems likely to take the child far enough away to effectively deny the other parent visitation rights, the court may place restrictions on custody. For example, the court may restrict the distance the child may travel, require that the custodial parent continue to live within a certain geographical area, or forbid the custodial parent to move without first giving written notice to the noncustodial parent, allowing time to seek a possible court modification of the visitation arrangements.

Sometimes the court may simply order that visitation be allowed at "reasonable" times and places, leaving the parents to work out the details. Such an arrangement between already-sparring ex-spouses is difficult, and some experts in family law recommend that parents specify their visitation arrangements at the start, lessening the areas of possible misunderstanding and resentment. More important, specifying visitation rights means that if the custodial parent denies visitation, the noncustodial parent can make a case for violation of a court order. With no arrangements specified, a noncustodial parent may have a difficult time proving in court that the custodial parent has denied "reasonable visitation."

Denial of visitation rights can be a serious problem. Noncustodial parents who are having difficulty seeing their children should carefully document their attempts to arrange for visitation, keep track of each precise meeting

Tips on Making Visitation Work

FOR BOTH PARENTS

- Be flexible and reasonable in making visitation arrangements.
- If the child must travel between parents, settle beforehand, as part of your original visitation arrangements, which parent pays which travel expenses.
- Do not try to pump the children about your ex-spouse's activities and friends.
- Do not try to turn the children against your ex-spouse.
- Do not use the children to pass messages between you and your ex-spouse.
- Do not use the visitation to talk or argue with your ex-spouse.
- Do not make unrealistic promises to children, or try to outdo your ex-spouse by promising something you cannot fulfill.
- Do not undermine your ex-spouse's discipline, or feed any tendency for the children to play one parent off against another.
- Understand that children may carry confusion and resentment into visitation and do not make such feelings the basis of argument with your ex-spouse; if such feelings persist, consider counseling for the whole family.
- Keep a separate date book purely for visitation arrangements, noting in it any visitation problems, such as failure to keep an appointment or denial of visitation; this can act as a record should there be future dispute over visitation.

FOR NONCUSTODIAL PARENTS

- Suggest reasonable visiting hours that do not put undue strain on the children or the custodial parent.
- Understand that older children increasingly have their own activities, and take them into account when arranging visitation.
- Pick up children promptly or, if necessary, call as soon as possible to alter arrangements.
- Return children promptly at the agreed-upon time.
- See the children regularly, so the children know they can count on you, rather than letting long stretches go by without contact.
- Spend at least some time with the children yourself alone, rather than always involving other relatives or friends, or dropping your children off with others.
- Do not insist that a new partner always be present during visitation.
- Try to bring the children into your everyday life and interests, rather than taking the children on a constant whirlwind of outings.
- Do not drink alcohol or use drugs while with the children; apart from the danger to the child, problems in this area can lose you visitation rights.
- See that children are kept reasonably clean and properly cared for; for example, see that cuts and scrapes are treated, rather than left untended.
- If a child has a rash or some other problem that seems to require a physical examination, protect yourself from possible charges of child abuse by having a third person present or taking the child to a doctor.
- If you are unable to avoid disagreeable discussion with your ex-spouse when picking up the children, try arranging to pick them up elsewhere, such as at a friend or relative's house or at school, or have a mutual friend pick them up for you.

FOR CUSTODIAL PARENTS

- Have children ready when agreed for pickup by your ex-spouse or, if necessary, call as soon as possible to alter arrangements.
- Be available at the agreed-upon time for the children's return.
- See that the children are reasonably clean and cared for at the time of visitation.
- Do not drink alcohol or use drugs while with the children; apart from the danger to the child, problems in this area can cause the court to reconsider custody.

Source: Adapted from materials from Parents Without Partners and other sources.

time agreed upon, and record every failure to make the child available as agreed—preferably having a third party available to testify that visitation was, indeed, denied. Sometimes a custodial parent denies visitation in an attempt to obtain overdue CHILD SUPPORT, and conversely some parents withhold child support when denied visitation, but courts in most states consider visitation and child support payments to be legally separate issues.

The parent who denies visitation may be considered in CONTEMPT OF COURT for disobeying a court order, and can be subject to fines or jail. But in practice, the court is reluctant to jail or fine a custodial parent, since that may harm the child. Some states provide for court-ordered MEDIATION in cases involving visitation disputes; others have special agencies or bureaus to help with visitation enforcement. In a model system in Michigan, a Friend of the Court system logs lost visitations, so that makeup visitations can be arranged.

In some cases, where parents have been unable to work out satisfactory visitation arrangements and the state has failed to enforce visitation rights, parents have resorted to parental kidnapping (see MISSING CHILDREN), to completely bar the other parent's access to the child. Under the CLEAN HANDS DOCTRINE, such parents risk losing all access to their children, and generally forfeit any future right to claim custody. (See CUSTODY; DIVORCE; also TIPS ON MAKING VISITATION WORK on page 617.)

visiting teacher (itinerant teacher), an educator who travels among several schools, providing special instructional services, or who teaches HOMEBOUND STUDENTS.

visual skills, a set of overlapping skills that involve the eyes, often in combination with MOTOR SKILLS.

Visual perception is the ability to interpret what is seen. Children with LEARNING DISABILITIES or some other DEVELOPMENTAL DISORDERS may have eyes that are physically normal, but still have defects that make objects and people appear to change, so they are unable to consistently judge size, shape, location, movement, and color. They are said to have a PERCEPTUAL HANDICAP. Such children, for example, may have difficulty putting together a puzzle or building with blocks.

Visual discrimination is the ability to look at objects or pictures and recognize whether they are the same or different. Children with learning disabilities or other developmental disabilities may show trouble in this area by having difficulty matching blocks, shapes, or line drawings, or in pointing out which object is unlike the others. This is a form of visual AGNOSIA.

Visual memory is the ability to remember for a short time objects and people in one's environment. Children with learning disabilities or other developmental disabilities may show visual memory problems by being unable to look at four familiar toys, close their eyes briefly, and then tell which toy has been removed.

Visual tracking is the ability to focus the eyes on one point and move them rhythmically from side to side, up and down, or diagonally, a skill crucial to learning how to read. Children with learning disabilities or other developmental disabilities may show tracking problems by shifting or jerking their eyes while watching activities that involve rhythmic movement, such as a rolling ball, a ping-pong game, or a running child.

Visual-motor integration is the ability to coordinate the eye and the hand, or the eye and the body, to carry out a desired action; this is also called *perceptual-motor skills* and includes *hand-eye coordination*, or *body-eye coordination*. Children with learning disabilities or other developmental disabilities may be unable to make their hands follow signals from their eyes, so they may have trouble copying simple designs and shapes, drawing, cutting and pasting, putting forms in a formboard, or putting together a puzzle.

A CHART OF NORMAL DEVELOPMENT (on page 637) indicates when between birth and age six children first *on the average* begin to develop the main visual skills. Children develop at individual and varying paces, but every child can benefit from activities designed to enhance their natural development. (Subscribers to the America Online computer service can find activities designed to develop children's skills in various areas, including visual skills, in the Moms Online Desk Reference section of Moms Online, under "Teaching Young Children.")

vitamin, any of a group of complex chemical compounds that are vital to the normal functioning of the body. They do not in themselves provide energy or build the body, but are necessary for the transformation of food into energy to perform those functions. Inadequate amounts of vitamins in the body can have serious consequences, often leading to disorders called DEFICIENCY DISEASES.

Vitamins are all made up largely of the same elements—carbon, hydrogen, oxygen, and sometimes nitrogen—but they have different chemical arrangements and functions in the body. Before the chemical makeup of vitamins was known, they were called by letters; in some cases (such as vitamin B), it was later found that several different vitamins were involved, so numbers were added as well (such as vitamin B_{12} and B_6). On the other hand, some substances originally thought to be vitamins turned out to be inessential, and so were dropped from the list, while sometimes different letters were given to vitamins that were later found to be the same. The result is various gaps in lettering and numbering.

The Food and Drug Administration's RECOMMENDED DAILY ALLOWANCES (RDAs) suggest how much of each vitamin a person should have each day, during infancy, early childhood, childhood through adulthood, and PREGNANCY. The amounts listed are those used on FOOD LABELS. Extremely small amounts of vitamins are necessary. Some vitamins are measured in international units (IUs), a scientific measure that indicates minute amounts of biological activity; others are expressed in milligrams (1/1000th of a gram) and micrograms (1/1000th of a milligram). The FDA notes that this means that just one ounce of vitamin B_{12} would supply the daily B_{12} needs of 4,724,921 people.

The FDA stresses the important of diet, rather than vitamin supplements, to meet vitamin needs, commenting in *Some Facts And Myths Of Vitamins*:

> A well-balanced diet will usually meet all the body's vitamin needs. So-called average or normal eaters probably never need supplement vitamins, although many think they do. Vitamin deficiency diseases are rarely seen in the U.S. population. People known to have deficient diets require supplemental vitamins, as do those recovering from certain illnesses or vitamin deficiencies.

The FDA recognizes that, "Many people, nevertheless, believe in being on the 'safe side' and thus take extra vitamins." If you do take vitamin supplements, the FDA notes that no special mix and proportion of vitamins has been shown to have any superiority, nor does timing make any difference (except daily).

Healthy women with normal pregnancies should generally meet their own and their babies' vitamin and mineral needs with an adequate and well-balanced diet through pregnancy and BREASTFEEDING. One notable exception is that many women have a low intake of folate, or VITAMIN B_{12}, which has been linked with development of neural tube defects (see SPINA BIFIDA). The doctor may advise additional folate and possibly other supplements, depending on a woman's health and current health recommendations.

Where the mother is in good health and well nourished, infants who are breastfed should receive most necessary vitamins. However, they may require some additional amounts of vitamins D and K, depending on doctor's advice and current health guidelines. Infants fed on properly prepared commercial FORMULA should also have an adequate vitamin intake.

For children in general, vitamin deficiency can lead to slow growth rates, inadequate mineralization of bones, and low body reserves of important nutrients. However, most children do not show signs of vitamin deficiency, and vitamin and mineral supplements are not generally regarded as necessary, except for children who are at high risk for deficiencies, especially those from poor families and those with poor appetites or eating habits.

Caution: The rule that, if a little is good, more is better, does not apply to vitamins. *Megadoses*, or amounts greatly in excess of the RDA for some of these vitamins, can cause serious health problems, BIRTH DEFECTS during pregnancy, and in some cases even death. The FDA puts it bluntly: "Taking excess vitamins is a complete waste, both in money and effect. In fact, excess amounts of any of several different vitamins can be harmful." This is especially true of vitamins (notably A, D, E, and K), which are *fat-soluble* and can be therefore build up in body fat.

Other vitamins, such as C and B vitamins, are *water-soluble*. In the body, these are used quickly or excreted in urine or perspiration, and so must be taken every day. Water-soluble vitamins also break down quickly, and their value can sometimes be lost through premature harvesting, poor storage, and overcooking, especially in water. For these kinds of vitamins, generally the fresher and least-cooked the fruits and vegetables, the greater the vitamins they contain.

FOR HELP AND FURTHER INFORMATION

Food and Drug Administration (FDA), 301–443–3170. (For full group information, see DRUG REACTIONS AND INTERACTIONS.)

American Institute for Cancer Research (AICR), 800–843–8114. Publishes *AICR Vitamin and Mineral Guide*. (For full group information, see CANCER.)

National Organization for Rare Disorders (NORD), 800–999–6673. (For full group information, see RARE DISORDERS.)

OTHER RESOURCES

The Vitamin and Mineral Encyclopedia. Sheldon Saul Hendler. Simon & Schuster, 1990.

Good Health with Vitamins and Minerals: A Complete Guide to a Lifetime of Safe and Effective Use. John Gallagher. Summit, 1990.

Drugs, Vitamins, Minerals in Pregnancy. Ann Karen Henry and Jill Feldhausen. Fisher Books, 1990.

(See also NUTRITION; RECOMMENDED DAILY ALLOWANCES; THIAMIN; NIACIN; FOLIC ACID; BIOTIN; PANTOTHENIC ACID; and other specific vitamins.)

vitamin A (retinol), a VITAMIN important for new cell growth, healthy tissue, and normal vision (especially at night). Signs of deficiency include night-blindness, DIARRHEA, dry skin, abnormally dry eyes (*xerophthalmia*), a tendency to intestinal infections, and impaired growth.

Because vitamin A is a *fat-soluble vitamin* that is stored in body fat, overconsumption can lead to a condition called *hypervitaminosis A*, which can have serious consequences. These include initially nausea and blurred vision, then headache, loss of HAIR, dry skin, and irregular MENSTRUATION, and more seriously impaired growth, enlargement of liver and spleen, bone pain, increased skull pressure mimicking presence of a BRAIN TUMOR.

In pregnant women, too much vitamin A can cause BIRTH DEFECTS. That is why women who are or may become pregnant are warned not to take the ACNE medication ACCUTANE, made from vitamin A, or to take more than the RECOMMENDED DAILY ALLOWANCES. Recent evidence, however, suggests that even the amount of vitamin A found in "one-a-day" style vitamins can be sufficient to cause birth defects. Women who are contemplating pregnancy should consult with their doctors for the most current information on this crucial question. Women who think they may be pregnant should stop taking any vitamin A supplements, except on a doctor's advice.

The body makes vitamin A from various foods containing the yellow pigment *carotene*; these include green and yellow vegetables and yellow fruits, including carrots, leafy green vegetables, sweet potatoes, squash, apricots, and cantaloupe. Vitamin A (*retinol*) itself may be found in liver, egg yolk, and dairy products, where other animals have formed the vitamin A from carotene; it is this form that can lead to hypervitaminosis A, if taken in excess. (See RECOMMENDED DAILY ALLOWANCES; VITAMINS.)

vitamin B_1 (thiamine), a VITAMIN that is important for normal digestion, growth, fertility, LACTATION, nerve-tissue functioning, and carbohydrate METABOLISM; part of a group of vitamins known as the vitamin B complex. Lack of vitamin B_1 causes the DEFICIENCY DISEASE *beriberi*, which involves disrupted functioning of the NERVOUS SYSTEM. Other symptoms of deficiency include loss of appetite, EDEMA (fluid buildup in the body), heart problems, nausea, VOMITING, and spastic muscle contractions. Vitamin B_1 is commonly found in meats such as pork and liver, whole grain and fortified grain products (including breads, cereals, and pasta), nuts, and beans. No problems of overconsumption are known, because the vitamin is water-soluble, so excess is flushed out of the body in urine. (See RECOMMENDED DAILY ALLOWANCES; VITAMINS.)

vitamin B_2 (riboflavin), a VITAMIN that is important in obtaining energy for the body from CARBOHYDRATES and PROTEINS; part of a group of vitamins known as the vitamin B complex. Vitamin B_2 is commonly found in leafy vegetables, enriched and whole-grain breads, liver, lean meats, eggs, milk, and cheese. Symptoms of vitamin B_2 deficiency are lip sores and cracks and dim vision. No problems of overconsumption are known, because the vitamin is water-soluble, so excess is excreted in urine. Certain kinds of drugs used to treat DEPRESSION and other MENTAL DISORDERS, and some ESTROGEN-containing BIRTH CONTROL PILLS can cause deficiency, as can digestive disorders affecting intestinal absorption of nutrients, as well as serious illness, injury, or surgery. (See RECOMMENDED DAILY ALLOWANCES; VITAMINS.)

vitamin B_6 (pyridoxine, pyridoxal, or pyridoxamine), a VITAMIN that exists in three forms, all important in the body's use of PROTEIN and for the proper growth and maintenance of body functions; part of a group of vitamins known as the vitamin B complex. Vitamin B_6 is abundant in liver, whole-grain cereals, red meats, green vegetables, and yellow corn. Symptoms of deficiency include soreness in the mouth, nausea, dizziness, weight loss, sometimes a type of ANEMIA and neurological disorders. Problems of overconsumption are rare, since vitamin B_6 is water-soluble and excess is normally excreted in urine; extreme excess has been linked with neuritis. (See RECOMMENDED DAILY ALLOWANCES; VITAMINS.)

vitamin B_{12} (cyanocobalamin), a VITAMIN important to the normal development of red blood cells and to the functioning of all cells, especially in the BONE MARROW, NERVOUS SYSTEM, and intestines; part of a group of vitamins known as the vitamin B complex. Severe deficiency causes pernicious ANEMIA and neurological disorders, in extreme cases eventually including degeneration of the spinal cord. Folic acid aids vitamin B_{12} in carrying out its functions; substances containing folic acids are called *folates*. Folic acid is very important in development of the FETUS, especially of the nervous system and red blood cells, and folate deficiency has been linked with increased risk of neural tube defects (see SPINA BIFIDA). Because Americans have a relatively low intake of vitamin B_{12}, pregnant women may be advised to take folate supplements.

Vitamin B_{12} is abundant in lean meats, organ meats (liver, kidney, heart), fish, shellfish, milk, and eggs, but is not present in any appreciable amounts in fruit and vegetables. As a result, the Food and Drug Administration recommends that people on a VEGETARIAN diet take vitamin B_{12} supplements. (See RECOMMENDED DAILY ALLOWANCES; VITAMINS.)

vitamin C (ascorbic acid), a VITAMIN that is important in promoting growth, including formation of teeth and bones, and repairing tissue, including healing of wounds. As a FOOD ADDITIVE, vitamin C also acts as a preservative. Lack of vitamin C causes the DEFICIENCY DISEASE *scurvy*, which involves bleeding, especially noticeable in gums and bruises, weakness, loss of weight, lassitude, and irritability. Vitamin C is abundant in many fruits and vegetables, especially turnip greens, green peppers, kale, broccoli, mustard greens, citrus fruits, strawberries, currants, and tomatoes. The Food and Drug administration notes; "You can get all the vitamin C your body needs by eating daily a 3- to 4-ounce serving of any of the foods named."

Though many people believe that large amounts of vitamin C can protect against the common cold, scientific research has so far failed to confirm that this is so, though there are indications that it may lessen severity and duration of symptoms, once the cold virus is active in the body. However, some researchers recommend that smokers take vitamin C supplements. Adults who do take MEGADOSES may, on discontinuing large supplements, briefly experience deficiency symptoms, as may newborns if pregnant women took too much vitamin C. (See RECOMMENDED DAILY ALLOWANCES; VITAMINS.)

vitamin D (calciferol), a VITAMIN existing in several forms, some from plant sources, some from animals, all of which are vital to the absorption of CALCIUM and PHOSPHORUS for bone formation. Vitamin D is formed in the skin by ultraviolet rays from sunlight. It is also abundant in canned and fresh fish (especially from salt water), egg yolk, and foods fortified with vitamin D, such as milk and margarine. Such fortified foods are especially important to infants and children with CHRONIC illnesses that keep them largely housebound. Others, who have normal outside activities usually have enough vitamin D from exposure to sunlight, though too much sunlight can increase the risk of SKIN CANCER.

Severe lack of vitamin D leads in children to the DEFICIENCY DISEASE called RICKETS, which results in skeletal deformities, including bowed legs, deformed spine, "pot belly" appearance, and flat feet. In adults, vitamin D deficiency leads to OSTEOMALACIA. Excess vitamin D is stored in the body, and too much vitamin D can cause nausea, weight loss, weakness, excessive urination, and more seriously hypertension (high BLOOD PRESSURE), calcification (hardening) of soft tissues, including the blood vessels and kidneys, and often bone deformities and multiple fractures. (See RECOMMENDED DAILY ALLOWANCES; VITAMINS.)

vitamin E, a VITAMIN (actually a group of substances) that acts as an *anti-oxidant,* helping to prevent oxygen from destroying other substances in the body, including other vitamins, such as VITAMIN A. Vitamin E has been used to treat a rare form of ANEMIA in infants. Effects of vitamin E deficiency are not clearly known, but are believed to include reduction of blood clotting and destruction of red blood cells, which can lead to anemia. Deficiencies are rare, but may result from digestive disorders, disrupting absorption of nutrients in the intestinal system; symptoms of deficiency in infants include irritability and fluid buildup (EDEMA). Symptoms of excess include abdominal pain, nausea, VOMITING, DIARRHEA, and reduced absorption of other vitamins, notably A, D, and K, leading to further vitamin deficiencies. Abundant sources of vitamin E are vegetables oils, beans, eggs, whole grains, liver, fruits, and vegetables. (See RECOMMENDED DAILY ALLOWANCES; VITAMINS.)

vitamin K, a VITAMIN that exists in several forms—variously produced by plant sources, animal sources, and bacteria in the intestines—all essential to proper clotting of blood. Vitamin K is abundant in spinach, lettuce, kale, cabbage, cauliflower, liver, and egg yolk. Synthetic forms are also available. Lack of vitamin K can cause HEMORRHAGE and liver problems. Vitamin K deficiency can result from long-term treatment with antibiotics, which kill vitamin K-producing bacteria in the intestines, or from digestive disorders disrupting intestinal absorption of vitamins. Human milk is low in vitamin K, so the American Academy of Pediatrics has recommended that vitamin K be routinely administered intravenously as part of PARENTERAL NUTRITION to all infants at birth, to prevent bleeding disorders. (See RECOMMENDED DAILY ALLOWANCES; VITAMINS.)

vitiligo, a SKIN DISORDER in which patches of skin are white and colorless, because of lack of skin cells called *melanocytes,* which produce the dark pigment *melanin.* (Another disorder, ALBINISM, results from melanocytes that are present but not functioning properly.) Of unknown origin, vitiligo may appear at any age, though usually in early adulthood. Some suggest that it is an AUTOIMMUNE DISORDER, while others think that some forms at least are GENETIC DISORDERS. It is sometimes associated with ADDISON'S DISEASE, DIABETES, pernicious ANEMIA, and THYROID DISORDERS. People with vitiligo are especially susceptible to sunburn. Sometimes pigment reappears in at least some portions of the affected skin. Among the treatments used for vitiligo is *PUVA,* a form of PHOTOTHERAPY combined with medications.

FOR HELP AND FURTHER INFORMATION

National Vitiligo Foundation (NVFI)
P.O. Box 6337
Tyler, TX 75711
903–534–2925
Fax: 903–534–8075
E-mail: 73071.33@compuserve.com (CompuServe: 73071,33)
Allen C. Locklin, President
Organization concerned with vitiligo; provides information and counseling; sponsors research; publishes semiannual newsletter *Vitiligo*; pamphlets *Vitiligo, Vitiligo: A Handbook for Patients, Vitiligo: A Manual for Physicians,* and *Vitiligo: A Handbook for Schools*; and *Guidelines for the Treatment of Patients with Vitiligo.*

National Arthritis and Musculoskeletal and Skin Diseases Information Clearinghouse (NAMSIC), 301–495–4484. Publishes information package *Vitiligo.* (For full group information, see ARTHRITIS.)

National Organization for Rare Disorders (NORD), 800–999–6673. (For full group information, see RARE DISORDERS.)

vocational rehabilitation (VR) services, education and training programs to help individuals with DISABILITIES become qualified for work, provided under SECTION 504 of the Rehabilitation Act of 1973 and under the AMERICANS WITH DISABILITIES ACT (ADA) of 1990. People with disabilities apply to their local VR agency, providing documentation of the disability, showing that they need VR services to obtain or keep a job commensurate with their strengths, capabilities, interests, and priorities. People found eligible will be given a priority status, depending on the severity of the disability; the agency will then assess what services might be needed to help them work or maintain jobs, a process that is supposed to be completed in 60 days, unless the individual agrees to an extension.

VR services focus on functional skills related to maximum independence and health (see OCCUPATIONAL THERAPIST). For children, these services are provided through the school system, and made part of their INDI-

VIDUALIZED EDUCATION PLAN (IEP). However, for teens in the years of transition to adulthood (ages fourteen to twenty-two), these programs are provided by the local VR services. Teens and their families should establish a relationship with the local rehabilitation counselors, so that VR services for working and independent living can be underway before graduation from HIGH SCHOOL. Some people with disabilities can achieve full independence, or nearly so; some will continue to require some assistance throughout their working lives, in what is called SUPPORTED EMPLOYMENT. It is important for parents, SURROGATE PARENTS, or others acting as advocate for a person with disabilities to make IEPs that are realistic and attainable, while encouraging the person to grow as much as possible in work beyond school (see ADVOCACY).

Under Section 504 and the ADA, employers are to make "reasonable accommodations" for qualified individuals with disabilities, providing these do not pose an "undue hardship" on the employer. These may include assistive technology, such as computers, and job coaching. Employers may have the costs of such accommodation covered by the local VR program, which may sometimes cover personal assistance services for the individual with disabilities, though these are not generally considered reasonable accommodations.

FOR HELP AND FURTHER INFORMATION

PACER Center (Parent Advocacy Coalition for Educational Rights), 612–827–2966, voice/TT. Publishes *Learn About Agencies Servicing Young Adults: Division of Rehabilitation Services (DRS) Counselors Can Be Important Team Members, Vocational Rehabilitation Appeal Procedures.* (For full group information, see HELP FOR SPECIAL CHILDREN on page 689.)

vocational schools, schools that provide a special CURRICULUM oriented to preparing students for employment after graduation from school; a type of MAGNET SCHOOL or SCHOOL OF CHOICE. Though the term has traditionally been used to refer to schools that focused on instruction for noncollege-bound students, such as automobile mechanics or printing trades, schools may also be termed vocational if they give intensive preparation in a subject area that will likely be pursued in college, such as performing arts or science. The U.S. Department of Education has increasingly recommended that parents exercise choice in finding the right school for their children. CHOOSING A SCHOOL FOR YOUR CHILD (on page 659) offers a checklist for evaluating schools. (See EDUCATION.)

volvulus, the twisting of an organ in the body, such as the intestines or stomach, often causing pain and obstruction and frequently requiring surgical correction. (See DIGESTIVE SYSTEM AND DISORDERS.)

vomiting, expulsion of the stomach's contents—partially digested food and digestive juices—through the esophagus and the mouth, by contractions of the diaphragm (see DIGESTIVE SYSTEM AND DISORDERS). Vomiting is often involuntary, occurring as a result of irritants in the stomach (as from too much food or alcohol), pressure in the brain (as from HYDROCEPHALUS or a BRAIN TUMOR), disturbance of the body's sense of balance (as in some EAR AND HEARING PROBLEMS), or other disorders or imbalances in the body, including APPENDICITIS and various digestive and METABOLIC DISORDERS. Vomiting can also be triggered deliberately, as in BULIMIA, where it is the "purge" part of the binge-purge syndrome. It is also frequently associated with PREGNANCY, as *morning sickness* (see VOMITING IN PREGNANCY on page 623).

If it persists, vomiting can cause damage and perhaps rupture of the esophagus. More important, it can leave the body short of vital nutrients. For how to handle vomiting in infants, see VOMITING AND YOUR BABY (page 623). It is important to have the underlying causes discovered and treated, if possible, especially if blood is being vomited as well (a condition called *hematemesis*).

FOR HELP AND FURTHER INFORMATION

No More Morning Sickness: A Survival Guide for Pregnant Women. Miriam Erick. NAL-Dutton, 1993.

(See also PREGNANCY.)

voucher system, a program under which school taxes go into a special fund, from which parents are given redeemable coupons (*vouchers*) that they can use to "purchase" education (up to a specified amount of money) for their children in the school of their choice, whether public or private. Under the traditional system, many parents whose children attend PRIVATE SCHOOL (approximately 1 in 8) pay TUITION out of their own pockets, while also paying school taxes to support the PUBLIC SCHOOLS, a situation proponents of the voucher system charge is unfair. Critics of the voucher system believe that parents should work to make the public schools responsive to the needs of all students, rather than opt out to private schools, and that the voucher system violates the constitutionally protected separation of church and state, since many of the private schools are religiously oriented or affiliated. The voucher plan has been tried only in limited areas, and often religious-affiliated private schools are not included.

FOR HELP AND FURTHER INFORMATION

Citizens for Educational Freedom (CEF)
927 South Walter Reed Drive, Suite 1
Arlington, VA 22204
703–486–8311
Fax: 703–486–3160
E-mail: cefvoucher@aol.com (America Online: CEFVoucher)
Patrick Reilly, Executive Director
Nonsectarian organization of parents and others interested in establishing free choice among educational alternatives, including religious schools, "without economic

Vomiting and Your Baby

Your baby may vomit during a cold or fever, or may have an illness which may have vomiting, or vomiting and diarrhea, as its only signs.

When your baby vomits, don't give anything to eat or drink for at least *one hour.* Then give half an ounce of water, sweet juice, or a commercially prepared clear liquid for rehydration. Repeat this half-ounce feeding every ten to fifteen minutes for an hour. Give 1-ounce feedings every ten to fifteen minutes for the next hour, and 2-ounce feedings as often as your baby wants them for the following hour.

If there is no more vomiting, it is okay to give small amounts of breastmilk, formula, cereal, crackers, or toast if your baby is eating solid foods, and then return to regular feeding. If vomiting happens more than two or three times, or your baby seems very sick and weak, you should call your doctor or clinic.

Source: Infant Care (1989). Prepared by the Bureau of Maternal and Child Health and Resources Development for the Public Health Service.

penalty"; supports voucher system for school tuition, as through an "Educard" credit card; encourages increased public participation in education; publishes various materials, including bimonthly *Parents' Choice, Handbook on Educational Vouchers: How to Get the CEF Educational Voucher Plan in Your State or District,* and *All You Ever Wanted to Know About Educational Vouchers—But No One Would Give You a Straight Answer.*

OTHER RESOURCES

The Effects of the California Voucher Initiative on Public Expenditures for Education. Michael A. Shires. Rand, 1994.

School Days: An Essay on the Hoover Institution Conference "Choice and Vouchers—The Future of American Education?" Peter Robinson. Hoover Institute, 1993.

Vomiting in Pregnancy

Nausea and vomiting are common complaints during the first months of pregnancy and are usually due to hormonal changes occurring in your body. About half of all pregnant women experience this problem. Nausea may start about the sixth or seventh week, but seldom continues beyond the end of the third month. Although often called morning sickness, nausea and vomiting may occur at any time of the day. If vomiting is severe and you cannot keep fluids down, report it to your doctor. Never take prescription drugs, over-the-counter medicines, or a home remedy unless recommended by your doctor.

You may find some relief by eating dry cereal, a piece of toast, or a cracker about half an hour before getting out of bed in the morning. Move slowly when you get up. Let plenty of fresh air into the house to get rid of cooking and other household odors.

Divide your food into five small meals a day rather than three large ones, since keeping food in your stomach seems to control nausea. Avoid greasy and highly spiced foods or any food that disagrees with you. Drinking liquids between meals instead of with your food may help.

The same suggestions may also help with symptoms of heartburn. Heartburn has nothing to do with your heart. It is a burning sensation caused by hormonal changes that slow down your digestive system and by the pressure of the growing uterus against your stomach. Food mixed with stomach acid is pushed up from your stomach and causes the burning, especially after meals. In addition, changing your sleeping position may also help relieve heartburn. Try sleeping with several pillows to raise your head or elevate the head of the bed a few inches. Note: Do *not* take baking soda (sodium bicarbonate) to relieve your heartburn. Remember, you should not take medicines unless your doctor recommends them.

Source: Prenatal Care (1989). Prepared by the Bureau of Health Care Delivery and Assistance, Division of Maternal and Child Health, for the Public Health Service.

(See also EDUCATION; SCHOOL OF CHOICE; also HELP ON LEARNING AND EDUCATION on page 659.)

vulnerable child syndrome, a pattern of behavior following a child's recovery from a life-threatening illness, in which parents continue to treat the child as if he or she were still at death's door. In some cases, the parents can create a SELF-FULFILLING PROPHECY, weakening the child's ability to grow toward independence; sometimes the child must consciously break out of the "gentle cage" to live a normal life. (Subscribers to the America Online computer service can find information on techniques for avoiding overdependence in young children, in the Moms Online Desk Reference section of Moms Online, under "Teaching Young Children.")

vulva, a female's external genitals (also called the *pudendum)*. These include the *mons veneris,* the mound of fatty tissue covering the pubic bone; the CLITORIS, the small organ of sexual stimulation between the pubic bone and the URETHRA; two sets of folded skin, the outer "lips" (*labia major*) and the inner (*labia minora*); and the opening to the VAGINA, between the urethra and the anus. It is the clitoris and sometimes parts of the labia that are sometimes removed in female CIRCUMCISION. During CHILDBIRTH, the *perineal tissue* toward the back of the vulva may be surgically cut in an EPISIOTOMY, or the region as a whole is sometimes anesthetized using a *pudendal block.*

A newborn girl's labia and clitoris are rather large at birth, due to the effect of the mother's HORMONES, but get slightly smaller over the next few weeks. The labia may sometimes be joined at birth, but generally separate naturally afterwards.

A female baby may also have a slight white or pinkish creamy discharge from the vagina in the first few weeks; this is normal and should gradually decline without irritating the skin. But if it becomes worse, or if she develops a discharge a week or two after birth, or if there is any bulge or lump in her genitals, she should be examined by a doctor or clinic staff.

FOR HELP AND FURTHER INFORMATION

American College of Obstetricians and Gynecologists (ACOG), 202–638–5577. Publishes *Diseases of the Vulva.* (For full group information, see PREGNANCY.)

(See also GENITALS.)

wage attachment, withholding of money from a person's paycheck to pay off debts, such as to pay CHILD SUPPORT or alimony. In some states, wage attachment laws are applied to everyone who has been ordered to pay child support. Sometimes an OBLIGATED PARENT may have wages voluntarily withheld to pay for child support.

walking, the act of moving the body by lifting the feet alternately in a chosen direction, with one foot returning to the ground before the next leaves it. Walking is actually a complicated set of movements controlled by the brain, in response to the body's signals about changes in position and balance (as monitored by the inner ear). Newborn infants exhibit a WALKING REFLEX—moving legs when help upright—and walking is one of the key MOTOR SKILLS learned by a young child (see CHART OF NORMAL DEVELOPMENT on page 637).

Most babies have legs and feet that look somewhat abnormal to adult eyes (see THOSE FUNNY-LOOKING LEGS, below), but they generally right themselves during early childhood. Some slight abnormalities may remain, but only severe cases will call for correction, by relatively minor surgery. Among the most common leg and foot abnormalities are:

- *Metatarsus varus* (*pigeon toes* or *toeing in*), in which the foot and toes point somewhat inward, because of rotation of the leg or foot.
- *Metatarsus valgus* (*duck walk* or *toeing out*), in which the foot and toes point somewhat outward, because of rotation of the leg or foot.
- *Genu valgum* (*knock-knees*), in which the legs bend inward, with the knees close together.
- *Genu varum* (*bowlegs*), in which the legs bend outward at the knees.

Many other conditions can affect walking, including CLUBFOOT (*talipes*) and PARALYSIS; infections that affect the balancing mechanism in the inner ear (see EAR AND HEARING PROBLEMS); and disorders that affect the muscles or the nerves communicating with the muscles, including MUSCULAR DYSTROPHY, POLIOMYELITIS, MULTIPLE SCLEROSIS, ATAXIA, and CHOREA, some of which are diagnosed partly by a characteristic walk. CONGENITAL DISLOCATION OF THE HIP is sometimes diagnosed first when a child begins to walk, though WELL-BABY EXAMINATIONS normally include checking the hip. Children with various kinds of ORTHOPEDIC DISABILITIES may need ORTHOPEDIC DEVICES such as crutches or braces to provide some of the support and balance needed for walking.

walking reflex, the automatic response of a baby, when held upright with feet touching the ground, to make stepping movements with alternate feet; also called a *stepping reflex*. This is a type of "primitive" REFLEX found only babies and disappearing in about two months, but reappears at about six months.

ward, a MINOR child, or an adult who has severe DISABILITIES and/or has been judged INCOMPETENT, whose CUSTODY and care are legally in the hands of a GUARDIAN, rather than a parent. A JUVENILE found to have committed DELINQUENT acts may under certain circumstances be made a ward of the court.

Those Funny-Looking Legs

Most babies' legs and feet don't look "normal" until the child has been walking for several years! Their feet seem to turn in or out in the first years of life. By the time they are 12 or 18 months old, their legs look bowed.

Almost all of these funny-looking feet and legs are perfectly normal and will gradually straighten out as babies run, play, and climb. If you can move your baby's foot easily into a "normal" looking position, and if the foot moves freely when the baby kicks and struggles, it is almost certainly a normal foot that developed a bend or twist while the baby was folded up inside during pregnancy.

You won't cause bowed legs by pulling your baby into a standing position or letting your baby walk or stand "too early." But remember, the baby will show you when he or she is ready to stand or walk—you can't make them do it.

Source: Infant Care (1989). Prepared by the Bureau of Maternal and Child Health and Resources Development for the Public Health Service.

weaning, the process of gradually substituting SOLID FOODS for BREASTFEEDING or BOTTLEFEEDING with FORMULA. (See BREASTFEEDING; SOLID FOODS.)

Wechsler Intelligence Scale for Children (WISC), a widely used INTELLIGENCE TEST, administered individually to children ages six to sixteen, similar in makeup to the WECHSLER PRESCHOOL AND PRIMARY SCALE OF INTELLIGENCE (WPPSI). Among the exceptions are that children are asked to arrange groups of pictures so they tell simple stories, to remember and repeat lists of digits, and to assemble three-dimensional objects (testing SYNTHETIC LEARNING), instead of geometric designs; also, the animal house is replaced by a coding exercise. The WISC exists in several forms: the 1949 edition (WISC), the revised edition (WISC-R), and a short form of the revised edition. Adolescents sixteen or older may also be given the original or revised adult version of these tests, the *Wechsler Adult Intelligence Scale-Revised* (WAIS or WAIS-R). (See WECHSLER PRESCHOOL AND PRIMARY SCALE OF INTELLIGENCE; TESTS; INTELLIGENCE TESTS.)

Wechsler Preschool and Primary Scale of Intelligence (WPPSI), a widely used INTELLIGENCE TEST, administered individually to children ages four and a half to six. The WPPSI is divided into verbal and performance tests, each with subtests.

In the verbal subtests, the specially trained examiner asks the child for:

- *General information*, about the body, money, or food, for example.
- *Vocabulary*, definitions of words, starting with simple ones and becoming more abstract.
- *Arithmetic*, counting, adding, and doing "takeaways."
- *Similarities*, such as what you can roll besides a ball, or how a pen and pencil are alike.
- *Comprehension*, calling for responses to social questions and relation to appropriate behavior.
- *Sentences*, having the child repeat progressively longer and more complex sentences.

On the performance side, the child is asked to complete pictures with a missing element, copy geometric designs, use blocks to reproduce designs on a picture card, work through a maze, and make an "animal house" following a model (a timed test). The "animal house" task may be done a second time during the test, if the child encountered problems the first time around.

After the test, the examiner totals the SCORES for the various subtests to give separate verbal and performance scores, as well as a total score; all three of these scores are then converted to scaled scores, using special tables. On the basis of the tables, the examiner then assigns a verbal designation based on the category in which a child's score falls, such as *average, bright average, superior*, or *very superior* (often considered GIFTED CHILDREN). Examiners do not usually report either numerical INTELLIGENCE QUOTIENTS (IQs) or PERCENTILES. For older children, ages six to sixteen, the WECHSLER INTELLIGENCE SCALE FOR CHILDREN (WISC) may be used, while adolescents may be given the *Wechsler Adult Intelligence Scale (WAIS)*.

FOR HELP AND FURTHER INFORMATION

The Baby Boards: A Parent's Guide to Preschool and Primary School Entrance Tests. Jacqueline Robinson. Arco, 1988. Gives a full description of the Wechsler tests and advice on how to "prepare" a child for one.

(See also TESTS; INTELLIGENCE TESTS.)

well-baby examination, any of a series of periodic medical examinations of a baby, not because of illness, but to try to ensure continuing good health. In well-baby examinations, medical professionals, often physicians but sometimes specially trained nurses, generally:

- Check the child's growth and development, as compared to established NORMS.
- Provide routine IMMUNIZATION.
- Perform SCREENING TESTS to try to detect early any signs of diseases, especially GENETIC DISORDERS, and begin immediate treatment as appropriate.
- Provide guidance to parents in areas such as NUTRITION, SAFETY, and accident prevention.
- Prepare parents for what to do for and expect from the child at various stages of growth and development.

The Public Health Service's recommendations for well-baby examinations are given in YOUR BABY'S HEALTH (page 627).

wet dream, an EJACULATION that occurs during sleep, often among adolescent males; also called a *nocturnal emission.*

whole word method, a general approach to teaching READING that focuses on teaching words as complete units, and only later breaking them down into parts, as opposed to the PHONICS METHOD in which words are broken down into letters associated with sounds; also called the *word-recognition method* or the *sight method.* For many students this works well, especially because the focus is strongly on the meaning and context of the words. However, for children who have trouble learning to read, especially those with LEARNING DISABILITIES, some version of the more traditional phonics method seems needed, at least as a supplement. Within the English language community, several approaches focus on teaching reading and WRITING by using the whole words in practical situations; collectively these are called the *whole language approach.* (See READING.)

whooping cough, a serious, highly contagious disease, medically known as *pertussis.* Caused by bacteria

Your Baby's Health

You may have chosen a doctor, nurse practitioner, or clinic for your baby before he or she was born. (If not, see SELECTING A DOCTOR OR CLINIC on page 455.) You will have many questions about your baby that can best be discussed with a person who is a health professional. The doctor or nurse will work with you and explain how you can help your baby grow and develop safely and healthily. Also, your baby should be checked from time to time for normal growth, development, and problems you may not notice. Every child needs certain shots (or "immunizations") and tests to avoid or detect and treat some illnesses. For all of these reasons, you should take your baby to the doctor or clinic several times during the first year.

GOING TO THE DOCTOR OR CLINIC

First, be sure to talk with the doctor who examines your baby in the hospital to find out if all is well. Ask questions and get answers!

Especially with a first baby, you will have more questions in the first days that you and your baby share than at any other time. Books and experienced and trusted friends or family members may be able to answer many of your questions, but don't hesitate to call the doctor, clinic, or hospital staff.

Most doctors and clinics will schedule the first checkup when your baby is between two weeks and one month old, and then plan further visits every four to eight weeks for three or four visits and less frequently after that. Your doctor will discuss the schedule with you.

Your conversation with the baby's doctor is the most important part of each visit. The doctor may actually examine your child only three or four times during the first year, but he or she will always want to know how your baby is growing, learning and developing, and whether you have noticed any problems. Between visits to the doctor or clinic, write down your questions and observations so you can be sure to remember them. But if something is pressing, don't wait until the next scheduled visit—call the office. A typical schedule of visits to the doctor of clinic is shown on the following chart:

	Age at Visit								
Procedures During Visit	in Hosp.	1 Mo.	2 Mos.	4 Mos.	6 Mos.	9 Mos.	12 Mos.	15 Mos.	18 Mos.
Discussion & questions	●	●	●	●	●	●	●	●	●
Examination	●	●	●	●	●	●	●	●	●
Measurements of length, weight, head size	●	●	●	●	●	●	●	●	●
DTP shot (diptheria-tetanus-pertussis)			●	●	○			○	○
Oral polio vaccine			●	●	○			○	○
MMR shot (measles, mumps and rubella)								●	
Blood test for anemia						●			
Test for lead exposure						○			
Tuberculin skin test							●		
H. Influenza B. Vaccine									●*

● usually done at this age
○ may be done at this age

(Note: Each doctor may have his or her own schedules, but you should expect it to include most of the items listed above. This schedule is only a general guide, current as of July 1989, which your doctor or clinic may change to fit your child's needs; the immunization schedule, in particular, changes with periodic new recommendations; for the recommendations as of mid-1996, see IMMUNIZATION.)

(continued)

(continued)

KEEPING RECORDS

You should keep a record of your baby's visits to the doctor or clinic. It is important to keep the record up-to-date in case you change doctors, or see someone else when your doctor is not available. You should take your record with you whenever you visit a doctor or clinic so that you can refer to it if you have any questions, and update it before you leave the office.

Because baby's first year is full of change, you might also want to keep a record of significant events in your baby's first year, such as when he or she first said a word or first crawled. Saving mementos, photos, and notes in a box or notebook will give you reminders to share with your child later on.

WHEN DOCTORS DISAGREE

Sometimes one doctor will give you different advice from another, or doctors may actually disagree with each other or with a book.

For many problems there are many good solutions; a particular book may mention only one. For some other problems, such as an ear infection, each doctor may choose a different medicine—and each may provide relief equally well. In other cases (for example, whether boys should be circumcised), there are real differences of opinion. When two doctors give you conflicting advice—or one doctor gives you advice you do not understand—you should ask for an explanation. Ask questions until you get the information that satisfies you. And if the best step to take is still unclear to you, you may need to ask another doctor for an opinion.

Source: Adapted from Infant Care (1989). Prepared by the Bureau of Maternal and Child Health and Resources Development, Public Health Service.

spread in droplets from the coughs and sneezes of infected people, it triggers violent, uncontrollable spells of coughing (with a characteristic "whooping" sound) that can interfere with eating, drinking, and breathing. Pertussis hits young children hardest; half of the cases are in children under age one, and two-thirds in children under five. The disease can last for weeks, and at least 40 percent of the children will need to be hospitalized. Common complications include pneumonia (in about 1 out of 6 cases; see LUNG AND BREATHING DISORDERS), CONVULSIONS, and ENCEPHALITIS (inflammation of the brain).

Once a leading killer of young children, pertussis is now largely preventable through IMMUNIZATION, generally in a series of five injections of the combination DTP VACCINE between ages two months and six years. As a result, a disease that once killed thousands of children every year has come under control. In recent years, concerns over side effects of the pertussis vaccine kept many parents from properly immunizing their young children, even though public health authorities strongly reported that the risk of the disease was far greater than the risk of vaccination. Partly because of inadequate immunization, the incidence of whooping cough in the United States increased by more than half between 1992 and 1993, and out of more than 6000 cases, eight children died. Epidemics have been more serious in other areas; in England, over 500 unimmunized children died of whooping cough between 1977 and 1983, and many others suffered brain damage. An improved pertussis vaccine has since been developed (see DTP VACCINE).

FOR HELP AND FURTHER INFORMATION

National Institute of Allergy and Infectious Diseases (NIAID), 301–496–5717. (For full group information, see ALLERGY.)

National Organization for Rare Disorders (NORD), 800–999–6673. (For full group information, see RARE DISORDERS.)

(See also DTP VACCINE.)

Wide Range Achievement Test (WRAT), a widely used type of ACHIEVEMENT TEST used for ages five to adult, focusing on the basic skills of word recognition (recognizing and naming letters and pronouncing printed words), spelling, and arithmetic. It is used for educational placement and also for identifying people with possible learning problems. While the reading part must be administered individually, the other parts may be given to groups; large-print editions are available for children with EYE AND VISION PROBLEMS. Tests are scored as compared to NORMS established by age. (See TESTS.)

Wilson's disease, a rare GENETIC DISORDER in which COPPER accumulates to toxic levels first in the liver, causing hepatitis and then cirrhosis of the liver (see LIVER AND LIVER PROBLEMS), and then in other parts of the body, including the blood, causing hemolytic ANEMIA, and in the brain, causing destruction of tissue and gradually intellectual impairment, tremors, muscle rigidity, DYSARTHRIA, and DEMENTIA. It is a GENETIC DISORDER of the AUTOSOMAL RECESSIVE type. Symptoms of Wilson's disease usually appear in adolescence, sometimes earlier. They include increasing tremors or rigidity, often leading to slurred, unintelligible speech, and abrupt personality change; the first symptom may be a mild illness, often misdiagnosed as hepatitis. Serious damage can be avoided if the disease is recognized quickly and the patient started on a lifelong course of penicillamine; in cases where the liver has been severely damaged, a TRANSPLANT may be required. If not properly recognized and treated, the disorder is generally fatal by age thirty.

In a related CONGENITAL disorder, *Menkes' syndrome*, the intestines are unable to absorb copper from the digestive system. Unusually kinky hair is the main early symptom. Brain degeneration, retarded GROWTH, and early death can result, unless the disorder is diagnosed early, and copper administered intravenously.

FOR HELP AND FURTHER INFORMATION

Wilson's Disease Association
P.O. Box 75324
Washington, DC 20013
703–743–1415
Carol A. Terry, President
Organization concerned with Wilson's disease or Menkes' syndrome; encourages family-to-family support; provides information and referrals; publishes quarterly newsletter and other materials.

National Center for the Study of Wilson's Disease
432 W. 58 St., Suite 614
New York, NY 10019
212–523–8717
Fax: 212–523–8708
I. Herbert Scheinberg, President
Organization studying Wilson's disease and related copper and metal metabolic disorders; supports research; maintains database; provides information; publishes brochure *What Is Wilson's Disease?*

National Digestive Disease Information Clearinghouse (NDDIC), 301–654–3810. (For full group information, see DIGESTIVE SYSTEM AND DISORDERS.)

National Institute of Child Health and Human Development (NICHD), 301–496–5133. (For full group information, see PREGNANCY.)

National Institute of Neurological Disorders and Stroke (NINDS), 800–352–9424. (For full group information, see BRAIN AND BRAIN DISORDERS.)

National Organization for Rare Disorders (NORD), 800–999–6673. (For full group information, see RARE DISORDERS.)

(See also LIVER AND PROBLEMS; METABOLIC DISORDERS.)

wisdom teeth, the four large third molars, the last of the adult set of permanent teeth to appear, generally around ages seventeen to twenty-one. Sometimes these teeth never erupt at all, or become blocked from erupting because the jaw is too small and overcrowded; such teeth are said to be IMPACTED. (See TEETH AND DENTAL PROBLEMS.)

witch's milk, a popular name for the milk sometimes produced by a newborn's enlarged BREASTS, in response to the mother's HORMONES.

Woodcock-Johnson Psychoeducational Battery (WJPEB), an individually administered test that seeks to measure cognitive ability, academic achievement, and interest level in children in grades K–12. It may be used as a DIAGNOSTIC ASSESSMENT TEST, to help diagnose LEARNING DISABILITIES, to help in CURRICULUM planning and class placement, and sometimes for occupational counseling and research. (See TESTS.)

word-attack skills, a set of PREREQUISITE skills that are vital to a child's ability to DECODE and understand new or unfamiliar words, and therefore to effective, independent READING. Among these word-attack skills are PHONICS, in which the child associates letters with sounds and "sounds out" the word; *structural analysis*, in which the child breaks the word down into meaningful parts, such as "read" and "-ing"; and *content analysis*, in which the child looks at the meaning of the word parts and the context in which they appear.

work-study program, a type of FINANCIAL AID in which students get help in meeting the costs of attending COLLEGE by working part-time, often in programs partly funded by federal money. The main federally funded program in this area is COLLEGE WORK-STUDY. Some colleges have *work-experience* or *cooperative work-study programs*, which are aimed less at providing aid than at giving students additional experience through off-campus work. (See FINANCIAL AID.)

writing, formation of letters and other symbols in such a way as to convey meaning; also the work produced. In ELEMENTARY SCHOOL, students are first taught *printing* (*manuscript writing*), in which each letter is formed separately. Only later do they learn *cursive writing*, in which the letters are joined together within words. The *Palmer method* is the traditional approach to teaching children how to write legibly. To these approaches have been added in recent years writing on computer, in which even very young children use a keyboard in writing, and as an aid to related skills of READING. Using various programs, available for home or school use, children can produce flyers, newsletters, newspapers, and even books of their own writings.

Students who have problems with ENCODING, such as those with LEARNING DISABILITIES or various communication problems (see COMMUNICATION SKILLS

AND DISORDERS), need extra help in learning to write clearly, and also in the related skill of learning the correct spellings of words. Difficulty in writing, especially in producing handwriting legible to others, is called *dysgraphia*; it generally results from problems with *visual-motor integration*, one of the key VISUAL SKILLS. Total inability to write is called *agraphia*, a type of APHASIA.

FOR HELP AND FURTHER INFORMATION

For parents and other adults

Story Games: Fun Activites for Teling, Creating, Collecting and Writing. Doug Lipman. Oryx, 1994

Preschoolers As Authors: Literacy Learning in the Social World of the Classroom. Deborah Rowe. Hampton, 1994.

Books by Kids! Helping Young Children Create Their Own Books. Karen Nelson. Fearon Teacher Aids, 1993

Kids Have All the Write Stuff: Inspiring Your Children to Put Pencil to Paper. Sharon A. Edwards and Robert W. Maloy. Viking Penguin, 1992.

For preteens and teens

What's Your Story: A Young Person's Guide to Writing Fiction. Marion Dane Bauer. Clarion, 1992.

How to Be a Better Writer. How to Built a Better Vocabulary. How to Make Grammar Fun—(And Easy!). How to Write Better Book Reports. Elizabeth A. Ryan. Troll, 1991.

Young Person's Guide to Becoming a Writer. Janet E. Grant. Shoe Tree Press, 1991.

Student's Guide to Good Writing: Building Writing Skills for Success in College. Rick Dalton and Marianne Dalton. College Entrance Examination Board, 1990.

Background works

Helping Young Writers Master the Craft: Strategy Instruction and Self-Regulation in the Writing Process. Karen R. Harris and Steven Graham. Brookline, 1992.

Written Language Disorders: Theory into Practice. Ann M. Bain and others, eds. PRO-ED, 1991.

(See also READING; also PRESCHOOL for school-preparation activities.)

X

xerostomia, a condition called dry mouth, resulting from temporary lack of saliva. Often associated with DIABETES, xerostomia may result from infection, some medicines, and radiation therapy (see CANCER) in the mouth area. Although helped by use of artificial saliva, dry mouth can cause trouble speaking and swallowing, and can lead to ULCERS in the gums and other dental problems. (For help and further information, see TEETH AND DENTAL PROBLEMS.)

X-linked (sex-linked or sex-limited), a gene that is located on the X chromosome, one of the two SEX CHROMOSOMES; also a trait or GENETIC DISORDER associated with such a gene. X-linked traits are RECESSIVE, meaning that the trait will be masked in the presence of a DOMINANT gene. As a result, X-linked traits rarely affect women because both of their X chromosomes must carry the defect; women who have just one abnormal gene are unaffected, but are called CARRIERS, because they can pass the trait on to their children.

X-linked disorders do not necessarily appear in every generation. In general, where a woman carries a single abnormal gene, an average of half of her male children will be affected by the disorder and half of her female children will be carriers. Female children are affected only if they receive the gene from both parents. Males cannot pass an X-linked gene on to male children. However, men have only one X chromosome (paired with a Y), so any X-linked defect will show itself. Among the most common X-linked genetic disorders are HEMOPHILIA, *agammaglobulinemia* (see IMMUNE SYSTEM), *color blindness* (see EYE AND VISION PROBLEMS), FRAGILE X SYNDROME, MUSCULAR DYSTROPHY (Duchenne), and spinal ATAXIA. During GENETIC COUNSELING, counselors will gather information from prospective parents or parents-to-be about their medical and genetic history, and put that information into the form of a PEDIGREE.

(See also GENETIC INHERITANCE; GENETIC COUNSELING.)

X-rays, in medicine and dentistry, pictures of the body taken by use of RADIATION, in some cases used for treatment. X-rays show what exists beneath the surface of the body and help health professionals identify problems, from IMPACTED TEETH or tooth decay to fractures to TUMORS. Though X-rays should not be overused, the benefits of their use in medicine and dentistry generally outweigh their associated risks, if they are used appropriately, with lead coverings protecting the vulnerable parts of the body not being X-rayed. However, X-rays should be used only when vital on a woman during PREGNANCY because of possible danger to the fetus and only sparingly with children because of possible long-term increase in rish of CANCER, especially of the BREAST.

XX, the genetic designation of a female child, referring to the possession of two X SEX CHROMOSOMES, one from the SPERM and one from the egg (OVUM).

XY, the genetic designation of a male child, referring to the possession of one X and one Y SEX CHROMOSOME, the X from the egg (OVUM) and the Y from the SPERM.

Y

year-round education (YRE), an instructional plan in which a school operates through the whole 12 months of the year. The school calendar may be organized in different ways.

The number of days in the school year may be increased, in what is called an *extended year.* Such an approach has the advantage in allowing more material to be taught more thoroughly. Indeed, the United States has a shorter school year (180 days) than any industrialized country except Belgium; the longest is Japan, at 240 days, while most European countries have a 220-day school calendar.

In a more common YRE approach, students attend the same number of days per year, but these are arranged differently, leading to more continuous learning, with more frequent breaks. For example, a student might be in school for nine weeks and on vacation for three; this is sometimes called the 45–15 calendar, since there are 45 weekdays in school and 15 weekdays on vacation. Other notable alternatives are a 60–20 plan, with students in school for 60 days, then on vacation for 20; a 90–30 plan; a 60–15 plan; a five-term plan, with five terms of 45 days each (of which a student is required to attend four) and a common three-week summer break; and an all-year plan, with school open for instruction for approximately 240 days, with the number of days required of a student set by each state.

In a *single-track* system, all students and teachers are in school and on vacation at the same time. In a *multiple track* system, the student body is divided into tracks, with at least one on vacation at all times. Students in a multiple-track system may attend classes in more than one track, called *cross-tracking.* The multiple-track system has some economic advantages, which has initially spurred acceptance of YRE in some quarters. The blocks of schooling can be staggered; for example, in a 45–15 system, only three-quarters of the total population will attend school at any one time. That way the school can accommodate one-third more students than under the traditional SEMESTER, TRIMESTER, or QUARTER systems. This approach allows school facilities to be used more efficiently and to meet rising student populations without building new schools.

Year-round schooling is also thought to have distinct advantages for learning, since with only a short period off at the end of each segment, instead of a whole summer, students forget less and classes need not waste time at the beginning of a new school year reviewing. A 1994 National Association for Year-Round Education (NAYRE) review of nineteen studies found that students in YRE programs did better on 48 of 58 measures, including performance on standard TESTS, such as CALIFORNIA ACHIEVEMENT TEST and IOWA TEST OF BASIC SKILLS.

Year-round education also has advantages for families where the parent or parents work, because it eliminates the need for summer-long CHILD CARE. Also older students do not spend long, fruitless, unsupervised summers. Partly for these reasons, the visionary 21ST CENTURY SCHOOL incorporates year-round education.

On the other hand, some people sharply criticize the move away from the traditional school schedule, with its predictable summer vacation. Those parents who normally have extensive summer vacation plans are particularly unhappy. So are some families with several children, in districts where the school system has not attempted to coordinate the schedules so that the children in a single family are on vacation at the same time. Year-round schooling is relatively new in practice, and its long-term attractiveness and success remains to be determined.

FOR HELP AND FURTHER INFORMATION

National Association for Year-Round Education (NAYRE)
P.O. Box 711386
San Diego, CA 92171–1386
619–292–3679
Fax: 619–571–5754
Charles Ballinger, Executive Director
Organization concerned with year-round education (YRE); operates information clearinghouse; publishes various materials, including *From Parent to Parent: A Look at Year-Round Education, Handbook for Implementing YRE in the High School, YRE: History, Philosophy and Future, The Great Lockout in America's Citizenship Plants, A Review of Recent Studies Relating to Academic Achievement of Students Enrolled in YRE Programs, YRE Calendar and Enrollment Plans,* a school-by-school listing of YRE programs, and annual directory.

PACER Center (Parent Advocacy Coalition for Educational Rights), 612–827–2966, voice/TT. Publishes *Extended School Year.* (For full group information, see HELP FOR SPECIAL CHILDREN on page 689.)

Council for Exceptional Children (CEC), 800–328–0272. Publishes special report *Extended School Year (ESY).* (For full group information, see HELP ON LEARNING AND EDUCATION on page 659.)

yeshiva, an ELEMENTARY SCHOOL for children of the Orthodox Jewish faith; also an advanced school where Jewish students study the Talmud and rabbinical law in preparation for becoming rabbis.

Z

zinc, a MINERAL needed in the body, though only in trace amounts, for a wide variety of functions, including normal growth and development, especially of the REPRODUCTIVE SYSTEM, manufacture of PROTEINS, and healing of wounds. Zinc is abundant in high-protein foods, such as meat (especially liver), seafood, milk and other dairy products, nuts, dried beans and peas, and whole-grain or enriched breads and cereals.

Deficiency is rare, except in cases of MALNUTRITION; disorders that hinder the body's ability to use zinc, such as MALABSORPTION, CYSTIC FIBROSIS, or cirrhosis of the liver (see LIVER AND LIVER PROBLEMS); or sharply increased need for zinc, as in cases of BURNS or sickle cell ANEMIA. Symptoms of zinc deficiency include loss of taste and appetite, slowed growth and sexual maturation in children, slow healing of wounds, and susceptibility to infection and injury. Low levels of zinc may also be linked to neural tube defects (see SPINA BIFIDA).

On the other hand, too much zinc, as from taking excessive amounts in mineral supplements, can cause gastrointestinal problems, including nausea, VOMITING, and DIARRHEA, which can also lead to loss of IRON and COPPER. Excess zinc among pregnant women can lead to PREMATURE delivery and STILLBIRTH. (For help and further information, see MINERALS; NUTRITION.)

zona pellucida, the outer protective layer of an OVUM (egg), which acts to protect the egg from being penetrated by multiple SPERM. After FERTILIZATION, the zona remains for a week or so to protect the resulting ZYGOTE or EMBRYO, and is normally shed as the embryo is about to implant itself in the UTERUS. Several new, still highly experimental REPRODUCTIVE TECHNOLOGIES, in general called ASSISTED FERTILIZATION, seek to facilitate fertilization by helping SPERM penetrate the zona pellucida; these include INTRACYTOPLASMIC SPERM INJECTION (ICSI), PARTIAL ZONA DISSECTION (PZD), and SUBZONAL SPERM INSERTION (SZI). In addition, ASSISTED HATCHING techniques focus on helping the embryo shed the zona pellucida, which it normally does before IMPLANTATION in the uterus wall.

zygote, a medical name for the fertilized egg (OVUM) up to the time it is implanted in the UTERUS. In relation to MULTIPLE BIRTHS, twins who grew from a single fertilized egg are termed *monozygotic* or *identical*, while those who developed from two separate fertilized eggs are termed *dizygotic*, *nonidentical*, or *fraternal*.

Special Help Section: General Parenting Resources

Basic Exercises for During and After Pregnancy

Exercise is very important to you and your baby. If you stay active you will feel better. Outdoor exercise and recreation give you a chance to get sunshine and fresh air. Walking is particularly good, because it strengthens some of the muscles you will use in labor.

If you normally are active in sports, continue to enjoy them. However, it's wise to stop when you get tired. Also, try team activities instead of individual games, and avoid strenuous workouts. Do things with your friends and family — swim in a pool, dance, go on a picnic, and participate in light sports that pose no danger of falling or being bumped. If you are thinking of trying a new sport or exercise, or have been using a specific exercise routine, talk it over with your doctor or someone at your clinic.

Avoid lifting heavy objects and moving furniture while you are pregnant. Stretching will not harm you or your baby, but don't reach for things from a chair or ladder, because you might lose your balance and fall. During the latter part of your pregnancy, you will probably begin to feel awkward, because your balance is affected by your increasing size. At this point you may want to substitute walking for more active sports.

Here are some exercises that are useful for strengthening muscles used in labor and delivery. They are quite simple to do and can be practiced whenever you have an opportunity to sit for a few minutes.

TAILOR SITTING

While seated on the floor, bring your feet close to your body and cross your ankles. Maintain this position as long as it is comfortable to do so.

TAILOR PRESS

While seated on the floor, bring the soles of your feet together as close to your body as is comfortable. Place your hands under your knees and press down with your knees while resisting the pressure with your hands. Count slowly to three, then relax. Gradually increase the number of presses until you are doing them ten times, twice each day.

TAILOR STRETCH

While seated on the floor and keeping your back straight, stretch your legs in front of you with your feet about a foot apart. Allow your feet to flop outward. Stretch your hands forward toward your left foot, then back; toward the center, then back; toward the right foot, then back. Gradually increase the set of stretches until you are doing ten of them twice a day.

KEGEL EXERCISE

This is sometimes called the Pelvic Floor Exercise, because it is designed to strengthen the muscles in your pelvis. After you have practiced it, you will be able to relax your pelvic muscles for delivery. First, sit down. Then contract the lowest muscles of the pelvis as tightly as you can. Tighten muscles higher in the pelvis until you are contracting the muscles at the top. Counting slowly to 10 helps, tightening additional muscles at each number. Release slowly, as you count back from 10 to 1. You are developing control of the muscles so that you can stop at any point.

These muscles are the same ones you use to stop the flow of urine. To see if you are doing the Kegel exercise correctly, try stopping the flow of urine while you are urinating. Practice the exercise for several minutes two or three times a day.

An alternate method of doing the Kegel exercises is to tighten first the pelvic muscles, then the anal muscle. Hold a few seconds, then release slowly in a reverse order.

BREATHING TECHNIQUES

There are breathing techniques that you can practice while you are pregnant to help you relax during labor. They also help reduce muscle tension that works against the contractions and causes pain. If you are able to relax, you will be able to use the rest periods between labor contractions to reduce fatigue and build up your energy.

- *Relaxation.* Lie down with your knees bent and feet on the floor. Breathe in once as deeply as possible, then hiss or blow the air out slowly through your mouth. Let yourself completely relax.
- *Practice Contraction.* Pretend that you are having a contraction that lasts about 30 to 45 seconds. At the beginning of the contraction, take a complete breath and blow it out. Then breathe deeply, slowly, and

rhythmically through the remainder of the practice contraction. Have your partner or coach go through this technique with you.

- *Abdominal Breathing.* This exercise helps keep the abdominal wall relaxed and keeps the uterus from pressing against the lining of the abdomen. Lie down and place your hands on your abdomen. Breathe in slowly and fully, allowing your abdominal wall to rise gently. Hold this position for four to six heartbeats. Breathe out slowly and smoothly through the mouth, allowing your abdomen to fall. Relax. Repeat four or five times.

You can learn about other breathing techniques in prenatal classes or from your doctor.

REST

Rest is just as important as exercise during pregnancy. Be sure to get plenty of sleep at night. Most pregnant women need about eight hours of sleep, but your needs may be different. You may also need to rest during the day.

There are some things you can do to keep from getting too tired. If your work requires you to be on your feet most of the day, try to sit down, put your feet up, and close your eyes whenever it is convenient. But if you spend most of your time sitting, get up and walk around for a few minutes every hour. When you are at home, take a nap during the day, especially if you have children who take naps. Plan a short rest period and really relax about the same time every day. When resting, you may find it more comfortable to use an extra pillow between your legs while on your side.

Try to find easier ways to do things, and ask other members of the family to share the workload. Perhaps someone else can help with the grocery shopping, laundry, and housework.

You should also know the best way to get out of bed:

- *Turn onto your side.*
- *While bending your knees, use your arms to raise yourself up.*
- *Lower your feet to the floor.*
- *Sit upright for a few moments and hold onto the side of the bed.*
- *Lean forward.*
- *Use the muscles in your legs to stand up.*

BACKACHE

As your pregnancy progresses, your posture changes, because your uterus is growing and pulls on your back muscles. Your pelvic joints also loosen. This may cause backache. To help prevent strain, wear low-heeled supporting shoes. Your doctor may suggest a maternity girdle that gives support without binding.

Good posture is important in preventing backaches. Try not to lift heavy objects, particularly if there is someone around who can lift them for you.

Here are several exercises that should help your back. Ask the nurse or someone at your clinic to help you do the exercises if you are not sure you are doing them correctly.

The following squatting exercise helps avoid back strain and strengthens muscles you will use in labor: Holding on to a heavy piece of furniture, squat down on your heels and allow your knees to spread apart. Keep your heels flat on the floor and your toes straight ahead. You may pick up the object from the floor by squatting, holding the object close to your body, and rising slowly, using your leg muscles. This position is a good one for reaching low drawers or for lifting a child or an object weighing 15 to 30 pounds.

Pelvic Rock exercises increase the flexibility of your lower back and strengthen your abdominal muscles. They not only relieve backache, but will help improve your posture and appearance. Here are three versions of the Pelvic Rock exercises:

- Standing up: When you practice the Pelvic Rock standing up, use a sturdy chair. Stand back 2 feet away from the back of the chair and bend slightly forward from your hips. Place your hands on the chair back and keep your elbows straight. Thrust your hips backward and relax your abdominal muscles. You now have a sway back. Bend your knees slightly, then slowly pull your hips forward. Tuck your buttocks under as if someone were pushing you from behind. Repeat.
- On your back: You can also practice the pelvic rock lying on your back with your knees bent and feet flat on the floor. Tighten your lower abdominal muscles and the muscles of the buttocks. This elevates your tailbone and presses the small of your back to the floor. Then relax your abdominal and buttock muscles. As you do this, arch your back as high as you can. Rest for a minute, then repeat.
- On all fours: In the third version of the Pelvic Rock, get down on all fours with your legs slightly apart and your elbows and back straight. While inhaling, arch your back using the muscles in your lower abdomen. As you exhale, slowly relax, allowing your back to sag. Return to the original position. Then repeat.

Practice all the versions several times every day. Try walking and standing with your pelvis lifted forward as described.

If you have a problem or pain doing these exercises, tell your doctor, nurse, or teacher.

Many community agencies, hospitals, and clinics offer special exercise classes for pregnant women. Exercises are also a part of most childbirth-preparation classes. Talk to your doctor or nurse about the benefits of such classes and how you can enroll.

VARICOSE VEINS

Varicose or enlarged veins usually occur in your lower legs but may extend into the pelvic area. They are caused by your enlarged uterus, which presses on your abdominal veins and interferes with the return of blood from your legs. Varicose veins usually shrink and disappear during the first few weeks after the baby is born. However, it is wiser to try to avoid varicose veins than to cure them.

You can help avoid varicose veins by not wearing tight garters, stockings, or socks. If at all possible, do not stand in one place for long periods of time. If your job requires you to stand, walk around at break time to improve circulation. If you can, sit down and put your feet up occasionally. Jobs in which you sit most of the day often aggravate varicose veins. Do not sit with your legs crossed or with the pressure of a chair under your knees. If traveling by car, take frequent rest stops and walk around. Support hose may also help you prevent varicose veins.

Here's a good position to take if you have varicose veins or swelling in your legs: Lie on a bed, couch, or floor and raise your feet and legs in the air, resting your heels against the wall. Take this position for two to five minutes several times a day.

If you have severe varicose veins, you may be advised to wear elastic stockings during the day. Support hose are not as effective as elastic stockings. Put the stockings on before you get out of bed in the morning, before your veins become swollen with blood, and take them off just before you go to bed. Wash them in mild soap after every wearing.

If you have varicose veins around your vaginal area, try to take frequent rest periods. Lie down with a pillow under your buttocks. This position elevates your hips and should give you some relief.

LEG CRAMPS

Leg cramps are more common during the latter months of your pregnancy and are generally due to pressure from the enlarged uterus. They frequently occur in bed. You can often get relief from leg cramps by heat, massage, or stretching the calf muscles. Here are two exercises that may help:

Begin by standing about six inches away from a sturdy chair and holding on to the back of it. Slide the foot of the leg that is cramping as far backward as you can while keeping your heel on the floor.

Bend the knee of your other leg as you slide the foot. Hold on to the chair and slide the foot back to the starting position. Repeat.

If you have someone to help you, lie down on the bed or floor and straighten your cramped leg. Have your helper push down against your knee with one hand and push up against the sole of your foot with the other hand so that your foot is at a right angle to your leg. Release and repeat several times. If cramps continue, tell your doctor.

GETTING BACK INTO SHAPE

Getting out of bed and walking around is the first "exercise" you will do after childbirth. Do this as soon as you feel up to it.

With the approval of your doctor or nurse-midwife, exercises may be started 24 hours after a normal delivery. Regular mild exercising will strengthen your muscles and help you get back into shape. Lying on your abdomen will help you uterus return to its normal position. Your doctor or nurse may give you some exercises, or you may want to try some of these.

The following exercises are designed to strengthen your abdominal muscles. You should begin by repeating each exercise about three times and gradually increasing the number as you feel more comfortable.

- Lie flat. Breathe in deeply from your abdomen. Exhale all the air. Rest. Repeat five times.
- Lie flat with your arms out at your sides. With your elbows stiff, raise your arms until they are straight over your head. Bring your palms together. Lower your arms. Rest. Repeat five times.
- Lie flat with your legs straight. Raise your head and one knee slightly. Reach toward that knee with the opposite hand. Relax, then repeat with the other hand and knee. Repeat the sequence five times.
- Lie flat with your arms at your sides. Slide your feet towards your buttocks. Arch your back while supporting yourself with arms, shoulders, and feet. Relax.
- Lie flat with your knees raised. Then lift your head while raising the pelvis and tightening buttock muscles. Relax.
- Lie on your back. Raise one knee and pull your thigh down onto your abdomen. Lower your foot to your buttock. Then raise the leg and straighten it. Lower slowly to the floor. Rest and repeat with the other leg.
- Lie flat on your back with toes extended outward. Raise the left leg using your abdominal muscles. Lower your leg slowly, then repeat with the right leg.
- Resting on all fours, arch your back while contracting the muscles in your buttocks and abdomen. Relax, then breathe deeply.
- Lie flat on your back. Lift both legs at once using the muscles in your abdomen. Lower your legs slowly.

Source: Adapted from Prenatal Care (1989). Prepared for the Public Health Service by the Health Resources and Services Administration, Bureau of Healthy Care Delivery and Assistance, Division of Maternal and Child Health.

Chart of Normal Development: Infancy to Six Years of Age

The chart of normal development on the next few pages presents children's achievements from infancy to six years of age in five areas:

- motor skills (gross and fine motor).
- cognitive skills.
- self-help skills.
- social skills
- communication skills (understanding language and speaking).

In each skill area, the age at which each milestone is reached *on the average* is also presented. This information is useful if you have a child who you suspect is seriously delayed in one or more skill areas.

However, it is important to remember that these milestones are only averages. From the moment of birth, each child is a distinct individual and develops in his or her unique manner. No two children have ever reached all the same developmental milestones at the exact same ages. The examples that follow show what we mean.

By nine months of age, Gi Lin had spent much of her time scooting around on her hands and tummy, making no effort to crawl. After about a week of pulling herself up on chairs and table legs, she let go and started to walk on her own. Gi Lin skipped the crawling stage entirely and scarcely said more than a few sounds until she was 15 months old. But she walked with ease and skill by 9-1/2 months.

Marcus learned to crawl on all fours very early and continued crawling until he was nearly 18 months old, when he started to walk. However, he said single words and used two-word phrases meaningfully before his first birthday.

Molly worried her parents by saying scarcely a word, although she managed to make her needs known with sounds and gestures. Shortly after her second birthday, Molly suddenly began talking in two- to four-word phrases and sentences. She was never again a quiet child.

All three children were healthy and normal. By the time they were three years old, there were no major differences among them in walking or talking. They had simply developed in their own ways and at their own rates. Some children seem to concentrate on one thing at a time—learning to crawl, to walk, or to talk. Other children develop across areas at a more even rate. As you read the chart of normal development, remember that children don't read baby books. They don't know they're supposed to be able to point out Daddy when they are a year old, or copy a circle in their third year. And even if they could read the baby books, they probably wouldn't follow them! Age-related development milestones are obtained by averaging out what many children do at various ages. No child is "average" in all areas. Each child is a unique person.

One final word of caution. As children grow, their abilities are shaped by the opportunities they have for learning. For example, although many five-year-olds can repeat songs and rhymes, the child who has not heard songs and rhymes many times cannot be expected to repeat them. All areas of development and learning are influenced by the child's experiences as well as by the abilities he or she is born with.

	Motor Skills		Communication
	Gross Motor Skills	Fine Motor Skills	Understanding Language
0–12 Months	Sits without support. Crawls. Pulls self to standing and stands unaided. Walks with aid. Rolls in a ball in imitation of an adult.	Reaches, grasps, puts objects in mouth. Picks things up with thumb and one finger (pincer grasp). Transfers objects from one hand to the other. Drops and picks up toys.	Responds to speech by looking at speaker. Responds differently to aspects of speaker's voice (for example, friendly or unfriendly, male or female). Turns to source of sound. Responds with gesture to "hi," "bye-bye," and "up," when these words are accompanied by appropriate gesture and tone. Stops ongoing action when told "no," when negative is accompanied by appropriate gestures and tone.
12–24 Months	Walks alone. Walks backward. Picks up toys from floor without falling. Pulls and pushes toys. Seats self in child's chair. Walks up and down stairs (hand-held). Moves to music.	Builds tower of three small blocks. Puts four rings on stick. Places five pegs in pegboard. Turns pages two or three at a time. Scribbles. Turns knobs. Throws small ball. Paints with whole arm movement, shifts hands, makes strokes.	Responds correctly when asked *where* (when question is accompanied by gesture). Understands prepositions *on, in,* and *under.* Follows request to bring familiar object from another room. Understands simple phrases with key words (for example, "Open the door," or "Get the ball"). Follows a series of two simple but related directions.

Skills

Spoken Language	Cognitive Skills	Self-Help Skills	Social Skills
Makes crying and non-crying sounds. Repeats some vowel and consonant sounds (babbles) when alone or when spoken to. Interacts with others by vocalizing after an adult. Communicates meaning through intonation. Attempts to imitate sounds.	Follows moving object with eyes. Recognizes differences among people. Responds to strangers by crying or staring. Responds to and imitates facial expressions of others. Responds to very simple directions (for example, raises arms when someone says, "Come," and turns head when asked, "Where is Daddy?"). Imitates gestures and actions (for example, shakes head no, plays peek-a-boo, waves bye-bye). Puts small objects in and out of a container with intention.	Feeds self a cracker. Holds cup with two hands. Drinks with assistance. Holds out arms and legs while being dressed.	Smiles spontaneously. Responds different to strangers than to familiar people. Pays attention to own name. Responds to "no." Copies simple actions of others.
Says first meaningful word. Uses single word plus a gesture to ask for objects. Says successive single words to describe an event. Refers to self by name. Uses "my" or "mine" to indicate possession. Has vocabulary of about 50 words for important people, common objects, and the existence, nonexistence, and recurrence of objects and events (for example, "more" and "all gone").	Imitates actions and words of adults. Responds to words or commands with appropriate action (for example: "Stop that." "Get down"). Is able to match two similar objects. Looks at storybook pictures with an adult, naming or pointing to familiar objects on request (for example: "What is that?" "Point to the baby"). Recognizes difference between *you* and *me*. Has very limited attention span. Accomplishes primary learning through own exploration.	Uses spoon, spilling little. Drinks from cup, one hand, unassisted. Chews food. Removes shoes, socks, pants, sweater. Unzips large zipper. Indicates toilet needs.	Recognizes self in mirror or picture. Refers to self by name Plays by self; initiates own play. Imitates adult behaviors in play. Helps put things away.

	Motor Skills		Communication
	Gross Motor Skills	Fine Motor Skills	Understanding Language
24–36 Months	Runs forward well. Jumps in place, two feet together. Stands on one foot, with aid. Walks on tiptoe. Kicks ball forward.	Strings four large beads. Turns pages singly. Snips with scissors. Holds crayon with thumb and fingers, not fist. Uses one hand consistently in most activities. Imitates circular, vertical, and horizontal strokes. Paints with some wrist action. Makes dots, lines, and circular strokes. Rolls, pounds, squeezes, and pulls clay.	Points to pictures of common objects when they are named. Can identify objects when told their use. Understands question forms *what* and *where.* Understands negatives *no, not, can't,* and *don't.* Enjoys listening to simple storybooks and requests them again.
36–48 Months	Runs around obstacles. Walks on a line. Balances on one foot for five to ten seconds. Hops on one foot. Pushes, pulls and steers wheeled toys. Rides (that is, steers and pedals) tricycle. Uses slide without assistance. Jumps over 15-centimeter (6-inch)-high object, landing on both feet together. Throws ball overhead. Catches ball bounced to him or her.	Builds tower of nine small blocks. Drives nails and pegs. Copies circle. Imitates cross. Manipulates clay materials (for example, rolls balls, snakes, cookies).	Begins to understand sentences involving time concepts (for example, "We are going to the zoo tomorrow"). Understands size comparatives such as *big* and *bigger.* Understands relationship expressed by *if ... then* or *because* sentences. Carries out a series of 2 to 4 related directions. Understands when told, "Let's pretend."

SKILLS

SPOKEN LANGUAGE	COGNITIVE SKILLS	SELF-HELP SKILLS	SOCIAL SKILLS
Joins vocabulary words together in two-word phrases. Gives first and last name. Asks *what* and *where* questions. Makes negative statements (for example, "Can't open it"). Shows frustration at not being understood.	Responds to simple directions (for example: "Give me the ball and the block." "Get your shoes and socks"). Selects and looks at picture books, names pictured objects, and identifies several objects within one picture. Matches and uses associated objects meaningfully (for example, given cup, saucer, and bead, puts cup and saucer together). Stacks rings on peg in order of size. Recognizes self in mirror, saying *baby* or own name. Can talk briefly about what he or she is doing. Imitates adult actions (for example, housekeeping play). Has limited attention span. Learning is through exploration and adult direction (as in reading of picture stories). Is beginning to understand functional concepts of familiar objects (for example, that a spoon is used for eating) and part/whole concepts (for example, parts of the body).	Uses spoon, spilling little. Gets drink from fountain or faucet unassisted. Opens door by turning handle. Takes off coat. Puts on coat with assistance. Washes and dries hands with assistance	Plays near other children. Watches other children; joins briefly in their play. Defends own possessions. Begins to play house. Symbolically uses objects, self in play. Participates in simple group activity (for example, sings, claps, dances). Knows gender identity.
Talks in sentences of 3 or more words, which take the form agent-action-object ("I see the ball") or agent-action-location ("Daddy sits on chair"). Tells about past experiences. Uses "s" on nouns to indicate plurals. Uses "ed" on verbs to indicate past tense. Refers to self using pronouns *I* or *me*. Repeats at least one nursery rhyme and can sing a song. Speech is understandable to strangers, but there are still some sound errors.	Recognizes and matches six colors. Intentionally stacks blocks or rings in order of size. Draws somewhat recognizable picture that is meaningful to child, if not to adult. Names and briefly explains picture. Asks questions for information (*why* and *how* questions requiring simple answers). Knows own age. Knows own last name. Has short attention span. Learns through observing and imitating adults, and by adult instruction and explanation. Is very easily distracted. Has increased understanding of concepts of the functions and groupings of objects (for example, can put doll-house furniture in correct rooms), and part-whole (for example, can identify pictures of hand and foot as parts of body). Begins to be aware of past and present (for example: "Yesterday we went to the park." "Today we go to the library").	Pours well from small pitcher. Spreads soft butter with knife. Buttons and unbuttons large buttons. Washes hands unassisted. Blows nose when reminded. Uses toilet independently.	Joins in play with other children. Begins to interact. Shares toys. Takes turns with assistance. Begins dramatic play, acting out whole scenes (for example, traveling, playing house, pretending to be animals).

	Motor Skills		Communication
	Gross Motor Skills	**Fine Motor Skills**	**Understanding Language**
48–60 Months	Walks backward toe-heel. Jumps forward 10 times, without falling. Walks up and down stairs alone, alternating feet. Turns somersault.	Cuts on line continuously. Copies cross. Copies square. Prints a few capital letters.	Follows three unrelated commands in proper order. Understands comparatives like *pretty, prettier*, and *prettiest.* Listens to long stories but often misinterprets the facts. Incorporates verbal directions into play activities. Understands sequencing of events when told them (for example, "First we have to go to the store, then we can make the cake, and tomorrow we will eat it").
60–72 Months	Runs lightly on toes. Walks on balance beam. Can cover 2 meters (6'6") hopping. Skips on alternate feet. Jumps rope. Skates.	Cuts out simple shapes. Copies triangle. Traces diamond. Copies first name. Prints numerals 1 to 5. Colors within lines. Has adult grasp of pencil. Has handedness well established (that is, child is left- or right-handed). Pastes and glues appropriately.	Demonstrates preacademic skills.

Skills

Spoken Language	Cognitive Skills	Self-Help Skills	Social Skills
Asks *when, how,* and *why* questions Uses modals like *can, will, shall, should,* and *might.* Joins sentences together (for example, "I like chocolate-chip cookies and milk"). Talks about causality by using *because* and *so.* Tells the content of a story but may confuse facts.	Plays with words (creates own rhyming words; says or makes up words having similar sounds). Points to and names four to six colors. Matches pictures of familiar objects (for example, shoe, sock, foot; apple, orange, banana). Draws a person with two to six recognizable parts, such as head, arms, legs. Can name and match drawn parts to own body. Draws, names, and describes recognizable picture. Rote counts to five, imitating adults. Knows own street and town. Has more extended attention span. Learns through observing and listening to adults as well as through exploration. Is easily distracted. Has increased understanding of concepts of function, time, and part/whole relationships. Function or use of objects may be stated in addition to names of objects. Time concepts are expanding. The child can talk about yesterday or last week (a long time ago), about today, and about what will happen tomorrow.	Cuts easy foods with a knife (for example, hamburger patty, tomato slice). Laces shoes.	Plays and interacts with other children. Dramatic play is closer to reality, with attention paid to detail, time, and space. Plays dress-up. Shows interest in exploring sex differences.
There are few obvious differences between child's grammar and adult's grammar. Still needs to learn such things as subject-verb agreement and some irregular past tense verbs. Can take appropriate turns in a conversation. Gives and receives information. Communicates well with family, friends, or strangers.	Retells story from picture book with reasonable accuracy. Names some letters and numerals. Rote counts to 10. Sorts objects by single characteristics (for example, by color, shape, or size if the difference is obvious). Is beginning to use accurately the concepts of *tomorrow* and *yesterday.* Uses classroom tools (such as scissors and paints) meaningfully and purposefully. Begins to relate clock time to daily schedule. Attention span increases noticeably. Learns through adult instruction. When interested, can ignore distractions. Concepts of function increase as well as understanding of why things happen. Time concepts are expanding into an understanding of the future in terms of major events (for example, "Christmas will come after two weekends").	Dresses self completely. Ties bow. Brushes teeth unassisted. Crosses street safely.	Chooses own friend(s). Plays simple table games. Plays competitive games. Engages with other children in cooperative play involving group decisions, role assignments, and fair play.

Source: Mainstreaming Preschoolers, *series of books prepared for the Head Start Bureau, Administration of Children, Youth and Family.*

Organizations offering help and information

ON PARENTING IN GENERAL

New Parents' Network
P.O. Box 44226
Tucson, AZ 85733–4226
520–327–1451
Fax: 520–881–8474
E-mail: moreinfo@npn.org or kstorek@npn.org
Internet Website:
http://www.indirect.com/www/kstorek/parents.html
Karen Storek, Chief Executive Officer
Organization offering information (through telecommunications services) on pregnancy and early childhood parenting, including safety concerns, child abuse prevention, hotlines, and disability information and services; pioneered touch-screen parenting information kiosks in public sites.

Parents Without Partners (PWP)
401 North Michigan Avenue
Chicago, IL 60611–4267
312–644–6610; 800–637–7974
Fax: 312–321–6869
Network of chapters for single parents; acts as advocate; provides information and referrals; offers group insurance, discount programs, and scholarships for PWP children; publishes various materials, including magazine *The Single Parent*; book *Mega Skills*; brochure *Practical Parenting... Tips to Grow By*; information sheets *Single Parents and the Schools*, *Never-Married Mothers*, and *Resource Organizations for Single Parent Families*; and *Never-Married Parent Reading List.*

American Academy of Pediatrics (AAP), 800–433–9016. Publishes brochures *Single Parenting*, *Television and the Family*, and *Temper Tantrums: A Normal Part of Growing Up*; book *Caring for Your Adolescent: Ages 12 to 21*; and video and booklet set *Baby Talk—The Videoguide for New Parents.* (For full group information, see HEALTH CARE.)

Families and Work Institute (FWI)
330 Seventh Avenue
New York, NY 10001
212–465–2044
Fax: 212–465–8637
Dana Friedman and Ellen Galinsky, Cofounders
Organization concerned with work and families and their effects on each other; provides information; conducts policy research; seeks to shape public policy; publishes numerous materials, including *The Family in Transition*, *Work and Family Trends*, *The Implementation of Flexible Time and Leave Policies*, and other works of analysis.

Effectiveness Training International
531 Stevens Avenue
Solana Beach, CA 92075–2093
619–481–8121; 800–628–1197
Fax: 619–481–8125
Organization offering courses in Parent Effectiveness Training (PET); publishes various books, including *Parent Effectiveness Training (P.E.T.)*, *P.E.T. in Action*, and *You Can Have a Family Where Everybody Wins.*

Johnson Institute, 800–231–5165, U.S. except MN. Publishes numerous materials, including:

- Booklets for parents: *A Job Description for Parents*, *A Job Description for Kids*, *Helping Kids Understand Their Feelings*, *Helping Kids Communicate*, *Helping Kids Learn Refusal Skills*, *Helping Kids Make Decisions*, *Helping Kids Be Responsible for Themselves*, *Helping Kids Feel Good About Themselves*, and *Avoiding Power Plays with Kids.*
- Books for parents: *Teaching Your Children Values*, *How to Talk So Kids Will Listen and Listen So Kids Will Talk*, and *How You Feel Is Up to You: The Power of Emotional Choice.*
- For preteens and teens: *Teen Esteem: A Self-Direction Manual for Young Adults*, *Fighting Invisible Tigers*, and *Changing Families: A Group Activities Manual for Middle and High School Students* (for divorced or troubled families).
- For children: books *Liking Myself* and *Stick Up for Yourself! Every Kid's Guide to Personal Power and Positive Self-Esteem*; and *Land of Many Shapes*, children's video and coloring book on different families.

(For full group information, see HELP AGAINST SUBSTANCE ABUSE on page 703.)

Family Resources Warmline, 412–641–4546; 800–641–4546, PA except Philadelphia; Fax: 412–422–9116. A parent-support service of the Magee-Women's Hospital in Pittsburgh; answers questions on parenting concerns.

Children's Defense Fund (CDF), 800–233–1200. Publishes *Helping Children by Strengthening Families*, *Adolescent and Young Adult Fathers: Problems and Solutions*, *The Family Support Act: How Can It Help Teen Parents?*, *The Adolescent and Young Adult Fact Book*, *Where to Find Data About Adolescents and Youths: A Guide to Sources*, *Latino Youths at a Crossroads*, *Tackling the Youth Employment Problem*, *Building Youth Corps*, and materials on programs for adolescents. (For full group information, see ADOLESCENT PREGNANCY.)

The Children's Foundation (TCF), 202–347–3300. Publishes *Stressbusters: Balancing Family and Job Commitments and Time* and *The Single Parent Experience.* (For full group information, see CHILD CARE.)

American Association of Family and Consumer Sciences (AAFCS)
1555 King Street
Alexandria, VA 22314
703–706–4600
Mary Jane Kolar, Executive Director
Organization for family and consumer science professionals; formerly American Home Economics Association (AHEA); acts as advocate; operates Center for the Family; publishes various materials, including newsletter *AAFCS Action*; quarterlies *Journal of Family and Consumer Sciences* and *Family and Consumer Sciences Journal*; *Where's Papa? Father's Role in Child Care*; *Families in Transition*; and *New Realities of the American Family.*

American Academy of Child and Adolescent Psychiatry (AACAP), 202–966–7300. Publishes information sheets *Normal Adolescent Development: A Fact Sheet, Stepfamily Problems, When Children Have Children,* and *Children and Family Moves.* (For full group information, see MENTAL DISORDERS.)

Family Initiative Council
1333 South Kirkwood Road
St. Louis, MO 63122
314–965–9000, ext. 1264 or 314–965–9917; Family Connection Office: 800–351–1001
Fax: 314–822–8307
Jim Schlie, Executive Director

Organization of family support groups linked with the Lutheran Church-Missouri Synod; among its Action Teams is one focusing on School and Early Childhood; the Family Connection line offers information and counseling on family problems, including parenting and sexuality; publishes newsletter *Family Connection* and other materials.

Planned Parenthood Federation of America (PPFA), 800–230–7526. Publishes pamphlet *How to Be a Good Parent.* (For full group information, see BIRTH CONTROL.)

Couple to Couple League (CCL), 513–471–2000. Publishes brochure *The First Three Years of Life.* (For full group information, see NATURAL FAMILY PLANNING.)

Childhelp USA, 818–953–7577. Publishes pamphlets *Test Your Parent IQ, How Do You Spell Motivation, Family Stress Juggling Act, Dads and Stress,* and *Moms and Stress.* (For full group information, see HELP AGAINST CHILD ABUSE AND NEGLECT on page 680.)

National Association for the Education of Young Children (NAEYC), 800–424–2460. Publishes books *Character Development: Encouraging Self-Esteem and Self-Discipline in Infants* and *Beyond Self-Esteem: Developing a Genuine Sense of Human Value.* (For full group information, see PRESCHOOL.)

Hazelden Foundation (HF), 800–262–5010. Publishes *Full Esteem Ahead: 100 Ways to Build Self-Esteem in Children and Adults* and *The Lovables in the Kingdom of Self-Esteem* (for children). (For full group information, see HELP AGAINST SUBSTANCE ABUSE on page 703.)

National Committee for Prevention of Child Abuse (NCPCA), 800–835–2671. Publishes *Growth and Development Through Parenting* and *What Every Parent Should Know.* (For full group information, see HELP AGAINST CHILD ABUSE AND NEGLECT on page 680.)

National Woman's Christian Temperance Union (WCTU), 800–755–1321. Publishes booklets *About Self-Esteem* and *Increasing Children's Self-Confidence.* (For full group information, see HELP AGAINST SUBSTANCE ABUSE on page 703.)

National Clearinghouse on Child Abuse and Neglect Information (NCCAN), 800–394–3366. Publishes annotated bibliography *Parenting.* (For full group information, see HELP AGAINST CHILD ABUSE AND NEGLECT on page 680.)

Alliance for Parental Involvement in Education (ALLPIE), 518–392–6900. Publishes *Adventuring with Children: The Complete Manual for Family Adventure Travel.* (For full group information, see HELP ON LEARNING AND EDUCATION on page 659).

ON PARENTING ADOLESCENTS

Child Welfare League of America (CWLA), 202–638–2952. Publishes *Independence: A Life Skills Guide for Teens, Preparing Adolescents for Life After Foster Care: The Central Role of Foster Parents, Independent-Living Services for At-Risk Adolescents, The One Girl in Ten: Self Portrait of the Teen-age Mother,* and *Parenting Curriculum.* (For full group information, see FOSTER CARE.)

Alexander Graham Bell Association for the Deaf (AGBAD), 202–337–5220, voice/TT. Publishes *Parenting Teens with Love and Logic: Preparing Adolescents for Responsible Adulthood.* (For full group information, see EAR AND HEARING PROBLEMS.)

National Institute of Mental Health (NIMH), 301–443–4513. Publishes *Adolescence.* (For full group information, see MENTAL DISORDER.)

National Mental Health Consumer Self-Help Clearinghouse, 800–553–4539. Publishes reprint packet on adolescence. (For full group information, see MENTAL DISORDERS.)

FOR TEEN PARENTS

March of Dimes Birth Defects Foundation (MDBDF), 914–428–7100. Publishes *Risks and Results: Making Responsible Life Choices,* and *Rockabye,* on teen parenting. (For full group information, see BIRTH DEFECTS.)

Educational Equity Concepts (EEC), 212–725–1803. Publishes video *Breaking Stereotypes: Teens Talk About Raising Children.* (For full group information, see HELP ON LEARNING AND EDUCATION on page 659.)

National Organization on Adolescent Pregnancy, Parenting, and Prevention (NOAPP), 301–913–0378. Publishes *Directory of Adolescent Pregnancy and Parenting Programs.*

Council for Exceptional Children (CEC), 800–328–0272. Publishes *Double Jeopardy: Pregnant and Parenting Youth in Special Education.* (For full group information, see HELP ON LEARNING AND EDUCATION on page 659.)

ON STEPFAMILIES

Step Family Foundation (SFF)
333 West End Avenue
New York, NY 10023
212–877–3244; 212–799-STEP [799–7837] (24 hours); Crisis Line: 212–744–6924
Fax: 212–362–7030
E-mail: stepfamily@delphi.com (Delphi: STEPFAMILY)
Jeannette Lofas, Executive Director
Organization concerned with stepfamilies; provides information, counseling, and training; publishes various materials, including quarterly newsletter *New American Family*; pamphlets *Ten Steps for Steps* and *The Dynamics of Step*; books *Living in Step* and *Stepparenting*; video *Family Matters: The Realities of Step* and *Step Relationships*; numerous audiotapes, including many for professional counselors.

Stepfamily Association of America (SAA)
215 Centennial Mall South, Suite 212
Lincoln, NE 68508–1834
402–477–7837; 800–735–0329
Fax: 402–477–8317
Jim Zolbe, Executive Director
Support network for stepfamilies; acts as advocate; provides information and referrals; publishes various materials, including quarterly *Stepfamilies*; manual *Stepfamilies Stepping Ahead, Support for Stepfamilies, Suggestions for Schools*; fact sheets, catalog of stepfamily resources, training manuals, and other materials.

Association of Family and Conciliation Courts (AFCC), 608–251–4001. Publishes pamphlet *Guide for Stepparents* and *Guide for a Successful Marriage.* (For full group information, see DIVORCE.).

ON OTHER SPECIAL FAMILY CONCERNS

National Mental Health Association (NMHA), 800–969–6642. Publishes *Helping a Child Build a Full Life with One Parent.* (For full group information, see MENTAL DISORDERS.)

Interracial Family Alliance (IFA)
P.O. Box 16248
Houston, TX 77222
713–586–8949
Organization for families that are interracial through marriage or adoption; offers support and encourages public acceptance; provides information; publishes various materials.

Big Brothers and Big Sisters of America (BB/BSA)
230 North 13th Street
Philadelphia, PA 19107
215–567–7000
Fax: 215–567–0394
Thomas M. McKenna, Executive Director
Network of local, volunteer agencies to provide an adult friend for children from single-parent homes. Publishes newsletter and other materials.

Lavender Families Resource Network, 206–325–2643, voice/TT. Publishes pamphlet *Introduction to Lesbian Families: A Fact Sheet;* and article reprints *This Child Does Have Two Mothers: Redefining Parenthood to Meet the Needs of Children in Lesbian-Mother and Other Nontraditional Families, Children of Lesbian and Gay Parents, Parenting by Gay Fathers, Adoption and Foster Parenting for Lesbians and Gay Men: Creating New Traditions in Family,* and other legal and social analyses. (For full group information, see HOMOSEXUALITY.)

ONLINE RESOURCES FOR PARENTS

Moms Online (America Online), a service offering information, resources, and a meeting place for mothers (and fathers) online. Offers the Moms Online Desk Reference, which includes most of this book, as well as *The Women's Desk Reference* and *What's New for Parents,* also by Irene Franck and David Brownstone. Other areas include MO Chat, which has structured and open forums on issues of interest to paarents; Ma'zine, a weekly online magazine for mothers; Daily Alexander, a series of day-by-day essays by a working mother about life with her baby boy; Mom-to-Mom, a place for mothers to meet and share advice, interests, and information, also offering a Symposium and a Resource Center; the Daily Sphinx, questions on moms-related trivia for building free online time; Moms Online Direct, a store offering products for parents and children; and three Message Boards: the Mother Board, on the whole range of parenting topics; Moms Across America, organized by state, for local sharing of experiences and recommendations; and the Public Eye, for general responses to Ma'zine and more general messages.

Parents' Information Network (America Online: PIN) Wide range of online services on parenting concerns; general interests areas include Parents' Newsstand, Parents' Exchange (for messages and conferences parent-to-parent or with AOL staff), Parents' Libraries, and Parents' Databases; includes special information on topics such as school choice, home schooling, child abuse, substance abuse, study skills, educational television, gifted children, and special children; includes information from the National Clearinghouse for Child Abuse and Neglect Information and U.S. Department of Education, as well as KidsNet.

Family Services Forum (CompuServe), meeting place for all family members to "talk" with others; maintains online libraries; holds separate online conferences for all (The Living Room), Just Us Two (for parents only), moms only, dads only, teens only, and kids only.

Internet: Genealogy. Collection of resources, including archives and software, including help for beginners. gopher://vienna.hh.lib.umich.edu

Internet. misc.kids Usenet newsgroup offering information and discussion about children and their behavior. Subscribe through newsread: news:misc.kids

Internet: ACS Gopher. Resource file on children, families, and child care, from Administration for Children and Families, of the U.S. Department of Health and Human Services. gopher://spike.acf.dhhs.gov

Internet: CYFERNET (Child, Youth, and Family Education Network). Public information service from the Youth Development Information Center at the National Agricultural Library. gopher://ra.esusda.gov/11/CYFER-net

Issues in Mental Health (America Online: IMH). Provides discussion forum and online library covering parenting issues. (For full information, see MENTAL DISORDERS.)

OTHER RESOURCES

On parenting babies

Dr. Miriam Stoppard's Complete Book of Baby and Child Care. Miriam Stoppard. Dorling Kindersley, 1995.

The Disney Encyclopedia of Baby and Childcare, 2 vols. Genell Subak-Sharpe, ed. Hyperion, 1995.

Baby Basics for New Parents: Quick Answers When You Need Them. Susan Limato. Avon, 1994.

Mayo Clinic Book of Pregnancy and Baby's First Year. Mayo Foundation for Medical Education and Research. Morrow, 1994.

Mothercare's New Guide to Pregnancy and Childcare: An Illustrated Guide to Caring for Your Child from Pregnancy through Age Five. Penny Stanway. Simon & Schuster, 1994.

Great Beginnings: An Illustrated Guide to You and Your Baby's First Year. Antonia Van der Meer. Dell, 1994.

The Baby Care Handbook: A Practical Guide to Infant Care from Birth to 12 Months. Shelby Clark. New Shoes, 1994.

What Every Mother Needs to Know about Babies. Brenda Hunter. Questar, 1994.

Babies First Year. Deb Mores. Crown, 1994.

Babies for Beginners. David Brizer. Writers and Readers, 1994.

Crib Notes. Heather King. Avon, 1994.

Newborn Joy. Linda Sunshine. Andrews and McMeel, 1994.

Baby Steps: A Parents' Guide to Understanding During the First Two Years. Claire B. Kopp and Donne L. Bean. Freeman, 1993.

Bringing Baby Home—An Owner's Manual for First-Time Parents. Laura Zahn. Down to Earth, 1993.

Baby and You. Claire Revelli. Pocket Books, 1993.

The Baby Book: Everything You Need to Know About Your Baby—From Birth to Age Two. William M. Sears and Martha Sears. Little, Brown, 1993.

My Baby Book. Janet Anastasio and Peter Gouck. Adams, 1993.

Caring for Your Baby and Young Child: Birth to Age 5. Steven P. Shelov. Bantam, 1993.

Help! for Parents of Children from Birth to Five: Tried-and-True Solutions to Parents' Everyday Problems, rev. ed. Jean I. Clarke, ed. HarperCollins, 1993. Originally titled: *Help! for Parents of Infants from Birth to Six Months*

You and Your Newborn Baby: A Guide to the First Months after Birth. Linda Todd. Harvard Common Press, 1993.

Your Baby's Development. Joan Miller. Atrium, 1993.

The Baby Journal. Matthew Bennett. Meadowbrook, 1993.

Baby Care Basics. Diane, 1993.

Checklist for Your New Baby. Dylan Landis. Berkley, 1993.

Dr. Spock's Baby and Child Care, 6th ed. Benjamin M. Spock and Michael B. Rothenburg. NAL-Dutton, 1992.

Hi Mom! Hi Dad!: The First Twelve Months of Parenthood, rev. ed. Lynn Johnston. Meadowbrook, 1992.

Baby's First Year. Marcia O'Levin. Random, 1992.

The First Twelve Months of Life Companion: A Personal Record of Your Baby's Early Development. Princeton Center for Infancy and Early Childhood Staff; Theresa Caplan, ed. Berkley, 1992.

Building Blocks: An Infant Toddler Handbook, rev. ed. Gail R. Quatmann and Patricia B. Ewen. G.-R. Quatmann, 1992.

The Complete Baby Check List: A Total Organizing System for Parents. Elyse Karlin and others. Avon, 1992.

Raising Baby Right: A Guide to Avoiding 20 Common Mistakes New Parents Make. Charles E. Schaefer. Crown, 1992.

A Doctor Discusses the Care and Development of Your Baby. May Guy and Miriam Gilbert. Budlong, 1992.

A Baby's Story: A Remarkable Photographic Account of a Baby's First Year. Nicola McClure. Simon & Schuster, 1992.

Conversations with Mr. Baby: A Celebration of New Life. Steve Chapple. Arcade, 1992.

Three Hundred Questions New Parents Ask: Answers about Pregnancy, Childbirth, and Infant and Child Care. William Sears and Martha Sears. NAL-Dutton, 1991.

Keys to Caring and Preparing for Your Newborn. William Sears. Barron's, 1991.

Babysense: A Practical and Supportive Guide to Baby Care, 2nd ed. Frances W. Burck. St. Martin's, 1991.

Bringing up Baby: The First Twelve Months. Ann Kishbaugh and Nevin Kishbaugh. Bonus, 1991.

Baby Talk-Parent Talk: Understanding Your Baby's Body Language. Sirgay Sanger. Doubleday, 1991.

Baby Tactics: Parenting Tips That Really Work. Barbara A. Hill. Avery, 1991.

Parent's Survival Guide: Ease into Parenthood with Parents' Survival Guide Birth to One Year. Margaret R. Spelman and Sandra L. Kosik. HealthProInk, 1991.

From Birth to Three: An Illustrated Journey Through Your Child's Early Development. Camilla Jessel. Dell, 1991.

The First Year of Life, rev. ed. Nina R. Lief and Mary E. Fahs. Walker, 1991.

Caring for Your Newborn Baby. Glenn R. Stoutt. Falsoft, 1990.

Diary of a Baby: What Your Child Sees, Feels and Experiences. Daniel N. Stern. Basic, 1990.

The Baby's Budget Book: Financial Planning for New Parents. Randolph W. Farmer and Robert V. Ling. Shadetree, 1990.

The Baby Kit: Everything You Need to Know About Caring for Your Newborn. Penelope Leach. Simon & Schuster, 1990.

I Wish Someone Had Told Me: Comfort, Support, and Advice for New Moms from More Than 60 Real-Life Mothers. Nina Barrett. Simon & Schuster/Fireside, 1990.

The First Weeks of Life. Miriam Stoppard. Ballantine, 1990.

Taking Care of Your New Baby: A Guide to the First Month of Parenting. Jeanne Watson Driscoll and Marsha Walker. Avery, 1990.

The Superbaby Syndrome: Escaping the Dangers of Hurrying Your Child. Jean Grasso Fitzpatrick. Harcourt Brace Jovanovich, 1990.

What to Expect the First Year. Arlene Eisenberg and others. Workman, 1988.

Activities for Babies

The New Beyond Peek-A-Boo and Pat-a-Cake: Activities for Baby's First 24 Months, 3rd ed. Evelyn M. Munger and Susan J. Bowdon. New Win, 1993.

Games to Play with Babies, rev. ed. Jackie Silberg. Gryphon House, 1993.

Babies Looking Book: Stimulation for the Newborn to Six Month Old Infant. Sharon K. Hyde. S. K. Hyde, 1992.

Baby and I Can Play and *Fun with Toddlers,* rev. ed. Karen Hendrickson. Parenting, 1990.

(See also PLAY GROUP; MOTOR SKILLS; HELP ON LEARNING AND EDUCATION on page 659.)

On Calming Babies

Twenty Ways to Calm a Crying Baby. Rebecca B. Barns. Thomasson-Grant, 1994.

Why Is My Baby Crying?: The Seven-Minute Program for Soothing the Fussy Baby. Bruce Taubman. Simon & Schuster, 1993.

Keys to Comforting the Fussy Baby. William Sears. Barron's, 1991.

The Crying Baby. Sheila Kitzinger. Penguin, 1990.

Baby Name Books

What's in a Name? The Heroes and Heroines Baby Name Book. Nancy Heffernan and Louis Judson. Prima, 1990.

The Baby Name Countdown: Meanings and Popularity Ratings for 50,000 Names. Janet Schwegel. Paragon, 1990.

The Worst Baby Name Book. Bob Glickman. Andrews and McMeel, 1990.

The Great Beginnings Baby Name Book: Illustrious Names from the Arts, History, Literature, Sports, Mythology, and Cultures Around the World. Sara L. Whitter. Contemporary, 1989.

On Buying Products for Children

The Natural Nursery: The Parent's Guide to Ecologically Sound, Nontoxic, Safe and Healthy Baby Care. Louis Pottkotter. Contemporary, 1994.

The Pink and Blue Baby Pages. Laurie S. Waldstein and Leslie F. Zinberg. Price Stern, 1994.

Baby's Best!: The Best Baby (and Toddler) Products to Make a Parent's Life Easier and More Fun. Susan Silver. Adams Hall, 1993.

Best Bets for Babies: Time-Saving, Trouble-Saving, Money-Saving Tips for Your Baby's First Two Years from the Real Experts—Parents. Brooke M. Beebe. Dell, 1993.

Baby Products Basics: The Busy Person's Guide to Baby Products on a Budget. Renee M. Rolle-Whatley. Sandcastle, 1991.

Bargains-by-Mail for Baby and You: Where to Buy for Your Baby, Nursery, Playroom, and Yourself at Mail-Order Wholesale Prices. Dawn Hardy. Prima, 1991.

Guide to Baby Products, 3rd ed. Sandy Jones and Werner Freitag. Consumer Reports, 1991.

The Childwise Catalog, rev. ed. Jack Gillis and Mary Ellen Fise. Harper & Row/Perennial, 1990.

On parenting toddlers and preschoolers

My Toddler: The Beginning of Independence and *My Preschooler: Ready for New Adventures.* Paul Warren. Nelson, 1995.

What to Expect the Toddler Years. Arlene Eisenberg and others. Workman, 1994.

Emotional Life of the Toddler. Alicia Lieberman. Free Press, 1993.

I Heard It Through the Playground: 616 Best Tips from the Mommy and Daddy Network for Raising a Happy, Healthy Child from Birth to Age Five. Carol Boswell. HarperCollins, 1993.

Keys to Parenting Your One-Year-Old. Meg Zweibach. Barron's, 1992.

The Incredible Years: A Trouble-Shooting Guide for Parents of Children Aged 3–8. Carolyn Webster-Stratton. Pacific Pipeline, 1992.

Kid Think. William Lee Carter. Word, 1992. On dealing with common behavioral problems by thinking from the child's point of view.

I Wanna Do It Myself: A Radical Three-Tiered Approach to Helping Your Child Achieve Independence. William Sammons. Hyperion, 1992.

The Second Year of Life, rev. ed, and *The Third Year of Life.* Nina R. Lief and Mary E. Fahs. Walker, 1991.

The Preschool Years: Family Strategies That Work—from Experts and Parents. Ellen Galinsky and Judy David. Ballantine, 1991.

Caring for Your Baby and Young Child: Birth to Age Five, Stephen P. Shelov and others, eds. Bantam, 1991.

Caring for Your Baby and Young Child: Birth Through 5. American Academy of Pediatrics Staff. American Academy of Pediatrics/Bantam, 1991.

Time Out for Toddlers. James W. Varni. Berkley, 1991.

The Inner Child: Understanding Your Child's Emotional Growth in the First Six Years of Life. H. Paul Gabriel and Robert Wool. Times Books, 1990.

Everyday Parenting: The First Five Years. Robin Goldstein with Janet Gallant. Penguin, 1990.

Your Baby and Child: From Birth to Age Five, rev. ed. Penelope Leach. Schocken, 1989.

Toddlers and Parents: A Declaration of Independence, rev. ed. T. Berry Brazelton. Delacorte, 1989.

Your One-Year-Old: The Fun-loving, Funny 12-to-24-month Old. Louise Bates Ames and others. Delacorte, 1982.

Your Two-Year-Old: Terrible or Tender. Your Three-Year-Old: Friend or Enemy. Your Four-Year-Old: Wild & Wonderful. Your Five-Year-Old: Sunny & Serene. Louise Bates Ames and Frances L. Ilg. Delacorte, 1979.

Activities for preschoolers

Success Before Six: One Hundred Step-by-Step Activities for Children under Six. Scot F. Carter. Scotland, 1995.

Kidstuff: Parent Activities for Your Preschooler. Deborah C. Harding. Eagle Press, 1994.

Pint-Size Science: Finding-Out Fun for You and Your Preschooler. Linda Allison and Martha Weston. Little, Brown, 1994.

Sing Us a Story: Using Music in Preschool and Family Story Times. Jane Marino. Wilson, 1994.

Entertain Me!. Riverside Mothers' Playgroup Staff. Claire Zion, ed. Pocket Books, 1993.

Slow and Steady, Get Me Ready: The How-to Book That Grows with the Child. June R. Oberlander and Clyde G. Oberlander. Bio-Alpha, 1992.

See What I Can Do Today: A Year's Worth of Fascinating Fun for Your Pre-Schooler. Margaret Joslin. STA-Kris, 1992.

Treasured Time with Your Toddler: A Monthly Guide to Activities. Jan Brennan. August House, 1991.

Preschool Power (1990). Educational music video for kids ages one to six. Also *More Preschool Power!* (1991), and *Preschool Power 3!* (1992). Concept Videos.

(See also PRESCHOOL for school-preparation activities.)

(Subscribers to the America Online computer service can find school preparation activities, in the Moms Online Desk reference section of Moms Online, under "Teaching Young Children.")

On parenting school-age children

Life's Little Miseries: Helping Your Child with the Disasters of Everyday Life: For Parents and Teachers of Children Ages 3–12. Diane Lynch-Fraser. Free Press, 1992.

Stop Struggling with Your Child: Quick-Tip Parenting Solutions That Will Work for You—and Your Kids Ages 4–12. Evonne Weinhaus and Karen Friedman. HarperCollins, 1991.

The Parenting Challenge: Your Child's Behavior from 6 to 12. Arnold Rincover. Pocket Books, 1991.

More Everyday Parenting: The Six-to-Nine-Year-Old. Robin Goldstein. Viking Penguin, 1991.

Your Six-Year-Old: Defiant but Loving. Louise Bates Ames and others. Delacorte, 1979.

Your Seven-Year-Old: Life in a Minor Key. Your Eight-Year-Old: Lively and Outgoing. Your Nine-Year-Old: Thoughtful and Mysterious. Louise Bates Ames and Carol Chase Haber. Delacorte, 1990.

Your Ten- to Fourteen-Year-Old. Louise Bates Ames and others. Delacorte, 1988.

Activities for preteens and teens

Peterson's Summer Opportunities for Kids and Teenagers. Peterson's, annual.

Surviving Summers with Kids: Funfilled Activities for All. Rita B. Herron. R & E Publishers, 1993.

One Hundred One Great Ways to Keep Your Child Entertained: While You Get Something Else Done. Danelle Hickman and Valerie Teurlay. St. Martin's, 1992.

50 Simple Things Kids Can Do to Save the Earth. The Earth Works Group. Andrews and McMeel, 1990.

What Would We Do Without You?: A Guide to Volunteer Activities for Kids. Kathy Henderson. Betterway, 1990.

On parenting girls

Teenage Girls: A Parent's Survival Manual. Lauren K. Ayers. Crossroad, 1994.

The Modern Girl: Girlhood and Growing Up. Lesley Johnson. Taylor and Francis, 1993.

The Little Girl Book. David Laskin and Kathleen O. Laskin. Ballantine, 1992.

Don't Stop Loving Me: A Reassuring Guide for Mothers of Adolescent Daughters. Ann F. Caron. HarperCollins, 1991.

On parenting boys

Strong Mothers, Strong Sons: Raising Adolescent Boys in the 90's. Ann Caron. Holt, 1994. Also published as *Strong Mothers, Strong Sons: Raising the Next Generation of Men.* HarperCollins, 1995.

Saving Our Sons: Raising Black Children in a Turbulent World. Marita Golden. Doubleday, 1995.

The Joy of Being a Boy. Elizabeth Noble and Leo Sorger. New Life Images, 1994.

Boys!. William Beausay. Nelson, 1994.

The Courage to Raise Good Men: A Manifesto for Change. Olga Silverstein and Beth Rashbaum. Viking Penguin, 1994.

How to Be Your Little Man's Dad: Three Hundred Sixty-Five Things to Do with Your Son. Dan Bolin and Ken Sutterfield. Pinon Press, 1993.

Boys Will Be Boys: Breaking the Link Between Masculinity and Violence. Myriam Miedzian. Doubleday, 1992.

On parenting in general

Getting Out of Your Kids' Faces and Into Their Hearts. Valerie Bell. Zondervan, 1995.

Wonderful Ways to Love a Child. Judy Ford. Conari, 1995.

Eight Weeks to a Well-Behaved Child: A Failsafe Program for Toddlers Through Teens. James Windell. Macmillan, 1994.

The ABCs of Parenting: A Guide to Help Parents and Caretakers Handle Childrearing Problems. Joan Barbuto. R & E Publishers, 1994.

How to Live with Your Kids: When You've Already Lost Your Mind. Ken Davis. Zondervan, 1994.

Parenting and Child Care, rev. ed. William Sears. Nelson, 1993. Originally titled: *Christian Parenting and Child Care.*

Parent Talk: Straight Answers to the Questions That Rattle Moms and Dads. Kevin Leman and Randy Carlson. Nelson, 1993.

Raising Good Kids. Louise B. Ames. Dell, 1993.

The Joys of Having a Child. Bill Adler and Gloria Adler, eds. Morrow, 1993.

The Thinking Parent: Understanding and Guiding Your Child. Anne Stokes. Twenty-Third, 1993.

Understanding Children: Infancy Through School-Age, 2nd ed., and *Understanding Children: School-Age and Adolescence,* 2nd ed. Judith Schickedanz. Mayfield, 1993.

What Next?: Understanding Your Child at Each Age and Stage. Robert E. Ripley and Marie J. Ripley. Carefree Press, 1993.

Questions Kids Wish They Could Ask Their Parents. Zoe Stern and Ellen S. Stern. Celestial Arts, 1993.

Bringing up Kids Without Tearing Them Down. Kevin Leman. Delacorte, 1993. By the author of *Keeping Your Family Together When the World Is Falling Apart* (1992).

Everything You Always Wanted to Tell Your Children. Dee Edward. Intrepid, 1993.

Little Kids, Big Questions. Judith E. Craig. Hearst, 1993.

What Is Happening to Our Children?: How to Raise Them Right. Mardel E. Gustafson. R & E Publishers, 1993.

Help! for Parents of Children from Birth to Five: Tried-and-True Solutions to Parents' Everyday Problems, rev. ed., and *Help! for Parents of School-Age Children and Teenagers: Tried-and-True Solutions to Parent's Everyday Problems,* rev. ed. Jean I. Clarke. HarperCollins, 1993. Originally titled: *Help! for Parents of Infants from Birth to Six Months* and *Help! for Parents of Children from Ages Six to Twelve Years.*

Family Encyclopedia of Child Psychology and Development: An Easy-to-Understand Parent's Guide. Frank J. Bruno. Wiley, 1992.

Party Shoes to School and Baseball Caps to Bed: The Parents' Survival Guide to Understanding Kids, Clothes, and Independence. Marilise Flusser. Simon & Schuster, 1992.

Helping Kids Help Themselves. E. Perry Good. New View, 1992.

Judicious Parenting. Forrest Gathercoal. Caddo Gap, 1992.

How to Stay Lovers While Raising Your Children. Anne Mayer. St. Martin's, 1992.

Tough Parenting for Dangerous Times. Andre Bustanoby. Zondervan, 1992.

Be Nice but Firm: A Down-to-Earth Approach to Child Management. Walter M. Block. Guild Press, 1992.

Fathers and Mothers. Robert Bly and others. Spring Publications, 1992. On breaking old habits of thinking about family.

The Measure of Our Success: A Letter to My Children and Yours. Marian Wright Edelman. Beacon, 1992.

Dr. Mom's Parenting Guide: Commonsense Guidance for the Life of Your Child. Marianne E. Neifert. Dutton,

1991. By the author of *Dr. Mom: A Guide to Baby and Child Care.* Putnam, 1986.

Oh No! Maybe My Child Is Normal. Cliff Schimmels. Shaw, 1991.

The Parenting Cookbook: Recipes for Raising Successful Children. Steven A. Szykula. Family First, 1991.

Raising Kids in a Changing World: Preschool Through the Teen Years. Dian G. Smith. Prentice Hall, 1991.

Parent and Child: Getting Through to Each Other. Lawrence Kutner. Morrow, 1991.

Guiding Your Family in a Misguided World. Anthony Evans. Focus Family, 1991.

Parent Power!: A Common-Sense Approach to Parenting in the '90s and Beyond. John Rosemond. Andrews and McMeel, 1991.

One Thousand Mother's Questions Answered: All You Need to Know about Child Care From Conception to School. Davina Lloyd and Ann Rushton. Thorsons, 1991.

How to Raise the Children You Wish Your Parents Had Raised. Carol Marsh. Gallopade, 1991.

Your Child's Development: From Birth Through Adolescence, a Complete Guide for Parents. Richard Lansdown and Marjorie Walker. Knopf, 1991.

Tough-Minded Parenting. Joe Batten and others. Broadman, 1991.

Parenting by Heart. Ron Taffel with Melinda Blau. Addison-Wesley, 1991.

The Parent's License. Film/video for purchase or rental. Pyramid Film & Video, 1991. (Address: Box 1048, Santa Monica, CA 90406)

The Family Contract: A Parent's Bill of Rights. Howard Leftin. PIA Press, 1990.

Go Ask Your Mother: Family Life and Other Impossible Situations. Thomas Trowbridge III. Morrow, 1990.

Experts Advise Parents: A Guide to Raising Loving, Responsible Children. Eileen Shiff, ed. Delacorte, 1990.

Compassionate Child-Rearing: An In-Depth Approach to Optimal Parenting. Robert W. Firestone. Plenum, 1990.

Families: Crisis and Caring. T. Berry Brazelton. Addison-Wesley, 1990.

PARENTING RESOURCE GUIDES

The Parents' Resource Almanac: Where to Write, Who to Call, What to Buy and How to Find Out Everything You Need to Know. Beth Defrancis. Adams, 1994.

What's New for Parents. Irene Franck and David Brownstone. Prentice-Hall/Simon & Schuster, 1993.

Who to Call: The Parent's Source Book. Dan Starer. Morrow, 1992.

Help for Children From Infancy to Adulthood, 5th ed. Miriam J. Williams Wilson. Rocky River, 1991. Directory of hotlines and organizations.

Positive Parenting Fitness: A Parent's Resource Guide to Nutrition, Stress Reduction, Total Exercise, and Practical Information. Sylvia Klein Olkin. Avery, 1991.

FOR AFRICAN-AMERICAN PARENTS

Saving Our Sons: Raising Black Children in a Turbulent World. Marita Golden. Doubleday, 1995.

Raising the Rainbow Generation. Darlene Powell Hopson and Derek Hopson. Simon & Schuster, 1993. On countering racial and ethnic stereotypes. By the authors of *Different and Wonderful: Raising Black Children in a Race-Conscious Society* (1992).

Raising Black Children: Questions and Answers for Parents and Teachers. James P. Comer and Alvin F. Poussaint. NAL-Dutton, 1992. By the authors of *Black Child Care: How To Bring Up a Healthy Black Child in America* (1975).

African American Parent's Guide: Raising Culturally Aware Children. Mary Sood. Amesbury, 1992.

ON WORKING PARENTS

Working Parents. Linda Ribaudo and Darlyne Walker. New Readers, 1994.

Parents' Jobs and Children's Lives. Toby L. Parcel and Elizabeth G. Menaghan. Aldine de Gruyter, 1994.

Making It Work: Finding the Time and Energy for Your Career, Marriage, Children, and Self. Victoria Houston. Contemporary, 1990.

Working Parent/Happy Child: You Can Balance Job and Family. Caryl Waller Krueger. Abingdon, 1990.

Taking Care of Your Child, rev. ed. Robert H. Pantell and others. Addison-Wesley, 1990.

ON BLENDED OR NONTRADITIONAL FAMILIES

The Living Together Kit, 7th ed. Toni Ihara and Ralph Warner. Nolo, 1994.

Cupid, Couples and Contracts: A Guide to Living Together, Prenuptial Agreements, and Divorce. Lester Wallman and Sharon McDonnell. MasterMedia, 1994.

The Living Together Trap: Everything Women and Men Should Know. Rosanne Rosen. New Horizon, 1993.

The Spousal Equivalent Handbook: A Legal and Financial Guide to Living Together. Johnette Duff and George G. Truitt. NAL-Dutton, 1992.

Divorce and New Beginnings: An Authoritative Guide to Recovery and Growth, Solo Parenting, and Stepfamilies. Genevieve Clapp. Wiley, 1992.

Raising Jewish Children in a Contemporary World: The Modern Parent's Guide to Creating a Jewish Home. Steven Carr Reuben. Prima, 1992. For both Jewish and interfaith parents.

Stepmothers: Keeping It Together with Your Husband and His Kids. Merry Bloch Jones and Jo Ann Schiller. Carol/Birch Lane, 1992.

Re-Married with Children: A Blended Couple's Journey to Harmony. Don Houck and Ladean Houck. Here's Life Publishers, 1991.

Love in the Blended Family: Step-Families: A Package Deal. Angela N. Clubb. Health Communications, 1991.

Wider Families: New Traditional Family Forms. Theresa D. Marciano and Marvin B. Sussman, eds. Haworth Press, 1991.

Practical Parenting—Blended Families: (Yours, Mine and Ours) (1991). Video on the myths and realities of stepfamilies, including such issues as divided loyalties, periods of adjustment, dealing with absent parents, maintaining family continuity, and handling discipline. (Address: United Learning, 6633 West Howard, Niles, IL 60648.)

Yours, Mine, and Ours: How Families Change When Remarried Parents Have a Child Together. Anne C. Bernstein. Norton, 1990.

Raising Your Jewish/Christian Child: How Interfaith Parents Can Give Children the Best of Both Their Heritages. Lee F. Gruzen. Newmarket, 1990.

For children, on family relationships

What Is A Family? (1991), *What Kind of Family Do You Have?* (1991), *Traditions* (1992), and *Sisters and Brothers* (1992). Gretchen Super. Twenty-First Century Books.

Free to Be...You and Me: A Different Kind of Book for Children and Adults to Enjoy Together. Conceived by Marlo Thomas; Carole Hart and others, eds., 1974. *Free to Be...A Family: A Book About All Kinds of Belonging.* 1987. Marlo Thomas and friends. Bantam.

Weird Parents. Audrey Wood. Dial, 1990.

Talking About Stepfamilies. Maxine B. Rosenberg. Bradbury, 1990.

Sam Is My Half Brother. Lizi Boyd. Viking, 1990.

Stepfamilies. Marilyn Bailey. Crestwood/Macmillan, 1990.

Stepfamilies. Elizabeth Hodder. Watts/Gloucester, 1990.

On parenting disagreements

Why Parents Disagree: How Men and Women Parent Differently and How We Can Work Together. Ron Taffel and Robert Israeloff. Morrow, 1994.

Mothering and Fathering: The Gender Differences in Child Rearing. Tine Thevenin. Avery, 1993.

On late parenting

Having a Baby in Your Forties: An Intimate, Touching Account of a Career Minded Woman Adjusting to Becoming a Mother. Patricia Mellon-Elibol. Lifetime, 1992.

The Long Awaited Stork: A Guide to Parenting after Infertility. Ellen Sarasohn Glazer. Lexington, 1990.

On single parenting

On Our Own: Living Happily As a Single-Parent Family. Marge Kennedy and Janet S. King. Crown, 1994.

A Single Parent's Guide: Providing Anchors for the Innocent. Gail C. Christopher. Noble, 1992.

Single Moms, Single Dads: Help and Hope for the One-Parent Family. David R. Miller. Chariot Family, 1992.

The Two-Parent Family Is Not the Best. June Stephenson. Diemer-Smith, 1991.

My Child, My Teacher, My Friend: Parenting in Recovery. Dwight Lee Wolter. CompCare, 1991.

Never a Day Off: Surviving Single Parenthood. Elizabeth H. Rigdon. Beacon Hill, 1991.

Complete Financial Guide for Single Parents. Larry Burkett. Dandelion House, 1991.

The Single Mother's Book: A Practical Guide to Managing Your Children, Career, Home, Finances and Everything Else. Joan Anderson. Peachtree, 1990.

Handbook for Single Parents. William Rabior and Vicki W. Bedard. Liguori Publications, 1990.

Single Moms, Single Dads: Help and Hope for the One-Parent Family. David R. Miller. Accent Books, 1990.

For children of single parents

My Kind of Family: A Book for Kids in Single-Parent Homes. Michele Lash and others. Waterfront, 1990.

This Is Me and My Single Parent: A Discovery Workbook for Children and Single Parents. Marla D. Evans. Magination, 1989.

Single-Parent Families. Marilyn Bailey. Crestwood, 1990.

On family patterns

Taming the Dragon in Your Child: Solutions for Breaking the Cycle of Family Anger. M. Eastman and S. C. Rozen. Wiley, 1994.

Family Cycles: How Understanding the Way You Were Raised Will Make You a Better Parent. Lee Carter. NavPress, 1993.

I'll Never Do to My Kids What My Parents Did to Me: A Guide to Conscious Parenting. Thomas Paris and Eileen Paris. Lowell House, 1992.

How to Avoid Your Parents' Mistakes When You Raise Your Children. Claudette Wassil-Grimm. Pocket, 1992.

Family Mirrors: What Our Children's Lives Reveal About Ourselves. Elizabeth Fishel. Houghton Mifflin, 1991.

On teaching values

Parent's Bible: Bringing up Ethical Children in a Changing World. Wayne Dosick. HarperCollins, 1995.

Teaching Your Children Joy. Linda Eyre. Simon & Schuster, 1994.

Bringing up a Caring Child: Teaching Your Child to Be Kind, Just, and Responsible. Michael Schulman and Eva Mekler. Doubleday, 1994.

Helping Your Child Learn Responsible Behavior. Diane, 1994.

Teaching Children Responsibility. Linda Eyre. Ballantine, 1993.

Raising Ethical Children: Ten Keys to Helping Your Children Become Moral and Caring. Steven C. Reuben. Prima, 1993.

Raising Responsible Kids. Jay Kesler. Avon, 1993.

Raising Kids Who Can: Using Family Meetings to Nurture Responsible, Cooperative, Caring, and Happy Children.

Betty L. Bettner and Amy Lew. HarperCollins, 1992.

Good Parents for Hard Times: Raising Responsible Kids in the Age of Drug Use and Sexual Promiscuity. Joanne B. Koch and Linda N. Freeman. Simon & Schuster, 1992.

Happier Families: Raising Responsible, Self-Managed Children. Michael B. Medland. Barcroft, 1992.

Familyhood: Nurturing the Values That Matter. Lee Salk. Simon & Schuster, 1992.

Something More: Nurturing Your Child's Spiritual Growth. Jean G. Fitzpatrick. Viking Penguin, 1992.

Parents' Guide to Raising Responsible Kids: Preschool through Teen Years. Karyn Feiden. Prentice Hall, 1991.

Why Kids Lie: How Parents Can Encourage Truthfulness. Paul Ekman. Viking Penguin, 1991.

To Raise a Jewish Child: A Guide for Parents. Hayim H. Donin. Basic Books, 1991.

Reclaiming America's Children: Raising and Educating Morally Healthy Kids, a Resource for Parents and Teachers. M. V. Willis. Ocean East, 1991.

Love and Twenty-Five Four-Letter Words to Teach Your Children. Clara W. Brooks. Feelings Unlimited, 1991.

ON HELPING CHILDREN BUILD SELF-ESTEEM

Things Will Be Different for My Daughter: A Practical Guide to Building Her Self-Esteem. Mindy Bingham and others. Viking Penguin, 1995.

Teaching Children Self-Esteem. Anne R. Smith. E. Mellen, 1994.

Five Hundred One Ways to Boost Your Child's Self-Esteem. Robert Ramsay. Contemporary, 1994.

All That She Can Be: Helping Your Daughter Maintain Her Self-Esteem During the Critical Years. Carol J. Eagle and Carol Colman. Simon & Schuster, 1993.

The Winning Family: Increasing Self-Esteem in Your Children and Yourself, rev. ed. Louise Hart. Celestial Arts, 1993.

Promoting Healthy Self-Esteem in Children. Jon Drescher. Bureau for At-Risk Youth, 1992.

The Six Vital Ingredients of Self-Esteem: And How to Develop Them in Your Child. Bettie B. Youngs. Macmillan, 1991.

How to Give Your Child a Great Self-Image: Proven Techniques to Build Confidence from Infancy to Adolescence. Debora Phillips and Fred Bernstein. NAL-Dutton, 1991.

A Parent's Guide to Building Children's Self-Esteem, 2nd ed. Waln K. Brown. W. Gladden, 1991.

Building Your Child's Self-Esteem. Gary Smalley and John Trent. NavPress, 1991.

Fifty-Two Simple Ways to Build Your Child's Self-Esteem. Jan Dargatz. Nelson, 1991.

How to Raise Teenagers' Self-Esteem, rev. ed. Reynold Bean and Harris Clemes. Price Stern, 1990.

FOR CHILDREN, ON SELF-ESTEEM

You Are Special: Words of Wisdom from America's Most Beloved Neighbor. Fred Rogers. Viking Penguin, 1994.

Just for Me: The Self-Esteem and Wellness Guide for Girls. Donna T. Wanner. Spiritseeker, 1994.

FOR PRETEENS AND TEENS, ON SELF-ESTEEM

Soy Joven! Soy Importante!—That Very Special Person—Me!: La Autoestima En la Adolescencia—Self-Esteem for Teens. Margaret Houk. Casa Bautista, 1993.

The How-to Book of Teen Self Discovery: Helping Teens Find Balance, Security and Esteem, 2nd ed. Doc L. Childre and others. Planetary Publications, 1992.

Teen Esteem. Sarah Radcliff. Targum Press, 1992.

What Do You Think of You?: A Teen's Guide to Finding Self-Esteem. Scott Sheperd. Hazelden, 1990.

ON CHILDREN AND TELEVISION

Abandoned in the Wasteland: Children, Television, and the First Amendment. Newton N. Minow and Craig L. LaMay. Hill & Wang, 1995.

Children's Television, 1947–1990: Over 200 Series, Games and Variety Shows, Cartoons, Educational Programs and Specials. Jeffery Davis. McFarland, 1995.

The Parent's Guide to Getting the Most Out of Television: How Use TV to Your Child's Advantage. Dorothy G. Singer and others. Acropolis, 1990.

Who Touched the Remote Control? Television and Christian Choices for Children and Adults Who Care About Children. Friendship Press, 1990.

ON CHILDREN AND MONEY

Money Doesn't Grow on Trees: A Parent's Guide to Raising Financially Reponsible Children. Neale S. Godfrey. Simon & Schuster, 1994.

Money-Making Ideas for Kids. Todd Temple and Melinda Douros. Nelson, 1994.

Simple Ways to Help Your Kids Become Dollar-Smart. Elizabeth Lewin and Bernard Ryan, Jr. Walker, 1994.

Raising Money-Smart Kids. Ron Blue and Judy Blue. Nelson, 1992.

The Teenage Entrepreneur's Guide: 50 Money-Making Business Ideas, 2nd ed. Sarah Riehm. Surrey Books, 1990.

ON HOUSEHOLD ACTIVITIES

Organize Your Family!: Simple Routines for You and Your Kids. Ronnie Eisenberg and Kate Kelly. Hyperion, 1993.

Do I Have To?: Children Who Do Too Little Around the House. Patricia H. Sprinkle. Zondervan, 1993.

How to Get Your Kids to Help at Home. Elva Anson. Ballantine, 1991.

ON CHILDREN AND GROOMING

Here's Looking at You, Kid!: A Busy Parent's Guide to Children's Grooming, Health, and Clothing Basics. Carol Straley. Holt, 1993.

Bringing Out Their Best: A Parent's Guide to Healthy Good Looks for Every Child. Wende D. Gates. Bantam, 1992.

On children and pets

Kids and Pets: A Family Guide to Living and Growing Together. Cook Rodgers and Clarice Rutherford. Alpine, 1993.

Adopting Cats and Kittens: A Care and Training Guide. Connie Jankowski. Howell, 1993.

On parenting active children

Raising Your Type A Child: How to Help Your Child Make the Most of an Achievement Oriented Personality. Steven Shelov and John Kelly. PocketBooks, 1992. On raising ambitious, aggressive children.

How to Raise a Healthy Achiever: Escaping the Type A Treadmill. Laurel Hughes. Abingdon, 1992.

Raising Your Spirited Child: A Guide for Parents Whose Child Is More Intense, Sensitive, Perceptive, Persistent, Energetic. Mary Sheedy Kurcinka. HarperCollins, 1991.

Children of Fast-Track Parents: Raising Self-Sufficient and Confident Children in an Achievement-Oriented World. Andrée Aelion Brooks. Penguin, 1990.

Living with the Active Alert Child: Groundbreaking Strategies for Parents. Linda S. Budd. Prentice Hall, 1990.

On children and stress

Stress and Your Child, a Parent's Guide to Symptoms, Strategies and Benefits. Ruth Arent. W. Gladden, 1994.

Teenage Stress. Charmaine Saunders. S. Milner/Sterling, 1993.

Stress and Your Child: Its Causes, Dangers and Prevention. Archibald D. Hart. Word, 1992.

Helping Kids Cope: A Parents' Guide to Stress Management. Arnold Burron. Chariot Family, 1992.

Helping Your Kids Handle Stress. H. Norman Wright. Here's Life, 1990.

On stress, for teens

Stress Stoppers: For Children and Adolescents. W. Gladden, 1994.

What, Me Worry? How to Hang in When Your Problems Stress You Out. Alice Fleming. Scribner's, 1992.

Teenage Stress. Daniel Cohen and Susan Cohen. Dell, 1992.

On children and peer pressure

Helping Children Handle Peer Pressure. Alan Dubro. Bureau for At-Risk Youth, 1992.

On peer pressure, for preteens and teens

Who Are My Real Friends? Peer Pressure: A Teen Survival Guide. Joe White. Questar, 1992.

Everything You Need to Know about Peer Pressure. Robyn M. Feller. Rosen, 1993.

On general emotional concerns

Words Every Child Must Hear: Emotional Nourishment for Children of All Ages. Cynthia Good. Longstreet, 1994.

Touchpoints—the Essential Reference: Your Child's Emotional and Behavioral Development. T. Berry Brazelton. Addison-Wesley, 1994.

The Emotional Problems of Normal Children: How Parents Can Understand and Help. Stanley K. Turecki and Sarah Wernick. Bantam, 1994.

Fifty Two Ways to Help Your Kids Deal with Fear and Feel Secure. Jan Dargatz. Nelson, 1994.

All My Feelings Are OK: An Innovative Program Using Stories, Skits, and Games to Help Families Identify and Express Their Feelings. Linda Kondracki. Revell, 1993.

The Anxious Parent. Michael Schwartzman with Judith Sachs. Simon & Schuster, 1990.

On parenting troubled children

Is Your Teenager Out of Control?: The Little Book of Solutions. Linda W. Friedman and Harry H. Friedman. Sulzburger and Graham, 1994.

Good Kids—Bad Habits. Charles E. Schaefer and Theresa F. DiGeronimo. Crown, 1993.

Leave Me Alone!: Helping Your Troubled Teenager. Belinda T. Mooney. McGraw-Hill, 1992.

When Love Is Not Enough: Parenting Through Tough Times. Stephen Arterburn and Jim Burns. Focus on the Family, 1992.

Smart Kids, Stupid Choices. Kevin Leman. Dell, 1992.

The Lost Child: Hope for Kids Without Hope. Tom Collins. Deaconess, 1992.

Coping with Angry, Acting-Out Children. Alan Dubro. Bureau for At-Risk Youth, 1992.

When Good Kids Do Bad Things: A Survival Guide for Parents. Katherine Gordy Levine. Norton, 1991.

Managing Behavior Problems in Children: A Guide for Parents. Reeta Peshawaria. S. Asia, 1991.

How to Find Help for a Troubled Kid: A Parent's Guide to Programs and Services for Adolescents. John Reaves and James B. Austin. HarperCollins, 1990.

Preventing Adolescent Relapse, a Guide for Parents, Teachers, and Counselors. Tammy L. Bell. Herald House, 1990.

On handling family problems

Who's in Charge Here? Overcoming Power Struggles with Your Kids. Robert G. Barnes, Jr. Word, 1990.

A Guide to a Happier Family: Overcoming the Anger, Frustration, and Boredom that Destroy Family Life. Andrew Schwebel and others. Tarcher, 1990.

When Parents Love Too Much: What Happens When Parents Won't Let Go. Laurie Asher and Mitch Meyerson. Morrow, 1990.

Fixing Your Frazzled Family. Dean Feldmeyer. Group Publishing, 1990.

The Co-Dependent Parent: A Recovery Program to Help You Stop Enabling Your Child's Worst Behavior. Barbara Cottman Becnel. Lowell House/Contemporary, 1990.

Adult Children Raising Children: Ending the Cycle of Co-Dependency for Your Children. Randy Rolfe. Health Communications, 1990.

For children, on family and social problems

What Should I Tell the Kids?: A Parent's Guide to Real Problems in the Real World. Ava L. Siegler. NAL-Dutton, 1993.

Knowing Where the Fountains Are: The Lives of Homeless Youth. Kevin Cwayna. Deaconess, 1993.

Changing Places: A Kid's View of Shelter Living. Margie Chalofsky. Gryphon, 1992.

Talking with Your Child about a Troubled World. Lynne S. Duman. Fawcett, 1992.

Place I Call Home: Faces and Voices of Homeless Teens. Lois Stavsky. Shapolsky, 1992.

I Cried, You Didn't Listen: The Story of Incarcerated Children. Dwight E. Abbott and Jack Carter. Feral House, 1991.

Tough Questions: Talking Straight with Your Kids About the Real World. Sheila Kitzinger and Celia Kitzinger. Harvard Common, 1991.

Raising an Earth Friendly Child: The Keys to Your Child's Happy, Healthy Future, Level 1. Debbie J. Tilsworth. Raven Press, 1991.

A Parent's Guide to Teens and Cults. Richard Altesman and Larry E. Dumont. PIA Press, 1990.

For preteens and teens, on family or social problems

The American Family: Can It Survive? Karen Bornemann Spies. Twenty-First Century Books, 1995.

Everything You Need to Know About Living in a Shelter. Julie Parker, 1995.

I Am Who I Am: Speaking Out about Multiracial Identity. Kathlyn Gay. Watts, 1995.

Everything You Need to Know About Being a Biracial/Biethnic Teen. Renea D. Nash. Rosen, 1995.

Erik Is Homeless. Keith E. Greenberg. Lerner, 1992.

When Andy's Father Went to Prison. Martha Whitmore Hickman. Whitman, 1990.

Cults. Sarah Stevens. Crestwood/Macmillan, 1992.

The Homeless. Laurie Beckelman. Crestwood, 1990.

On children's legal rights

The Best Interests of the Child. Philip Alston, ed. Oxford University Press, 1994.

Children's Rights. Lewis B. Sckolnick. Rector Press, 1994.

Teen Legal Rights: A Guide for the 90s. Kathleen A. Hempelman. Greenwood, 1994.

Kids, the Law, and You: Understanding and Using the Legal System to Protect Our Children. Robert C. Waters. Self-Counsel Press, 1994.

Nameless Persons: Legal Discrimination Against Non-Marital Children in the United States. Martha T. Zingo and Kevin E. Early. Greenwood, 1994.

Kids and the Law: A Parent's Guide. John Gilchrist. Pro Se, 1990.

Under Eighteen: Knowing Your Rights. Michael Kronenwetter. Enslow, 1993.

As a Child: Safeguarding Children's Rights. Elizabeth D. Shetina. Rourke, 1992.

Children, Rights, and the Law. Philip Alston and others, eds. Oxford University Press, 1992.

In Their Best Interest?: The Case Against Equal Rights for Children. Laura M. Purdy. Cornell University Press, 1992.

On other parenting concerns

Coping with Teen Gambling. Jane Haubrich-Casperson and Doug Van Nispen. Rosen, 1993.

Hey, Mom, I'm Home Again!: Strategies for Parents and Grown Children Who Live Together. Monica L. O'Kane. Marlor, 1992.

Helping Children Cope with Change. Barbara Y. Wollman and Ron Kerner. Bureau for At-Risk Youth, 1992.

Spoiled Rotten: Today's Children and How to Change Them. Fred G. Gosman. Villard, 1992.

Who's Calling the Shots? How to Respond Effectively to Children's Fascination with War Play and War Toys. Nancy Carlsson-Paige and Diane Levin. New Society, 1990.

For parents of teen parents

You Can Help Pregnant and Parenting Teens. Jeanne W. Lindsay. Morning Glory, 1993.

For teen parents

Teenage Couples—Coping with Reality: Handling Money, In-Laws, Babies and Other Details of Daily Life. Jeanne W. Lindsay. Morning Glory, 1995.

Young, Poor, and Pregnant: The Psychology of Teenage Motherhood. Judith S. Musick. Yale University Press, 1993.

Coping with Teen Parenting, rev. ed. Kay Beyer. Rosen, 1992.

Coping with Teenage Motherhood. Carolyn Simpson. Rosen, 1992.

Teenage Parents. John Glore. Rourke, 1990.

"Teens Parenting" series. Includes: *Your Pregnancy and Newborn Journey: How to Take Care of Yourself and Your Newborn When You're a Pregnant Teen.* Jeanne W. Lindsay and Jean Brunelli. 1991; *Discipline from Birth to Three: How to Prevent and Deal with Discipline Problems with Babies and Toddlers.* Jeanne W. Lindsay and Sally McCullough. *The Challenge of Toddlers: Parenting Your Child from One to Three.* Jeanne W. Lindsay. 1991. *Your Baby's First Year: A How-to-Parent Book Especially for Teenage Parents,* rev. ed. Jeanne W. Lindsay. Morning Glory, 1991.

For teen fathers

Everything You Need to Know about Teen Fatherhood. Eleanor Ayer. Rosen, 1993.

Teen Dads: Rights, Responsibilities and Joys. Jeanne W. Lindsay. Morning Glory, 1993.

Background works on teen parenting

Teen Mothers: Citizens or Dependents? Ruth Horowitz. University of Chicago Press, 1994.

When Children Want Children: An Inside Look at the Crisis of Teenage Parenthood. Leon Dash. Viking Penguin, 1990.

On parenting adolescents

Adolescence: The Survival Guide for Parents and Teenagers. Elizabeth Fenwick and Tony Smith. Dorling Kindersley, 1994.

Adolescence: Guiding Youth Through the Perilous Ordeal. Miller Newton. Norton, 1995.

Stop Treating Me Like a Kid: Everyday Parenting—the 10–13 Year Old. Robin Goldstein and Janet Gallant. Viking Penguin, 1994.

What Growing up Is All About: A Practical Guide to Help Parents Understand Children and Adolescents. Ann Vernon and Rahdi Al-Mabuk. Research Press, 1995.

Making Sense of Adolescence: How to Parent from the Heart. John Crudele and Dick Erickson. Liguori, 1995.

Coping with Your Adolescent. Larry Waldman. Hampton Roads, 1994.

Understanding Your Child From Birth to Sixteen. David Elkind. Allyn, 1994.

Getting Your Kids to Say "No" in the Nineties When You Said "Yes" in the Sixties. Victor Strasburger. Simon & Schuster, 1993.

Parenting Your Teenager in the Nineties. David Elkind. Modern Learning Press, 1993.

Safeguarding Your Teenager from the Dragons of Life: A Parent's Guide to the Adolescent Years. Bettie Youngs. Health Communications, 1993.

Just Say "No Car Keys": And Other Survival Tactics for Parents of Teenagers. Shelley Goldbloom. NAL-Dutton, 1993.

Teenagers Are Temporary. Charles L. Allen. Barbour, 1993.

How to Really Love Your Teenager, rev. ed. Ross Campbell. SP Publications, 1993.

What to Do until the Grownup Arrives: The Art and Science of Raising Teenagers. Joseph R. Novello. Hogrefe and Huber, 1993.

Keys to Parenting Your Teenager. Don H. Fontenelle. Barron's, 1992.

Parenting Teens with Love and Logic: Preparing Adolescents for Responsible Adulthood. Cline Foster and Jim Fay. Pinon Press, 1992.

The No-Nonsense Parents' Guide: What You Can Do about Teens and Alcohol, Drugs, Sex, Eating Disorders and Depression. Sheila Fuller and others. Parents Pipeline, 1992.

Surviving Your Adolescents: How to Manage and Let Go of Your 13 to 18 Year Olds, rev. ed. Thomas W. Phelan. Child Management, 1992.

What Teenagers Want to Know. Shideler Harpe and Wesley W. Hall. Budlong, 1992.

Parenting Teens, rev. ed. Bruce Narramore and Vern Lewis. Tyndale, 1992.

Don't Be Taken Hostage: A Workbook to Help You Survive Your Adolescent. John Jensen. Professional Resources, 1991.

Raising Responsible Teenagers. Tom Tozer. Group Publishing, 1991.

Crisis-Proof Your Teenager: How to Recognize, Prevent, and Deal with Risky Adolescent Behavior. Kathleen McCoy. Bantam, 1991.

Caring for Your Adolescent: Ages 12–21. American Academy of Pediatrics Staff; Donald E. Greydanus, ed. American Academy of Pediatrics/Bantam, 1991.

Teen Is a Four-Letter Word: A Survival Kit for Parents, 2nd ed. Joan Wester Anderson. Betterway, 1990.

You and Your Adolescent: A Parent's Guide for Ages 12 to 20. Laurence Steinberg and Ann Levine. Harper & Row, 1990.

You Can Say No to Your Teenager: And Other Strategies for Effective Parenting in the 1990's. Jeannette Shalov and others. Addison-Wesley, 1990.

Your Ten to Fourteen Year Old. Louise Bates Ames and others. Delacorte, 1988.

On the parent-adolescent relationship

Anticipating Adolescence: How to Cope with Your Child's Emotional Upheaval and Forge a New Relationship Together. H. Paul Gabriel and Robert Wool. Henry Holt, 1995.

How to Live with Your Kids When You've Already Lost Your Mind. Ken Davis. Zondervan, 1992. By the author of *How to Live with Your Parents Without Losing Your Mind* (1988).

Decoding Your Teenager: How to Understand Each Other During the Turbulent Years. Michael Desisto. Morrow, 1991.

"Get Out of My Life, but First Could You Drive Me and Cheryl to the Mall?" A Parent's Guide to the New Teenager. Anthony E. Wolf. Farrar/Noonday, 1991.

Parent-Teen Breakthrough: The Relationship Approach. Mira Kirshenbaum and Charles Foster. NAL-Dutton, 1991.

Teenagers and Parents: Ten Steps for a Better Relationship. Roger McIntire and Carol McIntire. Human Resources Development Press, 1991.

Story Power: Talking with Teens in Turbulent Times. John Alston and Brenda Richardson. Longmeadow, 1991.

I'm On Your Side: Resolving Conflict Between Parents and Teenagers. Jane Nelsen and Lynn Lott. Prima, 1990.

For teens, on the parent-adolescent relationship

Bringing up Parents, the Teenager's Handbook. Alex J. Packer. W. Gladden, 1994.

If You Print This, Please Don't Use My Name: Questions from Teens and Their Parents about Things That Matter. Nancy Keltner. Terra Nova, 1992.

Please Don't Tell My Parents. Dawson McAllister. Word, 1992. Explores "questions parents never hear from their kids."

Coping with Family Expectations. Margaret Hill. Rosen, 1990.

Coping with Overprotective Parents. Margot Webb. Rosen, 1990.

Straight Talk about Parents. Elizabeth A. Ryan. Facts on File, 1990.

The Emotional Incest Syndrome: What to Do When a Parent's Love Controls Your Life. Patricia Love with Jo Robinson. Bantam, 1990.

Adolescence: A Guide for Teenagers and Their Parents. Joel Engel. Tor, 1990.

For parents, on specific adolescent concerns

Adolescents and Their Music: If It's Too Loud, You're Too Old. Jonathon S. Epstein, ed. Garland, 1994.

A Parent's Guide to Coping with Adolescent Friendships: The Three Musketeer Phenomenon. M.C. Gore Camerer. C.C. Thomas, 1994.

The Teenage Book of Manners...Please!. Fred Hartley and family. Barbour, 1991. A book of practical advice.

General works on adolescence

Adolescence. Louise Kaplan. Simon & Schuster, 1995.

Surviving Adolescence. Larry Dumont. Random House, 1993.

Preparing for Adolescence. James C. Dobson. Tyndale, 1992.

Adolescence Is Not an Illness. Bruce Narramore. Revell, 1991.

Teens: A Fresh Look. Anne Pedersen and *Mothering* Magazine Staff. John Muir, 1991.

Teenage Pros and Cons. Matilda M. Naputi. Carlton, 1990.

For teens, on adolescence in general

Finding Our Way: The Teen Girls' Survival Guide. Allison Abner and Linda Villarosa. HarperCollins, 1995.

Adolescent Rights: Are Young People Equal under the Law. Keith Greenberg. Twenty-First Century Books, 1995.

Teenage Survival Manual: How to Reach '20' in One Piece (and Enjoy Every Step of the Journey), 4th ed. H. Samm Coombs. D.B. Inc., 1993.

Feeling Great: Reaching Out to the World, Reaching in to Yourself—Without Drugs, 2nd ed. Nancy S. Levinson and Joanne Rocklin. Hunter House, 1992.

Don't Check Your Brains at the Door. Josh McDowell and Bob Hostetler. Word, 1992.

Adolescence. Nicholas Tucker. Raintree Steck-Vaughn, 1991.

But You Don't Understand, rev. ed. Paul Borthwick. Nelson, 1991.

You and Your Family: A Survival Guide for Adolescence. You and Stress: A Survival Guide for Adolescence. You and School: A Survival Guide for Adolescence. Gail C. Roberts and others. Free Spirit, 1990.

Adolescence. Rebecca Stefoff. Chelsea House, 1990.

Surviving Adolescence: Or Growing up Oughta Be Easier Than This. Jim Burns. Word, 1990.

For teens, on social concerns

But Everyone Else Looks So Sure of Themselves: A Guide to Surviving the Teen Years. Denise V. Lang. Betterway, 1991.

Tips for Teens: Telephone Tactics, Petting Practices, and Other Milestones on the Road to Popularity. Benjamin Darling. Chronicle Books, 1994.

Social Savvy: A Teenager's Guide to Feeling Confident in Any Situation. Judith Ré with Meg Schneider. Summit, 1991.

Guys and Girls: Understanding Each Other. Linda Snyder. Group, 1991.

For teens, on preparing for independent living

The String on a Roast Won't Catch Fire in the Oven: An A-Z Encyclopedia of Common Sense for the Newly Independent Young Adult. Candice Kohl. Gylantic, 1993.

"Lifeskills Library," including *Setting Goals, Independent Living, Shopping Savvy, The World of Work, Great Grooming for Guys, Great Grooming for Girls, Staying Healthy,* and *Money Smarts.* Rosen Publishing, 1992.

Surviving after High School: Overcoming Life's Hurdles. Arthur J. Heine. J-Mart Press, 1991.

The Teenage Liberation Handbook: How to Quit School and Get a Real Life and Education. Grace Llewellyn. Lowry House, 1991.

On family history

Tracing, Charting and Writing Your Family History, rev. ed. Lois M. Skalka. Pilot Books, 1994.

Genealogy in the Computer Age: Understanding FamilySearch (Ancestral File, International Genealogical Index, Social Security Death Index), rev. ed. Elizabeth L. Nichols. Family History Education, 1994.

Genealogy Online: Researching Your Roots. Elizabeth P. Crowe. McGraw-Hill, 1994. With computer disk.

The Genealogist's Companion: Modern Methods for Researching Family History. Raymond S. Wright, III. ALA, 1994.

Parenthood Is Your Greatest Achievement: An Interactive Family, Education and Genealogical Resource Book and Diary. Benjamin A. Benson. Partners Education, 1993.

The Genealogist's Companion and Sourcebook. Emily A. Croom. Betterway, 1994. A companion to Croom's *Unpuzzling Your Past: A Basic Guide to Genealogy* (1989).

Writing the Family Narrative Workbook. Lawrence P. Gouldrup. Ancestry, 1993.
Roots Illustrated: How to Bring Your Family Tree to Life. Anne P. Dee. Juneberry, 1993.
Getting a Quick Start up Your Family Tree. How to Survive the Genealogy Bug Without Going Broke. Nancy E. Carlberg. Carlberg, 1993.
Record and Remember: Tracing Your Roots Through Oral History. Jane Lewit. Madison Books, 1993.
Family Tree and Book of Remembrance. Joseph R. Harris. Family Print, 1992.
The Oxford Guide to Family History. David Hey. Oxford University Press, 1993.
Lifelines: A New Way to Trace Your Family Tree and Discover Unknown Relatives. Noel M. Elliot. Firefly, 1992.
Your Self As History: Family History and Its Effect on Your Personality: A Research Guide. Valentine R. Winsey. Pace University Press, 1992.
In Search of Family History: A Starting Place. Paul Drake. Heritage, 1992.
Genealogy Quest: Tracing Your Family Tree. Elaine B. Bailey and James D. Griffin, Jr. J-Laina, 1991.
Unravelling Tangled Family Ties: A Guide for Amateur Genealogists. Marjorie Wolf. Carlton, 1992.
Researching Your Family and Heritage. Marilyn Lind. Linden Tree, 1991.
Secrets of Your Family Tree. Dave Carder. Moody, 1991.
Family History Is Fun. Billy L. Latta, ed. Ye Olde Genealogie Shoppe, 1992.
Tracing, Charting and Writing Your Family History, rev. ed. Lois M. Skalka. Pilot, 1991.
Genealogy Is More Than Charts. Lorna D. Smith. LifeTimes, 1991.

For children, on family history

Where in the World Did You Come From? Paul Nichols. Boyer-Caswell, 1993.
The Family Tree: A Family History Book. Elizabeth Ward and Neil Kagan, eds. Time Life, 1993.
My African Roots: A Child's Create Your Own Keepsake Book of Family History and African-Awareness. Jacqueline Galloway-Blake. Brown Sugar and Spice, 1992.
My Family History. Nancy Burgeson. Troll, 1992.
My First Family Tree Book. Catherine Bruzzone. Hambleton-Hill, 1992.
Kinship: It's All Relative. Jackie S. Arnold. Genealogical Publishing, 1991.
Do People Grow on Family Trees?: Genealogy for Kids and Other Beginners. Ira Wolfman. Workman, 1991.
My Family 'Tis of Thee: The Official Ellis Island Book of Genealogy for Kids. Ira Wolfman. Workman, 1990.

(See also GENETIC INHERITANCE.)

Background works on parenting

On Becoming a Family: The Growth of Attachment Before and After Birth, rev. ed. T. Berry Brazelton. Delacorte, 1992.
When Partners Become Parents: The Big Life Change for Couples. Carolyn Pape Cowan and Philip A. Cowan. Basic Books, 1992.
Taking Sides: Clashing Views on Controversial Issues in Family and Personal Relationships. Gloria Bird and Michael Sporakowski. Dushkin, 1992.
The Encyclopedia of Marriage, Divorce and Family. Margaret DiCanio. Facts on File, 1989.

(See also FATHER; MOTHER; DIVORCE; GRANDPARENTS'S RIGHTS; CUSTODY; CHILD SUPPORT; ADOLESCENCE.)

Help on Learning and Education

Choosing a School for Your Child

THINKING ABOUT YOUR CHILD AND YOUR FAMILY

Start your search for the best school by thinking about what you want a school to do for your child. After all, you know your son or daughter better than anyone else does.

First, think about your child's personality. What is the youngster like? Children who thrive on exploration and responsibility might flourish in an open school or an alternative school. Other students fare better in a traditional school, with closer direction and supervision from the teachers. Both kinds of schools can provide a rich curriculum and a firm foundation; the choice should depend on which situation your child will respond to better.

Another factor is your child's school experience to date. A child who is bored in school may need more challenging work. If your child has had difficulty keeping up, you will want a school with a strong commitment to helping every student learn. The best schools will build on your child's academic strengths and be able to help with any academic difficulties.

How does your child respond to large and small groups? Some youngsters might "fall through the cracks" in a large school; some students do best in the more intimate atmosphere of a small school. Other students can gain from attending a larger school, which can offer a program closely tailored to their needs.

Collecting Information on Available Schools

If you were looking at cars, vacuum cleaners, or refrigerators, you could quickly find information in consumer magazines and other published resources. Investigating schools is not quite so easy; you may have to make phone calls, collect written material from different schools, and look for reports in your local paper to get the information you need. The hard work will be worth your while if you find a school that brings out the best in your child.

If possible, start your investigation a year before you want your child to enroll at a new school. It may take some time to find schools that suit your needs; you will want to obtain written information, visit those schools, make a final choice, and have time to get your child admitted for the fall. Some schools stop accepting applications as early as January or February.

You will certainly want to know what the school will teach your child. Does it give enough focus to the basics? Is the curriculum enriched with any special programs that would be good for your child?

Some schools may emphasize specific subjects. Schools of choice are especially likely to stress a special field or topic, such as math and science, performing arts, international commerce, or communications. Religious teaching and moral development are likely to be a part of the focus in church-affiliated schools, and some private schools may provide extra study of the ethnic heritage shared by many of their students.

If a school has a special focus in its curriculum, you should check to be sure that other core subjects and skills are being taught as well, too. Asking to see test scores may give you some information; reviewing the curriculum and visiting classes can also help.

School Philosophy

Schools differ in their philosophies. You will want to find out what beliefs guide a school's teaching. What kind of learning does it consider most important? How does it believe students can learn best?

Two schools may have different philosophies and both be excellent from some students. For example, a traditional or back-to-basics school will provide clear standards and structure for the child who needs them, while an open school may allow extra freedom for a child who can use it well.

Many large public school systems offer an alternative school for high school students who are likely to drop out or who have found the regular program unchallenging. Often these schools are deliberately small and informal; they encourage students to feel like "members" who belong to the school community rather than merely attending. Yet a more traditional school with formal classes and wider offerings can bring out the best in most students, provided that school has high standards, clear expectations, and a well-planned program.

Some schools can provide you with written statements of their philosophy. In others, you will have to ask the principal and teachers to describe their goals. Most importantly, visit the school and talk to parents to see if the school's philosophy is working well in practice.

Important School Policies

In addition, you will probably want to know about some other school policies.

1. *Discipline.* The existence of written rules and clear penalties is one sign that a school is working on discipline issues. When you visit the school, you may want to watch carefully to see if those rules are being enforced fairly and firmly.
2. *Homework.* Researchers have found that regular homework can significantly increase student achievement. Find out if the school requires homework and how frequently it is given. Ask if teachers check, grade, and return the homework on a regular basis. Some schools also have hotlines to teachers, after-school clinics, or tutoring programs ready to help kids succeed.
3. *Grades and Feedback.* You will want to know how students' work is judged and how often you will receive report cards on your child's progress. You may also want to ask how else the school gives students feedback on how they are doing and how they can improve. Are there programs to recognize children who do well in school? Are there regular policies for helping children who are having trouble?

Proof of Results

Once you know what a school is trying to do, ask for some indicators about whether it succeeds. Here are some factors you may want to investigate.

1. *Test Scores.* Ask for information on the school's scores over the last few years. The school district or the school should be able to provide these to you. If the scores have been going down in recent years, you will want to ask the school's principal why this is so.

   If you are told that a school's scores are above the national average, be careful. A recent research report pointed out that "no state is below average on any of the six major nationally normed, commercially available tests." In other words, every state, and most districts, may be able to show you test results showing that their schools are above average. How is this possible? It may be that education has improved since the "national averages" were determined, but it may also be that the test designers set the norms too low at the start or that schools are "teaching to the test."

   The principal should be willing to share information about test scores. If an administrator refuses to give you information about test results, think very carefully about placing your child in that school.
2. *Attendance rates.* Another important measure is attendance. Parents should ask about attendance of both students and teachers. A school with a more than 10-percent absence rate for either may have some serious problems.
3. *Turnover and Graduation Rates.* You may want to find out how stable the student body is: How many students leave the school in a year? How many of those move or transfer? How many drop out? For high schools, graduation rates provide one indication of whether schools are providing an education their students value. On the other hand, remember that a diploma alone does not tell you what those students learned; gather other information to tell you whether a school's graduates got a sound education while enrolled there.
4. *Postgraduation Activities.* Some schools conduct surveys to determine how many students find jobs, join the military, or seek postsecondary education. Generally, high schools in affluent areas have a high percentage of graduates attending colleges and universities. However, some urban schools in poor neighborhoods pride themselves on encouraging students to continue their formal education. You may want to pay special attention to a school that sends many graduates from less wealthy homes on to colleges, universities, and technical training and business schools.
5. *Special Achievements.* Has the school had special successes in recent years? A school you are considering may have received an award for excellence, initiated an important new program, or dramatically improved its students' achievement. Staff members may have been recognized for superior teaching. Successes like these tell you what a school does well, and they may also show that the principal, teachers, and families at that school work together for good education.

School Facilities

Research indicates that fancy facilities do not always lead to higher achievement. Be sure to bear this in mind when you look into a school's resources. But a library and classroom books are always important. Children need to read many good books in order to learn independently and build their reading skills; textbooks are not enough. If a school does not have a wide variety of interesting books readily available to its students, that is a serious weakness.

VISITING A SCHOOL

Be sure to visit any school before you finally decide to send your child there. Make an appointment before you visit, calling the principal's office or, if the school has one, the admissions office. You will want to tour the school during regular school hours. If possible, you will want to visit a few classes. To get a real feeling for how the school usually operates, avoid visiting during the first or last week of a school term.

You will also want some scheduled time to talk to the principal and some teachers about the school. Ask for an appointment that will let you do all these things. Attending an open house, PTA meeting, or other school function could also give you valuable information about the attitudes of staff, students, and parents.

Things to Look For

As you walk around a school or visit some classrooms, you should ask yourself questions like the following: Do I feel comfortable walking into the school? How do the adults talk to children? Are they friendly or harsh? Are the children clearly interested in what they are doing? Is the overall atmosphere one that allows students to work hard and learn? Do pupils seem to have opportunity for quiet reading as well as group activities? Are there some areas of the school or some classrooms the tour guide avoids? Does the school display examples of excellent student work? Is the building tidy and well maintained?

In general, schools where students do best are clean, orderly, pleasant places. Staff members in good schools respect each other, their students, and their parents. They speak enthusiastically of the children. Teachers are clearly interested in the subjects they teach. Students are friendly and respectful, and you can tell that they are busy learning. Parents should hesitate before placing children in schools that do not have these characteristics.

A visit also lets you double check some of the information you may have collected earlier. Does the library appear both well stocked and well used? Do the disciplinary rules you read about really seem to be enforced? Do any special programs you were interested in appear to be working well?

CHECKLIST

(Make a photocopy for each school you consider.)

In looking at available schools, you may want to use the checklist below as a guide. During your school visit, you can confirm what you heard or read earlier. Once you select a school, you will want to double check the admissions information you collected to make sure you meet all the requirements.

CURRICULUM	YES	NO
1. Thorough coverage of basic subjects?	☐	☐
If no, which subjects are not covered completely?		
2. A special focus or theme to the curriculum?	☐	☐
What is it?		
3. Elective offerings (if appropriate):		
4. Extracurricular programs to enhance learning and character development:		

PHILOSOPHY

	YES	NO
5. Emphasis on a particular approach to teaching and learning?	☐	☐
6. Belief that every child can learn?	☐	☐
7. Encouragement of attributes of good character?	☐	☐

IMPORTANT POLICIES

8. Discipline:

9. Drugs:

10. Homework: How much per subject?

	YES	NO
11. Homework hotlines?	☐	☐
12. Tutoring?	☐	☐
If yes, by whom?		

13. Grades, feedback, and recognition:
    How often?

    What type?

14. Teacher opportunities and incentives:

Proof of Results

15. Standardized test scores:
    Current   Past

16. Attendance rate:
    Students   Teachers

17. Graduation rate:

18. How many leave school in a year?

    Why?

19. Special achievements or honors for the school:

School Resources

20. Staff backgrounds and qualifications:

	YES	NO
21. Library?	☐	☐
22. Classroom books for independent reading?	☐	☐
23. Auditorium or other meeting room?	☐	☐
24. Physical education facilities? If yes, what type? If no, what alternatives?	☐	☐

Parent and Community Involvement

25. Parent volunteers in school? Doing what?	☐	☐
26. Teachers enlist parent cooperation on home learning? If yes, how?	☐	☐
27. Other community members involved in school?	☐	☐

28. Partnerships with local businesses or other institutions:

Reputation

29. Views of parents with children in the school:

30. Views of friends and neighbors:

31. Views of community leaders:

Special Questions for Private and Church-affiliated Schools

Financial obligations

32. Tuition $__________________
33. Other fees $__________________

	YES	NO
34. Uniforms?	☐	☐
35. Book purchases?	☐	☐
36. Required participation in fund-raising?	☐	☐

Financial assistance

37. Scholarships up to what percent of tuition?

38. Loans?	☐	☐
39. Reduced fees if more than one child enrolls?	☐	☐
40. State aid available to families?	☐	☐
41. Apply how and when?		

Other

42. School's age and financial status:

43. Religious instruction and activities:

Admissions Requirements and Procedures

For a public, church-affiliated, or other private school of choice

44. List of materials to submit (application form, transcript, test scores, references, etc.):

	YES	NO
45. Interview required?	☐	☐

Date:

Time:

46. Date school will decide:

47. How will school select students?

For other public schools

48. Borders of the attendance area the school usually serves:

49. Does state law give you a right to transfer your child to another public school?	☐	☐

50. Tuition or other charges for transferring students:

51. Facts considered important in deciding whether to grant a request for a transfer:

52. When will a decision be made on transfer requests?

53. Names of district officials who can permit a child to transfer to a school outside that child's attendance area:

Source: Choosing a School for Your Child (1989). Prepared by the U.S. Department of Education. (See original for fuller discussion.)

ORGANIZATIONS OFFERING HELP AND INFORMATION

On families in education

National Congress of Parents and Teachers (National PTA)
330 North Wabash Avenue, Suite 2100
Chicago, IL 60611–3690
312–670–6782
Fax: 312–670–6783
Internet website, Children First!: http://www.pta.org/
Microsoft Network (MSN), Children First!: Go Children
Joan Dykstra, President
Organization seeking to improve education, health, and safety of children; acts as advocate; publishes various materials, including *PTA Today*, quarterly *National PTA Directory*, newsletter *What's Happening in Washington*, and other materials on topics such as parent-school relations, single parents, latchkey children, alcohol and drug abuse prevention, absenteeism, teenage sexuality, discipline, seatbelts, and parent education.

Center for Law and Education
1875 Connecticut Avenue NW
Washington, DC 20009
202–986–3000
Fax: 202–986–6648
For publication orders:
197 Friend Street, 9th Floor
Boston, MA 02114
617–371–1166
Organization acting as advocate on education issues relating to low-income families; publishes numerous materials, many originally from the now-dissolved National Committee for Citizens in Education (NCCE), including:

- Quarterly *Newsnotes*.
- General works: *Identifying Parental and Student Education Rights in Your State, Public School Choice: An Equal Chance for All?, Beyond the Bake Sale: An Educator's Guide to Working with Parents, Parents and Dropout Prevention*, and *The Middle School Years: A Parents' Handbook.*
- "Information for Parents" brochures: *Parent Involvement, Parent/Teacher Conference, Education of Handicapped Children, Educational Rights of Children with Disabilities: A*

Primer for Advocates, Overview: Educational Rights of Children with Disabilities under the Individuals with Disabilities Education Act and Section 504 of the Rehabilitation Act of 1973, Obtaining Appropriate Educational Services for Three Through Five Year Old Children with Disabilities: An Outline of Selected Issues, and *The Rights of Students with Limited English.*

- *Parent Rights Card* and *Annual Education Checkup Card.*
- Numerous materials on family involvement, vocational education, local action, and education for low-income families and homeless students, such as *Effective Schools for Poor Children: A Parent Handbook, Planning for Title I Programs: Guidelines for Parents, Advocates and Educators, Beyond the Open Door: A Citizens' Guide to Increasing Public Access to Local School Boards, How to Run a School Board Campaign—and Win,* and *A Workbook on Parent Involvement for District Leaders.*
- Numerous materials on education of homeless students.

Alliance for Parental Involvement in Education (ALLPIE)
P.O. Box 59
East Chatham, NY 12060–0059
518–392–6900
E-mail: allpiesr@aol.com (America Online: ALLPIESR)
Catharine Houk, Executive Director
Organization of parents involved with their children's education, in public or private school, including alternative or special education and home schooling; maintains mail-order lending library; sponsors workshops; provides information and referrals; publishes various materials, including:

- Newsletters: *Options in Learning* (national) and *New York State Home Education News.*
- Leaflets: *What Does a Friends School Have to Offer?* (on Quaker education), *Your Home Is Your Child's First School,* and *Volunteering in the Schools.*
- General books: *Dumbing Us Down: The Hidden Curriculum of Compulsory Schooling, The Exhausted School: The First National Grassroots Speakout on the Right to School Choice, Alternatives in Education, The Magic Feather: The Truth About "Special Education," Unicorns Are Real: A Right-Brained Approach to Learning,* and *Learning All the Time: How Small Children Begin to Read, Write, Count, and Investigate the World, Without Being Taught.*
- For families: *Families Writing, Family Math, Psychology for Kids: 40 Fun Tests that Help You Learn About Your Self,* and *Sharing Nature with Children: The Classic Parents' and Teachers' Nature Awareness Guidebook.*

Home and School Institute (HSI)
1500 Massachusetts Ave. NW
Washington, DC 20005
202–466–3633; 800-MEGAUSA [634–2872]
Fax: 202–833–1400
Dorothy Rich, President
Organization stressing the importance of home and community in education; develops methods and materials to assist parents in helping children learn at home, using household items and activities to teach basic educational and coping skills; operates MegaSkills® Education Center and Workshops; publishes *MegaSkills® Survival Guide for Today's Parents* (book and audiocassettes), *Get Smart: Advice for Teens, Careers and Caring,* and *Job Success Begins at Home.*

Institute for Responsive Education (IRE)
605 Commonwealth Avenue
Boston, MA 02215
617–353–3309
Fax: 617–353–8444
Tony Wagner, President
Organization advocating increased citizen participation in schools and educational decision-making; provides information; publishes various materials, including magazine *Equity and Choice.*

Parents Without Partners (PWP), 800–637–7974. Publishes information sheet *Single Parents and the Schools* and *Rights of Noncustodial Parents to Examine School Records.* (For full group information, see GENERAL PARENTING RESOURCES on page 634.)

Parents Rights Organization (PRO)
12571 Northwinds Drive
St. Louis, MO 63146
Phone and fax: 314-434-4171
Mae Duggan, President
Organization supporting freedom of choice in education; aims to gain legal recognition for parents' rights to control their children's education; seeks to educate public and influence public policy; publishes various materials, including *Parents Rights Newsletter.*

ON EDUCATIONAL IMPROVEMENT

Association for Childhood Education International (ACEI)
11501 Georgia Avenue, Suite 315
Wheaton, MD 20902
301–942–2443; 800–423–3563
Fax: 301–942–3012
Gerald Odland, Executive Director
Organization focusing on sound education for children from birth through early adolescence; encourages professional growth for educators; publishes various materials, including:

- *Childhood Education* (five times a year) and semiannual *Journal of Research in Childhood Education.*
- Educational series for young children: *Kelly Bear Feelings, Kelly Bear Behavior, Kelly Bear Health, Kelly Bear Activities,* and *Kelly Bear Drug Awareness.*
- General books: *Selecting Educational Equipment and Materials for School and Home* and *Teachers and Parents:*

Together for Children's Benefit; and reprints *Are Schools Really for Kids?*, *The Physically Unattractive Child*, and *The Child's Rights to the Expressive Arts*.

- Books on early arts, science, and math education: *Learning from the Inside Out: A Guide to the Expressive Arts*, *Earthways: Simple Environmental Activities for Young Children*, *Mudpies to Magnets: A Preschool Science Curriculum*, and *Mathematics Is More Than Counting*.
- Audiotapes and other professional materials.

Council for Basic Education (CBE)
1319 F St. NW, Suite 900
Washington, DC 20004
202–347–4171
Fax: 202–347–5047
A. Graham Down, Executive Director
Organization supporting liberal arts education; publishes various materials, including quarterly *Basic Education: Issues, Answers, and Facts*.

National Association for Year-Round Education (NAYRE), 619–292–3679. (For full group information, see YEAR-ROUND EDUCATION.)

Creative Education Foundation (CEF)
1050 Union Road
Buffalo, NY 14224
716–675–3181
Fax: 716–675–3209
John W. Meyerhoff, Executive Vice President and CEO
Organization fostering creative thinking in all areas of life; provides training programs, including some for preteens and teens; publishes numerous materials, including monthly newsletter *Creativity in Action*, quarterly newsletter *In Perspective*, quarterly *Journal of Creative Behavior* (JCB), and a *Creativity Catalog* containing books, videos, audiotapes, and periodicals from many sources, such as *Awakening Your Child's Natural Genius: Enhancing Curiosity, Creativity and Learning Ability*, *The Growing Person: How to Encourage Healthy Emotional Development in Children*, *Teaching Creative Behavior: How to Evoke Creativity in Children of All Ages*, and *What Would Happen If I Said Yes?: A Guide to Creativity for Parents and Teachers*.

Twin Services, 510–524–0863. Publishes *Twins in School: Together or Apart* and *When Teachers Recommend Holding One Twin Back in School*. (For full group information, see MULTIPLE BIRTH.)

On Equity in Education

Educational Equity Concepts (EEC)
114 East 32 Street, Suite 701
New York, NY 10016
212–725–1803
Fax: 212–725–0947
E-mail: 75507.1306@compuserve.com (CompuServe: 75507,1306)
Organization seeking learning environments and activities that are free from bias, such as that based on gender, race, ethnicity, or disability; addresses special challenges faced by girls and women with disabilities; operates resource center; develops early childhood programs and early elementary hands-on science programs; publishes numerous materials, including:

- General materials: *Non-Sexist Education for Young Children*, and videos *Equity Works* (two parts).
- On science equity: *What Will Happen If... Young Children and the Scientific Method*, *Hands On to Science*, and *Playtime Is Science: Implementing a Parent-Child Activity Program*.
- On inclusion: *Including All of Us: An Early Childhood Curriculum About Disability*, *Mainstreaming for Equity: Activity and Resource Kits* (to be integrated into curriculum for grades K–6), *Women with Disabilities in Postsecondary Education*, *Women and Girls with Disabilities: An Introductory Teaching Packet*, and *Inclusive Materials Mini Kit*, including equity-oriented games, wheelchair acessibility symbols, Braille alphabet chart, and other materials.

A Better Chance (ABC)
419 Boylston Street
Boston, MA 02116
617 421–0950; 800–562–7865
Fax: 617–421–0965
Organization of private and some public secondary schools to provide educational opportunity for talented minority students; finds and selects students for placement in special secondary school programs, preparatory to selective colleges and universities; provides financial and technical aid.

American Association of University Women (AAUW)
1111 16 Street NW
Washington, DC 20036
202–785–7700; for publications: 800–225–9998
Fax: 202–872–1425
Anne Bryant, Executive Director
Organization concerned with general equity for women, including education, civil rights, work, and self-development; sponsors AAUW Educational Foundation, offering grants and fellowships; publishes quarterly *Outlook*; *Shortchanging Girls, Shortchanging America*; *Hostile Hallways: The AAUW Survey on Sexual Harassment in America's Schools*; *The AAUW Report: How Schools Shortchange Girls*; video *Girls Can!*; and numerous issue briefs.

NAACP Legal Defense and Educational Fund (LDF)
99 Hudson Street, 16th Floor
New York, NY 10013
212–219–1900
Elaine R. Jones, Director-Counsel

Arm of the National Association for the Advancement of Colored People (NAACP) using the law to fight discrimination in many areas, including education; finances court actions; seeks to influence public policy; publishes various materials, including newsletter and watchdog reports.

Project on Equal Education Rights (PEER)
1413 K Street NW, 9th Floor
Washington, DC 20005
202–332–7337
Leslie R. Wolfe, Director
Arm of National Organization of Women (NOW), seeking to eliminate sex discrimination in schools; provides information; sponsors programs about problems for minority and disabled girls and women, especially in computer and other technical training; publishes various materials, including newsletter *Equal Education Alert* and policy papers, such as *Sex Bias at the Computer Terminal—How Schools Program Girls, Learning Her Place—Sex Bias in the Elementary Classroom,* and *Black Women in a High Tech World.*

National Black Child Development Institute (NBCDI)
1023 15 St. NW, Suite 600
Washington, DC 20005
202–387–1281; 800–556–2234
Fax: 202–234–1738
Evelyn K. Moore, Executive Director
Organization acting as advocate for Black children, including those with disabilities; offers programs on curriculum, play schools, materials, and equipment; publishes various materials including newsletters *Black Child Advocate* and *Child Health Talk*; booklets *Giving Your Child a Good Start in School,* and "Spirit of Excellent: Each One, Reach One" manuals, handbooks, resource guides, and videotape.

Organization for Equal Education of the Sexes (OEES)
P.O. Box 438
Blue Hill, ME 04614
207–374–2489
Fax: 207–374–2890
Lucy Picco Simpson, Director
Organization seeking education equity; provides teaching resource packets, including *Teaching About Women in American History* and *Teaching About Women and Girls with Disabilities,* and multicultural materials on women, including those with disabilities.

Women's Action Alliance (WAA)
370 Lexington Avenue, Room 603
New York, NY 10017
212–532–8330
Fax: 212–779–2846
Karel R. Amaranth, Director
Organization fostering "self-determination for all women"; provides information and referrals; runs several model programs, such as Resource Mothers Project, Project TELL (on sexual abuse and harassment) and Sexual Harassment Resource and Referral network, and BEST: Buddies Exploring Science Together (on girls in science); publishes various materials, including *Beginning Equal: A Manual About Nonsexist Childrearing for Infants and Toddlers, Nonsexist Education for Young Children: A Practical Guide, Equal Their Chances: Children's Activities for Nonsexist Learning,* and *Children of Single Parents and the Schools*; and works on equity in the areas of computers, science, and technology.

ON EDUCATION FOR CHILDREN WITH SPECIAL NEEDS

PACER Center (Parent Advocacy Coalition for Educational Rights), 612–827–2966, voice/TT. Publishes *Parent's Questions: Is Retention a Good Idea?, Preparing for Life: A Manual for Parents on the Least Restrictive Environment—Questions and Answers, Coping with School, Purposeful Integration Inherently Equal, Integration in Action: Successful Programs Based on Careful Planning and Preparation, Length-of-School-Day Rules Explained, Physical Education: An Important Part of Special Education, When Billy Doesn't Do His Homework,* and *Opening Doors,* on inclusion. (For full group information, see HELP FOR SPECIAL CHILDREN on page 689.)

Council for Exceptional Children (CEC)
1920 Association Drive
Reston, VA 22091–1589
703–620–3660, voice/TT; 800–328–0272
Fax: 703–264–9494
Membership: 800–845–6232
Publications: 703–264–9446, TT; 800-CEC-READ [232–7323]
Fax: 703–264–1637
Nancy Safer, Interim Executive Director
Organization concerned with children with disabilities and gifted children; offers training; maintains Exceptional Child Education Resources (ECER) database; operates information center that includes federally funded ERIC (Educational Resources Information Center) Clearinghouse on Disabilities and Gifted Education, ERIC/OSEP Special Project on research in special education, and National Clearinghouse for Professions in Special Education; also operates federally funded programs on gifted education and attention deficit disorder; publishes newsletter *CEC Today,* bimonthly *Exceptional Children* and quarterlies *Exceptional Child Education Resources* and *Teaching Exceptional Children*; general CEC publications also include:

- General works: *Preparing Children with Disabilities for School, Creating Schools for All Our Students: What 12 Schools Have to Say, Special Education Dropouts, Computer-Assisted Instruction for Students with Mild Handicaps, Issues and Options in Restructuring Schools and Special Education Programs, Beyond Drill and Practice:*

Expanding the Computer Mainstream, Hidden Youth: Dropouts from Special Education, Homeless and in Need of Special Education, and *How to Find Answers to Your Special Education Questions,* on searching in the ERIC (Educational Resources Information Center) database (see further in this list).

- On inclusion: *Regular Lives* and videos *Two Faces of Inclusion: The Concept and the Practice* and *Facing Inclusion Together.*
- Numerous materials on special education law, such as *P.L. 94–142, Section 504, and P.O. 99–457—Understanding What They Are and Are Not.*
- Numerous materials on language minorities and performance assessment, cooperative or collaborative teaching, and materials for special education teachers.
- "ERIC Basics" on how to use ERIC (see below, under "Public Resources") for research: *How to Use ERIC to Search Your Special Education Topic* and *Search Planning Worksheet and List of ERIC Clearinghouses.*

CEC maintains seventeen divisions, each focusing on an aspect of special education, maintaining its own programs, and publishing its own newsletters, journals, and books; these divisions include:

- Division for Research (CEC-DR), which publishes quarterly *Exceptionality* and triannual newsletter *Focus on Research.*
- Division on Career Development and Transition (DCDT), which publishes quarterly newsletter *DCDT Network,* semiannual *Career Development for Exceptional Individuals,* and other materials.
- CEC Pioneers Division (CEC-PD), which publishes triannual newsletter *Pioneers Press;* for longtime CEC members.
- Council of Administrators of Special Education (CASE), which publishes *CASE Newsletter* and semiannual *CASE IN POINT.*

(For other divisions, see COMMUNICATION SKILLS AND DISORDERS; EARLY INTERVENTION; EYE AND VISION PROBLEMS; GIFTED CHILD; LEARNING DISABILITIES; MENTAL DISORDERS; MENTAL RETARDATION; TESTS.)

National Information Center for Children and Youth with Disabilities (NICHCY), 800–695–0285, voice/TT. Publishes *Questions Often Asked About Special Education Services* (ages 3–21), *Education of Children and Youth with Special Needs: What Do the Laws Say?, Related Services for School-Aged Children with Disabilities, Promising Practices and Future Trends for Special Education,* and *Special Education and Related Services: Communicating Through Letter Writing.* (For full group information, see HELP FOR SPECIAL CHILDREN on page 689.)

The Arc, 817–261–6003. Publishes fact sheet *The Education of Students With Mental Retardation: Preparation for Life in the Community* and *Report Card to the Nation on Inclusion in Education of Students with Mental Retardation.* (For full group information, see MENTAL RETARDATION.)

National Association for Gifted Children (NAGC), 202–785–4268. Advises on curriculum development, counseling, and guidance; publishes *Some Thoughts on Acceleration, Smart Kids with School Problems: Things to Know and Ways to Help, Underachievement Syndrome, Directory of Special Schools/Programs,* and materials for educators. (For full group information, see GIFTED CHILD.)

National Federation of the Blind (NFB), 410–659–9314. Publishes *Focus on the Education of Blind Children, Competing on Terms of Equality as Blind Students, Education of the Handicapped Act (Public Law 94–142), Problems of Placement and Responsibility: Mainstreaming Revisited, Teaching Teachers About Civil Rights,* and *Literacy for the Blind at School and Work: A Panel Discussion.* (For full group information, see EYE AND VISION PROBLEMS.)

National Information Center on Deafness (NICD), 202–651–5051; 202–651–5052, TT. Publishes *Educating Deaf Children: An Introduction, Teacher's Activity Handbook,* and *Educating Deaf and Hard of Hearing Children: A Legal Perspective.* (For full group information, see EAR AND HEARING PROBLEMS.)

Autism Society of America (ASA), 800–328–8476. Publishes *Activities for Developing Pre-Skill Concepts in Children with Autism, Autism: Identification, Education, and Treatment, Preschool Issues in Autism, The Artistic Autistic, Some Interpersonal Social Skill Objectives and Teaching Strategies for People with Autism, Some Social Communication Skill Objectives and Teaching Strategies for People with Autism, Teaching Activities for Autistic Children,* and *Teaching Spontaneous Communication to Autistic and Communication Handicapped Children.* (For full group information, see AUTISM.)

Spina Bifida Association of America (SBAA), 800–621–3141. Publishes *Learning Among Children with Spina Bifida, Educational Issues among Children with Spina Bifida,* and *Parent/Teacher Packet.* (For full group information, see SPINA BIFIDA.)

Candlelighters Childhood Cancer Foundation (CCCF), 800–366–2223. Publishes *Educating the Child with Cancer.* (For full group information, see CANCER.)

American Juvenile Arthritis Organization (AJAO), Arthritis Foundation, 800–283–7800. Publishes *Educational Rights for Children with Arthritis: A Manual for Parents.* (For full group information, see ARTHRITIS).

Self-Help for Hard of Hearing People (SHHH), 301–657–2248; 301–657–2249, TT. Publishes *Our Forgotten Children: Hard of Hearing Pupils in Schools, A Personal Question for Education Excellence for a Hard of Hearing Child,* and *Teaching Hard of Hearing Students: Some Helpful Hints.* (For full group information, see EAR AND HEARING PROBLEMS.)

Hear You Are, Inc. (HYAI), 800–278–3277, voice/TT. Publishes *Otitis Media: Coping with the Effects in the Classroom, Early Communication Skills, Working with Children's Language, Working with Children's Phonology*, and *Activities and Ideas.* (For full group information, see EAR AND HEARING PROBLEMS.)

Center on Human Policy (CHP), 315–443–3851. Publishes information package *Resources on Inclusive Education.* (For full group information, see HELP FOR SPECIAL CHILDREN on page 689.)

National Center for Youth with Disabilities (NCYD), 800–333–6293. Publishes annotated bibliographies *Promoting Decision-Making Skills by Youth with Disabilities—Health, Educational, and Vocational Choices* and *Adolescents with Chronic Illnesses—Issues for School Personnel.* (For full group information, see HELP FOR SPECIAL CHILDREN on page 689.)

United Cerebral Palsy Association (UCPA), 800–872–5827. Publishes *Opening Doors: Strategies for Including All Students in Regular Education, Natural Supports in School, at Work, and in the Community for People with Severe Disabilities*, and *Connecting Students: A Guide to Thoughtful Friendship Facilitation for Educators and Families.* (For full group information, see CEREBRAL PALSY.)

Epilepsy Foundation of America (EFA), 800–332–1000. Publishes *Negotiating the Special Education Maze: A Guide for Parents and Teachers, School Planning for Children with Seizure Disorders* (book and video); and numerous materials for educating school and recreation personnel. (For full group information, see EPILEPSY.)

Alexander Graham Bell Association for the Deaf (AGBAD), 202–337–5220, voice/TT. Publishes *Negotiating the Special Education Maze: A Guide for Parents and Teachers.* (For full group information, see EAR AND HEARING PROBLEMS.)

National Mental Health Consumer Self-Help Clearinghouse, 800–553–4539. Publishes reprint packets on education, and on physical disability and mental illness. (For full group information, see MENTAL DISORDERS.)

Independent Living Research Utilization Program (ILRU), 713–520–0232. Publishes *Your Disabled Child's Right to a Free Education.* (For full group information, see HELP FOR SPECIAL CHILDREN on page 689.)

National Adoption Information Clearinghouse (NAIC), 301–231–6512. Publishes *Adoption and School Issues.* (For full group information, see ADOPTION.)

American Academy of Child and Adolescent Psychiatry (AACAP), 202–966–7300. Publishes information sheet *Children Who Won't Go to School.* (For full group information, see MENTAL DISORDERS.)

Child Welfare League of America (CWLA), 202–638–2952. Publishes *Evaluation Criteria for Special Education in Residential Schools.* (For full group information, see FOSTER CARE.)

On religion-based or value-oriented education

Character Education Institute
8918 Tesoro Drive, Suite 575
San Antonio, TX 78217–6153
210–829–1727; 800–284–0499
Fax: 210–829–1729
Louis J. Sanchez, Executive Director
Organization aiming to provide children basic values, through the Character Education Curriculum (CEC), a value-oriented, antiviolence, and drug abuse prevention program (pre-K–9); formerly American Institute for Character Education (AICE); trains and advises teachers; maintains library; publishes various materials, including quarterly *Character Accounts.*

National Association of Hebrew Day School PTAs
160 Broadway
New York, NY 10038
212–227–1000, ext. 115
Fax: 212–406–6934
E-mail: umesorah@aol.com (America Online: UMESORAH)
Joshua Fishman, Executive Vice-President
Organization of PTA associations of Hebrew elementary and secondary schools; publishes *Jewish Parent Connection.*

National Office of Catholic School Associations
3211 4 St. NE
Washington, DC 20017–1194
202–541–3009
Fax: 202–541–3390
Ken DuPre, Executive Director
Organization of Catholic parent groups and schools, an arm of National Catholic Educational Association; advises parents on at-home religious training and parents' rights in education; acts as advocate for government support of nonpublic schools; publishes quarterly *The Catholic Parent.*

On other special concerns

National Rural Education Association (NREA)
c/o Joseph T. Newlin, Executive Director
Office for Rural Education
230 Education Building
Colorado State University
Fort Collins, CO 80523–1588
970–491–7022
Fax: 970–491–1317
Organization concerned with education in rural and small schools; acts as advocate; encourages development of materials and programs for rural school children; publishes various materials, including quarterly *NREA News*, journal *The Rural Educator*, and *The Country Teacher.*

Lavender Families Resource Network, 206–325–2643, voice/TT. Publishes for educators *Diversity in Your Classroom: Tips for Teachers, Working with Lesbian and Gay Parents and Their Children, Penny's Question: "I Will Have a Child in My Class with Two Moms—What Do You Know About This?"*, and *A Complicated Bias.* (For full group information, see HOMOSEXUALITY.)

ON LEGAL CONCERNS

National Organization on Legal Problems of Education (NOLPE)
Southwest Plaza
3601 SW 29th Street, Suite 223
Topeka, KS 66614
913–273–3550
Fax: 913–273–2001
Robert M. Wagner, Executive Director
Organization serving as an information clearinghouse on law in the schools; publishes monthlies *NOLPE Notes* and *NOLPE School Law Reporters*; *Yearbook of Education Law*; books *Search and Seizure in the Public Schools, Pupil Transportation and the Law, Recent Developments in Public Education Law, A Legal Guide to Religion and Public Education,* and works on school and college administration; and NOLPE Case Citation Series, including *Pupil Issues, How Free Is Speech in Schools?*

National Association for Legal Support of Alternative Schools (NALSAS), 505–471–6928. (For full group information, see ALTERNATIVE SCHOOLS.)

Home School Legal Defense Association (HSDLA), 703–338–5600. (For full group information, see HOME SCHOOLING.)

Community Dispute Services (CDS)
140 West 51st Street, 9th Floor
New York, NY 10020
212–484–4000 (ask for CDS)
Fax: 212–765–4874
William Slate, President
Organization fostering use of mediation, arbitration, and fact-finding in community disputes, including those in schools; an arm of the American Arbitration Association; offers community training programs; provides neutral third parties, on request.

Children and Adults with Attention Deficit Disorder (CHADD), 305–587–3700. Publishes *Educational Rights of Children with ADD.* (For full group information, see ATTENTION DEFICIT HYPERACTIVITY DISORDER.)

National Alliance for the Mentally Ill (NAMI), 800–950–6264. Maintains online forum and libraries that cover children's educational rights. (For full group information, see MENTAL DISORDERS.)

PUBLIC RESOURCES

ERIC (Educational Resources Information Center)
Federally funded information system providing access to literature on schooling, education, and related topics, through 800 subscribing college and university libraries; special emphases covered under separate clearinghouses (see later in this entry). Abstracts of the more than 850,000 documents are available in university and many public libraries, and reprints of many articles can be obtained on paper or microfiche. The computer database is searchable by subject through subscribing libraries, through various commercial services, on CD-ROM, or online via the Internet. The clearinghouses and the main ways of accessing ERIC are:

ACCESS ERIC
Aspen Systems Corporation
1600 Research Boulevard
Rockville, MD 20850–4305
301–251–5264; 800-LET-ERIC [538–3742]
Fax: 301–251–5767
E-mail: acceric@inet.ed.gov

ERIC Processing and Reference Facility
1301 Piccard Drive, Suite 300
Rockville, MD 20850–4305
301–258–5500; 800–799–3742
Fax: 301–948–3695
E-mail: ericfac@inet.ed.gov

ERIC Document Reproduction Service (EDRS)
7420 Fullerton Road, Suite 110
Springfield, VA 22153–2852
703–440–1400; 800–443-ERIC [443–3742]
Fax: 703–440–1408
E-mail: edrs@gwuvm.gwu.edu

ERIC CLEARINGHOUSES:

Elementary and Early Childhood Education (PS)
University of Illinois, College of Education
805 West Pennsylvania Avenue
Urbana, IL 61801–4897
217–333–1386; 800–583–4135
Fax: 217–333–3767
E-mail: ericeece@ux1.cso.uiuc.edu

Disabilities and Gifted Education (EC)
Council for Exceptional Children
1920 Association Drive
Reston, VA 22091–1589
703–264–9474; 800–328–0272
Fax: 703–264–9494
E-mail: ericec@inet.ed.gov

Urban Education (UD)
Teachers College, Columbia University
Institute for Urban and Minority Education
Main Hall, Room 300, Box 40
525 West 120 Street
New York, NY 10027–9998
212–678–3433; 800–601–4868
Fax: 212–678–4048
E-mail: eric-cue@columbia.edus

Rural Education and Small Schools (RC)
Appalachia University
1031 Quarrier Street
P.O. Box 1348
Charleston, WV 25325–1348
304–347–0400; 800–624–9120
Fax: 304–347–0487
E-mail: u56e1@wvnvm.wwvnet.edu

Reading, English, and Communication (CS)
Indiana University
Smith Research Center, Suite 150
2805 East 10 Street
Bloomington, IN 47408–2698
812–855–5847; 800–759–4723
Fax: 812–855–4220
E-mail: ericcs@ucs.indiana.edu

Science, Mathematics, and Environmental Education (SE)
Ohio State University
1929 Kenny Road
Columbus, OH 43210–1080
614–292–6717; 800–276–0462
Fax: 614–292–0263
E-mail: ericse@osu.edu

Social Studies/Social Science Education (SO)
Indiana University
Social Studies Development Center
2805 East 10th Street, Suite 120
Bloomington, IN 47408–2698
812–855–3838; 800–266–3815
Fax: 812–855–0455
E-mail: ericso@ucs.indiana.edu

Languages and Linguistics (FL)
Center for Applied Linguistics
1118 22 Street NW
Washington, DC 20037–0037
202–429–9292; 800–276–9834
Fax: 202–659–5641
E-mail: eric@cal.org

Assessment and Evaluation (TM)
The Catholic University of America
209 O'Boyle Hall
Washington, DC 20064
202–319–5120; 800–464–3742
Fax: 202–319–6692
E-mail: eric_ae@cua.edu

Counseling and Student Services (CG)
ERIC/CASS, School of Education, Curry Building
University of North Carolina at Greensboro
Greensboro, NC 27412–5001
910–334–4114; 800–414–9769
Fax: 910–334–4116
E-mail: ericcass@iris.uncg.edu

Adult, Career, and Vocational Education (CE)
Ohio State University
Center on Education and Training for Employment
1900 Kenny Road
Columbus, OH 43210–1090
614–292–4353; 800–848–4815
Fax: 614–292–1260
E-mail: ericacve@magnus.acs.ohio-state.edu

Information and Technology (IR)
Syracuse University
4–194 Center for Science and Technology
Syracuse, NY 13244–4100315–443–3640;
800–464–9107
Fax: 315–443–5448
E-mail: eric@ericir.syr.edu
AskERIC (see later in this list): askeric@ericir.syr.edu

Teaching and Teacher Education (SP)
American Association of Colleges for Teacher Education
One Dupont Circle NW, Suite 610
Washington, DC 20036–1186
202–293–2450; 800–822–9229
Fax: 202–457–8095
E-mail: ericsp@inet.ed.gov

Community Colleges (JC)
3051 Moore Hall
University of California at Los Angeles (UCLA)
Los Angeles, CA 90024–1521
310–825–3931; 800–832–8256
Fax: 310–206–8095
E-mail: eeh3usc@mvs.oac.ucla.edu

Higher Education (HE)
George Washington Univesity
One Dupont Circle NW, Suite 630
Washington, DC 20036–1183
202–296–2597; 800–773–3742
Fax: 202–296–8379
E-mail: eriche@inet.ed.gov

Educational Management (EA)
University of Oregon
1787 Agate Street
Eugene, OR 97403–5207
503–346–5043; 800–438–8841
Fax: 503–346–2334
E-mail: ppiele@oregon.uoregon.edu

ONLINE ACCESS

ACCESS ERIC (America Online: ERIC), provides direct online access to the database (Location: Learning and Reference—Teacher's Information Network: Resource Pavilion).

AskERIC, an Internet-based question-and-answer service for parents and educators; answers to education-related questions are usually answered within 48 hours. AskERIC can be reached in various ways via Internet. For information, contact: E-mail: askeric@ericir.syr.edu

ERIC computer database can be searched through some libraries or, via the Internet, through the University of Saskatchewan. **ERIC Digests**, summaries of current education topics written by the ERIC clearinghouses, can be reached through the University of North Carolina's laUNCHpad. Contact AskERIC or other number above for more information.

ONLINE RESOURCES

Interactive Education Services (America Online: IES; Classes; Courses) Offers Academic Assistance Center for students, with regularly scheduled tutoring sessions on major academic subjects, including private sessions by appointment, and message boards providing group help at all hours. Special services include:

- Teacher Pager, which provides "nearly immediate" help.
- Exam Prep Center, which offers exam-taking tips, minilessons, and samples practice exams.
- Study Skills Service, which offers lessons on how to study, course content outlines, brochures for parents on helping their children learn, and information from the U.S. Department of Education.
- Academic Research Service provides help in locating references and information for papers and research projects.

IES also provides minicourses (generally eight weeks long) for people of all ages and a wide range of topics; some are self-study, while others include live, online lectures, message board and E-mail support, and libraries of supplementary materials. Subject-oriented meeting sites include The Bull Moose Tavern (on politics and history), The Afterwards Cafe (on arts and music), International House (on international culture and language; a different language is spoken every night and holidays are celebrated), and Coliseum 4.0 (offering educational contests, quizzes, and games).

Internet: K12Net Network of educational bulletin board systems (BBSs), allowing students, teachers, and parents internationally to discuss educational issues. gopher://woonext.dsrd.orul.gov/11/Docs/k12net

Internet: EDNET. Mailing list exploring the possibilities of education on the Internet. To subscribe, send this message "SUB Ednet [your first name] [your last name] to: gopher://ericir.syr.edu/00/askERIC/FullText/Lists/Messages/EDNET-List/README

Peterson's Education Center. Searchable information on colleges, programs (including summer programs), resources, college applications; includes e-mail addresses and a newsline. Internet address: http://www.petersons.com

ONLINE RESOURCES FOR PARENTS AND OTHER ADULTS

Parents' Information Network (America Online: PIN) Online forums and libraries include information on topics such as school choice, home schooling, study skills, educational television, gifted children, and special children; includes information from the U.S. Department of Education, as well as KidsNet. (For full information, see GENERAL PARENTING RESOURCES on page 634.)

College and Adult Students Forum (CompuServe: STUFOB). Provides meeting and discussion area for parents under "Parenting." (For full information, see COLLEGE.)

Education Forum (CompuServe: EDFORUM). Maintains discussions, conferences, and libraries for teachers, but may interest parents as well.

Association for Supervision and Curriculum Development (America Online: ASCD). Provides articles, research, and discussion areas on improving teaching, learning, curriculum, and school organization; for professionals and public.

Internet: Altlearn (Alternative Approaches to Learning). Provides discussion of learning strategies for all ages. To subscribe, send this message "SUB Altlearn [your first name] [your last name]" to: mailto:listserv@sjuvm.bitnet

National Alliance for the Mentally Ill Forum (America Online: NAMI). Online forum and libraries include children's educational rights. (For full group information, see MENTAL DISORDERS.)

ONLINE RESOURCES FOR CHILDREN AND TEENS

Homework Helper (Prodigy). Searchable database including contents of hundreds of books, magazines, newspapers, pictures, photographs, and maps. Note: As of this writing, available only for users of IBM-style PCs, not Macintosh users.

Kids Forum (CompuServe: STUPOC). Forum for children 12 and under, containing message areas, general discussions, libraries, and files on topics of current interest; provides separate chat places for very young children, older children, and preteens, allowing them to "talk" with kids their age from around the world.

Teens Forum (CompuServe: STUPOA). Forum for teenage students, containing chat places, message areas, general discussions, libraries, and files on topics of current interest.

KidsNet (America Online: PIN). Part of Parents' Information Network.

Internet: KIDLINK and KIDCAFE. Structured discussion group and forums (in different languages) for children aged 10–15 (read-only for others). gopher://kids/ccit/duq/edu

Internet: alt.kids-talk Usenet newsgroup for kids K–12. Subscribe through newsreader: news: alt.kids-talk

Internet: k12.chatjunior Usenet newsgroup for students K–8. Subscribe through newsreader: news:k12.chat.junior

Internet: k12.chatsenior Usenet newsgroup for high school students. Subscribe through newsreader: news:k12.chat.senior

Internet: Pen-pals. Monitored forum allowing children to correspond with each other. To subscribe, send E-mail message to: mailto:pen-pals@mainstream.com

College and Adult Students Forum (CompuServe: STUFOB). (For full information, see COLLEGE.)

ON SCIENCE AND MATH

Science/Math Forum (CompuServe: SCIENC), a meeting and discussion place for students, teachers, amateurs, and professionals; provides science update files in the Student's Library; encourages links to classrooms.

Internet: Chemistry Tutorial Information. Information for high school chemistry students, including text, data, pictures, and programs (Macintosh only). gopher://plaza.aarnet.edu.au@/micros/mac/umich/misc/chemistry/00index.txt

Internet: Sais-l (Science Awareness and Promotion). Forum for ideas on making science stimulating for students K–12. To subscribe, send this message: "SUB sais-l [your first name] [your last name] to: mailto:listserv@uub.ca

ON ARTS AND CULTURE

Foreign Languages Forum (CompuServe: FLEFO). Meeting and discussion place for people interested in foreign languages; maintains Student/Teachers section; allows students to communicate with others around the world.

Internet: The Human Languages Page. Provides international language resources, including dictionaries, spoken samples, and tutorials. http://www/willamette.edu/~tjones/Language-Page.html

OTHER RESOURCES

General works for parents

Your Child's Growing Mind: A Guide to Learning and Brain Development from Birth to Adolescence. Jane M. Healy. Doubleday, 1994.

Smart Questions on Child Education. D. Leeds. HarperCollins, 1994.

Your Child Is Smarter Than You Think. Wanda Draper. Macedon, 1993.

The Passionate Mind: Bringing Up an Intelligent and Creative Child. Michael Schulman. Free Press, 1991.

Your Baby's Mind. S.H. Jacob. Adams, 1991.

Learning All the Time. John Holt. Addison-Wesley, 1989.

You Are Your Child's First Teacher. Rahima Baldwin. Celestial Arts, 1989.

For parents as teachers of young children

Thirty Plus Games to Get Ready to Read: Teaching Kids at Home and in School. Toni S. Gould. Walker, 1994.

Helping Your Child to Learn. Gordon W. Green. Citadel/Carol, 1994.

Born to Fly: How to Discover and Encourage Your Child's Natural Gifts. Tom Black and Lynda R. Stephenson. Zondervan, 1994.

How to Teach Your Baby Math, 4th ed. Glenn Doman and Janet Doman. Avery, 1994.

Earth Child: Games, Stories, Experiments and Ideas about Living Lightly on Planet Earth, 2nd ed. Kathryn Sheehan and Mary Waidner. Council Oak Books, 1994.

A-B-C, 1–2–3: A Teacher–Parent *Resource for Teaching Beginning Concepts,* rev. ed. Sue Goldsmith. Incentive, 1993.

Age One—Part One: For Parents or Teachers of Children One Year of Age or Older. Solon W. McDonald. Vantage, 1993.

Science Everywhere: Opportunities for Very Young Children. Barbara Taylor. Harcourt Brace, 1993.

Snail Trails and Tadpole Tails: Nature Education for Young Children. Richard Cohen and others. Redleaf, 1993.

Family Learning: Help Your Child Love Learning Every Day. William F. Russell. Crown, 1993.

How to Make Your Child a Better Listener. How to Improve Your Child's Language and Thinking Skills. Florence Karnofsky and Trudy Weiss. Fearon Teacher Aids, 1993.

How to Maximize Your Child's Learning Ability: A Complete Guide to Choosing and Using the Best Games, Toys, Activities, Learning Aids. Lauren Bradway and Barbara A. Hill. Avery, 1993.

Head Start: Teach Your Toddler to Learn. Ken Adams. Seven Hills, 1993.

They Can but They Don't: Helping Students Overcome Work Inhibition. Jerome H. Bruns. Viking Penguin, 1993.

Understanding and Encouraging Your Child's Art: How to Enhance Confidence in Drawing, Ages 2–12. Mia Johnson. Lowell House, 1992.

Growing up Confident: How to Make Your Child's Early Years Learning Years. Melitta J. Cutright. Doubleday, 1992.

How to Multiply Your Baby's Intelligence. Glenn Doman. M. Evans, 1992.

The Giftedness in Your Child: Unlocking Every Child's Unique Talents, Strengths, and Potential. Rita Dunn and others. Wiley, 1992.

Growing Up Confident: How to Make Your Child's Early Years Learning Years. Melitte Cutright. Doubleday, 1992.

How to Develop Your Child's Intelligence: More Successful Adulthood by Providing More Adequate Childhood. G.N. Getman. VisionExtension, 1992.

How to Teach a Child to Learn. Anthony Coletta. Programs for Education, 1992.

How Your Child Is Smart: A Life-Changing Approach to Learning. Dawna Markova and Anne Powell. Conari, 1992.

Is Your Bed Still There When You Close the Door?...And Other Playful Ponderings. Jane M. Healy. Doubleday, 1992.

Teaching Children to Think: New Strategies for Parents and Teachers. David Perkins. Free Press, 1992.

Games for Learning: Ten Minutes a Day to Help Your Child Do Well in School—from Kindergarten to Third Grade. Peggy Kaye. Farrar, Straus & Giroux, 1991. By the author of *Games for Reading: Playful Ways to Help Your Child Read* (1984), and *Games for Math: Playful Ways to Help Your Child Do Math* (1988).

Awakening Your Child's Natural Genius: Enhancing Curiosity, Creativity and Learning Ability. Thomas Armstrong. Tarcher, 1991.

Raising Wise Children: How to Teach Your Child to Think. Carolyn Kohlenberger and Noel Wescombe. Multnomah, 1990.

(See also PRESCHOOL; also GENERAL PARENTING RESOURCES on page 634, under "Activities for babies" and "Activities for preschoolers.")

GENERAL GUIDES TO SCHOOL-BASED EDUCATION

Parents' Public School Handbook. Kenneth Shore. Simon & Schuster, 1994.

Parent Education: Parents As Partners. Dorothy Knopper. Open Space, 1994.

Planning for Your Child's Future: A Guide to Preserving Educational Choices After High School for Parents of Middle and Elementary School Students. Jim Montague. College Board, 1994.

Choosing Schools and Child Care Options: Answering Parents' Questions. Nancy H. Phillips. C.C. Thomas, 1994.

Your Public Schools: What You Can Do to Help Them. Barbara J. Hansen and Philip English Mackey. Catbird Press, 1993.

Survival Kit for Teachers and Parents, 2nd ed. Myrtle T. Collins and Susan J. Benjamin. Good Year Books, 1993.

School Years. Julie Karen. Longmeadow, 1993.

Raising Funds for Your Child's School: Over Sixty Great Ideas for Parents and Teachers. Cynthia F. Gensheimer. Walker, 1993.

A Parent's Guide to Innovative Education: Working with Teachers, Schools, and Your Children for Real Learning. Anne W. Dodd. Noble Press, 1992.

Tracking Your School's Success: A Guide to Sensible Evaluation. Joan L. Herman and Lynn Winters. Corwin, 1992.

Sense and Nonsense about Hothouse Children: A Practical Guide for Parents and Teachers. Michael J. Howe. Paul and Co., 1992.

Get Your Child the Best Possible Education at No Cost to You: A Parent's Manual. Dick Amann. Program Studies, 1992.

Helping Parents Cope with the Bewildering World of Public Schools. Bill Sanders. Wynwood, 1992. Stresses "Judeo-Christian values."

The School Book: Everything Parents Must Know about Their Child's Education, from Preschool through Eighth Grade. Mary Susan Miller. St. Martin's, 1991.

Erasing the Guilt: Play an Active Role in Your Child's Education No Matter How Busy You Are. Nancy S. Haug and Nancy D. Wright. Career Press, 1991.

How to Get the Best Public School Education for Your Child: A Parents Guide for the Nineties. Carol A. Ryan and others. Walker, 1991.

The National PTA Talks to Parents: How to Get the Best Education for Your Child. Melitta J. Cutright. Delacorte, 1989.

(See also CHOOSING A SCHOOL FOR YOUR CHILD on page 659.)

ON TEACHING CHILDREN STUDY SKILLS

How to Develop Your Child's Gifts and Talents Through the Elementary Years: A Gifted and Talented Book. Raelynne P. Rein and Rachel Rein. Lowell House, 1994.

The Active Learner. Carl B. Smith, ed. (1994) *The Confident Learner: Help Your Child Succeed in School.* Marjorie R. Simic and others. *The Curious Learner: Help Your Child Develop Academic and Creative Skills.* Margorie R. Simic. (1992) Grayson Bernard.

Starting Your Child on the Computer: A Guidebook for Parents and Teachers. Peter Silton. N.P. Financial Systems, 1994.

Teaching Tips for Parents. Stan Bippus. Applied Resources, 1993.

Helping Your Child Succeed in Public School. Cheri Fuller. Focus on the Family, 1993.

The Parent's Guide—Studying Made Easy: A Practical Step by Step Guide for Parents, to Study Skills That Work. Barbara Keller and Ray Keller. Eagles, 1993. Paperback and multimedia program.

Helping Your Child Succeed in School: With Activities for Children Aged 5 Through 11. Dorothy Rich. Diane, 1993.
How to Help Your Child Become an Excellent Student Today: A Guide for Parents. Linda M. Schroeder. Gratitude, 1993.
Active Learning: A Parent's Guide to Helping Your Teen Make the Grade in School. Peter D. Lenn. Viking Penguin, 1993.
Arrows Swift and Far: Guiding Your Child Through School. Nancy Devlin. Archeb, 1993.
Beyond Grades: A Parent's Handbook for Developing the Real Skills for School Success. Dick Socwell. Rudi, 1993.
Help Your Child Excel in Math: Easy, Practical Methods That Make Learning Fun. Margaret Berge and Philip Gibbons. Lifetime, 1992.
Failproof Children, rev. ed. Ivan Fitzwater. Watercress, 1992.
A Black Parent's Handbook to Educating Your Children: Outside of the Classroom. Baruti K. Kafele. Baruti, 1991.
More Parents Are Teachers, Too: Encouraging Your 6 to 12-Year-Old. Claudia Jones. Williamson, 1991.

On handling problems with schools

School Crisis Survival Guide. Suni Petersen and Ron L. Straub. W. Gladden, 1994.
The Parent's Guide to Solving School Problems: Kindergarten Through Middle School. Elaine K. McEwan. Shaw, 1992.
Common and Uncommon School Problems: A Parent's Guide. David Gross and Irl Extein. Berkley, 1990. Paperback edition of *The Parents Guide to Common and Uncommon School Problems.* PIA Press, 1989.

On elementary school

Basic Skills Every Kindergarten Student Should Know. Stan Bippus. Applied Resources, 1993. Other series titles cover first through fifth grades.
One Hundred One Educational Conversations You Should Have with Your Kindergartener–First Grader. Vito Perrone. Chelsea House, 1993. Other series titles cover second through fifth grades.
What Your First Grader Needs to Know: Fundamentals of a Good First Grade Education. E.D. Hirsch, Jr. Doubleday, 1993. Other series titles cover second through fifth grades.
How to Teach Your Child: Things to Know from Kindergarten Through Grade 6, rev. ed. Veltisezar B. Bautista. Bookhaus, 1992.
The School-Smart Parent: A Guide to Knowing What Your Child Should Know—from Infancy Through the End of Elementary School. Gene I. Maeroff. Times Books, 1989.
The Elementary School Handbook: Making the Most of Your Child's Education. Joanne Oppenheim. Pantheon, 1989.

For children

My New School. Harriet Hains. Dorling Kindersley, 1993.
Learning a Lesson: How You See, Think and Remember. Steve Parker. Watts, 1991.
Martha's New School. Danielle Steel. Delacorte, 1989.

(See also PRESCHOOL, for books on starting school.)

On middle school

Changing Middle Schools: How to Make Schools Work for Young Adolescents. Nancy L. Adams and Edward Miller. Jossey-Bass, 1994.
One Hundred One Educational Conversations You Should Have with Your Sixth Grader. 1994. *One Hundred One Educational Conversations You Should Have with Your Seventh Grader. One Hundred One Educational Conversations You Should Have with Your Eighth Grader.* Both 1991. Vito Perrone. Chelsea House.

For preteens and teens

Help! My Teacher Hates Me: A School Survival Guide for Kids 10–14 Years Old. Meg Schneider. Workman, 1994.
Your New School. Claudine G. Wirths and Mary Bowman-Kruhm. Holt, 1993.
Everything You Need to Know about Changing Schools. Susan Mernit. Rosen, 1992.
The Struggle for Equal Education. Clarence Lusane. Watts, 1992.

(See also HIGH SCHOOL.)

On homework

Taming the Homework Monster: How to Stop Fighting with Your Kids over Homework. Ellen Klavan. Simon & Schuster, 1992.
1,001 Ways to Improve Your Child's Schoolwork: An Easy-to-Use Reference Book of Common School Problems and Practical Solutions. Lawrence J. Greene. Dell, 1991.
Ending the Homework Hassle: How to Help Your Child Succeed Independently in School. John Rosemond. Andrews and McMeel, 1990.
The Homework Solution: Getting Kids to Do Their Homework. Linda Agler Sonna. Williamson, 1990.

For children, on homework and study skills

One Hundred One Ways to Do Better in School. Penny Colman. Troll, 1993.
How to Write a Great School Report. Elizabeth James and Carol Barkin. Morrow, 1993.

For preteens and teens, on homework and study skills

Everything You Need to Know about English Homework. Everything You Need to Know about American History Homework. Everything You Need to Know about Math Homework. Everything You Need to Know about Science Homework. Anne Zeman and Kate Kelly. Scholastic, 1994.
How to Study, 3rd ed. *Write Papers*, 2nd ed. *Improve Your Reading*, 2nd ed. *Take Notes*, 2nd ed. *Ace Any Test*,

2nd ed. *Improve Your Memory,* 2nd ed. *Manage Your Time,* 2nd ed. Ron Fry. Career Press, 1994.
School Smarts: Two Thousand Things Students Need to Know, Ages 10 Plus. Jay Amberg. Good Year Books, 1994.
Becoming an Achiever: A Student Guide. Carolyn Coil. Pieces of Learning, 1994.
How to Study Just Enough. Sue H. Cross. Kendall-Hunt, 1993.
Excellence Without Excuse: The Black Student's Guide to Academic Excellence. Charles W. Cherry, II. International Scholastic Press, 1993.
The Secret of Getting Straight A's: Learn More in Less Time with Little Effort. Brian Marshall. Hathaway, 1993.
Achieving Academic Success: A Learning Skills Handbook, 2nd ed. Elaine Cherney and others. Kendall-Hunt, 1993.
How to Get a 4.0, Easily: One Hundred Twenty-Seven Ways to Get A's. Allan Richards. Vector, 1993.
Getting Straight A's, rev. ed. Gordon W. Green. Lyle Stuart/Carol, 1993.
Get Smart Fast: A Handbook for Academic Success, rev. ed. Sondra Geoffrion. R & E Publishers, 1993.
How to Get up When Schoolwork Gets You Down. Claudine G. Wirths and Mary Bowman-Kruhm. Chariot Family, 1993.
How to Get Good Grades: And Still Keep Your Fabulous Reputation As a Cool Person. Kris Bearss. Zondervan, 1992.
Making the Grade: Raising Your GPA by Studying Smarter, Not Harder, 2nd ed. Meredith Gall and Joyce P. Gall. Prima, 1992.
What You Need to Know about Developing Study Skills, Taking Notes and Tests, Using Dictionaries and Libraries. Marcia Conan and Kathy Heavers. NTC Publishing Group, 1992.
Ways to Make A's. Karl Davidson. Team Effort, 1992.
Smarten Up! How to Increase Your Brain Power. Roger Yepsen. Little, Brown, 1990.
The Student's Guide to Good Writing: Building Writing Skills for Success in College. Rick Dalton and Marianne Dalton. College Board, 1990.
Improve Your Grades: Effective Study and Test-Taking Techniques Not Taught in School. Veltisezar B. Bautista. Bookhaus, 1989.
Succeed with Math: Every Student's Guide to Conquering Math Anxiety. Sheila Tobias. College Board, 1987. By the author of *Overcoming Math Anxiety.*

On school anxiety

Dealing with Math Anxiety. Anna N. Kitchens. Irwin, 1994.
Overcoming Math Anxiety. Sheila Tobias. Norton, 1994.
School Phobia and Other Anxieties in Youth. Ron Kerner. Bureau for At-Risk Youth, 1992.
Coping with Academic Anxiety, rev. ed. Allen J. Ottens. Rosen, 1991.
Math Anxiety: What It Is and What to Do about It. Mitchell Collins. Kendall-Hunt, 1991.
Math Panic. Laurie Buxton. Heinemann, 1991.
Where Do I Put the Decimal Point?: How to Conquer Math Anxiety and Let Numbers Work for You. Elisabeth Ruedy and Sue Nirenberg. Holt, 1990.

(See also SCHOOL PHOBIA.)

For parents, on special education

My Child Needs Special Services!: Parents Talk about What Helps...and What Doesn't. Nancy O. Wilson. Mills Sanderson, 1994.
You, Your Child, and Special Education: A Guide to Making the System Work. Barbara C. Cutler. P.H. Brookes, 1993.
Optimizing Special Education: How Parents Can Make a Difference. N.O. Wilson. Plenum, 1992.
The Special Education Handbook: A Comprehensive Guide for Parents and Educators. Kenneth Shore. Teachers College Press, 1986.

Personal experiences on special education

Experiencing Special Education: What Children with Special Needs Can Tell Us. Barrie Wade and Maggie Moore. Taylor and Francis, 1993.
Since Owen. Charles R. Callanan. Johns Hopkins, 1990.

Background works on special education

Exceptional Lives: Special Education in Today's Schools. Ann Turnbull. Merrill, 1994.
Special Education: Good Intentions Gone Awry. Edward Moscovitch. Pioneer Institute, 1993.
The History of Special Education: From Isolation to Integration. Margret A. Winzer. Gallaudet University Press, 1993.

On dropping out

Last Chance High: How Girls and Boys Drop In and Out of Alternative Schools. Deidre M. Kelly. Yale University Press, 1993.
Dropout Prevention Handbook: Apprenticeships and Other Solutions. William Callison. Technomic, 1993.
School Attendance, Truancy and Dropping Out. Marilyn Dreilinger. Bureau for At-Risk Youth, 1992.
Dropping Out: Issues and Answers. James A. Farmer and Yolanda Payne. C.C. Thomas, 1992.
School Dropouts: The Tragedy of America's Undereducated Youth. Carlos A. Bonilla and Jana L. Brazda. ICA Publishing, 1992.
Giving up on School: Student Dropouts and Teacher Burnouts. Margaret D. LeCompte and Anthony G. Dworkin. Corwin, 1991.

For preteens and teens, on dropping out

Dropping Out of School. Debra Goldentyer. Raintree Steck-Vaughn, 1993.

When I Was Young I Loved School: Dropping Out and Hanging In. Children's Express; Anne Sheffield and Bruce Frankel, eds. Meckler, 1989.

On other educational problems

School Girls: Young Women, Self-Esteem, and the Confidence Gap. Peggy Orenstein. Doubleday, 1994.
I'm New Here. Bud Howlett. Houghton Mifflin, 1993. On immigrant students and bilingual education.
Immigrant Students: Their Legal Right of Access to Public Schools, a Guide for Advocates and Educators, rev. ed. John W. Carrera. National Coalition of Advocates for Students, 1992.
Help??? Help!!!: Solving Learning Problems (Even Dyslexia). David Conway. Academic Reading/Nancibell, 1992.
Boosting the Adolescent Underachiever: How Parents Can Change a "C" Student into an "A" Student. Victor Cogen. Plenum, 1992.
Boosting the Underachiever: How Busy Parents Can Unlock Their Child's Potential. Victor Cogen. Plenum, 1990.
When Your Child Isn't Doing Well in School. Ann Thiel and others. Contemporary, 1988.
Smart Kids with School Problems: Things to Know and Ways to Help. Priscilla L. Vail. Dutton, 1987.
Is Your Child in the Wrong Grade?, rev. ed. Louise Bates Ames. Programs for Education, 1987.
What Am I Doing in This Grade? A Book for Parents about School Readiness. Louise Bates Ames. Programs for Education, 1985.
How Children Fail. John Holt. Delta, 1964.

On study abroad

The Exchange Student Survival Kit. Bettina Hansel. Intercultural Press, 1993.
Home from Home: Discover Other Cultures, Learn the Language, Experience the Way of Life. Central Bureau Staff, comp. Kuperard/Seven Hills Book Distributors, 1992.
Students Abroad—Strangers at Home: Education for a Global Society. Norman L. Kauffmann and others. Intercultural Press, 1992.

On failure of schools

Too Much Schooling, Too Little Education: A Paradox of Black Life in White Societies. Mwalimu J. Shujaa, ed. Africa World, 1994.
How to Trash Our Young via Public Education: A Practical Guide. Joseph Najavits. Open Vistas, 1993.
Schools Flunk...Kids Don't. Joe Petterle. Griffin, 1993.
Bad: or The Dumbing of America. Paul Fussell, Jr. Simon & Schuster, 1992.
The Learning Gap: Why Our Schools Are Failing and What We Can Learn from Japanese and Chinese Education. Harold W. Stevenson and James W. Stigler. Summit, 1992.
Savage Inequalities: Children in America's Schools. Jonathan Kozol. Crown, 1991.
In the Name of Excellence: The Struggle to Reform the Nation's Schools and Why It's Failing and What Should Be Done. Thomas Toch. Oxford University Press, 1991.
Why Children Reject School: Views From Seven Countries, Colette Chiland and J. Gerald Young, eds. Yale University Press, 1990.

On successful schools

The Nation's Best Schools: Blueprints for Excellence, Vol. 1: Elementary and Middle Schools. Evelyn H. Ogden and Vito Germinario. Technomic, 1994.
Schools That Work: America's Most Innovative Public Education Programs. George H. Wood. NAL-Dutton, 1993.
School Success: The Inside Story. Peter Kline and Laurence D. Martel. Great Ocean, 1993.
Classroom Crucible: What Really Works, What Doesn't, and Why. Edward Pauly. Basic Books, 1992.
America's Best Classrooms: How Award-Winning Teachers Are Shaping Our Children's Future. Daniel T. Seymour and Terrence J. Seymour. Peterson's Guides, 1992.
Schools That Work: America's Most Innovative Public Education Programs. George H. Wood. NAL-Dutton, 1992.
Smart Schools, Smart Kids: Why Do Some Schools Work? Edward B. Fiske. Simon & Schuster, 1991.

On improving schools

Not by Schools Alone: Sharing Responsibility for America's Education Reform. Sandra A. Waddock. Praeger/Greenwood, 1995.
School and Family Partnerships: Preparing Educators and Improving Schools. Joyce L. Epstein. Westview, 1995.
Making Schools Work: A View from the Firing Lines. Cheryl L. Fagnano and Katherine N. Hughes, eds. Westview, 1994.
Save Our Schools: 66 Things You Can Do to Improve Your School Without Spending an Extra Penny. Mary S. Miller. HarperCollins, 1993.
What Are We Trying to Teach Them Anyway?: A Father's Focus on School Reform. Ronald K. Pierce. ICS Press, 1993.
The Predictable Failure of Educational Reform: Can We Change Course Before It's Too Late? Seymour B. Sarason. Jossey-Bass, 1993.
We Must Take Charge: Our Schools and Our Future. Chester E. Finn, Jr. Free Press, 1993.
Making Schools Better: What Parents, Teachers, and Communities Can Do to Breathe New Life into America's Classrooms. Larry Martz. Times Books, 1992.
Parenting Our Schools: A Hands-On Guide to Education Reform. Jill Bloom. Little, Brown, 1992.
Reclaiming Our Schools: Creating Classrooms That Work. Larry Martz. Random, 1992.
Educating for the 21st Century: The Challenge for Parents and Teachers. Mark H. Mullin. Madison, 1991.
The Unschooled Mind: How Children Think and How Schools Should Teach. Howard Gardner. Basic Books, 1991. Proposals for school reform.

Improving Schools from Within: Teachers, Parents, and Principals Can Make a Difference. Roland S. Barth. Jossey-Bass, 1990.

Background books

Learning from the Past: What History Teaches Us about School Reform. Diane Ravitch and Maris Vinovskis, eds. Johns Hopkins, 1995.

Self and School Success: Voices and Lore of Inner-City Students. Edwin Farrell. State University of New York Press, 1994.

Separating School and State: How to Liberate America's Families. Sheldon Richman. Future of Freedom, 1994.

Seeking Effective Schools for African American Children. Bunyan Bryant and Alan H. Jones. Caddo Gap, 1993.

The Multi-Age Classroom: A Family of Learners. Wendy C. Kasten and Barbara K. Clarke. R. Owen, 1993.

Smart Kids: How Academic Talents Are Developed and Nurtured in America. William G. Durden and Arne E. Tangherlini. Hogrefe and Huber, 1993.

What America's Teachers Wish Parents Knew. Judy Privett and Tony Privett. Longstreet, 1993.

The Chalk Dust Report. Margaret DiPaul. Rudi, 1993.

The Children's Machine: Rethinking School in the Age of the Computer. Seymour Papert. Basic Books, 1993.

Thinking about Kids: An Agenda for American Education. Harold Howe, III. Free Press, 1993.

Teachers: Talking Out of School. Catherine Collins and Douglas Frantz. Little, Brown, 1993.

Smart Schools: From Educating Memories to Educating Minds. David D. Perkins. Free Press, 1992.

Small Districts, Big Problems: Making School Everbody's House. Richard A. Schmuck and Patricia A. Schmuck. Corwin, 1992.

Sex Equity and Sexuality in Education. Susan S. Klein, ed. State University of New York Press, 1992.

The Backcountry Classroom. Jack Drury and Bruce Bonney. ICS Books, 1992.

Early Years at Home: When Life Patterns Are Set. Theodore E. Wade, Jr. Gazelle, 1992.*Volunteers in Public Schools.* National Academy Press, 1990.

Endangered Brains: Why Our Children Can't Think. Jane Healy. Simon & Schuster, 1990.

Privatization and Educational Choice. Myron Lieberman. St. Martin's, 1989.

Innumeracy: Mathematical Illiteracy and Its Consequences. John Allen Paulos. Vintage, 1989.

(See also specific types or levels of schools, such as PRESCHOOL; MONTESSORI; HEAD START; KINDERGARTEN, HIGH SCHOOL, COLLEGE, PRIVATE SCHOOLS; ALTERNATIVE SCHOOLS; HOME SCHOOLING; SPECIAL EDUCATION; HOME STUDY; SCHOOL OF CHOICE; MASTERY LEARNING; LEARNING DISABILITIES; DISTANCE EDUCATION; also specific topics, such as DROPOUT; GIFTED CHILD; READING; WRITING; COGNITIVE DEVELOPMENT; LEARNING STYLE; MASTERY LEARNING; VOUCHER SYSTEM; CORPORAL PUNISHMENT; INDIVIDUALS WITH DISABILITIES EDUCATION ACT; INDIVIDUALIZED EDUCATION PLAN.)

Help Against Child Abuse and Neglect

ORGANIZATIONS OFFERING HELP AND INFORMATION

About Child Abuse and Neglect

National Center on Child Abuse and Neglect (NCCAN)
Administration for Children and Families
U.S. Department of Health and Human Services
P.O. Box 1182
Washington, DC 20013–1182
202–205–8586
Fax: 202–260–9351
David Lloyd, Director
Center established under the federal 1974 Child Abuse Prevention and Treatment Act; conducts research and gathers national statistics; operates National Clearinghouse on Child Abuse and Neglect Information (see next entry); provides technical assistance; funds pilot prevention, identification, and treatment projects, including parent self-help projects.

National Clearinghouse on Child Abuse and Neglect Information (NCCAN)
P.O. Box 1182
Washington, DC 20013–1182
703–385–7565; 800-FYI–3366 [394–3366]
Fax: 703–385–3206
E-mail: nccanch@clark.net
America Online: On Parents Information Network (PIN)
Clearinghouse funded by the National Center on Child Abuse and Neglect (see below); provides information and referrals; maintains and searches databases; publishes numerous materials, including:

- Fact sheets: *Child Abuse and Neglect: A Shared Community Concern*, *Child Abuse and Neglect*, and *National Center on Child Abuse and Neglect.*
- Annotated bibliographies on sexual abuse: *Sexual Abuse, Incest, Male Victims of Sexual Abuse, Sexual Abuse: Prevention, Sexual Abuse: Treatment for Victims, Sexual Abuse: Treatment for Perpetrators, Interviewing Techniques Used with Sexual Abuse Victims, Family Preservation, Sex Offenders, Adolescent Sex Offenders*, and *Characteristics of Abusive Parents.*
- Annotated bibliographies on victims and other types of abuse, such as *Risk Factors, Adolescent Abuse, Child Neglect, Emotional Maltreatment, Exploitation of Children, Generational Cycle of Abuse, Munchausen Syndrome, Perinatal Child Abuse, Physical Abuse, Ritual Abuse, Shaken Baby Syndrome, Substance Abuse, Adults Abused as Children, Characteristics of Abused Children, Child Fatalities, Child Abuse and Neglect in Homeless Communities, Child Witnesses, False Allegations*, and *Developmental Disabilities.*
- *Child Abuse and Neglect CD-ROM*
- Training manuals and research materials for professionals.

National Resource Center on Child Abuse and Neglect
63 Inverness Drive East
Englewood, CO 80112–5117
303–792–9900; 800–227–5242
Fax: 303–792–5333
Resource center funded by the National Center on Child Abuse and Neglect and operated by Children's Division of the American Humane Association; provides information, training, and technical assistance.

National Resource Center on Child Sexual Abuse (NRCCSA)
2204 Whitesburg Drive, Suite 200
Huntsville, AL 35801
205–534–6868; 800-KIDS–006 [543–7006] (For professional inquiries only)
Fax: 205–534–6883
Resource center for professionals who work with sexual abuse; funded by the National Center on Child Abuse and Neglect (see above); provides training and technical support, including customized complications; publishes *NRCCSA News*, information papers, monographs, bibliographies, and other professional materials.

Children's Division, American Humane Association
63 Inverness Drive East
Englewood, CO 80112–5117
303–792–9900; National Resource Center on Child Abuse and Neglect Information Line: 800–227–5242
Fax: 303–792–5333
Karen Farestad, Director, Children's Division
Division of the American Humane Association focusing on preventing child abuse and neglect; operates the National Resource Center on Child Abuse and Neglect (see above), which provides information, training, and technical assistance to community professionals; makes referrals; publishes quarterly magazine *Protecting Children*; quarterly newsletter *Child Protection Leader*; and various books and pamphlets, most oriented toward child welfare professionals.

C. Henry Kempe National Center for the Prevention and Treatment of Child Abuse and Neglect
University of Colorado Health Sciences Center
Department of Pediatrics
1205 Oneida Street
Denver, CO 80220–2944
303–321–3963

National Association of Counsel for Children
Tel: 303–322–2260
Fax: 303–329–3523
Center offering training, consultation, program development and evaluation, and research on all forms of child abuse and neglect; offers therapeutic preschool, family trauma survivor program, and other recovery and treatment projects; provides training to child advocates through the National Association of Counsel for Children, which publishes newsletter *The Guardian* and various books; publishes *Child Abuse and Neglect: The International Journal* and other materials, including:

- On general abuse: *Child Abuse, The Battered Child, Damaged Parents: An Anatomy of Child Neglect, The Child Abuse-Delinquency Connection, Chronic Acting-Out Students and Child Abuse: A Handbook for Intervention, Sibling Abuse: Hidden Physical, Emotional, and Sexual Trauma, Changing the Abusive Parent, Recognizing Child Abuse: A Guide for the Concerned, When a Child Kills: Abused Children Who Kill Their Parents, Child Abuse: A Community Concern, The Backlash: Child Protection Under Fire,* and *Protecting Children from Abuse and Neglect: Foundations for a New National Strategy.*
- On incest and other sexual abuse: *Betrayal of Innocence: Incest and Its Devastation, Conspiracy of Silence: The Trauma of Incest, Sexual Assault of Children and Adolescents, The Battle and the Backlash: The Child Sexual Abuse War, Sourcebook on Child Sexual Abuse, Sexual Abuse of Young Children, Nursery Crimes: Sexual Abuse in Daycare, Lasting Effects of Child Sexual Abuse, Males at Risk: The Other Side of Child Sexual Abuse,* and *Fuel on the Fire: An Inquiry into "Pornography" and Sexual Aggression in a Free Society.*
- Workbooks for sexually molested children: *Flip Flops* (ages 7–9), *Cartwheels* (ages 10–13), and *High Tops* (ages 14–17).
- Numerous professional works on assessment and treatment of abused children and of molesters (some of them juveniles who had themselves been sexually abused), including *Interviewing the Sexually Abused Child: Investigation of Suspected Abuse* and *Children Speak for Themselves.*

Childhelp USA
6463 Independence Avenue
Woodland Hills, CA 91367
818–953–7577; National Child Abuse Hot Line: 800–4-A-CHILD [422–4453]; 800–2-A-CHILD [222–4453], TT
Sara O'Meara, Chairman and Cofounder
Yvonne Fedderson, President and Cofounder
Organization concerned with child abuse; provides information and referrals; offers intervention and treatment services for abused children and families; sponsors research; acts as advocate; publishes various materials, including pamphlets such as *Child Abuse and You*...and list of recommended books for survivors of child abuse.

PACER Center (Parent Advocacy Coalition for Educational Rights), 612–827–2966, voice/TT. Sponsors "Let's Prevent Abuse" program and publishes *Risky Situations: Vulnerable Children, Celebrating Family Strengths: A Handbook for Families* (with preschool curriculum and newsletter), *LPA Prevention Handbook for Early Childhood Professionals and Families with Young Children, Resource Manual on Child Abuse,* and *Abuse Prevention.* (For full group information, see HELP FOR SPECIAL CHILDREN on page 689.)

National Committee for Prevention of Child Abuse (NCPCA)
332 South Michigan Avenue, Suite 1600
Chicago, IL 60604
312–663–3520; For publications: 800–835–2671
Anne Cohn Donnelly, Executive Director
Organization seeking to educate the public and shape policy regarding child abuse, sexual, physical, or emotional; provides information and referrals; conducts child abuse prevention programs and media campaigns; publishes various materials.

National Council on Child Abuse and Family Violence (NCCAFV)
1155 Connecticut Avenue NW, Suite 400
Washington, DC 20036
202–429–6695; HelpLine: 800–222–2000
Fax: 408–655–3930
Organization concerned with prevention and treatment of intergenerational family violence; provides information and makes referrals; publishes "Facts About" booklet *Child Abuse and Neglect.*

Child Welfare League of America (CWLA), 202–638–2952. Publishes *Confronting Child Sexual Abuse* (video training series, introduced by Oprah Winfrey), *What Only a Mother Can Tell You About Child Sexual Abuse, When I Was Little Like You* (on sexual abuse, for young children), *The Adoptive Family as a Healing Resource for the Sexually Abused Child: A Training Manual,* and *Tender Mercies: Inside the World of a Child Abuse Investigator.* (For full group information, see FOSTER CARE.)

Association for Childhood Education International (ACEI), 800–423–3563. Publishes videotape *Child Sexual Abuse: What Are You Going to Do About It?* and position paper *The Child's Right to Humane Treatment.*

(For full group information, see HELP ON LEARNING AND EDUCATION on page 659.)

Association of Family and Conciliation Courts (AFCC), 608–251–4001. Publishes books *Sexual Abuse Allegations.* (For full group information, see DIVORCE.)

Defense for Children International-United States of America (DCI-USA)
30 Irving Place, 9th Floor
New York, NY 10003
212–228–4773
Fax: 228–4275
Dorianne Beyer, Executive Director
Organization seeking to promote stronger protection for children's rights, as in cases of child abuse, sexual exploitation, parental kidnapping, and armed conflict; provides referrals; publishes quarterly newsletter *Children's Rights Outlook*; *In the Spirit of Peace: A Global Introduction to Children's Rights*, and other materials, many with an international focus.

Pediatric Projects, 800–947–0947. Publishes *Loss of Parental Support: A Form of Emotional Child Abuse* and *No Play Permitted: Indicator of Psychological Abuse.* (For full group information, see HOSPITAL.)

Center on Children and the Law
American Bar Association
740 15th Street NW
Washington, DC 20005
202–662–1720
Fax: 202–662–1755
E-mail: davidsonha@attmail.com or hn3788@connect.com
Hansnet: 3788, Child Welfare Forum
Howard Davidson, Director
Program of the American Bar Association's Young Lawyers Division; provides information on topics such as child custody and visitation, child abuse, child welfare, foster care, termination of parental rights, child support, child fatalities, juvenile delinquency, parental substance abuse, child advocates (guardians ad litem), and parental kidnapping; offers professional training and technical assistance; publishes numerous materials, including monthly *ABA Juvenile and Child Welfare Law Reporter* and numerous legal materials, such as *Handbook on Questioning Children: A Linguistic Perspective* and *The Prosecution of Child Sexual and Physical Abuse.*

National Center for Youth Law (NCYL)
114 Sansome Street, Suite 900
San Francisco, CA 94104
415–543–3307
Fax: 415–956–9024
Hansnet: 0366
John O'Toole, Director
Organization aiding legal services programs and lawyers in representing low-income young people in the U.S., in areas such as child abuse and neglect, termination of parental rights, foster care, juvenile delinquency, health problems, and housing discrimination due to children; provides consultation, training, research, drafting of legal documents, and aid in writing briefs; participates directly in litigation in certain cases; gathers and maintains library of legal and other materials relating to youth law; publishes bimonthly *Youth Law News.*

National Organization for Victim Assistance (NOVA)
1757 Park Road NW
Washington, DC 20010
202–393–6682; 24-hour hotline: 800-TRY-NOVA [879–6682]
Fax: 202–331–2225
Marlene A. Young, Executive Director
Organization focusing on victims of crime, especially violence and sexual assault against juvenile and minority victims; acts as advocate; provides information, direct aid, and referrals to victim assistance programs and other services; publishes various materials, including newsletter and *Victim Service Program Directory.*

Johnson Institute, 800–231–5165, U.S. except MN. Publishes video for children: *Tulip Doesn't Feel Safe* (on domestic violence) and *Teachers at Risk: Crisis in the Classroom* (on protecting against charges of abuse). (For full group information, see HELP AGAINST SUBSTANCE ABUSE on page 703.)

National Clearinghouse for Alcohol and Drug Abuse Information (NCADI), 301–468–2600. Publishes Prevention Resource Guide *Child Abuse.* (For full group information, see HELP AGAINST SUBSTANCE ABUSE on page 703.)

Council for Exceptional Children (CEC), 800–328–0272. Publishes *Abuse and Neglect of Exceptional Children.* (For full group information, see HELP ON LEARNING AND EDUCATION on page 659.)

Children's Defense Fund (CDF), 800–233–1200. Sponsors Child Watch Visitation program; publishes the annual *The State of America's Children.* (For full group information, see ADOLESCENT PREGNANCY.)

American Academy of Child and Adolescent Psychiatry (AACAP), 202–966–7300. Publishes information sheets *Child Abuse—The Hidden Bruises, Child Sexual Abuse*, and *Responding to Child Sexual Abuse.* (For full group information, see MENTAL DISORDERS.)

National Maternal and Child Health Clearinghouse (NMCHC), 703–821–8955. Publish *Responding to Child Abuse and Neglect: A Continuing Challenge.* (For full group information, see PREGNANCY.)

National Center for Women and Family Law, 212–674–8200. Publishes *Child Sexual Abuse and*

Intrafamily Custody/Visitation Disputes Packet, Legal Issues and Legal Options in Civil Child Sexual Abuse Cases: Representing the Protective Parent, Expert Testimony in Custody and Visitation Cases Involving Child Sexual Abuse, and other reference and legal materials. (For full group information, see CUSTODY.)

Parents and Children's Equality (PACE), 813–786–6911. (For full group information, see CUSTODY.)

New Parents' Network, 520–327–1451. Offers information (through telecommunications services) on child abuse. (For full group information, see GENERAL PARENTING RESOURCES on page 634.)

National Association for the Education of Young Children (NAEYC), 800–424–2460. Publishes book *Caring: Supporting Children's Growth,* on dealing with problems such as divorce, abuse, and death. (For full group information, see PRESCHOOL.)

Parents and Teachers Against Violence in Education (PTAVE), 510–831–1661. (For full group information, see CORPORAL PUNISHMENT.)

National Woman's Christian Temperance Union (WCTU), 800–755–1321. Publishes booklets *About Preventing Child Abuse, Child Abuse and Its Prevention, Child Abuse Digest, Child Sexual Abuse, Incest: A Family Tragedy,* and *Emotional Child Abuse.* (For full group information, see HELP AGAINST SUBSTANCE ABUSE on page 703.)

National Coalition Against Domestic Violence (NCADV), 303–839–1852. (For full group information, see VIOLENCE.)

End Violence Against the Next Generation (EVAN-G), 415–527–0454. (For full group information, see CORPORAL PUNISHMENT.)

ON CHILD SEXUAL ABUSE

Committee for Children (CFC)
2203 Airport Way South, Suite 500
Seattle, WA 98134–2027
206–343–1223; 800–634–4449
Fax: 206–343–1445
Alice-Ray-Keil, Executive Director
Organization that publishes child abuse and violence prevention curriculum for children K–12, including *Talking About Touching* (for various age groups, preschool-grade 5), *Personal Safety and Decision Making* (grades 6–8), and videos *Yes, You Can Say No* and *Identifying, Reporting and Handling Disclosure of the Sexually Abused Child.*

Parents United International
232 E. Gish Road, 1st Floor
San Jose, CA 95112
408–453–7676
Fax: 408–453–9064
Brian Abbott, Executive Director
Giarretto Institute
Child Sexual Abuse Treatment Program
Intake supervisor: 408–453–7616
Hank Giarretto, Founder and Director of Research and Development
Network of professionally guided groups for individuals and families with experience of child molestation; includes Daughters and Sons United, for sexually abused children (5–18) and their families, and Adults Molested as Children United (AMACU), for those over eighteen who were abused as children; makes referrals; provides family therapy and medical, legal, and vocational counseling. Affiliated Giarretto Institute operates Child Sexual Abuse Treatment Program (CSATP), a treatment program for sexually abused children and their families; offers training for professional therapists; publishes numerous materials, primarily for therapists.

Hazelden Foundation (HF), 800–262–5010. Publishes *Out of the Shadows: Understanding Sexual Addiction, Freedom Through Forgiving: A Workbook for Everyone Who Has Been Hurt by Someone,* and *Daybreak: Meditations for Women Survivors of Sexual Abuse.* (For full group information, see HELP AGAINST SUBSTANCE ABUSE on page 703.)

People Against Rape (PAR)
c/o S-Team Unlimited, Inc.
P.O. Box 5876
Naperville, IL 60567–5876
708–717–0310; 800-UR-SPCL–2 [877–3252]
Fax: 708–717–0391
Dan and Marie Lena, Founders and Program Presenters
Cindy Heider, National Programs Coordinator
Organization seeking to protect children from sexual abuse; offers self-defense training for children; publishes various materials, including booklet *Hands Off, I'm Special.*

SHARE, Inc.
P.O. Box 1342
Beverly Hills, CA 90213
310–274–5361
Judy Feder, President
Organization raising money for special programs for mentally retarded and abused children; funds diagnostic and counseling center, infant development and preschool programs, and special education for school-age children; Citizen Advocacy Program assigns a volunteer to represent each retarded person.

Society's League Against Molestation (SLAM)
c/o Women Against Rape/Childwatch
P.O. Box 346
Collingswood, NJ 08108
609–858–7800; 800–491-WATCH [491–92824] (NJ only)
Fax: 609–858–7063
Rita Unger, Director

Organization working to prevent sexual abuse and exploitation of children; acts as advocate; monitors court cases; provides information, referrals, and support to child molestation victims and their families; publishes newsletter.

National Adoption Information Clearinghouse (NAIC), 301–231–6512. Publishes *Parenting the Sexually Abused Child.* (For full group information, see ADOPTION.)

Child Care Action Campaign (CCAC), 212–239–0138. Publishes *Dealing with Sexual Abuse: A Guide for Parents* and *Do Criminal Record Checks Protect Children?* (For full group information, see CHILD CARE.)

Sexuality Information and Education Council of the United States (SIECUS), 212–819–9770. Publishes annotated bibliography *Child Sexual Abuse Education, Prevention, and Treatment.* (For full group information, see SEX EDUCATION.)

National Mental Health Consumer Self-Help Clearinghouse, 800–553–4539. Publishes reprint packet on sexual abuse. (For full group information, see MENTAL DISORDERS.)

VOICES in Action, Inc. (Victims of Incest Can Emerge Survivors)
P.O. Box 148309
Chicago, IL 60614
312–327–1500; 800–7-VOICE–8 [786–4238]
Network of support groups for victims of incest and others, to ease the transition from "victim" to "survivor"; acts as advocate; provides information and referrals; publishes various materials, including bimonthly newsletter *The Chorus*; books and booklets *How to File a Civil Suit*, and *How to Start a Self-Help Group*; and brochures *How to Confront Your Perpetrator, How to Choose a Therapist*, and *What Helps.*

About programs for child-abusing parents

Parents Anonymous (PA)
675 West Foothill Boulevard, Suite 220
Claremont, CA 91711
909–621–6184
Fax: 909–625–6304
E-mail: hn3831@hansnet.org (Hansnet: 3831)
Lisa Pion-Berlin, Executive Director
Organization aimed at rehabilitating child-abusing adults, modeled on Alcoholics Anonymous; publishes newsletter.

Sexaholics Anonymous (SA)
P.O. Box 111910
Nashville, TN 37222
615–331–6230
Fax: 615–331–6901
Network of support groups, modeled on Alcoholics Anonymous, for people addicted to destructive or self-destructive sexual behavior; publishes various materials, including *Essay Newsletter, Sexaholics Anonymous Manual*, and *SA Brochure—Problem, Solution and 20 Questions.*

ONLINE RESOURCES

Parents' Information Network (America Online: PIN) Online forums and libraries cover child abuse. (For full information, see GENERAL PARENTING RESOURCES on page 634.)

Internet: alt.sexual.abuse.recovery Usenet offering information and discussion about recovery. Subscribe through newsreader: news:alt.sexual.abuse.recovery

OTHER RESOURCES

For parents and other adults

The Assault on America's Children: Safeguarding Your Child from Becoming a Victim of Child Abuse. Donn Ferguson. Harbor House West, 1994.

Know and Tell: A Workbook for Parents and Children on How to Prevent Child Abuse, 2nd ed. Yvette K. Lehman. Y.K. Lehman, 1993.

Child Abuse: How and Where to Find Facts and Get Help. Robert D. Reed and Danek S. Kaus. R & E Publishers, 1993.

Seventy-Six Ways to Protect Your Child from Crime. J.L. Simmons and George J. McCall. Holt, 1992.

Child Abuse—The Parent's Guide to Protective Investigation and Foster Care. Janet V. Ward. Family Systems, 1992.

For Their Sake: Recognizing, Responding to and Reporting Child Abuse. For Kids Sake, Inc. Staff and Rebecca Cowan Johnson. American Camping Association, 1992.

Save the Family, Save the Child: What We Can Do to Help Children at Risk. Vincent J. Fontana and Valerie Moolman. NAL-Dutton, 1991.

Don't Make Me Go Back, Mommy. Doris Sanford. Multnomah, 1990. About abuse in a day-care center; with appendix for parents and caregivers.

Recognizing Child Abuse: A Guide for the Concerned. Douglas J. Besharov. Free Press/Macmillan, 1990.

For parents, on dealing with sexual abuse

Families in Recovery: Working Together to Heal the Damage of Childhood Sexual Abuse. Beverly Engel. Lowell House, 1994.

The Mother's Book: How to Survive the Molestation of Your Child, 2nd ed. Carolyn M. Byerly. Kendall-Hunt, 1993.

Mothers Surviving Child Sexual Abuse. Carol-Ann Hooper. Routledge, 1993.

From Trauma to Understanding: A Guide for Parents of Children with Sexual Behavior Problems. William Pithers and others. Safer Society, 1993.

Mothers of Incest Survivors: Another Side of the Story. Janis T. Johnson. Indiana University Press, 1992.

Helping Your Child Recover from Sexual Abuse. Caren Adams and Jennifer Fay. University of Washington Press, 1992.

Shifting the Burden of Truth: Suing Child Sexual Abusers—A Legal Guide for Survivors and Their Supporters. Joseph Crnich and Kimberly Crnich. Recollex, 1992.

For parents, on preventing child sexual abuse

Preventing Child Sexual Abuse: A Curriculum for Children Ages 5 Through 8. Kathryn G. Reid. Pilgrim, 1994.

I Like You to Make Jokes with Me, But I Don't Want You to Touch Me, 2nd ed. Ellen Bass. Lollipop Power, 1993.

A Better Safe Than Sorry Book: A Family Guide for Sexual Assault Prevention. Sol Gordon and Judith Gordon. Prometheus, 1992.

Protecting Children from Sexual Abuse. Marjorie S. Fink. Bureau for At-Risk Youth, 1992.

Preventing Child Sexual Abuse: Sharing the Responsibility. Sandy K. Wurtele and Cindy L. Miller-Perrin. University of Nebraska Press, 1992.

Teaching about Sexual Abuse. Pat Huggins. Sopris, 1991.

General works

Wounded Innocents: The Real Victims of the War Against Child Abuse, rev. ed. Richard Werler. Prometheus, 1995.

Licensing Parents: Can We Prevent Child Abuse and Neglect? Jack C. Westman. Plenum, 1994.

Disarming the Home: Nonviolent Strategies for Confronting Battering and Child Abuse. K. Louise Schmidt. New Society, 1994.

When the Victim Is a Child, 2nd ed. Debra Whitcomb. Diane, 1994.

The Facts about Child Physical Abuse. Bill Gillham. Cassell, 1994.

Breaking the Deadly Embrace of Child Abuse. E. Clay Jorgensen. Crossroad, 1993. Originally titled: *Child Abuse.*

The Abusing Family, rev. ed. Blair Justice and Rita Justice. Plenum, 1990.

Too Old to Cry: Abused Teens in Today's America. Robert J. Ackerman and Lee Marvin Joiner. TAB, 1990.

On incest and other child sexual abuse

Rocking the Cradle of Sexual Politics: What Happened When Women Said Incest. Louise Armstrong. Addison-Wesley, 1994. By the author of *Kiss Daddy Goodnight* (1978; 1987 sequel).

Child Sexual Abuse: How and Where to Find Facts and Get Help. Robert D. Reed and Danek S. Kaus. R & E Publishers, 1993.

Watch Out! We're Talking: Speaking Out about Incest and Abuse. Janice Mirikitani, ed. Glide Word, 1993.

What Only a Mother Can Tell You about Child Sexual Abuse. Karen L. Schaefer. Child Welfare, 1993.

Incest, 2nd ed. Adele Mayer. Learning Publications, 1993.

Sexual Abuse. Cynthia A. Kubetin and James D. Mallory, Jr. Rapha, 1992.

Child Sexual Abuse. Bill Gillham. Cassell, 1991.

Abused Boys: The Neglected Victims of Sexual Abuse. Mic Hunter. Fawcett, 1991.

The Best-Kept Secret: Sexual Abuse of Children. Florence Rush. TAB, 1991.

On ritual abuse

Ritual Child Abuse: How and Where to Find Facts and Get Help. Robert D. Reed and Danek S. Kaus. R & E Publishers, 1992.

Out of Darkness: Understanding Satanism and Ritual Abuse. David K. Sakheim and Susan Devine. Free Press, 1992.

Ritual Child Abuse: Discovery, Diagnosis, and Treatment. Pamela S. Hudson. R & E Publishers, 1991.

On the effects of abuse

Effects of Domestic Violence on Children. W. Gladden, 1994.

Spare the Child: The Religious Roots of Punishment and the Psychological Impact of Physical Abuse. Philip Greven. Random House, 1992.

Domestic Violence and Its Effect on Children. Barbara S. Fritz and Ron Kerner. Bureau for At-Risk Youth, 1992.

The Kasper Hauser Syndrome of "Psychosocial Dwarfism": Deficient Statural, Intellectual, and Social Growth Induced by Child Abuse. John Money. Promethueus, 1992.

The Effects of Child Abuse and Neglect: Issues and Research. Raymond H. Starr and David A. Wolfe, eds. Guilford, 1991.

On breaking the abuse cycle

Stopping Domestic Violence: A Counselor's Guide to Learning to Live Without Violence. Daniel J. Sonkin. Volcano, 1995.

Emotional Child Abuse: Breaking the Cycle. Dianne J. Moore. Write on Services, 1992.

Breaking the Cycle: Survivors of Child Abuse and Neglect. Pamela Fong. Norton, 1991.

On children's violence against parents

Why Kids Kill Parents: Child Abuse and Adolescent Homicide. Kathleen M. Heide. Ohio State University Press, 1992.

When a Child Kills: Abused Children Who Kill Their Parents. Paul A. Mones. PocketBooks, 1991.

For children

Hilde Knows: Someone Cries for the Children. Lisa Kent. Jalmar Press, 1994.

The Lost Boy. David J. Pelzer. Omaha Press, 1994. On abuse in foster care.

Sarah: Sexual Abuse. Illana Katz. Real Life Storybooks, 1994.

Something Happened to Me: Helping a Child to Become a Sexual Abuse Survivor. Sandy McCoy. Skyline, 1993.

Something Must Be Wrong with Me. Doris Sanford. Questar, 1993.

Promise Not to Tell. Carolyn Polese. Beech Tree/Morrow, 1993. Fiction.

Harpo's Horrible Secret. Barbara Kelley. Ozark, 1993. Fiction.

Secrets That Hurt and *Tough Times.* Jim Boulden and Joan Boulden. Boulden, 1993. Fiction.

Aaron Goes to the Shelter: A Story and Workbook Guide about Abuse, Placement and Protective Services. Phyllis Nasta. Whole Child, 1992.

It Happened to Me, Something Bad Happened, The World I See, Don't Go, I Can't Remember, and *All My Feelings.* Debra W. Alexander. Bureau for At-Risk Youth, 1992.

Sexual Abuse! What Is It?: An Informational Book for the Hearing Impaired. Alice LaBarre and others. Liberty, 1992.

Stranger Danger. Priscilla Larson. Tyndale, 1991.

So, You Have to Go to Court!: A Child's Guide to Testifying As a Witness in Child Abuse Cases, 3rd ed. Harvey Watson-Russell. Butterworth, 1991.

Daisy: A Book about Child Abuse. E. Sandy Powell. Carolrhoda, 1991.

No More Hurt. Wendy Deaton and Kendall Johnson. Hunter House, 1991.

Love Letters: Responding to Children in Pain. Doris Sanford and Graci Evans. Multnomah, 1991.

Child Abuse. rev. ed. Elaine Landau. Messner, 1990.

Child Abuse. Gail Stewart. Crestwood, 1990.

For preteens and teens

How Long Does It Hurt?: A Guide to Recovering from Incest for Teenagers, Their Friends, and Their Families. Cynthia L. Mather and Kristina E. Debye. Jossey-Bass, 1994.

Coping with Incest, rev. ed. Deborah Miller. Rosen, 1994.

Child Abuse. Tom Ito. Lucent, 1994.

Child Abuse: Opposing Viewpoints. Katie DeKoster and Karin L. Swisher, eds. Greenhaven, 1994.

If She Hollers. Cynthia Voigt. Scholastic, 1994. Fiction.

Laurie Tells. Linda Lowery. Carolrhoda, 1994. Fiction.

I Hadn't Meant to Tell You This. Jacqueline Woodson. Delacorte, 1994. Fiction.

Child Abuse: Fear in the Home. Nancy Jacobs, ed. Info Plus, 1994.

Shining Through: Pulling It Together after Sexual Abuse. Mindy B. Loiselle and Leslie B. Wright. Safer Society, 1994.

The Me Nobody Knows: A Guide for Teen Survivors. Barbara Bean and Shari Bennett. Free Press, 1993.

Growing up with Sexual Abuse. Rona D. Schenkerman. Bureau for At-Risk Youth, 1993.

Uncle Vampire. Cynthia D. Grant. Atheneum, 1993. Fiction.

Everything You Need to Know about Sexual Abuse, rev. ed. Evan Stark. Rosen, 1993.

Chelsea's Special Touch. Hilda Stahl. Crossway, 1993. Fiction.

Harper and Moon. Ramon R. Ross. Atheneum, 1993. Fiction.

Child Abuse, rev. ed. Edward F. Dolan. Watts, 1992.

Know about Abuse. Margaret O. Hyde. Walker, 1992.

Aidan's Fate. Jesse Harris. Borzoi Sprinters/Knopf, 1992. Fiction.

Everything You Need to Know about Incest. Karen Spies. Rosen, 1992.

My Father's Love. Jim Talley and Jane C. Baker. Nelson, 1992.

Coping with Sexual Abuse, rev. ed. Judith Cooney. Rosen, 1991.

How Can Children Be Protected from Abuse? Greenhaven, 1991.

Straight Talk about Child Abuse. Susan Mufson and Rachel Kranz. Facts on File, 1991.

Child Abuse: Detecting Bias. Stacey Tipp. Greenhaven, 1991.

No More Hurt. Wendy Deaton and Kendall Johnson. Hunter House, 1991.

For adult survivors of child abuse

The Courage to Heal: A Guide for Women Survivors of Child Sexual Abuse, 3rd ed. (1994) *Beginning to Heal: The First Book for Survivors of Child Sexual Abuse.* (1993) Ellen Bass and Laura Davis. HarperCollins.

The Healing Path: A Guide for Women Rebuilding Their Lives after Sexual Abuse. John P. Splinter. Nelson, 1993.

The Little Girl Within: Overcoming Memories of Childhood Abuse and Abandonment. Pamela Capone. R & E Publishers, 1992.

Wounded Boys, Heroic Men: A Man's Guide to Recovering from Child Abuse. Daniel J. Sonkin. Longmeadow, 1992.

Recovering from Sexual Abuse and Incest: A Twelve-Step Guide. Jean Gust and Patricia D. Sweeting. Mills Sanderson, 1992.

Pressing Toward the Mark: A Guide to Healing for Victims of Sexual Abuse: Incest, Child Molestation, Rape and Sexual Harassment. Jacqueline E. Nero. J.E. Nero, 1992.

A Secret That's Never Been Told: Healing the Wounds of Childhood Sexual Abuse. Tracy Hansen. Twenty-Third, 1992.

Breaking Down the Wall of Silence: The Liberating Experience of Facing the Painful Truth. Alice Miller. NAL-Dutton, 1991.

Pockets of Craziness: Identifying Yourself As an Adult Survivor of Incest. Kathryn Brohl. Free Press, 1991.

Becoming Whole Again: Help for Survivors of Childhood Sexual Abuse. Vera Gallagher. TAB, 1991.

Growing Beyond Abuse: A Workbook for Survivors of Sexual Exploitation or Childhood Sexual Abuse. Signe L. Nestingen and Laurel Lewis. Omni Recovery, 1991.

Inrage: Healing the Rage of Child Sexual Abuse. Linda Y. Callaghan. Neahtawanta Press, 1991.

The Sexual Healing Journey: A Guide for Survivors of Sexual Abuse. Wendy Maltz. HarperCollins, 1991.

Becoming Whole Again: Help for Women Survivors of Childhood Sexual Abuse. Vera Gallagher. McGraw-Hill, 1991.

Male Survivors: A Twelve-Step Recovery Program for Survivors of Childhood Sexual Abuse. Timothy L. Sanders. Crossing Press, 1991.

Escaping the Shadows, Seeking the Light: Christians in Recovery from Childhood Sexual Abuse. Connie Brewer. Harper-SanFrancisco, 1991.

Growing Through the Pain: The Incest Survivor's Companion. Anonymous. Prentice Hall, 1990.

Soul Survivors: A New Beginning for Adults Abused as Children. J. Patrick Gannon. Prentice Hall, 1990.

Adult Children of Abusive Parents: A Healing Program for Those Who Have Been Physically, Sexually, or Emotionally Abused. Steven Farmer. Ballantine, 1990.

Abused! A Guide to Recovery for Adult Survivors of Emotional/Physical Abuse. Dee Anna Parrish. Station Hill Press, 1990.

Strong at the Broken Places: Overcoming the Trauma of Childhood Abuse. Linda T. Sanford. Random, 1990.

Reclaiming the Heart: A Handbook of Help and Hope for Survivors of Incest. Mary Beth McLure. Warner, 1990.

Broken Boys/Mending Men: Recovery from Childhood Sexual Abuse. Stephen D. Grubman-Black. TAB Books, 1990.

Men Surviving Incest. T. Thomas. Launch, 1990.

Victims No Longer: Men Recovering from Incest and Other Childhood Sexual Abuse. Mike Lew. Harper/Perennial Library, 1990.

On repressed and recovered memories

Truth or Fantasy: The Danger of Recovered Memory Therapy and Decade-Delayed Accusations of Childhood Sexual Abuse. Claudette Wassil-Grimm. Overlook, 1995.

Victims of Memory: Incest Accusations and Shattered Lives. Mark Pendergrast. Upper Access, 1995.

When We Don't Remember: A Book about Discovering Incest. Lyda W. Hersloff. Distinctive, 1994.

Now I Remember: Recovered Memories of Sexual Abuse. Charles R. Kelley and Eric C. Kelley. K-R Publications, 1994.

The Myth of Repressed Memory: False Memories and the Accusations of Sexual Abuse. Elizabeth Loftus and Katherine Ketcham. St. Martin's, 1994.

Forgotten Memories: Treatment of Survivors of Sexual Abuse. Barbara Schave. Praeger/Greenwood, 1993.

The Hidden Legacy: Uncovering, Confronting and Healing Three Generations of Incest. Barbara S. Hamilton. Cypress House, 1993.

Repressed Memories: A Journey to Recovery from Sexual Abuse. Renee Fredrickson. Simon & Schuster, 1992.

True and False Accusations of Child Sex Abuse. Richard A. Gardner. Creative Therapeutics, 1992.

Secret Survivors: Uncovering Incest and Its Aftereffects in Women. E. Sue Blume. Ballantine, 1991.

On sexual abusers

From Generation to Generation: Learning about Adults Who Are Sexual with Children. Anne S. Hastings. Printed Voice, 1994.

Sins of the Father. Marianne Morris. Pacific Press, 1993.

When "The Other Woman" Is His Mother: Book I: Boys and Incest Victims, and Male Multiple Personality Disorder. Faithe Brodie. Winged Eagle, 1992.

Man-Child: An Insight into Child Sexual Abuse by a Convicted Molester, with a Comprehensive Resource Guide. Howard Hunter. McFarland, 1991.

On abuse in churches

A Gospel of Shame: Children, Sexual Abuse, and the Catholic Church. Elinor Burkett and Frank Bruni. Viking Penguin, 1993.

Sexual Abuse in Christian Homes and Churches. Carolyn H. Heggen. Herald Press, 1993.

When Child Abuse Comes to Church. Bill Anderson. Bethany House, 1992.

Lead Us Not into Temptation: Catholic Priests and the Sexual Abuse of Children. Jason Berry. Doubleday, 1992.

Sex in the Parish. Karen Lebacqz and Ronald G. Barton. Westminster/John Knox Press, 1991.

On abuse in schools

Behind the Playground Walls: Sexual Abuse in Preschools. Jill Waterman and others. Guilford, 1993.

Nap Time: The True Story of Sexual Abuse at a Suburban Day Care Center. Lisa Manshel. Morrow, 1990.

On abuse by other trusted authorities

Scout's Honor: Sexual Abuse in America's Most Trusted Institution. Patrick Boyle. Prima, 1994.

Patients As Victims: Sexual Abuse in Psychotherapy and Counselling. Derek Jehu. Wiley, 1994.

Sexual Abuse in Residential Treatment. Wander de C. Braga, ed. Haworth, 1993.

Personal experiences

Annie's Attic: Surviving Sexual Abuse... The Journey from Realization to Recovery. Sarah A. Stevens. Hubbard, 1994.

From Victim to Victory: Prescriptions from a Survivor of Child Abuse. Phil Quinn. Abingdon, 1994.

Childhood's Thief: One Woman's Journey of Healing from Sexual Abuse. Rose M. Evans. Lisa Drew/Macmillan, 1994.

The Thorn of Sexual Abuse: The Gripping Story of a Family's Courage and One Man's Struggle. Beth Sterling. Revell, 1994.

A Child's Story: Recovering Through Creativity. Pat Harris and Jeannette Batz. Cracom, 1993.

Come Here: A Man Copes with the Aftermath of Childhood Sexual Abuse. Richard Berendzen and Laura Palmer. Villard/Random, 1993.

Paperdolls: A True Story of Childhood Sexual Abuse in Mormon Neighborhoods. April Daniels and Carol Scott. RPI Publishing, 1993.

Daddy, Don't: Letters to My Father, A Story of Incest. Holly Broach-Sowels. Kehori, 1993.

The Someday Kid: A True Story of Sexual Abuse and Its Relationship to Pornography. Donna Ferguson. Harbor House West, 1993.

The Daughter of Incest. Josefina T. Torres. Vantage, 1993.

The Missing Voice: Writings by Mothers of Incest Victims. Sandi Ashley. Kendall-Hunt, 1992.

Daddy, Please Say You're Sorry. Amber. CompCare, 1992.

Mama, Why Didn't You Help Me? Amber B. Birts. K. Hughes, 1991.

Prisoner of Another War: A Remarkable Journey of Healing from Childhood Trauma. Marilyn Murray. PageMill Press, 1991.

Ghost Girl: The Story of a Child Who Refused to Talk. Torrey L. Hayden. Little, Brown, 1991. Teacher attempts to help a severely disturbed, emotionally neglected, sexually abused child.

Dancing with Daddy: A Childhood Lost and a Life Regained. Betsy Petersen. Bantam, 1991.

A Deadly Silence: The Ordeal of Cheryl Pierson: A Case of Incest and Murder. Dena Kleiman. Random House, 1991.

Not My Child: A Mother Confronts Her Child's Sexual Abuse. Patricia Crowley. Doubleday, 1990.

What Lisa Knew: The Truths and Lies of the Steinberg Case. Joyce Johnson. Putnam, 1990.

An Uncommon Hero: One Mother Who Went to Jail to Protect Her Child from Sexual Abuse. Stephen T. Curwood. Warner, 1990.

I Never Told Anyone: A Collection of Writings by Survivors of Child Sexual Abuse. Ellen Bass and Louise Thornton, eds. Harper & Row, 1983.

Personal experiences of an accused parent

Unpardonable Sins: A Father's Fight for Justice. Robert M. McQueeney and Bob Vacon. New Horizon, 1992.

Background works

The Child's Song: Religion and Child Abuse. Donald Capps. Westminster John Knox, 1995.

Female Sexual Abuse of Children: The Ultimate Taboo. Michele Elliott, ed. Guilford, 1994.

Emotional and Psychological Abuse of Children. Kieran O'Hagan. University of Toronto Press, 1993.

Child Abuse Errors: When Good Intentions Go Wrong. Dennis Howitt. Rutgers University Press, 1993.

Unequal Justice: The Prosecution of Child Sexual Abuse. Ellen B. Gray. Free Press, 1993.

Suffer the Children: A Pediatrician's Reflections on Abuse. Rosamond L. Murdock and Mariette Hartley. Health Press, 1992.

Too Scared to Cry: Psychic Trauma in Childhood. Lenore Terr. Basic Books, 1992.

Mothers of Incest Survivors: Another Side of the Story. Janis T. Johnson. Indiana University Press, 1992.

On Trial: America's Courts and their Treatment of Sexually Abused Children. Billie Wright Dziech and Charles B. Schudson. Beacon, 1991.

Sex Abuse Hysteria: Salem Witch Trials Revisited. Richard A. Gardner. Creative Therapeutics, 1991.

With the Best of Intentions: The Child Sexual Abuse Prevention Movement. Jill D. Berrick and Neil Gilbert. Guilford, 1991.

Breaking down the Wall of Silence: The Liberating Experience of Facing the Painful Truth. Alice Miller. NAL-Dutton, 1991.

Child Abuse and Neglect: An Information and Reference Guide. Timothy J. Iverson and Marilyn Segal. Garland, 1991.

(See also CORPORAL PUNISHMENT; DISCIPLINE; RAPE; VIOLENCE; POST-TRAUMATIC STRESS DISORDER; SAFETY; MISSING CHILDREN.)

Help for Special Children

ORGANIZATIONS OFFERING HELP AND INFORMATION

GENERAL ORGANIZATIONS FOR SPECIAL CHILDREN

National Information Center for Children and Youth with Disabilities (NICHCY)
P.O. Box 1492
Washington, DC 20013–1492
800–695–0285, voice/TT
Fax: 202–884–8441
SpecialNet User Name: NICHCY
E-mail: nichcy@capcon.net
Suzanne Ripley, Project Director
Information clearinghouse on disabilities and disability-related issues, focusing on children to age twenty-two; offers information about specific disabilities, early intervention, special education and related services, individualized education programs (IEPs), family issues, transition to adult life, multicultural issues, and legal issues; provides referrals and technical assistance; publishes numerous materials, including:

- Parent's guides such as *Accessing Parent Groups, Accessing the ERIC Resource Collection,* and *Doctors, Disabilities, and the Family.*
- Information on national resources, general information about disabilities, public agencies fact sheets, national toll free numbers, and state resource sheets.
- News digests, such as *Assistive Technology: Becoming an Informed Consumer, Having a Daughter with a Disability: Is It Different for Girls?, Estate Planning, Parenting a Child with Special Needs: Guide to Readings and Resources,* and *Directory of Organizations, Paying the Medical Bills,* and *Resources for Adults with Disabilities.*
- Fact sheets on many specific disabilities.

PACER Center (Parent Advocacy Coalition for Educational Rights)
4826 Chicago Avenue South
Minneapolis, MC 55417–1098
612–827–2966, voice/TT; 800–53PACER [537–2237], MN only
Fax: 612–827–3065
E-mail: hn2338@handsnet.org
Electronic bulletin boards on SpecialNet: Programs Involving Parents (PIP) and ADA.INDEPENDENT
Marge Goldberg and Paula F. Goldberg, Codirectors
Organization serving families of children and adults with disabilities, focusing on rights to education, services, and widest possible opportunities; operates various programs in support of children, parents, and grandparents; provides technical assistance through TAPP (Technical Assistance to Parent Projects; see full entry later in this listing), SEPT/TA (Supported Employment, Parents, Transition, and Technical Assistance), and TATRA (Technical Assistance on Training about the Rehabilitation Act); publishes various materials, including:

- Newsletters: *The Pacesetter, Early Childhood Connection,* and *Children's Mental Health Update,* and *PACER Advocate.*
- Family resources: *Parents Can Be the Key, Unlocking Doors, Hope for the Families, One Miracle at a Time: Getting Help for a Child with a Disability, Summer Vacation Ideas for Families and a Vacation Accessibility Checklist, Self-Injury: Answers to Questions for Parents, Teachers and Caregivers, Supplemental Security Income (SSI), Living Your Own Life: Student Handbook,* for adolescents, and resources on the Americans with Disabilities Act (ADA).
- Numerous materials on supported employment, transition, and multicultural resources, as well as many information handouts, such as *Adaptive Clothing Resources and Commercial Sources of Toys and Equipment for Children with Disabilities, A Checklist for Growing Children, Creating a Welcoming Environment for Persons with Disabilities of All Ages, The Evolution of a Parent: A Gradual Process, How Do You Combat Teasing?,* and *12 Commandments for Parents of Children with Disabilities.*

National Center for Youth with Disabilities (NCYD)
Adolescent Health Program
University of Minnesota, Box 721
420 Delaware Street SE
Minneapolis, MN 55455–0392
612–626–2825; 612–624–3939, TT; 800–333–6293
Fax: 612–626–2134
E-mail: ncyd@gold.tc.umn.edu
Nancy Okinow, Executive Director
Center focusing on youth with disabilities, including chronic illness; operates National Resource Library on Youth with Disabilities, including technical assistance and training materials; publishes:

- Newsletter: *Connections* and *Special Report: Teenagers at Risk;*
- Numerous annotated bibliographies, such as *An Introduction to Youth with Disabilities, Youth with Disabilities*

and Chronic Illnesses: An Introductory Guide for Youth and Parents, and *Self-Esteem: Issues for Adolescents with Chronic Illnesses and Disabilities.*

- "Issues for Adolescents with Chronic Illnesses and Disabilities" work such as *Race and Ethnicity, Developing Social Skills,* and *Legal Issues.*
- Periodic FYI Bulletins.

Parents Helping Parents (PHP)
3041 Olcott Street
Santa Clara, CA 95054–3222
408–727–5775
Fax: 408–727–0182
Florene Poyadue, Executive Director
Family resource center for children with special needs; operates programs for peer counseling, visiting parents, siblings, and family respite; offers workshops and training, as in planning individualized education plans (IEPs); maintains divisions focusing on specific disabilities or concerns, including autism, cleft lip and palate, learning disabilities, intensive care nursery parents (as of premature infants), Down syndrome, severe emotional disturbance, sickle cell anemia, parents of near drowning, and biochemical connections between diet and allergies and behavior; publishes various materials, including:

- Practical materials: *File It Once—Find It Everytime* (system for handling filing related to special needs), *Steps to Starting Self-Help* (on establishing a self-help group), and *P.I.E. Manual* (on early intervention).
- For children: *A Friend Like You—A Friend Like Me.*
- Information packets on near drownings (focusing on hospitalization and aftercare), and on needs of different age groups: infants, preschoolers, youth, and adults, as well as siblings.
- Materials for health professionals and peer counselors.

National Parent Network on Disabilities (NPND)
1727 King Street, Suite 305
Alexandria, VA 22314
703–684–6763, voice/TT
Fax: 703–836–1232
Patricia Magill Smith, Executive Director
Network of parent-oriented organizations concerned with children and adults with disabilities; acts as advocate; publishes various materials, including *Inclusion: A Parent's View,* video *What Is Inclusion?,* and manuals for parents' organizations.

Family Voices
P.O. Box 769
Algondones, NM 87001
505–867–2368
Fax: 505–867–6517
E-mail: famvO1r@wonder.em.cdc.gov
Polly Arango, Contact
Network of families and others concerned with children who have chronic illness or disabilities; provides information and referrals; urges universal community-based access to health care; publishes newsletter *Voices* and other materials on health care.

National Fathers' Network (NFN)
16120 North East 8th Street
Bellevue, WA 98008
206–747–4004
Fax: 206–747–1069
James May, Project Director
Organization for fathers and other male family members and friends concerned with children with special needs; fosters support programs; provides referrals; produces monthly column for *Exceptional Parent* magazine; publishes quarterly *National Fathers' Network Newsletter, Fathers of Children with Special Needs: New Horizons, Circles of Care and Understanding: Support Programs for Fathers of Children with Special Needs;* and videos *Special Dads, Special Kids: Fathers of Children with Disabilities* and *Health Care Delivery for African-American Fathers.*

Shriner's Hospitals for Crippled Children, 800–237–5055. Provides free medical care for children with orthopedic problems or severe burns. (For full group information, see BONE AND BONE DISORDERS.)

Educational Equity Concepts (EEC), 212–725–1803. Publishes *Bridging the Gap: A National Directory of Services for Women and Girls with Disabilities, Building Community: A Manual Exploring Issues of Women and Disability,* and *Including All of Us: An Early Childhood Curriculum About Disability.* (For full group information, see HELP ON LEARNING AND EDUCATION on page 659.)

National Federation of the Blind (NFB), 410–659–9314. Publishes *Plan to Achieve Self Support* and various materials on Social Security benefit programs. (For full group information, see EYE AND VISION PROBLEMS.)

Twin Services, TWINLINE: 510–524–0863. Publishes *When Twins Are Disabled.* (For full group information, see MULTIPLE BIRTH.)

Blind Children's Center, 800–222–3566. Publishes *Starting Points: Instructional Practices for Young Children Whose Multiple Disabilities Include Visual Impairment.* (For full group information, see EYE AND VISION PROBLEMS.)

Child Welfare League of America (CWLA), 202–638–2952. Publishes *When Love Is Not Enough—How Mental Health Professionals Can Help Special-Needs Adoptive Families,* and other materials for therapists. (For full group information and more titles, see FOSTER CARE.)

American Association on Mental Retardation (AAMR), 800–424–3688. Publishes *Recognizing Choices* *in Community Settings by People with Significant Disabilities, Pathways to Success: Training for Independent Living, Parent Involvement in Vocational Education of Special Needs Youth, Parent Training and Developmental Disabilities,* and numerous professional materials. (For full group information, see MENTAL RETARDATION.)

National Adoption Information Clearinghouse (NAIC), 301–231–6512. Publishes *Adopting Children with Developmental Disabilities, Adopting a Child with Special Needs,* and *Subsidized Adoption: A Source of Help for Children with Special Needs and Their Families.* (For full group information, see ADOPTION.)

National Information Center on Deafness (NICD), 202–651–5051; 202–651–5052, TT. Publishes *The Americans with Disabilities Act (ADA): Selected Resources for Deaf and Hard of Hearing People* and *Deaf Children with Multiple Disabilities.* (For full group information, see EAR AND HEARING PROBLEMS.)

The Children's Foundation (TCF), 202–347–3300. Publishes *Implications of the Americans with Disabilities Act of 1990 (ADA) for Family Day Care Providers.* (For full group information, see CHILD CARE.)

On siblings of children with special needs

Sibling Information Network
Connecticut's University Affiliated Program on Developmental Disabilities
University of Connecticut
249 Glenbrook Road, Box U–64
Storrs, CT 06268
203–486–3783
Kathleen Bradley, Coordinator
Organization concerned with siblings of people with disabilities; conducts research; provides information and referrals; publishes *Sibling Information Network Newsletter.*

Siblings for Significant Chance (SSC)
105 East 22 Street, 7th Floor
New York, NY 10010
212–420–0776
Gerri Zatlow, Director
Organization for siblings of people with disabilities; offers information, counseling, support, and legal aid; acts as advocate.

On health services for children with disabilities

National Information Clearinghouse (NIC) for Infants with Disabilities and Life-Threatening Conditions
The Center for Developmental Disabilities
University of South Carolina
Benson Building, 1st Floor
Columbia, SC 29208
803–777–4435; 800–922–9234, ext. 201, voice/TT
Fax: 803–777–6058
Organization concerned with infants born with life-threatening conditions; formerly National Information Center for Health Related Services; a joint program of the University of South Carolina's Center for Developmental Disabilities and the Association for the Care of Children's Health (see next entry), funded by the National Center on Child Abuse and Neglect (see HELP AGAINST CHILD ABUSE AND NEGLECT on page 680); provides information on support, resources, services, early intervention programs, protection and advocacy agencies, and special needs adoptions; publishes newsletter *Family-Centered Care Network*; fact sheets such as *Summary of Child Abuse Amendments of 1984* and *Primer of Disabilities, Health Conditions and Medical Terminology Related to Infants with Disabilities*; and bibliographies on the care of infants with disabilities, such as *Family and Psycho-Social Issues, Parental Experiences in the NICU,* and *Legal Issues.*

Association for the Care of Children's Health (ACCH)
7910 Woodmont Avenue, Suite 300
Bethesda, MD 20814–3015
301–654–6549; 800–808–2224
Fax: 301–986–4553
E-mail: acch@clark.net
Organization of pediatric health care professionals; cosponsors National Information Clearinghouse (NIC) for Infants with Disabilities and Life-Threatening Conditions (see earlier in this list); publishes various materials, including *How Can I Tell You? Secrecy and Disclosure with Children When a Family Member Has AIDS* and *Family-Centered Care for Children Needing Specialized Health and Developmental Services.*

Federation for Children with Special Needs (FCSN)
95 Berkeley Street, Suite 104
Boston, MA 02116
617–482–2915, voice/TT; 800–331–0688, voice/TT, MA only
Fax: 617–695–2939
P.O. Box 992
Westfield, MA 01086
413–562–3691
Martha H. Ziegler, Executive Director
Organization for parents of children with special needs; operates numerous programs, including:

- Parenting Training and Information (PTI), which offers information, assistance, training, and workshops on topics such as special education laws, due process, individualized education plans, transition, independent living, community integration, and parent/professional partnerships.

- Parent/Professional Advocacy League (PAL), which offers information and referral, coordinating a statewide (MA) network of parent support groups.
- Collaboration of Parents and Professionals (CAPP), which operates the National Parent Resource Center (NPRC).
- Early Intervention Parent Leadership Services, providing information and referrals and helping with the development and running of Early Intervention Parent Advisory Councils (EI-PACs).
- Technical Assistance for Parent Programs (TAPP).
- National Early Childhood Technical Assistance System (NEC*TAS), aiding states in planning and implementing early childhood special education programs, coordinating community-based services to families.
- Agent Orange Parent Network, offership workshops of topics related to children with special needs born of Vietnam Veteran families (1961–1972).

Publishes various materials, including *Federation Newsline.*

Technical Assistance for Parent Programs (TAPP). Federally funded network of parent-to-parent training and information centers, coordinated by the Federation for Children with Special Needs (see above) and established under the Individuals with Disabilities Education Act (IDEA), with grants to support Parent Training and Information (PTI) Centers; provides assistance on topics such as training and information, grant management, program development, and evaluation.

TAPP Regional Centers:

Midwest:

PACER Center
4826 Chicago Avenue South
Minneapolis, MN 55417–1098
612–827–2966, voice/TT; 800–53PACER
[537–2237], MN only
Fax: 612–827–3065
(For more information, see full entry above.)

Northeast:

Parent Information Center
51A Manchester Street
P.O. Box 1422
Concord, NH 03302–1422
603–224–7005, voice/TT; 800–232–0986, NH only
Fax: 603–224–4365

South:

The Arc/Georgia
2860 East Point Street, Suite 200
East Point, GA 30344
404–761–3150
Fax: 404–767–2258

West:

Washington State PAVE
6316 South 12th Street
Tacoma, WA 98465
206–565–2266, voice/TT; 800–5PARENT
[572–7368], voice/TT
Fax: 206–566–8052
E-mail: washingtonpave@aol.com (America Online: WASHINGTONPAVE)

TAPP Focus Centers:

Focus Center on Early Childhood
Pilot Parent Partnerships
2150 East Highland Avenue, Suite 105
Phoenix, AZ 85016
Phone and fax: 602–468–3001; 800–237–3007

Focus Center on Inclusion
PEAK Parent Center
6055 Lehman Drive, Suite 101
Colorado Springs, CO 80918
719–531–9400
Fax: 719–531–9452

Focus Center on Technology
PLUK (Parents Let's Unite for Kids)
1500 North 30th Street
Billings, MT 59101
406–657–2055; 800–222–7585 MT only
E-Mail: PLUKMT@aol.com

Children In Hospitals (CIH)
31 Wilshire Park
Needham, MA 02192
617–482–2915
Barbara Popper, Executive Director
Organization concerned with hospitalized children; encourages flexible parental visiting policies; provides support, information, and referrals; publishes various materials, including quarterly newsletter and *CIH Consumer Directory of Hospitals.*

National Foundation of Dentistry for the Handicapped (NFDH)
1800 Glenarm Place, Suite 500
Denver, CO 80202
303–298–9650
Larry Coffee, Executive Director
Organization of dental professionals concerned with special children.

Resource Center on Substance Abuse Prevention and Disability
1819 L Street NW, Suite 300
Washington, DC 20036
202–628–8080; 202–638–5862, TT; Toll-free: 202–628–8442
Fax: 202–628–3812

Organization concerned with alcohol and drug abuse among people with disabilities; provides information; publishes bimonthly newsletter, awareness video, and fact sheets, including *An Overview of Alcohol and Other Drug Abuse Prevention and Disability*, and "A Look at Alcohol and Drug Abuse Prevention and" series, including *Hidden Disabilities, Enabling, Americans with Disabilities, Mobility Limitations*, and *Health Implications*.

ERIC (Educational Resources Information Center) Clearinghouse on Disabilities and Gifted Education, 800–328–0272. (For full group information, see HELP ON LEARNING AND EDUCATION on page 659.)

General organizations and government agencies

National Easter Seal Society
230 W. Monroe Street, Suite 1800
Chicago, IL 60606–4802
312–726–6200; 312–726–4258, TT;
800–221–6827
Fax: 312–726–1494
James E. Williams, Jr., President and CEO
National network aiding people with disabilities of any kind; operates local rehabilitation centers; seeks to influence public policy; provides information and referrals; publishes *Making Life Better: A Catalog of Catalogs*; general brochures *Camps for Children With Disabilities: Make the Right Choice, The Americans with Disabilities Act, Yes You Can!* (for children), *Tips for Disability Awareness*, and *Tips for Portraying People with Disabilities in the Media*; brochures on many specific problems, such as CEREBRAL PALSY and DOWN SYNDROME; videos *Providing Public Transportation to Everyone, Diversity Equals Inclusion*, and *Friends Who Care® Teachers Kit* (for school curriculum); and other materials on employment, education, and housing.

National Rehabilitation Information Center (NARIC)
8455 Colesville Road, Suite 935
Silver Spring, MD 20910–3319
301–588–9284; 800–34NARIC [346–2742], voice/TT
Fax: 301–587–1967
E-mail: naric@capaccess.org
AbleInform BBS (electronic bulletin board):
301–589–3563 (settings 1200–9600 baud, 8-N–1)
Mark Odum, Director
Clearinghouse on services, research, and resources for people with disabilities, funded by the National Institute on Disability and Rehabilitation Research (NIDRR); provides information and makes referrals; maintains databases REHABDATA (on special topics) and ABLEDATA (commercially available assistive devices); publishes *NARIC Quarterly, Directory of National Information Sources on Disabilities, NIDRR Program Directory, NARIC Guide to Resources for the Americans with Disabilities Act (ADA), NARIC Guide to Disability and Rehabilitation Periodicals, ABLEDATA* CD-ROM (for IBM-style computers), and resource guides on spinal cord injury, head injury, stroke, and home modification.

American Association of University Affiliated Programs for Persons with Developmental Disabilities (AAUAP)
8630 Fenton Street, Suite 4010
Silver Spring, MD 20910
301–588–8252; 301–588–3319, TT
Fax: 301–588–2842
William E. Jones, Executive Director
Network of federally supported centers—University Affiliated Facilities (UAFs) or University Affiliated Programs (UAPs)—for assessment and treatment of developmental disabilities; some centers have specific focus, some treat whole range of problems; provides referrals to public and professionals.

Information Center for Individuals with Disabilities (ICID)
Fort Point Place
27–43 Wormwood Street
Boston, MA 02210–1606
617–727–5540; 617–345–9743, TT;
800–462–5015, MA only
Fax: 617–345–5318
J. Archer O'Reilly III, Executive Director
Organization providing information, referral, and problem-solving assistance on disability-related issues; maintains computerized database; publishes newsletter *Disability Issues*; numerous fact sheets on topics such as architectural accessibility, assistive technology, counseling, education, employment, finance, housing, law, personal care, recreation, transportation, and travel; and various bibliographies.

TASH: The Association for Persons with Severe Handicaps
29 West Susquehanna Avenue, Suite 210
Baltimore, MD 21204
410–828–8274; 410–828–6706, TT; 800–482-TASH [482–8274]
Fax: 410–828–1306
E-mail: 76023.1371@compuserve.com (CompuServe: 76023,1371)
Nancy R. Weiss, Executive Director
Organization concerned with improving the quality of life for people with severe disabilities; acts as advocate; provides information and referrals; publishes monthly *TASH Newsletter*, quarterly *Journal of the Association for Persons with Severe Handicaps*, and occasional books and monographs.

Gazette International Networking Institute (GINI)
4207 Lindell Boulevard, #110
St. Louis, MO 63108–2915

314–534–0475
Fax: 314–534–5070
Relay MO: 800–735–2966, TT; 800–735–2466. voice
Joan L. Headley, Executive Director
Organization concerned with severely disabled people, such as those who have effects from polio or spinal cord injuries, or who use ventilators; focuses on independent living as much as possible; acts as information clearinghouse and communications network; publishes biannual *Rehabilitation Gazette*, biannual *I.V.U.N. News*, for people who use ventilators, and *Ventilators and Muscular Dystrophy*.

Accent
c/o Cheever Publishing
P.O. Box 700
Bloomington, IL 61702
309–378–2961; 800–787–8444 (for orders)
Fax: 309–378–4420
Raymond C. Cheever, Publisher
Organization offering publications and products for people with disabilities; publishes magazine *Accent on Living*, annual *Accent Buyer's Guide*, and other materials, including:

- On family issues: *Parenting* (for parents with disabilities) and *Ideas for Kids on the Go* (on kids with physical disabilities).
- General materials: *It Feels Good to Be in Control, Yes You Can, Out of the Darkness, Accepting Disability, Crip Zen: A Manual for Survival, Accepting Disability, Earning a Living, Pacing Yourself—Steps to Save Energy*, and *How to Live Longer with a Disability*.
- Numerous materials on sexuality, travel, technical aids, home modifications, support services, and other products and services.

People First International (PFI)
P.O. Box 12642
Salem, OR 97309
503–362–0336
Mike Easterly, Executive Officer
Organization of and for people with developmental disabilities and mental retardation; acts as advocate; aids local groups; publishes various materials.

PRIDE Foundation—Promote Real Independence for the Disabled and Elderly
391 Long Hill Road
Groton, CT 06340
203–445–7320; 800–332–9022
Evelyn S. Kennedy, Executive Director
Organization to help people with disabilities dress and care for themselves at home independently, as through specially designed clothes and technical aids; provides training for handicapped people; disseminates information to other interested groups; publishes various materials, including *Dressing with Pride: Clothing Changes for Special Needs*.

American Amputee Foundation (AAF)
Box 250218
Hillcrest Station
Little Rock, AR 72225
501–666–2523
Fax: 501–666–8367
Jack M. East, Executive Director
Organization for amputees and their families; provides information and referrals; publishes *AAF Newsletter, National Resource Directory*; numerous self-help guides, such as *Children with Limb Loss* (*Birth to 5 Years Old; 6 to 12 Years Old, Adolescents*), *Crutches on the Go, Amputees' Guide* (*Above the Knee; Below the Knee*), and *What to Expect When You Lose a Limb: Psychological Aspects of Amputation*; and various articles and videos.

National Organization on Disability (NOD)
910 16 Street NW, Suite 600
Washington, DC 20006
202–293–5960, voice; 202–293–5968, TT
Fax: 202–293–7999
Alan A. Reich, President
Organization promoting fuller participation of people with disabilities in American life; publishes quarterly newsletter *REPORT*; *Guide to Organizing a Community Partnership Program; That All May Worship* (handbook and brochure); brochure *Loving Justice: Public Attitudes Towards People with Disabilities*; and fact sheets *Americans with Disabilities Act (ADA)* and *Jim Brady's "Calling on America" Campaign*.

Resources for Rehabilitation, 617–862–6455. Publishes books *Resources for People with Disabilities and Chronic Conditions* and *A Woman's Guide to Coping with Disability*. (For full group information, see EYE AND VISION PROBLEMS.)

United Cerebral Palsy Association (UCPA), 800–872–5827. Publishes *After the Tears: Parents Talk About Raising a Child with a Disability, I Wish: Dreams and Realities of Parenting a Special Needs Child, Natural Supports in School, at Work, and in the Community for People with Severe Disabilities, Enabling Romance: A Guide to Love, Sex, and Relationships for the Disabilities*, and *Breaking Ground: Ten Families Building Opportunities Through Integration*. (For full group information, see CEREBRAL PALSY.)

National Mental Health Consumer Self-Help Clearinghouse, 800–553–4539. Publishes reprint packet on physical disability and mental illness. (For full group information, see MENTAL DISORDERS.)

Spina Bifida Association of America (SBAA), 800–621–3141. Publishes *Planning Reasonable Accommodations: A Cost Effective Guide in a Legal Framework* (on the Americans with Disabilities Act), *Making the Workplace Accessible: Guidelines, Costs and Resources*, and *Accessible Gardening for People with Physical Disabilities*. (For full group information, see SPINA BIFIDA.)

Sexuality Information and Education Council of the United States (SIECUS), 212–819–9770. Publishes annotated bibliography *Sexuality and Disability.* (For full group information, see SEX EDUCATION.)

ON ACCESS TO EDUCATION, CULTURE, AND LIBRARY SERVICES

Center for Law and Education, 202–986–3000. Publishes "Information for Parents" brochure *Promoting Inclusion for All Students with Disabilities* and *Assistive Technology for Students with Disabilities: Rights Under Federal Law.* (For full group information, see HELP ON LEARNING AND EDUCATION on page 659.)

Council for Exceptional Children (CEC), 800–328–0272. Publishes *Rights and Responsibilities of Parents of Children with Handicaps, Rural, Exceptional, At Risk,* and special-topic reports *Disabilities: An Overview, Severe Disabilities,* and *Self-Management for Severely Handicapped Persons in Integrated Job Settings.* (For full group information, see HELP ON LEARNING AND EDUCATION on page 659.)

National Library Services for the Blind and Physically Handicapped, Library of Congress
1291 Taylor Street NW
Washington, DC 20542
202–707–5100; 202–707–0744, TT;
800–424–8567, U.S. except DC
Fax: 202–707–0712
E-mail: nls@loc.gov
Frank Kurt Cylke, Director
Federal service providing Braille or recorded books or magazines on free loan to anyone who cannot read standard print because of visual or physical disabilities; publishes numerous materials, including:

- Practical guides: *Physical Disabilities: National Organizations and Resources* and *Library Resources for the Blind and Physically Handicapped.*
- Information brochures: *Facts: Playback Machines and Accessories Provided on Free Loan to Eligible Individuals and Institutions, Talking Books for People with Physical Disabilities, Facts: Music for Blind and Physically Handicapped Individuals,* and *Reference and Information Services.*
- Catalogs and subject bibliographies of Braille and recorded books, and on accessibility, assistive technology, disability awareness and changing attitudes, and library and information services.
- Reference circulars in special topics for professionals.

Clearinghouse on Disability Information
U.S. Department of Education
Office of Special Education and Rehabilitative Services (OSERS)
Switzer Building, Room 3132
Washington, DC 20202–2425
202–205–8241; Publications: 202–205–8723
Organization providing information and referrals about services at all levels for people with disabilities; publishes numerous materials, including newsletter, *OSERS News in Print, Pocket Guide to Federal Help for Individuals with Disabilities;* and booklet *A Summary of Existing Legislation Affecting Persons with Disabilities.*

National Association of Private Schools for Exceptional Children (NAPSEC)
1522 K Street NW, Suite 1032
Washington, DC 20005–1202
202–408–3338
Fax: 202–408–3340
Sherry L. Kolbe, Executive Director
Organization of private schools with programs for children with special needs; provides information and referrals, based on the age, sex, and type of disability of the child, the region desired, and the type of facility (for example, day, residential, or summer); provides accreditation; publishes *NAPSEC News* and directory of member schools.

American Council on Rural Special Education (ACRES)
University of Utah
Department of Special Education
221 Milton Bennion Hall
Salt Lake City, UT 84112
801–585–5659
Fax: 801–581–5223
E-mail: acres@gse.utah.edu
Joan Sebastian and Jack Mayhew, Coordinators
Organization focusing education of rural children with disabilities; provides information and referrals; publishes bimonthly newsletter *ACRES RuraLink, Rural Special Education Quarterly,* and other materials.

Rural Institute on Disabilities
52 Corbin Hall
University of Montana
Missoula, MT 59812
406–243–5467; 406–243–4200, TT;
800–732–0323, voice/TT
Fax: 406–243–4730
E-mail: muarid@selway.umt.edu
R. Timm Vogelsberg, Director
Organization promoting full participation in rural life by individuals of all ages with disabilities; provides information and referrals; acts as advocate; conducts research and develops model programs; sponsors training; publishes various materials, including:

- Newsletters: quarterly *The Rural Exchange, MonTECH* on assistive technology, *Child Care Plus +,* and *MSED Quarterly,* on Montana Supported Employment Development Project.

- On general concerns: *Acceptance Is Only the First Battle* (booklet and video), *Robbie* (fiction about mother and child with disability), *Getting the Word Out* (on building community support), and *Seizure Disorders and Medications.*
- Various fact sheets and other materials on topics such as access, independent living, respite care, and assistive technology.

Henry Viscardi School
201 I.U. Willets Road
Albertson, NY 11507
516–747–5400; 516–747–5378
Edmund Cortez, President
Organization providing various special programs for handicapped people, Human Resources School for severely disabled, otherwise homebound students, K–12; formerly Human Resources Center (HRC); maintains library and seeks to educate public through tours and seminars; spreads information on model programs to other groups; publishes print and audiovisual materials.

National Challenged Homeschoolers Associated Network (NATHHAN), 206–857–4257. (For full group information, see HOME SCHOOLING.)

Very Special Arts (VSA)
Education Office
John F. Kennedy Center for the Performing Arts
Washington, DC 20566
202–628–2800; 202–737–0645, TT; 800–933–8721
Fax: 202–737–0725
Eileen Ceskaden, Acting Chief Executive Officer
Organization that provides arts and educational programs to people with disabilities, working with public and private groups; publishes newsletter *The Creative Spirit.*

National Maternal and Child Health Clearinghouse (NMCHC), 703–821–8955. Publishes *Children with Special Health Needs—A Resource Guide, Equals in This Partnership: Parents of Disabled and At-Risk Infants and Toddlers Speak to Professionals, The Open Door: Parent Participation in State Policymaking About Children with Special Health Needs, EPSDT: A Guide to Educational Programs, Pediatric Resources for Prehospital Care*; and numerous materials on family support programs and for professionals. (For full group information, see PREGNANCY.)

Alliance for Parental Involvement in Education (ALLPIE), 518–392–6900. Publishes *To a Different Drumbeat: A Practical Guide to Parenting Children with Special Needs.* (For full group information, see HELP ON LEARNING AND EDUCATION on page 659.)

National Clearinghouse for Alcohol and Drug Abuse Information (NCADI), 301–468–2600. Publishes *Life Transitions and Healthy Choices: Help Your Child with a Disability Adjust to the Changes in Life in a Healthy Way.* (For full group information, see HELP AGAINST SUBSTANCE ABUSE on page 703.)

Center for Safety in the Arts (CSA), 212–227–6220. Publishes fact sheet *Teaching Art Safely to the Disabled.* (For full group information, see ENVIRONMENTAL HAZARDS.)

ON SPECIAL SERVICES FOR YOUNG CHILDREN

Association for Childhood Education International (ACEI), 800–423–3563. Publishes position paper *Infants and Toddlers with Special Needs and Their Families.* (For full group information, see HELP ON LEARNING AND EDUCATION on page 659.)

National Association for the Education of Young Children (NAEYC), 800–424–2460. Publishes books *Including Children with Special Needs in Early Childhood Programs* and *A Place for Me: Including Children with Special Needs in Early Care and Education Settings*; and brochure *Understanding the Americans with Disabilities Act: Information for Early Childhood Programs.* (For full group information, see PRESCHOOL.)

Pediatric Projects, 800–947–0947. Publishes reprints *Children with Handicaps, Parent and Family Issues, Profoundly Disabled Children Learn by Touch,* and *The Theory Behind Stuffed Animals and Dolls That Have Disabilities, and Ideas on Using Them with Children.* (For full group information, see HOSPITAL.)

National Lekotek Center
2100 Ridge Avenue
Evanston, IL 60201
708–328–0001; 800–366-PLAY [366–7529]
Fax: 708–328:5514
E-mail: lekotek@aol.com or lekotek@interaccess.com
Network of centers offering play programs and toy-lending services for children with special needs.

Parent Care (PC), 317–872–9913. Publishes *For Families of Children with Special Needs: A Calendar of Resources.* (For full group information, see PREMATURE.)

ON HIGH SCHOOL AND BEYOND FOR PEOPLE WITH DISABILITIES

HEATH Resource Center, National Clearinghouse on Postsecondary Education for Individuals with Disabilities
One Dupont Circle, Suite 800
Washington, DC 20036
202–939–9320 (voice/TT); 800–544–3284 (voice/TT)
Fax: 202–833–4760
E-mail: heath@ace.nche.edu
Rhona C. Hartman, Director
National clearinghouse on postsecondary education for people with disabilities; operated by the American Coun-

cil on Education and supported by the U.S. Department of Education, under the Individuals with Disabilities Education Act; provides information on support services, policies, procedures, adaptations, and opportunities; publishes newsletter *Information from HEATH* and numerous other materials, including:

- Directories and guides: *HEATH Resource Directory*, *Transition Resource Guide*, and *Computers, Technology, and Disability*.
- Resource papers: *Young Adults with Learning Disabilities and Other Special Needs*, *Measuring Student Progress in the Classroom*, *Adults with Disabilities and Distance Learning*, *Strategies for Advising Students with Disabilities*, *After High School, What's Next?*, *High School Diploma Alternatives*, *Education for Employment*, and *Career Planning and Employment Strategies*;
- Newsletter reprints: *American with Disabilities Act*, *Facts You Can Use*, *Vocational Assessment*, *Social Security Work Incentives*, *Descriptive Summary of ETS Project*, *Keefe Technical School*, *Focus on Faculty*, and *Current Language*.

Scholastic Aptitude Test (SAT)
Admissions Testing Program (ATP) for Handicapped Students
CN 6603
Princeton, NJ 08541–6226
609–771–7137; 609–882–4118, TT
Catherine Nelson, Contact
Organization that offers special testing arrangements for students with documented learning disabilities, visual or hearing disabilities, or dyslexia, including untimed tests or additional time, tests in large type or braille, tests on tape cassette or read to student, scribe or interpreter, special answer sheets, extended testing time, flexible test dates, and rest breaks.

ACT Universal Testing
2255 North Dubuque Road
P.O. Box 4028
Iowa City, IO 52243–4028
319–337–1028; Special Testing: 319–337–1332; Arranged Testing: 319–337–1448; 319–337–1701, TT
Fax: 319–339–3020
Organization that offers special arrangements for students with documented physical or perceptual disabilities, as when students are unable to go to the test center, cannot complete the test using regular test booklets, or are confined to hospitals; offers individually administered tests and other accommodations, such as use of large-type or Braille test books or audiocassette tapes, or a scribe to record answers.

Foundation for Science and Disability (FSD)
236 Grand Street
Morgantown, WV 26505–7509
304–293–6363
E-mail, Bitnet: u0072@wvnvm
For grant information:
Rebecca F. Smith
115 South Brainard Avenue
La Grange, IL 60625
Organization of scientists and professionals, many with disabilities, who apply their skills to solving disability-related problems; offers guidance and referrals; seeks to ease access in universities and industry; provides some grants for college seniors or graduate students with disabilities; publishes *Able Scientists—Disabled Persons*.

ON LEGAL AND ECONOMIC ISSUES FOR PEOPLE WITH DISABILITIES

Disability Rights Education and Defense Fund (DREDF)
2212 Sixth Street
Berkeley, CA 94710
510–644–2555; 800–466–4ADA [466–4232], voice/TT
Fax: 510–841–8645
Robert J. Funk, Director
Organization seeking equal opportunity for people with disabilities, including access to education and training programs; acts as advocate; provides information, advice, and assistance; publishes various materials, including *Disability Rights Review*.

Estate Planning for Persons with Disabilities (EPPD)
P.O. Box 2606
Birmingham, AL 35202–2606
2801 Highway 280 South
Birmingham, AL 35223
205–879–9230; 800–934–1929
Fax: 800–880–9327
Organization providing low-cost estate planning services for families of people with disabilities; makes referrals to local legal and financial teams; offers seminars on planning.

Disabled and Alone/Life Services for the Handicapped, Inc.
352 Park Avenue South
New York, NY 10010
212–532–6740
Fax: 212–532–6740
Roslyn Brilliant, Executive Director
Organization concerned with long-term issues for people with disabilities, especially care after parents are gone; formerly Life Services for the Handicapped; helps families make financial plans for care of a surviving child with disabilities and establish trusts to pay for services for such surviving children, often working through local organizations and under direction of a family-chosen trustee, advocate, and guardian; publishes newsletter *Life Lines*, *"After We're Gone"*, and *Partnership Plan*.

Center on Human Policy (CHP)
c/o Syracuse University
805 South Crouse Avenue, Room 101
Syracuse, NY 13244–2280
315–443–3851
Fax: 315–443–4338
E-mail: razubal@sued.syr.edu
Steven Taylor, Director
Organization concerned with people who have severe physical or emotional disabilities, seeking to bring them into the mainstream as much as possible; acts as advocate; provides information on rights, regulations, laws, programs and other resources; publishes numerous materials, including:

- Information packages *Selected Issues in Family Support: A Compilation of Materials and Resources, Housing for People with Severe Disabilities: A Collection of Resource Materials, Multiculturalism and Disability: A Collection of Resources, Supported Employment: Issues and Resources, Personal Relationships and Social Networks: Facilitating the Participation of Individuals with Disabilities,* and *Women with Disabilities: Issues, Resources, Connections.*
- News bulletins *Families for all Children, Safeguards, Disability and Family Policy, Safeguards,* and *Social Relationships.*
- Site visit reports, collections of articles and papers, and resource materials, about experiences from around the country, on topics such as inclusion in schools and communities, integrated employment, family support, deinstitutionalization, model programs, and independent living.

National Alliance for the Mentally Ill (NAMI), 800–950-NAMI. Publishes book *Disability and the Family: A Guide to Decisions for Adulthood, Planning for the Future: Providing a Meaningful Life for a Child with Disability,* and *A Parent's Guide to Wills and Trusts.* (For full group information, see MENTAL DISORDERS.)

National Health Lawyers Association (NHLA)
1120 Connecticut Avenue NW, Suite 950
Washington, DC 20036–3902
202–833–1100
Fax: 202–833–1105
Marilou King, Executive Vice-President
Interdisciplinary organization of attorneys and health professionals working in health-related legal areas; publishes various materials, including weekly *The Federal Health Monitor,* monthly *Health Law Digest, United States Health Care Laws and Rules,* and *The Long Term Care Handbook: Legal Operational and Financial Guideposts.*

Mental Disability Legal Resource Center (MDLRC), American Bar Association, 202–331–2240. (For full group information, see MENTAL DISORDERS.)

National Center for Youth Law (NCYL), 415–543–3307. (For full group information, see HELP AGAINST CHILD ABUSE AND NEGLECT on page 680.)

Office of the Americans with Disabilities Act
Civil Rights Division
U.S. Department of Justice
P.O. Box 66118
Washington, DC 20035–6118
202–514–0301; 202–514–0381, TT;
202–514–0383, TT
Office for general information on the Americans with Disabilities Act (ADA). For specific concerns, see below:

Construction and alterations:

Architectural and Transportation Barriers Compliance Board
1331 F Street NW, Sutie 1000
Washington, DC 20004–1111
800-USA-ABLE [872–2253]

Employment:

Equal Employment Opportunity Commission
1801 L Street NW
Washington, DC 20507
800–669–3362; 800–872–3362, TT

Telecommunications:

Federal Communications Commission
1919 M Street NW
Washington, DC 20554
202–632–7260; 202–632–6999, TT

Transportation:

Department of Transportation
400 Seventh Street SW
Washington, DC 20590
202–366–9305; 202–755–7687, TT

ON SPORTS AND RECREATION PROGRAMS

Special Olympics International
1325 G Street NW, Suite 500
Washington, DC 20005–3104
202–628–3630
Fax: 202–824–0200
Telex: 650–284–1739 MCI
Sargent Shriver, President
Organization promoting sports training and athletic competition for children and adults with mental retardation; publishes fact sheets *What Is Special Olympics?, Mental Retardation,* and *Language Guidelines.*

National Center for Youth with Disabilities (NCYD), 800–333–6293. Publishes annotated bibliography *Sports and Athletics: Issues for Adolescents with Chronic Illnesses and Disabilities* and *Recreation and Leisure: Issues for Adolescents with Chronic Illnesses and Disabilities.* (For full group information, see HELP FOR SPECIAL CHILDREN on page 689.)

Center on Human Policy (CHP), 315–443–3851. Publishes information package *Resources on Integrated Recreation/Leisure Opportunities for Children and Teens with Developmental Disabilities.* (For full group information, see HELP FOR SPECIAL CHILDREN on page 689.)

National Therapeutic Recreation Society
3101 Park Center Drive, 12th Floor
Alexandria, VA 22302
703–820–4940, ext. 518
Dean Tice, Executive Director
Organization of people who specialize in organizing therapeutic recreational programs for people with disabilities; an arm of the National Recreation and Park Association; provides information and referrals.

National Library Services for the Blind and Physically Handicapped, Library of Congress, 800–424–8567, U.S. except DC. Publishes *Sports, Outdoor Recreation, and Games for Visually and Physically Impaired Individuals.* (For full group information, see HELP FOR SPECIAL CHILDREN on page 689.)

Amputees in Motion (AIM)
P.O. Box 2703
Escondido, CA 92033
619–454–9300
Bill Handler, President
Organization concerned with helping amputees reestablish active lives, including sports and recreation; offers special training and competitions; provides information on services and technical aids, such as driving attachments and special sports equipment; publishes newsletter.

Mobility International U.S.A. (MIUSA)
P.O. Box 10767
Eugene, OR 97440
503–343–1284, voice/TT
Fax: 503–343–6812
E-mail: miusa@igc.apc.org
Susan Sygall, Executive Director
Organization seeking "equal opportunities for persons with disabilities"; offers international exchange programs; provides information and referrals; acts as advocate; publishes quarterly newsletter *Over the Rainbow*; *A World of Options for the '90s: A Guide to International Educational Exchange, Community Service and Travel for Persons with Disabilities, A New Manual for Integrating Persons with Disabilities into International Exchange Programs, Global Perspectives on Disability—A Curriculum, Equal Opportunity in International Education Exchange*; videos *Mi Casa Es Su Casa* (*Let My Home Be Your Home*; about international exchanges by young people with disabilities), *Home Is in the Heart, Looking Back—Looking Forward,* and *Emerging Leaders*; and travel information sheets and other materials on various countries.

National Advisory Committee on Scouting for the Handicapped (NACOSH)
1325 West Walnut Hill Lane
Irving, TX 75038
214–580–2000
Jere Ratcliffe, Chief Scout Executive
Organization developing scouting programs for young people with disabilities, coordinating with other organizations; an arm of the Boy Scouts of America; publishes various materials, including newsletter.

Special Recreation, Inc. (SRI)
362 Koser Avenue
Iowa City, IA 52246–3038
319–337–7578
John A. Nesbit, President
Organization seeking to expand recreational opportunities for people with disabilities; provides information; publishes various materials.

Blind Outdoor Leisure Development (BOLD)
533 East Main Street
Aspen, CO 81611
970–923–3811
Organization that provides recreational vacations for the blind, with guides and instructors provided by local clubs; outdoor sports offered include skiing, golfing, skating, swimming, and camping.

National Hemophilia Foundation (NHF), 800–424–2634. Publishes *Hemophilia and Sports.* (For full group information, see HEMOPHILIA.)

American Amputee Foundation (AAF), 501–666–2523. Publishes *Sports for the Leg Amputee* and *Devices to Enable People with Amputation to Participate in Sports.* (For full group information, see HELP FOR SPECIAL CHILDREN on page 689.)

Winners on Wheels (WOW)
2842 Business Park Avenue
Fresno, CA 93727–1328
209–292–2171
Organization for children in wheelchairs.

Accent, 800–787–8444. Publishes *Recreation and Sports.* (For full group information, see HELP FOR SPECIAL CHILDREN on page 689.)

ON WISHES FOR TERMINALLY OR CHRONICALLY ILL CHILDREN

Make-a-Wish Foundation of America (MWFA)
100 West Clarendon, Suite 2200
Phoenix, AZ 85013–3518
602–279-WISH [279–9474]; 800–722-WISH [722–9474]
Fax: 602–279–0855
Stephen Torkelsen, President and CEO
Organization dedicated to granting a wish to children (under age eighteen) with life-threatening illnesses;

request may be made by the child, or a parent, guardian, or health professional, and is coordinated through local chapters.

Brass Ring Society (BRS), Inc.
314 South Main Street
Ottawa, Kansas 66067
913–242–1666; 800–666–9474
Ray Esposito, President
Organization dedicated to granting a wish to terminally ill children; publishes bimonthly *Carousel*.

Children's Wish Foundation International (CWFI)
32 Perimeter Center East NE, Suite 100
Atlanta, GA 30358
404–393-WISH [393–9474]; 800–323–9474
Fax: 404–393–0683
Arthur Stein, President
Organization dedicated to granting a wish to terminally ill children; publishes newsletters and other materials.

Starlight Foundation International
12424 Wilshire Boulevard, Suite 1050
Los Angeles, CA 90025
310–207–5558
Peter Samuelson, President
Organization funded by donations dedicated to granting a wish to terminally or chronically ill children.

Sunshine Foundation (SF)
2001 Bridge Street
Philadelphia, PA 19124
215–535–1413; 800–767–1976
Bill Sample, President
Organization dedicated to granting a wish to terminally or chronically ill children, often providing a vacation for children and their families.

Candlelighters Childhood Cancer Foundation (CCCF), 800–366–2223. Publishes list of wish fulfillment organizations. (For full group information, see CANCER.)

On techniques and services for independent living

Independent Living Research Utilization Program (ILRU)
2323 South Sheperd, Suite 1000
Houston, TX 77019
713–520–0232; 713–520–5136, TT
Fax: 713–520–5785
E-mail: ilru@tsbbso2.tnet.com
Lex Frieden, Director
Federally funded research, training, and resource center focusing on independent living issues and technical assistance; makes referrals; publishes various materials, including:

- Bimonthly newsletter and *Directory of Independent Living Programs.*
- Video *Ball Bearings and Bent Spokes: A Consumer's Guide to Manual Wheelchair Repair and Maintenance.*
- On independent living: *Independent Living Networks, Constructing a Barrier-Free Home, Dimensions in Peer Counseling: Observations from the National Evaluation of Independent Living Centers, Independent Living and Mental Retardation: The Role of Independent Living Programs, On the Right Track: Foundations for Operating an ILP, Disability Issues: Organizing Community Support,* and *Putting Advocacy Rhetoric into Practice.*
- On attendant-care: booklets *A Guide for the Person with a Disability, A Guide for the Personal Care Attendant,* and *A Message to Parents of Handicapped Youth*; and monographs on personal assistance services.

National Council on Independent Living (NCIL)
2111 Wilson Boulevard, Suite 405
Arlington, VA 22201
703–525–3406; 703–525–3407, TT
Fax: 703–525–3409
E-mail: hughey@tsbbs02.tnet.com
Anne-Marie Hughey, Executive Director
Organization of independent living centers; provides information and referrals, including advice on starting a center; acts as advocate; publishes quarterly newsletter and policy and legislative briefings.

National Institute for Rehabilitation Engineering
97 Decker Road
Butler, NJ 07405
201–853–6585
Organization that provides equipment to increase independence of people with disabilities; evaluates equipment, modifies or custom-makes equipment, and trains others in their use; sets fees on ability to pay; provides rebuilt used equipment to needy people.

Trace Research and Development Center on Communication, Control, and Computer Access for Handicapped Individuals
S–151 Waisman Center
University of Wisconsin-Madison
Madison, WI 53706
608–262–6966; 608–263–5408, TT
Organization focusing on use of computer technology to meet communication and other needs of people with disabilities; maintains reprint services, including *Trace Resource Book* of aids, systems, and modifications that have been developed and used; offers evaluations.

Center for Applied Special Technology (CAST)
39 Cross Street
Peabody, MA 01960
508–531–8555
Fax: 508–531–0192
E-mail: cast@cast.org
Organization seeking to use computers and related technology to allow fuller opportunities for children and

adults with disabilities; provides assessment and training services; sponsors summer camp.

Closing the Gap (CTG)
P.O. Box 68
Henderson, MN 56044
612–248–3294
Fax: 612–248–3810
Organization that focuses on using computers for special education and rehabilitation for people with disabilities; provides training to professionals in education and rehabilitation; publishes bimonthly newspaper.

ONLINE RESOURCES

Internet: Our-kids. Provides support and exchange of experiences for parents of children with developmental delays of whatever nature. To subscribe, send E-mail message to: mailto:our-kids-request@oar.net

Internet: Disability-Related Resources. Collection of resources on disabilities, including deafness and blindness. gopher://hawking.u.washington.edu

Internet: Cornucopia of Disability Information (CODI). Collection of information, including legal documents and directory of computer resources for people with disabilities; linked to National Rehabilitation Information Center. gopher://val-dor.cc.buffalo.edu

Internet: Family Village Web site. Central clearinghouse for parents of children with disabilities, providing resources for some 400 conditions. Operated by the Waisman Center at the University of Wisconsin at Madison. Allows parents to contact each other, exchange experiences, and provide support. http://www.familyvillage.wisc.edu

Internet: Disability Information. Collection of information about disabilities, with links to international resources. gopher://gopher.tamu.edu/.dir/disability.dir

Internet: Disability Reading Room. Collection of reading matter on disabilities, including many firsthand accounts. gopher://info.umd.edu

Internet: Handicap. Collection of files and programs, including Handicap BBS (Bulletin Board Services) list. ftp://handicap.shel.isc-br.com

Internet. misc.handicap. Usenet newsgroup for information and discussion. Subscribe through newsreader. news:misc.handicap

Parents' Information Network (America Online: PIN) Online forums and libraries cover special children. (For full information, see GENERAL PARENTING RESOURCES on page 634.)

Better Health and Medical Forum (America Online: Health, Medicine) Provides discussion areas and libraries covering various disorders and caregiving. (For full information, see HEALTH CARE.)

IBM/Special Needs Forum (CompuServe: IBMSPE), Online forums and libraries on computers and special needs.

OTHER RESOURCES

For parents and other adults

Your Child and Health Care: A "Dollars & Sense" Guide for Families with Special Needs. Lynn Robinson Rosenfeld. Paul H. Brookes, 1994.

Planning for the Future: Providing a Meaningful Life for a Child with a Disability after Your Death. Mark Russell and others. American, 1994.

Nobody's Perfect: Living and Growing with Children Who Have Special Needs. Nancy B. Miller. Brookes, 1993.

We Have a Problem: A Parent's Sourcebook. Jane Marks. HarperCollins, 1993.

Your Child Has a Handicap: A Practical Guide to Daily Care. Mark L. Batshaw. Little, Brown, 1993.

Deciphering the System: A Guide for Families of Young Children with Disabilities. Paula J. Beckman and Gayle Beckman Boyes. Brookline, 1993.

Shared Moments: Learning Games for Disabled Children. Sally M. Rogow and Julia L. Hass. Tudor, 1993.

Brothers and Sisters: A Special Part of Exceptional Families, 2nd ed. Thomas H. Powell and Peggy Ahrendold Ogle. Brookes, 1992.

Raising a Handicapped Child. Charlotte Thompson. Ballantine, 1991.

Resource guides

The Complete Directory for People with Disabilities, 1996. Grey House Publishing, 1995.

Caring for Kids with Special Needs 1994: Residential Programs for Children and Adolescents, 2nd ed. Michele Fetterolf, ed. Peterson's, 1994.

Periodicals

Exceptional Parent. Magazine published eight times a year for parents of special children. For subscription orders: 120 State Street, Hackensack, NJ 07601.

Report on Disability Programs. Biweekly newsletter on news relating to people with disabilities, including legislation. For subscription orders: Business Publishers, Inc., 951 Pershing Drive, Silver Spring, MD 20910; 301–587–6300; Fax: 301–587–1087.

Mainstream—The Magazine for the Able-Disabled. Published ten times a year. For subscription orders: Mainstream: P.O. Box 370598, San Diego, CA 92137–9882; 619–234–3138, voice/TT.

New Mobility, bimonthly magazine for people who use wheelchairs. For orders: Spinal Network, P.O. Box 4162, Boulder, CO 80306; 303–449–5412.

Sports 'n Spokes—The Magazine for Wheelchair Sports and Recreation. Bimonthly. For Subscriptions: Sports 'n Spokes, 2111 East Highland Avenue, Suite 180, Phoenix, AZ 85016–4702.

For children

Stories for Children with Problems and Wishes: A Therapeutic Workbook for Turning Problems into Gifts. Burt G. Wasserman. Educational Media, 1994.

Finding a Way: Living with Exceptional Brothers and Sisters. Maxine B. Rosenberg. Lothrop, Lee & Shepard, 1988.

For preteens and teens

How It Feels to Fight for Your Life. Jill Krementz. Joy Street/Little, Brown, 1989. Young people talk about dealing with life-threatening disorders.

Born Different: The Amazing Stories of Some Very Special People. Frederick Drimmer. Atheneum, 1988.

On transition

Transition Strategies That Work, Vol. 2, and *What's Working in Transition*, quarterly newsletter. Available from Institute on Community Integration, University of Minnesota, 6 Pattee Hall, 150 Pillsbury Drive SE, Minneapolis, MN 55455; 612–625–3863.

A Struggle for Choice: Students with Special Needs in Transition to Adulthood. Jenny Corbett and Len Barton. Routledge, 1993.

Bridging Early Services for Children with Special Needs and Their Families: A Practical Guide for Transition Planning. Sharon Rosenkoetter and others. P.H. Brookes, 1993.

Background works

Children's Understanding of Disability. Ann Lewis. Routledge, 1995.

An Exposure of the Heart. Rebecca Busselle. Penguin, 1990. About a year observing in an institution for those with developmental disabilities.

(See also SERVICE DOGS.)

Help Against Substance Abuse

Resource Materials on Substance Abuse

Following is an overview of signs of drug use, some suggestions of what parents might do to lessen the likelihood that a child will succumb to substance abuse, and descriptions of specific types of drugs and their effects.

Signs of Drug Use

Changing patterns of performance, appearance, and behavior may signal use of drugs. The items in the first category listed below provide direct evidence of drug use; the items in the other categories offer signs that may indicate drug use. Adults should watch for extreme changes in children's behavior, changes that together form a pattern associated with drug use.

Signs of Drugs and Drug Paraphernalia

- Possession of drug-related paraphernalia such as pipes, rolling papers, small decongestant bottles, eye drops, or small butane torches.
- Possession of drugs or evidence of drugs, such as pills, white powder, small glass vials, or hypodermic needles; peculiar plants or butts, seeds, or leaves in ashtrays or in clothing pockets.
- Odor of drugs, smell of incense or other "cover-up" scents.

Identification with Drug Culture

- Drug-related magazines, slogans on clothing.
- Conversation and jokes that are preoccupied with drugs.
- Hostility in discussing drugs.
- Collection of beer cans.

Signs of Physical Deterioration

- Memory lapses, short attention span, difficulty in concentrating.
- Poor physical coordination, slurred or incoherent speech.
- Unhealthy appearance, indifference to hygiene and grooming.
- Bloodshot eyes, dilated pupils.

Dramatic Changes in School Performance

- Marked downturn in student's grades — not just from C's to F's, but from A's to B's and C's; assignments not completed.
- Increased absenteeism or tardiness.

Changes in Behavior

- Chronic dishonesty (lying, stealing, cheating); trouble with the police.
- Changes in friends; evasiveness in talking about new ones.
- Possession of large amounts of money.
- Increasing and inappropriate anger, hostility, irritability, secretiveness.
- Reduced motivation, energy, self-discipline, self-esteem.
- Diminished interest in extracurricular activities and hobbies.

Instilling Responsibility

Recommendation #1:

Teach standards of right and wrong and demonstrate these standards through personal example.

Children who are brought up to value individual responsibility and self-discipline and to have a clear sense of right and wrong are less likely to try drugs than those who are not. Parents can help to instill these values by:

- Setting a good example for children and not using drugs themselves.
- Explaining to their children at an early age that drug use is wrong, harmful, and unlawful, and reinforcing this teaching through adolescence.
- Encouraging self-discipline by giving children regular duties and holding them accountable for their actions.
- Establishing standards of behavior concerning drugs, drinking, dating, curfews, and unsupervised activities, and enforcing them consistently and fairly.
- Encouraging their children to stand by their convictions when pressured to use drugs.*Recommendation*

Recommendation #2:

Help children to resist peer pressure to use alcohol and other drugs by supervising their activities, knowing who their friends are, and talking with them about their interests and problems.

When parents take an active interest in their children's behavior, they provide the guidance and support children need to resist drugs. Parents can do this by:

- Knowing their children's whereabouts, activities, and friends.
- Working to maintain and improve family communications and listening to their children.
- Being able to discuss drugs knowledgeably. It is far better for children to obtain their information from their parents than from their peers or on the street.
- Communicating regularly with the parents of their children's friends and sharing their knowledge about drugs with other parents.
- Being selective about their children's viewing of television and movies that portray drug use as glamorous or exciting.

In addition, parents can work with the school in its efforts to fight drugs by:

- Encouraging the development of a school policy with clear no-use message.
- Supporting administrators who are tough on drugs.
- Assisting the school in monitoring students' attendance and planning and chaperoning school-sponsored activities.
- Communicating regularly with the school regarding their children's behavior.

Recommendation #3:

Be knowledgeable about drugs and signs of drug use. When symptoms are observed, respond promptly.

Parents are in the best position to recognize early signs of drug use in their children. To inform and involve themselves, parents should take the following steps:

- Learn about the extent of the drug problem in their community and in their children's schools.
- Learn how to recognize signs of drug use.
- Meet with parents of their children's friends or classmates about the drug problem at their school. Establish a means of sharing information to determine which children are using drugs and who is supplying them.

Parents who suspect their children are using drugs often must deal with their emotions of anger, resentment, and guilt. Frequently they deny the evidence and postpone confronting their children. Yet, the earlier a drug problem is detected and faced, the less difficult it is to overcome. If parents suspect that their children are using drugs, they should take the following steps:

- Devise a plan of action. Consult with school officials and other parents.
- Discuss their suspicions with their children in a calm, objective manner. Do not confront a child while he or she is under the influence of alcohol or other drugs.
- Impose disciplinary measures that help remove the child from those circumstances where drug use might occur.
- Seek advice and assistance from drug treatment professionals and from a parent group.

SPECIFIC DRUGS AND THEIR EFFECTS

Alcohol

Alcohol consumption causes a number of marked changes in behavior. Even low doses significantly impair the judgment and coordination required to drive a car safely, increasing the likelihood that the driver will be involved in an accident. Low to moderate doses of alcohol also increase the incidence of a variety of aggressive acts, including spouse and child abuse. Moderate to high doses of alcohol cause marked impairments in higher mental functions, severely altering a person's ability to learn and remember information. Very high doses cause respiratory depression and death. If combined with other depressants of the central nervous system, much lower doses of alcohol will produce the effects just described.

Repeated use of alcohol can lead to dependence. Sudden cessation of alcohol intake is likely to produce withdrawal symptoms, including severe anxiety, tremors, hallucinations, and convulsions. Alcohol withdrawal can be life-threatening. Long-term consumption of large quantities of alcohol particularly when when combined with poor nutrition, can also lead to permanent damage to vital organs such as the brain and the liver.

Mothers who drink alcohol during pregnancy may give birth to infants with fetal alcohol syndrome. These infants have irreversible physical abnormalities and mental retardation. In addition, research indicates that children of alcoholic parents are at greater risk than other youngsters of becoming alcoholics.

Cannabis

All forms of cannabis have negative physical and mental effects. Several regularly observed physical effects of cannabis are a substantial increase in the heart rate, bloodshot eyes, a dry mouth and throat, and increased appetite.

Use of cannabis may impair or reduce short-term memory and comprehension, alter sense of time, and reduce ability to perform tasks requiring concentration and coordination, such as driving a car. Research also shows that students do not retain knowledge when they are "high." Motivation and cognition may be altered, making the acquisition of new information difficult. Marijuana can also produce paranoia and psychosis.

Because users often inhale the unfiltered smoke deeply and then hold it in their lungs as long as possible, marijuana is damaging to the lungs and pulmonary system. Marijuana smoke contains more cancer-causing agents than tobacco smoke.

Long-term users of cannabis may develop psychological dependence and require more of the drug to get the same effect. The drug can become the center of their lives.

Inhalants

The immediate negative effects of inhalants include nausea, sneezing, coughing, nosebleeds, fatigue, lack of coordination, and loss of appetite. Solvents and aerosol sprays also decrease the heart and respiratory rates and impair judgment. Amyl and butyl nitrate cause rapid pulse, headaches, and involuntary passing of urine and feces. Long-term use may result in hepatitis or brain damage.

Deeply inhaling the vapors, or using large amounts over a short time, may result in disorientation, violent behavior, unconsciousness, or death. High concentrations of inhalants can cause suffocation by displacing the oxygen in the lungs or by depressing the central nervous system to the point that breathing stop.

Long-term use can caught weight loss, fatigue, electrolyte imbalance, and muscle fatigue. Repeated sniffing of concentrated vapors over time can permanently damage the nervous system.

(See table on page 708.)

Cocaine

Cocaine stimulates the central nervous system. Its immediate effects include dilated pupils and elevated blood pressure, heart rate, respiratory rate, and body temperature. Occasional use can cause a stuffy or runny nose, while chronic use can ulcerate the mucous membrane of the nose. Injecting cocaine with contaminated equipment can cause AIDS, hepatitis, and other diseases. Preparation of freebase, which involves the use of volatile solvents, can result in death or injury from fire or explosion. Cocaine can produce psychological and physical dependency, a feeling that the user cannot function without the drug. In addition, tolerance develops rapidly.

Crack or freebase rock is extremely addictive,and its effects are felt within 10 seconds. The physical effects include dilated pupils, increased pulse rate, elevated blood pressure, insomnia, loss of appetite, tactile hallucinations, paranoia, and seizures.

The use of cocaine can cause death by cardiac arrest or respiratory failure.

Other Stimulants

Stimulants can cause increased heart and respiratory rates, elevated blood pressure, dilated pupils, and decreased appetite. In addition, users may experience sweating, headache, blurred vision, dizziness, sleeplessness, and anxiety. Extremely high doses can cause a rapid or irregular heartbeat, tremors, loss of coordination, and even physical collapse. An amphetamine injection creates a sudden increase in blood pressure that can result in stroke, very high fever, or heart failure.

In addition to the physical effects, users report feeling restless, anxious, and moody. Higher doses intensify the effects. Persons who use large amounts of amphetamines over a long period of time can develop amphetamine psychosis that includes hallucinations, delusions, and paranoia. These symptoms usually disappear when drug use ceases.

Depressants

The effects of depressants are in many ways similar to the effects of alcohol. Small amounts can produce calmness and relaxed muscles, but somewhat larger doses can cause slurred speech, staggering gait, and altered perception. Very large doses can cause respiratory depression, coma, and death. The combination of depressants and alcohol can multiply the effects of the drugs, thereby multiplying the risks.

The use of depressants can cause both physical and psychological dependence. Regular use over time may result in tolerance to the drug, leading the user to increase the quantity consumed. When regular users suddenly stop taking large doses, they may develop withdrawal symptoms ranging from restlessness, insomnia, and anxiety to convulsions and death.

Babies born to mothers who abuse depressants during pregnancy may be physically dependent in the drugs and show withdrawal symptoms shortly after they are born. Birth defects and behavioral problems also may result.

Hallucinogens

Phencyclidine (PCP) interrupts the functions of the neocortex, the section of the brain that controls the intellect and keeps instincts in check. Because the drug blocks pain receptors, violent PCP episodes may result in self-inflicted injuries.

The effects of PCP vary, but users frequently report a sense of distance and estrangement. Time and body movement are slowed down. Muscular coordination worsens and senses are dulled. Speech is blocked and incoherent.

Chronic users of PCP report persistent memory problems and speech difficulties. Some of these effects may last 6 months to a year following prolonged daily use. Mood disorders — depression, anxiety, and violent behavior — also occur. In later stages of chronic use, users often exhibit paranoid and violent behavior and experience hallucinations.

Large doses may produce convulsions and coma, as well as heart and lung failure.

Lysergic acid (LSD), mescaline, and psilocybin cause illusions and hallucinations. The physical effects may include dilated pupils, elevated body temperature, increased heart rate and blood pressure, loss of appetite, sleeplessness, and tremors.

Sensations and feelings may change rapidly. It is common to have a bad psychological reaction to LSD, mescaline, and psilocybin. The user may experience panic, confusion, suspicion, anxiety, and loss of control. Delayed effects, or flashbacks, can occur even after use has ceased.

Narcotics

Narcotics initially produce a feeling of euphoria that often is followed by drowsiness, nausea, and vomiting. Users also may experience constricted pupils, watery eyes, and itching. An overdose may produce slow and shallow breathing, clammy skin, convulsions, coma, and possible death.

Tolerance to narcotics develops rapidly and dependence is likely. The use of contaminated syringes may result in disease such as AIDS, endocarditis, and hepatitis. Addiction in pregnant woman can lead to premature, stillborn, or addicted infants who experience severe withdrawal symptoms.

Designer Drugs

Illegal drugs are defined in terms of their chemical formulas. To circumvent these legal restrictions, underground chemists modify the molecular structure of certain illegal drugs to produce analogs known as "designer drugs." These drugs can be several hundred times stronger than the drugs they are designed to imitate.

Many of the so-called drugs are related to amphetamines and have mild stimulant properties but are mostly euphoriants. They can produce severe neurochemical damage to the brain.

The narcotic analogs can cause symptoms such as those seen in Parkinson's disease: uncontrollable tremors, drooling, impaired speech, paralysis, and irreversible brain damage. Analogs of amphetamines and methamphetamines cause nausea, blurred vision, chills or sweating, and faintness. Psychological effects include anxiety, depression, and paranoia. As little as one dose can cause brain damage. The analogs of phencyclidine cause illusions, hallucinations, and impaired perception.

Anabolic Steroids

Anabolic steroids are a group of powerful compounds closely related to the male sex hormone testosterone. Developed in the 1930s, steroids are seldom prescribed by physicians today. Current legitimate medical uses are limited to certain kinds of anemia, severe burns, and some types of breast cancer.

Taken in combination with a program of muscle-building exercise and diet, steroids may contribute to increases in body weight and muscular strength. Because of these properties, athletes in a variety of sports have used steroids since the 1950s, hoping to enhance performance. Today, they are being joined by increasing numbers of young people seeking to accelerate their physical development.

Steroid users subject themselves to more than 70 side effects ranging in severity from liver cancer to acne and including psychological as well as physical reactions. The liver and cardiovascular and reproductive systems are most seriously affected by steroid use. In males, use can cause withered testicles, sterility, and impotence. In females, irreversible masculine traits can develop along with breast reduction and sterility. Psychological effects in both sexes include very aggressive behavior known as "roid rage" and depression. While some side effects appear quickly, others, such as heart attacks and strokes, may not show up for years.

Signs of steroid use include quick weight and muscle gains (if steroids are being used in conjunction with a weight training program); behavioral changes, particularly increased aggressiveness and combativeness; jaundice; purpose or red spots on the body; swelling of feet or lower legs; trembling; unexplained darkening of the skin; and persistent unpleasant breath odor.

Steroids are produced in tablet or capsule form for oral ingestion, or as a liquid for intramuscular injection.

Source: What Works: Schools Without Drugs. U.S. Department of Education.

Cannabis

TYPE	WHAT IS IT CALLED?	WHAT DOES IT LOOK LIKE?	HOW IS IT USED?
Marijuana	Pot Grass Weed Reefer Dope Mary Jane Sinsemilla Acapulco gold Thai sticks	Dried parsley mixed with stems that may include seeds	Eaten Smoked
Tetrahydro-cannabinol	THC	Soft gelatin capsules	Taken orally
Hashish	Hash	Brown or black cakes or balls	Taken orally
Hashish oil	Hash oil	Concentrated syrupy liquid varying in color from clear to black	Smoked—mixed with tobacco

Inhalants

TYPE	WHAT IS IT CALLED?	WHAT DOES IT LOOK LIKE?	HOW IS IT USED?
Nitrous Oxide	Laughing gas Whippets	Propellant for whipped cream in aerosol spray can Small 8-gram metal cylinder sold with a balloon or pipe (buzz bomb)	Vapors inhaled
Amyl Nitrite	Poppers Snappers	Clear yellowish liquid in ampules	Vapors inhaled
Butyl Nitrite	Rush Bold Locker room Bullet Climax	Packed in small bottles	Vapors inhaled
Chlorohydro-carbons		Aerosol sprays Aerosol paint cans Containers of cleaning fluid	Vapors inhaled
Hydrocarbons		Solvents Cans of aerosol propellants, gasoline, glue, paint thinner	Vapors inhaled

Cocaine

TYPE	WHAT IS IT CALLED?	WHAT DOES IT LOOK LIKE?	HOW IS IT USED?
Cocaine	Coke Snow Flake White Blow Nose candy Big C Snowbirds Lady	White crystalline powder, often diluted with other ingredients	Inhaled through nasal passages
Crack	Freebase rocks Rock	Light brown or beige pellets—or crystalline rocks that resemble coagulated soap; often packaged in small vials	Smoked

Other Stimulants

TYPE	WHAT IS IT CALLED?	WHAT DOES IT LOOK LIKE?	HOW IS IT USED?
Amphetamines	Speed Uppers Ups Black beauties Pep pills Copilots Bumblebees Hearts Benzedrine Dexedrine Footballs Biphetamine	Capsules Pills Tablets	Taken orally Injected Inhaled through nasal passages
Metham-phetamines	Crank Crystal meth Crystal methadrine Speed	White powder Pills A rock that resembles a block of paraffin	Taken orally Injected Inhaled through nasal passages
Additional stimulants	Ritalin Cylert Preludin Didrex Pre-State Voranil Tenuate Tepanil Pondimin Sandrex Plegine Ionamin	Pills Capsules Tablets	Taken orally Injected

Depressants

TYPE	WHAT IS IT CALLED?	WHAT DOES IT LOOK LIKE?	HOW IS IT USED?
Barbiturates	Downers Barbs Blue devils Red devils Yellow jacket Yellows Nembutal Seconal Amytal Tuinals	Red, yellow, blue, or red-and-blue capsules	Taken orally
Methaqualone	Quaaludes Ludes Sopors	Tablets	Taken orally
Tranquilizers	Valium Librium Equanil Miltown Serax Tranxene	Tablets Capsules	Taken orally

Hallucinogens

TYPE	WHAT IS IT CALLED?	WHAT DOES IT LOOK LIKE?	HOW IS IT USED?
Phencyclidine	PCP Angel dust Loveboat Lovely Hog Killer weed	Liquid Capsules White crystalline powder Pills	Taken orally Injected Smoked—can be sprayed on cigarettes, parsley, and marijuana
Lysergic acid diethylamide	LSD Acid Green or red dragon White lightning Blue heaven Microdot	Brightly colored tablets Impregnated blotter paper Thin squares of gelatin Clear liquid Sugar cubes	Taken orally Licked off paper Gelatin and liquid can be put in the eyes
Mescaline and Peyote	Mesc Cactus	Hard brown discs Buttons Tablets Capsules	Discs—chewed, swallowed, or smoked Tablets and capsules—taken orally
Psilocybin	Magic mushrooms 'shrooms	Fresh or dried mushrooms	Chewed and swallowed

Narcotics

TYPE	WHAT IS IT CALLED?	WHAT DOES IT LOOK LIKE?	HOW IS IT USED?
Heroin	Smack Horse Brown sugar Junk Mud Big H Black Tar	Powder, white to dark brown Tarlike substance	Injected Inhaled through nasal passages Smoked
Methadone	Dolophine Methadose Amidone	Solution	Taken orally Injected
Codeine	Epirin compound F with codeine Tylenol with codeine Codeine Codeine in cough medicines	Dark liquid varying in thickness Capsules Tablets	Taken orally Injected
Morphine	Pectoral syrup	White crystals	Injected Hypodermic tablets Taken orally Injectable solutions Smoked
Meperidine	Pethidien	White powder Demerol	Taken orally Solution Injected
Mepergan			Tablets
Opium	Paregoric Dover's powder Parepectolin	Dark brown chunks Powder	Smoked Eaten
Other narcotics	Perocet Percodan Tussionex Fentanyl Darvon Talwin Lomotil	Tablets Capsules Liquid	Taken orally Injected

Designer Drugs

TYPE	WHAT IS IT CALLED?	WHAT DOES IT LOOK LIKE?	HOW IS IT USED?
Analogs of Fentanyl (Narcotic)	Synthetic Heroin China White	White powder identically resembling heroin	Inhaled through nasal passages Injected
Analogs of Meperidine (Narcotic)	Synthetic Heroin MPTP (New Heroin) MPPP	White Powder	Inhaled through nasal passages Injected
Analogs of Amphetamines and Methamphetamines	MDMA (Ecstasy, XTC, Adam, Essence) MDM STP PMA 2,5-DMA TMA DOM DOB EVE	White powder Tablets Tablets Capsules	Taken orally Injected Injected Inhaled through nasal passages
Analogs of Phencyclidine (PCP)	PCPy PCE	White powder	Taken orally Injected Smoked

ORGANIZATIONS OFFERING HELP AND INFORMATION

ON SUBSTANCE ABUSE IN GENERAL

National Clearinghouse for Alcohol and Drug Abuse Information (NCADI)
P.O. Box 2345
5600 Fishers Lane, Room 10A–43
Rockville, MD 20857–2345
Address for mail orders:
P.O. Box 416
Kensington, MD 20795
301–468–2600, DC; 800–729–6686;
800–487–4889, TT
Children's line: 800-HI-WALLY [449–2559]
Customer Care Line: 301–622–3464; 800-NCADI–64 [622–3464]
Media Liaison Specialist: 800–487–4890
Internet website, PREVline (Prevention Online): www.health.org
E-mail: info@prevline.health.org
Other Internet access ("new" as User-ID; to reach information specialist, type "info" at E-mail prompt in main menu):
Telnet: ncadi.health.org
FTP: ftp.health.org
Gopher: gopher.health.org
Mosaic: www.health.org
For modems up to 14,400 baud, without Internet access: 301–770–0850; type "new" for User-ID;
Modem setting: N–8–1
Federally supported alcohol and drug abuse information clearinghouse; provides information; advises on setting up local groups to counter drug use; maintains Prevention Materials Database (PMD); publishes various materials, many from other agencies, including:
From **Center for Substance Abuse Prevention (CSAP)**:

- Bimonthly *Prevention Pipeline* and *Journal of Community Psychology.*
- For parents: *Helping Your Child Say "No": A Parent's Guide, Healthy Women/Healthy Lifestyles: Here's What You Should Know About Alcohol, Tobacco, and Other*

Drugs, What You Can Do About Drug Use in America, and *Pointers for Parents Card.*

- General materials, such as *Citizen's Alcohol and Other Drug Prevention Directory: Resources for Getting Involved, What You Can Do About Drug Use in America, Prevention Primer: An Encyclopedia of Alcohol, Tobacco, and Other Drug Prevention Terms, The Prevention Story: Programs That Make a Difference,* and *Drug-Free Community Series.*
- For teens: "Tips for Teens About" brochures, such as *Alcohol, Crack and Cocaine, Hallucinogens, Inhalants,* and *Marijuana*; and videos *Right Turns Only* and *Think About It; Be Smart! Don't Start.*
- "Making the Link" fact sheets, such as *Alcohol, Tobacco, and Other Drugs and the College Experience, Sex Under the Influence of Alcohol and Other Drugs, Alcohol, Tobacco, and Other Drugs in the Workplace,* and *Health Care Costs, the Deficit and Alcohol, Tobacco, and Other Drugs.*
- Numerous prevention materials, including newsletters in CSAP's "Put on the Brakes" campaign on college drinking.

From **U.S. Department of Education:**

- Newsletter *The Challenge,* on successful school-based drug prevention programs.
- For parents: *Growing Up Drug Free: A Parent's Guide for Prevention.*
- Videos for children and preteens: *The Drug Avengers, Fast Forward Future,* and *Lookin' Good.*
- Videos for teens: *Straight Talk, Hard Facts About Drugs: Alcohol, Marijuana, Cocaine and Crack: Speak-Up and Speak Out: Learning to Say No to Drugs,* and *Private Victories.*
- Prevention materials for educators, such as *Success Stories from Drug-Free Schools.*

From **National Institute for Alcohol Abuse and Alcoholism** (see later in this list):

- Alcohol Alert series, such as *Moderate Drinking, Alcohol and Minorities, Alcohol-Related Impairment, Assessing Alcoholism, Treatment Outcome Research,* and *Alcohol Research and Public Health Policy.*
- For scientists and researchers: *Alcohol Research: Promise for the Decade.*

From **National Institute on Drug Abuse** (see later in this list):

- For preteens and teens: videos *Straight At Ya, Straight Up, Remotely Science,* and *If You Change Your Mind* (for and by preteens, with related magazine and teacher's guide).
- For women: *Women and Drug Abuse* and *Women and Drug Abuse: You and Your Community Can Help.*
- NIDA Capsules on types of drugs: *Cocaine Abuse, Cocaine: The Big Lie, Heroin, Ibogaine, Inhalant Abuse, LSD (Lysergic Acid Diethylamide), Marijuana Update, MDMA Ecstasy, Methamphetamine Abuse, Designer Drugs, PCP (Phencyclidine),* and on drug use, prevention, and treatment.
- Materials for health professionals, including national surveys of drug use, research monographs, and clinical reports.

Substance Abuse and Mental Health Services Administration (SAMHSA)
Parklawn Building
5600 Fishers Lane
Rockville, MD 20857
301–443–6780
CSAP Drug-Free Workplace Helpline: 800–843–4971
Fax: 301–443–3031
Federal arm overseeing and providing public information on drug and alcohol use and abuse; formerly Alcohol, Drug Abuse, and Mental Health Administration (ADAMHA); conducts research and provides information; operates Center for Substance Abuse Prevention (CSAP), Center for Substance Abuse Treatment (CSAT), and RADAR Network of local assistance centers; all publish many materials (available through National Clearinghouse for Alcohol and Drug Abuse Information)

National Institute for Alcohol Abuse and Alcoholism (NIAAA)
Willco Building, Suite 409
6000 Executive Boulevard, MSC 7003
Bethesda, MD 20892–7003
301–443–3860
Federal organization, affiliated with the National Institute of Mental Health, conducting health, education, research, and planning programs on alcohol abuse and rehabilitation; publishes quarterly journal *Alcohol Health & Research World* and numerous other materials, available through National Clearinghouse for Alcohol and Drug Abuse Information.

National Women's Resource Center for the Prevention of Alcohol, Tobacco, Other Drug Abuse and Mental Illness
200 North Michigan Avenue, Suite 300
Chicago, IL 60601
800–354–8824

Internet (for PREVline, electronic information resource): www.health.org or Telnet: ncadi.health.org (press Enter, with used-ID: new)
PREVline technical assistance: 800–729–6686, ext. 300
Organization concerned with prevention and treatment of alcohol, tobacco, and other drug abuse and mental illness in women; provides information and referrals.

American Academy of Pediatrics (AAP), 800–433–9016. Publishes brochures *Marijuana: Your Child and Drugs, Cocaine: Your Child and Drugs, Alcohol: Your Child and Drugs,* and *Teens Who Drink and Drive: Reducing the Death Toll*; and video-and-booklet set *Adolescent Substance Abuse: The Inside Story.* (For full group information, see HEALTH CARE.)

American Academy of Child and Adolescent Psychiatry (AACAP), 202–966–7300. Publishes information sheets *Teens: Alcohol and Other Drugs, Children of Alcoholics,* and *Making Decisions About Substance Abuse Treatment.* (For full group information, see MENTAL DISORDERS.)

American Council on Science and Health (ACSH), 212–362–7044. Publishes *Alcohol: Defining the Parameters of Moderation, Does Moderate Alcohol Consumption Prolong Life?,* and *Cocaine Facts and Dangers.* (For full group information, see SAFETY.)

National Organization on Legal Problems of Education (NOLPE), 913–273–3550. Publishes *Drug and Alcohol Abuse in the Schools: A Practice Guide for Administrators and Educators for Combating Drug and Alcohol Abuse.* (For full group information, see HELP ON LEARNING AND EDUCATION on page 000.)

National Institute on Drug Abuse (NIDA), Drug Abuse Information and Treatment Referral Line, 800–662-HELP [662–4357]; in Spanish, 800–66A-YUDA, 9A.M.–3A.M. M–F; Noon–3A.M. Sat–Sun. Federal organization offering information and referrals on drug abuse and treatment; publishes various materials, available through National Clearinghouse for Alcohol and Drug Abuse Information.

800-COCAINE [262–2463]. For treatment referrals only; no counseling. Service of Phoenix House, 164 West 74 Street, New York, NY 10023.

Food and Drug Administration (FDA), 301–443–3170. Answers public queries about drug safety and proper drug use. (For full group information, see DRUG REACTIONS AND INTERACTIONS.)

National PRIDE (Parents' Resource Institute for Drug Education)
10 Park Place South, Suite 540
Atlanta, GA 30303
404–577–4500; 800–853–7867
Fax: 404–688–6937
PRIDE Parent Training
1240 Johnson Ferry Place, Suite F–10
Marietta, GA 30068
404–565–5257; 800–487-PRIDE [487–77433] [c/e: sic]
Fax: 404–565–4749
Thomas J. Gleaton, President
Organization seeking to counter drug use; encourages formation of community-based groups; offers PRIDE Parent Training prevention workshops (see above); provides information and referrals; acts as advocate; publishes newsletter and other materials, including pamphlets *What Parents Can Do* and *Parent Primer.*

National Center for Youth with Disabilities (NCYD), 800–333–6293. Publishes annotated bibliography *Substance Use by Youth with Disabilities.* (For full group information, see HELP FOR SPECIAL CHILDREN on page 689.)

Cottage Program International (CPI)
736 South 500 East
Salt Lake City, UT 84102
801–532–5185; 800–752–6102
Bernell Boswell, Executive Director
Organization focusing on use of behavior modification for prevention and treatment of alcohol and drug abuse; provides trained volunteers to aid families, schools, and other organizations in substance abuse prevention programs; publishes training programs and other materials.

National Council on Alcoholism and Drug Dependency (NCADD)
12 West 21 Street, 7th Floor
New York, NY 10010
212–206–6770; 800-NCA-CALL [622–2255]
Thomas Seessel, Executive Director
Network of organizations fighting substance abuse; provides information and referrals; publishes:

- Fact sheets *Alcohol-Related Birth Defects, Youth and Alcohol, Alcoholism and Alcohol-Related Poblems, Use of Alcohol and Other Drugs Among Women,* and *Alcohol and Other Drugs in the Workplace.*
- General pamphlets *The Disease of Alcoholism, What Are the Signs of Alcoholism? The NCADD Self-Test,* and *What Can You Do About Someone Else's Drinking?*

Thomas Seessel, Executive Director
Network of organizations fighting substance abuse; provides information and referrals; publishes:

- Fact sheets *Alcohol-Related Birth Defects, Youth and Alcohol, Alcoholism and Alcohol-Related Poblems, Use of Alcohol and Other Drugs Among Women,* and *Alcohol and Other Drugs in the Workplace.*
- General pamphlets *The Disease of Alcoholism, What Are the Signs of Alcoholism? The NCADD Self-Test,* and *What Can You Do About Someone Else's Drinking?*
- On prevention for young people: *Kids Talk to Kids About Alcohol, Girls! Straight Talk About Drinking and Drugs, Who's Got the Power? You Or Drugs?,* and *Wine Cooler? Not!.*

Narcotic Educational Foundation of America (NEFA)
5055 Sunset Boulevard
Los Angeles, CA 90027
213–663–5171
Henry B. Hall, Executive Director
Organization dedicated to educating young people and adults about hazards of drug abuse; gathers research data and maintains library; produces film and print materials, including student warning-reference sheets such as *Drugs and the Automotive Age, Amphetamine Abuse, Barbiturates and Other Sedative Drugs, Inhalants (Breathable Chemicals), The Cocaine Story, Phencyclidine=PCP=Peace Pill and Angel(Death?)Dust, Drug Dependence, The Heroin Story, A Very Potent Drug: Ethyl Alcohol, Glue Sniffing,* and *Some Things You Should Know About Prescription and Other Drugs.*

National Association for Families and Addiction Research and Education (NAFARE)
200 N. Michigan Avenue, Suite 300
Chicago, IL 60601
312–541–1272; 800–638-BABY [638–2229]
Fax: 312–541–1271
Ira Chasnoff, M.D., President
Organization concerned with perinatal addiction; formerly National Association for Perinatal Addiction Research and Education (NAPARE); supports research; operates clinic; acts as information clearinghouse; publishes quarterly *NAPARE Update,* brochure *Q & A for You and You Baby,* and a packet of materials for health professionals.

Center on Children and the Law, 202–662–1720. Publishes *A Judicial Benchbook on Drugs and Families.* (For full group information, see HELP AGAINST CHILD ABUSE AND NEGLECT on page 680.)

National Maternal and Child Health Clearinghouse (NMCHC), 703–821–8955. Publishes *Adolescent Substance Abuse: Risk Factors and Prevention Strategies.* (For full group information, see PREGNANCY.)

March of Dimes Birth Defects Foundation (MDBDF), 914–428–7100. Publishes pamphlets *Making the Right Choices: Facts About Drugs and Pregnancy* and *Teens Talk Drugs*; information sheet *Cocaine Use During Pregnancy*; and videos *Cocaine's Children* and *Smoking, Drinking and Drugs.* (For full group information, see BIRTH DEFECTS.)

Association of Family and Conciliation Courts (AFCC), 608–251–4001. Publishes videotape series on mediation in difficult situations, including *Boyd and Sheryl: A Family Recovering from Alcohol.* (For full group information, see DIVORCE.)

Healthy Mothers, Healthy Babies National Coalition (HMHB), 202–863–2458. Publishes resource list *Substance Use and Pregnancy.* (For full group information, see PREGNANCY.)

Women's Action Alliance (WAA), 212–532–8330. Publishes *Alcohol and Drugs Are Women's Issues* (2 vols). (For full group information, see HELP ON LEARNING AND EDUCATION on page 659.)

Child Welfare League of America (CWLA), 202–638–2952. Publishes *Children at the Front: A Different View of the War on Alcohol and Drugs, Crack and Other Addictions: Old Realities and New Challenges, Our Best Hope: Early Intervention with Prenatally Drug-Exposed Infants and Their Families,* and *That's What Drugs Took Me To. A Story of Addiction and Teen Pregnancy* (video and discussion guide). (For full group information, see FOSTER CARE.)

Council for Exceptional Children (CEC), 800–328–0272. Publishes *Alcohol and Other Drugs: Use, Abuse, and Disabilities* and *Born Substance Exposed, Educationally Vulnerable.* (For full group information, see HELP FOR SPECIAL CHILDREN on page 689.)

Resource Center on Substance Abuse Prevention and Disability, 202–628–8442. Publishes *A Look at Alcohol and Other Drug Abuse Prevention and the Family* and *A Look at Alcohol and Other Drug Abuse Prevention and Symptoms Checklist.* (For full group information, see HELP FOR SPECIAL CHILDREN on page 689.)

American College of Obstetricians and Gynecologists (ACOG), 202–638–5577. Publishes *The Negative Effects of Substance Abuse* and *Drugs and Pregnancy: Alcohol, Tobacco, and Other Drugs.* (For full group information, see PREGNANCY.)

National Information Center on Deafness (NICD), 202–651–5051; 202–651–5052, TT. Publishes *Alcoholism and Deafness* and *Programs and Resources for Deaf Alcoholics and Substance Abusers.* (For full group information, see EAR AND HEARING PROBLEMS.)

American Institute for Cancer Research (AICR), 800–843–8114. Publishes *Alcohol and Cancer Risk: Make the Choice for Health.* (For full group information, see CANCER.)

SPECIAL SUBSTANCE ABUSE PROGRAMS

Alcoholics Anonymous World Services (AA)
P.O. Box 459, Grand Central Station
New York, NY 10163
212–686–1100 (see white pages for local number); 212–870–3199, TT
Fax: 212–870–3003
Fax (for publication order): 212–870–3137 or 800–437–3584
International, nondenominational network of independent self-help groups aimed at helping individuals achieve and maintain sobriety; publishes numerous materials, including:

- The Big Book: *Alcoholics Anonymous,* also in audio or electronic form, Braille, or many other languages.
- General booklets: *Living Sober, Came to Believe, Letter to a Woman Alcoholic, Time to Start Living, The AA Member—Medications and Other Drugs, Do You Think You're Different?, Is There an Alcoholic in Your Life,* and *Problems Other Than Alcohol* (on drug addiction).
- On AA: *This Is AA, 44 Questions, Is AA for You?, Is AA for Me?, AA for the Woman, A Newcomer Asks, AA and the Gay/Lesbian Alcoholic, A Brief Guide to AA*; and videos *Alcoholics Anonymous—An Inside View* and *Hope: Alcoholics Anonymous.*
- For teens: *Young People and AA, Too Young?*; and videos *Young People and AA* and *AA—Rap with Us.*
- AA directories and numerous professional materials.

DrugAnon (DA)
443 West 50th Street
New York, NY
212–484–9095
Mary Lou Phippen, Secretary
Network of mutual-support, self-help groups of drug abusers, modeled on Alcoholics Anonymous (see above); formerly Pills Anonymous; offers Pil-Anon Family Program for family of drug abusers.

Narcotics Anonymous (NA)
P.O. Box 9999
Van Nuys, CA 91409
818–773–9999 (see telephone directory for local numbers, including hotlines in major cities)
Fax: 818–785–0923
George Hollahan and Anthony Edmondson, Co-Executive Directors
Network of mutual-support, self-help groups for recovering narcotic addicts, modeled on Alcoholics Anonymous (see above); publishes various materials, including:

- *NA Way Magazine.*
- Books: *Narcotics Anonymous, Just for Today: Daily Meditations for Recovering Addicts,* and *It Works: How and Why.*
- Booklets: *A Introductory Guide to Narcotics Anonymous, The Group Booklet,* and other booklets on the 12-step approach.
- Pamphlets: *Youth and Recovery, For the Newcomer, For Those in Treatment, Who, What, How, and Why, Another Look, Recovery and Relapse, Am I an Addict?, Self-Acceptance, Just for Today, Living the Program,* and *The Group.*

Hazelden Foundation (HF)
15251 Pleasant Valley Road
Box 176
Center City, MN 55012–0176
612–257–4010; Treatment programs:
800–262–5010, U.S. except MN and AK; Publications: 800–328–9000, U.S. except MN and AK;
800–257–0070, MN
Organization offering treatment and rehabilitation for people addicted to alcohol or drugs; services include Hazelden's Pioneer House Program for teenagers and young adults, group home for young male drug addicts, family programs, such as that of Hazelden Renewal Center, and outpatient or aftercare programs; trains professional counselors; gathers research data on abuse problems; publishes *From Survival to Recovery: Growing Up in an Alcoholic Home, Brave New Families: A Guide for Families in Recovery, Addictionary: A Primer of Recovery Terms and Concepts from Abstinence to Withdrawal, Fundamentals of Recovery* (12-Step pamphlets), *Alcoholism, The Complete Relapse Prevention Skills Program, Lifestyle Changes: 12 Step Recovery Nutrition and Diet Guide, The Addictive Personality: Roots, Rituals, and Recovery,* and other inspirational and supportive materials.

Johnson Institute
7205 Ohms Lane
Minneapolis, MN 55439–2159
612–831–1630; 800–231–5165, U.S. except MN;

800–247–0484, MN
Fax: 612–831–1631
Vernon Johnson, Founder and President Emeritus
Bud Remboldt, President
Organization concerned with people at risk because of alcohol, drugs, violence, or other problems; provides training and consultation for professionals; publishes numerous materials, including:

- Booklets for parents: *Helping Kids Learn Refusal Skills, Is Your Child Involved with Alcohol and Other Drugs?, Facts About Kids' Use of Alcohol and Other Drugs, Chemical Dependence and Recovery: A Family Affair*, and *How Chemical Dependence Differs for Adults and Teenagers.*
- Prevention programs for parents: *Parenting for Prevention: How to Raise a Child to Say No to Alcohol/Drugs* (book, with accompanying curriculum), *Choices and Consequences: What to Do When a Teenager Uses Alcohol/Drugs* (book and video), *Families for Prevention* (videos and books for prevention program), and *Co-Dependence: The Joy of Recovery* (video).
- Books for parents: *Helping Your Chemically Dependent Teenager Recover: A Guide for Parents and Other Concerned Adults, Breaking Away: Saying Good-bye to Alcohol/Drugs: A Guide to Help Teenagers Stop Using Chemicals, When Your Child Is Chemically Dependent, Recovery and Relapse Prevention for Parents of Chemically Dependent Children, The Alcoholic Family, Who Kids Turn to When They're in Trouble, Everything You Need to Know About Chemical Dependence: Vernon Johnson's Complete Guide for Families, Recovery Is a Family Affair*, and *Healing the Hurt: Rebuilding Relationships with Your Children.*
- Video materials on abuse and recovery, such as *Intervention: How to Help Someone Who Doesn't Want Help* and *The Enablers.*
- For children: books *Peter the Puppy Talks About Chemical Dependence in the Family, Kids' Power: Healing Games for Children of Alcoholics, My Dad Loves Me, My Dad Has a Disease: A Workbook for Children of Alcoholics, Dear Kids of Alcoholics* (with guidebook); video *Where's Shelley?*; video and coloring book sets *Twee Fiddle and Huff: A Fable About Young Children of Alcoholics* and *A Story About Feelings.*
- Books for preteens: *The Mouse, the Monster and Me* (on personal rights and responsibility), and *Tanya Talks About Chemical Dependence in the Family.*
- Videos for preteens and teens: *Another Chance to Change: A Teenager's Struggle with Relapse and Recovery*; on peer enablers: *An Attitude Adjustment for Ramie, Covering Up for Kevin*, and *Good Intentions, Bad Results: Am I an Enabler?: A Self-Assessment Guide for Teenagers* (with book); and on children of alcoholics: *Blaming Kitty, Different Like Me: A Book for Teens Who Worry About Their Parents' Use of Alcohol/Drugs* (with book), and *The Mirror of a Child.*
- Books for teens on peer groups: *Positive Peer Groups, How to Say No and Keep Your Friends: Peer Pressure Reversal for Teens and Preteens*, and *When to Say Yes! and Make More Friends.*
- Books for teens on fighting abuse: *How Chemical Use Becomes Chemical Dependence: And How to Tell if Someone You Know Has a Problem, Can I Handle Alcohol/Drugs?: A Self-Assessment Guide for Youth, When Chemicals Come to School: The Student Assistance Program Model, Drinking, Driving, and You, Stepping Stones to Recovery for Young People, How to Stay Clean and Sober: A Relapse Prevention Guide for Teenagers, Take Charge of Your Life*, and *Breaking Away: Saying Good-bye to Alcohol/Drugs: A Guide to Help Teenagers Stop Using Chemicals.*
- Numerous other general materials on abuse, treatment, and recovery, and works for professional therapists and counselors.

Toughlove, 215–348–7090. (For full group information, see DISCIPLINE.)

ON ANTISUBSTANCE ABUSE PROGRAMS FOR PARENTS AND COMMUNITY LEADERS

American Council for Drug Education (ACDE)
136 East 64th Street
New York, NY 10021
212–758–8060; 800–488-DRUG [488–3784]
Fax: 212–758–6784
Stacey Reynolds, Executive Director
Organizations concerned about drug abuse; distributes information; publishes numerous materials, including:

- For families: pamphlets *Drug Abuse: A Family Affair, Talking to Children About Alcohol and Drug Abuse, Teens and Drugs, Youthful Drug Use—A Physician Talks to Teens*, and *Youthful Drug Use—A Physician Talks to Parents*; book *Getting Tough on Gateway Drugs: A Guide for the Family*; and videos *Wasted—A True Story, Chasin' Life*, and *A Gift for Life*, on parent-child discussions about drugs.
- General pamphlets: *Drugs in Pregnancy, Drugs in Your Medicine Cabinet, Drugs in the Community, Enabling and Denial*, and *Drug and Alcohol Abuse at Work.*
- Numerous pamphlets on alcohol and other specific drugs, such as marijuana, cocaine, heroin, crack, LSD, PCP, and inhalants.
- Prevention materials and works for health professionals.

National Families in Action
2296 Henderson Mill Road, Suite 300
Atlanta, GA 30345

404–934–6364
Fax: 404–934–7137
Sue Rusche, Executive Director
Organization concerned with preventing drug abuse among children and adolescents; operates drug information center; publishes various materials, including quarterlies *Drug Abuse Update* and *Drug Abuse Update for Kids, You Have the Right to Know* training curriculum (three units: cocaine, alcohol, tobacco), *Crack Update, The American Prevention Movement, Twelve Tips for Helping Your Children Stay Drug-Free,* and *Twelve Reasons for Not Legalizing Drugs.*

U.S. Department of Education
Drug-Free Schools Staff
400 Maryland Avenue SW
Washington, DC 20202
202–732–4599
Special federal program helping local school districts and education agencies develop and coordinate alcohol and drug abuse prevention and education programs; provides technical assistance and training, through five regional centers:

National Woman's Christian Temperance Union (WCTU)
1730 Chicago Avenue–4585
Evanston, IL 60201
708–864–1396; Publications (Signal Press): 708–864–1322; 800–755–1321
Rachel B. Kelly, President
Organization concerned about the harmful effects of alcohol, narcotic drugs, and tobacco; seeks total abolition of alcohol; acts as advocate; operates youth abstinence training camps; provides information; maintains research library; makes video training materials available to organizations; publishes various materials, including:

- Monthly *Legislative Update,* bimonthlies *Promoter* and *The Union Signal,* children's magazine *Young Crusader.*
- Booklets on alcohol *About Addiction, Alcohol and You—Guide for Teenagers, Alcoholism and the Family, Alcoholics Victorious, Alcoholism—Medical Consequences,* and *Alcoholism in the Workplace.*
- Leaflets on alcohol *Alcohol Fact Sheet, Alcohol Facts for Women, Choices* (for teens), *Student Drinking, Teen Creed, Coach Dan's Chalk Talk About Alcohol, Ads vs. Reality, Alcohol and Other Drugs, How Much Is Drunk?, Is Alcoholism a Disease?, Parent's Nightmare, Party? Comments by a Teenager, Positive Approach—Total Abstinence, Six Established Facts, Staggering Statistics, Alcohol and the Body, Bible and Alcohol: Moderation or Abstinence, Don't Destroy Your Brain Cells,* and *Ten Reasons Why I Abstain.*
- Numerous booklets and leaflets about drugs in general, misuse of nonprescription drugs, and specific drugs, such as marijuana, cocaine, crack, heroin, LSD, and PCP.
- Various books and booklets on social issues, including teenage gambling.
- Numerous children's teaching materials, including coloring and activity books, think-and-do sheets, videos, story and puzzle pages, leaflets, contests, day camp material, and lesson kits for teachers.

Organizations Against Drunk Driving

Mothers Against Drunk Driving (MADD)
669 Airport Freeway, Suite 310
Hurst, TX 76053
817–595–0192; Hotline: 800–438–6233
D. E. Schaet, Executive Director
Organization against drunk driving; acts as advocate; refers survivors to bereavement groups; provides help in negotiating through the judicial system; publishes various materials, including newsletter.

RID-United States of America (Remove Intoxicated Drivers)
P.O. Box 520
Schenectady, NY 12301
Helpline: 518–393-HELP [393–4357]; Victims National Hotline: 518–372–0034
Fax: 518–370–4917
Doris Aiken, President
Organization seeking to keep drunk drivers off the highways; acts as advocate; offers emotional support for victims and their families; provides practical aid for negotiating through the judicial system; publishes various materials, including newsletter and *Victims Aid Network.*

Students Against Driving Drunk (SADD)
P.O. Box 800
Marlboro, MA 01752
508–481–3568
Fax: 508–481–5759
William Cullinane, Executive Director
Organization of students against underage drinking, drug abuse, and drunk driving; seeks stronger penalties for intoxicated drivers; publishes various materials, including quarterly *SADD On the Move,* fact sheets, middle and high school starter kits, and training manuals.

Citizens for Safe Drivers Against Drunk Drivers and Chronic Offenders (CSD)
5632 Connecticut Avenue NW
P.O. Box 42018

Washington, DC 20015
301–469–6282
Ken Nathanson, President
Organization of families of drunk-driving crash victims and others; seeks to strengthen drunk-driving penalties, licensing regulations, and use of U.S. Department of Transportation's national register of drivers whose licenses have been revoked; serves as information clearinghouse and as support network for victims' families.

Programs for Families and Friends of Substance Abusers

Al-Anon Family Group Headquarters (AAFGH)
P.O. Box 862, Midtown Station
New York, NY 10018–0862
212–302–7240 (see Alcoholics Anonymous in white pages for local number)
Fax: 212–869–3757
Network of self-help groups for family and friends of alcoholics, paralleling Alcoholics Anonymous; operates Alateen groups for teens (12–20); helps people deal with the problems resulting from another's drinking; publishes numerous materials on Al-Anon and other works, including:

- For parents: *How Can I Help My Children?, To the Mother and Father of an Alcoholic, Dear Mom and Dad,* and *Parents' Newcomer Packet.*
- For other adults: *From Survival to Recovery: Growing Up in an Alcoholic Home, Alcoholism, the Family Disease, Guide for the Family of the Alcoholic, So You Love An Alcoholic, What Do You Do About the Alcoholic's Drinking?, Understanding Ourselves and Alcoholism, Living with Sobriety: Another Beginning, Sexual Intimacy and the Alcoholic Relationship, Did You Grow Up with a Problem Drinker?,* and other general materials.
- For children: *What's "Drunk," Mama?*
- For teens: *Alateen: Hope for Children of Alcoholics, Alateen: A Day at a Time, Youth and the Alcoholic Parent, If Your Parents Drink Too Much, Facts About Alateen, Alateen: Is It for You?*; and video *Alateen Tells It Like It Is.*

Children of Alcoholics Foundation (CAF)
555 Madison Avenue, 20th Floor
New York, NY 10022
212–754–0656; 800–359-COAF [359–2623]
Fax: 212–754–0664
Richard Colon, Secretary
Organization concerned with the effects on children of alcohol and drug abuse in the family, including parents who are adult children of alcoholics; publishes various materials including:

- For parents and other adults: *Discovering Normal: A Parenting Course for Adult Children of Alcoholics and Their Partners, Story of Hope, Trying to Find Normal;* brochures *How You Can Help* and *For the One in Eight Americans Who Is the Child of an Alcoholic;* and videotape *FOCUS: Children of Alcoholics.*
- General materials: *Parental Consent: Helping Children of Addicted Parents Get Help, Suggested Readings to Help Students Understand Family Alcoholism, Help for Inner-City Children of Addicted Parents, Profiles: Ten Prevention Programs for Children of Alcoholics, Children of Alcoholics, Children of Alcoholics at Work,* and *Report of the Forum on Protective Factors, Resiliency, and Vulnerable Children.*
- For young children: *The Feel Better Book.*
- For preteens and teens: *Kids Talking to Kids, If You Think Your Parents Drink Too Much. . .,* and *What You Can Do to Help a Friend.*
- Educational programs and works on adult children of alcoholics in the workplace.

Families Anonymous (FA)
P.O. Box 3475
Culver City, CA 90231–3475
310–313–5800; 800–736–9805
Network of mutual-support groups for family and friends of people who abuse drugs or have related emotional problems, modeled after Al-Anon; provides information and referrals; publishes newsletter and other materials, including *A Guide for the Family of the Drug Abuser, A Father Faces Drug Abuse, Introduction to an FA Meeting, FA and Treatment Programs,* and *A Recovering Addict Comes Home.*

National Association for Children of Alcoholics (NACOA)
11426 Rockville Pike, Suite 100
Rockville, MD 20852
301–468–0985
Fax: 301–468–0987
Marcie Thompson, Executive Officer
Organization concerned with children of alcoholics (COAs); provides information and referrals; acts as advocate; publishes newsletter and other materials, including video *Poor Jennifer, She's Always Losing Her Hat,* videotape about children with a parent suffering from alcoholism.

National Safety Council (NSC), 800–621–7615. Publishes booklet *Substance Abuse, Alcohol and Drug Personal Action Guide,* video *Alcohol and Drugs,* and *Drugs: Look for Yourself* (educational program including video, teacher's guides, and student workbooks). (For full group information, see SAFETY.)

ONLINE RESOURCES

Better Health and Medical Forum (America Online: Health, Medicine) Provides discussion areas and libraries covering addictions and chemical dependencies. (For full information, see HEALTH CARE.)

Parents' Information Network (America Online: PIN) Online forums and libraries cover substance abuse. (For full information, see GENERAL PARENTING RESOURCES on page 000.)

Internet: alt.drugs Usenet newsgroup offering information and discussion. Subscribe through newsreader: news: alt.drugs

OTHER RESOURCES

GENERAL GUIDES FOR PARENTS AND OTHER ADULTS

A Parent's Guide to Alcoholism and Drug Abuse. Dennis Daley. Learning Publications, 1993.

Help! for Kids and Parents about Drugs. Jean I. Clarke and others. HarperCollins, 1993.

The No-Nonsense Parents' Guide: What You Can Do about Teens and Alcohol, Drugs, Sex, Eating Disorders and Depression. Sheila Fuller and others. Parents Pipeline, 1992.

Alcohol and Drug Education for Parents. Sally S. Crawford. Healthy Life, 1992.

How to Tell If Your Kids Are Using Drugs. Steve Carper and Timothy Dimoff. Facts on File, 1992.

Active Parenting Family Guide: Tobacco, Alcohol and Other Drugs. Nancy Ballance, ed. Active Parenting, 1992.

Early Warning: Recognizing the Signs of Addiction. Producer: Advanced American Communications, 1991. Video for sale or rental. (Address: MTI Film & Video, 108 Wilmot Road, Deerfield, IL 60015.)

Good News about Drugs and Alcohol: Curing, Treating and Preventing. Mark S. Gold. Random House, 1991.

Family Addictions: A Guide for Surviving Alcohol and Drug Abuse. Charles R. Norris, Jr. PIA Press, 1990.

ON PREVENTION, FOR PARENTS AND OTHER ADULTS

Help Your Child Say No to Alcohol, Tobacco and Drugs. Ruth Bowdoin. W. Gladden, 1994.

Drug and Alcohol Abuse: The Authoritative Guide for Parents, Teachers, and Counselors. H.T. Milhorn, Jr. Plenum, 1994.

Developing a Partnership to Eliminate Alcohol and Other Drugs in Your Community. Sally S. Crawford. Healthy Life, 1992.

Citizen's Alcohol and Other Drug Prevention Directory: Resources for Getting Involved. Diane, 1992.

Citizen's Alcohol and Other Drug Prevention Directory: Resources for Getting Involved. Gordon, 1992.

Straight Talk with Kids: Improving Communication, Building Trust, and Keeping Your Children Drug Free. Bantam, 1991. Project of the Scott Newman Center, founded by Paul Newman in memory of his son, whose death was drug-related.

Drug Free Zone: Keeping Drugs Out of Your Child's School. Carol Sager. TAB, 1991.

Keep Your Kids Straight: What Parents Need to Know about Drugs and Alcohol. Ronald Main and Judy Zervas. TAB, 1991.

GENERAL WORKS ON ALCOHOLISM

Alcoholism: The Facts, 2nd ed. Donald W. Goodwin. Oxford University Press, 1994.

Straight Talk about Alcoholism: A Doctor Explains Its Causes, Its Effects, and What You Can Do about It. Robert A. Liebelt. Pharos, 1992.

Teenagers and Alcohol: When Saying No Isn't Enough. Roger E. Vogler and Wayne R. Bartz. Charles, 1992.

Wellness: Alcohol Use and Abuse. Richard Schlaadt. Dushkin, 1992.

All about Underage Drinking. Charles Gleason and Maryanne Driscoll. Bur For At-Risk, 1992.

Runs in Your Family: Alcoholism. Ronald L. Rogers and C. Scott McMillin. Bantam, 1992.

Alcoholism and Codependency. Alexander C. Dejong. Tyndale, 1991.

Driving the Drunk Off the Road. Sandy Golden. Revell, 1990.

GENERAL WORKS ON ADDICTION AND SUBSTANCE ABUSE

Addicted? A Guide to Understanding Addiction. Tom O'Connell. Sanctuary, 1990.

Drug Dependence. Jason M. White. Prentice-Hall, 1990.

ON DEALING WITH SUBSTANCE ABUSE

Up and Down the Mountain: Helping Children Cope with Parental Alcoholism. Pamela L. Higgins. New Horizon, 1994.

End Their Drinking? Their Drug Taking? You Decide: A Black and White No Nonsense Guide for Those Who Fear Someone Is Drinking Or Drugging Too Much. Abyss, 1994.

Growing Up with Alcohol. Emma Fossey. Routledge, 1994.

Under Whose Influence? Judy Laik. Parenting Press, 1994.

When a Family Is in Trouble: Children Can Cope with Grief from Drug and Alcohol Addictions. Marge Heegaard. Woodland Press, 1993.

Seven Lessons for Children of Substance Abusive Families: A Survivor's Manual. Christena S. Jones. Learning Publications, 1993.

The Facts about Drug Use: Coping with Drugs and Alcohol in Your Family, at Work, in Your Community. Consumer Reports Books Editors; Barry Stimmel, ed. Haworth, 1992.

Children in Pain: Helping Chronically Addicted Adolescents. C.C. Nuckols. TAB, 1992.

Raising Healthy Children in an Alcoholic Home. Barbara L. Wood. Crossroad, 1992.

Clean and Sober Parenting: A Guide to Help Recovering Parents Rebuild Trust, Create Structure and Routine from Chaos, Improve Communication and Share Feelings, Learn Parenting Skills, and Give up Guilt and Shame. Jane Nelsen and others. Prima, 1992.

Corey's Dad Drinks Too Much. Anne Courtney. Tyndale, 1991.

When the Drug War Hits Home: Healing the Family Torn Apart by Teenage Drug Abuse. Laura Stamper. Deaconess, 1991.

Children of Alcoholics: A Sourcebook. Penny B. Page. Garland, 1991.

Growing Out of an Alcoholic Family. Karen Sandvig. Regal Books, 1990.

Lovebound: Recovering from an Alcoholic Family. Phyllis Hobe. NAL-Dutton, 1990.

Double Duty: Dual Dynamics Within the Chemically Dependent Home. Claudia Black. Ballantine, 1990. By the author of *It Will Never Happen to Me* (1982).

When Someone You Love Drinks Too Much: A Christian Guide to Addiction, Codependence and Recovery. Christina B. Parker. HarperSanFrancisco, 1990.

For children, on substance-abusing parents

Growing up with an Alcoholic Parent. Rona D. Schenkerman. Bur For At-Risk, 1993.

What You Should Know about a Parent Who Drinks Too Much. William L. Coleman. Augsburg Fortress, 1992.

For children, on substance abuse

The Gladden Book about Alcohol. Marnie Starbuck. W. Gladden, 1994.

Say No and Know Why: Kids Learn About Drugs. Wendy Wax. Walker, 1991.

What Are Drugs? Drugs and Our World. You Can Say No to Drugs. Gretchen Super. Troll Associates, 1990. On what drugs are, what they do in the body, the consequences of abuse, and the differences between medicines and illegal drugs.

For children, fiction on substance abuse

My Dad: Story and Pictures. Niki Daly. McElderry/Macmillan, 1995.

Lasso the Moon. Dennie Covington. Delacorte, 1995.

Blue-Eyed Son. Dreams in Black and White. Chris Lynch. HarperCollins, 1995.

Sometimes My Mom Drinks Too Much. Kevin Kenny. Raintree/Steck-Vaughn, 1993.

Safe at Home!. Peggy K. Anderson. Atheneum/Macmillan, 1992.

For preteens and teens, on substance-abusing parents

Dangerous Legacy: The Babies of Drug-Taking Parents. Ben Sonder. Watts, 1994.

Alcoholism and the Family. Gilda Berger. Watts, 1993.

Coping with an Alcoholic or Drug Abusing Parent. Alan Gadol. Bur For At-Risk, 1992.

Everything You Need to Know About an Alcoholic Parent. Nancy Shuker. Rosen, 1990. Large-type book for teens with reading difficulties.

Coping with an Alcoholic Parent. Kay Marie Porterfield. Rosen, 1990.

Living with a Parent Who Takes Drugs. Judith S. Seixas. Greenwillow/Morrow, 1989.

For preteens and teens, on substance abuse

Marijuana. Crack. Cocaine. Heroin. Drugs on Your Streets. Drugs and Your Brothers and Sisters. Drugs and Your Parents. Drugs and Your Friends. Rosen, 1993.

Straight Talk about Drugs and Alcohol. Alizabeth A. Ryan. Dell, 1992.

A Young Person's Guide to the Twelve Steps. Stephen Roos. Hazelden, 1992.

Drugs in the Body: Effects of Abuse. Mark Yoslow. Watts, 1992.

Dad: Are People Using Alcohol and Drugs As an Alternative to Problem Solving? Albert J. Tate, III. Unique Memphis, 1992.

Chemical Dependency: Opposing Viewpoints, Charles P. Cozic and Karin Swicher, eds. Greenhaven, 1991.

Focus on Opiates. Focus on Medicines. Drugs and the Family. Susan DeStefano. *Focus on Hallucinogens. Drugs and Crime. The Drug-Alert Dictionary and Resource Guide.* Jeffrey Shulman. *Drugs and Sports.* Katherine S. Talmadge. (All 1991.) *Focus on Drugs and the Brain.* David Friedman. *Focus on Alcohol.* Catherine O'Neill. *Focus on Marijuana.* Paula Klevan Zeller. *Focus on Cocaine and Crack.* Jeffrey Shulman. *Focus on Nicotine and Caffeine.* Robert Perry. (All 1990.) Twenty-First Century Books.

Compact Paperback Library of the Encyclopedia of Psychoactive Drugs, including individual volumes: *The Addictive Personality; Amphetamines; Barbiturates; Celebrity Drug Use; Cocaine; Drinking; Driving and Drugs; Drugs and Pregnancy; Drugs and Sports; Drugs and Women; Heroin; Marijuana;* and *Teenage Depression and Suicide.* Chelsea House, 1989.

For preteens and teens, on alcohol abuse

Teenage Drinking. Elaine Landau. Enslow, 1994.
Alcohol. Judy Monroe. Enslow, 1994.
Alcoholism. Carol Wekesser, ed. Greenhaven, 1994.
Coping with Drinking and Driving, rev. ed. Janet Grosshandler. Rosen, 1994.
Everything You Need to Know about Alcohol, rev. ed. Barbara Taylor. Rosen, 1993.
Alcohol. Ellen Wijnberg. Raintree/Steck-Vaughn, 1993.
Alcoholism. Chris Varley. Marshall Cavendish, 1993.
A Six Pack and a Fake I. D.: Teens Look at the Drinking Question. Susan Cohen and Daniel Cohen. Dell, 1992.
Alcohol and Alcoholism. Ross Fishman. Chelsea, 1992.
Alcohol: Teenage Drinking, rev. ed. Alan R. Lang. Chelsea House, 1992.
Alcohol and Alcoholism, rev. ed. Ross Fishman. *Alcohol: Customs and Rituals,* rev. ed. Thomas Babor. Chelsea House, 1992.
Alcoholism. Arthur Diamond. Lucent, 1992.
Alcoholism. Herma Silverstein. Watts, 1990.
Teen Alcoholism. Nancy Nielsen. Lucent, 1990.

For preteens and teens, on drug abuse

Drugs in Society: Are They Our Suicide Pill? John Salak. Twenty-First Century Books, 1995.
Drugs and AIDS. Barbara H. Draimin. Rosen, 1994.
Drugs in the Body: Effects of Abuse. Mark Yoslow. Watts, 1992.
Drug Abuse A-Z. Gilda Berger and Melvin Berger. Enslow, 1990.

For preteens and teens, fiction and first-hand accounts on substance abuse

A Share of Freedom. June R. Wood. Putnam, 1994.
Hannah in Between. Colby Rodowsky. Farrar, Straus & Giroux, 1994.
David and Della. Paul Zindel. HarperCollins, 1993.
No Guarantees: A Young Woman's Fight to Overcome Drug and Alcohol Addiction. Chris Campbell. New Discovery/Macmillan, 1993.
Binge. Charles Ferry. DaisyHill Press, 1992.
My Dad's Definitely Not a Drunk!. Elisa L. Carbone. Waterfront, 1992.
Burnt: A Teenage Addict's Road to Recovery. Craig Fraser and Deidre Sullivan. NAL-Dutton, 1990.

On recovery from substance abuse

Food for Recovery: The Next Step. Joseph D. Beasley and Susan Knightly. Crown, 1994. Nutrition for those recovering from substance abuse and eating disorders.
Under Your Own Power: A Guide to Recovery for Nonbelievers—and the Ones Who Love Them. Ronald L. Rogers and Chandler S. McMillin. Perigee/Berkley, 1993.
You've Got the Power: A Recovery Guide for Young People with Drug and Alcohol Problems. Edward M. Read and Dennis C. Daley. American Correctional Association, 1993.
The Small Book: A Revolutionary Alternative for Overcoming Alcohol and Drug Dependence. Jack Trimpey. Delacorte, 1992.
S.O.S. Sobriety: The Proven Alternative to 12-Step Programs. James Christopher. Prometheus, 1992.
How to Defeat Alcoholism Through Nutrition. Gordon, 1992.
Blessed Are the Addicts: The Spiritual Side of Alcoholism, Addiction, and Recovery. John A. Martin. HarperSanFrancisco, 1992.
Adolescent Relapse Prevention Workbook: A Guide to Staying Off Drugs and Alcohol. Dennis Daley and Charles Sproule. Learning Publications, 1991.
Recovery from Alcoholism: Beyond Your Wildest Dreams. Jerome D. Levin. Aronson, 1991.
Beyond AA: Dealing Responsibly with Alcohol. Clarence Barrett. Positive Attitudes, 1991.
Why Don't I Feel Better? Healing the Recovering Alcoholic. Joyce Bismack. Bear and Co., 1991.
Step Workbook for Adolescent Chemical Dependency Recovery: A Guide to the First Five Steps. Steven L. Jaffe. American Psychiatric Press, 1990.
Recovery from Addiction. John Finnegan and Daphne Gray. Celestial Arts, 1990.
Overcoming Chemical Dependency. Robert S. McGee. Word, 1990.

Recovery resource books

The Recovery Resource Book: The Best Available Information on Addictions and Co-Dependence. Barbara Yoder. Simon & Schuster/Fireside, 1990.
The 800-COCAINE Book of Drug and Alcohol Recovery. James Cocores. Villard Books, 1990.
Drug, Alcohol and Other Addictions: A Directory of Treatment Centers and Prevention Programs Nationwide. Katherine Clay. Oryx Press, 1989.

Peterson's Drug and Alcohol Programs and Policies at Four-Year Colleges. Janet Carney Schneider and Bunny Porter-Shirley, eds. Peterson's, 1989.

Background works

Alcohol, Culture, and Control: Preventing Alcohol Abuse. David J. Hanson. Greenwood, 1995.

Alcohol and Homicide: A Deadly Combination of Two American Traditions. Robert N. Parker and Linda-Anne Rebhun. State University of New York Press, 1995.

The Genetics of Alcoholism. Henri Begleiter and Benjamin Kissins, eds. Oxford University Press, 1995.

Dangerous Legacy: The Babies of Drug-Taking Parents. Ben Sonder. Watts, 1994.

Alcohol Use and Misuse by Young Adults. George S. Howard and Peter E. Nathan, eds. University of Notre Dame Press, 1994.

Encyclopedia of Drugs and Alcohol. Jerome Jaffe, ed. Macmillan, 1994.

Dictionary of Street Alcohol and Drug Terms, 4th ed. Peter Johnson and others. Diane, 1993.

Altered States: Alcohol and Other Drugs in America. Patricia M. Tice. Strong Museum, 1992.

A Handbook of Drug and Alcohol Abuse, 3rd ed. F. Hofman and others. Oxford University Press, 1992.

Psychedelics Encyclopedia, 3rd ed. Peter Stafford and others. Ronin, 1992.

Alcohol in America: Drinking Practices and Problems. Walter B. Clark and Michael E. Hilton, eds. State University of New York Press, 1991.

Encyclopedia of Alcoholism, 2nd ed. Glen Evans and others. Facts On File, 1991.

Illegal Drugs and Alcohol—America's Anguish. Carol D. Foster and others, eds. Information Plus, 1991.

Suicide in Alcoholism. George E. Murphy. Oxford University Press, 1992.

Cocaine Kids: The Inside Story of a Teenage Drug Ring. Terry Williams. Addison-Wesley, 1990.

Encyclopedia of Drug Abuse, 2nd ed. Glen Evans and others. Facts On File, 1990.

Adolescents Worlds: Drug Use and Athletic Activity. M.F. Stuck. Praeger/Greenwood, 1990.

(See also ALCOHOL ABUSE; DRUG ABUSE; FETAL ALCOHOL SYNDROME; STEROIDS.)

Index